ELENCHUS OF BIBLICAL BIBLIOGRAPHY

——————————— 18 ———————————

ROBERT ALTHANN S.J.

ELENCHUS OF BIBLICA

2002

EDITRICE PONTIFICIO ISTITUTO BIBLICO
ROMA 2005

© 2005 E.P.I.B. – Roma
ISBN: 88-7653-627-2

EDITRICE PONTIFICIO ISTITUTO BIBLICO
Piazza della Pilotta, 35 - 00187 Roma, Italia

ROBERT ALTHANN S.J.

ELENCHUS OF BIBLICA

2002

EDITRICE PONTIFICIO ISTITUTO BIBLICO
ROMA 2005

Urbes editionis—Cities of publication

AA	Ann Arbor	Lv(N)	Leuven (L-Neuve)
Amst	Amsterdam	M/Mi	Madrid/Milano
B	Berlin	Mkn	Maryknoll/
Ba/BA	Basel/Buenos Aires	Mp	Minneapolis
Barc	Barcelona	Mü/Müns('r)	München/Münster
Bo/Bru	Bologna/Brussel	N	Napoli
C	Cambridge, England	ND	NotreDame IN
CasM	Casale Monferrato	Neuk	Neukirchen/Verlag
Ch	Chicago	NHv	New Haven
CinB	Cinisello Balsamo	Nv	Nashville
CM	Cambridge, Mass.	NY	New York
ColMn	Collegeville MN	Oxf	Oxford
Da:Wiss	Darmstadt, WissBuchg	P/Pd	Paris/Paderborn
DG	Downers Grove	Ph	Philadelphia
Dü	Düsseldorf	R/Rg	Roma/Regensburg
E	Edinburgh	S	Salamanca
ENJ	EnglewoodCliffs NJ	Sdr	Santander
F	Firenze	SF	San Francisco
Fra	Frankfurt/M	Shf	Sheffield
FrB/FrS	Freiburg-Br/Schweiz	Sto	Stockholm
Gö	Göttingen	Stu	Stuttgart
GR	Grand Rapids MI	T/TA	Torino/Tel Aviv
Gü	Gütersloh	Tü	Tübingen
Ha	Hamburg	U/W	Uppsala/Wien
Heid	Heidelberg	WL	Winona Lake IN
Hmw	Harmondsworth	Wmr	Warminster
J	Jerusalem	Wsb	Wiesbaden
K	København	Wsh	Washington D.C.
L/Lei	London/Leiden	Wsz	Warszawa
LA	Los Angeles	Wu	Wuppertal
Lp	Leipzig	Wü	Würzburg
LVL	Louisville KY	Z	Zürich

Punctuation: To separate a subtitle from its title, we use a COLON (:). The *semicolon* (;) serves to separate items that in other respects belong together. Hence, at the end of an entry a *semicolon* indicates a link with the following entry. This link may consist in the two entries having the same author or in the case of multiauthor works having the same book title; the author will be mentioned in the first entry of such a group, the common book title in the last entry, that is the one which concludes with a fullstop [period] (.).
Abbreviations: These follow S.M. Schwertner, **IATG**[2] (De Gruyter; Berlin 1992) as far as possible. A list of **other** abbreviations appears below.
* An asterisk after a book review or an article indicates a reference to an electronic version.
Price of books: This is sometimes rounded off ($10 for $9.95).

Index systematicus — Contents

The present volume contains all the 2002 material of the Elenchus. Thanks are due the staff of the Editrice Pontificio Istituto Biblico which assures the publication of the Elenchus. I should also like to express gratitude to my colleague Fr. Jean-Noël Aletti, S.J. for his patience and readiness to help in matters electronic. I further thank graduates of the Institute for their valuable assistance.

The materials for this volume were gathered principally from the libraries of the Pontifical Biblical Institute, the Pontifical Gregorian University and the University of Innsbruck. I thank the staff of these libraries for their courtesy and unvarying willingness to help. The Department of Biblical Studies at the University of Innsbruck continues to be an important and dependable source of bibliographical information. We in turn supply the Department with lists of book reviews which may be accessed through the University's electronic catalogue, BILDI, at the following address: http://bildi.uibk.ac.at.

Acronyms: Periodica - Series (small). *8 fig.*=ISSN; *10 fig.*=ISBN.

A: in Arabic.
ABIG: Arbeiten zur Bibel und ihrer Geschichte; Lp.
AcBib: Acta Pontificii Instituti Biblici; R.
ACCS: Ancient Christian Commentary on Scripture; DG.
ACPQ: American Catholic Philosophical Quarterly; Wsh.
Acta Philosophica; R.
ActBib: Actualidad Bibliográfica; Barc.
AcTh(B): Acta Theologica; Bloemfontein.
Ad Gentes; Bo.
AETSC: Annales de l'Ecole Théologique Saint-Cyprien; Yaoundé, Cameroun.
AfR: Archiv für Religionsgeschichte; Stu.
Afrika Yetu; Nairobi.
AGWB: Arbeiten zur Geschichte und Wirkung der Bibel; Stu.
AHIg: Anuario de historia de la iglesia; Pamplona.
AJPS: Asian Journal of Pentecostal Studies;
AJSR: Association for Jewish Studies Review; Waltham, MA.
Ä&L: Ägypten und Levante; Wien.
Alei Etzion; Alon Shvut.
Al-Mushir [**Urdu**]; Rawalpindi.
Alpha Omega; R.
Alternativas; Managua.
AltOrF: Altorientalische Forschungen; B.
AnáMnesis; México.
AnBru: Analecta Bruxellensia; Bru.
Ancient Philosophy; Pittsburgh.
Ancient West & East; Lei.
ANESt [<Abr-n]: Ancient Near Eastern Studies; Melbourne.
Anime e corpi; Brezzo di Bedero, Va.
Annali Chieresi; Chieri.
Annals of Theology [**P.**]; Kráków.
AnnTh: Annales Theologici; R.
AnScR: Annali di Scienze Religiose; Mi.
Antologia Vieusseux; F.

APB: Acta Patristica et Byzantina; Pretoria.
Archaeology in the Biblical World; Shafter, CA.
ARET: Archivi reali di Ebla, testi; R.
ARGU: Arbeiten zur Religion und Geschichte des Urchristentums; Fra.
ARJ: The Annual of Rabbinic Judaism; Lei.
ASJ: Acta Sumerologica; Kyoto, Japan.
ATT: Archivo teologico torinese; Leumann (Torino).
AtT: Atualidade teológica; Rio de Janeiro.
Atualizaçâo; Belo Horizonte.
AuOr: Aula Orientalis (S: Supplement); Barc.
Auriensia; Ourense, Spain.
Aviso; Mü.
B&B: Babel und Bibel; Moscow.
BAIAS: Bulletin of the Anglo-Israel Archaeological Society; L.
Bailamme; Mi.
Barnabiti Studi; R.
Bazmavep; Venise.
BBR: Bulletin for Biblical Research; WL.
BCSMS: Bulletin of the Canadian Society for Mesopotamian Studies; Toronto.
BEgS: Bulletin of the Egyptological Seminar; NY.
Bib(L): Bíblica; Lisboa.
BiblInterp (BiblInterp): Biblical Interpretation; Lei.
Biblioteca EstB: Biblioteca de Estudios Bíblicos; S.
BnS: La bibbia nella storia; Bo.
Bobolanum [**P.**]; Wsz.
Bogoslovni Vestnik [**S.**]; Ljubljana.
BolT: Boletín teológico; BA.
BoSm: Bogoslovska Smotra; Zagreb.
BOTSA: Bulletin for Old Testament Studies in Africa; Stavanger.
BRT: The Baptist Review of Theology / La revue baptiste de théologie; Gormely, Ontario.
BSÉG: Bulletin de la Société d'Égyptologie; Genève.

BSGJ: Bulletin der Schweizerischen Gesellschaft für Judaistische Forschung; Z.

BSLP: Bulletin de la Société de Linguistique de Paris; P.

BuBB: Bulletin de bibliographie biblique; Lausanne.

Bulletin of Ecumenical Theology; Enugu, Nigeria.

Bulletin of Judaeo-Greek Studies; C.

Bulletin of Research of Christian Culture; Okayama, Japan.

BurH: Buried History; Melbourne.

BWM: Bibelwissenschaftliche Monographien; Gießen.

C: in Chinese.

CAH: Cambridge Ancient History[2]; Cambridge Univ.

Cahiers de l'Atelier; P.

Cahiers Ratisbonne; J.

CahPhRel: Cahiers de l'Ecole des Sciences philosophiques et religieuses; Bru.

Caietele Institutului Catolic; Bucureşti.

CAL.N: Comprehensive Aramaic Lexicon, Newsletter; Cincinatti.

CamArchJ: Cambridge Archaeological Journal; C.

Carmel(T); Toulouse.

Carmel(V); Venasque.

Carthaginensia; Murcia.

Catalyst; Goroka, Papua New Guinea.

Catechisti parrocchiali; R.

Cathedra; Bogotá.

Cathedra [H.]; J.

CBET: Contributions to biblical exegesis and theology; Lv.

Centro pro unione, Bulletin; R.

Chakana; Fra.

Chemins de Dialogue; Marseille.

Ching Feng; Hong Kong.

Choisir; Genève.

Chongshin Review; Seoul.

Christian Thought; Seoul.

Chronology and Catastrophism Workshop; Luton.

Cias; Buenos Aires.

CICat: Caietele Institutului Catolic; Bucharest.

CLEC: Common Life in the Early Church;

CLehre: Die Christenlehre; B.

CMAO: Contributi e Materiali di Archeologia Orientale; R.

Colloquium; Brisbane.

Comunidades; S.

ConAss: Convivium Assisiense; Assisi.

Confer; M.

ConnPE: Connaissances des Pères de l'Église; Montrouge.

Contacts; Courbevoie.

Contagion; Rocky Mount.

Convergência; São Paulo.

CoSe: Consacrazione e Servizio; R.

CQuS: Companion to the Qumran Scrolls; L.

CredOg: Credereoggi; Padova.

CritRR: Critical Review of Books in Religion; Atlanta.

Crkva u Svijetu; Split.

Croire aujourd'hui; P.

Crux: Vancouver.

CTrB: Cahiers de traduction bibli-que; Pierrefitte, France.

CuBR: Currents in biblical research; L.

CuesTF: Cuestiones Teológicas y Filosóficas; Medellin.

Cuestion Social, La; Mexico.

Cultura e libri; R.

CurResB: Currents in Research: Biblical Studies; Shf.

Daphnis; Amst.

D: Director dissertationis.

Diadokhē [ΔΙΑΔΟΧΗ]. Revista de Estudios de Filosofía Platónica y Cristiana; B.A.

Didascalia; Rosario, ARG.

Dimensioni e problemi della ricerca storica; R.

Direction; Fresno, CA.

DiscEg: Discussions in Egyptology; Oxf.

DissA: Dissertation Abstracts International; AA/L. -A [= US etc.]: 0419-4209 [C = Europe. 0307-6075].

Doctor Angelicus; Bonn.

DosB: Les Dossiers de la Bible; P.

DQ: Documenta Q; Leuven.

DSBP: Dizionario di spiritualità biblico-patristica; R.

DSD: Dead Sea Discoveries; Lei.
DT(B): Divus Thomas; Bo.
^E^: Editor, Herausgeber, a cura di.
Ecclesia orans; R.
Eccl(R): Ecclesia; R.
EfMex: Efemérides Mexicana; Tlalpan.
EgArch: Egyptian Archaeology, Bulletin of the Egypt Exploration Society; L.
Emmanuel; St. Meinrads, IN.
Emmaus; Gozo, Malta.
Encounters; Markfield, U.K.
Epimelia; BA.
ERSY: Erasmus of Rotterdam Society Yearbook; Lexington.
EscrVedat: Escritos del Vedat; Valencia.
Esprit; P.
EThF: Ephemerides Theologicae Fluminenses; Rijeka.
Ethical Perspectives; Lv.
Ethics & Medicine; Carlisle.
ETJ: Ephrem's Theological Journal; Satna, India.
ETSI Journal; Igbaja, Nigeria.
EurJT: European Journal of Theology; Carlisle.
Evangel; E.
Evangelizzare; Bo.
EyV: Evangelio y Vida; León.
Exchange; Lei.
^F^: Festschrift.
Faith & Mission; Wake Forest, NC.
FCNT:The feminist companion to the New Testament and early christian writings; L.
Feminist Theology; Shf.
FgNT: Filologia Neotestamentaria; Córdoba.
Filosofia oggi; Genova.
FIOTL: Formation and interpretation of Old Testament literature; Lei.
Firmana; Fermo.
Florensia; S. Giovanni in Fiore (CS).
FolTh: Folia theologica; Budapest.
Forum. Sonoma, CA.
Forum Religion; Stu.
FoSub: Fontes et Subsidia ad Bibliam perinentes; B.
Franciscanum; Bogotá.
Freiburger Universitätsblätter; FrB.
Fundamentum; Basel.

Furrow; Maynooth.
G: in Greek.
Gema; Yogyakarta.
Georgica; Konstanz.
Gnosis; SF.
Graphè; Lille.
H: in Hebrew.
Hagiographica; F.
Hamdard Islamicus; Karachi.
HBO: Hallesche Beiträge zur Orientwissenschaft; Halle.
Hekima Review; Nairobi.
Henoch; T.
Hermenêutica; Cachoeira, Brasil.
HlL: Das Heilige Land; Köln.
History of European Ideas; Oxf.
Ḥokhma; Lausanne.
Holy Land; J.
Horeb; Pozzo di Gotto (ME).
Horizons; Villanova, PA.
HorWi: Horizonty Wiary; Kraków.
Ho Theológos; Palermo.
IAJS: Index of Articles on Jewish Studies; J.
Ichthys ΙΧΘΥΣ; Aarhus.
ICMR: Islam and Christian-Muslim Relations; Birmingham.
ICSTJ: ICST Journal; Vigan, Philippines.
Igreja e Missão; Valadares, Cucujaes.
IHR: International History Review; Burnaby, Canada.
IJCT: International Journal of the Classical Tradition; New Brunswick, NJ.
IJSCC: International Journal for the Study of the Christian Church; E.
Image; Seattle.
INTAMS.R: INTAMS [International Academy for Marital Spirituality] review; Sint-Genesius-Rode, Belgium.
Inter Fratres; Fabriano (AN).
Interpretation(F). Journal of Political Philosophy; Flushing.
Iran; L.
Isidorianum; Sevilla.
IslChr: Islamochristiana; R.
ITBT: Interpretatie; Zoetermeer.
ITE: Informationes Theologiae Europae; Fra.

Iter; Caracas.

Itin(L): Itinerarium; Lisboa.

Itin(M): Itinerarium; Messina.

J: in Japanese.

JAAT: Journal of Asian and Asian American Theology; Claremont, Calif.

JAB: Journal for the Aramaic Bible; Shf.

JAGNES: Journal of the Association of Graduates in Near Eastern Studies; Berkeley, CA.

Jahrbuch Politische Theologie; Mü.

JANER: Journal of Ancient Near Eastern Religions; Lei.

Japan Mission Journal; Tokyo.

JATS: Journal of the Adventist Theological Society; Collegedale, Tennessee.

JBTSA: Journal of Black Theology in South Africa; Atteridgeville.

JCoS: Journal of Coptic Studies; Lv.

JEarlyC: Journal of Early Christian Studies; Baltimore.

JECS: Journal of Early Christian Studies; Baltimore.

Jeevadhara; Alleppey, Kerala.

JEGTFF: Jahrbuch der Europäischen Gesellschaft für theologische Forschung von Frauen; Mainz.

JGRChJ: Journal of Graeco-Roman Christianity and Judaism; Shf.

JHiC: Journal of Higher Criticism; Montclair, NJ.

Jian Dao; Hong Kong.

JIntH: Journal of interdisciplinary history; CM.

JISt: Journal of Interdisciplinary Studies; Pasadena, CA.

JJSS: Jnanatirtha (Journal of Sacred Scriptures); Ujjain, India.

JJTP: Journal of Jewish Thought & Philosophy; Ba.

JKTh: Jahrbuch für kontextuelle Theologien; Fra.

JMEMS: Journal of Medieval and Early Modern Studies; Durham, NC.

JNSL: Journal of Northwest Semitic Languages; Stellenbosch.

Jota; Lv.

Journal of Ancient History; Moscow.

Journal of Institutional and Theoretical Economics; Tü.

Journal of Interdisciplinary History, The; CM.

Journal of Medieval History; Amst.

Journal of Medieval Latin; Turnhout.

Journal of Psychology and Judaism; NY.

Journal of Social History; Fairfax, VA.

JPentec: Journal of Pentecostal Theology; Shf (S: Supplement).

JPersp: Jerusalem Perspective; J.

JPJRS: Jnanadeepa, Pune Journal of Religious Studies; Pune.

JProgJud: Journal of Progressive Judaism; Shf.

JRadRef: Journal from the Radical Reformation; Morrow, GA.

JRTI: Journal of Religious and Theological Information; Harrisburg, PA.

JRTR: Jahrbuch für Religionswissenschaft und Theologie der Religionen; FrB.

JSem: Journal for Semitics; Pretoria.

JSHS(.S): Journal for the study of the historical Jesus (Supplementary series); Shf.

JSQ: Jewish Studies Quarterly; Tü.

JSSEA: Journal of the Society for the Study of Egyptian Antiquities; Toronto.

JStAI: Jerusalem Studies in Arabic and Islam; J.

JTrTL: Journal of Translation and Textlinguistics; Dallas.

Jud.: Judaism; NY.

K: in Korean.

Kairos(G); Guatemala.

KaKe: Katorikku-Kenkyu [J.]; Tokyo.

Kerux; Escondido, CA.

KUSATU (KUSATU): Kleine Untersuchungen zur Sprache des Alten Testaments und seiner Umwelt; Waltrop.

Kwansei-Gakuin-Daigaku; Japan.

Labeo; N.

Landas. Journal of Loyola School of Theology; Manila.

Laós; Catania.
Leqach; Lp.
LingAeg: Lingua Aegyptia; Gö.
Literary and linguistic computing; Oxf.
Living Light; Wsh.
LSDC: La Sapienza della Croce; R.
Luther-Bulletin; Amst.
Luther Digest; Crestwood, Miss.
M: Memorial.
MAI: Masters Abstracts International; AA: 0898-9095.
MastJ: Master's Seminary Journal; Sun Valley, CA.
Mayéutica; Marcilla (Navarra).
MEAH: Miscellánea de Estudios Árabes y Hebraicos (**MEAH.A**: Árabe-Islam. **MEAH.H**: Hebreo); Granada.
Meghillot; J.
Mélanges carmélitains; P.
MESA.B: Middle East Studies Association Bulletin; Muncie, IN.
MethT: Method and Theory in the Study of Religion; Toronto.
Mid-Stream; Indianapolis.
Miles Immaculatae; R.
MillSt: Milltown Studies; Dublin.
Missionalia; Menlo Park, South Africa.
MissTod: Mission Today; Shillong, India.
Mitteilungen für Anthropologie und Re-l-i-gionsgeschichte; Saarbrücken.
Mondo della Bibbia, Il; T.
Moralia; M.
MST Review; Manila.
Muslim World Book Review; Markfield, UK.
NABU: Nouvelles Assyriologiques Brèves et Utilitaires; P.
NAC: New American Commentary; Nv.
Naval Research Logistics; NY.
NEA: Near Eastern Archaeology; Boston.
Nemalah; K.
Neukirchener Theologische Zeitschrift; Neuk.
NET: Neutestamentliche Entwürfe zur Theologie; Ba.
NewTR: New Theology Review; Ch.
NHMS: Nag Hammadi and Manichaean Studies; Lei.

NIBC: New International Biblical Commentary; Peabody.
Nicolaus; Bari.
NIntB: The New Interpreter's Bible; Nv.
NotesTrans: Notes on Translation; Dallas.
NTGu: New Testament Guides; Shf.
NTMon: New Testament Mo-no-graphs; Shf.
NTTRU: New Testament Textual Research Update; Ashfield NSW, Australia. 1320-3037.
Nuova Areopago, Il; Forlì.
Nuova Europa, La; Seriate (Bg).
Nuova Umanità; R.
Obnovljeni Život; Zagreb.
Oecumenica Civitas: Livorno.
Omnis Terra; R.
OrBibChr: Orbis biblicus et christianus; Glückstadt.
OrExp: Orient-Express, Notes et Nouvelles d'Archéologie Orientale; P.
Orient; Tokyo.
Orientamenti pastorali; Bo.
Orientamenti pedagogici; R.
P: in Polish.
Pacifica. Australian Theological Studies; Melbourne.
Paginas; Lima.
PaiC.: Paideia Cristiana; Rosario, ARG.
Paléorient; P.
Palestjinskji Sbornik [**R.**]; Moskva.
Parabola; NY.
Passaggi; Terni.
Path; Città del Vaticano.
Pensiero politico, Il; F.
Phase; Barc.
Philosophiques; Montréal.
Physis; F.
PJBR: The Polish Journal of Biblical Research; Kraków.
PKNT: Papyrologische Kommentare zum Neuen Testament; Gö.
PoeT: Poetics Today; Durham, NC.
PoST: Poznańskie studia teologiczne; Poznán.
PredOT: Prediking van het Oude Testament; Baarn.

Presbyteri; Trento.
Presbyterion; St. Louis.
PresPast: Presenza Pastorale, R.
Prism; St. Paul, MN.
ProcGLM: Proceedings of the Eastern Great Lakes and Midwest Bible Societies; Buffalo.
Pro dialogo; Città del Vaticano.
ProEc: Pro ecclesia; Northfield, MN.
Prooftexts; Baltimore.
Proverbium; Burlington, VT.
Proyección; Granada.
ProySal: Proyecto Centro Salesiano de Estudios; BA.
Prudentia [.S]; Auckland, NZ.
Przegląd Tomistyezny; Wsz.
PzB: Protokolle zur Bibel; Klosterneuburg.
Qol; México.
Qol(I); Novellara (RE).
Quaderni di azione sociale; R.
Quaderni di scienze religiose; Loreto.
Quinio; R.
Qumran Chronicle; Kraków.
QVC: Qüestions de Vida Cristiana; Barc.
R: in Russian.
R: *recensio*, book-review.
Ragion Pratica; Genova.
RANL.mor.: Rendiconti dell'Accademia Nazionale dei Lincei, Cl. di scienze morali; R.
RASM: Revue africaine des sciences de la mission; Kinshasa.
RBBras: Revista Bíblica Brasileira; Fortaleza.
RBLit: Review of Biblical Literature; Atlanta.
REAC: Ricerche di egittologia e di antichità copte; Bo.
Reason and the Faith, The; Kwangju.
Recollectio; R.
Reformation, The; Oxf (Tyndale Soc.).
Religion; L.
Religious Research; Wsh.
RelT: Religion and Theology; Pretoria.
RenSt: Renaissance Studies; Oxf.
ResB: Reseña Bíblica; Estella.
RevCT: Revista de cultura teológica; São Paulo.
Revista católica; Santiago de Chile.

Revue d'éthique et de théologie morale; P.
RF(CR): Revista de filosofia; San José, Costa Rica.
RF(UI): Revista de filosofia; México.
RGRW: Religions in the Graeco-Roman World; Lei.
Ribla: Revista de interpretação biblica latino-americana; Petrópolis.
RICAO: Revue de l'Institut Catholique de l'Afrique de l'Ouest; Abidjan.
Ricerche teologiche; Bo.
Rivista di archeologia; R.
Rivista di science religiose; R.
Rivista de storia della miniatura; F.
Roczniki Teologiczne; Lublin
Romania; P.
RRT: Reviews in Religion and Theology; L.
R&T: Religion and theology = Religie en teologie; Pretoria.
RTLit: Review of Theological Literature; Leiderdorp.
RTLu: Rivista Teologica di Lugano; Lugano.
S: Slovenian.
SAAA: Studies on the Apocryphal Acts of the Apostles; Kampen.
SAA Bulletin: State Archives of Assyria Bulletin; Padova.
SAAS: State Archives of Assyria, Studies; Helsinki.
Sacrum Ministerium; R.
Saeculum Christianum; Wsz.
San Juan de la Cruz; Sevilla.
Sapientia Crucis; Anápolis.
SaThZ: Salzburger Theologische Zeitschrift; Salzburg.
Satya Nilayam; Chennai, India.
SBL.SCSt: Society of Biblical Literature, Septuagint and Cognate Studies; Atlanta.
Science and Christian Belief; Carlisle.
Scriptura; Stellenbosch.
Scrittura e civiltà; F.
SdT: Studi di Teologia; R.
SEAP: Studi di Egittologia e di Antichità Puniche; Pisa.
Search; Dublin.

Sedes Sapientiae; Chéméré-le-Roi.
Segni e comprensione; Lecce.
SeK: Skrif en Kerk; Pretoria.
Semeia; Atlanta.
Seminarios; M.
Semiotica; Amst.
Sen.: Sendros; Costa Rica.
Servitium; CasM.
SetRel: Sette e Religioni; Bo.
Sevartham; Ranchi.
Sève; P.
Sewanee Theological Review; Sewanee, TN.
Shofar; West Lafayette, IN.
SIDIC: Service International de Documentation Judéo-Chrétienne; R.
Sinhak Jonmang; Kwangju, S. Korea.
SMEA: Studi micenei ed egeo-anatolici; R.
Società, La; Verona.
Soleriana; Montevideo.
Soundings; Nv.
Sources; FrS.
Spiritual Life; Wsh.
Spiritus(B); Baltimore.
Spiritus; P.
SPJMS: South Pacific Journal of Mission Studies; North Turramurra NSW.
SRATK: Studia nad Rodzina, Akademia Teologii Katolickiej; Wsz, 1429-2416.
STAC: Studien und Texte zu Antike und Christentum; Tü.
Stauros; Pescara.
StBob: Studia Bobolanum; Wsz.
StEeL: Studi epigrafici e linguistici; Verona.
Storia della storiografia; Mi.
St Mark's Review; Canberra.
StPhiloA: Studia Philonica Annual; Providence, RI.
StSp(K): Studies in Spirituality; Kampen.
Studi emigrazione; R.
Studia Textus Novi Testamenti; Osaka.
Studi Fatti Ricerche; Mi.
Studi sull'Oriente Cristiano; R.
Stulos. Theological Journal; Bandung, Indonesia.
StWC: Studies in World Christianity; E.

SUBB: Studia Universitatis Babeş-Bolyai; Cluj-Napoca, Romania.
Sudan & Nubia; L.
Synaxis; Catania.
T: Translator.
Tanima; Kochi, Kerala.
Teocomunicaçâo; Porto Alegre, Brasil.
Teologia Iusi; Caracas.
Ter Herkenning; 's-Gravenhage.
Tertium Millennium; R.
Testimonianze; Fiesole.
TGr.T: Tesi Gregoriana, Serie Teologia; R.
TEuph: Transeuphratène; P.
Themelios; L.
Theoforum; Ottawa.
Theologia Viatorum; Potenza.
Theologica & Historica; Cagliari.
Theologika; Lima.
Théologiques; Montréal.
Theologischer; Siegburg.
ThEv(VS): Théologie évangélique; Vaux-sur-Seine.
ThLi: Theology & Life; Hong Kong.
Theology for Our Times; Bangalore.
Theotokos; R.
ThirdM: Third Millennium: Pune, India.
T&K: Texte und Kontexte; Stu.
TMA: The Merton Annual; Shf.
TrinJ: Trinity Journal; Deerfield, IL.
TTE: The Theological Educator; New Orleans.
Tychique; Lyon.
Umat Baru; Yogyakarta, Indonesia.
Una Voce-Korrespondenz; Köln.
VeE: Verbum et Ecclesia; Pretoria.
Verbum Vitae; Kielce.
VeVi: Verbum Vitae; Kielce. P.
Viator; Turnhout.
Vie Chrétienne; P.
Vie, La: des communautés religieuses; Montréal.
Vita Sociale; F.
Vivar(C): Vivarium; Catanzaro.
Vivar(L): Vivarium; Lei.
VivH: Vivens Homo; F.

VO: Vicino Oriente; R.
Volto dei volti, Il; R.
Vox latina; Saarbrücken.
Vox Patrum; Lublin.
VoxScr: Vox Scripturae; São Paulo.
VTW: Voices from the Third World; Bangalore.
WaW: Word and World; St. Paul, Minn.
Way, The; L.
WBC: Word Biblical Commentary; Waco.
West African Journal of Ecclesial Studies; Ibadan, Nigeria.
WUB: Welt und Umwelt der Bibel; Stu.

YESW: Yearbook of the European Society of Women in Theological Research; Lv.
Yonsei Journal of Theology; Seoul.
ZAC: Zeitschrift für antikes Christentum; B.
ZAR: Zeitschrift für altorientalische und biblische Rechtsgeschichte; Wsb.
ZME: Zeitschrift für medizinische Ethik; Salzburg.
ZNT: Zeitschrift für Neues Testament; Tü.
ZNTG: Zeitschrift für neuere Theologiegeschichte; B.

I. Bibliographica

A1 Opera collecta .1 **Festschriften**, memorials

1 ACHTEMEIER, Paul J.: The forgotten God: perspectives in biblical theology. [E]**Das, A. Andrew; Matera, Frank J.**: LVL 2002, Westminster xv; 300 pp. $25. 0-664-22276-5. Essays in honor of Paul J. Achtemeier on the occasion of his 75th birthday; Bibl. Achtemeier 271-274.
2 AICHERN, Maximilian: Aufmerksame Solidarität: Festschrift für Bischof Maximilian Aichern zum siebzigsten Geburtstag. [E]**Hofer, Peter**: Rg 2002, Pustet 296 pp. €29.90. 3-7917-1846-0.
3 ASCHOFF, Diethard: Grenzgänge: Menschen und Schicksale zwischen jüdischer, christlicher und deutscher Identität: Festschrift für Diethard Aschoff. [E]**Siegert, Folker**: Münsteraner Judaistische Studien 11: Müns 2002, LIT 455 pp. 3-8258-5856-1. Bibl. Aschoff 423-438.
4 BARNETT, Paul: A review of the Greek inscriptions and papyri published in 1986-87. [E]**Llewelyn, S.R.**: New Documents Illustrating Early Christianity 9: GR 2002, Eerdmans xvi; 136 pp. $35/£25. 0-8028-4519-3. Bibl. xiii-xiv.
5 BECKER, Jürgen: Das Urchristentum in seiner literarischen Geschichte. [E]**Mell, Ulrich; Müller, Ulrich B**: BZNW 100: 1999 ⇒15,9; 17,4. [R]RBLit (2002)* (*Oehler, Markus*).
6 BERGER, Klaus: Religionsgeschichte des Neuen Testaments. [E]**Dobbeler, Axel von; Erlemann, Kurt; Heiligenthal, Roman**: 2000 ⇒16,9. [R]ZKTh 124 (2002) 238-239 (*Oberforcher, R.*).
7 BETZ, Hans Dieter: Antiquity and humanity: essays on ancient religion and philosophy. [E]**Collins, Adela Yarbro; Mitchell, Margaret M.**: 2001 ⇒17,5. [R]RHPhR 82 (2002) 219-220 (*Grappe, Ch.*).
8 BIANCHI, Ugo: Ugo Bianchi: una vita per la storia delle religioni. [E]**Casadio, Giovanni**: Biblioteca di storia delle religioni 3: R 2002, Il Calamo 525 pp. 88-88039-24-4. Bibl. Ugo Bianchi 469-496.
9 BOGAERT, Pierre-Maurice: Lectures et relectures de la bible. [E]**Auwers, Jean-Marie; Wénin, André**: BEThL 144: 1999 ⇒15,14...17,7. [R]JThS 53 (2002) 119-122 (*Hayward, Robert*); EThL 78 (2002) 180-181 (*Verheyden, J.*); JSJ 33 (2002) 314-315 (*Xeravits, Géza*); RivBib 50 (2002) 467-71 (*Bianchi, Francesco*); LASBF 52 (2002) 556-9 (*Casalini, Nello*).

10 BREKELMANS, C.H.W.: Deuteronomy and Deuteronomic literature. EVervenne, M.; Lust, J.: BEThL 133: 1997 ⇒13,17... 16,17. RRivBib 50 (2002) 209-222 (*Cardellini, Innocenzo*).

11 BUSSAGLI, Mario: Oriente & Occidente: convegno in ricordo di Mario Bussagli: Roma, 31 maggio-1 giugno 1999. EAntonini, Chiara S.; Alfieri, Bianca M.; Santoro, Arcangela: Pisa 2002, Istituti Editoriali e Poligrafici Internazionali 299 pp. 88-8147-254-6.

12 CANCIK, Hubert; CANCIK-LINDEMAIER, Hildegard: Ἐπτομή τῆς οἰκουμένης: Studien zur römischen Religion in Antike und Neuzeit EAuffarth, Ch.; Rüpke, J.: Potsdamer Altertumswissenschaftliche Beiträge 6: Wsb 2002, Steiner 284 pp. €48. 3-515-08210-7.

13 CARROLL, Robert P.: Sense and sensitivity: essays on reading the bible in memory of Robert Carroll. EDavies, Philip R.; Hunter, Alastair G.: JSOT.S 348: L 2002, Sheffield A. xix; 480 pp. £65. 0-8264-6049-6. Bibl. 457-462.

14 CATCHPOLE, David R.: Christology, controversy and community. EHorrell, David G.; Tuckett, Christopher: NT.S 99: 2000 ⇒16,25. RCBQ 64 (2002) 608-10 (*Martin, Francis*); BBR 12 (2002) 297-300 (*Evans, Craig A.*); RBLit 4 (2002) 299-301 (*Crook, Zeba Antonin*).

15 CIASCA, Antonia: Da Pyrgi a Mozia: studi sull'archeologia del Mediterraneo in memoria di Antonia Ciasca. EAmadasi Guzzo, Maria Giulia; Liverani, Mario; Matthiae, Paolo: Vicino Oriente—Quaderno 3/1-2: R 2002, "La Sapienza" 2 vols. Bibl. Antonia Ciasca vol. 1, iii-ix.

16 CLARKE, Ernest G.: Targum and scripture: studies in Aramaic translations and interpretation in memory of Ernest G. Clarke. EFlesher, Paul V.M.: Studies in the Aramaic interp. of Scripture 2: Lei 2002, Brill xxv; 327 pp. €99/$115. 90-04-12677-5. Bibl. 291-309, Clarke xv-xvii.

17 CLASSEN, Carl Joachim: Antike Rhetorik und ihre Rezeption. EDöpp, Siegmar: 1999 ⇒15,17. RLatomus 61 (2002) 231-233 (*Aubrion, Etienne*).

18 CROATTO, José Severino: Los caminos inexhauribles de la palabra. EHansen, Guillermo: 2000 ⇒17,20. RRevBib 64 (2002) 123-125 (*Conti, Cristina*).

19 CROSS, Frank Moore, Jr.: Frank Moore Cross volume. ELevine, Baruch A., al.: ErIs 26: 1999 ⇒15,20; 16,32. RCV 44 (2002) 198-202 (*Segert, Stanislav*).

20 CULLEY, Robert C.: The labour of reading. EBlack, Fiona C.; Boer, Roland; Runions, Erin: SBL Semeia Studies 36: 1999 ⇒15,21. RABR 50 (2002) 93-95 (*Elvey, Anne*).

21 DARIS, Sergio: Studium atque urbanitas: miscellanea in onore di Sergio Daris. ECapasso, Mario; Pernigotti, Sergio: Papyrologica Lupiensia 9: Galatina (Le) 2001, Congedo 410 pp. 88-8086-3878. Bibl. 399-405.

22 DAVID, Yona: Studies in Hebrew literature of the Middle Ages and Renaissance in honor of Prof. Yona David. ERosen, T.; Holtzman. A.: Te'uda 19: J 2002, Tel Aviv Univ. 386 + 60* pp.

23 DE GRUCHY, John W.: Theology in dialogue: the impact of the arts, humanities, and science on contemporary religious thought: essays in honor of John W. de Gruchy. EHolness, Lyn; Wüstenberg, Ralf K.: GR 2002, Eerdmans xxvi; 286 pp. £29/$40. 0-8028-3916-9.

24 DELOBEL, Joël: New Testament textual criticism and exegesis: Festschrift J. Delobel. EDenaux, Adelbert: BEThL 161: Lv 2002, Peeters xviii; 391 pp. €60. 90-429-1085-2. Bibl. xi-xviii. RSNTU.A 27 (2002) 276-278 (*Fuchs, Albert*).

25 DESROCHES NOBLECOURT, Christiane: La femme dans les civilisations orientales et miscellanea aegyptologica. ᴱCannuyer, Christian; Fredericq-Homes, D.: Acta Orientalia Belgica 15: 2001 ⇒17,22. ᴿMSR 59/2 (2002) 95-96 (*Nocquet, Dany*).

26 DEURLOO, Karel Adriaan: Unless some one guide me. ᴱVan Midden, P.J.: ACBET.S 2: 2001 ⇒17,23. ᴿEThL 78 (2002) 185-187 (*Lust, J.*).

27 DIAKONOFF, Igor Michailovitch: History and languages of ancient Orient: I.M. Diakonoff memorial volume. ᴱLivsis, V.A.; Medvedskaja, I.N.; Jakobson, V.A.: St. Petersburg 2002, Institute of Oriental Studies 412 pp. 5-85803-202-8. ᴿUF 34 (2002) 964-967 (*Heltzer, M.*).

28 DIETRICH, Manfried: Ex Mesopotamia et Syria Lux: Festschrift für Manfried Dietrich zu seinem 65. Geburtstag. ᴱLoretz, Oswald; Metzler, Kai Alexander; Schaudig, Hanspeter: AOAT 281: Müns 2002, Ugarit-Verlag xxxv; 950 pp. 3-927120-99-5. Bibl. xiii-xxxv.

29 DIETRICH, Wendell S.: Ethical monotheism, past and present. ᴱVial, Theodore M.; Hadley, Mark A.: BJSt 329: 2001 ⇒17,24. ᴿRBLit (2002)* (*Hamilton, Mark Wade*).

30 DION, Paul Eugène: The world of the Aramaeans. ᴱDaviau, Michèle; Wevers, John William; Weigl, Michael: JSOT.S 324-6: 2001 ⇒17, 25. ᴿThLZ 127 (2002) 1023-1027 (*Weippert, Manfred*).

31 DOTHAN, Trude: Mediterranean peoples in transition. ᴱGitin, Sy; Mazar, Amihai; Stern, Ephraim: 1998 ⇒14,23; 15,24. ᴿJNES 61 (2002) 148-149 (*Hallotte, Rachel S.*).

32 DUCHESNE-GUILLEMIN, Jacques: L'autre, l'étranger, sports et loisirs: Jacques Duchesne-Guillemin in honorem. ᴱCannuyer, Christian, al.: Acta Orientalia Belgica 16: Bru 2002, Société Belge d'Études Orientales xix; 248 pp.

33 EGGEBRECHT, Arne: Festschrift Arne Eggebrecht zum 65. Geburtstag am 12. März 2000. ᴱSchmitz, Bettina: HÄB 48: Hildesheim 2002, Gerstenberg xv; 143 pp. €39. 3-8067-8140-0. Bibl. Eggebrecht xi-xv.

34 ERNST, Josef: Schrift und Tradition: ᴱBackhaus, Knut; Untergaßmair, Franz Georg: 1996 ⇒12,23; 15,28. ᴿTheoforum 33 (2002) 239-240 (*Laberge, Léo*).

35 ESTRADA-VILARRASA, Alberto: Colores y palabras: homenaje a Alberto Estrada-Vilarrasa, editor de Aula Orientalis. ᴱOlmo Lete, Gregorio del: AuOr 20/1-2 (2002) 7-310.

36 FATUM, Lone: Køn & bibel: skrifterne, kvinderne og kristendommene. ᴱPetterson, Christina; Holst, Søren; Nielsen, Jesper Tang: K 2002, ANIS 223 pp [SEÅ 68,224s—Stenström, Hanna].

37 FEE, Gordon: Romans and the people of God. ᴱSoderlund, Sven K.; Wright, N.T.: 1999 ⇒15,29; 16,37. ᴿEThL 78 (2002) 222-223 (*Verheyden, J.*); EvQ 74 (2002) 181-183 (*Mohrmann, Douglas C.*).

38 FLANAGAN, James W.: 'Imagining' biblical worlds: studies in spatial, social and historical constructs in honor of James W. Flanagan. ᴱGunn, David M.; McNutt, Paula M.: L 2002, Sheffield A. ix; 336 pp. £75. 0-8264-6149-2. Bibl. 297-326, of Flanagan 10-12.

39 FOERSTER, Gideon: What Athens has to do with Jerusalem: essays on classical, Jewish, and early christian art and archaeology in honor of Gideon Foerster. ᴱRutgers, Leonard Victor: Interdisciplinary studies in ancient culture and religion 1: Lv 2002, Peeters ix; 600 pp. 90-429-1122-0. Bibl. 535-591.

40 FRERICHS, Ernest S.: Hesed ve-Emet: ᴱMagness, Jodi; Titin, Seymour: BJSt 320: 1998 ⇒14,28...17,33. ᴿBiOr 59 (2002) 126-129 (*Barstad, Hans M.*).

41 FUCHS, Albert: Forschungen zum Neuen Testament und seiner Umwelt: Festschrift für Albert Fuchs. ᴱNiemand, Christoph: Linzer Philosophisch-Theologische Beiträge 7: Fra 2002, Lang 424 pp. €60.30. 3-631-37714-2. Bibl. Albert Fuchs 419-422.

42 FUSCO, Vittorio: Mysterium regni ministerium verbi (Mc 4,11; At 6, 4). ᴱFranco, Ettore: SRivBib 38: 2000 ⇒16,40. ᴿVerbum Vitae 2 (2002) 306-309 (Witczyk, Henryk).

43 GALLO, Italo: Scritti in onore di Italo Gallo. ᴱTorraca, Luigi: Pubblicazioni dell'Univ. degli studi di Salerno; sezione atti, convegni, miscellanee 59: N 2002, Ed. Scientifiche Italiane 591 pp. 88-495-0171-4.

44 GELSTON, Anthony: New heaven and new earth prophecy and the millennium. ᴱHarland, Peter J.; Hayward, Robert: VT.S 77: 1999 ⇒15,35; 16,42. ᴿRBLit 4 (2002) 203-205 (Munoz, Francisco V.).

45 GEOLTRAIN, Pierre: Apocryphité: histoire d'un concept transversal aux religions du livre: en hommage à Pierre Geoltrain. ᴱMimouni, Simon C.: BEHE.R 113: Turnhout 2002, Brepols (8) 333 pp. 2-503-51349-2.

46 GILBERT, Maurice: Toute la sagesse du monde. ᴱMies, Françoise: 1999 ⇒15,36...17,35. ᴿRivBib 50 (2002) 86-93 (Milani, Marcello); CDios 215 (2002) 669-670 (Gutiérrez, J.);

47 Treasures of wisdom: studies in Ben Sira... Wisdom: ᴱCalduch Benages, Nuria; Vermeylen, Jacques: BEThL 143: 1999 ⇒15,37...17,34. ᴿBZ 46 (2002) 116-118 (Jüngling, Hans-Winfried); CDios 215 (2002) 318-319 (Gutiérrez, J.); LouvSt 27 (2002) 177-178 (Eynikel, Erik).

48 GNILKA, Christian: Alvarium: Festschrift für Christian Gnilka. ᴱBlümer, Wilhelm; Henke, Rainer; Mülke, Markus: JAC.E 33: Müns 2002, Aschendorff xii; (2) 405 pp. €73.50. 3-402-08119-9. Bibl. ix-xi.

49 GOPHNA, Ram: In quest of ancient settlements and landscapes: archaeological studies in honour of Ram Gophna. ᴱVan den Brink, Edwin C.M.; Yannai, Eli: J 2002, Ramot 288 pp. $36. 965-274-3445.

50 GREENFIELD, Jonas C.: Solving riddles and untying knots. ᴱZevit, Ziony; Gitin, Seymour; Sokoloff, Michael: 1995 ⇒11/1,11; 13,35. ᴿBASOR 325 (2002) 90-92 (Halpern, Baruch).

51 GREER, Rowan A.: Reading in christian communities: essays on interpretation in the early church. ᴱBobertz, Charles A.; Brakke, David: Christianity and Judaism in Antiquity 14: ND 2002, University of Notre Dame Press xi; 233 pp. $35/19. 0-268-03165-7/04017-6.

52 GRIFFIN, Miriam: Philosophy and power in the Graeco-Roman world: essays in honor of Miriam Griffin: ᴱClark, Gillian; Rajak, T.: Oxf 2002, OUP xvii; 348 pp. £45/$72. 0-1982-9990-7.

53 GÜNTHER, Hartmut: Wortlaute: Festschrift für Dr. Hartmut Günther. ᴱSchillhahn, Wolfgang; Schätzel, Michael: Groß Oesingen 2002, Harms 459 pp. 3-86147-225-8.

54 GÜTERBOCK, Hans Gustav: Recent developments in Hittite archaeology and history: papers in memory of Hans G. Güterbock. ᴱYener, K. Aslihan; Hoffner, Harry Angier: WL 2002, Eisenbrauns vi; 212 pp. 1-57506-053-1. Collab. Dhesi, Simrit.

55 HAAG, Ernst: Schöpfungsplan und Heilsgeschichte: Festschrift für Ernst Haag zum 70. Geburtstag. ᴱBrandscheidt, Renate; Mende, Theresia: Trier 2002, Paulinus 410 pp. €29.70. 3-7902-1299-7. Bibl. Ernst Haag 397-407.

56 HAGEN, Kenneth: Ad fontes Lutheri: toward the recovery of the real LUTHER. ᴱMaschke, Timothy; Posset, Franz; Skocir, Joan: 2001 ⇒ 17,40. ᴿSCJ 33 (2002) 1161-1163 (Haemig, Mary Jane).

57 HAMMANN, Gottfried: Histoire et herméneutique: mélanges offerts à Gottfried Hammann. ᴱ**Rose, M.**: HistSoc 45: Genève 2002, Labor et F. 443 pp. €39. 2-8309-1068-0.

58 HANSEN, Donald P.: Leaving no stones unturned: essays on the ancient Near East and Egypt in honor of Donald P. Hansen. ᴱ**Ehrenberg, Erica**: WL 2002, Eisenbrauns xii; 323 pp. $49.50. 1-57506-055-8.

59 HOHEISEL, Karl: Hairesis: Festschrift für Karl Hoheisel zum 65. Geburtstag. ᴱ**Hutter, Manfred; Klein, Wassilios; Vollmer, Ulrich**: JAC.E 34: Müns 2002, Aschendorff xix; 538 pp. €108. 3-402-08120-2.

60 HÜBNER, Hans: Paulinische Christologie. ᴱ**Schnelle, Udo; Söding, Thomas**: 2000 ⇒16,54. ᴿJThS 53 (2002) 250-253 (*Wedderburn, A.J.M.*).

61 IMPARATI, Fiorella: Anatolia Antica: studi in memoria di Fiorella Imparati. ᴱ**De Martino, Stefano; Pecchioli Daddi, Franca**: Eothen 11: F 2002, LoGisma 2 vols. 88-87621-22-5.

62 JACOBSEN, Thorkild: Riches hidden in secret places: ancient Near Eastern studies in memory of T...Jacobsen. ᴱ**Abusch, I.** Tzvi: WL 2002, Eisenbrauns xxvii; 333 pp. $45. 1-57506-061-2. Bibl. Jacobsen ix-xvii.

63 JANZEN, Waldemar: Reclaiming the Old Testament. ᴱ**Zerbe, Gordon**: 2001 ⇒17,54. ᴿCBQ 64 (2002) 602-3 (*Smith-Christopher, Daniel L.*).

64 JASTROW, Otto: 'Sprich doch mit deinen Knechten aramäisch, wir verstehen es!': 60 Beiträge zur Semitistik: Festschrift für O...Jastrow zum 60. Geburtstag. ᴱ**Arnold, Werner; Bobzin, Hartmut**: Wsb 2002, Harrassowitz xxii; 876 pp. 34470-44918 [WZKM 93,324s—S.Procházka].

65 KAISER, Otto: Gerechtigkeit und Leben im hellenistischen Zeitalter. ᴱ**Jeremias, Jörg**: BZAW 296: 2001 ⇒17,56. ᴿThLZ 127 (2002) 1027-1029 (*Sauer, Georg*).

66 KEMPINSKI, Aharon: Aharon Kempinski memorial volume: studies in archaeology and related disciplines. ᴱ**Aḥituv, Shmuel; Oren, Eliezer D.**: Beer-Sheva 15: Beer-Sheva 2002, Ben-Gurion Univ. Pr. viii; 526 pp. $65. 0334-2255. Num. ill.

67 KLAWEK, Aleksy: Mogilany 1995. ᴱ**Kapera, Zdzislaw J.**: Qumranica Mogilanensia 15: 1998 ⇒14,51; 15,51. ᴿCV 44 (2002) 195-198 (*Segert, Stanislav*).

68 KUHN, Heinz-Wolfgang: Das Ende der Tage und die Gegenwart des Heils. ᴱ**Becker, Michael; Fenske, Wolfgang**: AGJU 44: 1999 ⇒15, 56. ᴿDSD 9 (2002) 104-106 (*Swanson, Dwight D.*).

69 KURTH, Gottfried: Jericho und Qumran. ᴱ**Mayer, Bernhard**: ESt 45: 2000 ⇒16,65; 17,60. ᴿBiKi 57 (2002) 53-54 (*Then, Reinhold*); OLZ 97 (2002) 579-581 (*Ballhorn, Egbert*).

70 KYSAR, Robert: Word, theology, and community in John. ᴱ**Painter, John; Culpepper, R. Alan; Segovia, Fernando F.**: St. Louis, Missouri 2002, Chalice xii; 244 pp. $33. 0-8272-4246-8.

71 LAMBERT, Wilfred George: Wisdom, gods and literature. ᴱ**George, A.R.; Finkel, Irving L.**: 2000 ⇒16,66. ᴿBiOr 59 (2002) 98-103 (*Schwemer, Daniel*); Or. 71 (2002) 311-313 (*Dandamayev, M.A.*); OLZ 97 (2002) 358-361 (*Böck, Barbara*).

72 LAMBRECHT, Jan: Resurrection in the New Testament: Festschrift J. Lambrecht. ᴱ**Bieringer, Reimund; Koperski, Veronica; Lataire, Bianca**: BEThL 165: Lv 2002, Univ. Pr. xxxi; 551 pp. €70. 90-42912-14-6. Bibl. Lambrecht xv-xxxi.

73 LEENE, Hendrik: The new things: eschatology in Old Testament prophecy: Festschrift for Henk Leene. ᴱ**Postma, Ferenc; Spronk, Klaas; Talstra, Eep**: Amsterdamse cahiers voor exegese van de bijbel en zijn

tradities, Suppl. 3: Maastricht 2002, Shaker x; 296 pp. 90-423-0190-2. Bibl. Leene 269-275.

74 LEERTOUWER, Lammert: Modern societies & the science of religions: studies in honour of L...Leertouwer. ^EWiegers, Gerard Albert: SHR 95: Lei 2002, Brill viii; 397 pp. 90-04-11665-6. Collab. *Jan Platvoet.*

75 LEVI, Mario Attilio: Lóghios anér: studi di antichità in memoria di Mario Attilio Levi. ^EMichelotto, Pier Giuseppe: Quaderni di ACME 55: Mi 2002, Cisalpino xi; 516 pp. 88-323-4621-4.

76 LONG, Burke O.: "A wise and discerning mind": essays in honor of Burke O. Long. ^EOlyan, Saul M.; Culley, Robert C.: BJSt 325: 2000 ⇒16,70; 17,66. ^RJJS 53 (2002) 159 (*Williamson, H.G.M.*).

77 LÜHRMANN, Dieter: Text und Geschichte. ^EMaser, Stefan: MThSt 50: 1999 ⇒15,61. ^RSNTU.A 27 (2002) 278-280 (*Fuchs, Albert*).

78 MIKAT, Paul: Rom und das himmlische Jerusalem: die frühen Christen zwischen Anpassung und Ablehnung. ^EHaehling, Raban von: 2000 ⇒ 16,76; 17,72. ^RREA 104 (2002) 279 (*Maraval, Pierre*).

79 MILLAR, Fergus: Representations of Empire: Rome and the Mediterranean world. ^EBowman, Alan K.; Cotton, Hannah M.: Proceedings of the British Academy 114: Oxf 2002, OUP xii; 196 pp. £20. 0-19-726276-7. Conference 2000: London/Oxford; Bibl. Millar 181-188.

80 NEUMANN, Günter: Novalis indogermanica: Festschrift für Günter Neumann zum 80. Geburtstag. ^EZeilfelder, Susanne; Fritz, Matthias: Grazer Vergleichende Arbeiten 17: Graz 2002, Leykam v; 562 pp. 3701-1-0032-2.

81 NICKELSBURG, George W.E.: For a later generation: the transformation of tradition. ^EArgall, Randal A.; Bow, Beverly A.; Werline, Rodney Alan: 2000 ⇒16,79. ^RJEarlyC 10 (2002) 133-135 (*Kraus, Janice A.*); CBQ 64 (2002) 198-200 (*Murphy, Frederick J.*).

82 NILES, Daniel P.: Scripture, community, and mission: essays in honor of D. Preman Niles. ^EWickeri, Philip L.: Hong Kong 2002, Christian Conference of Asia xv; 367 pp. 962-7439-32-0. Bibl. Niles 363-365.

83 NISSEN, Hans Jörg: Material culture and mental spheres: Rezeption archäologischer Denkrichtungen in der vorderasiatischen Altertumskunde: internationales Symposium für Hans J. Nissen: Berlin Juni 2000. ^EHausleiter, Arnulf; Kerner, Susanne; Müller-Neuhof, Bernd: AOAT 293: Müns 2002, Ugarit-Verlag xii; 391 pp. €88. 39346-28222.

84 NORTH, J.L.: The Old Testament in the New Testament. ^EMoyise, Steve: JSNT.S 189: 2000 ⇒16,80; 17,79. ^RRBLit 4 (2002) 309-312 (*Albl, Martin C.*).

85 O'BRIEN, Peter: The gospel to the nations. ^EBolt, Peter; Thompson, Mark: 2000 ⇒16,82; 17,80. ^REvangel 20 (2002) 92-93 (*Van Neste, Ray*); SBET 20 (2002) 219-221 (*Adams, Edward*).

86 O'COLLINS, Gerald Glynn: The convergence of theology. ^EKendall, Daniel; Davis, Stephen T.: 2001 ⇒17,81. ^RDoLi 52 (2002) 441-442 (*Flanagan, Donal*).

87 PARROT, André: Recueil d'études à la mémoire d'André Parrot. ^ECharpin, Dominique; Durand, Jean-Marie: Florilegium Marianum 6; Mémoires de NABU 7: P 2002, SEPOA 570 pp.

88 PASQUATO, Ottorino: Historiam perscrutari: miscellanea di studi offerti al prof. Ottorino Pasquato. ^EMaritano, Mario: BSRel 180: R 2002, LAS 882 pp. €50. 88-213-0513-9. Pres. Card. P. Poupard [RTL 35, 106s—J.-M. Auwers.]

89 PATTE, Daniel: Reading communities reading scripture: essays in honor of Daniel Patte. ᴱPhillips, Gary A.; Duran, Nicole W.: Harrisburg, PA 2002, Trinity xvi; 393 pp. $47. 15633-83691. Bibl. Patte 383-91.

90 POMPEDDA, Mario Francesco: Studi in onore del Cardinale Mario Francesco Pompedda. ᴱCabizzosu, Tonino: Cagliari 2002, Della Torre xxvii; 394 pp. €30. 88-7343-357-X.

91 POPKO, Maciej: Silva Anatolica: Anatolian studies presented to Maciej Popko on the occasion of his 65th birthday. ᴱTaracha, Piotr: Wsz 2002, Agade xxviii; 369 pp. 83-87111-12-0. Bibl. Popko xix-xxviii.

92 POTGIETER, Pieter C.: Essentialia et hodierna: oblata P.C. Potgieter. ᴱTolmie, D. Francois: Acta Theologica Suppl. 3: Bloemfontein 2002, Univ. of the Free State xi; 186 pp. 0-8688-66725. Bibl. Potgieter 9-16.

93 PURY, Albert de: Jacob: commentaire à plusieurs voix de Gen 25-36. ᴱMacchi, Jean-Daniel; Römer, Thomas: MoBi 44: 2001 ⇒17,89. ᴿHebStud 43 (2002) 255-256 (Van Wolde, Ellen).

94 QUAEGEBEUR, Jan: Egyptian religion the last thousand years. ᴱClarysse, Willy; Schoors, Antoon; Willems, Harco: OLA 84-85: 1998 ⇒14,94; 16,91. ᴿDiscEg 53 (2002) 93-112 (Graindorge, Catherine).

95 QUISPEL, Gilles: From POIMANDRES to Jacob BÖHME: gnosis, hermetism and the christian tradition. ᴱVan den Broek, Roelof; Van Heertum, Cis: 2001 ⇒17,90. ᴿJThS 53 (2002) 323-325 (Wilson, R. McL.).

96 RATZINGER, Kardinal Josef [BENEDIKT XVI]: Weggemeinschaft des Glaubens: Kirche als Communio: Festgabe zum 75. Geburtstag. ᴱHorn, Otto; Pfnür, Vinzenz: Augsburg 2002, Sankt-Ulrich 325 pp. 3-929-246-805. FS32.10.

97 RÄISÄNEN, Heikki: Fair play: diversity and conflicts in early christianity: essays in honour of Heikki Räisänen. ᴱDunderberg, Ismo; Tuckett, Christopher M.; Syreeni, Kari A.: NT.S 103: Lei 2002, Brill xii; 592 pp. €120. 90-04-12359-8.

98 REINHARDT, Heinrich J.F.: Akktuelle Beiträge zum Kirchenrecht: Festgabe für Heinrich J.F. Reinhardt zum 60. Geburtstag. ᴱAlthaus, Rüdiger; Oehmen-Vieregge, Rosel; Olschewski, Jürgen: Adnotationes in ius canonicum 24: Fra 2002, Lang 346 pp. €50.10. 3-631-39133-1.

99 RICHARDSON, Peter: Text and artifact in the religions of Mediterranean antiquity. ᴱWilson, Stephen G.; Desjardins, Michel: 2000 ⇒16,97; 17,93. ᴿRBLit (2002)* (Stoutenburg, Dennis C.).

100 RIGAL, Jean: L'Église à la croisée des chemins: hommage amical à Jean Rigal. ᴱDebergé, P.: Théologies: P 2002, Cerf 241 pp. €29. 2-204-07030-0 [NRTh 125,647s—Detienne, P.].

101 RITSCHL, Dietrich: Metapher und Wirklichkeit: die Logik der Bildhaftigkeit im Reden von Gott, Mensch und Natur: Dietrich Ritschl zum 70. Geburtstag. ᴱBernhardt, Reinhold; Link-Wieczorek, Ulrike: Gö 1999, Vandenhoeck & R. 346 pp.

102 ROBERT, Fernand: Dieux, héros et médecins grecs. ᴱWoronoff, Michel; Follet, Simone; Jouanna, Jacques: Littératures et civilisations antiques: 2001 ⇒17,94. ᴿREA 104 (2002) 575-7 (Cusset, Christophe).

103 ROBINSON, James M.: From quest to Q. ᴱAsgeirsson, Jon Ma.; De Troyer, Kristin; Meyer, Marvin W.: BEThL 146: 2000 ⇒16,100; 17,96. ᴿBZ 46 (2002) 293-296 (Ettl, Claudio); SNTU.A 27 (2002) 273-276 (Fuchs, Albert).

104 ROETZEL, Calvin J.: Pauline conversations in context: essays in honor of Calvin J. Roetzel. ᴱAnderson, Janice Capel; Sellew, Philip; Setzer, Claudia J.: JSNT.S 221: L 2002, Sheffield A. xiv; 295 pp. $115. 1-84127-264-7. Bibl. 262-282.

105 ROLOFF, Jürgen: Kirche und Volk Gottes. ^E**Karrer, Martin; Kraus, Wolfgang; Merk, Otto**: 2000 ⇒16,102. ^RSNTU.A 27 (2002) 280-281 (*Fuchs, Albert*).

106 SANDELIN, Karl-Gustav: A bouquet of wisdom. ^E**Illman, Karl-Johan**: Religionsvetenskapliga skrifter 48: 2000 ⇒16,104. ^RStPhiloA 14 (2002) 238-239 (*Runia, David T.*).

107 SAUER, James A.: The archaeology of Jordan and beyond. ^E**Stager, Lawrence E.; Greene, Joseph A.; Coogan, Michael D.**: 2000 ⇒16, 105; 17,98. ^RRBLit (2002)* (*Ferrara, Enzo*).

108 SCHENKE, Hans-Martin: For the children, perfect instruction: studies in honor of Hans-Martin Schenke on the occasion of the Berliner Arbeitskreis für koptisch-gnostische Schriften's thirtieth year. ^E**Bethge, Hans-Gebhard**, *al.*, NHS 54: Lei 2002, Brill xiv; 447 pp. 90-04-12672-4. Bibl. Schenke 47-64.

109 SCHENKER, Adrian: La double transmission du texte biblique. ^E**Goldman, Yohanan; Uehlinger, Christoph**: OBO 179: 2001 ⇒17,100. ^RJNSL 28/1 (2002) 118-122 (*Cook, Johann*).

110 SCHNEIDER, Herbert: Led by the Spirit: Festschrift in honor of Herbert Schneider, SJ on the occasion of his 65th birthday. ^E**Locker, Markus Ekkehard**: Ch 2002, Loyola school of Theology xiii; 193 pp.

111 SCHOTTROFF, Luise: Transgressors: toward a feminist biblical theology. ^E**Janssen, Claudia; Ochtendung, Ute; Wehn, Beate**: ^T*Maloney, Linda M.*: ColMn 2002, Glazier xiv; 182 pp. $30. 0-8146-5094-5.

112 SIRAT, René-Samuel; SULTAN, Claude: Tracer le chemin': mélanges offerts aux professeurs René-Samuel Sirat et Claude Sultan. ^E**Iancu, Carol**: Montpellier 2002, Univ. Valéry 222 pp.

113 SMEND, Rudolf: Vergegenwärtigung des Alten Testaments: Beiträge zur biblischen Hermeneutik: Festschrift für Rudolf Smend zum 70. Geburtstag. ^E**Bultmann, Christoph; Dietrich, Walter; Levin, Christoph**: Gö 2002, Vandenhoeck & R. 496 pp. 3-525-53621-6.

114 SMITH, Harry S.: Studies on ancient Egypt. ^E**Leahy, Anthony; Tait, John Gavin**: Occasional Publications 13: 1999 ⇒15,86; 17,103. ^RAJA 106 (2002) 611-613 (*Smith, Stuart Tyson*).

115 STACHEL, Günter: Meditatio: Beiträge zur Theologie und Religionspädagogik der Spiritualität: Günter Stachel zum 80. Geburtstag. ^E**Simon, W.**: Forum Theologie und Pädagogik: Müns 2002, LIT viii; 429 pp. 3-8258-6035-3 [ThLZ 128,1145s—Christian Grethlein].

116 STECK, Odil Hannes: Schriftauslegung in der Schrift. ^E**Kratz, Reinhard G.; Krüger, Thomas; Schmid, Konrad**: BZAW 300: 2000 ⇒ 16,110. ^RBZ 46 (2002) 319-320 (*Jüngling, Hans-Winfried*).

117 STEINGRÍMSSON, Sigurdur Örn: "Wer darf hinaufsteigen zum Berg JHWHs?": Beiträge zu Prophetie und Poesie des Alten Testaments: Festschrift für Sigurdur Örn Steingrímsson zum 70. Geburtstag. ^E**Irsigler, Hubert**: ATSAT 72: St. Ottilien 2002, EOS x; 345 pp. 3-8306-71-24-5. Mitarbeit von *Kristinn Olason*; Bibl. Steingrímsson 343-345.

118 STENDAHL, Krister: Paul and politics. ^E**Horsley, Richard A.**: 2000 ⇒ 16,112. ^RCrossCur 52/1 (2002) 136-142 (*Chapman, G. Clarke*); Miss. 30 (2002) 420-421 (*Carriker, Tim*).

119 THOMA, Clemens: Lesarten des jüdisch-christlichen Dialoges: Festschrift zum 70. Geburtstag von Clemens Thoma. ^E**Käppeli, Silvia**: JudChr 20: Bern 2002, Lang 369 pp. 3-906769-53-4.

120 THOMPSON, William G.: The gospel of Matthew in current study. ^E**Aune, David Edward**: 2001 ⇒17,108. ^RVJTR 66 (2002) 783-786 (*Raj, M.I.*); RBLit (2002)* (*Vinson, Richard B.*).

121 TOWNER, W. Sibley: God who creates. ^EBrown, William P.; Mc-
Bride, S. Dean: 2000 ⇒16,115. ^RHebStud 43 (2002) 250-252 (Clifford, Richard J.).

122 TREVIJANO ETCHEVERRIA, Ramón: Plenitudo temporis: miscelánea homenaje al Prof. Dr. Ramón Trevijano Etcheverría. ^EFernández Sangrador, Jorge Juan; Guijarro Oporto, Santiago: BSal.E 249: S 2002,
Publicaciones Universidad Pontificia 560 pp. €23. 84-729-9544-5.

123 TUDDA, Francesco: Liber Scripturae: miscellanea in onore del prof. P.
Francesco Tudda ofm. ^ELopasso, Vincenzo; Parisi, Serafino: Teologia e teologi 3: Soveria Mannelli (Catanzaro) 2002, Rubbettino 217 pp.
88-498-0368-0.

124 VAN SETERS, John: Rethinking the foundations: historiography in the
ancient world and in the bible. ^EMcKenzie, Steven L.; Römer, Thomas: BZAW 294: 2000 ⇒16,117. ^RETR 77 2002) 120-121 (Vincent,
Jean M.); WO 32 (2002) 241-242 (Koenen, Klaus).

125 VEENHOF, Klaas R.: Veenhof anniversary volume: studies presented to
Klaas R. Veenhof on the occasion of his sixty-fifth birthday. ^EVan
Soldt, Wilfred Hugo: UNHAII 89: 2001 ⇒17,111. ^RBiOr 59 (2002)
344-348 (Lion, Brigitte).

126 VERSNEL, Hendrik Simon: Kykeon: studies in honour of H.S. Versnel.
^EHorstmanshoff, H.F.J.; Singor, H.W., al.: RGRW 142: Lei 2002,
Brill viii; 228 pp. 90-04-11983-3.

127 VOGLER, Werner: Leqach 1: Mitteilungen und Beiträge. 2001 ⇒17,
112. Forschungsstelle Judentum an der Theologischen Fakultät Leipzig. ^ROLZ 97 (2002) 396-398 (Wächter, Ludwig).

128 WAHL, Otto: Ein Gott für die Menschen: Festschrift für Otto Wahl
SDB zum 70. Geburtstag. Benediktbeurer Studien 9: Mü 2002, Don
Bosco 406 pp. €22.50. 3-7698-13642 [ZKTh 125,85—Fischer, Georg].

129 WALDENFELS, Hans: Faszination Gott: Hans Waldenfels zum 70. Geburtstag. ^ESonnemans, H.; Fößel, Th.: Pd 2002, Bonifatius 183 pp.
€12.90. 3-89710-233-1.

130 WALKER, Christopher: Mining the archives: Festschrift for Christopher
Walker on the occasion of his 60th birthday 4 October 2002.
^EWunsch, Cornelia: Babylonische Archive 1: Dresden 2002, Islet x;
374 pp. Bibl. Walker 365-368.

131 WALTKE, Bruce K.: The way of wisdom: essays in honor of Bruce K.
Waltke. ^EPacker, James I.; Soderlund, Sven K.: GR 2000, Zondervan xviii; 332 pp. 0-310-22728-3. Bibl. Waltke 327-332.

132 WEDDERBURN, Alexander J.M.: Paul, Luke and the Graeco-Roman
world: essays in honour of Alexander J.M. Wedderburn. ^EChristo-
phersen, Alf, al.: JSNT.S 217: L 2002, Sheffield A. xvi; 290 pp. £65.
1-84127-259-0.

133 WEIPPERT, Manfred: Kein Land für sich allein: Studien zum Kulturkontakt in Kanaan, Israel/Palästina und Ebirnâri für Manfred Weippert
zum 65. Geburtstag. ^EHübner, Ulrich; Knauf, Ernst Axel: OBO 186:
Gö 2002, Vandenhoeck & R. viii; 331 pp. FS98. 3-525-53043-9. Bibl.
Weippert 309-318.

134 WHITE, Reginald E.O.: Baptism, the New Testament and the church.
^EPorter, Stanley E.; Cross, Anthony R.: JSNT.S 171: 1999 ⇒15,99.
^REvQ 74 (2002) 272-275 (Griffith, Terry); LASBF 52 (2002) 575-579
(Casalini, Nello).

135 WILD, John Peter: The Roman textile industry and its influence: a
birthday tribute to John Peter Wild. ^EWalton, Penelope; Jorgensen,

Lisa Bender; Rast-Eicher, Antoinette: Oxf 2001, Oxbow xiii; 200 pp. $35. 1-84217-046-5. 127 fig.
136 WILKEN, Robert Louis: In dominico eloquio: in lordly eloquence: essays on patristic exegesis in honor of...Wilken. ᴱBlowers, Paul M., *al.*: GR 2002, Eerdmans xvi; 438 pp. $45. 0-8028-3882-0. Bibl. 427-438.

A1.2 Miscellanea *unius* auctoris

137 Adamo, David Tuesday Explorations in African biblical studies. 2001 ⇒17,116. ᴿOTEs 15 (2002) 551-553 (*Wendland, E.R.*).
138 Baeck, Leo Aus drei Jahrtausenden; das Evangelium als Urkunde der jüdischen Glaubensgeschichte. ᴱ*Friedlander, Albert H.; Klappert, Bertold; Licharz, Werner*: Leo Baeck Werke 4: 2000 ⇒17,119. ᴿSNTU.A 27 (2002) 283-284 (*Fuchs, Albert*).
139 Barbiero, Gianni Studien zu alttestamentlichen Texten. SBAB 34: Stu 2002, Katholisches Bibelwerk 303 pp. €41. 3-460-06341-6.
140 Bartelmus, Rüdiger Auf der Suche nach dem archimedischen Punkt der Textinterpretation: Studien zu einer philologisch-linguistisch fundierten Exegese alttestamentlicher Texte. Z 2002, Pano viii; 405 pp. €19.50. 3-9075-7643-8.
141 Barton, Stephen C. Life together: family, sexuality and community in the New Testament and today. 2001 ⇒17,121. ᴿJThS 53 (2002) 288-290 (*Meeks, Wayne A.*); HeyJ 43 (2002) 509-510 (*Briggs, Richard*); ASEs 19 (2002) 281-283 (*Balch, David*).
142 Bauckham, Richard God and the crisis of freedom: biblical and contemporary perspectives. LVL 2002, Westminster 221 pp. £13. 0-664-22479-2.
143 Beauchamp, Paul Testament biblique. 2001 ⇒17,124. ᴿÉtudes (Jan. 2002) 125-127 (*Madelin, Henri*); PastSc 21 (2002) 407-409 (*Arnaud, Richard*).
144 Beckwith, Roger T. Calendar and chronology, Jewish and christian. AGJU 33: 1996 ⇒12,112...14,1333. ᴿRB 109 (2002) 632-634 (*Nodet, Étienne*).
145 Blázquez, José María Los pueblos de España y el Mediterráneo en la antigüedad: estudios de arqueología, historia y arte. 2000 ⇒16,134. ᴿAt. 90 (2002) 674-675 (*Mazzocchi, Giuseppe*).
146 Borgen, Peder Early christianity and Hellenistic Judaism. 1996 ⇒12, 116... 16,135. ᴿEvQ 74 (2002) 189-190 (*Marshall, I. Howard*).
147 Bosse-Griffiths, Kate Amarna Studies and other selected papers. ᴱ*Griffiths, John Gwyn*: OBO 182: 2001 ⇒17,128. ᴿArOr 70 (2002) 243-245 (*Kořinková, Jana*); DiscEg 53 (2002) 113-114 (*Van Voss, M. Heerma*).
148 Brelich, Angelo Mitologia, politeismo, magia: e altri studi di storia delle religioni (1956-1977). ᴱ*Xella, Paolo*: Anthropos 38: N 2002, Liguori xii; 182 pp. 88-207-3415-X. Bibl. Brelich 165-172.
149 Breton, Stanislas The word and the cross. ᵀ*Porter, Jacquelyn*: Perspectives in continental philosophy 22: NY 2002 <1981>, Fordham Univ. Pr. xxvii; 154 pp. $35. 0-8232-2158-X [ThD 49,261—W. Charles Heiser].
150 Brox, Norbert Das Frühchristentum: Schriften zur Historischen Theologie. ᴱ*Dünzl, Franz; Fürst, Alfons; Prostmeier, Ferdinand R.*: 2000 ⇒16,136. ᴿThLZ 127 (2002) 772-773 (*Böttrich, Christfried*).

151 **Buber, Martin** Meetings: autobiographical fragments. [E]*Friedman, M. L* 2002, Routledge 113 pp. 0-415-28266-7.

152 **Bultmann, Rudolf Karl** Neues Testament und christliche Existenz: theologische Aufsätze. [E]*Lindemann, Andreas*: UTB 2316: Tü 2002, Mohr S. xxviii; 313 pp. €12.90. 3-8252-2316-7;

153 Theologie als Kritik: ausgewählte Rezensionen und Forschungsberichte. [E]*Dreher, Matthias; Müller, Klaus W.*: Tü 2002, Mohr S. xiv; 638 pp. €104. 31614-74066. [R]SNTU.A 27 (2002) 285-286 (*Fuchs, Albert*).

154 **Ceresko, Anthony R.** Prophets and Proverbs: more studies in Old Testament poetry and biblical religion. Quezon City, Philippines 2002, Claretian xiv; 160 pp. 971-501-929-3.

155 **Chirilă, Ioan** Fragmentarium exegetic (Exegetisches Bruchstück). 2001 ⇒17,134. [R]OrthFor 16 (2002) 266-267 (*Basarab, Mircea*).

156 **Clines, David J.A.** On the way to the postmodern: Old Testament essays, 1967-1998. JSOT.S 292-293: 1998 ⇒14,142; 15,112. [R]SEL 19 (2002) 161-164 (*Scagliarini, Fiorella*).

157 **Cross, Frank Moore** Leaves from an epigrapher's notebook: collected papers in Hebrew and West Semitic palaeography and epigraphy. Harvard Semitic Studies 51: WL 2001, Eisenbrauns xx; 371 pp. 1-57506-911-3.

158 **Davis, Ellen F.** Getting involved with God: rediscovering the Old Testament. 2001 ⇒17,138. [R]AThR 84 (2002) 772-74 (*O'Brien, Julia M.*).

159 **Dietrich, Walter** Theopolitik: Studien zur Theologie und Ethik des Alten Testaments. Neuk 2002, Neuk 297 pp. 3-7887-1914-1;

160 Von David zu den Deuteronomisten: Studien zu den Geschichtsüberlieferungen des Alten Testaments. BWANT 156: Stu 2002, Kohlhammer 280 pp. €35.50. 3-17-017260-3.

161 **Dossetti, Giuseppe** La parola di Dio seme di vita e di fede incorruttibile. Momenti della chiesa italiana: Bo 2002, EDB 232 pp. Ed. Piccola famiglia dell'Annunziata; Pref. *Luciano Monari* [RivBib 51,252s— Mela, Roberto].

162 **Ehrlich, Ernst Ludwig** Reden über das Judentum. [E]*Stegemann, Ekkehard W.*: 2001 ⇒17,140. [R]FrRu 9 (2002) 208-210 (*Mußner, Franz*).

163 **Fee, Gordon D.** To what end exegesis?: essays textual, exegetical, and theological. 2001 ⇒17,143. [R]RTR 61 (2002) 103-104 (*Hood, Jared*).

164 **Fitzmyer, Joseph A.** The Dead Sea scrolls and christian origins. 2000 ⇒16,156; 17,146. [R]DSD 9 (2002) 111-112 (*Hempel, Charlotte*); HeyJ 43 (2002) 362-363 (*King, Nicholas*); RBLit 4 (2002) 275-280 (*Lukaszewski, Albert L.*); LTP 58 (2002) 369-371 (*Poirier, Paul-Hubert*).

165 **Flusser, David** Esejské dobrodružství—židovské společenství od mrtvého moře: čeho si jze povšimnout u Ježíše, Pavla, Didaché a Martina Bubera. [T]*Sláma, Petr*: 1999 ⇒16,157. [R]CV 44 (2002) 122-125 (*Segert, Stanislav*). Czech.

166 **Forte, Bruno** La esencia del cristianismo. [T]*Carda, José María*: Verdad e imagen 159: S 2002, Sígueme 186 pp. €14. 84-301-1469-6.

167 **Freyne, Sean** Texts, contexts, and cultures: essays on biblical topics. Dublin 2002, Veritas 265 pp. €20. 1-85390-626-3;

168 Galilee and gospel: collected essays. WUNT 125: 2000 ⇒16,159; 17, 148. [R]TJT 18 (2002) 261-263 (*Kloppenberg Verbin, John S.*).

169 **Frye, Northrop** Northrop FRYE on religion: excluding 'The great code' and 'Words with power'. [E]*Lee, Alvin A.; O'Grady, Jean*: Collected works of Northrop Frye 4: 2000 ⇒16,160. [R]JR 82 (2002) 343-344 (*Marshall, Donald G.*).

170 **Gilbert, Maurice** Il a parlé par les prophètes. ^T*Pahk, Johan Yeong-Sik*: Seoul 2002, Bible & Life 3 vols. 89-8481-074-6. **K**.

171 **Gorman, Michael M.** Biblical commentaries from the early middle ages. Millennio Medievale 32; Reprints 4: Tavarnuzze (Firenze) 2002, SISMEL xiv; 513 pp. 88-8450-024-9.

172 **Grosby, Steven** Biblical ideas of nationality: ancient and modern. WL 2002, Eisenbrauns 271 pp. $29.50. 1-57506-065-5 [RivBib 51,249s— Mela, Roberto].

173 **Grottanelli, Cristiano** Kings & prophets. 1999 ⇒15,132...17,154. ^RAuOr 20/1-2 (2002) 283-285 (*Pórtulas, J.*).

174 **Haacker, Klaus** Versöhnung mit Israel: exegetische Beiträge. VKHW 5: Neuk 2002, Neuk 223 pp. €20. 3-7887-1836-6.

175 **Halliday, Michael A.K.** Linguistic studies of text and discourse. ^E*Webster, Jonathan*: Collected Works of M.A.K. Halliday 2: L 2002, Continuum x; 301 pp. 0-8264-5868-8. Bibl. 289-296.

176 **Hengel, Martin** Kleine Schriften I: Judaica et Hellenistica. WUNT 90: 1996 ⇒12,128... 17,160. ^RJThS 53 (2002) 305-306 (*Horbury, William*); GGA 254 (2002) 1-14 (*Walter, Nikolaus*);

177 Kleine Schriften II: Judaica, Hellenistica et Christiana. WUNT 109: 1999 ⇒15,139; 17,161. ^RJThS 53 (2002) 306-307 (*Horbury, William*); GGA 254 (2002) 14-18 (*Walter, Nikolaus*);

178 Kleine Schriften III: Paulus und Jakobus. WUNT 141: Tü 2002, Mohr S. xii; 587 pp. €159. 3-16-147710-3.

179 **Herrmann, Siegfried** Geschichte und Prophetie: kleine Schriften zum Alten Testament. ^E*Liwak, Rüdiger; Thiel, Winfried*: BWANT 157: Stu 2002, Kohlhammer viii; 262 pp. 317-0172-611. Bibl. Herrmann 257-8.

180 **Hofius, Otfried** Paulusstudien II. WUNT 143: Tü 2002, Mohr 294 pp. 3-16-147736-7. ^RLuThK 26 (2002) 106-107 (*Stolle, Volker*);

181 Neutestamentliche Studien. WUNT 132: 2000 ⇒16,174; 17,163. ^RJThS 53 (2002) 281-282 (*Morgan, Robert*); ThG 45 (2002) 221-223 (*Giesen, Heinz*).

182 **Holmes, Stephen R.** Listening to the past: the place of tradition in theology. GR 2002, Baker xiii; 167 pp. $18. 0-8010-2642-3 [ThD 50,271—Heiser, W. Charles].

183 **Holter, Knut** Yahweh in Africa: essays on Africa and the Old Testament. Bible and Theology in Africa 1: 2000 ⇒16,175; 17,164. ^RBgMiss 66 (2002) 321-322 (*Gieniusz, Andrzej*); VeE 23 (2002) 262-264 (*Boshoff, W.S.*).

184 **Jeremias, Joachim** Jesus and the message of the New Testament. ^E*Hanson, K.C.*: Mp 2002, Fortress xiii; 126 pp. $15. 0-8006-3469-1. Bibl. 111-116.

185 **Jossa, Giorgio** I gruppi giudaici ai tempi di Gesù. BCR 66: 2001 ⇒17, 5195. ^RHenoch 24 (2002) 355-365 (*Troiani, Lucio*).

186 **Kaiser, Otto** Gottes und der Menschen Weisheit. BZAW 261: 1998 ⇒ 14,166. ^RThRv 98 (2002) 108 (*Marböck, Johannes*);

187 Studien zur Literaturgeschichte des Alten Testamentes. FzB 90: 2000 ⇒16,176; 17,166. ^RETR 77 (2002) 264-265 (*Bauks, Michaela*).

188 **Kallai, Zecharia** Biblical historiography and historical geography. BEAT 44: 1998 ⇒14,167. ^RBASOR 327 (2002) 94-96 (*Vanderhooft, David S.*).

189 **Kampling, Rainer** Im Angesicht Israels: Studien zum historischen und theologischen Verhältnis von Kirche und Israel. ^E*Blum, Matthias*: SBB 47: Stu 2002, Kathol. Biblewerk vii; 274 pp. €40.90. 3-460-00471-1.

190 **Kim, Seyoon** Paul and the new perspective: second thoughts on the origin of Paul's gospel. WUNT 140: Tü 2002, Mohr xv; 336 pp. $25. 3-16-147692-1. Bibl. 298-317; =GR: Eerdmans 2002, 0-8028-4974-1. [R]RHPhR 82 (2002) 239-240 (*Grappe, Ch.*); RTR 61 (2002) 163-164 (*Goswell, Greg*); SNTU.A 27 (2002) 256-258 (*Wick, P.*).

191 **Kirsch, Jonathan** I raconti proibiti della bibbia. 2001 <1997> ⇒17, 168. [R]Hum(B) 57 (2002) 1051-1052 (*Capelli, Piero*).

192 **Landy, Francis** Beauty and the enigma. JSOT.S 312: 2001 ⇒17,171. [R]SR 31 (2002) 452-453 (*Parker, Kim Ian*); RBLit (2002)* (*Brenner, Athalya*).

193 **Lange, Günter** Bilder zum Glauben: christliche Kunst sehen und verstehen. Mü 2002, Kösel 351 pp. €20. 3-466-36589-9.

194 **Levine, Étan** Heaven and earth, law and love. BZAW 303: 2000 ⇒16, 179. [R]RBLit (2002)* (*Kaminsky, Joel S.*).

195 **Lewis, David M.** Selected papers in Greek and Near Eastern history. [E]*Rhodes, Peter John*: 1997 ⇒13,143 [R]JNES 61 (2002) 230-232 (*Vinson, Steve*).

196 **Lindbeck, George** The church in a postliberal age. [E]*Buckley, James J.*: L 2002, SCM vii; 300 pp. £16. 0-334-02880-0.

197 **Lohfink, Norbert** La opción por los pobres. 1999 ⇒16,182. [R]ITER 28 (2002) 164-165 (*Frades Gaspar, Eduardo*);

198 Studien zum Deuteronomium und zur dtr. Literatur, 4. SBAB 31: 2000 ⇒16,183; 17,177. [R]CBQ 64 (2002) 193-194 (*McConville, J.G.*);

199 A la sombra de tus alas: nuevo comentario de grandes textos bíblicos. Biblioteca Manual Desclée 30: Bilbao 2002, Desclée de B. 291 pp. 84-330-1692-X. [R]RevAg 43 (2002) 718-720 (*Tejerina Arias, Gonzalo*);
Church dreams: talking against the trend. 2000 ⇒349.

200 **Lohse, Eduard** Das Neue Testament als Urkunde des Evangeliums: exegetische Studien zur Theologie des Neuen Testaments III. FRLANT 192: 2000 ⇒16,184; 17,179. [R]ThLZ 127 (2002) 45-46 (*Holtz, Traugott*); BBR 12 (2002) 292-295 (*Ellis, E. Earle*); SNTU.A 27 (2002) 281-283 (*Fuchs, Albert*).

201 **Loretz, Oswald** Psalmstudien: Kolometrie, Strophik und Theologie ausgewählter Psalmen. BZAW 309: B 2002, De Gruyter x; 441 pp. €118. 3-11-017578-9. Bibl. 423-426.

202 **Luke, K.** The cultural background of the Old Testament. Bangalore 2002, Claretian 289 pp. [R]ETJ 6 (2002) 202-203 (*Parathanam, Thomas*).

203 **Mack, Burton L.** The christian myth: origins, logic, and legacy. 2001 ⇒17,181. [R]CBQ 64 (2002) 769-771 (*Perkins, Pheme*).

204 **Maggi, Alberto** Comment lire l'évangile sans perdre la foi. 1999 ⇒ 15,149; 16,187. [R]SR 31 (2002) 231-232 (*Mainville, Odette*).

205 **Malamat, Abraham** History of biblical Israel. 2001 ⇒17,182. [R]IEJ 52 (2002) 117-118 (*Cogan, Mordechai*); BASOR 327 (2002) 90-92 (*Fox, Nili S.*); ThLZ 127 (2002) 626 (*Soggin, J. Alberto*); JBL 121 (2002) 748-750 (*Burnett, Joel S.*).

206 **Malina, Bruce J.** El mundo social de Jesús y los evangelios: la antropología cultural mediterránea y el Nuevo Testamento. [T]*Lozano-Gotor Perona, José Manuel*: Presencia teológica 116: Sdr 2002, Sal Terrae 334 pp. €23.50. 84293-14415. [R]SalTer 90 (2002) 804-6 (*Alcaraz Moreno, Juan Pedro*); Communio 35 (2002) 501-502 (*Garzón, F. Javier*).

207 **Mazzoleni, Danilo** Epigrafi del mondo cristiano antico. Città del Vaticano 2002, Lateran Univ. Pr. 414 pp. 88-465-0231-0.

208 **Meeks, Wayne A.** In search of the early christians: selected essays. ᴱ*Hilton, Allen R.; Snyder, H. Gregory*: NHv 2002, Yale University Pr. xxviii; (2) 314 pp. $35. 0-300-09142-7. Bibl. 263-286.

209 **Meinhold, Arndt** Zur weisheitlichen Sicht des Menschen. ᴱ*Neumann, Thomas; Thon, Johannes*: ABIG 6: Lp 2002, Evangelischer x; 265 pp. €38. 3-374-01908-0.

210 **Miller, Patrick D.** Israelite religion and biblical theology. JSOT.S 267: 2000 ⇒16,191. ᴿSal. 64 (2002) 579-580 (*Vicent, R.*).

211 **Moloney, Francis J.** 'A hard saying': the gospel and culture. 2001 ⇒ 17,184. ᴿPacifica 15 (2002) 217-218 (*Loader, William*); NewTR 15/4 (2002) 89-90 (*Osiek, Carolyn*).

212 **Moran, William L.** The most magic word: essays on Babylonian and biblical literature. ᴱ*Hendel, Ronald S.*: CBQ.MS 35: Wsh 2002, Catholic Biblical Association of America x; 212 pp. $11.50. 0-915170-34-5.

213 **Mostert, Walter** Glaube und Hermeneutik. ᴱ*Bühler, Pierre; Ebeling, Gerhard*: 1998 ⇒14,179; 15,157. ᴿRHPhR 82 (2002) 91-93 (*Lehmkühler, K.*).

214 **Mussner, Franz** Jesus von Nazareth im Umfeld Israels und der Urkirche. ᴱ*Theobald, Michael*: WUNT 111: 1999 ⇒15,160...17,186. ᴿTThZ 111 (2002) 240-241 (*Müller, Paul-Gerhard*).

215 **Nicole, Roger** Standing forth: collected writings of Roger Nicole. Fearn, Rossshire 2002, Mentor (12) 492 pp. 1-85792-646-3.

216 **Nicolet, C.** Censeurs et publicains: économie et fiscalité dans la Rome antique. 2000 ⇒16,195. ᴿCIR 52 (2002) 122-123 (*Broadhead, William*).

217 **North, Robert** Medicine in the biblical background: and other essays on the origins of Hebrew. AnBib 142: 2000 ⇒16,196. ᴿRivBib 50 (2002) 240-4 (*Prato, Gian Luigi*); ATG 65 (2002) 318-20 (*Torres, A.*).

218 **O'Neill, John C.** The point of it all: essays on Jesus Christ. 2000 ⇒16, 198; 17,189. ᴿNBl 83 (2002) 205-206 (*Cry, Brian MacNeil*).

219 **Pathrapankal, Joseph** Dimensions of the word. 2000 ⇒16,199. ᴿIThQ 67 (2002) 173-174 (*Perry, Jim*);

220 Time and history: biblical and theological studies. Bangalore 2002, Asian Trading vi; 254 pp. 81-7086-287-6.

221 **Penna, Romano** Vangelo e inculturazione. 2001 ⇒17,193. ᴿFirmana 27 (2002) 128 (*Amato, Angelo*); RevAg 43 (2002) 720-721 (*Sánchez Navarro, Luis*).

222 **Perea Yébenes, Sabino** Entre occidente y oriente: temas de historia romana: aspectos religiosos. Graeco-Romanae Religionis Electa Collectio 4: 2001 ⇒17,194. ᴿAevum 76 (2002) 222-225 (*Ramelli, Ilaria*).

223 **Phillips, Anthony C.J.** Essays on biblical law. JSOT.S 344: L 2002, Sheffield A. xvi; 295 pp. £70. 0-8264-6147-6. Bibl. 269-278.

224 **Picard, Jean-Claude** Le continent apocryphe: essai sur les littératures apocryphes juives et chrétiennes. IP 36: 1999 ⇒15,163; 17,195. ᴿTEuph 24 (2002) 157-160 (*Sapin, J.*); LTP 58 (2002) 376-378 (*Côté, Dominique*).

225 **Pilhofer, Peter** Die frühen Christen und ihre Welt: Greifswalder Aufsätze 1996-2001. ᴱ*Frey, Jörg; Hengel, Martin; Hofius, Otfried*: WUNT 145: Tü 2002, Mohr xvi; 234 pp. €59. 3-16-147776-6.

226 **Puhvel, Jaan** Epilecta indoeuropaea: opuscula selecta annis 1978-2001 excusa imprimis ad res Anatolicas attinentia. Innsbrucker Beiträge zur Sprachwissenschaft 104: Innsbruck 2002, Institut für Sprachen und Literaturen xii; 309 pp. €88. 3-85124-684-5. Bibl. ix-xii.

227 **Quaglia, Rocco** I sogni della bibbia: un'interpretazione psicodinamica e altri scritti. R 2002, Borla 113 pp. 88-263-1434-9. Bibl. 107-112.

228 **Rajak, Tessa** The Jewish dialogue with Greece and Rome. AGJU 48: 2001 ⇒17,199. ᴿJThS 53 (2002) 176-180 (*Carleton Paget, James*); Zion 67 (2002) 337-341 (*Bohak, Gideon*); JSJ 33 (2002) 337-339 (*Geljon, A.C.*); SCI 21 (2002) 318-322 (*Gruen, Erich S.*); JJS 53 (2002) 387-390 (*Mendels, Doron*).

229 **Riede, Peter** Im Spiegel der Tiere: Studien zum Verhältnis von Mensch und Tier im alten Israel. OBO 187: Gö 2002, Vandenhoeck & R. 362 pp. €67. 3-525-53044-7. Bibl. 311-6 [ThQ 183,87—Groß, W.]

230 **Roberts, Jimmy Jack M.** The bible and the ancient Near East: collected essays. WL 2002, Eisenbrauns xiv; 434 pp. $42.50. 1-57506-066-3.

231 **Rofé, Alexander** Deuteronomy: issues and interpretation. Old Testament Studies: L 2002, Clark xiii; 258 pp. £30. 0-567-08754-9.

232 **Rossano, Pietro** Teologia cristiana delle religioni e della missione 'Ad Gentes': a dieci anni dalla morte di Pietro Rossano (1991-2001), Professore alla Pontificia Università Gregoriana, Roma (1967-1977). ᴱ*Dhavamony, Mariasusai*: DMis 27: R 2002, E.P.U.G. 249 pp. €32. 88-7652-906-3.

233 **Ruggieri, G.** Cristianesimo, chiese e vangelo. TRSR 30: Bo 2002, Mulino 373 pp. €26. 88-15-08910-1 [NRTh 126,141—Clarot, B.]

234 **Schaller, Berndt** Fundamenta Judaica: Studien zum antiken Judentum und zum Neuen Testament. ᴱ*Doering, Lutz; Steudel, Annette*: StUNT 25: 2001 ⇒17,206. ᴿRBLit (2002)* (*Chapman, David W.*).

235 **Schenker, Adrian** Recht und Kult im Alten Testament. OBO 172: 2000 ⇒16,206; 17,207. ᴿThLZ 127 (2002) 385-388 (*Reventlow, Henning Graf*).

236 **Schmidt, Werner H.** Zukunftsgewißheit und Gegenwartskritik: Studien zur Eigenart der Prophetie. BThSt 51: Neuk ²2002 <1973>, Neuk xxiv; 11-154 pp. €19.90. 3-7887-1892-7. Bibl. 147-148.

237 **Schner, George P.** Essays catholic and critical. ᴱ*Ziegler, Philip G.; Husbands, Mark*: Burlington 2002, Ashgate xix; 195 pp.

238 **Schroer, Silvia** Wisdom has built her house.ᵀ*Maloney, Linda M.; McDonough, William*: 2000 ⇒16,208; 17,210. ᴿPacifica 15 (2002) 84-86 (*Reaburn, Mary*); NewTR 15/1 (2002) 81-82 (*Bergant, Dianne*); RivBib 50 (2002) 366-367 (*Prato, Gian Luigi*); JBL 121 (2002) 356-358 (*Masenya, Madipoane*).

239 **Schüngel-Straumann, Helen** Anfänge feministischer Exegese: gesammelte Beiträge, mit einem orientierenden Nachwort und einer Auswahlbibliographie. Exegese in unserer Zeit 8: Müns 2002, LIT 319 pp. 3-8258-5753-0.

240 **Schweizer, Harald** '...Deine Sprache verrät dich!': Grundkurs Religiosität: Essays zur Sprachkritik. Forum Religionskritik 1: Müns 2002, LIT x; 399 pp. 3-8258-5869-3.

241 **Segovia, Fernando F.** Decolonizing biblical studies: a view from the margins. 2000 ⇒16,211. ᴿJAAR 70 (2002) 664-67 (*Smith, Abraham*).

242 **Sieben, Hermann-Josef** 'Manna in deserto': Studien zum Schriftgebrauch der Kirchenväter. ᴱ*Nyssen, Wilhelm; Schneider, Michael*: Cardo 92: Köln 2002, Koinonia O. 321 pp. 3-9333001-89-3 [ThPh 78, 281s—Fiedrowicz, M.].

243 **Slenczka, Reinhard** Altes und Neues. ᴱ*Herzog, Albrecht Immanuel*: 2000 ⇒16,214. ᴿThR 67 (2002) 262-266 (*Beißer, Friedrich*).

244 **Smend, Rudolf** Die Mitte des Alten Testaments: exegetische Aufsätze. Tü 2002 <1983>, Mohr S. (8) 279 pp. €29. 316-1477-162. Bibl. 263-4.

245 **Stuhlmacher, Peter** Biblische Theologie und Evangelium: Gesammelte Aufsätze. WUNT 146: Tü 2002, Mohr S. xiv; 341 pp. €89. 3-16-147768-5.

246 **Tosato, Angelo** Vangelo e ricchezza: nuove prospettive esegetiche. *EAntiseri, Dario; D'Agostino, Francesco; Petroni, Angelo*: La politica 46: Soveria Mannelli (Catanzaro) 2002, Rubbettino 611 pp. 88-498-0212-9.

247 **Tov, Emanuel** The Greek and Hebrew Bible. VT.S 72: 1999 ⇒15, 180; 17,220. ᴿJSJ 33 (2002) 114-116 (*Den Hertog, Cornelis G.*).

248 **Trevijano Etcheverría, Ramón** Estudios Paulinos. Plenitudo Temporis 8: S 2002, Publicaciones Universidad Pontificia 642 pp. €26.87. 84-7299-534-8. Bibl. 559-601.

249 **Troiani, Lucio** Il perdono cristiano e altri studi. StBi 123: 1999 ⇒15, 181; 17,221. ᴿProtest. 57 (2002) 246-247 (*Spanu, Alessandro*).

250 **Urbach, Ephraim E.** Collected writings in Jewish studies. *EBrody, Robert; Herr, Moshe D.*: 1999 ⇒15,182. ᴿJThS 53 (2002) 311-312 (*Horbury, William*).

251 **Van der Horst, Pieter Willem** Japheth in the tents of Shem: studies on Jewish Hellenism in antiquity. CBET 32: Lv 2002, Peeters 272 pp. €35. 90-429-1137-9.

252 **VanderKam, James C.** From revelation to canon: studies in the Hebrew Bible and second temple literature: JSJ.S 62: 2000 ⇒16,221. ᴿJSJ 33 (2002) 116-118 (*Lange, Armin*).

253 **Vanhoozer, Kevin J.** First theology: God, scripture and hermeneutics. DG 2002, IVP 384 pp. £18. 0-85111-267-6.

254 **Veijola, Timo** Moses Erben. BWAT 149: 2000 ⇒16,222. ᴿAnton. 77 (2002) 753-754 (*Volgger, David*); ThLZ 127 (2002) 39-41 (*Levin, Christoph*).

255 **Veltri, Giuseppe** Gegenwart der Tradition: Studien zur jüdischen Literatur und Kulturgeschichte. JSJ.S 69: Lei 2002, Brill xxvii; 319 pp. €103. 90-04-11686-9.

256 **Viviano, Benedict Thomas** Trinity—kingdom—church. NTOA 48: 2001 ⇒17,223. ᴿSEÅ 67 (2002) 181-182 (*Starr, James*).

257 **Vollenweider, Samuel** Horizonte neutestamentlicher Christologie: Studien zu Paulus und zur früchristlichen Theologie. WUNT 144: Tü 2002, Mohr viii; 425 pp. €89. 3-16-147791-X. ᴿFZPhTh 49 (2002) 520-523 (*Venetz, Hermann-Josef*).

258 **Warfield, Benjamin B.** La persona e l'opera di Cristo. 2001 ⇒17, 226. ᴿStudi di teologia 14 (2002) 208-209 (*Melini, Augusto*).

259 **Waschke, Ernst-Joachim** Der Gesalbte. BZAW 306: 2001 ⇒17,227. ᴿThLZ 127 (2002) 507-510 (*Reventlow, Henning Graf*).

260 **Wilhelm, Adolf** Kleine Schriften: Abteilung II: Abhandlungen und Beiträge zur griechischen Inschriftenkunde Teil IV. *EDobesch, Gerhard; Rehrenböck, Georg*: SÖAW.PH 691; Veröffentlichungen der Kleinasiatischen Kommission 11: W 2002, Verlag der Österreichischen Akademie der Wissenschaften 644 pp. 3-7001-3056-2. Mitwirkung von *Andreas Hofeneder*.

261 **Willi-Plein, Ina** Sprache als Schlüssel: gesammelte Aufsätze zum Alten Testament. *EPietsch, Michael; Präckel, Tilmann*: Neuk 2002, Neuk viii; 242 pp. €24.90. 3-7887-1912-5.

262 **Winston, David** The ancestral philosophy: Hellenistic philosophy in second temple Judaism. *ESterling, Gregory E.*: Studia Philonica Monographs 4; BJSt 331: 2001 ⇒17,228. ᴿJSJ 33 (2002) 344-347 (*Fox, Kenneth A.*); StPhiloA 14 (2002) 204-206 (*Collins, John J.*).

263 **Wrede, William** Gesammelte theologische Studien, 1 u. 2: [E]*Zager, W.*:
Theologische Studien-Texte 14: Waltrop 2002, Spenner xxxi; 460 +
xii; 502 pp. €49.50. 3-933688-66-3 [ThLZ 128,53—Niebuhr, K.-W.].

A1.3 *Plurium compilationes* biblicae

264 [E]**Abella, Josef** Salmi e letteratura sapienziale: pregare Dio nella vita.
Lettura pastorale della bibbia, parola-missione 6: Bo 2002, EDB 519
pp. 88-10-20146-9.

265 [E]**Adam, A.K.M.** Handbook of postmodern biblical interpretation.
2000 ⇒16,225. [R]BiblInterp 10 (2002) 76-79 (*Castelli, Elizabeth A.*);
ThTo 59 (2002) 456-457 (*Green, Joel B.*);

266 Postmodern interpretations of the bible: a reader. 2001 ⇒17,229.
[R]AThR 84 (2002) 771-72 (*Fontaine, Carole R.*); ThTo 59 (2002) 457-
458 (*Green, Joel B.*); CBQ 64 (2002) 604-606 (*Richey, Lance Byron*).

267 [E]**Aichele, George; Walsh, Richard** Screening scripture: intertextual
connections between scripture and film. Harrisburg 2002, Trinity 335
pp. $28. 1-56338-354-3.

268 [E]**Arblaster, Paul; Juhász, Gergely; Latré, Guido** TYNDALE's testament. Turnhout 2002, Brepols (8) 195 pp. 2503-51411-1. Bibl. 179-84.

269 [E]**Ådna, Jostein; Kvalbein, Hans** The mission of the early church to
Jews and Gentiles. WUNT 127: 2000 ⇒16,226; 17,233. [R]Sal. 64
(2002) 384-386 (*Vicent, R.*); ThG 45 (2002) 217-219 (*Giesen, Heinz*);
ThLZ 127 (2002) 512-514 (*Sänger, Dieter*).

270 [E]**Baker, David W.; Arnold, Bill T.** The face of Old Testament stud-
ies: a survey of contemporary approaches. 1999 ⇒15,192; 17,234.
[R]SBET 20 (2002) 98-99 (*Morrison, Hector*); EvQ 74 (2002) 353-354
(*Jenson, Philip*); RBLit (2002)* (*Haney, Randy Gayle*).

271 [E]**Balch, David L.** Homosexuality, science, and the 'plain sense' of
scripture. 2000 ⇒16,231; 17,8005. [R]HeyJ 43 (2002) 245-247 (*Hardy,
Richard P.*); RBLit (2002)* (*Hester, J. David*).

272 [E]**Bartholomew, Craig,** *al.,* A royal priesthood?: the use of the bible
ethically and politically: a dialogue with Oliver O'DONOVAN . Scripture and hermeneutics 3: Cheltenham 2002, Univ. of Gloucestershire
xxiv; 446 pp. £21.90. 1-84227-067-2 [RB 110,639].

273 [E]**Barton, John** The biblical world, 1-2. L 2002, Routledge xxiii; 525 +
viii; 539 pp. $225. 0-415-16105-3.

274 [E]**Ben Zvi, Ehud; Floyd, Michael H.** Writings and speech in Israelite
and ancient Near Eastern prophecy. 2000 ⇒16,238. [R]HebStud 43
(2002) 271-273 (*Person, Raymond F.*); RBLit 4 (2002) 200-203
(*Eades, Keith L.*).

275 [E]**Blasi, Anthony J.; Duhaime, Jean; Turcotte, Paul-André** Handbook of early christianity: social science approaches. Walnut Creek,
CA 2002, Alta Mira xxvii; 802 pp. $100. 07591-00152. Bibl. 705-751.

276 [E]**Borgen, Peder; Giversen, Søren** The New Testament and Hellenistic
Judaism. 1995 ⇒11/1,67... 16,241. [R]RevBib 61 (1999) 267-268 (*Levoratti, A.J.*)

277 [E]**Bortone, Giuseppe** La speranza: indagine biblico-teologico-letterari-
a: XXII Corso Biblico. Studio Biblico Teologico Aquilano 22:
L'Aquila 2002, ISSRA xiii; 345 pp.

278 [E]**Bottoni, Gianfranco; Nason, Luigi** Secondo le scritture: chiese cristiane e popolo di Dio. Ecumenismo: Bo 2002, EDB 384 pp. €30. 88-

10-40122-0. Bibl. 375-378. [R]PaVi 47/5 (2002) 61-63 (*Giavini, Giovanni*).

279 [E]**Braaten, Carl E.; Jenson, Robert W.** The last things: biblical and theological perspectives on eschatology. GR 2002, Eerdmans ix; 169 pp. $16. 0-8028-4878-8;

280 The strange new world of the gospel: re-evangelizing in the postmodern world. GR 2002, Eerdmans 176 pp. $23. 0-8028-3947-9.

281 [E]**Brenner, Athalya; Van Henten, Jan Willem** Bible translation on the threshold of the twenty-first century: authority, reception, culture and religion. JSOT.S 353; The Bible in the 21st century 1: Shf 2002, Sheffield A. x; 207 pp. £60. 0-82646-029-1.

282 **Briend, Jacques; Quesnel, Michel** La vie quotidienne aux temps bibliques. 2001 ⇒17,393. [R]RICP 82 (2002) 204-205 (*Brossier, François*).

283 [E]**Brown, William P.** Character and scripture: moral formation, community, and biblical interpretation. GR 2002, Eerdmans 432 pp. $34. 0-8028-4625-4 [ThD 50,66—Heiser, W. Charles].

284 [E]**Broyles, Craig C.** Interpreting the Old Testament: a guide for exegesis. 2001 ⇒17,248. [R]BS 159 (2002) 485-486 (*Chisholm, Robert B.*)

285 [E]**Calzolari Bouvier, Valentina; Kaestli, Jean-Daniel; Outtier, Bernard** Apocryphes arméniens: transmission, traduction, création, iconographie. 1999 ⇒15,205. [R]ThLZ 127 (2002) 884-886 (*Siegert, Folker*); BiOr 59 (2002) 615-617 (*Cox, Claude E.*)

286 [E]**Carnevale, Laura** La bibbia nelle comunità antiche: bilancio e prospettive di un'esperienza formativa. QVetChr 27: Bari 2002, Edipuglia 148 pp. 88-7228-342-6.

287 [E]**Carson, D.A.; O'Brien, Peter Thomas; Seifrid, Mark A.** Justification and variegated nomism, 1: the complexities of second temple Judaism. WUNT 2/140: 2001 ⇒17,251. [R]RHPhR 82 (2002) 208-209 (*Grappe, Ch.*); ETR 77 (2002) 599-600 (*Cuvillier, Elian*); SNTU.A 27 (2002) 284-285 (*Oberforcher, R.*); RBLit (2002)* (*Byron, John; Eisenbaum, Pamela*; BTB 32 (2002) 154 (*Sanders, James A.*).

288 [E]**Chilton, Bruce David; Evans, Craig A.** James the Just and christian origins. NT.S 98: 1999 ⇒15,208...17,255. [R]BiblInterp 10 (2002) 93-96 (*Riesner, Rainer*); RBLit (2002)* (*Batten, Alicia*).

289 [E]**Comba, Enrico** Profeti e profezie: un percorso attraverso culture e religioni. Popoli e culture delle Americhe 10: T 2001, Segnalibro 176 pp.

290 [E]**Conidi, Francesco** Weisheiten der Bibel. Gü 2002, Gü 127 pp. 3-57-9-02331-4.

291 [E]**Coogan, Michael D.** The Oxford history of the biblical world. 2001 ⇒17,258. [R]RExp 99 (2002) 117-118 (*Eddinger, Terry W.*).

292 [E]**Court, John M.** New Testament writers and the Old Testament. L 2002, SPCK 132 pp. £14.

293 [E]**Daecke, Sigard M.; Sahm, Peter R.** Jesus von Nazareth und das Christentum: braucht die pluralistische Gesellschaft ein neues Jesusbild?. Neuk. 2000, Neuk. 230 pp. €21.15. 3-7887-1767-X.

294 [E]**Das, A. Andrew; Matera, Frank J.** Perspectives in biblical theology. LVL 2002, Westminster xv; 300 pp. £20.

295 [E]**Davies, Philip R.** First person: essays in biblical autobiography. BiSe 81: Shf 2002, Sheffield A. 168 pp. £17. 1-84127-320-1. Bibl. 155-163.

296 [E]**Davies, Philip R.; Halligan, John M.** Second temple studies III: studies in politics, class and material culture. JSOT.S 340: L 2002, Sheffield A. ix; 246 pp. £55. 0-8264-6030-5. Bibl. 218-236.

297 ^E**Dekker, W.J.; Visser, P.J.** Om de verstaanbaarheid: over bijbel, geloof en kerk in een postmoderne samenleving. Zoetermeer 2002, Boekencentrum 273 pp. €17..90 90-2391-3159.

298 ^E**Dettwiler, Andreas; Zumstein, Jean** Kreuzestheologie im Neuen Testament. WUNT 151: Tü 2002, Mohr x; 367 pp. €84. 316-147775-8.

299 **Dillmann, Rainer; Grilli, Massimo; Paz, César Mira [! Mora]** Vom Text zum Leser: Theorie und Praxis einer handlungsorientierten Bibelauslegung. SBS 193: Stu 2002, Verlag Katholisches Bibelwerk 173 pp. 3-460-04931-6. Bibl. 163-173.

300 ^E**Dube, Musa W.** Other ways of reading: African women and the bible. 2001 ⇒17,260. ^RTheol. 105 (2002) 457-8 (*Sentamu, Margaret*).

301 ^E**Ebner, Martin** Gottes Kinder. JBTh 17: Neuk 2002, Neuk'er xi; 427 pp. 3-7887-1920-6.

302 ^E**Eckstein, Hans-Joachim; Welker, Michael** Die Wirklichkeit der Auferstehung. Neuk 2002, Neuk xvi; 351 pp. €24.90. 3-7887-1808-0.

303 ^E**Ego, Beate; Lange, Armin; Pilhofer, Peter** Gemeinde ohne Tempel: community without temple. WUNT 118: 1999 ⇒15,218...17,2879. ^RThG 45 (2002) 224-226 (*Giesen, Heinz*); DSD 9 (2002) 402-404 (*Grossman, Maxine*); RBLit 4 (2002) 96-100 (*Pietsch, Michael*).

304 ^E**Esler, Philip F.** The early christian world. 2000 ⇒16,256. ^RTS 63 (2002) 170-2 (*Casiday, A.M.*); JR 82 (2002) 277-9 (*Grant, Robert M.*).

305 ^E**Evans, Craig A.** The interpretation of scripture in early Judaism and christianity. JSPE.S 33: 2000 ⇒16,257; 17,264. ^RSal. 64 (2002) 150-151 (*Vicent, R.*); RHPhR 82 (2002) 215-216 (*Grappe, Ch.*); OLZ 97 (2002) 581-584 (*Böttrich, Christfried*).

306 ^E**Fernández Sangrador, Jorge Juan** Iglesias apostólicas: orígenes y diversidad. ResB 35 (2002) 1-61.

307 ^E**Flint, Peter W.** The bible at Qumran: text, shape, and interpretation. 2001 ⇒17,267. ^RDSD 9 (2002) 113-114 (*Crawford, Sidnie White*); RHPhR 82 (2002) 211-212 (*Grappe, Ch.*); RSR 90 (2002) 443-445 (*Paul, André*); ScEs 54 (2002) 238-240 (*Duhaime, Jean*); HebStud 43 (2002) 303-304 (*Lim, Timothy H.*); AUSS 40 (2002) 325-327 (*Johnston, Robert M.*); RBLit (2002)* (*Young, Ian; Schuller, Eileen*).

308 ^E**Fredriksen, Paula; Reinhartz, Adele** Jesus, Judaism and christian anti-Judaism: reading the NewTestament after the Holocaust. LVL 2002, Westminster xi; 129 pp. £15. 0-664-22328-1.

309 ^E**Freyne, Sean; Van Wolde, Ellen** As muitas vozes da bíblia. Petrópolis 2002, Vozes 135 pp. Conc(P) 294.

310 **Furnish, Victor Paul,** *al.*, Bibbia e omosessualità. ^E*Franzosi, Teresa*: Piccola collana etica 92: T 2002, Claudiana 173 pp. 88701-64217.

311 ^E**Gaventa, Beverly R.; Rigby, Cynthia L.** Blessed one: Protestant perspectives on Mary. LVL 2002, Westminster xii; 158 pp. $20. 0-66-422-438-5 [BiTod 41,199—Senior, Donald].

312 ^E**Gibert, Pierre; Marguerat, Daniel L.** Dieu, vingt-six portraits bibliques. P 2002, Bayard 350 pp. €23. 2-227-47088-7. Bibl. 323-333.

313 ^E**Gibert, Pierre; Theobald, Christoph** Le cas Jésus Christ: exégètes, historiens et théologiens en confrontation. P 2002, Bayard 475 pp [RThPh 135,286—Amsler, Frédéric].

314 ^E**Gibson, R.J.** Ripe for harvest: christian mission in the New Testament and in our world. 2000 ⇒16,265. ^REvangel 20 (2002) 89 (*Marshall, Howard*).

315 ^E**Giombi, Samuele** La sorgente e il roveto: la bibbia per il XXI secolo fra storia religiosa e scrittura letteraria. Manziana (R) 2002, Vecchiarelli 239 pp. €20. 88-8247-083-0.

316 ^E**Grabbe, Lester L.** Did Moses speak Attic?: Jewish historiography and scripture in the Hellenistic period. JSOT.S 317: 2001 ⇒17,270. ^RJBL 121 (2002) 359-361 (*Gruen, Erich S.*).

317 ^E**Grabbe, Lester L.; Haak, Robert D.** 'Every city shall be forsaken': urbanism and prophecy in Ancient Israel and the Near East. JSOT.S 330: 2001 ⇒17,271. ^RBiblInterp 10 (2002) 438-440 (*Edelman, Diana*); RBLit (2002)* (*Power, Bruce A.*).

318 ^E**Green, Joel B.; Turner, Max** Between two horizons: spanning New Testament studies and systematic theology. 2000 ⇒16,267; 17,272. ^RPacifica 15 (2002) 92-4 (*Roennfeldt, Ray C.W.*); HeyJ 43 (2002) 233-234 (*Turner, Geoffrey*); BS 159 (2002) 496-498 (*Kreider, Glenn R.*); HBT 24/2 (2002) 130-132 (*Sharbaugh, Patricia A.*); RBLit 4 (2002) 290-293 (*Johnson, Thomas F.*).

319 ^E**Griffiths, Richard** The bible in the Renaissance: essays on biblical commentary and translation in the fifteenth and sixteenth centuries. 2001 ⇒17,273. ^RTheol. 105 (2002) 474-475 (*Jeanes, Gordon*).

320 ^E**Guerriero, E.** Santi della bibbia: apostoli e profeti. CinB 2002, San Paolo 336 + 24 pp. €28.

321 ^E**Guijarro Oporto, Santiago** Los discípulos de Jesús. ResB 36 (2002) 1-53.

322 ^E**Habel, Norman C.; Balabanski, Vicky** The earth story in the New Testament. The Earth Bible 5: L 2002, Sheffield A. xx; 225 pp. £19. 0-8264-6060-7. Bibl. 193-211.

323 ^E**Habel, Norman C.** Readings from the perspective of earth. The Earth bible 1: 2000 ⇒16,270. ^RJRTI 5/2 (2002) 65-67 (*Snavely, Cynthia*).

324 ^E**Hagner, Donald A.** Conflicts and challenges in early christianity. 1999 ⇒15,236; 16,271. ^RRBLit 4 (2002) 293-296 (*Bowley, James E.*).

325 ^E**Hahn, Udo** Mein Jahr mit der Bibel. Gü 2002, Gü 408 pp. 3-579-02330-6.

326 ^E**Hallo, William; Younger, K. Lawson Jr.** The context of scripture, 3: archival documents from the biblical world. Lei 2002, Brill liv; 406 pp. $129. 90-04-10620-0. ^RUF 33 (2001) 717-720 (*Metzler, K.A.*).

327 **Hengel, Martin; Schwemer, Anna Maria** Der messianische Anspruch Jesu und die Anfänge der Christologie. WUNT 138: 2001 ⇒17, 276. ^RRHPhR 82 (2002) 232-3 (*Grappe, Ch.*); ThLZ 127 (2002) 1050-1051 (*Becker, Jürgen*); SNTU.A 27 (2002) 263-267 (*Fuchs, Albert*).

328 ^E**Hermans, Michel; Sauvage, Pierre** Bible et histoire. 2000 ⇒16,273; 17,277. ^RRevSR 76 (2002) 249-251 (*Laurent, Françoise A.-M.*); ScEs 54 (2002) 122-123 (*Mathieu, Yvan*).

329 ^E**Horrell, David G.** Social-scientific approaches to NT interpretation. 1999 ⇒15,241...17,975. ^REThL 78 (2002) 196-197 (*Verheyden, J.*).

330 ^E**Horsley, Richard A.** Paul and politics. 2000 ⇒16,275; 17,282. ^RNBl 83 (2002) 206-207 (*Ounsworth, Richard*).

331 ^E**Hossfeld, Frank-Lothar** Wieviel Systematik erlaubt die Schrift?: auf der Suche nach einer gesamtbiblischen Theologie. QD 185: 2001 ⇒17, 283. ^RThLZ 127 (2002) 1147-1151 (*Reventlow, Henning Graf*).

332 ^E**Howard-Brook, Wes; Ringe, Sharon H.** The New Testament—introducing the way of discipleship. Mkn 2002, Orbis x; 214 pp. $24. 1-57075-418-7 [BiTod 40,265—Senior, Donald].

333 ^E**Innocenti, Mario degli** La bibbia lacerata: l'interpretazione delle scritture, cammino di unione tra i cristiani. Mi 2002, Ancora 139 pp. €11.90.

334 **Isaacs, Ronald H.** Legends of biblical heroes: a sourcebook. Northvale, NJ 2002, Aronson x; 190 pp. 0-7657-6052-5. Bibl. 173.

335 ᴱIsasi-Díaz, Ada María; Matovina, Timoteo; Torres-Vidal, Nina
    M. Camino a Emaús: compartiendo el ministerio de Jesús. Mp 2002,
    Fortress 105 pp. $10.
336 ᴱJobling, David; Pippin, Tina; Schleifer, Ronald The postmodern
    bible reader. 2001 ⇒17,287. ᴿRRT 9 (2002) 306-309 (Moberly,
    Walter).
337 Johnson, Luke Timothy; Kurz, William S. The future of catholic
    biblical scholarship: a constructive conversation. GR 2002, Eerdmans
    xii; 299 pp. $24/£18. 0-8028-4545-2.
338 ᴱKnobloch, Frederick W. Biblical translation in context. Studies and
    texts in Jewish history and culture 10: Bethesda, MD 2002, University
    Press of Maryland xiii; 223 pp. 1-883053-40-4.
339 ᴱKorpel, Marjo C.A.; Oesch, Josef M. Studies in scriptural unit divi-
    sion. Pericope 3: Assen 2002, Van Gorcum viii; 288 pp. €70. 90-232-
    3840-0.
340 ᴱKörtner, Ulrich H.J. Glauben und Verstehen: Perspektiven herme-
    neutischer Theologie. 2000 ⇒16,284. ᴿThLZ 127 (2002) 889-895
    (Hübner, Hans).
341 ᴱKuntzmann, Raymond Typologie biblique: de quelques figures
    vives. LeDiv: P 2002, Cerf 278 pp. €22. 2-204-06997-3.
342 Lacocque, André C.; Ricoeur, Paul Pensar la biblia: estudios exegé-
    ticos y hermenéuticos. 2001 ⇒17,291. ᴿCTom 129 (2002) 423-424
    (Díaz Sariego, Jesús); CDios 215 (2002) 671-672 (Gutiérrez, J.);
    Communio 35 (2002) 498-499 (Garzón, F. Javier);
343 Come pensa la bibbia: studi esegetici ed ermeneutici. ᴱBassani, Fran-
    co: Introduzione allo studio della Bibbia, Suppl. 9: Brescia 2002, Pai-
    deia 421 pp. €39. 88-394-0638-7.
344 ᴱLemaire, André Prophètes et rois: Bible et Proche-Orient: LeDiv:
    2001 ⇒17,292. ᴿOLZ 97 (2002) 403-407 (Rose, Martin); BASOR 327
    (2002) 99-100 (Dion, Paul E.); Or. 71 (2002) 473-475 (Bonnet, Co-
    rinne).
345 ᴱLichtenberger, Hermann; Oegema, Gerbern S. Jüdische Schriften
    in ihrem antik-jüdischen und urchristlichen Kontext. Studien zu den Jü-
    dischen Schriften aus hellenistisch-römischer Zeit 1: Gü 2002, Gü'er
    511 pp. €115. 3-579-05360-4.
346 ᴱLinafelt, Tod Strange fire: reading the bible after the Holocaust. BiSe
    71: 2000 ⇒16,290; 17,293. ᴿRBLit 4 (2002) 121-124 (Greenspahn,
    Frederick E.);
347 A shadow of glory: reading the New Testament after the Holocaust.
    NY 2002, Routledge xi; 258 pp. $25. 0-415-93793-0.
348 ᴱLohfink, Norbert; Zenger, Erich The God of Israel and the nations:
    studies in Isaiah and the Psalms. ᵀKalin, Everett R.: 2000 ⇒16,291.
    ᴿRBLit (2002)* (Miller, Patrick D.).
349 Lohfink, Norbert Church dreams: talking against the trend. ᵀMaloney,
    Linda M.: 2000 ⇒16,292. ᴿTheoforum 33 (2002) 245-246 (McEvenue,
    Sean).
350 ᴱLongenecker, Bruce W. Narrative dynamics in Paul: a critical as-
    sessment. LVL 2002, Westminster vi; 253 pp. $25. 0-664-22277-3.
351 ᴱLong, V. Philips Israel's past in present research: essays on Ancient
    Israelite historiography. 1999 ⇒15,252; 16,293. ᴿCBQ 64 (2002) 194-
    196 (Williams, Tyler F.); RBLit 4 (2002) 163-165 (Becking, Bob).
352 ᴱLöning, Karl; Faßnacht, Martin Rettendes Wissen: Studien zum
    Fortgang weisheitlichen Denkens im Frühjudentum und im frühen

Christentum. AOAT 300: Müns 2002, Ugarit-Verlag x; 370 pp. 3-934-628-28-1.
353 ^E**Magnoni, Inere Filippo** Hipocrate e vangelo nella sanità che cambia. Bo 2002, Dehoniane 110 pp.
354 ^E**Mainville, Odette; Marguerat, Daniel L.** Résurrection: l'après-mort dans le monde ancien et le Nouveau Testament. Le monde de la Bible 45: 2001 ⇒17,296. ^RRHPhR 82 (2002) 192-193 (*Grappe, Ch.*).
355 ^E**Marguerat, Daniel** Quand la bible se raconte. LiBi 134: P 2002, Cerf 211 pp. €17. 2-204-07179-X.
356 **Martini, Carlo Maria,** *al.*, Il libro sacro: letture e interpretazioni ebraiche, cristiane e musulmane. Testi e pretesti: Mi 2002, Mondadori xxiii; 259 pp. 88-424-9386-4.
357 ^E**Mies, Françoise** Bible et droit: l'esprit des lois. Connaître et Croire 7: 2001 ⇒17,300. ^RActBib 39 (2002) 191-192 (*Boada, J.*); EeV 58 (2002) 9-12 (*Bony, Paul*);
358 Bible et sciences: déchiffrer l'univers. Le livre et le rouleau 15: Namur 2002, Presses Univ. 199 pp. €20. 2-87037-362-7.
359 ^E**Mulloor, Augustine** God of big dreams: Messianic texts in the O.T. and challenges. Kerala 2002, Jyotir Dharma xiii; 15-299 pp. Rs120.
360 ^E**Müller, Mogens; Tronier, Henrik** The New Testament as reception. JSNT.S 230; Copenhagen International seminar 11: Shf 2002, Sheffield A. xii; 226 pp. 1-84127-314-7.
361 ^E**Naluparayil, J.** Patheyasruti: biblical foundations of the eucharist. Kalady 2002, Emmaus 243 pp. Rs120.
362 ^E**Newman, Carey C.** Jesus & the restoration of Israel: a critical assessment of N.T. WRIGHT's Jesus and the victory of God. 1999 ⇒15,262. ^RProEc 11 (2002) 110-111 (*Fowl, Stephen*).
363 ^E**Oakes, Peter** Rome in the bible and the early church. Carlisle 2002, Paternoster xvii; 166 pp. $18. 1-84227-133-4. Bibl. 164-166.
364 ^E**O'Sullivan, Orlaith** The bible as book: the Reformation. 2000 ⇒16,307. ^RRHE 97 (2002) 708-709.
365 ^E**Otto, Eckart** Mose: Ägypten und das Alte Testament. SBS 189: 2000 ⇒16,307; 17,306. ^RRTL 33 (2002) 259-260 (*Wénin, A.*); CBQ 64 (2002) 795-796 (*Greifenhagen, Franz Volker*).
366 ^E**Otto, Eckart; Zenger, Erich** "Mein Sohn bist du" (Ps 2,7): Studien zu den Königspsalmen. SBS 192: Stu 2002, Kathol. Bibelwerk vi; 258 pp. €23.90. 3-460-04921-9.
367 ^E**Pokorny, Petr; Roskovec, Jan** Philosophical hermeneutics and biblical exegesis. WUNT 153: Tü 2002, Mohr x; 389 pp. €84. 3-16-147894-0.
368 The Polish Journal of Biblical Research, 1/2, December 2001. Kraków 2002, Enigma. ^RCoTh 72/4 (2002) 238-241 (*Chrostowski, Waldemar*).
369 ^E**Porter, Stanley E.; Stamps, Dennis L.** Rhetorical criticism and the bible. JSNT.S 195: Shf 2002, Sheffield A. 572 pp. $85. 1-84127-0938.
370 ^E**Quesnel, Michel; Gruson, Philippe** La biblia y su cultura, 1: Antiguo Testamento, 2: Jesús y el Nuevo Testamento. ^T*Díez Aragón, Ramón Alfonso; Pablo Otero, Gregorio de*: Sdr 2002, SalTer 575 + 606 pp. €85. 84-293-1432-2. ^RBiFe 28 (2002) 307-308 (*Salas, A.*); EstB 60 (2002) 428-429 (*Asurmendi, J.*); Proyección 207 (2002) 364-365 (*Sicre, J.L.*).
371 Rois et reines de la bible au miroir des Pères. Cahiers de Biblia Patristica 6: 1999 ⇒15,277; 16,319. ^RVetChr 39/1 (2002) 201-202 (*Veronese, Maria*).

372 **Rossi de Gasperis, Francesco; Carfagna, Antonella** Prendi il libro e mangia!, 3/2: dall'esilio alla nuova alleanza: pietà, poesia, sapienza. Bibbia e spiritualità 18: Bo 2002, EDB 390 pp. 88-10-21111-1.

373 ^E**Rowland, Christopher; Barton, John** Apocalyptic in history and tradition. JSPE.S 43: Shf 2002, Sheffield A. xvi; 332 pp. £85. 0-82646-208-1.

374 ^E**Römer, Thomas** The future of the Deuteronomistic History. BEThL 147: 2000 ⇒16,322; 17,2644. ^RNRTh 124 (2002) 275-276 (*Ska, Jean Louis*); RivBib 50 (2002) 364-365 (*Cortese, Enzo*); Lat. 68 (2002) 148-160 (*Cardellini, Innocenzo*); OLZ 97 (2002) 761-769 (*Veijola, Timo*); ET 113 (2002) 173-174 (*Auld, Graeme*).

375 ^E**Runia, David T.** The studia philonica annual: studies in Hellenistic Judaism. BJSt 323: Atlanta 1998, Scholars viii; 194 pp. ^RRBLit 4 (2002) 269-272 (*Bowley, James E.*).

376 ^E**Rutgers, Leonard Victor, al.**, The use of sacred books in the ancient world. 1998 ⇒14,263; 15,279. ^ROLZ 97 (2002) 76-82 (*Pinggéra, Karl*).

377 ^E**Schiffrin, Deborah; Tannen, Deborah; Hamilton, Heidi E.** The handbook of discourse analysis. Oxf 2001, Blackwell xx; 851 pp. 0-631-20595-0.

378 ^E**Shanks, Hershel** Ancient Israel: from Abraham to the destruction of the temple. ²1999 <1988> ⇒15,287; 17,321. ^RJNES 61 (2002) 149-150 (*Joffe, Alexander H.*).

379 ^E**Sieg, Franciszek; Kasilowski, P.** Studies on the bible: to commemorate the 400th anniversary of the publication of Jakub WUJEK's translation of the bible 1599-1999. 2000 ⇒16,333; 17,322. ^RLASBF 51 (2001) 399-401 (*Chrupcała, L.D.*).

380 **Studium Biblicum Franciscanum**, liber annuus 49. J 1999. ^RStFr 99 (2002) 169-174 (*Giovannetti, Ottaviano*).

381 **Das Studium des Neuen Testaments, 1-2.** ^E**Neudorfer, Heinz-Werner; Schnabel, Eckhard J.**: Bibelwissenschaftliche Monographien 5, 8: 1999-2000 ⇒15,261; 16,337. ^RNT 44 (2002) 189-92 (*Black, David*).

382 ^E**Sutter Rehmann, Luzia; Bieberstein, Sabine; Metternich, Ulrike** Sich dem Leben in die Arme werfen: Auferstehungserfahrungen. Gü 2002, Kaiser 199 pp. 3-579-05381-7.

383 ^E**Thompson, William M.; Morse, David Lee** VOEGELIN's Israel and revelation: an interdisciplinary debate and anthology. Marquette Studies in Theology 19: 2000 ⇒16,338; 17,328. ^RIThQ 67 (2002) 285-286 (*Hogan, Maurice*).

384 ^E**Tuckett, Christopher M.** The scriptures in the gospels. BEThL 131: 1997 ⇒13,234... 17,329. ^RDSD 9 (2002) 277-278 (*Evans, Craig*).

385 ^E**Watson, Duane F.** The intertexture of apocalyptic discourse in the New Testament. Symposium series 14: Atlanta 2002, SBL xiii; 299 pp. $40. 1-58983-041-5. Bibl. 243-263.

386 ^E**West, Gerald O.; Dube, Musa W.** The bible in Africa: transactions, trajectories and trends. 2000 ⇒16,342; 17,333. ^RMiss. 30 (2002) 117-118 (*Maclean, Iain S.*); Exchange 33 (2002) 302-303 (*Schaaf, Ype*).

387 ^E**Wimbush, Vincent** African Americans and the bible: sacred texts and social textures. 2000 ⇒16,344; 17,334. ^RTS 63 (2002) 388-390 (*Okoye, James Chukwuma*).

388 **Witczyk, Henryk, al.**, Kto bedzie zbawiony?. Verbum Vitae 1: Kielce 2002, VERBUM 299 pp. **P.**

A1.4 *Plurium compilationes* **theologicae**

389 ^E**Assmann, Jan; Bommas, Martin** Ägyptische Mysterien?. Kulte, Kulturen: Müns 2002, Fink 151 pp. €22.90. 3-7705-3650-9.

390 ^E**Assmann, Jan; Trauzettel, Rolf** Tod, Jenseits und Identität: Perspektiven einer kulturwissenschaftlichen Thanatologie. Veröffentlichungen des 'Instituts für Historische Anthropologie E.V.' 7: FrB 2002, Alber 831 pp. 3-495-47931-7.

391 ^E**Bauckham, Richard; Hart, Trevor** Hope against hope: christian eschatology in contemporary context. 1999 ⇒15,304...17,8215. ^RTrinJ 23 (2002) 136-138 (*Pennington, Jonathan T.*); SJTh 55 (2002) 482-484 (*Cosden, Darrell*).

392 ^E**Blickle, Peter,** *al.*, Macht und Ohnmacht der Bilder: reformatorischer Bildersturm im Kontext der europäischen Geschichte. HZ.B 33: Mü 2002, Oldenbourg x; 537 pp. 3-486-64433-5/56634-2.

393 ^E**Bongardt, Michael; Kampling, Rainer; Wörner, Markus** Verstehen an der Grenze: Beiträge zur Hermeneutik interkultureller und interreligiöser Kommunikation. Jerusalemer Theologisches Forum 4: Müns 2002, Aschendorff 236 pp. €37. 3-402-07503-2.

394 ^E**Bremmer, Jan Nicolaas; Veenstra, Jan R.** The metamorphosis of magic from late antiquity to the early modern period. Groningen Studies in Cultural Change 1: Lv 2002, Peeters xv; 317 pp. 90-429-1227-8. Bibl. 273-305.

395 ^E**D'Lima, Errol; Gonsalves, Max** What does Jesus Christ mean?. 2001 ⇒17,348. ^RLivWo 108 (2002) 234-235 (*Karikassery, Joseph*).

396 ^E**Diez de Velasco, Francisco; García Bazán, Francisco** El estudio de la religión. M 2002, Trotta 434 pp. 84-8164-554-0.

397 ^E**Diez de Velasco, Francisco** Miedo y religión. M 2002, Orto 380 pp. 84-7923-295-1.

398 ^E**Dorival, G.; Pralon, D.** Prières méditerranéennes hier et aujourd'hui. Textes et documents de la Méditerranée antique et médiévale 1: 2000 ⇒16,359. ^RREG 115 (2002) 435-436 (*Pouderon, Bernard*).

399 ^E**Ebach, Jürgen,** *al.*, Gretchenfrage: von Gott reden—aber wie?, 1. Jabboq 2: Gü 2002, Gü'er 193 pp. 3-579-05188-1.

400 ^E**Ferngren, Gary B.** The history of science and religion in the western tradition: an encyclopedia. Garland Reference Library 1833: 2000 ⇒ 16,361. ^RHeyJ 43 (2002) 375-377 (*Klaver, Jan Marten Ivo*).

401 ^E**Fiorensoli, Dario** Colpa e sacrificio: il sacrificio vicario nella storia delle religioni. La Vite e i Tralci 9: S. Pietro in Cariano (Verona) 2002, Il Segno dei Gabrielli 194 pp. 88-88163-03-4.

402 ^E**Fischer, Michael; Rothaug, Diana** Das Motiv des Guten Hirten in Theologie, Literatur und Musik. Mainzer Hymnologische Studien 5: Tü 2002, Francke 328 pp. €48. 3-7720-2915-9.

403 ^E**Frankemölle, Hubert** Christen und Juden gemeinsam ins dritte Jahrtausend: 'das Geheimnis der Erlösung heißt Erinnerung'. 2001 ⇒17, 352. ^RBiLi 75 (2002) 71-72 (*Himmelbauer, Markus*).

404 ^E**Fürst, Walther** Pastoralästhetik: die Kunst der Wahrnehmung und Gestaltung in Glaube und Kirche. QD 199: FrB 2002, Herder 348 pp. 3-4510-2199-4. Mitarb. Andreas Wittrahm; Ulrich Feeser-Lichterfield.

405 ^E**Geerlings, Wilhelm** Theologen der christlichen Antike: eine Einführung. Da:Wiss 2002, 226 pp. €29.90. 3-534-14736-7. ^RActBib 39 (2002) 219-220 (*Boada, J.*).

406 ^E**Gestrich, Christof** Die Aktualität der Antike: das ethische Gedächtnis des Abendlandes. BThZ.B, 2002: B 2002, Wichern 152 pp. 3-889-81-134-5. Bibl. 151-152.

407 ^E**Groß, Walter** Das Judentum. 2001 ⇒17,360. ^RJud. 58 (2002) 137-138 (*Morgenstern, Matthias*).

408 ^E**Hahn, Johannes** Religiöse Landschaften. AOAT 301: Müns 2002, Ugarit-Verlag vi (2); 227 pp. 3-9346-283-11. Mitarb. *Christian Ronning*.

409 ^E**Häfner, Gerd; Schmid, Hansjörg** Wie heute vom Tod Jesu sprechen?: neutestamentliche, systematisch-theologische und liturgiewissenschaftliche Perspektiven. FrB 2002, Katholische Akademie 191 pp. €18. 3-928698-20-6.

410 ^E**Helm, Paul; Trueman, Carl R.** The trustworthiness of God: perspectives on the nature of scripture. GR 2002, Eerdmans xiv; 289 pp. $28. 0-8028-4951-2.

411 ^E**Henriksen, Jan-Olav** Makt eiendom rettferdighet: bibelske moraltradisjoner i møte med vår tid. Oslo 2000, Gyldendal 272 pp. KR290. ^RRBLit 4 (2002) 103-105 (*Nissen, Johannes*).

412 ^E**Huxley, Andrew** Religion, law and tradition: comparative studies in religious law. L 2002, RoutledgeCurzon 240 pp. $105. 0-7007-1689-0.

413 **Jung, Patricia Beattie; Coray, Joseph Andrew** Sexual diversity and catholicism: toward the development of moral theology. 2001 ⇒17, 363. ^RBTB 32 (2002) 40 (*Salzmann, Todd*).

414 ^E**Katz, Steven T.** Mysticism and sacred scripture. 2000 ⇒16,369. ^RSpiritus 2/1 (2002) 108-109 (*McGinn, Bernard*).

415 ^E**Kinzig, Wolfram; Kück, Cornelia** Judentum und Christentum zwischen Konfrontation und Faszination: Ansätze zu einer neuen Beschreibung der jüdisch-christlichen Beziehungen. Judentum und Christentum 11: Stu 2002, Kohlhammer 221 pp. 3-17-017593-9.

416 ^E**Klöckener, Martin; Kranemann, Benedikt** Liturgiereformen: historische Studien zu einem bleibenden Grundzug des christlichen Gottesdienstes: Teil I: biblische Modelle und Liturgiereformen von der Frühzeit bis zur Aufklärung; Teil II: Liturgiereformen seit der Mitte des 19. Jahrhunderts bis zur Gegenwart. Liturgiewissenschaftliche Quellen und Forschungen 88: Müns 2002, Aschendorff 2 vols. 3-402-04067-0.

417 ^E**Kranemann, Benedikt; Sternberg, Thomas** Wie das Wort Gottes feiern?: der Wortgottesdienst als theologische Herausforderung. QD 194: FrB 2002, Herder 256 pp. €24.90. 3-451-02194-3.

418 ^E**Krebernik, Manfred; Van Oorschot, Jürgen** Polytheismus und Monotheismus in den Religionen des Vorderen Orients. AOAT 298: Müns 2002, Ugarit-Verlag (6); 269 pp. 3-934628-27-3. ^RUF 34 (2002) 954-957 (*Loretz, O.*).

419 ^E**Kreuzer, Siegfried; Lüpke, Johannes von** Gerechtigkeit glauben und erfahren: Beiträge zur Rechtfertigungslehre. VKHW 7: Neuk 2002, Neuk 287 pp. 3-406-482023.

420 ^E**Laplanche, Fr.** Histoire du christianisme des origines à nos jours, 14: anamnèsis: origines—perspectives—index. 2001 ⇒17,366. ^RNRTh 124 (2002) 317-318 (*Joassart, B.*).

421 ^E**Lehming, Hanna** Wendung nach Jerusalem: Friedrich-Wilhelm Marquardts Theologie im Gespräch. 1999 ⇒15,326. ^RLebZeug 57 (2002) 64-65 (*Petzel, Paul*).

422 La libertà. Firmana 28-29: Fermo 2002, Istituto Teologico Marchigiano 227 pp.

423 [E]**Malek, Roman** The Chinese face of Jesus Christ, 1. Monograph 50/1: Sankt Augustin 2002, Institut Monumenta Serica 391 pp. €40. 3-8050-0476-1. [R]BgMiss 66 (2002) 337-339 (*Müller, Wilhelm K.*).

424 [E]**Moriconi, Bruno** Antropologia cristiana: bibbia, teologia, cultura. 2001 ⇒17,371. [R]Ang. 79 (2002) 475-480 (*Mirri, Luciana Maria*).

425 [E]**Mursell, Gordon** The story of spirituality: two thousand years, from east to west. Mp 2001, Fortress 384 pp. $35. [R]RBLit 4 (2002) 476-479 (*Dreitcer, Andrew*).

426 [E]**Neuner, Peter** Glaubenswissenschaft?: Theologie im Spannungsfeld von Glaube, Rationalität und Öffentlichkeit. QD 195: FrB 2002, Herder 173 pp. 3-451-02195-1.

427 [E]**Neuner, Peter; Wenz, Gunther** Theologen des 19. Jahrhunderts: eine Einführung. Da:Wiss 2002, 242 pp. €29.90. 3-534-14962-9. [R]ActBib 39 (2002) 206-207 (*Boada, J.*);

428 Theologen des 20. Jahrhunderts: eine Einführung. Da:Wiss 2002, 239 pp. €29.90. 3-534-14963-7. [R]ActBib 39 (2002) 208-209 (*Boada, J.*).

429 [E]**Osten-Sacken, Peter von der** Das missbrauchte Evangelium: Studien zur Theologie und Praxis der Thüringer Deutschen Christen. B 2002, Institut Kirche und Judentum 432 pp.

430 [E]**Panimolle, Salvatore A.,** *al.*, Guerra e pace nei padri della chiesa: DSBP. I grandi temi della s. scrittura per la 'lectio divina' 33: R 2002, Borla 199 pp. €20.

431 [E]**Parsons, Susan Frank** The Cambridge companion to feminist theology. Cambridge Companions to Religion: NY 2002, CUP xviii; 268 pp. $55/20. 0-521-66327-X/80-6 [ThD 49,367—Heiser, W. Charles].

432 [E]**Perez de Laborda, Alfonso** Dios para pensar: El Escorial 2002. Presencia y diálogo 2: M 2002, Publicaciones de la Facultad de Teología "San Damaso" 237 pp. 84-932705-5-5.

433 [E]**Porter, Barbara Nevling** One God or many?: concepts of divinity in the ancient world. 2000 ⇒16,375; 17,375. [R]BiOr 59 (2002) 438-440 (*Tromp, Johannes*).

434 [E]**Porter, Stanley E.; Cross, Anthony R.** Dimensions of baptism: biblical and theological studies. JSNT.S 234: L 2002, Sheffield A. xvi; 401 pp. £80. 0-8264-6203-0. Bibl. 354-379.

435 **Possenti, Vittorio,** *al.*, Il monoteismo. Uomini e religioni, Saggi: Mi 2002, Mondadori 259 pp. 88-04-49023-3.

436 [E]**Riedel-Spangenberger, Ilona** Leitungsstrukturen der katholischen Kirche: kirchenrechtliche Grundlagen und Reformbedarf. QD 198: FrB 2002, Herder 256 pp. 3-451-02198-6.

437 [E]**Scarafoni, Paolo** Cristocentrismo: riflessione teologica. Collana di teologia: R 2002, Città N. 412 pp. 88-311-3343-8.

438 [E]**Schwikart, Georg** Was ist der Sinn meines Lebens?: Antworten aus den Religionen der Welt. GTBS 1170: Gü 2002, Gü'er 144 pp. 3-579-01170-7.

439 [E]**Shulman, David; Stroumsa, Guy G.** Self and self-transformation in the history of religions. NY 2002, OUP xii; 268 pp. 0-19-514450-3.

440 [E]**Stackhouse, John G.** What does it mean to be saved?: broadening evangelical horizons of salvation. GR 2002, Baker A. 198 pp. $18.

441 [E]**Williams, D.H.** The free church and the early church: bridging the historical and theological divide. GR 2002, Eerdmans xiii; 183 pp. 0-8028-4986-5.

442 [E]**Zeller, Dieter** Christentum, 1: von den Anfängen bis zur Konstantinischen Wende. Die Religionen der Menschheit 28: Stu 2002, Kohlhammer x; 474 pp. €89. 3-17-014787-0. Bibl. 7-11.

443 ^E**Zeller, Dieter** Religion und Weltbild. Marburger Religionsgeschichtliche Beiträge 2: Müns 2002, LIT 190 pp. 3-8258-6294-1.

A1.5 *Plurium compilationes* philologicae vel archaeologicae

444 ^E**Abusch, Tzvi; Van der Toorn, Karel** Mesopotamian magic: textual, historical, and interpretive perspectives. 1999 ⇒15,332. ^RSEL 19 (2002) 157-158 (*Xella, Paolo*).

445 ^E**Adams, J.N.; Janse, M.; Swain, S.** Bilingualism in ancient society: language contact and the written text. Oxf 2002, OUP x; 483 pp. £65. 0-19-924506-1.

446 ^E**Aldhouse-Green, Miranda; Webster, Peter** Artefacts and archaeology: aspects of the Celtic and Roman world. Cardiff 2002, Univ. of Wales Pr. xii; 276 pp 0-7083-1752-9.

447 ^E**Ariel, Donald T.** Excavations at the city of David 1978-1985 VI: inscriptions. Qedem 41: 2000 ⇒16,379; 17,389. ^RZDPV 118 (2002) 92-99 (*Weippert, Manfred*).

448 ^E**Biale, David** Cultures of the Jews: a new history. NY 2002, Schocken xxxiii; 1196 pp. 0-8052-4131-0.

449 ^{TE}**Bierling, Marilyn R.** The Phoenicians in Spain: an archaeological review of the eight-sixth centuries B.C.E.: a collection of articles translated from Spanish. WL 2002, Eisenbrauns xv; 304 pp. $39.50. 1-57506-056-6. *Gitin, Seymour* assoc. ed.; 122 ill. ^RRSO 76 (2002) 265-267 (*Garbini, Giovanni*).

450 ^E**Bispham, Edward; Smith, Christopher** Religion in archaic and republican Rome and Italy: evidence and experience. 2000 ⇒16,384. ^RPrudentia 34/1 (2002) 69-76 (*Stevenson, Tom*).

451 ^E**Blasius, Andreas; Schipper, Bernd Ulrich** Apokalyptik und Ägypten: eine kritische Analyse der relevanten Texte aus dem griechisch-römischen Ägypten. OLA 107: Lv 2002, Peeters x; 329 pp. 90-429-1113-1. 16 pl.; Bibl. 303-314.

452 ^E**Blench, Roger; Spriggs, Matthew** Archaeology and language, 1: theoretical and methodological orientations. 1997 ⇒15,335. ^RAJA 106 (2002) 111-112 (*Smith, Joanna S.*).

453 **Blum, Hartmut**, *al.*, Brückenland Anatolien?: Ursachen, Extensität und Modi des Kulturaustausches zwischen Anatolien und seinen Nachbarn. Tü 2002, Attempto vii; 400 pp. 3-89308-346-4.

454 ^E**Blumenfield-Kosinsky, Renate; Robertson, Duncan; Warren, Nancy Bradley** The vernacular spirit: essays on medieval religious literature. The New Middle Ages: NY 2002, Palgrave vii; 324 pp. £32.50. 0-312-29385-2 [JEH 55,367s—Alexandra Barratt].

455 ^E**Boer, Roland** Tracking the tribes of Yahweh: on the trail of a classic. JSOT.S 351: L 2002, Sheffield A. ix; 205 pp. £50. 0-8264-6050-X. Bibl. 186-201.

456 ^E**Borbein, Adolf H.; Hölscher, Tonio; Zanker, Paul** Klassische Archäologie: eine Einführung. 2000 ⇒16,385. ^RAJA 106 (2002) 115-116 (*Calder, William M.*).

457 **Bottero, Jean; Herrenschmidt, Clarisse; Vernant, Jean-Pierre** Ancestor of the west: writing, reasoning and religion in Mesopotamia, Elam and Greece. 2000 ⇒16,386. ^RJRH 26 (2002) 98-9 (*Ridley, R.T.*).

458 ^E**Chavalas, Mark William; Younger, K. Lawson** Mesopotamia and the bible: comparative explorations. JSOT.S 341: Shf 2002, Sheffield A. 395 pp. $30. 1-84127-252-3.

459 ^EColeman, John E.; Walz, Clark A. Greeks and Barbarians: essays on the interactions between Greeks and non-Greeks in antiquity and the consequences for Eurocentrism. 1997 ⇒13,272; 15,341. ^RAJA 106 (2002) 128-130 (*Malkin, Irad*).

460 ^ECollins, John J.; Sterling, Gregory E. Hellenism in the land of Israel. Christianity and Judaism in Antiquity 13: 2001 ⇒17,399. ^RSBET 20 (2002) 120-122 (*Gathercole, Simon*); JSJ 33 (2002) 290-313 (*Feldman, Louis H.*); CBQ 64 (2002) 410-412 (*Harrington, Daniel J.*).

461 ^ECoogan, Michael David The Oxford history of the biblical world. 1998 ⇒17,258. ^RCBQ 64 (2002) 187-188 (*Huddleston, John R.*).

462 ^ECowey, James M.S.; Maresch, Klaus Urkunden des Politeuma der Juden von Herakleopolis (144/3 - 133/2 v. Chr.) (P. Polit. Iud.): Papyri aus den Sammlungen von Heidelberg, Köln, München und Wien. PapyCol 29: 2001 ⇒17,400. ^RBiOr 59 (2002) 541-550 (*Falivene, Maria Rosaria*); JQR 93 (2002) 257-268 (*Kasher, Aryeh*).

463 ^EDahl, Östen Tense and aspect in the languages of Europe. Empirical approaches to language typology 20: 2000 ⇒16,395. ^RAGI 87 (2002) 120-124 (*Di Giovine, Paolo*).

464 ^EDe Angelis, Violetta Sviluppi recenti nella ricerca antichistica. Quaderni di ACME 54: Mi 2002, Cisalpino 407 pp. 88-323-4616-8. 75 tav., fig.

465 Denis, Albert-Marie, *al.*, Introduction à la littérature religieuse judéohellénistique. 2000 ⇒16,397; 17,402. ^RJSJ 33 (2002) 101-102 (*Hilhorst, A.*); EThL 78 (2002) 189-191 (*Verheyden, J.*); Sal. 64 (2002) 570-572 (*Vicent, R.*); AnBoll 120 (2002) 438-440 (*Lequeux, N.*); Apocrypha 13 (2002) 257-278 (*Roessli, Jean-Michel*); LTP 58 (2002) 618-619 (*Painchaud, Louis*).

466 ^EDirven, René; Porings, Ralf Metaphor and metonymy in comparison and contrast. Cognitive linguistics research 20: B 2002, De Gruyter xii; 605 pp. $118. 3-1101-7373-5 [Lg. 80,344—Xie, Chaoqun].

467 ^EDognini, Cristiano Kosmos: la concezione del mondo nelle civiltà antiche. Studi di storia greca e romana: T 2002, Dell'Orso 176 pp. 88-7694-610-1.

468 ^EEgelhaaf-Gaiser, Ulrike; Schäfer, Alfred Religiöse Vereine in der römischen Antike: Untersuchungen zu Organisation, Ritual und Raumordnung. STAC 13: Tü 2002, Mohr viii; 310 pp. €64. 3-16-147771-5.

469 Elayi, J.; Sapin, J. Quinze ans de recherche (1985-2000) sur la Transeuphratène à l'époque perse. TEuph.S 8: 2000 ⇒16,398. ^RETR 77 (2002) 432-433 (*Nocquet, Dany*); RSR 90 (2002) 244-245 (*Abadie, Philippe*).

470 ^EFforde, Cressida; Hubert, Jane; Turnbull, Paul The dead and their possessions: repatriation in principle, policy and practic.e One World Archaeology 43: L 2002, Routledge xix; 340 pp. 0-415-23385-2.

471 Frede, Simone, *al.*, Die phönizischen anthropoiden Sarkophage, 2: Tradition—Rezeption—Wandel. ^E*Schäfer, Pia; Schollmeyer, Patrick; Weber, Sabine*: Forschungen zur phönizisch-punischen und zyprischen Plastik 1/2: Mainz 2002, Von Zabern xi; 358 pp. 3805329385. 120 pl..

472 ^EGeerlings, Wilhelm; Schulze, Christian Der Kommentar in Antike und Mittelalter: Beiträge zu seiner Erforschung. Clavis Commentariorum Antiquitatis et Medii Aevi 2: Lei 2002, Brill vii; 371 pp. 90-0412-528-0.

473 ^EGignoux, Philippe Ressembler au monde: nouveaux documents sur la théorie du macro-microcosme dans l'antiquité orientale. BEHE.R 106: 1999 ⇒15,356. ^RApocrypha 13 (2002) 281-283 (*Roessli, J.-M.*).

474 ^E**Gordon, Cyrus H.; Rendsburg, Gary A.** Eblaitica: essays on the Ebla archives and Eblaite language, 4. Publications of the Center for Ebla Research at New York University 4: WL 2002, Eisenbrauns xvi; 269 pp. $39.50. 1-57506-060-4.

475 ^E**Gualandri, Isabella** Tra IV e V secolo: studi sulla cultura latina tardoantica. Quaderni di ACME 50: Mi 2002, Cisalpino xii; 331 pp. 883-23-4612-5.

476 ^E**Gyselen, Rika** La science des cieux: sages, mages, astrologues. Res orientales 12: Lv 1999, Peeters vi; 264 pp. €72 2-9508-2666-0. ^ROLZ 97 (2002) 362-365 (*Böck, Barbara*);

477 Charmes et sortilèges: magie et magiciens. Res Orientales 14: Bures-sur-Yvette 2002, Groupe pour l'Étude de la Civilisation du Moyen-Orient 304 pp. 2-9508266-8-7.

478 ^E**Hansen, Mogens Herman** A comparative study of thirty city-state cultures: an investigation conducted by the Copenhagen Polis Centre. 2000 ⇒16,407. ^RJESHO 45 (2002) 136-138 (*Liverani, Mario*).

479 ^E**Harrison, Thomas** Greeks and barbarians: Readings on the Ancient World: E 2002, University Pr. xv; 336 pp. 0-7486-1271-8. Bibl. 314-327.

480 ^E**Heinz, M.; Bonatz, Dominik** Bild—Macht—Geschichte: visuelle Kommunikation im Alten Orient. B 2002, Reimer 230 pp. €28. 3-496-01258-7 55. Ill.

481 ^E**Hellinger, Marlis; Bußmann, Hadumod** Gender across languages: the lingustic representation of women and men, 2. Impact 10: Amst 2002, Benjamins xiii; 348 pp. 90-272-1842-0.

482 ^E**Hempel, Charlotte; Lange, Armin; Lichtenberger, Hermann** The wisdom texts from Qumran and the development of sapiential thought. BEThL 159: Lv 2002, University Pr. xi; 502; 8 pp. €80. 9042-9101-00.

483 ^E**Hetzron, Robert** The Semitic languages. 1997 ⇒13,283; 16,408. ^RIOS 20 (2002) 501-510 (*Izre'el, Shlomo*).

484 ^E**Hodkinson, Stephen; Powell, Anton** Sparta: beyond the mirage. L 2002, Duckworth xx; 354 pp. 0-7156-31837.

485 ^E**Hoffmann, Adolf; Kerner, Susanne** Gadara—Gerasa und die Dekapolis. Zaberns Bildbände zur Archäologie: Mainz 2002, Von Zabern 150 pp. €37.50. 3-8053-2687-4.

486 ^E**Hopkins, David C.** Across the Anatolian Plateau: readings in the archaeology of ancient Turkey. AASOR 57, 2000: Oxf 2002, Oxbow x; 209 pp. £60. 0-89757-053-7.

487 ^E**Horowitz, Elliott; Orfali, Moises** The Mediterranean and the Jews: society, culture and economy in early modern times, 2. Ramat-Gan 2002, Bar-Ilan Univ. Pr. 266 pp. $38. 965-226-221-8 23. Ill.

488 ^E**Højte, Jakob Munk** Images of ancestors. Aarhus Studies in Mediterranean Antiquity (ASMA) 5: Aarhus 2002, University Pr. 308 pp. $35. 87-7288-948-9. Bibl. 259-290.

489 ^E**Klinger, Elmar; Böhm, Stephanie; Franz, Thomas** Paare in antiken religiösen Texten und Bildern: Symbole für Geschlechterrollen damals und heute. Wü 2002, Echter 211 pp. 3-429-02518-4.

490 ^E**Konradt, Matthias; Steinert, Ulrike** Ethos und Identität: Einheit und Vielfalt des Judentums in hellenistisch-römischer Zeit. Studien zu Judentum und Christentum: Pd 2002, Schöningh 192 pp. 35067-23618.

491 ^E**Koschel, Ansgar** Katholische Kirche und Judentum im 20. Jahrhundert. Müns 2002, LIT 176 pp. €17.90. 3-8258-5507-4. ^RSaThZ 6 (2002) 317-318 (*Winkler, Ulrich*).

492 ᴱ**Kratz, Reinhard G.** Religion und Religionskontakte im Zeitalter der Achämeniden. Veröffentlichungen der Wissenschaftlichen Gesellschaft für Theologie 22: Gü 2002, Gü'er 312 pp. €50. 3-579-05350-7.
493 ᴱ**Lana, Italo; Maltese, Enrico V.** Storia della civiltà letteraria greca e latina v.1, Dalle origini al IV secolo a.C.; v.2, dall'ellenismo all'età di Traiano; v.3, dall'età degli Antonini alla fine del mondo antico. 1998 ⇒14,346. ᴿÁsp. 49 (2002) 124-128 (*Di Palma, Gaetano*).
494 ᴱ**Lebrun, R.** Syro Anatolica scripta minora II. Muséon 115/1-2 (2002) 1-10.
495 ᴱ**Lehmann, Yves** Religions de l'antiquité. Premier cycle: 1999 ⇒16, 416. ᴿIst. 47 (2002) 416-421 (*Couteau, Elisabeth*).
496 ᴱ**Lemaire, André** Les routes du Proche-orient: des séjours d'Abraham aux caravanes de l'encens. 2000 ⇒16,417. ᴿTEuph 23 (2002) 207-209 (*Elayi, J.*).
497 ᴱ**Levy, Thomas E.; Van den Brink, Edwin C.M.** Egypt and the Levant: interrelations from the 4th through the early 3rd millennium BCE. L 2002, Leicester University Pr. xxi; 547 pp. $210. 0-7185-0262-0. Num. ill.
498 ᴱ**Lewin, Ariel** Gli ebrei nell'Impero Romano: saggi vari. 2001 ⇒17, 415. ᴿStudi Fatti Ricerche 97 (2002) 13-14 (*Menestrina, Giovanni*).
499 ᴱ**Lim, Timothy H.; MacQueen, Hector L.; Carmichael, Calum M.** On scrolls, artefacts and intellectual property. JSPE.S 38: 2001 ⇒17, 416. ᴿRSR 90 (2002) 437-438 (*Paul, André*).
500 ᴱ**Long, V. Philips; Baker, David W.; Wenham, Gordon J.** Windows into Old Testament history: evidence, argument, and the crisis of 'Biblical Israel'. GR 2002, Eerdmans viii; 204 pp. $22. 0-8028-3962-2. ᴿIgreja e Missão 55/1 (2002) 109-110 (*Couto, A.*); RTR 61 (2002) 167-168 (*Goswell, Greg*).
501 ᴱ**Loprieno, Antonio** Ancient Egyptian literature: history and forms. PÄ 10: 1996 ⇒12,230… 16,420. ᴿBiOr 59 (2002) 40-45 (*Shirun-Grumach, Irene*); OLZ 97 (2002) 43-55 (*Moers, Gerald*); JNES 61 (2002) 310-311 (*Foster, John L.*).
502 ᴱ**Luukkainen, Matti; Pyykkö, Riitta** Zur Rolle der Sprache im Wandel der Gesellschaft: the role of language in changes of society. STAT.Humaniora 317; AASF: Helsinki 2002, Finnish Society of Sciences and Letters 308 pp. 951-41-0908-2. Bibl. 304-305.
503 ᴱ**Macleod, R.** The library of Alexandria: centre of learning in the ancient world. 2000 ⇒16,421; 17,418. ᴿSCI 21 (2002) 280-283 (*Wasserstein, David J.*).
504 ᴱ**Mattingly, David J.; Salmon, John** Economies beyond agriculture in the classical world. 2001 ⇒17,419. ᴿHZ 275 (2002) 708 (*Möller, Astrid*).
505 ᴱ**Mirecki, Paul Allan; Meyer, Marvin W.** Magic and ritual in the ancient world. RGRW 141: Lei 2002, Brill xvii; 468 pp. 90-04-10406-2.
506 ᴱ**Mitchell, Kathleen; Wood, Ian N.** The world of Gʀᴇɢᴏʀʏ of Tours. Cultures, Beliefs and Traditions, Medieval and Early Modern Peoples 8: Lei 2002, Brill xx; 445 pp. 90-04-11034-8.
507 ᴱ**Nebes, Norbert** Tempus und Aspekt in den semitischen Sprachen. 1999 ⇒16,427. ᴿZDMG 152 (2002) 400-402 (*Fischer, Wolfdietrich*).
508 ᴱ**Neuhaus, Richard John** The chosen people in an almost chosen nation: Jews and Judaism in America. GR 2002, Eerdmans xii; 218 pp. 0-8028-4929-6.

509 ^E**Neusner, Jacob; Avery-Peck, Alan J.** Judaism in late antiquity, 3: where we stand: issues and debates in ancient Judaism, 3. HO 1/53: 2000 ⇒16,428. ^RJSJ 33 (2002) 316-317 (*Teugels, Lieve*);

510 Where we stand: issues and debates in ancient Judaism, 4: the special problem of the synagogue. HO 1/55: 2001 ⇒17,424. ^RJSJ 33 (2002) 318-320 (*Teugels, Lieve*);

511 Judaism in late antiquity, 5: the Judaism of Qumran. HO 1/56-57: 2001 ⇒17,425. ^RDSD 9 (2002) 394-399 (*Brooke, George J.*).

512 ^E**Oden, Amy G.** And you welcomed me: a sourcebook on hospitality in early christianity. Nv 2001, Abingdon 316 pp. 0-687-09671-5. Bibl. 304-314.

513 ^E**Olsson, Birger O.; Mitternacht, Dieter; Brandt, Olof** The synagogue of ancient Ostia and the Jews of Rome: interdisciplinary studies. 2001 ⇒17,427. ^RBASOR 328 (2002) 97-99 (*Meyers, Eric M.*).

514 ^E**Oppenheimer, Aharon** Jüdische Geschichte in hellenistisch-römischer Zeit: Wege der Forschung: vom alten zum neuen Schürer. 1999 ⇒15,376. ^RHZ 274 (2002) 421-423 (*Botermann, Helga*).

515 ^E**Oren, E.D.** The sea peoples and their world: a reassessment. 2000 ⇒ 16,429; 17,428, ^RBASOR 326 (2002) 94-96 (*Cline, Eric H.*); BiOr 59 (2002) 399-405 (*Smith, J.S.*).

516 ^E**Parayre, Dominique** Les animaux et les hommes dans le monde syro-mesopotamien aux époques historiques. Topoi Supplément 2: Lyon 2002, Maison de l'Orient Méditerranéen 506 pp. €23.

517 ^E**Porter, Stanley E.; Evans, Craig A.** The scrolls and the scriptures: Qumran fifty years after. JSPE.S 26: 1997 ⇒13,299... 16,432. ^RRBLit 4 (2002) 274-275 (*Kugler, Robert E.*).

518 ^E**Rowlandson, Jane** Women and society in Greek and Roman Egypt: a sourcebook. 1998 ⇒14,9678... 17,435. ^RLatomus 61 (2002) 470-471 (*Straus, Jean A.*).

519 ^E**Scarre, Chris** Monuments and landscape in Atlantic Europe: perception and society during the Neolithic and Early Bronze Age. L 2002, Routledge xiii; 210 pp. 0-415-27313-7. Bibl. 202-204.

520 ^E**Schäfer, Peter; Hezser, Catherine** The Talmud Yerushalmi and Graeco-Roman culture II. TSAJ 79: 2000 ⇒16,442. ^RSal. 64 (2002) 142-143 (*Vicent, R.*).

521 ^E**Schuol, Monika; Hartmann, Udo; Luther, Andreas** Grenzüberschreitungen: Formen des Kontakts zwischen Orient und Okzident im Altertum. Oriens et Occidens 3: Stu 2002, Steiner 415 pp. 3-515-07962-9.

522 Semitic linguistics: the state of the art at the turn of the twenty-first century. ^E**Izre'el, Shlomo**: IOS 20 (2002) 535 pp.

523 ^E**Setälä, P.; Savunen, L.** Female networks and the public sphere in Roman society. 1999 ⇒15,386; 16,443. ^RAnCl 71 (2002) 464-466 (*Raepsaet-Charlier, Marie-Thérèse*).

524 ^E**Siegert, Folker** Israel als Gegenüber: vom alten Orient bis in die Gegenwart: Studien zur Geschichte eines wechselvollen Zusammenlebens. SIJD 5: 2000 ⇒16,444. ^RThLZ 127 (2002) 639-641 (*Löhr, Hermut*).

525 ^E**Silberman, Neil Asher; Frerichs, Ernest S.** Archaeology and society in the 21st century. 2001 ⇒17,443. ^RCV 44 (2002) 217-219 (*Segert, Stanislav*); DSD 9 (2002) 268-271 (*Broshi, Magen*).

526 ^E**Swanson, R.N.** The Holy Land, holy lands, and christian history. SCH(L) 36: L 2000, Boydell & B. xxiv; 397 pp £40. 0-95297-3359.

527 ^E**Taplin, O.** Literature in the Greek and Roman worlds: a new perspective. 2000 ⇒16,446. ^RJRS 92 (2002) 225-226 (*Brady, Martin*).

528 ᴱTirosh-Samuelson, Hava Judaism and ecology: created world and revealed world. Religions of the world and ecology: CM 2002, Harvard Univ. Pr. lxii; 515 pp. $47/29. 0-945454-35-X/6-8. Bibl. 481-486 [ThD 50,274—Heiser, W. Charles].

529 ᴱToo, Yun Lee Education in Greek and Roman antiquity. 2001 ⇒17, 448. ᴿClR 52 (2002) 331-333 (Morgan, Teresa).

530 ᴱTschuggnall, Peter Religion—Literatur—Kunst II: ein Dialog. Im Kontext 14: Anif/Salzburg 2002, Mueller-Speiser xiv; 593 pp. 3-85145-061-2.

531 ᴱTsetskhladze, Gocha R. Ancient Greeks west and east. Mn.S 196: 1999 ⇒15,397; 17,447. ᴿAncient West & East 1/1 (2002) 13-17 (Ridgway, David).

532 ᴱTuplin, C.J.; Rihll, T.E. Science and mathematics in ancient Greek culture. Oxf 2002, OUP xvi; 379 pp. $80. 01981-52485. Bibl. 326-49.

533 ᴱValantasis, R. Religions of late antiquity in practice. 2000 ⇒16,448. ᴿClR 52 (2002) 384-385 (Lee, A.D.).

534 ᴱVogel, Petra M.; Comrie, Bernard Approaches to the typology of word classes. Empirical approaches to language typology 23: 2000 ⇒ 16,449. ᴿAGI 87 (2002) 109-115 (Ramat, Paolo).

535 ᴱWillinghöfer, Helga Die Hethiter und ihr Reich: das Volk der 1000 Götter. Stu 2002, Theiss 375 pp. 3-8062-1676-2. Ausstellung "Die Hethiter" vom 18. Januar bis 28. April 2002 Bonn.

536 ᴱWiseman, T.P. Classics in progress: essays on ancient Greece and Rome. Oxf 2002, OUP xvi; 451 pp. £45. 0-19-726270-8.

537 ᴱWorthington, Ian; Foley, John Miles Epea and grammata: oral and written communication in ancient Greece. Orality and Literacy in Ancient Greece 4; Mn.S 230: Lei 2002, Brill xi; 206 pp. 90-04-12455-1. Bibl. 191-201.

538 ᴱZwickel, Wolfgang Edelsteine in der Bibel. Mainz 2002, Von Zabern vii; 99 pp. €24.80. 3-8053-2912-1. 80 ill.

A2.1 Acta congressuum biblica

539 ᴱAbadie, Philippe; Lémonon, Jean-Pierre Le judaïsme à l'aube de l'ère chrétienne. LeDiv 186: 2001 ⇒17,450. 18e Congr. Assoc. Cath. Française pour l'étude de la bible, Lyon 1999. ᴿHumTeo 23/1 (2002) 118-121 (Carvalho, José Carlos); RSR 90 (2002) 432-434 (Paul, André); ScEs 54 (2002) 225-232 (Tremblay, Hervé); LTP 58 (2002) 366-367 (Poirier, Paul-Hubert).

540 ᴱAbbott, William M. The roles of woman and men in scripture in the context of family, church and society: proceedings of the third annual training center, Tagaytay City, 19-21 July 2002. Manila 2002, Catholic Biblical Association of the Philippines vi; 129 pp.

541 ᴱArmstrong, Donald Who do you say that I am?: christology and the church. 1999 ⇒15,401; 17,451. Symposium, Anglican Institute, Paris 1998. ᴿVJTR 66 (2002) 696-698 (Meagher, P.M.).

542 ᴱAvemarie, Friedrich; Lichtenberger, Hermann Auferstehung—Resurrection: the fourth Durham-Tübingen research symposium. WUNT 135: 2001 ⇒17,452. ᴿTThZ 111 (2002) 74-76 (Reiser, Marius); RHPhR 82 (2002) 191-192 (Grappe, Ch.); Sal. 64 (2002) 563-565 (Vicent, R.); CBQ 64 (2002) 606-608 (Perkins, Pheme); SEL 19 (2002) 168-171 (Lancellotti, Maria Grazia).

543 ^E**Berner, Christian; Wunenburger, Jean-Jacques** Mythes et philosophie: les traditions bibliques. P 2002, P.U.F. 270 pp. ^RRThPh 134 (2002) 97-98 (*Karakash, Clairette*).

544 ^E**Brooke, George J.** Jewish ways of reading the bible. JSSt.S 11: 2000 ⇒16,456. British Assoc. for Jewish Studies, Manchester 1999. ^RJJS 53 (2002) 168-169 (*Lange, Nicholas de*).

545 ^E**Casalegno, Alberto** Tempo ed eternità: in dialogo con Ugo Vanni S.I. RdT Library, Saggi 7: CinB 2002, San Paolo 399 pp. €20. 88-215-4632-2. 17th interdisciplinary seminar, Pontificia Facoltà Teologica dell'Italia Meridionale; Sezione san Luigi, Naples 2000.

546 ^E**Charlesworth, James H.** The Hebrew Bible and Qumran, 1. 2000 ⇒ 16,459. Proceedings of the Jubilee celebration at Princeton Theological Seminary. ^RDSD 9 (2002) 106-109 (*Gathercole, Simon J.*).

547 ^E**Charlesworth, James H.; Weaver, Walter P.** Jesus two thousand years later. 2000 ⇒16,458; 17,457. Biblical Symposium, Florida Southern 1998 ^RRBLit 4 (2002) 329-330 (*Vinson, Richard B.*).

548 ^E**Cook, Johann** Bible and computer: the Stellenbosch AIBI-6 Conference: "From Alpha to Byte," University of Stellenbosch 17-21 July, 2000. Lei 2002, Brill xxxv; 699 pp. 90-04-12495-0.

549 ^E**Dempsey, Carol J.; Loewe, William P.** Theology and sacred scripture. College Theol. Soc. Annual Publication. ser. 47: Mkn 2002, Orbis xv; 239 pp. $28. 15707-5411X. Conf. College Theology Society 2001.

550 ^E**Dietrich, Walter; Luz, Ulrich** The bible in a world context: an experiment in contextual hermeneutics. GR 2002, Eerdmans xii; 80 pp. $10. 0-8028-4988-1. Symposium, Univ. Bern 2000.

551 ^E**Donnelly, Doris** Jesus: a colloquium in the Holy Land. 2001 ⇒17, 461. ^RHorizons 29 (2002) 365-366 (*Crowley, Paul*).

552 ^E**Dunn, James D.G.** Paul and the Mosaic law. 2001 ⇒17,462. 3rd Durham-Tübingen Research Symposium 1994. ^RCThMi 29 (2002) 145-146 (*Linss, Wilhelm C.*); AUSS 40 (2002) 140-143 (*Burton, Keith Augustus*); RBLit (2002)* (*Nanos, Mark D.*).

553 ^E**Eriksson, Anders; Olbricht, Thomas H.; Übelacker, Walter** Rhetorical argumentation in biblical texts: essays from the Lund 2000 Conference. Emory studies in early christianity 8: Harrisburg 2002, Trinity 456 pp. $47. 1-56338-355-1. Bibl. 389-420.

554 ^E**Fédou, Michel** Le Fils unique et ses frères: unicité du Christ et pluralisme religieux. P 2002, Facultés Jésuites de Paris 164 pp. €12. 2-848-47001-1. Coll. Centre Sèvres 2001 [VJTR 67,467–Gispert-Sauch, G.].

555 ^E**Gourgues, Michel; Talbot, Michel** En ce temps-là... conceptions et expériences bibliques du temps. Montréal 2002, Médiaspaul 213 pp. $27. 2-89420-506-6. 58e congrès de l'ACÉBAC.

556 ^E**Green, Joel B.; Turner, Max** Between two horizons: spanning New Testament studies and systematic theology. 1999 ⇒16,267; 17,272. ^REvangel 20 (2002) 28-29 = 89-90 (*Marshall, I. Howard*).

557 ^E**Greenspoon, Leonard Jay; LeBeau, Bryan F.** Sacred text, secular times: the Hebrew Bible in the modern world. 2000 ⇒16,470; 17,467. ^RRBLit 4 (2002) 154-158 (*Tooze, George Andrew*).

558 ^E**Hafemann, Scott J.** Biblical theology: retrospect and prospect. DG 2002, InterVarsity 300 pp. $25. 0-8308-2684-X. Wheaton Theol. Conf., April 2000 [ThD 50,62—Heiser, W. Charles[..

559 ^E**Hahn, Johannes** Zerstörungen des Jerusalemer Tempels: Geschehen–Wahrnehmung–Bewältigung. WUNT 147: Tü 2002, Mohr viii; 279 pp. €89. 3-16-147719-7. Simposium Münster, 17-18 Nov. 2000.

560 ᴱHeller, J.; Talmon, S.; Hlaváčková, H. The Old Testament as inspiration in culture, international academic symposium, Prague, September 1995. 2001 ⇒17,470. ᴿCV 44 (2002) 132-135 (*Čapek, Filip*).

561 ᴱHofrichter, Peter Leander Für und wider die Priorität des Johannesevangeliums: Symposion Salzburg 10. März 2000. Theologische Texte u. Studien 9: Hildesheim 2002, Olms 320 pp. €40. 34871-16928.

562 ᴱHusherr, Cécile; Reiber, Emmanuel Figures bibliques, figures mythiques: ambiguités et réécritures. Coup d'essai: P 2002, Rue d'Ulm 128 pp. €18. Séminaire 1999-2000.

563 The interpretation of the bible: the international symposium in Slovenia. ᴱKrašovec, Jože: JSOT.S 289: 1998 ⇒14,388; 17,475. ᴿRBLit 4 (2002) 111-121 (*Becking, Bob*).

564 L'interpretazione della bibbia nella chiesa: atti del simposio promosso dalla Cong. per la Dottrina della Fede. 2001 ⇒17,471. ᴿPerTeol 34 (2002) 123-125 (*Koenings, Johan*); Path 1/1 (2002) 119-122 (*Amato, Angelo*); Annales Theologici 16 (2002) 278-280 (*Tábet, M.*); ED 55/3 (2002) 169-171 (*Biguzzi, Giancarlo*); Theoforum 33 (2002) 242-243 (*Vogels, Walter*); Alpha Omega 5 (2002) 373-377 (*Izquierdo, Antonio*); RevBib 64 (2002) 239-242 (*Ruiz, Eleuterio R.*).

565 ᴱIzquierdo, Antonio Scrittura ispirata: atti del simposio internazionale sull'ispirazione promosso dall'Ateneo Pontificio "Regina Apostolorum". Atti e Documenti 16: Città del Vaticano 2002, Libreria Editrice Vaticana 324 pp. €19. 88-209-7363-4.

566 ᴱJacob, Walter; Jürgensen, Almuth Die Exegese hat das erste Wort: Beiträge zu Leben und Werk Benno JACOBs. Stu 2002, Calwer 200 pp. €49. 3-7668-3745-1. Conf. Jerusalem & Hamburg [EuA 79,346— Hogg, Theodor].

567 ᴱKeel, Othmar; Zenger, Erich Gottesstadt und Gottesgarten: zu Geschichte und Theologie des Jerusalemer Tempels. QD 191: FrB 2002, Herder 288 pp. €24.90. 3-451-02191-9. Tagung deutschspr. kath. Alttestamentler, Mödling, August 2000.

568 ᴱLabahn, Michael; Zangenberg, Jürgen Zwischen den Reichen: Neues Testament und Römische Herrschaft: Vorträge auf der ersten Konferenz der European Association for Biblical Studies. TANZ 36: Tü 2002, Francke viii; 286 pp. €48. 3-7720-2828-4.

569 ᴱLeBeau, Bryan F.; Greenspoon, Leonard J.; Hamm, M. Dennis The historical Jesus through catholic and Jewish eyes. 2000 ⇒16,477; 17,476. Seminars, Creighton Univ., 1997, 1998. ᴿRBLit 4 (2002) 340-343 (*Just, Felix*); RBLit (2002)* (*Gilbert, Gary H.*).

570 ᴱLemaire, André Congress Volume Basel 2001. VT.S 92: Lei 2002, Brill vii; 409 pp. €108/$126. 90-04-12680-5.

571 ᴱLemaire, André; Saebo, Magne Congress Volume, Oslo 1998. VT.S 80: 2000 ⇒16,478. ᴿETR 77 (2002) 430-432 (*Bauks, Michaela*); CBQ 64 (2002) 404-406 (*Cahill, Michael*); RBLit (2002)* (*Power, Bruce*).

572 ᴱLeonardi, Claudio; Santi, Francesco; Valerio, Adriana La bibbia nell'interpretazione delle donne. Millennio Medievale 34; Atti di convegni 9: F 2002, Galluzzo xi; 249 pp. €62. 88-8450-073-7. Atti del convegno del Centro A. Pignatelli, Napoli 27-28.5.1999 [Il Tetto 233,80ss—Pernetti, Viviana].

573 ᴱLindemann, Andreas The sayings source Q and the historical Jesus. BEThL 158: 2001 ⇒17,477. ᴿRHPhR 82 (2002) 230-1 (*Grappe, Ch.*).

574 ᴱLuttikhuizen, Gerard P. Paradise interpreted: representations of biblical paradise in Judaism and Christianity. 1999 ⇒15,422...17,2066. Conf. 1998, Groningen. ᴿDSD 9 (2002) 417-423 (*Harding, James E.*).

575 ᴱMacDonald, Dennis R. Mimesis and intertextuality in antiquity and christianity. Harrisburg 2002, Trinity xi; 171 pp. $26. Conf. Claremont Univ. 1998 [BiTod 41,201—Senior, Donald].

576 ᴱMamiani, Maurizio Scienza e sacra scrittura nel XVII secolo. Biblioteca Europea 21: 2001 ⇒17,481. Convegno Univ. di Udine, 1995. ᴿGCFI (2002) 305-319 (*Lotti, Brunello*).

577 ᴱMarguerat, Daniel; Curtis, Adrian Intertextualités: la bible en échos. MoBi 40: 2000 ⇒16,481. Colloque Lausanne 1998. ᴿApocrypha 13 (2002) 315-317 (*Stoops, R.*); RBLit 4 (2002) 124-127 (*Brawley, Robert L.*).

578 ᴱMay, Gerhard; Greschat, Katharina MARCION und seine kirchengeschichtliche Wirkung: Marcion and his impact on church history: Vorträge der Internationalen Fachkonferenz zu Marcion, gehalten vom 15.-18. August 2001 in Mainz. TU 150: B 2002, De Gruyter xi; 333 pp. €94. 3-11-017599-1. Collab. *Martin Meiser*; Bibl. 313-322.

579 ᴱMeyer, Marvin; Hughes, Charles Jesus then and now: images of Jesus in history and christology. 2001 ⇒17,483. Conf. Chapman Univ., 1999. ᴿCBQ 64 (2002) 412-413 (*Mercer, Calvin R.*).

580 ᴱMimouni, Simon C. Le judéo-christianisme dans tous ses états: actes du colloque de Jérusalem 6-10 juillet 1998. LeDiv: 2001 ⇒17,484. ᴿREJ 161 (2002) 295-296 (*Maraval, Pierre*); RHPhR 82 (2002) 222-223 (*Grappe, Ch.*); Apocrypha 13 (2002) 293-294 (*Dubois, J.-D.*); RSPhTh 86 (2002) 129-131 (*Cerbelaud, Dominique*).

581 ᴱNaudé, J.A.; Van der Merwe, C.H.J. Contemporary translation studies and bible translations: a South African perspective. AcTh(B) 2: Bloemfontein 2002, UOVS vii; 290 pp. $22. 0-86886-661-X. Symposium 2001.

582 ᴱNewman, Carey C.; Davila, James R.; Lewis, Gladys S. The Jewish roots of christological monotheism: papers from the St. Andrews conference on the historical origins of the worship of Jesus. JSJ.S 63: 1999 ⇒15,424. ᴿRBLit (2002)* (*Oegema, Gerbern S.*).

583 ᴱNieuviarts, Jacques; Debergé, Pierre Les nouvelles voies de l'exégèse: en lisant le Cantique des cantiques: XIXe congrès de l'Association catholique pour l'étude de la bible (Toulouse, septembre 2001). LeDiv 190: P 2002, Cerf 374 pp. €29. 2-204-06932-9. ᴿBrot. 155 (2002) 430-431 (*Silva, I. Ribeiro da*).

584 ᴱNissinen, Martti Prophecy in its ancient Near Eastern context: Mesopotamian, Biblical, and Arabian perspectives. SBL.Symposium 13: 2000 ⇒16,483; 17,486. SBL Internat. Meeting, Lahti, Finland, 1999. ᴿThLZ 127 (2002) 1273-1275 (*Schart, Aaron*); HebStud 43 (2002) 269-271 (*Lemaire, André*); RBLit 4 (2002) 81-84 (*Becking, Bob*).

585 ᴱO'Kane, Martin Borders, boundaries and the bible. Shf 2002, Sheffield Academic 360 pp. £33.50. 1-84127-148-9. Papers of 2 conferences, Newman College: Reading the bible & Characters and heroes of the bible; Bibl. 334-347 [ScrB 32,117].

586 ᴱO'Loughlin, Thomas The scriptures and early medieval Ireland: proceedings of the 1993 Conference of the Society for Hiberno-Latin Studies on early exegesis and homiletics. IP 31: 1999 ⇒15,425. ᴿREAug 48 (2002) 216-219 (*M.-Gorman, Michael*); Apocrypha 13 (2002) 308-309 (*Zamagni, C.*).

587 ᴱPadovese, Luigi Atti del VII Simposio di Tarso su S. Paolo Apostolo. Turchia: la Chiesa e la sua storia 16; Simposio di Tarso su S. Paolo Apostolo 7: R 2002, Pontificio Ateneo Antoniano 440 pp.

588 ᴱ**Poffet, Jean-Michel** L'autorité de l'écriture. LeDiv: P 2002, Cerf 302 pp. €28. 2-204-07007-6. Colloque Jérusalem sept. 2000; Bibl. 294-298.

589 ᴱ**Porter, Stanley E.; Stamps, Dennis L.** The rhetorical interpretation of scripture: essays from the 1996 Malibu conference. JSNT.S 180: 1999 ⇒15,430. ᴿRBLit 4 (2002) 312-315 (*McGinn, Sheila E.*).

590 Proceedings from the first Pan-Hellenic Conference, 'Theoria and praxis of the psaltic art' (Athens, 3-5 Nov. 2000). Athens 2001, Institute of Byzantine Musicology 247 pp. 960-86798-3-4.

591 ᴱ**Puig i Tàrrech, Armand** Perdó i reconciliació en la tradició Jueva. Scripta Biblica 4: Montserrat 2002, Associació Bíblica de Catalunya 246 pp. 84-8415-402-5. Colloq. 1998.

592 **Räisänen, Heikki; Fiorenza, Elisabeth Schüssler,** *al.*, Reading the bible in the global village: Helsinki. 2000. ⇒16,485; 17,491. SBL International Meeting (1999:Helsinki). ᴿCBQ 64 (2002) 413-415 (*Bowe, Barbara E.*); JSSt 47 (2002) 320-322 (*Barton, John*); JBL 121 (2002) 533-536 (*Segovia, Fernando F.*).

593 ᴱ**Reventlow, Henning Graf; Hoffman, Yair** Creation in Jewish and christian tradition. JSOT.S 319: Shf 2002, Sheffield A. xiii; 356 pp. $90. 1-84127-162-4. Symposia Tel Aviv—Bochum; Bibl. 309-333.

594 ᴱ**Rollston, Christopher A.** The gospels according to Michael GOULD-ER: a North American response. Harrisburg, PA 2002, Trinity x; 165 pp. $19. 1-56338-378-0. Symposium 2000 Johns Hopkins.

595 ᴱ**Rowland, Chris; Vincent, John** Bible and practice. 2001 ⇒17,493. Conf., Institute for British Liberation Theology. ᴿRRT 9 (2002) 350-351 (*Cane, Anthony*).

596 ᴱ**Sandler, Willibald; Wandinger, Nikolaus** Der unbequeme Gott: Vorträge der zweiten Innsbrucker Theologischen Sommertage 2001. Theologische trends 11: Thaur 2002, Thaur. 3-85400-121-5.

597 SBL 1999 Seminar Papers: 135th Annual Meeting, 1999, Boston. SBL. SP 38: 1999 ⇒15,433. ᴿEThL 78 (2002) 193-194 (*Verheyden, J.*).

598 SBL.SP: 138th Annual Meeting November 23-26, 2002 Toronto. SBL.SPS 41: Atlanta, GA 2002, SBL viii; 327 pp. 1-58983-051-2.

599 ᴱ**Socci, S.** Il cinema e la bibbia: atti del congresso internazionale, Genova, 30 ott.-1 nov. 1999. 2001 ⇒17,496. Assoc. Laica di Cultura Biblica. ᴿAsp. 49 (2002) 286-287 (*Castello, Gaetano*).

600 ᴱ**Stefani, Piero; Minestrina, Giovanni** Pace e guerra nella bibbia e nel Corano. Brescia 2002, Morcelliana 263 pp. Congresso internazionale Torino 12-14.10.2001.

601 ᴱ**Stegemann, Wolfgang; Malina, Bruce J.; Theissen, Gerd** Jesus in neuen Kontexten. Stu 2002, Kohlhammer 288 pp. €20. 3-17-016311-6. Bibl. 255-288; 4th meeting Context Group, Tutzing 1999;

602 The social setting of Jesus and the gospels. Mp 2002, Fortress xvi; 404 pp. $24. 0-8006-3452-7. 4th meeting Context Group, Tutzing 1999.

603 ᴱ**Steinmetz, David C.** Die Patristik in der Bibelexegese des 16. Jahrhunderts. 1999 ⇒15,438...17,12509. ᴿRH 126 (2002) 199-202 (*Quantin, Jean-Louis*).

604 ᴱ**Swartley, Willard M.** Violence renounced: René GIRARD, biblical studies, and peacemaking. 2000 ⇒16,491. ᴿThTo 58 (2002) 639-640 (*Dawn, Marva J.*).

605 ᴱ**Taylor, David G.K.** Studies in the early text of the gospels and Acts. 1999 ⇒15,292; 17,1583. Birmingham Colloquium on the Textual Criticism of the NT 1997. ᴿEThL 78 (2002) 197-198 (*Verheyden, J.*).

606 ᴱTriacca, Achille M.; Pistoia, A. La liturgie, interprète de l'écriture I: les lectures bibliques pour les dimanches et fêtes: conférences Saint-Serge XLVIIIe Semaine d'Études Liturgiques, Paris, 25-28 Juin 2001. BEL.P 119: R 2002, Liturgiche 250 pp. €33.57. 88-7367-007-5.

607 Ukpong, Justin S., al., Reading the bible in the global village: Cape Town. Global perspectives on biblical scholarship 3: Atlanta 2002, SBL 221 pp. $25. 1-58983-025-3. SBL Internat. Meeting Cape Town 2000; Bibl. 199-217.

608 ᴱVan Henten, Jan Willem; Brenner, Athalya Families and family relations as represented in early Judaisms and early Christianities. 2000 ⇒16,495; 17, 502. NOSTER colloquium Amsterdam, 1998. ᴿThLZ 127 (2002) 1269-1271 (Kollmann, Bernd); RBLit 4 (2002) 105-108 = JBL 121 (2002) 364-366 (MacLean, Jennifer K. Berenson).

609 ᴱVerheyden, Joseph The unity of Luke-Acts. BEThL 142: 1999 ⇒15, 5410...17,5368. Colloquium Biblicum Lovaniense (47: 1998). ᴿBS 159 (2002) 376-377 (Bock, Darrell L.); LASBF 51 (2001) 429-430 (Bottini, G.C.); RBLit 4 (2002) 387-391 (Litwak, Kenneth D.).

610 ᴱWischmeyer, Wolfgang; Schwarz, Karl SOMEF, Teil 1: Kongress 1999: die Bedeutung der Theologie; Teil II: Kongress 2001: Bibel—Spiritualität—Gesellschaft. W 2002, Evangelischer P. 212 pp. 3-8507-3218-5 [BuBB 39,74].).

A2.3 Acta congressuum theologica

611 ᴱBateman, Herbert Authentic worship: hearing scripture's voice, applying its truths. GR 2002, Kregel 318 pp. $16. 0-8254-2092-X. Meeting Evang. Theol. Soc., WL 2001 [ThD 50,158–Heiser, W.C.].

612 ᴱBaumgarten, Albert I. Sacrifice in religious experience. SHR 93: Lei 2002, Brill viii; 329 pp. $105. 90-04-12483-7. Conf. Bar-Ilan Univ.

613 ᴱBeaude, Pierre-Marie: Fantino, Jacques Le discours religieux, son sérieux, sa parodie en théologie et en littérature: colloque de Metz 1999. 2001 ⇒17,506. ᴿETR 77 (2002) 296-8 (Despland, Michel).

614 ᴱBof, Giampiero; Battaglia, Vincenzo Gesù di Nazaret... figlio di Adamo, figlio di Dio. Cammini nello Spirito, Teologia 38: 2000 ⇒16, 499; 17,507. Congresso delle Associazioni Teologiche Italiane (CATI) 1. ᴿAsprenas 49 (2002) 438-444 (Scognamiglio, Edoardo).

615 ᴱBoralevi, Lea Campos; Quaglioni, Diego Politeia biblica. Il pensiero politico 35 (2002) 365-522. Conv. Trento 15-17.10.1998.

616 ᴱCalduch Benages, Nuria La Sagrada Familia en la vida consagrada y familiar: 5° congr. internac. sobre la Sagrada Familia, 2000. 2001 ⇒ 17,512. ᴿRevAg 43 (2002) 717-718 (Domínguez Sanabria, Jesús).

617 ᴱCanobbio, Giacomo La fede di Gesù: convegno Trento 1998. 2000 ⇒16,500 ᴿHum(B) 57/1 (2002) 161 (Montagnini, Felice).

618 ᴱCereti, G. Monoteismo cristiano e monoteismi. 2001 ⇒17,514. Corso 1997. ᴿPaVi 47/1 (2002) 59-60 (Giavini, Giovanni).

619 ᴱChialà, Sabino; Cremaschi, Lisa Giovanni CLIMACO e il Sinai: atti del IX convegno ecumenico internazionale di spiritualità ortodossa sezione bizantina, Bose, 16-18 settembre 2001. Spiritualità orientale: Magnano 2002, Qiqajon 398 pp. ᴿOCP 68 (2002) 546-550 (Poggi, V.).

620 ᴱCoda, Piero; Crociata, Mariano Il crocifisso e le religioni: compassione di Dio e sofferenza dell'uomo nelle religioni monoteiste. Collana di teologia 44: R 2002, Città Nuova 376 pp. €24. 88-311-3345-4.

621 ^ECollet, Giancarlo Weltdorf Babel: Globalisierung als theologische Herausforderung. Theologie und Praxis, B 11: Müns 2001, LIT 126 pp. €12.90. 3-8258-5580-5. Studienwoche Münster Nov. 2000.

622 ^EDal Covolo, Enrico; Uglione, Renato Chiesa e impero: da AUGUSTO a GIUSTINIANO. BSRel 170: 2001 ⇒17,517. Atti, Giornate Patristiche Torinesi, 1994, 1996. ^RItinerarium(Messina) 10 (2002) 266-269 (*Stelladoro, Gabriella*); Path 1 (2002) 388-389 (*Amato, Angelo*).

623 ^EDavis, Stephen; Kendall, Daniel; O'Collins, Gerald The Trinity 2000. ⇒16,503; 17,518. Symposium, Dunwoodie, 1998. ^RBS 159 (2002) 481-483 (*Burns, J. Lanier*);

624 The incarnation: an interdisciplinary symposium on the incarnation of the Son of God. Oxf 2002 OUP xxv; 404 pp. £35. 0-19-924845-1. Symposium, Easter 2000, NY.

625 ^EDe Fiores, S.; Strangio, G.; Vidau, E. Il mistero della croce e Maria: IV Colloquio internazionale di mariologia. Biblioteca di Theototkos 4: 2001 ⇒17,519. ^RAsprenas 49 (2002) 458-459 (*Piscopo, Salvatore*).

626 ^EDorival, Gilles; Pralon, Didier Nier les dieux, nier Dieu: actes du colloque Centre Paul-Albert Février (UMR 6125), avril 1999. Aix-en-Provence 2002, Public. de l'Univ. de Provence 420 pp. 2-85399-505-4.

627 ^EDreyer, Elizabeth A. The cross in christian tradition: from Paul to BONAVENTURE. 2000 ⇒16,506; 17,522. Seminars at St Mary's College, Notre Dame, 1996, 1997. ^RScEs 54 (2002) 115-117 (*Bigaouette, Francine*); IThQ 67 (2002) 180-182 (*Cunningham, Enda*).

628 ^EDrobner, Hubertus R.; Viciano, Alberto GREGORY of Nyssa: homilies on the Beatitudes: proc. 8th internat. coll. on Gregory of Nyssa (Paderborn, 1998). SVigChr 52: 2000 ⇒16,12641; 17,4876. ^RJEH 53 (2002) 126-127 (*Ludlow, Morwenna*); RSR 90 (2002) 267-268 (*Sesboüé, Bernard*); JEarlyC 10 (2002) 401-403 (*Harrison, Nonna Verna*).

629 ^EDunand, Françoise; Boespflug, François Voir les dieux, voir Dieu. Strasbourg 2002, Presses Univ. de Strasbourg 208 pp. €15. 2-8682-0185-7. Sém. Strasbourg [RHPhR 83,489—P. Prigent].

630 Ecumenismo e dialogo interreligioso: il contributo dei fedeli laici: seminario di studio Vaticano, 22-23 giugno 2001. Laici oggi 6: Città del Vaticano 2002, Libreria Editrice Vaticana 190 pp. 88-209-7362-6. Pontificium Consilium pro Laicis.

631 ^EEllis, George F.R. The far-future universe: eschatology from a cosmic perspective. Ph 2002, Templeton Foundation vii; 384 pp. $40. Conf. Rome Nov. 2000.

632 ^EFarina, M.; Marchi, M. Maria nell'educazione di Gesù Cristo e del cristiano, 1: la pedagogia interroga alcune fonti biblico-teologiche. Il Prisma 25: R 2002, LAS 234 pp. Atti del Seminario di studio promosso dalla Pontificia Facoltà di Scienze dell'Educazione 'Auxilium', Roma 14-15 dic. 2001.

633 Fe en Dios y ciencia actual: III jornadas de teología. Santiago de Compostela 2002, Instituto Teológico Compostelano 284 pp [Studium 44, 314—Marcos F. Manzanedo].

634 ^EFiloramo, Giovanni; Gianotto, Claudio Verus Israel: nuove prospettive sul giudeocristianesimo. BCR 65: 2001 ⇒17,524. Atti del Colloquio di Torino (4-5 novembre 1999). ^RRasIsr 68/2 (2002) 142-146 (*Davidzon, Irith*); SR 31 (2002) 424-427 (*Piovanelli, Pierluigi*).

635 ^EFinan, Thomas; Twomey, Vincent Studies in patristic christology. 1998 ⇒14,412...17,525. Proc.Third Maynooth Patristic Conference, 17-20 October 1996. ^RThPh 77 (2002) 248-250 (*Hainthaler, T.*).

636 ᴱGesche, A.; Scolas, P. Dieu à l'épreuve de notre CRI. 1999 ⇒15, 460. ᴿRevSR 76 (2002) 120-122 (*Thiel, Marie-Jo*).

637 ᴱGoergen, Donald J.; Garrido, Ann The theology of the priesthood. 2000 ⇒16,512. ᴿHeyJ 43 (2002) 370-372 (*Cooper, Adam G.*).

638 ᴱHengel, Martin; Mittmann, Siegfried; Schwemer, Anna Maria La cité de Dieu: actes 3e symposium Strasbourg, Tübingen, Uppsala, septembre 1998. WUNT 129: Tü 2002. Mohr 470 pp. €99. 316-1472-004.

639 ᴱHoward-Snyder, Daniel; Moser, Paul K. Divine hiddenness: new essays. C 2002, CUP 242 pp. $60. Conference.

640 ᴱIllanes, José Luis El Dios y Padre de nuestro Señor Jesucristo. 2000 ⇒16,513. Simposio Internacional de Teologia. ᴿCTom 129 (2002) 166-167 (*Luis Carballada, Ricardo de*).

641 ᴱIzquierdo, C. Escatología y vida cristiana. Pamplona 2002, Servicio de Pub. de la Univ. de Navarra xviii, 700 pp. 84-8081-007-6. XXII Simposio internacional de teología de la Univ. de Navarra. ᴿRTLi 36 (2002) 397-398 (*Sánchez R., Gustavo*).

642 ᴱJordan, D.R.; Montgomery, H.; Thomassen, E. The world of ancient magic: first international Eitrem Seminar May 1997. 1999 ⇒15, 463; 16,514. ᴿSMSR 68 (2002) 217-225 (*Gasparro, Giulia Sfameni*).

643 ᴱKoslowski, Peter Progress, apocalypse, and completion of history and life afer death of the human person in the world religions. A discourse of the world religions 4: Dordrecht 2002, Kluwer viii; 142 pp. $59. 1-4020-0647-0. 4th EXPO-Discourse Hanover, 2000 [ThD 50,87—Heiser, W. Charles].

644 ᴱLongenecker, Richard N. Community formation in the early church and in the church today. Peabody 2002, Hendrickson xix; 251 pp. $20. 1-56563-718-6. Birmingham Coll. McMaster 2000 [BiTod 41,201—Senior, Donald].

645 ᴱMarcos, Sylvia Gender/bodies/religions. 2000 ⇒16,518. Adjunct proceedings of the XVIIth Congress for the History of Religions. ᴿNumen 49 (2002) 347-348 (*Hernández Castillo, R. Aída*).

646 ᴱMazza, E. L'idea di sacrificio: un approccio di teologia liturgica. Bo 2002, EDB 154 pp. Simposio Trento, Maggio 2001.

647 ᴱMcEvoy, James; Dunne, Michael History and eschatology in John Scottus ᴇʀɪᴜɢᴇɴᴀ and his time: proceedings of the Tenth International Conference of the Society for the Promotion of Eriugenian Studies, Maynooth—Dublin. Lv 2002, Univ. Pr. 645 pp.

648 ᴱMcLoughlin, William M.; Pinnock, Jill Mary for earth and heaven: papers on Mary and ecumenism. Leominster 2002, Gracewing xvii; 386 pp. Conferences 1997-2001; Foreword Card. Cassidy.

649 Mysterium redemptionis: do sacrificio de Cristo à dimensao sacrificial da existência cristianâ: congresso internacional de Fátima. Fátima 2002, Santuário de Fátima.

650 ᴱParappally, Jacob; Monteiro, Evelyn Hope at the dawn of a new century: proceedings of the 22nd annual meeting of the Indian Theological Association, 24th-28th April 1999. 2000 ⇒16,521. ᴿVJTR 66 (2002) 945-946 (*Gispert-Sauch, G.*).

651 La parola di Dio tra scrittura e rito: atti della XXVIII settimana di studio dell'Associazione professori di liturgia–Calambrone, 27 agosto-1 settembre 2000. BEL.S 122: R 2002, CLV 232 pp. €20. 88736-7013X.

652 ᴱPeters, Ted; Russell, Robert John; Welker, Michael Resurrection: theological and scientific assessments. GR 2002, Eerdmans xviii; 326 pp. $39. 0-8028-0519-1. Conference Heidelberg 2001.

653 ᴱPizzolato, Luigi F.; Rizzi, Marco ORIGENE maestro di vita spirituale: Origen: master of spiritual life. SPMed 22: Mi 2001, Vita e P. xii; 313 pp. Congresso Milano, 13-15 sett. 1999.

654 ᴱPouderon, Bernard; Duval, Yves-Marie L'Historiographie de l'Église des premiers siècles. ThH 114: 2001 ⇒17,541. IIe colloque internat. d'études patristiques...française, Tours 2000. ᴿREJ 161 (2002) 506-508 (Debié, Muriel); LTP 58 (2002) 623-626 (Côté, Dominique).

655 ᴱPrades López, J.; Magaz, J.M. La razón creyente: actas del congreso internacional sobre la encíclica: Fides et Ratio, Madrid, 16-18 feb. 2000. Studia Theologica Matritensia 1: M 2002, Publicaciones de la Facultad de Teología "San Damaso" xiii; 615 pp. 84-932705-0-4.

656 Radici dell'antigiudaismo in ambiente cristiano: colloquio intra-ecclesiale: atti del simposio teologico-storico, Città del Vaticano, 30 ott. - 1 nov. 1997—Grande Giubileo dell'anno 2000. Atti e Documenti 8: 2000 ⇒16,524. ᴿPath 1 (2002) 384-385 (Dal Covolo, Enrico).

657 ᴱRalte, Lalrinawmi; Anderson-Rajkumar, Evangeline Feminist hermeneutics. Delhi 2002, Indian Women in Theology 164 pp. Rs125/ $12. 81-7214-710-4. Workshop Bangalore.

658 ᴱReboiras Domínguez, Fernando; Villalba Varneda, Pere; Walter, Peter Arbor scientiae Der Baum des Wissens vom Ramon Lull: Akten des Internationalen Kongresses aus Anlaß des 40-jährigen Jubiläums des Raimundus-Lullus-Instituts der Universität Freiburg i. Br. Instrumenta Patristica et Mediaevalia 42; Subsidia Lulliana 1: Turnhout 2002 Brepols (8) 372 pp. 2-503-51215-1.

659 ᴱRomagnani, Gian Paolo La bibbia, la coccarda e il tricolore: i valdesi fra due emancipazioni 1798-1848. 2001 ⇒17,542. 37 e 38 convegno di studi sulla Riforma... in Italia, Torre Pellice, 1997 e 1998. ᴿSocietà et Storia 25 (2002) 844-846 (Ferrara degli Uberti, Carlotta).

660 ᴱRuiz Sánchez, José-Leonardo Milenarismos: mesianismo y apocalipsis desde la historia y la religión. 2001 ⇒17,543. ᴿIsidorianum 21 (2002) 487-488 (Martín Riego, Manuel).

661 ᴱSchaber, Johannes Gemeinsame Wurzeln: der Gottesglaube im Judentum, Christentum und Islam. Schriftenreihe der Ottobeurer Studienwoche 3: Leutesdorf 2002, Johannes-Verl. 127 pp. 3-7794-1468-6.

662 ᴱSchmidt-Leukel, Perry Buddhist perceptions of Jesus: papers of the third conference of the European network of Buddhist-Christian studies (St. Ottilien 1999). 2001 ⇒17,544. ᴿPacifica 15 (2002) 226-228 (Johnston, William M.); RRT 9 (2002) 304-306 (Harris, Elizabeth J.); Milltown Studies 50 (2002) 153-159 (Mullins, Patrick).

663 ᴱSevrin, J.-M.; Haquin, A. La théologie entre deux siècles: bilan et perspectives. CRTL 34: Lv(N) 2002, Publications de la Faculté de théologie 187 pp. €25. 90-429-1169-7. Actes du colloque organisé à l'occasion du 575ᵉ anniversaire de l'Université catholique de Louvain. ᴿRTL 33 (2002) 565-568 (Étienne, Jacques).

664 ᴱSöding, Thomas Eucharistie: Positionen katholischer Theologie. Rg 2002, Pustet 279 pp. €22. 37917-17928. Tagung München Sept. 2001.

665 ᴱTeja, Ramón Actas del XIV seminario sobre historia del monacato: profecía, magia y adivinación en las religiones antiguas. 2001 ⇒17, 546. ᴿSef. 62 (2002) 214-216 (González Salinero, R.).

666 ᴱTernes, Charles-Marie; Ries, Julien Symbolisme et expérience de la lumière dans les grandes religions: actes du colloque tenu à Luxembourg du 29 au 31 mars 1996. Homo religiosus 1: Turnhout 2002, Brepols 276 pp. 2-503-51221-6. Bibl. 263-269.

667 ᴱTurner, John Douglas; Majercik, Ruth Dorothy Gnosticism and later platonism. SBL, Symposium 12: 2000 ⇒16,526; 17,548. ᴿJThS 53 (2002) 320-323 (*Wilson, R. McL.*); JR 82 (2002) 442-443 (*Brakke, David*); RMet 56/1 (2002) 207-209 (*Meconi, David Vincent*).

668 ᴱUglione, R. 'Millennium': l'attesa della fine nei primi secoli cristiani: atti delle III giornate patristiche torinesi (Torino 23-24 ottobre 2000). T 2002, CELID 311 pp. €18. 88-7661-540-7.

669 ᴱVaccaro, Luciano Storia religiosa della Grecia. Mi 2002, Centro Ambrosiano 511 pp. ᴿOCP 68 (2002) 515-516 (*Ruggieri, V.*).

670 ᴱVan den Broek, Roelof; Van Heertum, Cis From POIMANDRES to Jacob BÖHME: Gnosis, Hermetism and the christian tradition. Pimander 4: 2000 ⇒16,527; 17,90. ᴿNumen 49 (2002) 214-215 (*Stuckrad, Kocku von*); JEarlyC 10 (2002) 546-547 (*Brakke, David*).

671 ᴱVauchez, André L'attente des temps nouveaux: eschatologie, millé-narisme et visions du futur du moyen âge au XXe siècle. Turnhout 2002, Brepols 170 pp. €44. 2-503-51335-2. Conf. Oslo Aug. 2000 .

A2.5 *Acta* philologica et historica

672 ᴱAndorlini, Isabella; Bastianini, Guido Atti del XXII Congresso In-ternazionale di Papirologia, Firenze, 23-29 agosto 1998. 2001 ⇒17, 555. ᴿBiOr 59 (2002) 522-527 (*Verhoogt, Arthur*); BASPap 39 (2003) 213-227 (*Keenan, James G.*).

673 ᴱBarcelona, Antonio Metaphor and metonymy at the crossroads: a cognitive approach. Topics in English linguistics 30: B 2000, De Gruy-ter x; 356 pp. $42. 3-1101-75568. Conf. Amsterdam & Debrecen 1997.

674 ᴱBaurain, Claude; Bonnet, Corinne; Krings, Véronique Phoinikeia Grammata: lire et écrire en Méditerrané. 1991 ⇒9,9820. ᴿMaarav 9 (2002) 107-112 (*Daniels, Peter T.*).

675 ᴱBrodersen, K. Prognosis: Studien zur Funktion von Zukunftsvorher-sagen in Literatur und Geschichte seit der Antike. 2001 ⇒17,558. ᴿClR 52 (2002) 386-387 (*Scullion, Scott*).

676 ᴱCarruba, Onofrio; Meid, Wolfgang Anatolisch und Indogerma-nisch: Akten des Kolloquiums der Indogermanischen Gesellschaft, Pa-via, 1998. Innsbrucker Beiträge zur Sprachwissenschaft 100: Innsbruck 2001, Institut für Sprachwissenschaft der Univ. Innsbruck 428 pp. 385-124-679-9.

677 ᴱCartledge, P.; Cohen, E.E.; Foxhall, Lin Money, labour and land: approaches to the economies of ancient Greece. L 2002, Routledge xviii; 266 pp. £45. 0-415-19649-3. Conf. Cambridge 1997. ᴿEtCl 70 (2002) 314-315 (*Migeotte, L.*).

678 ᴱCerri, Giovanni La letteratura pseudepigrafa nella cultura greca e ro-mana: atti di un incontro di studi, Napoli, 15-17 gennaio 1998. AION, 22: 2000 ⇒16,534. ᴿAevum 76 (2002) 238-240 (*Ramelli, Ilaria*).

679 ᴱD'Alessio, Giovan Battista; Cannatà Fera, Maria I lirici greci: for-me della comunicazione e storia del testo: atti dell'Incontro di studi, Messina, 5-6 novembre 1999. Pelorias 8: Messina 2001, Di.Sc.A.M. 205 pp. 88-8268-007-X.

680 ᴱDeniaux, E. Rome antique: pouvoir des images, images du pouvoir: actes du Colloque de Caen (30 mars 1996). 2000 ⇒16,539. ᴿREA 104 (2002) 608-609 (*Hurlet, Frédéric*).

681 ᴱHorbury, William Hebrew study from Ezra to Ben-Yehuda. 1999 ⇒ 15,240; 17,566. Meeting British Assoc. for Jewish Studies, 1996.

^{R}JThS 53 (2002) 173-75 (*Williamson, H.G.M.*); HeyJ 43 (2002) 220-2 (*McNamara, Martin*): VT 52 (2002) 572-573 (*Gillingham, Susan E.*).

682 ^{E}**Laffineur, Robert; Hägg, Robin** Potnia: Deities and religion in the Aegean Bronze Age: 8th internat. Aegean conf. 2000. Aegaeum 22: 2001 ⇒17,567. ^{R}Archaeus 6 (2002) 461-463 (*Cursaru, Gabriela*).

683 ^{E}**Lebrun, René** Hethitica XV: panthéons locaux de l'Asie Mineure préchrétienne. BCILL 109: LvN 2002, Peeters 244 pp. 90-429-1199-9. Colloque Louis Delaporte—Eugène Cavaignac 1, Inst. Catholique de Paris 26-27 mai 2000.

684 ^{E}**Leder, Stefan,** *al.,* Studies in Arabic and Islam: proceedings of the 19th Congress, Union Européenne des Arabisants et Islamisants, Halle 1998. OLA 108: Lv 2002, Peeters ix; 541 pp. 90-429-1120-4.

685 **Lehnus, Luigi,** *al.,* Callimaque. Fondation Hardt, Entretiens 48: Genève 2002, Fondation Hardt xii; 322 pp. 2-600-00748-2.

686 ^{E}**Lo Cascio, E.; Rathbone, W.** Production and public powers in classical antiquity. 2000 ⇒16,546. 11th Intern. Economic History Congress, Milan 1994. ^{R}JRS 92 (2002) 201 (*Bruun, Christopher*).

687 ^{E}**MacDonald, Dennis R.** Mimesis and intertextuality in antiquity and christianity. 2001 ⇒17,568. Conf. Claremont Univ. ^{R}CBQ 64 (2002) 611-3 (*Brawley, Robert L.*); RBLit 4 (2002) 306-9 (*Litwak, Kenneth*).

688 ^{E}**Mooren, Leon** Politics, administration and society in the Hellenistic and Roman world: international colloquium, Bertinoro 1997. StHell 36: 2000 ⇒16,549. ^{R}BiOr 59 (2002) 527-530 (*Kehoe, Dennis P.*).

689 ^{E}**Morag, Shelomo; Bar-Asher, Moshe; Mayer-Modena, Maria** Vena Hebraica in Judaeorum Linguis: 2nd Int. Conf. on Hebr. & Aram. elements in Jewish Languages (Milan 1995). Studi Camito-Semitici 5: 1999 ⇒15,496. ^{R}BiOr 59 (2002) 599-601 (*Van Peuren, W.Th.*).

690 ^{E}**Moreau, A.; Turpin, J.C.** La magie: colloque international de Montpellier 25-27 mars 1999, 1-4. 2000 ⇒16,550. ^{R}CIR 52 (2002) 132-133 (*Ogden, Daniel*); AnCl 71 (2002) 380-381 (*Lecomte, Catherine*).

691 ^{E}**Muraoka, Takamitsu; Elwolde, J.F.** Sirach, scrolls, and sages: 2nd internat. symposium on the Hebrew of the Dead Sea scrolls, Ben Sira, and the Mishnah, Leiden University, 15-17 December 1997. StTDJ 33: 1999 ⇒15,497; 16,551. ^{R}BBR 12 (2002) 295-297 (*lund, Jerome A.*).

692 ^{E}**Nebes, Norbert** Neue Beiträge zur Semitistik. Jenaer Beiträge zum Vorderen Orient 5: Wsb 2002, Harrassowitz vi; 298 pp. €74. 3-447-04606-6. Erstes Arbeitstreffen der Arbeitsgemeinschaft Semitistik in der Deutschen Morgenländischen Gesellschaft September 2000, Jena.

693 ^{E}**Oliver, G.J.** The epigraphy of death: studies in the history and society of Greece and Rome. 2000 ⇒16,553. Symposium, Univ. of Liverpool, 1995. ^{R}AJA 106 (2002) 494-496 (*Davies, Penelope J.E.*).

694 **Parole, parole:** alle origini della comunicazione: atti del convegno internazionale, Milano, 27 gennaio 2001. Mi 2001, Centro Studi del Vicino Oriente 89 pp. Bibl. 88-89.

695 ^{E}**Peláez, J.** El Dios que hechiza y encanta: magia y astrologia en el mundo clásico y helenístico. Córdoba 2002, Almendro 294 pp. Actas del 1 Congreso Nacional, 4-6.11.1998, Córdoba.

696 ^{E}**Perez Jiménez, Aurelio; Casadesús Bordoy, Francesc** Estudios sobre PLUTARCO: misticismo y religiones mistéricas en la obra de Plutarco: actas del VII simposio español sobre Plutarco (Palma de Mallorca, 2-4 de noviembre de 2000). M 2002, Clásicas 577 pp. 84-7882-461-8.

697 ^{E}**Primmer, Adolf; Smolak, Kurt; Weber, Dorothea** Textsorten und Textkritik: Tagungsbeiträge. SÖAW.PH 693; VKCLK 21: W 2002,

Verlag der Österreichischen Akademie der Wissenschaften 260 pp. 3-7001-3062-7. Symposium CSEL, 15-17.2.2001, Wien.

698 ᴱReif, Stefan C. The Cambridge Genizah collections: their contents and significance. Genizah series 1: C 2002, CUP xiv, 241 pp. 0-52181-361-1. Assist. *Shulamit Reif*, Conf. Cambridge 1994.

699 ᴱRibichini, Sergio; Rocchi, Maria; Xella, Paolo La questione delle influenze vicino-orientali sulla religione greca: stato degli studi e prospettive della ricerca: atti del colloquio internazionale Roma, 20-22 maggio 1999. 2001 ⇒17,574. ᴿBASOR 328 (2002) 94-95 (*Lupu, Eran*); SMSR 68 (2002) 405-428 (*Lancellotti, Maria Grazia*).

700 ᴱRutter, N.K.; Sparkes, B.A. Word and image in ancient Greece. 2000 ⇒16,556. Conf. Univ. of Edinburgh, 1999. ᴿClR 52 (2002) 107-108 (*Lewis, Sian*).

701 ᴱStadter, Philip A.; Van der Stockt, Luc Sage and emperor: PLU-TARCH, Greek intellectuals, and Roman power in the time of TRAJAN (98-117 A.D.). Lv 2002, Leuven Univ. Pr. 357 pp. $86. 90-5867-2395. Conf. Univ. of N. Carolina, Chapel Hill.

702 ᴱValbelle, Dominique; Leclant, Jean Le décret de Memphis: colloque de la Fondation Singer-Polignac... bicentenaire découverte de la Pierre de Rosette. 2000 ⇒16,557. ᴿArOr 70 (2002) 426-27 (*Bareš, Ladislav*).

703 ᴱWildfang, Robin Lorsch; Isager, Jacob Divination and portents in the Roman world: colloquium Odense Univ., May 1998. OUCS 21: 2000 ⇒16,559. ᴿLatomus 61 (2002) 482-483 (*Montero, Santiago*).

704 ᴱZohari, Menahem Studies in Hebrew language and literature: Milan Congress. J 2002, Brit Ivrit Olamit 13; 157; xv pp. Proc. of the 15th Hebrew Scientific European Congress, Milan Sept. 2000. H.

A2.7 *Acta* orientalistica

705 ᴱAbusch, Tzvi, *al.*, Proceedings of the XLVe Rencontre Assyriolo-gique Internationale, 1: historiography in the cuneiform world. 2001 ⇒ 17,577. ᴿBiOr 59 (2002) 113-115 (*Popko, Maciej*).

706 ᴱBord, L.J.; Hamidovic, D. Jubilé...jubilés: actes du colloque tenu à Angers les 1ᵉʳ-2-3 mars 2000. P 2001, Cariscript 186 pp.

707 ᴱDurand, J.-M.; Lafont, B. Actes de la table ronde 'Les traditions amorrites et la bible', Paris, 20-21 juin 1997. RA 92-93/1: 1998-1999 ⇒15,506. ᴿBZ 46 (2002) 121-127 (*Uehlinger, Christoph*).

708 ᴱEmmel, Stephen Lewis; Krause, Martin Ägypten und Nubien in spätantiker und christlicher Zeit: Akten 6. Internat. Koptologenkongresses Münster, 1996. Sprachen und Kulturen des Christlichen Orients 6/1-2: 1999 ⇒15,507. ᴿOrChr 86 (2002) 290-293 (*Scholz, Piotr O.*).

709 ᴱEmmerick, Roland E.; Sundermann, Werner; Zieme, Peter Studia Manichaica, 4: internationaler Kongress zum Manichäismus. 2000 ⇒ 16,568; 17,579. Berlin, 14-18.7.1997. ᴿVigChr 56 (2002) 96-103 (*Taillieu, Dieter*); Apocrypha 13 (2002) 298-300 (*Dubois, J.-D.*).

710 ᴱFierro, Maríbel Judíos y musulmanes en al-Andalus y el Magreb: contactos intelectuales: seminario celebrado en la Casa de Velázquez (febrero de 1997). Coll. de la Casa de Velázquez 74; Judíos en tierras de Islam 1: M 2002, Casa de Velázquez xiv; 254 pp. 84-95555-23-9.

711 ᴱMelaerts, Henri; Mooren, Leon Le rôle et le statut de la femme en Égypte hellénistique, romaine et byzantine: actes du colloque interna-tional, Bruxelles-Leuven 27-29 novembre 1997. Lv 2002, Peeters xv; 396 pp. €80. 11 pl. ᴿAeg. 81 (2001) 363-366 (*Balconi, Carla*).

712 EParpola, Simo; Whiting, Robert M. Sex and gender in the ancient Near East: proceedings of the 47th Rencontre Assyriologique Internationale, Helsinki, July 2-6, 2001 Part I and II. Helsinki 2002, The Neo-Assyrian Text Corpus Project 2 vols. 965-45-9054-6.

713 EWhiting, Robert M. Mythology and mythologies. 2nd annual symposium of the Assyrian...Intellectual Heritage Project, Paris, 1999. 2001 ⇒17, 589. RArOr 70 (2002) 86-88 (Pečírková, Jana).

A2.9 Acta archaeologica

714 EAdams, Colin; Laurence, Ray Travel and geography in the Roman Empire. 2001 ⇒17,590. Roman archaeology conference, Durham 1999. RAJP 123 (2002) 529-534 (Talbert, Richard J.A.).

715 Eal-Maqdissi, Michel, al., The Syrian Jezira cultural heritage and interrelations: international conf. at Deir ez-Zor April 1996. Documents d'archéologie syrienne 1: Damascus Ministère de la culture 634 pp.

716 EAugé, C.; Duyrat, F. Les monnayages syriens: quel apport pour l'histoire du Proche-Orient hellénistique et romain? BAHI 162: Beyrouth 2002, Institut Français d'Archéologie du Proche-Orient 255 pp. 2-912738-17-2. Actes d'une Table Ronde, Damas, 1999; 10 pl..

717 EÅström, P. The chronology of base-ring ware and bichrome wheelmade ware: conf. Stockholm, 2000. 2001 ⇒17,593. RDiscEg 54 (2002) 115-27 (Hulin, Linda); BASOR 328 (2002) 87-8 (Frankel, David).

718 EBalty, Jean-Charles Rites et cultes dans le monde antique: actes de la table ronde du LIMC à la Villa Kérylos, Beaulieu-sur-Mer, 8-9 juin 2001. Cahiers de la Villa 'Kérylos' 12: P 2002, De Boccard x; 108 pp.

719 EBartlett, John Raymond Jews in the Hellenistic and Roman cities. L 2002, Routledge xi; 249 pp. £39.44/$65. 0-415-18638-2. Conf. Dublin 1997; Bibl. 221-238.

720 EBatsch, C.; Egelhaaf-Gaiser, U.; Stepper, R. Zwischen Krise und Alltag: antike Religionen im Mittelmeerraum. 1999 ⇒15,521; 17,595. Coll. Potsdam, June 1997. RHZ 274 (2002) 410-411 (Orth, Wolfgang).

721 EBeinlich, Horst, al., 5. Ägyptologische Tempeltagung: Wü, 23.-26. September 1999. ÄAT 33/3: Wsb 2002, Harrassowitz viii; 221 pp. €49.80. 3-447-04544-2.

722 EBerlin, A.; Overman, J. Andrew The first Jewish Revolt: archaeology, history, and ideology. L 2002, Routledge 272 pp. £48.55. 0-4152-5706-9. Conf. Twin Cities 1999.

723 EBietak, Manfred F.K.W.; Schwarz, Mario; Schwab, Angela Krieg und Sieg: narrative Wanddarstellungen von Altägypten bis ins Mittelalter. DÖAW 24; Untersuchungen der Zweigstelle Kairo des Österreichischen Archäologischen Institutes 20: W 2002, Verlag der Österreichischen Akad. der Wissenschaften 225 pp. 3-7001-3037-6. Internationales Kolloquium 29.-30. Juli 1997 im Schloß Haindorf, Langenlois.

724 EBlois, Lukas de; Rich, John The transformation of economic life under the Roman Empire. Amst 2002, Gieben xxii; 266 pp. €75. 9050-63-328-5. Proc. 2nd Workshop of the International Network Impact of Empire (Roman Empire, c.200 B.C.-A.D. 476) Nottingham July 2001.

725 EBlondé, Francine; Ballet, Pascale; Salles, Jean-François Céramiques héllénistiques et romaines: productions et diffusion en Mediterranée orientale (Chypre, Égypte et Côte Syro-Palestiniénne). Lyon 2002, Maison de l'Orient Mediterranéen-Jean Pouilloux 341 pp. 2-903264-77-5. 204 fig..

726 **Borrmans, M.**, *al.*, Il Corano: traduzioni, traduttori e lettori in Italia.
2000 ⇒16,579. Atti del convegno, Padova, nov. 1998. [R]Sal. 64 (2002)
377-380 (*Buzzetti, Carlo*).

727 [E]**Capelli, Piero; Perani, Mauro** Atti del XV. Convegno Internazionale dell'AISG, (Gabicce Mare, 3-5 sett. 2001). Materia giudaica 7/1: F
2002, Giuntina 207 pp. 88-8057-152-4.

728 [E]**Carruthers, Martin**, *al.*, TRAC 2001: proceedings of the eleventh
annual theoretical Roman archaeology conference, University of Glas-
gow 29-31 March 2001. Oxf 2002, Oxbow iv; 124 pp. 1-84217-075-9.

729 [E]**Ciraolo, Leda; Seidel, Jonathan** Magic and divination in the ancient
world. Ancient magic and divination 2: Lei 2002, Brill xii; 152 pp. 90-
04-12406-3. Colloquium Berkeley, Calif. 1994.

730 [E]**Clarke, Graeme** Identities in the eastern Mediterranean in antiquity:
conference, Canberra, 1997. 1998 ⇒14,469…17,604. [R]AJA 106
(2002) 322-323 (*Roller, Duane W.*).

731 [E]**Coppens, Filip** Abusir and Saqqara in the year 2001: proceedings of
the symposium (Prague, Sept. 25-27, 2001). ArOr 70/3: Praha 2002,
Oriental Institute 269-425 pp.

732 [E]**Davila, James R.** The Dead Sea scrolls as background to postbiblical
Judaism and early christianity: papers from an international conference
at St. Andrews in 2001. StTDJ 46: Lei 2002, Brill xv; 340 pp. €110.
90-04-12678-3.

733 [E]**Docter, Roald F.** Proceedings of the XVth international congress of
classical archaeology, Amsterdam, July 12-17, 1998, classical archaeology towards the third millennium: reflections and perspectives. 2000
⇒16,582. [R]RAr (2002/1) 80-82 (*Hellman, Marie-Christine*).

734 [E]**Drew-Bear, Thomas; Taşhalan, Mehemet; Thomas, Christine M.**
Actes du Ier congrès international sur Antioche de Pisidie. Archéologie
et histoire de l'antiquité 2.5: Lyon 2002, Univ. Lumière 457 pp. €49.
2-91-1971-04-3. 149 pl.; 35 fig..

735 [E]**Elm, Kaspar; Conseca, Cosimo Damiano** Militia sancti sepulcri:
idea e istituzioni. 1998 ⇒16,584. Coll. internazionale Pont. Univ. del
Laterane 1996. [R]HZ 275 (2002) 738-739 (*Favreau-Lilie, Marie-Luise*).

736 [E]**Fentress, Elizabeth** Romanization and the city: creation, transformations, and failures: conference American Acad. Rome to celebrate…
50th anniv. excavations at Coa, 1998. Journal of Roman Archaeology,
Suppl. 38: 2000 ⇒16,585. [R]AJA 106 (2002) 502 (*Anderson, James*).

737 [E]**Fossey, John M.** Boeotia antiqua, 6: 8th International Conference on
Boiotian antiquities, Loyola Univ. of Chicago, 24-26.5.1995. 1996 ⇒
15,534. [R]AJA 106 (2002) 130-131 (*Roller, Duane W.*).

738 [E]**Freeman, Philip**, *al.*, Limes XVIII: proceedings of the XVIIIth international congress of Roman frontier studies, Amman, Sept. 2000. Oxf
2002, Archaeopress 2 vols; xxxviii; 948 pp.

739 [E]**Gazda, Elaine K.** The ancient art of emulation: studies in artistic
originality and tradition from the present to classical antiquity. MAAR-
Suppl. 1: AA 2002, Univ. of Michigan Pr. xiii; 300 pp. $65. 0-472111-
89-2. Sem. Rome 1994; 125 fig..

740 [E]**Giversen, Søren; Petersen, Tage; Sørensen, Jørgen Podemann**
The Nag Hammadi texts in the history of religions: proc. internat. conference, Royal Academy of Sciences and Letters in Copenhagen, September 1995 on the occasion of the 50th anniversary of the Nag Hammadi discovery. DVSS.HF 26: K 2002, Reitzel 228 pp. 87-7876-283-9.

741 [E]**Goodblatt, David M.; Pinnick, Avital; Schwartz, Daniel R.** Historical perspectives: from the Hasmoneans to Bar Kokhba in light of the

Dead Sea Scrolls: 4th Internat. Symposium of the Orion Center for the Study of the Dead Sea Scrolls and Associated Literature, 1999. StTDJ 37: 2001 ⇒17,612. [R]RSR 90 (2002) 446-448 (*Paul, André*).

742 [E]**Hardmeier, Christof** Steine–Bilder–Texte: historische Evidenz außerbiblischer und biblischer Quellen. ABIG 5: 2001 ⇒17,613. Congress Greifswald 2000. [R]ThLZ 127 (2002) 747-8 (*Beyse, Karl-Martin*).

743 [E]**Harvey, Steven** The medieval Hebrew encyclopedias of science and philosophy. 2000 ⇒16,588. Symposium, Univ. Bar-Ilan, 1998. [R]REJ 161 (2002) 308-310 (*Rothschild, Jean-Pierre*).

744 [E]**Hausleiter, A.; Reiche, A.** Iron Age pottery in northern Mesopotamia, northern Syria and south-eastern Anatolia. Altertumskunde des Vorderen Orients 10: 1999 ⇒17,614. Meetings of the international 'table ronde' at Heidelberg (1995) and Nieborów (1997) and other contributions. [R]BASOR 325 (2002) 81-83 (*Lehmann, Gunnar*).

745 [E]**Hägg, Robin** Ancient Greek cult practice from the archaeological evidence: 4th international seminar on ancient Greek cult. Acta Instituti Atheniensis Regni Sueciae 15: 1998 ⇒14,482... 17,615. [R]RAr (2002/1) 75 (*Jost, Madeleine*);

746 Peloponnesian sanctuaries and cults: proceedings...9th international symposium...Swedish Institute...Athens, 11-13 June 1994. Acta Instituti Atheniensis Regni Sueciae 48: Sto 2002, Åström 232 pp.

747 [E]**Herfort-Koch, Marlene; Mandel, Ursula; Schädler, Ulrich** Hellenistische und kaiserzeitliche Keramik des östlichen Mittelmeergebietes: Kolloquium Frankfurt 24.-25. April 1995. 1996 ⇒12,312. [R]AJA 106 (2002) 340-341 (*Rosenthal-Heginbottom, Renate*).

748 [E]**Herrmann, Georgina** The furniture of western Asia, ancient and traditional. 1996 ⇒12,313...15,538. Papers..Inst.of Archaeology, University College London 1993. [R]JNES 61 (2002) 138-140 (*Biggs, Robert*).

749 [E]**Hickmann, Ellen; Eichmann, Ricardo** Studien zur Musikarchäologie, 1: Saiteninstrumente im archäologischen Kontext:. 2000 ⇒16,590. [R]AJA 106 (2002) 479-480 (*Mathiesen, Thomas J.*).

750 [E]**Hickmann, Ellen; Laufs, Ingo; Eichmann, Ricardo** Studien zur Musikarchäologie, 2: Musikarchäologie früher Metallzeiten. 2000 ⇒ 16,591. [R]AJA 106 (2002) 480-481 (*Mathiesen, Thomas J.*).

751 [E]**Hoff, Michael C.; Rotroff, Susan I.** The romanization of Athens: proceedings of an international conference held at Lincoln, Nebraska, April 1996. Oxbow Monograph 94: Oxf 1997, Oxbow 208 pp. 49 fig.; 4 tables. [R]AJA 106 (2002) 501-502 (*Anderson, James C.*).

752 [E]**Hope, Valerie M.; Marshall, Eireann** Death and disease in the ancient city. 2000 ⇒16,592; 17,616. Conf. Univ. of Exeter. [R]Latomus 61 (2002) 495-497 (*Le Blay, Frédéric*).

753 [E]**Karageorghis, Vassos; Morris, Christine E.** Defensive settlements of the Aegean and the eastern Mediterranean after c. 1200 B.C.: workshop Dublin, 1999. 2001 ⇒17,619. [R]BiOr 59 (2002) 163-166 (*Wright, G.R.H.*); BASOR 327 (2002) 92-93 (*Rutter, Jeremy B.*).

754 [E]**Karageorghis, Vassos** The white slip ware of late Bronze Age Cyprus. DÖAW 20: 2001 ⇒17,620. Conf. Nicosia 29-30 Oct. 1998. [R]OLZ 97 (2002) 744-748 (*Bartl, Karin*).

755 [E]**Kugel, James L.** Shem in the tents of Japhet: essays on the encounter of Judaism and Hellenism. JSJ.S 74: Lei 2002, Brill ix; 286 pp. €80. 90-04-12514-0. Conf. Bar Ilan Univ. 1998, Harvard 1999.

756 [E]**Labrique, Françoise** Religions méditerranéennes et orientales de l'antiquité: actes du colloque des 23-24 avril 1999, Institut des sciences

et techniques de l'antiquité (UMR 6048) Université de Franche-Comté,
à Besançon. Bibliothèque d'étude 135: Le Caire 2002, Institut Français
d'Archéologie Orientale vii; 243 pp. 2-7247-0314-6.
757 ᴱLinant de Bellefonds, Pascale Rites et cultes dans le monde antique.
P 2002, Acad. des Inscriptions et Belles Lettres x; 107 pp. €12. 2-87-
754-133-9. Table ronde du LIMC à Beaulieu-sur-Mer, 8-9.6.2001; ill..
758 ᴱMarc, Jean-Yves; Moretti, Jean-Charles Constructions publiques
et programmes édilitaires en Grèce entre le IIᵉ siècle av. J.-C. et le Iᵉʳ
siècle apr. J.-C.: actes du colloque, Athènes, mai 1995. BCH.S 39: P
2001, De Boccard viii; 587 pp.
759 ᴱMazar, Amihai Studies in the archaeology of the Iron Age in Israel
and Jordan. JSOT.S 331: 2001 ⇒17,625. ᴿBASOR 328 (2002) 95-97
(Herr, Larry G.).
760 ᴱMolin, M. Images et représentations du pouvoir et de l'ordre social
dans l'antiquité. 2001 ⇒17,627. Actes du colloque d'Angers, 28-29
mai 1999. ᴿCEg 153-154 (2002) 353-354 (Nachtergael, Georges).
761 ᴱMuller, B. 'Maquettes architecturales' de l'antiquité: colloque Strasbourg 1998. 2001 ⇒17,628. ᴿBiOr 59 (2002) 150-3 (Wright, G.R.H.).
762 ᴱNicolet, Claude; Ilbert, Robert; Depaule, Jean-Charles Mégapoles
méditerranéennes: géographie urbaine rétrospective. EFR 261: 2000 ⇒
16,601. Colloque Rome, du 8-11 mai 1996. ᴿLatomus 61 (2002) 498-
499 (Chevalier, Raymond).
763 ᴱNiklasson, Karin H. Cypriote archaeology in Göteborg: symposium
Göteborg, 20 May 1998. SIMA 157: 1999 ⇒15,549; 16,602. ᴿRAr
(2002/1) 76-77 (Fourrier, Sabine).
764 ᴱO'Mahony, Anthony The christian heritage in the Holy Land. 1995
⇒13,401. Conference, Jerusalem, 1994. ᴿOS 51 (2002) 163-164
(Bräuer, Martin).
765 ᴱPhilip, Graham; Baird, Douglas Ceramics and change in the early
Bronze Age of the southern Levant. 2000 ⇒16,605. Workshop, Durham, 1995. ᴿBASOR 327 (2002) 76-78 (London, Gloria).
766 ᴱRenfrew, Colin; Scarre, Chris Cognition and material culture: the
archaeology of symbolic storage. 1998 ⇒15,556. Conference, Cambridge, Sept. 1996. ᴿAJA 106 (2002) 318-320 (Trigger, Bruce G.).
767 ᴱSchäfer, Peter The Talmud Yerushalmi and Graeco-Roman culture,
3. TSAJ 93: Tü 2002, Mohr xviii; 486 pp. 31614-78525. Conf. Princeton 2000.
768 ᴱSchiffer, Michael Brian Social theory in archaeology. 2000 ⇒16,
608. Round table 1997. ᴿAJA 106 (2002) 317-318 (Barrett, John C.).
769 ᴱSchiffman, Lawrence H.; Tov, Emanuel; VanderKam, James C.
The Dead Sea scrolls fifty years after their discovery: Jerusalem
Congress, July 1997. 2000 ⇒16,609; 17,639. ᴿOLZ 97 (2002) 273-
276 (Rösel, Martin); ThLZ 127 (2002) 1168-1171 (Albani, Matthias).
770 ᴱSilvestri, Domenico; Marra, Antonietta; Pinto, Immacolata Saperi
e sapori mediterranei: la cultura dell'alimentazione e is suoi riflessi linguistici: atti del convegno internazionale, Napoli 13-16 ottobre 1999.
AIΩN 3: N 2002, L'Orientale 3 vols; 1296 pp.
771 ᴱStone, Michael Edward; Ervine, Roberta R.; Stone, Nira The Armenians in Jerusalem and the Holy Land. Hebrew University Armenian
Studies 4: Lv 2002, Peeters xii; 288 pp. €45. 90-429-1078-X. Collo-
quies May, June 1999, April 2000.
772 ᴱSwiny, Stuart; Hohlfelder, Robert L.; Swiny, Helena Wylde Res
Maritimae: Cyprus and the Eastern Mediterranean from prehistory to

late antiquity: 2nd Internat. Symposium "Cities on the Sea" Nicosia, Cyprus, October 1994. ASOR Archaeological Reports 4. 1998 ⇒14,- 491... 17,643. [R]IEJ 52 (2002) 118-120 (*Muhly, James D.*).

773 Traffico illecito del patrimonio archeologico: internazionalizzazione del fenomeno e problematiche di contrasto: 7° Convegno Internazionale Roma, Scuola Ufficiali Carabinieri, giugno 2001. Bollettino di numismatica, Suppl. 38: R 2002, Ministero per i Beni Culturali 499 pp.

774 [E]**Uehlinger, Christoph** Images as media: sources for the cultural history of the Near East and the eastern Mediterranean (Ist millennium BCE). OBO 175: 2000 ⇒16,611; 17,644. [R]BASOR 326 (2002) 96-98 (*Feldman, Marian H.*); JESHO 45 (2002) 376-380 (*Root, Margaret Cool*); AfO 48-49 (2001-2002) 268-269 (*Bahrani, Zainab*).

775 Il volto dei volti, 5: Cristo. 2001 ⇒17,647. Istit. internaz. di ricerca sul volto di Cristo. [R]Asp. 49 (2002) 265-269 (*Scognamiglio, Edoardo*).

776 [E]**Wilhelm, Gernot** Akten des IV. Internationalen Kongresses für Hethitologie: Würzburg, 4.-8. Oktober 1999. StBT 45: 2001 ⇒17,650. [R]BiOr 59 (2002) 581-586 (*Mouton, Alice*).

A3.1 *Opera consultationis*—Reference works *plurium* infra

777 Augustinus-Lexikon, 2. [E]**Mayer, Cornelius** Ba 1996-2002, Schwabe lvi; 1340 col. 3-7965-1929-6;

778 2/5-6: Donatistas (Contra)—Epistulae. [E]**Mayer, Cornelius**: 2001 ⇒ 17,652. [R]REAug 48 (2002) 375-378 (*Duval, Yves-Marie*);

779 2/7-8: Epistulae ad Romanos inchoata expositio–Fides. [E]**Mayer, Cornelius** Ba 2002, Schwabe 1057-1340 col. 3-7965-1928-8.

780 The Blackwell companion to the Hebrew Bible. [E]**Perdue, Leo G.**: 2001 ⇒17,653. [R]RRT 9 (2002) 121-123 (*Norton, Gerard J.*); ABR 50 (2002) 82-85 (*Gardiner, Anne*).

781 **CAH**[2]: The Cambridge ancient history, 11: the high empire, A.D. 70-192. [E]**Bowman, Alan K.; Garnsey, P.; Rathbone, D.**: 2000 ⇒17, 654. [R]BSAPap 39 (2002) 237-241 (*Whitehorne, John*).

782 **DBS**: Supplément au dictionnaire de la bible, vol. 13 [fasc. sans numéro]: Targum. **Le Déaut, Robert; Robert, Jacques.** [E]*Briend, Jacques; Quesnel, Michel*: P 2002, Letouzey & A. 1*-344* col. €88. 2-7063-0223-2;

783 13/73: Sumer-Suse. [E]**Briend, Jacques; Quesnel, Michel**: P 2002, Letouzey & A. 257-512 col. €55. 2-7063-0161-9.

784 **DHGE**: Dictionnaire d'histoire et de géographie ecclésiastiques, 28/164: Julien de Cividale-Kalamona. [E]**Aubert, R.**: P 2002, Letouzé et A. 513-718 col. €48.75. 2-7063-0217-8.

785 The encyclopedia of apocalypticism. [E]**Collins, John J.**: 1998 ⇒14, 507. [R]WThJ 64 (2002) 420-423 (*Carpenter, Craig B.*).

786 **LThK**[3]: Lexikon für Theologie und Kirche, 9: San bis Thomas. [E]**Kasper, Walter**: 2000 ⇒17,655. [R]CivCatt 153/1 (2002) 308-309 (*Capizzi, C.*);

787 11: Nachträge Register Abkürzungsverzeichnis. [E]**Kasper, Walter**: 2001 ⇒17,655. [R]CivCatt 153/1 (2002) 519-520 (*Capizzi, C.*).

788 Der neue Pauly 12/1: Tam-Vel. [E]**Cancik, Hubert; Schneider, Helmuth**: Stu 2002, Metzler xii; 1172 col. 3-476-01470-3;

789 12/2: Ven-Z; Nachträge. [E]**Cancik, Hubert; Schneider, Helmuth**: Stu 2002, Metzler xii; 1192 col. 3-476-01470-3;

790 15/2: Pae-Sch. ^E**Landfester, Manfred**: Stu 2002, Metzler ix; 1156 col. 3-476-01488-6.
791 New catholic encyclopedia. Detroit ²2002, Gale 15 vol. 0-7876-4004-2. Catholic University of America.
792 **RAC**: Reallexikon für Antike und Christentum, 19: Itinerarium-Kannibalismus. ^E**Dassmann, Ernst**: 2001 ⇒17,660. ^RVigChr 56 (2002) 321-323 (*Van Winden, J.C.M.*);
793 Supplement-Lieferung 9: Birkat ham-minim—Brücke. ^E**Schöllgen, Georg**, *al*.,: Stu 2002, Hiersemann 1-160 col.
794 **RGG⁴**: Religion in Geschichte und Gegenwart, 1-5. ^E**Betz, Hans Die-ter**: 1998-2002 ⇒14,496... 17,664. ^RFaith & Mission 19/1 (2002) 70-73 (*Sailhamer, John H.*);
795 3: F-H. ^E**Betz, Hans Dieter**: 2000 ⇒14,496...17,662. ^RETR 77 (2002) 453-4 (*Askani, Hans-Christoph*); RBLit 4 (2002) 60-2 (*Timbie, Janet*).
796 5: L-M. ^E**Betz, Hans Dieter**: Tü 2002, Mohr lxxiv pp; 1704 col. €214. 3-16-146945-3.
797 **TDOT**: Theological Dictionary of the Old Testament, 10: nâqam-ʿâzab. ^E**Botterweck, C. Johannes**, *al*., ^T*Stott, Douglas W.*: 1999 ⇒16, 625; 17,671. ^RHebStud 43 (2002) 233-234 (*Lyons, Michael A.*);
798 11: ʿzz-pânîm. ^T*Green, David E.*: 2000 ⇒16,626. ^RBS 159 (2002) 484-485 (*Chisholm, Robert B.*).
799 **TRE**: Theologische Realenzyklopädie, 33: Technik-Transzendenz. ^E**Müller, Gerhard**: B 2002, De Gruyter 810 pp. €198. 3-11-017132-5. ^RETR 77 (2002) 454-455 (*Reymond, Bernard*);
800 34: Trappisten/Trappistinnen-Vernunft II. ^E**Müller, Gerhard**: B 2002, De Gruyter 792 pp 3-11-017388-3.

A3.3 *Opera consultationis* biblica *non excerpta infra*—not subindexed

801 ^E**Alexander, T.D.; Rosner, Brian S.** The new dictionary of biblical theology. 2000 ⇒16,624; 17,668. ^RSBET 20 (2002) 90-91 (*Glover, Ian D.*); RBLit (2002)* (*Hawk, L. Daniel*).
802 ^E**Bock, Darrell L.** The bible knowledge key word study: the gospels. Colorado Springs 2002, Cook 430 pp. $40 [BS 160,500s–Zuck, Roy].
803 ^E**Bogaert, Pierre-Maurice**, *al*., Dictionnaire encyclopédique de la bible. Turnhout 2002 <1987, 2001>, Brepols 1373 pp. €169. 2-50351-310-7.
804 **Brueggemann, Walter** Reverberations of faith: a theological hand-book of Old Testament themes. LVL 2002, Westminster xiv; 256 pp. £15. 0-664-22231-5.
805 ^E**Evans, Craig A.; Porter, Stanley E.** Dictionary of New Testament background 2000. ⇒16,631; 17,674. ^RRBLit 4 (2002) 69-72 (*McLean, Bradley H.*).
806 ^E**Freedman, David Noel** Eerdmans dictionary of the bible. 2000 ⇒16, 633; 17,676. ^RHeyJ 43 (2002) 212-213 (*Briggs, Richard*); VJTR 66 (2002) 542-543 (*Meagher, P.M.*); ThLZ 127 (2002) 1183-1184 (*Nie-buhr, Karl-Wilhelm*); AUSS 40 (2002) 329-330 (*Stefanovich, Ranko*); RBLit 4 (2002) 64-69 (*Croy, N. Clayton; Konkel, A.H.*).
807 **Gillièron, Bernard** Les gens du Nouveau Testament: dictionnaire des personnes, des groupes et des institutions. Poliez-le-Grand 2002, Moulin 131 pp. €16. 2-88469-009-3.

808 **GLAT**: Grande lessico dell'Antico Testamento, 2: גלולים - חמץ. [E]**Bot-terweck, G. Johannes**, *al.*, ed. ital. [E]*Borbone, Pier Giorgio*: Brescia 2002, Paideia xvi pp; 1130 col. 88-394-0648-4.

809 [E]**Görg, Manfred; Lang, Bernhard** Neues Bibel-Lexikon, Lfg. 14/15: Täuferbewegung-Zyrene. 2001 ⇒17,677. [R]ThLZ 127 (2002) 493-500 (*Stahl, Rainer*).

810 [E]**Hayes, John H.** Dictionary of biblical interpretation. 1999 ⇒15,584 ...17,678. [R]EvQ 74 (2002) 72-74 (*Ellingworth, Paul*); JBL 121 (2002) 745-747 (*Hurtado, Larry W.*); SJTh 55 (2002) 480-481 (*Clarke, Andrew D.*).

811 **Labre, Chantal** Dictionnaire biblique, culturel et littéraire. P 2002, Colin 319 pp. 2-200-21828-1.

812 **Léon-Dufour, Xavier** Diccionario del Nuevo Testamento. Bilbao 2002, Desclée de B. 625 pp. 84-330-1694-6.

813 [E]**Metzger, Bruce M.; Coogan, Michael D.** The Oxford guide to ideas and issues of the bible. NY 2002, OUP 592 pp. $30 [BiTod 40,259— Bergant, Dianne].

814 Navigare nella bibbia: dizionario biblico illustrato. T 2001, Claudiana 240 pp. €24.79 [CivCatt 153/3,195s—Scaiola, D.].

815 **Patzia, Arthur G.; Petrotta, Anthony J.** Pocket dictionary of biblical studies. DG 2002, InterVarsity 128 pp. 0-8308-1467-1.

816 [E]**Rogerson, John William** The Oxford illustrated history of the bible. 2001 ⇒17,682. [R]JRTI 5/2 (2002) 70-75 (*Snavely, Iren L.*).

817 **Soulen, Richard N.; Soulen, R. Kendall** Handbook of biblical criticism. [3]2001 ⇒17,684. [R]EThL 78 (2002) 508-509 (*Van Belle, G.*).

818 **TDOT**: Theological Dictionary of the Old Testament, 10: nâqam-ʿâzab. [E]**Botterweck, G. Johannes**, *al.*, [T]*Stott, Douglas W.*: 1999 ⇒16, 625; 17,671. [R]HebStud 43 (2002) 233-234 (*Lyons, Michael A.*);

819 11: ʿzz-pânîm. [E]**Botterweck, G. Johannes**, *al.*, [T]*Green, David E.*: 2000 ⇒16,626. [R]BS 159 (2002) 484-485 (*Chisholm, Robert B.*).

820 [E]**Van der Toorn, Karel**, *al.*, Dictionary of deities and demons in the bible. [2]1999 <1995> ⇒15,596...17,685. [R]JNES 61 (2002) 140-141 (*Biggs, Robert D.*); JQR 92 (2002) 497-505 (*Hurowitz, Victor A.*).

821 [E]**Wigoder, G.** Nuevo Diccionario de la biblia. 2001 ⇒17,686. [R]RelCult 48 (2002) 524-525 (*Olmo Veros, Rafael del*).

A3.5 *Opera consultationis* **theologica** *non excerpta infra*

822 [E]**Barbaglio, Giuseppe; Bof, Giampiero; Dianich, Severino** Dizionari San Paolo: teologia. CinB 2002, San Paolo xxii; 1955 pp. €99. 88-215-4535-0.

823 The book of saints: a comprehensive dictionary. [E]**Watkins, Basil**: NY [7]2002, Continuum xiv; 640 pp. $50. 0-8264-1378-1 [ThD 50,260— Heiser, W. Charles].

824 **Bradshaw, Paul** The new Westminster dictionary of liturgy and worship. LVL 2002, Westminster xiii; 493 pp. $45. 0-664-22655-8.

825 [E]**Brouard, M.** Eucharistia: encyclopédie de l'eucharistie. P 2002, Cerf 814 pp.

826 [E]**Carey, Patrick W.; Lienhard, Joseph T.** Biographical dictionary of christian theologians. Westport 2002 <2000>, Greenwood 589 pp. $35. 1-56563-723-2. Bibl. 553-555.

827 [E]**Coenen, Lothar; Haacker, Klaus** Theologisches Begriffslexikon zum Neuen Testament: Registerband. Neuk 2002, Neuk 88 pp. 3-7887-1937-0 [EuA 79,435].

828 [E]**Cosi, Dario M.**, *al.*, Religioni del Mediterraneo e del Vicino Oriente. Antico Enciclopedia delle religioni 11: R 2002, Città N. 579 pp. €124. 88-311-9326-0.

829 [E]**Di Berardino, Angelo** Dicionário patrístico e de antigüidades cristãs. [T]*Andrade, Cristina*: Petrópolis 2002, Vozes 1483 pp [REB 248, 998].

830 Dictionnaire encyclopédique de la liturgie, 2: M-Z avec un lexique des principaux termes liturgiques. [E]**Sartore, Domenico; Triacca, Achille M.**; [T]*Delhougne, Henri*: Turnhout 2002, Brepols 575 pp. 2-503-50320-9 [QuLi 84,272—Michiels, G.].

831 Dizionario comparato delle religioni monoteistiche: Islam cristianesimo ebraismo a confronto. CasM 2002, Piemme Pocket 814 pp. €9.90 [RdT 43,158].

832 [E]**Döpp, Siegmar; Geerlings, Wilhelm** Dictionary of early christian literature. [T]*O'Connell, Matthew*: 2000 ⇒16,653. [R]RRT 9 (2002) 46-48 (*Taylor, David*); Faith & Mission 19/2 (2002) 103-04 (*Olsen, Robert*);

833 Lexikon der antiken christlichen Literatur: FrB [3]2002 <1998, 1999>, Herder xviii; 763 pp. €65. 3-451-27776-X. [R]OrdKor 43 (2002) 371 (*Schmitz, Josef*).

834 [E]**Elwell, Walter A.** Evangelical dictionary of theology. [2]2001 ⇒17, 694. [R]Faith & Mission 19/2 (2002) 85-87 (*Hammett, John S.*).

835 Encyclopedia of millennialism and millennial movements. 2000 ⇒16, 654. [R]RStT 20/2 (2002) 83-85 (*Gow, Andrew*).

836 [E]**Englert, Rudolf**, *al.*, Neues Handbuch religionspädagogischer Grundbegriffe. Mü 2002, Kösel 566 pp. €25.

837 [E]**Fahlbusch, Erwin; Bromiley, Geoffrey William** The encyclopedia of christianity, 2: E-I. 2001 ⇒17,696. [R]AUSS 40 (2002) 143-144 (*Knight, George R.*).

838 [E]**Gauvard, Claude; Libera, Alain de; Zink, Michel** Dictionnaire du Moyen-Âge. Quadrige: P 2002, P.U.F. 1548 pp. [R]RThPh 134 (2002) 373-374 (*Borel, Jean*).

839 [E]**Hastings, Adrian; Mason, Alistair; Pyper, Hugh** The Oxford companion to christian thought. 2000 ⇒16,660. [R]AThR 84 (2002) 1032-1033 (*Maclean, Iain S.*).

840 [E]**Kurian, George Thomas** Nelson's new christian dictionary. 2001 ⇒ 17,699. [R]SBET 20 (2002) 119-120 (*Rainey, David*).

841 Lexikon der Reformationszeit: Lexikon für Theologie und Kirche kompakt. [E]**Ganzer, K.; Steiner, B.**: FrB 2002, Herder 500 pp. €20.50. 34-51-22019-9 [ZKTh 125,301—Hell, Silvia].

842 [E]**McAuliffe, Jane Dammen** Encyclopaedia of the Qur'an, v.2: E-I. Lei 2002, Brill xxiv; 572 pp. €228/$278. 90-04-12035-1. 20 ill.

843 Metzler-Lexikon Religion: Gegenwart—Alltag—Medien, 4: Text- und Bildquellen. [E]**Auffarth, Christoph; Bernard, Jutta; Mohr, Hubert**: Stu 2002, Metzler x; 438 pp. €85.90. 3-476-01678-1.

844 **Noegel, Scott B.; Wheeler, Brannon M.** Historical dictionary of prophets in Islam and Judaism. Historical dictionaries of religions, philosophies, and movements 43: Lanham 2002, Scarecrow xxxvii; 522 pp. 0-8108-4305-6. Bibl. 376-480.

845 **Santa, Thomas M.** The essential bible handbook: a guide for catholics. Ligouri 2002, Ligouri 304 pp. $14 [BiTod 41,61—Bergant, D.].

846 [E]**Sbalchiero, P.** Dictionnaire des miracles et de l'extraordinaire chrétiens. P 2002, Fayard xxx; 880 pp. €59. 2-213-613949.

847 ᴱSodi, Manlio; Triacca, Achille M. Dizionario di omiletica. 1998 ⇒
14,533... 17,703. ᴿNicolaus 29/1 (2002) 229-233 (*Bux, Nicola; Muscedra, Emilia*).
848 ᴱSunquist, Scott, *al.*, A dictionary of Asian christianity. 2001 ⇒17,
706. ᴿRTR 61 (2002) 55-57 (*Burke, David*).

A3.6 *Opera consultationis* generalia

849 ᴱBearman, P.J. The encyclopaedia of Islam, new edition / Encyclopédie de l'Islam, Nouvelle édition: Index of subjects / Index des matières to Volumes / des Tomes I-X and to the Supplement, Fascicules / et du Supplément, Livraisons 1-6. Lei 2002, Brill 162 pp. 90-04-09739-2;
850 Index of proper names / index des noms propres to volumes / des tomes I-X and to the supplement, fascicules/ et du supplément, livraisons 1-6. ᴱVan Donzel, E.J.: Lei 2002, Brill 449 pp. 90-04-12107-2;
851 10: T–U. Lei 2002, Brill xvi; 1046 pp. $851. 90-04-12761-5.
852 Bierbrier, Morris L. Historical dictionary of ancient Egypt. 1999 ⇒
15,609. ᴿArOr 70 (2002) 242-243 (*Bareš, Ladislav*); JNES 61 (2002) 289-290 (*Yurco, Frank J.*).
853 ᴱCancik, Hubert; Schneider, Helmuth Brill's new Pauly: encyclopaedia of the ancient world, 1: antiquity volume 1: A-Ari. Lei 2002, Brill 90-04-12259-1.
854 The encyclopedia of the Middle Ages. ᴱVauchez, André: 2000 ⇒17,
722. ᴿCarmelus 49 (2002) 220-222 (*Copsey, Richard*).
855 Enzyklopädie des Märchens, 10: Nibelungenlied-Prozeßmotive. ᴱBrednich, Rolf Wilhelm, *al.*: B 2002, De Gruyter xvi; 1459 col. 311-0168-41-3.
856 ᴱGoodman, Martin; Cohen, Jeremy; Sorkin, David The Oxford handbook of Jewish studies. Oxf 2002, OUP xiv; 1037 pp. €80. 0-19-829996-6.
857 Heine, Bernd; Kuteva, Tania World lexicon of grammaticalization. C 2002, CUP xii; 387 pp. £50. 0-521-00597-3. Bibl. 351-387.
858 ᴱHorbury, William; Davies, W.D.; Sturdy, John The Cambridge history of Judaism, 3: the early Roman period. 1999 ⇒15,613...17, 712. ᴷHeyJ 43 (2002) 357-358 (*King, Nicholas*); RSR 90 (2002) 424-425 (*Paul, André*); JSSt 47 (2002) 346-349 (*Schlüter, Margarete*).
859 Millán Puelles, Antonio Léxico filosófico. M ²2002 <1984>, Rialp 636 pp.
860 ᴱNeusner, Jacob; Avery-Peck, Alan Jeffery; Green, William Scott The encyclopaedia of Judaism. 2000 ⇒16,674; 17,716. ᴿRBLit 4 (2002) 72-75 (*Wolf, Arnold Jacob*).
861 The new encyclopedia of Judaism. ᴱWigoder, Geoffrey; Skolnik, Fred; Himelstein, Shmuel: NY 2002, NY Univ. Pr. xv; 17-856 pp. 0-8147-9388-6. Bibl. 828-835.

A3.8 *Opera consultationis* archaeologica et geographica

862 Calderini, Aristide Dizionario dei nomi geografici e topografici dell' Egitto greco-romano. ᴱDaris, Sergio: Mi 1988- Cisalpino—Goliardica. Supplemento 1 (1935-1986); Supplemento 3 (1994-2001).
863 Darvill, Timothy The concise Oxford dictionary of archaeology. Oxf 2002, OUP xi; 506 pp. £25. 0-19-211649-5.

864 Dictionnaire de l'antiquité grecque et romaine. ᴱThuillier, Jean-Paul, al.,: Carré Histoire: P 2002, Hachette 287 pp. 2-01-145387-9.
865 ᴱLeschhorn, Wolfgang Lexikon der Aufschriften auf griechischen Münzen, Band 1: geographische Begriffe, Götter und Heroen. Veröffentlichungen der Kleinasiatischen Kommission 13: W 2002, Verl. der Österr. Akad. der Wissensch. 426 pp. €100. 37001-30821. Bibl. 15-19.
866 Lexicon of the Greek and Roman cities and place names in antiquity: ca 1500 B.C.-ca. A.D. 500, 6: Arados-Artanada. ᴿZahariade, Mihail: Amst 2002, Hakkert 801-960 col. 90-256-0985-6.
867 Lexikon der ägyptischen Götter und Götterbezeichnungen: v.I: '-y; v.II: e-b; v.III: p-nbw; v.IV: nbt-h; v.V: h-h; v.VI: h-s; v.VII: s-d. ᴱLeitz, Christian: OLA 110-116: Lv 2002, Peeters 90-429-.
868 ᴱMurray, Tim Encyclopedia of archaeology: the great archaeologists. Santa Barbara 1999, ABC-CLIO xxii; 950 pp. $150. ᴿRBLit 4 (2002) 62-64 (Krieger, William H.).
869 ᴱNegev, Avraham; Gibson, Shimon Archaeological encyclopedia of the Holy Land. 2001 ⇒17,730. ᴿRBLit (2002)* (Arav, Rami).
870 Neusner, Jacob The Halakhah: an encyclopaedia of the law of Judaism. Reference Library of Ancient Judaism 1/1-5: 2000 ⇒16,686. ᴿCBQ 64 (2002) 742-744 (Jacobs, Steven Leonard).
871 Pinch, Geraldine Handbook of Egyptian mythology. World mythology: Santa Barbara 2002, ABC-CLIO 257 pp. £42. 1-57607-242-8.
872 Rice, Michael Who's Who in Ancient Egypt. 1999 ⇒15,628. ᴿCEg 153-154 (2002) 128-129 (Karlshausen, C.).
873 Shaw, I.P.; Nicholson, P. The British Museum dictionary of Ancient Egypt. L 2002, British Museum Pr. 328 pp. £15. 0-7141-2179-7.

A4.0 Bibliographiae, *computers* biblicae

874 *Adair, J.R.* Creating and maintaining a premier electronic journal. Bible and computer. 2002 ⇒548. 135-145.
Alvoni, Giovanna Scienze dell'antichità per via informatica: banche dati, internet e risorse elettroniche nello studio dell'antichità classica. Bo 2002, CLUEB viii; 195 pp. ⇒922.
875 *Bergant, Dianne; Senior Donald* The bible in review. BiTod 40 (2002) 56-66, 126-136, 191-200, 256-268, 322-333, 394-404.
876 Bible Works 5.0. Norfolk, VA 2002, Bible Works.
877 Bibliographia carmelitana annualis 2001, IV: sacra scrittura. ᴱWaite, David: Carmelus 49 (2002) 237-249;
878 2002... Carmelus 50 (2002) 195-210.
879 BuBB: Bulletin de bibliographie biblique. ᴱKaestli, Jean Daniel: Lausanne 2002, Institut des sciences bibliques de l'Université de Lausanne. 3 issues a year.
880 *Bulkeley, Tim* Commentary beyond the codex: hyptertext and the art of biblical commentary. Bible and computer. 2002 ⇒548. 641-651.
881 *Debergé, Pierre* Chroniques: écrits du Nouveau Testament et naissance du christianisme. BLE 103 (2002) 97-114.
882 *Den Hollander, A.A.* A bibliography of bibles printed in the Netherlands and Belgium (BBNB). Bible and computer. 2002 ⇒548. 663-72.
883 DiTommaso, Lorenzo A bibliography of pseudepigrapha research 1850-1999. JSPE.S 39: 2001 ⇒17,739. ᴿRHPhR 82 (2002) 207 (Grappe, Ch.); Muséon 115 (2002) 470-472 (Stone, M.E.).

884 *Dugandžić, Ivan* Biblijska bibliografija (1990-2001). BoSm 72/1 (2002) 185-209. **Croatian**.

885 **Elliott, James Keith** A bibliography of Greek New Testament manuscripts. MSSNTS 109: ²2000 ⇒16,697; 17,740. ᴿJThS 53 (2002) 290-298 (*Birdsall, J. Neville*).

886 *Fabre, Véronique* Chronique d'Ecriture Sainte. VieCon 74 (2002) 415-423.

887 Gottes Volk auf CD-ROM: Bibel und Liturgie im Leben der Gemeinde. 2000 ⇒16,698. ᴿBiKi 57 (2002) 109-110 (*Holzer, Paul-Joseph*).

888 **IZBG**: International Review of Biblical Studies 47 (2000-2001): ᴱ**Lang, Bernhard**: 2002 ⇒16,701. ᴿTheol(A) 73 (2002) 755-756, 816-817 (*Simotas, Pan.N.*);

889 48 (2001-2002): ᴱ**Lang, Bernhard**: Lei 2003, Brill xii; 514 pp. €105/ $105. 90-04-12889-1.

890 *Luciani, Didier* Chronique d'Ecriture Sainte (A.T.). VieCon 74 (2002) 334-349.

891 ᴱ**Lumini, Antonella**: La bibbia: edizioni del XVI secolo. Biblioteca di Bibliografia Italiana 162: 2000 ⇒16,704. ᴿAevum 76 (2002) 850-852 (*Rozzo, Ugo*).

892 *Lust, Johann* Scriptura Sacra Veteris Testamenti. EThL 78 (2002) 152*-274*.

893 **NTAb**: New Testament Abstracts 46. ᴱ**Harrington, Daniel J.; Matthews, Christopher R.** CM 2002, Weston Jesuit School of Theology. 3 issues a year.

894 Old Testament Essays: index volume: volumes 1-15 (new series), volumes 1-5 (old series). ᴱ**Boshoff, W.S.; Cronjé, S.I.; Strydom, J. G.**: Pretoria 2002, OTSSA. 1010-9919.

895 **Ostański, Piotr** Bibliografia biblistyki polskiej 1945-1999. Bibliographica 1: Poznań 2002, Uniw. Mickiewicza 2 vols; 1716 pp.

896 **OTA**: Old Testament Abstracts 25. ᴱ**Begg, Christopher T.**: Wsh 2002, Catholic Biblical Association.. 3 issues a year.

897 *Rech, David Alan* Bible study software: what's right for you?. BArR 28/5 (2002) 60-63.

898 **Reinhardt, Klaus** Biblekommentare spanischer Autoren (1500-1700), 2: Autoren M-Z. Medievalia et humanistica 2: 1999 ⇒15,650. ᴿRevAg 43 (2002) 723-724 (*Sánchez Navarro, Luis*).

899 *Robinson, Bernard P.* Old Testament chronicle. PrPe 16 (2002) 38-41.

900 *Schmidl, Martin* BibleWorks 5.0. Journal of Biblical Studies 2/1 (2002).

901 The Society for Old Testament Study Book List 2002. ᴱ**Brooke, George J.**: L 2002: Clark. 240 pp. 18412-72949 [=JSOT 5 (2002) 1-271].

902 *Spronk, Klaas* Exegese en internet: je vindt altijd wat je niet zoekt. ITBT 10/4 (2002) 6 [Mt 10,5-42].

903 *Swart, Ignatius* The imperative of development: a third public challenge to computerised biblical scholarship. Bible and computer. 2002 ⇒548. 593-613.

904 ᴱ*Van der Grijp, Klaus* La biblia: traducciones protestantes o relacionadas con la historia del protestantismo en España. DiEc 37 (2002) 341-353.

905 *Van der Merwe, Christo H.J.* The bible and hypertext technology: challenges for maximizing the use of a new type of technology in biblical studies. JNSL 28/1 (2002) 87-102.

906 *Verheyden, Joseph* Scriptura Sacra Novi Testamenti. EThL 78 (2002)
     274*-348*.
907 **Worth, Roland H.** Biblical studies on the Internet: a resource guide.
     Jefferson, NC 2002, McFarland xi; 316 pp. 0-7864-1327-1.
908 ZAW 114: ᴱ**Waschke, Ernst-Joachim; Köckert, Matthias**: B 2002,
     De Gruyter 116-187; 270-338; 446-496.
909 ZNW 93: ᴱ**Wolter, Michael**: B 2002, De Gruyter 146-148; 288-290.

A4.2 *Bibliographiae* **theologicae**

910 Bibliografia internationalis spiritualitatis, 34: bibliografia anni 1999. R
     2002, Teresianum xxxi; 514 pp. 0084-7834.
911 **Biester, Björn** Harnack-Bibliographie: Verzeichnis der Literatur über
     Adolf von Harnack 1911-2002. Erfurt 2002, Biester Univ. vi; 126 pp
     [ZKTh 125,311—Neufeld, K.H.].
912 ᴱ**Conti, Beniamino** Sangue di Cristo, sangue dell'uomo: indici degli at-
     ti: sangue e antropologia; sangue e vita del Centro Studi Sanguis Chri-
     sti. R 2002, Pia Unione Preziosissimo Sangue 133 pp.
913 Elenchus bibliographicus. ᴱ**Auwers, J.-M.**, *al.*: EThL 78: Lv 2002,
     Peeters 831* pp.
914 **Keller, Adalbert** Translationes patristicae graecae et latinae: Biblio-
     graphie der Übersetzungen altchristlicher Quellen, 1: A-H. 1997 ⇒13,
     490; 15,658. ᴿRBLit 4 (2002) 76-78 = JBL 121 (2002) 388-390 (*Casi-
     day, Augustine M.*).
915 **Moulinet, Daniel** Guide bibliographique des sciences religieuses.
     2000 ⇒16,722. ᴿEThL 78 (2002) 179 (*Van Belle, G.*).
916 ᴱ**Nardin, Roberto** Indice generale 1976-2002 volumi XLII-LXVIII.
     Lat. (2002) 1-136.
917 ThD 48: Book survey. ᴱ*Heiser, W. Charles*: Duluth, MN 2002, Theol-
     ogy Digest. 4 times a year.
918 Theologie im Kontext 22. Aachen 2002, Missionswissenschaftliches
     Institut. 2 issues a year.
919 **Van Belle, Gilbert** Index generalis ETL/BETL 1982-1997. BEThL
     134: 1999 ⇒15,663...17,772. ᴿRivBib 50 (2002) 77-78 (*Prato, Gian
     Luigi*); LouvSt 27 (2002) 188-190 (*Harrington, Jay M.*).
920 ᴱ*Van der Grijp, Klaus* Ensayo de una bibliografía de la historia del
     protestantismo español. DiEc 37 (2002) 337-651.
921 **Žitnik, Maksimilijian** Sacramenta: bibliographia internationalis: con-
     tinuatio, 5: A-K; 6: L-Z; 7: Indices. R 2002, E.P.U.G. xi; 907 + 889 +
     350 pp. €60 + 60 + 28. 88-7652-914-4/22-5/36-5. ᴿCarmelus 49
     (2002) 202-203 (*Valabek, Redemptus Maria*).

A4.3 *Bibliographiae* **philologicae** et **generales**

922 **Alvoni, Giovanna** Scienze dell'antichità per via informatica: banche
     dati, internet e risorse elettroniche nello studio dell'antichità classica.
     Bo 2002, CLUEB viii; 195 pp. Contrib. *Ulrich Rausch;* introd. *Franco
     Montanari.*
923 *Berschin, Walter* An unpublished library catalogue from eighth-century
     Lombard Italy. Journal of Medieval Latin 11 (2001) 201-209 [RBen
     114,183—P.-M. Bogaert].

924 Bibliographie annuelle du Moyen-Âge Tardif 12. Turnhout 2002, Brepols 700 pp. 2-503-51276-3.

925 Bibliographie de l'année 2000 et compléments d'années antérieures. ᴱCorsetti, Pierre-Paul; Rebillard, Éric: AnPh 71 (2001-2002) lxi; 1733 pp.

926 *Domhardt, Yvonne* Auswahlbibliographie von Werken mit jüdisch-judaistischer Thematik, die seit Sommer 2001 bis Redaktionsschluss 2002 in Schweizer Verlagen erschienen sind bzw. durch Inhalt oder Verfasser/in die Schweiz betreffen. Bulletin der Schweizerischen Gesellschaft für Judaistische Forschung 11 (2002) 35-43.

927 *Gauthier, Philippe, al.*, Bulletin épigraphique. REG 115 (2002) 622-777.

928 **Kitchen, Kenneth A.** Documentation for ancient Arabia part II: bibliographical catalogue of texts. The World of Ancient Arabia 2: 2000 ⇒ 16,736. ᴿJSSt 47 (2002) 370-372 (*Potts, D.T.*); AfO 48-49 (2001-2002) 282-285 (*Sima, Alexander*).

929 Language: twentieth-century index 1925-2000 (volumes 1-76). ᴱSumner, Meghan; Aronoff, Mark: 2002, v; 1-597 pp.

A4.4 *Bibliographiae* orientalisticae

930 **Beinlich-Seeber, Christine** Bibliographie Altägypten; 1822-1946. ÄA 61: 1998 ⇒14,581; 16,739. ᴿJNES 61 (2002) 69-70 (*Teeter, Emily*).

931 *Jursa, M.; Weszeli, M.* Assyriologie, Register;

932 Mesopotamien und Nachbargebiete;

933 *Müller, Walter W.* Südarabien im Altertum: ausgewählte und kommentierte Bibliographie der Jahre 1998 und 1999. AfO 48-49 (2001-2002) 311-461; 462-505; 298-307.

934 *Neumann, Hans* Keilschriftbibliographie, 60. Or. 71 (2002) 1*-121*.

935 ᴱSoucek, Vladimír; Siegelová, Jana Systematische Bibliographie der Hethitologie 1915-1995. HO 1 A. 38: 1998 ⇒14,592; 15,676. ᴿAfO 48-49 (2001-2002) 250-254 (*Beal, Richard H.*).

A4.5 *Bibliographiae* archaeologicae

936 *Botto, M., al.*, Bibliografia 30 (1.1.2001-31.12.2001). RSFen 30 (2002) 237-270.

937 *Dollfus, Geneviève* Bibliographie générale annuelle. Paléorient 28/2 (2002) 157-200.

938 *Dupont, P., al.*, Bulletin archéologique: céramique. REG 115 (2002) 216-404.

939 *Elayi, J.; Sapin, J.* Syrie—Phénicie—Palestine: bibliographie. TEuph 24 (2002) 43-111.

940 *Garlan, Yvon* Bulletin archéologique: amphores et timbres amphoriques (1997-2001). REG 115 (2002) 149-215.

941 **Ninow, Friedbert** Index librorum de rebus Moabiticis conscriptorum. Beiträge zur Erforschung der antiken Moabitis (Ard el-Kerak) 1: Fra 2002, Lang 192 pp. 3-631-38769-5.

942 Rendiconti: Supplemento al volume LXXIII: indice generale dal 1966 al 2001. ᴱBuonocore, Marco: APARA (Serie III): Città del Vaticano 2002, Vaticana 145* pp.

II. Introductio

B1.1 *Introductio tota vel VT*—Whole Bible or OT

943 **Akenson, Donald Harman** Surpassing wonder: the invention of the bible and the talmuds. 1998 ⇒14,596...17,9382. [R]SR 31 (2002) 109-110 (*Gaston, LLoyd*).

944 *Barstad, Hans M.* Is the Hebrew Bible a Hellenistic book?: or: Niels Peter LEMCHE, HERODOTUS, and the Persians. TEuph 23 (2002) 129-151.

945 **Baslez, Marie-Françoise** Bibbia e storia: Giudaismo, ellenismo, cristianesimo. Introduzione allo studio della bibbia, Suppl. 8: Brescia 2002, Paideia 389 pp. 88-394-0640-9. Bibl. 369-374.

946 **Boshoff, W.S.; Scheffler, E.H.; Spangenberg, I.J.J.** Ancient Israelite literature in context. 2000 ⇒16,750; 17,797. [R]RBLit (2002)* (*Benjamin, Don C.*).

947 **Buzzetti, Carlo** Se l'Antico Testamento vale ancora: guida-base per l'apostolato biblico. Bibbia, proposte e metodi: Leumann (Torino)] 2002, Elle Di Ci 123 pp. 88-01-02636-6.

948 **Campbell, Antony F.** The study companion to the Old Testament literature: an approach to the writings of pre-exilic and exilic Israel. OT Studies 2: 1989 ⇒6,1159... 9,819. [R]RB 109 (2002) 136-138 (*Loza Vera, J.*).

949 **Ceresko, Anthony R.** Introduction to the Old Testament. 2001 <1992> ⇒17,802. [R]NewTR 15/2 (2002) 90-91 (*Cook, Joan E.*).

950 **Cimosa, Mario** L'ambiente storico-culturale delle scritture ebraiche. 2000 ⇒16,755; 17,804. [R]Annales Theologici 16 (2002) 212-215 (*Tábet, M.*); EfMex 20 (2002) 279-280 (*Junco Garza, Carlos*); RivBib 50 (2002) 476-478 (*Prato, Gian Luigi*); CoTh 72/4 (2002) 233-238 (*Chrostowski, Waldemar*).

951 **Coggins, Richard James** Introducing the Old Testament. [2]2001 ⇒17, 805. [R]RfR 61 (2002) 329-330 (*Asen, Bernhard A.*).

952 [E]**Dué, Andrea; Rossi, Renzo** La bibbia e la sua storia, 1: l'Antico Testamento. 2001 ⇒17,807. Nuova ed. [R]RivBib 50 (2002) 123-124 (*Mela, Roberto*).

953 **Gillingham, S.E.** One bible, many voices: different approaches to biblical studies. 1998 ⇒14,605... 16,763. [R]SJTh 55 (2002) 490-492 (*Pokrifka-Joe, Hyunhye June*).

954 **Kaiser, Otto** Die alttestamentlichen Apokryphen: eine Einleitung in Grundzügen. 2000 ⇒16,767; 17,817. [R]ThLZ 127 (2002) 1165-1167 (*Schmitt, Armin*).

955 *Mason, Rex* The Old Testament / Hebrew Bible. Biblical world, 1: 2002 ⇒273. 5-14.

956 **Meynet, Roland** Ler a bíblia. Biblioteca básica de Ciência e Cultura 102: Lisboa 2000, Instituto Piaget 137 pp. 972771479X. Bibl. 129-31.

957 **Motyer, Alec** The story of the Old Testament. L 2001, Candle 191 pp. £8. 1-85985-401-X.

958 **Nunes, Manuel** Querido sobrinho, explica-me a bíblia. Dinamização Bíblica 21: Lisboa 2002, Difusora Bíblica 259 pp.

959 **Potin, Jean** La bible rendue à l'histoire. 2000 ⇒16,776; 17,825. [R]LTP 58 (2002) 362-364 (*Crégheur, Eric*).
960 **Schmidt, Werner H.** Einführung in das Alte Testament. [5]1995 ⇒11/2, 1132. [R]RB 109 (2002) 139-140 (*Loza Vera, J.*).
961 **Shillington, V. George** Reading the sacred text: an introduction to biblical studies. L 2002, Clark x; 322 pp. £17. 0-567-08824-3. Bibl. 297-313.
962 **Smend, Rudolf** La formazione dell'Antico Testamento. 1993 ⇒9,850 ... 12,476. [R]RB 109 (2002) 138-139 (*Loza Vera, J.*).
963 [E]**Stone, Michael Edward; Bergren, Theodore A.** Biblical figures outside the bible. 1998 ⇒14,8207; 17,828. [R]SR 31 (2002) 498-500 (*Piovanelli, Pierluigi*).
964 **Tábet, Miguel Angel** Introduzione al pentateuco e ai libri storici dell' Antico Testamento: manuale di Sacra Scrittura. 2001 ⇒17,829. [R]PaVi 47/2 (2002) 61-62 (*De Virgilio, Giuseppe*); Asp. 49 (2002) 130-132 (*Castello, Gaetano*); RivBib 50 (2002) 479-481 (*Castello, Gaetano*); Annales Theologici 16 (2002) 512-515 (*De Virgilio, G.*); LASBF 51 (2001) 412-414 (*Kaswalder, P.*).
965 **Zwickel, Wolfgang** Einführung in die biblische Landes- und Altertumskunde. Da:Wiss 2002, 176 pp. €19.90. 3-534-15084-8 [EuA 79,78—Schwank, Benedikt]

B1.2 'Invitations' to Bible or OT

966 **Apel, William** Silent conversations: reading the bible in good company. Valley Forge, PA 2000, Judson xiii; 174 pp. $15. 0-8170-13202.
967 **Arnold, Bill T.; Beyer, Bryan E.** Readings from the ancient Near East. Encountering Biblical Studies: GR 2002, Baker 240 pp. $22. 08-010-2292-4. [R]RExp 99 (2002) 628-629 (*Nogalski, James D.*).
968 **Beauchamp, Paul** Biblische Lebensbilder. Stu 2002, Katholisches Bibelwerk 160 pp. 3-460-30212-7.
969 **Beretta, Roberto; Broli, Elisabetta** Gli undici comandamenti: equivoci, bugie e luoghi comuni sulla bibbia e dintorni. CasM 2002, Piemme x; 203 pp. 88-384-6491-X. Prefazione di *Gianfranco Ravasi.*
970 **Bergant, Dianne** People of the covenant: an invitation to the Old Testament. 2001 ⇒17,837. [R]Spiritual Life 48/1 (2002) 56-58 (*Gribble, Richard*); RfR 61 (2002) 327-328 (*Asen, Bernhard A.*).
971 Die Bibel: Geschichte und Gegenwart. Stu 2002, Kath. Bibelwerk 240 pp. €49.90. 3-460-30213-5. 400+ ill.
972 *Brossier, François* L'utilisation de l'Écriture dans les révisions de vie et les pratiques de partages. Cahiers de l'Atelier 495 (2001) 24-30.
973 **Cukrowski, Kenneth; Hamilton, Mark W.; Thompson, James W.** God's holy fire: the nature and function of scripture. The Heart of the Restoration 2: Abilene, TX 2002, ACU xiii; 303 pp. $15. 0-891-1203-78 [ThD 49,368—Heiser, W. Charles].
974 **Deselaers, Paul** Lebensweisheit aus der Bibel: biblische Frauen und Männer—Inspiration für heute. FrB 2002, Herder 222 pp. €14.90. 3-451-27320-9 [BiKi 57,170s—Zwingenberger, Uta].
975 **Eaton, Michael** Know the bible: a daily guide to searching the scriptures. L 2002, Hodder & S. 460 pp. $18 [BiTod 41,326—Bergant, D.].
976 **Ellsworth, Roger** The guide—the bible book by book. Darlington 2002, Evangelical 432 pp. £10. 0-85234-486-4.

977 *Feldkämper,Ludger* Sharing personal faith: the practice of bible-sharing. NewTR 15/1 (2002) 5-13.
978 **Fischer, Georg** Wege in die Bibel: Leitfaden zur Auslegung. 2000 ⇒ 16,790; 17,840. [R]ThPQ 150 (2002) 81-82 (*Böhmisch, Franz*).
979 **Hamel, Christopher F.R. de** The book: a history of the bible. 2001 ⇒ 17,842. [R]Theol. 105 (2002) 211-212 (*Coggins, Richard*); BiTr 53 (2002) 362-363 (*Ellingworth, Paul*).
980 **Hart, Maarten 't** De rebil van God: de Schrift betwist, deel II. Amst 2002, Arbeiderspers 240 pp. €12. 90-295-228-3.
981 **Jackman, David** Opening up the bible. North Pomfret, Vermont 2000, Hodder 240 pp. $15 [BiTod 42,187—Bergant, Dianne.].
982 **Lamp, Ida; Meurer, Thomas** Basiswissen Bibel. GTBS 673: Gü 2002, Gü'er 95 pp. €6.90. 3579-0067-38 [BiKi 58,190–Schapdick, S.].
983 **Lim, Johnson T.K.** A strategy for reading biblical texts. Studies in Biblical Literature 29: NY 2002, Lang xvii; 152 pp. $50. 0-8204-5028-6. Bibl. 131-152.
984 **Linden, Nico ter** Die schönsten Geschichten der Bibel. GTBS 1332: Gü 2002, Gü'er 157 pp. 3-579-01332-7.
985 **Merton, Thomas** Leggere la bibbia. Mi 2002, Garzanti 98 pp. €6.50;
986 Die Bibel öffnen: ein Essay. Z 2002, Theologischer 111 pp. 3-290-17243-0 [ThZ 60,189—Edgar Kellenberger].
987 **Philipps, James** Unlocking the treasures of the bible: a practical guide. Mystic, CONN 2002, Twenty-Third 138 pp. $13 [BiTod 41,196—Bergant, Dianne].
988 **Roberts, Vaughan** God's big picture: tracing the story-line of the bible. Leicester 2002, IVP 160 pp [SdT 16,85—Luigi Dalla Pozza].
989 **Robinson, Alan** Called by God: stories from the Jewish and christian bibles. Brighton 2002, Alpha viii; 136 pp. $18. 1-898595-40-2.
990 [E]**Rogerson, John William** Beginning Old Testament study. [2]1998 <1983> ⇒14,647. [R]SBET 20 (2002) 247-249 (*Rowlands, Eryl*).
991 **Schaube, Werner** Aufbrechen: Bibel-Impulse für junge Menschen. FrB 2002, Herder 125 pp. €9.90 [BiLi 76,224—Geiger, Georg].
992 **Vallet, Ronald E.** The steward living in covenant: a new perspective in Old Testament stories. 2001 ⇒17,852. [R]RBLit (2002)* (*Braaten, Laurie J.*).
993 **Vermeylen, Jacques** Ten keys for opening the bible. 2000 ⇒16,806. [R]RBLit 4 (2002) 183-184 (*Reed, Stephen A.*) .

B1.3 *Pedagogia biblica*—**Bible-teaching techniques**

994 [E]**Hennig, Peter** Die Bibel neu ins Spiel bringen: ein Werkbuch mit zahlreichen Projekten für die Gemeindearbeit. Gü 2002, Gü'er 160 pp. €19. 3-579-05590-9.
995 [E]**Scheidler, Monika; Hilberath, Bernd Jochen; Wildt, Johannes** Theologie lehren: Hochschuldidaktik und Reform der Theologie. QD 197: FrB 2002, Herder 263 pp. 3-451-02197-8.
996 **Bechtel, Carol M.** Teaching the "strange new world" of the bible. Interp. 56 (2002) 368-377.
997 **Bek, Birgit, Link, Paulin** Glauben erfahren und ausdrücken: ein Werkbuch zur Arbeit mit biblischen Erzählungen. Mü 2002, Bernward 95 pp. €12.70. 3-7698-1327-8 [OrdKor 44,126].

998 La biblia en la formación. Estella 2002, Verbo Divino 312 pp. €16. 84-8169-553-X. La Casa de la Biblia.

999 ^E**Bissoli, C.** Grandi temi della pastorale biblica. Proposte e metodi: T 2002, Elle Di Ci 269 pp. €12. Ufficio Catechistico Nazionale [PaVi 47/5,59—Gamba, Rosetta].

1000 *Bizer, Christoph* "Verstehst du, was du liesest?": Lesekompetenz in PISA und eine Erzählung aus dem Heiligen Land. Zeitschrift für Pädagogik und Theologie 54 (2002) 317-327 [Acts 8,26-40].

1001 ^E**Bortone, Giuseppe** La Provvidenza divina: approccio pluridisciplinare: XXI corso biblico. Studio Biblico Teologico Aquilano 21: 2001 ⇒17,864. ^RAnnales Theologici 16 (2002) 531-533 (*Tábet, M.*).

1002 **Boyer, Mark G.** Using film to teach New Testament. Lanham 2002, University Press of America x; 280 pp. $41. 0-7618-2242-9.

1003 *Böhlemann, Peter* Biblische Visionen für die Gemeindeentwicklung. Die Bibel neu ins Spiel bringen. 2002 ⇒994. 135-150.

1004 ^E**Brielmaier, Beate; Eltrop, Bettina** Bibelarbeit mit Kindern. Stu 2002, Kath. Bibelwerk 80 pp. €9.50. 3-460-25501-3. ^RBiKi 57 (2002) 230-231 (*Kaiser, Helga*).

1005 *Brink, Birgitt; Derksen, Nicolaas; Sieben, Franz* Wirksame Erinnerung: die Inszenierung des "Als-ob" im Bibliodrama. BiLi 75 (2002) 27-31.

1006 *Brueggemann, Walter* That the world may be redescribed. Interp. 56 (2002) 359-367.

1007 ^E**Burger, Ronna** Encounters & reflections: conversations with Seth Benardete: with Robert Berman, Ronna Burger, and Michael Davis. Ch 2002, University of Chicago Press x; 229 pp. 0-226-04278-2.

1008 *Cardona, Hernán Darío* La pastoral bíblica en medio de los jóvenes. Medellín 28 (2002) 79-96.

1009 *Cavalletti, Sofia* Die Katechese des Guten Hirten: ein Abenteuer. JBTh 17 (2002) 291-312.

1010 *Cook, Stephen L.* Teaching the bible at Virginia Seminary in late modern times. AThR 84/1 (2002) 37-47;

1011 Introduction: teaching the bible in a new millennium. AThR 84 (2002) 3-9.

1012 *Couto, António* Elementos de pedagogia evangélica. Theologica 37/1 (2002) 15-30.

1013 ^E**Currò, Salvatore; Dimonte, Roberto** Giovani in cammino con la bibbia. 2001 ⇒17,868. ^RSal. 64 (2002) 147-148 (*Buzzetti, Carlo*).

1014 *Dannemann, Christiane* "Muss es aus der Bibel sein?". JK 63/2 (2002) 2-5.

1015 *Delkurt, Holger* Erziehung nach dem Alten Testament. JBTh 17 (2002) 227-253.

1016 *Duncan, G.A.; Hofmeyr, J.W.* Leadership through theological education: two case studies in South African history;

1017 *Erasmus, J.A.; Klerk, B.J. de* Perspektiewe vanuit die psigologie en sosiale wetenskappe vir kerklike bediening aan die adolessent: 'n ondersoek na die ontwikkeling van die adolessent. VeE 23 (2002) 642-657/343-352.

1018 *Farmer, Kathleen A.; Dalton, Russell W.* Using multimedia resources in teaching the bible. Interp. 56 (2002) 387-397.

1019 *Festa, Riccardo* L'attenzione educativa ai giovani: testimonianza sull' applicazione del "principio biblico dell'educazione". [Card. Martini] Ambrosius 78/2 (2002) 135-140.

1020 *Fricke, Michael* Kain und Abel für Kinder?. KatBl 127 (2002) 10-18.
1021 **Giavini, Giovanni** Con Dio nel deserto: educare con la bibbia in mano. Mi 2002, IPL 121 pp. ᴿPaVi 47/5 (2002) 60-61 (*Ferrari, Pier
Luigi*).
1022 ᴱ**Grabner-Haider, Anton** Prontuario della bibbia. 2000 ⇒16,830.
ᴿVivH 13/1 (2002) 187-188 (*Tarocchi, Stefano*).
1023 **Griggs, Donald L.** The bible from scratch: the Old Testament for be-
ginners. LVL 2002, Westminster 135 pp. $10 [BiTod 40,397—Ber-
gant, Dianne].
1024 *Grill, Ingrid* Verwurzelung und Differenz: zum Umgang mit christlich-jüdischen Themen im Religionsunterricht. PTh 91 (2002) 460-
477.
1025 *Henao Mesa, Jairo Alberto* Visión profética de la pastoral bíblica de
la iglesia. Medellín 28 (2002) 51-62.
1026 *Hennig, Peter* Bibelausstellungen und Bibelzentren—ein touristisch-
pädagogischer Führer;
1027 Was man sonst noch machen kann;
1028 Die Bibel ernst nehmen;
1029 *Hessenauer, Gisela* Bibelarbeiten und Andachten gemeinsam gestalten Die Bibel neu ins Spiel bringen 2002 52-68/151-158/6-20/21-35.
1030 *Hügel, Sylvia* Die Bergpredigt als Lesestoff im 9. Schuljahr. Zeitschrift für Pädagogik und Theologie 54 (2002) 373-377 [Mt 5-7].
1031 ᴱ**Idinopulos, Thomas A.; Wilson, Brian C.** Reappraising Durkheim for the study and teaching of religion today. SHR 92: Lei 2002,
Brill xix; 192 pp. 90-04-12339-3. Bibl. 183-185.
1032 *Jones, Barry A.* Teaching bible studies from First and Second Samuel
in a congregational setting. RExp 99 (2002) 255-273.
1033 *Jung, Thomas* Das Wort Gottes schafft Lebensalternativen: Bibelarbeit im Bistum Pasto (Kolumbien). NZM 58 (2002) 281-296.
1034 **Kalloch, Christina** Das Alte Testament im Religionsunterricht der
Grundschule—Chancen und Grenzen alttestamentlicher Fachdidaktik
im Primarbereich. ᴰ*Göllner, Reinhard*: 2002 Diss.-Habil. Hildesheim
[ThRv 99/2,xii.].
1035 *Kang, S. Steve* The church, spiritual formation, and the kingdom of
God: a case for canonical-communion reading of the bible. ExAu 18
(2002) 137-151. Resp. *Paul Bramer* 152-154.
1036 **Kirchschläger, Walter** Grundkurs Bibel—Altes Testament. TOPOS
-plus-Taschenbücher 421: Mainz 2002, Matthias-Grünewald 124 pp.
3-7867-8421-3. Neuausg.;
1037 Neues Testament. TOPOS-plus-Taschenbücher 422: Mainz 2002,
Matthias-Grünewald 124 pp. 3-7867-8422-1. Neuausg.
1038 *Klöpper, Diana; Schiffner, Kerstin; Taschner, Johannes* Mut zur biblischen Geschichte. JK 63/2 (2002) 19-21.
1039 *Küster, Volker* Das Evangelium in Bildern erzählen: die Papierschnitt
-Zyklen von Fan Pu (China). NZM 58 (2002) 267-280.
1040 ᴱ**Lachmann, R.; Adam, G.; Reents, Chr.** Elementare Bibeltexte:
exegetisch—systematisch—didaktisch. 2001 ⇒17,892. ᴿBiKi 57
(2002) 171-172 (*Wunderlich, Reinhard*).
1041 *Langenhorst, Annegret* Sprich nicht darüber, meine Schwester Tamar. KatBl 127 (2002) 25-29.
1042 *Le Roux, Jurie; Lombaard, Christo* The Old Testament in a new
medium: graduate studies in the Old Testament via the internet at the
University of Pretoria. BOTSA 13 (2002) 12-15.

1043 ^E**Lessmann, Beate** Mein Gott, mein Gott: mit Psalmworten biblische Themen erschliessen: ein Praxisbuch für Schule und Gemeinde. Neuk 2002, Neuk'er 232 pp. €24.90. 3-7887-1851-X.

1044 *Lohkemper-Sobiech, Gudrun* Bibliodrama—ein Raum für holistische Heilungsprozesse?: Reflexion einer Unterrichtseinheit zur Heilung der gekrümmten Frau. rhs 45 (2002) 229-242 [Lk 13,11-17].

1045 **Mabundu Masamba, Fidèle** La lecture de la bible en pastorale: analyse d'expériences. ^D*Cheza, M.*: Diss. Louvain-la-Neuve 2002 [EThL 79,239].

1046 **Magirius, Georg** 99 Fragen aus der Bibel. Gütersloher Taschenbücher 1204: Gü 2002, Gü'er 144 pp. €7.90 [BiLi 75,214].

1047 *Martini, Carlo M.* Il principio biblico dell'educazione. Ambrosius 78/ 2 (2002) 95-105;

1048 Il valore educativo della scrittura. RCI 83 (2002) 376-385.

1049 *Meurer, Thomas* Bibeldidaktik als ästhetische Erfahrung: zu einem exegetisch und religionspädagogisch verantworteten Umgang mit der Bibel im RU. Orien. 66 (2002) 167-172;

1050 Begegnung mit der fremden Bibel. KatBl 127 (2002) 19-24;

1051 Das Fremde unmittelbar oder das Unmittelbare fremd machen?: Suchbewegungen in der Bibeldidaktik. RPäB 49 (2002) 3-16.

1052 *Mitchell Legg, Pamela* Understanding bible study curricula: theology, hermeneutics, and education in the congregation. Interp. 56 (2002) 398-409.

1053 *Moore, Michael S.* Searching in Sheba: the goal of christian education. RestQ 44/1 (2002) 33-42.

1054 *Moscatelli, Luca* Diventare adulti nella fede: la pedagogia della lettura biblica. [Card. Martini] Ambrosius 78/2 (2002) 117-129.

1055 *Nagel, Günter* Gegen die Harmlosigkeit gängigen Bibelunterrichts. KatBl 127 (2002) 4-9.

1056 *Naurath, Elisabeth* Auf dem Boden stehen und nach dem Himmel greifen: Bibliodrama als integrative Hermeneutik biblischer Texte. Diak. 33 (2002) 268-273.

1057 ^E**Naurath, Elisabeth; Pohl-Patalong, Uta** Bibliodrama: Theorie— Praxis—Reflexion. Stu 2002, Kohlhammer 192 pp. €25.

1058 *Neubrand, Maria* "Verstehst du, was du liest?" (Apg 8,30): neutestamentliche Wissenschaft und universitäre Lehre. Theologie lehren. QD 197: 2002 ⇒995. 83-96.

1059 *Niehl, Franz W.* Warum hat David keine Angst? oder: unter welchen Bedingungen fördern biblische Texte identitätsorientierendes Lernen?. rhs 45 (2002) 310-315.

1060 *Niemeyer, Günter* Die Bibel in der Seniorenarbeit. Die Bibel neu ins Spiel bringen. 2002 ⇒994. 118-134.

1061 **Otis, Jacques** La vie en abondance: une relecture des évangiles pour aujourd'hui. Ottawa 2002, Novalis 227 pp.

1062 *Phillips, Gary A.* The teaching of the biblical text: teaching as ethics and ethics as teaching. ^F PATTE, D. 2002 ⇒89. 15-36.

1063 *Porzelt, Burkard* Bibeldidaktik in posttraditionalen Zeiten. RPäB 49 (2002) 33-48.

1064 *Prichard, Robert W.* Biblical studies and the teaching of church history. AThR 84 (2002) 49-56.

1065 *Puttkammer, Annegret* Die Bibel in Frauengruppen. Die Bibel neu ins Spiel bringen. 2002 ⇒994. 85-102.

1066 *Richard, Pablo* Interpreting and teaching the bible in Latin America. Interp. 56 (2002) 378-386.

1067 *Schmid, Bruno; Kuld, Lothar* Biblische Dilemmageschichten. KatBl 127 (2002) 30-34.

1068 *Schoberth, Ingrid* Glauben-lernen heißt eine Sprache lernen: exemplarisch durchgeführt an einer Performance zu Psalm 120. rhs 45 (2002) 20-31.

1069 *Scullion, James* Actualization, inspiration, canonicity. NewTR 15/1 (2002) 14-20.

1070 **Simian-Yofre, H.** Metodología del Antiguo Testamento. ᵀ*Ortiz García, Alfonso*: 2001 ⇒17,914. ᴿSalm. 49 (2002) 241-242 (*Sánchez Caro, J.M.*); CTom 129 (2002) 189-190 (*González Blanco, Rafael*); Cart. 18 (2002) 547-548 (*Sanz Valdivieso, R.*); ActBib 39 (2002) 195-197 (*Sivatte, R. de*).

1071 *Smith, Carol* What was in the scripture knowledge syllabus at Bertie Wooster's prep school?. ᴹCARROLL, R.: JSOT.S 348: 2002 ⇒13. 395-415.

1072 **Smith, David I.; Shortt, John** The bible and the task of teaching. Nottingham 2002, Stapleford 171 pp. $14.

1073 **Snyder, H. Gregory** Teachers and texts in the ancient world: philosophers, Jews and christians. 2000 ⇒16,865; 17,915. ᴿJJS 53 (2002) 167-168 (*Lange, Nicholas de*); ChH 71 (2002) 168-169 (*Setzer, Claudia J.*); JEarlyC 10 (2002) 292-294 (*Scalise, Charles J.*); ClR 52 (2002) 289-290 (*Vanderspoel, John*); StPhiloA 14 (2002) 226-228 (*Fox, Kenneth A.*)

1074 *Steffe, Hans-Martin* Religionsunterricht für Erwachsene. Die Bibel neu ins Spiel bringen. 2002 ⇒994. 36-51.

1075 *Sternberger, Jean P.* Les bibles pour enfants ou les aventures de Targoum et Midrach. FV 101/4 (2002) 85-95.

1076 **Stubna, Kris D.** Opening the scriptures: a guide to the catechism for use with the Sunday readings. Huntington, IN 2002, Our Sunday Visitor xv;230 pp. $15. 1-59276-022-8 [ThD 51,88–W.C. Heiser].

1077 *Stypułkowska, Beata* Zagadnienie krytyki tekstu pisma świętego w katechezie biblijnej [The problem of biblical criticism in scriptural catechesis]. StBob 2 (2002) 157-166 Sum. 166. **P**.

1078 **Theis, Joachim** Die Bibel verstehen: eine bibeldidaktische Studie mit einer empirischen Untersuchung zum Gleichnis vom barmherzigen Samariter. ᴰ*Bitter, Gottfried*: 2002 Diss.-Habil. Bonn [ThRv 99, 350] [Lk 10,29-37].

1079 *Torres M., Fernando* Caminos de pastoral bíblica. ThX 52 (2002) 641-662.

1080 *Warns, Else Natalie* Die Bibel spielen. Die Bibel neu ins Spiel bringen. 2002 ⇒994. 69-84.

1081 *Weisensee H., Jesús Antonio* La pastoral bíblica—perspectivas. Medellín 28 (2002) 97-124.

1082 **Welborn, Amy** Jesus Prove it!. Huntington, IN 2002, Our Sunday Visitor 128 pp. $7. 0-87973-395-0 [ThD 50,94—Heiser, W.C.].

1083 *Welborn, Laurence L.* Vom Unterrichten der Bibel im "Ausnahmezustand": Reflexionen über die hermeneutische Aufgabe eines neutestamentlichen Historikers nach dem 11. September 2001. ZNT 10 (2002) 2-12.

1084 *Wetzel, Christoph* Die "Armenbibel"—eine Bilderbibel für Analphabeten?. Die Bibel: Geschichte und Gegenwart. 2002 ⇒971. 120-121.

1085 *Wills, Angela* A journey into the scriptures. PrPe 16 (2002) 302-306.

1086 *Wuckelt, Agnes* Annäherungen an die Turmbau-Geschichte in der Sekundarstufe I. KatBl 127 (2002) 269-273.

1087 zwölfmal bibel. entdecken: Stu 2002, Verl. Kath. Bibelwerk 144 pp.
      3-460-20033-2.

B2.1 Hermeneutica

1088 *Almond, Ian* The honesty of the perplexed: DERRIDA and IBN 'ARABI
      on 'bewilderment'. JAAR 70 (2002) 515-537.
1089 *Antón Pacheco, José Antonio* Sabiduría y hermenéutica: la interpre-
      tación como prática sapiencial. Isidorianum 21 (2002) 357-373.
1090 *Anum, Eric* Towards intercultural contextual bible study: a review of
      the adoption of contextual bible study (from South Africa) in the west
      of Scotland. IRM 91 (2002) 224-236.
1091 *Argárate, Pablo* Herméneutica y exégesis de los Padres de la iglesia.
      AnáMnesis 12/1 (2002) 25-38.
1092 *Arzt, Silvia* Reading the bible is a gendered act. Feminist Theology
      29 (2002) 32-39.
1093 ᴱ**Barton, John** The Cambridge companion to biblical interpretation.
      1998 ⇒14,699…16,890. ᴿRStT 20/2 (2002) 91-94 (*Linville, James*);
1094 La interpretación bíblica, hoy. Presencia teológica 113: 2001 ⇒17,
      931. ᴿEE 77 (2002) 163-166 (*Ramírez Fueyo, Francisco*); Salm. 49
      (2002) 214-216 (*Sánchez Caro, J.M.*); CTom 129 (2002) 191-192
      (*González Blanco, Rafael*).
1095 *Bayer, Oswald* Hermeneutical theology. Philosophical hermeneutics.
      WUNT 153: 2002 ⇒367. 103-120.
1096 *Bechmann, Ulrike* Wenn heilige Texte unheilig sind: Aspekte einer
      kritischen Bibelhermeneutik. BiKi 57 (2002) 208-214.
1097 *Bergant, Dianne* The challenge of hermeneutics: Lamentations 1:1-
      11: a test case. CBQ 64 (2002) 1-16.
1098 **Berger, Klaus** Hermenêutica do Novo Testamento. ᵀ*Schneider, Né-
      lio*: 1999 ⇒15,820; 17,934. ᴿPerTeol 34 (2002) 396-397 (*Marques,
      Valdir*);
1099 Sind die Berichte des Neuen Testaments wahr?: ein Weg zum Ver-
      stehen der Bibel. Gü 2002, Gü'er 212 pp. €19.95. 3-579-05193-8.
      ᴿSNTU.A 27 (2002) 287-288 (*Gmainer-Pranzl, F.*);
1100 Ermeneutica del Nuovo Testamento. 2001 ⇒17,935. ᴿAnnales Theo-
      logici 16 (2002) 204-209 (*Tábet, M.*); CivCatt 153/3 (2002) 338-339
      (*Scaiola, D.*).
1101 *Berlinerblau, Jacques* "Poor bird, not knowing which way to fly":
      biblical scholarship's marginality, secular humanism, and the lauda-
      ble occident. BiblInterp 10 (2002) 267-304.
1102 *Blanchard, Yves-Marie* Le texte dans son corpus: enjeux herméneu-
      tiques du canon scripturaire. Les nouvelles voies. LeDiv 190: 2002
      ⇒583. 295-319.
1103 *Bormann, Lukas* Bibelauslegung als Kraft gesellschaftlicher Ände-
      rung. ITE 11 (2002) 159-169.
1104 *Bourgeois, Jason* BALTHASAR's theodramatic hermeneutics: trinitari-
      an and ecclesial dimensions of scriptural interpretation. Theology and
      sacred scripture. 2002 ⇒549. 125-134.
1105 ᴱ**Bouteneff, Peter; Heller, Dagmar** Interpreting together: essays in
      hermeneutics. 2001 ⇒17,343. ᴿTheol. 105 (2002) 142-143 (*Tanner,
      Mary*); TS 63 (2002) 402-403 (*Riggs, Ann K.*); RRT 9 (2002) 100-
      102 (*Cöster, Henry*); ITS 39 (2002) 385-388 (*Legrand, L.*).

1106 *Braun, Bernhard* Im Schatten der Aufklärung: zum Ort des Lebens im Diskurs der Moderne. Religion—Literatur—Künste II. Im Kontext 14: 2002 ⇒530. 472-480.

1107 *Brito, Emilio* FICHTE et le Nouveau Testament. EThL 78 (2002) 79-107.

1108 *Broz, Jaroslav* From allegory to the four senses of scripture: hermeneutics of the church fathers and of the christian Middle Ages. Philosophical hermeneutics. WUNT 153: 2002 ⇒367. 301-309.

1109 *Bultmann, Rudolf* Die Bedeutung der "dialektischen Theologie" für die neutestamentliche Wissenschaft <1928>;

1110 Das Problem der Hermeneutik <1946>;

1111 Ist voraussetzungslose Exegese möglich? <1957>;

1112 Zum Problem der Entmythologisierung <1963>. NT und christliche Existenz. UTB 2316: 2002 ⇒152. 39-58/223-247/258-266/284-293.

1113 *Burgess, Margaret* From archetype to antitype: a look at Frygian archetypology. Semeia 89 (2002) 103-124.

1114 *Burrows, Mark S.* "To taste with the heart": allegory, poetics, and the deep reading of scripture. Interp. 56 (2002) 168-180.

1115 *Campbell, Antony F.* Invitation or ...?: the bible's role. ABR 50 (2002) 1-9.

1116 *Canale, Fernando L.* Deconstrucción y teologia: una propuesta metodológica. DavarLogos 1/1 (2002) 3-26 [BuBB 39,19].

1117 *Carroll, Benajah H.* Our articles of faith: article 1—the scriptures. SWJT 44/3 (2002) 3-13.

1118 *Carroll, Robert P.* Removing an ancient landmark: reading the bible as cultural production. Borders. JSOT.S 313: 2002 ⇒585. 6-14.

1119 *Chardel, Pierre-Antoine* Du primat du visage aux richesses inattendues de l'écriture: remarques sur l'herméneutique d'Emmanuel LÉVINAS. RPL 100/1-2 (2002) 186-211.

1120 *Clarke, Sathianathan* Viewing the bible through the eyes and ears of subalterns in India. BiblInterp 10 (2002) 245-266.

1121 *Clooney, Francis X.* Theology and sacred scripture reconsidered in the light of a Hindu text. Theology and sacred scripture. 2002 ⇒549. 211-236.

1122 **Coelho, Ivo** Hermeneutics and method: the 'universal viewpoint' in Bernard LONERGAN. 2001 ⇒17,948. ᴿTS 63 (2002) 398-400 (*Liddy, Richard M.*); IThQ 67 (2002) 390-391 (*Moloney, Raymond*).

1123 *Conrad, Edgar W.* How the bible was colonized. ᶠNILES, D. 2002 ⇒ 82. 92-105.

1124 *Conradie, E.M.* Biblical interpretation within the context of established bible study groups;

1125 A preface on empirical biblical hermeneutics;

1126 What are interpretative strategies?;

1127 *Conradie, E.M.; Jonker, L.C.* Determining relative adequacy in biblical interpretation. Scriptura 78 (2001) 442-447/333-339/429-441/448-455 [NTAb 47,209-210].

1128 **Cook, John G.** The interpretation of the New Testament in Greco-Roman paganism. Peabody 2002, Hendrickson 385 pp. $25. 1-56563-658-9. ᴿKerux 17/1 (2002) 76-79 (*Dennison, James T.*);

1129 2000 ⇒16,912; 17,954. ᴿCBQ 64 (2002) 154-156 (*Perkins, Pheme*); JR 82 (2002) 440-442 (*Asher, Jeffrey R.*).

1130 *Cording, Robert* The "something more" in the bible: a response to Robert Alter, David Gay, and Michael Dolzani. [Frye, N.] Semeia 89 (2002) 155-169.

1131 ^E**Corley, Bruce** Biblical hermeneutics: a comprehensive introduction to interpreting scripture. Nv ²2002, Broadman & H. xvii; 525 pp. $30. 0-8054-2492-X [ThD 49,260—W. Charles Heiser].

1132 *Davies, Philip R.* Introduction: autobiography as exegesis. First person. BiSe 81: 2002 ⇒295. 11-24.

1133 **De La Torre, Miguel** Reading the bible from the margins. Mkn 2002, Orbis ix; 196 pp. $20. 1570754101 [BiTod 40,264: Senior, D.]

1134 *De Monticelli, Roberta* Abramo e la fede prima dei libri. Il libro sacro. 2002 ⇒356. 207-213.

1135 *Dennison, James T.* What is the 'critical' reading of the bible?. Kerux 17/1 (2002) 3-24.

1136 *Dillmann, Rainer* Überlegungen zur Pragmatik. Vom Text zum Leser. SBS 193: 2002 ⇒299. 59-75.

1137 *Dormeyer, Detlev* Interkulturelle Exegese: der pragmalinguistische 'Kommentar für die Praxis' für Lateinamerika und Europa. Philosophical hermeneutics. WUNT 153: 2002 ⇒367. 270-98 [Acts 28,16-31].

1138 *Draper, Jonathan A.* "Less literate are safer": the politics of orality and literacy in biblical interpretation. AThR 84 (2002) 303-318;

1139 The bible as poison onion, icon and oracle: reception of the printed sacred text in oral and residual-oral South Africa. JTSA 112 (2002) 39-56.

1140 *Dube, Musa W.* Villagizing, globalizing, and biblical studies. Reading the bible in the global village. 2002 ⇒607. 41-63.

1141 *Dulk, Maarten den* Tussen buik en bijbel: epiloog bij de serie 'subjectief bijbellezen'. ITBT 10/2 (2002) 10-11.

1142 *Dusek, Jan* Saying 'true' according to A.J. GREIMAS. Philosophical hermeneutics. WUNT 153: 2002 ⇒367. 94-100.

1143 *Eriksson, Stefan* Refining the distinction between modern and postmodern theologies: the case of Lindbeck. StTh 56 (2002) 152-163.

1144 *Erlenwein, Peter* Bibliodrama : a modern body-mind hermeneutics. AJTh 16/2 (2002) 327-340.

1145 *Fortin, Anne* Lire le geste théologique des écritures. SémBib 105 (2002) 14-28.

1146 **Garagalza, Luis** Introducción a la hermenéutica contemporanea: cultura, simbolismo y sociedad. Barc 2002, Anthropos 233 pp. 84-7658-607-8.

1147 *Gay, David* "The humanized God": biblical paradigms of recognition in FRYE's final three books. Semeia 89 (2002) 39-57.

1148 *Geffré, Claude* La lettura fondamentalista della scrittura nel cristianesimo. FilTeo 16 (2002) 227-237 Sum. 227;

1149 La lecture fondamentaliste de l'Ecriture dans le christianisme. Etudes 397 (2002) 635-645;

1150 Credere e interpretare: la svolta ermeneutica della teologia. Giornale di teologia 288: Brescia 2002, Queriniana 199 pp. 88-399-0788-2.

1151 *Gibson, Arthur* Relations between rhetoric and philosophical logic. Rhetorical criticism. JSNT.S 195: 2002 ⇒369. 97-128.

1152 *Gielen, Marlis; Reiterer, Friedrich* Die Bibel—ein Modell interkultureller Theologie und Begegnung der Religionen. SaThZ 6 (2002) 125-140.

1153 *Giesen, Heinz* Zugänge zu einem besseren Verstehen des Neuen Testaments. ThG 45 (2002) 210-216.

1154 *Gottwald, Norman K.* The role of biblical politics in contextual theologies. Reading the Bible in the global village. 2002 ⇒607. 111-123.

1155 **Graafland, C.** Bijbels en daarom gereformeerd. 2001 ⇒17,965.
      RITBT 10/2 (2002) 33-34 (*Talstra, Eep*).
1156 *Grabbe, Lester L.* 'The comfortable theory': maximal conservatism
      and neo-fundamentalism revisited. MCARROLL, R.: JSOT.S 348: 2002
      ⇒13. 174-193.
1157 *Grech, Prosper* Inner-biblical reinterpretation and modern hermeneu-
      tics. Philosophical hermeneutics. WUNT 153: 2002 ⇒367. 221-237;
1158 La reinterpretazione intra-biblica e l'ermeneutica moderna. StPat 49
      (2002) 641-662.
1159 **Green, Garrett** Theology, hermeneutics and imagination: the crisis
      of interpretation at the end of modernity. 2000 ⇒16,946; 17,967.
      RIThQ 67 (2002) 278-281 (*Laughery, Gregory J.*); SJTh 55 (2002)
      369-371 (*Vidu, Adonis*).
1160 *Green, Joel B.* Scripture and theology: failed experiments, fresh per-
      spectives. Interp. 56 (2002) 5-20.
1161 *Greimann, Dirk* Grundriss einer sprechaktanalytischen Theorie der
      Wahrheit. ZPhF 56 (2002) 191-219.
1162 *Grenholm, Cristina* Scriptural criticism and the story of annunciation.
      FPATTE, D. 2002 ⇒89. 88-97.
1163 *Grilli, Massimo* Evento comunicativo e interpretazione di un testo
      biblico. Gr. 83 (2002) 655-678;
1164 Überlegungen zur Syntaktik. Vom Text zum Leser. SBS 193: 2002
      ⇒299. 31-39.
1165 *Grondin, Jean* GADAMER and BULTMANN. Philosophical hermeneu-
      tics. WUNT 153: 2002 ⇒367. 121-143.
1166 *Hathaway, William L.* Integration as interpretation: a hermeneutical-
      realist view. [Gadamer, H.] JPsC 21/3 (2002) 205-218.
1167 *Hayes, Diana L.* The art of interpretation: contexts, challenges and
      interconnections. Theology and sacred scripture. 2002 ⇒549. 24-31.
1168 *Hejdánek, Ladislav* Hermeneutik und die Zeit. Philosophical hermen-
      eutics. WUNT 153: 2002 ⇒367. 42-48.
1169 *Hempelmann, Heinzpeter* Plädoyer für eine Hermeneutik der Demut:
      zum Ansatz einer Schriftlehre, die von der Schrift selbst zu lernen
      sucht. ThBeitr 33 (2002) 179-196.
1170 **Henry, Michel** Paroles du Christ. P 2002, Seuil 158 pp. €15. 2-020-
      55758-4.
1171 **Hens-Piazza, Gina** The new historicism. Guides to Biblical Scholar-
      ship, OT: Mp 2002, Fortress viii: 94 pp. $11. 0-8006-2989-2. Bibl.
      91-94.
1172 *Himbaza, Innocent* La recherche scientifique et la contextualisation
      de la bible. BOTSA 13 (2002) 2-7.
1173 *Holter, Knut* Is it necessary to be black?. BOTSA 13 (2002) 7-8.
1174 EHorrell, **David G.** Social-scientific approaches to New Testament
      interpretation. 1999 ⇒15,241...17,975. REThL 78 (2002) 196-197
      (*Verheyden, J.*).
1175 *Hroch, Jaroslav* Hermeneutics and the contemporary Anglo-Ameri-
      can philosophy. Philosophical hermeneutics. WUNT 153: 2002 ⇒
      367. 49-58.
1176 *Hull, John M.* Open letter from a blind disciple to a sighted saviour.
      Borders. JSOT.S 313: 2002 ⇒585. 154-177.
1177 *Hübner, Hans* Dialog und Dialektik: zum wissenschaftstheoretischen
      Gespräch mit Heikki Räisänen. FRÄISÄNEN, H.: NT.S 103: 2002 ⇒
      97. 501-519;

1178 Zuspruch des Seyns und Zuspruch Gottes: die Spätphilosophie Martin HEIDEGGERs und die Hermeneutik des Neuen Testaments. Philosophical hermeneutics. WUNT 153: 2002 ⇒367. 144-175.

1179 *Jasper, David* Literature and the possibility of theology. ^MCARROLL, R.: JSOT.S 348: 2002 ⇒13. 331-342.

1180 *Jeanrond, Werner* Pluralismo biblico e teologico. Conc(I) 38/1 (2002) 146-160. Conc(E) 294,129-141; Conc(D) 38/1,99-108; Conc(P) 294, 120-131.

1181 *Jobling, David* Daniel Patte's 'tripolar' model for critical biblical studies: the case of 'Jubilee 2000'. ^FPATTE, D. 2002 ⇒89. 147-157.

1182 *Jobling, David* Biblical studies on a more capacious canvas: a response to Joe Velaidum and James M. Kee. [Frye, N.] Semeia 89 (2002) 139-146.

1183 *Johnson, Luke Timothy* What's catholic about catholic biblical scholarship?: an opening statement;

1184 Rejoining a long conversation;

1185 Imaging the world that scripture imagines;

1186 Response to Bill Kurz. The future of Catholic biblical scholarship. 2002 ⇒337. 3-34/35-63/119-142/249-259;

1187 Reading after the Holocaust: a New Testament scholar responds to Emil Fackenheim. A shadow of glory. 2002 ⇒347. 216-231.

1188 *Jonker, L.C.* Mapping the various factors playing a role in biblical interpretation. Scriptura 78 (2001) 418-428 [NTAb 47,213];

1189 Social transformation and biblical interpretation: a comparative study. Scriptura 77 (2001) 259-270 [NTAb 47,8].

1190 *Kattan, A.* Hermeneutics: a Protestant discipline for an Orthodox context?. ThRev 23/1 (2002) 47-57.

1191 *Kee, James M.* Northrop FRYE and the poetry in biblical hermeneutics. Semeia 89 (2002) 75-87.

1192 *King, Nicholas* Interpreting in our own context. PrPe 16 (2002) 317-321.

1193 *Kirwan, Michael* The limits of interpretation: the GADAMER-HABERMAS conversation and its implications for philosophical hermeneutics. Philosophical hermeneutics. WUNT 153: 2002 ⇒367. 68-82.

1194 *Kurz, William* Response to Luke Johnson;

1195 Voices in the church: preunderstandings in applying scripture. The future of Catholic biblical scholarship. 2002 ⇒337. 143-55/182-202.

1196 **Labuschagne, Casper J.** Numerical secrets of the bible: rediscovering the bible codes. 2000 ⇒16,976. ^RRB 109 (2002) 306-308 (*Langlamet, François*).

1197 *Labuschagne, K.* Geloofsekerheid in die kerk se geskiedenis van bybelinterpretasie. HTS 57 (2001) 959-988 [NTAb 46,431];

1198 's Ontleding van drie hoofstrominge van bybelinterpretasie wat onderliggend is aan geloofsekerheid. HTS 57 (2001) 989-1014 [NTAb 46,431.].

1199 **Lanci, John R.** Texts, rocks, and talk: reclaiming biblical christianity to counterimagine the world. ColMn 2002, Liturgical x; 290 pp. $20. 0-8146-5883-0 [Bibl. 275-286].

1200 *Lategan, Bernard C.* History, historiography and hermeneutics. Philosophical hermeneutics. WUNT 153: 2002 ⇒367. 204-218.

1201 *Lavik, Marta Høyland* Inculturation and liberation hermeneutics in African Old Testament studies. African Christian Studies 18/4 (2002) 5-33.

1202 *Lawrie, D.G.* Reading, interpretation, reinscription: three perspectives on engaging with texts. Scriptura 78 (2001) 399-417 [NTAb 47, 213].

1203 *Lee, Archie C.C.* Polyphonic voices in the bible. ^FNILES, D. 2002 ⇒ 82. 177-192.

1204 *Lefebvre, Solange* Hermeneutic, biblical texts and interdisciplinary dialogue: the question of creation and cosmology. Philosophical hermeneutics. WUNT 153: 2002 ⇒367. 340-344.

1205 *Levine, Amy-Jill* A particular problem: Jewish perspectives on christian bible study. Theology and sacred scripture. 2002 ⇒549. 12-23.

1206 *Liem, Johnson* Contemporary hermeneutics: bane or boon?. Evangel 20 (2002) 70-73.

1207 *Lies, Lothar* Zur Kategorie des Ästhetischen in Systematischer Theologie. Religion—Literatur—Künste II. 2002 ⇒530. 539-546.

1208 *Little, David L.* The aversion to biblical interpretation in the thought of David Lipscomb and Tolbert Fanning. RestQ 44/3 (2002) 159-164.

1209 *Loonstra, B.* Vrijgemaakte bezinning op het schriftgezag. ThRef 45 (2002) 362-367.

1210 **MacKenzie, Ian** Paradigms of reading: relevance theory and deconstruction. L 2002, Palgrave viii; 237 pp. 03339-68336. Bibl. 221-31.

1211 *Maggioni, Bruno* Attualizzare la scrittura. RCI 83 (2002) 178-187.

1212 *Malan, G.* Postmoderniteit: krisi of uitdaging?: die rol van teoloë se skrifbeskouing. HTS 57 (2001) 623-648 [NTAb 46,432].

1213 *Maluleke, Tinyiko S.* What if we are mistaken about the bible and christianity in Africa?. Reading the Bible in the global village. 2002 ⇒607. 151-172.

1214 *Mariaselvam, A.* Bible interpretation for India today. BiBh 28 (2002) 505-520.

1215 *Masenya, Madipoane* Response to Himbaza and Holter. BOTSA 13 (2002) 9-12.

1216 *Masoga, Alpheus* Redefining power: reading the bible in Africa from the peripheral and central positions. Reading the Bible in the global village. 2002 ⇒607. 95-109.

1217 *Mathauser, Zdenek* Verständnis und Gültigkeit: zu künstlerischen und biblischen Texten. Philosophical hermeneutics. WUNT 153: 2002 ⇒367. 29-41.

1218 *Meeks, Wayne A.* A hermeneutics of social embodiment. In search. 2002 ⇒208. 185-195.

1219 *Meurer, Thomas* Bibel macht Schule: aber schafft sie auch Glauben?: Anmerkungen zur aktuellen Diskussion. ThPQ 150 (2002) 393-404.

1220 *Minear, Paul S.* Wanted: an exegetical realism. ThTo 59 (2002) 178-189.

1221 *Moberly, R.W.L.* The use of scripture in *The desire of the nations*. ^FO'DONOVAN, O. 2002 ⇒272. 46-64.

1222 **Moore-Jumonville, Robert** The hermeneutics of historical distance: mapping the terrain of American biblical criticism, 1880-1914. Lanham 2002, University Press of America xxix; 236 pp. 0-7618-2462-6. Bibl. 197-231.

1223 **Muthuraj, J.G.** The significance of Mircea ELIADE for the study of the New Testament. Bangalore Theological Forum [Bangalore] 33/2 (2001) 38-59 [NTAb 46,432].

1224 *Nadar, Sarojini* The bible in Africa: transactions, trajectories and trends. JTSA 112 (2002) 99-104.

1225 **Neumann, Klaus** Das Fremde verstehen—Grundlagen einer kultur-anthropologischen Exeges, 1-2. Theologie 18/1-2: 2000 ⇒16,1000. [R]ThLZ 127 (2002) 1151-1153 (*Strecker, Christian*);

1226 Die Geburt der Interpretation: die hermeneutische Revolution des Historismus als Beginn der Postmoderne. Forum Systematik 16: Stu 2002, Kohlhammer 199 pp. 3-17-017596-3.

1227 **Nikolakopoulos, Konstantin** Die 'unbekannten' Hymnen des Neuen Testaments: die orthodoxe Hermeneutik und die historisch-kritische Methode. 2000 ⇒16,1001. [R]OrthFor 16 (2002) 47-52 (*Frey, Jörg*); ThLZ 127 (2002) 912-914 (*Söding, Thomas*).

1228 *Noble, Ivana* Apophatic elements in DERRIDA's deconstruction;

1229 The apophatic way in GREGORY of Nyssa. Philosophical hermeneutics. WUNT 153: 2002 ⇒367. 83-93/323-339.

1230 *O'Connor, Kathleen M.* Surviving the storm in a multi-cultural world. Theolcgy and sacred scripture. 2002 ⇒549. 3-11 [Acts 27].

1231 *O'Donovan, Oliver* Response to Walter Moberly. [F]O'DONOVAN, O. 2002 ⇒272. 65-68.

1232 Response to Peter Scott. [F]O'DONOVAN, O. 2002 ⇒272. 374-376.

1233 *Oeming, Manfred* Existenzerhellung: Karl JASPERS als Ausleger des Alten Testaments. Philosophical hermeneutics. WUNT 153: 2002 ⇒ 367. 176-190.

1234 **Palmer, Richard E.** ¿Qué es la hermenéutica?: teoría de la interpretación en SCHLEIERMACHER, DILTHEY, HEIDEGGER y GADAMER. [T]Domínguez, B.: Perspectivas: M 2002, Arco 331 pp. 84-7635-509-2.

1235 *Patte, Daniel* Reading with gratitude: the mysteries of 'Reading communities reading scripture'. [F]PATTE, D. 2002 ⇒89. 361-382.

1236 *Paz, César Mora* Einleitung;

1237 Überlegungen zur Semantik. Vom Text zum Leser. SBS 193: 2002 ⇒299. 13-30/41-57.

1238 *Pelletier, Anne-Marie* Le livre ouvert. Les nouvelles voies. LeDiv 190: 2002 ⇒583. 321-345.

1239 *Perkin, J. Russel* Reconfiguring the liberal imagination: a response to Margaret Burgess, Patricia Demers, and William Robins. [Frye, N.] Semeia 89 (2002) 147-153.

1240 *Pesce, Mauro* L'esegesi e i limiti dell'autonomia del testo. RivBib 50 (2002) 205-208.

1241 **Phillips, D.Z.** Religion and the hermeneutics of contemplation. 2001 ⇒17,1021. [R]Theol. 105 (2002) 221-222 (*Hyman, Gavin*).

1242 *Poffet, Jean-Michel* La bible au risque de la lecture et de la relecture. LASBF 51 (2001) 251-256.

1243 *Pokornÿ, Petr* Philosophische Hermeneutik und biblische Exegese: zum Wesen des hermeneutischen Prozesses. Philosophical hermeneutics. WUNT 153: 2002 ⇒367. 1-4.

1244 *Porter, Stanley E.; Stamps, Dennis L.* Introduction: rhetorical criticism and the Florence conference. Rhetorical criticism. JSNT.S 195: 2002 ⇒369. 17-21.

1245 *Prickett, Stephen* Polyphonic carrolling: heteroglossia, pluralism, and editing the bible. [M]CARROLL, R.: JSOT.S 348: 2002 ⇒13. 343-357.

1246 *Punt, J.* The call to rewrite the bible: some perspectives. Scriptura 77 (2001) 303-324 [NTAb 47,11].

1247 **Reinmuth, Eckart** Hermeneutik des Neuen Testaments: eine Einführung in die Lektüre des Neuen Testaments. UTB 2310: Gö 2002, Vandenhoeck & R. 118 pp. 3-8252-2310-8. Bibl. 114-116. [R]ZNT 5/2 (2002) 79-80 (*Alkier, Stefan*).

1248   *Robbins, Vernon K.* The rhetorical full-turn in biblical interpretation: reconfigurating rhetorical-political analysis. Rhetorical criticism. JSNT.S 195: 2002 ⇒369. 48-60.

1249   *Robert, Philippe de* Le trésor et le champ. ETR 77 (2002) 563-572.

1250   *Robins, William* Modeling biblical narrative: FRYE and D.H. LAWRENCE. Semeia 89 (2002) 125-135.

1251   **Sandy, D. Brent** Plowshares and pruning hooks. Leicester 2002, IVP 263 pp. £13. 0-85111-277-3.

1252   *Sánchez Navarro, Luis* Carácter testimonial de la sagrada escritura. RevAg 43 (2002) 349-369.

1253   *Schröter, Jens* Überlegungen zum Verhältnis von Historiographie und Hermeneutik in der neutestamentlichen Wissenschaft. Philosophical hermeneutics. WUNT 153: 2002 ⇒367. 191-203.

1254   *Scott, Peter* 'Return to the vomit of "legitimation"'?: scriptural interpretation and the authority of the poor. ᶠO'DONOVAN, O. 2002 ⇒272. 344-373.

1255   *Simsa, Martin* The question of understanding and its criteria in conservative and critical hermeneutics. Philosophical hermeneutics. WUNT 153: 2002 ⇒367. 59-67.

1256   *Ska, Jean Louis* Sacra Scrittura e parola di Dio. StPat 49 (2002) 7-23.

1257   **Smith, James K.A.** The fall of interpretation: philosophical foundations for a creational hermeneutic. 2000 ⇒16,1035. ᴿHeyJ 43 (2002) 365-367 (*Briggs, Richard*).

1258   *Snodgrass, Klyne* Reading to hear: a hermeneutics of hearing. HBT 24/1 (2002) 1-32.

1259   *Sölle, Dorothee* Die beiden Bücher Gottes. Die Bibel: Geschichte und Gegenwart. 2002 ⇒971. 182-189, 192-199.

1260   *Spangenberg, I.J.J.* Hoe dink vandag se mense oor die bybel?. VeE 23 (2002) 183-195.

1261   **Stemberger, Günter** Ermeneutica ebraica della bibbia. Studi Biblici 127: 2000 ⇒16,1038; 17,1040. ᴿRivBib 50 (2002) 374-376 (*Pesce, Mauro*); CivCatt 153/2 (2002) 90-92 (*Prato, G.L.*).

1262   *Sterling, Gregory E.* Making the past present: the roles of critical scholarship and faith in the interpretation of scripture. RestQ 44/2 (2002) 65-72.

1263   **Stiver, Dan R.** Theology after RICOEUR: new directions in hermeneutical theology. 2001 ⇒17,1041. ᴿTrinJ 23 (2002) 273-277 (*Pérez, Josué*).

1264   *Strauss, D.F.M.* Is it possible to do theology without philosophical presuppositions?. AcTh(B) 22/1 (2002) 146-164.

1265   *Struck, Peter T.* The poet as conjurer: magic and literary theory in late antiquity. Magic and divination. 2002 ⇒729. 119-131.

1266   *Stuhlmacher, Peter* Vom 'richtigen' Umgang mit der Bibel;

1267   Aus Glauben zum Glauben"—zur geistlichen Schriftauslegung <1995>;

1268   Anamnese—eine unterschätzte hermeneutische Kategorie <2000>. Biblische Theologie. WUNT 146: 2002 ⇒245. 233-250/215-232/191-214.

1269   *Sugirtharajah, R.S.* Postcolonial theory and biblical studies. ᶠRÄISÄNEN, H.: NT.S 103: 2002 ⇒97. 541-552.

1270   **Sugirtharajah, Rasiah S.** Postcolonial criticism and biblical interpretation. Oxf 2002, OUP ix; 231 pp. $18. 0-19-875269-5. Bibl. 208-224.

1271 *Synman, Gerrie* 'Who has the moral right to speak?': a reflection on a discourse within Old Testament studies. OTEs 15 (2002) 799-820.

1272 *Szücs, Ferenc* Reformed dogmatics as a hermeneutical circle: between exegesis and preaching. Philosophical hermeneutics. WUNT 153: 2002 ⇒367. 345-351.

1273 *Tapia Bahena, Toribio* Para una interpretación bíblica contextualizada. Qol 30 (2002) 77-85.

1274 *Thomasset, Alain* Biblical hermeneutics, the art of interpretation, and philosophy of the self: a tribute to Paul RICOEUR and Paul BEAUCHAMP. Ethical Perspectives 9 (2002) 48-55.

1275 **Tilliette, X.** I filosofi leggono la bibbia. ᵀ*Sansonetti, G.*: GdT 295: Brescia 2002, Queriniana 242 pp. €18.50 [StPat 50,572: Segalla, G.];

1276 Les philosophes lisent la bible. 2001 ⇒17,1047. ᴿBrot. 154 (2002) 415-416 (*Silva, I. Ribeiro da*).

1277 *Topel, John* What does systematic theology say to New Testament interpretation?. Theology and sacred scripture. 2002 ⇒549. 105-124.

1278 **Tracy, David** Pluralité et ambiguïté: herméneutique, religion, espérance. 1999 ⇒15,950. ᴿRTL 33 (2002) 273-274 (*Brito, E.*).

1279 *Ukpong, Justin S.* Reading the bible in a global village: issues and challenges from African readings. Reading the Bible in the global village. 2002 ⇒607. 9-39.

1280 *Van Dyk, Peet J.* A fuzzy interpretation of the bible: going beyond modernism and postmodernism. R&T 9/3 (2002) 163-182.

1281 *Van Nieuwenhove, Rik* De 'analogie' van het geloof: de relatie tussen bijbelexegese en theologie, geschiedenis en geloof. TTh 42 (2002) 361-377.

1282 **Vanhoozer, Kevin** Is there a meaning in this text?: the bible, the reader, and the morality of literary knowledge. 1998 ⇒14,847... 17, 1053. ᴿSBET 20 (2002) 213-215 (*Dow, Colin*).

1283 *Velaidum, Joe* Towards reconciling the solitudes. [Frye, N.] Semeia 89 (2002) 23-37.

1284 *Venard, Olivier-Thomas* Esquisse d'une critique des "méthodes littéraires". L'autorité de l'Écriture. LeDiv: 2002 ⇒588. 259-298.

1285 **Wallace, Ronald S.** On the interpretation and use of the bible: with reflections on experience. 1999 ⇒15,964; 17,1060. ᴿEvQ 74 (2002) 80-81 (*Barus, Armand*).

1286 **Walsh, Richard G.** Mapping myths of biblical interpretation. Playing the Texts 4: 2001 ⇒17,1061. ᴿRBLit (2002)* (*Moeser, Marion*).

1287 *Walton, J.H.* Inspired subjectivity and hermeneutical objectivity. MastJ 13/1 (2002) 65-77 [NTAb 46,436].

1288 **Watson, Francis** Agape, eros, gender: towards a Pauline sexual ethic. 2000 ⇒16,1064; 17,1063. ᴿTheol. 105 (2002) 57-58 (*Bonnington, Mark*); JThS 53 (2002) 256-261 (*Esler, Philip F.*); JPsT 30 (2002) 168-170 (*Hunter, William F.*); EvQ 74 (2002) 363-365 (*Ellingworth, Paul*).

1289 *West, Gerald* The bible as bola: among the foundations of African biblical apprehensions. JTSA 112 (2002) 23-37;

1290 Indigenous exegesis: exploring the interface between missionary methods and the rhetorical rhythms of Africa—locating local reading resources in the academy. Neotest. 36 (2002) 147-162;

1291 Unpacking the package that is the bible in African biblical scholarship. Reading the Bible in the global village. 2002 ⇒607. 65-94.

1292 *Wénin, A.* Des livres pour rendre la bible à la culture. RTL 33 (2002) 408-413.

1293 *Willi, Thomas* Hebraica veritas in Basel: christliche Hebraistik aus jüdischen Quellen. Congress volume Basel 2001. VT.S 92: 2002 ⇒ 570. 375-397.
1294 *Willi-Plein, Ina* Spuren der Unterscheidung von mündlichem und schriftlichem Wort im Alten Testament. Sprache als Schlüssel. 2002 <1996> ⇒261. 116-129.
1295 *Wimbush, Vincent L.* Response. Reading the Bible in the global village. 2002 ⇒607. 173-177.
1296 *Wire, Antoinette Clark* New ways of reading the bible. ᶠNILES, D. 2002 ⇒82. 106-122.
1297 *Wisse, Maarten* From cover to cover?: a critique of Wolterstorff's theory of the bible as divine discourse. IJPR 52 (2002) 159-173.
1298 *Yébenes Escardó, Zenia* La hermenéutica analógica y el simbolismo religioso. AnáMnesis 12/2 (2002) 101-110.
1299 *Zwiep, Arie* Hermeneutiek: een goed gesprek met vier deelnemers: vernieuwing in de evangelische theologie. ITBT 10/4 (2002) 7-12.

B2.4 *Analysis* narrationis *biblicae*

1300 *Andersson, Helen* The moment of a star: the ethics of narration. StTh 56 (2002) 44-63.
1301 **Balaguer, Vicente** La interpretación de la narración: la teoría de Paul RICOEUR. Anejos de RILCE 40: Pamplona 2002, EUNSA 204 pp. 84-313-1969-0. ᴿRevista de Literatura 64 (2002) 601-603 (*Pego Puigbó, Armando*).
1302 *Bourquin, Yvan* Bibliographie de contributions récentes en analyse narrative. ETR 77 (2002) 79-93.
1303 ᴱ**Brooke, George J.; Kaestli, Jean-Daniel** Narrativity in biblical and related texts. BEThL 149: 2000 ⇒16,1084. ᴿRTL 33 (2002) 422-423 (*Wénin, A.*).
1304 *Campbell, Antony F.* The storyteller's role: reported story and biblical text. CBQ 64 (2002) 427-441.
1305 *Chisholm, Robert B.* A rhetorical use of point of view in Old Testament narrative. BS 159 (2002) 404-414.
1306 **Crouch, Walter B.** Death and closure in biblical narrative. 2000 ⇒ 16,1086; 17,1073. ᴿBiblInterp 10 (2002) 201-203 (*Ward, Graham*).
1307 **Fokkelman, Jan P.** Reading biblical narrative: an introductory guide. 1999 ⇒15,983…17,1075. ᴿOTEs 15 (2002) 560-562 (*Nel, Philip J.*);
1308 Comment lire le récit biblique: une introduction pratique. Le livre et le rouleau 13: Bru 2002, Lessius 239 pp. €19. 2-87299-096-8. Traduit du néerlandais par les Cisterciennes de l'abbaye Notre-Dame de Clairefontaine.
1309 **Heimerdinger, Jean-Marc** Topic, focus and foreground in ancient Hebrew narratives. JSOT.S 295: 1999 ⇒15,984; 16,1095. ᴿThLZ 127 (2002) 745-747 (*Bartelmus, Rüdiger*); RBLit 4 (2002) 158-160 (*Bodner, Keith*).
1310 **Jensen, Hans Jørgen L.** Den fortaerende ild: strukturelle analyser af narrative og rituelle tekster i det Gamle Testamente [The devouring fire: structural analyses of narrative and ritual texts in the OT]. 2000 ⇒16,1098. ᴿRBLit 4 (2002) 167-170 (*Hallbaeck, Geert*).
1311 *Jensen, Hans J.L.* Svar til Carsten Pallesen. DTT 65 (2002) 180-183.

1312 **Marguerat, D.; Bourquin, Y.** Cómo leer los relatos bíblicos: iniciación al análisis narrativo. 2000 ⇒16,1104. ᴿEE 77 (2002) 169-170 (*Ramírez Fueyo, Francisco*);

1313 La bible se raconte: initiation à l'analyse narrative. 1998 ⇒14,875... 16,1103. ᴿRThom 102 (2002) 477-480 (*Devillers, Luc*); EThL 78 (2002) 509-510 (*Van Belle, G.*).

1314 *Marguerat, Daniel* Entrer dans le monde du récit. Quand la bible se raconte. 2002 ⇒355. 9-37.

1315 **Merenlahti, Petri** Poetics for the gospels?: rethinking narrative criticism. Studies of the New Testament and its world: L 2002, Clark xi; 174 pp. £30. 0-567-08851-0. Bibl. 147-160.

1316 **Minguzzi, Edi** L'idea di struttura: interpretazioni dello strutturalismo. Mi 2002, CUEM 82 pp. Bibl. 79-80.

1317 **Murphy, Francesca Aran** The comedy of revelation: paradise lost and regained in biblical narrative. 2000 ⇒17,1084. ᴿRRT 9 (2002) 242-245 (*Elkins, William Wesley*); PrPe 16 (2002) 249-250 (*O'Brien, Mark A.*).

1318 *Pallesen, Carsten* Det Gamle Testamente som kogebog: den systematisk-teologiske udfordring i Hans Jørgen Lundlager Jensen: "Den fortaerende ild. Strukturelle analyser af narrative og rituelle tekster i Det Gamle Testamente". DTT 65 (2002) 161-179.

1319 *Polak, Frank H.* On speaker status and dialogue in biblical narrative. BetM 172 (2002) 1-18 Sum. 96;

1320 Parameters for stylistic analysis of Biblical Hebrew prose texts. Bible and computer. 2002 ⇒548. 259-281.

1321 **Reinhartz, Adele** 'Why ask my name?': anonymity and identity in biblical narrative. 1998 ⇒14,883... 17,1088. ᴿJQR 92 (2001) 205-209 (*Gruber, Mayer I.*).

1322 *Schnittjer, Gary Edward* The narrative multiverse within the universe of the bible: the question of "borderlines" and "intertextuality". WThJ 64 (2002) 231-252.

1323 *Shaw, Suzanne* Letters to the editor of Genesis. First person. BiSe 81: 2002 ⇒295. 25-46.

1324 **Walsh, Jerome T.** Style and structure in Biblical Hebrew narrative. 2001 ⇒17,1091. ᴿRBLit (2002)* (*Savran, George W.*).

1325 *White, Hugh C.* Metaphor as performative. ᶠPATTE, D. 2002 ⇒89. 66-87.

1326 *Wigen, Tore* Narratives and references. StTh 56 (2002) 164-191.

B3.1 *Interpretatio ecclesiastica* **Bible and Church**

1327 ᴱ**Alberigo, Giuseppe** Historia del Concilio Vaticano II, 2: la formación de la conciencia conciliar: el primer periodo y la primera intersesión (oct. 1962-sept. 1963). ᵀ*Hernández Blanco, José María*: El peso de los días 28: S 2002, Sígueme 563 pp. 84-3011-4521;

1328 Histoire du Concile Vatican II (1959-1965), 4: l'église en tant que communion: la troisième session et la troisième intersession (Septembre 1964-Septembre 1965). ᵀ*Mignon, J.*: P 2002, Cerf 822 pp.

1329 *Betori, Giuseppe* Il vangelo nel tempo: leggere la parola nella storia. Asp. 49/3 (2002) 323-340.

1330 *Beutler, Johannes* Das jüdische Volk und seine Heilige Schrift in der christlichen Bibel: zu einem neueren Dokument der Päpstlichen Bibelkommission. BiKi 57 (2002) 158-165;

1331 Das jüdische Volk und die christliche Bibel: zu einem neuen Dokument der Päpstlichen Bibelkommission. StZ 220 (2002) 519-529;

1332 Il popolo ebraico e le sue sacre scritture: un nuovo documento della Pontificia Commissione Biblica. CivCatt 153/2 (2002) 445-457.

1333 ᴱᵀBéchard, Dean Philip The scripture documents: an anthology of official catholic teachings. ColMn 2002, Liturgical xvi; 352 pp. $30. 0-8146-2591-6. Foreword by *Joseph A. Fitzmyer, S.J.*.

1334 *Bieringer, Reimund* Biblical revelation and exegetical interpretation according to Dei Verbum 12. SNTU.A 27 (2002) 5-40.

1335 *Buzzetti, Carlo* Il popolo ebraico e le sue sacre scritture nella bibbia cristiana: il nuovo documento della Pontificia Commissione Biblica (2001): una presentazione schematica, per una prima lettura. Sal. 64 (2002) 513-523.

1336 *Carrón Pérez, Julián* La *Fides et ratio* y el problema de la exégesis. La razón creyente. 2002 ⇒655. 562-576.

1337 *Castello, Gaetano* Il popolo ebraico e le sue scritture: riflessioni sul documento della Pontificia Commissione Biblica. Asp. 49/2 (2002) 215-224.

1338 Commission biblique pontificale: Le peuple juif et ses saintes écritures dans la bible chrétienne. 2001 ⇒17,1104. ᴿSal. 64 (2002) 653-655 (*Dingida, Didier-André*); EeV 57 (2002) 13-15 (*Cothenet, Edouard*).

1339 *Davidson, Robert* The bible in church and academy. ᴹCARROLL, R.: JSOT.S 348: 2002 ⇒13. 161-173.

1340 *Davis, Ellen Frances* Reading the bible confessionally in the church. AThR 84 (2002) 25-35.

1341 *Döring, Heinrich* Die ekklesiale Dimension der Schriftinspiration: Überlegungen zur Selbstauslegungskraft des Wortes Gottes im Anschluss an das Dokument "Communio Sanctorum". Cath(M) 56/1 (2002) 1-27.

1342 *Dunn, James D.* The bible and scholarship: on bridging the gap between the academy and the church. Anvil 19/2 (2002) 109-118.

1343 L'élection d'Israël. NV 77/4 (2002) 27-33.

1344 *Farkasfalvy, Denis* The Pontifical Biblical Commission's document on Jews and Christians and their scriptures: attempt at an evaluation. Com(US) 29 (2002) 715-737.

1345 Il futuro dell'uomo: fede cristiana e antropologia: IV forum del progetto culturale. Oggi e domani 51: Bo 2002, EDB 318 pp. 88-10-14004-4. Servizio Nazionale per il Progetto Culturale della Conferenza Episcopale Italiana.

1346 Futuro dell'uomo e speranza cristiana: strumenti di riflessione e di lavoro. Leumann (Torino)] 2002, Elle Di Ci 141 pp. 88-01-02572-6. Servizio Nazionale per il progetto culturale della Conferenza Episcopale Italiana.

1347 *Graffy, Adrian* The bible as the word of God: the humanity of scripture. ScrB 32 (2002) 1-8.

1348 **Hamel, Christophe de** La bible: histoire du livre. P 2002, Phaidon 352 pp. €40. 0-7148-9339-0. 250 ill.

1349 *Jericó Bermejo, José Ignacio* Las expresiones de la sagrada escritura y las declaraciones de la iglesia: su autoridad en la enseñanza de la Escuela de Salamanca (1526-1584). Communio 35/1 (2002) 79-152, 359-396.

1350 *Johnson, Luke Timothy* Renewing catholic biblical scholarship. PrPe 16 (2002) 297-301.

1351 *Kereszty, Roch* The Jewish-Christian dialogue and the Pontifical Biblical Commission's document on 'The Jewish people and their sacred scriptures in the christian bible'. Com(US) 29 (2002) 738-745.

1352 *Leonardi, Giovanni* Dagli "articoli di fede certi" ai valori evangelici. StPat 49 (2002) 99-103.

1353 **Lerotholi, Gerard Tlali** The Acts of the Apostles and Ecclesia in Africa: an intertextual inquiry. ^D*Dumais, M.*: 2002 Diss. Ottawa [RTL 34,599.].

1354 **Lubac, Henri de** Die Göttliche Offenbarung: Kommentar zum Vorwort und zum ersten Kapitel der dogmatischen Konstitution "Dei Verbum" des Zweiten Vatikanischen Konzils. ThRom 26: 2001 ⇒ 17,1112. ^RFKTh 18 (2002) 152-154 (*Lochbrunner, Manfred*).

1355 **Maggioni, Bruno** 'Impara a conoscere il volto di Dio nelle parole di Dio'. 2001 ⇒17,1114. ^RCivCatt 153/4 (2002) 99-100 (*Scaiola, D.*).

1356 *Mejía, Jorge* Il mistero della parola scritta. Il libro sacro. 2002 ⇒ 356. 214-218.

1357 *Mitchell, William Liturgiam authenticam*:... towards a true liturgy?. BiTr 53 (2002) 343-353.

1358 *Murphy, Roland E.* The Biblical Commission, the Jews, and scriptures. BTB 32 (2002) 145-149.

1359 **Neuner, Josef; Dupuis, Jacques** La fede cristiana nei documenti dottrinali della chiesa cattolica. Abside 50: CinB 2002, San Paolo xviii; 1108 pp. 88-215-4512-1.

1360 Papieska Komisja Biblijna: Naród zydowski i jego Swiete Pisma w Biblii chrzescijanskiej. Kielce 2002, Verbum 177 pp. 83-915855-3-0.

1361 Pauselijke Bijbelcommissie: Het joodse volk en zijn heilige geschriften in de christelijke bijbel. Kerkelijke documentatie 30,9-10: Utrecht 2002, n.p. 103 pp.

1362 *Pawlak, Leonard* Biblijne podstawy duchowości rodziny w Adhortacji Apostolskiej *Familiaris consortio* [Biblical foundations of the spirituality of the family in the Apostolic Exhortation *Familiaris consortio*]. SRATK 10 (2002) 43-55. **P.**

1363 *Perera, James Dudley* Celibacy and priestly ministry: can the church separate what the church has joined together?: some biblical and theological considerations. VJTR 66 (2002) 754-766 [1 Cor 7].

1364 The Pontifical Biblical Commission: The Jewish people and their sacred scriptures in the christian bible. Città del Vaticano 2002, Libreria Editrice Vaticana 205 pp. 88-209-7919-0.

1365 Pontificia Comisión Bíblica: El pueblo Judío y sus escrituras sagradas en la biblia cristiana. Città del Vaticano 2002, Libreria Editrice Vaticana 215 pp. 88-209-7235-2.

1366 *Rogerson, John* Biblical criticism and the churches: a plus or a minus?. ET 113 (2002) 255-258.

1367 *Rurlander, Daniel* The bible in the academy and the church: why is the church being kept in ignorance of what is known in the academy about the bible?. RTR 61/3 (2002) 148-159.

1368 **Schaaf, Ype** On their way rejoicing: the history and role of the bible in Africa. Carlisle 2002, Regnum xi; 252 pp. £13. 1-870345-33-9 [Missionalia 32,140s—G.A. Duncan.].

1369 *Schützeichel, Heribert* Vom Hören und Sagen in der Kirche. TThZ 111 (2002) 148-160.

1370 *Snyman, S.D.* Die verstaan en funksie van die Ou Testament in die kerk (of: kan die kerk klaarkom sonder die Ou Testament?). AcTh(B) 22/2 (2002) 126-146, 147-162.

1371 *Tosato, Angelo* Lo statuto cattolico dell'interpretazione della bibbia. Vangelo e ricchezza. 2002 <1999> ⇒246. 25-124;

1372 Magistero pontificio e sacra scrittura (due pagine di storia). Vangelo e ricchezza. 2002 <1992, 1994> ⇒246. 125-186.

1373 Vatican II: l'intégralité. P 2002, Bayard xxiv; 1177 pp. €29. 2-227-47129-8. Edition bilingue révisée avec tables biblique et analytique et index des sources; introd. *Christoph Theobald.*

1374 *Wansbrough, Henry* The Jewish people and its holy scripture in the christian bible. ScrB 32 (2002) 49-63;

1375 IThQ 67 (2002) 265-275.

1376 *Wells, Arthur* Bishop Christopher BUTLER at Vatican II: his role in *Dei verbum.* DR 120 (2002) 129-154.

1377 *Werblowsky, R.J. Zwi* Dominus Iesus: christian, non-christian and Jewish readings. ᶠTHOMA, C.: JudChr 20: 2002 ⇒119. 321-327.

1378 *Williams, Stephen* Towards trust. The trustworthiness of God. 2002 ⇒410. 219-236.

1379 **Williamson, Peter S.** Catholic principles for interpreting scripture: a study of the Pontifical Biblical Commissions's The interpretation of the bible in the church. SubBi 22: 2001 ⇒17,1130. ᴿAnnales Theologici 16 (2002) 524-529 (*Tábet, M.*); Bib. 83 (2002) 434-439 (*Fitzmyer, Joseph A.*).

B3.2 *Homiletica*—The Bible in preaching

1380 ᴱ**Körtner, Ulrich H.J.** Jesus im 21. Jahrhundert: Bultmanns Jesus-buch und die heutige Jesusforschung. Neuk 2002, Neuk'er viii; 231 pp. €24.90. 3-7887-1898-6.

1381 *Abbott, William M.* The two sides of secrecy: 20 July 2002. The roles. 2002 ⇒540. 118-120 [Mic 1,1-5; Mt 12,14-21].

1382 *Achtemeier, Elizabeth* Preaching and ministry in the service of the God of the bible. ᶠACHTEMEIER, P. 2002 ⇒1. 249-266.

1383 **Ahlgrim, Ryan** Not as the scribes: Jesus as a model for prophetic preaching. Scottdale, PA 2002, Herald 155 pp. $17. 0-8361-9200-1 [ThD 50,157—Heiser, W. Charles].

1384 **Allen, Ronald J.; Bartholomew, Gilbert L.** Preaching verse by verse. LVL 1999, Westminster ix; 160 pp. $15. ᴿRBLit 4 (2002) 469-472 (*Starbuck, Scott R.A.*).

1385 **Allen, Ronald J.** Preaching: the essential guide. Nv 2002, Abingdon 135 pp. $16. 0-687-04516-9 [BiTod 41,261—Bergant, Dianne].

1386 **Babut, Etienne** Mais alors, que fait Dieu?: une parole adressée. LiBi 128: P 2002, Cerf 324 pp. €22. 2-204-07022-X.

1387 *Becking, Bob* Tussen unificatie en diversificatie: over bijbelse theologie en het probleem van de prediking van het Oude Testament. KeTh 53 (2002) 237-250.

1388 *Berenson Maclean, Jennifer K.* Micah 3:5-12. Interp. 56 (2002) 413-416.

1389 **Bergant, Dianne** Preaching the new lectionary: year A. 2001 ⇒17,1134. ᴿACR 79 (2002) 243-244 (*Trainor, Michael*).

1390 **Bériou, Nicole** L'Avènement des maîtres de la parole: la prédication à Paris au XIIIᵉ siècle. EAug.Moyen Âge 31-32: 1998 ⇒15,1028. ᴿRSPhTh 86 (2002) 150-154 (*Bataillon, Louis-Jacques*).

1391   Bond, L. Susan Acts 10:34-43. Interp. 56 (2002) 80-83.
1392   Bongartz, Heinz-Günter Zum Umgang mit fiktionalen biblischen Texten in der Predigt: Versuch einer Annäherung. BiLi 75 (2002) 32-37.
1393   Borsch, Frederick Houk, al., New proclamation: year B, 2002-2003: Advent through Holy Week. Mp 2002, Fortress 259 pp. $25.
1394   Brisson, E. Carson Matthew 25:14-30. Interp. 56 (2002) 307-310.
1395   Buttrick, David Speaking Jesus: homiletic theology and the Sermon on the Mount. LVL 2002, Westminster x; 230 pp. $20. 0-664-22602-7 [BiTod 41,267—Senior, Donald].
1396   Byars, Ronald P. Psalm 95. Interp. 56 (2002) 77-79.
1397   Campbell, Charles L. The word before the powers: an ethic of preaching. LVL 2002, Westminster 206 pp. $23. 0-664-22233-1.
1398   Carter, Warren Resisting and imitating the empire: imperial paradigms in two Matthean parables. Interp. 56 (2002) 260-272 [Mt 18, 23-35; 22,01-14].
1399   ETCavallotto, Stefano Filippo MELANTONE: predicazione evangelica: sermoni per le domeniche dell'anno. CasM 2001, Piemme 352 pp. €21.69. RCivCatt 153/4 (2002) 514-516 (Vanzan, P.).
1400   Chatham, James O. Enacting the word: using drama in preaching. LVL 2002, Westminster 71 pp. $9. 0-664-22570-5.
1401   Cilliers, J. Die geheim van die prediking: om na die stem van die teks te luister. VeE 23 (2002) 67-79.
1402   Coates, William L. A study of David, the thoroughly human man who genuinely loved God: selected texts for preaching and teaching from 2 Samuel. RExp 99 (2002) 237-253.
1403   Craddock, Fred B. Overhearing the gospel. St. Louis 2002, Chalice viii; 146 pp. $20. 0-8272-2717-5 [ThD 50,165—Heiser, W. Charles].
1404   Davis, John Isaiah 6: a biblical paradigm or model for all styles of corporate worship. Faith & Mission 19/2 (2002) 10-18.
1405   De Haes, René Prêchons-nous encore la parole de Dieu?. Telema 110-111 (2002) 7-17.
1406   Driscoll, Jeremy Preaching in the context of the eucharist: a patristic perspective. ProEc 11/1 (2002) 24-40.
1407   Duke, Paul D. First prayer from the ashes: a sermon on Job 7:7-21. RExp 99 (2002) 615-619.
1408   Edwards, Jonathan The salvation of souls: nine previously unpublished sermons on the call of ministry and the gospel. EBailey, Richard A.; Wills, Gregory A.: Wheaton, IL 2002, Crossway 190 pp. 1-58134-451-1.
1409   Eslinger, Richard L. The web of preaching: new options in homiletic method. Nv 2002, Abingdon 309 pp. $24 [BiTod 41,326—Bergant, Dianne].
1410   Findley, Gary F. Bridges or ladders?. Kerux 17/2 (2002) 3-21.
1411   Ford, Richard Q. Body language: Jesus' parables of the woman with the yeast, the woman with the jar, and the man with the sword. Interp. 56 (2002) 295-306 [Mt 13,33; Lk 13,20-21].
1412   Freund, Annegret Predigt und interaktionale Bibelarbeit: Studien zu einer praktisch-theologischen Hermeneutik in homiletisch-methodischem Interesse. DRaschzok, Klaus 2002, Diss.-Habil. Jena [ThRv 99/2,xii].
1413   Gipe, William Numbers 11:24-30. Interp. 56 (2002) 196-198.

1414 **Goldsworthy, Graeme** Preaching the whole bible as christian scripture. 2000 ⇒16,1159; 17,1150. ᴿHBT 24/2 (2002) 133-135 (*Stricklen, Teresa Lockhart*).

1415 *Graves, Mike* Followed by the sun: Matthew 14:22-33. RExp 99 (2002) 91-96.

1416 **Greidanus, Sidney** Preaching Christ from the Old Testament: a contemporary hermeneutical method. 1999 ⇒15,1037...17,1151. ᴿAtK 138 (2002) 607-609 (*Slawiński, Henryk*); ThLZ 127 (2002) 1037-1038 (*Dohmen, Christoph*).

1417 **Grevel, Jan Peter** Die Predigt und ihr Text: Grundlegung einer hermeneutischen Homiletik. Neuk 2002, Neuk x; 293 pp. €39.90. 3-7887-1905-2.

1418 **Gross, Nancy Lammers** If you cannot preach like Paul... GR 2002, Eerdmans xviii; 182 pp. $15. 0-8028-4938-5. Bibl. 172-177 [Acts 20,7-12; Rom 8,18-25; Col 2,8-3,4].

1419 *Heimbach-Steins, Marianne* Wie willst Du wissen, wer Du bist, wenn Du nicht weißt, woher Du kommst?: Predigt zum Stammbaum Jesu Mt 1. BiLi 75 (2002) 292-295.

1420 *Holmgren, Fredrick C.* Exodus 2:11-3:15. Interp. 56 (2002) 73-76.

1421 *Hunter, Scott F.* A heart for God's law: Matthew 3,1-2. Kerux 17/1 (2002) 36-42.

1422 **Janowiak, Paul** The holy preaching: the sacramentality of the word in the liturgical assembly. 2000 ⇒16,1163. ᴿHeyJ 43 (2002) 372-373 (*Cooper, Adam G.*).

1423 **Jeter, Joseph R.; Allen, Ronald J.** One gospel, many ears: preaching for different listeners in the congregation. Saint Louis 2002, Chalice 197 pp. $27. 0-8272-2716-7.

1424 *Juel, Donald H.* Encountering the sower: Mark 4:1-20. Interp. 56 (2002) 273-283.

1425 **Jung, Seung Ryong** An analytical study of the dominant methodology of contemporary Korean preaching in light of selected aspects of the methodology of Jesus' preaching. ᴰ*Fasol, A.*: 2002, 213 pp. Diss. Fort Worth [RTL 34,643].

1426 *Jüngel, Eberhard* Predigt über Psalm 46. ᶠSMEND, R.: 2002 ⇒113. 465-472.

1427 **Kendall, R.T.** The way of wisdom: patience in waiting on God; sermons on James 4-5. New Westminster Pulpit 2: Carlisle 2002, Paternoster xi; 372 pp. 1-84227-112-1.

1428 *Kim, Eunjoo Mary* Hermeneutics and Asian American preaching. Semeia 90/91 (2002) 269-290.

1429 *Koopmans, William T.* Vengeance and the fair trial venue: a sermon on Joshua 20. CTJ 37 (2002) 95-98.

1430 *Koperski, Veronica* Hebrews 10:16-25. Interp. 56 (2002) 202-204.

1431 **Krasowski, Andrzej** Sąd Ostateczny (Mt. 25,31-46) w posoborowym przepowiadaniu polskim: studium egzegetyczno-homiletyczne. ᴰ*Bielecki, S.*: 2002, 236 pp. Diss. Lublin [RTL 34,644]. **P.**

1432 **Larsen, David L.** The evangelism mandate: recovering the centrality of gospel preaching. GR 2002, Kregel 256 pp. $14.

1433 *Lategan, L.O.K.* "Voorberei en toegerus": P.C. Potgieter se beskouing van die opleiding van predikante in kritiese perspektief. ᶠPOTGIETER, P.: AcTh(B).S 3: 2002 ⇒92. 89-106.

1434 *Lawson, Steven J.* The passion of biblical preaching: an expository study of 1 Timothy 4:13-16. BS 159 (2002) 79-95.

1435 *MacDaniel, Judith M.* The place of the bible in the Virginia Seminary curriculum : homiletics. AThR 84 (2002) 57-65.

1436 [E]**Martin, Lawrence T.** Homiliarium Veronense. Scriptores Celtigenae 4: 2000 ⇒16,1167. [R]PIBA 25 (2002) 166-81 (*Rittmueller, Jean*).

1437 **Matera, Frank J.** Strategies for preaching Paul. 2001 ⇒17,1161. [R]Pacifica 15 (2002) 106-108 (*Woods, Laurie*).

1438 **Mathewson, Steven D.** The art of preaching Old Testament narrative. GR 2002, Baker 279 pp. $17. 0-8010-2296-7. Bibl. 261-270. [R]RExp 99 (2002) 638-639 (*Quicke, Michael*).

1439 **McKenzie, Alyce** Preaching biblical wisdom in a self-help society. Nv 2002, Abingdon 255 pp. $22. 0-687-09050-4.

1440 *Mears, Amy L.* Because everyone can use a little therapy: preaching 1 Samuel as community mental health. RExp 99 (2002) 223-234.

1441 *Meyer, Dietgard* Predigt zu Mk 7,31-37: 14. Sonntag nach Trinitatis: 14. September 1952, Bergen bei Frankfurt/Main. Jesus im 21. Jahrhundert. 2002 ⇒1380. 201-206.

1442 **Mohler, Robert A.** Preaching: the centrality of scripture. E 2002, Banner of Truth 21 pp.

1443 *Morrissey, Mary* Scripture, style and persuasion in seventeenth-century English theories of preaching. JEH 53 (2002) 686-706.

1444 **Nicol, Martin** Einander ins Bild Setzen: dramaturgische Homiletik. Gö 2002, Vandenhoeck & R. 160 pp. 3-525-60289-8.

1445 *Niewiadomski, Jozef* Rationalität des Opfers: Predigt beim Gottesdienst am Fest des Hl. Matthäus am 21. September 2000 zum Text Mt 9,9-13. Glaubenswissenschaft?. QD 195: 2002 ⇒426. 161-163.

1446 **O'Day, Gail R.** The word disclosed: preaching the gospel of John. St. Louis 2002, Chalice 151 pp. $20. 0-8272-4245-X. Rev. ed.

1447 [E]**Oeming, Manfred** Die Schrift kommt zu Wort: Predigten. Stu 2002, Calwer 184 pp. 3-7668-3752-4.

1448 *Perkins, Pheme* Mark 4:30-34. Interp. 56 (2002) 311-313.

1449 *Pierik, Martin* Clean flour from unclean yeast: closing mass, 21 Juli 2002. The roles. 2002 ⇒540. 121-125.

1450 **Pilarczyk, Daniel E.** Live letters: reflections on the second readings of the Sunday lectionary. Cincinnati 2002, St Anthony Messenger x; 485 pp. $25. 0-86716-399-2 [BiTod 40,403—Senior, Donald].

1451 *Prince, Robert* Top ten preaching texts from 1 Samuel. RExp 99 (2002) 207-222.

1452 **Saunders, Stanley P.; Campbell, Charles L.** The word on the street: performing the scriptures in the urban context. 2000 ⇒16, 1175. [R]CThMi 29 (2002) 291-292 (*Graham, Paul*).

1453 *Schöttler, Heinz-Günther* Leben in zwei Welten: die homiletische Inszenierung fiktionaler Schrifttexte. BiLi 75 (2002) 20-26.

1454 [TE]**Sheridan, J. Mark** RUFUS of Shotep: homilies on the gospels of Matthew and Luke: introduction, text, translation, commentary. 1998 ⇒14,951. [R]Muséon 115/1-2 (2002) 218-219 (*Brankaer, J.*).

1455 [E]**Souletie, Jean-Louis; Gagey, Henri-Jérôme** La bible, parole adressée. LeDiv 183: 2001 ⇒17,323. [R]RICP 82 (2002) 217-219 (*Tassin, Claude*).

1456 **Söding, Thomas** Exegese und Predigt: das Markus-Evangelium: Anregungen zum Lesejahr B. Wü 2002, Echter 100 pp. 3-429-02411-0.

1457 *Strübind, Kim* Was hat die Predigt mit dem Bibeltext zu tun?: Wahrheit und Freiheit einer "kanonischen" Theologie für die christliche Verkündigung. Zeitschrift für Theologie und Gemeinde 7 (2002) 90-124.

1458 *Taylor, Barbara B.* Treasure hunt: Luke 12:13-21. RExp 99 (2002) 97-104.

1459 *Theissen, Gerd* Defensa de una relación renovada entre exégesis y homilética: un nuevo 'primado' del texto en la predicación. SelTeol 41 (2002) 184-194 <ETR 75 (2000) 531-547.

1460 **Theißen, Gerd** Erlösungsbilder: Predigten und Meditationen. Gü 2002, Gü'er 192 pp. 3-579-05389-2.

1461 *Thompson, Philip E.* 2 Timothy 4:1-5. Interp. 56 (2002) 421-423.

1462 *Ulrich, Daniel W.* Exodus 33:12-23. Interp. 56 (2002) 410-412.

1463 *Van Rensburg, J. Janse* Narrative preaching—yet another perspective. AcTh(B) 22/2 (2002) 219-233.

1464 **Vieira, Antonio** Sermon du bon larron. ^T*Marquès, Guida*: P 2002, Alia 90 pp. €6.10. ^RMoBi 147 (2002) 67 (*Boyer, Frédéric*).

1465 *Walaskay, Paul W.* Matthew 5:17-20. Interp. 56 (2002) 417-420.

1466 **Wallace, James A.** Preaching to the hungers of the heart: the homily on the feasts and within the rites. ColMn 2002, Liturgical xii; 196 pp. $18 [BiTod 41,329—Bergant, Dianne].

1467 *Walters, Stanley D.* The costly gift: a monologue sermon on 2 Samuel 24. CTJ 37 (2002) 103-112.

1468 *Young, Robert D.* John 20:1-18. Interp. 56 (2002) 199-201..

B3.3 Inerrantia, inspiratio

1469 **Achtemeier, Paul J.** Inspiration and authority: nature and function of christian scripture. 1999 ⇒15,1063...17,1185. ^RRTR 61 (2002) 54-55 (*Foord, Martin*).

1470 *Amato, Angelo* Ispirazione biblica e 'ispirazione' dei libri sacri delle altre religioni. Scrittura ispirata. 2002 ⇒565. 167-190.

1471 *Artola, Antonio M.* Los nuevos métodos de exégesis y la comprensión de la inspiración bíblica. Scrittura ispirata. 2002 ⇒565. 132-166.

1472 *Barbeau, Jeffrey W.* NEWMAN and the interpretation of inspired scripture. TS 63 (2002) 53-67.

1473 **Barr, James** The scope and authority of the bible. SCM classics: L 2002, SCM xviii; 154 pp. 0-334-02879-5. Pref. *John Barton*:Bibl. 134-140.

1474 *Biguzzi, Giancarlo* Il problema della verità biblica nel Nuovo Testamento. Scrittura ispirata. 2002 ⇒565. 233-248.

1475 **Brossier, François** La bibbia dice il vero?: questa storia è vera o è una favola, come i miti dell'antichità?. BCR 5: Leumann (Torino) 2002, Elle Di Ci 156 pp. 88-01-02143-7.

1476 **Brueggemann, Walter; Blount, Brian K.; Placher, William Carl** Struggling with scripture. LVL 2002, Westminster v; (2) 69 pp. $10. 0-664-22485-7.

1477 **Bryan, Christopher** And God spoke: the authority of the bible for the church today. CM 2002, Cowley x; 149 pp. $12. 1-56101-201-7 [ThD 49,365—Heiser, W. Charles].

1478 *Busch, Eberhard* The one word of God: recollections of a reformed principle. IBSt 24 (2002) 72-96.

1479 *De Rosa, Giuseppe* La bibbia, parola di Dio in linguaggio umano: l'ispirazione della sacra scrittura. CivCatt 153/4 (2002) 554-566.

1480 **Draper, James T., Jr.; Keathley, Kenneth** Biblical authority: the critical issue for the body of Christ. Nv 2001, Broadman & H. 148 pp.

1481 *Fabris, Rinaldo* In che senso la sacra scrittura è testimonianza dell'
     ispirazione?. Scrittura ispirata. 2002 ⇒565. 41-60.
1482 *Frishman, Judith* Why a translation of the bible can't be authorita-
     tive: a response to John Rogerson. Bible translation. JSOT.S 353:
     2002 ⇒281. 31-35.
1483 *Gabel, Helmut* Inspiration und Wahrheit der Schrift (DV 11): neue
     Ansätze und Probleme im Kontext der gegenwärtigen wissenschaftli-
     chen Diskussion. ThG 45 (2002) 121-136.
1484 *Grech, Prosper* Che significa oggi 'ispirazione'?: una visione globa-
     le. Scrittura ispirata. 2002 ⇒565. 118-131.
1485 *Izquierdo García, Antonio* La escritura inspirada y la encarnación del
     Verbo. Alpha Omega 5/1 (2002) 103-136;
1486 Scrittura ispirata. 2002 ⇒565. 249-282.
1487 *Jones, L. Gregory* Formed and transformed by scripture: character,
     community, and authority in biblical interpretation. Character and
     scripture. 2002 ⇒283. 18-33.
1488 **Lancaster, Sarah Heaner** Women and the authority of scripture: a
     narrative approach. Harrisburg 2002, Trinity viii; 198 pp. $24. 1-56-
     338-356-X [ThD 50,80—Heiser, W. Charles].
1489 **Law, David R.** Inspiration. New century theology: 2001 ⇒17,1196.
     ᴿTheol. 105 (2002) 220-221 (*Goldingay, John*); RRT 9 (2002) 261-
     262 (*Williams, Jane*).
1490 *Mies, Françoise* Où est la parole de Dieu?. L'autorité de l'Écriture.
     LeDiv: 2002 ⇒588. 229-257.
1491 *Nicole, Roger* The nature of inerrancy <1980>;
1492 Induction and deduction with reference to inspiration <1976>;
1493 The inspiration and authority of scripture: J.D.G. Dunn versus B.B.
     Warfield <1983>. Standing forth. 2002 ⇒215. 27-49/151-8/159-222.
1494 *Pinchon, Michel* L'autorité de la bible. Cahiers de l'Atelier 497
     (2002) 64-74.
1495 *Pleasants, Phyllis Rodgerson Sola scriptura* in Zürich?. The free
     church. 2002 ⇒441. 77-99.
1496 *Poffet, Jean-Michel* Introduction. L'autorité de l'Écriture. LeDiv:
     2002 ⇒588. 7-19.
1497 *Prost, Gilbert R.* The liberal arts, language and transcendence. JIST
     14/1 (2002) 47-67.
1498 *Rodriguez, Angel M.* Paralelismos del antiguo Cercano Oriente y la
     biblia relacionados con el asunto de la revelación e inspiración. The-
     ologika 17/1 (2002) 2-41.
1499 *Rogerson, John* Can a translation of the Bible be authoritative?.
     Bible translation. JSOT.S 353: 2002 ⇒281. 17-30.
1500 *Scognamiglio, Edoardo* Religioni e ispirazioni. Asp. 49/3 (2002)
     341-380.
1501 *Scott, David A.* Teaching the authority of the bible. AThR 84 (2002)
     11-24.
1502 ᴱ**Sungenis, Robert A.** Not by scripture alone: a catholic critique of
     the protestant doctrine of sola scriptura. 1997 ⇒16,1204. ᴿBS 159
     (2002) 371-373 (*Powell, Charles E.*).
1503 *Tábet, Michelangelo* Ispirazione biblica e canonicità dei libri sacri.
     Scrittura ispirata. 2002 ⇒565. 80-117.
1504 **Tomei, Fernando** Conoscere meglio per amare di più: ispirazione
     biblica, sacramenti, sacrificio, sacerdozio. Biblioteca '80, Saggi: F
     2002, L'Autore Libri 197 pp. 88-517-0165-2. Bibl. 194-195.

1505 *Vassiliadis, Petros* Inspiration, canon and authority of scripture: an Orthodox hermeneutical perspective;
1506 *Vempeny, Ishanand* Non-biblical scriptures;
1507 *Vogels, Walter* Three possible models of inspiration. Scrittura ispirata. 2002 ⇒565. 193-210/211-232/61-79.
1508 **Ward, Timothy** Word and supplement: speech acts, biblical texts, and the sufficiency of scripture. NY 2002, OUP x; 332 pp. £50. 0-19-924438-3. Bibl. 310-326.
1509 *Ward, Timothy* The diversity and sufficiency of scipture. The trustworthiness of God. 2002 ⇒410. 192-218.
1510 **Whitlock, Jonathan** Schrift und Inspiration: Studien zur Vorstellung von inspirierter Schrift und inspirierter Schriftauslegung im antiken Judentum und in den paulinischen Briefen. Diss. Tübingen 1998/99. ᴰ*Stuhlmacher, Peter*: WMANT 98: Neuk 2002, Neuk'er xvi; 508 pp. €74. 3-7887-1918-4. Bibl. 457-491.
1511 *Younger, George D.* The authority of scripture for Baptists. ABQ 21/2 (2002) 146-155.

B3.4 **Traditio**

1512 *Bauckham, Richard* Authority and tradition. God and the crisis. 2002 <1988> ⇒142. 91-115.
1513 *Casale, Umberto* La relazione scrittura/tradizione: una prospettiva ecumenica. ATT 8 (2002) 339-361.
1514 *Gibbs, Lee W.* Richard HOOKER's Via Media doctrine of scripture and tradition. HThR 95 (2002) 227-235.
1515 *Hinison, E. Glenn* The authority of tradition: a Baptist view. The free church. 2002 ⇒441. 141-161.
1516 *Rösel, Martin, al.*, Tradition. TRE 33 (2002) 689-732.
1517 **Thiel, John E.** Senses of tradition: continuity and development in catholic faith. 2000 ⇒16,1215; 17,1219. ᴿHorizons 29 (2002) 299-321 (*Haight, Roger; Tanner, Kathryn; Espín, Orlando; Thiel, John*).
1518 *Van Slyke, Daniel* Is the end of the empire the end of the world?: exegetical traditions. Theology & sacr. scripture. 2002 ⇒549. 85-102.

B3.5 **Canon**

1519 ᴱ**McDonald, Lee Martin; Sanders, James A.** The canon debate. Peabody, MASS 2002, Hendrickson x; 662 pp. $40. 1-56563-517-5. Bibl. 599-623.

1520 **Aichele, George** The control of biblical meaning: canon as semiotic mechanism. 2001 ⇒17,1223. ᴿThTo 59 (2002) 113-115 (*Chapman, Stephen B.*).
1521 **Alter, Robert** Canon and creativity: modern writing and the authority of scripture. [Kafka, Franz; Bialik, Haim; Joyce, James] 2000 ⇒ 16,1217. ᴿJThS 53 (2002) 158-9 (*Drury, John*); HeyJ 43 (2002) 226-8 (*Loubse, J.A.*); MoTh 18/1 (2002) 131-133 (*Dawson, John David*).
1522 **Baird, Joseph Arthur** Holy word: the paradigm of New Testament formation. ᴱ*Evans, Craig A.; Porter, Stanley E.*: JSNT.S 224; Classics in biblical and theological studies.S 1: Shf 2002, Sheffield A. 268 pp. £55. 0-8264-6025-9. Collab. *Scott N. Dolff*.

1523 *Balla, Peter* Evidence for an early christian canon (second and third century). Canon debate. 2002 ⇒1519. 373-385.

1524 *Barker, Margaret* The bible Jesus knew. PrPe 16 (2002) 322-326.

1525 *Blanchard, Yves-Marie* Naissance du Nouveau Testament et canon biblique. L'autorité de l'Écriture. LeDiv: 2002 ⇒588. 23-50.

1526 *Bovon, François* The canonical structure of gospel and apostle. Canon debate. 2002 ⇒1519. 516-527.

1527 *Böhler, Dieter* Der Kanon als hermeneutische Vorgabe biblischer Theologie: über aktuelle Methodendiskussionen in der Bibelwissenschaft. ThPh 77 (2002) 161-178.

1528 **Chapman, Stephen B.** The law and the prophets: a study in OT canon formation. FAT 27: 2000 ⇒16,1226; 17,1230. ᴿETR 77 2002) 117-8 (*Vincent, Jean M.*); OLZ 97 (2002) 242-248 (*Schart, Aaron*); BZ 46 (2002) 297-301 (*Grund, Alexandra S.*); Sal. 64 (2002) 566-568 (*Vicent, R.*); JR 82 (2002) 617-618 (*Hagedorn, Anselm C.*); SvTK 78 (2002) 187-188 (*Starr, James*); ThLZ 127 (2002) 277-280 (*Reventlow, Henning Graf*); CBQ 64 (2002) 549-550 (*Owens, J. Edward*); Bib. 83 (2002) 409-412 (*Dohmen, Christoph*).

1529 *Clarke, Kent D.* The problem of pseudonymity in biblical literature and its implications for canon formation;

1530 *Dunn, James D.G.* Has the canon a continuing function?;

1531 *Epp, Eldon Jay* Issues in the interrelation of New Testament textual criticism and canon;

1532 *Evans, Craig A.* The scriptures of Jesus and his earliest followers. Canon debate. 2002 ⇒1519. 440-468/558-579/485-515/185-195.

1533 **Evans, Joseph Keith** Petrine authority in the formation of the New Testament canon. Diss. Pampelune 2002; ᴰ*Aranda, G.*: 453 pp [RTL 34,597].

1534 *Farmer, William R.* Reflections on Jesus and the New Testament canon. Canon debate. 2002 ⇒1519. 321-340.

1535 *Ferguson, Everett* Factors leading to the selection and closure of the New Testament canon: a survey of some recent studies;

1536 *Funk, Robert W.* The once and future New Testament;

1537 *Gamble, Harry Y.* The New Testament canon: recent research and the status questionis. Canon debate. 2002 ⇒1519. 295-320/541-557/ 267-294.

1538 *Gilbert, Maurice* Textes bibliques: dont l'église a défini le sens;

1539 Textes exclus, textes inclus: les enjeux. L'autorité de l'Écriture. LeDiv: 2002 ⇒588. 71-94/51-70.

1540 *Hahneman, Geoffrey Mark* The Muratorian fragment and the origins of the New Testament canon. Canon debate. 2002 ⇒1519. 405-415.

1541 *Herbst, Adrián* La canonización del Nuevo Testamento y la mishná judía. RevBib 62 (2000) 87-100.

1542 *Kalin, Everett R.* The New Testament canon of EUSEBIUS. Canon debate. 2002 ⇒1519. 386-404.

1543 *Kealy, Seán P.* Does the canonical order of the bible matter?. BiTod 40 (2002) 44-48.

1544 *Knauf, Ernst Axel* Der Kanon und die Bibeln: die Geschichte vom Sammeln heiliger Schriften. BiKi 57 (2002) 193-198.

1545 *Kraft, Robert A.* The codex and canon consciousness. Canon debate. 2002 ⇒1519. 229-233.

1546 *Kügler, Joachim* Moses, Jesus und der kleine Prinz?: die Bibel als Heilige Schrift des Gottesvolkes. BiKi 57 (2002) 188-192.

1547 *Lathuilière, Pierre* La bible des chrétiens. LV(L) 255 (2002) 81-93.
1548 *Lewis, Jack P.* Jamnia revisited. Canon debate. 2002 ⇒1519. 146-162.
1549 *Lightstone, Jack N.* The rabbis' bible: the canon of the Hebrew Bible and the early rabbinic guild. Canon debate. 2002 ⇒1519. 163-184.
1550 *Loader, James Alfred* Tenach and Old Testament—the same bible?. HTS 58 (2002) 1415-1430 [OTA 26,389].
1551 *McDonald, Lee Martin* Identifying scripture and canon in the early church: the criteria question. Canon debate. 2002 ⇒1519. 416-439.
1552 *McDonald, Patricia* From Malachi to Matthew: a gift of the tradition. Theology and sacred scripture. 2002 ⇒549. 53-68.
1553 (*a*) *Michollet, Bernard* Le statut du livre dans les monothéismes: quelques enjeux. LV(L) 255 (2002) 107-122.
      (*b*) *Nicole, Roger* The canon of the New Testament. Standing forth. 2002 <1997> ⇒215. 91-101.
1554 *Norris, Frederick W.* The canon of scripture in the church. The free church. 2002 ⇒441. 3-25.
1555 **Paul, André** Et l'homme créa la bible: d'HÉRODOTE à Flavius JO-SÈPHE. 2000 ⇒16,1245; 17,1245. ᴿSR 30 (2002) 253-254 (*Lavoie, Jean-Jacques*); LTP 58 (2002) 617-618 (*Crégheur, Eric*).
1556 *Perkins, Pheme* Gnosticism and the christian bible. Canon debate. 2002 ⇒1519. 355-371.
1557 *Pitta, Antonio* Der Kanon: die christologische Interpretation des Alten Testaments. Die Bibel: Geschichte und Gegenwart. 2002 ⇒971. 112-119, 122-127.
1558 *Potin, Jean-Michel* La page blanche de la chair. LV(L) 255 (2002) 95-105.
1559 *Quantin, Jean-Louis Apocryphorum nimis studiosi*?: DODWELL, MILL, GRABE et le problème du canon néo-testamentaire au tournant du XVIIᵉ et XVIIIᵉ siècle. ᶠGEOLTRAIN, P.: BEHE.R 113: 2002 ⇒ 45. 285-306 [BuBB 38,133].
1560 *Ricoeur, Paul* The canon between the text and the community. Philosophical hermeneutics. WUNT 153: 2002 ⇒367. 7-26.
1561 *Sanders, James A.* The issue of closure in the canonical process. Canon debate. 2002 ⇒1519. 252-263.
1562 *Sarfati, Georges-Elia* Qu'est-ce qu'un texte canonique?. L'autorité de l'Écriture. LeDiv: 2002 ⇒588. 177-192.
1563 *Sánchez Caro, José Manuel* Sobre la fecha del canon muratoriano. ᶠTREVIJANO ETCHEVERRÍA, R. 2002 ⇒122. 297-314.
1564 *Schmid, Ulrich* MARCIONs Evangelium und die neutestamentlichen Evangelien: Rückfragen zur Geschichte und Kanonisierung der Evangelienüberlieferung in arabischen Quellen. Marcion. 2002 ⇒578. 67-77.
1565 *Schmidt, Daryl D.* The Greek New Testament as a codex. Canon debate. 2002 ⇒1519. 469-484.
1566 (*a*) *Schneider, Katharina* Der Apologet ARISTIDES als Zeuge der neutestamentlichen Schriftwerdung. ᶠHOHEISEL, K.: JAC.E 34: 2002 ⇒ 59. 226-231.
      (*b*) *Stuhlmacher, Peter* Der Kanon und seine Auslegung. Biblische Theologie. WUNT 146: 2002 <1997> ⇒245. 167-190.
1567 *Trebolle Barrera, Julio C.* Origins of a tripartite Old Testament canon. Canon debate. 2002 ⇒1519. 128-145.
1568 *Trobisch, David* Das Neue Testament: eine Auswahl von Gottes Wort. BiKi 57 (2002) 200-203.

1569 **Trobisch, David** Die Endredaktion des Neuen Testaments: eine Untersuchung zur Entstehung der christlichen Bibel. NTOA 31: 1996 ⇒ 12,826 ... 15,1137. ᴿThLZ 127 (2002) 56-58 (*Maurer, Alexander*).

1570 *Ulrich, Eugene* The notion and definition of canon;

1571 The Jewish scriptural canon in cultural perspective. Canon debate. 2002 ⇒1519. 21-35./36-52.

1572 *Van Aarde, A.G.* The 'cause of Jesus' (*Sache Jesu*) as the canon behind the canon. HTS 57 (2001) 1229-1253 [NTAb 46,450].

1573 (a) *VanderKam, James C.* Questions of canon viewed through the Dead Sea scrolls. Canon debate. 2002 ⇒1519. 91-109.
(b) *Vassiliadis, Petros; Taylor, Justin* The canon of the bible, or the authority of scripture: from an orthodox perspective. L'autorité de l'Écriture. LeDiv: 2002 ⇒588. 113-135.

1574 *Veltri, Giuseppe* Tradent und Traditum im antiken Judentum: zu einer sog. Kanonformel <1998>;

1575 Voraussetzung der Kanonbildung und die Yavne-Legende <1990>. Gegenwart der Tradition. 2002 ⇒255. 3-22/23-37.

1576 *Wall, Robert W.* The significance of a canonical perspective of the church's scripture. Canon debate. 2002 ⇒1519. 528-540.

1577 **Wegner, Paul D.** The journey from texts to translations: 1999 ⇒16,783. ᴿRRT 9 (2002) 170-172 (*Norton, Gerard J.*).

1578 *Wells, M. Jay* Figural representation and canonical unity. Biblical theology. 2002 ⇒558. 111-125.

B4.1 *Interpretatio humanistica* **The Bible—man; health, toil, age**

1579 **Boni, Cesare** Dove va l'anima dopo la morte?: cosa accade, come comportarsi, come accompagnare il morente. I misteri: Morbio Inf. (CH) 2002, Elvetica 400 pp. 88-86639-09-0. Bibl. 393-399.

1580 *Brenner, Athalya* Age and ageism in the Hebrew Bible, in an autobiographical perspective. ᴹCARROLL, R.: 2002 ⇒13. 302-310.

1581 **Cassiday-Shaw, Aimee K.** Family abuse and the bible: the scriptural perspective. NY 2002, Haworth xii; 144 pp. $50/20. 0-7890-1576-5/ 7-3 [ThD 50,65—Heiser, W. Charles].

1582 *Johnson, E. Elizabeth* Apocalyptic family values. Interp. 56 (2002) 34-44.

1583 **Newman, Jay** Biblical religion and family values: a problem in the philosophy of culture. 2001 ⇒17,1277. ᴿJR 82 (2002) 663-664 (*Green, M. Christian*); SR 31 (2002) 239-240 (*Corneil, Richard*).

1584 *Penn, Michael* Performing family: ritual kissing and the construction of early christian kinship. JECS 10 (2002) 151-174.

1585 *Pilch, John* The family: status and roles. BiTod 40 (2002) 387-391.

1586 **Rashkow, Ilona N.** Taboo or not taboo: sexuality and family in the Hebrew Bible. 2000 ⇒16,1275; 17,1282. ᴿINTAMS Review 8/1 (2002) 118-119 (*Thatcher, Adrian*).

1587 *Rossano, Pietro* Religions and human advancement. Teologia cristiana. DMis 27: 2002 <1978> ⇒232. 437-440.

1588 **Vendrame, Calisto** Los enfermos en la biblia. Salud y Vida 3: M 2002, San Pablo 240 pp. 84-285-2404-1 [Theologica 38,170s—Coutinho, Jorge].

1589 *Vignolo, Roberto* 'Dal grembo di mia madre, tu sei il mio Dio'. RCl 83 (2002) 725-737.

1590 *Willett, Elizabeth* Infant mortality and family religion in the biblical periods. DavarLogos 1/1 (2002) 27-42.

B4.2 *Femina, familia*; **Woman in the Bible** [⇒B4.1; H8.8s]

1591 *Ackerman, Susan* Why is Miriam also among the prophets? (and is Zipporah among the priests?). JBL 121 (2002) 47-80.

1592 **Ackerman, Susan** Warrior, dancer, seductress, queen: women in Judges and Biblical Israel. AncB Reference Library: 1998 ⇒14, 1071. ᴿBib. 83 (2002) 574-576 (*Steinberg, Naomi*).

1593 **Aschkenasy, Nehama** Woman at the window: biblical tales of oppression and escape. 1998 ⇒14,1074; 16,1283. ᴿJQR 92 (2002) 589-593 (*Gruber, Mayer I.*).

1594 *Brenner, Athalya* Wide gaps, narrow escapes: I am known as Raḥab, the broad. First person. BiSe 81: 2002 ⇒295. 47-58.

1595 **Camp, Claudia V.** Wise, strange and holy: the strange woman and the making of the bible. JSOT.S 320: 2000 ⇒16,144; 17,1295. ᴿBiblInterp 10 (2002) 83-86 (*Rooke, Deborah W.*).

1596 **Chalier, Catherine** Le matriarche: Sara, Rebecca, Rachele e Lea. ᵀ*Ombrosi, Orietta*: Schulim Vogelmann 95: F 2002, Giuntina 276 pp. 88-8057-141-9. Pref. *Emmanuel Lévinas*.

1597 *Colijn, B.B.* A biblical theology of women in leadership. AThJ 34 (2002) 67-80 [NTAb 47,291].

1598 *Cunningham, Phillip J.* Those shady ladies in Jesus' family tree. BiTod 40 (2002) 184-188.

1599 *Friedlander, Albert* Frauen in der hebräischen Bibel. Die Bibel: Geschichte und Gegenwart. 2002 ⇒971. 70-71.

1600 **Frymer-Kensky, Tikva Simone** Reading the women of the bible. NY 2002, Schocken xxvii; 446 pp. 0-8052-4121-3.

1601 **Gaines, Janet Howe** Music in the old bones: Jezebel through the ages. 1999 ⇒15,1175; 16,1294. ᴿJR 82 (2002) 97-98 (*Mattox, Mickey L.*).

1602 *Gubler, Marie-Louise* Bathseba—oder: wie ist Gott?: Roman von Torgny Lindgren. KuI 17 (2002) 31-44.

1603 **Ilan, Tal** Integrating women into second temple history. TSAJ 76: 1999 ⇒15,1179...17,1303. ᴿJQR 92 (2002) 647-9 (*Satlow, Michael*).

1604 **James, Sharon** God's design for women: biblical womanhood for today. Darlington 2002, Evangelical 364 pp [SdT 15,239: Rendina, S.].

1605 **Kiesow, Anna** Löwinnen von Juda: Frauen als Subjekte politischer Macht in der judäischen Königszeit. 2000 ⇒16,1300. ᴿYESW 10 (2002) 241-242 (*Müllner, Ilse*).

1606 ᴱ**Knippenkötter, Anneliese; Langwald, Marie-Luise** FrauenGottesDienste: Modelle und Materialien 12: biblische Frauen. Ostfildern 2002, Schwabenverlag 88 pp. €7.80 [BiLi 75,211s—Penner, Ingrid.].

1607 *Lefebvre, Philippe* Riçpah, la dame du Lithostrôton (2 Sam XXI; Jn XIX). RB 109 (2002) 217-240.

1608 **McKenna, Megan** 'Déjala' (Juan 12,7): mujeres en la escritura. 2001 ⇒17,1307. ᴿSalTer 90 (2002) 177-178 (*Márquez, Carmen*).

1609 ᴱ**Meyers, Carol; Craven, Toni; Kraemer, Ross S.** Women in scripture: a dictionary of named and unnamed women in the Hebrew Bible, the apocryphal/deuterocanonical books, and the NT. 2000 ⇒ 16,1305; 17,1308. ᴿHebStud 43 (2002) 244-246 (*Fuchs, Esther*).

1610 *Peleg, Yitzhak* Did Pharaoh touch (*nag'a*) Sarai?: was the ancestress of Israel in danger?. BetM 172 (2002) 54-64 Sum. 92. **H.**

1611 *Pereira, Nancy C.* Tamborins, espelhos e sonhos: perguntando pela profecia de mulheres na Bíblia Hebraica. Estudos bíblicos 73 (2002) 67-75.

1612 *Piedad Sánchez, Jorge* El rol político de las mujeres en el Antiguo Testamento. Qol 28 (2002) 49-60.

1613 *Pyper, Hugh S.* Jezebel. First person. BiSe 81: 2002 ⇒295. 77-92.

1614 **Rapp, Ursula** Mirjam: eine feministisch-rhetorische Lektüre der Mirjamtexte in der hebräischen Bibel. [D]*Fischer, I.*: BZAW 317: B 2002, De Gruyter xiv; 434 pp. €100.93. 3-11-017384-0. Diss. Graz 2001; Bibl. 399-422.

1615 *Rosenbloom, William I.* Tamar times three. JBQ 30 (2002) 127-130.

1616 *Sanz Giménez-Rico, Enrique* Dos palabras, dos personajes: éxito y fracaso en la vida de Raquel y de Abraham. SalTer 90 (2002) 645-655.

1617 [E]**Spendel, Aurelia** Mit Frauen der Bibel den Glauben feiern: Modelle für Frauengottesdienste. FrB 2002, Herder 142 pp. €14.50 [BiLi 76,224—Jeller, Stefanie]..

1618 **Streete, Gail Corrington** The strange woman. 1997 ⇒13,1043... 16, 1317. [R]JQR 92 (2001) 210-215 (*Gruber, Mayer I.*).

1619 **Thompson, John Lee** Writing the wrongs: women of the Old Testament among biblical commentators from PHILO through the Reformation. 2001 ⇒17,1313. [R]RBLit (2002)* (*Hagelia, Hallvard*).

1620 **Ulterino, Gloria** Drawing from wisdom's well: stories, celebrations, and explorations of courageous women of faith. ND 2002, Ave Maria 223 pp. $18. 0-87793-954-3 [ThD 50,190—Heiser, W. Charles].

1621 *Van Boxel, Piet* Le Dieu de Rébecca. SIDIC 35/2-3 (2002 <1976>) 13-18.

1622 *Van Rensburg, J.F.* Intellect and/or beauty: a portrait of women in the Old Testament and extra biblical literature. JSem 11/1 (2002) 112-125.

1623 *Vielhaus, Brigitte* Frauenleben sind vielfältig: Überlegungen für die Praxis. AnzSS 111/10 (2002) 11-14.

1624 *Vivas A., María del Socorro* La misión de las mujeres en la biblia. ThX 52 (2002) 683-697.

1625 *West, Gerald* Reading abused female bodies in the bible: interpretative strategies for recognising and recovering the stories of women inscribed by violence but circumscribed by patriarchal text (2 Kings 5). OTEs 15 (2002) 240-258.

1626 *Willi-Plein, Ina* Michal und die Anfänge des Königtums in Israel. Sprache als Schlüssel. 2002 <1997> ⇒261. 79-96.

1627 **Zlotnick, Helena** Dinah's daughters: gender and Judaism from the Hebrew Bible to late antiquity. Ph 2002, University of Pennsylvania Pr. x; 248 pp. $20. 0-8122-3644-0. Bibl. 215-233.

B4.4 *Exegesis litteraria*—**The Bible itself as literature**

1628 *Abicht, Ludo* De bijbel is literatuur. Streven 69 (2002) 978-987.

1629 **Amit, Yairah** Reading biblical narratives: literary criticism and the Hebrew Bible. 2001 ⇒17,1320. [R]TJT 18 (2002) 255-256 (*Oeste, Gordon*).

1630 **Andersen, Øivind** Im Garten der Rhetorik: die Kunst der Rede in der Antike. 2001 ⇒17,1322. [R]ThLZ 127 (2002) 1156-1157 (*Reiser, Marius*).

1631   *Beentjes, Panc* De bijbel is literatuur: ja zeker, maar ook nog iets meer?. Streven 69 (2002) 988-991.

1632   *Berman, Joshua* The 'sword of mouths' (Jud iii 16; Ps. cxlix 6; Prov. v 4): a metaphor and its ancient Near Eastern context. VT 52 (2002) 291-303.

1633   *Bieberstein, Klaus* Geschichten sind immer fiktiv—mehr oder minder: warum das Alte Testament fiktional erzählt und erzählen muss. BiLi 75 (2002) 4-13.

1634   *Bieberstein, Sabine* "Warum hat uns das nie jemand gesagt ...?": Erfahrungen mit der Fiktionalität in der bibelpastoralen Arbeit. BiLi 75 (2002) 37-41.

1635   *Bodi, Daniel* Bible et littérature—Erich AUERBACH et les débuts de la méthode. REJ 161 (2002) 465-473.

1636   **Coenen, Hans Georg** Analogie und Metapher: Grundlegung einer Theorie der bildlichen Rede. De-Gruyter-Studienbuch: B 2002, De Gruyter x; 251 pp. 3-11-017343-3.

1637   **Corbineau-Hoffmann, Angelika** Die Analyse literarischer Texte: Einführung und Anleitung. UTB 2330: Tü 2002, Francke 201 pp. 3-8252-2330-2.

1638   **Danblon, Emmanuelle** Rhétorique et rationalité: essai sur l'emergence de la critique et de la persuasion. Bru 2002, Univ. de Bruxelles 276 pp. Préf. *M. Dominicy.*

1639   **Dancy, John** The divine drama: the Old Testament as literature. 2001 ⇒17,1327. [R]IBSt 24 (2002) 44-46 (*Amos, Clare*); RRT 9 (2002) 32-35 (*Norton, Gerard J.*).

1640   **Dundes, Alan** Holy writ as oral lit: the bible as folklore. 1999 ⇒15, 1206. [R]AUSS 40 (2002) 317-319 (*Sparing-Chavez, Margarethe*).

1641   *Évrard, Étienne* Sur quelques précautions en statistique littéraire. Bible and computer. 2002 ⇒548. 583-591.

1642   *Garhammer, Erich* Erzählen statt zählen: eine kleine Apologie der Fiktionalität. BiLi 75 (2002) 13-19.

1643   *Grau, Marion* Erasing "economy": DERRIDA and the construction of divine economies. CrossCur 52 (2002) 360-370.

1644   **Grelot, Pierre** Le langage symbolique dans la bible: enquête de sémantique et d'exégèse. Initiations bibliques: 2001 ⇒17,1335. [R]Brot. 155 (2002) 429-430 (*Silva, I. Ribeiro da*); ITS 39 (2002) 91-93 (*Legrand, L.*); ThLZ 127 (2002) 489-491 (*Schenk, Wolfgang*).

1645   **Haines-Eitzen, Kim** Guardians of letters: literacy, power, and the transmitters of early christian literature. 2000 ⇒16,1325; 17,1337. [R]NT 44 (2002) 404-407 (*Rodgers, Peter R.*); ASEs 19 (2002) 292-295 (*Mazza, Roberta*); CBQ 64 (2002) 575-576 (*Pascuzzi, Maria*).

1646   *Hardmeier, Christof* Literaturwissenschaft, biblisch. RGG 5. 2002 ⇒ 796. 425-429.

1647   *Hülst, Dirk* Der Symbolbegriff in der neueren soziologischen Kunsttheorie. Symb. 15 (2002) 11-27.

1648   **Jacobs, Jonathan** Measure for measure as literary and ideological tool in the biblical story telling. [D]*Garsiel, M.*: 2002: 289 pp. Diss. Bar Ilan [RTL 34,591].

1649   **Johnson, Marshall D.** Making sense of the bible: literary type as an approach to understanding. GR 2002, Eerdmans ix; 161 pp. $12/£9. 0-8028-4919-9. Bibl. 151-155. [R]ScrB 32 (2002) 100-101 (*Turner, Geoffrey*).

1650   *Köpf, Ulrich, al.*, Literaturgeschichte/Literaturgeschichtsschreibung. RGG 5. 2002 ⇒796. 403-425.

1651 *Marshall, Ian H.* Living in the "flesh". BS 159 (2002) 387-403.

1652 **Moreschini, Claudio; Norelli, Enrico** Histoire de la littérature chrétienne antique grecque et latine, 1: de Paul à l'ère de Constantin. [T]*Rousset, Madeleine*: 2000 ⇒16,1333; 17,1348. [R]AnCl 71 (2002) 352-355 (*Savon, Hervé*).

1653 **Niditch, Susan** A prelude to biblical folklore: underdogs and tricksters. [2]2000 <1987> ⇒16,1337. [R]RBLit 4 (2002) 174-176 (*Bakke, Janice B.*).

1654 **Norton, David** A history of the English Bible as literature. 2000 ⇒ 16,1339. [R]ThTo 59 (2002) 150-152 (*Daniell, David*); Reformation 7 (2002) 217-221 (*Daniell, David*); RBLit 4 (2002) 130-133 (*Aichele, George*).

1655 *Nouillez, Lucien* Bible et poésie, deux paroles aimantées par le sens. CCicst 64 (2002) 150-164.

1656 *Paul, Shalom M.* The shared legacy of sexual metaphors and euphemisms in Mesopotamian and biblical literature;

1657 *Philip, Tarja* Woman in travail as a simile to men in distress in the Hebrew Bible. Sex and gender. 2002 ⇒712. 489-498/499-505.

1658 **Prickett, Stephen** Narrative, religion and science: fundamentalism versus irony 1700-1999. C 2002, CUP viii; 281 pp. 0-521-00983-9. Bibl. 264-273.

1659 *Roberts, J.J.M.* The bible and the literature of the ancient Near East. The bible and the ANE. 2002 <1988> ⇒230. 44-58.

1660 *Sand, Ephraim* Two dialogue documents in the bible: Genesis chapter 23:3-18 and 1 Kings chapter 5:15-25. ZAR 8 (2002) 88-130.

1661 *Sandler, Willibald* Christentum als grosse Erzählung: Anstöße für eine narrative Theologie. Religion—Literatur—Künste II. Im Kontext 14: 2002 ⇒530. 523-538.

1662 **Schmidt, Karl Ludwig** The place of the gospels in the general history of literature. [T]*McCane, Byron R.*: Columbia, South Carolina 2002, Univ. of South Carolina Pr. xxxv; 88 pp. $25. 1-57003-430-3.

1663 **Schmitz, Thomas A.** Moderne Literaturtheorie und antike Texte: eine Einführung. Da:Wiss 2002, 261 pp. €34.90. 3-534-15204-2.

1664 *Schwager, Raymund* Erinnerung in Theologie und Literatur;

1665 *Sedmak, Clemens* 'Sie alle suchen den Schuldigen': Semiotik und Theologie und andere crime stories;

1666 *Siebenrock, Roman A.* Poesie und Reflexion: Beobachtungen und Überlegungen zu den Sprachen im Werk Karl RAHNERS als Grundbestimmungen theologischer Rechenschaft des Glaubens. Religion—Literatur—Künste II. 2002 ⇒530. 515-522/447-456/490-504.

1667 **Stenger, Hermann M.** Im Zeichen des Hirten und des Lammes: Mitgift und Gift biblischer Bilder. 2000 ⇒16,1343; 17,1359. [R]GuL 75 (2002) 230 (*Steinmetz, Franz-Josef*).

1668 *Tschuggnall, Peter* Dialogizität—Intertextualizität—Alterität: mögliche Ausgangspunkte komparatistischer Analysen. Religion—Literatur—Künste II. Im Kontext 14: 2002 ⇒530. 18-29.

1669 **Van Tillo, Gerard** De metaforische betekenis van bijbelteksten. Amst 2002, Husserl-Stichting 44 pp. €7. 90-75701-15-2 [ITBT 11/1, 29—Sneller, Rico].

1670 **Whedbee, J. William** The bible and the comic vision. Mp 2002 <1998>, Fortress xii; 315 pp. $20. 0-8006-3486-1.

B4.5 **Influxus biblicus in litteraturam profanam,** *generalia*

1671 **Anderson, Graham** Fairytale in the ancient world. 2000 ⇒16,1354.
ᴿAJP 123 (2002) 287-289 (*De Luce, Judith*); CIR 52 (2002) 34-36
(*Whitmarsh, Tim*).

1672 *Ashton, John* BROWNING on FEUERBACH and RENAN;

1673 *Bach, Alice* Alice's adventures in wonderland: a girl in the guild.
ᴹCARROLL, R.: JSOT.S 348: 2002 ⇒13. 374-384/385-394.

1674 **Beccaria, Gian Luigi** Sicuterat: il latino di chi non lo sa: bibbia e liturgia nell'italiano e nei dialetti. 1999 <2001> ⇒15,1247. ᴿRAMi 71
(2002) 174-175 (*Spera, Salvatore*).

1675 *Brunn, Albert von* Kain und Abel in Manaus: zum Roman Zwei
Brüder von Milton Hatoum. Orien. 66 (2002) 228-230.

1676 **Campanella, Nicoletta** Salomè... quel che resta di una principessa:
senso e valore del mito di Salomè in una rilettura contemporanea. R
2001, Armando 96 pp. €10.33.

1677 *Campos Boralevi, Lea* La *Respublica Hebraeorum* nella tradizione
olandese. Il Pensiero Politico 35 (2002) 431-463.

1678 *Cardellino, Lodovico* Ermeneutica ed esegesi biblica nella Divina
Commedia. BeO 44 (2002) 88-126.

1679 *Cremascoli, Giuseppe* L'oblio della bibbia. La sorgente. 2002 ⇒315.
215-226.

1680 **Flinker, Noam** The Song of Songs in English Renaissance literature:
kisses of their mouth. Studies in Renaissance Literature 3: 2000 ⇒
16,1361. ᴿSCJ 33 (2002) 1098-1100 (*Swan, Jesse G.*).

1681 *Gojny, Tanja; Deeg, Alexander; Nicol, Martin* Vernetzte Texte: Bibel und moderne Lyrik im Wechselspiel. Praktische Theologie 37
(2002) 298-311.

1682 *Hartman, Michelle* Jesus, Joseph and Job: reading rescriptings of
religious figures in Lebanese women's fiction. Literaturen im Kontext
12: Wsb 2002, Reichert 177 pp. €39. 3-89500-298-4.

1683 *Kerner, Max* Vor einer nachchristlichen Welt?: die Entdeckung des
Himmels (Harry Mulisch). Jesus von Nazareth und das Christentum.
2000 ⇒293. 97-106.

1684 **King, Jeannette** Women and the word: contemporary women novel-
ists and the bible. NY 2000, Palgrave 207 pp. $60. ᴿJAAR 70 (2002)
653-655 (*Cullinan, Colleen Carpenter*).

1685 *Klaghofer, Wolfgang* Gott ist Unterscheidung: die biblischen Romane von Thomas MANN und Franz WERFEL. IKaZ 31 (2002) 66-81.

1686 ᴱ**Knight, Alan E.** Les mystères de la procession de Lille: le pentateuque. Textes littéraires français 535: 2001 ⇒17,1398. ᴿMA 108
(2002) 707-708 (*Ritch, K. Janet*).

1687 *Langenhorst, Georg* Wie von Gott reden?: Schriftsteller als theologische Sprachlehrer. Religion—Literatur—Künste II. Im Kontext 14:
2002 ⇒530. 43-56.

1688 **Leplay, Michel** La bible entre le culte et la culture: vingt siècles de
vitalité et de résistance. Ecritures saintes des religions du Livre: Poliez-le-Grand 2002, Moulin 96 pp. €11. 28846-90115 [BCLF 645,22].

1689 *Liew, Tat-siong Benny* Writing new and joyful songs: con-versing
with Joy Kogawa. Semeia 90/91 (2002) 195-209.

1690 **Maier, Paul** Pilatus: historischer Roman. 2001 ⇒17,1403. ᴿStr. 69
(2002) 283-285 (*Beentjes, Panc*).

1691 *McConvery, Brendan* Matthews, Mark and Molly: Mark 8:22-26 and 10:46-52 in two contemporary Irish dramas. PIBA 25 (2002) 69-80.

1692 ᴱᵀ**Mengozzi, Alessandro** Israel of Alqosh and Joseph of Telkepe: a story in a truthful language, religious poems in vernacular Syriac (North Iraq, 17th Century): v.1, text and glossary; v.2, introduction and translation. CSCO 589-590; CSCO.S 230-231: Lv 2002, Peeters 2 vols v.1.90-429-1022-4, v.2.90-429-1021-6. Bibl. vol. 2, 125-136.

1693 *Pelletier, Anne-Marie* Lectures culturelles de la bible: un malentendu?. La sorgente. 2002 ⇒315. 227-239.

1694 *Pichetto, Maria Teresa* La 'Respublica Hebraeorum' nella rivoluzione americana. Il Pensiero Politico 35 (2002) 481-500.

1695 *Sánchez Salor, Eustaquio* Reflejo de la biblia en la cultura profana latino-medieval. RevAg 43 (2002) 99-139.

1696 *Sisley, Joy* Heroes of the promised land: translating American frontier myths into biblical epics;

1697 *Stocker, Margarita* On the frontier: Judith and Esther in the myth of America. Borders. JSOT.S 313: 2002 ⇒585. 274-291/229-253.

1698 **Viejo Sánchez, Maria Luisa** La relación marido-miujer en la tradición literaria española (1254-1583) a la luz de los códigos de deberes familiares del NuevoTestamento. Cum laude: Valencia 2002, Pont. Inst. Juan Pablo II 175 pp [AnVal 29/1,169s—Calatayud, Rafael].

B4.6 *Singuli auctores*—Bible influence on individual authors

1699 AMICHAI, Y: *Ferrari, Sara* 'Io voglio confondere la bibbia': la tradizione biblica nella poesia di Yehuda Amichai. Acme 55/3 (2002) 127-188.

1700 BECKETT S: *Cascetta, Annamaria* Il sottotesto biblico nella dramaturgia di Samuel Beckett. La sorgente. 2002 ⇒315. 177-191.

1701 BODIN J: *Lazzarino del Grosso, Anna Maria* La 'Respublica Hebraeorum' come modello politico 'scientifico' nella *Methodus* di Jean Bodin. Il Pensiero Politico 35 (2002) 382-398.

1702 BÖLL H: ᴱ**Langenhorst, Georg** 30 Jahre Nobelpreis Heinrich Böll: zur literarisch-theologischen Wirkkraft Heinrich Bölls. Müns 2002, LIT 250 pp. €19.90. ᴿOrien. 66 (2002) 255-62 (*Gellner, Christoph*).

1703 BUBER M: *Quaglioni, Diego* La '*Politeia* biblica' in Martin Buber. Il Pensiero Politico 35 (2002) 501-521.

1704 CAMPBELL A: *Celsor, Scott* The Old Testament in the formation of Alexander Campbell's apocalyptic worldview. RestQ 44/4 (2002) 213-231.

1705 CHESSEX J: **Molla, Serge** Jacques Chessex et la bible: parcours à l'orée des écritures. Genève 2002, Labor et Fides 210 pp. €22.

1706 CONRAD J: *Kreitzer, Larry J.* 'The horror! the whore!': the abomination of desolation and Conrad's *Heart of darkness*. Apocalyptic. JSPE.S 43: 2002 ⇒373. 284-318.

1707 DANTE: **Hawkins, Peter S.** Dante's testaments: essays in scriptural imagination. 1999 ⇒15,1294; 17,1441. ᴿAThR 84 (2002) 459-461 (*Petersen, William H.*); ASEs 19 (2002) 508-511 (*Ledda, Giuseppe*);

1708 *Manica, Raffaele* Alla lettera: su *Commedia* e *bibbia*. La sorgente. 2002 ⇒315. 83-98.

1709 DIDEROT; D'ALEMBERT: *Suppa, Silvio* L'ebraismo nell'"Encyclopédie" di Diderot e D'Alembert: ovvero regole, scrittura e memoria, in un ordine senza stato. Il Pensiero Politico 35 (2002) 464-480.

1710 DOSTOEVSKIj: **Salvestroni, Simonetta** Dostoevskij e la bibbia. 2000
      ⇒16,1389. ᴿRivBib 50 (2002) 119-121 (*Balzaretti, Claudio*); Pro-
      test. 57 (2002) 344-345 (*Spanu, Alessandro*).
1711 GEORGE S: *Würffel, Stefan Bodo* Sakralisation, postfigurale Gestal-
      tung und Prophetie in der Dichtung Stefan Georges. Religion—Li-
      teratur—Künste II. Im Kontext 14: 2002 ⇒530. 163-117.
1712 HEINE H: **Kuschel, Karl-Josef** Gottes grausamer Spaß?: Heinrich
      Heines Leben mit der Katastrophe. Dü 2002, Patmos 359 pp. 3-491-
      70350-6.
1713 HERDER J: *Deneken, Michel* Quand Dieu apprend à parler aux
      hommes: Herder et la bible. RSR 90 (2002) 487-508.
1714 HUGO V: *Bordet, Gaston* Victor Hugo et la bible. MoBi 45/147
      (2002) 6-9.
1715 IUVENCUS: **Heinsdorff, Cornel** Die Gespräche Christi mit Nikode-
      mus und mit der Samaritanerin (Ioh. 3 und 4) in der Bibeldichtung
      von Juvencus: Kommentar zu Iuvenc. 2.177/327. 2002, 399 pp. Diss.
      Bonn [RBen 114,204—P.-M. Bogaert].
1716 KAFKA F: *Battisti, Siegfried* Gottesfrage in zeitgenössischer Litera-
      tur: Versuch einer religiösen Interpretation von Kafkas Roman *Das
      Schloss* als Ort der Gnade. Religion—Literatur—Künste II. Im Kon-
      text 14: 2002 ⇒530. 178-189.
1717 KIPLING R: *Kreitzer, Larry J.* 'The son of God goes forth to war': bib-
      lical imagery in Ruyard Kipling's 'The man who would be king.' Bor-
      ders. JSOT.S 313: 2002 ⇒585. 99-125.
1718 KLOPSTOCK F: *Venier, Elio* Il 'Messias' di F.G. Klopstock 'il patriar-
      ca della letteratura'. Il volto dei volti 5/2 (2002) 56-71. Som. 71.
1719 LEOPARDI G: *Castronuovo, David* 'Templi deformi': le preghiere re-
      toriche di Giacomo Leopardi. La sorgente. 2002 ⇒315. 163-176.
1720 LEWIS C: *Walker, Andrew* Scripture, revelation and Platonism in C.S.
      Lewis. SJTh 55 (2002) 19-35.
1721 MANN T: *Frühwald, Wolfgang* Thomas Manns "Moses-Phantasie":
      zu der Erzählung "Das Gesetz" (1943). ᶠSMEND, R. 2002 ⇒113.
      296-309;
1722 **Golka, Friedemann W.** Joseph—biblische Gestalt und literarische
      Figur: Thomas Manns Beitrag zur Bibelexegese. Stu 2002, Calwer
      220 pp. €19.90. 3-7668-3788-5 [EuA 79,434];
1723 —; SINGER I: *Kurz, Paul Konrad* Die Gestalt des Büßers: in Roma-
      nen von Hermann Hesse, Thomas Mann, Albert Camus, Isaac B. Sin-
      ger. GuL 75 (2002) 98-110.
1724 MARGUERITE de Navarre: ᴱ**Marczuk, Barbara** Marguerite de Na-
      varre: les comédies bibliques. 2000 <1547> ⇒16,1399. ᴿBHR 64
      (2002) 214-217 (*Reyff, Simone de*); SCJ 33 (2002) 253-254 (*Rey-
      nolds-Cornell, Régine*).
1725 MILTON J: **Shoulson, Jeffrey** Milton and the rabbis: Hebraism, Hel-
      lenism, and christianity. 2001 ⇒17,1463. ᴿSCJ 33 (2002) 847-848
      (*Weidhorn, Manfred*);
1726 *Tournu, Christophe* John Milton, Dieu et la liberté. RHPhR 82/1
      (2002) 33-59;
1727 **Wood, Derek N.C.** Exiled from divine light: law, morality, and
      violence in Milton's *Samson Agonistes*. 2001 ⇒17,1464. ᴿSCJ 33
      (2002) 917-918 (*Spurr, Barry*).
1728 MORSELLI G: *Pierangeli, Fabio* Guido Morselli e l'uomo carità. La
      sorgente. 2002 ⇒315. 192-200.

1729 NONNOS P: ^{ET}**De Stefani, Claudio** Nonno di Panopoli: parafrasi del vangelo di S. Giovanni: canto I. Eikasmos 6: Bo 2002, Pàtron 260 pp. Introd., testo critico, trad., commento [Jn 1,1-18–REByz 61,266]

1730 O'CONNOR F: *Faricy, Robert* Apocalypse in the stories of Flannery O'Connor. Studies in Spirituality 12 (2002) 178-188.

1731 SADE D. de: **Schmid, Muriel** Le soufre au bord de la chair: Sade et l'évangile. 2001 ⇒17,1472. ^RETR 77 (2002) 288-290 (*Causse, Jean-Daniel*).

1732 SANTA CRUZ C: *Pereira, Armando de Sousa* Motivos bíblicos na historiografia de Santa Cruz de Coimbra dos finais do século XII. Lus-Sac 13-14 (2001-2002) 315-336.

1733 SCHILLER F: *Mor, Lucia* Il 'progetto' di Mosè: *Die Sendung Moses* di Friedrich Schiller fra misteri massonici e deismo. Hum(B) 57 (2002) 527-539;

1734 ^T*Frola, Maria Franca* Friedrich Schiller: La missione di Mosè. Hum(B) 57 (2002) 540-554.

1735 SIGONIO C: *Conti, Vittorio* Carlo Sigonio e il *De Republica Hebraeorum.* Il Pensiero Politico 35 (2002) 399-408.

1736 SPENSER E: **Kaske, Carol** Spenser and biblical poetics. 1999 ⇒15, 1317; 16,1411. ^RJR 82 (2002) 340-341 (*Wilson-Okamura, David S.*).

1737 TOLKIEN J: *Garbowski, Christopher* Tolkien's eschatology of hope: from Ragnarok to joyous subcreation. Apocalyptic. JSPE.S 43: 2002 ⇒373. 271-283.

1738 TOURNIER M: *Boitani, Piero* La sorgente e il roveto: il ritorno a Mosè di Michel Tournier. La sorgente. 2002 ⇒315. 201-213.

1739 UCHIDA Y: *Matsuoka, Fumitaka* America seen through a different lens: the bible in the works of Yoshiko Uchida. Semeia 90/91 (2002) 181-193.

1740 WALZER M: *Riva, Franco* Morali dell'Esodo in Michael Walzer. Hermeneutica (2002) 263-281.

1741 WERFEL F: *Palaver, Wolfgang* Gnade und Schuld in Franz Werfels Roman *Eine blassblaue Frauenschrift.* Religion—Literatur—Künste II. Im Kontext 14: 2002 ⇒530. 202-216.

B4.7 *Interpretatio* **psychiatrica**

1742 *Boer, Roland* MARX, method and Gottwald. Tracking the tribes. JSOT.S 351: 2002 ⇒455. 98-156.

1743 *Fenn, Richard K.* Dread of the community?: a psychoanalytical study of fratricidal conflict in the context of first-century Palestine. Handbook of early christianity. 2002 ⇒275. 599-618.

1744 *Gottwald, Norman K.; Boer, Roland* Political activism and biblical scholarship: an interview;

1745 *Gottwald, Norman K.* Response to the contributors. Tracking the tribes. JSOT.S 351: 2002 ⇒455. 157-171/172-185.

1746 **Kille, D. Andrew** Psychological biblical criticism. 2000 ⇒16,1423. ^RRBLit 4 (2002) 108-110 (*Mandolfo, Carleen*).

1747 *Kille, D. Andrew* Psychology and the bible: three worlds of the text. PastPsy 51/2 (2002) 125-134 [NTAb 47,8].

1748 **Merkur, Dan** The mystery of manna: the psychedelic sacrament of the bible. 2000 ⇒16,1425; 17,1496. ^RRBLit 4 (2002) 170-173 (*Hodges, Horace Jeffrey*).

1749   *Mosala, Itumeleng* The politics of debt and the liberation of the scriptures. Tracking the tribes. JSOT.S 351: 2002 ⇒455. 77-84.

1750   **Pfeifer, Samuel** Die Schwachen tragen: moderne Psychiatrie und biblische Seelsorge. Ba 2002 <1988>, Brunnen 220 pp. €19.80. 3-7655-1266-4 [RTL 35,116s—Ph. Weber].

1751   *Philipp, Thomas* In Beziehung mit dem Text: psychologische Auslegungen und deren Reichweite. [Drewermann, E.] Orien. 66 (2002) 127-131, 137-140 [Mk 5].

1752   **Polka, Brayton** Depth psychology interpretation and the bible: an ontological essay on FREUD. 2001 ⇒17,1498. [R]SR 31 (2002) 474-477 (*Rollins, Wayne G.*).

1753   *Quaglia, Rocco* L'uomo biblico in FREUD e JUNG. I sogni. 2002 ⇒ 227. 99-106.

1754   *Rashkow, I.N.* The hermeneutical agenda: between text and reader. PastPsy 51/2 (2002) 151-155 [NTAb 47,11].

1755   **Rollins, Wayne Gilbert** Soul and psyche: the bible in psychological perspective. 1999 ⇒15,1326; 17,1499. [R]PastPsy 51/2 (2002) 135-149 (*Underwood, R.L.*); PastPsy 51/2 (2002) 119-123 (*Ellens, J.H.*).

1756   *Rollins,W.G.* The bible in psycho-spiritual perspective: news from the world of biblical scholarship. Pastoral Psychology 51/2 (2002) 101-118.

1757   *Wahl, Heribert* L'uomo FREUD e il suo *Mosè* monoteistico. Hum(B) 57 (2002) 555-575.

B5 Methodus exegeticus

1758   *Anderson, R. Dean* The use and abuse of LAUSBERG in biblical studies. Rhetorical argumentation. 2002 ⇒553. 66-76.

1759   *Barton, John* Thinking about reader-response criticism. ET 113 (2002) 147-151.

1760   *Bormann, Lukas* Bibelauslegung als Kraft gesellschaftlicher Änderung. ITE 11 (2002) 159-169.

1761   *Bressolette, Michel* La lecture de la bible à l'Université: enjeux et défis. Les nouvelles voies. LeDiv 190: 2002 ⇒583. 57-71.

1762   *Briggs, Richard S.* The implied author and the creation of the world: a test case in reader-response criticism. ET 113 (2002) 264-270.

1763   **Brown, Raymond E.** Croire en la bible, à l'heure de l'exégèse. [T]*Degorce, Jean-Bernard*: Lire la bible 123: P 2002, Cerf 224 pp. €18. 2-204-06791-1 [R]Brot. 154 (2002) 407-408 (*Silva, I. Ribeiro da*).

1764   *Bultmann, Rudolf* Das Problem einer theologischen Exegese des Neuen Testaments. NT und christliche Existenz. UTB 2316: 2002 <1925> ⇒152. 13-38.

1765   **Buss, Martin J.** Biblical form criticism in its context. JSNT.S 274: 1999 ⇒15,1341; 16,1440. [R]JBL 121 (2002) 150-152 (*Sweeney, Marvin A.*).

1766   **Classen, Carl Joachim** Rhetorical criticism of the New Testament. WUNT 128: 2000 ⇒16,145; 17,1510. [R]ThG 45 (2002) 298-300 (*Giesen, Heinz*).

1767   *Daley, Brian E.* Is patristic exgesis still usable?: reflections on the early christian interpretation of the Psalms. Com(US) 29/1 (2002) 185-216.

1768   *Debergé, Pierre* L'exégèse aujourd'hui: déplacements et ouvertures. Les nouvelles voies. LeDiv 190: 2002 ⇒583. 349-356.

1769 **Deist, Ferdinand** Ervaring, rede en metode in skrifuitleg: 'n weten-skaps-historiese ondersoek na skrifuitleg in die Ned. Geref. Kerk 1840-1990. 1994 ⇒13,1158; 14,1186. [R]Scriptura 78 (2001) 467-478 (*Lombaard, Christo J.S.*).

1770 *Dorival, Gilles* Exégèse juive et exégèse chrétienne. Der Kommentar. 2002 ⇒472. 131-150.

1771 **Dreytza, M.; Hilbrands, W.; Schmid, H.** Das Studium des Alten Testaments: eine Einführung in die Methoden der Exegese. BWM 10: Wu 2002, Brockhaus 213 pp.

1772 *Duval, Danièle; Kuntzmann, Raymond* Synthèse finale. Typologie biblique. LeDiv: 2002 ⇒341. 267-274.

1773 **Fee, Gordon D.** New Testament exegesis: a handbook for students and pastors. LVL [3]2002, Westminster xxviii; 195 pp. 0-664-22316-8.

1774 **Gillingham, Susan E.** The image, the depths and the surface: multi-valent approaches to biblical study. JSOT.S 354: Shf 2002, Sheffield A. xi; 147 pp. 1-84127-297-3. Bibl. 128-137.

1775 **Gorman, Michael J.** Elements of biblical exegesis: a basic guide for students and ministers. 2001 ⇒17,1518. [R]RBLit 4 (2002) 100-102 (*Campbell, William Sanger*).

1776 *Haacker, Klaus* Par la foi ou par la vue?: une alternative fondamentale pour la méthodologie des sciences bibliques. Hokhma 78 (2001) 22-34 [BuBB 39,47]..

1777 *Hall, Stuart George* Typologie. TRE 34. 2002 ⇒800. 208-224.

1778 *Halligan, John M.* 'Where angels fear to tread..': an account of the development of the social-scientific approach to the study of the ancient world. [F]FLANAGAN, J.: JSOT.S 359: 2002 ⇒38. 202-218.

1779 *Holmes, Jeremy* The spiritual sense of scripture. DR 120 (2002) 113-128.

1780 *Husser, Jean-Marie* La typologie comme procédé de composition dans les textes de l'Ancien Testament. Typologie biblique. LeDiv: 2002 ⇒341. 11-34.

1781 **Jonker, Louis Cloete** Exclusivity and variety: perspectives on multi-dimensional exegesis. CBET 19: 1996 ⇒12,958... 16,1460. [R]Scriptura 78 (2001) 467-478 (*Lombaard, Christo J.S.*).

1782 *Jódar Estrella, Carlos* La búsqueda del evento en la estructura testimonial de la revelación bíblica. RevAg 43 (2002) 371-390.

1783 *Kannengiesser, Charles* A key to the future of patristics: the 'senses' of scripture. [F]WILKEN, R.: 2002 ⇒136. 90-106.

1784 *Kerbs, Raúl* El método histórico-crítico en teología: en busca de su estructura básica y de las interpretaciones filosóficas subyacentes (parte 1). DavarLogos 1 (2002) 105-123.

1785 *Kraus, Manfred* Theories and practice of the enthymeme in the first centuries B.C.E. and C.E. Rhetorical argumentation. 2002 ⇒553. 95-111 [Rom 2,21-23].

1786 [E]**Kreuzer, Siegfried,** *al.,* Proseminar—Altes Testament: ein Arbeits-buch. 1999 ⇒15,1365; 17,1528. [R]OTEs 15 (2002) 295-296 (*Van der Merwe, C.H.J.*).

1787 **Krispenz, Jutta** Literarkritik und Stilstatistik im Alten Testament: eine Studie zur literarkritischen Methode, durchgeführt an Texten aus den Büchern Jer., Ezech. und 1 Kön.. BZAW 307: 2001 ⇒17,1529. [R]BZ 46 (2002) 316-319 (*Stipp, Hermann-Josef*); OLZ 97 (2002) 544-550 (*Stahl, Rainer*); RBLit (2002)* (*Premstaller, Volkmar*).

1788 *Langner, Córdula* La exégesis como testimonio fe. Qol 29 (2002) 3-24.

1789   *Lombaard, Christo; Le Roux, Jurie* Wat dateer ons?: enkele opmerk-
       ings rondom die datering van bybelse tekste. HTS 58 (2002) 1855-
       1867 [OTA 26,412].
1790   *Marchadour, Alain* La lecture de la bible hier et aujourd'hui: état de
       la question. Les nouvelles voies. LeDiv 190: 2002 ⇒583. 25-55.
1791   *Mathewson, Daniel B.* A critical binarism: source criticism and
       deconstructive criticism. JSOT 98 (2002) 3-28.
1792   *Matson, Mark A.* False dichotomies in gospel studies. RestQ 44/3
       (2002) 129-138.
1793   *Meynet, Roland* The question at the center: a specific device of
       rhetorical argumentation in scripture. Rhetorical argumentation. 2002
       ⇒553. 200-214.
1794   *Naluparayil* Reader-response criticism: a theoretical framework for
       multiple interpretations of biblical texts. BiBh 28 (2002) 558-564.
1795   *Naro, Massimo* Mistica e interpretazione della scrittura: i fondamenti
       dell'esegesi spirituale di Divo Barsotti. Ho Theológos 20 (2002) 43-
       68.
1796   *Noble, Paul R.* Esau, Tamar, and Joseph: criteria for identifying
       inner-biblical allusions. VT 52 (2002) 219-252.
1797   *Pilhofer, Peter* Zur lokalgeschichtlichen Methode. Die frühen Chri-
       sten. WUNT 145: 2002 <1998> ⇒225. 1-57.
1798   **Reis, Pamela Tamarkin** Reading the lines: a fresh look at the He-
       brew Bible. Peabody, MASS 2002, Hendrickson x; 227 pp. $25. 1-
       56563-696-1.
1799   **Reiser, Marius** Sprache und literarische Formen des Neuen Testa-
       ments: eine Einführung. UTB für Wissenschaft 2197: 2001 ⇒17,
       1543. ᴿBZ 46 (2002) 273-274 (*Wehr, Lothar*).
1800   *Robbins, Vernon K.* Argumentative textures in socio-rhetorical inter-
       pretation. Rhetorical argumentation. 2002 ⇒553. 27-65.
1801   *Roberts, J.J.M.* Historical-critical method, theology, and contempo-
       rary exegesis. The bible and the ANE. 2002 <1995> ⇒230. 393-405.
1802   *Rösel, Martin; Merk, Otto* Traditionskritik/Traditionsgeschichte.
       TRE 33. 2002 ⇒799. 732-750.
1803   *Sanders, John* On heffalumps and heresies. Journal of Biblical
       Studies 2/1 (2002)*.
1804   *Smelik, Klaas A.* Verwijzingen in de Hebreeuwse Bijbel. AnBru 7
       (2002) 184-197.
1805   **Talstra, Eep** Oude en nieuwe lezers: een inleiding in de methoden
       van uitleg van het Oude Testament. Kampen 2002, Kok 320 pp. 90-
       435-0502-1 [Streven 70,179s—Beentjes, Panc].
1806   *Telford, William R.* Modern bible interpretation. Biblical world, 2.
       2002 ⇒273. 427-449.
1807   *Thurén, Lauri* Is there biblical argumentation?;
1808   *Van Emeren, Frans H.* Argumentation theory: an overview of ap-
       proaches and research themes. Rhetorical argumentation. 2002 ⇒
       553. 77-92/7-26.
1809   *Wendland, Ernst R.* Aspects of rhetorical analysis applied to New
       Testament texts. Handbook of early christianity. 2002 ⇒275. 169-95.
1810   **Weren, Wim J.C.** Finestre su Gesù: metodologia dell'esegesi dei
       vangeli. ᵀ*Soggin, Thomas*: Strumenti 8: 2001 ⇒17,1558. ᴿTer. 53
       (2002) 608-611 (*Pasquetto, Virgilio*).
1811   *Weyermann, Maja* The typologies of Adam-Christ and Eve-Mary,
       and their relationship to one another. AThR 84 (2002) 609-626.

1812 *Wortham, Robert A.* Statistical textual analysis: a special technique. Handbook of early christianity. 2002 ⇒275. 147-167.
1813 **Young, Frances Margaret** Biblical exegesis and the formation of christian culture. 1997 ⇒13,1219... 15,1408. [R]Religion 32 (2002) 147-148 (*Bauman-Martin, Betsy J.*).

III. Critica Textus, Versiones

D1 Textual Criticism

1814 [E]**Sharpe, John L.; Van Kampen, Kimberly** The bible as book, 1: the manuscript tradition. L 2002, British Library xi; 260 pp. 0-7123-4522-1. Rpr.

1815 *Clarkson, Christopher* Some representations of the book and book-making, from the earliest codex forms to Jost Amman;
1816 *Hamel, Christopher de* Books of hours: 'imaging' the word;
1817 *Hunt, Lucy-Anne* Cultural transmission: illustrated biblical manuscripts from the medieval eastern christian and Arab worlds. The bible as book. 2002 ⇒1814. 197-203/137-143/123-136.
1818 *Letis, Theodore P.* From lower criticism to higher criticism: Joseph PRIESTLEY and the use of conjectural emendation. JHiC 9/1 (2002) 31-48.
1819 **Letis, Theodore P.** The ecclesiastical text: text criticism, biblical authority and the popular mind. [2]2000 <1997> ⇒16,1506; 17,1561. [R]EvQ 74 (2002) 78-80 (*Gribben, Crawford*).
1820 *Louth, Andrew* The theology of the Word made flesh. The bible as book. 2002 ⇒1814. 223-228.
1821 *Lust, Johan* Textual criticism of the Old and New Testaments: step-brothers?. [F]DELOBEL, J.: BEThL 161: 2002 ⇒24. 15-31.
1822 *Nolcken, Christina von* Lay literacy, the democratization of God's law, and the Lollards. The bible as book. 2002 ⇒1814. 177-195.
1823 **Parker, David C.** The living text of the gospels. 1997 ⇒13,1273... 16,1508. [R]EvQ 74 (2002) 359-361 (*Head, Peter M.*).
1824 *Pattie, Thomas S.* The creation of the great codices;
1825 *Sharpe, John; McKendrick, Scot; Van Kampen, Kimberly* Introduction. The bible as book. 2002 ⇒1814. 61-72./1-8.
1826 *Spottorno, Maria Victoria* The textual significance of Spanish polyglot bibles. Sef. 62 (2002) 375-392.
1827 *Van der Kooij, Arie; Aland, Barbara* Textgeschichte/Textkritik der Bibel. TRE 33. 2002 ⇒799. 148-168.
1828 *Verey, Christopher* A Northumbrian text family. The bible as book. 2002 ⇒1814. 105-122.
1829 *Wetzel, Christoph* Prachthandschriften der Bibel;
1830 *Ziehr, Wilhelm* Die Bibel: Gottes Wort;
1831 Buchrollen und Codices. Die Bibel: Geschichte und Gegenwart. 2002 ⇒971. 174-175/8-13, 16-23, 26-33/14-15.

D2.1 *Biblia Hebraica* Hebrew text

1832   *Breuer, Mordechai* Three editions of the bible. Leš. 64/1-2 (2002) 33-50. Sum. I. **H.**

1833   **Chiesa, Bruno** Filologia storica della bibbia ebraica, 1:da ORIGENE al Medioevo. StBi 125: 2000 ⇒16,1515(a). ᴿCivCatt 153/1 (2002) 409-411 (*Prato, G.L.*);

1834   2: dall'età moderna ai giorni nostri. StBi 135: Brescia 2002, Paideia 241-501 pp. €20. 88-394-0644-1 [RB 110,154].

1835   *Clines, David J.A.* What remains of the Hebrew Bible?: its text and language in a postmodern age. StTh 56 (2002) 76-95.

1836   ᴱ**Dotan, Aron** Biblia Hebraica Leningradensia: prepared according to the vocalization, accents, and masora of Aaron ben Moses ben Asher in the Leningrad Codex. 2001 ⇒17,1565. ᴿSWJT 45/1 (2002) 76-77 (*Johnson, Rick*).

1837   *Freedman, David Noel; Dolansky Overton, Shawna* Omitting the omissions: the case for haplography in the transmission of the biblical texts. ᶠFLANAGAN, J.: JSOT.S 359: 2002 ⇒38. 99-116 [Dt 7,1].

1838   *Gottlieb, Leeor* Repetition due to homoeoteleuton. Textus 21 (2002) 21-43.

1839   *Herbst, Adrián* Los textos de Qumrán, el pentateuco samaritano y la crítica textual de la biblia hebrea. RevBib 63 (2001) 129-151,

1840   JPS Hebrew-English Tanakh: the traditional Hebrew text and the new JPS translation. ²1999 <1985> ⇒15,1593; 17,1570. ᴿRBLit 4 (2002) 180-182 (*Sweeney, Marvin A.*).

1841   **Kelley, Page H.; Mynatt, Daniel Stephen; Crawford, Timothy G.** The Masorah of Biblia Hebraica Stuttgartensia: introduction and annotated glossary. 1998 ⇒14,1245...17,1571. ᴿSWJT 45/1 (2002) 78 (*Johnson, Rick*).

1842   *Kreuzer, Siegfried* Text, Textgeschichte und Textkritik des Alten Testaments: zum Stand der Forschung an der Wende des Jahrhunderts. ThLZ 127 (2002) 127-155.

1843   *Levinson, Bernard M.* Textual criticism, assyriology, and the history of interpretation: Deuteronomy 13:7a as a test case in method. JBL 120 (2001) 211-243.

1844   *Loader, James Alfred* The finality of the Old Testament 'final text'. OTEs 15 (2002) 739-753.

1845   *Mashiah, Rahel; Sharvit, Uri* Two issues regarding the biblical accents of the '21 books': a linguistic-ethnomusicological interdisciplinary study. Tarbiz 71 (2002) 433-447. Sum. viii. **H.**

1846   *McCarthy, Carmel* Text and versions: the Old Testament. Biblical world, 1. 2002 ⇒273. 207-228.

1847   *Ofer, Yosef* A new edition of the bible. Leš. 64/3-4 (2002) 181-206. Keter Yerushalayim; Sum. I. **H.**;

1848   A Masoretic note in the Aleppo codex concerning the composite words. Textus 21 (2002) 209-233.

1849   *Penkower, Jordan S.* A sheet of parchment from a 10th or 11th century Torah scroll: determining its type among four traditions (Oriental, Sefardi, Ashkenazi, Yemenite). Textus 21 (2002) 235-264.

1850   *Pilocane, Chiara* Frammenti di un antico manoscritto biblico italiano (Sec. XI) dagli archivi modenesi. Materia giudaica. 2002 ⇒727. 38-46.

1851 *Ramirez, Rojohn Bernardino* The eternal word in dead language: a study of the Masoretic Text and cryptology. ICSTJ 4 (2002) 64-82.

1852 *Schorch, Stefan* Die hebräische Sprachgeschichte und die Vokalisierung(en) der Hebräischen Bibel. KUSATU 3 (2002) 55-70.

1853 *Sed-Rajna, Gabrielle* The image as exegetical tool: paintings in medieval Hebrew manuscripts of the bible. The bible as book. 2002 ⇒1814. 215-221.

1854 *Tov, Emanuel* Copying of a biblical scroll. JRH 26 (2002) 189-209;

1855 The status of the Masoretic Text in modern text editions of the Hebrew Bible: the relevance of canon. Canon debate. 2002 ⇒1519. 234-251.

1856 **Tov, Emmanuel** Textual criticism of the Hebrew Bible. ²2001 ⇒17, 1581. ᴿRSR 90 (2002) 441-443 (*Paul, André*); LASBF 51 (2001) 401-412 (*Pierri, R.*); RBLit (2002)* (*Konkel, Gus*).

1857 *Turan, Sinai* The history of Hebrew punctuation—introductory chapters. Tarbiz 71 (2002) 449-530. Sum. ix. **H**.

1858 *Ulrich, Eugene* The text of the Hebrew scriptures at the time of Hillel and Jesus. Congress vol. Basel 2001. VT.S 92: 2002 ⇒570. 85-108.

1859 ᴱ**Weil, Gérard E.** Massorah Gedolah: iuxta codicem Leningradensem B19a, 1: catalogi. 2001 <1971> ⇒17,1582. ᴿATG 65 (2002) 316-317 (*Torres, A.*).

1860 *Weis, R.D. Biblia Hebraica Quinta* and the making of crirical editions of the Hebrew Bible. TC: a journal of biblical textual criticism [http://purl.org/TC] 7 (2002) pars. 1-42 [NTAb 47,534].

1861 *Zatelli, Ida* The collection of 16th century bibles in the Central National Library of Florence: the importance of Jewish culture. Studies in Hebrew language and literature. 2002 ⇒704. 80-85. Sum. x. **H**.

D2.2 Targum

1862 ᴱ**Girón Blanc, Luis-Fernando** Narraciones bíblicas de la creación: edición y estudio comparativo. Revista de Ciencias de las Religiones 7: M 2002, Univ. Complutense 139 pp .

1863 *Alarcon Sainz, Juan José* Targum: las versiones arameas de la biblia hebrea. Narraciones bíblicas. 2002 ⇒1862. 63-73 [BuBB 37,9] [Gen 1,1-2,4].

1864 *Alexander, Philip S.* Notes on some targums of the targum of the Song of Songs. ᶠCLARKE, E. 2002 ⇒16. 159-174.

1865 *Beattie, Derek R.G.* The targum of Ruth: a preliminary edition. ᶠCLARKE, E. 2002 ⇒16. 231-290.

1866 **Bengstsson, Per Å.** Passover in Targum Pseudo-Jonathan Genesis. 2001 ⇒17,1586. ᴿJSJ 33 (2002) 92-94 (*Houtman, Alberdina*); JQR 92 (2002) 317-319 (*Tabory, Joseph*).

1867 *Bernstein, Moshe J.* The Aramaic versions of Deuteronomy 32: a study in comparative targumic theology;

1868 *Brady, Christian M.M.* Targum Lamentations 1:1-4: a theological prologue;

1869 *Campbell, R.M.* Parashiyyot and their implications for dating the fragment-targums;

1870 *Chilton, Bruce* 'HEBR. 75' in the Bibliothèque Nationale;

1871 *Cook, Edward M.* The Psalms Targum: introduction to a new translation, with sample texts. [F]CLARKE, E. 2002 ⇒16. 29-52/175-183./105-114/141-148/185-201.
DBS: Suppl. au dictionnaire de la bible: Targum 2002 ⇒782.

1872 *Díez Merino, L.* Translation of proper names: a targumic method of hermeneutics in Targum Esther. [F]CLARKE, E. 2002 ⇒16. 203-223.

1873 *Fine, Steven* 'Their faces shine with the brightness of the firmament': study houses and synagogues in the targumim to the pentateuch. Biblical translation. 2002 ⇒338. 63-92.

1874 [E]**Flesher, Paul V.M.** Targum Studies, II: Targum and Peshitta. SF-SHJ 165: 1998 ⇒14,238...17,266. [R]RBLit 4 (2002) 283-285 (*Garber, Zev*).

1875 *Flesher, Paul V.M.* Targum as scripture. [F]CLARKE, E. 2002 ⇒16. 61-75 [Gen 4].

1876 **Grossfeld, Bernard** Targum Neofiti, 1:an exegetical commentary to Genesis including full rabbinic parallels. [E]**Schiffman, Lawrence H.** 2000 ⇒16,1547; 17,1597. [R]JSJ 33 (2002) 331-333 (*Ribera-Florit, Josep*); JSSt 47 (2002) 352-355 (*McNamara, Martin*); REJ 161 (2002) 505-506 (*Rothschild, Jean-Pierre*); Bib. 83 (2002) 296-301 (*Díez Merino, Luis*).

1877 *Hayward, C.T.R.* Targum Pseudo-Jonathan and the bread of the presence. [F]CLARKE, E. 2002 ⇒16. 115-128 [Exod 25,30].

1878 *Himbaza, Innocent* Le poème acrostiche sur Exode xx 1-5 dans le targum fragmentaire (MS G). VT 52 (2002) 42-50.

1879 *Klein, Michael L.* Targumic studies and the Cairo Genizah. The Cambridge Genizah collections. 2002 ⇒698. 47-58.

1880 *Kvam, Bjørn Olav Grüner* "Come, let the two of us go out into the field": the Targum supplement to Genesis 4:8a—a text-immanent reading?. [F]CLARKE, E. 2002 ⇒16. 97-103.

1881 *Le Déaut, Roger* Targum et Nouveau Testament. SIDIC 35/2-3 (2002 <1976>) 37-39.

1882 *Mangan, Celine* Blessing and cursing in the prologue of Targum Job;
1883 *McNamara, Martin* Towards an English synoptic presentation of the pentateuchal targums. [F]CLARKE, E. 2002 ⇒16. 225-229/3-27.

1884 [E]**Moor, Johannes de** A bilingual concordance to the targum of the prophets 9: Isaiah 1: ' (Aleph) - z (Zajin). Lei 2002, Brill vi; 348 pp. €114/$133. 90-04-12636-8;

1885 10: Isaiah 2: ḥ (Hêt) - s (Samek). Lei 2002, Brill 375 pp. €114/$133. 90-04-12637-6;

1886 10: Isaiah 3: ' (Ajin) - t (Tâw). Lei 2002, Brill 486 pp. €114/$133. 90-04-12638-4.

1887 *Mortensen, Beverly P.* Pseudo-Jonathan's temple, symbol of Judaism. [F]CLARKE, E. 2002 ⇒16. 129-137.

1888 *Penkower, Jordan S.* The textual transmission of Targum: Jonathan and KIMHI's commentary on Ezekiel 23:20 and 34:18. Shnaton 13 (2002) 247-270. **H**.

1889 *Ribera-Florit, Josep* Some doctrinal aspects of the targum of Ezekiel. [F]CLARKE, E. 2002 ⇒16. 149-156.

1890 *Smelik, Willem F.* How to grow a tree: computerised stemmatology and variant selection in targum studies. Bible and computer. 2002 ⇒548. 495-518.

1891 *Stuckenbruck, Loren T.; Freedman, David Noel* The fragments of a targum to Leviticus in Qumran cave 4 (4Q156): a linguistic comparison and assessment. [F]CLARKE, E. 2002 ⇒16. 79-95.

1892 *Syrén, Roger* Text and community: the case of the targums. [F]CLARKE, E. 2002 ⇒16. 53-59 [Ex 4,24-26].

1893 **Van Staalduine-Sulman, Eveline** The Targum of Samuel. [D]*Moor, J.C. de*: Studies in the Aramaic interpretation of Scripture 1: Lei 2002, Brill xiv; 767 pp. €139/$162. 90-04-12164-1. Diss. Kampen.

1894 *Veltri, Giuseppe* Eine targumische Übersezung zur Zeit Esras?: eine sprachgeschichtliche und historische Frage <1993>; .

1895 Der griechische Targum Aquilas. Gegenwart der Tradition. 2002 <1994> ⇒255. 55-74/75-103.

D3.1 *Textus graecus*—Greek NT

1896 *Aland, Barbara* Kriterien zur Beurteilung kleinerer Papyrusfragmente des Neuen Testaments. [F]DELOBEL, J.: BEThL 161: 2002 ⇒24. 1-13.

1897 [E]**Black, David Alan** Rethinking New Testament textual criticism. GR 2002, Baker 157 pp. $17. 0-8010-2280-0;

1898 *Black, David Alan* Introduction. Rethinking... 11-15.

1899 [E]**Brown, Andrew J.** Novum Testamentum ab ERASMO recognitum, 2: evangelium secundum Iohannem et Acta Apostolorum. Opera Omnia 6/2: Amst 2001, Elsevier 516 pp. €204. 0-444-50942-9.

1900 *Clarke, Kent D.* Textual certainty in the United Bible Societies' Greek New Testament. NT 44 (2002) 105-133.

1901 *Ehrman, B.D.* Text and tradition: the role of New Testament manuscripts in early christian studies. TC: a journal of biblical textual criticism [http://purl.org/TC] 5 (2000) pars. 1-62 (part 1), pars. 1-64 (part 2) [NTAb 47,428].

1902 *Elliott, J.K.* The case for thoroughgoing eclecticism. Rethinking NT textual criticism. 2002 ⇒1897. 101-124.

1903 *Emmel, Stephen* The christian book in Egypt: innovation and the Coptic tradition. The bible as book. 2002 ⇒1814. 35-43.

1904 *Epp, Eldon Jay* Issues in New Testament textual criticism: moving from the nineteenth century to the twenty-first century. Rethinking NT textual criticism. 2002 ⇒1897. 17-76.

1905 Greek-English New Testament. [E]**Aland, Kurt; Aland, Barbara**: Stu 2001, Dt. Bibelges. x; 46, 812 pp. 3-438-05408-6 9. rev. ed.; Greek text Novum Testamentum Graece, in the tradition of Nestle; Engl. text 2nd ed. of the RSV.

1906 *Hohnjec, Nikola* Predstavljanje Vatikanskog kodeksa B. Papina donacija faksimil izdanja za zadarska zbirku Biblija: (Vat. Graec. 1209, B). BoSm 72 (2002) 521-541. **Croatian**.

1907 *Holmes, Michael W.* The case for reasoned eclecticism. Rethinking NT textual criticism. 2002 ⇒1897. 77-100.

1908 *Maisano, Riccardo* Filologia neotestamentaria e filologia bizantina: riflessioni sulle problematiche comuni e gli indirizzi attuali. RdT 43 (2002) 892-909.

1909 [E]**Nestle, E.; Aland, Kurt** Novum Testamentum Graece. [27]2001 ⇒ 17,1609. 8th repr. [R]NT 44 (2002) 297-301 (*Elliott, J.K.*).

1910 *Nicklas, Tobias* Zur historischen und theologischen Bedeutung der Erforschung neutestamentlicher Textgeschichte. NTS 48 (2002) 145-158.

1911 *O'Reilly, Jennifer* Gospel harmony and the names of Christ: insular images of a patristic theme. The bible as book. 2002 ⇒1814. 73-88.

1912   *Parker, David* Text and versions: the New Testament. Biblical world,
       1. 2002 ⇒273. 229-249.
1913   *Parker, D.C.; Morrill, M.B.* Some new manuscripts of the Greek
       New Testament in Boston and Cambridge. HThR 95 (2002) 237-244.
1914   **Perrier, Pierre** Évangiles de l'oral à l'écrit. Évangiles de l'oral à
       l'écrit 1: P 2000, Éd. du Jubilé 304 pp. 2-86679-2963. Bibl. 267-269.
1915   *Robinson, Maurice A.* Crossing boundaries in New Testament textual
       criticism: historical revisionism and the case of Frederick Henry Am-
       brose Scrivener. TC: a journal of biblical textual criticism [http://
       purl.org/TC] 7 (2002) pars. 1-77 [NTAb 47,429];
1916   New Testament textual criticism: the case for Byzantine priority. TC:
       a journal of biblical textual criticism [http://purl.org/TC] 6 (2001)
       pars. 1-113 [NTAb 47,429];
1917   The case for Byzantine priority;
1918   *Silva, Moisés* Response. Rethinking NT textual criticism. 2002 ⇒
       1897. 125-139/141-150.
1919   *Spencer, M.; Wachtel, K.; Howe, C.J.* The Greek Vorlage of the Syra
       Harclensis: a comparative study on method in exploring textual
       genealogy;
1920   *Thorpe, J.C.* Multivariate statistical analysis for manuscript classifi-
       cation. TC: a journal of biblical textual criticism [http://purl.org/TC]
       7 (2002) pars. 1-46, 1-65 [NTAb 47: 429, 430].
1921   *Trobisch, David* From New Testament manuscripts to a central elec-
       tronic database. Bible and computer. 2002 ⇒548. 427-433.
1922   **Trobisch, David** The first edition of the New Testament. 2000 ⇒16,
       1584. [R]JThS 53 (2002) 298-305 (*Parker, D.C.*).
1923   *Zamagni, Claudio* Un art de l'"optimisme textuel" néotestamentaire?:
       étude critique d'après un travail de K.D. Clarke. RivBib 50 (2002)
       421-443.

D3.2 *Versiones graecae*—**VT, Septuaginta etc.**

1924   *Baumgarten, Albert I.* Bilingual Jews and the Greek Bible. Shem.
       JSJ.S 74: 2002 ⇒755. 13-30.
1925   **Beck, John A.** Translators as storytellers: a study in Septuagint trans-
       lation technique. Studies in biblical literature 25: 2000 ⇒16,1586;
       17,1621. [R]CBQ 64 (2002) 368-369 (*O'Loughlin, Thomas*).
1926   *Bons, Eberhard* Das Projekt "Septuaginta Deutsch" im Kontext ge-
       genwärtiger Septuaginta-Forschung. BiLi 75 (2002) 274-282;
1927   Ein Blick in die Werkstatt der Septuaginta Deutsch. BiLi 75 (2002)
       282-287 [Ps 7].
1928   *Bruin, Wim de* Interpreting delimiters: the complexity of text delimi-
       tation in four major Septuagint manuscripts. Studies in scriptural unit
       division. Pericope 3: 2002 ⇒339. 66-89.
1929   *Cardona Ramírez, Hernán* La biblia de los Setenta de ayer a hoy.
       CuesTF 29 (2002) 319-342.
1930   *Clancy, Frank* The date of LXX. SJOT 16 (2002) 207-225.
1931   **Collins, Nina L.** The library in Alexandria and the Bible in Greek.
       VT.S 82: 2000 ⇒16,1589. [R]JSJ 33 (2002) 97-101 (*Fernández
       Marcos, N.*).
1932   *Cook, Johann* NETS—a new English translation for the Septuagint.
       OTEs 15 (2002) 600-615.

1933 *Dafni, Evangelia G.* Theologie der Sprache der Septuaginta. ThZ 58 (2002) 315-328.
1934 *Evans, Trevor V.* Some alleged confusions in translation from Hebrew to Greek. Bib. 83 (2002) 238-248.
1935 *Fernández Marcos, Natalio* The other Septuagint: from the letter of Aristeas to the letter of Jeremiah. JNSL 28/2 (2002) 27-41.
1936 **Fernández Marcos, Natalio** Introducción a las versiones griegas de la Biblia. TECC 64: [2]1998 ⇒14,1301...17,1634. [R]RBLit (2002)* (*Floyd, Michael H.*);
1937 La bibbia dei Settanta: introduzione alle versioni greche della bibbia. [E]*Zoroddu, Donatella*: Introduzione allo studio della bibbia, supplementi 6: 2000 ⇒16,1594; 17,1635. [R]Asprenas 49 (2002) 433-436 (*Di Palma, Gaetano*); CivCatt 153/1 (2002) 100 (*Scaiola, D.*);
1938 The Septuagint in context: introduction to the Greek versions of the bible. [T]*Watson, Wilfred G.E.*: 2000 ⇒16,1595. [R]JSJ 33 (2002) 103-104 (*Hilhorst, A.*); ThGl 92 (2002) 291-292 (*Herr, Bertram*).
1939 **Hengel, Martin** The Septuagint as christian scripture: its prehistory and the problem of its canon. [T]*Biddle, Mark E.*: Old Testament studies: E 2002, Clark xvi; 153 pp. £25. 0-567-08737-9. Assistance of *Roland Deines*; introduction by *Robert Hanhart*; Bibl. xv-xvi.
1940 **Jobes, Karen H.; Silva, Moisés** Invitation to the Septuagint. 2000 ⇒16,1601; 17,1648. [R]JSJ 33 (2002) 105-107 (*Hilhorst, A.*); TS 63 (2002) 162-164 (*Knobloch, Frederick W.*); CBQ 64 (2002) 138-140 (*Williams, Tyler F.*); NT 44 (2002) 407-409 (*Elliott, J.K.*); AUSS 40 (2002) 333-35 (*Taylor, Bernard*); TrinJ 23 (2002) 257-260 (*DeRouchie, Jason S.*); RBLit 4 (2002) 7-32 [Resp. BIOSCS 35 (2002) 43-46] (*Barr, James*); LASBF 52 (2002) 542-556 (*Pierri, Rosario*).
1941 *Joosten, Jan* Biblical Hebrew as mirrored in the Septuagint: the question of influence from spoken Hebrew. Textus 21 (2002) 1-19.
1942 *Larsson, Gerhard* Septuagint versus Massoretic chronology. ZAW 114 (2002) 511-521.
1943 *McLay, R. Timothy* Beyond textual criticism: the use of the Septuagint in NT research. JNSL 28/1 (2002) 69-85.
1944 **Muraoka, Takamitsu** A Greek-English lexicon of the Septuagint: chiefly of the pentateuch and twelve prophets. Lv 2002, Peeters xxxii; 613 pp. €75. 90-429-1182-4. Bibl.xxii-xxx.
1945 *Nagel, Peter* Die Septuaginta in den Nag Hammadi-Teksten. The Nag Hammadi texts. DVSS.HF 26: 2002 ⇒740. 164-182.
1946 *Pietersma, Albert* A new paradigm for addressing old questions: the relevance of the interlinear model for the study of the Septuagint. Bible and computer. 2002 ⇒548. 337-364.
1947 **Polak, Frank; Marquis, Galen** A classified index of the minuses of the Septuagint: v.1: Introduction; v.2: The Pentateuch. CATSS Basic Tools 4-5: Stellenbosch 2002, CATSS Project 2 vols. 0-7972-0886-0/7-9. Hebrew University Bible Project. [R]OTEs 15 (2002) 569-572 (*Naudé, J.A.*).
1948 [ET]**Raurell, Frederic** Carta d'Aristeas: introducció, text revisat, traducció i notes. Literatura Intertestamentària, Supplementa 1: Barc 2002, Fundació Bíblica Catalana 149 pp. 84-7225-805-X. Bibl. 57-59. [R]RCatT 27 (2002) 499-500 (*Alegre, Xavier*).
1949 [E]**Sollamo, Rajia; Sipilä, Seppo** Helsinki perspectives on the translation technique of the Septuagint: proceedings of the IOSCS congress in Helsinki 1999. SESJ 82: 2001 ⇒17,1617. [R]EThL 78 (2002) 184-185 (*Lust, J.*).

1950 *Sundberg, Albert C., Jr.* The Septuagint: the bible of Hellenistic Judah. Canon debate. 2002 ⇒1519. 68-90.

1951 **Tov, Emanuel** The Greek and Hebrew Bible: collected essays on the Septuagint. VT.S 72: 1999 ⇒15,180; 17,220. ᴿJSJ 33 (2002) 114-116 (*Den Hertog, Cornelis G.*).

1952 *Trebolle Barrera, Julio C.* La tradición textual griega y latina: texto e interpretación: unidad y pluralidad. Narraciones bíblicas. 2002 ⇒ 1862. 35-62 [BuBB 37,10].

1953 *Veltri, Giuseppe* Die Entstehung der LXX in der jüdischen Historiographie des Mittelalters <1992>;

1954 Ein Fasttag wegen der LXX <1991/1992>? Gegenwart der Tradition. 2002 ⇒255. 120-143/144-150.

1955 *Wergeland, Andrew* Kva står det på gresk?: Septuaginta og GT-tekstkritikk. Ung teologi 35/3 (2002) 7-19.

1956 *Wright, Benjamin G., III* The Jewish scriptures in Greek: the Septuagint in the context of ancient translation activity. Biblical translation. 2002 ⇒338. 3-18.

D4 Versiones orientales

1957 *Cannuyer, Christian* Alte orientalische Bibelübersetzungen. WUB Sonderheft (2002) 32-37.

1958 *Jenner, Konrad D.; Talstra, Eep* CALAP and its relevance for the translation and interpretation of the Syriac Bible: the presentation of a research programme on the computer assisted linguistic analysis of the Peshitta. Bible and computer. 2002 ⇒548. 681-699.

1959 *Kate, A.A.S. ten* Un témoin arménien de la tradition 'césaréenne' des évangiles. Muséon 115/1-2 (2002) 157-169.

1960 *Malzoni, Cláudio Vianney* L'ancienne tradition syriaque des évangiles, sa place et sa signification. L'autorité de l'Écriture. LeDiv: 2002 ⇒588. 95-112.

1961 *Merian, Sylvie L.* The Armenian bookmaking tradition in the christian east: a comparison with the Syriac and Greek traditions. The bible as book. 2002 ⇒1814. 205-214.

1962 **Schmid, Ulrich** 'Unum ex quattor': Genealogie und Rezeption von Evangelienharmonien am Beispiel der lateinischen Tatianüberlieferung. ᴰ*Benad, Matthais*: 2002 Diss.-Habil. Bethel [ThRv 99/2,xi].

1963 ᴱ**Schüssler, Karlheinz** Das sahidische Alte und Neue Testament: vollständiges Verzeichnis mit Standorten sa 93-120. Biblia Coptica 1/4: 2000 ⇒16,1623; 17,1697. Lfg. 4. ᴿOLZ 97 (2002) 353-357 (*Feder, Frank*).

1964 *Torijano Morales, Pablo* La versión armenia de la biblia. Narraciones bíblicas. 2002 ⇒1862. 101-110 [BuBB 37,10].

1965 **Weitzman, Michael Perry** The Syriac version of the Old Testament: an introduction. UCOP 56: 1999 ⇒15,1552...17,1704. ᴿETR 77 (2002) 265-266 (*Sternberger, Jean-Pierre*).

1966 **Wilson, E. Jan** The Old Syriac gospels: studies and comparative translations. Eastern Christian Studies 1-2: Piscataway, NJ 2002, Gorgias 2 vols. 1-931956-17-0 v.1, 1-931956-18-9 v.2 Syriac Transcriptions by *George A. Kiraz*.

1967 *Zipor, Moshe A.* Towards an annotated English translation of the Peshitta. JNSL 28/2 (2002) 63-82.

D5.0 **Versiones latinae**; *Citationes apud Patres*—**The Patristic Bible**

1968 ^E**Nolden, Reiner** Die Touronische Bibel der Abtei St. Maximin vor Trier: Faksimile der erhaltenen Blätter: Farbtafeln mit den Initialen: Aufsätze. Trier 2002, Gesellschaft für nützliche Forschungen zu Trier iv; 252 pp. Bibl. von *Anna Boeck* 243-245 [RBen 114,184—P.-M. Bogaert].

1969 *Alidori, Laura* Motivi classici nella Bibbia Edili 125-126 della Biblioteca Mediceo-Laurenziana. Rivista de storia della miniatura 4 (1999) 39-48. 17 pl. [RBen 114,186—P.-M. Bogaert].

1970 *Bogaert, Pierre-Maurice* Bulletin de la Bible Latin VII. RBen 112 (2002) 152-175.

1971 **Burton, Philip** The Old Latin gospels: a study of their texts and language. Oxford Early Christian Studies: 2000 ⇒16,1632. ^RRBen 112 (2002) 167-168 (*Bogaert, P.-M.*); JEarlyC 10 (2002) 420-421 (*Cahill, Michael*); JRS 92 (2002) 265 (*Clackson, James*). [rpr. 2002].

1972 *Ceccanti, Melania* Una ricostruita bibbia fiorentina del quattrocento: prime considerazioni. Rivista di storia della miniatura 5 (2000) 97-108. 14 pl. [RBen 114,189—P.-M. Bogaert].

1973 *De Floriani, Anna* Note sulla miniatura dell'ultimo quarto del Duecento tra Bologna e Padova: la Bibbia di Albenga riconsiderata. Rivista di storia della miniatura 3 (1998) 25-58. 27 pl. [RBen 114, 189—P.-M. Bogaert].

1974 **Denzinger, Götz** Die Handschriften der Hofschule KARLs des Grossen: Studien zu ihrer Ornamentik. Langwaden 2001, Bernardus 37 pp [RBen 114,203—P.-M. Bogaert].

1975 **Dutton, Paul Edward; Kessler, Herbert L.** The poetry and paintings of the first bible of CHARLES the Bald. AA 1998, Univ. of Michigan Pr. xii; 137 pp. 42 pl. [RBen 114,184—P.-M. Bogaert].

1976 *Ferrari, Michele C.* Bibelhandschriften im Frühmittelalter. Die Touronische Bibel. 2002 ⇒1968. 185-203 RBen 114,184—P.-M. Bogaert.

1977 ^E**Fingernagel, Andreas** Die Admonter Riesenbibel (Wien, ÖNB, Cod. Ser. n. 2701 und 2702). Codices illuminati 1: Graz 2001, Akademische 68 pp. 3201017639. 45 pl. [RBen 114,187: P.-M. Bogaert].

1978 *Froehlich, Karlfried* An extraordinary achievement: the *glossa ordinaria* in print. The bible as book: the first printed editions. 1999 ⇒ 15,442. 15-21 [RBen 114,189—P.-M. Bogaert].

1979 *Fuchs, Robert; Oltrogge, Doris; Hahn, Oliver* Farbmittel und Maltechnik der Bibel von St. MAXIMIN. Die Touronische Bibel. 2002 ⇒ 1968. 239-242 [RBen 114,184—P.-M. Bogaert].

1980 *Gameson, Richard* The insular gospel book at Hereford cathedral. Scr. 56 (2002) 48-79 [Ps 54-55];

1981 Why did EADFRITH write the Lindisfarne gospels?. Belief and cultures in the Middle Sages: studies presented to Henry MAYR-HARTING. ^E*Gameson, Richard; Leyser, Henrietta*: NY 2001, OUP 45-59. 3 pl. [RBen 114,202—P.-M. Bogaert].

1982 *Gros, Miquel S.* Les fragments de l'épistolier latin du Sinaï: étude liturgique. EO 19 (2002) 391-404 [RBen 114,192—P.-M. Bogaert].

1983 ^E**Gryson, Roger** Vetus Latina 2000: 46. Arbeitsbericht der Stiftung; 35. Bericht des Instituts. FrB 2002, Herder 52 pp.

1984 *Gumbert, J.P.* The layout of the bible gloss in manuscript and early print. The bible as book: the first printed editions. 1999 ⇒15,442. 1999 7-13. Pl. 1-7 [RBen 114,189—P.-M. Bogaert].

1985 ᴱ**Heitzmann, Christian; Santos Noya, Manuel** The Bibelsammlung der Württembergischen Landesbibliothek: Abteilung 1, Bd. 4,1-3: Lateinische Bibeldrucke 1454-2001. BSWLB 1/4/1-3: Stu 2002, Frommann-Holzboog xxxiii; 1396 pp. €1995. 3-7728-2207-X. Mitarbeit *Imgard Schauffler* u. *Eberhard Zwink*; Teil 1: 1454-1564; Teil 2: 1565-1738; Teil 3: 1740-2001 [EuA 78,418];

1986 *Lo Cicero, Carla* RUFINO traduttore di BASILIO: emulazione e citazione bibliche. Tra IV e V secolo. 2002 ⇒475. 97-117 [RBen 114,190—P.-M. Bogaert].

1987 *Magrini, Sabina* 'Per difetto del legatore...': storia delle rilegature della Bibbia Amiatina in Laurenziana. Quinio 3 (2001) 137-167 [RBen 114,182—P.-M. Bogaert].

1988 *Marsden, Richard* 'Ask what I am called': the Anglo-Saxons and their bibles. The bible as book. 2002 ⇒1814. 145-176.

1989 *McKitterick, Rosamond, al.*, The Rorigo Bible in its ninth-century context. Scritti in onore di Girolamo ARNALDI. ᴱ**Rinaldi, Rossella**: R 2001, Istituto Storico Italiano per il Medio Evo 409-422 [RBen 114,183—P.-M. Bogaert].

1990 *Mielle de Becdelièvre, Dominique* D'une bible à l'autre... la réalisation des deux premières bibles de la Grande Chartreuse au XIIᵉ siècle. RMab 13 (2002) 161-188.

1991 *Mütherich, Florentine* Der ornamentale Schmuck der Bibel von St. MAXIMIN.;

1992 *Nolden, Reiner* Die Fragmente der Touronischen Bibel von St. MAXIMIN vor Trier. Die Touronische Bibel. 2002 ⇒1968. 233-238/205-232 [RBen 114,184—P.-M. Bogaert].

1993 *Oliver, Judith* Chaos in the scriptorium: the Parc Bible of 1263. 'Als ich can': liber amicorum in memory of Professor Dr. Maurits SMEYERS, 2. ᴱ**Cardon, Bert; Van der Stock, Jan; Vanwijnsberghe, Dominique**: Corpus of Illuminated Manuscripts 11-12: Lv 2002, Peeters 1059-1078 [RBen 114,188—P.-M. Bogaert].

1994 *Pfisterer, Andreas* Cantilena Romana: Untersuchungen zur Überlieferung des gregorianischen Chorals. Beiträge zur Geschichte der Kirchenmusik 11: Pd 2002, Schöningh 349 pp [RBen 114,193—P.-M. Bogaert].

1995 *Reilly, Diane J.* French romanesque giant bibles and their English relatives: blood relatives or adopted children?. Scr. 56 (2002) 294-311.

1996 *Russo, Antonio* Su alcune novità per la Bibbia di Corradino. Rivista di storia della miniatura 5 (2000) 51-64. 18 pl. [RBen 114,189—P.-M. Bogaert].

1997 *Smith, Joseph J.* Liturgiam authenticam: the authority of the Vulgate and the Neo-Vulgate. Landas 16 (2002) 124-133.

1998 *Telesko, Werner* Die 'Riesenbibeln' und das Problem des 'Reformstils' in der Salzburger Buchmalerei des späten 11. und frühen 12. Jahrhunderts: Überlegungen zur Bedeutung der Admonter Bibelhandschriften C-E und der St.Florianer Riesenbibel. ZHVSt 89-90 (1998-1999) 9-29 [RBen 114,187—P.-M. Bogaert].

1999 *Verdejo Sánchez, Maria Dolores* El léxico de las glosas de 'Vetus Latina' en manuscritos de vulgatas españoles. Actas del Congresso Internacional 'Cristianesimo y tradición latina'. ᴱ**Alberte González,**

Antonio; **Macías Villalobos, Cristóbal**: M 2001, Laberinto 323-330 [RBen 114,194—P.-M. Bogaert].
2000 *Verdejo Sánchez, Maria Dolores, al.*, Rasgos de latin hispánico encontrados en glosas de Vetus Latina en manuscritos de Vulgata españoles. Sub luce florentis calami: homenaje a Manuel C. DÍAZ Y DÍAZ. ᴱ**Domínguez García, Manuela**: Santiago di Compostela 2002, Universidade [RBen 114,194—P.-M. Bogaert].
2001 Vetus Latina Database. BVLI 46 (2002) 44.

D6 Versiones modernae .1 *romanicae*, romance

2002 **Alonso Schökel, Luis** Biblia breve del peregrino. Bilbao 2002, Mensajero 406 pp. €12. 84-271-2451-1;
2003 Bíblia do peregrino. ᵀ*Storniolo, Ivo; Bortolini, José; Vidigal, José Raimundo*: São Paulo 2002, Paulus 3056; xiv pp. 85-349-2006-0.
2004 *Alves, Herculano* Memorando de uma tradução da bíblia em português. HumTeo 23/1 (2002) 108-115.
2005 **Auwers, Jean-Marie**, *al.*, La bible en français: guide des traductions courantes. ConBib 11/12: Bru 2002, Lumen Vitae 144 pp. €9.41. 2-87324-170-5. Éd. revue [RTL 33,572—Wénin, A.].
2006 **Avenoza, G.** La Biblia de Ajuda y la Megl.lat Antiochus en romance. Biblioteca de filología hispánica 25: M 2001, CSIC xvi; 215 pp.
2007 *Barbieri, Edoardo* 'Misurare' la bibbia: bibliografia e ricezione del testo biblico in volgare. La sorgente. 2002 ⇒315. 99-108.
2008 Bibbia Ebron: nuovissima versione dai testi originali. CinB 2002, San Paolo 1543 pp. 88-215-4022-7. 64 pl.
2009 Bible d'étude: version du Semeur 2000: traduite en français d'après les textes originaux hébreu et grec. 2001 ⇒17,1726. ᴿEvTh(VS) 1/2 (2002) 90-92 (*Margot, Jean-Claude*).
2010 La Bible de Jérusalem: édition de référence avec notes et augmentée de clefs de lectures. 2001 ⇒17,1725. ᴿLV(L) 256 (2002) 121-122 (*Lémonon, Jean-Pierre*).
2011 La bible: nouvelle traduction. ᵀ*Boyer, Frédéric; Prévost, Jean-Pierre; Sevin, Marc*: 2001 ⇒17,1724. ᴿUna Voce Korrespondenz 32 (2002) 48-49 (*Schönberger, Andreas*); Com(F) 27 (2002) 85-104 (*Joyeux, Béatrice*); RSPhTh 86 (2002) 301-302 (*Jossua, Jean-Pierre*); ScEs 54 (2002) 205-223 (*Gourgues, Michel*); LTP 58 (2002) 387-388 (*Poirier,Paul-Hubert*).
2012 Bíblia de Jerusalém. São Paulo 2002, Paulus 2206 pp. ᴿEstudos Bíblicos 76 (2002) 79-81 (*Pereira, Ney Brasil*); RBBras 19 (2002) 324-6 (*Minette de Tillesse, Gaëtan*) & 340-344 (*Pereira, Ney Brasil*).
2013 Bíblia Sagrada. São Paulo ²2002, Ave Maria 14 + 1490 pp. Trad. da CNBB, com introd. e notas. ᴿRBBras 19 (2002) 327-339 (*Pereira, Ney Brasil*).
2014 *Bonilla A., Plutarco* El Nuevo Testamento: la Biblia textual Reina-Valera: reseña crítica. RevBib 64 (2002) 89-122. Cf. la traducción del NT publicada por la Sociedad Biblica Iberoamericana, 2001.
2015 *Brunet, Éttienne* [!] Un texte sacré peut-il changer?: variations sur l'évangile. Bible and computer. 2002 ⇒548. 79-98.
2016 ᴱ**Coronado, Florencio** Sagrada biblia quechua-castellano. GR 2002, Diócesis de Huancavelica 2496 pp. Tomada de la biblia argentina 'El libro del pueblo de Dios'.

2017 ^E**Costecalde, Cl.-B.; Hassonville, Henry de; Hari, A.** Nouveau T.:
le Nouveau Testament traduit du grec en français courant. 2000 ⇒
16,1654. ^RSR 31 (2002) 213-214 (*Cazelais, Serge*).

2018 *Danieli, Giuseppe* Revisione della traduzione della Bibbia CEI:
storia, criteri, esiti della collaborazione ABI-CEI. RStB 14/1-2
(2002) 313-318.

2019 **Fellous, Sonia** Histoire de la bible de Moïse ARRAGEL: quand un
rabbin interprète la bible pour les chrétiens, Tolède, 1422-1433. 2001
⇒17,1731. ^RMÂ 108 (2002) 424-425 (*Schatzmiller, Joseph*).

2020 *Gourgues, Michel* Le Nouveau Testament dans la nouvelle traduction
de la bible en français. ScEs 54 (2002) 205-223.

2021 *Konings, Johan* Segunda edição da "Bíblia da CNBB". REB 62
(2002) 911-912.

2022 ^E**Leonardi, Lino** La bibbia in italiano tra Medioevo e Rinascimento.
1998 ⇒14,390; 16,1658. ^RCrSt 23 (2002) 219-220 (*Gilmont, Jean-
François*).

2023 La Nouvelle Bible Segond. P 2002, Alliance Biblique Universelle
1886 pp. €45. 2-85300-172-5. ^RLV(L) 256 (2002) 122-124 (*Lémonon, Jean-Pierre*); EvTh(VS) 1/3 (2002) 88-89 (*Tricard, François*).

2024 Sagrada Biblia: Antiguo Testamento, 4: libros proféticos: traducción,
notas. Pamplona 2002, EUNSA 1355 pp. 84-313-1952-6 [ActBib 39,
194—Boada, J.].

2025 *Sánchez Caro, José Manuel* Intervención de la iglesia en la labor tra-
ductora: el caso de la biblia en España. Salm. 49 (2002) 387-432.

2026 *Schönberger, Andreas* Ein Bibel-Skandal in Frankreich. Una Voce-
Korrespondenz 32 (2002) 48-49.

2027 *Zardin, Danilo* Tra latino e volgare: la 'Dichiarazione dei salmi' del
PANIGAROLA e i filtri di accesso alla materia biblica nell'editoria della controriforma. La sorgente. 2002 ⇒315. 109-149.

D6.2 *Versiones anglicae*—English Bible Translations

2028 ^T**Barnstone, Willis** The New Covenant, commonly called the New
Testament, 1: the four gospels and Apocalypse. NY 2002, Riverhead
(10); 577 pp. 1-57322-182-1. Bibl. 572-576.

2029 *Berlin, Adele* On bible translations and commentaries. Bible translation. JSOT.S 353: 2002 ⇒281. 175-191.

2030 The catholic answer bible. Huntington, IN 2002, Fireside xxix; 1394;
xii pp. $22. 1-931709-60-2 [ThD 50,62—Heiser, W. Charles].

2031 ^E**Cooper, W.R.** William TYNDALE: The New Testament: the text of
the Worms ed. of 1526 in original spelling. 2000 ⇒16,1666.
^RCrossCur 51 (2002) 554-556 (*Madsen, Catherine*);

2032 The WYCLIFFE New Testament (1388): an edition in modern spelling
with an introduction, the original prologues and the Epistle to the
Laodiceans. L 2002, The British Library xv; 528 pp. 0-7123-4728-3.

2033 *Davies, Philip R.; Thomson, Claire E.* The Wycliffite Bible: an electronic resource. Bible and computer. 2002 ⇒548. 677-680.

2034 *Dempsey, Deirdre* The New American Bible: generational differences. Biblical translation. 2002 ⇒338. 155-164.

2035 *Fox, Michael V.* Translation and mimesis;

2036 *Greenspoon, Leonard* Top dollar, bottom line?: marketing English-
language bibles within the Jewish community. Biblical translation.
2002 ⇒338. 207-220/115-133;

2037 Jewish bible translation. Biblical world, 2. 2002 ⇒273. 397-412.
2038 **Gutjahr, Paul C.** An American Bible: a history of the Good Book in the United States, 1777-1880. 1999 ⇒15,1591...17,1744. ^RReformation 6 (2001-2002) 212-215 (*Corner, Martin*).
2039 Holman christian standard bible, New Testament. 2001 ⇒17,1762. ^RJRTI 5 (2002) 64-66 (*Artz, James I.*).
2040 *Hope, Andrew* The Antwerp origins of the Coverdale Bible: investigations from the 1884 <u>Athenaeum</u> controversy to the present day. Tyndale's testament. 2002 ⇒268. 39-54.
2041 *Korsak, Mary Phil* Translating the bible: bible translations and gender issues. Bible translation. JSOT.S 353: 2002 ⇒281. 132-146.
2042 *Longman, Tremper, III* Accuracy and readability: warring impulses in Evangelical translation tradition. Biblical translation. 2002 ⇒281. 165-175.
2043 **Mackenzie, Cameron A.** The battle for the bible in England, 1557-1582. NY 2002, Lang xi; 338 pp. $66. 0-8204-58104. Bibl. 309-333.
2044 **Martin, Robert** Accuracy of translation: the primary criterion in evaluating bible versions with special reference to the New International Version. 1997 ⇒15,1596. ^RSBET 20 (2002) 113-115 (*Macgregor, Alan*).
2045 **McGrath, Alister E.** In the beginning: the story of the King James Bible and how it changed a nation, a language, and a culture. 2001 ⇒17,1750. ^RCTJ 37 (2002) 122-124 (*Boonstra, Harry*);
2046 L 2002, Hodder x (2); 340 pp. 0-340-78585-3. Bibl. 317-328.
2047 **Morey, James H.** Book and verse: a guide to Middle English biblical literature. 2000 ⇒16,1678; 17,1751. ^RSpec. 77 (2002) 608-610 (*Bestul, Thomas H.*).
2048 **Norton, David** A history of the English Bible as literature. 2000 ⇒ 16,1339. ^RThTo 59 (2002) 150-152 (*Daniell, David*); Reformation 7 (2002) 217-221 (*Daniell, David*); RBLit 4 (2002) 130-133 (*Aichele, George*).
2049 *Ohlhausen, Sidney K.* Folio editions of English catholic bibles and testaments: a comprehensive bibliography. ReH 26 (2002) 259-290.
2050 **Poythress, Vern S.; Grudem, Wayne A.** The gender-neutral bible controversy: muting the masculinity of God's words. 2000 ⇒16, 1685. ^RAUSS 40 (2002) 155-157 (*Running, Leona Glidden*); TrinJ 23 (2002) 111-118 (*Siebenthal, Heinrich von*); RTR 61 (2002) 162-163 (*Davies, John*).
2051 *Raabe, Paul R.* The problem of facile translations. Biblical translation. 2002 ⇒281. 195-205.
2052 *Rashkow, Ilona N.* Art as text—text as art: apparatus as a translation tool. SBL.SP 2002. SBL.SPS 41: 2002 ⇒598. 182-189.
2053 *Rendsburg, Gary A.* The literary approach to the bible and finding a good translation. Biblical translation. 2002 ⇒281. 179-194.
2054 **Ryken, Leland** The word of God in English: criteria for excellence in bible translation. Wheaton, IL 2002, Crossway 336 pp. $16. 1-58134-464-3.
2055 Student bible: Good News translation with deuterocanonicals. ^E**Yancey, Philip; Stafford, Tim**: GR 2002, Zondervan xv; 1613 pp. $35. 0-310-92261-5. Notes [ThD 50,259—Heiser, W. Charles].
2056 *Sugirtharajah, R.S.* Marketing the testaments: Canongate and their pocket-sized bibles. BiblInterp 10 (2002) 221-244.

2057 **Thuesen, Peter J.** In discordance with the scriptures: American Protestant battles over translating the bible. 1999 ⇒15,1606...17, 1756. ᴿJR 82 (2002) 105-107 (*Hillis, Bryan*).

2058 Today's New International Version New Testament. GR 2001, Zondervan vii; 367 pp. $17. 0-3109-5592-0.

2059 *Vander Stichele, Caroline* Murder she wrote or why translation matters: a response to Mary Phil Korsak's 'Translating the bible'. Bible translation. JSOT.S 353: 2002 ⇒281. 147-155.

D6.3 *Versiones germanicae*—**Deutsche Bibelübersetzungen**

2060 ᵀ**Berger, Klaus; Nord, Christiane** Das Neue Testament und frühchristliche Schriften. ⁵2001 ⇒17,1765. ᴿBiLi 75 (2002) 287-290 (*Scholtissek, Klaus*).

2061 *Beutel, Albrecht* LUTHER's translation of the bible and the consequences. ᵀᴱ*Vondey, Wolfgang*: Luther Digest 10 (2002) 2-4 <EvTh 59 (1999) 13-24.

2062 *Erne, Thomas* Die Kinderbibel als Medium religiöser Überlieferung. ThLZ 127 (2002) 471-490.

2063 ᴱ**Fricke, K.D.; Meurer, S.** Die Geschichte der Lutherbibelrevision: von den Anfängen 1850 bis 1984. 2001 ⇒17,1763. ᴿThLZ 127 (2002) 886-889 (*Stolt, Birgit*).

2064 *Gillman, Abigail E.* Between religion and culture: MENDELSSOHN, BUBER, ROSENZWEIG and the enterprise of biblical translation. Biblical translation. 2002 ⇒281. 93-114.

2065 *Gretler, Trix; Schellenberg, Annette* Die neue Zürcher Bibel: eine Zwischenbilanz nach 15 Jahren Übersetzungsarbeit;

2066 *Haubeck, Wilfrid* Neue kommunikative Übersetzungen auf dem deutschen Markt: Gute Nachricht Bibel, Hoffnung für alle und Neue Genfer Übersetzung: ein Vergleich am Beispiel von Matthäus 5-7 und Römer 3-5. BiLi 75 (2002) 231-237/251-264.

2067 *Hotze, Gerhard* Die "Interlinearübersetzung" und das "Münchener Neue Testament"—zwei nicht alltägliche Bibelausgaben. BiLi 75 (2002) 243-250.

2068 ᴱ**Joerg, Urs; Hoffmann, David Marc** Die Bibel in der Schweiz: Ursprung und Geschichte. 1997 ⇒13,1378... 16,1703. ᴿThR 67 (2002) 383-384 (*Perlitt, Lothar*).

2069 *Köhler, Hanne* Bibel in gerechter Sprache. BiLi 75 (2002) 238-243.

2070 *Leutzsch, Martin* Probleme gerechter Bibelübersetzung. JK 63/2 (2002) 31-39.

2071 *Millard, Matthias* Die Lutherbibel(n). BiLi 75 (2002) 223-231.

2072 *Wellmann, Bettina* Einheitübersetzung, quo vadis?. BiLi 75 (2002) 290-292.

2073 *Wenz, Armin* Schriftgemäße Bibelübersetzung?: kritische Anmerkungen zur "Guten Nachricht" (1997). Lutherische Beiträge 7/3 (2002) 157-186.

2074 *Zenger, Erich* Neues Licht auf alte Weisheit: was die Gute Nachricht Bibel an Verständnishilfen über die traditionellen Bibelübersetzungen hinaus bringt. BiLi 75 (2002) 264-268.

2075 *Ziehr, Wilhelm* Erste volkssprachliche Bibeltexte;

2076 Die Übersetzung der Bibel. Die Bibel: Geschichte und Gegenwart. 2002 ⇒971. 190-191/24-25.

D6.4 **Versiones africanae** *et variae*

2077 *Chakkuvarackal, T. Johnson* Translating the bible in the Indian context. BiBh 28 (2002) 656-671.

2078 Important issues in the translation of the bible in the Indian context. Bangalore Theological Forum [Bangalore] 34/1 (2002) 163-175 [NTAb 47,17].

2079 *Combrink, B.* The Afrikaans translation of the bible for the deaf. Scriptura 77 (2001) 297-302 [NTAb 47,17].

2080 **Garzaniti, Marcello** Die altslavische Version der Evangelien: Forschungsgeschichte und zeitgenössische Forschung. 2001 ⇒17,1802. ^ROCP 68 (2002) 540-542 (*Uchanova, E.B.*).

2081 *Hermanson, E.A.* A brief overview of bible translation in South Africa. Contemporary translation studies. AcTh(B).S 2: 2002 ⇒581. 6-18.

2082 *Hong, Joseph* Revision of the Chinese Union Version Bible (CUV): assessing the challenges from an historical perspective. BiTr 53 (2002) 238-248.

2083 ^E**Irudayam, Susai Michael; Robinson Levi, Y.** History of Tamil bible translation. Arasaradi, Madurai 2002, Theological Education through Living Literature (10); 79 pp.

2084 *Janse, S.* Krijgt de NBV al handen en voeten?. KeTh 53 (2002) 145-154.

2085 *Knüppel, Michael* Die christlich-türkischen Transkriptionstexte bei Hieronymus MEGISER (um 1553-1619): ein Beitrag zur Geschichte der türkischen Bibelübersetzung. ZKG 113 (2002) 237-245.

2086 *Kors, Mikel M.* De Historiebijbel van 1361: een poging tot reconstructie. OGE 76 (2002) 3-14.

2087 **Laukkanen, Pauli Vilhelm** Rough road to dynamism: bible translating in northern Namibia, 1954-1987: Kwanyama, Kwangali and Ndonga. 2002 Diss. Helsinki [StTh 57,78].

2088 *Laurant, Sophie* La Bible de Novgorod. MoBi 145 (2002) 6-9.

2089 *Nikolaenko, Dina* Old church Slavonic versions of the gospels: computer-aided classification and the choice of variants. Bible and computer. 2002 ⇒548. 475-493.

2090 Pismo Swiete: Starego i Nowego Testamentu. ^T**Tynieckich, Benedyktynów**: Poznan 2002, Wydawnictwo Pallottinum 1468 pp. 83-7014-419-5. **P**.

2091 *Ponelis, F.* The language ecology of a new Afrikaans Bible. Contemporary translation studies. AcTh(B).S 2: 2002 ⇒581. 280-289.

2092 *Punt, Jeremy* Translating the bible in southern Africa: contested ownership?: owning, owing, and owning up. SBL.SP 2002. SBL.SPS 41: 2002 ⇒598. 156-181.

2093 *Sardushkin, Valery M.* Is 'God' in Albanian feminine or masculine?. BiTr 53 (2002) 137-143.

2094 *Schäferdiek, Knut* Der vermeintliche Arianismus der Ulfila-Bibel: zum Umgang mit einem Stereotyp. ZAC 6 (2002) 320-329.

2095 *Shae, Gam Seng* The portrait of Jesus in the Burmese gospels. BiTr 53 (2002) 202-210.

2096 *Teter, Magdalena* 'Lost in the translation': the London Missionary Society's Mongolian Pentateuch. Biblical translation. 2002 ⇒281. 145-154.

2097 *Weber, E.A.* Bibelübersetzungen in afrikanischen Sprachen. Lutherische Beiträge 7/3 (2002) 187-206.
2098 *Zetzsche, Jost* Die Übersetzung der Bibel ins Chinesische. WUB Sonderheft (2002) 62-63.

D7 *Problema vertentis*—Bible translation techniques

2099 **Askani, Hans-Christoph** Das Problem der Übersetzung dargestellt an Franz ROSENZWEIG: die Methoden und Prinz.pien der Rosenzweigschen und Buber-Rosenzweig. Übersetzungen. HUTh 35: 1997 ⇒13,1403; 14,1479. ᴿGGA 254 (2002) 289-303 *(Bader, Günter).*
2100 *Babut, Jean M.* La traduction par équivalence dynamique. FV 101/4 (2002) 19-30.
2101 *Berlin, Adele* Text, translation, commentary. Biblical translation. 2002 ⇒281. 135-144.
2102 *Blois, K.F. de; Mewe, T.* Functional equivalence and the new Dutch translation project. Contemporary translation studies. AcTh(B).S 2: 2002 ⇒581. 214-227.
2103 *Brenner, Athalya* 'Between lying and blasphemy': responding to Robert Carroll. Bible translation. JSOT.S 353: 2002 ⇒281. 65-69.
2104 *Briffard, Colette* Gammes sur l'acte de traduire. FV 101/4 (2002) 13-18.
2105 *Buzzetti, Carlo* Il mitico traduttore-traditore e il caso della bibbia. AnScR 7 (2002) 73-84;
2106 Per valutare una traduzione della bibbia: una mappa. RivBib 50 (2002) 385-400.
2107 *Carroll, Robert P.* Between lying and blasphemy or on translating a four-letter word in the Hebrew Bible: critical reflections on bible translation. Bible translation. JSOT.S 353: 2002 ⇒281. 53-64.
2108 **Chaudhuri, Sukanta** Translation and understanding. Oxf 2002, OUP (8); 89 pp. 0-19-564877-3.
2109 *Crisp, Simon* Icon of the ineffable?: an orthodox view of language and its implications for bible translation. Bible translation. JSOT.S 353: 2002 ⇒281. 36-49.
2110 *Deile, Volkmar* Mehr verschieden als versöhnt. JK 63/2 (2002) 6-9.
2111 *Dieterlé, Christiane* La bible au risque des traductions. FV 101/4 (2002) 31-40.
2112 *Dohmen, Christoph* Treue zum Text: jüdische Bibelübersetzungen. BiLi 75 (2002) 269-273.
2113 *Ellingworth, Paul* 'You can say you to him': t- and v-forms in common language translations of the New Testament;
2114 Theology and translation: a survey and a proposal. BiTr 53 (2002) 143-153/302-307.
2115 *Fougeras, Didier* Nommer Dieu en traduction biblique: quelques réflexions autour de la "Nouvelle Bible Segond". FV 101/4 (2002) 41-52.
2116 *Fox, Everett* The translation of Elijah: issues and challenges. Bible translation. JSOT.S 353: 2002 ⇒281. 156-169 [2 Kgs 2].
2117 *Greenspahn, Frederick E.* How Jews translate the bible. Biblical translation. 2002 ⇒281. 43-61.
2118 *Guilmin, Serge* D'une bible à l'autre. FV 101/4 (2002) 79-84.
2119 *Harris, John* Innovations in translating for the deaf. BiTr 53 (2002) 233-238.

2120 *Joosten, Jan* Lire la bible en traduction: une perspective historique. FV 101/4 (2002) 3-13.

2121 *Jordaan, G.J.C.* Problems in the theoretical foundation of the functional-equivalent approach. Contemporary translation studies. AcTh(B).S 2: 2002 ⇒581. 19-28.

2122 *Josipovici, Gabriel* Vibrant spaces. ᴹCARROLL, R.: JSOT.S 348: 2002 ⇒13. 358-373.

2123 *Joubert, S.J.* No culture shock?: addressing the Achilles heel of modern bible translation. Contemporary translation studies. AcTh(B).S 2: 2002 ⇒581. 30-43.

2124 *Joyeux, Béatrice* L'écriture et les Écritures. Com(F) 37/1 (2002) 85-104.

2125 *Kaiser, Ursula Ulrike* Brian WALTON und die Londoner Polyglotte: ein Beispiel für die bisweilen schwierigen äußeren Umstände von Editions- und Übersetzungsprojekten. ꟳSCHENKE, H.: NHS 54: 2002 ⇒108. 425-437.

2126 *Konings, Johan* Traduzindo a bíblia (no Brasil). Convergência 37 (2002) 53-64.

2127 *Köhler, Hanne* Der Nerv unseres Glaubens. JK 63/2 (2002) 26-30.

2128 *Krašovec, Jože* Prevodi Svetega pisma v evfropske jezike [Translation of the bible into European languages]. Bogoslovni Vestnik 62 (2002) 529-549 Sum. 548. Š.

2129 *Kruger, A.* Corpus-based translation research: its development and implications for general, literary and bible translations. Contemporary translation studies. AcTh(B).S 2: 2002 ⇒581. 70-106.

2130 *Launderville, Dale* The art of translating. BiTod 40 (2002) 38-43.

2131 *Lis, Marek; Buzzetti, Carlo Transmediatio*: traduzione della Bibbia nei media audiovisivi: perché e con quale terminologia?. Sal. 64 (2002) 29-59.

2132 *Lombaard, Christo* Elke vertaling is 'n vertelling: opmerkings oor vertaalteorie, geïllustreer aan die hand van die chokmatiese *ratio interpretationis*. OTEs 15 (2002) 754-765 [Prov 1,7].

2133 **Long, Lynne** Translating the Bible: from the 7th to the 17th century 2001 ⇒17,1833. ᴿMAe 71 (2002) 311-312 (*Shell, Alison*).

2134 *Lys, Daniel* La bible en quête de langage(s). FV 101/4 (2002) 65-78.

2135 **Metzger, Bruce Manning** The bible in translation: ancient and English versions. 2001 ⇒17,1836. ᴿSBET 20 (2002) 206-207 (*Meredith, David C.*); OTEs 15 (2002) 296-298 (*Naudé, J.A.*).

2136 *Mojola, A.O.* Bible translation in Africa: what implications does the new UBS perspective have for Africa?: an overview in the light of the emerging new UBS translation initiative. Contemporary translation studies. AcTh(B).S 2: 2002 ⇒581. 202-213.

2137 *Mundhenk, Norman A.* Translating the 'gods'. BiTr 53 (2002) 218-225.

2138 **Nida, Eugene A.; Rayburn, William D.** Significado y diversidad cultural. Miami 1998, Sociedades Bíblicas Unidas 149 pp. ᴿRevBib 62 (2000) 127-128 (*Levoratti, J.*).

2139 *Noorda, Sijbolt* New and familiar: the dynamics of bible translations. Bible translation. JSOT.S 353: 2002 ⇒581. 8-16.

2140 *Nord, C.* Bridging the cultural gap: bible translation as a case in point. AcTh(B) 22/1 (2002) 98-116.

2141 *Noss, Philip A.* Translators' words and theological readings. BiTr 53 (2002) 331-343.

2142   *Ogden, Graham S.* Translation as a theologizing task;
2143   *Omanson, Roger L.* Theology, interpretation, and translation. BiTr
       53 (2002) 308-316/353-362.
2144   *Ortíz García, Javier* Éléments (con)textuels dans la traduction. RICP
       81 (2002) 193-204.
2145   *Plooy, H. du* Listening to the wind in the trees: meaning, interpreta-
       tion and literary theory. Contemporary translation studies. AcTh(B).S
       2: 2002 ⇒581. 266-279.
2146   *Punt, Jeremy* Translating the bible in South Africa: challenges to re-
       sponsibility and contextuality;
2147   *Regt, Lénart J. de* Otherness and equivalence in bible translation: a
       response to Simon Crisp. Bible translation. JSOT.S 353: 2002 ⇒581.
       94-124/50-52.
2148   *Römer, Thomas* Traductions et paratexte: sur le problème des annota-
       tions dans les bibles modernes. FV 101/4 (2002) 53-64.
2149   **Salevsky, Heidemarie** Translationswissenschaft: ein Kompendium.
       Fra 2002, Lang xx; 660 pp. 3-631-31413-2.
2150   **Sallis, John** On translation. Studies in continental thought: Bloom-
       ington, IND 2002, Indiana Univ. Pr. xii (2) 125 pp. 0-253-34156-6.
2151   *Smith, K.* Translation as secondary communication: the relevance
       theory perspective of Ernst-August Gutt. Contemporary translation
       studies. AcTh(B).S 2: 2002 ⇒581. 107-117.
2152   *Strandenaes, Thor* Translation as interpretation. NT as reception.
       JSNT.S 230: 2002 ⇒360. 181-200.
2153   ᴱ**Tymoczko, Maria; Gentzler, Edwin** Translation and power. Am-
       herst 2002, Univ. of Massachusetts Pr. xxviii; 244 pp. 1-55849-358-
       1. Bibl. 219-235.
2154   *Van der Merwe, C.H.J.* An overview of recent developments in the
       description of Biblical Hebrew relevant to bible translation;
2155   *Van der Watt, J.G.* Some considerations on bible translation as com-
       plex process;
2156   What happens when one picks up the Greek text?. Contemporary
       translation studies. AcTh(B).S 2: 2002 ⇒581. 228-245/118-139/246-
       265.
2157   *Veltri, Giuseppe* Die heilige Sprache: Sprachphilosophien und Über-
       setzungstheorien. Gegenwart der Tradition. 2002 <1994> ⇒255. 38-
       52.
2158   *Verheij, A.J.C.* 'The translation of Elijah': a response to Everett Fox.
       Bible translation. JSOT.S 353: 2002 ⇒581. 170-174 [2 Kgs 2].
2159   *Voinov, V.* Pronominal theology in translating the gospels. BiTr 53
       (2002) 210-218.
2160   *Wansbrough, Henry* Christian bible translation. Biblical world, 2.
       2002 ⇒273. 413-426.
2161   *Wendland, E.R.* Towards a 'literary' translation of the scriptures: with
       special reference to a 'poetic' rendition. Contemporary translation
       studies. AcTh(B).S 2: 2002 ⇒581. 164-201.
2162   *Wendland, Ernst R.* 'Theologizing' in bible translation with special
       reference to study notes in Chichewa. BiTr 53 (2002) 316-330.
2163   *Weren, Wim J.C.* Translation, interpretation and ideology: a response
       to Jeremy Punt. Bible translation. JSOT.S 353: 2002 ⇒581. 125-
       131.
2164   *Wilt, T.* A new framework for bible translation Contemporary transla-
       tion studies. AcTh(B).S 2: 2002 ⇒581. 140-163.

D8 *Concordantiae, lexica specialia*—**Specialized dictionaries, synopses**

2165 **Brisman, Shimeon** History and guide to Judaic dictionaries and concordances. Jewish research literature 3,1: 2000 ⇒16,1753. [R]REJ 161 (2002) 291-292 (*Rothschild, Jean-Pierre*).

2166 [E]**Coenen, Lothar; Haacker, Klaus** Theologisches Begriffslexikon zum Neuen Testament, 1-2. 1997-2000 ⇒ [R]ThG 45 (2002) 210-212 (*Giesen, Heinz*).

2167 [E]**Coenen, Lothar; Haacker, Klaus** Theologisches Begriffslexikon zum Neuen Testament, 1: A-H. Wu 1997, Brockhaus 3-417-24841-8. Neubearbeitete Ausgabe;

2168 2: I-Z. 2000 ⇒16,1756. [R]ThLZ 127 (2002) 54-56 (*Lindemann, Andreas*) [vol. 1-2].

2169 **Laurentin, René** Nouveau Diatesseron: 'les quatre évangiles en un seul'. P 2002, Fayard 418 pp. €22. 2-213-61445-8 [LV.F 58,352— Beernaert, M.].

2170 [E]**Marshall, I. Howard** Concordance to the Greek New Testament. L 2002, Clark xxi; 1121 pp. £60. 0-567-08571-6. Sixth edition; Moulton & Geden.

2171 **Militarev, Alexander; Kogan, Leonid**, *al.*, Semitic etymological dictionary, vol. 1: anatomy of man and animals. AOAT 278/1: 2000 ⇒16,1760. [R]WZKM 92 (2002) 234-237 (*Podolsky, B.*).

IV. Exegesis generalis VT vel cum NT

D9 Commentaries on the whole Bible or OT

2172 [E]**Barton, John; Muddiman, John** The Oxford bible commentary. 2001 ⇒17,1860. [R]Theol. 105 (2002) 212-214 (*Moore, Elizabeth*); PrPe 16 (2002) 348-350 (*King, Nicholas*); ET 113 (2002) 388-389 (*McDonald, J. Ian*); Anvil 19/3 (2002) 209-213 (*Seddon, Philip*).

2173 [E]**Ghezzi, Bert** The New Jerusalem Bible: Saints' devotional edition. L 2002, Darton, L. & T. xiv; (4) 1610 pp. 0-232-52458-0.

2174 **Halbfas, Hubertus** Die Bibel: erschlossen und kommentiert. [2]2001 ⇒17,1864. [R]ThPQ 150 (2002) 200-201 (*Hubmann, Franz*); Anton. 77 (2002) 173-174 (*Ballhorn, Egbert*).

2175 [E]**Kroeger, Catherine Clark; Evans, Mary J.** The IVP women's bible commentary. DG 2002, InterVarsity xxxvii; 874 pp. $30. 0-83-08-1437-X [BiTod 40,324—Bergant, Dianne].

2176 [E]**Mills, Watson Early; Wilson, Richard Francis** Deuterocanonicals/Apocrypha. Mercer Commentary on the Bible 5: Macon, GA 2002, Mercer Univ. Pr. lxxviii; 208 pp. $20. 0-86554-510-3.

2177 The Navarre Bible: Joshua-Kings: the Books of Joshua, Judges, Ruth, 1 and 2 Samuel and 1 and 2 Kings in the Revised Standard Version and New Vulgate. Dublin 2002, Four Courts 640 pp. $40. 1-85182-676-9. Comment. members Fac. Theology Univ. of Navarre.

V. Libri historici VT

E1.1 Pentateuchus, Torah *Textus, commentarii*

2178 [E]**Alexander, T. Desmond; Baker, David W.** Dictionary of the Old Testament: pentateuch. DG 2002, InterVarsity xxii; 954 pp. $50. 0-8308-1781-6 [ThD 50,69—Heiser, W. Charles].

2179 [E]**Brenner, Athalya; Fontaine, Carole R.** Exodus to Deuteronomy. The Feminist Companion to the Bible 5: 2000 ⇒16,1772. [R]CBQ 64 (2002) 401-402 (*Laffey, Alice L.*).

2180 [E]**Dogniez, Cécile; Harl, Marguerite** La Bible d'Alexandrie: la Bible des Septante. Le pentateuque d'Alexandrie: texte grec et traduction. 2001 ⇒17,1616. [R]ASEs 19 (2002) 499-503 (*Neri, Camillo*); RBBras 19 (2002) 345-346 (*Minette de Tillesse, Gaëtan*).

2181 **Evans, Trevor V.** Verbal syntax in the Greek pentateuch: natural Greek usage and Hebrew interference. 2001 ⇒17,1879. [R]RBLit (2002)* (*Mclay, Tim*).

2182 *Giron Blanc, Luis F.* La versión samaritana del pentateuco. Narraciones bíblicas. 2002 ⇒1862. 75-82 [BuBB 37,9].

Herbst, Adrián ...Qumrán, el pentateuco samaritano ⇒1839.

2183 [E]**Kreisel, Ḥayyīm** Rabbi Nɪssɪᴍ Massilitani Liber Maʿase Nissim: commentarius in pentateuchum. J 2000, Nirdamim yud-alef; 515 pp.

2184 *Lienhard, Joseph T.* The christian reception of the pentateuch: patristic commentaries on the books of Moses. JECS 10 (2002) 373-388.

2185 *Polak, Frank H.* Pluses and minuses of the LXX on the pentateuch: textual transmission and gradual expansion. Bible and computer. 2002 ⇒548. 395-412.

2186 [E]**Pury, Albert de; Römer, Thomas** Le pentateuque en question: les origines et la composition des cinq premiers livres de la Bible à la lumière des recherches récentes. MoBi 19: Genève [3]2002 <1989, 1991>, Labor et F. xxxix; 4-429 pp. €40. 2-8309-1046-X.

2187 [E]**Sparks, Kenton L.** The pentateuch: an annotated bibliography. Bibliographies 1: GR 2002, Baker A. 160 pp. $17. 0-8010-2398-X [BiTod 41,197—Bergant, Dianne].

2188 **Van Seters, John** The pentateuch: a social-science commentary. 1999 ⇒15,1689...17,1892. [R]ThR 67 (2002) 130-134 (*Otto, Eckart*); ZAR 8 (2002) 407-411 (*Otto, Eckart*).

E1.2 *Pentateuchus* Introductio: Fontes JEDP

2189 [E]**Gertz, Jan Christian; Schmid, Konrad; Witte, Markus** Abschied vom Jahwisten: die Komposition des Hexateuch in der jüngsten Diskussion. BZAW 315: B 2002, De Gruyter xi; 345 pp. €98. 3-11-017121-X.

2190 **Alexander, T. Desmond** From paradise to the promised land: an introduction to the pentateuch. Carlisle 2002, Paternoster xxi; 339 pp. $20. 0-8010-2597-4 [ThD 50,59—Heiser, W. Charles].

2191 **Artus, Olivier** O pentateuco. [T]*Lopes, Joaquim Ferreira*: Cadernos Bíblicos 81: Lisboa 2002, Difusora Bíblica 64 pp.

2192 Ausgewählte Bibliographie zum Problem des 'jahwistischen Geschichtswerks' innerhalb des Pentateuchs/Hexateuchs. Abschied vom Jahwisten. BZAW 315: 2002 ⇒2189. 325-335.

2193 **Berkowitz, Ariel; Berkowitz, D'vorah** De tora: ontdek opnieuw wat de eerste vijf bijbelboeken betekenen voor de gemeente en voor U. Hoornaar 2002, Gideon 204 pp. 90-6067-8567.

2194 **Blenkinsopp, Joseph** El pentateuco: introducción a los cinco primeros libros de la biblia. 1999 ⇒15,1694; 17,1895. ᴿITER 28 (2002) 160-161 (*González C., Francisco Javier*).

2195 *Blenkinsopp, Joseph* A post-exilic lay source in Genesis 1-11;

2196 *Blum, Erhard* Die literarische Verbindung von Erzvätern und Exodus: ein Gespräch mit neueren Endredaktionshypothesen. Abschied vom Jahwisten. BZAW 315: 2002 ⇒2189. 49-61/119-156.

2197 *Breuer, Mordechai* Das Studium der Tora nach der Bibelkritik. Jud. 58 (2002) 154-171.

2198 *Brzegowy, Tadeusz* Duchowość kapłanów i lewitów w tradycji kapłańskiej (P) pięcioksięgu [La spiritualité des prêtres et des lévites selon la tradition sacerdotale du pentateuque]. ACra 34 (2002) 131-146. **P.**;

2199 Najnowsze teorie na temat powstania Piecioksiegu-próba oceny. CoTh 72/1 (2002) 11-44. **P.**;

2200 Kapłani i lewici w tradycji kapłańskiej (P) Piecioksiegu. CoTh 72/3 (2002) 5-32. **P.**

2201 **Fonsatti, José Carlos** O pentateuco. Cademos temáticos para evangelização 7: Petrópolis 2002, Vozes 44 pp.

2202 **Frevel, Christian** Mit Blick auf das Land die Schöpfung erinnern: zum Ende der Priestergrundschrift. Herders Biblische Studien 23: 2000 ⇒16,1789; 17,1900. ᴿThR 67 (2002) 128-130 (*Otto, Eckart*).

2203 **Graupner, Axel** Der Elohist: Gegenwart und Wirksamkeit des transzendenten Gottes in der Geschichte. WMANT 97: Neuk 2002, Neuk'er xiii; 459 pp. €69. 3-7887-1916-8. Bibl. 415-442.

2204 *Houk, Cornelius B.* Statistical analysis of Genesis sources. JSOT 27 (2002) 75-105.

2205 **Janowski, Bernd** Sühne als Heilsgeschehen: Studien zur Sühnetheologie der Priesterschrift. WUNT 55: 2000 ⇒16,1796. ᴿETR 77 2002) 122-123 (*Vincent, Jean M.*).

2206 *Johnstone, William* The use of the reminiscences in Deuteronomy in recovering the two main literary phases in the production of the pentateuch. Abschied vom Jahwisten. BZAW 315: 2002 ⇒2189. 247-273 [Ex 15,22-19,2; Num 32,32-42; Dt 1,6-4,40; 05-11; 29-30; 31,1-32,47].

2207 *King, Greg A.* La hipótesis documentaria. Theologika 17/1 (2002) 94-112.

2208 *Knauf, Ernst Axel* Towards an archaeology of the hexateuch. Abschied vom Jahwisten. BZAW 315: 2002 ⇒2189. 275-294 .

2209 *Kratz, Reinhard G.* Der vor- und der nachpriesterschriftliche Hexateuch. Abschied vom Jahwisten. BZAW 315: 2002 ⇒2189. 295-323.

2210 **Kratz, Reinhard Gregor** Die Komposition der erzählenden Bücher des Alten Testaments: Grundwissen der Bibelkritik. UTB 2157: 2000 ⇒16,1800; 17,1904. ᴿThR 67 (2002) 152-155 (*Otto, Eckart*); ThLZ 127 (2002) 623-625 (*Knauf, Ernst Axel*); BBR 12 (2002) 300-302 (*Moore, Michael S.*).

2211 *Larson, Gerhard* A system of biblical dates. SJOT 16 (2002) 184-206.

2212 *Levinson, Bernard M.* GOETHE's analysis of Exodus 34 and its influence on WELLHAUSEN: the Pfropfung of the documentary hypothesis. ZAW 114 (2002) 212-223.
2213 **McDermott, John J.** Reading the pentateuch: a historical introduction. Mahwah 2002, Paulist 250 pp. $20. 0-8091-4082-9 [BiTod 41, 128—Bergant, Dianne].
2214 *Moenikes, Ansgar* Die Tora des Mose: Beispiel eines kanongeschichtlichen Prozesses in der antiken Religionsgeschichte. [F]HOHEISEL, K.: JAC.E 34: 2002 ⇒59. 19-32.
2215 **Nicholson, Ernest** The pentateuch in the twentieth century. 1998 ⇒ 14,1584... 17,1907. [R]AsbTJ 56/2-57/1 (2001-2002) 146-149 (*Arnold, Bill T.*).
2216 *Otto, Eckart* Forschungen zum nachpriesterschriftlichen Pentateuch. ThR 67 (2002) 125-155.
2217 **Rofé, Alexander** Introduction to the composition of the pentateuch. BiSe 58: 1999 ⇒15,1712; 17,1910. [R]JJS 53 (2002) 381-382 (*Nahkola, Aulikki*).
2218 *Römer, Thomas* Nouvelles recherches sur le pentateuque: à propos de quelques ouvrages récents. ETR 77 (2002) 69-78;
2219 Le pentateuque toujours en question: bilan et perspectives après un quart de siècle de débat. Congress volume Basel 2001. VT.S 92: 2002 ⇒570. 343-374.
2220 *Schmidt, Ludwig* Die Kundschaftererzählung in Num 13-14 und Dtn 1,19-46: eine Kritik neuerer Pentateuchkritik. ZAW 114 (2002) 40-58.
2221 *Ska, Jean Louis* The Yahwist, a hero with a thousand faces: a chapter in the history of modern exegesis. Abschied vom Jahwisten. BZAW 315: 2002 ⇒2189. 1-23.
2222 **Ska, Jean Louis** Introduzione alla lettura del pentateuco: chiavi per l'interpretazione dei primi cinque libri della bibbia. Collana biblica: Bo 2002, EDB 315 pp. 88-10-22101-X;
2223 Introduction à la lecture du pentateuque. [T]*Vermorel, Frédéric*: 2000 ⇒16,1808; 17,1913. [R]JThS 53 (2002) 129-131 (*Nicholson, Ernest*); ScEs 54 (2002) 127-129 (*Laberge, Léo*); ThLZ 127 (2002) 33-36 (*Schmitt, Hans-Christof*); RBLit 4 (2002) 184-187 (*Carr, David M.*);
2224 Introducción a la lectura del Pentateuco. [T]*Gordón, Francisco*: 2001 ⇒17,1915. [R]ResB 33 (2002) 66-69 (*Sevilla Jiménez, Cristóbal*).
2225 *Sonnet, Jean-Pierre* "Lorsque Moïse eut achevé d'écrire" (Dt 31,24): une "théorie narrative" de l'écriture dans le pentateuque. RSR 90 (2002) 509-524.
2226 *Tin-sheung, Wong* Tetrateuch? pentateuch? hexateuch?: analysis of torah criticism. Jian Dao 18 (2002) 21-46 Sum. 44. **C.**
2227 [E]**Watts, James Washington** Persia and torah: the theory of imperial authorization of the pentateuch. SBL.Symposium 17: 2001 ⇒17, 1919. [R]ZAR 8 (2002) 411-413 (*Otto, Eckart*).

E1.3 *Pentateuchus*, themata

2228 **Domański, Adam** The figure of Caleb in the OT tradition: its role and importance. [D]*Agius, Joseph A.*: Łowicz 2002, 258 pp. Diss. Pont. Univ. S. Thomae; Bibl. 229-248.
2229 **Greifenhagen, F.V.** Egypt on the pentateuch's ideological map: constructing Biblical Israel's identity. [D]*Crenshaw, J.L.* :JSOT.S 361: L

2002, Sheffield A. xi; 325 pp. £65. 0-8264-6211-1. Diss. Duke; Bibl. 277-306.

2230 *Loader, James Alfred* 'Law' and 'gospel' in the pentateuch organization. HTS 57 (2001) 70-85 [OTA 25,439].

2231 *Mathew, Alex* God's healing dreams: pentateuch and messianic hope. God of big dreams. 2002 ⇒359. 78-105.

2232 *McBride, S. Dean, Jr.* The God who creates and governs: pentateuchal foundations of biblical theology. ^FACHTEMEIER, P. 2002 ⇒1. 11-28.

2233 *Pardes, Ilana* Imagining the birth of ancient Israel: national metaphors in the bible. Cultures. 2002 ⇒448. 9-41.

2234 *Phillips, Anthony* The attitude of torah to wealth. Essays on biblical law. JSOT.S 344: 2002 <1986> ⇒223. 148-163 [Dt 8,11-18].

2235 *Warning, Wilfried* Terminological patterns and the noun ʿrlh 'foreskin' in the pentateuch. ScrB 32 (2002) 93-99.

E1.4 **Genesis**; *textus, commentarii*

2236 **Brodie, Thomas L.** Genesis as dialogue: a literary, historical, & theological commentary. 2001 ⇒17,1938. ^RRRT 9 (2002) 212-216 (*Norton, Gerard J.*); TS 63 (2002) 840-841 (*Simkins, Ronald A.*).

2237 **Brueggemann, Walter** Genesi. ^E*Franzosi, Teresa*: Strumenti—Commentari 9: T 2002, Claudiana 483 pp. €34. 88-7016-414-4. Bibl. 471-475.

2238 **Cappelletto, Gianni** Genesi (Capitoli 12-50). Dabar—Logos—Parola, AT: Padova 2002, Messaggero 240 pp. Bibl.

2239 **Hartley, John E.** Genesis. NIBCOT: 2000 ⇒16,1828. ^RTheoforum 33 (2002) 235-6 (*Vogels, Walter*); RBLit (2002)* (*Petersen, David*).

2240 **Hendel, Ronald S.** The text of Genesis 1-11. 1998 ⇒14,1618...17, 1942. ^RRBLit (2002)* (*Greenspoon, Leonard J.*).

2241 *Knobloch, Frederick W.* 'Transcription technique' and the text of the Greek Genesis. BIOSCS 35 2002 (2002) 97-109.

2242 ^E**Louth, Andrew** Genesis I-II [! 1-11]. ACCS.OT 1: 2001 ⇒17, 1948. ^RFaith & Mission 19/2 (2002) 79-81 (*Moseley, N. Allan*).

2243 ^E**MacGinty, Gerard** The reference bible—das Bibelwerk: pauca problemata de enigmatibus ex tomis canonicis... Libri de Pentateucho Moysi. CChr.CM 173; Scriptores Celtigenae Pars 3. 2000 ⇒16, 1833. ^RAevum 76 (2002) 267-270 (*Löfstedt, Bengt*).

2244 ^E**McGrath, Alister; Packer, J.I.** Genesis by John CALVIN. Wheaton 2001, Crossway 384 pp. $20. 1-581-343-019.

2245 ^T**Meschonnie, Henri** Au commencement: traduction de la Genèse. Ecritures saintes des religions du livre: P 2002, Desclée de B. 370 pp. €22. 2-220-05092-0. Bibl. 23-24, 220 [BCLF 641,24].

2246 **Minissale, Antonino** Alle origini dell'universo e dell'uomo (Gn 1-11): interrogativi esistenziali dell'antico Israele. La Bibbia nelle nostre mani 36: CinB 2002, S. Paolo 92 pp. €5. 88-215-4517-2. Bibl. 89. ^RLaós 9/2 (2002) 99-100 (*Calambrogio, Leone*).

2247 **O'Loughlin, Thomas** Teachers and code-breakers: the Latin Genesis tradition, 430-800. StPatr 35: 1999 ⇒15,1766...17,1951. ^RRSR 90 (2002) 148-149 (*Dulaey, Martine*).

2248 **Rogerson, John William; Moberly, R.W.L.; Johnstone, William** Genesis and Exodus. OTGu N.S. 1-2: 2001 ⇒17,1952. ^RRBLit (2002)* (*Steinberg, Naomi; Yarchin, William*).

2249   **Ruppert, Lothar** Genesis: ein kritischer und theologischer Kommentar, 2: 11,27 - 25,18. FzB 98: Wü 2002, Echter 657 pp. €36.80. 3-429-02461-7. ᴿThLZ 127 (2002) 1287-1290 (*Seebass, Horst*).
2250   **Seebass, Horst** Genesis. 1996-2000. ⇒12,1408... 16,2168. ᴿThLZ 127 (2002) 30-33 (*Gertz, Jan Christian*).
2251   ᴱ**Sheridan, Mark** Genesis 12-50. ACCS.OT 2: DG 2002, InterVarsity xxxix; 392 pp. 0-8308-1472-8. Bibl. 370-373.
2252   *Stroumsa, Sarah* From the earliest known Judaeo-Arabic commentary on Genesis. JStAI 27 (2002) 375-395.
2253   *Tharedkadavil, Antony* Is Genesis a confusion?: the organization of the pre-flood primeval history (Gen 1,1-6,8) and its message. BiBh 28 (2002) 595-631.
2254   ᴱ**Wénin, André** Studies in the book of Genesis: literature, redaction and history. BEThL 155: 2001 ⇒17,1936. ᴿCart. 18 (2002) 552-553 (*Sanz Valdivieso, R.*); ETR 77 (2002) 587-589 (*Bauks, Michaela*).
2255   *Zeytounian, Andranik* Des traces non-Origéniques dans le texte arménien classique de 'La Genèse'. BAZMAVEP 160 (2002) 142-149.
2256   *Zipor, Moshe A.* Some notes on the Greek text of Genesis in the common editions. BIOSCS 35 (2002) 121-126.

E1.5 *Genesis*, topics

2257   **Borgman, Paul** Genesis: the story we haven't heard. DG 2001, InterVarsity 252 pp. $15 [BS 161,243—Chisholm, Robert B.].
2258   **Carr, David M.** Reading the fractures of Genesis: historical and literary approaches. 1996 ⇒12,1345... 16,1847. ᴿOLZ 97 (2002) 554-560 (*Pietsch, Michael*).
2259   *Couto, António* Da cobiça à aliança: uma leitura de Gn 4-11. Igreja e Missão 55/1 (2002) 3-21.
2260   *Davidson, Jo Ann* Genesis matriarchs engage feminism. AUSS 40 (2002) 169-178.
2261   *De Benedetti, Paolo* Globalizzazione al negativo e al positivo nel pensiero biblico. RTM 135 (2002) 335-338 [Gen 11].
2262   ᴱ**Dozzi, Dino** Genesi: cantico della creazione cantico della creatura. Itinerari di fede: Bo 2002, EDB 168 pp. €10.60. 88-1062113-1.
2263   **Gardner, Bruce K.** The Genesis calendar: the synchronistic tradition in Genesis 1-11. 2001 ⇒17,1965. ᴿDSD 9 (2002) 254-258 (*Stern, Sacha*) [Gen 5,1-32; 11,10-26].
2264   *Gnuse, Robert K.* A process theological interpretation of the primeval history in Genesis 2-11. Horizons 29/1 (2002) 23-41.
2265   ᴱ**Habel, Norman C.; Wurst, Shirley** The earth story in Genesis. 2000 ⇒16,1848. ᴿBiblInterp 10 (2002) 81-83 (*Mullen, E. Theodore*); JRTI 5/2 (2002) 65-67 (*Snavely, Cynthia*); RBLit (2002)* (*Swenson-Méndez, Kristin*).
2266   **Humphreys, W. Lee** The character of God in the book of Genesis: a narrative appraisal. Old Testament Studies: 2001 ⇒17,1968. ᴿRRT 9 (2002) 123-126 (*Brummitt, Mark*); Theol. 105 (2002) 357-358 (*Dell, Katherine J.*).
2267   *Janecko, Benedict* Forgiveness and reconciliation in Genesis. BiTod 40 (2002) 5-11.
2268   **Lim, Johnson T.K.** Grace in the midst of judgment: grappling with Genesis 1-11. BZAW 314: B 2002, De Gruyter ix (2); 262 pp. €68. 3-11-017420-0. Bibl. 231-248.

2269 *Schultz, Richard* What is 'canonical' about a canonical biblical theology?: Genesis as a case study of recent Old Testament proposals. Biblical theology. 2002 ⇒558. 83-99.
2270 *Van der Horst, Pieter W.* Antediluvian knowledge: Graeco-Roman and Jewish speculations about wisdom from before the flood. Japheth. CBET 32: 2002 <2000> ⇒251. 139-158.
2271 *Warning, Wilfried* Terminologische Verknüpfungen in der Urgeschichte. ZAW 114 (2002) 262-269.
2272 *Wénin, André* Lire la Genèse comme un récit: quelques clés. Quand la bible se raconte. 2002 ⇒355. 39-66.
2273 *William, Lawrence John* Violence in the patriarchal history. Jeevadhara 32 (2002) 85-94.
2274 **Williams, Michael James** Deception in Genesis. Studies in Biblical Literature 32: 2001 ⇒17,1976. [R]BiblInterp 10 (2002) 455-458 (*Steinberg, Naomi*).
2275 **Witte, Markus** Die biblische Urgeschichte: redaktions- und theologiegeschichtliche Beobachtungen zu Genesis 1,1-11,26. BZAW 265 1998 ⇒14,1640... 17,1977. [R]ThR 67 (2002) 134-136 (*Otto, Eckart*); WO 32 (2002) 236-238 (*Richter, H.-F.*); RB 109 (2002) 422-426 (*Vera, J. Loza*).

E1.6 **Creatio**, *Genesis 1s*

2276 *Alomía, Haroldo* Sujeción del planeta en Génesis 1:26-28 y su mensaje ecológico vinculado con el mensaje de la Iglesia Adventista del Séptimo Día. Theologika 17/1 (2002) 42-92.
2277 *Alvarez-Pedrosa Nuñez, Juan Antonio* La versión eslava más antigua de Génesis 1: introducción: historia del texto. Narraciones bíblicas. 2002 ⇒1862. 111-117 [BuBB 37,9].
2278 *Annoni, Maurizio* Ascolto la voce dei dimenticati;
2279 *Ardigò, Achielle* La politica dei valori. Genesi: cantico. 2002 ⇒ 2262. 56-59/63-64.
2280 *Bauks, Michaela* Le shabbat: un temple dans le temps. ETR 77 (2002) 473-490.
2281 *Blum, Erhard* Urgeschichte. TRE 34. 2002 ⇒800. 436-445.
2282 *Bolewski, Jacek* Chaos i początek [Chaos and the beginning]. StBob 2 (2002) 79-98 Sum. 98. P.
2283 **Borella, Jean** Le poème de la création: traduction de la Genèse 1-3. Genève 2002, Ad Solem 45 pp. €10. 2-88482-000-0 [RTL 33,570s— Wénin, A.].
2284 *Brandscheidt, Renate* 'Es ist nicht gut, daß der Mensch allein ist' (Gen 2,18): zur Tradition und Interpretation von Gen 2,18-24. [F]HAAG, E. 2002 ⇒55. 29-60.
2285 *Butkus, Russell A.* Creation-in-crisis: biblical creation theology and the disclosure of God. Theology and sacred scripture. 2002 ⇒549. 35-52.
2286 *Carlo, Giuseppe de* Raccantando le fondamenta dal presente;
2287 *Casadio, Alessandro* Dalla fine al principio. Genesi: cantico. 2002 ⇒ 2262. 9-14/36-38.
2288 *Clasen, Norbert* Die Vernunft des biblischen Schöpfungsglaubens und Menschenbildes. Theologisches 32 (2002) 247-260.
2289 *Dattrino, Lorenzo* Gen 1,26-27 e Gen 2,7 nella interpretazione patristica (le scuole "asiatica" e "alessandrina"). TyV 43 (2002) 196-204.

2290 *Dozzi, Dino* Ivi è perfetta letizia;
2291 Lavorare liberi di lavorare. Genesi: cantico. 2002 ⇒2262. 21-25/48-52.
2292 *Dumbrell, William J.* Genesis 2:1-17: a foreshadowing of the new creation. Biblical theology. 2002 ⇒558. 53-65.
2293 **Euvé, François** Penser la création comme jeu. CFi: 2000 ⇒16,1871. [R]TS 63 (2002) 405-406 (*Guarino, Thomas G.*).
2294 *Gallego, María Ángeles; Abumalham, Montserrat* La versión judeo-árabe. Narraciones bíblicas. 2002 ⇒1862. 83-90 [BuBB 37,9].
2295 *Geldbach, Erich* The concept of creation in the conciliar process of justice, peace and the integrity of creation. Creation in Jewish and christian tradition. JSOT.S 319: 2002 ⇒593. 291-308.
2296 *Giron Blanc, Luis F.; Abumalham, Montserrat* La comparación de versiones. Narraciones bíblicas. 2002 ⇒1862. 119-139 [BuBB 37,9].
2297 **Goldberg, Sylvie Anne** La Clepsydre: essai sur la pluralité des temps dans le judaïsme. 2000 ⇒16,1876. [R]JQR 92 (2002) 598-601 (*Harvey, Warren Zev*).
2298 *Gonzalez Casado, Pilar; Abumalham, Montserrat* Génesis 1-2,4 en la biblia árabe cristiana. Narraciones bíblicas. 2002 ⇒1862. 91-100 [BuBB 37,9].
2299 *Gordon, Cyrus H.* Gnostic light on Genesis 1 and 2 via Maśśa'. Eblaitica 4. 2002 ⇒474. 197-198 [Prov 30].
2300 *Greenstein, Edward L.* God's golem: the creation of the human in Genesis 2;
2301 *Gruenwald, Ithamar* The creation of the world and the shaping of ethnos and religion in ancient Israel. Creation in Jewish and christian tradition. JSOT.S 319: 2002 ⇒593. 219-239/179-218.
2302 **Hayes, Zachary** The gift of being: a theology of creation. 2001 ⇒ 17,1997. [R]Pacifica 15 (2002) 97-98 (*Darragh, Neil*); HeyJ 43 (2002) 235-236 (*Northway, Eric W.*).
2303 **Herzfeld, Noreen L.** In our image: artificial intelligence and the human spirit. Mp 2002, Fortress 135 pp. $16. 0-8006-3476-4. [R]Anton. 77 (2002) 754-757 (*Oviedo, Lluís*) [Gen 1,26].
2304 *Hoffman, Yair* The first creation story: canonical and diachronic aspects. Creation in Jewish and christian tradition. JSOT.S 319: 2002 ⇒593. 32-53.
2305 *Knauf, Ernst Axel* 'Seine Arbeit, die Gott geschaffen hat, um sie auszuführen': Syntax und Theologie in Gen 2,3. BN 111 (2002) 24-27.
2306 *Kok, Johnson L.* Explication of an exegetical enigma in Genesis 1:1-3. AJTh 16/2 (2002) 301-314.
2307 *Lafratta, Lucia* L'ultimo tilt della pallina. Genesi: cantico. 2002 ⇒2262. 65-67.
2308 *Lode, Lars* The two creation stories in Genesis chapters 1 to 3. JOTT 14 (2002) 1-32, 33-52.
2309 *Lorenzetti, Luigi* Quello che sta nel mezzo;
2310 Viventi in chi dà vita. Genesi: cantico. 2002 ⇒2262. 60-62/29-31.
2311 *Merino, José Antonio* Sfogliando il libro delle armoni;
2312 *Monti, Stefania* A immagine del settimo giorno. Genesi: cantico. 2002 ⇒2262. 26-28/45-47.
2313 **Morales, José** Creation theology. 2001 ⇒17,2005. [R]Ang. 79 (2002) 740-741 (*Paluch, Michał*).
2314 *Motta, Giovanni* Il lieto operare perpetuo. Genesi: cantico. 2002 ⇒ 2262. 53-55.

2315 *Núñez, Miguel A.* "Feminino": origen ideológico de una palabra. DavarLogos 1/1 (2002) 81-83 [Gen 1,26-27].

2316 *Oh, Jeffrey* A reflection on Genesis 1-11 as a missiological preface. MissTod 4 (2002) 242-253.

2317 *O'Neill, J.C.* How early is the doctrine of creatio ex nihilo?. [Philo] JThS 53 (2002) 449-465 [Prov 8,24; 2 Macc 7,28; Rev 4,11].

2318 *Polak, Frank H.* Poetic style and parallelism in the creation account (Genesis 1.1-2.3). Creation in Jewish and christian tradition. JSOT.S 319: 2002 ⇒593. 2-31.

2319 *Raffaeli, Barbara* Alternative di un 'doppio lavoro'. Genesi: cantico. 2002 ⇒2262. 68-70.

2320 *Ravasi, Gianfranco* Bereshît... en archè: Genesi 1-3: il canto della creazione e della redenzione. Il libro sacro. 2002 ⇒356. 1-18.

2321 **Rödding, Gerhard** Die Schöpfungsgeschichte: wie ich sie heute verstehen kann. Gü 2002, Gü 144 pp. 3-579-06020-1.

2322 *Sarti, Eugenio* Il pilota dell'universo. Genesi: cantico. 2002 ⇒2262. 32-35.

2323 *Sokol, Jan* Der zweifache Schöpfungsbericht als hermeneutischer Schlüssel. Philosophical hermeneutics. WUNT 153: 2002 ⇒367. 238-244.

2324 **Van Wolde, Ellen J.** Racconti dell'inizio: Genesi 1-11 e altri racconti di creazione. BiBi(B) 24: 1999 ⇒15,1838; 16,1908. [R]Asp. 49 (2002) 148-149 (*Villano, Francesco*).

2325 *Watson, Timothy* Is HESCHEL's sabbath biblical?. AUSS 40 (2002) 265-272.

2326 *Weimar, Peter* Struktur und Komposition der priesterschriftlichen Schöpfungserzählung (Gen 1,1-2,4a*). [F]DIETRICH, M. 2002 ⇒28. 803-843.

2327 **Wilkinson, David** The message of creation: encountering the Lord of the universe. The Bible Speaks Today: Leicester 2002, Inter-Varsity Pr. 296 pp. £10. 0-85111-269-2.

E1.7 *Genesis 1s*: **Bible and myth [⇒M3.8]**

2328 *Aires, Joarez V.* A linguagem mítica no Gênesis. Estudos bíblicos 75 (2002) 52-60.

2329 *Berquist, Jon L.* Critical spatiality and the construction of the ancient world. [F]FLANAGAN, J.: JSOT.S 359: 2002 ⇒38. 14-29.

2330 **Costa, Alcindo** Génesis—das lendas e mitos da criação à fé no Deus Criador. Dinamização Bíblica 5: Lisboa 2002, Difusora Bíblica 158 pp.

2331 *Gerlitz, Peter* Ursprungsmythen. TRE 34. 2002 ⇒800. 450-458.

2332 **Keel, Othmar; Schroer, Silvia** Schöpfung: Biblische Theologien im Kontext altorientalischer Religionen. Gö 2002, Vandenhoeck & R. 302 pp. €32. 3-525-53500-7. Bibl. 259-281. [R]RBBras 19 (2002) 379-381 (*Minette de Tillesse, Gaëtan*).

2333 *Malter, Rudolf* Die Kritik der Philosophie am Weltbild der Religion. Religion und Weltbild. 2002 ⇒443. 179-191.

2334 *Metzler, Kai Alexander* Tod, Weiblichkeit und Ästhetik im mesopotamischen Weltschöpfungsepos *Enūma eliš*. Sex and gender. 2002 ⇒ 712. 393-411;

2335 Perfekta im jungbabylonischen Weltschöpfungsepos. [F]DIETRICH, M. 2002 ⇒28. 435-495.

2336 *Michel, Diethelm* Die Funktion von Weltbildvorstellungen im Alten Testament. Religion und Weltbild. 2002 ⟹443. 31-48.
2337 *Rechenmacher, Hans* Gott und das Chaos: ein Beitrag zum Verständnis von Gen 1,1-3. ZAW 114 (2002) 1-20.
2338 *Roberts, J.J.M.* Myth versus history: relaying the comparative foundations. The bible and the ANE. 2002 <1976> ⟹230. 59-71.
2339 *Sjöberg, Åke W.* In the beginning. ᴹJACOBSEN, T. 2002 ⟹62. 229-247.
2340 *Strobel, August* Zur antiken Theorie der Einheit der Welt. JETh 16 (2002) 69-73.
2341 *Vermeylen, Jacques* Les représentations du cosmos dans la bible hébraïque. Bible et sciences. 2002 ⟹358. 59-102.
2342 *Wolff, Günter* O projeto do jardim x o projeto da serpente (Gn 2,4-3,24). Estudos bíblicos 74 (2002) 52-64.
2343 *Zeller, Dieter* Einführung Religion und Weltbild. 2002 ⟹443. 5-12.
2344 **Zimmerman, Anthony** The primeval revelation in myths and in Genesis: a dynamic subject much neglected by theologians. 1999 ⟹15, 1854. ᴿHPR 102/4 (2002) 78-79 (*Kalpakgian, Mitchell*).

E1.8 *Gen 1s, Jos 10,13*...: **The Bible, the Church and science**

2345 **Aviezer, Nathan** Fossils and faith: understanding torah and science. Hoboken, NJ 2002, KTAV xv; 270 pp. 0-88125-607-2.
2346 *Bogaert, Pierre-Maurice* 'Le soleil s'arrête à Gabaon': interprétations de la bible et avancée des sciences. Bible et sciences. Le livre et le rouleau 15: 2002 ⟹358. 157-177 [Josh 10,12-15].
2347 *Buitendag, J. Karl* Heim se verstaan van ruimte in die debat tussen die teologie en natuurwetenskap. VeE 23 (2002) 291-304.
2348 **Buonfiglio, Michele** La creazione nella bibbia e nella scienza. F 2002, Pagnini e M. 158 pp. €13.50.
2349 **Davis, John Jefferson** The frontiers of science & faith: examining questions from the big bang to the end of the universe. DG 2002, InterVarsity 199 pp. $15. 0-8308-26645 [ThD 49,265: W.C. Heiser].
2350 *Euvé, François* L'imaginaire biblique des scientifiques: regard d'un théologien. Bible et sciences. 2002 ⟹358. 103-123.
2351 **Facchini, Fiorenzo** Origini dell'uomo ed evoluzione culturale: profili scientifici, filosofici, religiosi. Di fronte e attraverso, 588: Le origini dell'uomo: Mi 2002, Jaca 311 pp. €23. 8816-40588-0. Bibl. 287-311.
2352 *Gräb, Wilhelm* Creation or nature?: about dialogue between theology and natural sciences. Creation in Jewish and christian tradition. JSOT.S 319: 2002 ⟹593. 277-290.
2353 **Griffin, David Ray** Religion and scientific naturalism: overcoming the conflicts. 2000 ⟹16,1937; 17,2034. ᴿZygon 37 (2002) 985-990 (*Pailin, David A.*).
2354 ᴱ**Hayward, James L.** Creation reconsidered: scientific, biblical, and theological perspectives. 2000 ⟹16,1939. ᴿAUSS 40 (2002) 148-150 (*Standish, Timothy*).
2355 **Howell, Kenneth J.** God's two books: Copernican cosmology and biblical interpretation in early modern science. ND 2002, Univ. of Notre Dame Pr. viii; 319 pp. $40. 0-268-01045-5. ᴿIsis 93 (2002) 482-483 (*Harrison, Peter*).
2356 *Lambert, Dominique* TEILHARD et la bible. Bible et sciences. Le livre et le rouleau 15: 2002 ⟹358. 125-156.

2357 ^E**Lerner, Michel-Pierre** Tommaso CAMPANELLA: apologia pro GA-
LILEO: apologie de Galilée. 2001 ⇒17,2038. ^RRThPh 134 (2002) 79-
80 (*Suarez-Nani, Tiziana*); RPL 100 (2002) 818-820 (*Stoffel, Jean-
François*); SCJ 33 (2002) 1154-1155 (*Kelter, Irving A.*).

2358 **Lidsey, James E.** The bigger Bang. C 2002, CUP ix; 134 pp. 0-521-
01273-2.

2359 **Lucas, Ernest** Can we believe Genesis today?: the bible and the
questions of science. 2001 ⇒17,2040. ^RSBET 20 (2002) 112-113
(*McIntosh, Alex*).

2360 **Moore, John A.** From Genesis to genetics: the case of evolution and
creation. Berkeley 2002, Univ. of California Pr. xvi; 224 pp.

2361 *Müller, Helmut* Evolution und Schöpfung—eine nicht ausgestandene
Kontroverse. FKTh 18/2 (2002) 106-121.

2362 *Pascual, Rafael* Algunas consideraciones sobre el *caso Galileo*.
Ecclesia 16 (2002) 201-210.

2363 *Roberts, Michael* The Genesis of John Ray and his successors. EvQ
74 (2002) 143-163.

2364 **Rose, Seraphim** Genesis, creation and early man. 2000 ⇒16,1946.
^RSVTQ 46 (2002) 365-390 (*Theokritoff, George; Theokritoff, Eliza-
beth*).

2365 **Rowland, Wade** GALILEO's mistake: the archeology of a myth. 2001
⇒17,2046. ^RHPR 102/8 (2002) 78-79 (*DeMarco, Donald*).

2366 *Sandorfi, A.M.; Khandaker, M.* Modern cosmology and the Judeo-
Christian and Islamic creation accounts. JJSS 2 (2002) 7-43.

2367 *Trublet, Jacques* La science dans la bible: méthode et résultats. Bible
et sciences. Le livre et le rouleau 15: 2002 ⇒358. 11-58.

2368 **Wahrman, Miryam Z.** Brave new Judaism: when science and scripture collide. Hanover, NH 2002, Brandeis University Press xix (2)
287 pp. 1-58465-031-1. Bibl. 265-275.

2369 **Wise, Kurt P.** Faith, form, and time: what the bible teaches and
science confirms about creation and the age of the universe. Nv 2002,
Broadman & H. 287 pp. $15. 08054-24628]ThD 50,95: Heiser, W.].

2370 **Witham, Larry A.** Where DARWIN meets the bible: creationists and
evolutionists in America. NY 2002, OUP vi; 330 pp. $30. 0-1951-
5045-7.

E1.9 *Peccatum originale*, the sin of Eden, *Genesis 2-3*

2371 *Alexandre, Jean* Sur les deux noms du Dieu de Genèse 2/4b-3/24 ou
la 'théo-logique' d'un Dieu critique. ETR 77 (2002) 415-420.

2372 **Alexandre, Jean** Eden, huis clos: une parabole du Dieu critique, lecture du récit biblique de Genèse 2,4b-4,1. Sémantiques: P 2002,
L'Harmattan 180 pp. €15. 2-7475-2824-3.

2373 *Boato, Michele* Storie di benzene e promesse di serpente. Genesi:
cantico. 2002 ⇒2262. 39-41.

2374 *Brassiani, Itacir* "O diabo não há! Existe é homem humano!" : apon-
tamentos sobre o demônio em "Grande Sertão: Veredas". Estudos
bíblicos 74 (2002) 11-22.

2375 **Callender, Dexter E.** Adam in myth and history: ancient Israelite
perspectives on the primal human. HSSt 48: 2000 ⇒16,1957; 17,
2056. ^RBib. 83 (2002) 583-586 (*Noegel, Scott B.*).

2376   *Dafni, Evangelia* G. שֹׁנָח—ὄφις: Genesis 3 und Jesaja 27,1 auch im Lichte von I Kön. 22,19-23; Hi. 1,6-12; 2,1-7 und Sach 3,1-2. BIOSCS 35 (2002) 47-54.

2377   *Dietrich, Manfried* Der "Garten Eden" und die babylonischen Parkanlagen im Tempelbezirk: vom Ursprung des Menschen im Gottesgarten, seiner Verbannung daraus und seiner Sehnsucht nach Rückkehr dorthin. Religiöse Landschaften. AOAT 301: 2002 ⇒408. 1-29.

2378   **Enzo, Carlo** Adamo, dove sei?. La Cultura 557: Mi 2002, Il Saggiatore 443 pp. 88-428-0984-5. Introd. *Romano Màdera*; Bibl. 418.

2379   **Fernandez, D.** Il peccato originale: un problema antico da interpretare in modo nuovo. Barzago 2002, Vicenza 60 pp.

2380   *Gooder, Paula* Eden and beyond: images of paradise in biblical and extra-biblical literature. NBl 83 (2002) 3-15.

2381   *Gosse, Bernard* L'inclusion de l'ensemble Genèse-II Rois, entre la perte du jardin d'Eden et celle de Jérusalem. ZAW 114 (2002) 189-211.

2382   **Grillo, Roberta** Il principe di questo mondo: il diavolo nella storia, nelle religioni, nei documenti, nelle testimonianze. Smeraldi 3: Mi 2002, Ares 413 pp. 88-8155-233-7. Bibl. 385-388.

2383   *Harrison, Peter* Original sin and the problem of knowledge in early modern Europe. JHI 63/2 (2002) 239-259.

2384   *Kilpp, Nelson* Os poderes demoníacos no Antigo Testamento. Estudos bíblicos 74 (2002) 23-36.

2385   *Klein, Wassilios, al.*, Teufel. TRE 33. 2002 ⇒799. 113-147.

2386   *Kübel, Paul* Die Ablehnung einer Muttergottheit als Hintergrund von Gen 3,19f. BN 113 (2002) 24-28 [Job 1,21; Qoh 5,14].

2387   *Levine, Nachman* The curse and the blessing: narrative discourse syntax and literary form. JSOT 27 (2002) 189-199 [Gen 3,11-14].

2388   *Léon-Dufour, Xavier* El diablo. SelTeol 41 (2002) 347-354 <Etudes 396 (2002) 349-363.

2389   *Malamud, Martha* Writing original sin. [Prudentius] JECS 10 (2002) 329-360.

2390   *Matura, Thaddée* Ritorno al paradiso. Genesi: cantico. 2002 ⇒2262. 18-20.

2391   *McMahon, Kevin A.* Man and woman at the moment of creation: a covenantal study of the first sin. Com(US) 29 (2002) 506-523.

2392   *Meinhold, Arndt* Frau und Mann in biblischen Schöpfungstexten. Zur weisheitlichen Sicht. 2002 ⇒209. 35-47 [BuBB 37,10].

2393   *Mende, Theresia* Sieger über Satan: zur glaubensgeschichtlichen Entstehung der Deutung von Gen 3,15 als Protoevangelium. ᶠHAAG, E. 2002 ⇒55. 87-121.

2394   *Monti, Stefania* Liberi e imperfetti. Genesi: cantico. 2002 ⇒2262. 15-17.

2395   *Müller, Hans-Peter* Eva und das Paradies. ᶠDIETRICH, M. 2002 ⇒28. 501-510 [Gen 3,20].

2396   *Nash, Peter T.; Neuenfeldt, Elaine G.* De magias e demônios: os processos de exclusão e marginalização do/a outro/a. Estudos bíblicos 74 (2002) 70-78.

2397   *Navone, John* Death, Satan, and sin. BiTod 40 (2002) 366-373.

2398   *Novák, Mirko* The artificial paradise: programme and ideology of royal gardens. Sex and gender. 2002 ⇒712. 443-460.

2399 **Ognibeni, Bruno** Dominare la moglie?: a proposito di Gn 3,16. Pontificio Istituto Giovanni Paolo II, Cathedra: R 2002, Lateran Univ. Pr. 46 pp. 88-465-0208-6.

2400 **Ojewole, Afolarin** The seed in Genesis 3:15: an exegetical and intertextual study. ^D*Davidson, R.M.*: 2002 537 pp. Diss. Andrews [RTL 34,593].

2401 *Ouro, Roberto* The Garden of Eden account: the chiastic structure of Genesis 2-3. AUSS 40 (2002) 219-243.

2402 *Pinzetta, Inácio* O mal e suas determinaçãoes na história. Estudos bíblicos 74 (2002) 37-41.

2403 *Porath, Renatus* Lúcifer—a evoluç̃ao de um simbolismo do mal. Estudos bíblicos 74 (2002) 42-51.

2404 *Porro, Carlo* Il peccato originale: prospettive teologiche. RCI 83 (2002) 296-311.

2405 *Rilloma, N.C.* Biography of the devil: an alternative approach to the cosmic conflict. JATS 13/2 (2002) 136-150 [NTAb 47,300].

2406 *Rossé, Gérard* Riflessioni sul rapporto uomo-donna in Genesi 2-3. Nuova Umanità 24 (2002) 743-760.

2407 *Russouw, Tiana* 'I will greatly increase your toil and your pregnancies': alternate perspectives on Genesis 3:16. OTEs 15 (2002) 149-163 {Genesis}03,16.

2408 *Schmid, Konrad* Die Unteilbarkeit der Weisheit: Überlegungen zur sogenannten Paradieserzählung Gen 2f. und ihrer theologischen Tendenz. ZAW 114 (2002) 21-39.

2409 *Schüngel-Straumann, Helen* Feministische Exegese ausgewählter Beispiele aus der Urgeschichte: Rückblick auf ein Vierteljahrhundert feministische Auslegung von Gen 2 und 3. Congress volume Basel 2001. VT.S 92: 2002 ⇒570. 205-223.

2410 **Stordalen, Terje** Echoes of Eden: Genesis 2-3 and symbolism of the Eden garden in biblical Hebrew literature. 2000 ⇒16,1987; 17,2075. ^ROLZ 97 (2002) 386-392 (*Bauks, Michaela*); ThLZ 127 (2002) 36-39 (*Witte, Markus*); Bib. 83 (2002) 268-273 (*Morla, Victor*).

2411 **Vaz, Armindo dos Santos** A visão das origens em Gen 2,4b-3,24 como coere*ncia temática e unidade literária. 1996 ⇒12,1557; 14, 1757. ^RRTL 33 (2002) 424-425 (*Wénin, A.*).

2412 **Wiley, Tatha** Original sin: origins, developments, contemporary meanings. Mahwah 2002, Paulist vii; 276 pp. $20. 0-8091-4128-0 [ThD 50,194—Heiser, W. Charles].

2413 *Willi-Plein, Ina* Sprache als Schlüssel zur Schöpfung: Überlegungen zur sogenannten Sündenfallgeschichte in Gen 3. Sprache als Schlüssel. 2002 <1995> ⇒261. 24-40.

E2.1 Cain and Abel; *gigantes, longaevi; Genesis 4s*

2414 *Dietrich, Walter* "Wo ist dein Bruder?": zu Tradition und Intention von Genesis 4. Theopolitik. 2002 <1976> ⇒159. 159-172.

2415 *Gilboa, R.* Who 'fell down' to our earth?: a different light an Genesis 6:1-4. BN 111 (2002) 66-75 [Gen 6,1-04].

2416 *Kvanvig, Helge S.* Gen 6,1-4 as an antediluvian event. SJOT 16 (2002) 79-112.

2417 *Reis, Pamela Tamarkin* What Cain said: a note on Genesis 4.8. JSOT 27 (2002) 107-113.

2418   *Stuckenbruck, Loren T.* Genesis 6:1-4 as the basis for divergent readings during the second temple period. Henoch 24 (2002) 99-106.

E2.2 *Diluvium*, the Flood; *Gilgameš (Atraḫasis)*; Genesis 6...

2419   *Accrocca, Felice* Le eredità di un testamento. Genesi: cantico. 2002
⇒2262. [S. Franceso] 79-81 [Gen 11].
2420   *Alster, Bendt ilū awīlum : we-e i-la,* 'gods : men' versus 'man : god':
punning and the reversal of patterns in the Atrahasis epic. ^MJacobsen,
T. 2002 ⇒62. 35-40.
2421   *Berges, Ulrich* Die befreiende Gabe der Vielfalt. KatBl 127 (2002)
248-253 [Gen 11,1-9].
2422   *Carlo, Giuseppe de* Andate e popolate la terra;
2423   *Casadio, Alessandro* Ed è subito sear;
2424   *Cavaleri, Pietro* Isole nella corrente. Genesi: cantico. 2002 ⇒2262.
73-75/95-97/91-94 [Gen 11].
2425   *Cohen, Aviezer* The 'drunkenness of Noah'—the source of the
'Hamitic hypothesis'?. BetM 169 (2002) 152-170 Sum. 189 [Gen
9,18-29]. **H.**
2426   **Cohn, Norman** Noah's Flood: the Genesis story in western thought.
1999 ⇒15,1926. ^RJRH 26 (2002) 97-98 (*Almond, Philip C.*).
2427   *Cooper, Jerrold S.* Buddies in Babylonia: Gilgamesh, Enkidu, and
Mesopotamian homosexuality. ^MJACOBSEN, T. 2002 ⇒62. 73-85.
2428   *Dozzi, Dino* Il linguaggio universale dell'accoglienza [Gen 11];
2429   Il testamento scritto dalla vita. Genesi: cantico. 2002 ⇒2262. 82-84/
107-110.
2430   **Ebach, Jürgen** Noah: die Geschichte eines Überlebenden. 2001 ⇒
17,2100. ^RThLZ 127 (2002) 1161-1162 (*Witte, Markus*);
2431   Noè: la storia di un sopravissuto. T 2002, Claudiana 239 pp.
2432   *Fontana, Raniero* I precetti di Noè. BeO 44 (2002) 65-87.
2433   *Görg, Manfred* Zur Diskussion um das Land Put. BN 113 (2002) 5-
11 [Gen 10,6; 1 Chr 1,8].
2434   **Hirsch, Hans** Gilgamesch-Epos und Erra-Lied: zu einem Aspekt des
Verbalsystems. AfO.B 29: W 2002, Institut für Orientalistik der
Univ. Wien iv; 257 pp. €62. 3-900345-09-0.
2435   *Kilmer, Anne Draffkorn* The investiture of Enkidu in the epic of Gilgamesh tablet III. Sex and gender. 2002 ⇒712. 283-288.
2436   *Klein, Jacob* A new look at the 'oppression of Uruk' episode in the
Gilgameš epic. ^MJACOBSEN, T. 2002 ⇒62. 187-201.
2437   *Levin, Yigal* Nimrod the mighty, king of Kish, king of Sumer and Ak-
kad. VT 52 (2002) 350-366 [Gen 10,8-12].
2438   *Lorenzetti, Luigi* La regula d'oro di ogni cultura. Genesi: cantico.
2002 ⇒2262. 85-87 [Gen 11].
2439   *Marcus, David* The mission of the raven (Gen. 8:7). JANES 29
(2002) 71-80;
2440   God shut Noah in (Genesis 7:16), but who shut Utnapishtim in?.
Maarav 9 (2002) 53-59.
2441   *Monti, Stefania* La lallazione dello Spirito. Genesi: cantico. 2002 ⇒
2262. 76-78 [Gen 11].
2442   *Moran, William L.* RILKE and the Gilgamesh epic <1980>;
2443   The creation of man in Atrahasis I 192-248 <1970>;
2444   The epic of Gilgamesh: a document of ancient humanism <1991>;

2445 OVID's *Blanda voluptas* and the humanization of Enkidu <1991>;
2446 Atrahasis: the Babylonian story of the Flood <1971>;
2447 Some considerations of form and interpretation in Atrahasis <1987>;
2448 A Mesopotamian myth and its biblical transformation. The most magic word. 2002 ⇒212. 1-4/75-86/ 5-20/23-32/33-45/ 46-58/59-74.
2449 *Nault, François* Un dieu érotique: en revisitant le mythe de Babel. ETR 77 (2002) 385-400 [Gen 11,1-9].
2450 *Niehl, Franz W.* Die Verwirrung der Sprache oder der misslungene Turmbau. KatBl 127 (2002) 242-247 [Gen 11,1-9].
2451 *Oberthür, Rainer* Kinder begegnen der Geschichte von Babelturm und Sprachverwirrung. KatBl 127 (2002) 260-268 [Gen 11,1-9].
2452 **Rizzi, Giovanni, Caglioni, Adriano; Redaelli, Raffaella** Il patto con Noè: tradizioni bibliche, giudaiche, cristiane e coraniche a confronto. Sintesi e proposte 21: 2001 ⇒17,2112. [R]Ho Theológos 20 (2002) 305-307 (*Naro, Massimo*).
2453 *Salonia, Giovanni* Il cantico della creazione. Genesi: cantico. 2002 ⇒2262. 88-90 [Gen 11,1-9].
2454 *Saporetti, Claudio* Breve revisione di un sogno di Gilgameš. [M]IMPARATI, F. 2002 ⇒61. 695-704.
2455 *Savasta, Carmelo* Il Diluvio (Gen 5,28-29.32; 6,5-8.11-22.7,1-24; 8,1-22; 9,1-19). BeO 44 (2002) 3-41.
2456 **Schrott, Raoul** Gilgamesh: Epos. 2001 ⇒17,2114. [R]ArOr 70 (2002) 101-103 (*Hruška, Blahoslav*).
2457 *Ska, Jean Louis* La creazione del mondo o la speranza di Dio (Gn 1-11). La speranza. 2002 ⇒277. 1-31.
2458 *Smend, Rudolf* 'Das Ende ist gekommen': ein Amoswort in der Priesterschrift. Die Mitte des A.T. 2002 <1981> ⇒244. 238-243 [Gen 6,13].
2459 *Spero, Shubert* Why was God optimistic after the Flood?. JBQ 30 (2002) 235-241.
2460 *Stander, H.F.* Die (reën)boog na die sondvloed (Gen 9:12-17). HTS 58 (2002) 1447-1458 [OTA 26,443].
2461 **Van Stiphout, Herman** Het epos van Gilgameš. Roeselare 2002, Roularta 302 pp. €24.50. 90-5466-619-6. [R]Akkadica 123 (2002) 200 (*Tanret, Michel*).
2462 *Villiers, G. de; Prinsloo, G.T.M.* Gilgamesh sees the deep: from shame to honour. JSem 11/1 (2002) 23-44.

E2.3 Patriarchae, Abraham; *Genesis 12s*

2463 *Bonari, Luca* Camminare per far camminare. Genesi: cantico. 2002 ⇒2262. 115-117.
2464 *Bordreuil, Pierre* Rupture religieuse et identité ethnique;
2465 *Briend, Jacques* Hébron, un lieu de mémoire et de traditions;
2466 *Caillet, Jean-Pierre* Le patriarche saisi par l'image. MoBi 140 (2001) 26-31/20-25/40-47.
2467 *Cohen, Jeffrey M.* Displacement in the matriarchal home: a psychological study of the Abraham-Sarah marriage. JBQ 30 (2002) 90-96.
2468 *Crüsemann, Frank* Abraham und die Bewohner des Landes: Beobachtungen zum kanonischen Abrahambild. EvTh 62 (2002) 334-348 [Gen 12,1-9].
2469 *Dall'Osso, Maria Teresa* La scuola della commozione. Genesi: cantico. 2002 ⇒2262. 121-124.

2470 **Feiler, Bruce S.** Abraham: a journey to the heart of three faiths. NY 2002, Morrow xii; 224 pp. 0-380-97776-1.
2471 *Frisch, Amos R.* Jacob Zvi MEKLENBURG's method in the issue of the patriarch's sins. JJS 53 (2002) 107-119.
2472 *Gibert, Pierre* La nécessité du père unique. MoBi 140 (2001) 48-53.
2473 *Goshen-Gottstein, Alon* Abraham and 'Abrahamic religions' in contemporary interreligious discourse: reflections of an implicated Jewish bystander. Studies in interreligious dialogue 12 (2002) 165-183.
2474 *Gosse, Bernard* Abraham comme figure de substitution à la royauté davidique, et sa dimension internationale à l'époque postexilique. Theoforum 33/2 (2002) 163-186 [Gen 14].
2475 *GuillénTorralba, Juan* Ciclo de Jacob y sus hijos. Isidorianum 21 (2002) 33-63.
2476 *Halpérin, Jean* Abramo nel cuore della scrittura. Il libro sacro. 2002 ⇒356. 219-224.
2477 **Heard, R. Christopher** Dynamics of diselection: ambiguity in Genesis 12-36 and ethnic boundaries in post-exilic Judah SBL Semeia Studies 39 2001 ⇒17,2134. [R]CBQ 64 (2002) 350-351 (*Bellavance, Éric*); RBLit (2002)* (*Mullen, E.T.*).
2478 **Imbach, Josef** Mit Abraham unterwegs: vom Abenteuer des Glaubens. Wü 2002, Echter 112 pp. 3-429-02454-4.
2479 *Lafratta, Lucia* Le certezze dei piccoli Abramo. Genesi: cantico. 2002 ⇒2262. 125-126.
2480 *Loeff, Yoav; Stökl, Daniel* Two chronological texts from an Armenian manuscript (M451). Muséon 115/1-2 (2002) 171-189.
2481 *Lorenzetti, Luigi* L'energia del dono;
2482 *Marconi, Nazzareno* Un Dio troppo grande per non essere dono;
2483 *Monti, Stefania* Leggere la vita oltre di essa. Genesi: cantico. 2002 ⇒2262. 118-120/101-103/104-106.
2484 **Nauerth, Thomas** Untersuchungen zur Komposition der Jakoberzählungen: auf der Suche nach der Endgestalt des Genesisbuches. BEAT 27: 1997 ⇒13,1772; 15,1976. [R]ThR 67 (2002) 137-8 (*Otto, Eckart*).
2485 *Pabst, Irene* Szenen zweier Ehen: Beobachtungen zu den Erzelternpaaren Rebekka und Isaak und Rahel/Lea und Jakob. Paare 2002 ⇒ 489. 93-131.
2486 *Platti, Emilio* L'islam, 'la religion d'Abraham'. MoBi 140 (2001) 39.
2487 *Quesnel, Michel* Visages d'Abraham dans le Nouveau Testament. MoBi 140 (2002) 32-36.
2488 *Ramsey, George W.* Israel's ancestors: the patriarchs and matriarchs. Biblical world, 2. 2002 ⇒273. 175-193.
2489 *Remaud, Michel* Abraham dans la littérature rabbinique. MoBi 140 (2001) 37-38.
2490 *Rota Scalabrini, Patrizio* Una vita colma di bene: le tradizioni patriarcali. PSV 45 (2002) 27-40.
2491 *Römer, Thomas* Figures d'un ancêtre. MoBi 140 (2001) 14-19;
2492 Typologie exodique dans les récits patriarcaux. Typologie biblique. LeDiv: 2002 ⇒341. 49-76.
2493 *Ruppert, Lothar* Abraham und Lot—zwei ungleiche 'Brüder'. [F]HAAG, E. 2002 ⇒55. 235-250;
2494 Abraham als Stammvater und Vorbild Israels. [F]FUCHS, A.: 2002 ⇒ 41. 15-29.
2495 *Salonia, Giovanni* Uno solo è il Padre vostro. Genesi: cantico. 2002 ⇒2262. 111-114.

2496 **Ska, Jean-Louis** Abraham et ses hôtes: le patriarche et les croyants au Dieu unique. L'autre et les autres 3: Bru 2002, Lessius 151 pp. 2-87299-121-2. Bibl. 131-139;

2497 Abramo e i suoi ospiti: il patriarca e i credenti nel Dio unico. Collana biblica. Bo 2002, EDB 153 pp. €11. 88-10-22119-2. Bibl. 127-140.

2498 **Thompson, Thomas L.** The historicity of the patriarchal narratives: the quest for the historical Abraham. Harrisburg ²2002 <1974>, Trinity x; 392 pp. $28. 1-56338-389-6 [ThD 50,190—Heiser, W.C.].

2499 *Toaff, Elio* La figure d'Abraham dans la tradition juive. SIDIC 35/2-3 (2002 <1982>) 7-13.

2500 *Vogel, Dan* Forget not your forebears!. JBQ 30 (2002) 164-170.

E2.4 **Melchisedech**: *Genesis 14*

2501 ᴱ**Charlesworth, James H.** The Dead Sea scrolls: Hebrew, Aramaic, and Greek texts with English translations: 6B, Pesharim, other commentaries, and related documents: songs of the Sabbath sacrifices. The Princeton Theological Seminary Dead Sea Scrolls Project: Tü 2002, Mohr xxv; 384 pp. €109. 3-16-147426-0.

2502 *Davila, James R.* Melchizedek, the "youth," and Jesus. Dead Sea scrolls as background. StTDJ 46: 2002 ⇒732. 248-274.

2503 **Lyons, William John** Canon and exegesis: canonical praxis and Sodom narrative. JSOT.S 352: Shf 2002, Sheffield A. x; 317 pp. 1-84127-295-7. Bibl. 276-303.

2504 *Roberts, J.J.M.* Melchizedek (11Q13=11QMelchizedek=11QMelch). The Dead Sea scrolls: texts. 2002 ⇒2501. 264-273 [Lev 25,9; 25,13; Dt 15,2; Ps 82,1-2; 7,8-9].

2505 *Stolz, Gerhard P.J.; Breytenbach, A.P.B.* Genesis 14—'n redaksiekritiese ondersoek. HTS 57 (2001) 1312-1343 [OTA 25,450].

E2.5 **The Covenant** (alliance, Bund): *Foedus, Genesis 15...*

2506 *Auffret, Pierre* La justice pour Abram: étude structurelle de Gen 15. ZAW 114 (2002) 342-354.

2507 *Drey, Philip R.* The role of Hagar in Genesis 16. AUSS 40 (2002) 179-195.

2508 *Ephros, Abraham* Nineveh and Sodom juxtaposed: contrasts and parallels. JBQ 30 (2002) 242-246 [Gen 18-19].

2509 *Gertz, Jan Christian* Abraham, Mose und der Exodus: Beobachtungen zur Redaktionsgeschichte von Gen 15. Abschied vom Jahwisten. BZAW 315: 2002 ⇒2189. 63-81.

2510 *Goodnick, Benjamin* Is incest with a daughter permissible?. JBQ 30 (2002) 41-44 [Gen 19,30-38].

2511 *Görg, Manfred* Ismael: Wüstenbewohner und Bogenschütze (Gen 21,20). BN 114/115 (2002) 34-37.

2512 **Ha, John** Genesis 15: a theological compendium of pentateuchal history. BZAW 181: 1989 ⇒5,2372... 9,2146. ᴿThR 67 (2002) 136-137 (*Otto, Eckart*).

2513 *Hepner, Gershon* The sacrifices in the covenant between the pieces allude to the law of Leviticus and the covenant of the flesh. BN 112 (2002) 38-73 [Gen 4,2-4; 15,13-16];

2514   The affliction and divorce of Hagar involves violations of the covenant and deuteronomic codes. ZAR 8 (2002) 166-206 [Gen 16].
2515   *Jarrell, R.H.* The birth narrative as female counterpart to covenant.
       JSOT 97 (2002) 3-18 [Gen 16].
2516   *Kahn, Pinchas* The mission of Abraham: Genesis 18:17-22:19. JBQ
       30 (2002) 155-163.
2517   *Lang, Bernhard* Im Zeichen des Bundes mit Gott: jüdisches Brauchtum in biblischer Zeit. Die Bibel: Geschichte und Gegenwart. 2002
       ⇒971. 44-45.
2518   **Lyons, William John** Canon and exegesis: canonical praxis and the
       Sodom narrative. JSOT.S 352: Shf 2002, Sheffield A. x; 317 pp. 1-
       84127-295-7 [Gen 19].
2519   *Mizrahi, Noam* The derivation of Abraham's name (Gen 17:5). Tarbiz 71 (2002) 337-352 Sum. v. H.
2520   **Rendtorff, Rolf** La "formula dell'alleanza": ricerca esegetica e teologica. ᴱ*Garrone, Daniele*: StBi 128: 2001 ⇒17,2177. ᴿCivCatt 153/4
       (2002) 207-208 (*Scaiola, D.*).
2521   *Siegelová, Jana* Blendung als Strafe für den Eidbruch. ᴹIMPARATI, F.
       2002 ⇒61. 735-737.
2522   *Smend, Rudolf* Die Bundesformel. Die Mitte des A.T. 2002 <1963>
       ⇒244. 1-29.
2523   **Williamson, Paul R.** Abraham, Israel and the nations: the patriarchal
       promise and its covenantal development in Genesis. JSOT.S 315:
       2000 ⇒16,2083. ᴿCBQ 64 (2002) 149-150 (*Mandell, Sara R.*); BS
       159 (2002) 491-492 (*Chisholm, Robert B.*); ThLZ 127 (2002) 631-
       633 (*Seebass, Horst*) [Gen 15; 17].

E2.6 The 'Aqedâ, Isaac, Genesis 22...

2524   ᴱ**Noort, Edward; Tigchelaar, Eibert** The sacrifice of Isaac: the
       Aqedah (Genesis 22) and its interpretations. Themes in biblical narrative 4: Lei 2002, Brill xiii; 230, [8] pp. €105/$122. 90-04-12434-9.

2525   *Bauer, Uwe F.* "Poesie des Raumes" in Gen 22,1-19. CV 44 (2002)
       225-234.
2526   *Boehm, Omri* The binding of Isaac: an inner-biblical polemic on the
       question of "disobeying" a manifestly illegal order. VT 52 (2002) 1-
       12 [Gen 22].
2527   **Burger, Hilde** De zandloper van Genesis: de visie van Benno JACOB
       op Genesis 22 in het licht van zijn tijd en van de traditie. ᴰ*Deurloo,
       K.*: Zoetermeer 2002, Boekencentrum 256 pp. €24.90. 90-239-1187-
       3. Diss. Amsterdam [Streven 70,661—Beentjes, Panc].
2528   *Dassmann, Ernst* "Bindung" und "Opferung" Isaaks in jüdischer und
       patristischer Auslegung. ᶠHOHEISEL, K.: JAC.E 34: 2002 ⇒59. 1-18
       [Gen 22,1-19].
2529   *Feldman, Louis H.* PHILO's version of the 'Aqedah. StPhiloA 14
       (2002) 66-86 [Gen 22,1-19]
2530   *Fitzmyer, Joseph A.* The sacrifice of Isaac in Qumran literature. Bib.
       83 (2002) 211-229 [Gen 22,1-19].
2531   **Gathmann, Stefan** "Klippenabsturz zu Gott " Gen 22,1-19: sprachwissenschaftliche Notizen. ATSAT 71: St. Ottilien 2002, EOS xiv;
       164 pp. 3-8306-7107-5. Bibl. 156-164 [Gen 22,1-19].

2532 *Hälbig, Klaus W.* Der Aufstieg zum Sehen Gottes in der Schöpfung: Isaaks Opferung und das Kreuzesopfer Christi im Zeichen des kosmischen Chi (X). ZKTh 124 (2002) 145-176 [Gen 22,1-19].

2533 *Hilhorst, Anton* The Bodmer poem on the sacrifice of Abraham. Aqedah. 2002 ⇒2524. 96-108 [Gen 22,1-19].

2534 *Kessler, Edward* The sacrifice of Isaac (the Akedah) in the christian and Jewish tradition: artistic representations. Borders. JSOT.S 313: 2002 ⇒585. 74-98 [Gen 22,1-19].

2535 **Kundert, Lukas** Die Opferung, Bindung Isaaks: 1. Gen 22,1-19 im Alten Testament, im Frühjudentum und im NT. WMANT 78: 1998 ⇒14,1894...17,2191. RFrRu 9 (2002) 145-46 (*Oberforcher, Robert*).

2536 **Mandrella, Isabelle** Das Isaak-Opfer: historisch-systematische Untersuchung zu Rationalität und Wandelbarkeit des Naturrechts in der mittelalterlichen Lehre vom natürlichen Gesetz. BGPhMA 62: Müns 2002, Aschendorff 331 pp. €44. 3-402-04013-1.

2537 *Noort, Ed* Genesis 22: human sacrifice and theology in the Hebrew Bible. Aqedah. 2002 ⇒2524. 1-20.

2538 *Norin, Stig* Aqedat Jiṣḥaq—1 Mos 22:1-19: på jakt efter ett retoriskt centrum. SEÅ 67 (2002) 5-18.

2539 *Paseggi, Marcos R.* Lazos de sangre : una aproximación literaria a la "Aqueda". DavarLogos 1/1 (2002) 43-61 [Gen 22,1-19].

2540 *Popović, M.* Bibliography of recent studies. Aqedah. 2002 ⇒2524. 211-223 [Gen 22,1-19].

2541 *Sanders, Andy F.* KIERKEGAARD's reading of the sacrifice of Isaac. Aqedah. 2002 ⇒2524. 166-181 [Gen 22,1-19].

2542 *Ska, Jean-Louis* Genèse 22 ou l'épreuve d'Abraham. Quand la bible se raconte. 355. 2002 67-84.

2543 **Steins, Georg** Die "Bindung Isaaks" im Kanon (Gen 22). Herders Biblische Studien 20: 1999 ⇒15,2011; 16,2094. RJBL 121 (2002) 152-154 (*Crenshaw, James L.*).

2544 *Van Bekkum, Wout Jac.* The Aqedah and its interpretations in Midrash and Piyyut. Aqedah. 2002 ⇒2524. 86-95 [Gen 22,1-19].

2545 *Vandermeersch, Patrick* Isaac threatened by the knife of psychoanalysis?. Aqedah. 2002 ⇒2524. 198-210 [Gen 22,1-19].

2546 *Van Ruiten, Jacques* Abraham, Job and the book of Jubilees: the intertextual relationship of Genesis 22:1-19, Job 1:1-2:13 and Jubilees 17:15-18:19. Aqedah. 2002 ⇒2524. 58-85.

2547 *Vries, Jan de* 'Leid on niet in verzoeking...': over Genesis 22. ITBT 10/4 (2002) 13-14.

2548 *Zorgdrager, Heleen* The sacrifice of Abraham as a (temporary) resolution of a descent conflict?: a gender-motivated reading of Gen 22. Aqedah. 2002 ⇒2524. 182-197.

2549 *Warning, Wilfried* Terminological patterns and Genesis 24. EstB 60 (2002) 51-76.

E2.7 **Jacob** and Esau: ladder dream; *Jacob, somnium, Gen 25...*

2550 *Dauzat, Pierre-Emmanuel* Ein Klettersteig zum Himmel?: Jakobs Leiter in der Lesart der ersten Christen. WUB 26 (2002) 35-37 [Gen 28,12].

2551 *Quaglia, Rocco* Il sogno di Jacov. I sogni. 2002 ⇒227. 73-79 [Gen 28,10-17].

2552 *Sicre Diaz, Jose Luis* Las tradiciones de Jacob: búsqueda y rechazo de la propria identidad. EstB 60 (2002) 443-478.

2553 **Taschner, Johannes** Verheissung und Erfüllung in der Jakoberzählung (Gen 25,19 - 33,17). Herders biblische Studien 27: 2000 ⇒16, 2113. [R]ThLZ 127 (2002) 168-170 (*Wahl, Harald*).

2554 *Theißen, Gerd* Das Schweigen der Engel oder Jakobs Traum in Bethel (Gen 28,10-22). Erlösungsbilder. 2002 ⇒1460. 14-18.

2555 *Willi-Plein, Ina* Genesis 27 als Rebekkageschichte: zu einem historiographischen Kunstgriff der biblischen Vätergeschichten. Sprache als Schlüssel. 2002 <1989> ⇒261. 41-59.

2556 *Zabka, Andreas P.* Jakob, Esau und die Himmelsleiter: Predigt über Genesis 28,10-22. Zeitschrift für Theologie und Gemeinde 7 (2002) 337-344.

E2.8 Jacob's wrestling, the Angels: *Gen 31-36 & 38*

2557 *Dietrich, Walter* Jakobs Kampf am Jabbok Theopolitik 2002 <2001> ⇒159. 173-183 [Gen 32,23-33].

2558 *Fischer, Irmtraud* Jabboq: der Fluss, der die Geschichte Israels spaltet. Gretchenfrage. Jabboq 2: 2002 ⇒399. 172-190 [Gen 32].

2559 *Fleischman, Joseph* Socio-legal aspects of Genesis 34. Shnaton 13 (2002) 141-155. H.

2560 **Hannah, Darrel D.** Michael and Christ: Michael traditions and angel christology in early christianity. WUNT 2/109: 1999 ⇒15,2032; 17, 2250. [R]ThG 45 (2002) 293-294 (*Giesen, Heinz*).

2561 *Homan, Michael M.* Date rape: the agricultural and astronomical background of the Sumerian sacred marriage and Genesis 38. SJOT 16 (2002) 283-292.

2562 *Kok, Flordia de; Lensink,Erna* Recht van spreken: Genesis 34 volgens Dina. ITBT 10/6 (2002) 27-28.

2563 *Leu, Philippe* Genèse 38: l'ascendance ombreuse et paternelle du Messie. Lire et Dire 54 (2002) 4-16 [BuBB 39,73].

2564 *Leutzsch, Martin* Eine rettende Beziehung: biblische Hinweise auf die Wirksamkeit der Boten Gottes. Zeitschrift für Pädagogik und Theologie 54 (2002) 242-260.

2565 *Lux, Rüdiger* Der Deuteengel und der Prophet: biblisch-hermeneutische Aspekte der Angelologie. Zeitschrift für Pädagogik und Theologie 54 (2002) 235-242.

2566 *Parry, Robin* Feminist hermeneutics and evangelical concerns: the rape of Dinah as a case study. TynB 53 (2002) 1-28 [Gen 34].

2567 *Petercă, Vladimir* The attack against Jacob at Iabboq. Caietele Institutului Catolic 3/1 (2002) 25-37 Zsfg. 36s [Gen 32,23-33].

2568 *Ravid, Dalia* האפקט הטראגי של סיפור יהודה ותמר [The tragic effect of the story of Judah and Tamar (Gen 38)]. BetM 170 (2002) 257-266 Sum. 285. H.

2569 *Van Wolde, Ellen* The Dinah story: rape or worse?. OTEs 15 (2002) 225-239 [Gen 34].

E2.9 Joseph; Jacob's blessings; *Genesis 37; 39-50*

2570 *Accrocca, Felice* La determinate semplicità di un Poverello. Genesi: cantico. 2002 ⇒2262. 139-141.

2571 *Beauchamp, Paul* Joseph et ses frères: offense, pardon, réconciliation. SémBib 105 (2002) 3-13.

2572 *Biguzzi, Giancarlo* La sovversione della provvidenza. Genesi: cantico. 2002 ⇒2262. 129-131.

2573 *Blumenthal, Fred* Jacob's blessing for Dan. JBQ 30 (2002) 107-109 [Gen 49,16-18].

2574 *Carlo, Giuseppe de* Poco meno degli angeli;

2575 *Casadio, Alessandro* I have a dream. Genesi: cantico. 2002 ⇒2262. 132-134/156-158.

2576 *Docherty, Susan* Joseph the patriarch: representations of Joseph in early post-biblical literature. Borders. JSOT.S 313: 2002 ⇒585. 194-216.

2577 *Dozzi, Dino* Per sempre in vasi de creta. Genesi: cantico. 2002 ⇒ 2262. 135-138.

2578 **Fung, Yiu-Wing** Victim and victimizer: Joseph's interpretation of his destiny. JSOT.S 308: 2000 ⇒16,2150. [R]BiblInterp 10 (2002) 86-89 (*Moberly, Walter*); Bib. 83 (2002) 119-120 (*Ackerman, James S.*); RBLit (2002)* (*Wallace, Howard Neil*) [Gen 45,5-11].

2579 **Goldman, Shalom** The wiles of women/the wiles of men: Joseph and Potiphar's wife in anc. Near Eastern, Jewish...Islamic folklore. 1995 ⇒11/1,503... 15,2048. [R]Islam 79 (2002) 369-71 (*Hörner, Karin*).

2580 *Heltzer, Michael* A guarantee hostage in the story of Joseph (Gen. 42-44) and in middle-Assyrian times. ZAR 8 (2002) 207-210.

2581 **Hoop, Raymond de** Genesis 49 in its literary and historical context. OTS 39: 1999 ⇒15,2050...17,2275. [R]BiOr 59 (2002) 377-385 (*Timm, S.*).

2582 *Huddlestun, John R.* Divestiture, deception, and demotion: the garment motif in Genesis 37-39. JSOT 98 (2002) 47-62.

2583 *La Perna Pisana, Agata* La rispota soffia nel vento;

2584 *Lorenzetti, Luigi* Un concilio che parla di noi. Genesi: cantico. 2002 ⇒2262. 152-155/145-148.

2585 **Lux, Rüdiger** Josef: der Auserwählte unter seinen Brüdern. Biblische Gestalten 1: 2001 ⇒17,2280. [R]BiKi 57 (2002) 107-108 (*Doering, Lutz*); ThLZ 127 (2002) 161-163 (*Utzschneider, Helmut*).

2586 *Merli, Alvaro* Incoscienti per amore. Genesi: cantico. 2002 ⇒2262. 142-144.

2587 *Naor, Bezalel* Joseph and Daniel: court Jews and dreamers. JBQ 30 (2002) 10-16 [Dan 2].

2588 *Nocquet, Dany* Genèse 37 et l'épreuve d'Israël: l'intention du cycle de Joseph. ETR 77 (2002) 13-35.

2589 **Pirson, Ron** The lord of the dreams: a semantic and literary analysis of Genesis 37-50. JSOT.S 355: L 2002, Sheffield A. xi; 168 pp. £50. 0-8264-6209-X. Bibl. 149-157.

2590 *Prickett, Stephen* The idea of character in the bible: Joseph the dreamer. Borders. JSOT.S 313: 2002 ⇒585. 180-193.

2591 *Quaglia, Rocco* I sogni di Faraone [Gen 41];

2592 I sogni di Josèf [Gen 37];

2593 I sogni degli ufficiali di Faraone [Gen 40]. I sogni. 2002 ⇒227. 47-55/57-71/65-71.

2594 *Rachaman, Yosefa* Sheaves, ears and Pharaoh's birthday: how did Joseph interpret Pharaoh's dreams?. BetM 170 (2002) 267-275 Sum. 285 [Gen 41]. **H.**

2595 *Schmid, Konrad* Die Josephsgeschichte im Pentateuch. Abschied vom Jahwisten. BZAW 315: 2002 ⇒2189. 83-118.

2596 *Toloni, Giancarlo Šuppîm, muppîm, ḥuppîm* nelle genealogie de la bibbia ebraica. EstB 60 (2002) 189-210 [Gen 46,12; 1 Chr 7,12].
2597 *Toschi, Massimo* La storia a cielo aperto. Genesi: cantico. 2002 ⇒ 2262. 149-151.
2598 *Viljoen, D.A.; Breytenbach, A.P.B.* Genesis 38 binne die Josefverhal: 'n literêr-sosiologiese perspektief. HTS 58 (2002) 1795-1827 [OTA 26,449].
2599 *Wénin, André* Le temps dans l'histoire de Joseph (Gn 37-50): repères temporels pour une analyse narrative. Bib. 83 (2002) 28-53.
2600 *Willi-Plein, Ina* Historiographische Aspekte der Josefsgeschichte. Sprache als Schlüssel. 2002 <1979> ⇒261. 60-78.

E3.1 Exodus event and theme; *textus, commentarii*

2601 **Benedetti, P.** Il loro grido salì a Dio: commento all'Esodo. Brescia 2002, Morcelliana 111 pp.
2602 *Bosman, H.L.* The Exodus and the spade: the impact of archaeology on the interpretation of the book of Exodus. HTS 58 (2002) 1487-1497 [OTA 26,450].
2603 *Carbajosa, Ignacio '...con mano fuerte y brazo extendido*: el testimonio de la salida de Egipto en los libros del Éxodo y Deuteronomio. RevAg 43 (2002) 391-412.
2604 *Clifford, Richard J.* The Exodus in the christian bible: the case for "figural" reading. TS 63 (2002) 345-361.
2605 *Cnockaert, André* Le salut, la route et la marche: promenade spirituelle dans un champ de métaphores bibliques. Telema 110-111 (2002) 66-77.
2606 **Collins, Andrew; Ogilvie-Herald, Chris** Tutankhamun: the Exodus conspiracy: the truth behind archaeology's greatest mystery. L 2002, Virgin xii (2); 338 pp. 1-85227-972-9. Bibl. 325-333.
2607 *Craig, Judith Lapkin* Text and textile in Exodus: toward a clearer understanding of מעשה חֹשֵׁב. JANES 29 (2002) 17-30.
2608 **Dykstra, Laurel A.** Set them free: the other side of Exodus. Mkn 2002, Orbis xvi; 254 pp. $24. 1-57075-441-1. Bibl.238-248.
2609 **Gabriel, Richard A.** Gods of our fathers: the memory of Egypt in Judaism and christianity. Contributions to the study of religion 67: Westport, CONN 2002, Greenwood xix; 242 pp. 0-313-31286-9. Foreword by *Mordechai Gichon.*
2610 **Gertz, Jan** Christian Tradition und Redaktion in der Exoduserzählung: Untersuchungen zur Endredaktion des Pentateuch. FRLANT 186: 2000 ⇒16,2191; 17,2303. ᴿThR 67 (2002) 139-141 (*Otto, Eckart*); RThPh 134 (2002) 388-389 (*Nihan, Christophe*).
2611 **Heither, Theresia; Reemts, Christiana** Schriftauslegung, 4: das Buch Exodus bei den Kirchenvätern. Neuer Stuttgarter Kommentar: AT 33/4: Stu 2002, Verl. Kath. Bibelwerk 221 pp. €22.90. 3-460-07-334-9. Bibl. 220-221.
2612 **Hoffmeier, James Karl** Israel in Egypt: the evidence for the authenticity of the Exodus tradition. 1997 ⇒13,1912... 16,2194. ᴿMSR 59/ 2 (2002) 83-85 (*Cannuyer, Christian*).
2613 **Houtman, Cornelis** Exodus, 3: chapters 20-40. ᵀ*Woudstra, Sierd*: Historical commentary on the OT: 2000 ⇒16,2179; 17,2307. ᴿOLZ 97 (2002) 560-563 (*Reventlow, Henning Graf*); BiOr 59 (2002) 602-604 (*Otto, Eckart*); RBLit 4 (2002) 189-191 (*Propp, William*).

2614 **Isbell, Charles David** The function of Exodus motifs in biblical narratives: theological didactic drama. SBEC 52: NY 2002, Mellen xv; 184 pp. 0-7734-6994-X. Bibl. 169-173.

2615 **Jacob, Benno** Das Buch Exodus. *EMayer, Shlomo*: 1997 ⇒13,1883; 15,2069. *R*FrRu 4 (2002) 297-299 (*Schwendemann, Wilhelm*).

2616 **Janzen, Waldemar** Exodus. 2000 ⇒16,2181. *R*CBQ 64 (2002) 137-8 (*Dozeman, Thomas B.*); RExp 99 (2002) 455-56 (*Biddle, Mark E.*).

2617 **Larsson, Göran** Bound for freedom: the book of Exodus in Jewish and Christian traditions. 1999 ⇒15,2088; 16,2196. *R*AsbTJ 56/2-57/1 (2001-2002) 149-150 (*Mead, James K.*); IThQ 67 (2002) 284-285 (*Hogan, Maurice*); SEÅ 67 (2002) 155-156 (*Bengtsson, Håkan*).

2618 *McHatten, Mary Timothy* Israel and Egypt during the Exodus. BiTod 40 (2002) 141-147.

2619 **Nepi, Antonio** Esodo, v.1: cap. 1-15. Dabar, AT: Padova 2002, Messaggero 288 pp. €11.50. 88-250-1086-9.

2620 **Ortega Monasterio, María Teresa** Las masoras del libro de Éxodo: Códice M1 de la Universidad Complutense de Madrid. TECC 67: M 2002, Inst. de Filolog., C.S.I.C., Dept Filolog. 238 pp. 84000-80181.

2621 **Oswald, Wolfgang** Israel am Gottesberg: eine Untersuchung zur Literargeschichte der vorderen Sinaiperikope Ex 19-24 und deren historischem Hintergrund. OBO 159: 1998 ⇒14,2069... 16,2184. *R*ThR 67 (2002) 141-143 & ZAR 8 (2002) 398-400 (*Otto, Eckart*).

2622 *Pattarumadathil, Henry* Life-deal and death-deal: an interpretation of violence in Exodus. Jeevadhara 32 (2002) 108-118.

2623 **Propp, William H.C.** Exodus 1-18. AncB 2: 1999 ⇒17,2318. *R*ArOr 70 (2002) 88-91 (*Segert, Stanislav*); ABR 50 (2002) 80-81 (*Treloar, Richard*); IEJ 52 (2002) 267-268 (*Aḥituv, Shmuel*).

2624 **Raimondi, Enzo** Esodo il vangelo dell'Antico Testamento. Sussidi per i gruppi biblici: Bo 2002, EDB 168 pp. €12.40. 88-10-90451-6.

  Rogerson, John W., *al.*, Genesis and Exodus 2001 ⇒2248.

2625 *T***Rottzoll, Dirk U.** Abraham IBN ESRAS langer Kommentar zum Buch Exodus. SJ 17,1-2: 2000 ⇒16,2188; 17,2322. *R*BZ 46 (2002) 119-121 (*Ego, Beate*); RBLit 4 (2002) 262-265 (*Gruber, Mayer I.*).

2626 **Sanz Giménez-Rico, Enrique** Cercanía del Dios distante: imagen de Dios en el libro del Éxodo. *D*Sicre Díaz, J.L.: Estudios 84: M 2002, Depart. de Publicaciones, Univ. Pontificia Comillas 476 pp. €33.65. 8484680525. Diss. Comillas 1999-2000; Bibl. 439-76 [RB 110,159].

2627 *Wheeler, Gerald* Ancient Egypt's silence about the Exodus. AUSS 40 (2002) 257-264.

2628 **Zornberg, Avivah Gottlieb** The particulars of rapture: reflections on Exodus. 2001 ⇒17,2330. *R*ETR 77 2002) 113-115 (*Vincent, Jean M.*); AThR 84 (2002) 151-152 (*Davis, Ellen F.*).

E3.2 Moyses—Pharaoh, Goshen—*Exodus 1...*

2629 **Assmann, Jan** Mosè l'Egizio. 2000 ⇒16,2209. *R*Hum(B) 57 (2002) 576-584 (*Zenger, Erich*);

2630 Moïse l'égyptien. *T*Bernardi, Laure: 2001 ⇒17,2333. *R*MSR 59/2 (2002) 85-86 (*Cannuyer, Christian*).

2631 *Barbiero, Gianni* Der Glaubensweg des jungen Mose als Synthese der sprituellen Erfahrung des Exodus. Studien. SBAB 34: 2002 <1995> ⇒139. 199-220.

2632 *Brink, Aldert* Die gebeure en karakters in Eksodus 2: 'n studie van die storie-aspekte in die narratiewe teks van Eksodus 2. OTEs 15 (2002) 335-349.

2633 *Chinitz, Jacob* Moses: intermediary or teacher?. JBQ 30 (2002) 196-200.

2634 **Finkelstein, Israel; Silberman, Neil Asher** Le tracce di Mosè: la bibbia tra storia e mito. Saggi 14: R 2002, Carocci 409 pp. 88-43021-30-3. Bibl. 371-391.

2635 *Gertz, Jan Christian* Mose und die Anfänge der jüdischen Religion. ZThK 99 (2002) 3-20.

2636 *Gosse, B.* Les mentions de Moïse en Isaïe 63,7-64,11 et Psaumes 90-106, et les relations entre le livre d'Isaïe, le Psautier et les Cantiques. TEuph 24 (2002) 23-39.

2637 **Krauss, Rolf** Das Moses-Rätsel: auf den Spuren einer biblischen Erfindung. 2000 ⇒16,2221. ᴿThLZ 127 (2002) 1285-1287 (*Schipper, Bernd U.*).

2638 **Lierman, John D.** The New Testament Moses in the context of ancient Judaism. ᴰ*Horbury, W.*: Diss. Cambridge 2002 [TynB 53,317-320].

2639 *Marín ı Torner, Joan Ramon* 'Vulgues perdonar el seu pecat': Moisès intercedeix davant del Senyor pel pecat del poble (Ex 32-34; Nm 13-14; Dt 9-10). Perdó i reconciliació. 2002 ⇒591. 39-91.

2640 *Meinhold, Arndt* Mose und Elia am Gottesberg and am Ende des Prophetenkanons. Leqach 2 (2002) 22-38 [Dt 6,4].

2641 *Minkoff, Harvey* Moses and Samuel: Israel's era of charismatic leadership. JBQ 30 (2002) 257-261.

2642 *Nigosian, Solomon A.* Images of Moses: a comparative inquiry. ThRev 23/1 (2002) 27-46.

2643 *Otto, Eckart, al.,* Mose. RGG 5: 2002 ⇒796. 1534-1543.

2644 *Rechenmacher, Hans* Das Mosebild im chronistischen Geschichtswerk. RB 109 (2002) 57-65.

2645 **Rozier, Gilles** Moïse fiction. 2001 ⇒17,2343. ᴿEeV 54 (2002) 28-29 (*Grelot, Pierre*).

2646 **Römer, Thomas** Moïse, 'Lui que Yahvé a connu face à face'. Découvertes Religions 424: P 2002, Gallimard 127 pp. €11.60. 2-0707-6480-X [ETL 78,293s].

2647 *Siebert-Hommes,Jopie* Mozes, wie heeft jou aangesteld? (Exodus 2 en 3). ITBT 10/1 (2002) 21-22.

2648 *Theißen, Gerd* Konspiration für das Leben: die Rettung jüdischer Kinder vor Pharao (Ex 1,1-2,10). Erlösungsbilder. 2002 ⇒1460. 19-30.

2649 **Vanhoomissen, Guy** En commençant par Moïse: de l'Égypte à la Terre Promise. Écritures 7: Bru 2002, Lumen Vitae 254 pp. €25. 28-7324-167-5. Bibl. 247-249.

2650 *Van Seters, John* Moses. Biblical world, 2. 2002 ⇒273. 194-207.

2651 **Vogels, Walter** Moïse aux multiples visages: de l'Exode au Deutéronome. LiBi 114: 1998 ⇒14,2013. ᴿRTL 33 (2002) 96-7 (*Wénin, A.*).

2652 *Williams, Margaret H.* The case for Jewish use of Moses as a personal name in Graeco-Roman antiquity. ZPE 140 (2002) 279-283.

E3.3 Nomen divinum, Tetragrammaton; *Exodus 3,14*...Plagues

2653 *Bartelmus, Rüdiger* Ex 3,14 und die Bedeutung von היה. Auf der Suche. 2002 ⇒140. 383-402.

2654 *Berlingieri, Giovanni* Il nome Yhwh nel contesto dell'esodo. ^FTUD-DA, F.: 2002 ⇒123. 27-36.

2655 *Brünenberg, Esther* Der Gott, der aus dem Feuer spricht. BN 112 (2002) 12-15 [Ex 3,1-6].

2656 **Burnett, Joel S.** A reassessment of biblical Elohim. SBL.DS 183: 2001 ⇒17,2355. ^RJBL 121 (2002) 538-540 (*Wiggins, Steve A.*).

2657 *Dietrich, Walter* Über Werden und Wesen des biblischen Monotheismus: religionsgeschichtliche und theologische Perspektiven. Theopolitik. 2002 <1994> ⇒159. 71-83.

2658 *Feller, Penina Galpaz* 'And I will give this people favour in the sight of the Egyptians' (Exodus 3:22). BetM 169 (2002) 133-142 Sum. 190. **H.**

2659 *Folliet, Georges Inquilina* uel *concellaria* (Exode 3,22): deux leçons de la *Vetus Latina* confrontées par AUGUSTIN. Aevum 76 (2002) 143-149.

2660 *Galpaz-Feller, Pnina* Silver and gold, Exodus 3:22. RB 109 (2002) 197-209;

2661 Egyptological motifs in the sign of the serpent (Exodus 4:2-5; 7:8-14). BetM 171 (2002) 322-335 Sum. 383. **H.**;

2662 The hidden and revealed in the sign of the serpent (Exodus 4:2-5; 7: 8-14). BN 114/115 (2002) 24-30.

2663 *Glatt-Gilad, David A.* Yahweh's honor at stake: a divine conundrum. JSOT 98 (2002) 63-74 [Dt 32].

2664 *Grosby, Steven* Religion and nationality in antiquity: the worship of Yahweh and ancient Israel. Biblical ideas 2002 <1991> ⇒172. 13-51.

2665 *Heltzer, M.* A unique Jewish religious (?) symbol in the Achaemenid period (résumé). TEuph 23 (2002) 153-154.

2666 *Hertog, Cornelis den* The prophetic dimension of the divine name: on Exodus 3:14a and its context. CBQ 64 (2002) 213-228.

2667 *Kellenberger, Edgar* Theologische Eigenarten der Verstockung Pharaos in Ex 4-14. ThZ 58 (2002) 109-113.

2668 *Lemmelijn, Bénédicte* The so-called 'priestly' layer in Exod 7,14-11,10: 'source' and/or/nor 'redaction'?. RB 109 (2002) 481-511.

2669 *Marchadour, Alain* Dieu de l'exode. Dieu, vingt-six portraits. 2002 ⇒312. 215-225.

2670 *Phillips, Anthony* The origin of 'I Am' in Exodus 3.14. Essays on biblical law. JSOT.S 344: 2002 <1998> ⇒223. 261-263.

2671 *Pury, Albert de* Gottesname, Gottesbezeichnung und Gottesbegriff: 'Elohim als Indiz zur Entstehungsgeschichte des Pentateuch. Abschied vom Jahwisten. BZAW 315: 2002 ⇒2189. 25-47.

2672 *Roberts, J.J.M.* The king of glory. The bible and the ANE. 2002 <1980> ⇒230. 104-109.

2673 **Rosenbaum, Stanley Ned** Understanding biblical Israel: a reexamination of the origins of monotheism. Macon, GA 2002, Mercer Univ. Pr. xii; 338 pp. 0-86554-702-5. Bibl. 327-338.

2674 **Soler, Jean** L'invention du monothéisme: aux origines du Dieu unique. P 2002, Fallois 281 pp. 2-87706-437-9. Préf. de *Jean Perrot*.

2675 *Timor, Edna* Adoption and redemption—a novel approach based on an adoption document from Nuzi. BetM 169 (2002) 143-151 Sum. 190 [Lev 25,25-28; Ruth 4; Jer 32,6-14].

2676 *Vries, Anneke de; Kalsky, Manuela* Ein Name, der ein Geheimnis bleibt. JK 63/2 (2002) 22-25.

2677 *Wachter, Rudolf* Jahwe, Pharao und Nomothetes: Gedanken zu einigen antiken Sprachschöpfungsmythen. ThZ 58 (2002) 1-14.

2678 **Williams, Catrin H.** I am He: the interpretation of 'Anî Hû' in Jewish and early christian literature. WUNT 2/113: 2000 ⇒16,2248. ᴿJThS 53 (2002) 207-210 (*Casey, Maurice*); CBQ 64 (2002) 398-399 (*Harrington, Wilfrid J.*).

E3.4 *Pascha, sanguis, sacrificium*: **Passover, blood, sacrifice**, *Ex 11*...

2679 ᴱ**Gittlen, Barry Melvin** Sacred time, sacred place: archaeology and the religion of Israel. WL 2002, Eisenbrauns xii; 228 pp. $29.50. 1-57506-054-X.

2680 ᴱ**Ochs, Peter W.; Levene, Nancy** Textual reasonings: Jewish philosophy and text study at the end of the twentieth century. Radical traditions: L 2002, SCM x; 310 pp. £16. 0-334-02881-7.

2681 *Alvarez Valdes, Ariel* ¿Cómo cruzaron los Israelitas el Mar Rojo?. CuesTF 29 (2002) 407-412.

2682 *Bachra, Bernard N.* Structural regularities in the story of the passage through the sea (Exod 13,17-22 and Exod 14). SJOT 16 (2002) 246-263.

2683 *Barbiero, Gianni mamleket kohanîm* (Ex 19,6a): die Priester an die Macht?. Studien. SBAB 34: 2002 <1989> ⇒139. 11-27.

2684 **Cardellini, Innocenzo** I sacrifici dell'antica alleanza. 2001 ⇒17, 2379. ᴿVerbum Vitae 2 (2002) 291-295 (*Malina, Artur*).

2685 **Cohen, Jeffrey M.** Let my people go: insights to Passover and the Haggadah. Northvale, NJ 2002, Aronson xviii; 193 pp. 07657-62048.

2686 *Davies, Graham I.* Some christian uses and interpretations of the Song of Moses (Exodus 15:1-18). ᶠSMEND, R. 2002 ⇒113. 179-195.

2687 *Davies, John A.* A royal priesthood: literary and intertextual perspectives on an image of Israel in Exodus 19:6. TynB 53 (2002) 157-159.

2688 *Eberhart, Christian* Beobachtungen zum Verbrennungsritus bei Schlachtopfer und Gemeinschafts-Schlachtopfer. Bib. 83 (2002) 88-96.

2689 **Eberhart, Christian** Studien zur Bedeutung der Opfer im Alten Testament: die Signifikanz von Blut- und Verbrennungsriten im kultischen Rahmen. ᴰ*Rendtorff, Rolf*: WMANT 94: Neuk 2002, Neuk xviii; 462 pp. €79. 3-7887-1887-0. Diss. Heidelberg 2000; Bibl. 403-444.

2690 **Frankel, David** The murmuring stories of the priestly school: a retrieval of ancient sacerdotal lore. VT.S 89: Lei 2002, Brill x; 385 pp. €102/$119. 90-04-12368-7. Bibl. 365-372 [Ex 16; Num 16-18; 20].

2691 *Frymer-Kensky, Tikva* Revelation revealed: the doubt of torah. Textual reasonings. 2002 ⇒2680. 68-75 [Ex 19].

2692 *Garrone, Daniele* Il sacrificio nell'Antico Testamento. Colpa. 2002 ⇒401. 71-79.

2693 **Hauge, Martin Ravndal** The descent from the mountain: narrative patterns in Exodus 19-40. JSOT.S 323: 2001 ⇒17,2382. ᴿCBQ 64 (2002) 134-135 (*Miscall, Peter D.*); NTT 103 (2002) 166-173 (*Berge, Kåre*).

2694 *Human, D.J.* Monolatries-monoteïstiese perspektiewe in die Psalms: konsep vir 'n teologiese ontwerp uit Eksodus 15:1b-18. HTS 58 (2002) 1605-1624 [OTA 26,452].

2695 *Kohl, Karl-Heinz* Weltbild, Ritual und Sozialstruktur: zur kosmologischen Bedeutung des Opfers in Ost-Flores. Religion und Weltbild. Marburger religionsgeschichtliche Beiträge 2: 2002 ⇒443. 135-150.

2696 *Lemaire, André* Dieu du Sinaï. Dieu, vingt-six portraits. 2002 ⇒312. 227-236.

2697 *Lemardelé, Christophe* Le sacrifice de purification: un sacrifice ambigu?. VT 52 (2002) 284-289.

2698 *Levine, Baruch A.* Ritual as symbol: modes of sacrifice in Israelite religion. Sacred time. 2002 ⇒2679. 125-135.

2699 *Locci, Adolfo* `Amaleq e i mille volti del male. VM 56/222 (2002) 9-19 [Ex 17,8-16].

2700 *Phillips, Anthony* A fresh look at the Sinai pericope. Essays on biblical law. JSOT.S 344: 2002 <1984> ⇒223. 25-48 [Ex 20,22-23; 32 - 34].

2701 *Rau, Michael* Im Blut ist das Leben!: eine kritische Nachfrage nach der biblischen Begründung des theologischen Denkmusters vom "stellvertretenden Sühnetod". Deutsches Pfarrerblatt 102/3 (2002) 121-125.

2702 **Russell, Brian Douglas** The Song of the Sea: the date and theological significance of Exodus 15:1-21. ^D*McBride, S.D., Jr.*: 2002 Diss. Virginia, Union [RTL 34,593].

2703 *Vanoni, Gottfried* Wer ist König?: Untersuchungen zum Nominalsatztyp von Exodus 19,6a. ^FSTEINGRIMSSON, S.: ATSAT 72: 2002 ⇒ 117. 333-339.

2704 *Warnke, Annekatrin* Die Verbformen mit dem Suffix "ומ-" als Kernelemente der Textstruktur von Ex 15,1b-18. Bib. 83 (2002) 399-408.

2705 *Wénin, André* La théophanie du Sinaï (Ex 19,9-20,21): une approche narrative. Voir les dieux. 2002 ⇒629. 57-77.

2706 *Willi-Plein, Ina* Opfer und Ritus im kultischen Lebenszusammenhang. Sprache als Schlüssel. 2002 <2000> ⇒261. 209-230.

E3.5 Decalogus, *Ex 20=Dt 5; Ex 21ss*; Ancient Near Eastern Law

2707 *Arbib, Roberto* Il pericolo della teocrazia e le Dieci Parole. VM 56/222 (2002) 21-30.

2708 *Bartelmus, Rüdiger* Die samaritanische Fassung des Dekalogs und die Frage der Endredaktion des Pentateuchs am Beispiel des Anfangs der Sinai-Perikope (Ex 19-24). Auf der Suche. 2002 ⇒140. 287-306.

2709 *Chouraqui, André* I dieci comandamenti e la Dichiarazione universale dei diritti dell'uomo. Il libro sacro. 2002 ⇒356. 136-164.

2710 *DiGrazia, Ottavio* Il rapporto tra le Dieci Parole e la teocrazia. VM 56/222 (2002) 31-47.

2711 **Freedman, David Noel** The nine commandments: uncovering a hidden pattern of crime and punishment in the Hebrew Bible. 2000 ⇒ 16,2286; 17,2410. ^RStudia Canonica 35 (2002) 554-555 (*Vogels, Walter*).

2712 *Himbaza, Innocent* Le Décalogue de Papyrus Nash, PHILON, 4QPhyl G, 8QPhyl 3 et 4QMez A. RdQ 20 (2002) 411-428.

2713 **Holbert, John C.** The ten commandments: a preaching commentary. Nv 2002, Abingdon 143 pp. 0-687-09048-2. Bibl. 143.

2714 **John, Frère de Taizé** Vers une terre de liberté: une relecture des dix commandements. Taizé 2002, Presses de Taizé 174 pp. €12.50. 2-85-040-203-6 [Choisir 520,42—Carrillo, Francine].

2715 *Löhr, Hermut* Der Dekalog im frühesten Christentum und seiner jüdischen Umwelt. Judentum und Christentum. 2002 ⇒415. 29-43.
2716 *Luf, Gerhard* Die zehn Gebote und die Menschenrechte. Österreichisches Archiv für Recht und Religion 49 (2002) 177-189.
2717 *Miller, Patrick D.* The good neighborhood: identity and community through the commandments. Character and scripture. 2002 ⇒283. 55-72.
2718 **Pahk, Johan Yeong-Sik** The decalogue. Seoul 2002, The Catholic University of Korea Pr. 255 pp. 89-7108-104-X. Bibl. 231-239.
2719 *Phillips, Anthony* The decalogue: ancient Israel's criminal law. Essays on biblical law. JSOT.S 344: 2002 <1983> ⇒223. 2-24.
2720 **Pronzato, Alessandro** Ritorno ai dieci comandamenti. Mi 2002, Gribaudi 2 vols; 328+288 pp [Hum(B) 58,542—Montagnini, Felice].
2721 **Ravasi, G.** I comandamenti: nelle antiche dieci parole è scritta la via maestra. CinB 2002, San Paolo 176 pp. €27.
2722 *Ro, He W.* The Exodus decalogue in Deuteronomistic redaction. AJTh 16/2 (2002) 315-326.
2723 *Tedeschi, Gianfranco* I dieci comandamenti. VM 56/222 (2002) 5-8.

2724 *Miller, Patrick D.* The story of the first commandment: the book of Exodus. ABQ 21/2 (2002) 234-246.
2725 *Eliav, Yaron Z.* Viewing the sculptural environment: shaping the second commandment. The Talmud Yerushalmi, 3. TSAJ 93: 2002 ⇒ 767. 411-433.
2726 *Keel, Othmar* Das biblische Kultbildverbot und seine Auslegung im rabbinisch-orthodoxen Judentum und im Christentum. Macht und Ohnmacht. HZ.B 33: 2002 ⇒392. 65-96.
2727 *Nepi, Antonio* Le maschere e il volto: il divieto dell'idolatria in Es 20,1-7. PSV 46 (2002) 11-27 [Ex 20,1-7].
2728 *Nicole, Émile* La faute des pères. ThEv(VS) 1/3 (2002) 47-50 [Ex 20,5; Dt 5,9].
2729 *Phillips, Anthony* The case of the woodgatherer reconsidered. Essays on biblical law. JSOT.S 344: 2002 <1969> ⇒223. 235-238 [Ex 20,4-5; Num 15,32-36; Dt 19,19].
2730 *Pritchard, Elizabeth A.* Bilderverbot meets body in Theodor W. ADORNO's inverse theology. HThR 95 (2002) 291-318.
2731 *Sasson, Jack M.* On the use of images in Israel and the ancient Near East: a response to Karel van der Toorn. Sacred time. 2002 ⇒2679. 63-70.
2732 *Elßner, Thomas R.* Das dekalogische Namensmißbrauch-Verbot (Ex 20,7 / Dtn 5,11). BN 114/115 (2002) 61-70.
2733 **Elßner, Thomas R.** Das Namensmißbrauch-Verbot (Ex 20,7, Dtn 5,11): Bedeutung, Entstehung und frühe Wirkungsgeschichte. EThSt 75: 1999 ⇒15,2215; 16,2316. [R]TS 63 (2002) 161-2 (*North, Robert*).
2734 *Meinhold, Arndt* Jüdische Stimmen zum dritten Gebot. Zur weisheitlichen Sicht. 2002 ⇒209. 71-80 [BuBB 37,29] [Ex 20,7].
2735 *Bartelmus, Rüdiger* Sabbat und Arbeitsruhe im Alten Testament. Auf der Suche. 2002 ⇒140. 159-200.
2736 **Jungbauer, Harry** "Ehre Vater und Mutter": der Weg des Elterngebots in der biblischen Tradition. [D]*Jeremias, G.*: WUNT 2/146: Tü 2002, Mohr S. xiv (2); 445 pp. €69. 3-16-147680-8. Diss. Tübingen 2001; Bibl. 375-411 [Ex 20; Dt 5].
2737 *Meinhold, Arndt* Zum Verständnis des Elterngebotes. Zur weisheitlichen Sicht. 2002 ⇒209. 61-70 [BuBB 37,29] [Ex 20,12].

2738 *Phillips, Anthony* Another look at adultery. Essays on biblical law. JSOT.S 344: 2002 <1981> ⇒223. 74-95 [Ex 20,14; Lev 18,29; 20,10; Dt 22,22].

2739 **Levinson, Bernard Malcolm** Deuteronomy and the hermeneutics of legal innovation. 1997 ⇒13,2083... 16,2339. ^RThR 67 (2002) 303-305 (*Veijola, Timo*) [Ex 20,22-23,33; Dt 12-26].

2740 **Lucrezi, Francesco** L'uccisione dello schiavo in diritto ebraico e romano: studi sulla 'Collatio', 1. T 2001, Giappichelli vii; 136 pp. ^RRivista internazionale di diritto romano e antico 52 (2001) 290-300 (*Garofalo, L.*)

2741 *Phillips, Anthony* Some aspects of family law in pre-exilic Israel <1980> [Ex 21,18-19; 22,15-16];

2742 The laws of slavery: Exodus 21.2-11 <1984>;

2743 Another look at murder <1977>. Essays on biblical law. JSOT.S 344: 2002 ⇒223. 111-126/96-110/49-73 [Ex 21,12-17].

2744 **Rothenbusch, Ralf** Die kasuistische Rechtssammlung im 'Bundesbuch' (Ex 21,2-11.18-22,16) und ihr literarischer Kontext im Licht altorientalischer Parallelen. AOAT 259: 2000 ⇒16,2343; 17,2445. ^RWZKM 92 (2002) 245-249 (*Steymans, Hans Ulrich*).

2745 *Sasson, Jack M.* Ritual wisdom?: on 'Seething a kid in its mothers milk'. ^FWEIPPERT, M.: OBO 186: 2002 ⇒133. 294-308 [Ex 23,19].

2746 *Bartor, Asnat* Prophet versus king—'juridical dialogue': juridical analysis of three sections. BetM 169 (2002) 105-132 Sum. 191 [1 Sam 13,11-14; 15,13-31; 1 Kgs 21,17-29]. **H.**

2747 **Beauchamp, Paul** La legge di Dio. 2000 ⇒16,8073. ^RCivCatt 153/1 (2002) 314-315 (*Scaiola, D.*).

2748 **Cohen, Orah** Proximity of sexes: Jewish law and custom. ^D*Sperber, D.*: 2002: 270 pp. Diss. Bar Ilan [RTL 34,595].

2749 *Cook, Johann* The law of Moses as a fence and a fountain. ^MCARROLL, R.: JSOT.S 348: 2002 ⇒13. 280-288.

2750 **Crüsemann, Frank** A torá: teologia e história social da lei do Antiguo Testamento. ^T*Reimer, Haroldo*: Petrópolis 2002, Vozes 599 pp. 85-326-2360-3.

2751 *Dietrich, Walter* Rache: Erwägungen zu einem alttestamentlichen Thema. Theopolitik. 2002 <1976> ⇒159. 117-136;

2752 '... den Armen das Evangelium zu verkünden": vom befreienden Sinn biblischer Gesetze. Theopolitik. 2002 <1985> ⇒159. 184-193.

2753 **Doorly, William J.** The laws of Yahweh: a handbook of biblical law. Mahwah 2002, Paulist xi; 171 pp. $20. 0-8091-4037-3. Bibl. 149-150. ^RStCan 36 (2002) 551-552 (*Vogels, Walter*).

2754 *Ferrari, Silvio* Canon law as a religious legal system. Religion, law. 2002 ⇒412. 49-60 [BuBB 38,93].

2755 **Fitzpatrick-McKinley, Anne** The transformation of Torah from scribal advice to law. JSOT.S 287: 1999 ⇒15,1728...17,2436. ^RJNES 61 (2002) 295-6 (*Westbrook, Raymond*); JSSt 47 (2002) 327-333 (*Jackson, B.S.*); RBLit 4 (2002) 187-189 (*Crenshaw, James L.*).

2756 **Friedmann, Daniel** To kill and take possesion: law, morality, and society in biblical stories. Peabody, MA 2002, Hendrickson xv; 327 pp. $30. 1-56563-641-4 [ThD 50,169—Heiser, W. Charles].

2757 **Grünwaldt, Klaus** Auge um Auge, Zahn um Zahn: das Recht im Alten Testament. Mainz 2002, Matthias-Grünewald 171 pp. €19.80. 3-7867-2370-2.

2758 **Jackson, Bernard S.** Studies in the semiotics of biblical law. JSOT.S 314: 2000 ⇒16,2293; 17,2440. ᴿCBQ 64 (2002) 353-354 (*Patrick, Dale*).

2759 *Köckert, Matthias* Wie kam das Gesetz an den Sinai?. ᶠSMEND, R.: 2002 ⇒113. 13-27.

2760 *Martens, Elmer A.* How is the christian to construe Old Testament law?. BBR 12 (2002) 199-216 [Lev 19].

2761 *McDermott, John J.* Strange laws and good theology. BiTod 40 (2002) 117-122.

2762 *Milgrom, Jacob* Were the firstborn sacrificed to Yhwh?: to Molek?: popular practice or divine demand?. Sacrifice in religious experience. 2002 ⇒612. 49-55.

2763 *Phillips, Anthony* Torah and mishpat: a light to the peoples <1979>;
2764 Respect for life in the Old Testament. Essays on biblical law <1983>;
2765 The undetectable offender and the priestly legislators <1985> [Lev 5, 20-26; Num 15,30-31]. Essays on biblical law. JSOT.S 344: 2002 ⇒ 223. 179-200/139-147/255-260.

2766 **Porten, Bezalel** The Elephantine papyri in English: three millennia of cross-cultural continuity and change. DMOA 22: 1996 ⇒12,2009 ...15,2252. ᴿJBL 121 (2002) 159-160 (*Smith-Christopher, David L.*).

2767 *Rofé, Alexander* Methodological aspects of the study of biblical law. Deuteronomy. 2002 <1986> ⇒231. 205-219.

2768 *Schenker, Adrian* Die Verwandtschaft zwischen dem Gebot der Elternehrung und den Inzestverboten im Alten Testament: Dekalog Ex 20:12; Dt 5:16 und die Liste Lev 18:6-23. Anthropotes 18/1 (2002) 33-42.

2769 *Smend, Rudolf* Das Gesetz im Alten Testament. Die Mitte des A.T. 2002 <1981> ⇒244. 115-147.

2770 *Wagner, Volker* Ein Indiz für die praktische Verwendung der kasuistischen Rechtssatzsammlungen des Pentateuchs im Rechtsleben. ZAR 8 (2002) 211-241.

2771 *Wyschogrod, Michael* La tora en tant que loi dans le judaïsme. SIDIC 35/2-3 (2002 <1986>) 18-24.

2772 *Zipor, Moshe A.* עיון בנוסחות ההתייצגות של האל, עם הפלגה לויקרא כ 22-27, כן 42-45 [A study of God's self-introducing formulas and the cases of Leviticus 20:22-27 and 26:42-45]. BetM 170 (2002) 199-207 Sum. 288 [Ex 20,02]. H.

2773 *Altman, Amnon* On some basic concepts in the law of people seeking refuge and sustenance in the ancient Near East. ZAR 8 (2002) 323-342.

2774 *Bouzon, Emanuel* Einige Bemerkungen zum §60 der Hammurapi-Stele. ᶠDIETRICH, M.: 2002 ⇒28. 73-87.

2775 *Cardellini, Innocenzo* Problematica sui principi costitutivi del "diritto" e della "giustizia" in ambito mesopotamico. RStB 14/1-2 (2002) 39-45.

2776 *Faist, Betina* Die Rechtsordnung in Syrien nach der hethitischen Eroberung: Wandel und Kontinuität. Brückenland Anatolien?. 2002 ⇒ 453. 129-146.

2777 *Goddeeris, Anne* An adoption document from the Kisurra Collection in the British Museum. ᶠWALKER, C. 2002 ⇒130. 93-97.

2778 *Greengus, Samuel* Redefining 'inchoate marriage' in Old Babylonian contexts. ^{M}JACOBSEN, T.: 2002 ⇒62. 123-139.

2779 *Haase, Richard* Minima ad Codicem Hethaerorum pertinenta. ZAR 8 (2002) 308-322.

2780 *Hallo, William W.* A model court case concerning inheritance. ^{M}JA-COBSEN, T.: 2002 ⇒62. 141-154.

2781 **Hölkeskamp, Karl-Joachim** Schiedsrichter, Gesetzgeber und Gesetzgebung im archaischen Griechenland. 1999 ⇒15,2265; 16,2367. ^{R}At. 90 (2002) 614-617 (*Bearzot, Cinzia*).

2782 *Jacobson, V.A.* Laws and legality in OB Mesopotamia. ^{M}DIAKONOFF, I.: 2002 ⇒27. 344-352.

2783 ^{E}**Joannès, Francis** Rendre la justice en Mésopotamie, archives judiciaires du Proche-Orient ancien (IIIe-I^e millénaires avant J.-C.). 2000 ⇒16,2368. ^{R}RAr (2002/1) 73-74 (*Rede, Marcelo*).

2784 **Lafont, Sophie** Femmes, droit et justice dans l'antiquité orientale. OBO 165: 1999 ⇒15,2266...17,2470. ^{R}ZAR 8 (2002) 389-398 (*Yaron, Reuven*).

2785 *Oelsner, Joachim* Frühneubabylonische Rechtsurkunden: die Schlußklauseln. ^{F}DIETRICH, M.: 2002 ⇒28. 527-545.

2786 *Otto, Eckart* Gerechtigkeit in der orientalischen und okzidentalen Antike: Aspekte für den ethischen Diskurs in der Moderne im Spannungsfeld zwischen Max WEBER und Ernst TROELTSCH. Aktualität der Antike. 2002 ⇒406. 44-64.

2787 *Selz, Gebhard J.* "Streit herrscht, Gewalt droht"—zu Konfliktregelung und Recht in der frühdynastischen und altakkadischen Zeit. WZKM 92 (2002) 155-203.

2788 **Snell, Daniel C.** Flight and freedom in the ancient Near East. 2001 ⇒17,10270. ^{R}BiOr 59 (2002) 342-344 (*Limet, Henri*); JBL 121 (2002) 337-339 (*Moore, Michael S.*).

2789 **VerSteeg, Russ** Law in ancient Egypt. Durham 2002, Carolina Academic 241 pp. $27.50. 0-89089-978-9.

2790 *Waerzeggers, Caroline* Endogamy in Mesopotamia in the Neo-Babylonian period. ^{F}WALKER, C.: 2002 ⇒130. 319-342.

2791 ^{E}**Westbrook, Raymond; Jasnow, Richard** Security for debt in ancient Near Eastern law. Culture and history of the Ancient Near East 9: 2001 ⇒17,649. ^{R}OLZ 97 (2002) 537-39 (*Van de Mieroop, Marc*).

2792 *Wilcke, Claus* Der Kodex Urnamma (CU): Versuch einer Rekonstruktion. ^{M}JACOBSEN, T.: 2002 ⇒62. 291-333.

2793 *Wunsch, Cornelia* 'Du hast meinen Sohn geschlagen!'. ^{F}WALKER, C. 2002 ⇒130. 355-364.

E3.6 **Cultus**, *Exodus 24-40*

2794 **Alexander, Kelly D.** Ark of the covenant: simplified information for lay-persons. Lanham 2002, University Press of America xvii; 132 pp. 0-7618-2197-X. Bibl. 127-128.

2795 **Balentine, Samuel Eugene** The Torah's vision of worship. 1999 ⇒ 15,2274; 17,2479. ^{R}JR 82 (2002) 269-270 (*Lieber, Laura*).

2796 *Barbiero, Gianni* "... ma certo non lascia il colpevole senza punizione": la "giustizia" di Dio e di Mosè in Es 32-34. RStB 14/1-2 (2002) 55-79;

2797 '... aber gewiss lässt er den Schuldigen nicht ungestraft": die Gerechtigkeit Gottes und Moses in Ex 32-34;

2798 Ex. xxxiii 7-11: eine synchrone Lektüre <2000>. Studien. SBAB 34: 2002 ⇒139. 255-282/80-92.

2799 **Cardellini, Innocenzo** I "Leviti", l'esilio e il tempio: nuovi elementi per una rielaborazione storica. R 2002, Lateran Univ. Pr. 50 pp. €6. 88-465-0219-1.

2800 **Chilton, Bruce David** Redeeming time: the wisdom of ancient Jewish and Christian festal calendars. Peabody, MASS 2002, Hendrickson viii; 132 pp. $20. 1-56563-380-6. Bibl. 115-120.

2801 *Doan, William; Gannon, Terry* Masking God: the application of drama theory to biblical texts. ProcGLM 22 (2002) 127-145.

2802 **Franz, Matthias** Der barmherzige und gnädige Gott: die Gnadenrede vom Sinai (Exodus 34,6f) und ihre parallelen Aussagen im Alten Testament und seiner Umwelt. ᴰ*Kessler, Rainer*: 2002 Diss. Marburg [ThRv 99/2,ix].

2803 **Gabai, Hyman** Judaism, mathematics, and the Hebrew calendar. Northvale, NJ 2002, Aronson xii; 420 pp. 0-7657-6144-0.

2804 *Karagiannis, Christos G.* The ark of the covenant. Theol(A) 73 (2002) 247-304, 651-693.

2805 *Klingbeil, Gerald A.* "Quebrar la ley": algunas notas exegéticas acerca de Éxodo 32:19. DavarLogos 1/1 (2002) 73-81.

2806 **Körting, Corinna** Der Schall des Schofar: Israels Feste im Herbst. BZAW 285: 1999 ⇒15,2285. ᴿThRv 98 (2002) 484-486 (*Braulik, Georg*).

2807 **LaRocca-Pitts, Elizabeth C.** "Of wood and stone": the significance of Israelite cultic items in the bible and its early interpreters. HSM 61: 2001 ⇒17,2491. ᴿCBQ 64 (2002) 354-355 (*Dick, Michael B.*); BiOr 59 (2002) 386-388 (*Dion, Paul E.*).

2808 *Long, Burke O.* Embodies typology: modeling the Mosaic tabernacle. ᶠFLANAGAN, J.: JSOT.S 359: 2002 ⇒38. 117-138.

2809 **Olyan, Saul M.** Rites and rank: hierarchy in biblical representations of cult. 2000 ⇒16,2397. ᴿCBQ 64 (2002) 141-142 (*Shafer, Byron E.*); JSSt 47 (2002) 335-336 (*Jenson, Philip*); JQR 92 (2002) 269-271 (*Brettler, Marc Z.*).

2810 **Reingold, Edward M.; Dershowitz, Nachum** Calendrical tabulations. C 2002, CUP xxx; 606 pp. 0-521-78253-8.

2811 *Schmitt, Hans-Christoph* Das sogenannte jahwistische Privilegrecht in Ex 34,10-28 als Komposition der spätdeuteronomistischen Endredaktion des Pentateuch. Abschied vom Jahwisten. BZAW 315: 2002 ⇒2189. 157-171.

2812 **Scoralick, Ruth** Gottes Güte und Gottes Zorn: die Gottesprädikationen in Exodus 34,6F und ihre intertextuellen Beziehungen zum Zwölfprophetenbuch. ᴰ*Zenger, Erich*: Herders Biblische Studien 33: FrB 2002, Herder ix; 246 pp. €40. 3-451-27849-9. Diss.-Habil. Münster; Bibl. 221-241.

2813 *Semen, Petre* La signification du pain et du vin dans les livres de l'Ancien Testament. Theol(A) 73/1 (2002) 109-120.

2814 **Soggin, J. Alberto** Israel in the biblical period: institutions, festivals, ceremonies, rituals. ᵀ*Bowden, John*: 2001 ⇒17,2506. ᴿBiblInterp 10 (2002) 446-447 (*Lang, Bernhard*).

2815 *Stefani, Piero* La gloria sul volto di Mosè nella tradizione ebraica. RSEc 20 (2002) 251-260 [Ex 34,29-33].

2816 **Volgger, David** Israel wird feiern: Untersuchung zu den Festtexten in Exodus bis Deuteronomium. ATSAT 73: St. Ottilien 2002, EOS (6) vii; 327 pp. 3-8306-7154-7. Bibl. 312-319.

2817 *Wellmann, Bettina* "Mein Angesicht wird mitgehen": Exodus 33,1-34,3: Januar—Neubeginn. zwölfmal bibel entdecken. 2002 ⇒1087. 8-15 {Exodus}33,12 - 34,03.

2818 *Wessner, Mark D.* Toward a literary understanding of Moses and the Lord "face to face" (panîm 'el-panîm) in Exodus 33:7-11. RestQ 44/2 (2002) 109-116.

2819 *Zwickel, Wolfgang* Die Edelsteine im Brustschild des Hohenpriesters und beim himmlischen Jerusalem. Edelsteine. 2002 ⇒538. 50-70 [Ex 28,17-20].

E3.7 Leviticus, *Jubilee*

2820 **Balentine, Samuel E.** Leviticus. LVL 2002, Westminster xiv; 220 pp. $25. 0-8042-3103-6 [ThD 50,257—Heiser, W. Charles].

2821 *Barnard, Willem* Leviticus lezen in de Advent. ITBT 10/7 (2002) 27-30.

2822 **Douglas, Mary** Leviticus as literature. 1999 ⇒15,2306...17,2514. ᴿCTJ 37 (2002) 344-346 (*Van der Weele, Steven J.*);

2823 NY 2002 <1999>, OUP xv; 280 pp. $17. 0-199244-197]BiTod 41, 58 —Bergant, Dianne].

2824 *Jürgens, Benedikt* Wiederherstellung der Schöpfungsordnung: Levitikus (Teil 1): Erzählung und Ritual. BiLi 75 (2002) 55-59;

2825 (Teil 2): rituelle Kommunikation. BiLi 75 (2002) 133-137;

2826 (Teil 3): Konstitution einer Lebensordnung durch Differenzierung. BiLi 75 (2002) 200-204.

2827 (Teil 4): der Sabbat als Prinzip der Schöpfung. BiLi 75 (2002) 301-305.

2828 **Koster, Albert** Toen riep hij / in de steppe / de woorden: een woord-voor-woordvertaling uit het Hebreeuws van Leviticus, Numeri en Deuteronomium. Eindhoven 2002, Aproges 302 pp. €22. 90-5733-0-13-X [Streven 70,757—Beentjes, Panc].

2829 *Kułaczkowski, Jerzy* Zasady świetości zycia małzeńskiego i rodzinnego w Kodeksie Świetości Ksiegi Kapłańskiej. CoTh 72/4 (2002) 5-35. **P.**

2830 **Lowery, Richard H.** Sabbath and jubilee. 2000 ⇒16,2449. ᴿRBLit 4 (2002) 165-167 (*Gorman, Frank H.*).

2831 **Maccoby, Hyam** Ritual and morality: the ritual purity system and its place in Judaism. 1999 ⇒15,2310... 17,2520. ᴿJQR 92 (2002) 286-292 (*Hayes, Christine*).

2832 **Milgrom, Jacob** Leviticus 17-22. AncB 3A: 2000 ⇒16,2417. ᴿRBLit (2002)* (*Brown, Walter E.*);

2833 Leviticus 23-27. AncB 3B: 2001 ⇒17,2522. ᴿJThS 53 (2002) 134-138 (*Bray, Jason*); JJS 53 (2002) 383-385 (*Davies, Graham*); IThQ 67 (2002) 281-282 (*McConvery, Brendan*);

2834 Leviticus 17-22; 23-27. AncB 3A-3B 2001 ⇒17,2521. ᴿNRTh 124 (2002) 276-277 (*Luciani, D.*); IThQ 67 (2002) 281-282 (*McConvery, Brendan*);

2835 **North, Robert** The Biblical Jubilee:...after fifty years. AnBib 145: 2000 ⇒16,2455; 17,2523. ᴿRivBib 50 (2002) 94-98 (*Prato, Gian Luigi*).

2836 ᴱ**Plaut, W. Gunther** Die Tora: in jüdischer Auslegung, 3: Wajikra: Levitikus. ᵀ*Böckler, Annette*: 2001 ⇒17,2525. ᴿJud. 58 (2002) 134-135 (*Ego, Beate*).

2837   **Ross, Allen P.** Holiness to the Lord: a guide to the exposition of the book of Leviticus. GR 2002, Baker 496 pp. $33. 0-8010-2285-1.
2838   **Schwartz, Baruch J.** The Holiness legislation: studies in the Priestly Code. 1999 ⇒15,2357; 17,2527. [R]RB 109 (2002) 604-607 (*Levine, Baruch A.*).
2839   *Shead, Andrew G.* An Old Testament theology of the sabbath year and jubilee. RTR 61/1 (2002) 19-33.
2840   **Sherwood, Stephen K.** Leviticus, Numbers, Deuteronomy. Berit Olam: ColMn 2002, Liturgical xviii; 306 pp. $40. 0-8146-5046-5. Bibl. 286-292. [R]RBLit (2002)* (*Wagenaar, Jan A.*).
2841   *Volschenk, G.J.* 'n Literêr-kritiese ondersoek na die belang van die jubilee in die bybel. HTS 58 (2002) 185-211 [OTA 26,140].

2842   *Hepner, Gershon* Jacob's oath causes Rachel's death: reflecting the law in Lev. 5:4-6. ZAR 8 (2002) 131-165.
2843   **Klingbeil, Gerald A.** A comparative study of the ritual of ordination as found in Leviticus 8 and Emar 369. 1998 ⇒14,2195; 15,2349. [R]JNES 61 (2002) 227-228 (*Sparks, Kent*); JQR 92 (2002) 604-608 (*Hurowitz, Victor Avigdor*).
2844   *Hess, Richard S.* Leviticus 10:1: strange fire and an odd name. BBR 12 (2002) 187-198.
2845   *Ages, Arnold* The subtle grammar of the biblical dietary laws. JBQ 30 (2002) 80-89 {Leviticus}11.
2846   *Douglas, Mary* The compassionate God of Leviticus and his animal creation. Borders. JSOT.S 313: 2002 ⇒585. 61-73 [Lev 11].
2847   **Moskala, Jirí** The laws of clean and unclean animals of Leviticus 11: their nature, theology, and rationale (an intertextual study). 2000 ⇒16,2474. [R]JThS 53 (2002) 131-134 (*Houston, Walter*).
2848   *Warning, Wilfried* Terminologische Verknüpfungen und Leviticus 11. BZ 46 (2002) 97-102.
2849   *Ostrer, Boris* Leviticus 13:13 and its Mishnaic parallel. JJS 53 (2002) 18-26.
2850   *Staubli, Thomas* Die Symbolik des Vogelrituals bei der Reinigung von Aussätzigen (Lev 14,4-7). Bib. 83 (2002) 230-237.
2851   *Carmichael, Calum M.* Religious claims about biblical law. Religion, law. 2002 ⇒412. 20-33 [BuBB 37,34] [Lev 16].
2852   **Jürgens, Benedikt** Heiligkeit und Versöhnung: Levitikus 16 in seinem literarischen Kontext. Herders Biblische Studien 28: 2000 ⇒16, 2479. [R]ThLZ 127 (2002) 899-901 (*Herrmann, Wolfram*).
2853   *Stökl, Daniel Johannes* The christian exegesis of the scapegoat between Jews and pagans. Sacrifice in religious experience. 2002 ⇒ 612. 207-232 [Lev 16].
2854   **James, Randall Craig** An analysis of the ethical implications of the interpersonal relationships in the Holiness Code. [D]*Hunt, H.*: 2002: 180 pp. Diss. Fort Worth [RTL 34,591] [Lev 17-26].
2855   *Kaiser, Otto* Freiheit und Bindung in der attischen Demokratie und der jüdischen Theokratie: ein Beitrag zur Bestimmung der Aufgabe der Religion in der modernen Zivilgesellschaft. [F]SMEND, R. 2002 ⇒ 113. 448-464 [Lev 17-26].
2856   *Melcher,, Sarah J.* Kinship and enculturation: shaping the generations in Leviticus 18. ProcGLM 22 (2002) 63-77.
2857   *Walsh, Jerome T.* Leviticus 18:22 and 20:13: who is doing what to whom?. JBL 120 (2001) 201-209.

2858 *Master, John R.* The place of chapter 24 in the structure of the book of Leviticus. BS 159 (2002) 415-424.
2859 **Lefèbvre, Jean-François** Un mémorial de la création et de la rédemption: le jubilé biblique en Lv 25. ConBib 23: 2001 ⇒17,2545. ᴿEeV 50 (2002) 24-25 (*Bony, Paul*).
2860 *Ssemakula, Luke* The Hebrew jubilee year in Leviticus 25: a paradigm for an African spirituality. African Christian Studies 18/1 (2002) 5-33.

E3.8 *Numeri*; Numbers, Balaam

2861 **Brown, Raymond** The message of Numbers: journey to the Promised Land. The bible speaks today: Leicester 2002, IVP 308 pp. £10. 0-85111-491-1. Bibl. 11-13.
2862 **Douglas, Mary** Nel deserto: la dottrina della contaminazione nel libro dei Numeri. ᴱ*Destro, Adriana*: Collana di studi religiosi: 2001 ⇒17,2552. ᴿVetChr 39 (2002) 407-408 (*Colantuono, Gaetano*).
     Koster, A. Woord-voor-woordvertaling...Numeri 2002 ⇒2827.
2863 *Leveen, Adriane B.* Variations on a theme: differing conceptions of memory in the book of Numbers. JSOT 27 (2002) 201-221.
2864 *Quesada, Jan Jaynes* Body piercing: the issue of priestly control over acceptable family structure in the book of Numbers. BiblInterp 10 (2002) 24-35.
2865 *Römer, Thomas* Das Buch Numeri und das Ende des Jahwisten: Anfragen zur 'Quellenscheidung' im vierten Buch des Pentateuch. Abschied vom Jahwisten. BZAW 315: 2002 ⇒2189. 215-231.
2866 **Seebass, Horst** Numeri [19,1-21,9]. BK IV/2 Lfg. 4: Neuk 2002, Neuk'er 241-320 pp. 3-7887-1475-1;
2867 [21,9-22,1] BK IV/2 Lfg. 5: Neuk 2002, Neuk'er 321-374; i-viii pp. 3-7887-1475-1
     Sherwood, S.K. Leviticus, Numbers... 2002 ⇒2840.
2868 ᴱ**Van Midden, P.J.** In de woestijn: Numeri. ACEBT 20: Maastricht 2002, Shaker viii; 155 pp. €15.50. 90-423-0208-9 [RB 110,312].
2869 **Wevers, John William** Notes on the Greek text of Numbers. SBL. SCS 46: 1998 ⇒14,2244; 16,2503. ᴿBIOSCS 35 (2002) 40-42 (*Flint, Peter W.*).

2870 *Knohl, Israel* The guilt offering of the 'Holiness School'. Tarbiz 71 (2002) 327-335 Sum. v [Num 5,5-8]. **H.**
2871 *Endmann, Philipp* Der sogenannte aaronitische Segen: eine Auslegung zu Num 6,22-27. ThGl 92 (2002) 518-537.
2872 *Dehn, Ulrich* Biblische Besinnung: Friede sei mit euch!: der aaronitische Segen (Numeri 6,24-26). ZMiss 28 (2002) 334-336.
2873 *Waaler, Erik* A revised date for pentateuchal texts?: evidence from Ketef Hinnom. TynB 53 (2002) 29-55 [Num 6,24-26].
2874 *Gertel, Elliot B.* Moses, Elisha and transferred spirit: the height of biblical prophecy?. JBQ 30 (2002) 73-79, 171-177 [Num 11].
2875 *Williams, Jacqueline* 'And she became 'snow white': Numbers 12:1-16. OTEs 15 (2002) 259-268.
2876 **Artus, Olivier** Études sur le livre des Nombres: récit, histoire et loi en Nombres 13,1-20,13. OBO 157: 1997 ⇒13,2217; 15,2382. ᴿThR 67 (2002) 144-146 (*Otto, Eckart*).

2877 *Frick, Frank S.* Ritual and social regulation in ancient Israel: the importance of the social context for ritual studies and a case study— the ritual of the red heifer. [F]FLANAGAN, J.: JSOT.S 359: 2002 ⇒38. 219-232 [Num 19].

2878 *Lim, Johnson T.K.* What has the sin of Moses in Numbers to do with Ezekiel?. ITS 39 (2002) 116-125 [Num 20,1-13].

2879 **Schüle, Andreas** Israels Sohn—Jahwes Prophet: ein Versuch zum Verhältnis von kanonischer Theologie und Religionsgeschichte anhand der Bileam-Perikope (Num 22-24). 2001 ⇒17,2575. [R]Bib. 83 (2002) 577-579 (*Moore, Michael S.*).

2880 *Wolf-Monzon, Tamar* "נופל וגלוי עיניים" תנודות בנקודות התצפית כמפתח לאירגונה הקומפוזיציוני של "פרשת בלעם" ['Falling into a trance, but having his eyes open': transitions between points of view as a key to the compositional organization of the Balaam episode]. BetM 170 (2002) 237-256. Sum. 286. H.

2881 *Auld, A. Graeme* Samuel, Numbers, and the Yahwist-question. Abschied vom Jahwisten. BZAW 315: 2002 ⇒2189. 233-246 [Num 22-24; 11,24-30].

2882 *Burrus, Virginia* Revelation revealed or reveiled?: 'Jewish' and 'christian' interpretation in late antiquity. Textual reasonings. 2002 ⇒ 2680. 76-81 [Num 25].

2883 *Litke, John D.* The daughters of Zelophehad. CThMi 29 (2002) 207-218 [Num 27,1-11].

2884 *Nwaoru, Emmanuel O.* The case of the daughters of Zelophehad (Num 27:1-11) and African inheritance rights. AJTh 16/1 (2002) 49-65.

2885 *Schmidt, Ludwig* Die Ansiedlung von Ruben und Gad im Ostjordanland in Numeri 32,1-38. ZAW 114 (2002) 497-510;

2886 Leviten-und Asylstädte in Num xxxv und Jos. xx; xxi 1-42. VT 52 (2002) 103-121.

E3.9 Liber Deuteronomii

2887 *Auld, Graeme* Deuteronomy, history and the Hebrew Bible. ET 113 (2002) 173-174.

2888 **Bennett, Harold V.** Injustice made legal: Deuteronomic law and the plight of widows, strangers, and orphans in Ancient Israel. The Bible in Its World: GR 2002, Eerdmans xiii; 209 pp. $50. 0-8028-3909-6. Bibl. 177-200.

2889 [E]**Beretta, Piergiorgio** Deuteronomio: ebraico, greco, latino, italiano. [T]*Doveri, C.*: Bibbia Ebraica Interlineare 5: CinB 2002, San Paolo 19*; 235 pp. 88-215-4705-1. Testo ebr.: BHS, testo greco: Settanta, ed. *Rahlfs*; testo latino: Vulgata Clementina; testo ital.: Nuovissima.

2890 *Bovati, Pietro* Deuterosi e compimento. Teol(Br) 27 (2002) 20-34. [F]BREKELMANS, C.: Deuteronomy and Deuteronomic literature 1997 ⇒10.

2891 **Carrière, Jean-Marie** Le livre du Deutéronome. La Bible tout simplement: P 2002, L'Atelier 192 pp. €15. 2-7082-3606-7.

2892 **Christensen, Duane L.** Deuteronomy: v.2, ch. 21:10-34:12. WBC 6B: Nv 2002, Nelson 464-915 pp. $40. 0-8499-1032-3.

2893 *Connor, George E.* Covenants and criticism: Deuteronomy and the American founding. BTB 32 (2002) 4-10.

2894 *Dahmen, Ulrich* Neu identifizierte Fragmente in den Deuteronomium-Handschriften vom Toten Meer. RdQ 20 (2002) 571-581.

2895 **Dahmen, Ulrich** Leviten und Priester im Deuteronomium: literarkritische und redaktionsgeschichtliche Studien. BBB 110: 1996 ⇒12, 2180; 14,2280. [R]ThR 67 (2002) 313-315 (*Veijola, Timo*).

2896 *Finsterbusch, Karin* Die kollektive Identität und die Kinder: Bemerkungen zu einem Programm im Buch Deuteronomium. JBTh 17 (2002) 99-120.

2897 *Garribba, Dario* Deuteronomismo e sapienza: la riscrittura dell'identità culturale e religiosa di Israele. RdT 43 (2002) 253-264.

2898 **Gertz, Jan Christian** Die Gerichtsorganisation Israels im deuteronomischen Gesetz. FRLANT 165: 1994 ⇒10,2400; 12,2185. [R]ThR 67 (2002) 309-312 (*Veijola, Timo*).

2899 **Gomes de Araújo, Reginaldo** Theologie der Wüste im Deuteronomium. ÖBS 17: 1999 ⇒15,2410. [R]ThR 67 (2002) 299-300 (*Veijola, Timo*).

2900 *Houtman, Cees* An der Schwelle zum Eschaton: prophetische Eschatologie im Deuteronomium. [F]LEENE, H. 2002 ⇒73. 119-128;

2901 Die ursprünglichen Bewohner des Landes Kanaan im Deuteronomium: Sinn und Absicht der Beschreibung ihrer Identität und ihres Charakters. VT 52 (2002) 51-65.

Koster, A. Woord-voor-woordvertaling...Deut. 2002 ⇒2827.

2902 **Krinetzki, Günter** Rechtsprechung und Amt im Deuteronomium: zur Exegese der Gesetze Dtn 16,18-20; 17,8-18,22. 1994 ⇒10,2427; 13,2252 [R]ThR 67 (2002) 308-309 (*Veijola, Timo*).

2903 *McCarthy, Carmel* Moving in from the margins: issues of text and context in Deuteronomy. Congress volume Basel 2001. VT.S 92: 2002 ⇒570. 109-137.

2904 **McConville, James Gordon** Deuteronomy. Apollos Old Testament commentary 5: Leicester 2002, Apollos 544 pp. £22. 0-85111-779-1. Bibl. 480-510.

2905 *McConville, J.G.* Singular address in the Deuteronomic law and the politics of legal administration. JSOT 97 (2002) 19-36.

2906 *McKenzie, Steven L.* The theological legacy of Deuteronomy. [F]SMEND, R.: 2002 ⇒113. 28-43.

2907 *Millar, J. Gary* 'A faithful God who does no wrong': history, theology, and reliability in Deuteronomy. The trustworthiness of God. 2002 ⇒410. 3-17.

2908 *Moran, William L.* The ancient Near Eastern background of the love of God in Deuteronomy. The most magic word. 2002 <1963> ⇒212. 170-181.

2909 **Nelson, Richard D.** Deuteronomy: a commentary. OTL: LVL 2002, Westminster xv; 424 pp. $45. 0-664-21952-7. Bibl. xi-xv.

2910 **Nielsen, Eduard** Deuteronomium. HAT 1/6: 1995 ⇒11/1,824; 12, 2166. [R]ThR 67 (2002) 287-288 (*Veijola, Timo*).

2911 **Norrback, Anna** The fatherless and the widow in the deuteronomic covenant. 2001 ⇒17,2599. [R]SEÅ 67 (2002) 156-158 (*Norin, Stig*).

2912 **Otto, Eckart** Das Deuteronomium: politische Theologie und Rechtsreform in Juda und Assyrien. BZAW 284: 1999 ⇒15,2417...17, 2600. [R]ThR 67 (2002) 292-298 (*Veijola, Timo*);

2913 Das Deuteronomium im Pentateuch und Hexateuch: Studien zur Literaturgeschichte von Pentateuch und Hexateuch im Lichte des Deuteronomiumrahmens. FAT 30: 2000 ⇒16,2550. [R]ThR 67 (2002) 146-

148 (*Otto, Eckart*); Anton. 77 (2002) 749-752 (*Volgger, David*);
ThLZ 127 (2002) 165-168 (*Reventlow, Henning Graf*);
2914 Gottes Recht als Menschenrecht: rechts- und literaturhistorische Studien zum Deuteronomium. ZAR.Beiheft 2: Wsb 2002, Harrassowitz vii; 331 pp. €78. 3-447-04276-1. Bibl. 277-315 [RB 110,158].
2915 *Perlitt, Lothar* LUTHERs Deuteronomium-Auslegung. FSMEND, R. 2002 ⇒113. 211-225.
2916 **Pressler, Carolyn** The view of women found in the deuteronomic family laws. BZAW 216: 1993 ⇒9,2536; 11/2,1762. RThR 67 (2002) 315-316 (*Veijola, Timo*).
2917 *Rofé, Alexander* The book of Deuteronomy: a summary <1986/7>;
2918 Qumranic paraphrases, the Greek Deuteronomy and the late history of the biblical נשיא <1988>;
2919 The arrangement of the laws in Deuteronomy <1988>;
2920 The strata of the law about the centralization of worship in Deuteronomy and the history of the Deuteronomic movement <1972>;
2921 The laws of warfare in the book of Deuteronomy: their origins, intent and positivity <1985>;
2922 Review of M. Weinfeld, *Deuteronomy and the Deuteronomic school* <1974>. Deuteronomy. 2002 ⇒231. 1-13/37-46/55-77/97-101/149-167/221-230.
2923 **Rose, Martin** 5. Mose. ZBK.AT 5: 1994 ⇒10,2392; 12,2167/8. RThR 67 (2002) 284-287 (*Veijola, Timo*).
2924 **Seijas de los Ríos-Zarzosa, María Guadalupe** Las masoras del libro de Deuteronomio: Códice M1 de la Universidad Complutense de Madrid. TECC 68: M 2002, Consejo Superior de Investigaciones Científicas, Instituto de Filología 226 pp. 84-00-08056-4.
       Sherwood, S.K. ... Deuteronomy 2002 ⇒2840.
2925 ESiquans, Agnethe Der Deuteronomiumkommentar des THEODORET von Kyros. DBraulik, G.: ÖBS 19: Fra 2002, Lang 381 pp. €56.60. 3-631-38868-3. Diss. Wien 2001; Bibl. 375-381.
2926 **Sonnet, Jean-Pierre** The book within the book: writing in Deuteronomy. Bibl.Interp. 14: 1997 ⇒13,2258... 15,2420. RThR 67 (2002) 323-327 (*Veijola, Timo*).
2927 *Veijola, Timo* Deuteronomismusforschung zwischen Tradition und Innovation. ThR 67 (2002) 273-327, 391-424.
2928 **Wilson, Ian** Out of the midst of the fire: divine presence in Deuteronomy. SBLDS 151: 1995 ⇒11/1,866... 15,2422. RThR 67 (2002) 302-303 (*Veijola, Timo*).

2929 *Braulik, Georg* Deuteronomium 1-4 als Sprechakt. Bib. 83 (2002) 249-257.
2930 **Lohfink, Norbert** The book of Deuteronomy: Moses' first address (Deut 1-4). R 2002, E.P.I.B. 100 pp. Collab. *A.M. Ahurwendeire*.
2931 *Hertog, Cornelius G. den* The contribution of the daughter translations to the lexicography of the Septuagint: with special emphasis on the Sahidic translation of Deuteronomy 1-10. JNSL 28/1 (2002) 57-67.
2932 *Moran, William L.* The end of the unholy war and the anti-Exodus. The most magic word. 2002 <1963> ⇒212. 148-157 [Dt 2,14-16].
2933 *Ninow, Friedbert* In search of the 'city which is in the middle of the valley'. AUSS 40 (2002) 125-129 [Dt 2,36].
2934 *Sanz Giménez-Rico, Enrique* Se convertirá Israel al entrar en la Tierra Prometida?: en torno a Dt 3,21-22. EE 77 (2002) 361-383 [Ex 14].

2935 *Talstra, Eep; Van der Merwe, Christo H.J.* Analysis, retrieval and the demand for more data: integrating the results of a formal textlinguistic and cognitive based pragmatic approach to the analysis of Deut 4:1-40. Bible and computer. 2002 ⇒548. 43-78.

2936 *Rofé, Alexander* The monotheistic argumentation in Deuteronomy 4:32-40: contents, composition and text <1985>;

2937 The history of the cities of refuge in biblical law <1986>. Deuteronomy. 2002 ⇒231. 15-24/121-147 [Dt 4,41-43; 19,1-13].

2938 *Haraguchi, Takaaki* A rhetorical study of the Deuteronomic decalogue (Deut 5:1-33). AJTh 16/2 (2002) 276-285.

2939 *Rofé, Alexander* Deuteronomy 5.28-6.1: composition and text in the light of Deuteronomic style and three *tefillin* from Qumran (4Q 128, 129, 137). Deuteronomy. 2002 <1985> ⇒231. 25-36.

2940 *Bord, Lucien-Jean; Hamidović, David* Écoute Israël (Deut. vi 4). VT 52 (2002) 13-29.

2941 *Donner, Herbert* 'Höre, Israel: unser Gott ist ein Jahwe'. Leqach 2 (2002) 12-21 [Dt 6,4].

2942 *Van Oorschot, Jürgen* 'Höre Israel ...!' (Dtn 6,4f.)—der eine und einzige Gott Israels im Widerstreit. Polytheismus. AOAT 298: 2002 ⇒ 418. 113-135.

2943 *Barbiero, Gianni* 'Höre Israel' (Dtn 6,4-25). Studien zu alttestamentlichen Texten. SBAB 34: 2002 ⇒139. 93-167.

2944 *Finsterbusch, Karin* Bezüge zwischen Aussagen von Dtn 6,4-9 und 6,10-25. ZAW 114 (2002) 433-437.

2945 *Rofé, Alexander* The tenth commandment in the light of four Deuteronomic laws. Deuteronomy. 2002 <1990> ⇒231. 79-96 [Dt 7,25].

2946 *Rüterswörden, Udo* Dtn 13 in der neueren Deuteronomiumforschung. Congress volume Basel 2001. VT.S 92: 2002 ⇒570. 185-203.

2947 *Venter, P.M.* The dietary regulations in Deuteronomy 14 within its literary context. HTS 58 (2002) 1240-1462 [OTA 26,459].

2948 **Morrow, William S.** Scribing the center: organization and redaction in Deuteronomy 14:1-17:13. SBL.MS 49: 1995 ⇒11/1,887; 16,2581. ᴿThR 67 (2002) 305-307 (*Veijola, Timo*).

2949 *Guillaume, Ph.* Thou shalt not curdle milk with rennet. UF 34 (2002) 213-215 [Dt 14,21].

2950 *Hoppe, Leslie J.* Deuteronomy on tithing. BiTod 40 (2002) 279-283 [Dt 14,22-29].

2951 **Hamilton, Jeffries** M. Social justice and Deuteronomy: the case of Deuteronomy 15. 1992 ⇒8,2706... 13,2271. ᴿThR 67 (2002) 307-308 (*Veijola, Timo*).

2952 *Rofé, Alexander* The organization of the judiciary in Deuteronomy (Deuteronomy 16.18-20; 17.8-13; 19.15; 21.22-23; 24.16; 25.1-3). Deuteronomy. 2002 <2001> ⇒231. 103-119.

2953 *Dutcher-Walls, Patricia* The circumscription of the king: Deuteronomy 17:16-17 in its ancient social context. JBL 121 (2002) 601-616 [Acts 2].

2954 *Schmidt, Brian B.* Canaanite magic vs. Israelite religion: Deuteronomy 18 and the taxonomy of taboo. Magic and ritual. RGRW 141: 2002 ⇒505. 242-259.

2955 *Phillips, Anthony* Prophecy and law. Essays on biblical law. JSOT.S 344: 2002 <1982> ⇒223. 164-178 [Dt 18,15-22].

2956 *Setio, Robert* The text of war in the context of war: a functional reading. ᴹCARROLL, R.: JSOT.S 348: 2002 ⇒13. 289-301 [Dt 20].

2957 *Rofé, Alexander* Family and sex laws in Deuteronomy and the book of the covenant. Deuteronomy 2002. <1987> ⇒231. 169-192 [Ex 21-22; Dt 21-25].

2958 **Willis, Timothy M.** The elders of the city: a study of the elders-laws in Dt. SBL.MS 55: 2001 ⇒17,2606. [R]RBLit (2002)* (*Hagedorn, Anselm C.*) [Dt 21,18-21; 25,4-10; 21,1-9; 22,13-21; 19,1-13].

2959 *Phillips, Anthony* Uncovering the father's skirt. Essays on biblical law. JSOT.S 344: 2002 <1980> ⇒223. 245-250 [Dt 23,1].

2960 *Volgger, David* Dtn 25,5-10—per Gesetz zur Ehe gezwungen?. BN 114/115 (2002) 173-188.

2961 **Raccah, William** Close kin relationship and economical dimensions in the stipulation of the law of the levirate as articulated in Deuteronomy 25,5-10. [D]*Langevin, P.-É.*: 2002 Diss. Laval [RTL 34,593].

2962 *Flury-Schölch, André* Israel weiht seine Erträge Gott: Dtn 26,1-13: Oktober—Erntedank. zwölfmal bibel. 2002 ⇒1087. 108-117.

2963 **Steymans, Hans Ulrich** Deuteronomium 28 und die *Adê* zur Thronfolgeregelung Asarhaddons: Segen und Fluch im Alten Orient und in Israel. OBO 145: 1995 ⇒11/1,902... 13,2283. [R]ThR 67 (2002) 289-292 (*Veijola, Timo*).

2964 *Rofé, Alexander* The covenant in the land of Moab: Deuteronomy 28.69-30.20: historico-literary, comparative and form critical considerations. Deuteronomy. 2002 <1985> ⇒231. 193-203.

2965 **Welikadaarachchi, Daya Andrew Shelton** Transition of leadership from Moses to Joshua: an exegetico-theological study of Deuteronomy 31:1-8. [D]*Deiana, Giovanni*: R 2002, vi; 129 pp. Extr. Diss. Urbaniana 2002.

2966 *Schweitzer, Steven* Deuteronomy 32 and 33 as proto-Deuteronomic texts. ProcGLM 22 (2002) 79-98.

2967 **Sanders, Paul** The provenance of Deuteronomy 32. OTS 37: 1996 ⇒12,2231... 14,2308. [R]ThR 67 (2002) 317-319 (*Veijola, Timo*).

2968 *McCarthy, Carmel* Masoretic undertones in the Song of Moses. PIBA 25 (2002) 29-44 [Dt 32; 31,28-31].

2969 *Hanhart, Robert* Die Söhne Israels, die Söhne Gottes und die Engel in der Masora, in Qumran und in der Septuaginta: ein letztes Kapitel aus "Israel in hellenistischer Zeit". [F]SMEND, R. 2002 ⇒113. 170-178 [Dt 32,8].

2970 *Himbaza, Innocent* Dt 32,8, une correction tardive des scribes: essai d'interprétation et de datation. Bib. 83 (2002) 527-548.

2971 *Rofé, Alexander* The end of the Song of Moses (Deuteronomy 32. 43). Deuteronomy. 2002 <2000> ⇒231. 47-54.

2972 **Beyerle, Stefan** Der Mosesegen im Deuteronomium: eine text-, kompositions- und formkritische Studie zu Deuteronomium 33. BZAW 250: 1997 ⇒13,2290...16,2597. [R]ThR 67 (2002) 319-320 (*Veijola, Timo*).

2973 *Mattingly, Keith* Joshua's reception of the laying on of hands, part 2: Deuteronomy 34:7[9!] and conclusion. AUSS 40 (2002) 89-103.

2974 *Sanders, Seth L.* Old light in Moses' shining face. VT 52 (2002) 400-406 [Dt 34,10].

E4.1 *Origo Israelis in Canaan: Deuteronomista*; **Liber Josue**

2975 *Ceresko, Anthony R.* Potsherds and pioneers: recent research on the origins of Israel. Prophets and proverbs. 2002 <1997> ⇒154. 73-86.

2976 **Finkelstein, Israel; Silberman, Neil Asher** The bible unearthed: archaeology's new vision of Ancient Israel and the origin of its sacred texts. 2001 ⇒17,2625. ᴿBASOR 327 (2002) 63-73 (*Finkelstein, Israel; Silberman, Neil Asher*).

2977 *Ignatius, Peter* Interpretative theories of Israelite settlement. Jeevadhara 32 (2002) 95-107.

2978 *Malul, Meir* The origins of the Israelite people in its self-perception: the motif of the other and the foundling. Zion 67/1 (2002) 5-18. Sum. V. H.

2979 *Nápole, Gabriel M.* Los orígenes del Israel bíblico: una cuestión abierta. RevBib 62 (2000) 33-65.

2980 *Rösel, Hartmut N.* The emergence of Ancient Israel—some related problems. BN 114/115 (2002) 151-160.

2981 **Sasson, Jack M.** Hebrew origins: historiography, history, faith of Ancient Israel. Chuen King Lecture Series 4: Hong Kong 2002 Theology Division, Chung Chi College xiii; 163 pp. 962-7137-25-1. Comments by *Archie C.C. Lee, Craig Y.S. Ho* and *Fook Kong Wong*; Bibl. 133-161.

2982 **Schmid, Konrad** Erzväter und Exodus: Untersuchungen zur doppelten Begründung der Ursprünge Israels innerhalb der Geschichtsbücher des Alten Testaments. WMANT 81: 1999 ⇒15,2463...17,2627. ᴿThR 67 (2002) 150-152 (*Otto, Eckart*).

2983 **Campbell, Antony F.; O'Brien, Mark A.** Unfolding the Deuteronomistic History: 2000 ⇒16,2612; 17, 2631. ᴿVJTR 66 (2002) 227-28 (*Raj, M.J.*); TS 63 (2002) 382-383 (*Niditch, Susan*); BS 159 (2002) 245-246 (*Merrill, Eugene H.*); Pacifica 15 (2002) 215-17 (*Johnston, Ann*); ABR 50 (2002) 81-82 (*Stamp, H. Arthur*); ThLZ 127 (2002) 738-42 (*Dietrich, Walter*); Bib. 83 (2002) 111-115 (*Ska, Jean Louis*).

2984 *Dietrich, Walter* Martin NOTH und die Zukunft des deuteronomistischen Geschichtswerkes <1994>;

2985 Geschichte und Gesetz: deuteronomistische Geschichtsschreibung und deuteronomistisches Gesetz am Beispiel des Übergangs von der Richter- zur Königszeit <1996>;

2986 Prophetie im deuteronomistischen Geschichtswerk <2000>;

2987 Niedergang und Neuanfang: die Haltung der Schlussredaktion des deuteronomistischen Geschichtswerkes zu den wichtigsten Frager ihrer Zeit. Von David. BWANT 156: 2002 <1999> ⇒160. 81-198/ 217-235/236-251/252-271.

2988 **Dziadosz, Dariusz** Gli oracoli divini in 1 Sam 8-2 Re 25: redazione e teologia nella storia deuteronomistica dei re. ᴰ*Pisano, Stephen*: R 2002, E.P.I.B. 387 pp. 83-88522-07-8. Diss.Pont. Bibl. Institute; Sum. AcBib 10,984-986; Bibl. 301-348.

2989 **Hamilton, Victor P.** Handbook on the historical books: Joshua, Judges, Ruth, Samuel, Kings, Chronicles, Ezra-Nehemiah, Esther. 2001 ⇒17,2635. ᴿOTEs 15 (2002) 829-830 (*Branch, R.G.*).

2990 **Klaus, Nathan** Pivot patterns in the Former Prophets. JSOT.S 247: 1999 ⇒15,2480; 17,2637. ᴿThLZ 127 (2002) 281-283 (*Conrad, Joachim*); RBLit 4 (2002) 191-193 (*Bodner, Keith*).

2991 ᴱ**Knoppers, G.N.; McConville, J.G.** Reconsidering Israel and Judah: recent studies on the Deuteronomistic History. 2000 ⇒16, 282. ᴿJJS 53 (2002) 157-158 (*Williamson, H.G.M.*); JSSt 47 (2002) 322-323 (*Mayes, A.D.H.*); JNSL 28/1 (2002) 117-118 (*Stipp, Hermann-Josef*); RBLit (2002)* (*Pyeon, Yohan*).

Kratz, R. Komposition der erzählenden Bücher 2000 ⇒2210.
2992 *Leder, Arie C.* Paradise lost: reading the former prophets by the rivers of Babylon. CTJ 37 (2002) 9-27.
2993 **Pakkala, Juha** Intolerant monolatry in the deuteronomistic history. SESJ 76: 1999 ⇒15,2488; 17,2640. [R]ThZ 58 (2002) 189-190 (*Kellenberger, Edgar*); RBLit (2002)* (*Stone, Ken*).
2994 **Person, Raymond Franklin, Jr.** The Deuteronomic School: history, social setting, and literature. Studies in Biblical Literature 2: Atlanta 2002, SBL x; 175 pp. $30. 1-58983-024-5. Bibl. 153-170.
2995 **Richter, Sandra L.** The Deuteronomistic History and the name theology: le'šakken šmo šam in the bible and the ancient Near East. BZAW 318: B 2002, De Gruyter xiii; 246 pp. 3-11-017376-X. Bibl. 219-241.
2996 [E]**Römer, Thomas** The future of the deuteronomistic history. BEThL 147: 2000 ⇒16,322; 17,2644. [R]NRTh 124 (2002) 275-276 (*Ska, Jean Louis*); RivBib 50 (2002) 364-365 (*Cortese, Enzo*); Lat. 68 (2002) 148-160 (*Cardellini, Innocenzo*); OLZ 97 (2002) 761-769 (*Veijola, Timo*); ET 113 (2002) 173-174 (*Auld, Graeme*).
2997 *Smend, Rudolf* Das Gesetz und die Völker: ein Beitrag zur deuteronomistischen Redaktionsgeschichte. Die Mitte des A.T. 2002 <1971> ⇒244. 148-161.
2998 *Thiel, Winfried* God as creator and lord of nature in the deuteronomistic literature. Creation in Jewish and christian tradition: JSOT.S 319: 2002 ⇒593. 54-71.

2999 **Boulhol, Pascal** CLAUDE de Turin: un évêque iconoclaste dans l'Occident carolingien: étude suivie de l'édition du *Commentaire sur Josué*. EAug.Moyen Âge 38: P 2002, Institut des Études Augustiniennes 568 pp [RBen 114,191—P.-M. Bogaert].
3000 **Fritz, Volkmar** Das Buch Josua. HAT 1/7: 1994 ⇒10,2467... 13, 2331. [R]ThR 67 (2002) 392-394 (*Veijola, Timo*).
3001 **Gangel, Kenneth O.** Joshua. Holman OT Commentary: Nv 2002, Broadman & H. 328 pp. $20.
3002 **Harris, J. Gordon: Brown, Cheryl A.; Moore, Michael S.** Joshua, Judges, Ruth. NIBCOT: 2000 ⇒16,2646. [R]Theoforum 33 (2002) 236-238 (*Vogels, Walter*); HebStud 43 (2002) 256-258 (*Schneider, Tammi J.*).
3003 **Hawk, L. Daniel** Joshua. Berit Olam: 2000 ⇒16,2647; 17,2651. [R]Pacifica 15 (2002) 213-14 (*Barry, Romuald J.*); HebStud 43 (2002) 258-261 (*Hubbard, Robert L.*); RBLit (2002)* (*Nelson, Richard D.*).
3004 *Hertog, Cornelis G. den* Eschatologisierung in der griechischen Übersetzung des Buches Josua. [F]LEENE, H.: 2002 ⇒73. 107-117.
3005 **Nelson, Richard Donald** Joshua: a commentary. 1997 ⇒13,2333... 15,2496. [R]ThR 67 (2002) 394-396 (*Veijola, Timo*).
3006 **Pressler, Carolyn** Joshua, Judges, and Ruth. Westminster Bible companion: LVL 2002, Westminster xii; 312 pp. $25. 0-664-25526-4. Bibl. 311-312.
3007 *Rösel, Martin* the Septuagint-version of the book of Joshua. SJOT 16 (2002) 5-23.
3008 **Sicre Diaz, José Luis** Josué. Nueva Biblia Española, comentario teológico y literario: Historia. Estella (Navarra) 2002, Verbo Divino 520 pp. 84-8169-488-6. Bibl. 70-76.

3009 *Dietrich, Walter* Bannkriege in der frühen Königszeit. Von David. BWANT 156: 2002 <1996> ⇒160. 146-156.

3010 *Dozeman, Thomas B.* Geography and ideology in the wilderness journey from Kadesh through the Transjordan. Abschied vom Jahwisten. BZAW 315: 2002 ⇒2189. 173-189 [Num 20-21; 33; Dt 1-3; Judg 11].

3011 *Granados R., Juan Manuel* 'Guerra santa' en el Antiguo Testamento y en el Corán. ThX 52/1 (2002) 15-30.

3012 *Greenspoon, Leonard J.* Joshua: a man for all seasons?. Archaeus 6 (2002) 141-155.

3013 *Hess, Richard S.* The book of Joshua as a land grant. Bib. 83 (2002) 493-506.

3014 *Levesque, G.C.; Breytenbach, A.P.B.* Die boek Josua gelees teen 'n naeksilese agtergrond. HTS 58 (2002) 1761-1794 [OTA 26,461].

3015 *Mayes, A.D.H.* Israel and the covenant people of Yahweh. PIBA 25 (2002) 45-57.

3016 *Reinmuth, Eckart* Zwischen Investitur und Testament: Beobachtungen zur Rezeption des Josuabuches im Liber Antiquitatum Biblicarum. SJOT 16 (2002) 24-43.

3017 **Rowlett, Lori L.** Joshua and the rhetoric of violence: a new historicist analysis. JSOT.S 226: 1996 ⇒12,2292... 14,2359. ᴿThR 67 (2002) 401-402 (*Veijola, Timo*).

3018 *Smend, Rudolf* Das uneroberte Land. Die Mitte des A.T. 2002 <1983> ⇒244. 162-173.

3019 *Stone, Lawson G.* On historical authenticity, historical criticism, and biblical authority: reflections on the case of the book of Joshua. AsbTJ 56/2-57/1 (2001-2002) 83-96.

3020 *Strange, John* The book of Joshua—origin and dating. SJOT 16 (2002) 44-51.

3021 **Bieberstein, Klaus** Josua—Jordan—Jericho: Archäologie, Geschichte und Theologie der Landnahmeerzählung Josua 1-6. OBO 143: 1995 ⇒11/1,948... 16,2601. ᴿThR 67 (2002) 398-400 (*Veijola, Timo*).

3022 *Moran, William L.* The repose of Rahab's Israelite guests. The most magic word. 2002 <1967> ⇒212. 158-169 [Josh 2].

3023 *Stek, John H.* Rahab of Canaan and Israel: the meaning of Joshua 2. CTJ 37 (2002) 28-48.

3024 *Butticaz, Simon* Josué et la rhétorique de la violence: le cas de la prise d'Aï en Jos 8/1-29. ETR 77 (2002) 421-427.

3025 *Breytenbach, A.P.B.* Die letterlike vertolking van metaforiese taal in Josua 10:12-14. HTS 58 (2002) 1337-1355 [OTA 26,462].

3026 *Szpek, Heidi M.* Achsah's story: a metaphor for societal transition. AUSS 40 (2002) 245-256 [Josh 15,13-19].

3027 **Vos, Jacobus Cornelis de** Das Los Judas: über Entstehung und Ziele der Landbeschreibung in Josua 15. ᴰ*Noort, E.*: Culemborg 2002, xii; 414 pp. Diss. Groningen [EThL 79,256].

3028 *Knight, Douglas A.* Joshua 22 and the ideology of space. ᶠFLANAGAN, J.: JSOT.S 359: 2002 ⇒38. 51-63.

3029 *Goldstein, Ronnie* Joshua 22:9-34: a priestly narrative from the second temple period. Shnaton 13 (2002) 43-81. **H.**

E4.2 *Liber Judicum*: **Richter, Judges**

3030 **Brettler, Marc Zvi** The book of Judges. L 2002, Routledge xv; 144
pp. $26. 0-415-16216-5. Bibl. 123-136.
3031 **Görg, Manfred** Richter. NEB.AT 31: 1993 ⇒9,2618. ᴿThR 67
(2002) 396-397 (*Veijola, Timo*).
      Harris, J., *al.*, Joshua, Judges, Ruth. NIBCOT: 2000 ⇒3002.
3032 **McCann, J. Clinton** Judges. Interpretation: LVL 2002, Westminster
x; 146 pp. $23. 0-8042-3107-9.
      Pressler, C. Joshua, Judges, and Ruth 2002 ⇒3006.
3033 **Schneider, Tammi J.** Judges. Berit Olam: 2000 ⇒16,2680;
17,2678. ᴿCBQ 64 (2002) 746 (*Christianson, Eric S.*).

3034 **Andersson, Greger** The book and its narratives: a critical examination of some synchronic studies of the book of Judges. 2001 ⇒ 17,
2679. ᴿSEÅ 67 (2002) 158-160 (*Sjöberg, Mikael*).
3035 *Guillaume, Philippe* From a post-monarchical to the pre-monarchical
period of the Judges. BN 113 (2002) 12-17 [Judg 19-21; Neh 9; Ps
106].
3036 **Guillaume, Philippe** Saviours, judges, losers and rogues: the formation of the book of Judges in historical perspective. ᴰ*Pury, A. de*:
2002 330 pp. Diss. Genève [RTL 34,591].
3037 *Miller, Robert D.* Deuteronomistic theology in the book of Judges?.
OTEs 15 (2002) 411-416.
3038 *Moltz, Howard* Story and plot in the book of Judges. Interpreta-
tion(F) 30/1 (2002) 3-19.
3039 *Scham, Sandra* The days of the Judges: when men and women were
animals and trees were kings. JSOT 97 (2002) 37-64.
3040 *Thompson, John L.* Preaching texts of terror in the book of Judges:
how does the history of interpretation help?. CTJ 37 (2002) 49-61.
3041 *Winther-Nielsen, Nicolai* Fact, fiction, and language use: can modern
pragmatics improve on Halpern's case for history in Judges?. Windows. 2002 ⇒500. 44-81.

3042 *Stevenson, Jeffery S.* Judah's successes and failures in holy war: an
exegesis of Judges 1:1-20. RestQ 44/1 (2002) 43-54.
3043 *Ogden, Graham S.* Irony or humor?—the case of Ehud in Judges
3.12-30. BiTr 53 (2002) 442-444.
3044 *Scherer, Andreas* Simson und Schamgar: zur Frage nach der ursprünglichen Position der Schamgarnotiz im Richterbuch. ZAW 114
(2002) 106-109 [Judg 3,31].
3045 **Neef, Heinz-Dieter** Deboraerzählung und Deboralied: Studien zu
Jdc 4,1-5,31. BThSt 49: Neuk 2002, Neuk xii; 216 pp. €34. 3-7887-
1890-0. Bibl. 192-205.
3046 *Abela, Anthony* Two short studies on Judges 5. BiTr 53 (2002) 133-
137.
3047 *Auffret, Pierre* En ce jour-là Debora et Baraq chantèrent: étude structurelle de Jg 5,2-31. SJOT 16 (2002) 113-150.
3048 *Derby, Josiah* Gideon and the Ephraimites. JBQ 30 (2002) 118-120
[Judg 6-8].
3049 *Bluedorn, Wolfgang* Yahweh Versus Baalism: a theological reading
of the Gideon-Abimelech narrative. JSOT.S 329: 2001 ⇒17,2702.
ᴿOLZ 97 (2002) 563-568 (*Scherer, Andreas*) [Judg 6-9].

3050 *Lee, Bernon* Fragmentation of reader focus in the preamble to battle in Judges 6.1-7.14. JSOT 97 (2002) 65-86.

3051 **Kustono, Antonius Hari** Abimelech and the tragic end of his kingship: a narrative-theological study of Judges 8,33-9,57. ᴰ*Conroy, Charles*: R 2002, 110 pp. Extr. Diss. Gregoriana.

3052 *Livni, Michael* The parable of Jotham: the question of authority in Judaism. JBQ 30 (2002) 247-252 [Judg 9,1-6].

3053 *Álvarez Barredo, Miguel* Aspectos sintácticos de Jueces 10,1-12,15. Anton. 77 (2002) 211-233;

3054 Enfoques literarios de Jue 10,1-12,15. Cart. 18 (2002) 1-40.

3055 *Shveka, Avi* '*Watiqzar nafsho baʾamal yisrael*' (Jud. 10:16): a new understanding. BetM 172 (2002) 77-86 Sum. 90. **H.**

3056 *Wénin, André* À quoi Jephté sacrifie-t-il sa fille?: lecture de Juges 11, 29-40. Quand la bible se raconte. 2002 ⇒355. 85-103.

3057 **Ingram, Beryl A.** A feminist rereading of the sacrifice of Jephthah's daughter (Judges 11:29-40) in sacred text and representation. ᴰ*Harrison, B.*: 2001-2002. Diss. New York, Union [RTL 34,591].

3058 *Alvarez Barredo, Miguel* Acción de Dios en las hazañas de Sansón?: enfoque teológico de Jueces 13-16. VyV 60 (2002) 471-498.

3059 **Meurer, Thomas** Die Simson-Erzählungen: Studien zu Komposition und Entstehung, Erzähltechnik und Theologie von Ri 13-16. BBB 130: 2001 ⇒17,2717. ᴿThQ 182 (2002) 367-369 (*Groß, Walter*).

3060 *Starke, Robert A.* Samson—the last judge. Kerux 17/3 (2002) 11-28 [Judg 13-16].

3061 *Weitzman, Steven* The Samson story as border fiction. BiblInterp 10 (2002) 158-174 [Judg 13-16].

3062 *Yadin, Azzan* Samson's *ḥîdâ*. VT 52 (2002) 407-426 [Judg 14].

3063 *Van Wieringen, Willien* Mogelijk blijvend letsel: een uitleg van Richteren 15:8. ITBT 10/2 (2002) 17-19.

3064 *Exum, J. Cheryl* Lethal woman 2: reflections on Delilah and her incarnation as Liz Hurley. Borders. JSOT.S 313: 2002 ⇒585. 254-273. [Judg 16,4-22].

3065 *Amit, Yairah* I, Delilah: a victim of interpretation. First person. BiSe 81: 2002 ⇒295. 59-76 [Judg 16,4-22].

3066 **Mueller, E. Aydeet** The Micah story: a morality tale in the book of Judges. Studies in Biblical Literature 34: 2001 ⇒17,2724. ᴿRBLit (2002)* (*Premstaller, Volkmar*) [Judges 17-18].

3067 *Derby, Josiah* Who was Jonathan son of Gershom in Judges 18:30?. JBQ 30 (2002) 191-195.

3068 *Coetzee, J.H.* The 'outcry' of the dissected woman in Judges 19-21: embodiment of a society. OTEs 15 (2002) 52-63.

3069 *Stadler-Sutskover, Talia* The leading word and its roles in Judges 19-21. Bible and computer. 2002 ⇒548. 295-307.

E4.3 **Liber Ruth**, '*V Rotuli*', the Five Scrolls

3070 **Fischer, Irmtraud** Rut. HThK.AT: 2001 ⇒17,2733. ᴿYESW 10 (2002) 236-238 (*Leijnse, Barbara*).

3071 *Gesche, Bonifatia* Ruth. BVLI 46 (2002) 13-14.

　　　Harris, J., *al.*, Joshua, Judges, Ruth. NIBCOT: 2000 ⇒3002.

3072 **Linafelt, Tod; Beal, Timothy Kandler** Ruth and Esther. Berit Olam: 1999 ⇒15,2556; 17,2735. ᴿVJTR 66 (2002) 547-549 (*Meagher, P.M.*); RBLit 4 (2002) 241-243 (*Laniak, Timothy S.*).

3073 **Ljungberg, Bo-Krister** Verbal meaning: a linguistic, literary, and theological framework for interpretive categories of the Biblical Hebrew verbal system as elaborated in the book of Ruth. 2001 ⇒17, 2736. [R]SEÅ 67 (2002) 161-163 (*Eskhult, Mats*).

3074 **Lowden, John** The making of the bibles moralisées, 1: the manuscripts; 2: the book of Ruth. 2000 ⇒16,2705; 17,2737. [R]HeyJ 43 (2002) 250-252 (*Tanner, Norman*); Spec. 77 (2002) 586-588 (*Rouse, Mary A.*); JR 82 (2002) 281-282 (*McGinn, Bernard*); CCMéd 45 (2002) 190-195 (*Skubiszewski, Piotr*); RMab 13 (2002) 362-364 (*Heck, Christian*).

3075 [T]**Nardoni, Fulvio** Rut e Ester. Einaudi tascabili, Religioni 856: T 2001, Einaudi 89 pp. 88-06-15425-7. Introd. *Dacia Maraini*; consulenza generale *Paolo De Benedetti*; appendice storico-critica di *Agnese Cini Tassinario*; Bibl. 79.

3076 *Pazzini, Massimo* La massorah del libro di Rut (BHS). LASBF 51 (2001) 31-53.

3077 **Pazzini, Massimo** Il libro di Rut la Moabita: analisi del testo siriaco. ASBF 60: J 2002, Franciscan Printing Press 107 pp. 965-516-048-3. Bibl. 8.

      Pressler, C. Joshua, Judges, and Ruth 2002 ⇒3006.

3078 **Roop, Eugene F.** Ruth, Jonah, Esther. Believers Church Bible Commentary: Scottdale, PA 2002, Herald 304 pp. 0-8361-9199-4. Bibl. 285-296.

3079 **Zakovitch, Yair** Das Buch Rut: ein jüdischer Kommentar. SBS 177: 1999 ⇒15,2560...17,2740. [R]BiKi 57 (2002) 110-111 (*Bohlen, Reinhold*); ThZ 58 (2002) 368-369 (*Veronesi, Elvira*).

3080 *Bons, Eberhard* Le vocabulaire de la servitude dans la Septante du livre de Ruth. JSJ 33 (2002) 153-163.

3081 *Carfagna, Antonella* Rut: il rotolo della delicatezza dell'amore. Prendi il libro. Bibbia e spiritualità 18: 2002 ⇒372. 9-30.

3082 *Cespedes, Raùl, al.*, Tema 6: semina comune, raccolta di Dio: libro di Rut. Salmi e letteratura sapienziale. 2002 ⇒264. 227-252.

3083 *Erbele-Küster, Dorothea* Imigration [!] and gender issues in the book of Ruth. VFTW 25/1 (2002) 32-39.

3084 *Giudici, Maria Pia* Rut: la straniera totalmente aperta ad amare. CoSe 51/3 (2002) 37-43.

3085 **Naffah, Joseph** La solidarité dans le livre de Ruth. [D]*Breton, S*.: R 2002, 126 pp. Extr. Diss. Gregoriana.

3086 **Nielsen, Kirsten; Jensen, Hans J.** Ludager Ruths Bog, Esters Bog og Højsangen. K 1998, Danske Bibelselskab 197 pp. DK160. [R]RBLit 4 (2002) 237-240 (*Jones, Ray Carlton*).

3087 *Ostriker, Alicia* The book of Ruth and the love of the land. BiblInterp 10 (2002) 343-359.

3088 *Phillips, Anthony* The book of Ruth: deception and shame. Essays on biblical law. JSOT.S 344: 2002 <1986> ⇒223. 201-220 [Ruth 1,16; Neh 5].

3089 *Rösener, Christiane* 'Your people shall be my people, and your God my God': the shared life of Ruth and Naomi as a model for women transgressing intercultural boundaries. [F]SCHOTTROFF, L. 2002 ⇒111. 1-8.

3090 *Sakenfeld, Katharine Doob* At the threshing floor: sex, reader response, and a hermeneutic of survival. OTEs 15 (2002) 164-178.

3091 *Shuchat, Raphael B.* The use of symbolism and hidden messages in the book of Ruth. JBQ 30 (2002) 110-117.
3092 *Thomas, Nancy J.* Weaving the words: the book of Ruth as missiologically effective communication. Miss. 30/2 (2002) 155-169.
3093 *Van Dyk, Alta C.; Van Dyk, Peet J.* HIV/AIDS in Africa, suffering women and the theology of the book of Ruth. OTEs 15 (2002) 209-224.
3094 *Varadi, Max* Ruth: una lettura. RasIsr 68/2 (2002) 107-114.
3095 **Wénin, André** O livro de Rute, uma abordagem narrativa. ^T*Leite, Joaquim Ferreira*: Cadernos Bíblicos 80: Lisboa 2002, Difusora Bíblica 64 pp.

3096 *Kinukawa, Hisako* '...and your God my God': how we can nurture openness to other faiths: Ruth 1:1-19 read from a feminist perspective of a multi-faith community. ^FNILES, D.: 2002 ⇒82. 193-203.
3097 *Menu, Blaise* Ruth 2: à l'ombre des blés... Lire et Dire 54 (2002) 28-40 [BuBB 39,73].
3098 *Ogden, Graham S.* A traditional note on Ruth 2.8-9. BiTr 53 (2002) 444-445.
3099 *Fischer-Yinon, Yochi* The original bundlers: Boaz and Ruth, and seventeenth-century English courtship practices. Journal of Social History 35 (2002) 683-705 [Ruth 3].

E4.4 1-2 Samuel

3100 ^T**Fox, Everett** Give us a king: Samuel, Saul, and David: a new translation of Samuel I and II. 1999 ⇒15,2596. ^RRBLit 4 (2002) 193-197 (*Niccacci, Alviero*).
3101 ^T**Grillet, Bernard; Lestienne, Michel** La Bible d'Alexandrie: 9,1: premier livre des Règnes. 1997 ⇒13,2415; 15,2597. ^REstB 60 (2002) 265-267 (*Urbán, A.*).
3102 **Holland, Martin** Das erste Buch Samuel. WStB.AT: Wu 2002, Brockhaus 320 pp. 3-417-25238-5. Bibl. 319-320.
3103 **Morrison, Craig, E.** The character of the Syriac version of the first book of Samuel. MPIL 11: 2001 ⇒17,2761. ^RCBQ 64 (2002) 741-742 (*Mathews, Edward G.*).
3104 **Orde, Klaus vom** Das zweite Buch Samuel. WStB.AT: Wu 2002, Brockhaus 320 pp. 3-417-25240-7. Bibl. 316-320.
3105 **Tábet, Miguel Ángel** Il secondo libro di Samuele. Guide spirituali all'Antico Testamento: R 2002, Città N. 143 pp. 88-311-3748-4. Bibl. 33-37.

3106 *Brooks, Simcha Shalom* The *Habiru/ʿApiru* and *ʿibrim* and the connection with I Samuel. BAIAS 19-20 (2001-2002) 65-70.
3107 *Dietrich, Walter* Arten der Geschichtsdarstellung in den Samuelbüchern. Von David. BWANT 156: 2002 ⇒160. 134-145.
3108 *Keown, Gerald L.* Prophecy in 1 and 2 Samuel. RExp 99 (2002) 175-184.
3109 *Walters, Stanley D.* Reading Samuel to hear God. CTJ 37 (2002) 62-81 .

3110 *Cartledge, Tony W.* Hannah asked, and God heard. RExp 99 (2002) 143-144 [1 Sam 1].

3111 **Cook, Joan E.** Hannah's desire, God's design: early interpretations of the story of Hannah. JSOT.S 282: 1999 ⇒15,2612. ᴿNewTR 15/1 (2002) 79-80 (*Hensell, Eugene*) [{1 Sam 1,1-2,21].
3112 *Mulzac, Ken* Hannah: the receiver and giver of a great gift. AUSS 40 (2002) 207-217 [1 Sam 1].
3113 **Wallace, Ronald S.** Hannah's prayer and its answer: an exposition for bible study. GR 2002, Eerdmans xiv; 113 pp. £10. 0-946069-86-0 [1 Sam 1-7].
3114 *Segal, Michael* 1 Samuel 2:3: text, exegesis, and theology. Shnaton 13 (2002) 83-95. H.
3115 *Lenchak, Timothy A.* Puzzling passages: 1 Samuel 2:25. BiTod 40 (2002) 54-55.
3116 **Adair, James R.** An inductive method for reconstructing the biblical text: illustrated by an analysis of 1 Samuel 3. JNSL.MS 2: 2000 ⇒ 16,2731. ᴿJNSL 28/2 (2002) 151-154 (*Polak, Frank*).
3117 **Seow, Choon Leong** Myth, drama, and the politics of David's dance. HSM 44: 1989 ⇒5,2777...9,2741. ᴿThR 67 (2002) 419-20 (*Veijola, Timo*) [1 Sam 4-6; 2 Sam 6].
3118 **Brueggemann, Walter** Ichabod toward home: the journey of God's glory. GR 2002, Eerdmans ix; 150 pp. £11/$15. 0-8028-3930-4. ᴿScrB 32 (2002) 103-104 (*Corley, Jeremy*); RExp 99 (2002) 458 (*Biddle, Mark E.*) [1 Sam 4,6].
3119 *Firth, David G.* Parallelismus memborum in prose narrative: the function of repetition in 1 Samuel 5-6. OTEs 15 (2002) 647-656.

E4.5 *1 Sam 7...Initia potestatis regiae*, **Origins of kingship**

3120 *Dietrich, Walter* Zwischen Gott und Volk: das Königtum in der Sicht des Alten Testaments. Theopolitik 2002 <1998> ⇒159. 137-156.
3121 **Forthomme, B.** La folie du roi Saül. P 2002, Empêcheurs 282 pp. €18. 2-84671-048-1.
3122 *Green, Barbara* King Saul's struggles. PrPe 16 (2002) 312-316.
3123 *McConville, J. Gordon* Law and monarchy in the Old Testament. ꜰO'DONOVAN, O. 2002 ⇒272. 69-88.
3124 **Nicholson, Sarah** Three faces of Saul: an intertextual approach to biblical tragedy. JSOT.S 339: Shf 2002, Sheffield A. 276 pp. £64.71. 1-84127-248-5. Bibl. 265-270.
3125 *O'Donovan, Oliver* Response to Gordon McConville. ꜰO'DONOVAN, O. 2002 ⇒272. 89-90.
3126 *Pigott, Susan M.* Wives, witches and wise women: prophetic heralds of kingship in 1 and 2 Samuel. RExp 99 (2002) 145-173.

3127 *Bianchin, Lucia* Politica e scrittura in ALTHUSIUS: il diritto regale nell'interpretazione di *1 Sam.* 8,11-18 e *Deut.* 17,14-20. Il Pensiero Politico 35 (2002) 409-430.
3128 **Ignatius, Peter** 1 Sam 9,1-16: have the Davidic propagandists capitalized on the folktales about Saul to enhance the image of David?. BiBh 28 (2002) 632-655.
3129 *Van den Eynde, Sabine* Ik zie, ik zie wat jij niet ziet (eenblik op 1 Samuël 16:1-13). ITBT 10/2 (2002) 22-23.

E4.6 *1 Sam 16...2 Sam: Accessio Davidis.* **David's Rise**

3130 *Alibert, Dominique* Figures du David carolingien. ᶠGEOLTRAIN, P.:
      BEHE.R 113: 2002 ⇒45. 203-227.
3131 *Arnold, Bill T.* What has Nebuchadnezzar to do with David?: on the
      Neo-Babylonian period and Early Israel. Mesopotamia and the bible.
      JSOT.S 341: 2002 ⇒458. 330-355.
3132 *Bodenheimer, Alfred* Gottes Erwählter: Davids Herrschaftslegitima-
      tion und Dynastiegründung—eine Reflexion, ausgehend von Stefan
      Heyms Roman "Der König David Bericht". KuI 17 (2002) 20-30.
3133 *Bodner, Keith* Is Joab a reader-response critic?. JSOT 27 (2002) 19-
      35.
3134 *Bowman, Richard G.* The complexity of character and the ethics of
      complexity: the case of King David. Character and scripture. 2002 ⇒
      283. 73-97.
3135 **Brueggemann, Walter** David's truth in Israel's imagination and
      memory. Mp ²2002 <1985>, Fortress xx; 153 pp. $15. 0-8006-3461-
      6. Bibl. 137-143. ᴿCTJ 37 (2002) 343-344 (*Bergsma, John*).
3136 **Dallmeyer, Hans-Jürgen; Dietrich, Walter** David—ein Königs-
      weg: psychoanalytisch-theologischer Dialog über einen biblischen
      Entwicklungsroman. Gö 2002, Vandenhoeck & R 256 pp. €28. 3-52-
      5016-247.
3137 ᴱ**Desrousseaux, Louis; Vermeylen, Jacques** Figures de David à
      travers la bible. LeDiv 177: 1999 ⇒15,410...17,2788. ᴿEstB 60
      (2002) 267-271 (*Urbán, A.*).
3138 *Deurloo, Karel A.* King and temple: David in the eschatology of the
      prophets. ᶠLEENE, H. 2002 ⇒73. 49-60.
3139 *Dietrich, Walter* Das biblische Bild der Herrschaft Davids;
3140 Das Ende der Thronfolgegeschichte <2000>;
3141 Der Name 'David' und seine inschriftliche Bezeugung <1997>;
3142 Die David-Abraham-Typologie im Alten Testament <2000>;
3143 Von einem, der zuviel wußte: Versuch über Stefan Heyms 'König
      David Bericht' <1976>;
3144 Gott, Macht und Liebe: drei neue Romane über die Davidszeit
      <1989>.Von David. BWANT 156: 2002 ⇒160. 9-31/32-57/74-87/
      88-99/100-112/113-119.
3145 *Frolov, Serge* Succession narrative: a "document" or a phantom?.
      JBL 121 (2002) 81-104.
3146 *George, Mark K.* Yhwh's own heart. CBQ 64 (2002) 442-459.
3147 **Halpern, Baruch** David's secret demons: messiah, murderer, traitor,
      king. 2001 ⇒17,2791. ᴿTS 63 (2002) 383-385 (*Collins, John J.*);
      JBL 121 (2002) 540-543 (*Ash, Paul S.*).
3148 *Herrmann, Siegfried* 'Realunion' und 'charismatisches Königtum':
      zu zwei offenen Fragen der Verfassungen in Juda und Israel. Ge-
      schichte und Prophetie. BWANT 157: 2002 <1993> ⇒179. 101-111.
3149 *Jones, Gwilym H.* David and Solomon. Biblical world, 2: 2002 ⇒
      273. 208-222.
3150 **Klein, Johannes** David versus Saul: ein Beitrag zum Erzählsystem
      der Samuelbücher. BWANT 158: Stu 2002, Kohlhammer 220 pp.
      €30. 3-17-017352-9. Bibl. 200-215.
3151 *Na'aman, Nadav* In search of reality behind the account of David's
      wars with Israel's neighbours. IEJ 52 (2002) 200-224.

3152   **Nitsche, Stefan Ark** König David: sein Leben—seine Zeit—seine
       Welt. Gü 2002 <1994>, Kaiser 319 pp. €25. 3-5790-5191-1 [ThLZ
       129,33s—Joachim Conrad].
3153   *Oredsson, Dag* David-kung eller shejk?: en forskningsöversikt över
       arkeologins ifrågasättande av det enade kungariket. SEÅ 67 (2002)
       27-35.
3154   *Pyper, Hugh S.* Reading David's mind: inference, emotions and the
       limits of language. ᴹCARROLL, R.: JSOT.S 348: 2002 ⟹13. 73-86.
3155   **Seiler, Stefan** Die Geschichte von der Thronfolge Davids (2 Sam 9-
       20; 1 Kön 1-2): Untersuchungen zur Literarkritik und Tendenz.
       BZAW 267: 1998 ⟹14,2469... 17,2804. ᴿThR 67 (2002) 411-416
       (*Veijola, Timo*).
3156   *Stott, Katherine* HERODOTUS and the Old Testament: a comparative
       reading of the ascendancy stories of King Cyrus and David. SJOT 16
       (2002) 52-78.
3157   *Vandergriff, Ken* Re-creating David: the David narratives in art and
       literature. RExp 99 (2002) 193-205.
3158   **Vermeylen, Jacques** La loi du plus fort: histoire de la rédaction des
       récits davidiques, de 1 Samuel 8 à 1 Rois 2. BEThL 154: 2000 ⟹16,
       2784. ᴿOLZ 97 (2002) 571-575 (*Seiler, Stefan*); RivBib 50 (2002)
       482-486 (*Bianchi, Francesco*); ThLZ 127 (2002) 629-631 (*Rose,
       Martin*).
3159   *Willi-Plein, Ina* Frauen um David: Beobachtungen zur Davidshausge-
       schichte. Sprache als Schlüssel. 2002 <1995> ⟹261. 97-115.

3160   *Aurelius, Erik* Wie David ursprünglich zu Saul kam (1 Sam 17).
       ᶠSmend, R. 2002 ⟹113. 44-68.
3161   *Dietrich, Walter* Die Erzählung von David und Goliat in 1Sam 17.
       Von David. BWANT 156: 2002 <1996> ⟹160. 58-73;
3162   Der Fall des Riesen Goliat: biblische und nachbiblische Erzählversu-
       che. Von David. 2002 <1995> ⟹160. 120-133 [1 Sam 17].
3163   *Van Wolde, Ellen* A leader led by a lady: David and Abigail in I
       Samuel 25. ZAW 114 (2002) 355-375.
3164   *Biddle, Mark E.* Ancestral motifs in 1 Samuel 25: intertextuality and
       characterization. JBL 121 (2002) 617-638.
3165   **Kleiner, Michael** Saul in En-Dor Wahrsagung oder Totenbeschwö-
       rung?: eine synchrone und diachrone Untersuchung zu 1 Sam 28.
       EThSt 66: 1995 ⟹11/1,1125... 14,2459. ᴿThR 67 (2002) 421-423
       (*Veijola, Timo*).
3166   *Theißen, Gerd* Die Humanität der Hexe und die Verzweiflung des
       Königs Saul (1 Sam 28,3-25). Erlösungsbilder. 2002 ⟹1460. 31-38.
3167   *Blenkinsopp, Joseph* Saul and the mistress of the spirits (1 Samuel
       28.3-25). ᴹCARROLL, R.: JSOT.S 348: 2002 ⟹13. 49-62.

3168   *Ceresko, Anthony R.* The identity of 'the blind and the lame' (*'iwwēr
       ûpissēah*) in 2 Samuel 5:8b. Prophets and proverbs. 2002 <2001>
       129-137.
3169   **Avioz, Michael** The negotiations between David and Nathan con-
       cerning the temple building (2 Samuel 7) and its echoes in the bibli-
       cal historiography. ᴰ*Garsiel, M.*: 2002, 256 pp. Diss. Bar Ilan [RTL
       34,590].
3170   **Gakuru, Griphus** An inner-biblical exegetical study of the Davidic
       covenant and the dynastic oracle. 2000 ⟹16,2804. ᴿBetM 171
       (2002) 373-380 H. (*Aviuz, Michael*) [2 Sam 7].

3171 *George, Mark K.* Fluid stability in Second Samuel 7. CBQ 64 (2002) 17-36.

3172 *Herrmann, Siegfried* 2 Samuel VII in the light of the Egyptian Königsnovelle—reconsidered. Geschichte und Prophetie. BWANT 157: 2002 <1985> ⇒179. 113-120.

3173 *Carillo-Guelbert, Francine; Schach, Michel* 2 Samuel 11: tel est pris qui croyait prendre!. Lire et Dire 54 (2002) 17-27 [BuBB 39,72].

3174 *Schiffner, Kerstin* Von Männern und Macht—ihrem Missbrauch und ihrem Verlust: 2. Samuel 12,1-15a. JK 63/4 (2002) 57-60.

3175 *Phillips, Anthony* The interpretation of 2 Samuel 12.5-6. Essays on biblical law. JSOT.S 344: 2002 <1966> ⇒223. 232-234.

3176 *Lescow, Theodor* Die Komposition der Tamar-Erzählung II Sam 13,1-22. ZAW 114 (2002) 110-111.

3177 *Bodner, Keith* Motives for defection: Ahitophel's agenda in 2 Samuel 15-17. SR 31 (2002) 63-78.

3178 *Yiu-wing, Fung* A portrayal of Hushai, David's friend. Jian Dao 17 (2002) 191-201 Sum 201 [2 Sam 17,1-14]. C.

3179 **Klement, Herbert H.** II Samuel 21-24: context, structure and meaning in the Samuel conclusion. EHS.T 682: 2000 ⇒16,2816. [R]OTEs 15 (2002) 831-833 (*Firth, David G.*).

3180 *Auld, A. Graeme* Bearing the burden of David's guilt. [F]SMEND, R. 2002 ⇒113. 69-81 [2 Sam 24; 1 Chr 21].

3181 *Briffard, Colette* 2 Samuel 24: un parcours royal: du pire au meilleur. ETR 77 (2002) 95-103.

E4.7 *Libri Regum*: Solomon, Temple: 1 Kings...

3182 **Balzaretti, Claudio** I libri dei Re. Guide spirituali all'Antico Testamento: R 2002, Città N. 222 pp. €15. 88-311-3749-2. Bibl. 19.

3183 **Brueggemann, Walter** 1 and 2 Kings: Smith & Helvys bible commentary. 2000 ⇒16,2824. [R]TS 63 (2002) 841-842 (*Penchansky, David*).

3184 **Buis, Pierre** O livri dos Reis. [T]*Silva, Vítor Arantes da*: Cadernos Bíblicos 77: Lisboa 2002, Difusora Bíblica 68 pp.

3185 *Kitchen, Kenneth A.* The controlling role of external evidence in assessing the historical status of the Israelite united monarchy. Windows. 2002 ⇒500. 111-130.

3186 *Łach, Józef* Z problematyki literackiej 1-2 Krl. CoTh 72/1 (2002) 45-56. P.

3187 *Larsson, Gerhard* The chronology of the kings of Israel and Judah as a system. ZAW 114 (2002) 224-235.

3188 **Rendsburg, Gary A.** Israelian Hebrew in the book of Kings. Occasional Publ. of the Dept. of Near East. Studies... Cornell University 5: Bethesda, MD 2002, CDL 186 pp. 1-883053-69-2. Bibl. 157-166.

3189 *Sals, Ulrike* Das literarisierte Königspaar Ahab und Isebel im Geflecht von Traditionen und Beziehungen. Paare. 2002 ⇒489. 133-62.

3190 **Turkanik, Andrzej Szymon** Issues in text and translation technique in the gamma-gamma section of 3 Reigns (1 Kings). [D]*Gordon, Robert P.*: Diss. Cambridge 2002 [TynB 55,157-160].

3191 [T]**Vogüé, Adalbert de** GRÉGOIRE le Grand (Pierre de Cava): commentaire sur le premier livre des Rois tome III (III,38-IV,78). SC 432: 1998 ⇒14,2499... 17,2855. [R]VetChr 39/1 (2002) 206-207 (*Sansone, Gilda*).

3192 **Werlitz, Jürgen** Die Bücher der Könige. Neuer Stuttgarter Kommentar, AT 8: Stu 2002, Kathol. Bibelwerk 364 pp. €31. 3-460-070-81-1. Bibl. 361-364.

3193 *Dietrich, Walter* Das harte Joch (1Kön 12,4): Fronarbeit in der Salomo-Überlieferung. Von David. BWANT 156: 2002 <1986> ⇒160. 157-163.

3194 *Niemann, Hermann Michael* Taanach und Megiddo: Überlegungen zur strukturell-historischen Situation zwischen Saul und Salomo. VT 52 (2002) 93-102 [Judg 5,19; 1 Kgs 4,8-17].

3195 **Snyder, Jason** The literary ambiguity of the Solomon narratives in First Kings. ^D*Aitken, K.T.*: 2002 Diss. Aberdeen [RTL 34,594].

3196 *Steiner, Margreet* Mesha versus Solomon: two models of economic organisation in Iron Age II. SEÅ 67 (2002) 37-45.

3197 **Torijano, Pablo A.** Solomon the esoteric king: from king to magus, development of a tradition. JSJ.S 73: Lei 2002, Brill xiv; 333 pp. €104/$121. 90-04-11941-8. Bibl. 317-330.

3198 **Wälchli, Stefan** Der weise König Salomo: eine Studie zu den Erzählungen von der Weisheit Salomos in ihrem alttestamentlichen und altorientalischen Kontext. BWANT 141: 1999 ⇒14,2506; 17,2868. ^RCBQ 64 (2002) 363-364 (*Launderville, Dale*).

3199 **Adna, Jostein** Jerusalemer Tempel und Tempelmarkt im 1. Jahrhundert n. Chr. ADPV 25: 1999 ⇒15,2698. ^RZRGG 54 (2002) 79-80 (*Horn, Friedrich W.*).

3200 *Albertz, Rainer* Die Zerstörung des Jerusalemer Tempels 587 v. Chr.: historische Einordnung und religionspolitische Bedeutung. Zerstörungen. WUNT 147: 2002 ⇒559. 23-39.

3201 *Averbeck, Richard E.* Sumer, the bible, and comparative method: historiography and temple building. Mesopotamia and the bible. JSOT.S 341: 2002 ⇒458. 88-125.

3202 **Bedford, Peter Ross** Temple restoration in early Achaemenid Judah. JSJ.S 65: 2001 ⇒17,2873. ^RJThS 53 (2002) 147-151 (*Tollington, Janet E.*); BiOr 59 (2002) 388-392 (*Albertz, Rainer*); CBQ 64 (2002) 734-735 (*Patton, Corrine L.*); Bib. 83 (2002) 432-434 (*Blenkinsopp, Joseph*).

3203 *Berlejung, Angelika* Notlösungen—altorientalische Nachrichten über den Tempelkult in Nachkriegszeiten. ^FWEIPPERT, M.: OBO 186: 2002 ⇒133. 196-230.

3204 *Bloch-Smith, Elizabeth* Solomon's temple: the politics of ritual space. Sacred time. 2002 ⇒2679. 83-94.

      ^E*Ego, B., al.*, Gemeinde ohne Tempel 1999 ⇒303.

3205 **Faßbeck, Gabriele** Der Tempel der Christen: traditionsgeschichtliche Untersuchungen zur Aufnahme des Tempelkonzepts im frühen Christentum. TANZ 33: 2000 ⇒16,2847; 17,2881. ^RThRv 98 (2002) 308-310 (*Müller, Christoph G.*).

3206 *Golzio, Karl-Heinz, al.*, Tempel. TRE 33. 2002 ⇒799. 42-72.

3207 *Hahn, Johannes* Kaiser JULIAN und ein dritter Tempel?: Idee, Wirklichkeit und Wirkung eines gescheiterten Projektes. Zerstörungen. WUNT 147: 2002 ⇒559. 237-262.

3208 *Halligan, John* Unsolved mysteries: the second temple. ^MCARROLL, R.: JSOT.S 348: 2002 ⇒13. 142-158 [Ezra 6,3].

3209 *Janowski, Bernd* Die heilige Wohnung des Höchsten: kosmologische Implikationen der Jerusalemer Tempeltheologie;

3210 *Keel, Othmar* Der salominische Tempelweihspruch: Beobachtungen zum religionsgeschichtlichen Kontext des Ersten Jerusalemer Tempels [1 Kgs 8,12-13]. Gottesstadt. QD 191: 2002 ⇒567. 24-68/9-23.

3211 *Lichtenberger, Hermann* Der Mythos von der Unzerstörbarkeit des Tempels. Zerstörungen. WUNT 147: 2002 ⇒559. 92-107.

3212 *Lücking, Stefan* Die Zerstörung des Tempels 70 n. Chr als Krisenerfahrung der frühen Christen. Zerstörungen. WUNT 147: 2002 ⇒559. 140-165.

3213 **MacCormick, Clifford Mark** Palace and temple: a study of architectural and verbal icons. BZAW 313: B 2002, De Gruyter x; 221 pp. €68. 3-11-017277-1. Bibl. 197-214.

3214 *Matthiae, Paolo* Una nota sul tempio di Salomone e la cultura architettonica neosiriana. ᴹCIASCA, A. 2002 ⇒15. 337-342.

3215 *Mayer, Walter* Die Zerstörung des Jerusalemer Tempels 587 v. Chr. im Kontext der Praxis von Heiligtumszerstörungen im antiken Vorderen Orient. Zerstörungen. WUNT 147: 2002 ⇒559. 1-22.

3216 *Mazor, Lea* The correlation between the garden of Eden and the temple. Shnaton 13 (2002) 5-42. H.

3217 **Paesler, Kurt** Das Tempelwort Jesu: die Traditionen von Tempelzerstörung und Tempelerneuerung im NT. FRLANT 184: 1999 ⇒15, 2719; 17,2888. ᴿCBQ 64 (2002) 176-177 (*Mowery, Robert L.*).

3218 *Panzram, Sabine* Der Jerusalemer Tempel und das Rom der Flavier;

3219 *Pohlmann, Karl-Friedrich* Religion in der Krise—Krise einer Religion: die Zerstörung des Jerusalemer Tempels 587 v. Chr. Zerstörungen. WUNT 147: 2002 ⇒559. 166-182/40-60.

3220 *Reidinger, Erwin* Die Tempelanlage in Jerusalem von Salomo bis Herodes aus der Sicht der Bautechnischen Archäologie. BN 114/115 (2002) 89-150.

3221 **Schwartz, Max** The biblical engineer: how the temple in Jerusalem was built. Hoboken, NJ 2002, KTAV xxv; 166 pp. 0-88125-710-9. Bibl. 160-166.

3222 **Stevens, Marty E.** Tithes and taxes: the economic role of the Jerusalem temple in its ancient Near Eastern context. ᴰMcBride, S.D., Jr.: 2002 Diss. Virginia, Union [RTL 34,594].

3223 *Villeneuve, Estelle* Simulation in Echtzeit—Rundgang durch eine virtuellen Tempel. WUB 25 (2002) 65.

3224 **Wolfe, George** Inner space as sacred space: the temple as metaphor for the mystical experience. CrossCur 52 (2002) 400-411.

3225 *Zevit, Ziony* Preamble to a temple tour. Sacred time. 2002 ⇒2679. 73-81.

3226 *Bartelmus, Rüdger* Sachverhalt und Zeitbezug: pragmatisch-exegetische Anwendung eines noetischen Theorems auf 1 Kön 1. Auf der Suche. 2002 <2001> ⇒140. 355-383.

3227 *Van Peursen, Wido* Morphosyntactic and syntactic issues in the Syriac text of 1 Kings 1. Bible and computer. 2002 ⇒548. 99-111.

3228 *Stoebe, Hans-Joachim* Überlegungen zum Aufbau von I Kön 1-12. ThZ 58 (2002) 97-108.

3229 **Schenker, Adrian** Septante et texte massorétique dans l'histoire la plus ancienne du texte de 1 Rois 2-14. CRB 48: 2000 ⇒16,2859; 17, 2897. ᴿRivBib 50 (2002) 227-231 (*Passoni dell'Acqua, Anna*).

3230 *Mena López, Maricel* Donne sagge in *1 Re* 3-11. Conc(I) 38/1 (2002) 34-44. Conc(E) 294,27-35; Conc(D) 38/1,17-25; Conc(P) 294,25-33.

3231 *Fortin, Anne; Pénicaud, Anne* L'énonciation au service du jugement de Salomon (I Rois, 3,16-28). SémBib 107 (2002) 3-49.
3232 *Garsiel, Moshe* Revealing and concealing as a narrative strategy in Solomon's judgment (1 King 3:16-28). CBQ 64 (2002) 229-247.
3233 *Hoppe, Leslie J.* The afterlife of a text: the case of Solomon's prayer in 1 Kings 8. LASBF 51 (2001) 9-30.
3234 *Schipper, Bernd Ulrich* Nocheinmal zur Pharaonentochter—ein Gespräch mit Karl Jansen-Winkeln. BN 111 (2002) 90-98 [1 Kgs 9,16-24; 2 Chr 8,11].

3235 *Arbach, Mounir* La reine de Saba entre légendes et réalité historique d'après les inscriptions sudarabiques préislamiques [1 Kgs 10,1-13];
3236 *Baude, Jeanne M.* Balkis entre présence et absence dans "La Reine de Saba" de Jean GROSJEAN;
3237 *Berthier, Patrick* La reine de Saba d'un conteur romantique: "La fée aux miettes" de NODIER (1832);
3238 *Cannyuer, Christian* La reine de Saba dans les traditions de l'église copte: une troublante inconnue. Graphè 11 (2002) 69-82/151-165/137-149/61-68 [1 Kings 10,1-13].
3239 **Chuecas Saldías, Ignacio Javier** 'Y la reina de Sabá vio toda la sabiduría de Salomón': un estudio sincrónico del texto de 1 Reyes 10, 1-13. ^D*Conroy, Charles*: R 2002, 128 pp. Extr. Diss. Gregoriana.
3240 *Gomez-Geraud, Marie C.* La reine de Saba au rendez-vous de la Croix: avatars typologiques du discours légendaire;
3241 *Haelewyck, Jean C.* La reine de Saba et les apocryphes salomoniens: "Testament de Salomon" et "Questions de la reine de Saba". Graphè 11 (2002) 123-135/83-99 [1 Kgs 10,1-13].
3242 *Lemaire, André* La reine de Saba à Jérusalem: la tradition ancienne reconsidérée. ^FWEIPPERT, M.: OBO 186: 2002 ⇒133. 43-55 [1 Kgs 10,1-13].
3243 *Lobrichon, Guy* La Dame de Saba: interprétations médiévales d'une figure impossible. Graphè 11 (2002) 101-122 [1 Kgs 10,1-13]
3244 *Niemann, Hermann Michael* Salomo und die Königin von Saba: heiliger Text zwischen Theologie und Historizität, Literatur und Archäologie. BiKi 57 (2002) 220-223 [1 Kgs 10,1-13].
3245 *Notter, Annick* La reine de Saba: fortune d'une iconographie;
3246 *Pelletier, Anne M.* Les femmes de Salomon: pour relire l'histoire de la reine de Saba. Graphè 11 (2002) 167-181/29-44 [1 Kgs 10,1-13].
3247 *Pennacchietti, Fabrizio A.* La regina di Saba, il pavimento di cristallo e il tronco galleggiante. La sorgente. 2002 ⇒315. 32-48 [1 Kgs 10, 1-13].
3248 *Pérès, Jacques N.* Jérusalem et Axoum ou la reine de Saba et l'arche d'alliance: mythe fondateur et traditions religieuses et politiques en Éthiopie. Graphè 11 (2002) 45-59 [1 Kgs 10,1-13].
3249 *Vermeylen, Jacques* La visite de la reine de Saba à Salomon: une lecture de 1 Rois 10,1-13. Graphè 11 (2002) 11-28.

3250 *Talshir, Zipora* 1 Kings and 3 Kingdoms—origin and revision case study: the sins of Solomon (1 Kgs 11). Textus 21 (2002) 71-105.
3251 *Van Keulen, P.S.F.* A case of ancient exegesis: the story of Solomon's adversaries (1 Kgs. 11:14-25) in Septuaginta, Peshitta, and JOSEPHUS. Bible and computer. 2002 ⇒548. 555-571.
3252 *Pakkala, Juha* Jerobeam's sin and Bethel in Kgs 12:25-33. BN 112 (2002) 86-94.

3253 *Bosworth, David* Revisiting Karl BARTH's exegesis of 1 Kings 13. BiblInterp 10 (2002) 360-383.

E4.8 *1 Regum 17-22: Elias,* **Elijah**

3254 *Chávez, Emilio G.* La huída de Elías al Horeb. AnáMnesis 12/1 (2002) 5-15 [1 Kgs 19].
3255 *Hauser, Alan J.* Should Ahab go to battle or not?: ambiguity as a rhetorical device in 1 Kings 22. Rhetorical argumentation. 2002 ⇒553. 141-154.
3256 **Otto, Susanne** Jehu, Elia und Elisa: die Erzählung von der Jehu-Revolution und die Komposition der Elia-Elisa-Erzählungen. BWANT 152: 2001 ⇒17,2928. RThLZ 127 (2002) 1042-1045 (*Stipp, Hermann-Josef*); FZPhTh 49 (2002) 518-520 (*Schenker, Adrian*).
3257 **Poirot, Soeur Éliane** Élie, archétype du moine: pour un ressourcement prophétique de la vie monastique. SpOr 65: 1995 ⇒11/1,1252 ... 13,2612. RIst. 47 (2002) 423-425.
3258 *Roberts, J.J.M.* A new parallel to 1 Kings 18:28-29. The bible and the ANE. 2002 <1970> ⇒230. 102-103.
3259 *Schlosser, Marianne* "Princeps noster Elias": der Prophet Elija als Vorbild monastischen Lebens. Edith-Stein-Jahrbuch 8 (2002) 48-64.
3260 *Smend, Rudolf* Der biblische und der historische Elia <1975>;
3261 Das Wort Jahwes an Elia: Erwägungen zur Komposition von 1Kön 17-19 <1975>. Die Mitte des A.T. 2002 ⇒244. 188-202/203-218.
3262 *Soroudi, Sorour* Sofreh of Elijah the prophet: a pre-Islamic Iranian ritual?. JStAI 27 (2002) 463-474.
3263 *Talstra, Eep* Signs, design and signification: the example of 1 Kings 21. Bible and computer. 2002. ⇒548. 147-166.
3264 **Thiel, Winfried** Könige 1 17ff. BK IX/2 Lfg. 2: Neuk 2002, Neuk'er 81-160 pp. 3-7887-1714-9. .
3265 *Tinambunan, Edison R.L.* Elijah according to the Fathers of the church. Carmelus 49 (2002) 85-116.
3266 *Toni, Roberto* In cammino con Elia e Maria. Horeb 11/2 (2002) 100-105.
3267 *Williams, P.J.* Lying spirits sent by God?: the case of Micaiah's prophecy. The trustworthiness of God. 2002 ⇒410. 58-66.

E4.9 **2 Reg 1**... *Elisaeus, Elisha*... Ezechias, Josias

3268 **Cohn, Robert L.** 2 Kings. Berit Olam: 2000 ⇒16,2902. RPacifica 15 (2002) 83-84 (*Barry, Rom J.*); HebStud 43 (2002) 261-262 (*Long, Burke O.*).
3269 *Dietrich, Walter* Der eine Gott als Symbol politischen Widerstands: Religion und Politik im Juda des 7. Jahrhunderts. Theopolitik. 2002 <1994> ⇒159. 204-223.
3270 **Sweeney, Marvin Alan** King Josiah of Judah: the lost Messiah of Israel. 2001 ⇒17,2938. RJThS 53 (2002) 144-147 (*Clements, R.E.*); JJS 53 (2002) 160-161 (*Reimer, David J.*); HebStud 43 (2002) 262-265 (*Laato, Antti*); CBQ 64 (2002) 558-559 (*Seibert, Eric A.*).

3271 *Abadie, Philippe* Mit Pferdestärken in den Himmel: die Entrückung Elijas—eine Prophetensymbolik. WUB 26 (2002) 38-41 [2 Kgs 2].

3272 *George, P.G.* Plight of urban youth: a practical interpretation of 2 Kings 2,23-25. BiBh 28 (2002) 672-681.
3273 *Berlyn, Patricia* The wrath of Moab. JBQ 30 (2002) 216-226 [2 Kgs 3].
3274 *Hasel, Michael G.* The destruction of trees in the Moabite campaign of 2 Kings 3:4-27: a study in the laws of warfare. AUSS 40 (2002) 197-206.
3275 *Tropper, Josef* Elischa und die 'große' Frau aus Schunem (2 Kön 4,8-37). KUSATU 3 (2002) 71-80.
3276 *Axskjöld, Carl-Johan* Altaret från Damaskus: en ideologisk förståelse. SEÅ 67 (2002) 19-25 [2 Kgs 5; 16].
3277 *Tronina, Antoni* Dobra nowina u bram Samarii (2 Krl 7) [The good news at the gates of Samaria (2 Kgs 7)]. Verbum Vitae 2 (2002) 19-30 Som. 30. **P.**
3278 *Dietrich, Walter* Jehus Kampf gegen den Baal von Samaria. Von David. BWANT 156: 2002 <2001> ⇒160. 164-180 [2 Kgs 9-10].
3279 *McKinlay, Judith E.* Negotiating the frame for viewing the death of Jezebel. BiblInterp 10 (2002) 305-323 [2 Kgs 9,30-37].
3280 *Dyk, Janet* Linguistic aspects of the Peshitta version of 2 Kings 18 and 19. Bible and computer. 2002 ⇒548. 519-543.
3281 *Swanson, Kristin A.* A reassessment of Hezekiah's reform in light of jar handles and iconographic evidence. CBQ 64 (2002) 460-469 [2 Kgs 18,4].
3282 *Kelly, Brian E.* Manasseh in the books of Kings and Chronicles (2 Kings 21:1-18; 2 Chron 33:1-20). Windows. 2002 ⇒500. 131-146.
3283 *Dietrich, Walter* Josia und das Gesetzbuch (2Kön 22). Von David. BWANT 156: 2002 <1977> ⇒160. 199-216.
3284 **Barrick, W. Boyd** The king and the cemeteries: toward a new understanding of Josiah's reform. VT.S 88: Lei 2002, Brill xiii; 274 pp. €63/$85. 90-04-12171-4. Bibl. 222-256. [R]JBL 121 (2002) 543-546 (*Roddy, Nicolae*) [1 Kgs 13; 2 Kgs 22-23; 2 Chr 34,1-36,1].
3285 *Van den Berg, Evert* Visies op de ondergang van Juda: een structurele analyse van 2 Koningen 24-25 en Jeremia 36-45. ITBT 10/3; 10/4 (2002) 4-6; 27-28.
3286 *Lipschits, Oded* Jehoiakim slept with his fathers' (II Kings 24:6): did he?. Journal of Hebrew Scriptures 4 (2002)*.
3287 *Murray, Donald F.* Of all the years the hopes—or fears?: Jehoiachin in Babylon (2 Kings 25:27-30). JBL 120 (2001) 245-265.

E5.2 *Chronicorum libri*—The books of Chronicles

3288 *Abadie, Philippe* Le livre des Chroniques comme oeuvre littéraire. RSR 90 (2002) 525-553.
3289 **Abadie, Philippe** O livro das Crónicas. [T]*Silva, Vítor Arantes da*: Cadernos Bíblicos 76: Lisboa 2002, Bíblica 68 pp.
3290 **Beentjes, P.C.** 1 Kronieken. Verklaring van de Hebreeuwse Bijbel: Kampen 2002, Kok 286 pp. €29.90. 90-435-0574-9.
3291 *Ben Zvi, Ehud* The book of Chronicles: another look. SR 31 (2002) 261-281.
3292 *Duke, Rodney K.* The strategic use of enthymeme and example in the argumentation of the books of Chronicles. Rhetorical argumentation. 2002. ⇒553. 127-140.

3293 *Glatt-Gilad, David A.* The root *knᶜ* and historiographic periodization in Chronicles. CBQ 64 (2002) 248-257.

3294 ᴱ**Graham, Matt Patrick; McKenzie, Steven L.** The Chronicler as author. JSOT.S 263: 1999 ⇒15,235; 17,2967. ᴿRSR 90 (2002) 241-42 (*Abadie, Philippe*); EvQ 74 (2002) 354-355 (*Johnstone, William*).

3295 **Hanspach, Alexander** Inspirierte Interpreten: das Prophetenverständnis der Chronikbücher und sein Ort in der Religion und Literatur zur Zeit des zweiten Tempels. ATSAT 64: 2000 ⇒16,2944. ᴿRTL 33 (2002) 260-261 (*Wénin, A.*); ThLZ 127 (2002) 898-899 (*Willi, Thomas*).

3296 *Hoglund, Kenneth G.* The priest of praise: the Chronicler's David. RExp 99 (2002) 185-191.

3297 **Hooker, Paul** First and Second Chronicles. Westminster Bible companion: 2001 ⇒17,2968. ᴿRExp 99 (2002) 624-625 (*Biddle, Mark*).

3298 **Japhet, Sara** The ideology of the book of Chronicles and its place in biblical thought. ᵀ*Barber, Anna*: BEAT 9: ²1997 ⇒13,2646. ᴿHeyJ 43 (2002) 213-214 (*McNamara, Martin*);

3299 1 Chronik. ᵀ*Mach, Dafna*: HThK.AT: FrB 2002, Herder 472 pp. 34-51-26816-7. Bibl. 12-23.

3300 **Jarick, John** 1 Chronicles. Readings: L 2002, Sheffield A. vii; 167 pp. $30. 0-8264-6202-2. Bibl. 158-159.

3301 **Johnstone, William** 1 and 2 Chronicles. JSOT.S 253-254: 1997 ⇒ 13,2647... 17,2969. ᴿThR 67 (2002) 71-72 (*Willi, Thomas*); HeyJ 43 (2002) 214-215 (*McNamara, Martin*).

3302 *Kalimi, Isaac* The view of Jerusalem in the ethnographical introduction of Chronicles (1 Chr 1-9). Bib. 83 (2002) 556-562.

3303 **Kalimi, Isaac** The book of Chronicles: historical writing and literary devices. 2000 ⇒17,2970. ᴿJQR 92 (2001) 200-201 (*Glatt-Gilad, David A.*).

3304 *Knoppers, Gary N.; Harvey, Paul B.* Omitted and remaining matters: on the names given to the book of Chronicles in antiquity. JBL 121 (2002) 227-243.

3305 *Lucca, Paolo* 1-2 Cronache nella versione armena della bibbia: dipendenze testuali e tecniche di traduzione della prima versione armena. BAZMAVEP 160 (2002) 150-187 Rés. 186.

3306 **McKenzie, Steven L.** The Chronicler's use of the Deuteronomistic History. 1985 ⇒1,2913... 4,3009. ᴿThR 67 (2002) 78-80 (*Willi, Thomas*).

3307 *Mitchell, Christine* Transformations in meaning: Solomon's accession in Chronicles. Journal of Hebrew Scriptures 4 (2002)*.

3308 **Shaver, Judson R.** Torah and the Chronicler's history work. 1989 ⇒ 6,3141; 9,2880. ᴿThR 67 (2002) 74-76 (*Willi, Thomas*).

3309 **Steins, Georg** Die Chronik als kanonisches Abschlußphänomen: Studien zur Entstehung und Theologie von 1/2 Chronik. BBB 93: 1995 ⇒11/1,1314... 17,2977. ᴿThR 67 (2002) 76-78 (*Willi, Thomas*).

3310 **Tuell, Steven Shawn** First and Second Chronicles. Interpretation: 2001 ⇒17,2979. ᴿHBT 24/2 (2002) 111-112 (*McCann, J. Clinton*).

3311 *Van den Berg, Evert* De profeet, de koning, de tempel en het volk: de ondergang van Jeruzalem in 2 Kronieken. ITBT 10/7 (2002) 8-10.

3312 *Willi, Thomas* Zwei Jahrzehnte Forschung an Chronik und Esra-Nehemia. ThR 67 (2002) 61-104.

3313   *Knoppers, Gary N.* Intermarriage, social complexity, and ethnic di-
       versity in the genealogy of Judah. JBL 120 (2001) 15-30 [1 Chr 2, 3-
       4,23].
3314   *Heard, R. Christopher* Echoes of Genesis in 1 Chronicles 4:9-10: an
       intertextual and contextual reading of Jabez's prayer. Journal of
       Hebrew Scriptures 4 (2002)*.
3315   **Wilkinson, Bruce** The prayer of Jabez. 2000 ⇒16,2953. RBS 159
       (2002) 112-117 (*Zuck, Roy B.*) [1 Chr 4,9-10].
3316   *Diller, Carmen* Der Kompositpsalm 1 Chr 16,8-36 als theologisches
       Kompendium. FSTEINGRIMSSON, S.: ATSAT 72: 2002 ⇒117. 173-
       203.
3317   *Graham, M. Patrick* A character ethics reading of 1 Chronicles 29:1-
       25. Character and scripture. 2002 ⇒283. 98-120.

3318   *Kuntzmann, Raymond* La définition d'un type au fil d'une lecture in-
       tertextuelle (2 Ch 20,5-13). Typologie biblique. LeDiv: 2002 ⇒341.
       35-47.
3319   *Becker, Joachim* Gegen Textverbesserungen in 2 Chr 20,25;
3320   'Söhne' oder 'Bauleute' der Atalja in 2 Chr 24,7?. BN 114/115 (2002)
       11-16/5-11.
3321   **Vaughn, Andrew G.** Theology, history, and archaeology in the
       Chronicler's account of Hezekiah. 1999 ⇒15,2814...17,2984. RThR
       67 (2002) 91-92 (*Willi, Thomas*); BASOR 325 (2002) 86-88 (*Zorn,
       Jeffrey R.*); HebStud 43 (2002) 267-269 (*Van Wyk, Wouter C., Jr.*);
       JSSt 47 (2002) 333-335 (*Hess, Richard S.*); JQR 92 (2001) 202-204
       (*Glatt-Gilad, David A.*) [2 Chr 29-32].
3322   *Jonker, Louis* Completing the temple with the celebration of Josiah's
       passover?. OTEs 15 (2002) 381-397 [2 Chr 35,1-19].

E5.4 *Esdrae libri*—**Ezra, Nehemiah**

3323   *Bedford, Peter R.* Diaspora: homeland relations in Ezra-Nehemiah.
       VT 52 (2002) 147-165.
3324   *Blum, Erhard* Esra, die Mosetora und die persische Politik. Religion
       und Religionskontakte. 2002 ⇒492. 231-256.
3325   **Bodi, Daniel** Jérusalem à l'époque perse: 'levons-nous et bâtissons!'
       (Néhémie 2,18). P 2002, Geuthner 320 pp. €38. 2-7053-3718-0 [FV
       102,101s—Marx, Alfred].
3326   *Böhler, Dieter* Das Gottesvolk als Altargemeinschaft: die Bedeutung
       des Tempels für die Konstituierung kollektiver Identität nach Esra-
       Nehemia. Gottesstadt. QD 191: 2002 ⇒567. 207-230.
3327   *Douglas, Mary* Responding to Ezra: the priests and the foreign
       wives. BiblInterp 10 (2002) 2-23.
3328   *Farisani, Elewani* The ideological biased use of Ezra-Nehemiah in a
       quest for an African theology of reconstruction. OTEs 15 (2002)
       628-646.
3329   *Janz, Timothy* A system of unit division from Byzantine manuscripts
       of Ezra-Nehemiah. Studies in scriptural unit division. Pericope 3:
       2002 ⇒339. 121-143.
3330   **Karrer, Christiane** Ringen um die Verfassung Judas: eine Studie zu
       den theologisch-politischen Vorstellungen im Esra-Nehemia-Buch.
       BZAW 308: 2001 ⇒17,2994. RJBL 121 (2002) 750-754 (*Siedlecki,
       Armin*).

3331 *Nápole, Gabriel M.* La *Oratio Esdrae* (IV Esd VIII,20-36): análisis exegético. RevBib 62 (2000) 67-85.

3332 **Schaper, Joachim** Priester und Leviten im achämenidischen Juda: Studien zur Kult- und Sozialgeschichte Israels in persischer Zeit. FAT 31: 2000 ⇒16,2971; 17,2999. [R]OLZ 97 (2002) 392-396 (*Willi, Thomas*); HebStud 43 (2002) 292-296 (*Klingbeil, Gerald A.*); SEÅ 67 (2002) 173-174 (*Nurmela, Risto*).

3333 **Schniedewind, William M.** The word of God in transition: from prophet to exegete in the Second Temple period. JSOT.S 197: 1995 ⇒11/2,2086; 13,2682. [R]ThR 67 (2002) 72-74 (*Willi, Thomas*).

3334 *Van Wyk, Wouter C., Jr.; Breytenbach, A.P.B.* The nature of conflict in Ezra-Nehemiah. HTS 57 (2001) 1254-1263 [OTA 25,479].
    Willi, T. Forschung an Chr. u. Esr.-Neh. 2002 ⇒3312.

3335 *Porten, B.* Theme and structure of Ezra 1-6: from literature to history. TEuph 23 (2002) 27-44.

3336 *Segal, Michael* Numerical discrepancies in the list of vessels in Ezra i 9-11. VT 52 (2002) 122-129.

3337 **Schwiderski, Dirk** Handbuch des nordwestsemitischen Briefformulars: ein Beitrag zur Echtheitsfrage der aramäischen Briefe des Esrabuches. BZAW 295: 2000 ⇒16,2978. [R]ThLZ 127 (2002) 1290-1292 (*Rösel, Martin*) [Ezra 4].

3338 *Sérandour, A.* Remarques sur Esdras 6,19-22. TEuph 23 (2002) 59-75 [Ezra 1,1-11].

3339 *Fewell, Danna Nolan* The genesis of Israelite identity: a narrative speculation on postexilic interpretation. [F]PATTE, D.: 2002 ⇒89. 111-118 [Ezra 9-10].

3340 **Janzen, David** Witch-hunts, purity and social boundaries: the expulsion of the foreign women in Ezra 9-10. JSOT.S 350: Shf 2002, Sheffield A. x; 179 pp. 1-84127-292-2. Bibl. 164-172.

3341 **Reinmuth, Titus** Der Bericht Nehemias: zur literarischen Eigenart, traditionsgeschichtlichen Prägung und innerbiblischen Rezeption des Ich-Berichts Nehemias. OBO 183: FrS 2002, Univ.-Verl. xiii; 383 pp. FS75. 3-7278-1377-6. Bibl. 350-377 [Neh 1-7; 11].

3342 *Williams, Gary R.* Contextual influences in readings of Nehemiah 5: a case study. TynB 53 (2002) 57-74.

3343 *Heltzer, Michael* The question of $m^{e^{3}}at$ $kesef$ reconsidered. [F]DIETRICH, M.: 2002 ⇒28. 169-170 [Neh 5,11].

3344 **Duggan, Michael W.** The covenant renewal in Ezra-Nehemiah (Neh 7:72B-10:40): an exegetical literary, and theological study. SBL.DS 164: 2001 ⇒17,3005. [R]CBQ 64 (2002) 550-551 (*Kelly, Brian E.*); JBL 121 (2002) 754-756 (*Siedlecki, Armin*).

3345 *Lipschits, Oded* Literary and ideological aspects of Nehemiah 11. JBL 121 (2002) 423-440.

3346 *Bergren, Theodore A.* The list of leaders in 5 Ezra 1:39-40. JBL 120 (2001) 313-327.

3347 *De Troyer, Kristin* Zerubbabel and Ezra: a revided and revised Solomon and Josiah?: a survey of current 1 Esdras research. CuBR 1/1 (2002) 30-60.

3348 **Hamilton, Alastair** The apocryphal Apocalypse: the reception of the second book of Esdras (4 Ezra) from the Renaissance to the Enlight-

enment. OWS: 1999 ⇒15,2864...17,3012. ᴿHeyJ 43 (2002) 88-90
(*McNamara, Martin*).
3349 *Harrington, Daniel J.* Afterlife expectations in Pseudo-Philo, 4 Ezra,
and 2 Baruch, and their implications for the New Testament. ᶠLAM-
BRECHT, J.: BEThL 165: 2002 ⇒72. 21-34.
3350 **Hogan, Karina** Theologies in conflict in 4 Ezra: wisdom debate and
apocalyptic solution. 2002 Diss. Chicago [RTL 34,595].
3351 ᴱᵀ**Monferrer Sala, Juan Pedro** Scripta arabica orientalia: dos estudios de literatura árabe cristiana. Textos y estudios de la literatura
árabe cristiana 2: 1999 ⇒15,2858 [1 Esdras; Acts]. ᴿEstB 60 (2002)
131-132 (*Urbán, Á.*).
3352 *Schmid, Konrad* Die Zerstörung Jerusalems und seines Tempels als
Heilsparadox: zur Zusammenführung von Geschichtstheologie und
Anthropologie im Vierten Esrabuch. Zerstörungen. WUNT 147:
2002 ⇒559. 183-206.
3353 **Talshir, Zipora** I Esdras: from origin to translation. SBL.SCSt 47:
1999 ⇒15,2859...17,3014. ᴿJSSt 47 (2002) 343-345 (*Grabbe,
Lester L.*).

E5.5 Libri Tobiae, Judith, Esther

3354 **Vílchez Líndez, José** Tobías y Judit. 2000 ⇒16,3003. ᴿThLZ 127
(2002) 903-904 (*Kessler, Rainer*).

3355 *Auwers, Jean-Marie* Tobit. BVLI 46 (2002) 15-19.
3356 *Ego, Beate* Tobit (Buch). TRE 33. 2002 ⇒799. 573-579;
3357 Heimat in der Fremde": zur Konstituierung einer jüdischen Identität
im Buch Tobit. Jüdische Schriften. 2002 ⇒345. 270-283.
3358 *Haag, Ernst* Das Tobitbuch und die Tradition von Jahwe, dem Heiler
Israels (Ex 15,26). TThZ 111 (2002) 23-41.
3359 **Otzen, Benedikt** Tobit and Judith. Guides to the Apocrypha and
Pseudepigrapha 11: L 2002, Sheffield A. xiii; 162 pp. £15. 0-8264-
6053-4. Bibl. 143-153.
3360 *Rossi de Gasperis, Francesco* 'Vita' di un santo del periodo postesili-
co: il libro di Tobia. Prendi il libro. Bibbia e spiritualità 18: 2002 ⇒
372. 239-250.
3361 **Schüngel-Straumann, Helen** Tobit. HThK.AT: 2000 ⇒16,3000.
ᴿBN 112 (2002) 28-32 (*Schmitt, Armin*); ThLZ 127 (2002) 505-507
(*Kaiser, Otto*); CBQ 64 (2002) 556-557 (*Skemp, Vincent*).
3362 *Skemp, Vincent T.M.* JEROME's Tobit: a reluctant contribution to the
genre rewritten bible. RBen 112 (2002) 5-35.
3363 *Stuckenbruck, Loren T.* The book of Tobit and the problem of "magic". Jüdische Schriften. 2002 ⇒345. 258-269.

3364 *Bogaert, Pierre-Maurice* Judith. BVLI 46 (2002) 19-20.
3365 ᴱ**Bogaert, Pierre-Maurice** Judith, 1: introduction. VL 7/2: 2001 ⇒
17, 3028. ᴿREAug 48 (2002) 197-198 (*Milhau, Marc*).
3366 *Carfagna, Antonella* Giuditta: una figlia d'Israele, gloria di Gerusalemme e vanto del suo popolo. Prendi il libro. Bibbia e spiritualità
18: 2002 ⇒372. 251-273.
3367 *Carvelli, Simona* La *Vulgata*, i decreti tridentini e la *Iudit* di Federico
della VALLE. La sorgente. 2002 ⇒315. 150-161.

3368 **Corradino, Saverio** Judith: il libro di una vita. [E]*Stancari, Pino*: Letture bibliche 9: Soveria Mannelli (Catanzaro) 2002, Rubbettino 161 pp. 88-498-0439-3. Bibl. 11-12.

3369 *Efthimiadis-Keith, Helen* Text and interpretation: gender and violence in the book of Judith, scholar commentary and the visual arts from the Renaissance onward. OTEs 15 (2002) 64-84.

3370 *Esler, Philip F.* Ludic history in the book of Judith: the reinvention of Israelite identity?. BiblInterp 10 (2002) 107-143.

3371 **Gallazzi, Sandro; Rizzante, Ana Maria** Judite: a mão da mulher na história do povo. Comentário Bíblico/AT: 2001 ⇒17,3034. [R]Estudos Biblicos 74 (2002) 107-111 (*Pereira, Ney Brasil*); REB 62 (2002) 456-461 (*Pereira, Ney Brasil*).

3372 **Arzt, Silvia** Frauenwiderstand macht Mädchen Mut: die geschlechtsspezifische Rezeption einer biblischen Erzählung. Innsbruck 1999, Tyrolia 160 pp. Diss. Salzburg [Esther]. [R]RBLit 4 (2002) 244-247 (*Labahn, Antje*).

3373 *Bahar, Shlomo* Expressions of sympathy to the clan of King Saul in the scroll of Esther. BetM 172 (2002) 42-53 Sum. 93. **H.**

3374 *Bar-Asher, Moshé* איש יהודי היה בשושן הבירה Il y avait à Suse un homme juif. REJ 161 (2002) 227-231 [Esth 2,5].

3375 **Bechtel, Carol M.** Esther. Interpretation: LVL 2002, Westminster 120 pp. $19. 0-8042-3113-3 [BiTod 41,262—Bergant, Dianne].

3376 **Beckett, Michael** Gospel in Esther. Carlisle 2002, Paternoster xv; 156 pp. £8. 1-8422-7137-7. Foreword *Stephen Sykes*.

3377 **Berlin, Adele** The book of Esther and ancient storytelling. JBL 120 (2001) 3-14.

3378 **Berlin, Adele** Esther: the traditional Hebrew text with new JPS translation. The JPS Bible Commentary: 2001 ⇒17,3042. [R]RBLit (2002)* (*Premstaller, Volkmar*).

3379 **Bodea, Cornelia** Treasures of Jewish art: the 1673 illuminated scroll of Esther offered to a Romanian hierarch. Iasi 2002, Center for Romanian Studies 72 pp. 973-9432-38-7.

3380 *Davies, Philip R.* Haman the victim. First person. BiSe 81: 2002 ⇒ 295. 137-154.

3381 *De Troyer, Kristin* The letter of the king and the letter of Mordecai. Textus 21 (2002) 175-207 [Esth 8,9-13].

3382 **De Troyer, Kristin M.L.L.** The end of the alpha text of Esther: translation and narrative technique in MT 8:1-17, LXX 8:1-17, and AT 7:14-41. SBL.SCSt 48: 2000 ⇒16,3029; 17,3045. [R]CBQ 64 (2002) 560-561 (*McLay, R. Timothy*).

3383 **Fountain, Allison Kay** Literary and empirical readings of the books of Esther. Studies in Biblical Literature 43: NY 2002, Lang xiii; 314 pp. 0-8204-5570-9. Bibl. 301-305.

3384 **Franke, Birgit** Assuerus und Esther am Burgunderhof: zur Rezeption des Buches Esther in den Niederlanden (1450-1530). 1998 ⇒15, 2905. [R]Francia 28/1 (2002) 397-398 (*Boone, Marc*).

3385 *Frolov, Serge* Two eunuchs, two conspiracies, and one loyal Jew: the narrative of botched regicide in Esther as text- and redaction-critical test case. VT 52 (2002) 304-325 [Esth 2,21-33].

3386 **Haberman, Bonna D.** Unmasking a global masquerade: or "stop the traffic". JFSR 18/1 (2002) 99-105.

3387 *Haelewyck, Jean-Claude* Esther. BVLI 46 (2002) 20-23.

3388 *Herman, Dov* The halakhah in the Aramaic targum of the book of Esther: nonnormative halakhah?. BetM 171 (2002) 336-351 Sum. 382. **H.**

3389 *Kasher, Hannah* On the book of Esther as an allegory in the works of Joseph IBN KASPI: a response to R. Eisen in *REJ* 160/3-4. REJ 161 (2002) 459-464.

3390 **Kossman, Ruth** Die Esthernovelle: vom Erzählten zur Erzählung: Studien zur Traditions- und Redaktionsgeschichte des Estherbuches. VT.S 79: 2000 ⇒16,3020. ᴿThRv 98 (2002) 33-35 (*Uehlinger, Christoph*); ThLZ 127 (2002) 502-505 (*Wahl, Harald*).

3391 *Larsson, Gerhard* Is the book of Esther older than has been believed?. VT 52 (2002) 130-131.

3392 **Limentani, Giacoma** Regina o concubina?: Ester. Mi 2001, Paoline 98; lxix pp. 88-315-2201-9. Disegni di *Francesco Pennisi*.

3393 **Linafelt, Tod; Beal, Timothy Kandler** Ruth and Esther. Berit Olam: 1999 ⇒15,2556; 17,2735. ᴿVJTR 66 (2002) 547-549 (*Meagher, P.M.*); RBLit 4 (2002) 241-243 (*Laniak, Timothy S.*).

3394 *Murphy, George L.* Providence and passion in Esther. CThMi 29 (2002) 122-127.

ᵀ**Nardoni, F.** Rut e Ester 2001 ⇒3075.

Nielsen, K., *al.*, Ruths Bog, Esters Bog...1998 ⇒3086.

3395 *Passoni dell'Acqua, Anna* Gli editti di liberazione nella letteratura giudaico-ellenistica: intento storico ed apologetico. Materia giudaica. 2002 ⇒727. 55-66.

Roop, Eugene F. Ruth, Jonah, Esther 2002 ⇒3078.

3396 *Rossi de Gasperis, Francesco* Ester: una figlia di Giuda nel turbine dell'esilio e nelle fauci degli imperi delle genti. Prendi il libro. Bibbia e spiritualità 18: 2002 ⇒372. 113-123.

3397 *Shemesh, Yael* The metamorphoses of Vashti: bible, aggadah, feminist exegesis, and modern feminist midrash. BetM 171 (2002) 356-372 Sum. 381. **H.**

3398 *Snyman, Gerrie* Identification and the discourse of fundamentalism: reflections on a reading of the book of Esther. Rhetorical criticism. JSNT.S 195: 2002 ⇒369. 160-208.

3399 *Warning, Wilfried* Terminological patterns and the book of Esther. OTEs 15 (2002) 489-503.

3400 *Weiland, Forrest S.* Historicity, genre, and narrative design in the book of Esther. BS 159 (2002) 151-165;

3401   Plot structure in the book of Esther. BS 159 (2002) 277-287;

3402   Literary conventions in the book of Esther. BS 159 (2002) 425-435.

3403 *Ziffer, Irit* Four new belts from the land of Ararat and the feast of the women in Esther 1:9. Sex and gender. 2002 ⇒712. 645-657.

E5.8 *Machabaeorum libri,* **1-2[3-4] Maccabees**

3404 *Aguilar, Mario I.* Time, communion, and ancestry in African biblical interpretation: a contextual note on 1 Maccabees 2:49-70. BTB 32 (2002) 129-144.

3405 *Brodersen, Kai* Die Makkabäerbücher als historische Quelle. BiKi 57 (2002) 80-81.

3406 **Cañas Reíllo, José Manuel** Glosas marginales de *Vetus Latina* en biblias vulgatas españolas:1-2 Macabeos. TECC 65: 2000 ⇒16,

3030. [R]RBen 112 (2002) 162-163 (*Bogaert, P.-M.*); RBLit 4 (2002) 255-257 (*Trebolle, Julio*).

3407 *Dobbeler, Stephanie von* Geschichte und Geschichten: der theologische Gehalt und die politische Problematik von 1 und 2 Makkabäer. BiKi 57 (2002) 62-67.

3408 **Gadecki, Stanislaw** Grecko-lacinsko-polska synopsa do Pierwszej i Drugiej Ksiegi Machabejskiej. Prymasowska Seria Biblijna: Wsz 2002, "Vocatio" xlix; 450 pp. 83-7146-169-0. Bibl. 449-450.

3409 *Gauger, Jörg-Dieter* Der "Tod des Verfolgers": Überlegungen zur Historizität eines Topos. JSJ 33 (2002) 42-64.

3410 *Geiger, Joseph* The Hasmonaeans and Hellenistic succession. JJS 53 (2002) 1-17.

3411 *Lieu, Judith* Not Hellenes but Philistines?: the Maccabees and JOSEPHUS defining the 'other'. JJS 53 (2002) 246-263.

3412 *Maier, Johann* Glaube gegen Unglaube?: jüdische Richtungskämpfe zur Makkabäerzeit im Lichte der Qumranschriften. BiKi 57 (2002) 73-78.

3413 *Manns, Frédéric* The prayers of the books of Maccabees and the Shemone Ezre. LASBF 51 (2001) 109-132.

3414 *Mayer, Reinhold; Rühle, Inken* Die makkabäische Bewegung im Talmud und im jüdischen Gebetbuch. BiKi 57 (2002) 89-92.

3415 *Oppen, Eberhard von* "See, the conqu'ring hero comes ...": der Makkabäer-Stoff in Musik und Geschichte. BiKi 57 (2002) 93-94.

3416 *Schwartz, Daniel R.* Antiochus the *nbl* (1 Maccabees 1:24). Shnaton 13 (2002) 185-197. **H.**

3417 *Thiel, Wolfgang* Zwischen Widerstand und Anpassung: archäologische Zeugnisse der Makkabäerzeit. BiKi 57 (2002) 95-103.

3418 *Van Henten, Jan Willem* Makkabäerbücher. RGG 5. 2002 ⇒796. 702-705;

3419 Die Märtyrer als Helden des Volkes. Jüdische Schriften. 2002 ⇒345. 102-133.

3420 *Williams, David S.* A literary encircling pattern in 1 Maccabees 1. JBL 120 (2001) 140-142.

3421 **Williams, David Salter** The structure of 1 Maccabees. CBQ.MS 31: 1999 ⇒15,2935...17,3074. [R]RBLit 4 (2002) 257-260 (*DesCamp, Mary Therese*).

3422 *Bauer, Dieter* Der Tod von Märtyrern und die Hoffnung auf die Auferstehung. BiKi 57 (2002) 82-86.

3423 *Frenkel, Diana Lea* La presencia de lo literario en el prólogo de *II Macabeos*. RevBib 64 (2002) 217-224.

3424 *Nicklas, Tobias* Der Historiker als Erzähler: zur Zeichnung des Seleukidenkönigs Antiochus in 2 Makk. ix. VT 52 (2002) 80-92.

3425 *Knöppler, Thomas* Die Gottesvorstellung des 3. Makkabäerbuches. Jüdische Schriften. 2002 ⇒345. 209-221.

3426 *Krieger, Klaus-Stefan* Das 3. und 4. Makkabäerbuch. BiKi 57 (2002) 87-88.

VI. Libri didactici VT

E6.1 *Poesis metrica*, **Biblical** and Semitic **versification**

3427 *Desnitskij, A.S.* Poetry and prose in the Old Testament. Journal of Ancient History 240 (2002) 68-87 Sum. 87. **R**.

3428 **Fokkelman, J.P.** Major poems of the Hebrew Bible: at the interface of prosody and structural analysis, 2: 85 psalms and Job 4-14. SSN 41: 2000 ⇒16,3051; 17,3087. ᴿBib. 83 (2002) 115-118 (*Berry, Donald K.*);

3429 Reading biblical poetry: an introductory guide. ᵀ*Smit, Ineke*: 2001 ⇒ 17,3088. ᴿKerux 17/3 (2002) 52-55 (*Dennison, James T.*); RBLit (2002)* (*Franke, Chris*).

3430 *Loretz, Oswald* Einleitung: das Verhältnis der Psalmen zur altsyrisch-kanaanäischen Poesie: Metrik und *Parallelismus membrorum* contra Kolometrie?. Psalmstudien. 2002 ⇒201. 1-9.

3431 ᴱ**Orton, David E.** Poetry in the Hebrew Bible: selected studies from Vetus Testamentum. Brill's readers in biblical studies 6: 2000 ⇒16, 3046. ᴿRBLit 4 (2002) 177-180 (*Bliese, Loren F.*).

3432 *Raphael, Rebecca* That's no literature, that's my bible: on James Kugel's objections to the idea of biblical poetry. JSOT 27 (2002) 37-45.

3433 ᴱ**Wendland, Ernst R.** Discourse perspectives on Hebrew poetry in the scripture. 1994 ⇒14,3646; 16,4152. ᴿKerux 17/1 (2002) 62-63 (*Dennison, James T.*).

E6.2 **Psalmi, textus**

3434 *Andrei, Filippo* Il salterio glossato di San ROMUALDO. Ben. 49/1 (2002) 23-52.

3435 ᴱ**Barberi, Claudio** Psalterium EGBERTI: fascimile del ms. CXXXVI del Museo Archeologico Nazionale di Cividale del Friuli 2000 ⇒16, 3074 1. ᴿStMed 43 (2002) 437-439 (*Fornasari, Giuseppe*).

3436 Salterio di Santa ELISABETTA: fascimile del ms. CXXXVII del Museo Archeologico Nazionale di Cividale del Friuli. Udine 2002, Ministero per i Beni 319 pp. Col. fasc. 356 pp; CD-Rom.

3437 ᵀ**Bianchi, Enzo** I salmi. 2001 ⇒17,3100. ᴿFirmana 27 (2002) 189 (*Nepi, Antonio*).

3438 ᵀ**Browne, Gerald** The abbreviated psalter of the Venerable BEDE. GR 2002, Eerdmans 92 pp. $18 [BiTod 41,57—Bergant, D.].

3439 ᵀ**Cadiot, Olivier; Sevin, Marc** Psaumes. P 2002, Bayard 345 pp. €25. Bible Bayard [DosB 97,34—Billon Gérard].

3440 *Caviness, Madeline H.* Conflicts between Regnum and Sacerdotium as reflected in a Canterbury Psalter of ca 1215. **Id**. Art in medieval west and its audience. CStS 718: Aldershot 2001, Ashgate. 1-27. ms. Paris, BNF, lat. 770 [RBen 114,199—P.-M. Bogaert].

3441 *Cox, Claude E.* The "Songs of Zion" in Armenian. Armenians in Jerusalem. Hebrew University Armenian studies 4: 2002 ⇒771. 33-59.

3442 **Devens, Monica S.** A concordance to Psalms in the Ethiopic version. ÄthF 59: 2001 ⇒17,3105. ᴿOLZ 97 (2002) 674-676 (*Voigt, Rainer*).

3443 *Dorival, Gilles* Septante et Texte Massorétique: le cas des Psaumes. Congress volume Basel 2001. VT.S 92: 2002 ⇒570. 139-161.

3444 **Fischer, Norman** Opening to you: Zen-inspired translations of the Psalms. NY 2002, Viking xxix; 175 pp. 0-670-03061-9.

3445 **Flint, Peter W.** The Dead Sea Psalms scrolls and the book of Psalms. StTDJ 17: 1997 ⇒13,2757... 17,3106. ᴿWZKM 92 (2002) 239-241 (*Steymans, Hans Ulrich*).

3446 **Fokkelman, Jan P.** The Psalms in form: the Hebrew Psalter in its poetic shape. Tools for Biblical Study 4: Lei 2002, Deo 172 pp. $47. 90-5854-017-0.

3447 **Haney, Kristin** The St. Albans psalter: an Anglo-Norman song of faith. StHu 60: Bern 2002, Lang xvi; 683 pp.

3448 ᵀ**Hartley, Vivian Maria** The psalter according to the seventy. ᴱ*Vachon, Pierre; Kamperidis, Lambros*: Westport, Ont. 2001, Wordsmith xxiv; 350 pp. 0-9688-8180-7.

3449 *Kloppers, E.* 'Woorde in die mond gelê'?: Psalmomdigting en die proses van kanonvormig. AcTh(B) 22/1 (2002) 42-56.

3450 **Knesebeck, Harald Wolter von dem** Der Elisabethpsalter in Cividale del Friuli: Buchmalerei für den Thüringer Landgrafenhof zu Beginn des 13. Jahrhunderts. 2001 ⇒17,3111. ᴿMAe 71 (2002) 132-133 (*Palmer, Nigel F.*).

3451 *Lust, J.* A lexicon of Sʏᴍᴍᴀᴄʜᴜs' special vocabulary in his translation of the Psalms. TC: a journal of biblical textual criticism [http://purl.org/TC] 5 (2000) pars. 1-19 [NTAb 47,530].

3452 ᴱ**Mares, Franz W.** Psalterii Sinaitici pars nova: (monasterii s. Catharinae codex slav. 2/N). 1997 ⇒13,2761. ᴿCCMéd 45 (2002) 385-388 (*Arranz, Miguel*).

3453 *McNamara, Martin* The psalms in the Irish church: the most recent research on text, commentary, and decoration—with emphasis on the so-called Psalter of Charlemagne. The bible as book. 2002 ⇒364. 89-103.

3454 *Netzer, Amnon* An early Judeao[!]-Persian fragment from Zefreh: Psalms 44:24-27, 45:1-9 and 55:2-16. JStAI 27 (2002) 419-438.

3455 **Reuben, Catherine** La traduction des Psaumes de David par Clément Mᴀʀᴏᴛ: aspects poétiques et théologiques. 2000 ⇒16,3097. ᴿBHR 64 (2002) 209-211 (*Skupien Dekens, Carine*); SCJ 33 (2002) 1121-1123 (*Mentzer, Raymond A.*).

3456 **Rüsen-Weinhold, Ulrich** Der Septuagintapsalter im Neuen Testament: eine textgeschichtliche Untersuchung. ᴰ*Karrer, Martin*: 2002, 392 pp. Diss. Wuppertal [ThRv 99/2,xi].

3457 *Sanders, Paul* The colometric layout of Psalms 1 to 14 in the Aleppo Codex. Studies in scriptural unit division. 2002 ⇒339. 226-257.

3458 *Sandler, Lucy Freeman* The illustration of the Psalms in fourteenth-century English manuscripts: three psalters of the Bohun family. Reading texts and images: essays in medieval and Renaissance art and patronage, in honour of Margaret M. Manion. ᴱ**Muir, Bernard J.**: Exeter 2002, Univ. of Exeter Press. 123-151 [RBen 114,199—P.-M. Bogaert].

3459 **Tov, Lika** Tehiliem: twintig psalmen uit de nieuwe bijbelvertaling. Heerenveen 2002, Nederlands Bijbelgenootschap 64 pp. 90-6126-8508.

3460 **Van Rooy, H.F.** Studies on the Syriac apocryphal psalms. JSSt.S 7: 1999 ⇒15,2972; 17,3129. ᴿHebStud 43 (2002) 308-311 (*Kitchen, Robert A.*).

E6.3 **Psalmi, introductio**

3461   **Brueggemann, Walter** El mensaje de los salmos. 1999 ⇒16,3104.
       ᴿITER 28 (2002) 161-164 (*Frades Gaspar, Eduardo*).
3462   **Bullock, C.** Hassell Encountering the book of Psalms: a literary and
       theological introduction. 2001 ⇒17,3135. ᴿRTR 61 (2002) 111-112
       (*Harman, Allan M.*); SBET 20 (2002) 210-211 (*MacKay, John L.*);
       OTEs 15 (2002) 825-828 (*Branch, R.G.*).
3463   **Crenshaw, James L.** The Psalms: an introduction. 2001 ⇒17,3136.
       ᴿInterp. 56 (2002) 205-206 (*Brown, William P.*); IThQ 67 (2002)
       174-176 (*Maher, Michael*); CBQ 64 (2002) 343-344 (*Johnson,
       Timothy J.*); AUSS 40 (2002) 314-315 (*Fanwar, Wann M.*).
3464   *Kizhakkeyil, S.* The Psalms: their use and content. JJSS 2 (2002) 147-
       176.
3465   **Magirius, Georg** Die Psalmen: wie ich sie heute verstehen kann. Gü
       2002, Gü 126 pp. 3-579-06019-8.
3466   **McNamara, Martin J.** The Psalms in the early Irish church. JSOT.S
       165: 2000 ⇒16,3110. ᴿCV 44 (2002) 291-293 (*Gale, Tara*); RBLit
       (2002)* (*Gay, David E.*).
3467   *Radermakers, J.* Les Psaumes et nous: quelques ouvrages récents.
       NRTh 124 (2002) 630-639.
3468   ᴱ**Reid, Stephen Breck** Psalms and practice: worship, virtue, and
       authority. 2001 ⇒17,3131. ᴿWorship 76 (2002) 476-478 (*Polan,
       Gregory J.*).
3469   **Schäfer, Brigitte; Steiner, Erika; Zanetti, Claudia** Vom Klagen
       zum Jubeln: Psalmen und ihre bewegende Kraft. Werkstattbibel 2:
       Stu 2002, Kathol. Bibelwerk 96 pp. €11.80/10.70. 3-460-08502-9.
3470   **Trebolle Barrera, Julio Cesar** Libro de los Salmos: religión, poder
       y saber. 2001 ⇒17,3127. ᴿCDios 215 (2002) 317-318 (*Gutiérrez,
       J.*); Cart. 18 (2002) 553-554 (*Sanz Valdivieso, R.*); CBQ 64 (2002)
       731-733 (*Bautch, Richard J.*).
3471   **Wénin, André** Entrare nei Salmi. CSB 41: Bo 2002, EDB 159 pp.
       88-10-40742-3.

E6.4 **Psalmi, commentarii**

3472   **Allen, Leslie C.** Psalms 101-150. WBC 21: Nv ²2002 <1983>, Nel-
       son xxiv; 423 pp. $35. 0-7852-4773-4. Bibl. xvii-xx.
3473   **Bortolini, José** Conocer y rezar los salmos: comentario popular para
       nuestros días. M 2002, San Pablo 750 pp. ᴿEphMar 52 (2002) 345-
       346 (*Largo Domínguez, Pablo*).
3474   **Broyles, Craig C.** Psalms. NIBC.OT: 1999 ⇒15,2985; 17,3148.
       ᴿRSR 90 (2002) 233-234 (*Abadie, Philippe*); SEÅ 67 (2002) 165-
       166 (*Eriksson, LarsOlov*).
3475   ᵀ**Cattani, Luigi** David KIMCHI: commento ai Salmi, 3: Sal 101-150.
       R 2001, Città Nuova 527 pp. ᴿCivCatt 153/2 (2002) 507-508
       (*Scaiola, D.*).
3476   **Cimosa, Mario** Lampada ai miei passi è la tua parola: commento
       esegetico-spirituale dei salmi (salmi 101-150). Città del Vaticano
       2002, LEV 384 pp.
3477   **Clifford, Richard J.** Psalms 1-72. Abingdon OT Commentaries: Nv
       2002, Abingdon 338 pp. $28. 0-687-02711-X. Bibl. 337-338.

3478 **Davidson, Robert** The vitality of worship: a commentary on the book of Psalms. 1998 ⇒14,2710; 15,2986. ^RJThS 53 (2002) 153-155 (*Gillingham, S.*).

3479 **Fiedrowicz, Michael** Psalmus vox totius Christi: Studien zu AUGU-STINS 'Enarrationes in Psalmos'. 1997 ⇒13,2799; 14,2711. ^RThPQ 150 (2002) 311-313 (*Böhmisch, Franz*).

3480 **Gerstenberger, Erhard S.** Psalms, part 2 and Lamentations. FOTL 15: 2001 ⇒17,3150. ^RBZ 46 (2002) 312-315 (*Zenger, Erich*); CBQ 64 (2002) 347-348 (*Murphy, Roland E.*); LASBF 51 (2001) 414-416 (*Cortese, E.*).

3481 ^E**Gori, Franco** AUGUSTINUS: Enarrationes in Psalmos 101-150, pars 3: enarrationes in Psalmos 119-133. CSEL 95/3: 2001 ⇒17,3151. ^RRSR 90 (2002) 125-126 (*Dulaey, Martine*);

3482 ^E**Gori, Franco; Recanatini, Francisca** AUGUSTINUS: Enarrationes in Psalmos 101-150, pars 4: enarrationes in Psalmos 134-140. CSEL 95/4: W 2002, Österr. Akad. der Wiss. 232 pp. €55. 3-7001-3132-1.

3483 **Goulder, Michael D.** Studies in the psalter, IV: the psalms of the return (Book V, Psalms 107-150). JSOT.S 258: 1998 ⇒14,2714... 17,3152. ^RRBLit 4 (2002) 231-232 (*Ballard, H. Wayne, Jr.*).

3484 ^T**Gruber, Mayer Irvin** RASHI's commentary on Psalms 1-89 (Books I-III): with English translation, introduction and notes. SFSHJ 161: 1998 ⇒14,2715; 16,3126. ^RREJ 161 (2002) 300-301 (*Kogel, Judith*).

3485 ^T**Hill, Robert Charles** THEODORET of Cyrus: commentary on the Psalms, 1-2: Psalms 1-72; 73-150. FaCh 101-102: 2000-2001. ⇒16, 3127; 17,3153. ^RJECS 10 (2002) 294-296 (*Blowers, Paul M.*).

3486 ^E**Holt, Else K.; Nielsen, Kirsten** Dansk kommentar til Davids salmer, 1-3. K 2002, Anis 256+267+302 pp. DKK800.

3487 **Hossfeld, Frank L.; Zenger, Erich** Die Psalmen, 2: Psalm 51-100. NEB.AT 40: Wü 2002, Echter 319-530 pp. €24.50. 3-429-02359-9;

3488 1-2: Psalm 1-100. NEB.AT: 1993-2002. ^RRBBras 19 (2002) 390-391 (*Minette de Tillesse, Gaëtan*);

3489 Psalmen 2: 51-100. HThK.AT: 2000 ⇒16,3128; 17,3156. ^RThRv 98 (2002) 481-484 (*Spieckermann, Hermann*).

3490 **Hunter, Alastair G.** Psalms. Old Testament readings: 1999 ⇒15, 2991. ^RCBQ 64 (2002) 135-136 (*Kuntz, J. Kenneth*).

3491 **Limburg, James** Psalms. Westminster Bible companion: 2000 ⇒16,3131; 17,3158. ^RBBR 12 (2002) 150-152 (*Broyles, Craig C.*); RBLit (2002)* (*Power, Bruce A.*).

3492 ^T**Ní Riain, Ide M.** Commentary of Saint AMBROSE on twelve psalms. 2000 ⇒16,3133. ^RIThQ 67 (2002) 392-396 (*Clancy, Finbarr G.*).

3493 **Oeming, Manfred** Das Buch der Psalmen, v.1, Psalm 1-41. 2000 ⇒ 16,3135; 17,3162. ^RRBLit 4 (2002) 228-230 (*Schorn, Ulrike*).

3494 **Schaefer, Konrad** Psalms. Berit Olam: 2001 ⇒17,3165. ^RRBLit (2002)* (*Mandolfo, Carleen R.*).

3495 **Scippa, Vincenzo** Salmi, 1: introduzione e commento. Dabar AT: Padova 2002, Messaggero 261 pp. €11.50. 88-250-1165-2. Bibl. 250-251.

3496 **Tromp, Nico** Psalmen 101-150. Belichting van het Bijbelboek: 's-Hertogenbosch 2002, Katholieke Bijbelstichting 320 pp. €16.50. 90-6173-894-6 [EThL 79,194—Lust, J.].

E6.5 **Psalmi, themata**

3497 **Achenbach, Reinhard** Unheilsdrohung und Erlösungshoffnung: zum
      Sitz im Leben mesopotamischer und altisraelitischer Klagegebete.
      ^D*Otto, Eckart*: 2002 Diss.-Habil. München [ThRv 99/2,xii].
3498 *Auwers, Jean-Marie* La numérotation des psaumes dans la tradition
      hébraïque: une enquête dans le fonds hébreu de la Bibliothèque
      Nationale. RB 109 (2002) 343-370.
3499 **Auwers, Jean-Marie** La composition littéraire du Psautier: un état
      de la question. CRB 46: 2000 ⇒16,3144; 17,3172. ^RTEuph 23
      (2002) 180-184 (*Gosse, B.*).
3500 *Barbiero, Gianni* Amore del nemico nei Salmi?. Horeb 11/1 (2002)
      47-52.
3501 *Blumenthal, David R.* Liturgies of anger. CrossCur 52 (2002) 178-
      199.
3502 *Bons, Eberhard* L'approche canonique du livre des psaumes: à
      propos de deux monographies récentes. RevSR 76 (2002) 371-381.
3503 **Bouzard, Walter C., Jr.** We have heard with our ears, O God:
      sources of the communal laments in the Psalms. SBL.DS 159: 1997
      ⇒13,2817... 17,3176. ^RThZ 58 (2002) 81-83 (*Weber, Beat*).
3504 **Brown, William P.** Seeing the Psalms: a theology of metaphor. LVL
      2002, Westminster xiii; 274 pp. $25. 0-664-22502-2.
3505 *Camarero, Lorenzo, al.*, Tema 8: quando il povero grida, Dio lo aiu-
      ta: Salmi 1-41. Salmi e letteratura sapienziale. 2002 ⇒264. 355-385.
3506 *Cisterna, Félix, al.*, Tema 9: fino a quando, Signore, dimenticherai il
      tuo popolo?: Salmi 73-80; Lamentazioni 1-5;
3507 Tema 11: Cantate al Signore un canto nuovo: Salmi 42-72; 90-105.
      Salmi e letteratura sapienziale. 2002 ⇒264. 389-409/447-467.
3508 **Conti, Martino** La vita fatta preghiera nei salmi di lamentazione
      individuale. Spicilegium 37: R 2002, Antonianum 411 pp. 88-7257-
      051-4. ^RAnton. 77 (2002) 393-394 (*Calvo, Gaspar*).
3509 *Cova, Gian D.* L'esigenza di giustizia nei salmi imprecatori. RStB
      14/1-2 (2002) 111-117.
3510 *Culley, Robert C.* The kingship of Yahweh psalms. ^FPATTE, D.: 2002
      ⇒89. 258-270 [Ps 47; 93; 95-99].
3511 *Darwin, George* God the servant and king: psalmic images of Mes-
      siah. God of big dreams. 2002 ⇒359. 230-252.
3512 *Day, John* The imprecatory psalms and christian ethics. BS 159
      (2002) 166-186 [Ps 58].
3513 **Doeker, Andrea** Die Funktion der Gottesrede in den Psalmen: eine
      poetologische Untersuchung. BBB 135: B 2002, Philo xi; 335 pp. 3-
      8257-0287-1. Bibl. 316-333.
3514 *Ego, Beate* Wasser, Fels und preisende Sterne: Aspekte der Relation
      von Weltbild und Lebenswelt am Beispiel der Psalmen. BZ 46
      (2002) 222-238.
3515 **Eissler, Friedmann** Königspsalmen und karäische Messiaser-
      wartung: Jefet ben ELIs Auslegung von Ps 2.72.89.110.132 im
      Vergleich mit SAADJA Gaons Deutung. TSMJ 17: Tü 2002, Mohr S.
      xxi; 700 pp. 3-16-147706-5. Bibl. 663-677.
3516 *Geller, Stephen A.* Wisdom, nature and piety in some biblical psalms.
      ^MJACOBSEN, T. 2002 ⇒62. 101-121.
3517 *Gillingham, Sue* From liturgy to prophecy: the use of psalmody in
      second temple Judaism. CBQ 64 (2002) 470-489.

3518 *Gillmayr-Bucher, Susanne* Spuren Sauls in den Psalmen. PzB 11 (2002) 33-46 [Ps 18; 52; 54; 57; 59];

3519 Relecture of biblical psalms: a computer aided analysis of textual relations based on semantic domains. Bible and computer. 2002 ⇒ 548. 309-321.

3520 *Gosse, Bernard* Le quatrième livre du Psautier, Psaumes 90-106, comme réponse à l'échec de la royauté davidique. BZ 46 (2002) 239-252.

3521 **Gzella, Holger** Lebenszeit und Ewigkeit: Studien zur Eschatologie und Anthropologie des Septuaginta-Psalters. ^D*Zenger, Erich*: BBB 134: B 2002, Philo 434 pp. €60. 3-8257-0286-3. Diss. Münster 2000/01 [Bibl. 367-403].

3522 **Haney, Randy G.** Text and concept analysis in royal psalms. NY 2002, Lang xix; 244 pp. 0-8204-5048-0.

3523 *Jeppesen, Knud* The Psalter in canon. ^FSTEINGRIMSSON, S.: ATSAT 72: 2002 ⇒117. 265-278.

3524 *Joffe, Laura* The answer to the meaning of life, the universe and the Elohistic psalter. JSOT 27 (2002) 223-235.

3525 **Klingbeil, Martin** Yahweh fighting from heaven: God as warrior and as God of heaven in the Hebrew Psalter and ancient Near Eastern iconography. OBO 169: 1999 ⇒15,3023. ^RJThS 53 (2002) 155-158 (*Gillingham, S.*).

3526 **Kombi, Ngwese** Vocabulaire des Psaumes de supplication: hébreu-anglais-français-swahili. Kinshasa 2002, Baobab 94 pp.

3527 **Kwakkel, Gert** 'According to my righteousness': upright behaviour as grounds for deliverance in psalms 7, 17, 18, 26, and 44. ^D*Noort, Ed*: OTS 46: Lei 2002, Brill x; 342 pp. €100/$116. 90-04-12507-8. Diss. Groningen 2001.

3528 *Landon, Michael* The Psalms as mission. RestQ 44/3 (2002) 165-175.

3529 *Loretz, Oswald* Politische Theologie des Königtums in Ugarit, Klein-asien, Assur und Israel: das juridische Theorem 'The King's two bodies'. Psalmstudien. 2002 <cf. 2001> ⇒201. 381-402;

3530 Zur Zitat-Vernetzung zwischen Ugarit-Texten und Psalmen: Anmer-kungen zu einem Werk von Y. Avishur. Psalmstudien. 2002 <1994> ⇒201. 403-421.

3531 *MacEwen, Alastair* The suffering of God's servants in the Psalms. VR 67 (2002) 3-23.

3532 *Mandolfo, Carleen* Finding their voices: sanctioned subversion in psalms of lament. HBT 24/2 (2002) 27-52 [Ps 7];

3533 God in the dock: dialog tension in the psalms of lament. JSOT.S 357: L 2002, Sheffield A. x; 222 pp. £50. 0-8264-6200-6. Bibl. 207-214.

3534 *Mays, James Luther* The God who reigns: the book of Psalms. ^FACH-TEMEIER, P. 2002 ⇒1. 29-38.

3535 *McCann, J. Clinton, Jr.* 'The way of the righteous' in the Psalms: character formation and cultural crisis. Character and scripture. 2002 ⇒283. 135-149.

3536 *Monroy, Agostino, al.*, Tema 10: ogni vivente dia lode al signore: Salmi 107-150. Salmi e letteratura sapienziale. 2002 ⇒264. 413-444.

3537 *Nielsen, Kirsten* The variety of metaphors about God in the psalter: deconstruction and reconstruction?. SJOT 16 (2002) 151-159.

3538 *Otto, Eckart* Politische Theologie in den Königspsalmen zwischen Ägypten und Assyrien: die Herrscherlegitimation in den Psalmen 2

und 18 in ihren altorientalischen Kontexten. 'Mein Sohn bist du'. SBS
192: 2002 ⇒366. 33-65.

3539   *Paximadi, Giorgio* Strutture retoriche in tre salmi (Sal 24; 3; 122): e
       punti di partenza per un cammino interpretativo. RTLu 7 (2002) 71-
       83.

3540   *Peels, H.G.L.* 'Gelukkig hij die uw kinderen zal grijpen': hermeneuti-
       sche en bijbels-theologische positionering van de Oudtestamentische
       vloekbede. AcTh(B) 22/1 (2002) 117-134.

3541   **Poovathinkal, Shaji** Matthew 'Let your face shine, O God': theolog-
       ical crisis and call to commitment in the Psalms of Asaph. *DSimian-
       Yofre, Horacio*: 2002 Diss. Gregorian [RTL 34,593].

3542   *Roberts, J.J.M.* The enthronement of Yhwh and David: the abiding
       theological significance of the kingship language of the psalms. CBQ
       64 (2002) 675-686.

3543   **Rösel, Christoph** Die messianische Redaktion des Psalters: Studien
       zu Entstehung und Sammlung Ps 2-89*. CThM.BW 19: 1999 ⇒15,
       3036...17,3215. ᴿWZKM 92 (2002) 241-245 (*Steymans, Hans Ul-
       rich*); VT 52 (2002) 142-143 (*Gillingham, Susan*).

3544   **Scaiola, Donatella** "Una cosa ha detto Dio, due ne ho udite": feno-
       meni di composizione appaiata nel Salterio Masoretico. *DBovati, Pie-
       tro*: Studia 47: Città del Vaticano 2002, Urbaniana University Press
       554 pp. €30. 88-401-1047-X. Diss. Pont. Ist. Biblico 2000; Bibl.
       425-516. ᴿStPat 49 (2002) 248-249 (*Lorenzin,Tiziano*); CivCatt 153/
       3 (2002) 442-443 (*Segalla, G.*).

3545   **Schnocks, Johannes** Vergänglichkeit und Gottesherrschaft: Studien
       zu Psalm 90 und dem vierten Psalmenbuch. *DFabry, Heinz-Josef*:
       BBB 140: B 2002, Philo 322 pp. 3-8257-0321-5. Diss. Bonn; Bibl.
       293-315.

3546   **Starbuck, Scott R.A.** Court oracles in the Psalms: the so-called royal
       psalms in their ancient Near Eastern context. SBL.DS 172: 1999 ⇒
       15,3039...17,3220. ᴿZAR 8 (2002) 405-407 (*Arneth, Martin*).

3547   **Sticher, Claudia** Die Rettung der Guten durch Gott und die Selbst-
       zerstörung der Bösen: ein theologisches Denkmuster im Psalter.
       DSchwienhorst-Schönberger, L.: BBB 137: B 2002, Philo 379 pp.
       €56. 3-8257-0289-8. Diss. Passau [Bibl. 345-379].

3548   *Thompson, Thomas L.* Kingship and the wrath of God: or teaching
       humility. RB 109 (2002) 161-196 [Ps 2; 89].

3549   *Van Rooy, H.F.* Towards a critical edition of the headings of the
       psalms in the different Syriac traditions;

3550   *Vegas Montaner, Luis* Towards a computer-assisted classification of
       discourse types in the Psalms. Bible and computer. 2002 ⇒548. 545-
       554/189-208.

3551   **Vesco, Jean-Luc** Psaumes: cris d'hommes et voix de Dieu. Marseille
       2002, La Thune 191 pp. €19. 2-913847-15-3 [RB 110,317].

3552   *Warren, Andy* Modality, reference and speech acts in the psalms.
       TynB 53 (2002) 149-152.

3553   *Weber, Beat* Akrostichische Muster in den Asaph-Psalmen. BN 113
       (2002) 79-93 [Ps 50; 73-83].

3554   *Wiesmüller, Wolfgang* Psalm-Gedichte: Aspekte eines Dialogs zwi-
       schen zwei Gattungen. Religion—Literatur—Künste II. Im Kontext
       14: 2002 ⇒530. 91-106.

3555   *Wilson, Gerald H.* Psalms and psalter: paradigm for biblical theol-
       ogy. Biblical theology. 2002 ⇒558. 100-110.

3556 *Zenger, Erich* "Ich liebe den Ort, da deine Herrlichkeit wohnt" (Ps 26,8): tempeltheologische Semiotisierung des Alltags im Psalter. Gottesstadt. QD 191: 2002 ⇒567. 180-206.w

E6.6 *Psalmi: oratio, liturgia*—Psalms as prayer

3557 **Aparicio, Ángel; García Paredes, José** Los salmos, oración de la comunidad. M [5]2002, Claretianas 516 pp.

3558 **Beauchamp, Paul** Salmer—nat og dag. [T]*Christiansen, Erik*: 1999 ⇒ 16,3190. [R]SEÅ 67 (2002) 164-165 (*Eriksson, LarsOlov*);

3559 Salmi notte e giorno. [T]*Natalini, Giampaolo*: Orizzonti biblici: Assisi [2]2002 <1983>, Cittadella (4) 282 pp. €16.50. 88-308-0336-7.

3560 *Black, Jonathan* Psalm uses in Carolingian prayerbooks: ALCUIN and the preface to *De psalmorum usu*. MS 64 (2002) 1-60.

3561 *Brenninckmeijer, Zuster Imelda* Psallite sapienter!: spiritualiteit van het psalmgebed in de getijden. ITBT 10/1 (2002) 11-14.

3562 **Brueggemann, Walter** Spirituality of the Psalms. Facets: Ph 2002, Fortress xvi; 76 pp. $6. 0-8006-3450-0. Bibl. 75-76.

3563 *Büttner, F.O.* Mit Bildern beten: der Psalter war im Mittelalter ein Buch mit Bildern und ein Bilderbuch von einzigartiger Vielfalt. Aviso 3 (2001) 38-51 [RBen 114,199—P.-M. Bogaert].

3564 *Coetzee, Johan H.* Politeness strategies in the so-called 'enemy psalms': an inquiry into Israelite prayer rhetoric. Rhetorical criticism. JSNT.S 195: 2002 ⇒369. 209-236.

3565 **Colón, M. Juanita** The Manhattan Psalter: the *lectio divina* of Sister Juanita Colón. ColMn 2002, Liturgical 223 pp. $16. 0-8146-2771-4.

3566 *Endres, John C.* Praising God the creator: praying with Psalms during the *Spiritual exercises* of IGNATIUS. ExAu 18 (2002) 93-115. Resp. C.C. *Mariottini* 116-119;

3567 Psalms and spirituality in the 21st century. Interp. 56 (2002) 143-154.

3568 **Erbele-Küster, Dorothea** Lesen als Akt des Betens: eine Rezeptionsästhetik der Psalmen. WMANT 87: 2001 ⇒17,3239. [R]BZ 46 (2002) 109-111 (*Zenger, Erich*).

3569 *Fidanzio, Marcello* I salmi per pregare: la proposta del cardinale Carlo Maria MARTINI. Ambrosius 78/3 (2002) 245-251.

3570 **Gariepy, Henry** Treasures from the Psalms: 100 meditations from the devotional treasury of the ages. GR 2002, Eerdmans 273 pp. $22.

3571 **Gillmayr-Bucher, Susanne** Die Psalmen im Spiegel der Lyrik Thomas Bernhards. [D]*Hubmann, Franz*: SBB 48: Stu 2002, Verl. Kath. Bibelwerk 412 pp. €45.90. 3-460-00481-9. Diss. Linz 2001; Bibl. 396-411.

3572 **Hopkins, Denise Dombkowski** Journey through the Psalms. St. Louis [2]2002, Chalice 176 pp. $27. 0-8272-1714-5.

3573 *Kizhakkeyil, S.* The Psalms: the prayerbook of the bible. JJSS 2 (2002) 81-96.

3574 **Lämmlin, Georg** Die Lust am Wort und der Widerstand der Schrift: homiletische Re-Lektüre des Psalters. Heidelberger Studien zur Praktischen Theologie 4: Müns 2002, Lit 437 pp. 3-8258-5982-7. Diss.-Habil. Heidelberg [ETR 79,117s—Fritz Lienhard].

3575 **Limburg, James** Psalms for sojourners. Mp 2002, Fortress 128 pp. $9 [BiTod 40,195—Bergant, Dianne].

3576 [E]**Marin, Marcello**, *al.*, I salmi nell'esegesi patristica. La bibbia nelle comunità antiche. 2002 ⇒286. 87-93.

3577 *Marshall, Molly T.* Plowing the soil of the heart: the psalter and spirituality. ABQ 21 (2002) 499-509.

3578 **Martin, Jean-Marie** Psaumes d'Israël et harmonies chrétiennes: prier en église dans le Christ. 2001 ⇒17,3250. [R]EeV 56 (2002) 29-30 (*Cyrille, Sr.*).

3579 **Martini, Carlo Maria** Il desiderio di Dio: pregare i salmi. [E]*Fidanzio, Marcello*: Mi 2002, Centro Ambrosiano 205 pp. 88-8025-316-6.

3580 *Marx, Tsvi* Emoties in de Tehilim: psalmen gelezen vanuit de rabbijnse traditie. ITBT 10/2-3 (2002) 26-27, 22-24.

3581 **Muñoz Iglesias, Salvador** La espiritualidad de los salmos. M 2002, Espiritualidad 280 pp [REsp 61,654].

3582 *Murphy, Roland E.* Reading/reciting the psalms: some reflections. RfR 61 (2002) 631-639.

3583 *Nieścior, O.* Leon Psalmy w procesie wewnetrznej ewangelizacji chrześcijanina: metoda *antyrretyczna* EWAGRIUSZA z Pontu [The Psalms and the process of internal evangelization of a christian...Evagrius of Pontus]. Verbum Vitae 2 (2002) 243-251 Zsfg. 251. **P.**

3584 *Oeming, Manfred* An der Quelle des Gebets: neuere Untersuchungen zu den Psalmen. ThLZ 127 (2002) 367-384 [Ps 31; 102].

3585 **Paulsell, William O.** Let my prayer rise to God: a spirituality for praying the psalms. St. Louis 2002, Chalice v; 113 pp. $17. 0-8272-2133-9 [ThD 50,179—Heiser, W. Charles].

3586 **Rainoldi, Felice** Il miele dalla pietra (Sal 80,17): guida liturgico-pastorale al canto dei salmi. Cantate et psallite 3: R 2002, C.L.V. 305 pp. 88-7367-009-1.

3587 *Ramos, Felipe F.* La oración en los salmos (I), NatGrac 49 (2002) 403-449.

3588 *Rizzi, Basilio* Salmodia e preghiera. Ambrosius 78/4 (2002) 513-529.

3589 *Rossi de Gasperis, Francesco; Carfagna, Antonella* I Salmi: preghiera del Messia, di Israele suo popolo e della sua chiesa. Prendi il libro. Bibbia e spiritualità 18: 2002 ⇒372. 233-237.

3590 *Scarpa, Marco* Una comunità consegna ai suoi giovani la preghiera dei salmi. Ambrosius 78/4 (2002) 531-544.

3591 *Schuman, Nick* Het gebedenboek van Jezus: vroegchristelijke messianisering van de psalmen. ITBT 10/1 (2002) 4-6.

3592 **Stier, Fridolin** Mit Psalmen beten. [E]*Beck, Eleonore*: Stu 2001, Katholisches Bibelwerk 102 pp. €16.50 [StZ 220,502—A. Batlogg].

3593 **Stuhlmueller, Carroll** The spirituality of the Psalms. [E]*Dempsey, Carol J.; Lenchak, Timothy A.*: ColMn 2002, Liturgical viii; 208 pp. $20. 0-8146-2599-1. Foreword by *Donald Senior.* [R]HPR 103/1 (2002) 78-79 (*Miller, Michael J.*).

3594 *Vos, C.J.A.; Olivier, G.C.* Die Psalms in die liturgie met verwysing na Psalm 8 as liedteks. HTS 58 (2002) 1431-1446 [OTA 26,478].

3595 *Weber, Beat* Die Psalmen als Wort zu Gott und als Wort von Gott: über den Sondercharakter des Psalmenbuchs innerhalb der Heiligen Schrift. JETh 16 (2002) 7-11.

3596 **Weeda, Robert** Le psautier de CALVIN: l'histoire d'un livre populaire au XVIe siècle (1551-1598). Turnhout 2002, Brepols 229 pp. €40. 2-503-51343-3.

3597 *Wit, Hans de* Van de bron naar de zee: Psalmen gelezen in Latijns-Amerika en Afrika. ITBT 10/1 (2002) 18-20.

3598 *Wuellner, Flora S.* The book of Psalms and our spiritual health. ᶠTHOMA, C.: JudChr 20 (2002) 329-335.

3599 *Zenger, Erich* "Du thronst auf den Psalmen Israels" (Ps 22,4): von der Unverzichtbarkeit der jüdischen Psalmen im christlichen Wortgottesdienst. Wie das Wort Gottes feiern?. QD 194: 2002 ⇒417. 16-40.

E6.7 *Psalmi: versiculi*—Psalms by number and verse

3600 *Loretz, Oswald* Psalm 1: poetologische und theologische *Vor*urteile in der Psalmenauslegung. Psalmstudien. 2002 ⇒201. 11-29.

3601 *Cole, Robert* An integrated reading of Psalm 1 and 2. JSOT 98 (2002) 75-88.

3602 *Loretz, Oswald* Psalm 2. Psalmstudien. 2002 ⇒201. 31-54;

3603 Psalm 3: ein historisiertes Klagelied eines Einzelnen mit Belagerungsmotivik. Psalmstudien. 2002 <2000> ⇒201. 55-73;

3604 Psalm 6: Klagelied eines Einzelnen: Totenklage im Keret-Epos und Weinen in Ps 6,7b-8 und Ps 55,4: zu ugaritisch-hebräisch *mṭt/mṭh, ʿq/*cj. *ʿqh und ʿtq/ʿtq. Psalmstudien. 2002 ⇒201. 75-102.

3605 *Auffret, Pierre* Qu'est-ce que l'homme, que tu t'en souviennes?: étude structurelle du Psaume 8. ScEs 54 (2002) 25-35.

3606 *Barlow, Michel* Le psaume 8: hymne à la gloire de Dieu et à la grandeur de l'homme. Unité chrétienne 146 (2002) 11-14.

3607 *De Simone, Giuseppe* Il commento di CASSIODORO al Salmo 8. ᶠTUDDA, F. 2002 ⇒123. 117-132.

3608 *Theißen, Gerd* Von der Schwierigkeit, den Schöpfer am Grab zu loben (Psalm 8). Erlösungsbilder. 2002 ⇒1460. 47-50.

3609 *Thomson, Thomas L.* From the mouth of the babes, strength: Psalm 8 and the book of Isaiah. SJOT 16 (2002) 226-245 [Isa 49,15; Jer 31,15-22; Mt 21,9].

3610 *Loretz, Oswald* Psalm 11: Gottes Thron in Tempel und Himmel: von der altorientalischen zur biblischen Tempeltheologie <1994>;

3611 Psalm 13: der altorientalische rechtliche Hintergrund der biblischen 'Klage des Einzelnen': 'Fortschrittsglaube' in der kanonischen Auslegung des Psalters. Psalmstudien. 2002 ⇒201. 103-130/131-170.

3612 *Auffret, P.* 'Mon seigneur c'est toi': étude structurelle du Psaume 16. OTEs 15 (2002) 310-319.

3613 *Häusl, Maria* Ps 17—Bittgebet einer kinderlosen Frau?. ᶠSTEIN-GRIMSSON, S.: ATSAT 72: 2002 ⇒117. 205-222.

3614 *Kruger, Peter* "Die hemel vertel die eer van God": natuur, skriftuur en die bidder in Psalm 19. VeE 23 (2002) 111-124.

3615 *Meinhold, Arndt* Psalm 19 und der Gegenstand der Theologie des Alten Testaments. Zur weisheitlichen Sicht. 2002 ⇒209. 49-60 [BuBB 37,113].

3616 **Avril, Anne-Catherine,** *al.*, Mon Dieu, pourquoi m'as-tu abandonné?. Psaume 22. CEv.S 121: 2002. 3-177 pp.

3617 *Hartmut, Günther* The hidden God in the passion: psalm 22 in the exposition of LUTHER. ᵀ*Krause, Sibylle G.*: Luther Digest 10 (2002) 25-29 <LuThK 23 (1999) 113-125.

3618 *Vall, Gregory* Psalm 22: Vox Christi or Israelite temple liturgy?. Thom. 66 (2002) 175-200.

3619 *Roberts, J.J.M.* A new root for an old crux, Psalm 22:17c. The bible and the ANE. 2002 <1973> ⇒230. 257-261.

3620 *Barbiero, Gianni* Die Eucharistie der '*anawîm*: Ps 22,23-32. Studien. SBAB 34: 2002 ⇒139. 168-184.
3621 *Oñoro, Fidel* Comentario al salmo 23. Revista católica 102 (2002) 7-11.
3622 *Ruiz, Delio* Estética y poesía de la palabra: Salmo 23 (22). RevBib 64 (2002) 225-232.
3623 **Schuman, Niek** Pastorale: Psalm 23 in bijbel en liturgie verwoord en uitgebeeld. Zoetermeer 2002, Meinema 204 pp. €18.50. 90-211-375-1-8 [Streven 70,856s—Beentjes, Panc].
3624 *Siertsema, Bettine* 'Psalm van kindsbeen af': Psalm 23 in moderne poëzie. ITBT 10/1 (2002) 7-10.
3625 *Theuer, Gabriele* Gott sorgt für uns: Psalm 23: Juli—Ferien I. zwölfmal bibel. 2002 ⇒1087. 72-81.
3626 *Vos, Cas* De beeldende taal van psalm 23. ITBT 10/2 (2002) 12-14.
3627 *Auffret, Pierre* "Mais YHWH m'accueillera": nouvelle étude structurelle du Psaume 27. EstB 60 (2002) 479-492.
3628 *Oñoro, Fidel* Salmo 27: Yahvé, confianza del peregrino. Revista Católica 102 (2002) 183-191.
3629 **Vivaldelli, Gregorio** 'Il Signore è mia luce e mia salvezza': il salmo 27 e il suo contributo per una teologia biblica della fiducia in Dio. ᴰ*Odasso, G.*: 2002 Diss. Lateranum [RTL 34,594].
3630 *Auffret, Pierre* Yoix de YHWH dans le splendeur!: étude structurelle de psaume 29. BN 112 (2002) 5-11.
3631 *Oñoro, Fidel* Salmo 29: 'Voz de Yahvé'. Revista Católica 102 (2002) 95-99.
3632 *La'da, Csaba; Papathomas, Amphilochios* Ein neues Papyrusamulett mit dem Septuaginta-Psalm 30,3d-4a. Aeg. 81 (2001) 37-46.
3633 *Auffret, Pierre* Que se rassure votre coeur!: étude structurelle du Psaume 31. StEeL 19 (2002) 59-76.
3634 *Witte, Markus* Das neue Lied—Beobachtungen zum Zeitverständnis von Psalm 33. ZAW 114 (2002) 522-541.
3635 *Hurowitz, Victor Avigdor* Additional elements of alphabetical thinking in Psalm xxxiv. VT 52 (2002) 326-333.
3636 *Roberts, J.J.M.* The young lions of Psalm 34:11. The bible and the ANE. 2002 <1973> ⇒230. 262-265.
3637 *Theißen, Gerd* Religionskritik und Gottesbild: das Lob Gottes in den Psalmen als Argument im Streit um Gott (Ps 36,6-10). Erlösungsbilder. 2002 ⇒1460. 51-60.
3638 *Vos, C.J.A.* A hermeneutical-homiletic reading of Psalm 37 with reference to H.J.C. Pieterse's homiletics. VeE 23 (2002) 575-585.
3639 *Siqueira, Tércio M.* A saudade de Jerusalém (Sl 42-43);
3640 *Nakanose, Shigeyuki* Nosso ventre está grudado no chão! (Sl 44). Estudos bíblicos 76 (2002) 11-20/21-32.
3641 **Grünbeck, Elisabeth** Christologische Schriftargumentation und Bildersprache: zum Konflict zwischen Metapherninterpretation und dogmatischen Schriftbeweistraditionen in der patristischen Auslegung des 44. (45.) Psalms. SVigChr 26: 1994 ⇒10,3013... 14,2833. ᴿThQ 182 (2002) 191-194 (*Vogt, Hermann J.*).
3642 *Lobato Casado, Abelardo* El misterio de Cristo y de la iglesia en el comentario de Santo TOMÁS al salmo, 44 (45);
3643 ᵀ*Lobato Casado, Abelardo* Me brota del corazón un poema bello: comentario al salmo 44 (45) de Santo TOMÁS de Aquino. Communio 35/1 (2002) 5-34/35-61.

3644 *Silva, Valmor da* Rei pela causa da verdade, da pobreza e da justiça (Sl 45). Estudos bíblicos 76 (2002) 33-43.

3645 *Siqueira, Tercio M.* Jerusalém vista pelos coraítas (Sl 46). Estudos bíblicos 76 (2002) 44-51.

3646 *Roberts, J.J.M.* The religio-political setting of Psalm 47. The bible and the ANE. 2002 <1976> ⇒230. 266-273.

3647 *Zabatiero, Júlio P.* Um reinado universal antiimperialista (Sl 47);

3648 *Garmus, Ludovico* Meditando em tua misericórdia no meio do teu templo (Sl 48). Estudos bíblicos 76 (2002) 52-57/58-68.

3649 *Veras, Lilia L.* Elohim resgatará minha alma do xeol (Sl 49). Estudos bíblicos 76 (2002) 69-78.

3650 *Spero, Shubert* Was Psalm 50 misplaced?. JBQ 30 (2002) 26-31.

3651 *Niclós, Josep Vicent* El comentari al salm 51 i la litúrgia del perdó: RASHI i la invitació a la penitència. Perdó i reconciliació. 2002 ⇒ 591. 233-244.

3652 *Oñoro, Fidel* Salmo 51. Revista Católica 102 (2002) 281-287.

3653 *Godoy Fernández, Cristina* Una inscripció musiva amb el salm LIII precedent de Thelepte: un petit testimoni de la liturgía africana a l'antiguitat. Misel.lània Litúrgica Catalana, 10: Barc 2001, Institut d'Estudis Catalans. 119-125 [RBen 114,193—P.-M. Bogaert].

3654 *Auffret, Pierre* Certes il y a un Dieu jugeant sur la terre!: étude structurelle du Psaume 58. JANES 29 (2002) 1-15.

3655 *De Feo, Francesco* Desiderio di giustizia nell'architettura poetica del salmo 58. Anton. 77 (2002) 649-681.

3656 *Loretz, Oswald* Der juridische Begriff *niḫlatum/nḥlt/naḥᵃlāh* 'Erbbesitz' als amurritisch-kanaanäischer Hintergrund von Psalm 58. UF 34 (2002) 453-479.

3657 *Botha, P.J.* The textual strategy and social background of Psalm 64 as keys to its interpretation. JSem 11/1 (2002) 64-82. Errata rectified on pp. 282-284.

3658 *Loretz, Oswald* Der ugaritisch-hebräische Parallelismus *rkb ʿrpt ‖ rkb bʿrbwt* in Psalm 68,5. UF 34 (2002) 521-526.

3659 *Strawn, Brent A.* *wĕnilʾā(h)*, 'O Victorious One,' in Ps 68,10. UF 34 (2002) 785-798.

3660 *Loth, Heinz-Jürgen* Ps. 68,31: "Ethiopia shall soon stretch out her hands unto God": ein Beitrag zur Rezeption und Wirkungsgeschichte des Begriffs Ethiopia im afroamerikanischen Kontext. ᶠHOHEISEL, K.: JAC.E 34: 2002 ⇒59. 398-411.

3661 *Groenewald, Alphonso* Psalm 69:23a-30b and divine retribution—a question of Ma'at?. OTEs 15 (2002) 657-674.

3662 *Arneth, Martin* Psalm 72 in seinen altorientalischen Kontexten. 'Mein Sohn bist du'. SBS 192: 2002 ⇒366. 135-172.

3663 **Arneth, Martin** 'Sonne der Gerechtigkeit': Studien zur Solarisierung der Jahwe-Religion im Lichte von Psalm 72. ZAR.B 1: 2000 ⇒ 16,3276; 17,3319. ᴿBiOr 59 (2002) 122-123 (*Spronk, Klaas*); RivBib 50 (2002) 357-362 (*Lorenzin, Tiziano*); ThLZ 127 (2002) 501-502 (*Hermann, Wolfram*).

3664 *Human, D.J.* An ideal for leadership—Psalm 72: the (wise) king—royal mediation of God's universal reign. VeE 23 (2002) 658-677.

3665 *Janowski, Bernd* Die Frucht der Gerechtigkeit: Psalm 72 und die judäische Königsideologie. 'Mein Sohn bist du'. SBS 192: 2002 ⇒366. 94-134.

3666 *Loretz, Oswald* Der anthologische Psalm 72: messianische Interpretation amurritisch-kanaanäischer Traditionen in nachexilischer Zeit.
Psalmstudien. 2002 ⇒201. 171-213.
3667 *Zenger, Erich* 'Es sollen sich niederwerfen vor ihm alle Könige' (Ps
72,11): redaktionsgeschichtliche Beobachtungen zu Psalm 72 und
zum Programm des messianischen Psalters 2-89. 'Mein Sohn bist du'.
SBS 192: 2002 ⇒366. 66-93.
3668 *Duthie, Alan S.* A note on Ernst Wendland's paper on Psalm 73 in
BTT January 1999. BiTr 53 (2002) 153-155.
3669 *Nordin, John P.* 'There is nothing on earth that I desire': a commentary on Psalm 73. CThMi 29 (2002) 258-264.
3670 **Cole, Robert L.** The shape and message of book III:(Psalms 73-89).
JSOT.S 307: 2000 ⇒16,3282; 17,3320. ᴿRSR 90 (2002) 234-236
(Abadie, Philippe).
3671 *Witte, Markus* Auf dem Weg in ein Leben nach dem Tod: Beobachtungen zur Traditions- und Redaktionsgeschichte von Psalm 73,24-
26. ThZ 58 (2002) 15-30.
3672 *Cordes, Ariane; Hansberger, Therese; Zenger, Erich* Die Verwü-
stung des Tempels—Krise der Religion?: Beobachtungen zum Volks-
klagepsalm 74 und seiner Rezeption in der Septuaginta und im Midrasch Tehillim. Zerstörungen. WUNT 147: 2002 ⇒559. 61-91.
3673 *Roberts, J.J.M.* Of signs, prophets, and time limits: a note on Psalm
74:9. The bible and the ANE. 2002 <1977> ⇒230. 274-281.
3674 *Botha, Phil J.* 'The honour of the righteous will be restored': Psalm
75 in its social context. OTEs 15 (2002) 320-334.
3675 *Kselman, John S.* Janus parallelism in Psalm 75:2. JBL 121 (2002)
531-532 [Acts 2].
3676 **Burger, Matthias** Psalm 76: Zionslied und Asafpsalm. ᴰ*Seybold, K.*:
2002, 200 pp. Diss. Basel [RTL 34,590].
3677 *Franz, Matthias* Wer die Wunder vergisst, wird auch die Gebote
missachten: das Rätsel des Psalms 78. ThBeitr 33 (2002) 155-163.
3678 *Bazak, Jacob* The structure and contents of Ps 80. BetM 172 (2002)
69-76. Sum. 91. **H.**
3679 *Loretz, Oswald* Psalm 81: Neujahrs- und Laubhüttenfest mit Exodus.
Psalmstudien. 2002 <1999> ⇒201. 215-250;
3680   Psalm 82: Gott als Richter über Götter und Engelsfürsten: der
Rechtsfall der Götterversammlung vor Jahwe. Psalmstudien. 2002 ⇒
201. 251-283.
3681 **Vorndran, Jürgen** "Alle Völker werden kommen": Studien zu
Psalm 86. BBB 133: B 2002, Philo 292 pp. 3-8257-0263-4. Bibl.
278-292.
3682 *Loretz, Oswald* Psalm 88: die Psalmenforschung H. GUNKELs und M.
DAHOODs im Licht der Ugarit-Texte. Psalmstudien. 2002 ⇒201.
285-309.
3683 *Ruiz, Eleuterio R.* El salmo 88 y el enigma del sufrimiento humano.
RevBib 61 (1999) 209-247.
3684 *Hossfeld, Frank-Lothar* Ps 89 und das vierte Psalmenbuch (Ps 90-
106). 'Mein Sohn bist du'. SBS 192: 2002 ⇒366. 173-183.
3685 *Steymans, Hans Ulrich* 'Deinen Thron habe ich unter den großen
Himmeln festgemacht': die formgeschichtliche Nähe von Ps 89,4-5.
20-38 zu Texten vom neuassyrischen Hof. 'Mein Sohn bist du'. SBS
192: 2002 ⇒366. 184-251.
3686 **Van Ek, G.** Tijd en ruimte, een studie over Psalm 92. Zoetermeer
2002, Meinema 151 pp. €17.34. 90-211-3881-6.

3687 Dziewas, Ralf "Gott wird vergelten": Predigt über Psalm 94,16-23. Zeitschrift für Theologie und Gemeinde 7 (2002) 345-348.

3688 Bazyliński, Stanisław Opiewać Boże panowanie (Ps 96) [Singing God's reign (Ps 96)]. Verbum Vitae 2 (2002) 65-87 Sum. 87. P.

3689 Auffret, Pierre Dans la colonmne de nuée il leur parlait: étude structurelle du psaume 99. BN 114/115 (2002) 5-10.

3690 Villiers, Francois T. de Psalm 100:3 a short note. OTEs 15 (2002) 616-619.

3691 Ebach, Jürgen "Eine Grenze hast du bestimmt, dass sie die nicht überschreiten" (Psalm 104,9). JK 63/2 (2002) 10-14,16-18.

3692 Golovanow, Iouri Historiotwórcza rola Słowa Bożego w Ps 105 [Le rôle créateur de la Parole de Dieu dans l'histoire, dans le Psaume 105]. ᴰTronina, A.: 2002, 229 pp. Diss. Lublin [RTL 34,591]. P.

3693 Meinhold, Arndt Psalm 109 in LUTHERs "Vier tröstliche Psalmen an die Königin zu Ungarn". ᶠSMEND, R. 2002 ⇒113. 226-241.

3694 Leene, Henk Psalm 113 als intonatie van het Hallel. ITBT 10/1 (2002) 15-17.

3695 ᴱDoignon, Jean HILARIUS Pictaviensis: Tractatus super Psalmos: in Psalmum CXVIII. CChr.SL 61 A: Turnhout 2002, Brepols xvi; 227 pp. 2-503-00613-2. Iuvamen praestante R. Demeulenaere.

3696 Mark, Martin Meine Stärke und mein Schutz ist der Herr: poetologisch-theologische Studie zu Psalm 118. FzB 92: 1999 ⇒15,3160; 17,3351. ᴿBZ 46 (2002) 315-316 (Zenger, Erich).

3697 Zenger, Erich Das schöne Confitemini: Perspektiven christlicher Psalmenhermeneutik am Beispiel des 118. Psalms. ᶠSMEND, R. 2002 ⇒113. 112-126.

3698 Leonhard, Clemens ISHODAD of Merw's exegesis of the Psalms 119 and 139-147: a study of his interpretation in the light of the Syriac translation of THEODORE of Mopsuestia's commentary. CSCO.Sub 107; CSCO 585: 2001 ⇒17,3355. ᴿPOC 52 (2002) 444-445 (Maier, Thomas).

3699 Auffret, Pierre Là montent les tribus: étude structurelle de la collection des Psaumes des Montées, d'Ex 15,1-18 et des rapports entre eux. BZAW 289: 1999 ⇒15,3165; 17,3356. ᴿTEuph 23 (2002) 175-180 (Gosse, B.) [Ex 15,1-18].

3700 Saint, Jean M. "D'où le secours me viendra t-il?": lecture du psaume 121. FV 101/2 (2002) 73-77.

3701 Van den Berg, Bas Sjalom voor Jeroesjalajim. ITBT 10/7 (2002) 5-7 [Ps 122].

3702 Loretz, Oswald Psalm 127 im Vergleich mit syllabischen und alphabetischen Keilschrifttexten. Psalmstudien. 2002 <1997> ⇒201. 311-329.

3703 Waaijman, Kees Schroom: wederkerigheid in Psalm 128. ITBT 10/3 (2002) 13-15.

3704 Botha, P.J. A social-scientific reading of Psalm 129. HTS 58 (2002) 1401-1414 [OTA 26,483].

3705 Prinsloo, Gert T.M. Psalm 130: poetic patterns and social significance. OTEs 15 (2002) 453-469.

3706 Booij, Thijs Psalm 133: "Behold, how good and how pleasant". Bib. 83 (2002) 258-267.

3707 Wirth, Morand O quam bonum et quam jucundum... lettura salesiana del salmo 133. PalCl 2 (2002) 311-326.

3708 Scoralick, Ruth Hallelujah für einen gewalttätigen Gott?: zur Theologie von Psalm 135 und 136. BZ 46 (2002) 253-272.

3709   *Loretz, Oswald* Psalm 137: ein Gespräch mit B. DUHM und H. GUN-
KEL über textologische Vorurteile. Psalmstudien. 2002 <1994> ⇒
201. 331-350.
3710   *Irsigler, Hubert* Psalm 139 als Gebetsprozess. ᶠSTEINGRIMSSON, S.:
ATSAT 72: 2002 ⇒117. 223-264.
3711   *Ortkemper, Franz-Josef* "Du siehst in mein Herz": Psalm 139: Febru-
ar—Fasching. zwölfmal bibel. 2002 ⇒1087. 18-25.
3712   *Lenchak, Timothy A.* Puzzling passages: Ps 139,21-22. BiTod 40
(2002) 320-321.
3713   *Maier, Johann* Die Feinde Gottes: auslegungsgeschichtliche Beobachtungen zu Ps. 139,21f. ᶠHOHEISEL, K.: JAC.E 34: 2002 ⇒59.
33-47.
3714   *Nachtergael, Georges* Un verset du *Psaume* 140 sur un encensoir du
Musée Copte du Caire. ZPE 141 (2002) 148.
3715   *Loretz, Oswald* Psalm 149: H. GUNKELs Historismus—'kanonische'
Auslegung des Psalters. Psalmstudien. 2002 <cf. 1993> ⇒201. 351-
380.
3716   *Auffret, Pierre* Par le tambour et la danse: étude structurelle du
Psaume 150. ETR 77 (2002) 257-261.

3717   *Segal, Michael* The literary development of Psalm 151: a new look at
the Septuagint version. Textus 21 (2002) 139-158.

E7.1 **Job,** *textus, commentarii*

3718   ᴱ**Marconi, Gilberto; Termini, Cristina** I volti di Giobbe: percorsi
interdisciplinari. Biblica: Bo 2002, Dehoniane 328 pp. €22.50. 88-
10-22117-6.

3719   **Alonso Schökel, Luis; Sicre Diaz, José-Luis** Job: comentario teológico y literario. M ²2002, Cristiandad 808 pp. [EstAg 38,157—
Mielgo, C.].
3720   *Bartoli, Marco* L'expositio super Iob ad litteram di TOMMASO
d'Aquino. I volti di Giobbe. 2002 ⇒3718. 147-160.
3721   *Bartolomei Romagnoli, Alessandra* GREGORIO Magno davanti a
Giobbe: fondamenti di un'antropologia medioevale;
3722   *Bianco, Maria Grazia* Interpretazioni di Giobbe nella patristica delle
origini. I volti di Giobbe. 2002 ⇒3718. 127-145/101-125.
3723   *Doyle, B.* Colloquium on the book of Job. EThL 78 (2002) 299-300.
Amsterdam, 18-19 April 2002.
3724   **Gradl, Felix** Das Buch Ijob. Neuer Stuttgarter Kommentar. AT 12:
Stu 2001, Kathol. Bibelwerk 366 pp. €30.90. 3-460-07121-4 [BiKi
59,103—Michael Hartmann].
3725   **Jung, Carl Gustav** Answer to Job. ᵀ*Hull, R.F.C.*: Routledge classics: L 2002, Routledge xvi; 153 pp. 0-415-28996-3.
3726   **Pahk, Johan Yeong-Sik** The book of Job. Wisdom Literature 5:
Seoul 2002, St Pauls 343 pp. 89-8015-457-7. **K.**
3727   **Ravasi, Gianfranco** Il libro di Giobbe. Conversazioni bibliche: Bo
2002, EDB 92 pp. 88-10-70981-0.
3728   ᴱ**Röll, Walter** Die jiddischen Glossen des 14.-16. Jahrhunderts zum
Buch 'Hiob' in Handschriftenabdruck und Transkription, 1: Einleitung und Register, 2: Edition. Texte und Textgeschichte 52: Tü
2002, Niemeyer viii; 381 + 835 pp. €256. 3-484-36052-6.

3729 **Sitaramayya, K.B.** The marvel and the mystery of pain: a new interpretation of the book of Job. 2001 ⇒17,3382. ᴿVJTR 66 (2002) 468-470 (*Raj, M.I.*).

3730 ᴱ**Terra, João Evangelista Martins** Estudos sobre o livro de Jó. RCB 25/103-104 (2002) 3-161.

3731 *Terra, João Evangelista Martins* Introdução ao livro de Jó. RCB 25/103-104 (2002) 9-14;

3732 Jó. RCB 25/103-104 (2002) 15-25.

3733 **Vattioni, Francesco** Per il testo di Giobbe. AION.S 89: 1996 ⇒12, 2929. ᴿEstB 60 (2002) 136-138 (*Urbán, Á.*).

3734 **Vogels, Walter** Giobbe: l'uomo che ha parlato bene di Dio. 2001 ⇒ 17,3385. ᴿAlpha Omega 5 (2002) 370-373 (*Izquierdo, Antonio*).

E7.2 *Job: themata*, **Topics**... *Versiculi*, **Verse numbers**

3735 *Angelotto, José Roberto* A mensagem do livro de Jó. RCB 25/103-104 (2002) 87-100.

3736 *Balentine, Samuel E.* Job as priest to the priests. ExAu 18 (2002) 29-52. Resp. *D.R. Magary* 53-56;

3737 Job's "struggle for the last truth about God";

3738 Have you considered my servant Job?. RExp 99 (2002) 579-580/495-501;

3739 "My servant Job shall pray for you". ThTo 58 (2002) 502-518.

3740 **Berrigan, Daniel** Job: and death no dominion. 2000 ⇒16,3348; 17, 3389. ᴿAThR 84 (2002) 147-148 (*Sharp, Carolyn J.*).

3741 *Bombazar, Dilsomar* Os discursos de Eliú e o diálogo de Iahweh. RCB 25/103-104 (2002) 131-142.

3742 *Caira, Rossana Maria* Il Giobbe di Riccardo Bacchelli. I volti di Giobbe. 2002 ⇒3718. 239-251.

3743 *Carfagna, Antonella* Il libro di Giobbe. Prendi il libro. Bibbia e spiritualità 18: 2002 ⇒372. 181-231.

3744 *Cotta, Gabriella* Giobbe e LUTERO e il problema del male radicale. I volti di Giobbe. 2002 ⇒3718. 161-170.

3745 *Crenshaw, James L.* Some reflections on the book of Job;

3746 *Edwards, Cliff* Greatest of all the people in the East: venturing east of Uz. RExp 99 (2002) 589-595/529-540.

3747 *Fava Guzzetta, Lia* La figura di Giobbe in alcune pagine di letteratura moderna. I volti di Giobbe. 2002 ⇒3718. 229-238.

3748 *Fàbrega, Valentí* El libro de Job: planteamientos y discrepancias. ActBib 38/1 (2002) 5-15.

3749 *Feliciano, Deibes* Un amigo no livro de Jó: o autor;

3750 *Flores, Alexis Guanipa* Jó e o mistério da providência. RCB 25/103-104 (2002) 143-149/81-85.

3751 *Frades, Eduardo, al.*, Tema 2: perché il dolore, Dio mio?: libro di Giobbe. Salmi e letteratura sapienziale. 2002 ⇒264. 87-121.

3752 **Fyall, Robert S.** Now my eyes have seen you: images of creation and evil in the book of Job. New Studies in Biblical Theology 12: Leicester 2002, Apollos 208 pp. £11. 0-85111-498-9. Bibl. 195-201.

3753 *Gaiffi, Francesco* Giobbe nella teologia contemporanea;

3754 *Gallo, Marco* Giobbe "rursus resurrecturus cum quibus dominus resurgit": note sull'iconografia della Discesa di Cristo agl'inferi e sulla figura di Giobbe in area veneta tra la fine del XV e l'inizio del XVI secolo;

3755 *Gallottini, Angela* Ma Giobbe era solo paziente?: l'iconografia paleo-cristiana di Giobbe. I volti di Giobbe. 2002 ⇒3718. 287-309/183-216/171-182.

3756 *Geller, Stephen A.* Nature's answer: the meaning of the book of Job in its intellectual context. Judaism and ecology. 2002 ⇒528. 109-132.

3757 *Godwin, Gail; Scott, Bar* Turning to Job. RExp 99 (2002) 505-527.

3758 *Gonçalves, Humberto M.* Jó 1-2 e 42,7-17: a pessoa humana manipulada por Deus e satanás ou sujeito da história junto ao Deus da vida?. Estudos bíblicos 74 (2002) 79-87.

3759 *Green, William Scott* Stretching the covenant: Job and Judaism. RExp 99 (2002) 569-577.

3760 **Grimm, Markus** "Dies Leben ist der Tod": Vergänglichkeit in den Reden Ijobs—Entwurf einer Textsemantik. ATSAT 62: 1998 ⇒14, 2945. [R]ZKTh 124 (2002) 123-124 (*Vonach, Andreas*).

3761 *Halpern, Baruch* Assyrian and pre-Socratic astronomies and the location of the book of Job. [F]WEIPPERT, M.: OBO 186: 2002 ⇒133. 255-264.

3762 *Hornik, Heidi J.* The Venetian images by BELLINI and CARPACCIO: Job as intercessor or prophet?. RExp 99 (2002) 541-568.

3763 *Janzen, J.G.* Job's oath. RExp 99 (2002) 597-605.

3764 **Köhlmoos, Melanie** Das Auge Gottes: Textstrategie im Hiobbuch. FAT 25: 1999 ⇒15,3210; 16,3362. [R]RBLit 4 (2002) 233-237 (*Pietsch, Michael*).

3765 *Maarschalk, R.; Viviers, H.* Die godsredes in die boek Job: ideologie en eko-teologie. VeE 23 (2002) 125-140.

3766 **MacNiccoll, Patricia Aldrich** Questioning the character of God: a study of subversion in the book of Job. [D]*Towner, W.S.*: 2002, Diss. Virginia, Union [RTL 34,592]..

3767 *Maldaner, Plínio* Deus e o diabo na roça : explicação popular do mal e seu embate teológico no meio: confronto com o livro de Jó. Estudos bíblicos 74 (2002) 65-69.

3768 *Marconi, Gilberto* La nascita della pazienza di Giobbe I [⇒3791]. I volti di Giobbe. 2002 ⇒3718. 69-80.

3769 *Mellado, Pablo Beltrán* Jó e a gratuidade de Deus. RCB 25/103-104 (2002) 101-120.

3770 *Moran, William L.* The Babylonian Job. The most magic word. 2002 ⇒212. 182-200.

3771 *Murphy, Roland E.* The last truth about God. RExp 99 (2002) 581-587.

3772 *Müller, Hans-Peter* Tun—Ergehens—Zusammenhang, Klageerhörung und Theodizee im biblischen Hiobbuch und in seinen babylonischen Parallelen. Wisdom texts. BEThL 159: 2002 ⇒482. 153-171.

3773 *Negri, Antonio* Il lavoro di Giobbe. Le esche 27: R 2002, Manifesto libri 158 pp. 88-7285-307-9. Bibl. 156-158.

3774 **Negri, Antonio** Job, la force de l'esclave. [T]*Revel, Judith*: P 2002, Bayard 188 pp. 2-227-47049-6. Bibl. 183-186.

3775 *Newsom, Carol A.* The book of Job as polyphonic text. JSOT 97 (2002) 87-108;

3776 Narrative ethics, character, and the prose tale of Job. Character and scripture. 2002 ⇒283. 121-134.

3777 *Nicole, Émile* Trois lecteurs de Job contemporains. ThEv(VS) 1/1 (2002) 3-14.

3778 *Passaro, Angelo* Domande e risposte sulla giustizia in Giobbe. RStB
      14/1-2 (2002) 119-136.
3779 **Perraymond, Myla** La figura di Giobbe nella cultura paleocristiana
      tra esegesi patristica e manifestazioni iconografiche. SAC: Città del
      Vaticano 2002, Pont. Ist. di Archeologia Cristiana 138 pp. 88-85991-
      31-9.
3780 *Ramos, Darlei* Livro de Jó—uma síntese. RCB 25/103-104 (2002)
      151-161.
3781 *Riede, Peter* 'Ein Spinnenhaus ist sein Vertrauen' (Hi 8,14): Tiere in
      der Bildsprache der Hiobdialoge Teil II: der Frevler und sein Ge-
      schick. Im Spiegel der Tiere. 2002 ⇒229. 133-152;
3782 Ich bin ein Bruder der Schakale' (Hi 30,29): Tiere als Exponenten
      der gegenmenschlichen Welt in der Bildsprache der Hiobdialoge. Im
      Spiegel der Tiere. 2002 ⇒229. 120-132.
3783 *Roberts, J.J.M.* Job and the Israelite religious tradition. The bible and
      the ANE. 2002 <1977> ⇒230. 110-116.
3784 **Rohr, Richard** Hiobs Botschaft: vom Geheimnis des Leidens. Mü
      2000, Claudius 223 pp. €12.70. 3-532-62250-5 [BiKi 59,104s—Mi-
      chael Hartmann].
3785 *Romagnoli, Gian Cesare* La psicologia economica dello Universal
      Bogey. I volti di Giobbe. 2002 ⇒3718. 271-286.
3786 *Salvati, Giuseppe Marco* Giobbe e il parlare di Dio. I volti di Giob-
      be. 2002 ⇒3718. 311-318.
3787 *Santos, José Marcos dos* Atualidade de Jó;
3788 *Santos, Marino de Souza* O livro de Jó e o problema do sofrimento
      humano. RCB 25/103-104 (2002) 51-62/121-129.
3789 *Scaiola, Donatella* Giobbe, piccola murena o cattedrale?;
3790 Creazione e antropologia;
3791 *Scarpa, Anna Maria* La nascita della pazienza di Giobbe II [⇒3768].
      I volti di Giobbe. 2002 ⇒3718. 11-24/45-55/81-99.
3792 *Schwendemann, Wilhelm* God's answer to Job. ᶠSCHOTTROFF, L.:
      2002 ⇒111. 155-162.
3793 *Siniscalchi, Claudio* Samuel BECKETT: Giobbe alle soglie della post-
      modernità. I volti di Giobbe. 2002 ⇒3718. 217-227.
3794 *Stefani, Piero* 'Metto la mano sulla bocca' (Gb 40,4): quando il dolo-
      re diventa innocente?. Il crocifisso. 2002 ⇒620. 113-123.
3795 *Termini, Cristina* Il filo della contesa giuridica nel libro di Giobbe. I
      volti di Giobbe. 2002 ⇒3718. 25-43.
3796 *Terra, João Evangelista Martins* A composição dramática do livro
      de Jó. RCB 25/103-104 (2002) 27-49.
3797 *Van Zyl, Danie C.* Missiological dimensions in the book of Job. IRM
      91 (2002) 24-30.
3798 *Veijola, Timo* Abraham und Hiob: das literarische und theologische
      Verhältnis von Gen 22 und der Hiob-Novelle. ᶠSMEND, R.: 2002 ⇒
      113. 127-144.
          Verdejo Sánchez, M.D. Rasgos de latin hispánico encontrados
      en glosas de Vetus Latina 2002 ⇒2000.
3799 *Verrienti, Virginia Joseph* ROTH: il Giobbe di Zuchnow. I volti di
      Giobbe. 2002 ⇒3718. 253-269.
3800 *Wechsler, Michael G.* Shared reflections of early Jewish exegetical/
      targumic tradition in the peshitta text of Job and the targum from
      Qumran (11QTgJob). Muséon 115/1-2 (2002) 77-128.
3801 *Williams, Peter* From despair to hope. Bromley 2002, Day One 220
      pp. £8. 1903-087-295 [Sermons on Job] [Evangel 21/1,29: Dray, S.].

3802 *Willi-Plein, Ina* Hiobs immer aktuelle Frage. Sprache als Schlüssel. 2002 <1979> ⇒261. 146-158.
3803 *Würmser, Rudolf* Fragen zu Hiob: Aspekte der Theaterarbeit George TABORIs. Religion—Literatur—Künste II. 2002 ⇒530. 81-90.
3804 *Yao, Vicent M'bra* O drama de Jó. RCB 25/103-104 (2002) 63-80.

3805 *Snoek, Hans* Stilte na de ramp: Job 2:13. ITBT 10/2 (2002) 7-9.
3806 *Cho, Eun S.* Job 3 in the creation of God: an exegetical essay from a Korean perspective. AJTh 16/1 (2002) 66-115.
3807 *Forstman Pettys, Valerie* Let there be darkness: continuity and discontinuity in the 'curse' of Job 3. JSOT 98 (2002) 89-104.
3808 *Tsoi, Jonathan T.P.* The vision of Eliphaz (Job 4:12-21)—an irony of human life. ThLi 25 (2002) 155-182.
3809 **Egger-Wenzel, Renate** 'Von der Freiheit Gottes, anders zu sein': die zentrale Rolle der Kapitel 9 und 10 für das Ijobbuch. FzB 83: 1998 ⇒14,2984…17,3421. [R]BiOr 59 (2002) 606-07 (*Holman, Jan*).
3810 *Roberts, J.J.M.* Job's summons to Yahweh: the exploitation of a legal metaphor. The bible and the ANE. 2002 <1974> ⇒230. 117-122 [Job 9,27-35; 23,3-9].
3811 *Remmert, Hans-Joachim* "Ich bin nicht Ijob!" Ijob 10: November—Totengedenken. zwölfmal bibel. 2002 ⇒1087. 120-129.
3812 *Theißen, Gerd* Hiob und Anti-Hiob: über unseren Umgang mit Vergänglichkeit und Leid (Hiob 14,1-15). Erlösungsbilder. 2002 ⇒1460. 39-46.
3813 *Mies, Françoise* Dieu contre toute espérance. Dieu, vingt-six portraits. 2002 ⇒312. 193-202 [Job 14,7-17].
3814 *Kruger, Paul A.* Job 18:11B: a conceptualisation of the emotion of fear?. JNSL 28/2 (2002) 143-149.
3815 **Tremblay, Hervé** Job 19,25-27 dans la Septante et chez les pères grecs: unanimité d'une tradition. EtB 47: P 2002, Gabalda 571 pp. €75. 2-85021-1403. Diss. Collège Dominicain, Ottawa; Bibl. 515-67.
3816 **Tchimboto, Bonifácio** Os privados de Deus: Jb 24 e as tradições bíblicas sobre o pobre. [D]*Rizzi, G.*: R 2002, xiii; 206 pp. Diss. Urbaniana 2002.
3817 *Riede, Peter* Spinnennetz oder Mottengespinst?: zur Auslegung von Hiob 27,18. Im Spiegel der Tiere. 2002 <2001> ⇒229. 107-119.
3818 *Taylor, Barbara B.* On not being God. RExp 99 (2002) 609-613 [Job 38].
3819 *Termini, Cristina* JHWH risponde dalla tempesta (Gb 38-41). I volti di Giobbe. 2002 ⇒3718. 57-67.
3820 *Johnson, Timothy* Implied antecedents in Job xl 2b and Proverbs iii 6a. VT 52 (2002) 278-284.
3821 *Glazov, Gregory Yuri* The significance of the 'hand on the mouth' gesture in Job xl 4. VT 52 (2002) 30-41.
3822 *Mathis, Claudia* 'Sieh doch den Behemot': die zweite Gottesrede Ijob 40,6-41,26. BN 112 (2002) 74-85.
3823 *Reed, Annette Yoshiko* Job as Jobab: the interpretation of Job in LXX Job 42:17b-e. JBL 120 (2001) 31-55.

E7.3 *Canticum Canticorum*, **Song of Songs, Hohelied,** *textus, comm.*

3824 **Bosetti, Elena** Cantico dei Cantici: "Tu che il mio cuore ama". [T]*Pahk, Johan Yeong-Sik*: Seoul 2002, St. Paul 167 pp. 89-8015-474-7. **K.**

3825 **DeSimone, Russell J.** The bride and the bridegroom of the Fathers: an anthology of patristic interpretations of the Song of Songs. SuPa 10: 2000 ⇒16,3405. ᴿRSLR 38 (2002) 540-544 (*Bossina, Luciano*).

3826 **Drijvers, Pius; Renkema, Jan** Hooglied. Baarn 2002, Ten Have 92 pp. €20. 90-806-8837-1 [Streven 70,756—Beentjes, Panc].

3827 **Ghi, Pierino** Il Cantico dei Cantici: una lettura spirituale. Mi 2001, Ancora 137 pp. 88-7610-938-2. Pres. *Aldo Giordano*; nota psicologica *Massimo Schinco*.

3828 *Guglielmetti, Rossana* 'Super Cantica canticorum': note sulla tradizione dei commenti di RUPERTO di Deutz, BERNARDO di Clairvaux, GUGLIELMO di Saint-Thierry, BEDA e ALCUINO. StMed 43 (2002) 277-286.

3829 *Hamblenne, Pierre* APPONIUS: le moment, une patrie. Aug. 41 (2001) 425-464 [RBen 114,202—P.-M. Bogaert] [⇒3838].

3830 **Langeac, Robert de** L'amour fort comme la mort, un commentaire spirituel du Cantique des Cantiques. Vie intérieure: Toulouse 2002, Carmel 247 pp.

3831 **Longman, Tremper** Song of Songs. NIC: 2001 ⇒17,3441. ᴿRTR 61 (2002) 58-59 (*Harman, Allan M.*); RExp 99 (2002) 284-285 (*Biddle, Mark E.*); Faith & Mission 19/1 (2002) 73-76 (*Rooker, Mark*); OTEs 15 (2002) 566-569 (*Branch, R.G.*); RBLit (2002)* (*Davis, Ellen Frances*).

3832 **Lorenzin, Tiziano** Cantico dei Cantici: introduzione e commento. 2001 ⇒17,3442. ᴿRdT 43 (2002) 138-139 (*Grandis, Giancarlo*); CivCatt 153/2 (2002) 619-620 (*Scaiola, D.*).

3833 **Mathieu, Bernard** La poésie amoureuse de l'Égypte ancienne: recherches sur un genre littéraire au Nouvel Empire. Bibliothèque d'étude 115: 1996 ⇒12,3026... 15,3254. ᴿJNES 61 (2002) 309-310 (*Foster, John L.*).

3834 **Murphy, Roland E.; Huwiler, Elizabeth** Proverbs, Ecclesiastes, Song of Songs. NIBC.OT 12: 1999 ⇒15,3284; 17,3443. ᴿRSR 90 (2002) 238-239 (*Abadie, Philippe*).

3835 **Pelletier, Anne-Marie** O Cântico dos Cânticos. ᵀ*Lopes, Joaquim Ferreira*: Cadernos Bíblicos 75: Lisboa 2002, Bíblica 64 pp.

3836 *Perrin, Louis* Lecture du Cantique des Cantiques. SémBib 108 (2002) 3-20.

3837 *Schulz-Flügel, Eva* Canticum Canticorum. BVLI 46 (2002) 23-28.

3838 ᵀᴱ**Vregille, Bernard de; Neyrand, Louis** APPONIUS: commentaire sur le Cantique des Cantiques Tome I-III. SC 420, 421, 430: 1997-1998 ⇒13,3083... 16,3416. ᴿRSLR 38 (2002) 156-159 (*Ruggiero, Fabio*).

E7.4 **Canticum**, *themata, versiculi*

3839 *Abécassis, Armand* Espaces de lecture du Cantique des cantiques en contexte juif. Les nouvelles voies. LeDiv 190: 2002 ⇒583. 185-196.

3840 *Alvarez Valdes, Ariel* ¿Contiene la biblia un libro erótico?. CuesTF 29 (2002) 413-419.

3841 *Autié, Dominique* La patine du monde: un écrivain éveille le texte;

3842 *Auwers, Jean-Marie* Lectures patristiques du Cantique des cantiques. Les nouvelles voies. LeDiv 190: 2002 ⇒583. 219-229/129-157.

3843 *Bastiaensen, Antoon A.R.* Die Anfänge der christlichen Hoheliedauslegung. ᶠGNILKA, C.: JAC.E 33: 2002 ⇒48. 27-38.

3844 *Battaglia, Vincenzo* La Passione di Cristo nei commenti al Cantico dei Cantici, 5: il medioevo latino. LSDC 17/1 (2002) 7-23 Sum. 23.

3845 *Bennett, Stephen J.* Love over gold: the Song of Songs for Aotearoa-New-Zealand. IRM 91 (2002) 31-40.

3846 *Berder, Michel* La lettre retrouvée?: lectures actuelles du Cantique et sens littéral. Les nouvelles voies. LeDiv 190: 2002 ⇒583. 103-128.

3847 *Cabestrero, Teófilo, al.*, Tema 7: l'amore, fuoco divino: Cantico dei cantici. Salmi e letteratura sapienziale. 2002 ⇒264. 255-292.

3848 *Causse, Jean-Daniel* Le geste de la lecture entre signification et signifiance. Les nouvelles voies. LeDiv 190: 2002 ⇒583. 279-294.

3849 **Elliott, Mark W.** The Song of Songs and christology in the early church 381-451. Studies in Antiquity & Christianity 7: 2000 ⇒16, 3430. [R]HeyJ 43 (2002) 506-507 (*Cooper, Adam G.*).

3850 **Ena Tardi, Jean Emmanuel de** Le conflit des interprétations sur le sens du Cantique des Cantiques: essai théorique et pratique d'une herméneutique articulée du sens au texte: sens textuel, sens directionnel et cadre du texte. [D]*Schenker, Adrian*: 2002, Diss. Fribourg [ThRv 99/2, vii]..

3851 [E]**Guglielmetti, Rossana** GILBERTUS Stanfordensis: tractatus super Cantica Canticorum: l'amore di Dio nella voce di un monaco del XII secolo. Per verba 16: F 2002, Galluzzo cxv; 336 pp. €49. 88-8450-037-0. Bibl. cix-cxiv.

3852 **Horine, Steven C.** Interpretive images in the Song of Songs. 2001 ⇒ 17,3454. [R]OTEs 15 (2002) 562-564 (*Viviers, H.*).

3853 **Lacocque, André** Romance she wrote: a hermeneutical essay on Song of Songs. 2000 ⇒16,3437. [R]RCatT 27/1 (2002) 241-242 (*Solà, Teresa*).

3854 *Linafelt, Tod* Biblical love poetry (...and God). JAAR 70 (2002) 323-345.

3855 *Lobrichon, Guy* Les nouvelles voies du Cantique des cantiques dans l'Occident médiéval (IXe-XVe siècle). Les nouvelles voies. LeDiv 190: 2002 ⇒583. 197-216.

3856 *Luzarraga, Jesús* El Cantar de los cantares en el canon bíblico. Gr. 83 (2002) 5-63.

3857 *Meinhold, Arndt* Göttlichkeit der Liebe?: Affinität und Spannung zwischen Theomorphie und Allegorisierung des Hohenliedes im Zusammenhang seiner Kanonisierung. Zur weisheitlichen Sicht. 2002 ⇒209. 87-98 [BuBB 37,134].

    Nielsen, K., *al.*, Ruths Bog...Højsangen 1998 ⇒3086.

3858 *Nieuviarts, Jacques* L'éveil des voix: l'exégèse au rendez-vous de l'histoire. Les nouvelles voies. LeDiv 190: 2002 ⇒583. 13-22.

3859 *Pelletier, Anne-Marie* Le Cantique des cantiques: un texte et ses lectures. Les nouvelles voies. LeDiv 190: 2002 ⇒583. 75-101.

3860 *Puttkammer, Annegret* Preist die Zeit der Liebe: Hoheslied: August —Ferien II. zwölfmal bibel. 2002 ⇒1087. 84-93.

3861 *Rossi de Gasperis, Francesco* Il Cantico dei cantici. Prendi il libro. Bibbia e spiritualità 18: 2002 ⇒372. 31-65.

3862 *Roubaud, Jacques* L'étrangeté du texte. Les nouvelles voies. LeDiv 190: 2002 ⇒583. 231-246.

3863 **Schwab, George M.** The Song of Songs' cautionary message concerning human love. Studies in biblical literature 41: NY 2002, Lang xviii; 221 pp. 0-8204-5566-0.

3864 *Seidl, Theodor* Das Hohelied in der musikalischen Avantgarde: zwei Vertonungen des 'Canticum Canticorum' am Ausgang des 20. Jahrhunderts. [F]STEINGRIMSSON, S.: ATSAT 72: 2002 ⇒117. 279-288.

3865 *Sonnet, Jean-Pierre* Le Cantique: la fabrique poétique. Les nouvelles voies. LeDiv 190: 2002 ⇒583. 159-184.

3866 **Sujecka, Ewa** Umiłowanie ziemi ojczstej w Pieśni nad Pieśniami [L'amour de la terre paternelle dans le Cantique des cantiques]. [D]*Chrostowski, W.*: 2002, 312 pp. Diss. Warsaw [RTL 34,594].

3867 *Viviers, Hendrik* The rhetoricity of the 'body' in the Song of Songs. Rhetorical criticism. JSNT.S 195: 2002 ⇒369. 237-254.

3868 **Walsh, Carey Ellen** Exquisite desire: religion, the erotic, and the Song of Songs. 2000 ⇒16,3449; 17,3467. [R]BiblInterp 10 (2002) 194-196 (*Linafelt, Tod*).

3869 *Wénin, André* Les nouvelles lectures synchroniques: une chance pour le texte?. Les nouvelles voies. LeDiv 190: 2002 ⇒583. 247-275.

3870 *Wojciechowska, Kalina* Das Hohelied als lyrisches Werk: gattungstheoretische Anmerkungen. STV 40/2 (2002) 147-165.

3871 *Maher, Michael* Anti-Jewish bias in the patristic interpretation of Cant 1:1. PIBA 25 (2002) 150-162.

3872 *Seidl, Theodor* 'Mein Geliebter gehört mir und ich gehöre ihm': zu den sprachlichen Ausdrucksmitteln der Paarbeziehung in Hld 2,8-17 und 3,1-5. BN 114/115 (2002) 161-172.

3873 *Barbiero, Gianni* Die Liebe der Töchter Jerusalems: Hld 3,10b MT im Kontext von 3,6-11. Studien. SBAB 34: 2002 <1995> ⇒139. 56-65.

3874 *Klopper, Frances* The rhetoric of conflicting metaphors: a fountain desired in the Song of Songs but abhorred in Leviticus. OTEs 15 (2002) 675-686 [Lev 12,6-7; 20,18; Cant 4,12-15];

3875 *Barbiero, Gianni* Die 'Wagen meines edlen Volkes' (Hld 6,12): eine strukturelle Analyse. Studien. SBAB 34: 2002 <1997> ⇒139. 66-79 [Cant 6,12; 6,4-7,11].

3876 *Reich, Ronny* The beauty and the king?: an interpretation of Song of Songs 7:6. Shnaton 13 (2002) 173-174. **H.**

3877 *Barbiero, Gianni* 'Leg mich wie ein Siegel auf dein Herz—fliehe, mein Geliebter': die Spannung in der Liebesbeziehung nach dem Epilog des Hohenliedes. Studien. SBAB 34: 2002 ⇒139. 185-198 [Cant 8,5-14].

E7.5 *Libri sapientiales*—Wisdom literature

3878 *Aldama-Andrade, Abelardo* La sabiduría en el mundo de hoy. Qol 29 (2002) 57-69.

3879 *Bartholomew, Craig G.* A time for war, and a time for peace: Old Testament wisdom, creation and O'Donovan's theological ethics. [F]O'DONOVAN, O.: 2002 ⇒272. 91-112;

3880 A God for life, and not just for Christmas!: the revelation of God in the Old Testament wisdom literature. The trustworthiness of God. 2002 ⇒410. 39-57.

3881 *Beauchamp, Paul* Sagesse et torah: accomplissement et folie. Typologie biblique. LeDiv: 2002 ⇒341. 223-239.

3882 *Bellia, Giuseppe; Passaro, Angelo* La sapienza donata dall'alto. Ho Theológos 20 (2002) 445-452.

3883 **Bergant, Dianne** Israel's wisdom literature: a liberation-critical reading. 1997 ⇒13,3118. [R]HeyJ 43 (2002) 504-506 (*McNamara, Martin*).

3884 *Carfagna, Antonella* La sapienza in Israele. Prendi il libro. Bibbia e spiritualità 18: 2002 ⇒372. 127-162.

3885 **Ceresko, Anthony R.** Introduction to Old Testament wisdom: a spirituality for liberation. 1999 ⇒15,3300; 16,3461. [R]HeyJ 43 (2002) 83-84 (*Corley, Jeremy*).

3886 **Clements, Ronald E.** Wisdom in theology. 1992 ⇒8,3458... 11/2, 1088 [R]ThR 67 (2002) 7-9 (*Kottsieper, Ingo*).

3887 **Clifford, Richard J.** The Wisdom literature. 1998 ⇒14,3062. [R]HeyJ 43 (2002) 502-503 (*McNamara, Martin*).

3888 *Clifford, Richard J.* The God who makes people wise. [F]ACHTEMEIER, P. 2002 ⇒1. 57-74.

3889 **Collins, John Joseph** Jewish wisdom in the Hellenistic age. 1997 ⇒ 13,3129... 17,3478. [R]HebStud 43 (2002) 296-298 (*Chesnutt, Randall D.*).

3890 *Constas, Nicholas* "Vanity of vanities"?: Solomon's trilogy and the patristic subversion of scripture. Shem. JSJ.S 74: 2002 ⇒755. 241-259.

3891 **Conti, Martino** La sapienza personificata negli elogi veterotesta- mentari (Pr 8; Gb 28; Sir 24; Bar 3; Sap 7). SPAA 36: 2001 ⇒17, 3479. [R]CivCatt 153/4 (2002) 312-313 (*Scaiola, D.*).

3892 *Coughenour, Robert A.* The sage and the pastoral counselor. RefR(H) 56/2 (2002) 147-158.

3893 *Dell, Katharine* Wisdom. Biblical world, 1. 2002 ⇒273. 107-128.

3894 *Doran, Robert* Jewish education in the Seleucid period. Second temple studies III. JSOT.S 340: 2002 ⇒296. 116-132. [Sir 6,32-37; 8,8-9; 39,1-5].

3895 **Fischer, James A.** A lighthearted view of wisdom in the bible: how to read the inspired books. Mahwah 2002, Paulist 145 pp. $13 [BiTod 40,257—Bergant, Dianne].

3896 **Fontaine, Carole R.** Smooth words: women, proverbs and per- formance in biblical wisdom. JSOT.S 356: Shf 2002, Sheffield A. xv; 296 pp. £60. 0-8264-6024-0. Bibl. 272-285.

3897 **Gesche, Petra D.** Schulunterricht in Babylonien im ersten Jahrtau- send v. Chr. AOAT 275: 2001 ⇒17,3484. [R]Or. 71 (2002) 462-465 (*Dandamayev, M.A.*).

3898 *Gilbert, Maurice* Les livres sapientiaux de l'Ancien Testament: con- clusion générale. EeV 61 (2002) 16-21.

3899 *Gismondi, Gualberto* Riflessione sapienziale biblica e spiritualità della ricerca scientifica. Convivium Assisiense 4/1 (2002) 13-38.

3900 *Harris, James I.* The king as public servant: towards an ethic of pub- lic leadership based on virtues suggested in the wisdom literature of the Older Testament. JTSA 113 (2002) 61-73.

3901 *Hess, Richard S.* Literacy in Iron Age Israel. Windows. 2002 ⇒500. 82-102.

3902 **Jamieson-Drake, David W.** Scribes and schools in monarchic Ju- dah. JSOT.S 109: 1991 ⇒7,e676... 11/2,c669. [R]ThR 67 (2002) 224-225 (*Kottsieper, Ingo*).

3903 [E]*Leanza, Sandro, al.*, I libri sapienziali nell'esegesi patristica. La bib- bia nelle comunità antiche. 2002 ⇒286. 75-85.

3904 *Loader, James Alfred* Lebensgestaltung als weisheitliche Lebensver- antwortung. OTEs 15 (2002) 715-738.

3905   **Lux, Rüdiger** Die Weisen Israels. 1992 ⇒8,3473; 10,3213. ᴿThR 67
       (2002) 5-7 (*Kottsieper, Ingo*).
3906   **Morgan, Donn F.** The making of sages: biblical wisdom and con-
       temporary culture. Harrisburg, Pennsylvania 2002, Trinity xxv; 182
       pp. $22. 1-56338-328-4. Bibl. 171-173.
3907   **Murphy, Roland E.** The tree of life: an exploration of biblical wis-
       dom literature. GR ³2002, Eerdmans 291 pp. $24 0-8028-3965-7.
3908   *Nel, Philip Johannes* The rhetorics of wisdom's ethics. OTEs 15
       (2002) 435-452.
3909   *Niccacci, Alviero* An overview of the wisdom books and their theol-
       ogy. JJSS 1 (2001) 209-218.
3910   *O'Donovan, Oliver* Response to Craig Bartholomew. ᶠO'DONOVAN,
       O. 2002 ⇒272. 113-115.
3911   **Perdue, Leo G.** Wisdom and creation: the theology of wisdom litera-
       ture. 1994 ⇒10,3224... 12,3085. ᴿThR 67 (2002) 9-12 (*Kottsieper,
       Ingo*).
3912   *Popielewski, Wojciech* Slowo Boże konieczne w drodze do szczęścia
       [The word of God is necessary on the way to happiness]. Verbum Vi-
       tae 2 (2002) 89-106 Rés. 105. P.
3913   *Thomas, Jesse J.* Wisdom literature and higher education. Journal of
       interdisciplinary studies 14 (2002) 117-140.
3914   *Torre, Gonzalo de la* Introduzione ai libri sapienziali. Salmi e lettera-
       tura sapienziale. 2002 ⇒264. 9-44.
3915   *Venter, P.M.* The connection between wisdom literature, apocalypses
       and canon. OTEs 15 (2002) 470-488.
3916   **Weber, Beat** Weisheiten aus der Bibel für ein gelingendes Leben.
       Gü 2002, Quell 160 pp. 3-579-03421-9.

E7.6 Proverbiorum liber, *themata, versiculi*

3917   *Bady, Guillaume; Tchernetskạ, Natalie* Un nouveau témoin direct
       des *Scholies aux Proverbes* d'ÉVRAGE le Pontique (*Cambridge Trin-
       ity College* 0.1.55). RHT 32 (2002) 63-72.
3918   **Boström, Lennart** The God of the sages: the portrayal of God in the
       book of Proverbs. CB.OT 29: 1990 ⇒6,3578... 10,3248. ᴿThR 67
       (2002) 212-213 (*Kottsieper, Ingo*).
3919   *Camarero, Lorenzo, al.*, Tema 1: cammino de vita: l'equità: libro dei
       Proverbi. Salmi e letteratura sapienziale. 2002 ⇒264. 51-83.
3920   *Carfagna, Antonella* Il libro dei Proverbi. Prendi il libro. Bibbia e
       spiritualità 18: 2002 ⇒372. 163-179.
3921   *Ceresko, Anthony R.* The function of 'order' (*ṣedeq*) and 'creation' in
       the book of Proverbs, with some implications for today. Prophets and
       proverbs. 2002 <1995> ⇒154. 23-46.
3922   **Cherix, Pierre** Lexique analytique du parchemin pBodmer VI ver-
       sion copte du livre des Proverbes 2000 ⇒16,3512 ᴿBiOr 59 (2002)
       557-558 (*Poirier, P.-H.*).
3923   *Cook, Johann* Unit delimitation in the book of Proverbs: in the light
       of the Septuagint of Proverbs. Studies in scriptural unit division.
       Pericope 3: 2002 ⇒339. 46-65;
3924   Towards a computerised exegetical commentary on the Septuagint of
       Proverbs. Bible and computer. 2002 ⇒548. 413-425.
3925   *Davies, Philip R.* The 'false pen of scribes': intellectuals then and
       now. ᴹCARROLL, R.: JSOT.S 348: 2002 ⇒13. 117-126.

3926 *Davis, Ellen F.* Preserving virtues: renewing the tradition of the sages. Character and scripture. 2002 ⇒283. 183-201.

3927 **Delkurt, Holger** Ethische Einsichten in der alttestamentlichen Spruchweisheit. BThSt 21: 1993 ⇒8,3501; 9,3352. [R]ThR 67 (2002) 210-211 (*Kottsieper, Ingo*).

3928 **Dell, Katharine** Seeking a life that matters: wisdom for today from the book of Proverbs. L 2002, Darton L. & T. 120 pp. £9. 0-2325-2402-5 [PrPe 18,83—Robinson, B.].

3929 *Estes, Todd K.* The principles of education in the Old Testament with a focus on the word *musar*. Faith & Mission 19/1 (2002) 20-30.

3930 **Frydrych, Tomás** Living under the sun: examination of Proverbs and Qoheleth. VT.S 90: Lei 2002, Brill xv; 255 pp. €68/$79. 90-04-12315-6. Bibl. 231-246.

3931 **Fuhs, Hans Ferdinand** Sprichwörter. NEB: Kommentar zum Alten Testament mit der Einheitsübersetzung, Lfg. 35. 2001 ⇒17,3520. [R]OrdKor 43 (2002) 358-359 (*Heinemann, Franz Karl*).

3932 *Gimeno Granero, José Carlos* Proverbios: una oferta de Sabiduría. EsVe 32 (2002) 81-110.

3933 [T]*Hamonville, David-Marc d'* La Bible d'Alexandrie, 17: Les Proverbes. 2000 ⇒16,3520; 17,3524. [R]CBQ 64 (2002) 131-132 (*Heskett, Randall*); ETR 77 (2002) 429-430 (*Bauks, Michaela*); RSR 90 (2002) 450-452 (*Paul, André*); JNSL 28/1 (2002) 103-115 (*Cook, Johann*).

3934 **Hausmann, Jutta** Studien zum Menschenbild der älteren Weisheit: (Spr 10ff.). FAT 7: 1995 ⇒11/1,1958...13,3170. [R]Sal. 64 (2002) 149-50 (*Cimosa, Mario*); ThR 67 (2002) 208-210 (*Kottsieper, Ingo*).

3935 *Hopkins, Simon* On the Vorlage of an early Judaeo-Arabic translation of Proverbs. JStAI 27 (2002) 369-374.

3936 *Kimilike, Lechion Peter* Friedemann W. Golka and African proverbs on the poor. ZAW 114 (2002) 255-261.

3937 *Kottsieper, Ingo* Alttestamentliche Weisheit: Proverbia und Kohelet (I). ThR 67 (2002) 1-34, 201-237.

3938 **Krispenz, Jutta** Spruchkompositionen im Buch Proverbia. EHS.T 349: 1989 ⇒5,3315... 7,3018. [R]ThR 67 (2002) 203-204 (*Kottsieper, Ingo*).

3939 **Lelièvre, André; Maillot, Alphonse** Commentaire des Proverbes, 3: chapitres 1-9. LeDiv Comment. 8: 2000 ⇒16,3523. [R]EstB 60 (2002) 545-547 (*Calduch-Benages, Nuria*);

3940 Proverbes, 1-3. LeDiv Comment. 1, 4, 8: 1993-2000 ⇒10,3241... 16, 3523. [R]BZ 46 (2002) 111-116 (*Scoralick, Ruth*).

3941 **Longman, Tremper** How to read Proverbs. DG 2002, InterVarsity 174 pp. 0-87784-942-0.

3942 **Meinhold, Arndt** Die Sprüche. ZBK.AT 16: 1991 ⇒7,3041... 10, 3242. [R]ThR 67 (2002) 21-23 (*Kottsieper, Ingo*).

3943 **Murphy, Roland E.; Huwiler, Elizabeth** Proverbs, Ecclesiastes, Song of Songs. NIBC.OT 12: 1999 ⇒15,3284; 17,3443. [R]RSR 90 (2002) 238-239 (*Abadie, Philippe*).

3944 **Murphy, Roland Edmund** Proverbs. WBC 22: 1998 ⇒14,3101... 17,3530. [R]HeyJ 43 (2002) 85-86 (*McNamara, Martin*).

3945 **Perdue, Leo G.** Proverbs. 2000 ⇒16,3531. [R]Interp. 56 (2002) 88-89 (*Bland, Dave*); HBT 24 (2002) 126-128 (*Brown, William P.*).

3946 *Sekine, Seizo* Research note: Proverbs as a catalogue of virtues: a comparison with Nicomachean ethics. AJBI 28 (2002) 55-86.

3947 *Solecka, K.; Stachowicz, E.* Mądrość przysłów ludowych, czyli jak
się zostaje Mistrzem [Comment devenir maître ou la sagesse des
Proverbes]. AtK 560 (2002) 116-125. **P.**

3948 **Steiert, Franz-Josef** Die Weisheit Israels—ein Fremdkörper im Alten Testament?: eine Untersuchung zum Buch der Sprüche auf dem
Hintergrund der ägyptischen Weisheitslehren. FThSt 143: 1990 ⇒6,
2573... 10,3231. ᴿThR 67 (2002) 218-219 (*Kottsieper, Ingo*).

3949 **Storøy, Solfrid** Sound and syllable: studies in monosyllabic words as
a poetic device in the book of Proverbs with special reference to the
words rash and dal. ᴰ*Barstad, H.M.*: 2002 Diss. Oslo, 363 pp [StTh
57,80].

3950 **Tauberschmidt, Gerhard** Secondary parallelism: a study of translation technique in LXX Proverbs. ᴰ*Watson, F.B.*: 2002 Diss. Aberdeen [RTL 34,594].

3951 **Vigini, Giuliano** L'Antico Testamento: Proverbi. Bibbia Paoline; Testi 8: Mi 2002, Paoline 187 pp. 88-315-2402-X. Testo e note di commento a cura di *Giuliano Vigini*; consulenza di *Tiziano Lorenzin*;
Bibl. 175-176.

3952 **Washington, Harold C.** Wealth and poverty in the instruction of
Amenemope and the Hebrew Proverbs. SBL.DS 142: 1994 ⇒12,
3124... 14,3106. ᴿThR 67 (2002) 215-218 (*Kottsieper, Ingo*).

3953 **Westermann, Claus** Wurzeln der Weisheit: die ältesten Sprüche Israels und anderer Völker. 1990 ⇒6,3597... 9,3370. ᴿThR 67 (2002)
221-223 (*Kottsieper, Ingo*).

3954 **Whybray, R. Norman** The composition of the book of Proverbs.
JSOT.S 168: 1994 ⇒10,3255... 13,3159. ᴿThR 67 (2002) 201-202
(*Kottsieper, Ingo*).

3955 **Baumann, Gerlinde** Die Weisheitsgestalt in Proverbien 1-9: traditionsgeschichtliche und theologische Studien. FAT 16: 1996 ⇒12,
3130... 15,3364. ᴿThR 67 (2002) 28-30 (*Kottsieper, Ingo*).

3956 *Carfagna, Antonella* Pr 1-9: il prologo del libro dei Proverbi. Prendi
il libro. Bibbia e spiritualità 18: 2002 ⇒372. /309-378.

3957 **Fox, Michael V.** Proverbs 1-9: AncB 18A: 2000 ⇒16,3518; 17,
3538. ᴿAUSS 40 (2002) 144-146 (*Caesar, Lael*); RExp 99 (2002)
110-111 (*Biddle, Mark E.*); BS 159 (2002) 492-493 (*Chisholm,
Robert B.*); HBT 24 (2002) 126-128 (*Brown, William P.*); RBLit
(2002)* (*Sandoval, Timothy*).

3958 **Gorges-Braunwarth, Susanne** 'Frauenbilder—Weisheitsbilder—
Gottesbilder' in Spr 1-9: die personifizierte Weisheit im Gottesbild
der nachexilischen Zeit. ᴰ*Fischer, Irmtraud*: Exegese in unserer Zeit
9: Müns 2002, LIT xiii; 464 pp. €25.90. 3-8258-5782-4. Diss. Bonn
2001.

3959 **Maier, Christl Margarethe** Die "fremde Frau": eine exegetische
und sozialgeschichtliche Studie zu Proverbien 1-9. OBO 144: 1995
⇒11/1,1936... 13,3182. ᴿThR 67 (2002) 27-28 (*Kottsieper, Ingo*).

3960 *Meinhold, Arndt* Vierfaches: Strukturprinzip und Häufigkeitsfigur in
Prov 1-9;

3961 Der Gewaltmensch als abschreckendes Beispiel in Proverbien 1-9.
Zur weisheitlichen Sicht. 2002 ⇒209. 119-141/151-164 [BuBB 37,
131].

3962 *Moss, Alan* Proverbs with Solomon: a critical revision of the pre-
critical commentary tradition in the light of a biblical intertextual
study. HeyJ 43 (2002) 199-211 [Prov 1-9].

3963 **Müller, Achim** Proverbien 1-9. BZAW 291: 2000 ⇒16,3543; 17, 3540. ᴿThLZ 127 (2002) 163-165 (*Krispenz, Jutta*).
3964 **Schäfer, Rolf** Die Poesie der Weisen: Dichotomie als Grundstruktur der Lehr- und Weisheitsgedichte in Proverbien 1-9. WMANT 77: 1999 ⇒15,3369...17,3542. ᴿThR 67 (2002) 31-32 (*Kottsieper, Ingo*).
3965 **Signoretto, Martino** Metafora e didattica in Prv 1-9. ᴰ*Calduch Benages, N.*: 2002 Diss. Gregoriana [RTL 34,594].
3966 **Yoder, Christine Roy** Wisdom as a woman of substance: a socioeconomic reading of Proverbs 1-9 and 31:10-31. BZAW 304: 2001 ⇒17,3543. ᴿRSR 90 (2002) 237-238 (*Abadie, Philippe*); ThLZ 127 (2002) 390-391 (*Schroer, Silvia*); RBLit (2002)* (*Maier, Christl*).

3967 *Lenchak, Timothy A.* Puzzling passages: Proverbs 1:7. BiTod 40 (2002) 392-393.
3968 *Meinhold, Arndt* Gott und Menschen in Proverbien III. Zur weisheitlichen Sicht. 2002 ⇒209. 143-150 [BuBB 37,131].
3969 *Potgieter, J.H.* The (poetic) rhetoric of wisdom in Proverbs 3:1-12. HTS 58 (2002) 1357-1374 [OTA 26,487].
3970 *Prinsloo, G.T.M.* Reading Proverbs 3:1-12 in its social and ideological context. HTS 58 (2002) 1375-1400 [OTA 26,487].
3971 *Barbiero, Gianni* Der masoretische Text von Spr 3,34. Studien. SBAB 34: 2002 <1982> ⇒139. 38-55 [Prov 3,27-35].
3972 *Pentiuc, Eugen J.* A self-offering God and his begotten wisdom (Proverbs 8:22-24). GOTR 46 (2001) 255-265.
3973 **Cerbelaud, Dominique**, *al.*, La figure de la sagesse: Proverbes 8,22-31. CEv.S 120: P 2002, Cerf 75 pp. 0222-9706.
3974 *Dowling, Maurice* Proverbs 8:22-31 in the christology of the early fathers. IBSt 24 (2002) 99-117.
3975 **Scoralick, Ruth** Einzelspruch und Sammlung: Komposition im Buch der Sprichwörter, Kapitel 10-15. BZAW 232: 1995 ⇒11/1,1953; 13, 3196. ᴿThR 67 (2002) 204-205 (*Kottsieper, Ingo*).
3976 **Heim, Knut Martin** Like grapes of gold set in silver: an interpretation of proverbial clusters in Proverbs 10:1-22:16. BZAW 273: 2001 ⇒17,3550. ᴿOLZ 97 (2002) 83-87 (*Scherer, Andreas*); CBQ 64 (2002) 351-353 (*Murphy, Roland E.*); ThLZ 127 (2002) 1282-1285 (*Krispenz, Jutta*); JBL 121 (2002) 546-549 (*Steinmann, Andrew E.*).
3977 **Scherer, Andreas** Das weise Wort und seine Wirkung: eine Untersuchung zur Komposition und Redaktion von Proverbia 10,1-22,16. WMANT 83: 1999 ⇒15,3377...17,3551. ᴿThR 67 (2002) 205-207 (*Kottsieper, Ingo*).
3978 *Brown, William P.* The pedagogy of Proverbs 10:1-31:9. Character and scripture. 2002 ⇒283. 150-182.
3979 *Kselman, John S.* Ambiguity and wordplay in Proverbs xi. VT 52 (2002) 545-548 [Prov 11,5-6].
3980 *Meinhold, Arndt* Das Wortspiel רזון - רצון in Prov 14,28-35. Zur weisheitlichen Sicht. 2002 ⇒209. 165-166 [BuBB 37,132].
3981 *Scoralick, Ruth* Salomos griechische Gewänder: Beobachtungen zur Septuagintafassung des Sprichwörterbuches. Rettendes Wissen. AOAT 300: 2002 ⇒352. 43-75 [Prov 15,27-16,9].
3982 *Meinhold, Arndt* Zur strukturellen Eingebundenheit der JHWH-Sprüche in Prov 18;
3983 Zur weisheitlichen Sicht des Menschen (vornehmlich nach dem Sprüchebuch, speziell Spr 20,2-30). Zur weisheitlichen Sicht. 2002 ⇒ 209. 167-176/177-187 [BuBB 37,132].

3984 **Moro, Caterina** "Ascolta la mia parola": analisi testuale di Proverbi 22,17-24,22. SS 17: R 2002, Università degli Studi di Roma "La Sapienza" xxxiv (2) 336 pp. Bibl. 320-336.

3985 **Römheld, Diethard** Wege der Weisheit: die Lehre Amenemopes und Proverbien 22,17-24,22. BZAW 184: 1989 ⇒6,3600*... 8,3525. ᴿThR 67 (2002) 214-215 (*Kottsieper, Ingo*).

3986 **Naré, Laurent** Proverbes solomoniens et proverbes mossi: étude comparative à partir d'une nouvelle analyse de Pr 25-29. EHS.T 283: 1986 ⇒2,2516...5,3329. ᴿThR 67 (2002) 223-224 (*Kottsieper, Ingo*).

3987 *Meinhold, Arndt* Der Umgang mit dem Feind nach Spr 25,21f als Massstab für das Menschsein. Zur weisheitlichen Sicht. 2002 ⇒209. 189-197 [BuBB 37,132].

3988 *Har-El, Menashe* 'The north wind driveth away rain' (Proverbs 25:23). BetM 169 (2002) 97-104 Sum. 192. **H.**

3989 *Wendland, E.R.* 'How to answer a fool': the wisdom of rhetoric and the rhetoric of wisdom in Proverbs 26:1-12, with special reference to bible translation. OTEs 15 (2002) 504-538.

3990 *Santos, Bartolome* The prayer of Proverbs 30:7-9. ICSTJ 4 (2002) 44-54.

3991 *Wechsler, Michael G.* The Arabic translation and commentary of YEFET ben ʿEli on Proverbs 31:1-9. REJ 161 (2002) 393-409.

3992 **Boyd, Mary Petrina** The house that wisdom wove: an analysis of the functions of household in Proverbs 31:10-31. ᴰ*Brown, W.P.*: 2002 Diss. Virginia, Union [RTL 34,590].

3993 *Rofé, Alexander* The valiant woman, γυνὴ συνετή, and the redaction of the book of Proverbs. ᶠSMEND, R. 2002 ⇒113. 145-155 [Prov 31, 10-31].

3994 *Lo Prinzi, Daniele* Una moglie che teme il Signore è degna di lode (Pro 31,30): לֵל תִּתְהַ הִיא יה יְרָאַת־יָה שֶׁה אָ. Laós 9/2 (2002) 23-49.

E7.7 *Ecclesiastes—Qohelet*; *textus, themata, versiculi*

3995 ᴱ**Bellia, Giuseppe; Passaro, Angelo** Il libro del Qohelet: tradizione, redazione, teologia. Cammini nello Spirito, Biblica 44: 2001 ⇒17, 453. ᴿItinerarium(Messina) 10 (2002) 275-77 (*Montanti, Calogero*); HebStud 43 (2002) 287-289 (*Hobbins, John F.*); Vivens Homo 13 (2002) 415-6; RevAg 43 (2002) 709-11 (*Granados García, Carlos*).

3996 ᵀ**Brunner, Fernand** Maître ECKHART: sermons et leçons sur 'L'Ecclésiastique'. P 2002, Ad Solem 154 pp. €20. 2-940090-74-2. Texte établi avec la collaboration éditoriale de *Alain de Libera*. ᴿRThPh 134 (2002) 253-254 (*Suarez-Nani, Tiziana*);

3997 **Burkes, Shannon** Death in Qoheleth and Egyptian biographies of the late period. SBL.DS 170: 1999 ⇒15,3400; 17,3590. ᴿRBLit (2002)* (*Christianson, Eric S.*); JNES 61 (2002) 71-73 (*Clemens, D.M.*).

3998 *Carfagna, Antonella* Qoelet e la ricerca del senso della vita. Prendi il libro. Bibbia e spiritualità 18: 2002 ⇒372. 67-112.

3999 *Christianson, Eric S.* The ethics of narrative wisdom: Qoheleth as test case. Character and scripture. 2002 ⇒283. 202-210.

4000 *Fischer, Stefan* Qohelet and 'heretic' Harpers' songs. JSOT 98 (2002) 105-121.

4001 **Fox, Michael Vass** A time to tear down and a time to build up: a re-reading of Ecclesiastes. 1999 ⇒15,3405...17,3599. ᴿJNES 61

(2002) 319-320 (*Reymond, Eric*); RBLit 4 (2002) 247-249 (*Bodner, Keith*).

4002 **Frades, Eduardo** Tema 3: non varrà l'uomo più della sua vita?: Ecclesiaste (Qoelet). Salmi e letteratura sapienziale. 2002 ⇒264. 125-158.

4003 **Frydrych, Tomás** Living under the sun: examination of Proverbs and Qoheleth. VT.S 90: Lei 2002, Brill xv; 255 pp. €68/$79. 90-04-12315-6. Bibl. 231-246.

4004 *Gilbert, Maurice* Qohélèt. EeV 49; 50 (2002) 11-15; 16-21.

4005 **Kamano, Naoto** Cosmology and character: Qoheleth's pedagogy from a rhetorical-critical perspective. BZAW 312: B 2002, De Gruyter xvi; 308 pp. $97. 3-11-017242-9. Bibl. 255-291.

4006 **Keddie, Gordon J.** The guide—Ecclesiastes. Darlington 2002, Evangelical 347 pp. £7. 0-85234-485-6.

4007 **Kieling, Michał** Terrena non amare sed coelestia: Theologie der Welt in ALKUINS Commentaria super Ecclesiasten. EHS.T 732: Fra 2002, Lang xii; 289 pp. €52. 3-631-38017-8. Bibl. 222-238.

4008 *Koprek, Ivan* Philosophical reflections on the book of Ecclesiastes: 'Keep thy foot when thou goest to the house of God, and be more ready to hear...' (Eccl. 4:17). Obnov. Život 57 (2002) 421-427 Sum. 426. **Croatian**.

4009 *Kottsieper, Ingo* Alttestamentliche Weisheit: Proverbia und Kohelet (I). ThR 67 (2002) 1-34, 201-237.

4010 **Laras, Giuseppe** Il libro di Qohelet. Storia della filosofia ebraica: Mi 2002, CUEM 152 pp.

4011 *Mazzinghi, Luca* Qohelet and Enochism: a critical relationship. Henoch 24 (2002) 157-167;

4012 'Gioisci, giovane, nella tua giovinezza!': il libro del Qohelet e la gioia del vivere. La vita del credente. PSV 45 (2002) 41-54.

4013 **Mazzinghi, Luca** "Ho cercato e ho esplorato": studi sul Qohelet. 2001 ⇒17,3605. ᴿAlpha Omega 5 (2002) 382-384 (*Furlong, Jude*).

4014 **Miller, Douglas B.** Symbol and rhetoric in Ecclesiastes: the place of 'Hebel' in Qohelet's work. Academia Biblica 2: Atlanta 2002, SBL xviii; 238 pp. $33. 1-58983-029-6. Bibl. 195-215.

     Murphy, R., *al.*, Proverbs, Ecclesiastes 1999 ⇒3943.

4015 *Niccacci, Alviero* Qohelet o la gioa come factica e dono di Dio a chi lo teme. LASBF 52 (2002) 29-102.

4016 *Prior, John M.* 'When all the singing has stopped': Ecclesiastes: a modest mission in unpredictable times. IRM 91 (2002) 7-23.

4017 *Putnam, Ruth Anna* Die Einsamkeit Kohelets. DZPh 50 (2002) 749-762.

4018 *Rudman, Dominic* Determinism and anti-determinism in the book of Koheleth. JBQ 30 (2002) 97-106.

4019 **Rudman, Dominic** Determinism in the book of Ecclesiastes. JSOT.S 316: 2001 ⇒17,3611. ᴿJBL 121 (2002) 549-551 (*Sneed, Mark*).

4020 **Salyer, Gary D.** Vain rhetoric: private insight and public debate in Ecclesiastes. JSOT.S 327: 2001 ⇒17,3612. ᴿBib. 83 (2002) 412-416 (*Schoors, Antoon*).

4021 **Schellenberg, Annette** Erkenntnis als Problem: Qohelet und die alttestamentliche Diskussion um das menschliche Erkennen. OBO 188: Gö 2002, Vandenhoeck & R. xii; 333 pp. FS98. 3-525-53045-5. Bibl. 301-321.

4022 *Schoors, Antoon* God in Qoheleth. ᶠHAAG, E. 2002 ⇒55. 251-270.

4023 *Schwartzmann, Julia* The commentator as editor: GERSONIDES' commentary on Ecclesiastes. JewSt 41 (2002) 169-186.
4024 **Schwienhorst-Schönberger, Ludger** 'Nicht im Menschen gründet das Glück' (Koh 2,24): Kohelet im Spannungsfeld jüdischer Weisheit und hellenistischer Philosophie. 1994 ⇒10,3302... 14,3177. ᴿThR 67 (2002) 229-232 (*Kottsieper, Ingo*).
4025 *Talstra, Eep* Second Isaiah and Qohelet: could one get them on speaking terms?. ᶠLEENE, H. 2002 ⇒73. 225-236.
4026 **Támez, Elsa** Cuando los horizontes se cierran: relectura del libro de Eclesiastés o Qohelet. 1998 ⇒16,3606. ᴿThX 52 (2002) 579-580 (*Román, Carlos Eduardo*).
4027 ᵀ**Vinel, Françoise** L'Ecclésiaste: traduction de la Septante. La Bible d'Alexandrie 18: P 2002, Cerf 186 pp. €25. 2-204-06903-5.
4028 *Virgili Dal Pra, Rosanna* Speranza e non speranza: il libro del Qohelet. La speranza. 2002 ⇒277. 41-67.
4029 **Zimmer, Tilmann** Zwischen Tod und Lebensglück: eine Untersuchung zur Anthropologie Kohelets. BZAW 286: 1999 ⇒15,3430; 17, 3583. ᴿThR 67 (2002) 232-234 (*Kottsieper, Ingo*).

4030 *Ortkemper, Franz-Josef* Alles hat seine Stunde: Koh 3,1-15: September – Arbeitsbeginn. zwölfmal bibel. 2002 ⇒1087. 96-103.
4031 *Lavoie, Jean-Jacques* Puissance divine et finitude humaine selon Qohélet 3,10-15. SR 31 (2002) 283-296.
4032 *D'Alario, Vittoria* Qohelet e l'apocalittica: il significato del termine 'ôlām in Qo 3,11. Tempo ed eternità. 2002 ⇒545. 73-88.
4033 *Frevel, Christian* Bei Zeiten—vom Nutzen des Augenblicks: die Zeitsignatur des Daseins bei Kohelet. WuA(M) 43 (2002) 135-137 [Qoh 3,11].
4034 **Laurent, Françoise** Les biens pour rien en Qohéleth 5,9-6,6 ou la traversée d'un contraste. ᴰ*Gilbert, Maurice*: BZAW 323: B 2002, De Gruyter xii; 281 pp. €78. 3-11-017498-7. Diss. Strasbourg 2000; Bibl. 253-267.
4035 *Mizrahi, Noam* Qoheleth 6:5b in light of 4 QQohᵃ ii 2 and rabbinic literature. Textus 21 (2002) 159-174.
4036 *Choi, John H.* The doctrine of the golden mean in Qoh 7,15-18: a universal human pursuit. Bib. 83 (2002) 358-374.
4037 *García Bachmann, Mercedes* A study of Qoheleth (Ecclesiastes) 9:1-12. IRM 91 (2002) 382-394.
4038 *Homan, Michael M.* Beer production by throwing bread into water: a new interpretation of Qoh. xi 1-2. VT 52 (2002) 275-278.

E7.8 *Liber Sapientiae*—Wisdom of Solomon

4039 *Burkes, Shannon* Wisdom and apocalypticism in the Wisdom of Solomon. HThR 95 (2002) 21-44.
4040 *Burns, Camilla* The ways of Wisdom. BiTod 40 (2002) 360-365.
4041 *Cabestrero, Teófilo, al.*, Tema 5: la sapienza, compagna in tempo di crisi: libro della Sapienza. Salmi e letteratura sapienziale. 2002 ⇒ 264. 195-224.
4042 *Ceresko, Anthony R.* The encounter of cultures and the growth of the biblical tradition: examples from the books of Wisdom and Sirach. Prophets and proverbs. 2002 <2000> ⇒154. 115-127.

4043 *Collins, John J.* Apocalyptic eschatology in philosphical dress in the
      Wisdom of Solomon. Shem. JSJ.S 74: 2002 ⇒755. 93-107.
4044 *Georgi, Dieter* Interpretation of scriptures in Wisdom of Solomon.
      Jüdische Schriften. 2002 ⇒345. 304-332.
4045 *Gilbert, Maurice* Les livres sapientiaux de l'Ancien Testament: la Sa-
      gesse de Salomon. EeV 58; 59; 60 (2002) 13-17; 10-14; 23-27.
4046 **Gilbert, Maurice** Mądrość Salomona. ᵀ*Kobiałka, Stanisław*: Mysl
      Teologiczna 37-38: Kraków 2002, WAM 2 vols; 200 + 172 pp. 83-
      7318-036-2/7-0. Bibl. v.II, 143-159. **P.**
4047 **Hecking, Detlev; Waldmüller, Gabriela; Wäffler, Angela** Sehn-
      sucht nach Gerechtigkeit: Denken und Handeln nach dem Buch der
      Weisheit. Werkstattbibel 3: Stu 2002, Kathol. Bibelwerk 96 pp.
      €11.80/10.70. 3-460-08503-7.
4048 **Hübner, Hans** Die Weisheit Salomons: Liber Sapientiae Salomonis.
      ATD, Apokryphen 4: 1999 ⇒15,3442...17,3634. ᴿRBLit 4 (2002)
      249-251 (*Premstaller, Volkmar*).
4049 *Kolarcik, Michael* The Wisdom of Solomon: justice and creation.
      BiTod 40 (2002) 341-347.
4050 **McGlynn, Moyna** Divine judgement and divine benevolence in the
      book of Wisdom. WUNT 2/139: 2001 ⇒17,3636. ᴿBib. 83 (2002)
      416-419 (*Gilbert, Maurice*).
4051 *Nowell, Irene* Immortality in Wisdom. BiTod 40 (2002) 355-359.
4052 **Pereira, Ney Brasil** Livro da Sabedoria: aos governantes, sobre a
      justiça. Comentário Bíblico AT: 1999 ⇒15,3443; 17,3637. ᴿRevBib
      61 (1999) 263-266 (*Andiñach, Pablo*).
4053 *Polan, Gregory J.* Literary creativity in the Wisdom of Solomon.
      BiTod 40 (2002) 349-353.
4054 *Reymond, Eric D.* The poetry of the Wisdom of Solomon recon-
      sidered. VT 52 (2002) 385-399.
4055 *Rossi de Gasperis, Francesco* Il libro della Sapienza: lo Spirito Santo
      sa parlare anche in greco in un libro deuterocanico che tende la mano
      al Nuovo Testamento. Prendi il libro. Bibbia e spiritualità 18: 2002
      ⇒372. 289-306.
4056 **Schenker, Adrian** El libro de la Sabiduría. Guía espiritual del Anti-
      guo Testamento 14: M 2002, Ciudad N. 138 pp. €9.50. 84-9715-015-
      5. ᴿRevAg 43 (2002) 711-712 (*Granados García, Carlos*).
4057 *Spieckermann, Hermann* Der Gerechten Seelen sind in Gottes Hand:
      die Bedeutung der Sapientia Salomonis für die Biblische Theologie.
      ᶠSMEND, R. 2002 ⇒113. 345-368.
4058 *Winston, David* PHILO and the Wisdom of Solomon on creation,
      revelation, and providence: the high-water mark of Jewish Hellenistic
      fusion. Shem. JSJ.S 74: 2002 ⇒755. 109-130.

4059 *Priotto, Michelangelo* Violenza e persecuzione contro il giusto (Sap
      2,1b-20). RStB 14/1-2 (2002) 137-146.
4060 *Mazzinghi, Luca* Come nasce un idolo (Sap 14,11-21 e 15,7-13).
      PSV 46 (2002) 61-76.
4061 *Backhaus, Franz-Josef* "Denn du hast Macht über Leben und Tod"
      (Weish 16,13): "Rettendes Wissen" am Beispiel von Weish 16,5-14.
      Rettendes Wissen. AOAT 300: 2002 ⇒352. 77-113.
4062 *Scaiola, Donatella* Il tema della manna nel libro della Sapienza: un
      esempio di inculturazione. ED 55 (2002) 41-62 [Wis 16,15-29;
      19,21].

E7.9 *Ecclesiasticus, Siracides*; **Wisdom of Jesus Sirach**

4063 [E]**Egger-Wenzel, Renate** Ben Sira's God: proceedings of the International Ben Sira Conference, Durham—Ushaw College 2001. BZAW 321: B 2002, De Gruyter viii; 393 pp. €91.59. 3-11-017559-2.

4064 *Aitken, James K.* Divine will and providence. Ben Sira's God. BZAW 321: 2002 ⇒4063. 282-301.

4065 *Argall, Randal A.* Competing wisdoms: *1 Enoch* and *Sirach*. Henoch 24 (2002) 169-178.

4066 *Becker, Eve M.* "Jesus Sirach Deutsch": über die Chancen und Schwierigkeiten einer modernen deutschen Übersetzung. Deutsches Pfarrerblatt 102/1 (2002) 18-20;

4067 Jesus Sirach und das Luthertum des 16.Jahrhunderts: über Inhalt und Funktion eines schlesischen Katechismus von 1561. Ben Sira's God. BZAW 321: 2002 ⇒4063. 352-360.

4068 *Beentjes, Pancratius C.* God's mercy: '*racham*' (pi.), '*rachum*', and '*rachamim*' in the book of Ben Sira. Ben Sira's God. BZAW 321: 2002 ⇒4063. 101-117;

4069 Errata et corrigenda zu *The book of Ben Sira in Hebrew. A text edition of all extant Hebrew manuscripts and a synopsis of all parallel Hebrew Ben Sira texts*, VTS 68; Leiden: Brill, 1997. Ben Sira's God. BZAW 321: 2002 ⇒4063. 375-377.

4070 *Cabestrero, Teófilo, al.*, Tema 4: Attenzione alla tradizione: valori e limiti: libro di Gesù, figlio di Sira (Ecclesiastico). Salmi e letteratura sapienziale. 2002 ⇒264. 161-192.

4071 *Ceresko, Anthony R.* Love ('*aheb*) and covenant in the teachings of Jesus son of Sirach and Jesus of Nazareth. The roles. 2002 ⇒540. 70-82 = Prophets and Proverbs. ⇒154. 139-150;

4072 The liberative strategy of Ben Sira: the sage as prophet. Prophets and proverbs. 2002 <1996> ⇒154. 53-71.

4073 **Coggins, Richard J.** Sirach. 1998 ⇒14,3228...16,3647. [R]HeyJ 43 (2002) 86-88 (*McNamara, Martin*).

4074 *Corley, Jeremy* God as merciful father in Ben Sira and the New Testament. Ben Sira's God. BZAW 321: 2002 ⇒4063. 33-38.

4075 **Corley, Jeremy** Ben Sira's teaching on friendship. BJSt 316: Providence 2002, Brown Univ. xv; 297 pp. $40. 1-930675-09-7. Bibl. 229-255.

4076 *DiLella, Alexander A.* God and wisdom in the theology of Ben Sira: an overview. Ben Sira's God. BZAW 321: 2002 ⇒4063. 3-17.

4077 [E]**Egger-Wenzel, Renate; Krammer, Ingrid** Der Einzelne und seine Gemeinschaft bei Ben Sira. BZAW 270: 1998 ⇒14,3230; 16,3656. [R]RBLit 4 (2002) 251-254 (*Wright, Benjamin G., III*).

4078 *Egger-Wenzel, Renate* Originalität des Ben Sira?: ein unveröffentlichter Beitrag Rabbi ALTMANNs. Ben Sira's God. BZAW 321: 2002 ⇒4063. 345-351.

4079 *Gilbert, Maurice* La Sagesse de Ben Sira. EeV 51; 52; 53; 54; 55; 56; 57 (2002) 19-24; 11-15; 19-23; 18-23; 14-18; 14-18; 16-20.

4080 *Harrington, Daniel J.* Two early Jewish approaches to wisdom: Sirach and Qumran sapiential work A. Wisdom texts. BEThL 159: 2002 ⇒482. 263-275.

4081 *Hayward, Robert C.T.* El elyon and the divine names in Ben Sira. Ben Sira's God. BZAW 321: 2002 ⇒4063. 180-198.

4082   *Jenner, Konrad; Van Peursen, Wido* Unit delimitation and the text of Ben Sira. Studies in scriptural unit division. Pericope 3: 2002 ⇒339. 144-201.

4083   *Kaiser, Otto* Die Furcht und die Liebe Gottes: ein Versuch, die Ethik Ben Siras mit der des Apostels Paulus zu vergleichen. Ben Sira's God. BZAW 321: 2002 ⇒4063. 39-75.

4084   *Kister, Menahem* Genizah manuscripts of Ben Sira. The Cambridge Genizah collections. 2002 ⇒698. 36-46.

4085   *Levene, David S.* Theology and non-theology in the rabbinic Ben Sira. Ben Sira's God. BZAW 321: 2002 ⇒4063. 305-320.

4086   *Liesen, Jan* "With all your heart": praise in the book of Ben Sira. Ben Sira's God. BZAW 321: 2002 ⇒4063. 199-213.

4087   **Obruśnik, Marian** Wychowanie człowieka według Księgi Syracydesa [L'éducation de l'homme selon le livre du Siracide]. ᴰ*Rubinkiewicz, R.*: 2002, 288 pp. Diss. Lublin [RTL 34,593].

4088   *Reif, Stefan C.* Prayer in Ben Sira, Qumran and Second Temple Judaism: a comparative overview;

4089   *Reiterer, Friedrich V.* Opferterminologie in Ben Sira;

4090   Gott und Opfer. Ben Sira's God. BZAW 321: 2002 ⇒4063. 321-341/ 371-374/136-179.

4091   *Rossi de Gasperis, Francesco* Il Siracide (Ecclesiastico): l'ultimo sapiente dell'ebraismo della terra d'Israele nel canone delle scritture della chiesa. Prendi il libro. 2002 ⇒372. 275-288.

4092   *Roure, Damià* L'obtenció del perdó en Ben Sira i en FILÓ d'Alexandria. Perdó i reconciliació. 2002 ⇒591. 209-221.

4093   **Sauer, Georg** Jesus Sirach / Ben Sira. ATD.Apokryphen 1: 2000 ⇒ 16,3650; 17,3647. ᴿCBQ 64 (2002) 144-145 (*Murphy, Roland E.*).

4094   **Schreiner, Josef** Jesus Sirach 1-24. NEB.AT 38: Wü 2002, Echter 134 pp. €17.40. 3-429-02355-6. ᴿCBQ 64 (2002) 747 (*Murphy, Roland E.*).

4095   ᴱ**Talmon, Shemaryahu** Masada VI, the Yigael Yadin excavations 1963-1965 final reports [1] Hebrew fragments from Masada; [2] the Ben Sira Scroll from Masada. The Masada Reports: 1999 ⇒15,3482 ...17,3648. ᴿDSD 9 (2002) 274-276 (*Aitken, James K.*).

4096   *Thiele, Walter* Sirach/Ecclesiasticus. BVLI 46 (2002) 28-33.

4097   *Horsley, Richard A.* Ben Sira and the sociology of the second temple. Second temple studies III. JSOT.S 340: 2002 ⇒296. 74-107.

4098   *Van Peursen, Wido* Progress report: three Leiden projects on the Syriac text of Ben Sira;

4099   *Wicke-Reuter, Ursel* Ben Sira und die Frühe Stoa: zum Zusammenhang von Ethik und dem Glauben an eine göttliche Providenz. Ben Sira's God. BZAW 321: 2002 ⇒4063. 361-370/268-281.

4100   **Wicke-Reuter, Ursel** Göttliche Providenz und menschliche Verantwortung bei Ben Sira und in der frühen Stoa. BZAW 298: 2000 ⇒ 16,3670; 17,3659. ᴿThLZ 127 (2002) 388-390 (*Sauer, Georg*); RivBib 50 (2002) 455-465 (*Prato, Gian Luigi*).

4101   *Wischmeyer, Oda* Theologie und Anthropologie im Sirachbuch. Ben Sira's God. BZAW 321: 2002 ⇒4063. 18-32.

4102   *Wright, Benjamin G., III Sirach and 1 Enoch*: some further considerations. Henoch 24 (2002) 179-187.

4103   *Gilbert, Maurice* God, sin and mercy: Sirach 15:11-18:14. Ben Sira's God. BZAW 321: 2002 ⇒4063. 118-135.

4104 *Rossetti, Marco* Le aggiunte ebraiche e greche a Sir 16,1-16. Sal. 64 (2002) 607-648.

4105 *Linder, Agnes* Il galateo della bocca: studio sulla struttura dei capp. 27-28 del libro di Ben Sira. Ang. 79 (2002) 273-301 [Sir 24,1-32,13].

4106 *Calduch-Benages, Núria* Abans perdonar que guardar rancúnia: estudi de Siràcida 27,30-28,7. Perdó i reconciliació. 2002 ⇒591. 175-95.

4107 *Lenchak, Timothy* Puzzling passages: Sirach 33:12 .BiTod 40 (2002) 189-190.

4108 *Rollston, Chris A.* Ben Sira 38:24-39:11 and the *Egyptian satire of the trades*: a reconsideration. JBL 120 (2001) 131-139.

4109 *Calduch-Benages, Núria* God, creator of all (Sir 43:27-33);

4110 *Brown, Teresa R.* God and men in Israel's history: God and idol worship in praise of the fathers (Sir 44-50). Ben Sira's God. BZAW 321: 2002 ⇒4063. 79-100/214-220.

4111 *Camp, Claudia V.* Storied space, or, Ben Sira 'tells' a temple. ᶠFLANAGAN, J.: JSOT.S 359: 2002 ⇒38. 64-80 [Sir 44-50].

4112 *Goshen-Gottstein, Alon* Ben Sira's praise of the fathers: a canon-conscious reading [Sir 50];

4113 *Mulder, Otto* Two approaches: Simon the high priest and YHWH God of Israel / God of all in Sirach 50. Ben Sira's God. BZAW 321: 2002 ⇒4063. 235-267/221-234.

4114 *Aslanov, Cyril* L'apocryphe réintégré: une réminiscence de Siracide 50,1-21 dans l'hymnologie juive. ᶠGEOLTRAIN, P.: BEHE.R 113: 2002 ⇒45. 31-43 [BuBB 37,156].

VII. Libri prophetici VT

E8.1 Prophetismus

4115 ᴱ**Zenger, Erich** Wort JHWHs, das geschah ..." (Hos 1,1): Studien zum Zwölfprophetenbuch. Herders biblische Studien 35: FrB 2002, Herder vi; 222 pp. 3-451-27493-0.

4116 **Abma, R.** Bonds of love: methodic studies of prophetic texts with marriage imagery (Isaiah 50:1-3 and 54:1-10, Hosea 1-3, Jeremiah 2-3). SSN 40: 1999 ⇒15,3522; 16,3686. ᴿHebStud 43 (2002) 273-276 (*Leneman, Helen*); RBLit 4 (2002) 209-211 (*Bulkeley, Tim*).

4117 *Ampazhathinal, Shaji* God the moulder of human lives: messianic hope in Daniel and Ezekiel. God of big dreams. 2002 ⇒359. 210-229.

4118 *Asurmendi, Jésus* Au-delà de la loi: le prophète. Revue d'éthique et de théologie morale.Suppl. 223 (2002) 25-37.

4119 *Auld, Graeme* Prophecy. Biblical world, 1. 2002 ⇒273. 88-106.

4120 *Bailpão, Marcos P.* Profetas e curandeiros. Estudos bíblicos 73 (2002) 20-25.

4121 **Baumann, Gerlinde** Liebe und Gewalt: die Ehe als Metapher für das Verhältnis JHWH—Israel in den Prophetenbüchern. SBS 185: 2000 ⇒16,3692; 17,3681. ᴿBiKi 57 (2002) 106-107 (*Schüngel-Straumann, Helen*); BZ 46 (2002) 304-309 (*Wacker, Marie-Theres*).

4122 *Beal, Timothy K.* Spectres of Moses: overtures to biblical hauntology. ^FFLANAGAN, J.: JSOT.S 359: 2002 ⇒38. 171-187.

4123 **Behrens, Achim** Prophetische Visionsschilderungen im Alten Testament: sprachliche Eigenarten, Funktion und Geschichte einer Gattung. AOAT 292: Müns 2002, Ugarit-Verlag xii; 413 pp. 3-934628-21-4. Bibl. 387-405.

4124 *Bingham Kolenkow, Anitra* Persons of power and their communities. Magic and divination. 2002 ⇒729. 133-144.

4125 *Bonnet, Corinne; Merlo, Paolo* Royal prophecy in the Old Testament and in the ancient Near East: methodological problems and examples. StEeL 19 (2002) 77-86.

4126 *Britt, Brian* Prophetic concealment in a biblical type scene. CBQ 64 (2002) 37-58 [Ex 34; 1 Kgs 19].

4127 **Brueggemann, Walter** The prophetic imagination. ²2001 <1978> ⇒ 17,3685. ^RRBLit (2002)* (*Swenson-Mendez, Kristin*).

4128 **Butting, Klara** Prophetinnen gefragt: die Bedeutung der Prophetinnen im Kanon aus Tora und Prophetie. Biblisch-feministische Texte 3: 2001 ⇒17,3687. ^RBZ 46 (2002) 302-304 (*Fischer, Irmtraud*); YESW 10 (2002) 234-236 (*Rakel, Claudia*).

4129 *Cañellas, Gabriel* Las tentaciones: teología del profetismo. BiFe 84 (2002) 337-361.

4130 *Caramelo, Francisco* Algumas reflexões teoréticas sobre o profetismo. LusSac 13-14 (2001-2002) 625-631.

4131 **Caramelo, Francisco** A linguagem profética na Mesopotâmia Mari e Assiria. Carnaxide 2002, Cascais 392 pp. 9727440568 [RB 110,475].

4132 *Carbajosa Pérez, Ignacio* Las imágenes sapienciales en el discurso profético. VyV 60 (2002) 97-116.

4133 **Chittinappilly, Paul** Reimagining prophetic alternatives: towards a historical reconstruction of the ancient Israelite prophecy & the early Jesus and Buddhist movements. ^D*De Schrijver, G.*: 2002, lv; 348 pp. Diss. Leuven 2002 [EThL 79,237].

4134 *Clines, David J.A.* He-prophets: masculinity as a problem for the Hebrew prophets and their interpreters. ^MCARROLL, R.: JSOT.S 348: 2002 ⇒13. 311-328.

4135 *Crüsemann, Frank 'th*—'Jetzt': Hosea 4-11 als Anfang der Schriftprophetie 'Wort JHWHs, das geschah'. Herders biblische Studien 35: 2002 ⇒4115. 13-31.

4136 **Dempsey, Carol J.** Hope amid the ruins: the ethics of Israel's prophets. 2000 ⇒16,3709. ^RHBT 24/2 (2002) 113-14 (*Gowan, Donald*).

4137 **Eaton, John** Mysterious messengers: a course on Hebrew prophecy from Amos onwards. 1997 ⇒14,3284. ^RRBLit (2002)* (*Bodner, Keith*); RBLit 4 (2002) 197-200 (*Bodner, Keith*).

4138 *Ferry, Joëlle* Les récits de vocation prophétique. EstB 60 (2002) 211-224.

4139 **Fischer, Charis** Die Fremdvölkersprüche bei Amos und Jesaja: Studien zur Eigenart und Intention in Am 1,3-2, 3.4f. und Jes 13,1-16,14. BBB 136: B 2002, Philo 247 pp. €42. 3-8257-0288-X. Bibl. 199-247.

4140 **Fischer, Irmtraud** Gotteskünderinnen: zu einer geschlechterfairen Deutung des Phänomens der Prophetie und der Prophetinnen in der Hebräischen Bibel. Stu 2002, Kohlhammer 298 pp. €20. 3-17-01745-7-6.

4141 **García de la Fuente, O.** Ezequiel, Daniel, Oseas y otros profetas de Israel. Analecta malacitana 38: Málaga 2001, Univ. de Málaga 506 pp.

4142 **Glazov, Gregory Yuri** The bridling of the tongue and the opening of the mouth in biblical prophecy. JSOT.S 311: 2001 ⇒17,3701. [R]CBQ 64 (2002) 737-738 (*Cook, Stephen L.*).

4143 *Gretcha, Job* Tradition et prophétisme. Revue d'éthique et de théologie morale.Suppl. 223 (2002) 39-49.

4144 **Griffin, William Paul** The God of the prophets: an analysis of divine action. JSOT.S 249: 1997 ⇒13,3393. [R]ThLZ 127 (2002) 280-281 (*Koch, Klaus*).

4145 **Hayes, Katherine Murphey** "The earth mourns": prophetic metaphor and oral aesthetic. Academia Biblica 8: Atlanta, GA 2002, SBL xiv; 286 pp. $40. 1-58983-034-2. Bibl. 247-261.

4146 *Herrmann, Siegfried* Ursprung und Funktion der Prophetie im alten Israel <1976>;

4147 Prophetie in Israel und Ägypten: Recht und Grenze eines Vergleichs <1963>. Geschichte und Prophetie. BWANT 157: 2002 ⇒179. 121-172/173-189.

4148 **Junco Garza, Carlos** Palabra sin fronteras: los profetas de Israel. 2000 ⇒16,3707. [R]RLAT 19 (2002) 89-91 (*Sivatte, Rafael de*).

4149 **Lange, Armin** Vom prophetischen Wort zur prophetischen Tradition: Studien zur Traditions- und Redaktionsgeschichte innerprophetischer Konflikte in der Hebräischen Bibel. [D]*Janowski, Bernd*: FAT 34: Tü 2002, Mohr S. xi; 371 pp. €74. 3-16-147732-4. Diss.-Habil. Tübingen 2000; Index von *K.F.D. Römfeld*; Bibl. 321-358.

4150 *Magarik, Larry* Three rationalist explanations of prophecy. JBQ 30 (2002) 32-40.

4151 **Matthews, Victor Harold** Social world of the Hebrew prophets. 2001 ⇒17,3722. [R]WThJ 63 (2002) 207-210 (*Kelly, Michael*).

4152 [E]**Mayhue, Richard L.; Thomas, Robert L.** The Master's perspective series, 4: the Master's perspective on biblical prophecy. GR 2002, Kregel 290 pp. $13. 0-8254-3182-4 [ThD 49,381: Heiser, W.].

4153 **McConville, J. Gordon** Exploring the Old Testament, 4: a guide to the prophets. DG 2002, InterVarsity xxxii; 272 pp. $25. 0-8308-2554-1 [ThD 50,81—Heiser, W. Charles].

4154 **McLaughlin, John** The marzeah in the prophetic literature: references and allusions in light of extra-biblical evidence. VT.S 39: 2001 ⇒17,3725. [R]SR 31 (2002) 234-235 (*Matthews, Victor H.*).

4155 *Meagher, Paddy* Violence in the prophetic books. Jeevadhara 32 (2002) 119-135.

4156 *Merlo, Paolo* Profezia neoassira e oracoli di salvezza biblici: motivazioni, forme e contenuti di un possibile confronto. RivBib 50 (2002) 129-152.

4157 *Miller, Patrick D.* 'Slow to anger': the God of the prophets. [F]ACHTEMEIER, P.: 2002 ⇒1. 39-55.

4158 *Moran, William L.* New evidence from Mari on the history of prophecy. The most magic word. 2002 <1969> ⇒212. 98-139;

4159 An ancient prophetic oracle. The most magic word. 2002 <1993> ⇒212. 140-147.

4160 **Mowinckel, Sigmund Olaf Plytt** The Spirit and the word: prophecy and tradition in Ancient Israel. [E]*Hanson, Kenneth C.*: Fortress Classics in Biblical Studies: Mp 2002, Fortress xiv; 174 pp. $16. 0-8006-3487-X. Bibl. 155-162.

4161   *Mulloor, Augustine* Hope: semantic implications in the prophecies
       and pragmatic challenges today. God of big dreams. 2002 ⇒359. 15-
       76.
4162   **Nissinen, Martti** Reference to prophecy in neo-Assyrian sources.
       SAAS 7: 1998 ⇒14,3311; 15,3579. ^RAfO 48-49 (2001-2002) 211-
       212 (*Lambert, W.G.*).
4163   *Nissinen, Martti* Prophets and the divine council. ^FWEIPPERT, M.:
       OBO 186: 2002 ⇒133. 4-19 [Jer 23,18].
4164   *Oberforcher, Robert* Die Opposition Gottes: Ringen der Propheten
       um authentischen Glauben und wahre Humanität. Der unbequeme
       Gott. ThTr 11 (2002) 11-34.
4165   **Parpola, Simo** Assyrian prophecies. 1997 ⇒13,3409... 17,3729.
       ^ROr. 71 (2002) 1-54 (*Weippert, Manfred*); JSSt 47 (2002) 312-313
       (*Postgate, J.N.*); AfO 48-49 (2001-2002) 208-211 (*Lambert, W.G.*);
       JQR 92 (2001) 227-232 (*Kwasman, Theodore*).
4166   *Patton, Corrine L.* The prophets and the nations. BiTod 40 (2002)
       149-153.
4167   **Petersen, David L.** The prophetic literature: an introduction. LVL
       2002, Westminster xii; 260 pp. $30. 0-664-25453-5. ^RRExp 99
       (2002) 627 (*Biddle, Mark E.*).
4168   *Pérez Sánchez, Francisco* El testimonio profético en el A.T. Teolo-
       gía y Catequesis 81 (2002) 9-16.
4169   **Pilch, John J.** The cultural world of the prophets: the first reading
       and responsorial psalm: Sunday by Sunday, Year B, ColMn 2002,
       Liturgical xiv; 127 pp. 0-8146-2787-0. Bibl. 126-127.
4170   **Podhoretz, Norman** The prophets: who they were, what they are.
       NY 2002, The Free Press ix; 390 pp. $30. 0-7432-1927-9.
4171   *Raabe, Paul R.* The particularizing of universal judgment in prophet-
       ic discourse. CBQ 64 (2002) 652-674.
4172   *Ramón, Lucía* Las profetas bíblicas: mujeres proféticas en estado de
       buena esperanza. TE 46 (2002) 143-166.
4173   **Renaud, Bernard** Nouvelle où éternelle alliance?: le message des
       prophètes. LeDiv 189: P 2002, Cerf 378 pp. €38. 2-204-06931-0.
       Bibl. 343-358. ^RRTL 33 (2002) 571-572 (*Bogaert, P.-M.*).
4174   *Roberts, J.J.M.* Does God lie?: divine deceit as a theological problem
       in Israelite prophetic literature <1988>;
4175   The Mari prophetic texts in transliteration and English translation;
4176   A christian perspective on prophetic prediction <1979>. The bible
       and the ANE. 2002 ⇒230. 123-131/157-253/406-418.
4177   **Rofé, Alexander** Introduzione alla letteratura profetica. StBi 111:
       1995 ⇒11/1,2151...13,3417. ^RRTL 33 (2002) 261-62 (*Di Pede, E.*).
4178   **Schultz, Richard L.** The search for quotation: verbal parallels in the
       prophets. JSOT.S 180: 1999 ⇒15,3588...17,3738. ^RCBQ 64 (2002)
       147-148 (*Parunak, H. Van Dyke*).
4179   *Sherwood, Yvonne* 'Darke texts needs notes': on prophetic prophecy,
       John DONNE and the baroque. JSOT 27 (2002) 47-74.
4180   **Smith, William Robertson** The prophets of Israel and their place in
       history. New Brunswick, NJ 2002, Transaction cxxii; 446 pp. 0-
       7658-0748-3. With a new introduction by *Robert Alun Jones*.
4181   *Spreafico, Ambrogio* I libri profetici e la profezia biblica. RdT 43
       (2002) 805-820.
4182   **Steck, Odil Hannes** The prophetic books and their theological wit-
       ness. 2000 ⇒16,3756. ^RRBLit 4 (2002) 207-208 (*O'Brien, Julia
       Myers*).

4183 *Stiebert, Johanna* Le ricchezze in Isaia ed Ezechiele: un esempio di inversione profetica. Conc(I) 38/1 (2002) 45-55; Conc(E) 294,37-45; Conc(D) 38/1,26-33; Conc(P) 294,34-42;

4184 The maligned patriarch: prophetic ideology and the 'bad press' of Esau. ^MCARROLL, R.: JSOT.S 348: 2002 ⇒13. 33-48.

4185 **Stiebert, Johanna** The construction of shame in the Hebrew Bible: the prophetic contribution. JSOT.S 346: Shf 2002, Sheffield A. x; 196 pp. £50. 1-84127-268-X. Bibl. 174-187. ^ROTEs 15 (2002) 837-839 (*Branch, R.G.*).

4186 *Stiglmair, Arnold* 'Prophet'und Gottesherrschaft. ^FHAAG, E.: 2002 ⇒ 55. 319-328 [Isa 6,1-13; Jer 1,4-10].

4187 **Vanderhooft, David Stephen** The Neo-Babylonian empire and Babylon in the latter prophets. HSM 59: 1999 ⇒15,3600...17,3746. ^RBASOR 326 (2002) 100-101 (*Sommer, Benjamin D.*); ZDPV 118 (2002) 179-183 (*Berlejung, Angelika*); BiOr 59 (2002) 579-580 (*Jong, M.J. de*); RBLit (2002)* (*Sweeney, Marvin A.*).

4188 **Wischnowsky, Marc** Tochter Zion: Aufnahme und Überwindung der Stadtklage in den Prophetenschriften des Alten Testaments. WMANT 89: 2001 ⇒17,3748. ^RBZ 46 (2002) 309-311 (*Berges, Ulrich*).

E8.2 **Proto-Isaias,** *textus, commentarii*

4189 **Berges, Ulrich** Das Buch Jesaja: Komposition und Endgestalt. 1998 ⇒14,3328...17,3750. ^RThRv 98 (2002) 30-32 (*Kaiser, Otto*); RBLit 4 (2002) 211-214 (*Sweeney, Marvin A.*).

4190 **Beuken, Willem A.M.** Isaiah, part 2, vol. 2: Isaiah chapters 28-39. ^T*Doyle, Brian*: Historical Commentary on the OT: 2000 ⇒16,3772; 17,3751. ^RRBLit (2002)* (*Sweeney, Marvin A.*).

4191 **Blenkinsopp, Joseph** Isaiah 1-39. AncB 19: 2000 ⇒16,3773; 17, 3752. ^RBS 159 (2002) 247-248 (*Chisholm, Robert B.*); AUSS 40 (2002) 134-135 (*Mulzac, Kenneth D.*); IThQ 67 (2002) 73-74 (*Hill, Robert C.*); Interp. 56 (2002) 320, 322 (*Sweeney, Marvin A.*); ThLZ 127 (2002) 275-277 (*Höffken, Peter*); JSSt 47 (2002) 324-326 (*Williamson, H.G.M.*); BBR 12 (2002) 147-148 (*Watts, John D.W.*); Bib. 83 (2002) 273-277 (*Beuken, Willem A.M.*); OTEs 15 (2002) 555-556 (*Cronjé, S.I.*).

4192 **Brueggemann, Walter** Isaiah. 1998 ⇒15,3705...16,3774. ^RHeyJ 43 (2002) 216-218 (*McNamara, Martin*).

4193 **Childs, Brevard Springs** Isaiah. 2000 ⇒16,3776; 17,3755. ^RZKTh 124 (2002) 121-122 (*Paganini, Simone*); Bib. 83 (2002) 579-583 (*Sommer, Benjamin D.*); RBLit 4 (2002) 214-217 = JBL 121 (2002) 351-353 (*Everson, A. Joseph*); NBl 83 (2002) 101-103 (*O'Brien, Mark A.*); RBLit (2002)* (*Sweeney, Marvin A.*); RRT 9 (2002) 127-128 (*Norton, Gerard J.*); ThTo 59 (2002) 121-122, 124 (*Williamson, H.G.M.*); ProEc 11 (2002) 235-237 (*McGinnis, Claire R. Mathews*); CBQ 64 (2002) 126-127 (*Redditt, Paul L.*); Interp. 56 (2002) 424, 426 (*Melugin, Roy F.*; BS 159 (2002) 493-494 (*Merrill, Eugene H.*); ThLZ 127 (2002) 1159-1161 (*Höffken, Peter*).

4194 **De Zan, Renato** Isaia [1-39]. Dabar... AT: 2001 ⇒17,3756. ^RLat. 68 (2002) 147-148 (*Ognibeni, Bruno*).

4195 ^E**Goshen-Gottstein, Moshe H.** The book of Isaiah. 1995 ⇒11/1, 2177... 15,3609. ^RRB 109 (2002) 459-461 (*Gonçalves, Francolino*).

4196   **Holladay, William Lee** Unbound by time: Isaiah still speaks. CM 2002, Cowley xx; 188 pp. $13. 1-56101-204-1 [ThD 50,76—Heiser, W. Charles].
4197   **Kaiser, Otto** Isaia (capp. 13-39). ᵀ*Audisio, A.*: Antico Testamento 18: Brescia 2002, Paideia 500 pp. €36.50. 88-394-0643-3.
4198   **Kalas, J. Ellsworth** A study of Isaiah: through suffering to hope. Bible Readers: Nv 2002, Abingdon 54 pp. $5.50 [BiTod 41,195— Bergant, Dianne].
4199   **Motyer, Alec** Isaia—introduzione e commentario. Commentari all'Antico Testamento: R 2002, GBU 665 pp;
4200   Isaiah: an introduction and commentary. Tyndale OT Commentaries: 1999 ⇒15,3614. ᴿVeE 23 (2002) 264-265 (*Venter, P.M.*).
4201   *O'Brien, Mark A.* Reading the book of Isaiah. PrPe 16 (2002) 307-311.
4202   **Quinn-Miscall, Peter D.** Reading Isaiah: poetry and vision. 2001 ⇒17,3762. ᴿRExp 99 (2002) 460-461 (*Biddle, Mark E.*).

E8.3 **Isaias 1-39,** *themata, versiculi*

4203   **Becker, Uwe** Jesaja—von der Botschaft zum Buch. FRLANT 178: 1997 ⇒13,3463...16,3788. ᴿOTEs 15 (2002) 554-555 (*Cronjé, S.I.*).
4204   *Blenkinsopp, Joseph* The formation of the Hebrew Bible canon: Isaiah as a test case. Canon debate. 2002 ⇒1551. 53-67.
4205   *Conrad, Edgar W.* Yehoshua GITAY: 'what is *he* doing?'. JSOT 27 (2002) 237-241.
4206   *Gosse, Bernard* Ex 15, Ps 120-134 et le livre d'Isaïe, le salut d'Israël et celui du psalmiste. BeO 44 (2002) 129-159, 193-206;
4207   L'évolution des rapports entre le salut (*yšw'h*) et le jugement (*mšpt*), dans les rédactions d'ensemble du livre d'Isaïe et du psautier et le rôle des cantiques bibliques. RB 109 (2002) 323-342.
4208   *Howell, Maribeth* A light to the nations. BiTod 40 (2002) 205-210.
4209   **Klouda, Sheri Lynn** An analysis of the significance of Isaiah's use of Psalms 96-99. ᴰ*Klein, G.*: 2002, 197 pp. Diss. Fort Worth [RTL 34,592].
4210   **Kustár, Zoltán** "Durch seine Wunden sind wir geheilt": eine Unter-suchungen zur Metaphorik von Israels Krankheit und Heilung im Je-sajabuch. BWANT 154: Stu 2002, Kohlhammer 259 pp. €35. 3-17-016973-4. Bibl. 227-250.
4211   *Landy, Francis* Ghostwriting Isaiah. First person. BiSe 81: 2002 ⇒ 295. 93-114.
4212   **Leclerc, Thomas L.** Yahweh is exalted in justice: solidarity and con-flict in Isaiah. 2001 ⇒17,3780. ᴿRBLit (2002)* (*Berges, Ulrich*).
4213   *Lepore, Luciano* "Un resto ritornerà" (Shear-Yashûb). BeO 44 (2002) 207-233.
4214   *Liss, Hanna* Undisclosed speech: patterns of communication in the book of Isaiah. Journal of Hebrew Scriptures 4 2002*.
4215   *Peter, Jeeva* Led by the empowering hands: Isaiah's dream of an alternate society. God of big dreams. 2002 ⇒359. 151-164.
4216   *Roberts, J.J.M.* Blindfolding the prophet: political resistance to First Isaiah's oracles in the light of ancient Near Eastern attitudes toward oracles. The bible and the ANE. 2002 <1997> ⇒230. 282-291;
4217   The divine king and the human community in Isaiah's vision of the future. The bible and the ANE. 2002 <1983> ⇒230. 348-357.

4218 *Sawyer, John F.A.* Isaiah and Zionism. ^MCARROLL, R.: JSOT.S 348: 2002 ⇒13. 246-260.

4219 *Schmid, Konrad* Herrschererwartungen und -aussagen im Jesajabuch: Überlegungen zu ihrer synchronen Logik und zu ihren diachronen Transformationen. ^FLEENE, H. 2002 ⇒73. 175-209.

4220 *Seijas de los Ríos-Zarzosa, Guadalupe* Towards a computer-assisted classification of discourse types in the Proto-Isaiah. Bible and computer. 2002 ⇒548. 245-258.

4221 *Sweeney, Marvin A.* On the road to DUHM: Isaiah in nineteenth-century critical scholarship. SBL.SP 2002. SBL.SPS 41: 2002 ⇒598. 191-211.

4222 *Williamson, Hugh G.M.* Biblical criticism and hermeneutics in Isaiah 1:10-17. ^FSMEND, R. 2002 ⇒113. 82-96.

4223 *Sigurvinsson, Jón Ásgeir* Die syntaktischen Verhältnisse des Verb יסף in Jes 1,12-13 im Hinblick auf die kolometrische und illokutionäre Struktur von Jes 1,10-20. ^FSTEINGRIMSSON, S.: ATSAT 72: 2002 ⇒ 117. 123-143.

4224 *Van Wieringen, Archibald L.H.M.* The day beyond the days: Isaiah 2:2 within the framework of the book Isaiah. ^FLEENE, H. 2002 ⇒73. 253-259.

4225 *Bruin, Willem M. de* De afbakening van Jesaja 2:5 in het licht van de oude tekstgetuigen. NedThT 56/4 (2002) 280-298.

4226 *Troxel, Ronald L.* Economic plunder as a leitmotif in LXX-Isaiah. Bib. 83 (2002) 375-391 [Isa 3,12-15; 5,5; 5,17; 6,13; 9,3-4].

4227 *Bartelmus, Rüdiger* Beobachtungen zur literarischen Struktur des sog. Weinbergslieds (Jes 5,1-7): Möglichkeiten und Grenzen der formgeschichtlichen Methode bei der Interpretation von Texten aus dem corpus propheticum. Auf der Suche. 2002 <1998> ⇒140. 319-336.

4228 *Borgonovo, Giantonio* Isaia 6: chiave di volta del pensiero isaiano. AnScR 7 (2002) 129-150.

4229 *Passoni Dell'Acqua, Anna* 'Ma io li guarirò!': la versione dei LXX di *Isaia* 6. AnScR 7 (2002) 151-168.

4230 *Vergani, Emidio Isaia* 6 nella letteratura siriaca: due autori del V secolo: BALAI e GIOVANNI il Solitario. AnScR 7 (2002) 169-192.

4231 *Sacchi, Paolo* Isaia 6 e la concezione di impurità nel medio giudaismo. Vivens Homo 13/1 (2002) 55-77 [Job 1,1-4].

4232 **Lehnert, Volker A.** Die Provokation Israels: die paradoxe Funktion von Jes 6,9-10 bei Markus und Lukas: ein textpragmatischer Versuch im Kontext gegenwärtiger Rezeptionsästhetik und Lesetheorie. 1999 ⇒15,3673...17,3809. ^RJBL 121 (2002) 369-371 (*Holm, Tawny*) [Mk 4,10-13; Lk 8,9-10].

4233 *Landy, Francis* Prophetic intercourse. ^MCARROLL, R.: JSOT.S 348: 2002 ⇒13. 261-279 [Isa 8,1-4; 12].

4234 *Roberts, J.J.M.* Whose child is this?: reflections on the speaking voice in Isaiah 9:5. The bible and the ANE. 2002 <1997> ⇒230. 143-156.

4235 *Van der Kooij, Arie* Wie heißt der Messias?: zu Jes 9,5 in den alten griechischen Versionen. ^FSMEND, R. 2002 ⇒113. 156-169.

4236 *Beuken, Willem André Maria* 'Lebanon with its majesty shall fall. A shoot shall come forth from the stump of Jesse' (Isa 10:34-11:1): interfacing the story of Assyria and the image of Israel's future in Isaiah 10-11. ^FLEENE, H. 2002 ⇒73. 17-33.

4237 *Groß, Walter* Syntax, Pragmatik, Stilistik in Jes 11,1-10: Vergleich und Kritik deutscher Übersetzungen. ^FSTEINGRIMSSON, S.: ATSAT 72: 2002 ⇒117. 25-43.

4238 *Haag, Emil* Ja, Gott ist meine Rettung: Predigt zur Jahreslosung 2002 (Jesaja 12,2). ThBeitr 33 (2002) 1-3.

4239 *Ittzés, János* "Ja, Gott ist meine Rettung, ihm will ich vertrauen, und niemals verzagen" (Jesaja 12,2a): zur Jahreslosung für 2002. LKW 49 (2002) 9-12.

4240 *Schöpflin, Karin* Ein Blick in die Unterwelt (Jesaja 14). ThZ 58 (2002) 299-314.

4241 **Shipp, R. Mark** Of dead kings and dirges: myth and meaning in Isaiah 14:4b-21. Academia Biblica 11: Atlanta, GA 2002, SBL xiv; 197 pp. $30. 1-58983-038-5. Bibl. 167-177.

4242 **Jones, Brian C.** Howling over Moab: irony and rhetoric in Isaiah 15-16. SBL.DS 157: 1996 ⇒12,3381... 15,3693. ^RJNES 61 (2002) 228-230 (*Hunt, Joel H.*).

4243 *Baruch, Eli* Isaiah's prophecy against Shebna. Shnaton 13 (2002) 97-110. **H.** [Isa 22,15-25].

4244 *Doyle, Brian* Fertility and infertility in Isaiah 24-27. ^FLEENE, H. 2002 ⇒73. 77-88.

4245 **Doyle, Brian** The Apocalypse of Isaiah metaphorically speaking: a study of the use, function and significance of metaphors in Isaiah 24-27. BEThL 151: 2000 ⇒16,3835. ^ROLZ 97 (2002) 568-571 (*Höffken, Peter*); ThLZ 127 (2002) 1279-1282 (*Nitsche, Stefan Ark*).

4246 *Smit, Peter-Ben* Appetite for destruction: a note on Isa 25:8a. BN 111 (2002) 44-47.

4247 *Snoek, J.* (Dis)continuity between present and future in Isaiah 26:7-21. ^FLEENE, H. 2002 ⇒73. 211-218.

4248 *Jenner, Konrad D.* The worship of YHWH on the holy mountain in light of the idea of the return: a short note on the confrontation of theology of the Old Testament and comparative and applied science of religion. ^FLEENE, H. 2002 ⇒73.129-133 [Isa 27,12-13].

4249 *Roberts, J.J.M.* Yahweh's foundation in Zion (Isaiah 28:16). The bible and the ANE. 2002 <1987> ⇒230. 292-310.

4250 *Thompson, Michael E.W.* Vision, reality and worship: Isaiah 33. ET 113 (2002) 327-333.

4251 *Cronjé, S.I.* Jesaja 36-39—sinkroniese en diakroniese lees van 'n teks. VeE 23 (2002) 305-318.

E8.4 **Deutero-Isaias 40-52**: *commentarii, themata, versiculi*

4252 **Baltzer, Klaus** Deutero-Isaiah: a commentary on Isaiah 40-55. ^T*Kohl, Margaret*: Hermeneia: 2001 ⇒17,3832. ^RRRT 9 (2002) 126-127 (*Norton, Gerard J.*); JThS 53 (2002) 139-141 (*Seitz, C.R.*); RBLit 4 (2002) 1-6 (*Sommer, Benjamin D.*).

4253 *Berges, Ulrich* Gottesgarten und Tempel: die neue Schöpfung im Jesajabuch. Gottesstadt. QD 191: 2002 ⇒567. 69-98.

4254 **Blenkinsopp, Joseph** Isaiah 40-55: a new translation with introduction and commentary. AncB 19A: NY 2002, Doubleday xvii; 411 pp. $45. 0-385-49717-2. ᴿIThQ 67 (2002) 282-284 (*Hill, Robert C.*).

4255 *Cajot, Rodel* The new exodus in Second Isaiah. PhilipSac 37 (2002) 43-56.

4256 **De Zan, Renato** Isaia 40-66. Dabar... AT: Padova 2002, Messaggero 204 pp. Bibl.

4257 *Hermisson, Hans-Jürgen* 'Deuterojesaja' und 'Eschatologie'. ᶠLEENE, H.: 2002 ⇒73. 89-105.

4258 **Hermisson, Hans-Jürgen** Deuterojesaja [48,1-11 (cont.) - 49,1-13]. Neuk 2002, Neuk'er 241-320 pp. 3-7887-1258-9.

4259 **Koole, Jan Leunis** Isaiah III,1-2: Isaiah 40-48; Isaiah 49-55. 1998 ⇒13,3538... 17,3834. ᴿOTEs 15 (2002) 564-566 (*Cronjé, S.I.*).

4260 *Luiz, Johnson* God the liberator: exilic hope according to 2ⁿᵈ and 3ʳᵈ Isaiah. God of big dreams. 2002 ⇒359. 180-209.

4261 **Oswalt, John N.** The book of Isaiah: chapters 40-66. NIC.OT: 1998 ⇒14,3409...16,3863. ᴿCBQ 64 (2002) 142-43 (*Sommer, Benjamin*).

4262 *Polliack, Meira* Deutero-Isaiah's typological use of Jacob in the portrayal of Israel's national renewal. Creation in Jewish and christian tradition. JSOT.S 319: 2002 ⇒593. 72-110.

4263 *Ramis ı Darder, Francesc* Perdó i reconciliació en Isaïes 40-55. Perdó i reconciliació. 2002 ⇒591. 145-173.

4264 *Simian-Yofre, Horacio* La critica agli idoli nel Deuteroisaia. PSV 46 (2002) 51-59.

4265 **Sommer, Benjamin D.** A prophet reads scripture: allusions in Isaiah 40-66. 1998 ⇒14,3413... 17,3848. ᴿRBLit 4 (2002) 217-219 (*Pyeon, Yohan*).

Talstra, E. Second Isaiah and Qohelet 2002 ⇒4025.

4266 **Zapff, Burkard M.** Jesaja 40-55. NEB: 2001 ⇒17,3838. ᴿBiOr 59 (2002) 124-126 (*Labahn, Antje*); OrdKor 43 (2002) 355-356 (*Heinemann, Franz Karl*); RivBib 50 (2002) 368-369 (*Marconcini, Benito*); ThLZ 127 (2002) 391-393 (*Höffken, Peter*).

4267 *Barstad, Hans M.* Isa. 40,1-11: another reading. Congress volume Basel 2001. VT.S 92: 2002 ⇒570. 225-240.

4268 *Phillips, Anthony* Double for all her sins. Essays on biblical law. JSOT.S 344: 2002 <1982> ⇒223. 251-254 [Isa 40,2].

4269 **Ramis Darder, Francesc** El triunfo de Yahvé sobre los ídolos (Is 40,12-44,23): "en vez de zarzas crecerá el ciprés". Sant Pacià 75: Barc 2002, Facultat de Teologia de Catalunya 374 pp. 84-86065-73-9. Bibl. 347-368.

4270 *Dijkstra, Meindert* 'He who calls the eras from the beginning' (Isa 41:4): from history to eschatology in Second Isaiah;

4271 *Van der Woude, Annemarieke* What is new in Isaiah 41:14-20?: on the drama theories of Klaus Baltzer and Henk Leene. ᶠLEENE, H. 2002 ⇒73. 61-76/261-267.

4272 *Chung, Paul* "A light to the nations" from an Asian perspective. JAAT 5 (2002) 81-102 [Isa 42,6-7].

4273 *Bons, Eberhard* Y a-t-il une typologie de l'Exode en Isaïe 43,16-23?. Typologie biblique. LeDiv: 2002 ⇒341. 77-102.

4274 *Fried, Lisbeth S.* Cyrus the messiah?: the historical background to Isaiah 45:1. HThR 95 (2002) 373-393.

4275 *Blocher, Henri* Glorious Zion, our mother: readings in Isaiah (conspectus, or abridged). EurJT 11 (2002) 5-14 [Isa 49,14-23; 54; 65-66].

4276 *Lemański, Janusz* Dobra Nowina według Deutero-Izajasza (Iz 52,7-10) [The good news according to Deutero-Isaiah (Isa 52,7-10).] Verbum Vitae 2 (2002) 49-64 Sum. 64. P.

E8.5 *Isaiae 53ss. Carmina Servi YHWH*: Servant Songs

4277 *Ashby, G.* Suffering, sacrifice and servanthood in Israel. OTEs 15 (2002) 11-22.

4278 *Ceresko, Anthony R.* The rhetorical strategy of the fourth Servant Song (Isaiah 52:13-53:12): poetry and the Exodus—new Exodus. Prophets and proverbs. 2002 <1994> ⇒154. 1-14.

4279 *Cortese, Enzo* Il "Servo di JHWH" (SdJ). RStB 14/1-2 (2002) 81-98.

4280 ᴱ**Gryson, Roger** VL 12: Esaias, pars 2, fasc. 8-11, Is 54,17-fin; conclusion: histoire du texte; correction et compléments; index des témoins; table des matières 1996-1997 ⇒14,3434; 16,3897. ᴿRB 109 (2002) 462-463 (*Gonçalves, Francolino J.*).

4281 **Schenker, Adrian** Douceur de Dieu et violence des hommes: le quatrième chant du Serviteur de Dieu et le Nouveau Testament. ᵀ*Hugo, Philippe; Riga, Brigitte*: Bru 2002, Lumen Vitae 80 pp.

4282 *Stuhlmacher, Peter* Der messianische Gottesknecht. Biblische Theologie. WUNT 146: 2002 <1993> ⇒245. 119-140.

4283 *Silva, A.A. da* Die teksfunksie en boodskap van Jesaja 49:1-6. HTS 58 (2002) 1323-1336 [OTA 26,502].

4284 *Oosting, Reinoud* Returning (to) Zion: Isaiah 52:8 in light of verbal valency patterns. ᶠLEENE, H.: 2002 ⇒73. 159-166.

4285 *Fritsch, Marc* Esaïe 52,12-53: nouveau départ sur le chemin du salut. Lire et Dire 53 (2002) 3-16 [BuBB 39,72].

4286 *Goulder, M.* "Behold my servant Jehoiachin". VT 52 (2002) 175-190 [Isa 52,13 - 53,12].

4287 *Mello, Alberto* Il Servo sofferente nella tradizione ebraica. Il crocifisso. 2002 ⇒620. 99-112.

4288 *Nakanose, Shigeyuki; Pedro, Enilda P.* A missão profética do povo sofredor: leitura do quarto Cântico do Servo Sofredor: Isaías 52,13-53,12. Estudos bíblicos 73 (2002) 26-41.

4289 *Manfredi, Silvana* Problematicità della figura del 'Servo' in *Isaia* 53. Il crocifisso. 2002 ⇒620. 11-28.

4290 **Schenker, Adrian** Knecht und Lamm Gottes (Jesaja 53): Übernahme von Schuld im Horizont der Gottesknechtslieder. SBS 190: 2001 ⇒ 17,3864. ᴿCBQ 64 (2002) 145-146 (*Laberge, Léo*); ThPQ 150 (2002) 422-423 (*Hubmann, Franz D.*).

4291 *Winandy, Jacques* Une traduction communément reçue et pourtant indéfendable. RB 109 (2002) 321-322 [Isa 53,3].

4292 *Seeligmann, Isac L.* δεῖξαι αὐτῷ φῶς. Textus 21 (2002) 107-128 [Isa 53,11].

4293 *Theißen, Gerd* Glauben als Überlebenskraft: der Bund meines Friedens für bedrohte Menschen und Völker (Jes 54,1-10). Erlösungsbilder. 2002 ⇒1460. 61-68.

4294 **Paganini, Simone** Der Weg zur Frau Zion, Ziel unserer Hoffnung: Aufbau, Kontext, Sprache, Kommunikationsstruktur und theologische Motive in Jes 55,1-13. *DFischer, Georg*: SBB 49: Stu 2002, Verl. Kath. Bibelwerk 232 pp. €41. 3-460-00491-6. Diss. Innsbruck. Bibl. 202-218.

E8.6 [Trito]Isaias 56-66

4295 **Croatto, J.** Isaías: a palava profética e sua releitura hermenêutica, 3: 56-66. *TOrth, Lúcia M.E.*: Comentário Bíblico: Petrópolis 2002, Vozes 415 pp. 85-326-2714-5.
4296 *Croatto, J. Severino* Cómo empezar a leer el Tercer Isaías. RevBib 63 (2001) 119-125.
4297 **Grant-Henderson, Anna L.** Inclusive voices in post-exilic Judah. ColMn 2002, Liturgical xxi; 178 pp. $18. 0-8146-5387-1. Bibl. 143-152.
4298 *Grenzer, Matthias* A proximidade de Deus na eliminação da opressão e na caridade ao pobre: um estudo de Isaías 56-66. Estudos bíblicos 73 (2002) 55-66.
4299 *Kratz, Reinhard G.* Tritojesaja. TRE 34. 2002 ⇒800. 124-130.
4300 **Ruszkowski, Leszek** Volk und Gemeinde im Wandel: eine Untersuchung zu Jesaja 56-66. FRLANT 191: 2000 ⇒16,3918; 17,3875. *RJThS* 53 (2002) 142-144 (*Williamson, H.G.M.*); RBLit (2002)* (*Wells, Roy, D.*).

4301 *Clauss, Bertrand; Thallinger, Jean-Matthieu* Esaïe 58,1-12: alors la lumière poindra comme l'aurore. Lire et Dire 53 (2002) 17-27 [BuBB 39,72].
4302 *Ballhorn, Egbert* Ein Fasten, das Gott gefällt: Jesaja 58,1-14: März— Fasten. zwölfmal bibel. 2002 ⇒1087. 28-37.
4303 **Mouw, Richard J.** When the kings come marching in: Isaiah and the New Jerusalem. GR ²2002, Eerdmans xi; 131 pp. $14. 0-8028-3996-7 [Isa 60; Rev 21-22].
4304 *Osborne, Thomas P.* Lumière contre lumières: une étude d'Ésaïe 60. Symbolisme et expérience. 2002 ⇒666. 135-147.
4305 *Edelmann, Karl* "Auf, werde licht, Jerusalem ...": Jesaja 60,1-6: die 1. Lesung der Epiphanieliturgie. BiHe 38 (2002) 103-106.
4306 *Berges, Ulrich* Der neue Himmel und die neue Erde im Jesajabuch: eine Auslegung zu Jesaja 65:17 und 66:22. *FLEENE, H.*: 2002 ⇒73. 9-15.
4307 *Gardner, Anne E.* The nature of the new heavens and new earth in Isaiah 66:22. ABR 50 (2002) 10-27.
4308 *Clements, Ronald E.* Isaiah: a book without an ending?. JSOT 97 (2002) 109-126 [Isa 66,24].

E8.7 Jeremias

4309 *Amphoux, Christian* La forme du livre de Jérémie à l'époque greque. Nier les dieux. 2002 ⇒626. 147-167.
4310 *Antony, Joseph* A fallen tree and a new sprout: Messianic hope in Jeremiah. God of big dreams. 2002 ⇒359. 165-179.

4311 E**Ausloo, Hans** Jeremia: profeet tussen hoop en wanhoop. Lv 2002, Acco 221 pp. €19.50. 90-334-5136-0 [Streven 70,757—Beentjes, Panc].

4312 *Barstad, Hans M.* Prophecy in the book of Jeremiah and the historical prophet. MCARROLL, R.: JSOT.S 348: 2002 ⇒13. 87-100.

4313 *Bauer, Angela* Death, grief, agony and a new creation: re-reading gender in Jeremiah after September 11. WaW 22 (2002) 378-386.

4314 *Bracke, John M.* Justice in the book of Jeremiah;

4315 *Brueggemann, Walter* Meditation upon the abyss: the book of Jeremiah. WaW 22 (2002) 387-395/340-350.

4316 E**Dal Covolo, Enrico; Maritano, Mario** Omelie su Geremia: lettura origeniana. BSRel 165: 2001 ⇒17,3902. RTer. 53 (2002) 598-599 (*Sánchez, Manuel Diego*); Itinerarium(Messina) 10 (2002) 269-270 (*Stelladoro, Gabriella*).

4317 **Dearman, J. Andrew** Jeremiah, Lamentations. NIV Application Commentary: GR 2002, Zondervan 488 pp. $28.

4318 T**Egawa, Augustine,** *al.,* The holy bible: the book of Jeremiah. Tokyo 2002, San Paolo vi; 412; 2*; vii pp. ¥4500. 4-8056-1011-5. Annotated; Studium Biblicum Franciscanum [RB 110,154].

4319 E**Feder, Frank** Biblia Sahidica: Ieremias, Lamentationes (Threni), Epistula Ieremiae et Baruch. TU 147: B 2002, De Gruyter xv; 249 pp. 3-11-017404-9. Bibl. xi-xv.

4320 **Fischer, Georg** El libro de Jeremías. T*Villanueva Salas, Marciano*: Guía espiritual del Antiguo Testamento: 1997 <1996> ⇒12,3453... 15,3785. RBrot. 154 (2002) 83-84 (*Silva, I. Ribeiro da*).

4321 *Fischer, Georg* Werfel als Interpret: zur Jeremia-Deutung in seinem Roman *Höret die Stimme*. Religion—Literatur—Künste II. Im Kontext 14: 2002 ⇒530. 217-243.

4322 *Fretheim, Terence E.* The character of God in Jeremiah. Character and scripture. 2002 ⇒283. 211-230.

4323 **Fretheim, Terence** Jeremiah. Macon 2002, Smyth & H. 704 pp. $65. 1-57312-072-3. Incl. CD.

4324 **Greenberg, Gillian** Translation technique in the Peshitta to Jeremiah. MPIL 13: Lei 2002, Brill xiii; 242 pp. €64/$75. 90-04-11980-9. Bibl. 221-225.

4325 *Herrmann, Siegfried* Die Bewältigung der Krise Israels: Bemerkungen zur Interpretation des Buches Jeremia <1977>;

4326 Jeremia—der Prophet und die Verfasser des Buches Jeremia <1981; 1997>;

4327 Der Beitrag des Jeremiabuches zur biblischen Theologie <1991>. Geschichte und Prophetie. BWANT 157: 2002 ⇒179. 191-203/ 205-222/223-242.

4328 *Hill, John* The book of Jeremiah MT and early second temple conflicts about prophets and prophecy. ABR 50 (2002) 28-42 [Zech 13,2-6].

4329 *Holladay, William L.* Indications of Jeremiah's psalter. JBL 121 (2002) 245-261.

4330 *Huffmon, Herbert B.* Gender subversion in the book of Jeremiah. Sex and gender. 2002 ⇒712. 245-253.

4331 **Laha, Robert R. Jr.** Jeremiah. Interpretation Bible studies: LVL 2002, Westminster viii; 94 pp. $8. 0-664-22581-0. Bibl. 83. ROTEs 15 (2002) 833-834 (*Wessels, W.J.*).

4332 *Langenhorst, Georg* Jeremia als literarische Identifikationsfigur: jüdische Selbst- und Zeitdeutung bei Stefan ZWEIG und Franz WERFEL.
KuI 17 (2002) 45-61.

4333 *Lopasso, Vincenzo* Geremia: il profeta e il libro. BeO 44 (2002) 161-
178;

4334 La data della vocazione di Geremia. [F]TUDDA, F.: 2002 ⇒123. 37-50.

4335 **Maier, Christl** Jeremia als Lehrer der Tora: soziale Gebote des Deu-
teronomiums in Fortschreibungen des Jeremiabuches. FRLANT 196:
Gö 2002, Vandenhoeck & R. 422 pp. €74. 3-525-53880-4. Bibl. 373-
402.

4336 **Maier, Michael P.** Ägypten—Israels Herkunft und Geschick: Studie
über einen theo-politischen Zentralbegriff im hebräischen Jeremiabuch. [D]*Conroy, Charles*: ÖBS 21: Fra 2002, Lang 355 pp. 3-631-50-
383-0. Diss. Gregoriana 2000; Bibl. 313-340.

4337 *McConville, Gordon* Divine speech and the book of Jeremiah. The
trustworthiness of God. 2002 ⇒410. 18-38.

4338 *Minette de Tillesse, Caetano* Jeremias. RBBras 19/1-2 (2002) 3-179.

4339 *Nikolsky, Ronit* The history of the Rechabites and the Jeremiah literature. JSPE 13 (2002) 185-207.

4340 *O'Connor, Kathleen M.* Surviving disaster in the book of Jeremiah.
WaW 22 (2002) 369-377.

4341 **Parke-Taylor, Geoffrey H.** The formation of the book of Jeremiah:
doublets and recurring phrases. SBL.MS 51: 2000 ⇒16,3949; 17,
3914. [R]JSSt 47 (2002) 326-327 (*McKane, William*).

4342 *Pietersma, Albert* 'Επίχειρον in Greek Jeremiah. JNSL 28/2 (2002)
101-108.

4343 *Regt, Lénart J. de* The prophet in the old and the new edition of Jeremiah: increased dramatisation. [F]LEENE, H.: 2002 ⇒73. 167-174.

4344 *Roberts, J.J.M.* The motif of the weeping God in Jeremiah and its
background in the lament tradition of the ancient Near East. The
bible and the ANE. 2002 <1992> ⇒230. 132-142.

4345 *Rouger, Denise* La figure christique de Jérémie à l'époque romaine.
Nier les dieux. 2002 ⇒626. 169-183.

4346 *Scalise, Pamela J.* The way of weeping: reading the path of grief in
Jeremiah. WaW 22 (2002) 415-422.

4347 *Searcy, Edwin* "A people, a name, a praise, and a glory": false and
true faith in Jeremiah. WaW 22 (2002) 333-339.

4348 *Simundson, Daniel J.* Preaching from Jeremiah: challenges and opportunities. WaW 22 (2002) 423-432.

4349 *Sivatte, Rafael de* El regreso siempre posible a Dios y al hermano: la
conversión en Jeremías. Perdó i reconciliació. 2002 ⇒591. 115-143.

4350 *Ung'eyowun, Etienne* La mission du prophète Jérémie dans le contexte national et international. RASM 17 (2002) 44-63.

4351 **Virgili, Rosanna** Geremia, l'incendio e la speranza: la figura e il
messaggio del profeta. 1998 ⇒14,3473. [R]Firmana 27 (2002) 190-191
(*Miola, Gabriele*).

4352 *Viviano, Pauline A.* Characterizing Jeremiah. WaW 22 (2002) 361-8.

4353 *Sérandour, Arnaud* Le cadre institutionnel du livre de Jérémie: notes
de lecture sur le prologue (Jr 1-2). Nier les dieux. 2002 ⇒626. 129-
145.

4354 *Wittenberg, Gunther H.* "... to build and to plant" (Jer. 1:10): the
message of Jeremiah as a source of hope for the exilic community

and its relevance for community building in South Africa. JTSA 112 (2002) 57-67.

4355 *Herrmann, Siegfried* Die Herkunft der 'ehernen Mauer': eine Miszelle zu Jeremia 1,18 und 15,20. Geschichte und Prophetie. BWANT 157: 2002 <1987> ⇒179. 243-249.

4356 *Macwilliam, Stuart* Queering Jeremiah. BiblInterp 10 (2002) 384-404 [Jer 2-3].

4357 *Barbiero, Gianni kî 'al kol 'ellæh* (Jer 2,34bB): eine kontextuelle Lektüre. Studien. SBAB 34: 2002 <1992> ⇒139. 28-37.

4358 **Manfredi, Silvana** Geremia in dialogo: nessi con le tradizioni profetiche e originalità in Ger 4,5-6,30. *DGonçalves, F.J.*: Facoltà Teologica di Sicilia, Studi 6: Caltanisetta 2002, Sciascia 443 pp. €20. 88-82-41-113-3. Diss. École Biblique de Jérusalem 2001; Bibl. 389-409.

4359 *Snyman, S.D.* A structural-historical investigtion of חמס ושׁד in Jeremiah 6:1-8. HTS 58 (2002) 1593-1603 [OTA 26,503].

4360 *Zatelli, Ida hnwh whmʿngh dmyty bt-ṣywn* 'ad un tenero prato paragona la figlia di Sion' (Ger. 6,2): una similitudine biblica controversa. MIMPARATI, F.: 2002 ⇒61. 891-893.

4361 *Villiers, Gerda de* Where did she come from, and where did she go to? (the queen of heaven in Jeremiah 7 and 44). OTEs 15 (2002) 620-627.

4362 *Henderson, Joseph M.* Who weeps in Jeremiah viii 23 (ix 1)?: identifying dramatic speakers in the poetry of Jeremiah. VT 52 (2002) 191-206.

4363 **Rayappan, Arasakumar** The divine struggle: divine—cosmic—human relationship in Jer IX. *DFischer, Georg*: 2002 Diss. Innsbruck [ThRv 99/2,viii].

4364 *Baumann, Gerlinde* Jeremia, die Weisen und die Weisheit: eine Untersuchung von Jer 9,22f. ZAW 114 (2002) 59-79.

4365 *Williams, H.H.* Of rags and riches: the benefits of hearing Jeremiah 9: 23-24 within James 1:9-11. TynB 53 (2002) 273-282.

4366 *Floss, Johannes P.* 'Warum bist du wie ein Fremder im Land, wie ein Reisiger, der nur zum Übernachten einkehrt?'. FSTEINGRIMSSON, S.: ATSAT 72: 2002 ⇒117. 291-304 [Jer 14,8].

4367 *Hubmann, Franz D.* "Synoptisches" aus dem Jeremiabuch. FFUCHS, A.: 2002 ⇒41. 403-417 [Jer 15,11-14; 17,3-4].

4368 *Barbiero, Gianni* Vom Schnee des Libanon und fremden Wassern: eine strukturorientierte Interpretation von Jer 18,14. ZAW 114 (2002) 376-390.

4369 *Fretheim, Terence E.* Caught in the middle: Jeremiah's vocational crisis. WaW 22 (2002) 351-360 [Jer 20,7-18].

4370 *Irudaya, Raj* A prophetic call against war: a politico-theological study of Jeremiah 21:1-14. VJTR 66 (2002) 796-808.

4371 *Aejmelaeus, Anneli* Jeremiah at the turning point of history: the function of Jer. xxv 1-14 in the book of Jeremiah. VT 52 (2002) 459-482.

4372 *Susaimanickam, J* Jeremiah, spokesperson of the people: intercession as a prophetic function in the light of Jer 27,18. BiBh 27 (2002) 317-345.

4373 *Becking, Bob* Petuʾah and setumah in Jeremiah 30-31. Studies in scriptural unit division. Pericope 3: 2002 ⇒339. 1-45.

4374 *Ferry, Joëlle* "YHWH crée du nouveau": restauration et nouveauté dans le livre de Jérémie (lecture de Jr 30-31). EstB 60 (2002) 381-404.

4375 Hughes, Tomaz "Há uma esperança para o seu futuro" (Jr 31,7-22). Estudos bíblicos 75 (2002) 77-84.

4376 Niedner, Frederick A. Rachel's lament. WaW 22 (2002) 406-414 [Jer 31,15].

4377 Pereira, Alvaro ¡Vuelve, doncella Israel!: lectura exegética de Jeremías 31,15-22. Isidorianum 21 (2002) 65-100.

4378 Vitório, Jaldemir 'Há uma esperança para o teu futuro' (Jr 31,17): despontar do novo para além das agruras do presente. Convergência 37 (2002) 538-557.

4379 Auld, Graeme Counting sheep, sins and sour grapes: the primacy of the primary history?. ^MCARROLL, R.: JSOT.S 348: 2002 ⇒13. 63-72 [1 Sam 24; 2 Chr 33,12-20; Jer 31,28-30; Ezek 18].

4380 Theißen, Gerd Der neue Bund: Gott und das Projekt der Moderne (Jer 31,31-34). Erlösungsbilder. 2002 ⇒1460. 69-72.

4381 Tita, Hubert "Ich hatte meine Tora in ihre Mitte gegeben": das Gewicht einer nicht berücksichtigten Perfektform in Jer. xxxi 33. VT 52 (2002) 551-556.

4382 Cisneros, Marcelo El derecho a la esperanza Jeremías 32. RevBib 62 (2000) 1-32.

4383 **Pardo Izal, José Javier** Pasión por un futuro imposible: estudio literario-teológico de Jeremías 32. TGr.T 76: 2001 ⇒17,3936. ^RCBQ 64 (2002) 555-556 (Laberge, Léo).

4384 **Shead, Andrew G.** The open book and the sealed book: Jeremiah 32 in its Hebrew and Greek recensions. JSOT.S 347; The Hebrew Bible and its Versions 3: Shf 2002, Sheffield A. 316 pp. 1-84127-274-4. Bibl. 270-295.

4385 Begin, Ze'ev B. Does Lachish letter 4 contradict Jeremiah xxxiv 7?. VT 52 (2002) 166-174.

4386 Jacobson, Rolf A. A freedom that is no freedom: Jeremiah 34 and the sabbatical principle. WaW 22 (2002) 396-405.

4387 Knights, Chris Rechabites ancient and modern: a study in the use of scripture. ET 113 (2002) 333-337 [2 Kgs 10; Jer 35].

4388 Migsch, Herbert Die Interpretation von Jeremia 35,14a und die Vugatalesart. BN 111 (2002) 28-33.

4389 Brummitt, Mark; Sherwood, Yvonne The tenacity of the word: using Jeremiah 36 to attempt to construct an appropriate edifice to the memory of Robert Carroll. ^MCARROLL, R.: JSOT.S 348: 2002 ⇒13. 3-29.

4390 Stipp, Hermann-Josef Baruchs Erben: die Schriftprophetie im Spiegel von Jer 36. ^FSTEINGRIMSSON, S.: ATSAT 72: 2002 ⇒117. 145-170.

4391 Mena López, Maricel Ebed-melec, o cuchita, salva Jeremias da cisterna: um testemunho de seguimento profético no tempo do cerco e queda de Jerusalém (Jeremias 38,7-13 e 39,15-18). Estudos bíblicos 73 (2002) 42-54.

4392 Müller, Hans-Peter Das 'Haus des Volkes' von Jer 39,8. ZAW 114 (2002) 611-617.

4393 **Huwyler, Beat** Jeremia und die Völker: Untersuchungen zu den Völkersprüchen in Jeremia 46-49. FAT 20: 1997 ⇒13,3694; 15,3877. ^RRBLit 4 (2002) 220-223 (Sweeney, Marvin A.).

4394 Smith, Jannes Jeremiah 52: Thackeray and beyond. BIOSCS 35 (2002) 55-96.

E8.8 Lamentations, *Threni*; Baruch

4395 **Berges, Ulrich** Klagelieder. HThK.AT: FrB 2002, Herder 312 pp. €60. 3-451-26840-X. Bibl. 13-28.

4396 **Berlin, Adele** Lamentations: a commentary. OTL: LVL 2002, Westminster xxvi; 135 pp. $40. 0-664-21849-0. Bibl. xv-xxvi. ᴿHBT 24/2 (2002) 115-117 (*Lee, Nancy C.*).
       Dearman, J.A. Jeremiah, Lamentations 2002 ⇒4317.

4397 **Dobbs-Allsopp, F.W.** Lamentations. Interpretation: LVL 2002, Knox xiv; 159 pp. $40. 0-8042-3141-9. Bibl. 155-159.
       ᴱ**Feder, F.** Biblia Sahidica: ...Lamentationes 2002 ⇒4319.

4398 *Fernández Marcos, Natalio; Fernández Tejero, Emilia* ¿QUEVEDO hebraísta?: *Lágrimas de Hieremías castellanas*. Sef. 62 (2002) 309-328.

4399 *Ferrer, Joan* Pecat i reconciliació en l'Apocalipsi siríac de Baruc. Perdó i reconciliació. 2002 ⇒591. 223-232.

4400 *Frevel, Christian* Zerbrochene Zier: Tempel und Tempelzerstörung in den Klageliedern (Threni). Gottesstadt. QD 191: 2002 ⇒567. 99-153.
       Gerstenberger, E. Psalms, part 2...Lamentations 2001 ⇒3480.

4401 *Labahn, Antje* Trauern als Bewältigung der Vergangenheit zur Gestaltung der Zukunft: Bemerkungen zur anthropologischen Theologie der Klagelieder. VT 52 (2002) 513-527.

4402 **Lee, Nancy C.** The singers of Lamentations: cities under siege, from Ur to Jerusalem to Sarajevo... BiblInterp 60: Lei 2002, Brill xiii; 231 pp. 90-04-12312-1. Bibl. 205-213.

4403 *Linafelt, Tod* The refusal of a conclusion in the book of Lamentations. JBL 120 (2001) 340-343.

4404 *Miller, C.W.* The book of Lamentations in recent research. CuBR 1/1 (2002) 9-29.

4405 **O'Connor, Kathleen** Lamentations and the tears of the world. Mkn 2002, Orbis xvi; 156 pp. $20. 1-57075-399-7. Bibl. 149-156.

4406 *Reichardt, Michael* Klagelieder und Krisenbewältigung: alttestamentliche Texte und Psychologie im Gespräch. Theologie lehren. QD 197: 2002 ⇒995. 226-240.

4407 *Reimer, David J.* Good grief?: a psychological reading of Lamentations. ZAW 114 (2002) 542-559.

4408 ᵀᴱ**Shute, Daniel** PETER MARTYR: commentary on the Lamentations of the prophet Jeremiah. SCES 55; Peter Martyr library 1/6: Kirksville, MO 2002, Truman State Univ. Pr. lxviii; 223 pp. $45. 0-9435-4964-7 [ThD 50,191—Heiser, W. Charles].

4409 *Bail, Ulrike* Die entsetzte Leserin: ein Essay vom Ort Gottes in der Gewalt (Klgl 1,12-13). Gretchenfrage. Jabboq 2 (2002) 100-110.

4410 *Van Hecke, Pierre J.P.* Lamentations 3,1-6: an anti-Psalm 23. SJOT 16 (2002) 264-282.

4411 **Kabasele Mukenge, André** L'unité littéraire du livre de Baruch. 1998 ⇒14,3526; 15,3895. ᴿRTL 33 (2002) 555-561 (*Auwers, Jean-Marie*).

4412 *Klijn, A. Frederick J.* The character of the Arabic version of the Apocalypse of Baruch. Jüdische Schriften. 2002 ⇒345. 204-208.

E8.9 **Ezekiel**: *textus, commentarii; themata, versiculi*

4413 **Eichrodt, Walther** Ezechiele. Antico Testamento 22/1-2: 2001 ⇒
17,3973. [R]CivCatt 153/1 (2002) 625-626 (*Scaiola, D.*).
4414 *Gindin, Thamar E.* Three fragments of an early Judaeo-Persian *tafsīr*
of Ezekiel. JStAI 27 (2002) 396-418 [Ezek 1,27-2,6; 21,2-9; 23,41-
24,4].
4415 *Lund, J.A.* Converse translation in Peshitta Ezekiel. TC: a journal of
biblical textual criticism [http://purl.org/TC] 6 (2001) pars. 1-31
[NTAb 47,530]..
4416 [E]**Odell, Margaret S.; Strong, John T.** The book of Ezekiel: theological and anthropological perspectives. SBL Symposium 9: 2000
⇒16,4021. [R]BiblInterp 10 (2002) 196-199 (*Galambush, Julie*);
HebStud 43 (2002) 276-279 (*Renz, Thomas*); RBLit 4 (2002) 223-
226 (*Findlay, James D.*).
4417 *Olley, John* Paragraphing in the Greek text of Ezekiel in P967: with
particular reference to the Cologne portion. Studies in scriptural unit
division. Pericope 3: 2002 ⇒339. 202-225.
4418 **Pohlmann, Karl-Friedrich** Das Buch des Propheten Hesekiel (Ezechiel) Kapitel 20-48. ATD 22/2: 2001 ⇒17,3975. [R]OrdKor 43
(2002) 356-357 (*Heinemann, Franz Karl*);
4419 ATD 22/1-2: 1996-2001 ⇒12,3539...17,3975. [R]LuThK 26 (2002)
199-201 (*Behrens, Achim*).
4420 [E]**Ribera Florit, Josep** Targum Jonatán de los profetas posteriores en
tradición babilónica: Ezequiel. TECC 62: 1997 ⇒13,3715. [R]RBLit 4
(2002) 286-288 (*Sweeney, Marvin A.*).
4421 **Sedlmeier, Franz** Das Buch Ezechiel: Kapitel 1-24. Neuer Stuttgarter Kommentar, AT 21/1: Stu 2002, Kath. Bibelwerk 335 pp. €28.90.
3-460-07211-3.
4422 *Vermeylen, Jacques* Ézéchiel: le livre et le prophète. LV(L) 256
(2002) 23-41.
4423 *Zurro Rodríguez, E.* Notas lexicográficas al libro de Ezequiel. EstB
60 (2002) 169-188.

4424 *Abadie, Philippe* Ézéchiel et l'apocalyptique;
4425 *Demaison, Michel* Un labyrinthe, un guetteur. LV(L) 256 (2002) 63-
83/7-21.
4426 **Drewermann, Eugen** '...auf dass ihr wieder leben sollt': die Botschaft des Propheten Ezequiel. 2001 ⇒17,3980. [R]ActBib 38/1 (2002)
38-39 (*Boada, J.*).
4427 *Duquoc, Christian* Responsabilité personelle et destin collectif.
LV(L) 256 (2002) 53-62.
4428 *Gruenenwald, Michèle Martin* La gloire de Yahvé et le guetteur: en-
racinement et régulation de la responsabilité chez Ezéchiel. LV(L)
256 (2002) 85-101.
4429 *Hosch, Harold E.* Rûah in the book of Ezekiel: a textlinguistic analysis. JOTT 14 (2002) 77-125.
4430 *Kohn, Risa Levitt* A prophet like Moses?: rethinking Ezekiel's relationship to the torah. ZAW 114 (2002) 236-254.
4431 **Kohn, Risa Levitt** A new heart and a new soul: Ezekiel, the exile
and the torah. JSOT.S 358: Shf 2002, Sheffield A. xii; 148 pp. £45.
0-8264-6057-7. Bibl. 119-125.

4432 **Kutsko, John F.** Between heaven and earth: divine presence and absence in the book of Ezekiel. 2000 ⇒16,4032; 17,3987. ᴿRBLit 4 (2002) 226-228 (*Sommer, Benjamin D.*).

4433 *Lust, Johan* The 'rekenaar' and the Septuagint: LXX Ezekiel a case study. Bible and computer. 2002 ⇒548. 365-393.

4434 **Mein, Andrew** Ezekiel and the ethics of exile. Oxford Theological Monographs: 2001 ⇒17,3990. ᴿTheol. 105 (2002) 296-297 (*Rodd, C.S.*).

4435 *Mercier, Philippe* Responsabilité personelle ou critique du fatalisme?. LV(L) 256 (2002) 43-51.

4436 *Nobile, Marco* Il principio della retribuzione in Ezechiele. RStB 14/ 1-2 (2002) 99-109;

4437 La visione della nuova Gerusalemme in Ezechiele. La speranza. 2002 ⇒277. 33-40.

4438 **Schöpflin, Karin** Theologie als Biographie im Ezechielbuch: ein Beitrag zur Konzeption alttestamentlicher Prophetie. ᴰ*Spieckermann, H.*: FAT 36: Tü 2002, Mohr ix; 392 pp. 3-16-147869-X. Diss.-Habil. Göttingen; Bibl. 359-377.

4439 **Virgili, Rosanna** Ezechiele: il giorno dopo l'ultimo. 2000 ⇒16, 4043. ᴿFirmana 27 (2002) 191-192 (*Miola, Gabriele*); EfMex 20 (2002) 283-284 (*Junco Garza, Carlos*).

4440 **Wong, Ka Leung** The idea of retribution in the book of Ezekiel. VT. S 87: 2001 ⇒17,3995. ᴿBib. 83 (2002) 277-280 (*Becker, Joachim*).

4441 **Pikor, Wojciech** La comunicazione profetica alla luce di Ez 2-3. ᴰ*Bovati, Pietro*: TGr.T 88: R 2002, E.P.U.G. 316 pp. €20. 88-7652-940-3. Diss. Gregoriana; Bibl. 279-305.

4442 *Pikor, Wojciech* "I bedziesz niemy" (Ez 3,26): milczenie Ezechiela jako Boze słowo. CoTh 72/1 (2002) 57-68. **P**.

4443 *Premstaller, Volkmar* A problematic treatment of Ezekiel?: observations on the relationship between YHWH and his prophet. BN 114/ 115 (2002) 53-56 [Ezek 3,14-15].

4444 *Pilch, John J.* The nose and altered states of consciousness: Tascodrugites and Ezekiel. HTS 58 (2002) 708-720 [OTA 26,307] [Ezek 8, 17; Lk 22,43-44].

4445 *Van Rooy, H.F.* Disappointed expectations and false hopes: the message of Ezekiel 13:1-16 in a time of change. HTS 58 (2002) 1499-1511 [OTA 26,505].

4446 *Israel, Felice* Der Amurriter in Ezechiel 16. ᶠWEIPPERT, M.: OBO 186: 2002 ⇒133. 231-242.

4447 *Odendaal, Marietjie* A South African anotation to shame in Ezekiel 16. Scriptura 78 (2001) 479-489 [OTA 26,307].

4448 *Malamat, A.* The politics of bipolarity in the guise of sexual relations: the case of Ezekiel 16 and 23. Sex and gender. 2002 ⇒712. 355-357.

4449 *Stiebert, Johanna* The woman metaphor of Ezekiel 16 and 23: a victim of violence, or a symbol of subversion?. OTEs 15 (2002) 200-208.

4450 *Monari, Luciano* Una storia d'idolatria: Ez 20. PSV 46 (2002) 41-50.

4451 *Pikor, Wojciech* Skuteczność przepowiadania prorockiego w świetle Ez 24,15-27 [The effectiveness of prophetic foretelling in light of Ez 24,15-27]. Verbum Vitae 2 (2002) 31-47 Som. 47. **P**.

4452 **Corral, Martin Alonso** Ezekiel's oracles against Tyre: historical reality and motivations. BibOr 46: R 2002, E.P.I.B. xi; 249 pp. €16/

$16. 88-7653-349-4. Diss. New York Univ. 2000; Bibl. 179-237.
^RBiOr 59 (2002) 604-606 (*Lipiński, E.*); SEL 19 (2002) 164-165
(*Zamora, José-Ángel*) [Ezek 26,1-28,19].

4453 *Mosis, Rudolf* Ezechiel 27,14: Auferweckung des Volkes—Auferweckung der Toten. ^FHAAG, E.: 2002 ⇒55. 123-173.

4454 *Sedlmeier, Franz* Wider die Selbstvergottung: der Fürst von Tyrus
und sein Selbstverständnis nach Ez 28,1-10. ^FHAAG, E.: 2002 ⇒55.
271-297.

4455 *Vincent, J.M.* Ez 28,11-19—un détournement d'oracle?. TEuph 23
(2002) 89-100.

4456 *Kuyvenhoven, Rosalie* De goede herder: beeld en tegenbeeld in Ezechiël 34. ITBT 10/2 (2002) 15-16.

4457 *Van der Meer, Michaël N.* A new spirit in an old corpus?: text-
critical, literary-critical and linguistic observations regarding Ezekiel
36:16-38. ^FLEENE, H.: 2002 ⇒73. 147-158.

4458 *Ebach, Jürgen* Ich bringe Ruach in euch!: Ezechiels Auferstehungs-
vision (Ez 37) auf der Jerusalemer Menora. BiHe 38 (2002) 67-69.

4459 *Rossier Buri, Kristin* Ezéchiel 37,1-14: la vision des ossements. Lire
et Dire 51 (2002) 5-14 [BuBB 39,73].

4460 *Weissert, David* Qal versus Nifʻal in Ezekiel 37:8. Textus 21 (2002)
129-138.

4461 *Wong, Ka Leung* The Masoretic and Septuagint texts of Ezekiel 39,
21-29. EThL 78 (2002) 130-147.

4462 *Lust, Johan* The spirit of the Lord, or the wrath of the Lord?: Ezekiel
39,29. EThL 78 (2002) 148-155.

4463 *Konkel, Michael* Die zweite Tempelvision Ezechiels (Ez 40-48): Di-
mensionen eines Entwurfs. Gottesstadt. QD 191: 2002 ⇒567. 154-
179.

4464 **Konkel, Michael** Architektonik des Heiligen: Studien zur zweiten
Tempelvision Ezechiels (Ez 40-48). BBB 129: 2001 ⇒17,4014.
^RThPQ 150 (2002) 313-314 (*Reinhartz, Wilhelm*); ThLZ 127 (2002)
1038-41 (*Liwak, Rüdiger*); ZAR 8 (2002) 384-9 (*Rudnig, Thilo A.*).

4465 *Peek-Horn, Margret* Der Reformentwurf von Ez 40-48: Beobachtungen und Anfragen im Hinblick auf die theologische Dimension von
Liturgiereform. Liturgiereformen. 2002 ⇒416. 25-67.

4466 **Rudnig, Thilo Alexander** Heilig und profan. BZAW 287: 2000
⇒16,4069; 17,4015. ^RAnton. 77 (2002) 351-354 (*Volgger, David*);
OLZ 97 (2002) 755-761 (*Fechter, F.*); ZAR 8 (2002) 357-383
(*Konkel, Michael*) [Ezek 40-48].

E9.1 Apocalyptica VT

4467 *Becking, Bob* Expectations about the end of time in the Hebrew
Bible: do they exist?. Apocalyptic. JSPE.S 43: 2002 ⇒373. 44-59.

4468 *Bedenbender, Andreas* Jewish apocalypticism: a child of mantic wisdom. Henoch 24 (2002) 189-196;

4469 Als Mose und Henoch zusammenfanden: die Entstehung der frühjüdischen Apokalyptik als Reaktion auf die Religionsverfolgung unter
Antiochus IV. Epiphanes. Jüdische Schriften. 2002 ⇒345. 182-203.

4470 **Bedenbender, Andreas** Der Gott der Welt tritt auf den Sinai: Entstehung, Entwicklung und Funktionsweise der frühjüdischen Apokalyptik. ANTZ 8: 2000 ⇒16,4076. ^RTThZ 111 (2002) 73-74 (*Haag,*

Ernst); ThLZ 127 (2002) 634-636 (*Zager, Werner*); REJ 161 (2002) 498-499 (*Lemaire, André*).

4471 *Blasius, Andreas; Schipper, Bernd Ulrich* Apokalyptik und Ägypten?: Erkenntnisse und Perspektiven. Apokalyptik und Ägypten. OLA 107: 2002 ⇒451. 277-302.

4472 *Bryan, David J.* Exile and return from Jerusalem. Apocalyptic. JSPE.S 43: 2002 ⇒373. 60-80.

4473 ᴱ**Bull, Malcolm** Apocalypse theory and the end of the world. 1995 ⇒11/1,2436; 12,3588. ᴿHeyJ 43 (2002) 510-511 (*McNamara, Martin*).

4474 *Collins, John J.* Temporality and politics in Jewish apocalyptic literature. Apocalyptic. JSPE.S 43: 2002 ⇒373. 26-43;

4475 Ethos and identity in Jewish apocalyptic literature. Ethos und Identität. 2002 ⇒490. 51-65.

4476 **Collins, John Joseph** The apocalyptic imagination: an introduction to Jewish apocalyptic literature. Biblical Resource: ²1998 ⇒14,3581 ... 17,4020. ᴿDSD 9 (2002) 109-111 (*Gathercole, Simon J.*).

4477 *Ego, Beate* Ein Engel öffnete mir die Tore des Himmels: Jenseitsreisen und Himmelfahrten im Antiken Judentum. WUB 26 (2002) 43-47.

4478 *Fiddes, Paul S.* Millennium and utopia: images of a fuller presence. Apocalyptic. JSPE.S 43: 2002 ⇒373. 7-25.

4479 *Garcia Martinez, Florentino* Guerra e pace in prospettiva escatologica e apocalittica. Pace e guerra. 2002 ⇒600. 47-64.

4480 *Hanson, Paul D.* Prophetic and apocalyptic politics. The last things. 2002 ⇒279. 43-66.

4481 **Hoffmann, Heinrich** Das Gesetz in der frühjüdischen Apokalyptik. StUNT 23: 1999 ⇒15,3956; 17,2439. ᴿCBQ 64 (2002) 163-164 (*Nickelsburg, George W.E.*).

4482 **Koenen, Klaus; Kühschelm, Roman** Zeitenwende: Perspektiven des Alten und Neuen Testaments. 1999 ⇒15,3957...17,4023. ᴿBiLi 75 (2002) 69-70 (*Hasitschka, Martin*).

4483 *Nel, M.; Human, D.J.* Historiese en sosiale oorspong(e) van apokaliptiek. HTS 58 (2002) 1056-1075 [OTA 26,507].

4484 *Nel, M.* Die hellenisties-romeinse wêreld en die ontstaan van apokaliptiek en gnostisisme. VeE 23 (2002) 452-467.

4485 *Rowland, Christopher* Apocalypticism. Biblical world, 1. 2002 ⇒ 273. 129-148.

4486 *Sacchi, Paolo* La teologia dell'enochismo antico e l'apocalittica. Materia giudaica. 2002 ⇒727. 7-13.

4487 *Schipper, Bernd Ulrich; Blasius, Andreas* Die 'apokalyptischen' Texte aus Ägypten: ein Forschungsüberblick;

4488 *Schipper, Bernd Ulrich* 'Apokalyptik', 'Messianismus', 'Prophetie': eine Begriffsbestimmung. Apokalyptik und Ägypten. OLA 107: 2002 ⇒451. 7-20/21-40.

4489 *Willi-Plein, Ina* Das Geheimnis der Apokalyptik. Sprache als Schlüssel. 2002 <1977> ⇒261. 159-176.

E9.2 **Daniel**: *textus, commentarii: themata, versiculi*

4490 ᴱ**Collins, John Joseph; Flint, Peter W.** The book of Daniel: composition and reception. VT.S 83/1-2: 2001 ⇒17,4028. ᴿJBL 121 (2002) 552-556 (*Suter, David Winston*).

4491　**Gowan, Donald E.** Daniel. Abingdon Old Testament Commentaries: 2001 ⇒17,4033. ᴿRExp 99 (2002) 277-278 (*Biddle, Mark E.*).

4492　**Koch, Klaus; Rösel, Martin** Polyglottensynopse zum Buch Daniel. 2000 ⇒16,4093; 17,4036. ᴿAUSS 40 (2002) 338-341 (*Pröbstle, Martin*).

4493　(*a*) **Lucas, Ernest** Daniel. Apollos Old Testament commentary 20: Leicester 2002, Apollos 359 pp. £20. 0-85111-780-5. Bibl. 327-339. ᴿVeE 23 (2002) 591-593 (*Nel, M.*).
　　(*b*) ᴱ**Mills, Watson E.** Daniel. Bibliographies for Biblical Research, OT: Lewiston 2002, Mellen xviii; 103 pp. $90.

4494　*Beckwith, Roger T.* Early traces of the book of Daniel. TynB 53 (2002) 75-82.

4495　**Fernando, Ajith** Spiritual living in a secular world: applying the book of Daniel today. GR 2002, Monarch 192 pp. $12. 1-85424-578-3 [ThD 50,168—Heiser, W. Charles].

4496　*Floß, Johannes P.* Menschensohn—Reich Gottes—Auferstehung im Buch Daniel. Jesus von Nazareth und das Christentum. 2000 ⇒293. 153-170.

4497　*Munnich, Olivier* Le roi impie dans le livre de *Daniel*. Nier les dieux. 2002 ⇒626. 199-210.

4498　*Nel, M.; Human, D.J.* Die Daniëlboek se twee *Sitze im Leben*. HTS 58 (2002) 1726-1746 [OTA 26,507].

4499　*Quaglia, Rocco* I sogni di Nabucodonosor. I sogni. 2002 ⇒227. 17-42. Nota sul sogno 43-45.

4500　*Santa Cruz, Luis* El mensaje de las profécias de Daniel. Theologika 17 (2002) 210-222.

4501　*Segert, Stanislav* Aramaic poetry in the Old Testament. ArOr 70 (2002) 65-79 [Jer 10,11].

4502　*Steinmann, Andrew* The chicken and the egg: a new proposal for the relationship between the Prayer of Nabonidus and the book of Daniel. RdQ 20 (2002) 557-570.

4503　*Valeta, David* The satirical nature of the book of Daniel. Apocalyptic. JSPE.S 43: 2002 ⇒373. 81-93.

4504　*Nel, M.* Daniël 1 as wysheidsliteratuur: bevestiging van die vergeldingsleer. OTEs 15 (2002) 780-798;

4505　A literary-historical analysis of Daniel 2: two powers in opposition. AcTh(B) 22/1 (2002) 77-97.

4506　(*a*) *Treiyer, Enrique B.* Los pies de hierro y arcilla y la Unión Europea: Daniel 2:41-43. Theologika 17 (2002) 192-208.
　　(*b*) *Perkams, Matthias* Die Erzählung von den Jünglingen im Feuerofen (Daniel 3) in der Auseinandersetzung der antiochenischen Kirche mit Kaiser Jᵤₗᵢₐₙ. ᶠHoʜᴇɪsᴇʟ, K.: JAC.E 34: 2002 ⇒59. 64-71.

4507　**Helbling, Dominik** Transzendierung der Geschichte: Dan 3,57-90 LXX als hymnische Exegese. BN.B 14: Mü 2002, Manfred Görg 74 pp. Bibl. 63-66.

4508　**Henze, Matthias** The madness of King Nebuchadnezzar: the ancient Near Eastern origins and early history of interpretation of Daniel 4. JSJ.S 61: 1999 ⇒15,3992; 17,4084. ᴿJThS 53 (2002) 151-153 (*Mastin, B.A.*); JSJ 33 (2002) 333-334 (*Martone, Corrado*); CBQ 64 (2002) 738-739 (*Grabbe, Lester L.*); RBLit (2002)* (*Becking, Bob*).

4509 *Willi-Plein, Ina* Daniel 6 und die persische Diaspora. Sprache als Schlüssel. 2002 <1991> ⇒261. 177-188.
4510 **Roloff, Jürgen** Die Adaptation der Tiervision (Daniel 7) in frühjüdischer und frühchristlicher Apokalyptik. Bayerische Akad. der Wiss., Phil.-hist. Kl. Sitzungsberichte 2002,2: Mü 2002, Verlag der Bayerischen Akademie der Wissenschaft 53 pp. 3-7696-1620-0.
4511 *Theißen, Gerd* Die Humanisierung der Geschichte: der Übergang vom Tier zum Menschen in der Vision des Daniel (Dan 7,1-14). Erlösungsbilder. 2002 ⇒1460. 73-76.
4512 **Eggler, Jürg** Influences and traditions underlying the vision of Daniel 7:2-14:the research history from the end of the 19th century to the present. OBO 177: 2000 ⇒16,4117. ᴿRivBib 50 (2002) 233-236 (*Marconcini, Benito*); AUSS 40 (2002) 321-325 (*Pröbstle, Martin*); JBL 121 (2002) 156-158 (*Collins, John J.*).
4513 *Fauth, Wolfgang* Der 'Alte der Tage' (Dan 7,9-14.22). ᶠDIETRICH, M. 2002 ⇒28. 133-157.
4514 *Dunn, Geoffrey D.* TERTULLIAN and Daniel 9:24-27: a patristic interpretation of a prophetic time-frame. ZAC 6 (2002) 352-367.
4515 *Adler, William* 'What the Hebrews say': translation, authority, and the story of Susanna and the elders. Biblical translation. 2002 ⇒281. 19-39 [Dan 13].

E9.3 *Prophetae Minores*, **Dōdekaprophetōn...Hosea, Joel**

4516 *Albertz, Rainer* Exile as purification: reconstructing the book of the Four (Hosea, Amos, Micah, Zephaniah). SBL.SP 2002. SBL.SPS 41: 2002 ⇒598. 213-233.
4517 **Barton, John** Joel and Obadiah: a commentary. OTL: 2001 ⇒17, 4102. ᴿCBQ 64 (2002) 733-734 (*Baker, David W.*); RExp 99 (2002) 279-280 (*Biddle, Mark E.*).
4518 **Clark, David J.; Hatton, Howard A.** A handbook on Haggai, Zechariah, and Malachi. UBS Handbook: NY 2002, UBS xii; 501 pp. $30.
4519 *Conrad, Edgar W.* Forming the Twelve and forming canon. SBL.SP 2002. SBL.SPS 41: 2002 ⇒598. 234-247.
4520 *Dietrich, Walter* Ninive in der Bibel. Theopolitik. 2002 ⇒159. 239-254 [Nah 1,14; 3,4; Zeph 2,3-15].
4521 *Fabry, Heinz-Josef* Die Nahum- und Habakuk-Rezeption in der LXX und in Qumran. 'Wort JHWHs, das geschah'. Herders biblische Studien 35: 2002 ⇒4115. 159-190.
4522 **Floyd, Michael H.** Minor prophets, part 2. FOTL 22: 2000 ⇒16, 4130; 17,4112. ᴿHeyJ 43 (2002) 218-219 (*Slattery, Joseph A.*); CBQ 64 (2002) 344-345 (*Jones, Barry Alan*).
4523 *House, Paul R.* Endings as new beginnings: returning to the Lord, the Day of the Lord, and renewal in the book of the Twelve. SBL.SP 2002. SBL.SPS 41: 2002 ⇒598. 258-284.
4524 *Jeremias, Jörg* Gelehrte Prophetie: Beobachtungen zu Joel und Deuterosacharja. ᶠSMEND, R. 2002 ⇒113. 97-111.
4525 *Kessler, Rainer* Nahum-Habakuk als Zweiprophetenschrift;
4526 *Lux, Rüdiger* Das Zweiprophetenbuch: Beobachtungen zu Aufbau und Struktur von Haggai und Sacharja 1-8 .'Wort JHWHs, das geschah'. Herders bibl. Studien 35: 2002 ⇒4115. 149-158/191-217.

4527 ^ENogalski, James; Sweeney, Marvin Alan Reading and hearing the Book of the Twelve. SBL Symposium 15: 2000 ⇒16,4140. ^RHeb-Stud 43 (2002) 281-283 (*Coote, Robert B.*).

4528 *Punnakal, James* Blooming future: hope in Amos, Hoseah, Micah and Joel. God of big dreams. 2002 ⇒359. 133-150.

4529 *Raurell, Frederic* El perdó, victòria de l'amor. Perdó i reconciliació. 2002 ⇒591. 93-113.

4530 *Rendtorff, Rolf* Der 'Tag Jhwhs' im Zwölfprophetenbuch. 'Wort JHWHs, das geschah'. Herders bibl. Studien 35: 2002 ⇒4115. 1-11.

4531 **Sweeney, Marvin A.** The Twelve Prophets, 1: Hosea... Jonah; 2,: Micah... Malachi. Berit Olam: 2000 ⇒16,4150; 17,4123. ^RPacifica 15 (2002) 81-83 (*Campbell, Antony F.*); HebStud 43 (2002) 279-281 (*Redditt, Paul L.*).

4532 **Sykes, Seth** Time and space in Haggai-Zechariah 1-8: a Bakhtinian analysis of a prophetic chronicle. Studies in Biblical Literature 24: NY 2002, Lang xiv; 172 pp. 0-8204-4596-7. Bibl. 151-165.

4533 *Thomson* Let us dare to dream: messianic images in Haggai and Malachi. God of big dreams. 2002 ⇒359. 273-293.

4534 *Vanoni, Gottfried* Elija, Jona und das Dodekapropheton: Grade der Intertextualität. 'Wort JHWHs, das geschah'. Herders biblische Studien 35: 2002 ⇒4115. 113-121.

4535 *Zenger, Erich* 'Wie ein Löwe brüllt er ...' (Hos 11,10): zur Funktion poetischer Metaphorik im Zwölfprophetenbuch. 'Wort JHWHs, das geschah'. Herders biblische Studien 35: 2002 ⇒4115. 33-45.

4536 ^TBons, Eberhard; Joosten, Jan; Kessler, Stephan Les Douze Prophètes: Osée: traduction du texte grec de la Septante. Bible d'Alexandrie 23/1: P 2002, Cerf 194 pp. €27. 2-204-06901-9. Introd. gen. aux Douze Prophètes de *Takamitsu Muraoka*. ^RIgreja e Missão 55/1 (2002) 108-109 (*Couto, A.*).

4537 **Bulgarelli, Valentino** L'immagine della rugiada nel libro di Osea: uso molteplice di una figura nella Bibbia Ebraica e nella Settanta. SRivBib 39: Bo 2002, EDB 196 pp. 88-10-30227-3.

4538 **Fuß, Barbara** "Dies ist die Zeit, von der geschrieben ist...":die expliziten Zitate aus dem Buch Hosea in den Handschriften von Qumran und im Neuen Testament. NTA 37: 2000 ⇒16,4158; 17,4129. ^RBZ 46 (2002) 128-130 (*Häfner, Gerd*); ThLZ 127 (2002) 284-286 (*Wilk, Florian*).

4539 **Gisin, Walter** Hosea: ein literarisches Netzwerk beweist seine Authentizität. BBB 139: B 2002, Philo (6) 332 pp. €49.80. 3-8257-0320-7. Bibl. 325-332.

4540 **Pennacchio, Maria Cristina** Propheta insaniens: l'esegesi patristica di Osea tra profezia e storia. SEAug 81: R 2002, Institutum Patristicum Augustinianum 326 pp. 88-7961-012-0. Bibl. 301-310.

4541 *Pentiuc, Eugen J.* Messianism in the book of Hosea in the light of patristic interpretations. GOTR 46 (2001) 35-56.

4542 **Pentiuc, Eugen J.** Long-suffering love: a commentary on Hosea with patristic annotations. Brookline, MASS 2002, Holy Cross Orthodox Pr. xiii; 221 pp. $16. 1-885652-58-5. Bibl. 215-221.

4543 **Pfeiffer, Henrik** Das Heiligtum von Bethel im Spiegel des Hoseabuches. FRLANT 183: 1999 ⇒15,4023; 17,4136. ^RThZ 58 (2002) 83-84 (*Weber, Beat*).

4544 **Simian-Yofre, Horacio** El desierto de los dioses: teología e historia en el libro de Oseas. 1993 ⇒9,3854... 13,3843. ᴿRBLit (2002)* (*Floyd, Michael H.*).

4545 *Boshoff, Willem* The female imagery in the book of Hosea: considering the marriage metaphor in Hosea 1-2 by listening to female voices. OTEs 15 (2002) 23-41.

4546 *Cooper, Gillian; Goldingay, John* Hosea and Gomer visit the marriage counsellor [Hos 1-3];

4547 *Magonet, Jonathan* Gomer's revenge [Hos 1-3]. First person. BiSe 81: 2002 ⇒295. 119-136/115-118.

4548 *Scibona, Rocco* Temporalità ed eternità in Os 1-3 'come la sabbia del mare (kᵉḥol hayyām = כְּחוֹל הַיָּם)': la metaforizzazione nel discorso di Dio. Tempo ed eternità. 2002 ⇒545. 89-128 [Hos 1-3].

4549 *Schwantes, Milton* "A lua nova devorará suas heranças": observações sobre Oséias 5,1-7. Estudos bíblicos 73 (2002) 8-19.

4550 *Utzschneider, Helmut* Situation und Szene: Überlegungen zum Verhältnis historischer und literarischer Deutung prophetischer Texte am Beispiel von Hos 5,8-6,6. ZAW 114 (2002) 80-105.

4551 *Schütte, Wolfgang* Hosea 6,5—eine Revision und eine ikonographische Deutung. BN 111 (2002) 40-43;

4552 Hosea 9,7-9—eine crux interpretum?. BN 114/115 (2002) 57-60.

4553 *Kwakkel, Gert* 'But I passed by her fair neck': on threshing and yoking in Hosea 10:11. ᶠLEENE, H.: 2002 ⇒73. 141-146.

4554 *Ólason, Kristinn* El und sein himmlischer Hofstaat im Hoseabuch?: einige Beobachtungen zu Hos 12,1-2;

4555 *Berge, Kåre* Weisheitliche Hosea-Interpretation?: zur Frage nach Kohärenz und literarischem Horizont von Hosea 14,6-10. ᶠSTEINGRIMSSON, S.: ATSAT 72: 2002 ⇒117. 101-121/3-23.

4556 *Croatto, J. Severino* Las langostas del libro de Joel a la luz de los textos de Mari. RevBib 61 (1999) 249-260.

4557 *Scoralick, Ruth* 'Auch jetzt noch' (Joel 2,12a): zur Eigenart der Joelschrift und ihrer Funktion im Kontext des Zwölfprophetenbuches. 'Wort JHWHs, das geschah'. Herders biblische Studien 35: 2002 ⇒ 4115. 47-69.

E9.4 Amos

4558 *Barco del Barco, Francisco Javier del* Towards a computer-assisted classification of discourse types in Amos. Bible and computer. 2002 ⇒548. 283-293.

4559 **Barriocanal Gómez, José Luis** La relectura de la tradición del Éxodo en el libro de Amós. TGr.T 58: 2000 ⇒16,4184. ᴿCBQ 64 (2002) 340-341 (*Ben Zvi, Ehud*).

4560 **Carroll R., M. Daniel** Amos—the prophet and his oracles: research on the book of Amos. LVL 2002, Westminster xiv; 224 pp. $33. 0-664-22455-5.

4561 *Dietrich, Walter* JHWH, Israel und die Völker beim Propheten Amos. Theopolitik. 2002 <1992> ⇒159. 194-203.

4562 **Etim, Leo Efiong** Social justice in the prophet Amos and today. ᴰBoschi, B.G.: 2002, 182 pp. Extr. Diss.Angelicum 2002.

4563 *Gelston, A.* Some Hebrew misreadings in the Septuagint of Amos. VT 52 (2002) 493-500.

4564 *Limburg, Klaus* La intervención personal de Dios en la historia de Israel: el "yo" de Yahvéh en el libro de Amós. ScrTh 34 (2002) 463-504.

4565 *Paas, Stefan* Seeing and singing: visions and hymns in the book of Amos. VT 52 (2002) 253-274.

4566 **Pierri, Rosario** Parole del profeta Amos: il libro di Amos secondo i LXX. SBFA 59: J 2002, Franciscan Printing Press 161 pp. $20. 965-516-037-8. Bibl. 11-24.

4567 *Rathinam, Selva* Universalism in Amos. VJTR 66 (2002) 725-738.

4568 **Simian-Yofre, Horacio** Amos. I Libri Biblici, Primo Testamento 15: Mi 2002, Paoline 242 pp. €23. 88-315-2307-4. Bibl. 217-230.

4569 *Smend, Rudolf* Das Nein des Amos. Die Mitte des A.T. 2002 <1963> ⇒244. 219-237.

4570 *Spreafico, Ambrogio* Amos: il povero come giusto in un contesto di ingiustizia. RStB 14/1-2 (2002) 47-54.

4571 **Wood, Joyce Rilett** Amos in song and book culture. JSOT.S 337: Shf 2002, Sheffield A. 249 pp. $80. 1-84127-244-2. Bibl. 218-234.

4572 *Ceresko, Anthony R.* Janus parallelism in Amos's 'oracles against the nations' (Amos 1:3-2:16). Prophets and proverbs. 2002 <1994> ⇒ 154. 15-21.

4573 *Backhaus, Franz Josef* 'So lege ich Feuer an die Mauer ...' (Am 1,14 / Jer 49,27). 'Wort JHWHs, das geschah'. Herders biblische Studien 35: 2002 ⇒4115. 71-111.

4574 *Brandscheidt, Renate* Die Stunde des Amos (Am 3,1-8): zur bleibenden Aktualität des Gerichtspropheten. TThZ 111 (2002) 1-22.

4575 *Zalcman, Lawrence* Laying *dmšq 'rš* to rest (Amos iii 12). VT 52 (2002) 557-559.

4576 *Barco del Barco, Francisco Javier del* Text in context: a textual-linguistic approach to Amos 4:7-8. Sef. 62 (2002) 227-240.

4577 *Mulzac, Kenneth D.* Amos 5:18-20 in its exegetical and theological context. AJTh 16/2 (2002) 286-300.

4578 *Virgili dal Prà, Rosanna* Il culto tra idolatria e ortodossia (lettura di Am 5,18-27). PSV 46 (2002) 29-40.

4579 *Hyman, Ronald T.* Amos 5:24 prophetic, chastising, surprising, poetic. JBQ 30 (2002) 227-234.

4580 *Lößl, Josef* Amos 6:1: notes on its text and ancient translations. JNSL 28/2 (2002) 43-61.

4581 *Pinker, Aron* Observations on some cruxes in Amos—part V. JBQ 30 (2002) 51-58 [Amos 7,1; 7,7-9; 8,8].

E9.5 Jonas

4582 *Akpan, Celestine U.* Jonah and pre-existing legends of sea monsters (Jonah 1:17; 2:10). Hekima Review 27 (2002) 9-18.

4583 *Antoniotti, Guido* Jonás y la 'difícil' misericordia de Dios. ResB 33 (2002) 30-42.

4584 *Álvarez Valdés, Ariel* ¿Fue el profeta Jonás tragado por una ballena?;

4585 *García Domene, Juan Carlos* Jonás para todos los públicos. ResB 33 (2002) 5-11/60-65.

4586 *Hunter, Alastair G.* Creating waves: why the fictionality of Jonah matters. ^MCARROLL, R.: JSOT.S 348: 2002 ⇒13. 101-116 [Ex 15].

4587 *Hyman, Ronald T.* Seeking vindication, especially in Jonah. JBQ 30 (2002) 17-25.

4588 *Ignatius, Peter* Aramaism in the book of Jonah: a case study for a methodology in philological study of the text. BiBh 28/2 (2002) 489-499.

4589 **Kamp, A.** Innerlijke werelden: een cognitief taalkundige benadering van het bijbelboek Jona [Des mondes intérieurs: une approche de linguistique cognitive du livre de Jonas]. ^D*Van Wilde, E.*: 2002 294 pp. Diss. Tilburg [RTL 34,592].

4590 *Kochalumkal, Peter* I challenge my jealous nature: Jonah's antipathy towards the Ninevites. Third Millennium 5/2 (2002) 86-94.

4591 *Kroeze, Jan H.* Developing a multi-level analysis of Jonah using HTML. Bible and computer. 2002 ⇒548. 653-662.

4592 *Magonet, Jonathan* Le livre de Jonas et le jour des expiations. SIDIC 35/2-3 (2002) <1985> 32-37.

4593 *Mulzer, Martin* Satzgrenzen im Jonabuch im Vergleich von hebräischer und griechischer Texttradition. BN 113 (2002) 61-68;

4594 Die Gottesbezeichnungen im Jonabuch. ^FSTEINGRIMSSON, S.: ATSAT 72: 2002 ⇒117. 45-62.

4595 **Murray, Paul** A journey with Jonah: the spirituality of bewilderment. Dublin 2002, Columba 69 pp. €6. 1-85607-363-7. ^RDoLi 52 (2002) 446-448 (*Jackson, Michael*); MillSt 50 (2002) 115-116 (*Agnew, Una*).

4596 *Oesch, Josef M.* Der Dialog mit dem biblischen Jonabuch in der deutschsprachigen Literatur nach 1945: eine intertextuelle Studie. Religion—Literatur—Künste II. Im Kontext 14: 2002 ⇒530. 107-22.

4597 *Pazzini, Massimo* La massorah del libro di Giona (BHS). LASBF 52 (2002) 103-116.

4598 *Peri, Chiara* Tra mare e deserto: il viaggio di Giona. Materia giudaica. 2002 ⇒727. 14-23.

4599 *Pérez Fernández, Miguel* El midrás de Jonás. ResB 33 (2002) 48-59.

4600 **Roop, Eugene F.** Ruth, Jonah, Esther. Believers Church Bible Commentary: Scottdale, PA 2002, Herald 304 pp. 0-8361-9199-4. Bibl. 285-296.

4601 ^E**Sevilla Jiménez, Cristóbal** Jonás. ResB 33 (2002) 2-65.

4602 *Sevilla Jiménez, Cristóbal* Del mar a la tierra firme. ResB 33 (2002) 13-22.

4603 **Sherwood, Yvonne** A biblical text and its afterlives: the survival of Jonah in western culture. 2000 ⇒16,4221. ^RCBQ 64 (2002) 148-149 (*Cook, Joan E.*); AThR 84 (2002) 422-424 (*Sharp, Carolyn J.*); RBLit (2002)* (*Landes, George M.*).

4604 **Simon, Uriel** Jonah. ^T*Schramm, Lenn J.*: JPS Bible Commentary: 1999 ⇒15,4087; 17,4184. ^RJQR 92 (2002) 644-6 (*Sasson, Jack M.*).

4605 *Steenbrink, Karel* Jonah: from a prophetic mission in reverse to interreligious dialogue. IRM 91 (2002) 41-51.

4606 *Tadiello, Roberto* Historia de una conversión. ResB 33 (2002) 23-29.

4607 *Vanoni, Gottfried* Spuren übergreifender Redaktionsarbeit im Jonabuch? 'Wort JHWHs, das geschah'. Herders biblische Studien 35: 2002 ⇒4115. 123-137.

4608 *Vermeylen, Jacques* Le livre de Jonas: un écrit politico-religieux?. ScEs 54 (2002) 287-297.

4609 *Lichtert, Claude* Par terre et par mer!: analyse rhétorique de Jonas 1. EThL 78 (2002) 5-24 .

4610 *Wendland, E.* Song from the seabed—how sweet does it sound?: aspects of the style, structure, and transmission of Jonah's "psalm". JSem 11/2 (2002) 211-244.

4611 *Dogniez, Cécile* Les dires de Jonas au bord de l'abîme: Jonas 2,5 selon les Septante: le doute ou la foi?. Nier les dieux. 2002 ⇒626. 185-197.

4612 *Mulzer, Martin* Die Buße der Tiere in Jona 3,7f und Jdt 4,10. BN 111 (2002) 76-89.

E9.6 *Micheas*, **Micah**

4613 **Andersen, Francis I.; Freedman, David Noel** Micah. AncB 24E: 2000 ⇒16,4237; 17,4191. ^RBS 159 (2002) 248-250 (*Chisholm, Robert B.*); AUSS 40 (2002) 132-133 (*Mulzac, Kenneth D.*); JBL 121 (2002) 353-356 (*Wagenaar, Jan A.*).

4614 **Ben Zvi, Ehud** Micah. FOTL 21B: 2000 ⇒16,4238; 17,4192. ^RHebStud 43 (2002) 284-287 (*Cuffey, Kenneth H.*).

4615 **García, Miguel Angel** Ethiopian biblical commentaries on the prophet Micah. ÄthF 52: 1999 ⇒15,4095. ^ROrChr 86 (2002) 254-257 (*Wehrle, Josef*).

4616 **Hahn, Noli B.** A profecia de Miquéias e "meu povo": memórias, vozes e experiências. Estudos bíblicos 73 (2002) 92-101.

4617 **Jacobs, Mignon R.** The conceptual coherence of the book of Micah. JSOT.S 322: 2001 ⇒17,4193. ^RCBQ 64 (2002) 136-137 (*Dempsey, Carol J.*); RBLit (2002)* (*Cuffey, Kenneth H:*).

4618 *Kessler, Rainer* Micha/Michabuch. RGG 5. 2002 ⇒796. 1201-1203;
4619 Das Buch Micha als Mitte des Zwölfprophetenbuchs: Einzeltext, redaktionelle Intention und kontextuelle Lektüre. 'Wort JHWHs, das geschah'. Herders biblische Studien 35: 2002 ⇒4115. 139-148.

4620 **Wagenaar, Jan A.** Judgement and salvation: the composition and redaction of Micah 2-5, VT.S 85: 2001 ⇒17,4198. ^KCBQ 64 (2002) 361-363 (*Biddle, Mark E.*).

4621 *Moor, Johannes C. de* The structure of Micah 2:1-13: the contribution of the ancient witnesses. Studies in scriptural unit division. Pericope 3: 2002 ⇒339. 90-120.

4622 *Becking, Bob* The exile does not equal the eschaton: an interpretation of Micah 4:1-5. ^FLEENE, H. 2002 ⇒73. 1-7.

4623 *Moor, Johannes C. de* Workshop on unit delimitation: Micah 4:14-5:8. Studies in scriptural unit division. 2002 ⇒339. 258-275.

4624 *Wessels, Willie* Meeting Yahweh's requirements—a proposed reading of Micah 6:1-8. OTEs 15 (2002) 539-550.

E9.7 *Abdias, Sophonias...***Obadiah, Zephaniah, Nahum**

4625 *Almada, Samuel E.* Abdías: la injusticia no quedará impune. RevBib 63 (2001) 153-167.

4626 *Dietrich, Walter* Die Kontexte des Zefanjabuches. Theopolitik. 2002 <1996> ⇒159. 224-238.

4627 **Fernandes, Leonardo Agostini** A dimensao escatológica do Yôm YHWH em Sf 1,14-18. Rio de Janeiro 2002, Pontifícia Universidade Católica do Rio de Janeiro (4) x; 195 pp. Bibl. 184-195.
4628 **Irsigler, Hubert** Zefanja. HThK.AT: FrB 2002, Herder 440 pp. 3-451-26851-5. Bibl. 16-29.
4629 *Zechmeister, Martha* "Das also ist die fröhliche Stadt...!". Orien. 66 (2002) 1-3..

4630 *Bosman, J.P.* The good, the bad and the Belial: traces of wisdom in the prophetic rhetoric of Nahum. OTEs 15 (2002) 589-599.
4631 *Johnston, Gordon H.* Nahum's rhetorical allusions to neo-Assyrian conquest metaphors. BS 159 (2002) 21-45.
4632 **O'Brien, Julia M.** Nahum. Readings: Shf 2002, Sheffield A. 162 pp. 1-84127-299-X. Bibl. 149-155.
4633 *Wandermurem, Marli* A feminilização de Nínive—Naum 3,1-7. Estudos bíblicos 73 (2002) 82-91.

E9.8 *Habacuc*, **Habakkuk**

4634 **Andersen, Francis I.** Habakkuk. AncB 25: 2001 ⇒17,4214. [R]BS 159 (2002) 495 (*Merrill, Eugene H.*); RExp 99 (2002) 625-626 (*Jones, Barry A.*); Bib. 83 (2002) 419-422 (*Sawyer, John F.A.*).
4635 *Dietrich, Walter* Habakuk—ein Jesajaschüler. Theopolitik. 2002 <1994> ⇒159. 255-269.
4636 *Everson, A. Joseph* The canonical location of Habakkuk. SBL.SP 2002. SBL.SPS 41: 2002 ⇒598. 248-257.
4637 *Holladay, William L.* Plausible circumstances for the prophecy of Habakkuk. JBL 120 (2001) 123-142.

4638 *Pinker, Aron* Better bitter river. ZAW 114 (2002) 112-115 [Hab 1,6];
4639 Castanets. ZAW 114 (2002) 618-621 [Hab 2,9-11].
4640 *Prinsloo, G.T.M.* Reading Habakkuk 3 in its literary context: a worthwile exercise or futile attempt?. JSem 11/1 (2002) 83-111.

E9.9 *Aggaeus*, **Haggai**—*Zacharias*, **Zechariah**—*Malachias*, **Malachi**

4641 **Kessler, John** The book of Haggai: prophecy and society in early Persian Yehud. VT.S 91: Lei 2002, Brill xx; 334 pp. €97/$113. 90-04-12481-0. Bibl. 281-307.
4642 *Rendtorff, Rolf* Haggai im Zwölfprophetenbuch: einige vorläufige Überlegungen. 'Wort JHWHs, das geschah'. Herders biblische Studien 35: 2002 ⇒4115. 219-222.
4643 *Kessler, John* Building the second temple: questions of time, text, and history in Haggai 1.1-15. JSOT 27 (2002) 243-256.
4644 *Pinto, Carlos O.* História en interpretação em Ageu 2:20-23, 2. parte. VoxScr 11/1 (2002) 5-22.

4645 *Michael, Rajeev* Finally God will triumph in spite of...: messianic dream in Zechariah. God of big dreams. 2002 ⇒359. 253-272.
4646 **Delkurt, Holger** Sacharjas Nachtgesichte: zur Aufnahme und Abwandlung prophetischer Traditionen. BZAW 302: 2000 ⇒16,4274. [R]LuThK 26 (2002) 201-204 (*Behrens, Achim*) [Zech 1,7-6,8].

4647 **Kunz, Andreas** Zions Weg zum Frieden: jüdische Vorstellungen vom endzeitlichen Krieg und Frieden in hellenistischer Zeit am Beispiel von Sacharja 9-14. Beiträge zur Friedensethik 33: 2001 ⇒17, 4231. ^ROLZ 97 (2002) 575-579 (*Kellermann, Ulrich*).

4648 **Hill, Andrew E.** Malachi. AncB 25D: 1998 ⇒14,3761...16,4292. ^RIEJ 52 (2002) 105-106 (*Ahituv, Shmuel*).

4649 **Meinhold, Arndt** Maleachi. BK XIV/8 Lfg. 2: Neuk 2002, Neuk'er 81-160 pp. 3-7887-1715-7.

4650 *Niccacci, Alviero* Poetic syntax and interpretation of Malachi. LASBF 51 (2001) 55-107.

4651 **Weyde, Karl William** Prophecy and teaching: prophetic authority, form problems, and the use of traditions in the book of Malachi. BZAW 288: 2000 ⇒16,4295; 17,4234. ^RThLZ 127 (2002) 1292-1294 (*Schart, Aaron*).

4652 *Drost, Daniela* Maleachi 2,10-16: eine Vorstufe zur christlichen Ehetheologie?. ^FREINHARDT, H. 2002 ⇒98. 89-104.

4653 *Hurowitz, Victor Avigdor* אכל in Malachi 3:11—caterpillar. JBL 121 (2002) 327-330.

4654 *Frizzell, Lawrence* Elie, l'artisan de paix: interprétation de Malachie 3,23-24 dans le judaïsme et dans le christianisme primitif. SIDIC 35/2-3 (2002 <1984>) 25-32.

VIII. NT Exegesis generalis

F1.1 New Testament introduction

4655 ^E**Keck, Leander E.**, *al.*, NIntB 10: The Acts of the Apostles; Introduction to epistolary literature; The letter to the Romans; The first letter to the Corinthians. Nv 2002, Abingdon xviii; 1011 pp. 0-687-27823-6.

4656 **Achtemeier, Paul J.; Green, Joel B.; Thompson, Marianne Meye** Introducing the New Testament. 2001 ⇒ 17,4235. ^RRRT 9 (2002) 172 (*Wansbrough, Henry*); VJTR 66 (2002) 543-545 (*Meagher, P.M.*); CTJ 37 (2002) 339-340 (*Deppe, Dean*); AUSS 40 (2002) 307-308 (*Reeve, Teresa*); RBLit (2002)* (*Croy, N. Clayton*).

4657 *Bouttier, Michèle* Qu'est-ce que le Nouveau Testament. ETR 77 (2002) 313-328.

4658 **Broer, Ingo** Einleitung in das Neue Testament: 1. die synoptischen Evangelien, die Apostelgeschichte und die johanneische Literatur. NEB.NT Ergänzungsband 2/1: 1998 ⇒14,3774; 15,4167. ^RCart. 18 (2002) 556-557 (*Sanz Valdivieso, R.*);

4659 2: die Briefliteratur, die Offenbarung des Johannes und die Bildung des Kanons. NEB Erg. Bd. z. N.T. 2/2: 2001 ⇒17,4237. ^RZKTh 124 (2002) 237-238 (*Oberforcher, R.*); Cart. 18 (2002) 556-557 (*Sanz Valdivieso, R.*); SNTU.A 27 (2002) 213-214 (*Fuchs, Albert*).

4660 **Brown, Raymond E.** Que sait-on du Nouveau Testament?. ^T*Mignon, Jacques*: 2000 ⇒16,4303. ^RLTP 58 (2002) 358-59 (*Cazelais, Serge*);

4661   Introduzione al Nuovo Testamento. ^{E}*Boscolo, Gastone*: 2001 ⇒17,
       4238. ^{R}HumTeo 23/1 (2002) 121-122 (*Carvalho, José Carlos*); Civ-
       Catt 153/3 (2002) 319-320 (*Scaiola, D.*).

4662   **Bull, Klaus-Michael** Bibelkunde des Neuen Testaments: die kanoni-
       schen Schriften und die apostolischen Väter: Überblicke, Themakapi-
       tel, Glossar. Neuk ^{2}2002, Neuk 198 pp. €14.90. 3-7887-1622-3
       [BuBB 39,5].

4663   **Burkett, Delbert R.** An introduction to the New Testament and the
       origins of christianity. C 2002, CUP xv; 600 pp. £20. 0-521-00720-8.

4664   **Casalini, Nello** Lettere Cattoliche, Apocalisse di Giovanni: intro-
       duzione storica, letteraria, teologica. SBFA 58: J 2002. Franciscan
       Printing Press 368 pp. $30. 965-516-033-5;

4665   Iniziazione al Nuovo Testamento. ASBF 53: 2001 ⇒17,4239. ^{R}StFr
       99 (2002) 177-182 (*Giovannetti, Ottaviano*).

4666 ^{E}**Du Toit, A.B.** The New Testament milieu. ^{T}*Briggs, D. Roy*: Guide
       to the NT 2: 1998 ⇒14,3781. ^{R}RBLit 4 (2002) 326-329 (*Malherbe,
       Abraham*).

4667   **Ellis, Edward Earle** The making of the New Testament documents.
       Bibl. Interp. 39: 1999 ⇒15,4171...17,4243. ^{R}CBQ 64 (2002) 158-
       160 (*Talbert, Charles H.*); BBR 12 (2002) 302-306 (*Schnabel, Eck-
       hard*).

4668   **Fusco, Vittorio** Le prime comunità cristiane: tradizioni e tendenze
       nel cristianesimo delle origini. 1997 ⇒13,3980; 15,4173. ^{R}Protest.
       57 (2002) 80-81 (*Noffke, Eric*).

4669   Gesù per amico: un percorso evangelico con i disabili mentali. Mi
       2002, Leonardo international 214 pp. 88-86482-88-4.

4670   **Johnson, Luke Timothy** The writings of the New Testament: an
       interpretation. L ^{2}2002 <1986>, SCM xvi; 694 pp. £29.91. With CD-
       ROM; collab. *Todd Penner*.

4671   **Junkins, B.E.** A fresh parenthetical version of the New Testament.
       Lanham 2002, University Press of America xi; 742 pp. 07618-23972.

4672   **Koester, Helmuth** Introduction to the New Testament, 2: history
       and literature of early christianity. B 2000 De Gruyter 375 pp. €49/
       $68.55; €30/$30. 3-11-014971-0/0-2. ^{R}RBLit (2002)* (*Dupertuis,
       Rubén René*).

4673 ^{E}**Mainville, Odette** Escritos e ambiente do Novo Testamento—uma
       introdução. ^{T}*Orth, Lúcia Mathilde Endlich*: Petrópolis 2002, Vozes
       324 pp. 85-326-2694-7 [REB 62,748].

4674 ^{E}**Marguerat, Daniel L.** Introduction au Nouveau Testament: son
       histoire, son écriture, sa théologie. Le monde de la bible 41: 2000 ⇒
       16,4322; 17,4248. ^{R}ThLZ 127 (2002) 292-295 (*Broer, Ingo*).

4675   **Marshall, I. Howard; Travis, Steven; Paul, Ian** Exploring the New
       Testament, 2: a guide to the letters & Revelation. DG 2002, InterVar-
       sity xv; 336 pp. $25. 0-8308-2556-8 [ThD 49,381—Heiser, W.C.].

4676   **Moule, Charles Francis Digby** The birth of the New Testament.
       Black's NT Commentaries: L ^{3}2002, Continuum xii; 382 pp. 0-7136-
       2133-8.

4677   **Schnelle, Udo** Einleitung in das Neue Testament. UTB 1830; UTB.
       W: Gö ^{4}2002, Vandenhoeck & R. 616 pp. 3-8252-1830-9.

4678   **Scott, J. Julius, Jr.** Jewish backgrounds of the New Testament. GR
       2000, Baker 416 pp. $25. Reprint of Customs and controversies:
       intertestamental Jewish backgrounds of the NT ⇒11/2,2203...
       15,4195. ^{R}RBLit 4 (2002) 319-322 (*Lukaszewski, A.*).

4679 **Tarazi, Paul Nadim** The New Testament: introduction, 1: Paul and Mark. Crestwood, NY 2000, St Vladimir Seminary Pr. 249 pp. ⇒16, 4330. [R]ThRev 23/1 (2002) 61-62 (*Mrad, Nicolas Abou*);

4680 2: Luke and Acts. 2001 ⇒17,4257. [R]ThRev 23/1 (2002) 62-63 (*Mrad, Nicolas Abou*).

4681 **Theissen, Gerd** A theory of primitive christian religion. 1999 ⇒15, 4201...17,4258. [R]HeyJ 43 (2002) 92-93 (*Taylor, N.H.*);

4682 Das Neue Testament. Wissen 2192: Mü 2002, Beck 128 pp. €8.20. 3-406-47992-8.

4683 *Thomas, John C.* "Pentecostal explorations of the New Testament": teaching New Testament introduction in a Pentecostal seminary. JPentec 11/1 (2002) 120-129.

4684 *Tuckett, Christopher* The New Testament. Biblical world, 1. 2002 ⇒ 273. 28-37.

4685 **Vouga, F.** Il cristianesismo delle origini: scritti, protagonisti, dibattiti. Strumenti, Biblica 7: 2001 ⇒17,4261. [R]RSEc 22/1 (2002) 112-114 (*Abbà, Maurizio*); Islam and Christian-Muslim Relations 13 (2002) 485-486 (*Robinson, Neal*); IslChr 28 (2002) 302-303 (*Borrmans, Maurice*); RBLit (2002)* (*Räisänen, Heikki*).

4686 *Wall, Robert W.* Introduction to the epistolary literature. NIntB 10. 2002 ⇒4655. 369-391.

4687 **Wenham, David; Walton, Steve** Exploring the New Testament, 1: a guide to the Gospels and Acts. 2001 ⇒17,4263. [R]RBLit (2002)* (*Litwak, Kenneth D.*).

F1.2 *Origo Evangeliorum*, the origin of the Gospels

4688 **Black, David Alan** Why four gospels?: the historical origins of the gospels. 2001 ⇒17,4265. [R]TrinJ 23 (2002) 125-127 (*Sweeney, James*); RBLit (2002)* (*Percer, Leo*).

4689 **Hengel, Martin** The four gospels and the one gospel of Jesus Christ: an investigation of the collection and origin of the canonical gospels. 2000 ⇒16,4337; 17,4267. [R]CThMi 29 (2002) 53-54 (*Danker, Frederick W.*); CTJ 37 (2002) 120-122 (*Crump, David M.*); VJTR 66 (2002) 695-696 (*Meagher, P.M.*); BS 159 (2002) 498-499 (*Bock, Darrell L*); RBLit 4 (2002) 337-340 = JBL 121 (2002) 366-368 (*Jeal, Roy R.*).

4690 **Houlden, Leslie** The strange story of the gospels: finding doctrine through narrative. L 2002, SPCK x; 133 pp. £10. 0-281-05436-3. Bibl. 124-126.

4691 *Hurley, Robert* Le genre 'évangile' en fonction des effets produits par la mise en intrigue de Jésus. LTP 58 (2002) 243-257.

4692 *Muddiman, John* The gospels. Biblical world, 1, 2002 ⇒273. 162-187.

4693 *Petersen, William L.* The genesis of the gospels. [F]DELOBEL, J.: BEThL 161: 2002 ⇒24. 33-65.

4694 **Senior, Donald P.**, *al.*, Invitation to the gospels. Mahwah 2002, Paulist x; 406 pp. $20. 0-8091-4072-1. Foreword *Lawrence Boadt*.

4695 **Sicre, José Luis** O quadrante, 1: a busca—introdução aos evangelhos; 2, a aposta—o mundo de Jesus; 3, o encontro—o quarto evangelho. 2000 ⇒16,4342. [R]REB 248 (2002) 977-982 (*Fonseca, Fabiano José*).

4696 **Sonnabend, Holger** Geschichte der antiken Biographie: von ISOK-
RATES bis zur Historia Augusta. Stu 2002, Metzler x; 246 pp. 3-476-
01914-4.
4697 **Stanton, Graham** The gospels and Jesus. Oxford Bible: NY ²2002,
OUP xii; 324 pp. $25. 0-1992-4616-5 [ThD 49,391—Heiser, W.C.].
4698 **Theissen, Gerd** La redacción de los evangelios y la política eclesial:
un enfoque socio-retórico. Estella 2002, Verbo Divino 216 pp.
€15.60. 84-8169-508-4.

F1.3 **Historicitas,** *chronologia* **Evangeliorum**

4699 **Byrskog, Samuel** Story as history—history as story: the gospel tradition in the context of ancient oral history. WUNT 123: 2000 ⇒16,
4343; 17,4277. ᴿJR 82 (2002) 270-271 (*Kelber, Werner H.*); RHPhR
82 (2002) 225-227 (*Grappe, Ch.*); ThG 45 (2002) 223-224 (*Giesen,
Heinz*); JBL 121 (2002) 175-177 (*Matthews, Christopher R.*).
4700 **Carrón Pérez, J.; García Pérez, J.M.** Cuándo fueron escritos los
evangelios: el testimonio de Pablo. Studia semitica NT 7: 2001 ⇒17,
4278. ᴿVyV 60 (2002) 189-192 (*Sanz Valdivieso, Rafael*).
4701 *Dschulnigg, Peter* Wann sind die Evangelien entstanden?. ᶠFUCHS,
A.: 2002 ⇒41. 31-51.
4702 *García Chavarín, Daniel* El pavor de lo nuevo: anotaciones sobre la
historicidad de los evangelios. Qol 28 (2002) 75-96.
4703 **Graffy, Adrian** Trustworthy and true: the gospels beyond 2000.
2001 ⇒17,4279. ᴿPIBA 25 (2002) 163-165 (*Vallely, Brighde*).
4704 **Heckel, Theo K.** Vom Evangelium des Markus zum viergestaltigen
Evangelium. WUNT 120: 1999 ⇒15,4220; 17,4280. ᴿCBQ 64
(2002) 377-378 (*Kelhoffer, James A.*); ThRv 98 (2002) 486-488
(*Scholtissek, Klaus*); ThLZ 127 (2002) 757-760 (*Schnelle, Udo*).

F1.4 *Jesus historicus*—**The human Jesus**

4705 ᴱ**Schröter, Jens; Brucker, Ralph** Der historische Jesus: Tendenzen
und Perspektiven der gegenwärtigen Forschung. BZNT 114: B 2002,
De Gruyter viii; 472 pp. €110.28. 3-11-017511-8.

4706 **Adinolfi, Marco** A tavola con Gesù di Nazaret. 2001 ⇒17,4285.
ᴿLASBF 52 (2002) 559-560 (*Bottini, G. Claudio*).
4707 **Akenson, Donald Harman** Saint Saul: a skeleton key to the historical Jesus. 2000 ⇒16,6315; 17,6291. ᴿRB 109 (2002) 300-303
(*Murphy-O'Connor, Jerome*); SR 31 (2002) 400-402 (*Megivern,
James J.*); RBLit (2002)* (*Mitchell, Matthew W.*).
4708 *Amato, Angelo* Il volto di Gesù nella ferialità della sua vita.
Orientamenti pastorali 1 (2002) 21-25.
4709 *Aune, David E.* Assessing the historical value of the apocryphal Jesus
traditions: a critique of conflicting methodologies. Der historische Jesus. BZNW 114: 2002 ⇒4705. 243-272.
4710 *Bartchy, S. Scott* The historical Jesus and honor reversal at the table.
The social setting. 2002 ⇒601. 175-183;
4711 Der historische Jesus und die Umkehr der Ehre am Tisch. Jesus in
neuen Kontexten. 2002 ⇒602. 224-229.

4712 *Baum, Armin D.* Das Schriftverständnis Jesu: ein exegetisches Mosaik JETh 16 (2002) 13-32.

4713 **Bénétreau, Samuel** Les prières de Jésus: l'unique et l'imitable. 2000 ⇒16,4363. [R]EvTh(VS) 1/2 (2002) 104-106 (*Carrez, Maurice*).

4714 [E]**Blackmore, V.; Hyatt, J.; Robson, J.** Jesús 2000: un estudio sobre la figura más fascinante de la historia. Estella 2000, Verbo Divino 239 pp.

4715 *Blanco, Severiano* Tema ausiliare 1: Gesù maestro, sapienza di Dio;
4716 Tema ausiliare 2: Gesù che prega ci insegna a pregare. Salmi e letteratura sapienziale. 2002 ⇒264. 295-326/471-506.

4717 **Bock, Darrell L.** Studying the historical Jesus: a guide to sources and methods. GR 2002, Baker 230 pp. $19. 0-8010-2451-X. Bibl. 217-220 [BiTod 40,329—Senior, Donald];

4718 Jesus according to scripture: restoring the portrait from the gospels. GR 2002, Baker 704 pp. $40. 080102370X [ThD 50,63: Heiser, W.].

4719 [E]**Bockmuehl, Markus** The Cambridge companion to Jesus. 2001 ⇒ 17,5087. [R]Theol. 105 (2002) 217-218 (*Houlden, Leslie*); Pacifica 15 (2002) 337-339 (*Byrne, Brendan*).

4720 *Bonilla, Max* The Jesus seminar, its methodology and philosophy: a challenge to catholic biblical theology. ScEs 54 (2002) 313-335.

4721 **Boscione, Franco** I gesti di Gesù: la comunicazione non verbale nei vangeli. Mi 2002, Ancora 135 pp.

4722 *Bos, R.* De gepredikte Jezus—de prediking aangaande Jezus Christus tussen theologie en historie. VeE 23 (2002) 274-290.

4723 *Bruni, Giancarlo M.* In tutto simile agli uomini: Gesù di Nazareth. Horeb 11/3 (2002) 16-20.

4724 *Bultmann, Rudolf* Brief an Dietgard Meyer. Jesus im 21. Jahrhundert. 2002 ⇒1380. 207-208.

4725 **Bultmann, Rudolf Karl** Historia de la tradición sinóptica. [T]*Ruis-Garrido, Constantino*: Biblioteca de estudios bíblicos 102: 2000 ⇒ 16,4375; 17,4298. [R]NatGrac 49/1 (2002) 345-347 (*Villalmonte, A.*); EstAg 37 (2002) 590-591 (*Tirado, Pablo*); REsp 61 (2002) 643-644 (*Castro, Secundino*).

4726 *Burnet, Régis* Une vision radicale du Jésus historique, le *Jesus Seminar*. Com(F) 37/2 (2002) 27-33.

4727 *Cadavid, Alvaro* La investigación sobre la vida de Jesús. TyV 43 (2002) 512-540.

4728 **Cain, Marvin** Jesus the man: an introduction for people at home in the modern world. 1999 ⇒16,4377. [R]TJT 18 (2002) 257-258 (*Damm, Alex*).

4729 *Carrasco Rouco, Alfonso* Historia y revelación: acceso crítico a la figura de Jesucristo. Dios para pensar 2002 ⇒432. 119-134.

4730 **Chavot, Pierre; Potin, Jean** L'ABCdaire de Jésus. ABCdaire: P 2000, Flammarion 120 pp. 2-08-012681-4 [NRTh 126,471—Wargnies, Ph.].

4731 **Childs, Hal** The myth of the historical Jesus and the evolution of consciousness. SBL.DS 179: 2000 ⇒16,4379; 17,4302. [R]RBLit 4 (2002) 330-333 (*Brown, Stephen H.*).

4732 *Craffert, P.F.* Historical-anthropological Jesus research: the status of authentic pictures beyond authentic material. HTS 58 (2002) 440-471 [NTAb 47,231];

4733 Appropriating historical Jesus research in Africa. R&T 9/3-4 (2002) 199-224.

4734 **Cserháti, Márta** Methods and models in the third quest of the historical Jesus. ^{D}*Dunn, J.D.G.*: 266 pp. Diss. Durham 2001 [RTL 34,596].

4735 *Cuvillier, Elian* Jésus de l'histoire et Christ de la foi: quelques publications récentes. ETR 77 (2002) 187-192.

4736 *Danieli, Giuseppe* La pastorale di Gesù. Orientamenti pastorali 1 (2002) 32-37.

4737 **Dawes, Gregory W.** The historical Jesus question: the challenge of history to religious authority. 2001 ⇒17,4312. ^{R}Jian Dao 17 (2002) 205-209 [C.] (*Wong, Eppie Y.*); Theol. 105 (2002) 299-301 (*Harvey, A.E.*).

4738 **De Mier, Francisco** Los encuentros de Jesús. 2001 ⇒17,4313. ^{R}Ter. 53 (2002) 606-607 (*Pasquetto, Virgilio*).

4739 *Deneken, Michel* Jésus de Nazareth fondement atypique de la typologie chrétienne. Typologie biblique. LeDiv: 2002 ⇒341. 241-266.

4740 *Depuydt, Leo* The date of the death of Jesus of Nazareth. JAOS 122 (2002) 466-480 [BuBB 38,13].

4741 *Destro, A.; Pesce, M.* Between family and temple: Jesus and sacrifices. HTS 58 (2002) 472-501 [NTAb 47,231].

4742 *Dhavamony, Mariasusai* Jesus and the gentiles. StMiss 51 (2002) 167-218.

4743 **Dirnbeck, Josef** Falsches Zeugnis wider Jesus: Jesusfälscher auf dem Prüfstand. Salzburg 2002, Müller 272 pp. €18. 3-7013-1050-5 [BiKi 58,183].

4744 *Duling, Dennis C.* The Jesus movement and network analysis. The social setting. 2002 ⇒601. 301-332.

4745 *Dulling [!—Duling], Dennis C.* Die Jesusbewegung und die Netzwerkanalyse. Jesus in neuen Kontexten. 2002 ⇒602. 135-157.

4746 **Dunn, James D.G.** Jesus and purity: an ongoing debate. NTS 48 (2002) 449-467;

4747 "All that glisters is not gold": in quest of the right key to unlock the way to the historical Jesus. Der historische Jesus. BZNW 114: 2002 ⇒4705. 131-161.

4748 *Dupuy, Michel* Les mystères de Jésus. Com(F) 37/2 (2002) 35-42.

4749 *Du Toit, David* Erneut auf der Suche nach Jesus: eine kritische Bestandsaufnahme der Jesusforschung am Anfang des 21. Jahrhunderts. Jesus im 21. Jahrhundert. 2002 ⇒1380. 91-134;

4750 Der unähnliche Jesus: eine kritische Evaluierung der Entstehung des Differenzkriteriums und seiner geschichts- und erkenntnistheoretischen Voraussetzungen. Der historische Jesus. BZNW 114: 2002 ⇒ 4705. 89-129.

4751 *Ebner, Martin* Die Mähler Jesu im Kontext der Gleichnisse vom Säen und Ernten, Brotbacken und -schenken, Einladen und Feiern. BiKi 57 (2002) 9-14.

4752 *Elliott, James K.* Research on the sayings of Jesus. CV 44 (2002) 174-181.

4753 *Evans, Craig A.* The ministry of Jesus in the gospels. Community formation. 2002 ⇒644. 59-72.

4754 *Fiensy, David A.* Jesus and debts: did he pray about them?. RestQ 44/4 (2002) 233-239.

4755 *Fiorenza, Elisabeth Schüssler* Der wirkliche Jesus?—feministische Anfragen an die sozialwissenschaftliche Jesusforschung. Jesus in neuen Kontexten. 2002 ⇒602. 23-32.

4756 *Fischer, Johannes* Zur Hermeneutik christologischer Aussagen. Jesus im 21. Jahrhundert. 2002 ⇒1380. 189-198.

4757 *Fletcher-Louis, Crispin H.T.* Jesus, the temple and the dissolution of heaven and earth. Apocalyptic. JSPE.S 43: 2002 ⇒373. 117-141.

4758 **Fredriksen, Paula** Jesus of Nazareth King of the Jews: a Jewish life and the emergence of christianity. 1999 ⇒15,4281...17,4328. [R]JThS 53 (2002) 180-185 (*Bryan, Steven M.*).

4759 **Freke, Timothy; Gandy, Peter** Os mistérios de Jesus: seria o Jesus original um deus pagão?. Mem Martins 2002, Europa-America 340 pp [Brot. 156,96—F. Pires Lopes].

4760 *Frey, Jörg* Der historische Jesus und der Christus der Evangelien. Der historische Jesus. BZNW 114: 2002 ⇒4705. 273-336.

4761 **Fricker, Denis** Le 'masculin-féminin' e le parallélisme dans les sentences de Jésus. [D]*Schlosser, J.*: 2002: 385 pp. Diss. Strasbourg [RTL 34,597].

4762 **Funk, Robert W.** A credible Jesus: fragments of a vision. Santa Rosa, CA 2002, Polebridge 184 pp. $18. 0-944344-88-7. Bibl. 179-180. [R]RBLit (2002)* (*Chancey, Mark Alan*).

4763 *Guijarro Oporto, Santiago* La investigación sobre el Jesús histórico. Did(L) 32/2 (2002) 3-30;

4764 Jesús y sus discípulos. ResB 36 (2002) 5-12.

4765 *Guillet, Jacques* Le Christ et l'avenir. Études (Jan. 2002) 63-72.

4766 *Haacker, Klaus* Jesus—Messias Israels?;

4767 Jesus unter den Messiaskandidaten des antiken Judentums <1998>. Versöhnung mit Israel. VKHW 5: 2002 ⇒174. 49-64/ 65-74.

4768 *Hanson, K.C.* Jesus und die "Freibeuter": eine sozialwissenschaftliche Studie. Jesus in neuen Kontexten. 2002 ⇒602. 123-134;

4769 Jesus and the social bandits. The social setting. 2002 ⇒601. 283-300.

4770 *Heiligenthal, Roman* Starb Jesus in Indien?. WUB Sonderheft (2002) 83-85.

4771 **Heiligenthal, Roman; Dobbeler, Axel von** Menschen um Jesus: Lebensbilder aus neutestamentlicher Zeit. 2001 ⇒17,4342. [R]ActBib 38/1 (2002) 46-48 (*Boada, J.*).

4772 **Heyer, C.J. den** Opnieuw: wie is Jezus?: balans van 150 jaar onderzoek naar Jezus. Zoetermeer 2002, Meinema 253 pp. €18.50. 90-211-3907-3;

4773 La storicità di Gesù. [T]*Soggin, Thomas*: 2000 ⇒16,4428; 17,4346. [R]Oecumenica Civitas 2/1 (2002) 117-118 (*Fattorini, Lucia*).

4774 *Hobbs, T. Raymond* The political Jesus: discipleship and disengagement. The social setting. 2002 ⇒601. 251-281.

4775 *Holmberg, Bengt* Karisma som sociologisk förklaringsmodell i tolkningen av Jesus. SEÅ 67 (2002) 61-77.

4776 **Holmén, Tom** Jesus and Jewish covenant thinking. BiblInterp 55: 2001 ⇒17,4348. [R]RBLit (2002)* (*Bateman, Herbert W.*).

4777 [E]**Hoover, Roy W.** Profiles of Jesus. Santa Rosa, CA 2002, Polebridge viii; 256 pp. $20. 0-944344-94-1. Bibl. 247-253.

4778 *Horsley, Richard A.* Jesus gegen die neue römische Ordnung. WUB 24 (2002) 27-31.

4779 **Horsley, Richard A.; Silberman, Neil Asher** A mensagem e o reino. [T]*Lambert, Barbara Theoto*: Bíblica Loyola 29: 2000 ⇒16,4433. [R]REB 62 (2002) 468-473 (*Andrade, William César de*).

4780 **Horsley, Richard A.** Jesus and empire: the kingdom of God and the new world disorder. Mp 2002, Fortress vii; 178 pp. $17. 0-8006-349-0-X [ThD 50,172—Heiser, W. Charles].

4781 **Jenkins, Philip** Hidden gospels: how the search for Jesus lost its way. 2001 ⇒17,4353. ᴿWorship 76 (2002) 189-91 (*Sloyan, Gerard*); Theol. 105 (2002) 361-362 (*Burridge, Richard A.*); JEH 53 (2002) 765-766 (*Elliott, J.K.*); SJTh 55 (2002) 498-500 (*Graham, Gordon*).

4782 *Jeremias, Joachim* The search for the historical Jesus. Jesus and the message. 2002 <1958> ⇒184. 1-17.

4783 **Johnson, Luke Timothy** Jésus sans parti pris: la quête chimérique du Jésus historique et la vérité des évangiles. ᵀ*Witt, Fabienne*: 2000 ⇒16,4439; 17,4355. ᴿETR 77 (2002) 435-436 (*Lienhard, Fritz*).

4784 *Kalsky, Manuela* Vom einsamen Helden zur messianischen Gemeinschaft: feministische Versuche, die Bedeutung Jesu neu zu erschließen. Diak. 33 (2002) 98-104.

4785 **Kazen, Thomas** Jesus and purity halakhah: was Jesus indifferent to impurity?. ᴰ*Syreeni, K.*: CB.NT 38: Sto 2002, Almqvist & W. xii; 402 pp. SEK301. 91-22-01964-2. Diss. Uppsala 2000; Bibl. 354-85.

4786 *Kelber, Werner H.* Der historische Jesus: Bedenken zur gegenwärtigen Diskussion aus der Perspektive mittelalterlicher, moderner und postmoderner Hermeneutik. Der historische Jesus. BZNW 114: 2002 ⇒4705. 15-66.

4787 **Kieffer, René** Evangeliernas Jesus—myt och verklighet. 2001 ⇒17, 4360. ᴿSEÅ 67 (2002) 175 (*Fornberg, Tord*).

4788 *Kuttianimattathil, Jose* Jesus the eminent dialogue partner. VJTR 66 (2002) 506-523 [Mt 8,5-13; Mk 7,24-30; Jn 4,1-42].

4789 *Lamerson, Samuel* Evangelicals and the quest for the historical Jesus. CuBR 1/1 (2002) 61-87.

4790 **Laurentin, René** Vida autêntica de Jesus Cristo, 1: narrativa; 2, fundamentos, provas e justificação. ᵀ*Valério, Paulo F.*: São Paulo 2002, Paulinas 548 + 248 pp [REB 248, 1008].

ᴱ**LeBeau, B.**, *al.*, The historical Jesus through catholic and Jewish eyes 2000 ⇒569.

4791 *Lee, S.M.* Beyond ideologies, toward unification in the light of the ethos of the Jesus movement. JAAT 5 (2002) 36-64 [NTAb 47,443].

4792 *Lémonon, Jean-Pierre* Au sujet des frères et soeurs de Jésus. CEv 121 (2002) 64-65;

4793 *Jésus de Nazareth: prophète et sage. CEv 119 (2002) 5-59.*

4794 *Leutzsch, Martin* Jesus der Galiläer. WUB 24 (2002) 7-13.

4795 *Lindemann, Andreas* Zur Einführung: die Frage nach dem historischen Jesus als historisches und theologisches Problem. Jesus im 21. Jahrhundert. 2002 ⇒1380. 1-21.

4796 **Loader, William** Jesus' attitude towards the law: a study of the gospels. GR ³2002, Eerdmans x; 563 pp. $50. 0-8028-4903-2 [BiTod 40,402—Senior, Donald];

4797 Jesus and the fundamentalism of his day. 2001 ⇒17,4370. ᴿEThL 78 (2002) 510-512 (*Van Belle, G.*); AThR 84 (2002) 1040-1041 (*Chilton, Bruce*); RBLit 4 (2002) 344-347 (*Novakovic, Lidija*).

4798 *Löhr, Hermut* Jesus und der Nomos aus der Sicht des entstehenden Christentums: zum Jesus-Bild im ersten Jahrhundert n. Chr. und zu unserem Jesus-Bild. Der historische Jesus. BZNW 114: 2002 ⇒ 4705. 337-354.

4799 **Ludwig, Ralph** Basiswissen Jesus. GTBS 674: Gü 2002, Gü 96 pp. 3-579-00674-6.

4800 *Luz, Ulrich* Warum zog Jesus nach Jerusalem?. Der historische Jesus. BZNW 114: 2002 ⇒4705. 409-427.

4801 *Lüdemann, Gerd* Fakten und Fantasien in der neuen Jesus-Literatur und im Neuen Testament. Jesus von Nazareth und das Christentum. 2000 ⇒293. 130-152.

4802 **Lüdemann, Gerd** Jesus after 2000 years: what he really said and did. 2000 ⇒16,4348; 17,4372. [R]Dialog 41 (2002) 253-254 (*Martin, Thomas W.*); Apocrypha 13 (2002) 289-291 (*Amsler, F.*).

4803 *MacGuckian, Michael C.* What kind of historicity do we have?. HPR 103/3 (2002) 8-17.

4804 *Maggioni, Bruno* Gesù poeta. PSV 45 (2002) 71-79.

4805 *Malina, Bruce J.* Sozialwissenschaftliche Methodik in der historischen Jesusforschung. Jesus in neuen Kontexten. 2002 ⇒602. 11-22;

4806 Social-scientific methods in historical Jesus research. The social setting. 2002 ⇒601. 3-26.

4807 [E]**Marguerat, Daniel; Norelli, Enrico; Poffet, Jean-Michel** Jésus de Nazareth: nouvelles approches d'une énigme. MoBi 38: 1998 ⇒14, 253... 17,298. [R]EThL 78 (2002) 203-205 (*Verheyden, J.*).

4808 *Martin, Dale B.* "Sex and the single savior". SEÅ 67 (2002) 47-60.

4809 **Martinez Garcia, Jesús** Quién es Jesús?. Libros mc 95: 2000 ⇒16, 4471. [R]RelCult 48/1 (2002) 196 (*Dujo, Eleuterio del*).

4810 *Matthey, Jacques* Jésus, un être de dialogue. Spiritus 43 (2002) 514-525.

4811 **McIver, Robert K.** The four faces of Jesus: four gospel writers, four unique perspectives, four personal encounters, one complete picture. 2000 ⇒16,4474. [R]ABR 50 (2002) 86-87 (*Squires, John T.*); RBLit 4 (2002) 347-348 (*Jackson, Glenna S.*).

4812 **Meier, J.P.** Un ebreo marginale: ripensare il Gesù storico, 1: le radici del problema e della persona. Btc 117: 2001 ⇒17,4388. [R]HumTeo 23/1 (2002) 124-126 (*Carvalho, José Carlos*);

4813 2: mentore, messagio e miracoli. [T]*Nepi, Antonio; Ferrari, Laura; Gatti, Enzo*: Btc 120: Brescia 2002, Queriniana 1338 pp. €99.50. 88-399-0420-4 [RdT 43,159];

4814 A marginal Jew: rethinking the historical Jesus, 3: companions and competitors. 2001 ⇒17,4387. [R]AThR 84 (2002) 418-419 (*Adam, A. K.M.*); CBQ 64 (2002) 771-773 (*Harrington, Daniel J.*); RExp 99 (2002) 459-460 (*Vickery, Jeffrey D.*); RBLit (2002)* (*Wilson, Alistair I.*).

4815 A marginal Jew: rethinking the historical Jesus, 1-3. 1991-2001. ⇒ 7,3667... 17,4387. [R]NBl 83 (2002) 504-513 (*McMahon, Christopher*); HTS 57 (2001) 230-246, 1179-1212 [on vols 1-2] (*Geyser, P.A.*);

4816 **Men, Alexander** Jesús, el Maestro de Nazaret. [T]*Conejo López-Lago, M.*: M 2002, Ciudad Nueva 380 pp. €18. 84-9715-019-8 [EstAg 38, 180—Sala, R.].

14817 *Merklein, Helmut* Wie hat Jesus seinen Tod verstanden?. LS 53 (2002) 86-96.

4818 *Merz, Annette* Das "Meer von Galiläa" und die Jesusbewegung. WUB 24 (2002) 32-39.

4819 *Mesters, Carlos* Gesù formatore. Vita Con 38 (2002) 339-350.

4820 *Miller, Robert J.* The (non-)apocalyptic Jesus: what is at stake?. ProcGLM 22 (2002) 109-126 .

4821 **Miller, Robert J.** The Jesus seminar and its critics. 1999 ⇒15,153. [R]TJT 18 (2002) 258-259 (*Damm, Alex*).

4822 *Mimouni, Simon* Jésus de Nazareth: personnage prophétique ou messianique?. Nier les dieux. 2002 ⇒626. 225-252.

4823 ^E**Mistrorigo, Antonio** Il vangelo unificato: per la prima volta dalla unione dei 4 vangeli l'intera vita di Gesù. CasM 2002, Piemme 198 pp. €12.90. 88-384-6955-5 [RdT 43,159].

4824 **Morales, J.** Jesús de Nazaret. M 2002, Rialp 274 pp.

4825 **Mordillat, G.; Prieur, J.** Jesús contra Jesús. Alzira 2002, Algar 378 pp.

4826 *Morgan, Robert* Jesus. Biblical world, 2. 2002 ⇒273. 223-257.

4827 **Moschetta, Jean-Marc** Jésus, fils de Joseph: comment comprendre aujourd'hui la conception virginale de Jésus?. P 2002, L'Harmattan 336 pp. €28. 2-7475-3450-2.

4828 *Moxter, Michael* Erzählung und Ereignis: über den Spielraum historischer Repräsentation. Der historische Jesus. BZNW 114: 2002 ⇒ 4705. 67-88.

4829 *Mulloor, Augustine* Jesus and violence. Jeevadhara 32 (2002) 136-145.

4830 **Müller, Norbert** Welchen Jesus hätten Sie gern?: Mosaik einer Biographie. 1996 ⇒15,4353. ^RThRv 98 (2002) 25-26 (*Biser, Eugen*).

4831 *Naro, Massimo* Il Dio di Gesù Cristo e i monoteismi. Ho Theológos 20 (2002) 453-457.

4832 ^E**Newman, Carey C.** Jesus & the restoration of Israel: a critical assessment of N.T. WRIGHT's Jesus and the victory of God. 1999 ⇒ 15,262. ^RProEc 11 (2002) 110-111 (*Fowl, Stephen*).

4833 **Nouwen, Henri J.M.** Jesus: a gospel. ^E*O'Laughlin, Michael*: 2001 ⇒17,4399. ^RVJTR 66 (2002) 232-233 (*Meagher, P.M.*).

4834 **Paul, André** Jésus-Christ, la rupture: essai sur la naissance du christianisme. 2001 ⇒17,4402. ^RHum(B) 57 (2002) 850-851 (*Montagnini, Felice*); EeV 52 (2002) 16-17 (*Cothenet, Edouard*).

4835 *Penna, Romano* Il nuovo Adamo e la danza della vita. PSV 45 (2002) 95-109.

4836 *Perrot, Charles* Enquêtes sur Jésus de Nazareth. Com(F) 37/2 (2002) 15-25.

4837 *Pilch, John J.* Ereignisse eines veränderten Bewusstseinszustandes bei den Synoptikern. Jesus in neuen Kontexten. 2002 ⇒602. 33-42;

4838 Altered states of consciousness in the synoptics. The social setting. 2002 ⇒601. 103-115.

4839 *Pokorný, Petr* Jesus von Nazareth als Problem der historischen Forschung und ihrer theologischen Interpretation. CV 44 (2002) 137-38;

4840 Lexikalische und rhetorische Eigentümlichkeiten der ältesten Jesustradition. Der historische Jesus. BZNW 114: 2002 ⇒4705. 393-408.

4841 **Porter, Stanley E.** The criteria for authenticity in historical-Jesus research: previous discussion and new proposals. JSNT.S 191: 2000 ⇒16,4507; 17,4409. ^RBS 159 (2002) 125-127 (*Bock, Darrell L.*); TrinJ 23 (2002) 120-124 (*McKnight, Scot*); ABR 50 (2002) 88-89 (*Sim, David C.*); ThLZ 127 (2002) 397-399 (*Scriba, Albrecht*).

4842 **Price, Robert M.** Deconstructing Jesus. 2000 ⇒16,4512; 17,4412. ^RRBLit 4 (2002) 348-351 (*Brown, H. Stephen*).

4843 *Raskin, Jay* A discovery, the Crucified, Simon, Zealots, and Essenes. JHiC 9/1 (2002) 94-124.

4844 **Rau, Eckhard** Jesus Freund von Zöllnern und Sündern: eine methodenkritische Untersuchung 2000 ⇒16,4518; 17,4415. ^RThPQ 150 (2002) 86-88 (*Niemand, Christoph*); ZKTh 124 (2002) 106-109 (*Neufeld, Karl H.*); ThRv 98 (2002) 108-110 (*Roloff, Jürgen*); ThLZ 127 (2002) 300-302 (*Fiedler, Peter*).

4845 **Reed, Jonathan L.** Archaeology and the Galilean Jesus: a re-examination of the evidence. Harrisburg, Pennsyl. 2002, Trinity xiii; 253 pp. 1-56338-394-2/24-1 [Lk 11,29-32].

4846 *Richard, Pablo* I diversi volti di Gesù nei vangeli sinottici. Conc(I) 38/1 (2002) 56-65; Conc(E) 294,49-56; Conc(D) 38/1,34-41; Conc(P) 294, 43-50.

4847 *Rieske-Braun, Uwe* Das Wesen des Christentums: ein Jahrhundert nach der Vorlesung Adolf von HARNACKs. Jesus von Nazareth und das Christentum. 2000 ⇒293. 107-129.

4848 *Rohrbaugh, Richard* Ethnozentrismus und geschichtliche Fragen: die Frage nach dem messianischen Bewusstsein Jesu. Jesus in neuen Kontexten. 2002 ⇒602. 212-223;

4849 Ethnocentrism and historical questions about Jesus. The social setting. 2002 ⇒601. 27-43;

4850 Semiotic behavior in Luke and John. HTS 58 (2002) 746-766 [NTAb 47,249].

4851 **Roloff, Jürgen** Jesus. Mü 2002, Beck 126 pp. €7.90. 3-406-44742-2 [BiKi 58,184].

4852 *Sanders, E.P.* Jesus' Galilee. FRÄISÄNEN, H.: NT.S 103: 2002 ⇒97. 1-41.

4853 *Schiwy, Günther* War Jesus Esoteriker?: esoterische Aspekte des Christentums. Jesus von Naz. u. das Christentum. 2000 ⇒293. 80-95.

4854 **Schlosser, Jacques** Gesù di Nazaret. Nuove vie dell'esegesi. R 2002, Borla 315 pp. €22.50. 88-263-1448-9.

4855 *Schmithals, Walter* Jesus verkündigt das Evangelium: BULTMANNS Jesus-Buch. Jesus im 21. Jahrhundert. 2002 ⇒1380. 23-60.

4856 **Schot, M.** La invención de Cristo: génesis de una religión. 1998 ⇒ 15,4397. RStudium 42 (2002) 154-155 (*López, L.*).

4857 *Schreiter, Robert J.* Die Botschaft Jesu: wozu sollen wir glauben?. Die Bibel: Geschichte und Gegenwart. 2002 ⇒971. 80-91.

4858 *Schröter, Jens* Von der Historizität der Evangelien: ein Beitrag zur gegenwärtigen Diskussion um den historischen Jesus;

4859 *Schröter, Jens; Brucker, Ralph* Einleitung. Der historische Jesus. BZNW 114: 2002 ⇒4705. 163-212/1-14.

4860 **Schweitzer, Albert** The quest of the historical Jesus. EBowden, John: 2000 ⇒16,4531; 17,4434. First complete edition. RJJS 53 (2002) 391-392 (*Vermes, Geza*).

4861 **Schweizer, E.** Jesús, parábola de Dios: ¿Qué sabemos realmente de la vida de Jesús?. TOlasagasti, Manuel: 2001 ⇒17,4436. RCTom 129 (2002) 192-193 (*González Blanco, Rafael*).

4862 *Segert, Stanislav* The languages of historical Jesus. CV 44 (2002) 161-173.

4863 **Sölle, Dorothee; Schottroff, Luise** Jesus von Nazareth. 2000 ⇒16, 4538. RBiKi 57 (2002) 55-56 (*Kosch, Daniel*);

4864 Jesus of Nazareth. TBowden, John: LVL 2002, Westminster 158 pp. $15. 0-664-22500-4.

4865 *Stefani, Piero* Violenza e nonviolenza nel linguaggio di Gesù. Pace e guerra. 2002 ⇒600. 79-88.

4866 *Stegemann, Wolfgang* Die Jesusbewegung als Armenbewegung Galiläas. WUB 24 (2002) 40-44.

4867 **Taylor, Justin** Where did christianity come from?. 2001 ⇒17,4444. RWorship 76 (2002) 282-285 (*Launderville, Dale*); Pacifica 15 (2002) 340-2 (*Coloe, Mary*); NewTR 15 (2002) 87-8 (*McDonald, Patricia*).

4868   *Theissen, Gerd* The political dimension of Jesus' activities. The social setting. 2002 ⇒601. 225-250;

4869   Die politische Dimension des Wirkens Jesu. Jesus in neuen Kontexten. 2002 ⇒602. 112-122.

4870   **Theissen, Gerd; Merz, Annette** Il Gesù storico: un manuale. BiBi(B) 25: 1999 ⇒15,4417; 16,4546. ᴿRivBib 50 (2002) 493-496 *(Fabris, R.)*.

4871   **Theissen, Gerd; Winter, Dagmar** The quest for the plausible Jesus: the question of criteria. LVL 2002, Westminster xxiii; 344 pp. £25. 0-664-22537-3. Bibl. 317-336.

4872   *Tuckett, Christopher M.* Q and the historical Jesus. Der historische Jesus. BZNW 114: 2002 ⇒4705. 213-241.

4873   *Van Aarde, A.G.* The 'cause of Jesus' *(Sache Jesu)* as the canon behind the canon. HTS 57 (2001) 1229-1253 [NTAb 46,450];

4874   Methods and models in the quest for the historical Jesus: historical criticism and/or social scientific criticism. HTS 58 (2002) 419-439 [NTAb 47,234].

4875   Jesus als vaterloses Kind: eine kulturübergreifende und sozialpsychologische Perspektive. Jesus in neuen Kontexten. 2002 ⇒602. 98-111;

4876   Jesus as fatherless child. The social setting. 2002 ⇒601. 65-84.

4877   **Van Aarde, Andries** Fatherless in Galilee: Jesus as child of God. 2001 ⇒17,4454. ᴿASEs 19 (2002) 300-301 *(Rescio, Mara)*; HTS 58 (2002) 77-99 *(Le Roux, Jurie H.)*.

4878   **Van Voorst, R.** Jesus outside the New Testament: an introduction to the ancient evidence. 2000 ⇒16,4555; 17,4457. ᴿThLZ 127 (2002) 192-193 *(Heiligenthal, Roman)*; LASBF 51 (2001) 444-447 *(Chrupcała, L.D.)*.

4879   *Vargas-Machuca, Antonio* La investigación actual sobre el Jesús histórico. EE 77 (2002) 3-71.

4880   *Verdoodt, Albert* Jesus und Paulus: was wir von sozialwissenschaftlichen Modellen lernen können. Jesus in neuen Kontexten. 2002 ⇒ 602. 230-236;

4881   The gospels in comparison with the Pauline letters: what we can learn from social-scientific models. The social setting. 2002 ⇒601. 367-377.

4882   **Vicent Cernuda, Antonio** Jesús perseguido a muerte: estudios exegéticos sobre las personas y los hechos. Monografías 82: M 2002, Fundación Universitaria Española 365 pp. 84-7392-509-2 [RB 110, 640].

4883   *Vignolo, Roberto* La convivialità di Gesù. PSV 45 (2002) 81-94.

4884   *Villiers, Pieter G.R. de* Geskiedenis, geloof en di evangelies: perspektiewe op die verhouding tussen geskiedenis en teologie in die bybelwetenskappe. Scriptura 80 (2002) 161-172 [NTAb 47,439].

4885   *Walter, Nikolaus* Johannes und Jesus—zwei eschatologische Propheten: das Selbstbild Jesu im Spiegel seines Bildes vom Täufer nach Q/ Lk 7,24-35. Jesus im 21. Jahrhundert. 2002 ⇒1380. 135-151.

4886   *Waters, C.J.* Healing in the context of ministry. ET 113 (2002) 372-374.

4887   **White, R.E.O.** Listening carefully to Jesus. GR 2002, Eerdmans vi; 108 pp. $12 [BiTod 41,68—Senior, Donald].

4888   **Wilckens, Ulrich** Theologie des Neuen Testaments, 1: Geschichte der urchristlichen Theologie, 1: Geschichte des Wirkens Jesu in Galiläa. Neuk 2002, Neuk xvi; 343 pp. €29.90. 3-7887-1894-3.

4889 *Williams, Catrin H.* Interpretations of the identity and role of Jesus. Biblical world, 2. 2002 ⇒273. 332-356.
4890 **Witherington, Ben, III** Jesus the seer: the progress of prophecy. 1999 ⇒15,4433...17,4466. [R]RevBib 63 (2001) 221-3 (*Croatto, J.S.*).
4891 *Wolter, Michael* "Gericht" und "Heil" bei Jesus von Nazareth und Johannes dem Täufer: semantische und pragmatische Beobachtungen. Der historische Jesus. BZNW 114: 2002 ⇒4705. 355-392.
4892 **Wright, Nicholas Thomas** The contemporary quest for Jesus. Facets: Mp 2002, Fortress 104 pp. $6. 0-8006-3482-9 [ThD 49,268—W. Charles Heiser];
4893 The challenge of Jesus. 1999 ⇒16,4566. [R]ProEc 11 (2002) 109-110 (*Fowl, Stephen*).
4894 *Zangenberg, Jürgen* "Jesus-Archäologie" zwischen Apologetik und Sensationalismus. WUB 24 (2002) 67-69.

F1.5 *Jesus et Israel*—Jesus the Jew

4895 [E]**Chilton, Bruce; Evans, Craig A.; Neusner, Jacob** The missing Jesus: rabbinic Judaism and the New Testament. Boston 2002, Brill xv; 175 pp. 0-391-04183-5.

4896 **Alonso Ávila, Ángeles** Sentir la historia: un acercamiento al judío Jesús. Graeco-Romanae Religionis Electa: M 2002, Signifer L. 246 pp. 84-932043-66.
4897 **Baeck, Leo** Les evangiles, une source juive. [T]*Hayoun, Maurice-Ruben*: P 2002, Bayard 150 pp. €23. 2-227-31737-X. [R]SR 31 (2002) 404-405 (*Lavoie, Jean-Jacques*).
4898 **Barbaglio, Giuseppe** Gesù ebreo di Galilea: indagine storica. La Bibbia nella storia 11: Bo 2002, EDB 671 pp. €45.98. 8810-40270-7.
4899 *Basser, Herbert W.* The gospels and rabbinic literature. The missing Jesus, 2002 ⇒4895. 77-99.
4900 *Bogaert, Pierre-Maurice* L'identité juive de Jésus: une question d'actualité. RTL 33 (2002) 351-370.
4901 [E]**Bruteau, Beatrice** Jesus through Jewish eyes. 2001 ⇒17,4467. [R]RRT 9 (2002) 199-200 (*Wollaston, Isabel*).
4902 **Calimani, R.** Jésus juif—les racines juives du christianisme. Toulouse 2002, Privat 256 pp. 2-7089-5694-9.
4903 [E]**Charlesworth, J.H.** L'ebraicità di Gesù. Piccola biblioteca teologica 56: T 2002, Claudiana 328 pp. €23.50. 88-7016-397-0. [R]RSEc 20 (2002) 495-496 (*Morandini, Simone*).
4904 *Chilton, Bruce* Mapping a place for Jesus;
4905 Getting it right: James, Jesus, and questions of sanctity;
4906 Conclusion: Jesus within Judaism. The missing Jesus, 2002 ⇒4895. 41-44/107-123/135-156.
4907 **Chilton, Bruce** Rabbi Jesus: an intimate biography. NY 2002 <2000>, Doubleday xxii; 330 pp. 0-385-49793-8. ⇒16,4604; 17,4535. [R]EvQ 74 (2002) 59-66 (*Burge, Gary M.*); Review of Rabbinic Judaism 5 (2002) 95-101 (*Lang, B.*).
4908 *Chouraqui, Jean-Marc* Gedanken eines Juden über Jesus. FrRu 9 (2002) 181-191.
4909 [E]**Copan, Paul; Evans, Craig A.** Who was Jesus?: a Jewish-Christian dialogue. 2001 ⇒17,4476. [R]Theol. 105 (2002) 365-366 (*Braybrooke, Marcus*); NBl 83 (2002) 494-495 (*Marshall, Gordian*).

4910 **Ehrman, B.D.** Jesús, el profeta judío apocalíptico. 2001 ⇒17,4478.
      [R]RF 245 (2002) 389-390 (*Sanjosé, Jesús*); EfMex 20 (2002) 427 (*Zesati Estrada, Carlos*).
4911 *Evans, Craig A.* Introduction: finding a context for Jesus;
4912 The misplaced Jesus: interpreting Jesus in a Judaic context;
4913 Reconstructing the halakah of Jesus: appropriating early and late sources. The missing Jesus, 2002 ⇒4895. 1-9/11-39/101-106.
4914 **Heller, Agnes** Die Auferstehung des jüdischen Jesus. B 2002, Philo 118 pp. €14.90. 3-8257-0243-X [BiKi 58,187].
4915 *Herion, Gary* Neusner's "contexts of comparison". The missing Jesus. 2002 ⇒4895. 69-75.
4916 **Heschel, Susannah** Der jüdische Jesus und das Christentum: Abraham GEIGERs Herausforderung an die christliche Theologie. [T]*Wiese, Ch.*: 2001 ⇒17,4484. [R]ThLZ 127 (2002) 636-639 (*Bodendorfer, Gerhard*).
4917 **Isaac, Jules** MARX Gesù e Israele. Radici 16: 2001 ⇒17,4486. [R]CivCatt 153/2 (2002) 509-511 (*Prato, G.L.*).
4918 *Kampling, Rainer* "Und er ging nach seiner Gewohnheit am Sabbat in die Synagoge": Jesuanisches zur Frage nach dem Ursprung des christlichen Antijudaismus. Im Angesicht. SBB 47: 2002 <1999> ⇒ 189. 101-119.
4919 **Kelley, Shawn** Racializing Jesus: race, ideology and the formation of modern biblical scholarship. Biblical Limits: L 2002, Routledge xvi; 254 pp. $80. 0-415-15402-2. Bibl. 237-250.
4920 **Kroll, Gerhard** Auf den Spuren Jesu: sein Leben—sein Wirken—seine Zeit. Lp [12]2002, Benno 472 pp. €49. 3-7462-1550-1. Num. ill..
4921 *Langston, Scott* Dividing it right: who is a Jew and what is a christian?. The missing Jesus, 2002 ⇒4895. 125-134.
4922 **McKnight, Scot** A new vision for Israel: the teachings of Jesus in national context. 1999 ⇒15,4448...17,4494. [R]SNTU.A 27 (2002) 269-271 (*Repschinski, Boris*).
4923 **Moberly, R.W.L.** The bible, theology, and faith: a study of Abraham and Jesus. 2000 ⇒16,4581; 17,4495. [R]BiblInterp 10 (2002) 89-91 (*Barton, John*); JR 82 (2002) 121-123 (*Tanner, Kathryn*); JThS 53 (2002) 122-125 (*Chave, Peter*); MoTh 18 (2002) 411-413 (*Bockmuehl, Markus*); RBLit 4 (2002) 127-130 (*Pascuzzi, Maria*).
4924 *Moxnes, Halvor* Jesus the Jew: dilemmas of interpretation. [F]RÄISÄNEN, H.: NT.S 103: 2002 ⇒97. 83-103.
4925 *Oegema, Gerbern S.* Der historische Jesus und das Judentum. Jesus im 21. Jahrhundert. 2002 ⇒1380. 61-90;
4926 The historical Jesus and Judaism: a methodological inquiry. Jüdische Schriften.. 2002 ⇒345. 449-469.
4927 *Röhser, Günter* Jesus und Paulus—ein unüberwindlicher Gegensatz?. Jesus von Nazareth und das Christentum. 2000 ⇒293. 194-208.
4928 *Sanders, E.P.* Jesus, ancient Judaism, and modern christianity: the quest continues. Jesus, Judaism. 2002 ⇒308. 31-55.
4929 *Schröter, Jens* Der historische Jesus in seinem jüdischen Umfeld: eine Bestandsaufnahme angesichts der neueren Diskussion. Bib. 83 (2002) 563-573.
4930 *Scott, Leonard C.* A mystical explanation of the real historical Jesus. Religion 32 (2002) 273-276.
4931 *Segal, Alan F.* The Incarnation: the Jewish milieu. The incarnation. 2002 ⇒624. 116-139.

4932 *Stefani, Piero* Gesù ebreo. Hum(B) 57 (2002) 585-596.
4933 *Stegemann, Ekkehard W.* Jesu Stellung im Judentum seiner Zeit. Jesus in neuen Kontexten. 2002 ⇒602. 237-245.
4934 *Theissen, Gerd; Merz, Annette* Der umstrittene historische Jesus: oder: wie historisch ist der historische Jesus?. Jesus von Nazareth und das Christentum. 2000 ⇒293. 171-193.
4935 **Tomson, Peter J.** 'If this be from heaven...': Jesus and the New Testament authors in their relationship to Judaism. BiSe 76: 2001 ⇒17, 4509. ᴿTheol. 105 (2002) 363-365 (*Griffith-Jones, Robin*); JSJ 33 (2002) 347-352 (*Hogeterp, Albert*); JBL 121 (2002) 562-565 (*Elliott, Mark Adam*).
4936 **Van der Linden, Ewout** Wie is die man?: joodse visies op Jezus. Baarn 2002, Ten Have 293 pp. 90-259-5338-7.
4937 **Vermes, Geza** The changing faces of Jesus. 2000 ⇒16,4585; 17, 4512. ᴿJSSt 47 (2002) 361-362 (*Lim, Timothy H.*); ET 113 (2002) 203-205 (*Knights, Chris*);
4938 La religione di Gesù l'ebreo: una grande sfida al cristianesimo. ᵀ*Rizzi, A.*: Studi Cristologici: Assisi 2002, Cittadella 302 pp. €25.50. 88-30-8-0720-6. Pres. di *Giuseppe Segalla*; Bibl. 270-277. ᴿAng. 79 (2002) 992-994 (*Garuti, Paolo*); Annales Theologici 16 (2002) 521-524 (*Tábet, M.*);
4939 Ieder zijn eigen Jezus. Baarn 2002, Ten Have 336 pp. €24.90. 90-259-5306-9.
4940 *Wengst, Klaus* Der Jesus der Evangelien und die Chassidim in der rabbinischen Literatur. Jesus in neuen Kontexten. 2002 ⇒602. 246-254.

F1.6 *Jesus in Ecclesia*—The Church Jesus

4941 *Annunziata di Gesù* Il più piccolo di tutti i semi: Gesù di Nazareth. Horeb 11/3 (2002) 21-27.
4942 *Banks, R.H.* Scripture in memory: Jesus as a model for spiritual formation. JATS 13/2 (2002) 67-80 [NTAb 47,230].
4943 *Bellia, Giuseppe* 'Rimasero scandalizzati di lui'. Presbyteri 36 (2002) 91-102.
4944 *Bieler, Martin* The mysteries of Jesus' public life: stages on the way to the cross. Com(US) 29/1 (2002) 47-61.
4945 *Haight, Roger* Jesus, symbol of God: criticism and response. LouvSt 27 (2002) 389-405.
4946 **Javierre, J. Maria** Busco a Jesús de Nazaret. S 2002, Sígueme 282 pp [EstAg 37,632—Natal, D.].
4947 *Langenhorst, Georg* Urvorbild Jesus: unerreichbar, abschreckend, Orientierung gebend?. rhs 45 (2002) 295-302.
4948 **Nouwen, Henri J.M.** Gesù: un vangelo. Spiritualità 103: Brescia 2002, Queriniana 240 pp. €16.50. Introd. *Michael O'Laughlin.*
4949 **Placher, William C.** Jesus the savior: the meaning of Jesus Christ for christian faith. 2001 ⇒17,4525. ᴿRExp 99 (2002) 634-635 (*Sharp, Douglas*).
4950 *Schütz, Christian* The mysteries of the life of Jesus as a prism of faith. Com(US) 29/1 (2002) 28-38; Com(I) 181,8-20.
4951 *Sfameni Gasparro, Giulia* Magie et magiciens: le débat entre chrétiens et païens aux premiers siècles de notre ère. Charmes et sortilèges. 2002 ⇒477. 239-266.

4952　**Snyder, Graydon F.** Irish Jesus, Roman Jesus: the formation of early Irish christianity. Harrisburg 2002, Trinity vi; 280 pp. $24. 1-5-6338-385-3. Bibl. 261-270 [BiTod 41,67—Senior, Donald].

F1.7 *Jesus 'annormalis'*: **to atheists, psychoanalysts, romance...**

4953　*Baugh, Lloyd* Un'analisi critica del recente film *Jesus* di Roger Young. CoSe 2 (2002) 57-70.
4954　**Dias, Mário Simões** A vida de Jesus na poesia portuguesa. Coimbra 2002, Dias, Mário Simões 202 pp. 972-98461-9-7 [Theologica 37, 409—Coutino, Jorge].
4955　*Henning, Klaus* Das Kommen Gottes in Jesus Christus: Konsequenzen für Alltag und Beruf. Jesus von Nazareth und das Christentum. 2000 ⇒293. 25-36.
4956　*Jacques, Georges* Le Jésus des romanciers: un visage caché. RTL 33 (2002) 239-249.
4957　**Jaschke, Helmut** Jesus der Mystiker. 2000 ⇒16,4607. [R]ThRv 98 (2002) 205-207 (*Biser, Eugen*).
4958　*Kampling, Rainer* Else Lasker-Schülers jüdischer Jesus. [F]ASCHOFF, D. 2002 ⇒3. 245-254.
4959　**Klint, Stefan** Romanen och evangeliet: former för Jesusgestaltning i Pär LAGERKVISTs prosa [The novel and the gospel: giving forms to the character of Jesus in the writings of Pär Lagerkvist]. 2002 Diss. Uppsala [StTh 57,82].
4960　**Kreitzer, Larry Joseph** Gospel images in fiction and film: on reversing the hermeneutical flow. BiSe 84: Shf 2002, Sheffield A. 234 pp. £18. 1-84127-266-3. Bibl. 189-223.
4961　**Maqsood, Ruqaiyyah Waris** The mysteries of Jesus. 2000 ⇒16, 4612. [R]Islam and Christian-Muslim Relations 13 (2002) 486-488 (*Bennett, Clinton*).
4962　**Miles, Jack** Jesus: der Selbstmord des Gottessohnes. [T]*Griese, Friedrich*: 2001 ⇒17,4542. [R]GuL 75 (2002) 154 (*Kurz, Paul Konrad*);
4963　Christ: a crisis in the life of God. 2001 ⇒17,4543. [R]CrossCur 52/1 (2002) 131-136 (*Madsen, Catherine*).
4964　*Ortiz, Gaye* Jesus, Mary and Joseph!: (Holy) Family values in film. Borders. JSOT.S 313: 2002 ⇒585. 292-306.
4965　**Sahm, Peter R.** Brauchen wir im Raumfahrtzeitalter ein neues Jesusbild?: auf dem Weg zu einer entdimensionalisierten Religion. Jesus von Nazareth und das Christentum. 2000 ⇒293. 11-24.
4966　[E]**Scharpe, Martin** Jesus unter Dichtern: ein literarisches Evangelium. Stu 2002, Radius 157 pp. €18. 3-87173-252-4 [ActBib 11,199].
4967　**Schmitt, Eric-Emmanuel** Il vangelo secondo Pilato: romanzo. CinB 2002, San Paolo 235 pp.
4968　**Tiemann, Manfred** Jesus comes from Hollywood: religionspädagogische Arbeiten mit Jesus-Filmen. Gö 2002, Vandenhoeck & R. 199 pp. €28. 3-525-61396-2. [R]Diak. 33 (2002) 145-147 (*Bobert, Sabine*).
4969　*Viganò, Dario E.* La figura di Gesù nel cinema contemporaneo. Orientamenti pastorali 1 (2002) 45-48.

F2.2 *Unitas VT-NT*: The Unity of OT-NT

4970 **Albl, Martin C.** "And scripture cannot be broken": the form and function of the early christian testimonia collections. NT.S 96: 1999 ⇒15,4162...17,4550. [R]ASEs 19 (2002) 279-280 (*Falcetta, Alessandro*).

4971 *Beaude, Pierre-Marie* Accomplissement des écritures et intertextualité. [F]HAAG, E. ⇒55. 2002 13-28.

4972 *Bultmann, Rudolf* Die Bedeutung des Alten Testaments für den christlichen Glauben. NT und christliche Existenz. UTB 2316: 2002 <1933> ⇒152. 148-171.

4973 **Büttner, Matthias** Das Alte Testament als erster Teil der christlichen Bibel: zur Frage nach theologischer Auslegung und 'Mitte' im Kontext der Theologie Karl BARTHs. BEvTh 120: Gü 2002, Kaiser 276 pp. €54. 3-579-05329-9. Bibl. 259-271.

4974 *Del Agua, Agustín* Jewish procedures of bible interpretation in the gospels: a proposal for a systematic classification. EstB 60 (2002) 77-106.

4975 *Dietrich, Walter; Luz, Ulrich* Universalität und Partikularität im Horizont des biblischen Monotheismus: eine Skizze. [F]SMEND, R.: 2002 ⇒113. 369-411.

4976 *Fenske, Wolfgang* Aspekte Biblischer Theologie dargestellt an der Verwendung von Ps 16 in Apostelgeschichte 2 und 13. Bib. 83 (2002) 54-70.

4977 *Ghiberti, Giuseppe* Documento della Pontifica Commissione Biblica sul popolo ebraico e le sue sacre scritture nella bibbia cristiana. LASBF 51 (2001) 213-232.

4978 [E]**Green, Joey** Jesus and Moses: the parallel sayings. Berkeley, CA 2002, Ulysses 208 pp. $19.

4979 *Hays, Richard B.* Can the gospels teach us how to read the Old Testament?. ProEc 11/4 (2002) 402-418.

4980 **König, Adrio** Die helfte is my nooit oor Jesus vertel nie: 'n nuwe kyk op Een wat jou lewe verander. 2001 ⇒17,7573. [R]VeE 23 (2002) 266-269 (*Spangenberg, I.J.J.*); AcTh(B) 22/2 (2002) 281-283 (*Van Tonder, Danie*).

4981 **Longenecker, Richard N.** Biblical exegesis in the apostolic period. [2]1999 ⇒15,12274; 16,4631. [R]LASBF 51 (2001) 449-451 (*Chrupcala, L.D.*).

4982 **Longman, Tremper, III** Immanuel in our place: seeing Christ in Israel's worship. Phillipsburg 2001, P & R 232 pp.

4983 *Loza Vera, J.* El pueblo judío y sus escrituras en la biblia cristiana. Qol 28 (2002) 69-73;

4984 L'Ancien Testament dans l'église: perspectives du récent document de la Commission Biblique Pontificale. LASBF 51 (2001) 233-250.

4985 *Macleod, Donald* Jesus and scripture. The trustworthiness of God. 2002 ⇒410. 69-95.

4986 **Margerie, Bertrand de** Les saints prophètes du Christ prophète. P 2002, De Guibert 184 pp. €19.

4987 *Marx, Tsvi* Emoties in de tehilim: psalmen gelezen vanuit de rabbijnse traditie. ITBT 10/3; 10/4 (2002) 22-24; 29-30.

4988 *Müller, Mogens* The New Testament reception of the Old Testament. NT as reception. JSNT.S 230: 2002 ⇒360. 1-14.

4989   *Neubrand, Maria* Brauchen Christinnen und Christen das Alte Testament?. ThG 45 (2002) 97-106.
4990   *Nicole, Roger* Patrick FAIRBAIRN and biblical hermeneutics as related to the quotations of the Old Testament in the New <1984>;
4991   The New Testament use of the Old Testament. Standing forth. 2002 <1959; 1984> ⟹215. 79-90/223-242.
4992   *Niemand, Christoph* Die christliche Bibel—Altes und Neues Testament: Überlegungen vor dem Hintergrund des christlich-jüdischen Dialogs. ᶠAICHERN, M. 2002 ⟹2. 205-225.
4993   *Perrin, Nicholas* Dialogic conceptions of language and the problem of biblical unity. Biblical theology. 2002 ⟹558. 212-224.
4994   *Radner, Ephraim* Sublimity and providence: the spiritual discipline of figural reading. ExAu 18 (2002) 155-170 Resp. *H. Cepero* 171-73.
4995   *Schoon, Simon* Lezen joden en christenen dezelfde bijbel?. ITBT 10/3 (2002) 16-19.
4996   *Seitz, Christopher R.* Two testaments and the failure of one tradition history. Biblical theology. 2002 ⟹558. 195-211.
4997   **Seitz, Christopher R.** Figured out: typology and providence in christian scripture. 2001 ⟹17,4577. ᴿAThR 84 (2002) 1048, 1050-1051 (*Cummins, S.A.*); RExp 99 (2002) 456-457 (*Biddle, Mark E.*).
4998   **Spawn, Kevin L.** "As it is written" and other citation formulae in the Old Testament: their use, development, syntax, and significance. BZAW 311: B 2002, De Gruyter xvii; 301 pp. 3-11-017161-9. Bibl. 259-276.
4999   *Vleugels, Gie* The Jewish scriptures in Galatians and Romans. AnBru 7 (2002) 156-163.

F2.3 *Unitas interna*—NT—**Internal unity**

5000   **Aletti, Jean-Noël** Jesu-Cristo ¿factor de unidad del Nuevo Testamento?. ᵀ*Lera Barrientos, Jeremías*: Agape 22: 2000 ⟹16,4648. ᴿCivCatt 153/1 (2002) 207-209 (*Scaiola, D.*).
5001   *Köstenberger, Andreas J.* Diversity and unity in the New Testament. Biblical theology. 2002 ⟹558. 144-158.

F2.5 *Commentarii*—**Commentaries on the whole NT**

5002   ᴱ**Bray, Gerald** La biblia comentada por los padres le la iglesia: Nuevo Testamento, 11: Santiago, 1-2 Pedro, 1-3 Juan, Judas. ᵀ*Merino Rodríguez, Marcelo*: M 2002, Ciudad N. 362 pp. €30. 849-715-0201;
5003   James, 1-2 Peter, 1-3 John, Jude. ACCS.NT 11: 2000 ⟹16,4650. ᴿEThL 78 (2002) 512-514 (*Yates, J.*).
5004   ᴱ**Gorday, P.; Oden, Th.C.** La biblia comentada por los padres de la iglesia, Nuevo Testamento, 9: Colosenses, 1-2 Tesalonicenses, 1-2 Timoteo, Tito, Filemón. ᵀ*Merino Rodríguez, Marcelo*: M 2002, Ciudad Nueva 500 pp. €30. 84-9715-020-1. ᴿRelCult 48 (2002) 795-796 (*Langa, Pedro*);
5005   ᴱ**Gruson, Philippe** Les évangiles: textes et comentaires. 2001 ⟹17,4589. ᴿSR 31 (2002) 437-438 (*Cazelais, Serge*).
        ᴱ**Keck, L.**, *al.*, NIntB 10: Acts of the Apostles; letter to the Romans; first letter to the Corinthians 2002 ⟹4655.

5006 ^E**Merklein, Helmut** Stuttgarter Neues Testament: Einheitsübersetzung mit Kommentar und Erklärungen. Stu 2002, Kathol. Bibelwerk
589 pp. €21.50. 3-920609-43-3.

5007 **Wright, Tom** Paul for everyone: the prison letters: Ephesians, Philippians, Colossians, and Philemon. L 2002, SPCK xi; 227 pp. £9. 0-
281-05303-0.

IX. Evangelia

F2.6 Evangelia Synoptica: *textus, synopses, commentarii*

5008 ^E**Hoffmann, Paul; Hieke, Thomas; Bauer, Ulrich** Synoptic concordance: a Greek concordance to the first three gospels in synoptic
arrangement, statistically evaluated, including occurences in Acts,
2:E—I; 3:K—O; 4. P—Omega. 2000 ⇒16,4666; 17,4594. ^RNT 44
(2002) 95-96 (*Elliott, J.K.*); ZKTh 124 (2002) 233-234 (*Huber, Konrad*); ThG 45 (2002) 213-214 (*Giesen, Heinz*).

5009 **Mangatt, George** Jesus: the good news: the works of Jesus. 1998 ⇒
15,4541. ^RVJTR 66 (2002) 698-699 (*Meagher, P.M.*).

5010 **Meynet, Roland** Un'introduzione ai vangeli sinottici. 2000 ⇒16,
4668. ^RVivH 13/1 (2002) 193-194 (*Tarocchi, Stefano*).
^E**Mistrorigo, A.** Il vangelo unificato ⇒4823.

5011 **Neves, Joaquim Carreira das** Evangelhos sinópticos. Estudos Teológicos 16: Lisboa 2002, Univ. Católica 405 pp. 972-54-0038-X.
^RTheologica 37 (2002) 405-406 (*Correia, João Alberto Sousa*).

5012 *Ometto, Franco* KHATUN ABADI: the Ayatollah who translated the
gospels. IslChr 28 (2002) 55-72.

5013 **Stein, Robert H.** Studying the synoptic gospels: origin and interpretation. ²2001 ⇒17,4601. ^RSWJT 45/1 (2002) 82 (*Wicker, Jim*).

F2.7 *Problema synopticum*: The Synoptic Problem

5014 **Allison, Dale C.** The intertextual Jesus: scripture in Q. 2000 ⇒16,
4670. ^RCBQ 64 (2002) 150-151 (*Derrenbacker, Robert A.*); JBL 121
(2002) 168-172 (*Kloppenborg, John S.*).

5015 ^T**Amsler, Frédéric** L'évangile inconnu: la source des paroles de
Jésus (Q). Essais bibliques 30: 2001 ⇒17,4605. ^RETR 77 (2002)
593-594 (*Cuvillier, Elian*); SR 31 (2002) 402-404 (*Cazelais, Serge*);
EeV 50 (2002) 22-23 (*Cothenet, Edouard*).

5016 **Arnal, William Edward** Jesus and the village scribes: Galilean conflicts and the setting of Q. 2001 ⇒17,4606. ^RThLZ 127 (2002) 1295-
1296 (*Hieke, Thomas*); CBQ 64 (2002) 751-752 (*Luomanen, Petri*);
JBL 121 (2002) 762-766 (*Moreland, Milton*).

5017 ^E**Black, David Alan; Beck, David R.** Rethinking the synoptic prob-
lem. 2001 ⇒17,4608. ^RKerux 17/1 (2002) 64-66 (*Dennison, James
T.*); SWJT 45/1 (2002) 83-84 (*Wicker, Jim*); RBLit (2002)* (*Matson,
Mark A.*).

5018 *Bridge, Steven L.* Literary source and redaction criticism. Handbook
of early christianity. 2002 ⇒275. 125-146.

5019 ^E**Carruth, Shawn** Q 12:49-59: children against parents—judging the time—settling out of court Documenta Q: the database of the International Q Project 1997 ⇒13,4447... 15,4613 ^RRBLit (2002)* (*Parrott, Douglas M.*).

5020 **Casey, Maurice** An Aramaic approach to Q: sources for the gospels of Matthew and Luke. MSSNTS 122: C 2002, CUP x; 210 pp. $60. 0-521-81723-4. Bibl. 191-205.

5021 *Derrenbacker, Robert A., Jr.; Kloppenborg Verbin, John S.* Self-contradiction in the IQP?: a reply to Michael Goulder. JBL 120 (2001) 57-76.

5022 **Dungan, David Laird** A history of the synoptic problem. AncB Reference Library: 1999 ⇒15,4559...17,4615. ^RSJTh 55 (2002) 373-377 (*Goodacre, Mark*).

5023 *Eve, Eric* Challenging Q. ET 113 (2002) 408-409.

5024 *Farnell, F.D.* How views of inspiration have impacted synoptic problem discussions. MastJ 13/1 (2002) 33-64 [NTAb 46,453].

5025 *Finnern, Sönke* Die Traditionshypothese als Alternative zur Zweiquellentheorie: ihre neueren Vertreter, ihre Argumente, ihre Beurteilung. JETh 16 (2002) 33-67.

5026 *Foster, Paul* In defence of the study of Q. ET 113 (2002) 295-300.

5027 *Freyne, Seán* In search of Q: a conversation with the work of John S. Kloppenborg. PIBA 25 (2002) 116-132.

5028 **Goodacre, Mark** The case against Q: studies in Markan priority and the synoptic problem. Harrisburg 2002, Trinity x; 228 pp. $30. 1-56-338-334-9. Bibl. 191-209. ^RRBLit (2002)* (*Percer, Leo; Kloppenborg, John S.*).

5029 *Goulder, Michael* The Derrenbacker-Kloppenborg defense. JBL 121 (2002) 331-336.

5030 **Han, Kyu Sam** Jerusalem and the early Jesus movement: the Q community's attitude toward the temple. JSNT.S 207: Shf 2002, Sheffield A. 248 pp. £55. 1-84127-183-7. Bibl. 214-236.

5031 *Hermant, Dominique* Les redites chez Marc et les deux autres synoptiques. RB 109 (2002) 528-555.

5032 *Hildenbeutel, Paul* Matthäus und Markus. Theologisches 32 (2002) 410.

5033 ^E**Hoffmann, Paul; Heil, Christoph** Die Spruchquelle Q: griechisch und deutsch. Da:Wiss 2002, 185 pp. €19.90. 3-534-16484-9.

5034 **Hultgren, Stephen** Narrative elements in the double tradition: a study of their place within the framework of the gospel narrative. BZNT 113: B 2002, De Gruyter xviii; 420 pp. €91.59. 3-11-017525-8. Bibl. 355-390.

5035 **Hüneburg, Martin** Jesus als Wundertäter in der Logienquelle: ein Beitrag zur Christologie von Q. Arbeiten zur Bibel und ihrer Geschichte 4: 2001 ⇒17,4635. ^RThLZ 127 (2002) 395-396 (*Sato, Migaku*).

5036 *Jervis, L. Ann* Suffering for the reign of God: the persecution of disciples in Q. NT 44 (2002) 313-332;

5037 All for Jesus: the cause, character and role of discipleship suffering in Q. ProEc 11/1 (2002) 41-56.

5038 **Johnson-DeBaufre, Melanie J.** It's the end of the world as we know it: eschatology, Q, and the contruction of christian origins. Diss. Harvard 2002 [HTHR 95,463].

5039 *Kiilunen, Jarmo* "Minor Agreements" und die Hypothese von Lukas' Kenntnis des Matthäusevangeliums. [F]RÄISÄNEN, H.: NT.S 103: 2002 ⇒97. 165-202.

5040 **Kirk, Alan** The composition of the sayings source: genre, synchrony, and wisdom redaction in Q. NT.S 91: 1998 ⇒14,4142...17,4637. [R]ThLZ 127 (2002) 288-289 (*März, Claus-Peter*).

5041 *Kloppenborg Verbin, John S.* Goulder and the new paradigm: a critical appreciation of Michael Goulder on the synoptic problem. Gospels according to Goulder. 2002 ⇒594. 29-60.

5042 **Kloppenborg Verbin, John S.** Excavating Q: the history and setting of the sayings gospel. 2000 ⇒16,4690; 17,4639. [R]ThLZ 127 (2002) 1301-1303 (*März, Claus-Peter*); Apocrypha 13 (2002) 288-289 (*Amsler, F.*).

5043 [E]**Labahn, Michael; Schmidt, Andreas** Jesus, Mark and Q: the teaching of Jesus and its earliest records. JSNT.S 214: 2001 ⇒17, 4283. [R]CBQ 64 (2002) 610-611 (*Powell, Mark Allan*); RBLit (2002)* (*Morton, Russell S.*).

5044 *McIver, Robert K.; Carroll, Marie* Experiments to develop criteria for determining the existence of written sources, and their potential implications for the synoptic problem. JBL 121 (2002) 667-687.

5045 *Miller, Robert J.* Q and the non-apocalyptic Jesus: assessing the evidence. FORUM n.s. 3 (2002) 223-245.

5046 **Neville, David** Mark's gospel—prior or posterior?: a reappraisal of the phenomenon of order. JSNT.S 222: Shf 2002, Sheffield A. xiv; 388 pp. 1-84127-265-5.

5047 *Nodet, Etienne* A proposito de la teoría de las dos fuentes. Qol 30 (2002) 3-29.

5048 [E]**Peabody, David B.; Cope, O. Lamar; McNicol, Allan J.** One gospel from two: Mark's use of Matthew and Luke: a demonstration by the research team of the International Institute for Renewal of Gospel Studies. Harrisburg, Pennsylvania 2002, Trinity xvi; 426 pp. $26. 1-56338-352-7. Bibl. 392-407.

5049 *Robinson, James M.; Heil, Christoph* P.Oxy. 655 und Q: zum Diskussionsbeitrag von Stanley E. Porter. [F]SCHENKE, H.: NHS 54: 2002 ⇒108. 411-423 [Mt 6,28; Lk 12,22-31].

5050 [E]**Robinson, James M.; Hoffmann, Paul; Kloppenborg, John S.** The critical edition of Q: synopsis including the gospels of Matthew and Luke, Mark and Thomas. 2000 ⇒16,4698; 17,4666. [R]RTL 33 (2002) 101-102 (*Focant, C.*); Salm. 49 (2002) 197-201 (*Guijarro Oporto, Santiago*); CBQ 64 (2002) 391-392 (*Fleddermann, Harry T.*); OLZ 97 (2002) 769-773 (*Labahn, Michael*);

5051 The sayings gospel Q in Greek and English with parallels from the gospels of Mark and Thomas. CBET 30: 2001 ⇒17,4667. [R]RBBras 19 (2002) 417-418 (*Minette de Tillesse, Gaëtan*);

5052 El documento Q en griego y en español, con paralelos del evangelio de Marcos y del evangelio de Tomás. Biblioteca de Estudios Bíblicos: S 2002, Sígueme 234 pp. €17.50.

5053 [E]**Robinson, James M.** The sayings of Jesus: the sayings of gospel Q in English. Facets: Ph 2002, Fortress xviii; 35 pp. 0-8006-3451-9. Bibl. 33-35.

5054 *Rodd, C.S.* The theology of Q yet again: a reply to the responses of Christopher Tuckett and Paul Foster. ET 114 (2002) 80-85.

5055   *Schiavo, Luigi* The temptation of Jesus: the eschatological battle and
       the new ethic of the first followers of Jesus in Q. JSNT 25 (2002)
       141-164 [Mt 4,1-11; Lk 4,1-13].
5056   *Schmidt, Daryl D.* Finding a non-apocalyptic Jesus: issues and
       reconsiderations. FORUM n.s. 3 (2002) 247-275.
5057   *Sisson, Russell B.* The interaction of social and scribal intertexture in
       Q's apocalyptic discourse. Intertexture. SBL.Symposium 14: 2002 ⇒
       385. 69-85.
5058   *Tuckett, Christopher* The search for a theology of Q: a dead end?. ET
       113 (2002) 291-294.
5059   *Vassiliadis, Petros* Paul's *theologia crucis* as an intermediate state of
       the trajectory from Q to Mark. VII Simposio di Tarso. 2002 ⇒587.
       47-55.
5060   *Villegas, Bertrán* En busca de Q: la fuente común de Mt y Lc. TyV
       43 (2002) 602-683.

F2.8 *Synoptica*: **themata**

5061   *Bissoli, Giovanni* Dio Padre nei sinottici. LASBF 52 (2002) 117-124.
5062   **De Virgilio, G.** Il messaggio dei vangeli sinottici. 2000 ⇒16,4706.
       ᴿAnnales Theologici 16 (2002) 274-275 (*Sampaio, B.A. de C.*).
5063   *Dreyer, Y.* Son-of-God traditions in the synoptic gospels: Ferdinand
       HAHN's diachronic perspective. HTS 57 (2001) 506-530 [NTAb 46,
       453].
5064   *Helewa, Giovanni* Credete al vangelo: la fede nel messaggio nuovo
       dei sinottici. RVS 56 (2002) 125-154.
5065   *Köber, Berthold W.* Jesus—der Heilige Gottes: die Heiligkeit Jesu im
       Zeugnis der Synoptiker in ihrer Bedeutung für Theologie und Glau-
       ben. EvTh 62 (2002) 304-317 [Mk 1,21-28; Jn 6,69].
5066   **Laaksonen, Jari** Jesus und das Land: das Gelobte Land in der Ver-
       kündigung Jesu. Abo 2002, Abo Akademis Förlag (8) 433 pp. 951-7-
       65-090-6. Diss. Abo Akademi Univ. 2002 [Bibl. 379-433].
5067   **Laato, Timo** De ignorantia Christi: zur Parusieverzögerung in den
       synoptischen Evangelien. Hormisto 2002, Evangelisk Litteraturmis-
       sion Scriptura. 114 pp. 91-631-2522-6. Bibl. 89-108.
5068   **Levine, Amy-Jill** Matthew, Mark and Luke: good news or bad?. Je-
       sus, Judaism. 2002 ⇒308. 77-98.
5069   **Liebenberg, Jacobus** The language of the Kingdom and Jesus: para-
       ble, aphorism, and metaphor in the sayings material common to the
       synoptic tradition and the gospel of Thomas. BZNW 102: 2001 ⇒17,
       4681. ᴿRBLit (2002)* (*Arnal, William E.*).
5070   *Mekkattukunnel, Andrews* Walking in the way of the Lord: a study of
       the ethics of synoptic gospels. Jeevadhara 32 (2002) 499-508.
5071   **Meynet, Roland** Jésus passe: testament, jugement, exécution et ré-
       surrection du Seigneur Jésus dans les évangiles synoptiques. Rhéto-
       rique Biblique 3: 1999 ⇒15,4623. ᴿNRTh 124 (2002) 281-282 (*Ra-
       dermakers, J.*);
5072   La Pasqua del Signore: testamento, processo, esecuzione e risurrezio-
       ne di Gesù nei vangeli sinottici. Retorica biblica 5: 2001 ⇒17,4688.
       ᴿCivCatt 153/4 (2002) 620-621 (*Scaiola, D.*).
5073   *Navone, John* The compassion of Jesus in the synoptics. BiTod 40
       (2002) 242-247.

5074 *Salas, Antonio* Las tentaciones de Jesús: síntesis teológico-catequética. BiFe 84 (2002) 439-447.

5075 *Stansell, Gary* Gabe und Reziprozität: zur Dynamik von Gaben in den synoptischen Evangelien. Jesus in neuen Kontexten. 2002 ⇒602. 185-196.

5076 *Stansell, Gary* Gifts, tributes, and offerings. The social setting. 2002 ⇒601. 349-364.

5077 **Subramanian Johnson, Samuel** The prophetic reading of the Psalms in the synoptic gospels, in the context of second temple Judaism. ᴰ*Westerholm, S.*: 2002, 247 pp. Diss. McMaster [RTL 34,601].

5078 **Tiwald, Markus** Wanderradikalismus: Jesu erste Jünger—ein Anfang und was davon bleibt. ᴰ*Küschelm, Roman*: ÖBS 20: Fra 2002, Lang xviii; 331 pp. 3-631-39192-7. Diss. Wien.

5079 **Wilk, Florian** Jesus und die Völker in der Sicht der Synoptiker. BZNT 109: B 2002, De Gruyter 360 pp. €100..21. 3-11-017179-1. Bibl. 293-311.

F3.1 **Matthaei evangelium**: *textus, commentarii*

5080 **Black, Stephanie L.** Sentence conjunction in the gospel of Matthew: Kai, de, tote, gar, syn and asyndeton in narrative discourse. JSNT.S 216; Studies in New Testament Greek 9: Shf 2002, Sheffield A. 420 pp. £60. 1-84127-255-8. Bibl. 396-408.

5081 **Bonnard, Pierre** L'évangile selon saint Matthieu. CNT 1: Genève ³2002 <1911>, Labor et F. 465 pp. €36.45. 2-8309-1040-0. ᴿEstB 60 (2002) 422-425 (*Sánchez Navarro, Luis*).

5082 **Buetow, Harold A.** The new out of the old: St Matthew meditations: homilies for weeks 10 through 21 of ordinary time. NY 2002, Alba lxii; 311 pp. $19. 0-8189-0931-5.

5083 **Carter, Warren C.** Matthew and the margins: a socio-political and religious reading. JSNT.S 204: 2000 ⇒16,4723. ᴿCBQ 64 (2002) 564-566 (*Wainwright, Elaine M.*); HBT 24 (2002) 144-145 (*Powell, Mark Allan*).

5084 *Childers, Jeff W.* Patristic citations and versional evidence: the Syriac version(s) of CHRYSOSTOM's homilies on Matthew and the Old Syriac text. Muséon 115/1-2 (2002) 129-156.

5085 ᵀ**Granados, José; Nieva, Javier** CROMACIO de Aquileya: comentario al evangelio de Mateo. Biblioteca de Patrística 58: M 2002, Ciudad Nueva 445 pp. €23. 84-9715-021-X. Bibl. 45-49.

5086 **Heras Oliver, Gloria** Jesús según San Mateo: análisis narrativo del primer evangelio. 2001 ⇒17,4705. ᴿCTom 129 (2002) 193-194 (*González Blanco, Rafael*); Ang. 79 (2002) 984-986 (*De Santis, Luca*); Studium 42 (2002) 427-428 (*López, L.*); Annales Theologici 16 (2002) 496-498 (*Caballero, J.L.*); RCatT 27 (2002) 501-502 (*Borrell, Agustí*).

5087 **Keener, Craig S.** A commentary on the gospel of Matthew. 1999 ⇒ 15,4652...17,4707. ᴿTrinJ 23 (2002) 127-129 (*Turner, David L.*); AUSS 40 (2002) 337-338 (*McIver, Rob*); LouvSt 27 (2002) 411-413 (*Harrington, Joy M.*).

5088 **Lafont, Ghislain** Jésus, un pauvre parmi les pauvres: une lecture de l'évangile de saint Mathieu. P 2002, Parole et Silence 221 pp. €14. 2-84573-129-9 [RTL 34,107—Houdart, M.-A.].

5089 **Linden, Nico ter** The story goes...Mark's story and Matthew's story,
     2. 1999 ⇒15,4655. ᴿVJTR 66 (2002) 302-304 (*Meagher, P.M.*).
5090 ᴱ**Löfstedt, Bengt** HRABANUS Maurus: expositio in Matthaeum.
     CChr.CM 174-174A: 2000 ⇒16,12888 v.1:I-IV; v.2:V-VIII.
     ᴿREAug 48 (2002) 209-211 (*Perrin, Michel Jean-Louis*).
5091 *Luz, Ulrich* Matthäusevangelium. RGG 5. 2002 ⇒796. 916-920.
5092 **Luz, Ulrich** Das Evangelium nach Matthäus, 4: Mt 26-28. Evang.-
     kath. Komm. z. NT 1/4: Z 2002, Benziger xii; 483 pp. €79. 3-7887-
     1681-9;
5093 Matthew 8-20: a commentary. ᵀ*Crouch, James E.*: Hermeneia: 2001
     ⇒17,4712. ᴿCBQ 64 (2002) 171-173 (*Carter, Warren*); JR 82
     (2002) 430-431 (*Brown, Michael Joseph*); HBT 24 (2002) 139-140
     (*Siker, Judy Yates*); JBL 121 (2002) 766-769 (*Hagner, Donald A.*);
5094 El evangelio según San Mateo, 2: Mt 8-17. BEB 103: 2001 ⇒17,
     4713. ᴿCart. 18 (2002) 559-560 (*Sanz Valdivieso, R.*); RevAg 43
     (2002) 714-715 (*Sánchez Navarro, Luis*); Communio 35 (2002) 497-
     498 (*Garzón, F. Javier*).
5095 ᴱ**Mills, Watson Early** The gospel of Matthew. Bibliographies for
     biblical research, periodical literature for the study of the NT 1:
     Lewiston, NY 2002, Mellen xvii; 153 pp. 0-7734-2494-6.
5096 **Minear, Paul Sevier** The good news according to Matthew: a train-
     ing manual for prophets. 2000 ⇒16,4734. ᴿRBLit 4 (2002) 356-359
     (*Spencer, F. Scott*).
5097 **Schnackenburg, Rudolf** The gospel of Matthew. ᵀ*Barr, Robert R.*:
     GR 2002, Eerdmans vii; 329 pp. $24. 0-8028-4438-3.
5098 **Senior, Donald** Matthew. 1998 ⇒14,4199... 16,4740. ᴿRBLit 4
     (2002) 359-361 (*Moreland, Milton C.*).
5099 *Senior, Donald* Invitation to Matthew. Invitation to the gospels. 2002
     ⇒4694. 1-105.
5100 ᴱ**Simonetti, Manlio** ACCS: NT 1a: Matthew 1-13. Ch 2002 <2001>,
     Dearborn lii; 326 pp. 0-8308-1489-8;
5101 1b: Matthew 14-28. Ch 2002, Dearborn xv; 344 pp. 0-8308-1469-8.
     ᴹTHOMPSON, W. Matthew in current study 2001 ⇒120.
5102 **Wright, Tom** Matthew for everyone: part 1: chapters 1-15; part 2:
     chapters 16-28. L 2002, SPCK 2 vols; ix; 223; xi; 227 pp. £9 + £9. 0-
     281-05-3014/4878.
5103 **Zuurmond, Rochus** Novum Testamentum Aethiopice: part III: the
     gospel of Matthew. ÄthF 55: 2001 ⇒17,4727. ᴿOrChr 86 (2002)
     257-260 (*Kropp, Manfred*).

F3.2 **Themata** *de Matthaeo*

5104 *Aichele, George* Translation as de-canonization: Matthew's gospel
     according to PASOLINI. CrossCur 51 (2002) 524-534.
5105 ᴱ**Balch, David L.** Social history of the Matthean community. 1991
     ⇒7,415d... 11/1,2842. ᴿVJTR 66 (2002) 780-783 (*Raj, M.I.*).
5106 **Beaton, Richard** Isaiah's Christ in Matthew's gospel. MSSNTS 123:
     C 2002, CUP xv; 242 pp. $60. 0-521-81888-5. Bibl. 198-224.
5107 *Blomberg, Craig L.* Interpreting Old Testament prophetic literature in
     Matthew: double fulfillment. TrinJ 23 (2002) 17-33.
5108 *Borghi, Ernesto* La giustizia dell'uomo nel vangelo di Matteo. RTM
     135 (2002) 339-343.

5109 **Bosetti, E.** Matteo un cammino di speranza. Bo 2002, EDB 328 pp. [Clar. 43,400s—García Castro, Florencio].

5110 **Brown, Jeannine K.** The disciples in narrative perspective: the portrayal and function of the Matthean disciples. Academia Biblica 9: Atlanta, GA 2002, SBL xii; 171 pp. $30. 15898-30482. Bibl. 153-61.

5111 *Byrne, Brendan* The messiah in whose name "the gentiles will hope" (Matt 12:21): gentile inclusion as an essential element of Matthew's christology. ABR 50 (2002) 55-73.

5112 **Byrskog, Samuel** Jesus the only teacher: didactic authority and transmission in ancient Israel: ancient Judaism and the Matthean community. CB.NT 24: 1994 ⇒10,4301... 13,4495. [R]Verbum Vitae 2 (2002) 309-313 (*Wróbel, Mirosław*).

5113 *Byrskog, Samuel* Jesus as messianic teacher in the gospel according to Matthew: tradition history and/or narrative christology. NT as reception. JSNT.S 230: 2002 ⇒360. 83-100.

5114 **Caldevilla Portilla, Juan José** Jesús el Mesías: trasfondo mesiánico judio y novedad cristiana en el evangelio de Mateo. [D]*Pikaza, X.*: 2002, 74 pp. Extr. Diss. Salamanca [RTL 34,596].

5115 **Castaño Fonseca, Adolfo M.** Δικαιοσύνη en Mateo: una interpretación teológica a partir de 3,15 y 21,32. TGr.T 27: 1997 ⇒13,4497; 15,4674. [R]RevBib 64 (2002) 243-245 (*Macin, Angel José*).

5116 *Castaño Fonseca, Adolfo M.* Las 'citas de cumplimiento' en el evangelio de Mateo. Qol 29 (2002) 89-103.

5117 **Charette, Blaine B.** Restoring presence: the Spirit in Matthew's gospel. JPentec.S 18: 2000 ⇒16,4749; 17,4734. [R]RBLit 4 (2002) 353-356 (*Whitt, R. Keith*).

5118 **Cousland, J.R.C.** The crowds in the gospel of Matthew. NT.S 102: Lei 2002, Brill xiii; 361 pp. €105. 90-04-12177-3. Bibl. 309-332.

5119 *Crosby, Michael H.* Matthew's gospel: the disciples' call to justice. NT: introducing. 2002 ⇒332. 16-39.

5120 *Duling, D.C.* Matthew as marginal scribe in an advanced agrarian society. HTS 58 (2002) 520-575 [NTAb 47,238].

5121 *Foster, Robert* Why on earth use 'Kingdom of Heaven'?: Matthew's terminology revisited. NTS 48 (2002) 487-499.

5122 *Giesen, Heinz* Jesu Sendung zu Israel und die Heiden im Matthäusevangelium. [F]FUCHS, A. 2002 ⇒41. 123-156.

5123 *Goulder, Michael D.* Matthew's gospel round the year. Gospels according to Goulder. 2002 ⇒594. 1-11.

5124 *Jacob, Emmanuel M.* Discipleship and mission: a perspective on the gospel of Matthew. IRM 91 (2002) 102-110.

5125 **Kowalski, Telesfor** L'opera messianica di Gesù nella teologia matteana alla luce di κηρυσσω, διδασκω e θεραπευω. [D]*Grilli, Massimo*: 2002, 92 pp. Extr. Diss. Gregoriana 2002.

5126 *Luomanen, Petri* The "sociology of sectarianism" in Matthew: modeling the genesis of early Jewish and christian communities. [F]RÄISÄNEN, H.: NT.S 103: 2002 ⇒97. 107-130.

5127 **Luz, Ulrich** La storia di Gesù in Matteo. StBi 134: Brescia 2002, Paideia 191 pp. €18 [Asp. 51,440—Gaetano Di Palma].

5128 *Manicardi, Ermenegildo* Maria e la Trinità nel vangelo secondo Matteo. Mar. 64 (2002) 17-50 [Mt 1,1-2,13; 12,15-21; 13,53-58].

5129 *Matthey, Jacques* Pilgrims, seekers and disciples: mission and dialogue in Matthew. IRM 91 (2002) 120-134 [Mt 2,1-12; 8,5-13; 15,21-28].

5130 **Mattila, Helena Talvikki** Citizens of kingdom: followers in Matthew from a feminist perspective. SESJ 83: Gö 2002, Vandenhoeck & R. 208 pp. 3-525-53622-4. Bibl. 192-207; Diss. Helsinki.

5131 **Miler, Jean** Les citations d'accomplissement dans l'évangile de Matthieu: quand Dieu se rend présent en toute humanité. AnBib 140: 1999 ⇒15,4697…17,4758. ᴿEThL 78 (2002) 206-7 (*Verheyden, J.*).

5132 **Mora, Vincent** La symbolique de Matthieu, 2: les groupes. LeDiv 187: 2001 ⇒17,4759. ᴿFV 101/2 (2002) 85-86 (*Gerber, Daniel*); Brot. 154 (2002) 409-410 (*Silva, I. Ribeiro da*); EeV 53 (2002) 24-25 (*Cothenet, Edouard*).

5133 **Moss, Charlene McAfee** Zechariah and the gospel of Matthew: the use of a biblical tradition. ᴰ*Stuckenbruck, L.T.*: 2002, 289 pp. Diss. Durham [RTL 34,599].

5134 *Mowery, Robert L.* Son of God in Roman imperial titles and Matthew. Bib. 83 (2002) 100-110.

5135 **Müller, Markus** Jüngerschaft im Reich des Menschensohnes: ein Beitrag zur Eschatologie des Matthäusevangeliums. ᴰ*Roloff, Jürgen*: 2002 Diss.-Habil. Erlangen [ThRv 99/2,xi].

5136 *Nissen, Johannes* Matthew, mission and method. IRM 91 (2002) 73-86.

5137 *Oborji, Francis Anekwe* Poverty and the mission-charity trend: a perspective from Matthew. IRM 91 (2002) 87-101.

5138 **Orsatti, Mauro; Manicardi, Ermenegildo** Matteo: alcuni percorsi. Sussidi biblici 74: Reggio Emilia 2002, San Lorenzo 191 pp. 88-807-1-126-1.

5139 **Parambi, Baby** The discipleship of the women in the gospel according to Matthew: an exegetical theological study of Matt 27:51b-56, 57-61 and 28:1-10. ᴰ*Martinez, E.R.*: R 2002, E.P.U.G. 270 pp. Diss. Gregorian [RTL 34,600].

5140 Pereira, Ney B. A não retaliação, o perdão, o amor dos inimigos: três salutares desafios do Evangelho. Estudos bíblicos 75 (2002) 28-37.

5141 *Phillips, Gary A.* The killing fields of Matthew's gospel. A shadow of glory. 2002 ⇒347. 232-247.

5142 *Puig i Tàrrech, Armand* Dolcesa i humilitat de cor en l'evangeli segons Mateu. QVC 208 (2002) 7-18.

5143 **Repschinski, Boris** The controversy stories in the gospel of Matthew. FRLANT 189: 2000 ⇒16,4784; 17,4767. ᴿSNTU.A 27 (2002) 215-220 (*Fuchs, Albert*).

5144 *Sánchez Navarro, Luis* Complacencia y deseo del Padre. EstB 60 (2002) 31-50 [Mt 11,26].

5145 *Sim, David C.* Matthew and the gentiles: a response to Brendan Byrne. ABR 50 (2002) 74-79.

5146 **Sim, David C.** The gospel of Matthew and christian Judaism: the history and social setting of the Matthean community. 1998 ⇒14,4253… 16,4789. ᴿSNTU.A 27 (2002) 220-222 (*Fuchs, Álbert*).

5147 *Sim, D.C.* The social setting of the Matthean community: new paths for an old journey. HTS 57 (2001) 268-280 [NTAb 46,455];

5148 Matthew's anti-Paulinsm: a neglected feature of Matthean studies. HTS 58 (2002) 767-783 [NTAb 47,238].

5149 **Vahrenhorst, Martin** "Ihr sollt überhaupt nicht schwören": Matthäus im halachischen Diskurs. ᴰ*Karrer, Martin*: WMANT 95: Neuk 2002, Neuk xiii; 465 pp. €74. 3-7887-1889-7. Diss. Wuppertal; Bibl. 420-450 [Mt 5,33-37; 23,16-22].

5150 *Van Aarde, Andries* Matthew and apocalypticism as the 'mother of christian theology': Ernst KÄSEMANN revisited. HTS 58 (2002) 118-142 [NTAb 47,33].

5151 **Wainwright, Elaine Mary** Shall we look for another?: a feminist re-reading of the Matthean Jesus. 1998 ⇒14,4259; 15,4718. [R]AThR 84 (2002) 424-425 (*Good, Deirdre*).

5152 *Welzen, Huub* Aankondiging, uitstel en crisis in Matteüs. ITBT 10/6 (2002) 22-26.

5153 *Wielenga, Bob* Poverty and the mission-charity trend: a perspective from Matthew. IRM 91 (2002) 87-101;

5154 Mission and the apocalyptic: a perspective from Matthew. IRM 91 (2002) 111-119.

5155 *Wilmshurst, S.M.B.* The historic present in Matthew's gospel: a survey and analysis focused on Matthew 13.44. LJ 52 (2002) 269-287.

F3.3 *Mt 1s (Lc 1s⇒F7.5) Infantia Jesu*—Infancy Gospels

5156 *Alvarez Valdés, Ariel* In che anno è nato Gesù?. TS(I) 78 (2002) 41-47.

5157 **Bagni, Arcangelo** I racconti dell'infanzia di Gesù (Mt 1-2 e Lc 1-2). Dabar... NT: Padova 2002, Messagero 216 pp.

5158 [E]**Billon, Gérard** Joseph le charpentier. DosB 91 (2002) 7-30.

5159 *Böttrich, Christfried* Die vergessene Geburtsgeschichte: Mt 1-2 / Lk 1-2 und die wunderbare Geburt des Melchisedek in slHen 71-72. Jüdische Schriften. 2002 ⇒345. 222-248.

5160 **Davidsen, Ole** Kristi fødsel: tekster og tolkninger år to tusind [The birth of Christ: texts and interpretations year two thousand]. Højberg 2000, Hovedland xiii; 608 pp. KR598. [R]RBLit 4 (2002) 334-337 (*Iversen, Gertrud Yde*).

5161 *Gallego, Epifanio* Nacimiento y niñez de Jesús. BiFe 82 (2002) 135-170.

5162 **Molnar, Michael R.** The star of Bethlehem: the legacy of the Magi. 2000 ⇒16,4820. [R]ET 114 (2002) 96-98 (*Birdsall, J. Neville*).

5163 *Navia Velasco, Carmiña* Jesús de Nazaret: miradas femeninas. Qol 30 (2002) 103-108.

5164 *Pikaza, Xabier* Los orígenes de Jesús: lecturas básicas del Nuevo Testamento. BiFe 82 (2002) 40-77.

5165 **Prigent, Pierre** Écoute... c'est Noël: narrations bibliques. P [2]2002 <1995>, Bergers 223 pp. €19. 2-85304-183-2.

5166 *Quelle Parra, Constantino* La figura de María en los evangelios de la infancia. BiFe 82 (2002) 106-134.

5167 *Ramis Darder, Francesc* Los evangelios de la infancia: apreciaciones críticas. BiFe 82 (2002) 7-39.

5168 **Romaniello, Giuseppe** La scrittura apocrifa dei primi due capitoli del vangelo secondo Matteo e controrevisione della datazione della nascita di Cristo. 2000 ⇒16,4806. [R]Emerita 70 (2002) 343-344 (*Cañas Reíllo, José Manuel*).

5169 *Scheidegger, Gabriele* Das Neugeborene und der Teufel: Kindheitsgeschichte als Reinheitsgeschichte. AKuG 84 (2002) 259-291.

5170 *Williams, Ritva H.* An illustration of historical inquiry: histories of Jesus and Matthew I.I[!]-25. Handbook of early christianity: 2002 ⇒ 275. 105-123.

5171 *Dodson, Derek S.* Dreams, the ancient novels, and the gospel of Matthew: an intertextual study. PRSt 29/1 (2002) 39-52 [Mt 1,18-24; 2, 13-15; 2,19-20].
5172 *Frey-Logean, Isabelle* Matthieu 1,18-25: Joseph à la croisée des chemins. Lire et Dire 54 (2002) 41-52 [BuBB 39,72].
5173 *Lehmeier, Karin* Von der unheiligen Familie zur heiligen Familie: Matthäus 1,18-25. JK 63/6 (2002) 58-61.

5174 *Albani, Matthias* Stars und Sterne: der Stern des Messias und die Sterne der Könige. WUB 26 (2002) 26-33 [Mt 2].
5175 *Tubach, Jürgen* Die Weisen aus dem Morgenland in einer Erzählung aus der Turfan-Oase. HBO 34 (2002) 323-345 [Mt 2].
5176 *Baumann, Rolf* Die Sterndeuter aus dem Osten;
5177 "Wir haben seinen Stern aufgehen sehen": die Magiererzählung und die heutige Exegese. BiHe 38 (2002) 94-95/96-101 [Mt 2, 1-12].
5178 *Birdsall, J. Neville* The star of Bethlehem. ET 114 (2002) 96-98 [Mt 2,1-12].
5179 **Chopitel, Jean; Gobry, Christiane** Les rois mages: histoire, légende et enseignements. Grenoble 2002, Mercure D. 158 pp. 2-913-826-24-5 [RHPhR 84,238—Grappe, C.] [Mt 2,1-12].
5180 *Eicher, Peter* Das kosmische Zeichen;
5181 *Fendrich, Herbert* Wirklich unmöglich. BiHe 38 (2002) 101-102/107-112 [Mt 2,1-12].
5182 **Reily, Suzel Ana** Voices of the Magi: enchanted journeys in southeast Brazil. Ch 2002, Univ. of Chicago Pr. xvii; 266 pp. $40/21 [Mt 2,1-12].
5183 **Stenschke, Christoph W.** Der Stern von Bethlehem: ein kritisches Gespräch mit Konradin Ferrari d'Occhieppo. R & T 9/3 (2002) 309-326 [Mt 2,1-12].
5184 *Wellmann, Bettina* Fragereise mit den Sterndeutern. BiHe 38 (2002) 116-118 [Mt 2,1-12].
5185 *McIvor, Robert S.* The star of Messiah. IBSt 24 (2002) 175-183 [Mt 2,2].
5186 **Valensi, Lucette** La fuite en Egypte: histoires d'Orient et d'Occident. P 2002, Seuil 336 pp. €26. 2-02-054145-9. ᴿMoBi 145 (2002) 60 (*Pouthier, Jean-Luc*) [Mt 2,13-15].

F3.4 *Mt 3...Baptismus Jesu*, **Beginnings of the Public Life**

5187 *Alonso Díaz, José* El mensaje del Bautista. BiFe 28 (2002) 209-233.
5188 *Alvarez Valdes, Ariel* ¿Fue Jesús discípulo de Juan el Bautista?. CuesTF 29 (2002) 197-203.
5189 *Axe, Anthony* A voice crying in the wilderness: the biblical hero in opera with specific reference to John the Baptist. Borders. JSOT.S 313: 2002 ⇒585. 307-333.
5190 *Cañellas, Gabriel* El bautismo de Jesús: conciencia mesiánica. BiFe 28 (2002) 234-258.
5191 *Chilton, B.* John the purifier: his immersion and his death. HTS 57 (2001) 247-267 [NTAb 46,445];
5192 John the Baptist: his immersion and his death. Dimensions of baptism. JSNT.S 234: 2002 ⇒434. 25-44.

5193 **Chung, Eul Kee** The background of John's baptism in light of the Old Testament. ^D*Wolfe, P.*: 2002, 184 pp. Diss. Fort Worth [RTL 34, 596].

5194 *Dube, Christopher* From ecstasy to ecstasis: a reflection on prophetic and Pentecostal ecstasy in the light of John the Baptizer. JPentec 11/1 (2002) 41-52.

5195 *Evans, Craig A.* The baptism of John in a typological context. Dimensions of baptism. JSNT.S 234: 2002 ⇒434. 45-71.

5196 *Gerstenberger, Erhard S.* Wasser—Chaos und Leben. JK 63/4 (2002) 37-44.

5197 *Hutchison, John C.* Was John the Baptist an Essene from Qumran?. BS 159 (2002) 187-200.

5198 *Jesudasan, I.* Baptism—a gospel meditation. VJTR 66 (2002) 288-292.

5199 *Manrique, Andrés* El bautismo de Jesús: experiencia de lo divino. BiFe 28 (2002) 259-274.

5200 **Müller, Ulrich B.** Johannes der Täufer: jüdischer Prophet und Wegbereiter Jesu. Biblische Gestalten 6: Lp 2002, Evangelische 230 pp. €14.80. 3-374-01993-5. Bibl. 224-228.

5201 *Serrano, Vicente* La tentación: experiencia del desierto. BiFe 84 (2002) 319-336.

5202 *Vázquez Allegue, Jaime* El bautismo judío en la época del segundo templo. BiFe 28 (2002) 181-208.

5203 **Tavardon, Paul** Les métamorphoses de l'Esprit: une exégèse du logion des deux baptêmes: Mt 3,10-12 et parallèles. ^D*Schlosser, J.* 2002, Diss. Strasbourg.

5204 *Gibbs, Jeffrey A.* Israel standing with Israel: the baptism of Jesus in Matthew's gospel (Matt 3:13-17). CBQ 64 (2002) 511-526.

5205 *Haidostian, Paul* When the tempter is made to leave!. ThRev 23/2 (2002) 143-149 [Mt 4,1-11].

5206 *Hasitschka, Martin* Der Sohn Gottes—geliebt und geprüft: Zusammenhang von Taufe und Versuchung Jesu bei den Synoptikern. ^FFUCHS, A. 2002 ⇒41. 71-80 [Mt 4,1-11].

5207 *Petraglio, Renzo* Gesù tentato?. PSV 46 (2002) 79-96 [Mt 4,1-11].

5208 *Salas, Antonio* Las tentaciones de Jesús: perspectiva de Mateo. BiFe 84 (2002) 386-409 [Mt 4,1-11].

5209 *Schlosser, Jacques* Les tentations de Jésus et la cause de Dieu (Q 4,1-13). RevSR 76 (2002) 403-425 [[Mt 4,1-11; Lk 4,1-13].

F3.5 Mt 5...Sermon on the Mount [...plain, Lk 6,17]

5210 ^T**Alichoran, Francis Y.** L'évangile en araméen: l'enseignement de Jésus au sommet de la montagne (Matthieu 5-7). SpOr 80: Bégrolles en Mauges 2002, Abbaye de Bellefontaine 201 pp. Traduction de la Peshitta et commentaire; Prés. *Claire Mazas*; collab. *Pierre Scheffer*; Avant-propos *Bernard Dupuis*.

5211 *Beutler, Johannes* Die Bergpredigt—Magna Charta christlicher Friedensethik. Gerechter Friede. Idstein 2002, Meinhardt. 67-83. Ed. Katholische Akademie Rabanus Maurus [AcBib 10,910].

5212 ^E**Dulk, M. den** De Bergrede: steunpunt van de vrijheid. 2001 ⇒17, 4850. ^RCHR 88 (2002) 79-80 (*Peerbolte, Bert Jan Lietaert*).

5213 *Dulk, Maarten den* De coulissen van de bergrede. ITBT 10/1 (2002) 26-27.

5214 **Hughes, R. Kent** The Sermon on the Mount. 2001 ⇒17,4851. [R]RExp 99 (2002) 629-631 (*Cranford, Lorin L.*).

5215 *Jeremias, Joachim* The Sermon on the Mount. Jesus and the message. 2002 <1961> ⇒184. 18-38.

5216 **Loader, William R.G.** Jesus' attitude towards the law: a study of the gospels. WUNT 2/97: 1997 ⇒13,4622... 16,4843. [R]StPat 49 (2002) 259-260 (*Segalla, Giuseppe*).

5217 **Pathrapankal, Joseph** The christian programme: a theological and pastoral study of the Sermon on the Mount. 1999 ⇒15,4781; 16, 4847. [R]VJTR 66 (2002) 699-701 (*Meagher, P.M.*).

5218 **Pelikan, Jaroslav** Divine rhetoric: the Sermon on the Mount as message and as model in AUGUSTINE, CHRYSOSTOM, and LUTHER. 2001 ⇒17,4855. [R]OCP 68 (2002) 523-525 (*Farrugia, E.G.*).

5219 **Petersen, Walter** Zur Eigenart des Matthäus: Untersuchung zur Rhetorik in der Bergpredigt. 2001 ⇒17,4856. [R]BZ 46 (2002) 131-133 (*Dobbeler, Stephanie*); ThLZ 127 (2002) 762-764 (*Meiser, Martin*).

5220 **Royster, Dmitri** Il regno di Dio: il sermone della montagna. Ecumene 17: Gorle 2000, Servitium 119 pp.

5221 **Stiewe, Martin; Vouga, François** Le Sermon sur la Montagne: un abrégé de l'évangile dans le miroitement de ses interprétations. Genève 2002, Labor et F. 302 pp. €36/FS53. 2-8309-1059-1.

5222 [E]**Trummer, Peter; Pichler, Josef** Kann die Bergpredigt Berge versetzen?. Graz 2002, Styria 277 pp. €22.90. 3-222-12970-3 [GuL 76, 151s—Baur, Franz Joseph].

5223 **Zeilinger, Franz** Zwischen Himmel und Erde: ein Kommentar zur "Bergpredigt" Matthäus 5-7. Stu 2002, Kohlhammer 251 pp. €19.80. 3-17-017268-9.

5224 *Thraede, Klaus* JUVENCUS: der Übergang zur 'Bergpredigt' des Matthäusevangeliums. [F]GNILKA, C.: JAC.E 33: 2002 ⇒48. 377-384 [Mt 5,1-2].

5225 *Charles, J. Daryl* Garnishing with the 'greater righteousness': the disciple's relationship to the law (Matthew 5:17-20). BBR 12 (2002) 1-15.

5226 *Kudiyiruppil, J.* Reflections on Mt 5,38-48. JJSS 2 (2002) 115-118.

5227 *Rivas, Luis Heriberto* El 'pacifismo' del sermón de la montaña (Mt 5, 39-40 y 44-48; Lc 6,27-38). RevBib 64 (2002) 5-52.

5228 *De Virgilio, Giuseppe* Mt 6,19-34: Provvidenza divina e realismo cristiano. RivBib 50 (2002) 3-29.

5229 *Leske, Adrian M.* Matthew 6.25-34: human anxiety and the natural world. Earth story. 2002 ⇒322. 15-27.

5230 *Rubiolo, Sergio* Las preocupaciones cotidianas y la providencia de Dios: exégesis de Mt 6,25-34. RevBib 63 (2001) 1-45.

5231 *Dennison, Charles G.* Invitations and warnings: Matthew 7:7-29. Kerux 17/1 (2002) 27-33.

5232 *Sánchez Navarro, Luis* La ley del corazón (Mt 7,12). EstB 60 (2002) 255-264.

F3.6 **Mt 5,3-11 (Lc 6,20-22) Beatitudines**

5233 *Barbaglia, Silvio* Le beatitudini di Matteo: 'carta d'identità' del discepolo. RCI 83 (2002) 543-552.

5234 *Botey, Jaume* Les benaurances, anunci del regne, i el compromís polític. QVC 208 (2002) 90-113.

5235 [E]**Drobner, Hubertus R.; Viciano, Alberto** GREGORY of Nyssa: homilies on the Beatitudes: an English version with commentary and supporting studies: proceedings 8th internat. colloquium on Gregory of Nyssa (Paderborn 1998). SVigChr 52: 2000 ⇒16,12641; 17,4876. [R]JEH 53 (2002) 126-127 (*Ludlow, Morwenna*); RSR 90 (2002) 267-268 (*Sesboüé, Bernard*); JEarlyC 10 (2002) 401-403 (*Harrison, Nonna Verna*).

5236 *Fabry, Heinz-Josef* Die Seligpreisungen in der Bibel und in Qumran. Wisdom texts. BEThL 159: 2002 ⇒482. 189-200.

5237 **Fernández-Paniagua, J.** Las bienaventuranzas, una brújul para encontrar el norte. M 2002, Narcea 94 pp. 84-277-1396-7.

5238 **Green, H. Benedict** Matthew, poet of the beatitudes. JSNT.S 203: 2001 ⇒17,4877. [R]ScrB 32 (2002) 37-39 (*Robinson, Bernard P.*); NT 44 (2002) 301-306 (*Doble, Peter*); EstB 60 (2002) 275-278 (*Sánchez Navarro, Luis*); CBQ 64 (2002) 375-376 (*Heil, John Paul*); ThLZ 127 (2002) 1048-1050 (*Konradt, Matthias*).

5239 **Johnson, Terry L.** When grace transforms: the character of Christ's disciples envisioned in the Beatitudes. Fearn 2002, Christian Focus 176 pp. £8. 1-85792-770-2.

5240 **Philippe, Marie-Dominique** Un feu sur la terre: entretiens autour des béatitudes. 2001 ⇒17,4881. [R]EeV 56 (2002) 30-31 (*Debarge, Louis*).

5241 *Strübind, Kim* Hunger und Durst nach Gerechtigkeit: Predigt über Matthäus 5,1-12. Zeitschrift für Theologie und Gemeinde 7 (2002) 349-354.

5242 *Vugdelija, Marijan* Beatitudine dei poveri (Mt 5,3; Lc 6,20);
5243 'Beati i poveri in spirito, perchè di essi è il regno dei cieli!' (Mt 5,3). Crkva u Svijetu 37 (2002) 8-37/172-198. **Croatian.**

5244 *Matteo, Armando* Ι πτωχοὶ τῷ πνεύματι della prima beatitudine di Matteo (Mt 5,3a). BeO 44 (2002) 245-254.

5245 **Talbot, Michel** "Heureux les doux, car ils héritont la terre": (Mt 5,4[5]). [D]*Gourgues, M.:* EtB 46: P 2002, Gabalda 454 pp. €62. 2-85021-139-7. Diss. Collège dominican Ottawa; Bibl. 382-414 [Isa 61; Mt 11,29; 21,5; 1 Peter 3,4].

5246 *Atlan, Gabrielle* Les juifs et le divorce: droit, histoire et sociologie du divorce religieux. Berne 2002, Lang xviii; 317 pp. Préf. *Jean Carbonnier.*

5247 *Guenther, Allen R.* The exception phrases: except porneia, including porneia or exluding porneia? (Matthew 5:32; 19:9). TynB 53 (2002) 83-96.

5248 **Instone-Brewer, David** Divorce and remarriage in the bible: the social and literary context. GR 2002, Eerdmans xi; 355 pp. $26. 0-8028-4943-1. Bibl. 315-333.

5249 **Kodithottam, George** Interreligious marriage and indissolubility: Jesus' prohibition of divorce: a law for christians or a gospel for all?. [D]*Rotter, Hans:* Diss. Insbruck 2002 [ZKTh 124,492].

5250 **Sutter Rehmann, Luzia** Konflikte zwischen ihm und ihr: sozialgeschichtliche und exegetische Untersuchungen zur Nachfolgeproblematik von Ehepaaren. Gü 2002, Gü'er 248 pp. €24.95. 3-579-05380-9. Diss.-Habil. Basel 2001 [Mk 10,1-12; 1 Cor 7].

F3.7 *Mt 6,9-13 (Lc 11,2-4)* **Oratio Jesu,** *Pater Noster,* **Lord's Prayer**

5251 *Black, C. Clifton* The education of human wanting: formation by
       Pater noster. Character and scripture. 2002 ⇒283. 248-263.
5252 *Boretti, Giancarlo* Per celebrare il Padre nostro. Ambrosius 78/3
       (2002) 355-361.
5253 **Clément, Olivier; Standaert, Benoît** Pregare il Padre nostro. 1998
       ⇒15,4815. ᴿEccl(R) 16 (2002) 117-118 (*Izquierdo, A.*).
5254 **Crosby, Michael H.** The prayer that Jesus taught us. Mkn 2002,
       Orbis 208 pp. $19. 1-57075-409-8. ᴿAmerica 187/13 (2002) 24
       (*Carmody, Denise Lardner*).
5255 *Delattre, Alain* Un 'Notre-Père' en copte à Médinet Abou. BASPap
       39 (2002) 13-16.
5256 *Föhr, Nikolaus* Mit Jesu Worten beten: das Gebet des Herrn im Got-
       tesdienst der Kirche: Praxis und Alternativen. ᶠHAAG, E. 2002 ⇒55.
       341-360.
5257 *French, Henry* The Lord's Prayer: a primer on mission in the way of
       Jesus. WaW 22/1 (2002) 18-26.
5258 **Gourgues, Michel** Le Pater: parole sur Dieu, parole sur nous. Con-
       naître la bible 26: Bru 2002, Lumen Vitae 80 pp. €9. 2-87324-169-1.
5259 **Hahn, Scott** Understanding 'Our Father': biblical reflections on the
       Lord's Prayer. Steubenville, OH 2002, Emmaus 146 pp $16. 1-
       931018-15-4 [ThD 50,269—Heiser, W. Charles].
5260 *Hammerling, Roy* GREGORY of Nyssa's sermons on the Lord's Prayer:
       lessons from the classics. WaW 22/1 (2002) 64-70.
5261 *Hinkle, Mary E.* The Lord's Prayer: empowerment for living the
       Sermon on the Mount. WaW 22/1 (2002) 9-17.
5262 *Jacobson, Karl N.* A word in season: preaching the Lord's Prayer.
       WaW 22/1 (2002) 88-93.
5263 *Jeremias, Joachim* The Lord's Prayer. Jesus and the message. 2002
       <1960> ⇒184. 39-62.
5264 **Körner, Reinhard** Das Vaterunser: Spiritualität aus dem Gebet Jesu.
       Lp 2002, St. Benno 254 pp. €14.90. 3-7462-1566-8 [GuL 76,150—
       Leenen, Maria Anna].
5265 *Luz, Ulrich; Leonhard, Clemens; Seitz, Manfred* Vaterunser. TRE
       34. 2002 ⇒800. 504-529.
5266 ᴱ**Martínez Ruiz, Carlos Mateo** Comentarios franciscanos al padre-
       nuestro. Ichthys 24: S 2002, Sígueme 198 pp. €11. 84-301-1450-5.
5267 *Meredith, Anthony* ORIGEN and GREGORY of Nyssa on the Lord's
       prayer. HeyJ 43 (2002) 344-356.
5268 *Minear, Paul S.* But whose prayer is it?. Worship 76 (2002) 324-338.
5269 ᴱ**Moreno García, Abdón; Nocon, Arkadiusz** [Pedro de Valencia:]
       El Padrenuestro de un humanista: un manuscrito inédito. 1999 ⇒15,
       4827; 16,4888. ᴿBurg. 43 (2002) 562 (*Pérez Herrero, Fco.*).
5270 *Oñoro, Fidel* El Padre Nuestro, una oracion comunitaria (Mt 6,9-13).
       Revista Católica 102 (2002) 100-102.
5271 **Philonenko, Marc** Das Vaterunser: vom Gebet Jesu zum Gebet der
       Jünger. ᵀ*Lehmkühler, Catherine; Lehmkühler, Karsten*: Tü 2002,
       Mohr S. 142 pp. €12.90. 3-8252-2312-4.
5272 *Riedl, Alfons* Vergib uns unsere Schuld—wie auch wir vergeben un-
       seren Schuldigern. LS 53 (2002) 110-115.
5273 *Ripamonti, Bruno; Sirboni, Silvano; Siliprandi, Antonella* Per una
       catechesi sul Padre nostro. Ambrosius 78/3 (2002) 335-353.

5274 **Schmemann, Alexander** Our Father. [T]*Vinogradov, Alexis*: Crestwood, NY 2002, St Vladimir's Seminary Pr. 93 pp. $10. 0-88141-234-1 [ThD 49,389—Heiser, W. Charles].

5275 *Siliprandi, Antonella* Sussidi per aiutare a pregare il Padre nostro. Ambrosius 78/3 (2002) 363-377.

5276 *Sölle, Dorothee* I pray, therefore I am. WaW 22/1 (2002) 6-8.

5277 [T]**Tolve-Vincenza, Umberto Antonio**, *al.*, S. Francesco Antonio FASANI: Secondo commento al 'Padre Nostro' (Expositio brevis). 1997 ⇒13,4691. [R]Ter. 53 (2002) 626-627 (*Croce, Giovanna della*).

5278 **Wackenheim, M.** Découvrir le Notre Père, P 2002, Salvator 96 pp. €10. 2-7067-0335-0 [NRTh 126,163s—Navez, G.].

5279 *Westhelle, Vítor* On displacing words: the Lord's Prayer and the new definition of justice. WaW 22/1 (2002) 27-35.

5280 **Nwagbala, Edmund Amobi** Matthew 6:12 in the exegesis of the early fathers. [D]*Schöllgen, Georg*: Diss. Bonn 2002 [ThRv 99,347].

5281 *Theißen, Gerd* Der Hauptmann von Kapernaum—ein Homosexueller?: eine diskrete biblische Geschichte und deren indiskrete Exegese (Mt 8,5-13). Erlösungsbilder. 2002 ⇒1460. 77-81.

F4.1 *Mt 9-12: Miracula Jesu*—The Gospel miracles

5282 [E]**Beavis, Mary Ann L.** The lost coin: parables of women, work and wisdom. BiSe 86: Shf 2002, Sheffield A. 344 pp. $20. 1-84127-313-9. Bibl. 313-327.

5283 [E]**Aguirre, Rafael** Los milagros de Jesús: perspectivas metodológicas plurales. Estella 2002, Verbo Divino 270 pp. €20.80. 84-8169-502-5.

5284 *Alvarez Valdes, Ariel* ¿Cómo hacía Jesús sus milagros?. CuesTF 29 (2002) 205-211.

5285 *Bartolomé, Juan J.* Jesús de Nazaret, 'ese varón acreditado por Dios con hechos prodigiosos' (Hch 2,22): una reseña de la investigación crítica sobre los milagros de Jesús. CuesTF 29 (2002) 345-382.

5286 [ET]**Brodersen, Kai** PHLEGON von Tralleis: das Buch der Wunder und Zeugnisse seiner Wirkungsgeschichte. TzF 79: 2002, Da:Wiss 138 pp. 3-534-15985-3. Bibl. 138.

5287 *Bultmann, Rudolf* Zur Frage des Wunders NT und christliche Existenz. UTB 2316: 2002 <1933> ⇒152. 84-98.

5288 *Dube, Musa W.* Healing where there is no healing: reading the miracles of healing in an AIDS context. [F]PATTE, D.: 2002 ⇒89. 121-133.

5289 **Earman, John** HUME's abject failure: the argument against miracles. 2000 ⇒16,4904. [R]JR 82 (2002) 302-303 (*Sweek, Joel*).

5290 *Erdozain, Luis* Los milagros. EE 77 (2002) 141-162.

5291 *Jimenez, Edilberto C.* 'Jesus, Son of David, have mercy on me!': prayers to Jesus in the miracle narratives. Landas 16 (2002) 51-64.

5292 **Kollmann, Bernd** Neutestamentliche Wundergeschichten: biblisch-theologische Zugänge und Impulse für die Praxis. Urban-Taschenbücher 477: Stu 2002, Kohlhammer 224 pp. 3-17-017175-5.

5293 *Lang, Walter* Die Existenz von Wundern und ihre Bedeutung für das Heilsgeschehen. Theologisches 32 (2002) 367-374.

5294 **Sorensen, Eric** Possession and exorcism in the New Testament and early christianity. [D]*Collins, A.Y.*: WUNT 2/157: Tü 2002, Mohr S. xiii; 295 pp. €49. 3-16-147851-7. Diss. Chicago [Bibl. 227-251].

5295 *Strecker, Christian* Jesus und die Besessenen: zum Umgang mit Alte-rität im Neuen Testament am Beispiel der Exorzismen Jesu. Jesus in neuen Kontexten. 2002 ⇒602. 53-63;
5296 Jesus and the demoniacs. The social setting. 2002 ⇒601. 117-133.
5297 **Vendrame, Calisto** A cura dos doentes na Bíblia. 2001 ⇒17,4935. [R]PerTeol 34 (2002) 129-130 (*Taborda, Francisco*).

5298 **Landmesser, Christof** Jüngerberufung und Zuwendung zu Gott: ein exegetischer Beitrag zum Konzept der matthäischen Soteriologie im Anschluß an Mt 9,9-13. WUNT 133: 2001 ⇒17,4940. [R]TS 63 (2002) 385-386 (*Viviano, Benedict T.*); ThLZ 127 (2002) 1188-1190 (*Feldmeier, Reinhard*); CBQ 64 (2002) 767-768 (*Bridge, Steven L.*); RBLit (2002)* (*Gundry, Robert H.*).
5299 *Love, Stuart L.* Jesus: der Heiler der blutflüssigen Frau im Matthäuse-vangelium: eine sozialwissenschaftliche Untersuchung. Jesus in neuen Kontexten. 2002 ⇒602. 86-97 [Mt 9,20-22];
5300 Jesus heals the hemorrhaging woman. The social setting. 2002 ⇒ 601. 85-101 [Mt 9,20-22].
5301 *Sisson, Russell B.* Instructions for 'broker' apostles: a socio-rhetori-cal analysis of Matthew's mission discourse. Rhetorical argumenta-tion. 2002 ⇒553. 174-187 [Mt 9,35-10,42].
5302 *Stuhlmacher, Peter* "Gehilfen der Wahrheit werden": Predigt über Matthäus 9,35-10,8. ThBeitr 33 (2002) 255-259.
5303 *Welzen, Huub* Geroepen en gezonden: mystiek in de zendingsrede van Matteüs. ITBT 10/4 (2002) 18-20 [Mt 10,5-42].
5304 **Lybaek, Lena** New and old in Matthew 11 - 13: normativity in the development of three theological themes. FRLANT 198: Gö 2002, Vandenhoeck & R. 269 pp. €54. 3-525-53882-0. Bibl. 250-269.
5305 *Visser, Paul J.* Aanbidding en nodiging. ThRef 45/3 (2002) 193-197 [Mt 11,25-30].
5306 *Humphrey, Edith M.* The enigma of the yoke: declining in parables (Mt. 11.28-30). The lost coin. BiSe 86: 2002 ⇒5282. 268-286.
5307 *Valleskey, D.J.* Matthew 11:29, 30—what is Christ's 'yoke'?. WLQ 99/3 (2002) 207-209 [NTAb 47,35].
5308 *Calambrogio, Leone* Rivoluzione in Mt 12. Laós 9/2 (2002) 51-57.
5309 *Cardellino, Lodovico* Il segno di Giona (Mt 12,38-42; Lc 11,16.29-32). BeO 44 (2002) 235-244.
5310 *Plisch, Uwe-Karsten* Was ist "das Zeichen des Jona"?. [F]SCHENKE, H.: NHS 54: 2002 ⇒108. 399-409 [Mt 12,38-42].
5311 *Mora, Vincent* El signo de Jonás. ResB 33 (2002) 43-47 [Mt 12,38-44].

F4.3 **Mt 13...***Parabolae Jesu*—**The Parables**

5312 Alle origini dell'occidente: parabole e personaggi del vangelo. Bres-cia 2002, Morcelliana 159 pp. 88-372-1873-7. Presentazione di *Pao-lo Corsini*; premessa di *Giulio Cittadini*.
5313 **Arzani, Paolo** Parabole di trasformazione. Amore e psiche 18: Bergamo 2002, Moretti & V 125 pp. 88-7186-196-5.
5314 **Ball, Michael** The foolish risks of God. L 2002, Mowbray x; 108 pp. 0-8264-6395-9.

5315 *Banschbach Eggen, Renate* The reception of the parables of Jesus in the synoptic gospels. NT as reception. JSNT.S 230: 2002 ⇒360. 58-82.

5316 *Bösen, Willibald* Die Figurenwelt der Gleichnisse. WUB 24 (2002) 60-66.

5317 *Bravo, Luis* La pedagogía de las parábolas: una perspectiva psicológica. TyV 43 (2002) 503-511.

5318 **Capon, Robert Farrar** Kingdom, grace, judgment: paradox, outrage, and vindication in the parables of Jesus. GR 2002, Eerdmans ix; 522 pp. $26. 0-8028-3949-5.

5319 *Crossan, John Dominic* The parables of Jesus. Interp. 56 (2002) 247-259.

5320 *Curkpatrick, Stephen* Between mashal and parable: "likeness" as a metonymic enigma. HBT 24/1 (2002) 58-71.

5321 **Erlemann, Kurt** Gleichnisauslegung: ein Lehr- und Arbeitsbuch. UTB.W; UTB 2093: 1999 ⇒15,4904. [R]BZ 46 (2002) 130-131 (*Lehnert, Volker A.*); ThLZ 127 (2002) 41-43 (*Mell, Ulrich*).

5322 *Evans, Craig A.* Jesus' rhetoric of criticism: the parables against his friends and critics. Rhetorical criticism. JSNT.S 195: 2002 ⇒369. 256-279.

5323 **Gourgues, Michel** Le parabole di Gesù in Marco e Matteo, dalla sorgente alla foce. Leumann 2002, Ldc 240 pp. [R]PaVi 47/5 (2002) 57-58 (*Giavini, Giovanni*).

5324 **Hultgren, Arland J.** The parables of Jesus: a commentary. 2000 ⇒ 16,4943; 17,4956. [R]ScrB 32 (2002) 110-111 (*Dale, John*); ABR 50 (2002) 87-88 (*Pryor, John W.*); ThLZ 127 (2002) 286-288 (*Mell, Ulrich*); HBT 24 (2002) 132-134 (*Allison, Dale C.*); TrinJ 23 (2002) 260-263 (*Sweeney, James P.*).

5325 **Johnson, Sylvester** Jesus and his parables. Delhi 2002, ISPCK xvi; 128 pp. Rs65/$7. 81-7214-647-7. [R]MissTod 4 (2002) 382-383 (*Fernandez, Francis*).

5326 **Jones, Peter Rhea** Studying the parables of Jesus. 1999 <1982> ⇒ 15,4472...17,7565. [R]RExp 99 (2002) 285-286 (*Cranford, Lorin L.*).

5327 **Kistemaker, Simon J.** The parables: understanding the stories Jesus told. GR 2002, Baker 271 pp. 0-8010-6391-4. Bibl. 268-270.

5328 [E]**Longenecker, Richard N.** The challenge of Jesus' parables. 2000 ⇒16,4929; 17,4957. [R]RTR 61 (2002) 102-103 (*Bird, Anthony E.*); ThLZ 127 (2002) 1054-1056 (*Hirsch-Luipold, Rainer*).

5329 *Neusner, Jacob* Contexts of conparison: reciprocally reading gospels' and rabbis' parables. The missing Jesus. 2002 ⇒4895. 45-68.

5330 **Oldenhage, Tania** Parables for our time: rereading New Testament scholarship after the Holocaust. AAR.Cultural Criticism: NY 2002, OUP (10) 189 pp. 0-19-515052-X. Bibl. 177-183.

5331 Parábolas de vida: el rostro di Dios Padre revelado por Jesús a todos los 'pequeños' que acogen su reino. Sdr 2002, Sal Terrae 175 pp. 84-293-1443-1.

5332 *Parris, David P.* Imitating the parables: allegory, narrative and the role of mimesis. JSNT 25/1 (2002) 33-53.

5333 *Piedad Sánchez, Jorge* La ironía en las parábolas. Qol 30 (2002) 87-98.

5334 **Raja, John Joshua** Facing the reality of communication: culture, church and communication. 2001 ⇒17,4966. [R]VJTR 66 (2002) 386-389 (*John, V.J.*) [Lk 10,25-37].

5335 *Reinstorf, D.; Van Aarde, Andries* Reflections on Jesus' parables as metaphorical stories past and present. HTS 58 (2002) 721-745 [NTAb 47,237].

5336 **Thielicke, Helmut** Das Bilderbuch Gottes: Reden über die Gleichnisse Jesu. Gü ⁷2002, Quell 304 pp. 3-579-03464-2.

5337 *Venetz, Hermann J.* Zeit der Königsherrschaft Gottes: irritierend, anregend, befreiend: ein Blick auf die Gleichnisse Jesu. WuA(M) 43/3 (2002) 104-111.

5338 *Weber, Christin Lore* Gathering: a mythic parable. The lost coin. BiSe 86: 2002 ⇒5282. 308-312.

5339 **Young, Bradford H.** The parables: Jewish tradition and christian interpretation. 1998 ⇒14,4451... 17,4973. ᴿJSJ 33 (2002) 119-121 (*Frey, Jörg*).

5340 **Wierzbicka, Anna** What did Jesus mean?: explaining the Sermon on the Mount and the parables in simple and universal human concepts. 2001 ⇒17,4973. ᴿProEc 11 (2002) 99-102 (*Oakes, Edward T.*); RRT 9 (2002) 173-174 (*Wansbrough, Henry*).

5341 *Manzi, Franco; Pagazzi, Giovanni Cesare* "Il regno dei cieli è simile a un tesoro nascosto" (Mt 13,44): la singolarità dell'immaginazione di Gesù. ScC 130/1 (2002) 9-42.

5342 *Camacho Acosta, Fernando* Las parábolas del tesoro y de la perla (Mt 13,44-46): matices interpretativos. Isidorianum 21 (2002) 101-117.

5343 **Hartmann, Michael** Der Tod Johannes' des Täufers: eine exegetische und rezeptionsgeschichtliche Studie auf dem Hintergrund narrativer, intertextueller und kulturanthropologischer Zugänge. SBB 45: 2001 ⇒17,4977. ᴿBZ 46 (2002) 276-277 (*Dobbeler, Stephanie von*); ThLZ 127 (2002) 907-909 (*Tilly, Michael*) [Mt 14,3-12].

5344 **Jackson, Glenna S.** 'Have mercy on me': the story of the Canaanite woman in Matthew 15.21-28. JSNT.S 228; Copenhagen International Seminar 10: L 2002, Sheffield A. xiv; 197 pp. $115. 0-8264-6148-4. Bibl. 160-182.

5345 *Love, Stuart L.* Jesus, healer of the Canaanite woman's daughter in Matthew's gospel: a social-scientific inquiry. BTB 32 (2002) 11-20 [Mt 15,21-28].

5346 *Mouton, E.* Die kanaänitiese vrou van Matteus 15: *hervormer* in eie reg. Scriptura 80 (2002) 220-225 [NTAb 47,452].

5347 *Nortjé-Meyer, L.* The homosexual hody without apology: a positive link between the Canaanite woman in Matthew 15:21-28 and homosexual interpretation of biblical texts. R&T 9/1-2 (2002) 118-134 [NTAb 47,241].

5348 *Hock, Ronald F.* Romancing the parables of Jesus. PRSt 29/1 (2002) 11-37 [Mt 18,23-35; 20,1-16; Lk 15,11-32].

F4.5 **Mt 16...***Primatus promissus*—**The promise to Peter**

5349 *Aguirre Monasterio, Rafael* Simón Pedro, el primero entre los apóstoles. ResB 36 (2002) 13-20.

5350 **Böttrich, Christfried** Petrus: Fischer, Fels und Funktionär. Biblische Gestalten 2: 2001 ⇒17,4986. ᴿBiKi 57 (2002) 108 (*Doering, Lutz*); ThLZ 127 (2002) 173-174 (*Pesch, Rudolf*).

5351 *Burnet, Régis; Bizot, Catherine* Pierre, apôtre entre Judas et le disciple bien-aimé. ETR 77 (2002) 105-111.
5352 *Doering, Lutz* Schwerpunkte und Tendenzen der neueren Petrus-Forschung. BThZ 19 (2002) 203-223.
5353 **Gibert, Pierre** Simon Pierre, apôtre et compagnon. 2001 ⇒17,4988. RSR 31 (2002) 430-432 (*Steigerwald, Diane*).
5354 **Gnilka, Joachim** Petrus und Rom: das Petrusbild in den ersten zwei Jahrhunderten FrB 2002 Herder 286 pp €24.90 3-451-27492-2 RThPh 77 (2002) 561-563 (*Schatz, Klaus*).
5355 **Perkins, Pheme** Peter: apostle for the whole church. ²2000 <1994> ⇒16,4976; 17,4990. RJR 82 (2002) 107-108 (*Martin, Troy W.*); ThLZ 127 (2002) 184-186 (*Doering, Lutz*).
5356 **Pesch, Rudolf** La primauté dans l'église: les fondements bibliques. THoffmann, Joseph: LiBi 125: P 2002, Cerf 172 pp. €17. 2-204-069-30-2;
5357 I fondamenti biblici del primato. Brescia 2002, Queriniana 174 pp. €14.50. 88-399-0791-2;
5358 Die biblischen Grundlagen des Primats. QD 187: 2001 ⇒17,4991. RLat. 68 (2002) 177-182 (*Rossetti, C. Lorenzo*).
5359 **Waldmann, Helmut** Petrus und die Kirche: Petri Versuchung (Mat 16: 'Weiche von mir, Satan!... Was nützt es dem Menschen...') und der Kampf der Kirche mit dem Kaisertum um die Weltherrschaft. 1999 ⇒15,4956. RThQ 182 (2002) 52-56 (*Vogt, Hermann J.*).
5360 **Wiarda, Timothy** Peter in the gospels: pattern, personality and relationship. WUNT 2/127: 2000 ⇒16,4979; 17,4994. RThLZ 127 (2002) 1058-60 (*Doering, Lutz*); CBQ 64 (2002) 593-4 (*Thompson, Mary R.*).

5361 *Montfort, Christian* Matthieu 16,13-28: suivre Jésus, un appel, une aventure et une promesse. Lire et Dire 53 (2002) 28-40 [BuBB 39, 73].
5362 *Rastoin, Marc* Pierre 'fils de la colombe' en Mt 16,17?. Bib. 83 (2002) 549-555.
5363 *Del Corro, Annie* To put or not to put a footnote: Matthew 16.19. BiTr 53 (2002) 226-233.
5364 *Ghiberti, Giuseppe* 'Vade retro, Satana' (Mt 16,23; Mc 8,33): ripulsa o chiamata al discepolato?. VII Simposio di Tarso. 2002 ⇒587. 115-129.
5365 *Norris, Frederick W.* The transfiguration of Christ: the transformation of the church. FGREER, R. 2002 ⇒51. 188-198 [Mt 17,1-3].
5366 *Fisichella, Rino* Valore teologico della trasfigurazione. Com(I) 181 (2002) 21-30 [Mt 17,1-8].
5367 **Heil, John Paul** The transfiguration of Jesus: narrative meaning and function of Mark 9:2-8, Matt 17:1-8 and Luke 9:28-36. AnBib 144: 2000 ⇒16,4984; 17,4995. RATG 65 (2002) 314-315 (*Rodríguez Carmona, A.*); ThLZ 127 (2002) 174-176 (*Mell, Ulrich*); Bib. 83 (2002) 121-125 (*Gundry, Robert H.*).
5368 *Dobbeler, Stephanie von* Die Versammlung 'auf meinen Namen hin' (Mt 18,20) als Identitäts- und Differenzkriterium. NT 44 (2002) 209-230.
5369 *Orsatti, Mauro* Perdono, il nome nuovo della giustizia difficile, ma sovrabbondante (Mt 18,21-35 e il suo contesto). RStB 14/1-2 (2002) 169-207.

5370 *Reid, Barbara E.* Puzzling passages: Matthew 18:35. BiTod 40
(2002) 123-124.
5371 *Norris, Frederick W.* 'As yourself': a least love. ^FWILKEN, R.: 2002
⇒136. 107-117 [Mt 19,19].

F4.8 Mt 20...*Regnum eschatologicum*—Kingdom eschatology

5372 *Avemarie, Friedrich* Das Gleichnis von den Arbeitern im Weinberg
(Mt 20,1-15)—eine soziale Utopie?. EvTh 62 (2002) 272-287.
5373 *Lamoureux, Patricia Ann; Zilonka, Paul* The workers in the vineyard: insights for the moral life. RfR 61 (2002) 57-69 [Mt 20,1-15].
5374 *Theißen, Gerd* Christen und Moslems oder die Souveränität der
Gnade Gottes (Mt 20,1-16). Erlösungsbilder. 2002 ⇒1460. 82-85.
5375 **Nieuviarts, Jacques** L'entrée de Jésus à Jérusalem (Mt 21,1-17):
messianisme et accomplissement des écritures en Matthieu. LeDiv
176: 1999 ⇒15,4976...17,5010. ^REstB 60 (2002) 138-140 (*Urbán,
A.*).
5376 **Ådna, Jostein** Jesu Stellung zum Tempel: die Tempelaktion und das
Tempelwort als Ausdruck seiner messianischen Sendung. WUNT 2/
119: 2000 ⇒16,4990; 17,5011. ^RThG 45 (2002) 219-221 (*Giesen,
Heinz*) [Mt 21,12-13; 24].
5377 *Elliott, James Keith* The parable of the two sons: text and exegesis.
^FDELOBEL, J.: BEThL 161: 2002 ⇒24. 67-77 [Mt 21,28-32].
5378 *Bara, Shailendra* The parable of the vineyard and the tenants (Mt
21:33-46; Mk 12:1-12; Lk 20:9-19). Sevartham 27 (2002) 43-55.
5379 *Turner, David L.* Matthew 21:43 and the future of Israel. BS 159
(2002) 46-61.
5380 *Pfandl, G.* Israel and the church. JATS 13/2 (2002) 15-29 [NTAb 47,
242] [Mt 21,43].
5381 *Lagorio, Gina* Venite, tutto è pronto. Il libro sacro. 2002 ⇒356. 165-
184 [Mt 22; Lk 14].
5382 *Uchida, K.* Does the parable of the feast (Matt. 22:1-14) teach salvation after 'hell'?. Exegetica [Tokyo] 13 (2002) 73-96. J.
5383 *Wielenga, Bob* Mission and the apocalyptic: a perspective from Matthew. IRM 91 (2002) 111-119 [Mt 24].
5384 *Hasitschka, Martin* "Nahe gekommen ist das Reich der Himmel":
faszinierende und zugleich "unbequeme" Botschaft Jesu nach dem
Matthäusevangelium. Der unbequeme Gott. ThTr 11: 2002 ⇒596.
35-46 [Mt 24-25].
5385 *Pettegrew, L.D.* Interpretive flaws in the Olivet discourse. MastJ 13/2
(2002) 173-190 [NTAb 47,242] [Mt 24-25].
5386 *Shea, William H.* The sabbath in Matthew 24:20. AUSS 40 (2002)
23-35.
5387 *Sim, D.C.* The dissection of the wicked servant in Matthew 24:51.
HTS 58 (2002) 172-184 [NTAb 47,36].
5388 *Jüngel, Eberhard* Sermon on Matthew 25:1-12. TJT 18 (2002) 13-
19.
5389 *Balabanski, Vicky* Opening the closed door: a feminist rereading of
the 'wise and foolish virgins' (Mt. 25.1-13). The lost coin. BiSe 86:
2002 ⇒5282. 71-97.
5390 *Eltrop, Bettina* Problem girls: a transgressive reading of the parable
of the ten virigins (Matthew 25:1-13). ^FSCHOTTROFF, L. 2002 ⇒111.
163-171.

5391 *Orsatti, Mauro* Il mio nome è 'Gregorio': la parabola delle dieci vergini (Mt 25,1-13). VitaCon 38 (2002) 576-583.

5392 *Pérès, Jacques-Noël* L'interprétation de la parabole des dix vierges dans l'Épître des apôtres. ᶠGEOLTRAIN, P.: BEHE.R 113: 2002 ⇒45. 183-190 [BuBB 40,17] [Mt 25,1-13].

5393 *Zimmermann, Ruben* Das Hochzeitsritual im Jungfrauengleichnis: sozialgeschichtliche Hintergründe zu Mt 25.1-13. NTS 48 (2002) 48-70.

5394 *Nielsen, Helge Kjaer* Ist der "faule" Knecht faul?: zur Übersetzung von ὀκνηρός in Mt 25,26. ᶠFUCHS, A.: 2002 ⇒41. 157-173.

5395 **Fumagalli, Anna** Gesù crocifisso, straniero fino alla fine dei tempi: una lettura di Mt 25,31-46 in chiave comunicativa. EHS.T 707: 2000 ⇒16,5013; 17,5020. ᴿThRv 98 (2002) 211-213 (*Dormeyer, Detlev*).

5396 *Pinciroli, Erminio* La figura dei 'minimi' in Mt 25,31-46: storia della interpretazione recente ed esempi di utilizzazione del testo. ᶠTUDDA, F. 2002 ⇒123. 133-151.

5397 *Pond, Eugene W.* The background and timing of the judgment of the sheep and goats. BS 159 (2002) 201-220 [Mt 25,31-46].

5398 *Wendland, E.* Whose side are you on?: structure and rhetoric in Christ's parable of the sheep and the goats (Matthew 25:31-46), with special reference to bible translation. Scriptura 80 (2002) 307-317 [NTAb 47,453].

5399 *Pond, Eugene W.* Who are "the least" of Jesus' brothers in Matthew 25:40?. BS 159 (2002) 436-448.

F5.1 *Redemptio*, **Mt 26**, *Ultima coena*; **The Eucharist** [⇒H7.4]

5400 *Balzer, Chris* The Lord's Supper—meal or sacrament?. RTR 61/3 (2002) 117-130.

5401 *Bradshaw, Paul F.* Did the early eucharist ever have a sevenfold shape?. HeyJ 43 (2002) 73-76.

5402 *Bremmer, Jan N.* Sacrificing a child in ancient Greece: the case of Iphigeneia. Aqedah. 2002 ⇒2524. 21-43.

5403 *Cahill, Michael* Drinking blood at a kosher eucharist: the sound of scholarly silence. BTB 32 (2002) 168-181.

5404 **Cingolani, Gabriele** He loved them to the end: meditations on the gospels of the Passion. NY 2002, Alba xiii; 226 pp. $15 [BiTod 40, 399—Senior, Donald].

5405 **Clark, Stephen, B.** Catholics and the eucharist: a scriptural introduction. 2000 ⇒16,5022; 17,5027. ᴿHPR 103/1 (2002) 77-78 (*Merdinger, Philip*).

5406 *Klawans, Jonathan* Interpreting the Last Supper: sacrifice, spiritualization, and anti-sacrifice. NTS 48 (2002) 1-17.

5407 **Koenig, John** The feast of the world's redemption: eucharistic origins and christian mission. 2000 ⇒16,5033; 17,5037. ᴿProEc 11 (2002) 245-247 (*Johnson, Maxwell E.*); CBQ 64 (2002) 168-169 (*Smith, Dennis E.*); RBLit 4 (2002) 303-306 (*Daneels, John W., Jr.*).

5408 *Lang, Walter* Ist die Eucharistie Mahl oder Opfer?. Theologisches 32 (2002) 421-428.

5409 *LaVerdiere, Eugene* The loaves and fish, a eucharistic banquet. BiTod 40 (2002) 229-235 [Mk 6,34-44].

5410 *Luz, Ulrich* The Lord's Supper in the NT. ThD 49 (2002) 239-243 < BiKi 57 (2002) 2-8;

5411 Das Herrenmahl im Neuen Testament. BiKi 57 (2002) 2-8.
5412 *Mazza, Enrico* À propos de la dérivation de l'eucharistie chrétienne de la *birkat ha-mazon* juive. QuLi 83 (2002) 233-239.
5413 *Niemand, Christoph* Jesu Abendmahl: Versuch zur historischen Rekonstruktion und theologischen Deutung. [F]FUCHS, A. 2002 ⇒41. 81-122 [Mk 14,22-25; 1 Cor 11,23-26].
5414 *Renaud, Bernard* Jésus et la (nouvelle) alliance dans les récits de l'institution eucharistique. Typologie biblique. 2002 ⇒341. 119-139.
5415 *Routledge, Robin* Passover and Last Supper. TynB 53 (2002) 203-21.
5416 **Stewart-Sykes, Alistair** The Lamb's high feast: MELITO, Peri Pascha and the Quartodeciman Paschal Liturgy at Sardis. SVigChr 42: 1998 ⇒14,4532; 17,5044. [R]VigChr 56 (2002) 103-111 (*Petersen, William L.*).
5417 *Strahm Bernet, Silvia* Mahl feiern: wozu bloß?. BiKi 57 (2002) 57.
5418 *Tomasi, Giovanni* Le parole dell'Ultima Cena sono soltanto un oracolo profetico?. MF 102 (2002) 207-230.
5419 *Wuckelt, Agnes* "Dein Brot teilen ...": eine Dia-Reihe als Zugang zur Feier des Abendmahls und der Eucharistie. BiKi 57 (2002) 28-30;
5420 Ein Opfermahl?: Überlegungen aus feministisch-theologischer Perspektive. BiKi 57 (2002) 40-45.

5421 *Sanz Giménez-Rico, Enrique* La Palabra y su palabra: omisión en Mt 26,17-35. EE 77 (2002) 99-114.

F5.3   Mt 26,30...//*Passio Christi*; Passion narrative

5422 *Austriaco, Nicanor P.* Was Jesus happy on the cross?. HPR 102/5 (2002) 24-30.
5423 *Brueggemann, Walter* Reading from the day 'in between'. A shadow of glory. 2002 ⇒347. 105-116.
5424 **Centini, Massimo** Giuda Iscariota: la vita ribelle e la misteriosa morte dell'apostolo che tradì Gesù Cristo. Profili: Genova 2002, ECIG 215 pp. 88-7545-925-8. Bibl. 209-212.
5425 **Cohn Chaim** Processo e morte di Gesù: un punto di vista ebraico. 2000 ⇒16,5055. [R]Hum(B) 57 (2002) 597-614 (*Menestrina, Giovanni*).
5426 *Crossan, John Dominic* The passion after the Holocaust. A shadow of glory. 2002 ⇒347. 171-184.
5427 *Diebner, Bernd Jørg* "Pontius Pilatus" in der postkanonischen Literatur: ein Beitrag zur Funktion und Rezeption der seit 2000 Jahren meisterwähnten Figur der Geschichte. Jüdische Schriften. 2002 ⇒ 345. 429-448.
5428 **Farcy, Gérard-Denis** Le sycophante et le rédimé ou le mythe de Judas. 1999 ⇒15,5025. [R]RSPhTh 86 (2002) 305-306 (*Jossua, Jean-Pierre*).
5429 *Feldman, Steven; Roth, Nancy E.* The short list: the New Testament figures known to history. BArR 28/6 (2002) 34-37.
5430 *Haacker, Klaus* Wer war schuld am Tode Jesu? Versöhnung mit Israel. VKHW 5 (2002) <1994> 33-48.
5431 **Jaroš, Karl** In Sachen Pontius Pilatus. Kulturgeschichte der antiken Welt 93: Mainz 2002, Zabern 144 pp. €18. 3-8053-2876-1. 27 ill.
5432 **Jossa, Giorgio** Il processo di Gesù. StBi 133: Brescia 2002, Paideia 146 pp. €13. 88-394-0639-5.

5433 *Kalaïtzidis, Pantélis* La tentation de Judas: église, nation et identités: de l'histoire de l'économie divine à l'histoire de la renaissance nationale. Contacts 54/1 (2002) 24-48.

5434 *Krieg, Matthias* Schöner trauriger Judas: Typologie einer literarischen Figur. KuI 17 (2002) 76-85.

5435 ^E**Mantovani, Piera Arata** Gesù: inchiesta sulla sua morte e sulla sua risurrezione. Mondo della bibbia 62 (2002) 3-50.

5436 **Nodet, Étienne** Le Fils de Dieu: procès de Jésus et évangiles. Josèphe et son temps 4: P 2002, Cerf xvii; 346 pp. €28. 2-204-06929-9. Bibl. xi-xvii. ^RBrotéria 155/1 (2002) 94-96 (*Silva, I. Ribeiro da*).

5437 **Scheidgen, Andreas** Die Gestalt des Pontius Pilatus in Legende, Bibelauslegung und Geschichtsdichtung vom Mittelalter bis in die frühe Neuzeit: Literaturgeschichte einer umstrittenen Figur. Mikrokosmos 68: Fra 2002, Lang 348 pp. £30. 3-631-39003-3.

5438 *Schmidt, Johann Michael* Das Verständnis der Passionsdarstellungen in den Evangelien. FrRu 9 (2002) 192-204.

5439 **Schmidt, Thomas** A scandalous beauty: the artistry of God and the way of the cross. GR 2002, Brazos 127 pp. $15. 1-58743-017-7 [ThD 49,286—W. Charles Heiser].

5440 *Scordato, Cosimo* Le sette parole di Gesù in croce. Ho Theológos 20 (2002) 21-42.

5441 *Siegert, Folker* "Zerstört diesen Tempel...!": Jesus als "Tempel" in den Passionsüberlieferungen. Zerstörungen. WUNT 147: 2002 ⇒ 559. 108-139.

5442 *Steinmetz, Franz-Josef* Leben aus dem Tod?: die sieben Worte Jesu am Kreuz. GuL 75 (2002) 117-131.

5443 *Strola, Germana* Guardare oltre: le donne al mattino di Pasqua. Horeb 11/2 (2002) 18-24.

5444 ^T**Tomàs, Assumpta** TOMÀS More: L'agonia de Crist: cartes desde la presó. Clàssics del cristianisme 92: Barc 2002, Proa 211 pp. Introd. *Joan Bada*.

5445 *Vázquez Allegue, Jaime* Judas Iscariote. ResB 36 (2002) 45-53.

5446 *Warner, Anita R.* Fulfilling all righteousness: the death of Jesus in Matthew. CThMi 29 (2002) 12-19.

5447 *White, R.E.O.* That 'cry of dereliction' ...?. ET 113 (2002) 188-189.

5448 **Williams, Rowan** Christ on trial: how the gospel unsettles our judgment. GR 2000, Eerdmans xvi; 141 pp. $16.

5449 *Zucchi, Pierluigi* Il volto dolente di Cristo: algos e pathos nel Gethsemani. Il volto dei volti 5/2 (2002) 46-55 Som. 55.

5450 *Mays, James L.* "Now I know": an exposition of Genesis 22:1-19 and Matthew 26:36-46. ThTo 58 (2002) 519-525.

5451 *Welzen, Huub* Getsemane, de laatste fase van een mystieke weg. ITBT 10/2 (2002) 28-30 [Mt 26,39-44].

5452 *Bond, Helen K.* Caiaphas: reflections on a High Priest. ET 113 (2002) 183-187 [Mt 26,57].

5453 *Menken, Maarten J.J.* The Old Testament quotation in Matthew 27, 9-10: textual form and context. Bib. 83 (2002) 305-328 [Zech 11,13].

5454 *Haacker, Klaus* "Sein Blut über uns": Erwägungen zu Matthäus 27,25. Versöhnung mit Israel. VKHW 5: 2002 <1986> ⇒174. 29-32.

5455 *Jacobs, Steven L.* Blood on our heads: a Jewish response to Saint Matthew. A shadow of glory. 2002 ⇒347. 57-67 [Mt 27,25].

5456 **Crowder, Stephanie R. Buckhanon** Simon of Cyrene: a case of Roman conscription. Studies in Biblical Literature 46: NY 2002, Lang xv; 130 pp. 0-8204-5686-1. Bibl. 115-125 [Mt 27,32].

5457 **Rigato, Maria-Luisa** Il titolo della croce di Gesù: confronto tra i vangeli e la tavoletta-reliquia della Basilica Eleniana a Roma. ᴰ*Beutler, Johannes*: 2002, 72 pp. Exc. Diss. Gregoriana 2002 [Mt 27,37].

5458 *Niskansen, Paul* The last words of Jesus. HPR 102/6 (2002) 23-25 [Mt 27,46].

5459 *Denaux, Adelbert* Matteus' verhaal van Jezus' begrafenis en verrijzenis (Mt 27,57-28,20). Coll. 32/1 (2002) 25-46.

5460 *Troxel, Ronald L.* Matt 27.51-4 reconsidered: its role in the passion narrative, meaning and origin. NTS 48 (2002) 30-47.

F5.6 Mt 28//: Resurrectio

5461 **Abrahamsson, Magnus** Jesu uppståndelse som historiskt problem: en studie av Rudolf BULTMANNs och Wolfhart PANNENBERGs tolkningar [The resurrection of Jesus as a historical problem: an examination of Rudolf Bultmann's and Wolfhart Pannenberg's interpretations]. 2002 Diss. Uppsala [StTh 57,81].

5462 *Adam, Jens* Das leere Grab als Unterpfand der Auferstehung Jesu Christi: der Beitrag Hans VON CAMPENHAUSENs. Die Wirklichkeit. 2002 ⇒302. 59-75 [2 Cor 1,12-24].

5463 *Araújo, José Wiliam Corrêa de* O conteúdo da fé na ressurreição de Jesus. Revista de espiritualidade 56 (2002) 25-48.

5464 *Biser, Eugen* Der Weg vom Bild ins Wort. LebZeug 57 (2002) 244-256.

5465 **Bony, Paul** La risurrezione di Gesù: inizio di una nuova umanità. Fame e sete della parola 39: CinB 2002, San Paolo 212 pp. 88-215-46-13-6. Bibl. 207-208.

5466 *Braun, Ute* Anhang: das Zeugnis der Auferstehung Jesu nach den vier Evangelien: ein synoptischer Vergleich;

5467 *Burmeister, Luise* Auferstehung in die Nachfolge: Dietrich BONHOEFFERs nicht-religiöse Interpretation der Auferstehung. Die Wirklichkeit. 2002 ⇒302. 333-342/111-119.

5468 ᴱ**Chareire, Isabelle** La résurrection... avenir du crucifié. LV(L) 253 (2002) 1-83.

5469 *Craffert, Pieter F.* "Seeing" a body into being: reflections on scholarly interpretations of the nature and reality of Jesus' resurrected body. R & T 9/1 (2002) 89-107.

5470 *Dalferth, Ingolf U.* Volles Grab, leerer Glaube?: zum Streit um die Auferweckung des Gekreuzigten. Die Wirklichkeit. 2002 ⇒302. 277-309.

5471 *Del Agua, Agustín* El testimonio narrativo de la resurrección de Cristo. EE 77 (2002) 241-273.

5472 *Deneken, Michel* Les apparitions du ressuscité: de la théophanie à la christophanie. Voir les dieux. 2002 ⇒629. 79-94.

5473 *Dettmar, Werner* Auferweckung Jesu: das älteste christliche Bekenntnis. Deutsches Pfarrerblatt 102/2 (2002) 54-57.

5474 *Dunn, James D.G.* Beyond the historical impasse?: in dialogue with A.J.M. Wedderburn. ᶠWEDDERBURN, A.: JSNT.S 217: 2002 ⇒132. 250-264.

5475 *Eckstein, Hans-Joachim* Die Wirklichkeit der Auferstehung Jesu: Lukas 24,34 als Beispiel früher formelhafter Zeugnisse;
5476 *Eckstein, Hans-Joachim; Welker, Michael* Einleitung;
5477 *Etzelmüller, Gregor* "Ich lebe, und ihr sollt auch leben!": die Leiblichkeit des Auferstandenen und ihre Bedeutung für die Eschatologie;
5478 *Fetzer, Antje* Auferstanden ins Kerygma?: Rudolf BULTMANNs existentiale Interpretation der Auferstehung. Die Wirklichkeit. 2002 ⇒ 302. 1-30/v-xvi/221-235/93-110.
5479 **Frosini, Giordano** La risurrezione inizio del mondo nuovo. Teologia viva 42: 2001 ⇒17,5097. ᴿEstTrin 36 (2002) 381-382 (*Pikaza, Xabier*).
5480 *Hoover, Roy W.* Realities and illusions: resurrection and life after death. FORUM n.s. 3 (2002) 277-306.
5481 *Jonge, Henk Jan de* Visionary experience and the historical origins of christianity. ᶠLAMBRECHT, J.: BEThL 165: 2002 ⇒72. 35-53.
5482 *Kendel, André* "Die Historizität der Auferstehung ist bis auf weiteres vorauszusetzen": Wolfhart PANNENBERGs Verständnis der Auferstehung und seine Bewertung der einschlägigen biblischen Überlieferungen. Die Wirklichkeit. 2002 ⇒302. 2002 139-163.
5483 *Kirby, Peter* The case against the empty tomb. JHiC 9/2 (2002) 175-202.
5484 **Kowalski, Th.** Les témoins de la résurrection de Jésus: du tombeau vide à l'ascension; Les apparitions de reconnaissance. Cahiers de l'École Cathédrale 51: P 2002, Parole et S. 130 pp. €12.50. 2-84573-09-2-6.
5485 ᴱ**Longenecker, R.N.** Life in the face of death: the resurrection message of the New Testament. 1998 ⇒14,252... 16,5103. ᴿRBLit (2002)* (*Van der Watt, Jan G.*).
5486 **Lorenzen, T.** Resurrección y discipulado: modelos interpretativos, reflexiones bíblicas y consecuencias teológicas. ᵀTosaus Abadía, José Pedro: 1999 ⇒15,5080... 17,5104. ᴿCTom 129 (2002) 187-189 (*Rodríguez, Eliseo*).
5487 **Lüdemann, Gerd; Özen, Alf** La resurrección de Jesús: historia, experiencia, teología. ᵀTosaus, José-Pedro: 2001 ⇒17,5106. ᴿActBib 38/1 (2002) 54-55; CTom 129 (2002) 194-197 (*González Blanco, Rafael*).
5488 ᴱ**Mainville, Odette; Marguerat, Daniel L.** Résurrection: l'après-mort dans le monde ancien et le Nouveau Testament. Le monde de la Bible 45: 2001 ⇒17,296. ᴿRHPhR 82 (2002) 192-93 (*Grappe, Ch.*).
5489 ᴱ**Mantovani, Piera Arata** Gesù: inchiesta sulla sua morte e sulla sua risurrezione. Mondo della bibbia 62 (2002) 3-50.
5490 *McDonald, Ian* Resurrection narratives in pastoral perspective. ET 113 (2002) 219-223.
5491 **Meynet, Roland** Morto e risorto secondo le scritture. Collana biblica: Bo 2002, EDB 133 pp. €8.50. 88-10-22118-4.
5492 *Miggelbrink, Ralf* Der Glaube an die Auferstehung der Toten im Kontext der Gegenwart .LebZeug 57 (2002) 178-189.
5493 *Munteanu, Daniel* Die universale Bedeutung der Auferstehung Christi in der Orthodoxie: die neopatristische SyntheseDumitru STANILO-AEs. Die Wirklichkeit. 2002 ⇒302. 121-138.
5494 *Myllykoski, Matti* What happened to the body of Jesus?. ᶠRÄISÄNEN, H.: NT.S 103: 2002 ⇒97. 44-82.
5495 *Navone, John* Il mistero pasquale. RdT 43 (2002) 165-180.

5496 *Oberdorfer, Bernd* "Was sucht ihr den Lebendigen bei den Toten?":
      Überlegungen zur Realität der Auferstehung in Auseinandersetzung
      mit Gerd Lüdemann. Die Wirklichkeit. 2002 ⇒302. 165-182.
5497 *Pilhofer, Peter* Die Auferstehung Jesu: Bemerkungen zu einer über-
      flüssigen Debatte. Die frühen Christen. WUNT 145: 2002 ⇒225. 92-
      105.
5498 *Rese, Martin* Exegetische Anmerkungen zu G. Lüdemanns Deutung
      der Auferstehung Jesu. ^FLAMBRECHT, J.: BEThL 165: 2002 ⇒72.
      55-71.
5499 *Rey, Bernard* Le défi de la foi en la résurrection. LV(L) 253 (2002)
      7-14.
5500 *Sawicki, Marianne* Catechesis and resurrection. Die Wirklichkeit.
      2002 ⇒302. 77-91.
5501 **Schmid, Johannes Heinrich** Die Auferweckung Jesu aus dem Grab.
      2000 ⇒17,5121. ^REvTh(VS) 1/2 (2002) 97-99 (*Blocher, Henri*).
5502 *Schüle, Andreas* Gottes Handeln als Gedächtnis: Auferstehung in kul-
      turtheoretischer und biblisch-theologischer Perspektive. Die Wirk-
      lichkeit. 2002 ⇒302. 237-275.
5503 **Simonis, Walter** Auferstehung und ewiges Leben?: die wirkliche
      Entstehung des Osterglaubens. Dü 2002, Patmos 151 pp. 3-491-703-
      45-X.
5504 *Standaert, Benoît* Raconter la résurrection: une paradoxe narratif.
      ^FLAMBRECHT, J.: BEThL 165: 2002 ⇒72. 73-91.
5505 *Thomas, Günter* "Er ist nicht hier!": die Rede vom leeren Grab als
      Zeichen der neuen Schöpfung. Die Wirklichkeit. 2002 ⇒302. 183-
      220.
5506 *Tissot, Yves* Redécouvrir le tombeau vide. LV(L) 253 (2002) 41-54.
5507 *Tolstoy, Margie* Woman as witness in a post-holocaust perspective.
      A shadow of glory. 2002 ⇒347. 117-127.
5508 *Vollenweider, Samuel* Ostern—der denkwürdige Ausgang einer Kri-
      senerfahrung. Horizonte. WUNT 144: 2002 <1993> ⇒257. 105-123.
5509 **Wedderburn, Alexander J.M.** Beyond resurrection. 1999 ⇒15,
      5098...17,5124. ^RBiblInterp 10 (2002) 215-7 (*Longenecker, Bruce*).
5510 *Welker, Michael* Die Wirklichkeit der Auferstehung. Die Wirklich-
      keit. 2002 ⇒302. 311-331.
5511 *Willems, Gerard F.* Dura-Europos en de oudste voorstellingen van
      Jezus' verrijzenis. KeTh 53 (2002) 125-138.
5512 **Winling, Raymond** La résurrection et l'exaltation du Christ dans la
      littérature de l'ère patristique. Théologies: 2000 ⇒16,5116; 17,5125.
      ^RTheoforum 33 (2002) 243-244 (*Provencher, Normand*).
5513 *Wright, N.T.* Jesus' resurrection and christian origins. Gr. 83 (2002)
      615-635.
5514 *Zeller, Dieter* Erscheinungen Verstorbener im griechisch-römischen
      Bereich. ^FLAMBRECHT, J.: BEThL 165: 2002 ⇒72. 1-19.

5515 *Denaux, Adelbert* Matthew's story of Jesus' burial and resurrection
      (Mt 27,57-28,20). ^FLAMBRECHT, J.: BEThL 165: 2002 ⇒72. 123-45.
5516 *Leicht, Barbara D.* Frauen am Grab: Matthäus 28,1-10: April—
      Ostern. zwölfmal bibel. 2002 ⇒1087. 40-45.
5517 *Sieg, Franciszek* Ewangelista Mateusz o zmartwychwstaniu Jezusa
      (Mt 28,1-10.16-20) [The evangelist Matthew on the resurrection of
      Jesus (Mt 28,1-10.16-20)]. StBob 2 (2002) 5-23 Sum. 23. **P**.

5518 *Weren, Wim J.C.* "His disciples stole him away" (Mt 28,13): a rival interpretation of Jesus' . ^FLAMBRECHT, J.: BEThL 165: 2002 ⇒72. 147-163.

5519 *Abromeit, Hans-Jürgen* "Alle Tage!": Predigt über Matthäus 28,16-20. ThBeitr 33 (2002) 113-116.

5520 *Grilli, Massimo* Das Testament des Auferstandenen: Untersuchung zu Mt 28,16-20. Vom Text zum Leser. SBS 193: 2002 ⇒299. 79-103.

5521 *Stuhlmacher, Peter* Zur missionsgeschichtlichen Bedeutung von Mt 28,16-20. Biblische Theologie. WUNT 146: 2002 <1999> ⇒245. 88-118.

F6.1 Evangelium Marci—*Textus, commentarii*

5522 *Achtemeier, Paul J.* Invitation to Mark. Invitation to the gospels. 2002 ⇒4694. 107-210.

5523 **Babut, Jean-Marc** Actualité de Marc. P 2002, Cerf 342 pp.

5524 *Bagni, Arcangelo* Il vangelo secondo Marco. CredOg 131-132 (2002) 7-27.

5525 ^E**Billon, Gérard** Jésus selon saint Marc. DosB 94 (2002) 3-30.

5526 **Black, C. Clifton** Mark: images of an apostolic interpreter. Studies on personalities of the N.T.: ^Z2001 <1994> ⇒17,5137. ^RLASBF 52 (2002) 567-571 (*Casalini, Nello*).

5527 **Blount, Brian K.; Charles, Gary W.** Preaching Mark in two voices. LVL 2002, Westminster 273 pp. $25. 0-664-22393-1.

5528 **Boismard, Marie-Émile** L'évangile de Marc: sa préhistoire. EtB 26: 1995 ⇒10,4740... 15,5108. ^RIst. 47 (2002) 410-411.

5529 **Broadhead, Edwin K.** Mark. 2001 ⇒17,5139. ^RRBLit (2002)* (*Malbon, Elizabeth Struthers*).

5530 **Buetow, Harold A.** Thirst for life: St Mark meditations: homilies for weeks 1 through 9 of ordinary time. NY 2002, Alba xlvii; 222 pp. $16. 0-8189-0930-7.

5531 *Collins, Adela Yarbro* Markusevangelium. RGG 5. 2002 ⇒796. 842-846.

5532 **Cuvillier, Elian** L'évangile de Marc. Bible en face: P 2002, Bayard 324 pp. €23. 2-227-47089-8.

5533 **Donahue, John R.; Harrington, Daniel** The gospel of Mark. Sacra Pagina 2: ColMn 2002, Liturgical xv; 488 pp. $40. 0-8146-5804-0. Bibl. 50-57. ^RScrB 32 (2002) 111-112 (*Boxall, Ian*); PhilipSac 37 (2002) 396-397 (*Ofilada, Macario*); LASBF 52 (2002) 561-564 (*Casalini, Nello*).

5534 **Dowling, Edward T.** Have you heard the good news?: reflections on the Sunday gospels, cycle B. NY 2002, Alba xiii; 192 pp. $13. 0-81-89-0926-9.

5535 **Edwards, James R.** The gospel according to Mark. Pillar NT Commentary: GR 2002, Eerdmans xxvi; 552 pp. $40. 0-85111-778-3. ^RRExp 99 (2002) 107-109 (*Vinson, Richard B.*).

5536 **Evans, Craig A.** Mark 8:27-16:20. 2001 ⇒17,5142. ^RCTJ 37 (2002) 346-348 (*Deppe, Dean*).

5537 **France, Richard Thomas** The gospel of Mark: a commentary on the Greek text. The New International Greek Testament Commentary (NIGTC). GR 2002, Eerdmans xxxvii; 719 pp. $55. 0-8028-2446-3. Bibl. xvii-xxxvii. ^RLASBF 52 (2002) 564-567 (*Casalini, Nello*).

5538 **Francis, Leslie J.; Atkins, Peter** Exploring Mark's gospel: an aid for readers and preachers using Year B of the Revised Common Lectionary. L 2002, Continuum 248 pp. £13.

5539 **Geddert, Timothy J.** Mark. 2001 ⇒17,5143. ᴿRExp 99 (2002) 109-110 (*Vinson, Richard B.*).

5540 **Liew, Tat-Siong Benny** Politics of parousia: reading Mark inter-(con)textually. BiblInterp. 42: 1999 ⇒15,5126. ᴿCBQ 64 (2002) 583-584 (*Barta, Karen A.*).

      Linden, N. ter The story goes...Mark's story 1999 ⇒5089.

5541 **Malbon, Elizabeth Struthers** Hearing Mark: a listener's guide. Harrisburg, PA 2002, Trinity xi; 114 pp. $13. 1-56338-379-9.

5542 **Marcus, Joel** Mark 1-8. AncB 27: 2000 ⇒16,5137; 17,5149. ᴿInterp. 56 (2002) 90, 92 (*Dowd, Sharyn*); JThS 53 (2002) 191-196 (*Telford, W.R.*).

5543 **Mateos, Juan; Camacho, Fernando** El evangelio de Marcos: análisis lingüístico y comentario exegético II. 1993 ⇒16,5140. ᴿEstB 60 (2002) 125-128 (*Rodríguez Ruiz, M.*) [Mk 6,7-10,31].

5544 **Moloney, Francis** The gospel of Mark: a commentary. Peabody 2002, Hendrickson xviii; 398 pp. $30. 1-56563-682-1. Bibl. 363-384 [RB 110,477].

5545 ᴱ**Oden, Thomas C.; Hall, Christopher Alan** Evangelio según San Marcos. La Biblia comentada por los Padres de la Iglesia, NT 2: 2000 ⇒16,5142; 17,5154. ᴿRTLi 36 (2002) 119-122 (*Kraft Auchter, Tomás*).

5546 **Paciorek, Antoni** Ewangelie synoptyczne, 3: ewangelia według św. Marka. Academica 57: Tarnów 2002, Biblos 164 pp. ᴿAtK 138 (2002) 634-636 (*Eckmann, Augustyn*).

5547 **Pellegrini, Silvia** Elija—Wegbereiter des Gottessohnes: eine textsemiotische Untersuchung im Markusevangelium. Herders Biblische Studien 26: 2000 ⇒16,5143. ᴿThLZ 127 (2002) 181-184 (*Schenk, Wolfgang*).

5548 **Pronzato, Alessandro** Nunca hemos visto nada semejante: comentario al evangelio de Marcos. S 2002, Sígueme 315 pp.

5549 **Reichert, Jean-Claude** Catéchèse pour temps de rupture: lecture initiatique de l'évangile de Marc. P 2002, Bayard 160 pp. €21. 2-227-47127-1 [RB 110,477].

5550 **Reid, Stephen Robert** Preaching Mark. 1999 ⇒16,5144. ᴿCTJ 37 (2002) 411-415 (*Overduin, Nick*).

5551 *Rius-Camps, Josep* Les variants del text occidental de l'evangeli de Marc (X) (Mc 6,6b-31). RCatT 27 (2002) 185-202;

5552 (XI) (Mc 6,32-52). RCatT 27 (2002) 451-464.

5553 **Runacher, Caroline** Saint Marc. 2001 ⇒17,5155. ᴿRICP 82 (2002) 213-215 (*Berder, Michel*).

5554 *Ruysschaert, Tine* 'Lezer, let goed op!': rond de vertaling van het Markusevangelie door Frans Van Bladel—een gesprek met Tine Ruysschaert. Streven 69 (2002) 501-506.

5555 **Sabin, Marie Noonan** Reopening the word: reading Mark as theology in the context of early Judaism. NY 2002, OUP xx; 294 pp. $50. 0-19-514359-0. Bibl. 263-275.

5556 **Sacchi, Alessandro** Un vangelo per i lontani: come leggere Marco. 1999 ⇒15,5136; 16,5146. ᴿTer. 53 (2002) 279-280 (*Pasquetto, Virgilio*).

5557 **Schnackenburg, Rudolf** Vangelo secondo Marco. Guide spirituali del Nuovo Testamento: R ²2002 <1969>, Città Nuova 469 pp. €29. ᴿCivCatt 153/4 (2002) 419-420 (*Scaiola, D.*).

5558 **Soares, Sebastião A.rmando Gameleira; Correia, João Luiz** Evangelho de Marcos, 1: 1-8. Comentario Bíblico/NT: Petrópolis 2002, Vozes 300 pp.

5559 **Stock, Klemens** Vangelo secondo Marco: introduzione e commento. Lectio divina popolare: Padova 2002, Messagero 227 pp [AcBib 10, 1032].

5560 *Suhl, Alfred* Das Evangelium nach Markus: eine Einführung. BiHe 38 (2002) 36-39.

5561 **Thurston, Bonnie Bowman** Preaching Mark. Fortress Resources for Preaching: 2001 ⇒17,5156. ᴿCTJ 37 (2002) 411-5 (*Overduin, Nick*).

5562 **Trainor, Michael F.** The quest for home: the household in Mark's community. 2001 ⇒17,5157. ᴿCBQ 64 (2002) 780-781 (*Osiek, Carolyn*).

5563 **Trocmé, Étienne** L'Evangile selon saint Marc. 2000 ⇒16,5150; 17, 5158. ᴿScEs 54 (2002) 129-131 (*Bonneau, Guy*).

5564 *Vironda, Marco* La trama di Marco: la manifestazione segreta del Figlio di Dio. CredOg 131-132 (2002) 29-65.

5565 **Witherington, Ben** The gospel of Mark: a socio-rhetorical commentary. 2001 ⇒17,5160. ᴿTrinJ 23 (2002) 129-132 (*Bayer, Hans F.*); CBQ 64 (2002) 399-400 (*Thomas, Carolyn*); SWJT 45/1 (2002) 74-76 (*Wicker, Jim*); ThLZ 127 (2002) 918-919 (*Pokorný, Petr*).

F6.2 *Evangelium Marci,* Themata

5566 *Aichele, George* The Son of Man and the sons of men. ᶠPATTE, D. 2002 ⇒89. 311-323.

5567 *Bauer, Dieter* Nicht Quantität, sondern Qualität: vom Umgang mit der Zeit im Markusevangelium. BiHe 38 (2002) 43-45.

5568 *Bedenbender, Andreas* Neue Beobachtungen zum Markusevangelium. TeKo 25/1 (2002) 17-98 [Mk 6,30-9,10].

5569 *Bobertz, Charles A.* Prolegomena to a ritual/liturgical reading of the gospel of Mark. ᶠGREER, R. 2002 ⇒51. 174-187.

5570 *Castro Sánchez, Secundino* La misión en Marcos. REsp 61 (2002) 355-390.

5571 *Cuvillier, Élian* Die "Kreuzestheologie" als Leseschlüssel zum Markusevangelium. Kreuzestheologie. WUNT 151: 2002 ⇒298. 107-50.

5572 *Danove, Paul L.* A rhetorical analysis of Mark's construction of discipleship. Rhetorical criticism. JSNT.S 195: 2002 ⇒369. 280-296.

5573 **Dawson, Anne** Freedom as liberating power: a socio political reading of the ἐχουσία texts in the gospel of Mark. NTOA 44: 2000 ⇒16, 5166; 17,5177. ᴿBZ 46 (2002) 133-134 (*Scholtissek, Klaus*); CBQ 64 (2002) 567-568 (*Witherup, Ronald D.*).

5574 *Ebner, Martin* Kreuzestheologie im Markusevangelium. Kreuzestheologie. WUNT 151: 2002 ⇒298. 151-168.

5575 **Feneberg, Rupert** Der Jude Jesus und die Heiden: Biographie und Theologie Jesu im Markusevangelium. 2000 ⇒16,5173; 17,5186. ᴿLebZeug 57 (2002) 65-66 (*Petzel, Paul*); CrSt 23 (2002) 490-494 (*Dautzenberg, Gerhard*).

5576 **Fenton, John** More about Mark. 2001 ⇒17,5188. ᴿNBl 83 (2002) 207-208 (*Viviano, Benedict Thomas*).

5577 *Focant, Camille* Vers une maison de prière pour toutes les nations (Mc 11-15). RTL 33 (2002) 3-27.
5578 *Franco, Ettore* Le scritture d'Israele nel vangelo secondo Marco. CredOg 131-132 (2002) 137-148.
5579 *Garcia, José Miguel* Per la storicità dei vangeli: miracoli e risurrezione di Gesù secondo Marco. Nuovo Areopago 21/3-4 (2002) 73-83.
5580 **Geyer, Douglas W.** Fear, anomaly, and uncertainty in the gospel of Mark. ATLA.MS 47: Lanham 2002, Scarecrow Pr. xi; 340 pp. $58. 0-8108-4202-5. Bibl. 303-327.
5581 *Gicnolo, Roberto* I titoli cristologici nel vangelo di Marco. CredOg 131-132 (2002) 67-88.
5582 *Gundry, Robert H.* A rejoinder to Joel F. Williams's 'Is Mark's gospel an apology for the cross?'. BBR 12 (2002) 123-139.
5583 **Hanson, James S.** The endangered promises: conflict in Mark. SBL.DS 171: 2000 ⇒16,5175. [R]RBLit 4 (2002) 361-363 (*Dowd, Sharyn*).
5584 **Harrington, Wilfred** John Mark: realistic theologian: the Jesus of Mark. Dublin [2]2002 <1996>, Columba 150 pp. €12. 1-85607-390-4. Bibl. 148-149.
5585 **Hatina, Thomas R.** In search of a context: the function of scripture in Mark's narrative. JSNT.S 232; Studies in scripture in early Judaism and Christianity 8: Shf 2002, Sheffield Academic xii; 428 pp. £65. 0-8264-6067-4.
5586 *Hatton, Stephen B.* The gospel of Mark as comedy. DR 120 (2002) 33-56.
5587 *Heckel, Theo K.* Der Gekreuzigte bei Paulus und im Markusevangelium. BZ 46 (2002) 190-204.
5588 *Hensell, Eugene* Discouragement viewed through Mark's gospel. RfR 61 (2002) 522-534.
5589 **Herranz Marco, Mariano; García Pérez, José Miguel** Milagros y resurrección de Jesús según San Marcos. Studia Semitica Novi Testamenti 8: 2001 ⇒17,5191. [R]VyV 60 (2002) 192-193 (*Sanz Valdivieso, Rafael*).
5590 *Hieke, Thomas* Literatur setzt Literatur voraus: das Alte Testament im Markusevangelium. BiHe 38 (2002) 51-53.
5591 *Hofrichter, Peter Leander* Zur Komposition des Markusevangeliums auf der Grundlage des Hellinistenbuches. Priorität. 2002 ⇒561. 161-181.
5592 **Horsley, Richard A.** Hearing the whole story: the politics of plot in Mark's gospel. 2001 ⇒17,5192. [R]JSNT 85 (2002) 126-127 (*Kelhoffer, James A.*); CTJ 37 (2002) 348-351 (*Overduin, Nick*); CBQ 64 (2002) 576-577 (*Liew, Tat-siong Benny*); ET 113 (2002) 306-308 (*McDonald, J. Ian*).
5593 **Jaśko, Andrzej** Gesù e la sua famiglia: contributo allo studio del discepolato nel contesto della parentela con Gesù nel vangelo di Marco. R 2002, 191 pp. Diss. Angelicum 2001.
5594 *John, V.J.* Literary structure of Mark and the concerns of ecology: search for a connection. BiBh 28 (2002) 521-545.
5595 **John, V.J.** The ecological vision of Jesus: nature in the parables of Mark. Thiruvalla 2002, Christava Sahitya Samithy 408 pp. Rs150. [R]BiBh 28 (2002) 682-685 (*Thaikkattil, Saijo*).
5596 *Kampling, Rainer* Das Gesetz im Markusevangelium. Im Angesicht. SBB 47: 2002 <1995> ⇒189. 21-52 [Mk 7; 10; 12,28-34].

5597 *Katz, Paul* Wie einer der Propheten?: das biblische Markusevangelium als Darbietung eines 'Vorevangeliums'. ThZ 58 (2002) 46-60.

5598 *Kingsbury, Jack Dean* 'God' within the narrative world of Mark. ᶠACHTEMEIER, P. 2002 ⇒1. 75-89.

5599 **Klumbies, Paul-Gerhard** Der Mythos bei Markus. BZNW 108: 2001 ⇒17,5200. ᴿETR 77 (2002) 592-593 (*Gloor, Daniel A.*); ThLZ 127 (2002) 1187-1188 (*Lührmann, Dieter*).

5600 *Leinhäupl-Wilke, Andreas* Jünger, Gegner, Frauen ... Figurenkonstellationen im Markusevangelium. BiHe 38 (2002) 48-50.

5601 *Leonardi, Giovanni* Le cristologie degli altri vangeli a confronto con quella di Marco. CredOg 131-132 (2002) 149-162.

5602 **MacDonald, Dennis Ronald** The Homeric epics and the gospel of Mark. 2000 ⇒16,5180; 17,5204. ᴿJThS 53 (2002) 196-198 (*Hooker, Morna D.*); RBLit 4 (2002) 363-367 (*Hock, Ronald F.*); RBLit (2002)* (*Gilmour, Michael*).

5603 **Malbon, Elizabeth Struthers** In the company of Jesus: characters in Mark's Gospel. 2000 ⇒16,5182; 17,5206. ᴿJThS 53 (2002) 199-202 (*Bolt, Peter G.*); BiblInterp 10 (2002) 203-208 (*Telford, W.R.*); JR 82 (2002) 618-619 (*Darr, John A.*).

5604 **Malina, Artur** Gli scribi nel vangelo di Marco: studio del loro ruolo nella sua narrazione e teologia. ᴰ*Stock, Klemens*: Katowice 2002, Wydawnictwo Uniwersytetu Slaskiego 322 pp. €35. 83-226-1206-0. Diss. Pont. Ist. Biblico 2001; Bibl. 285-312.

5605 *Matjaž, Maksimilijan* Wegmetaphorik im Markusevangelium. Bogoslovni vestnik 62 (2002) 175-186 Sum. 186.

5606 *Mazzucco, Clementina* I miracoli e la fede. CredOg 131-132 (2002) 101-118.

5607 *Meyer, Marvin W.* Taking up the cross and following Jesus: discipleship in the gospel of Mark. CTJ 37 (2002) 230-238.

5608 **Moeser, Marion C.** The anecdote in Mark, the classical world and the rabbis. JSNT.S 227: L 2002, Sheffield A. x; 288 pp. £55. 0-8264-6059-3. Bibl 258-275 [Mk 8,27-10,45].

5609 *Monari, Luciano* Il discepolato e i discepoli nella narrazione marciana. CredOg 131-132 (2002) 89-100.

5610 **Mpevo Mpilo, Aimé** Genre, sens, position et fonction littéraire des récits marciens de surdi-mutité et cécité (Mc 7,31-37; Mc 8,22-26; Mc 9,14-29; Mc 10,46-52): critique de rédaction et analyse structurelle. ᴰ*Buetubela, P.*: 2002 Diss. Kinshasa [RTL 34,599].

5611 *Myers, Ched* Mark's gospel: invitation to discipleship. NT: introducing. 2002 ⇒332. 40-61.

5612 **Naluparayil, Jacob Chacko** The identity of Jesus in Mark: an essay on narrative christology. SBFA 49: 2000 ⇒16,5191; 17,5214. ᴿCDios 215 (2002) 672-673 (*Gutiérrez, J.*); ThLZ 127 (2002) 760-762 (*Müller, Peter*); CBQ 64 (2002) 587-588 (*Watts, Rikki E.*); JJSS 2 (2002) 123-126 (*Ammanathukunnel, K.*).

5613 *Navarro Puerto, Mercedes* Cruzando fronteras, rompiendo estructuras: estudio narrativo del itinerario de María de Nazareth en Mc. EphMar 52/2 (2002) 191-224.

5614 **Palachuvattil, Joy** "He saw": the significance of Jesus' seeing denoted by the verb εἰδεν in the gospel of Mark. TGr.T 84: R 2002, E. P.U.G. 307 pp. $19. 88-7652-918-7. Bibl. 277-296.

5615 **Peterson, Dwight N.** The origins of Mark: the Markan community in current debate. BiblInterp 48: 2000 ⇒16,5196. ᴿRBLit 4 (2002) 367-369 (*Evans, Craig A.*).

5616 *Quelle, Constantino* Las tentaciones de Jesús: perspectiva de Marcos. BiFe 84 (2002) 362-385 [Mk 1,13].

5617 *Quiñones Benítez, Raúl Arturo* El significado de la casa en el evangelio según Marcos. Qol 30 (2002) 109-112.

5618 *Raja, A. Maria Arul* Breaking hegemonic boundaries: an intertextual reading of Madurai Veeran legend and Mark's story of Jesus. BiBh 28 (2002) 546-557.

5619 **Reiser, William** Jesus in solidarity with his people: a theologian looks at Mark. 2000 ⇒16,5204; 17,5224. ᴿScrB 32 (2002) 112-113 (*Boxall, Ian*).

5620 **Rhoads, David; Dewey, Joanna; Michie, Donald** Marcos como relato: introducción a la narrativa de un evangelio. ᵀ*Martín Vegas, Rosa Ana*: Biblioteca de estudios bíblicos 104: S 2002, Sígueme 222 pp. €14. 84-301-1471-8.

5621 *Robbins, Vernon K.* The intertexture of apocalyptic discourse in the gospel of Mark. Intertexture. SBL.Symp. 14: 2002 ⇒385. 11-44.

5622 **Rolin, Patrice** Les controverses dans l'évangile de Marc. ÉtB 43: 2001 ⇒17,5226. ᴿThLZ 127 (2002) 1192-1194 (*Weiß, Wolfgang*).

5623 **Rowe, Robert D.** God's kingdom and God's son: the background to Mark's christology from concepts of kingship in the psalms. AGJU 50: Lei 2002, Brill xvii; 435 pp. €109. 90-04-11888-8. Diss. London Bible College 1990; Bibl. 315-367.

5624 *Scholtissek, Klaus* "Augen habt ihr und seht nicht und Ohren habt ihr und hört nicht?" (Mk 8,18): Lernprozesse der Jünger Jesu im Markusevangelium. ᶠFUCHS, A. 2002 ⇒41. 191-222 [Mk 8,14-21].

5625 *Smith, C. Drew* "This is my beloved son; listen to him": theology and christology in the gospel of Mark. HBT 24/2 (2002) 53-86.

5626 *Stuckenbruck, Loren T.* 'Spiritual formation' and the gospel according to Mark. ExAu 18 (2002) 80-92.

5627 **Suk, Won Sik** Erzählte Welt und erfahrbare Wirklichkeit: zu den Heilungen und Exorzismen Jesu im Markusevangelium. ᴰ*Lindemann, Andreas*: 2002 Diss. Bethel [ThRv 99/2,v].

5628 *Trocmé, Étienne* How to get people moving: Mark and its readers. ᶠPATTE, D. 2002 ⇒89. 271-276.

5629 *Tuckett, Christopher* The disciples and the messianic secret in Mark. ᶠRÄISÄNEN, H.: NT.S 103: 2002 ⇒97. 131-149.

5630 **Van Oyen, Geert** The interpretation of the feeding miracles in the gospel of Mark. CBRA 4: 1999 ⇒15,5208; 17,5236. ᴿEstB 60 (2002) 415-417 (*Urbán, Á.*) [Mk 6,30-44; 8,1-9].

5631 **Vines, Michael E.** The problem of Markan genre: the gospel of Mark and the Jewish novel. Academia biblica 3: Lei 2002, Brill x; 220 pp. $30. 90-04-12693-7. Bibl. 165-205.

5632 **Watts, Rikki E.** Isaiah's new exodus in Mark. 2000 ⇒13,5106...17, 5240. ᴿCTJ 37 (2002) 131-133 (*Overduin, Nick*).

5633 *Wellmann, Bettina* Licht aus, Spot an!: die Schauplätze des Markusevangeliums. BiHe 38 (2002) 40-42.

5634 *Williams, Joel F.* Is Mark's gospel an apology for the cross?. BBR 12 (2002) 97-122.

5635 **Wördemann, Dirk** Das Charakterbild im bios nach PLUTARCH und das Christusbild im Evangelium nach Markus. SGKA.Mon. 19: Pd 2002, Schöningh 309 pp. €59. 3-506-79069-2.

F6.3 Evangelii Marci versiculi

5636 *Samuel, Simon* The beginning of Mark: a colonial/postcolonial conundrum. BiblInterp 10 (2002) 405-419 [Mk 1,1].

5637 *Klingbeil, Gerald A.* "Up, down, in, out, through and back": space and movement in Old Testament narrative, ritual and legal texts and their application for the study of Mark 1:1-3:12. EstB 60 (2002) 283-309.

5638 *Guijarro Oporto, Santiago* ¿Por qué comienza así el evangelio de Marcos?. [F]TREVIJANO ETCHEVERRÍA, R. 2002 ⇒122. 133-151 [Mk 1,1-15].

5639 *Loader, William* Good news—for the earth?: reflections on Mark 1.1-15. Earth story. 2002 ⇒322. 28-43.

5640 *DeMaris, Richard E.* Die Taufe Jesu im Kontext der Ritualtheorie. Jesus in neuen Kontexten. 2002 ⇒602. 43-52 [Mk 1,9-11];

5641 The baptism of Jesus: a ritual-critical approach. The social setting. 2002 ⇒601. 137-157 [Mk 1,9-11].

5642 *Kotecki, Dariusz* "Nawracjacie sie i wierzcie w Ewangelie (Mk 1,15) —fundament zycia chrześcijańskiego. CoTh 72/3 (2002) 33-53 [Mt 16,15-16]. **P.**

5643 *Greger, Barbara* הלך אהרי und die Folgen. BN 111 (2002) 23 [Mk 1, 17].

5644 **Peron, Gian Paolo** Seguitemi!: vi farò diventare pescatori di uomini (Mc 1,17): gli imperativi ed esortativi di Gesù ai discepoli come elementi di un loro cammino formativo. 2000 ⇒16,5226; 17,5249. [R]Ter. 53 (2002) 281-283 (*Pasquetto, Virgilio*).

5645 *Landgrave G., Daniel R.* La curación de la suegra de Pedro: Mc 1, 29-31//Mt 8,14-15//Lc 4,38-39 (una meditación bíblica). Qol 28 (2002) 61-67.

5646 *Fournier, Alain* De la communauté à la distance: deux récits de l'évangile de Marc. SémBib 106 (2002) 3-11 [Mk 1,29-31; 4,35-41].

5647 *Carrón Pérez, Julián* Curación de un leproso: la extraña ira de Jesús (Mc 1,40.43). [F]TREVIJANO ETCHEVERRÍA, R. 2002 ⇒122. 153-171.

5648 *Landgrave Gándara, Daniel* La purificación de un leproso (Mc 1,40-45): implicationes sociales del proyecto de Jesús: un análisis exegético-teológico. EfMex 20 (2002) 361-396.

5649 *López Villanueva, Mariola* Tocar al leproso: Mc 1,40-45: una aproximación al ministerio de la compasión. EE 77 (2002) 115-139.

5650 *Esselbach, Anne* Horizontalité / verticalité: deux dimensions de l'espace pour une mise en discours de la foi: une lecture sémiotique de Mc 2,1-12: la guérison du paralytique. SémBib 108 (2002) 21-37.

5651 *Derrett, J. Duncan M.* The teacher as physician: Mark 2,17 and Milindapañha vi.6. BeO 44 (2002) 43-55.

5652 *Klinghardt, Matthias* Boot und Brot: zur Komposition von Mk 3,7-8, 21. BThZ 19 (2002) 183-202.

5653 **Rüegger, Hans-Ulrich** Verstehen, was Markus erzählt: philologisch-hermeneutische Reflexionen zum Übersetzen von Markus 3,1-6. WUNT 2/155: Tü 2002, Mohr S. (10) 167 pp. 3-16-1477892-4. Bibl. 133-156.

5654 *Stasiak, Slawomir Jan* Controversia in Galilea e guarigione dell'uomo con la mano inaridita (analisi sincronica di Mc 3,1-6). Anton. 77 (2002) 617-647.

5655 *Rabuske, Irineu J.* O programa de Jesus: amarrar of forte satanás (Mc 3,20-30). Estudos bíblicos 74 (2002) 88-95.

5656 **Schlaepper, Carlos Frederico** A dinâmica da casa em Marcos 3,20-35: estar dentro ou fora como sinal da tensão entre unidade e divisão. ᴰ*Mazzarolo, Isidoro*: 2002 Diss. Pont. Univ. Católica, Rio de Janeiro [REB 64,492s].

5657 *Guijarro, Santiago* Die politische Wirkung der Exorzismen Jesu: gesellschaftliche Reaktionen und Verteidigungsstrategien in der Beelzebul-Kontroverse. Jesus in neuen Kontexten. 2002 ⇒602. 64-74 [Mk 3,22-27];

5658 The politics of exorcism. The social setting. 2002 ⇒601. 159-174 [Mk 3,22-27].

5659 *Malina, Artur* Ewangelia a bluźnierstwo przeciw Duchowi Świętemu (Mk 3,29; 12,40) [The gospel and blasphemy against the Holy Spirit (Mk 3,29: 12,40)]. Verbum Vitae 2 (2002) 109-126 Som. 126. **P.**

5660 *Fontana, Andrea* Marco 4: il mistero del regno compreso da chi accoglie Gesù. CredOg 131-132 (2002) 119-135.

5661 *Meza, Ramón* La citación de Isaías 6,9-10 en Marcos 4,12. RevBib 63 (2001) 47-71.

5662 **I Made Miasa, Kristinus** Paura e fede in Mc 4,35-41. ᴰ*Biguzzi, G.*: 2002, 150 pp. Diss. Urbaniana [RTL 34,598].

5663 *Maluleke, Tinyiko S.* The graveyardman, the "escaped convict" and the girl-child: a mission of awakening, an awakening of mission: bible study. IRM 91 (2002) 550-557 [Mk 5].

5664 **Correia, João Luiz** O poder de Deus em Jesus: um estudo de duas narrativas de milagres em Mc 5,21-43. Bíblia e História: 2000 ⇒16, 5247. ᴿREB 62 (2002) 727-729 (*Cavalcanti, Tereza Maria*).

5665 *Silva R., Santiago* Jesús, liberador de Israel: Mc 5,21-43. Revista Católica 102 (2002) 293-296.

5666 *Duran, Nicole Wilkinson* Return of the disembodied: how John the Baptist lost his head. ᶠPATTE, D. 2002 ⇒89. 277-291 [Mk 6,14-29].

5667 *Sacchi, Paolo* Marco 7: Gesù e la nuova concezione dell'impurità. CredOg 131-132 (2002) 179-198.

5668 *Untergaßmair, Franz Georg* Jesus und die jüdische Gesetzestradition im Lichte urchristlicher Interpretation (Mk 7,1-13). FUCHS, A. 2002 ⇒41. 175-190.

5669 **Svartvik, Jesper** Mark and mission: Mk 7:1-23 in its narrative and historical contexts. CB.NT 32: 2000 ⇒16,5256; 17,5277. ᴿJR 82 (2002) 98-99 (*Park, Eung Chun*); CBQ 64 (2002) 180-181 (*Maloney, Elliott C.*); BiblInterp 10 (2002) 452-455 (*Marcus, Joel*) {Mark}07,01-23; BBR 12 (2002) 290-292 (*Chilton, Bruce*); Bib. 83 (2002) 281-284 (*Fleddermann, Harry T.*); RBLit 4 (2002) 369-371 (*Evans, Craig A.*).

5670 *Rudolph, David J.* Jesus and the food laws: a reassessment of Mark 7:19b. EvQ 74 (2002) 291-311.

5671 *Rosik, Mariusz* Jesus and the daughter of the Syro-Phoenician woman (Mk 7,24-30): the raising to the dignity of God's child. STV 40/2 (2002) 139-145.

5672 *Zani, Lorenzo* Gesù stesso supera le preferenze con la donna sirofenicia. Presbyteri 36 (2002) 183-194 [Mk 7,24-30].

5673 *Delorme, Jean* Pas de signe pour cette génération (Mc 8:11): une sémiotique implicite dans le second évangile. ᶠPATTE, D. 2002 ⇒89. 98-110.

5674 *Loraschi, Celso* E não tinham senão um pão com eles mesmos: a incompreensão dos discípulos em Mc 8,14-21. Estudos bíblicos 75 (2002) 61-76.

5675 *Guttenberger, Gudrun* Why Caesarea Philippi of all sites?: some reflections on the political background and implications of Mark 8:27-30 for the christology of Mark. Zwischen den Reichen. TANZ 36: 2002 ⇒568. 119-131.

5676 *Theißen, Gerd* Wer ist Christus?: wer ist ein Christ?: Versuch einer Maximal- und Minimaldefinition (Mk 8,27-30). Erlösungsbilder. 2002 ⇒1460. 86-89.

5677 *Pérez Rodríguez, Gabriel* Estructura y mensaje de Mc 8,31-10,52. ᶠTREVIJANO ETCHEVERRÍA, R. 2002 ⇒122. 173-189.

5678 *Lambrecht, Jan* A note on Mark 8.38 and Q 12.8-9. JSNT 85 (2002) 117-125.

5679 *Souza Nogueira, Paulo Augusto de* Visionary elements in the transfiguration narrative. Apocalyptic. JSPE.S 43: 2002 ⇒373. 142-150 [Mk 9,2-8].

5680 *Kasiłowski, Piotr* Przemienienie Jezusa (Mk 9,2-9) [The Transfiguration of Jesus (Mk 9,2-9)]. StBob 2 (2002) 25-44 Sum. 44. **P.**

5681 **Ansaldi, Jean; Cuvillier, Elian** Il fut transfiguré devant eux: une oasis rafraîchissante sur le chemin de la foi. Poliez-le-Grand 2002, Moulin 90 pp. €10.37. 2-88469-010-7 [Mk 9,2-10].

5682 **Brandt, Pierre-Yves** L'identité de Jésus et l'identité de son disciple: le récit de la transfiguration comme clef de lecture de l'Évangile de Marc. ᴰ*Gemünden, P. von*: NTOA 50: Gö 2002, Vandenhoeck & R. xviii; 365 pp. FS108. 3-525-53951-7. Diss. Geneva 2001; Bibl. 347-365 [Mk 9,2-10].

5683 *Aitken, James K.* The proposed Aramaic background to Mark 9:11. JThS 53 (2002) 75-80.

5684 *Printz, Othon* Quelques réflexions sur l'épilepsie à partir des récits de la guérison de l'enfant épileptique: Marc 9,14-29 et les récits parallèles de Matthieu 17,14-21 et Luc 9,37-43. RHPhR 82 (2002) 391-400.

5685 *Cargal, Timothy B.* 'If your salt should become non-salt' (Mark 9:33-50): exclusion in an inclusive community. ᶠPATTE, D. 2002 ⇒89. 134-146.

5686 *Stowasser, Martin* διάκονος πάντων: eine Untersuchung zur ekklesialen Intention von Mk 9,33-50. BZ 46 (2002) 48-70.

5687 *Lambrecht, Jan* Scandal and salt: is Mark dependent on Q in 9,42-50?. ᶠFUCHS, A. 2002 ⇒41. 223-234.

5688 *Long, Timothy M.S.* Mark 10:1-12 and marriage, divorce and remarriage in South Africa today. Neotest. 36 (2002) 1-19.

5689 *Ebner, Martin* 'Kinderevangelium' oder markinische Sozialkritik?: Mk 10,13-16 im Kontext. JBTh 17 (2002) 315-336.

5690 *Janse, S.* Kinderzegening en kinderdoop: over de ecclesiologische implicaties van Mar. 10:13-16 par. ThRef 45/3 (2002) 242-255.

5691 *Schwankl, Otto* Machtwille und Dienstbereitschaft: zur Jüngerbelehrung in Mk 10,35-45. ᶠFUCHS, A. 2002 ⇒41. 235-257.

5692 *Silva R., Santiago* Jesús y las condiciones del seguimiento: Mc 10,35-52. Revista Católica 102 (2002) 297-313.

5693 *Stone, C.F.* Allusion to Isa 11.10 LXX in Mark 10.42b. NTS 48 (2002) 71-83.

5694 *Ntumba Kapambu, Valentin* 'Mon Maître, que je voie!': lecture narrative de Mc 10,46-52. RASM 17 (2002) 5-22.

5695 *Brown, Scott G.* Mark 11:1-12:12: a triple intercalation?. CBQ 64 (2002) 78-89.

5696 **Chávez, Emilio G.** The theological significance of Jesus' temple action in Mark's gospel. TST 87: Lewiston 2002, Mellen (16), v; 250 pp. $110. 0-7734-7141-3. Diss. Angelicum; Bibl. 189-219. [R]LASBF 51 (2001) 419-422 (*Bissoli, G.*) [Mk 11,15-17].

5697 *Kloppenborg Verbin, John S.* Egyptian viticultural practices and the citation of Isa 5:1-7 in Mark 12:1-9. NT 44 (2002) 134-159;

5698 Ideology and ideological readings of the parable of the tenants. BCSBS 61 (2001-2002) 5-24 [Mk 12,1-12].

5699 *Kozar, Joseph V.* Complementary insight: a scribe's approval of the 'most important' commandment in Mark 12:28-34. ProcGLM 22 (2002) 35-45.

5700 *Mazza, Roberta* "Vale più di tutti gli olocausti e i sacrifici": considerazioni intorno a Mc 12,33. ASEs 19 (2002) 23-42.

5701 *Cronjé, Schalk W.* The false Christs of Mark 13: the theios aner ("divine man") contention: can it be that in refutation of such a heresy Mark wrote his gospel?: if not, what then?. APB 13 (2002) 66-96.

5702 *Dyer, Keith D.* When is the end not the end?: the fate of earth in biblical eschatology (Mark 13). Earth story. 2002 ⇒322. 44-56.

5703 *Malina, Bruce J.* Exegetical eschatology, the peasant present and the final discourse genre: the case of Mark 13. BTB 32 (2002) 49-59.

5704 *Béré, Paul* 'What wonderful stones!'—a historical grounding of Mk 13:1-2. Hekima Review 28 (2002) 35-49.

5705 **Villota Herrero, Salvador** 'Palabras sin ocaso': estudio lingüístico-semántico sobre el valor interpretativo de Mc 13,28-37. Extr. Diss. Pont. Ist. Biblico. [D]*Stock, Klemens*: R 2002, E.P.I.B. 105 pp. Sum. AcBib 10,1093-1097; Bibl. 79-99.

F6.8 Passio secundum Marcum, 14,1...[F5.3]

5706 *Loza Vera, José* Pasión y resurrección de Jesús según Marcos. Qol 30 (2002) 31-54.

5707 **O'Brien, Kelli** The use of scripture in the Markan passion narrative. [D]*VanderKam, J.*: 2001, 353 pp. Diss. Notre Dame [RTL 34,600].

5708 **Pérez Herrero, Francisco** Pasión y pascua de Jesús según san Marcos. 2001 ⇒17,5308. [R]Cart. 18 (2002) 558-559 (*Sanz Valdivieso, R.*); ThX 52 (2002) 730-733 (*Escalante Molina, Luis Alfredo*); EstB 60 (2002) 548-550 (*Sánchez Navarro, Luis*).

5709 *Theis, Joachim* Die Passionsgeschichte nach Markus als religionspädagogische Aufgabe. RPäB 49 (2002) 17-32.

5710 *Butting, Klara* Die Salbung in Betanien—ein Liebesgedicht: Markus 14,3-11. JK 63/1 (2002) 54-56.

5711 *Frey, Jörg* Leidenskampf und Himmelsreise: das Berliner Evangelienfragment (Papyrus Berolinensis 22220) und die Gethsemane-Tradition. BZ 46 (2002) 71-96 [Mk 14,32-42].

5712 *Garuti, Paolo* Manus iniecerunt: dalla variante marciana ἐπέβαλον τὰς χεῖρας αὐτῷ (Mc 14,46) ad una possibile allusione al diritto romano volgarizzato nei racconti d'arresto neotestamentari. Ang. 79 (2002) 513-536.

5713 **Borrell, Augustí** The good news of Peter's denial: a narrative and rhetorical reading of Mark 14:54.66-72. 1998 ⇒14,4808...17,5319. ᴿRivBib 50 (2002) 98-103 (*Grasso, Santi*).

5714 **Bock, Darrell L.** Blasphemy and exaltation in Judaism and the final examination of Jesus: a philological-historical study of the key Jewish themes impacting Mark 14:61-64. WUNT 2/106: 1998 ⇒16, 5306; 17,5318. ᴿEvQ 74 (2002) 74-75 (*France, R.T.*).

5715 *Dannemann, Irene* The slave woman's challenge to Peter. ᶠSCHOT-TROFF, L. 2002 ⇒111. 53-57 [Mk 14,66-72].

5716 *Seitz, Erich* Das rätselhafte ἐπιβαλὼν: zu Mk 14,72. SNTU.A 27 (2002) 199-211.

5717 *Whitters, Mark F.* Why did the bystanders think Jesus called upon Elijah before he died (Mark 15:34-36)?: the Markan position. HThR 95 (2002) 119-124.

5718 *Kampling, Rainer* Henker—Zeuge—Bekenner?: Fragen zur Auslegung von Mk 15,39. Im Angesicht. SBB 47: 2002 <1993> ⇒189. 3-20.

5719 **Hanhart, Karel** Het open graf: Marcus' nieuwe versie van de opstanding. Zoetermeer 2002, Meinema 268 pp. €25. 90-211-3874-3 [ITBT 11/1,29—Hoet, Hendrik].

5720 *Hall, Stuart* How did Mark end?: an alternative. Theol. 105 (2002) 45-46. *John Fenton* replies 47s.

5721 *Bauer, Dieter* ... und alle Fragen offen?: der Schluss des Markuse-vangeliums. BiHe 38 (2002) 54-55 [Mk 16,1-8].

5722 *Cuvillier, Elian* La résurrection dans l'évangile de Marc, ou: la finale courte... et puis avant?. Quand la bible se raconte. 2002 ⇒355. 105-122 [Mk 16,1-8].

5723 *Dettwiler, Andreas* Le mystère de la résurrection: considérations thé-ologiques à propos de Marc 16,1-8. ᶠHAMMANN, G. 2002 ⇒57. 139-150 [BuBB 38,113].

5724 *Pérez Herrero, Francisco* Mc 16,1-8: un final que es el verdadero comienzo del evangelio. ᶠTREVIJANO ETCHEVERRÍA, R. 2002 ⇒122. 191-206.

5725 *Focant, Camille* Un silence qui fait parler (Mc 16,8). ᶠDELOBEL, J.: BEThL 16: 2002 ⇒24. 79-96.

5726 *Hall, Stuart G.* How did Mark end?: an alternative. Theol. 105 (2002) 45-48 [Mk 16,8-20].

5727 **Burgon, John William** The last twelve verses of Mark: vindicated against recent critical objectors & established. Collingswood, NJ 2002 <1871>, Dean Burgon Society 350 pp. $15 [Mk 16,9-20].

5728 **Kelhoffer, James A.** Miracle and mission: the authentication of missionaries and their message in the longer ending of Mark. WUNT 2/112: 2000 ⇒16,8316. ᴿCBQ 64 (2002) 167-168 (*Bridge, Steven L.*) [Mk 16,9-20].

5729 *Manicardi, Ermenegildo* La 'finale lunga' del vangelo secondo Marco: Mc 16,9-20: un altro testo. CredOg 131-132 (2002) 163-177.

5730 *Frey, Jörg* Zu Text und Sinn des Freer-Logion. ZNW 93 (2002) 13-34 [Mk 16,14].

X. Opus Lucanum

F7.1 *Opus Lucanum*—Luke-Acts

5731 **ᴱLeonardi, Giovanni; Trolese, Francesco G.B.** San Luca evangelista testimone della fede che unisce: atti del congresso internazionale,
Padova, 16-21 ottobre 2000: vol 1: l'unità letteraria e teologica
dell'opera di Luca (Vangelo e Atti degli apostoli). FRSEP 28: Padova
2002, Istituto per la Storia Ecclesiastica Padovana 637 pp. €50. Bibl.
1980-2000: pp 585-615.

5732 **ᴱLevine, Amy-Jill** A feminist companion to Luke. FCNT 2: Shf
2002, Sheffield A. 261 pp. $18. 1-84127-174-8 [BiTod 40,331—
Senior, Donald].

5733 *Barbi, Augusto* La morte di Gesù e la condanna del giusto nell'opera
lucana. RStB 14/1-2 (2002) 209-234 [Lk 23,47; Acts 3,14; 7,52; 22,
14].

5734 *Baum, Armin Daniel* Die lukanische und die chronistische Quellen-
benutzung im Vergleich: eine Teilanalogie zum synoptischen Problem. EThL 78 (2002) 340-357.

5735 *Betori, Giuseppe* L'unità letteraria e narrativa di Luca-Atti: indicazi-
oni dalla struttura. San Luca evangelista. FRSEP 28: 2002 ⇒5731.
71-93.

5736 *Bloomquist, L. Gregory* The intertexture of Lukan apocalyptic discourse. Intertexture. SBL.Symposium 14: 2002 ⇒385. 45-68;

5737 The role of the audience in the determination of argumentation: the
gospel of Luke and the Acts of the Apostles. Rhetorical argumentation. 2002 ⇒553. 157-173.

5738 **Bonz, Marianne Palmer** The past as legacy: Luke-Acts and ancient
epic. 2000 ⇒16,5321; 17,5332. ᴿRBLit 4 (2002) 374-378 (*Young,
George W.*); JBL 121 (2002) 178-181 (*Young, George W.*).

5739 **Böhm, Martina** Samarien und die Samaritai bei Lukas: eine Studie
zum religionshistorischen und traditionsgeschichtlichen Hintergrund
der lukanischen Samarientexte und zu deren topographischer Verhaf-
tung. WUNT 2/111: 1999 ⇒15,5319; 17,5333. ᴿJSJ 33 (2002) 94-97
(*Dexinger, F.*); ZRGG 54 (2002) 80-81 (*Beltz, Walter*); RBLit 4
(2002) 372-374 (*Morton, Russell*) [Lk 9,1-56; 10,25-37; 17,11-19;
Acts 8,4-25].

5740 *Bucher, Otto* The gospel for the first-century world. BiTod 40 (2002)
159-165.

5741 **Cadbury, Henry J.** The making of Luke-Acts. 1999 <1927, 1958>
⇒15,5322; 16,5326. ᴿOCP 68 (2002) 251-253 (*Farrugia, E.G.*).

5742 *Carroll, John T.* The God of Israel and the salvation of the nations:
the gospel of Luke and the Acts of the Apostles. ꜰACHTEMEIER, P.
2002 ⇒1. 191-106.

5743 **Cho, Young-Mo** Spirit and kingdom in the writings of Luke and
Paul. ᴰ*Clarke, A.D.*: 2002 Diss. Aberdeen [RTL 34,596].

5744 **Crump, David** Jesus the intercessor: prayer and christology in Luke-
Acts. 1999 <1992> ⇒15,5326. ᴿCTJ 37 (2002) 333-337 (*Deppe,
Dean B.*).

5745 *Curkpatrick, Stephen* 'Real and fictive' widows: nuances of independence and resistance in Luke. LexTQ 37/4 (2002) 215-224 [BuBB 38,129].

5746 *D'Angelo, Mary Rose* The ἀνήρ question in Luke-Acts: imperial masculinity and the deployment of women in the early second century. A feminist companion to Luke. FCNT: 2002 ⇒5732. 44-69.

5747 *De Virgilio, Giuseppe* L'impiego di 'evangelizzare' (εὐαγγελίζεσθαι) nell'opera di Luca;

5748 *Fabris, Rinaldo* Lo scopo principale dell'opera di Luca (Lc-At). San Luca evangelista. FRSEP 28: 2002 ⇒5731. 283-297/55-70.

5749 **Fletcher-Louis, Crispin H.T.** Luke-Acts: angels, christology and soteriology. WUNT 2/94: 1997 ⇒13,5226... 15,5335. ᴿEvQ 74 (2002) 361-363 (*Marshall, I. Howard*).

5750 **Fusco, Vittorio** Da Paolo a Luca: studi su Luca-Atti, 1. StBi 124: 2000 ⇒16,5333; 17,5337. ᴿVivH 13/1 (2002) 194-195 (*Tarocchi, Stefano*).

5751 **Ganser-Kerperin, Heiner** Das Zeugnis des Tempels: Studien zur Bedeutung des Tempelmotivs im Lukanischen Doppelwerk. NTA 36: 2000 ⇒16,5334; 17,5338. ᴿBZ 46 (2002) 134-137 (*Müller, Christoph G.*).

5752 *Giurisato, Giorgio* 'Ho deciso di scrivere con ordine' (Lc 1,3): struttura del vangelo di Luca e degli Atti degli Apostoli. San Luca evangelista. FRSEP 28: 2002 ⇒5731. 219-242.

5753 *Gregory, Andrew* The reception of Luke and Acts in the period before IRENAEUS. TynB 53 (2002) 153-156.

5754 **Heil, John Paul** The meal scenes in Luke-Acts: an audience-oriented approach. SBL.MS 52: 1999 ⇒15,5342. ᴿCBQ 64 (2002) 161-162 (*Karris, Robert J.*).

5755 **Heusler, Erika** Kapitalprozesse im Lukanischen Doppelwerk: die Verfahren gegen Jesus und Paulus in exegetischer und rechtshistorischer Analyse. NTA 38: 2000 ⇒16,5341. ᴿThLZ 127 (2002) 1184-1186 (*Böttrich, Christfried*); RBLit 4 (2002) 296-299 (*Skinner, Matthew L.*); JBL 121 (2002) 181-183 (*Skinner, Matthew L.*).

5756 *Hill, Craig C.* Restoring the kingdom to Israel: Luke-Acts and christian supersessionism. A shadow of glory. 2002 ⇒347. 185-200.

5757 **Janzen, Anna** Der Friede im lukanischen Doppelwerk vor dem Hintergrund der Pax Romana. EHS.T 752: Fra 2002, Lang 296 pp. 3-631-50395-4.

5758 *Kampling, Rainer* Erinnernder Anfang: eine bibeltheologische Besinnung zur Relevanz der lukanischen Kirchenkonzeption für eine christliche Israeltheologie. Im Angesicht. SBB 47: 2002 <1996> ⇒ 189. 239-259.

5759 *Karris, Robert J.* Women and discipleship in Luke;

5760 *Koperski, Veronica* Women and discipleship in Luke 10.38-42 and Acts 6.1-7: the literary context of Luke-Acts. A feminist companion to Luke. FCNT: 2002 ⇒5732. 23-43/161-196.

5761 *Leonardi, Giovanni* Congresso internazionale su San Luca evangelista e il vol. degli atti: "L'unità letteraria e teologica dell'opera" (Padova 2000-02). StPat 49 (2002) 693-709;

5762 *Comunità destinatarie dell'opera di Luca e identità dell'autore;*

5763 *Bibliografia scelta sull'opera di Luca (Vg ed At) 1980-2000. San Luca evangelista. FRSEP 28: 2002 ⇒5731. 187-215/585-615.

5764 **Leppä, Heikki Tapio** Luke's critical use of Galatians. 2002 Diss. Helsinki [StTh 57,78].

5765 *Levine, Amy-Jill* Introduction. A feminist companion to Luke. FCNT: 2002 ⇒5732. 1-22.
5766 *Meiser, Martin* Lukas und die römische Staatsmacht. Zwischen den Reichen. TANZ 36: 2002 ⇒568. 175-193.
5767 *Meynet, Roland* Composito o composto?: contributo dell'analisi retorica allo studio del vangelo di Luca: qualche esempio. San Luca evangelista. FRSEP 28: 2002 ⇒5731. 243-253.
5768 **Mount, Christopher** Pauline christianity: Luke-Acts and the legacy of Paul. NT.S 104: Lei 2002, Brill x; 207 pp. €92/$79. 90-04-12472-1. Diss. Chicago; Bibl. 181-195.
5769 **Müller, Christoph Gregor** Mehr als ein Prophet: die Charakterzeichnung Johannes des Täufers im lukanischen Erzählwerk. Herders Bibl. Studien 31: 2001 ⇒17,5353. ᴿBZ 46 (2002) 278-280 (*Bendemann, Reinhard von*); SNTU.A 27 (2002) 222-224 (*Fuchs, Albert*).
5770 **Nave, Guy D.** The role and function of repentance in Luke Acts. Academia biblica 4: Lei 2002, Brill viii; 241 pp. $33. 90-04-12694-5. Bibl. 227-241.
5771 **Neagoe, Alexandru** The trial of the gospel: an apologetic reading of Luke's trial narratives. ᴰ*Turner, Max*: MSSNTS 116: C 2002, CUP xiv; 253 pp. $60. 0-521-80948-7. Diss. Brunel 1998; Bibl. 228-242.
5772 **Nielsen, Anders E.** Until it is fulfilled: Lukan eschatology according to Luke 22 and Acts 20. WUNT 2/126: 2000 ⇒16,5357. ᴿThLZ 127 (2002) 295-297 (*Bendemann, Reinhard von*).
5773 **Orth, Burkhard** Lehrkunst im frühen Christentum: die Bildungsdimension didaktischer Prinzipien in der hellenistisch-römischen Literatur und im lukanischen Doppelwerk. Beiträge zur Erziehungswissenschaft und biblischen Bildung 7: Fra 2002, Lang 336 pp. €50.10. 3-631-39507-8. Diss. Kiel.
5774 **Owczarek, Krzysztof** Sons of the Most High: love of enemies in Luke-Acts: teaching and practice. ᴰ*O'Toole, Robert*: Nairobi 2002, Paulines 360 pp. $10. Diss. Gregoriana.
5775 *Panimolle, Salvatore A.* Grazia divina e divinizzazione dell'uomo nel terzo vangelo e negli Atti degli apostoli. DSBP 30 (2002) 102-144.
5776 *Pilhofer, Peter* Lukas als ἀνὴρ Μακεδών: zur Herkunft des Evangelisten aus Makedonien. Die frühen Christen. WUNT 145: 2002 <1999> ⇒225. 106-112;
5777 Was wußte Lukas über das pisidische Antiochien?. Die frühen Christen. WUNT 145 2002 <2000> ⇒225. 113-122 [Acts 13-14].
5778 *Pokorný, Petr* Der Evangelist Lukas und die theologische Bedeutung seines Werkes;
5779 *Rigato, Maria-Luisa* Luca originario giudeo, forse di stirpe levitica, seguace dei 'testimoni oculari' (Lc 1,2-3): una rilettura delle fonti più antiche con riscontri nell'opera di Luca. San Luca evangelista. FRSEP 28: 2002 ⇒5731. 255-264/391-422.
5780 **Sánchez, Héctor** Das lukanische Geschichtswerk im Spiegel heilsgeschichtlicher Übergänge. PaThSt 29: Pd 2002, Schöningh 196 pp. €34.80. 3-506-76279-6.
5781 *Segalla, Giuseppe* Etica ed escatologia futura: escatologia presenziale ed etica nell'opera lucana. San Luca evangelista. FRSEP 28: 2002 ⇒5731. 165-178.
5782 *Speckman, McGlory T.* Healing and wholeness in Luke-Acts as foundation for economic development: a particular reference to ὁλοκληρία in Acts 3:16. Neotest. 36 (2002) 97-109.

5783 *Spinetoli, Ortensio da* Qualche riflessione su 'la salvezza' nell'opera
       lucana (vangelo e Atti). San Luca evangelista. FRSEP 28: 2002 ⇒
       5731. 265-281.
5784 **Stenschke, Christoph W.** Luke's portrait of gentiles prior to their
       coming to faith. WUNT 2/108: 1999 ⇒15,5396...17,5365. [R]CBQ 64
       (2002) 178-179 (*Gowler, David B.*); Missionalia 30 (2002) 475-477
       (*Saayman, Willem*).
5785 *Taylor, Justin* St Luke and Flavius JOSEPHUS. San Luca evangelista.
       FRSEP 28: 2002 ⇒5731. 549-553.
5786 *Tomson, Peter J.* Luke-Acts and the Jewish scriptures. AnBru 7
       (2002) 164-183.
5787 *Tremolada, Pierantonio* Il valore salvifico della morte di Gesù nell'
       opera di s. Luca. San Luca evangelista. FRSEP 28: 2002 ⇒5731.
       179-186.
5788 *Van Zyl, H.C.* The soteriological meaning of Jesus' death in Luke-
       Acts: a survey of possibilities. VeE 23 (2002) 533-557.
5789 *Walton, Steve* The state they were in: Luke's view of the Roman
       empire. Rome in the bible. 2002 ⇒363. 1-41.
5790 *Wilcox, Max* Semitisms in Luke-Acts in the light of the Tobit mss
       from Qumram [!] and the Babatha archive (P. Yadin). San Luca
       evangelista. FRSEP 28: 2002 ⇒5731. 555-565.
5791 **Woods, Edward J.** The 'Finger of God' and pneumatology in Luke-
       Acts. JSNT.S 205: 2001 ⇒17,5369. [R]RTR 61 (2002) 52-53 (*Dum-
       brell, Bill*); ThLZ 127 (2002) 653-654 (*Horn, Friedrich W.*).

F7.3 *Evangelium Lucae*—Textus, commentarii

5792 **Bovon, François** Luke 1: a commentary on the gospel of Luke 1:1-
       9:50. [T]*Thomas, Christine M.*: Hermeneia: Mp 2002, Fortress xxxvi;
       442 pp. $59. 0-8006-6044-7. [R]RBLit (2002)* (*Tannehill, Robert C.*);
5793 El evangelio según San Lucas, 2: (Lc 9,51-14,35). [T]*Ortiz García,
       Alfonso*: S 2002, Sígueme 664 pp. €28.80. 84-301-1405-X. [R]SalTer
       90 (2002) 715-716 (*Sanz Giménez-Rico, Enrique*); Cart. 18 (2002)
       561-562 (*Sanz Valdivieso, R.*); CTom 129 (2002) 658-659 (*González
       Blanco, Rafael*);
5794 L'Évangile selon Saint Luc, 1-3: (Lk 1,1-19,27). Commentaire du
       Nouveau Testament 3a-c: 1991-2001 ⇒7,4439...17,5375/7. [R]RBBras
       19 (2002) 413-415 (*Minette de Tillesse, Gaëtan*).
5795 **Buetow, Harold A.** Rejoicing in hope: St Luke meditations: homilies
       for weeks 22 through 34 of ordinary time. NY 2002, Alba xlix; 344
       pp. $20. 0-8189-0932-3.
5796 **Butler, Trent C.** Luke. Holman NT Commentary: Nv 2000, Holman
       431 pp. $17. [R]RBLit 4 (2002) 378-380 (*Marler, Stephen W.*).
5797 **Craddock, Fred B.** Luca. [E]*Tomasetto, Domenico*: Strumenti—Com-
       mentari 10: T 2002, Claudiana 411 pp. €29.50. 88-7016-432-2. Bibl.
       379-382.
5798 **Decloux, Simon** L'Esprit Saint viendra sur toi: retraite de huit jours
       avec saint Luc. Namur 2002, Fidélité 177 pp. [R]Telema 110-111
       (2002) 122-124 (*Williams, Dhelonga*).
5799 **Gillman, John** Luke: stories of joy and salvation. NY 2002, New
       City 214 pp. $13. 1-56548-173-9 [BiTod 40,401—Senior, Donald.].

5800 **Hendrickx, Herman** The third gospel for the third world, 3-A, B: travel narrative—I-II (Luke 9:51-13:21, 13:22-17:10). 2000 ⇒16, 5390, 5391. ᴿMiss. 30 (2002) 106-107 (*Anderson, Justice*).
5801 ᵀ**Karris, Robert J.** Works of BONAVENTURE, 8/1: commentary on the gospel of Luke: chapters 1-8. 2001 ⇒17,5382. ᴿCBQ 64 (2002) 579-580 (*O'Toole, Robert F.*).
5802 *Karris, Robert J.* Invitation to Luke. Invitation to the gospels. 2002 ⇒4694. 211-324.
5803 **Osculati, Roberto** L'evangelo di Luca. Mi 2002, IPL 286 pp.
5804 *Radl, Walter* Lukasevangelium. RGG 5. 2002 ⇒796. 546-550.
5805 **Riera, Francesc** Jesús de Nazaret, el evangelio de Lucas (1), escuela de justicia y misericordia: una historia de Dios subversiva y fascinante. Bilbao 2002, Desclée de B. 266 pp. €12 [EstJos 57,141— Llamas, Román].
5806 **Shellard, Barbara** New light on Luke: its purpose, sources and literary context. JSNT.S 215: Shf 2002, Sheffield Á. 340 pp. $115. 1-8412-7236-1. ᴿBib. 83 (2002) 586-589 (*Tannehill, Robert C.*); RBBras 19 (2002) 416-417 (*Minette de Tillesse, Gaëtan*).

F7.4 *Lucae themata*—Luke's Gospel, topics

5807 *Baarlink, Heinrich* Jezus als dienaar (Lc 22,27) of als verzoener (Mc 10,45)?: een exegetische speurtocht door het evangelie naar Lucas. GThT 102 (2002) 16-28.
5808 **Bormann, Lukas** Recht, Gerechtigkeit und Religion im Lukasevangelium. StUNT 24: 2001 ⇒17,5376. ᴿOrdKor 43 (2002) 112-113 (*Giesen, Heinz*).
5809 **Byrne, Brendan** The hospitality of God: a reading of Luke's gospel. 2000 ⇒16,5409; 17,5396. ᴿPacifica 15 (2002) 86-88 (*Lawson,Veronica*).
5810 *Derrenbacker, Robert A., Jr.* Greco-Roman writing practices and Luke's gospel: revisiting 'The order of a crank'. Gospels according to Goulder. 2002 ⇒594. 61-83.
5811 *Edwards, James R.* The gospel of the Ebionites and the gospel of Luke. NTS 48 (2002) 568-586.
5812 *Elvey, Anne* Legacies of violence toward the other: toward a consideration of the outsider within the Lukan narrative. Colloquium 34/1 (2002) 21-34.
5813 **Forbes, Greg W.** The God of old: the role of the Lukan parables in the purpose of Luke's gospel. JSNT.S: 198: 2000 ⇒16,5410. ᴿJThS 53 (2002) 205-207 (*Beck, Brian E.*).
5814 *Gorman, Michael M.* Source marks and chapter divisions in BEDE's Commentary on Luke. RBen 112 (2002) 246-290.
5815 **Gourgues, Michel** Luc: de l'exégèse à la prédication. P 2002, Cerf 177 pp [Brotéria 156,404—Silva, I. Ribeiro da].
5816 ᴱ**Gómez-Acebo, Isabel; Navarro Puerto, Mercedes; Pikaza Ibarrondo, Xabier** Relectura de Lucas. En clave de mujer: 1998 ⇒14, 4896. ᴿRelCult 48 (2002) 791-792 (*Moral, Alejandro*).
5817 **Hyères, Sylvie Chabert d'** Des jours de lumière, I: chronologie de la vie de Jésus en Luc; II: Marie, témoin de la Parole en Luc. Sillery (Québec) 1998, Sigier 2 vols; 172 + 154 pp. 2-89129-300-2. ᴿRB 109 (2002) 294-295 (*Boismard, Marie-Émile*).

5818 *Kowalski, Beate* Forschungsgeschichtlicher Überblick: Sprache und Stil des Lukasevangeliums. SNTU.A 27 (2002) 41-83.

5819 **Kurth, Christina** "Die Stimmen der Propheten erfüllt": Jesu Geschick und "die" Juden nach der Darstellung des Lukas. BWANT 148: 2000 ⇒16,5415. ᴿThLZ 127 (2002) 645-647 (*Müller, Peter*).

5820 **LaVerdière, Eugène** Comer en el reino de Dios: los orígenes de la eucaristía en el evangelio de Lucas. ᵀ*Tosaus Abadía, José Pedro*: Sdr 2002, Sal Terrae 229 pp. €18.50. 84-293-1460-1 [RF 246,378—J.A. Irazabal].

5821 **Lee, David** Luke's stories of Jesus: theological reading of gospel narrative and the legacy of Hans FREI. JSNT.S 185: 1999 ⇒15,5455; 16,5416. ᴿRBLit 4 (2002) 384-387 (*McEntire, Mark*).

5822 *Lehtipuu, Outi* The imagery of the Lukan afterworld in the light of some Roman and Greek parallels. Zwischen den Reichen. TANZ 36: 2002 ⇒568. 133-146.

5823 *Lombardi, Michela* Aspetti innovativi della diegesi nel vangelo di Luca. Orpheus 23 (2002) 50-73.

5824 *Oñoro Consuegra, Fidel* Elementos característicos de la pedagogía de Jesús en el evangelio de Lucas. Medellín 28 (2002) 5-49.

5825 *Perroni, Marinella* Le donne e Maria madre di Gesù in Luca. San Luca evangelista. FRSEP 28: 2002 ⇒5731. 115-129.

5826 **Petracca, Vincenzo** Gott und das Geld: die Besitzethik des Lukasevangeliums. ᴰ*Erlemann, Kurt*: 2002 Diss. Wuppertal [ThRv 99/2,xi].

5827 *Poppi, Angelico* Luca e il problema sinottico. San Luca evangelista. FRSEP 28: 2002 ⇒5731. 131-147.

5828 *Reid, Barbara E.* Beyond petty pursuits and wearisome widows: three Lukan parables. Interp. 56 (2002) 284-294 [Lk 13,20-21; 15,8-10; 18,1-8].

5829 *Riesner, Rainer* Versuchung und Verklärung (Lukas 4,11-13; 9,28-36; 10,17-20; 22,39-53 und Johannes 12,20-36). ThBeitr 33 (2002) 197-207.

5830 *Ringe, Sharon H.* Luke's gospel: "good news to the poor" for the non-poor. NT: introducing. 2002 ⇒332. 62-79.

5831 *Tremolada, Pierantonio* Gesù e lo Spirito nel vangelo di Luca: annotazioni esegetiche per *una cristologia secondo lo Spirito*. ScC 130/1 (2002) 117-160.

5832 **Varkey, Saji** 'Den Armen gehört das Reich Gottes': lukanische Impulse für eine Dalit-Theologie. ᴰ*Ritt, Hubert*: 2002 Diss. Regensburg [ThRv 99,349].

5833 **Zovkić, Mato** Isus u evanđelju po Luki. Biblioteka Radovi 5: Sarajevo 2002, Vrhbosanska katolička teologija 557 pp. **Serbo-Croatian**.

F7.5 *Infantia, cantica*—**Magnificat, Benedictus: Luc. 1-3**

5834 *Álvarez Frías, Emilio* Los anuncios del ángel. BiFe 82 (2002) 78-105.

5835 **Coleridge, Mark** Nueva lectura de la infancia de Cristo: la narrativa como cristología en Lucas 1-2. ᵀ*Valiente, J.*: 2000 ⇒16,5439; 17,5425. ᴿEE 77 (2002) 166-168 (*Ramírez Fueyo, Francisco*).

5836 **García Pérez, José Miguel; Herranz Marco, Mariano** La infancia de Jesús según san Lucas. 2000 ⇒16,5441. ᴿBeO 44 (2002) 57-58 (*Stramare, Tarcisio*); CBQ 64 (2002) 373-374 (*Phillips, Thomas E.*).

5837 *Kampling, Rainer* "Gepriesen sei der Herr, der Gott Israels": zur Theozentrik von Lk 1-2. Im Angesicht. SBB 47: 2002 <1996> ⇒189. 53-83.

5838 *Serra, Aristide* 'Maria conservava tutte queste cose' (Lc 2,19: cfr. 2,51b): la madre di Gesù, fonte di informazione per l'evangelo dell'infanzia?: scrittura e tradizione a confronto. San Luca evangelista. FRSEP 28: 2002 ⇒5731. 425-438.

5839 *Valentini, Alberto* I cantici di Lc 1-2 nel contesto dell'opera lucana. San Luca evangelista. FRSEP 28: 2002 ⇒5731. 367-389.

5840 *Kahl, Brigitte* Reading Luke against Luke: non-uniformity of text, hermeneutics of conspiracy and the 'scripural principle' in Luke 1. A feminist companion to Luke. FCNT: 2002 ⇒5732. 70-88.

5841 *Aune, David E.* Luke 1.1-4: historical or scientific *prooimion?*. ᶠWEDDERBURN, A:. JSNT.S 217: 2002 ⇒132. 138-148.

5842 *Moessner, David P.* DIONYSIUS's narrative 'arrangement' (οἰκονομία) as the hermeneutical key to Luke's re-vision of the 'many.' ᶠWEDDER-BURN, A.: JSNT.S 217: 2002 ⇒132. 149-164 [Lk 1,1-4].

5843 *Fornberg, Tord* The annunciation: a study in reception history. NT as reception. JSNT.S 230: 2002 ⇒360. 157-180 [Lk 1,26-38].

5844 *Theißen, Gerd* Das Erlösungsprojekt: die Suche nach einer Sprache des Himmels (Lk 1,26-38). Erlösungsbilder. 2002 ⇒1460. 90-96.

5845 *Wiegard, Jesaja Michael* Ein Hauch von Himmel: Lukas 1,26-38: Mai—Marienmonat. zwölfmal bibel. 2002 ⇒1087. 48-57.

5846 *Cernuda, Antonio Vicent* La inquietud de María y las garantías del ángel (Lc 1,34s). Mar. 64 (2002) 113-135.

5847 *Broline, Robert L.* The meeting of Mary and Elizabeth: an eschatological encounter (Luke 1:39-56). Kerux 17/3 (2002) 32-48.

5848 **Ruiz López, Demetria** El Magnificat: un cántico para el tercer milenio. 2000 ⇒16,5451. ᴿSalm. 49 (2002) 212-214 (*Sánchez Caro, J.M.*) [Lk 1,46-55].

5849 *Porter, Stanley E.* The reason for the Lukan census. ᶠWEDDERBURN, A.: JSNT.S 217: 2002 ⇒132. 165-188 [Lk 2,1-5].

5850 *Gergolet, José Luis* Lc 2,1-20: ensayo de análisis narrativo. RevBib 64 (2002) 175-192.

5851 *Van Soom, Willy* Meer dan een geboorteverhaal: Lc 2,1-20. Coll. 32 (2002) 405-427.

5852 *Eltrop, Bettina* Simeon und Hanna: Lk 2,22-40: Dezember—Weihnachten. zwölfmal bibel. 2002 ⇒1087. 132-139.

5853 *Stramare, Tarcisio* Il 'mistero salvifico' della presentazione al tempio e la 'porneia' come idolatria: annotazioni in Lc 2,22-50 e At 15, 20. San Luca evangelista. FRSEP 28: 2002 ⇒5731. 493-503.

5854 *Serra, Aristide M.* "E anche a te una spada trapasserà l'anima": Luca 2,35a alla luce dell'antica tradizione giudaico-cristiana. Mar. 64 (2002) 51-111.

5855 *Christudhas, M.* The passover visit to the temple: a model for leadership in mission (Lk 2:41-52). MissTod 4 (2002) 124-139.

5856 *Grelot, P.* Joseph, père de Jésus. NRTh 124 (2002) 619-29 [Lk 2,48].

5857 *Voulgaris, Christos Sp.* The nature and significance of St. Luke's human genealogy of Jesus Christ. San Luca evangelista. FRSEP 28: 2002 ⇒5731. 567-573 [Lk 3,23-38].

F7.6 Evangelium Lucae 4,1...

5858 *Lefebvre, Philippe* Le Verbe en chair: méditation sur Jésus prêcheur (Lc 4). VS 156 (2002) 789-797.

5859 *Keller, Miguel Ángel* Las tentaciones de Jesús: perspectiva de Lucas. BiFe 84 (2002) 410-438 [Lk 4,1-13].

5860 **Osadare, Philip Oluwabusuyi** The temptation of Jesus in Luke 4,1-13. ᴰ*Biguzzi, G.*: 2002, 258 pp. Diss. Urbaniana [RTL 34,600].

5861 *Rosik, Mariusz; Onwukeme, Victor* Function of Isa 61,1-2 and 58,6 in Luke's programmatic passage (Lk 4,16-30). PJBR 2/1 (2002) 67-82.

5862 *O'Toole, Robert F.* Il giubileo, la 'buona notizia' (Lc 4,18-19) in Luca-Atti oggi: è per tutti, specie per i poveri e gli ultimi. San Luca evangelista. FRSEP 28: 2002 ⇒5731. 151-163.

5863 *Nicklas, Tobias* Das Agraphon vom "Sabbatarbeiter" und sein Kontext: Lk. 6:1-11 in der Textform des Codex Bezae Cantabrigiensis (D). NT 44 (2002) 160-175.

5864 *Berg, David* 'Blessed are they upon God's holy mountain': reflections on Luke 6:17-26. CThMi 29 (2002) 452-455.

5865 *Dillmann, Rainer* Wider die Habsucht und Raffgier der Reichen: syntaktische, semantische und pragmatische Aspekte zur lukanischen Feldrede. Vom Text zum Leser. SBS 193: 2002 ⇒299. 145-162 [Lk 6,20-49].

5866 *Colette, Jacques* La pécheresse et le pardon. RSPhTh 86 (2002) 185-203 [Lk 7].

5867 *Gourgues, Michel* Du centurion de Capharnaüm au centurion de Césarée: Luc 7,1-10 et sa fonction proleptique par rapport à Actes 10,1-11,18. ᶠ*Fuchs, A.*: 2002 ⇒41. 259-270.

5868 ᴱ**Johnson, Steven R.** Documenta Q: reconstructions of Q through two centuries of gospel research: excerpted, sorted, and evaluated: Q 7:1-10: the centurion's faith in Jesus' word. Lv 2002, Peeters xxxv; 418 pp. €70. 2-87723-604-8.

5869 *Harvey, Susan Ashbrook* Why the perfume mattered: the sinful woman in Syriac exegetical tradition. ᶠ*Wilken, R.*: 2002 ⇒136. 69-89 [Lk 7,36-50].

5870 *Hornsby, Teresa J.* The woman is a sinner / the sinner is a woman. A feminist companion to Luke. FCNT: 2002 ⇒5732. 121-132 [Lk 7, 36-50].

5871 *Reid, Barbara E.* 'Do you see this woman?': a liberative look at Luke 7.36-50 and strategies for reading other Lukan stories against the grain. A feminist companion to Luke. FCNT: 2002 ⇒5732. 106-120.

5872 *Baarda, Tjitze* A "non-canonical version" of Luke 7,42B?: the reading τινα [αὐτων] πλειον ἠγαπησεν ascribed to the Diatessaron. ᶠ*Delobel, J.*: BEThL 161: 2002 ⇒24. 97-129.

5873 *Witherington, Ben, III* On the road with Mary Magdalene, Joanna, Susanna, and other disciples-Luke 8.1-3. A feminist companion to Luke. FCNT: 2002 ⇒5732. 133-139.

5874 *Weissenrieder, Annette* Die Plage der Unreinheit?: das antike Krankheitskonstrukt "Blutfluss" in Lk 8,43-48. Jesus in neuen Kontexten. 2002 ⇒602. 75-85;

5875 The plague of uncleanness?: the ancient illness construct 'issue of blood' in Luke 8:43-48. The social setting. 2002 ⇒601. 207-222.

5876   *Stacy, R.W.* Glimpses of glory: Luke 9:28-36. RExp 99 (2002) 71-87.

F7.7   *Iter hierosolymitanum—Lc 9,51...*—**Jerusalem journey**

5877   **Bendemann, Reinhard von** Zwischen ΔΟΧΑ und ΣΤΑΥΡΟΣ: eine
exegetische Untersuchung der Texte des sogenannten Reiseberichts
im Lukasevangelium. BZNW 101: 2001 ⇒17,5462. ᴿThLZ 127
(2002) 171-173 (*Reinmuth, Eckart*).
5878   *Loubser, J.A.* What is biblical media criticism?: a media-critical reading of Luke 9:51-56. Scriptura 80 (2002) 206-219 [NTAb 47,464].
5879   *Allison, Dale C., Jr.* Rejecting violent judgment: Luke 9:52-56 and
its relatives. JBL 121 (2002) 459-478.
5880   *Cadwallader, Alan H.* Swords into ploughshares: the end of war?
(Q/Luke 9.62). Earth story. 2002 ⇒322. 57-75.
5881   *Vollenweider, Samuel* "Ich sah den Satan wie einen Blitz vom Himmel fallen" (Lk 10,18). Horizonte. WUNT 144: 2002 <1988> ⇒257.
71-87.

5882   *Goßmann, Hans C.* Der barmherzige Samariter von Zschopau. JK 63/
6 (2002) 26-28 [Lk 10,25-37].
5883   *Scheffler, E.* Die kommunikasie van die gelykenis van die barmharti-
ge Samaritaan in konteks. HTS 57 (2001) 318-343 [NTAb 46,466]
[Lk 10,25-37].
5884   *Mayemba K.-B., Bienvenu* Pharaon, Josué ou le bon samaritain: quel
salut pour une Afrique en péril?. Telema 110-111 (2002) 51-65 [Lk
10,29-37].
5885   **Pronzato, Alessandro** Sulle tracce del samaritano: pellegrinaggio al
santuario dell'uomo. Mi 2000, Gribaudi 117 pp. 88-7152-566-3 [Lk
10,29-37].
5886   *Esler, Philip F.* Jesus und die Reduzierung von Gruppenkonflikten:
das Gleichnis vom barmherzigen Samaritaner im Rahmen der Theorie der sozialen Identität. Jesus in neuen Kontexten. 2002 ⇒602.
197-211 [Lk 10,29-37];
5887   Jesus and the reduction of intergroup conflict. The social setting.
2002 ⇒601. 185-205 [Lk 10,29-37].
5888   *Alexander, Loveday C.* Sisters in adversity: retelling Martha's story.
A feminist companion to Luke. FCNT: 2002 ⇒5732. 197-213 [Lk
10,38-42].
5889   *Carter, Warren* Getting Martha out of the kitchen: Luke 10.38-42
again. A feminist companion to Luke. FCNT: 2002 ⇒5732. 214-231.
5890   *Ssemakula, Luke* Luke 10:38-42, Martha and Mary: a history of interpretation. African Christian Studies 18/3 (2002) 22-43.
5891   *Thimmes, Pamela* The language of community: a cautionary tale
(Luke 10.38-42). A feminist companion to Luke. FCNT: 2002 ⇒
5732. 232-245.
5892   *Stubbs, John* A certain woman raised her voice: the use of grammatical structure and the origins of texts. Neotest. 36 (2002) 21-37 [Lk
11,27-28].
5893   *Dagron, Alain* Luc 12,7-14. SémBib 105 (2002) 40-49.
5894   *Orr, Mary C.* Luke 12:13-23. Interp. 56 (2002) 314-316.
5895   *Elvey, Anne* Storing up death, storing up life: an earth story in Luke
12.13-24. Earth story. 2002 ⇒322. 95-107.

5896   *Reiser, Marius* Spaßkultur und Todeskultur: das Gleichnis vom reichen Narren (Lk 12,13-34)—damals und heute. EuA 78 (2002) 437-451.

5897   *Gundry, Robert H.* Spinning the lilies and unravelling the ravens: an alternative reading of Q 12.22b-31 and P. Oxy. 655. NTS 48 (2002) 159-180 [Lk 12,22-31].

5898   *Core, Deborah* Who is the faithful steward?: Luke 12.41-45. The lost coin. BiSe 86: 2002 ⇒5282. 196-204.

5899   *Kilgallen, John* The parable of the fig tree (Luke 13,6-9). San Luca evangelista. FRSEP 28: 2002 ⇒5731. 439-449.

5900   *Derrett, J. Duncan M.* Choosing the lowest seat: Lk 14,7-11. EstB 60 (2002) 147-168.

5901   *Dagron, Alain* "Perdu-trouvé": Luc 15,1-32. SémBib 106 (2002) 41-49.

5902   *LaHurd, Carol Schersten* Re-viewing Luke 15 with Arab christian women. A feminist companion to Luke. FCNT: 2002 ⇒5732. 246-268.

5903   *Milne, Douglas J.W.* The father with two sons: a modern reading of Luke 15. Themelios 27/1 (2001) 12-21.

5904   **Troyer, Franz** Gott sucht den Menschen: der Hirte, die Frau und der Vater in Lukas 15 als Metapher für den Gott Jesu Christi. [D]*Hasitschka, Martin*: 2002, 292 pp. Diss. Innsbruck [ThRv 99/2,ix].

5905   *Wolter, Michael* Lk 15 als Streitgespräch. EThL 78 (2002) 25-56.

5906   *Beavis, Mary Ann* 'Making up stories': a feminist reading of the parable of the Prodigal Son (Lk. 15.11b-32). The lost coin. BiSe 86: 2002 ⇒5282. 98-122.

5907   **Contreras Molina, Francisco** Un padre tenía dos hijos. 1999 ⇒15, 5555. [R]EstB 60 (2002) 431-439 (*Urbán, Á.*).

5908   *Crois, Théodossios-Marie de la* Das Gleichnis vom verlorenen Sohn. Una Voce-Korrespondenz 32 (2002) 157-162 [Lk 15,11-32].

5909   **Holgate, David A.** Prodigality, liberality and meanness in the parable of the prodigal son: a Greco-Roman perspective on Luke 15.11-32. JSNT.S 187: 1999 ⇒15,5558; 17,5495. [R]EvQ 74 (2002) 178-179 (*Graham, Gordon*); RBLit 4 (2002) 381-383 (*Thompson, Richard P.*); RBLit (2002)* (*Sheeley, Steven M.*).

5910   *Jean-Gabriel, Frère* Le 'père prodigue': Dieu riche en miséricorde. Carmel 103 (2002) 7-21 [Lk 15,11-32].

5911   *Landmesser, Christof* Die Rückkehr ins Leben nach dem Gleichnis vom verlorenen Sohn (Lukas 15,11-32). ZThK 99 (2002) 239-261.

5912   **Nouwen, H.J.M.** Dalla paura all'amore: riflessioni quaresimali sulla parabola del figliuol prodigo. Brescia 2002, Queriniana 104 pp. €8 [Lk 15,11-32].

5913   *Paz, César Mora* Das Problem von Struktur und Komposition: pragmalinguistische Analyse von Lukas 16. Vom Text zum Leser. SBS 193: 2002 ⇒299. 105-143.

5914   *Lygre, John G.* Of what charges? (Luke 16:1-2). BTB 32 (2002) 21-28.

5915   **Cheong, C.-S. Abraham** A dialogic reading of the steward parable (Luke 16:1-9). Studies in Biblical Literature 28: 2001 ⇒17,5500. [R]CBQ 64 (2002) 566-567 (*Kuhn, Karl A.*).

5916   *Dormandy, Richard* Unjust steward or converted master?. RB 109 (2002) 512-527 [Lk 16,1-13].

5917   *Boismard, Marie-Émile* La parabole de l'intendant infidèle en Lc
       16,1-9: au verset 8, qui est désigné par l'expression 'ho Kyrios'?.
       San Luca evangelista. FRSEP 28: 2002 ⇒5731. 451-454.
5918   *Galvão, Antônio M.* O rico e o pobre: estudo da parábola do rico in-
       sensível e do pobre Lázaro (Lc 16,19-31). REB 62 (2002) 52-77.
5919   *Regalado, Ferdinand O.* The Jewish background of the parable of the
       Rich Man and Lazarus. AJTh 16/2 (2002) 341-348 [Lk 16,19-31].
5920   *Dagron, Alain* "Il n'y a que cet étranger ...": Luc 17,11-19. SémBib
       108 (2002) 39-46.
5921   *Pokorný, Petr* Lukas 17,33parr.—die Geschichte Jesu und ein (da-
       mals) bekanntes Sprichwort. ᶠSCHENKE, H.: NHS 54: 2002 ⇒108.
       387-398.
5922   *Curkpatrick, Stephen* Dissonance in Luke 18:1-8. JBL 121 (2002)
       107-121.
5923   *Weaver, Dorothy Jean* Luke 18:1-8. Interp. 56 (2002) 317-319.
5924   *Matthews, Mary W.; Shelley, Carter; Scheele, Barbara* Proclaiming
       the parable of the persistent widow (Lk. 18.2-5). The lost coin. BiSe
       86: 2002 ⇒5282. 46-70.
5925   *Mußner, Franz* Die Skepsis des Menschensohnes: zu Lk 18,8b.
       ᶠFUCHS, A.: 2002 ⇒41. 271-275.
5926   *Alana, Olu E.* "Today salvation has come to this house ..." (Lk 19:1-
       10). VeE 23 (2002) 1-17.
5927   *Denaux, Adelbert* The parable of the king-judge (Lk 19,12-28) and
       its relation to the entry story (Lk 19,29-44). ZNW 93 (2002) 35-57.
5928   *Derrett, J. Duncan M.* Stones crying out (Luke 19:40). ET 113
       (2002) 187-188.
5929   *Croatto, J. Severino* La elaboración lucana de la alegoría de la viña
       de Isaías 5,1-7 (Lucas 20,9-19). RevBib 64 (2002) 175-192.
5930   *Vulliamy, Brigitte* Luc 20,27-40: sept maris à la résurrection?. Lire et
       Dire 51 (2002) 15-26 [BuBB 39,73].

F7.8 **Passio**—Lc 22...

5931   *Crüsemann, Frank* Schrift und Auferstehung: Beobachtungen zur
       Wahrnehmung des auferstandenen Jesus bei Lukas und Paulus und
       zum Verhältnis der Testamente. KuI 17 (2002) 150-162.
5932   **Matson, Mark A.** In dialogue with another gospel?: the influence of
       the fourth gospel on the passion narrative of the gospel of Luke. SBL.
       DS 178: 2001 ⇒17,5513. ᴿJR 82 (2002) 620-621 (*Trumbower, Jef-
       frey A.*); CBQ 64 (2002) 584-585 (*Patella, Michael*).
5933   **Megbelayin, Ibiolu Oluseyi Jerome** A socio-rhetorical analysis of
       the Lukan narrative of the Last Supper. ᴰ*Bloomquist, G.* 2002, 430
       pp. Diss. Ottawa [RTL 34,599] [Lk 22,7-38].
5934   *Clivaz, Claire* Douze noms pour une main: nouveaux regards sur
       Judas à partir de Lc 22.21-2. NTS 48 (2002) 400-416.
5935   *Montagnini, Felice* Il corollario lucano dell'ultima cena (Lc 22,24-
       38): un abbozzo di ecclesiologia. San Luca evangelista. FRSEP 28:
       2002 ⇒5731. 455-460.
5936   *Tuckett, Christopher M.* Luke 22,43-44: the "agony" in the garden
       and Luke's gospel. ᶠDELOBEL, J.: BEThL 161: 2002 ⇒24. 131-144.
5937   **Harrington, Jay M.** The Lukan passion narrative: the Markan mate-
       rial in Luke 22,54-23,25: a historical survey: 1891-1997. NTTS 30:

2000 ⇒16,5547; 17,5520. ᴿJThS 53 (2002) 202-205 (*Tuckett, C.M.*); CBQ 64 (2002) 763-764 (*Carroll, John T.*).

5938 *Brož, Jaroslav* Le parole di Gesù in croce (Lc 23): compendio della preghiera di Gesù secondo il vangelo di Luca. San Luca evangelista. FRSEP 28: 2002 ⇒5731. 315-326.

5939 *Schreiber, Stefan* "Ars moriendi" in Lk 23,39-43: ein pragmatischer Versuch zum Erfahrungsproblem der Königsherrschaft Gottes. ᶠFUCHS, A. 2002 ⇒41. 277-297.

5940 *Durussel, Michel; Mizzi, Arielle; Roland Korber, Evelyne* Luc 23,54-24,12: Fabienne... contribution à partir d'une improvisation. Lire et Dire 51 (2002) 27-37 [BuBB 39,72].

5941 *Decock, Paul B.* The breaking of bread in Luke 24. Neotest. 36 (2002) 39-56.

5942 *Gillman, John* The Emmaus story in Luke-Acts revisited. ᶠLAM-BRECHT, J.: BEThL 165: 2002 ⇒72. 165-188 [Lk 24].

5943 *Johnson, Andy* Ripples of the resurrection in the triune life of God: reading Luke 24 with eschatological and trinitarian eyes. HBT 24/2 (2002) 87-110;

5944 Our God reigns: the body of the risen Lord in Luke 24. WaW 22 (2002) 133-143.

5945 *Marion, Jean-Luc* "They recognized him; and he became invisible to them". MoTh 18 (2002) 145-152 [Lk 24].

5946 *Read-Heimerdinger, Jenny; Rius-Camps, Josep* Emmaous or Oulam-maous?: Luke's use of the Jewish scriptures in the text of Luke 24 in Codex Bezae. RCatT 27/1 (2002) 23-42 Sum. 42.

5947 *Vinzent, Markus* Der Schluß des Lukasevangeliums bei MARCION. Marcion. 2002 ⇒578. 79-94 [Lk 24].

5948 *Seim, Turid Karlsen* Conflicting voices, irony and reiteration: an exploration of the narrational structure of Luke 24:1-35 and its theological implications. ᶠRÄISÄNEN, H.: NT.S 103: 2002 ⇒97. 151-164.

5949 *Rigato, Maria-Luisa* "'Remember" ... then they remembered': Luke 24.6-8. A feminist companion to Luke. FCNT: 2002 ⇒5732. 269-80.

5950 *Neirynck, Frans* Luke 24,12: an anti-docetic interpolation?. ᶠDELO-BEL, J.: BEThL 161: 2002 ⇒24. 145-158.

5951 *Reece, Steve* Seven stades to Emmaus. NTS 48 (2002) 262-266 [Lk 24,13-35].

5952 *Reymond, Sophie* Une histoire sans fin: les pèlerins d'Emmaüs (Luc 24,13-35). Quand la bible se raconte. 2002 ⇒355. 123-141.

5953 *Phillips, Jane E.* On the road to Emmaus: ERASMUS' paraphrase of Luke 24:27. ERSY 22 (2002) 68-80.

5954 *Meynet, Roland* "Commençant à partir de Jérusalem, vous êtes les témoins de cela!" (l'annonce du kérygme aux nations en Lc 24,33b-53). StMiss 51 (2002) 1-22.

5955 *Grasso, Santi* Fattori ermeneutici per la codificazione delle parole del risorto all'interno del vangelo lucano (24,36-43.44-49). San Luca evangelista. FRSEP 28: 2002 ⇒5731. 299-313.

5956 *Prete, Benedetto* 'Aprì loro la mente all'intelligenza delle scritture' (Lc 24,45). San Luca evangelista. FRSEP 28: 2002 ⇒5731. 461-475.

5957 *Mekkattukunnel, Andrews George* The priestly blessing of the risen Lord in Lk 24,50-53. BiBh 27 (2002) 346-373.

5958 **Mekkattukunnel, Andrews George** The priestly blessing of the risen Christ: an exegetico-theological analysis of Luke 24,50-53. EHS.T 714: 2001⇒17,5528. ᴿLASBF 51 (2001) 422-426 (*Chrupcała, L.D.*).

F8.1 *Actus Apostolorum*, **Acts**—*text, commentary, topics*

5959   Atos dos Apóstolos. RCB 43 (2002) 49-111.
5960   *Aletti, Jean-Noël* Świadkowie zmartwychwstałego: Duch Święty i
       świadectwo w Dziejach Apostolskich [Witnesses of the resurrected
       Christ: the Holy Spirit and witness in the Acts of the Apostles]. Ver-
       bum Vitae 2 (2002) 127-149 Sum. 149. **P**.
5961   *Asso, Philippe* Raconter pour persuader: discours et narration des
       Actes des Apôtres. RSR 90 (2002) 555-571.
5962   **Avemarie, Friedrich** Die Tauferzählungen der Apostelgeschichte:
       Theologie und Geschichte. *DHengel, Martin*: WUNT 139: Tü 2002,
       Mohr S. xii: 546 pp. €104. 3-16-147639-5. Diss.-Habil. 2000; Bibl.
       479-515. RRHPhR 82 (2002) 236-237 (*Grappe, Ch.*).
5963   *Barbi, Augusto* Koinonia, soluzione dei conflitti e rapporti tra chiese:
       un aspetto dell'ecclesiologia degli Atti. San Luca evangelista. FRSEP
       28: 2002 ⇒5731. 95-113.
5964   **Barrett, Charles Kingsley** The Acts of the Apostles: a shorter com-
       mentary. E 2002, Clark xc; 434 pp. 0-567-08817-0.
5965   *Bartchy, S. Scott* Divine power, community formation, and leadership
       in the Acts of the Apostles. Community formation. 2002 ⇒644. 89-
       104.
5966   *Blümer, Wilhelm* Apostelgeschichte. BVLI 46 (2002) 36-37.
5967   *Bottini, G. Claudio; Casalini, Nello* Informazione e ricostruzione in
       Atti degli Apostoli. LASBF 52 (2002) 125-174.
5968   *Bottino, Adriana* La missione 'fino all'estremità della terra' e is suoi
       protagonisti negli Atti degli Apostoli. San Luca evangelista. FRSEP
       28: 2002 ⇒5731. 335-350.
5969   *Casalini, Nello* Nuovi commenti agli Atti degli Apostoli: saggio bib-
       liografico. LASBF 52 (2002) 175-216.
5970   **Czachesz, I.** Apostolic commission narratives in the canonical and
       apocryphal acts of the Apostles. *DLuttikhuizen, G.P.*: Lv 2002, Pee-
       ters vi; 296 pp. Diss. Groningen 2002 [EThL 79,255].
5971   **Dumais, Marcel** Communauté et mission: une lecture des Actes des
       Apôtres. 2000 ⇒17,5538. RSR 31 (2002) 218-220 (*Mainville,
       Odette*).
5972   *Gaventa, Beverly R.* Witnessing to the gospel in the Acts of the
       Apostles: beyond the conversion or conversation dilemma. WaW 22
       (2002) 238-245.
5973   *Gisana, Rosario* La paternità spirituale di Anania e Barnaba. Horeb
       11/2 (2002) 25-34.
5974   **Gonzalez, Justo L.** Acts: the gospel of the Spirit. 2001 ⇒17,5546.
       RCBQ 64 (2002) 759-760 (*Miller, Robert J.*).
5975   *Gonzáles, Justo L.* Acts of the Apostles: also known as Acts of the
       Holy Spirit. NT: introducing. 2002 ⇒332. 103-121.
5976   *Green, Joel B.* Doing repentance: the formation of disciples in the
       Acts of the Apostles. ExAu 18 (2002) 1-23. Resp. *D.B. Laytham* 24-
       28;
5977   The nature of conversion in the Acts of the Apostles. San Luca evan-
       gelista. FRSEP 28: 2002 ⇒5731. 327-334;
5978   'She and her househould were baptized' (Acts 16.15): household bap-
       tism in the Acts of the Apostles. Dimensions of baptism. JSNT.S
       234: 2002 ⇒434. 72-90;

5979   The book of Acts as history/writing. LexTQ 37/3 (2002) 119-127 [BuBB 40,70].
5980   **Green, Michael** 30 years that changed the world: a fresh look at the book of Acts. Leicester 2002, Inter-Varsity 287 pp. 0-85111-482-2.
5981   *Haacker, Klaus* Das Bekenntnis des Paulus zur Hoffnung Israels nach der Apostelgeschichte des Lukas. Versöhnung mit Israel. VKHW 5: 2002 <1985> ⇒174. 77-94.
5982   *Hengel, Martin* Zwischen Jesus und Paulus: die "Hellenisten", die "Sieben" und Stephanus (Apg 6,1-15; 7,54-8,3). Paulus und Jakobus. WUNT 141: 2002 <1975> ⇒178. 1-67.
5983   **Hoet, H.** Daarvan zijn wij allen getuigen. Antwerpen 2002, Halewijn 102 pp.
5984   *Hyldahl, Niels* The reception of Paul in the Acts of the Apostles. NT as reception. JSNT.S 230: 2002 ⇒360. 110-119.
5985   **Johnson, Luke Timothy** Septuagintal midrash in the speeches of Acts. The Père Marquette Lecture in Theology 2002: Milwaukee, WI 2002, Marquette Univ. Pr. vii; 76 pp. 0-87462-582-3.
5986   **Kanachikuzhy, Augustine** The theology of Paul in the Acts of the Apostles. ᴰ*Kilgallen, John J.*: Mumbai 2002, St Pauls 115 pp. Extr. Diss. Gregoriana 2000.
5987   *Kisirinya, S.K.* Re-interpreting the major summaries (Acts 2:42-46; 4:32-35; 5:12-16). African Christian Studies 18/1 (2002) 67-74.
5988   **Klauck, Hans-Josef** Magic and paganism in early christianity: the world of the Acts of the Apostles. ᵀ*McNeil, Brian* 2000 ⇒16,5601. ᴿJThS 53 (2002) 225-229 (*Twelftree, Graham H.*); ABR 50 (2002) 91 (*Palmer, Darryl W.*).
5989   **Marguerat, Daniel** La première histoire du christianisme: les Actes des Apôtres. 1999 ⇒15,5357...17,5568. ᴿRivBib 50 (2002) 115-116 (*Penna, Romano*); EstB 60 (2002) 552-560 (*Rodríguez Ruiz, Miguel*);
5990   The first christian historian: writing the 'Acts of the Apostles'. ᵀ*McKinney, Ken; Laughery, Gregory J.; Bauckham, Richard*: MSSNTS 121: C 2002, CUP xii; 299 pp. £45. 0-521-81650-5. Bibl. 257-281;
5991   La prima storia del cristianesimo: gli Atti degli Apostoli. CinB 2002, San Paolo 298 pp.
5992   **Martin, François** Actes des Apôtres: lecture sémiotique. Lyon 2002, Profac 283 pp. 2-85317-091-8.
5993   **Martín-Asensio, Gustavo** Transitivity-based foregrounding in the Acts of the Apostles: a functional-grammatical approach to the Lukan perspective. Studies in New Testament Greek 8; JSNT.S 202: 2000 ⇒16,5608. ᴿRBLit 4 (2002) 403-409 (*Graber, Philip L.; Matthews, Christopher R.*); JBL 121 (2002) 371-373 (*Graber, Philip L.;*).
       ᴱᵀ**Monferrer Sala, J.** Scripta arabica orientalia 1999 ⇒3351.
5994   *Núñez Regodón, Jacinto* Antioquía de Siria. Iglesias apostólicas. ResB 35 (2002) 19-26.
5995   *O'Fearghail, Fearghus* The Jews in the Hellenistic cities of Acts. Jews in... cities. 2002 ⇒719. 39-54.
5996   *Panimolle, Salvatore A.* Vita di comunione e tensioni nella chiesa delle origini (At 1-15). San Luca evangelista. FRSEP 28: 2002 ⇒ 5731. 351-365.
5997   **Pao, David W.** Acts and the Isaianic new Exodus. WUNT 2/130: 2000 ⇒16,5614. ᴿHBT 24 (2002) 137-138 (*Phillips, Thomas E.*).;

5998 GR 2002, Baker A. 311 pp. $35. 0-8010-2496-X.
5999 *Parisi, Serafino* Atti degli Apostoli e modelli storiografici. ᶠTUDDA, F. 2002 ⇒123. 97-114.
6000 *Phillips, Thomas E.* Narrative characterizations of Peter and Paul in early Christianity. Arc 30 (2002) 139-157.
6001 *Pilhofer, Peter* Antiochien und Philippi: zwei römische Kolonien auf dem Weg des Paulus nach Spanien. Die frühen Christen. WUNT 145: 2002 <2000> ⇒225. 154-165.
6002 **Pimentel, Stephen** Witnesses of the Messiah: on Acts of the Apostles 1-15. Steubenville, OH 2002, Emmaus Road 141 pp. $10.
6003 **Read-Heimerdinger, Jenny** The Bezan text of Acts: a contribution of discourse analysis to textual criticism. JSNT.S 236: L 2002. Sheffield A. xi; 379 pp. £75. 0-82646-212-X. Diss. Wales, 1994; Bibl. 356-365.
6004 **Reimer, Andy M.** Miracle and magic: a study in the Acts of the Apostles and the Life of APOLLONIUS of Tyana. JSNT.S 235: L 2002, Sheffield A. xiii; 277 pp. £60. 0-82646-210-3. Bibl. 253-265.
6005 **Richard, P.** El movimiento de Jesús antes de la iglesia: una interpretación liberadora de los Hechos de los Apóstoles. 2000 ⇒16,5618. ᴿEE 77 (2002) 168-169 (*Ramírez Fueyo, Francisco*).
6006 *Richard, P.* The pluralistic experiences of the first christian communities according to the Acts of the Apostles. Dei Verbum [Stuttgart] 62-63 (2002) 24-31 [NTAb 47,474].
6007 **Riddle, Jeffrey Todd** Paul as prophet in the Acts of the Apostles. ᴰ*Carroll, J.T.* 2002. Diss. Virginia, Union [RTL 34,601].
6008 *Rius-Camps, Josep; Read-Heimerdinger, Jenny* The message of the book of Acts in the Alexandrian tradition and in Codex Bezae. San Luca evangelista. FRSEP 28: 2002 ⇒5731. 575-584.
6009 **Roloff, Jürgen** Gli Atti degli Apostoli. NT 5: Brescia 2002, Paideia 502 pp. €41.50. 883-940-645-X.
6010 **Santos, Carlos César dos** Atos dos Apóstolos: ação criadora e criativa do Espírito. Petrópolis 2002, Vozes 84 pp [REB 248,998].
6011 *Serrano, Vicente* El bautismo: praxis de las primeras comunidades cristianas. BiFe 28 (2002) 275-298.
6012 **Smith, David E.** The canonical function of Acts: a comparative analysis. ColMn 2002, Liturgical 136 pp. $16. 0-8146-5103-8. Bibl. 129-136.
6013 **Tavardon, Paul** Sens et enjeux d'un conflit textuel: le texte occidental et le texte alexandrin des Actes des Apôtres. CRB 44: 1999 ⇒15, 5614. ᴿCBQ 64 (2002) 183-184 (*Gignac, Francis T.*).
6014 *Taylor, Justin* Witness in the book of Acts. PrPe 16 (2002) 129-133.
6015 **Taylor, Justin** Les Actes des deux apôtres, 4: commentaire historique (Act. 1,1-8,40). EtB 41: 2000 ⇒16,5584. ᴿCBQ 64 (2002) 184-185 (*Turro, James C.*); ThLZ 127 (2002) 650-653 (*Roloff, Jürgen*); Bib. 83 (2002) 131-133 (*Elliott, James Keith*).
6016 *Trevijano Etcheverría, Ramón* Éfeso. Iglesias apostólicas. ResB 35 (2002) 37-44.
6017 *Varickasseril, Jose* Roots in the Acts: a study of the beginnings of religious life in the Acts of the Apostles. MissTod 4 (2002) 344-362.
6018 **Wall, Robert W.** The Acts of the Apostles: introduction, commentary, and reflections. NIntB 10: 2002 ⇒4655. 1-368.
6019 **Wander, Bernd** Timorati di Dio e simpatizzanti: studio sull'ambiente pagano delle sinagoghe della diaspora. Studi sulla Bibbia e il suo

ambiente 8: CinB 2002, San Paolo 334 pp. €26.86. 88-215-4548-2. Bibl. 279-306.

6020 *Wedderburn, A.J.M.* The 'we'-passages in Acts: on the horns of a dilemma. ZNW 93 (2002) 78-98.

6021 *Wolff, Christian* λαλεῖν γλώσσαις in the Acts of the Apostles. [F]WEDDERBURN, A.: JSNT.S 217: 2002 ⇒132. 189-199.

F8.3 *Ecclesia primaeva Actuum*—Die Urgemeinde

6022 *Bauckham, Richard* The early Jerusalem church, Qumran, and the Essenes. Dead Sea scrolls as background. StTDJ 46: 2002 ⇒732. 63-89.

6023 *Estévez López, Elisa* Jerusalén. Iglesias apostólicas. ResB 35 (2002) 5-18.

6024 *Gerdmar, Anders* Hebreer och hellenister i urförsamlingen—ett receptionskritiskt perspektiv. SEÅ 67 (2002) 105-119.

6025 **Gnilka, Joachim** Die frühen Christen: Ursprünge und Anfang der Kirche. HThK.S 7: 1999 ⇒15,5656; 17,5603. [R]StBob 2/1 (2002) 169-174 (*Kasiłowski, Piotr*).

6026 **Lüdemann, Gerd** Das Urchristentum: eine kritische Bilanz seiner Erforschung. ARGU 12: Fra 2002, Lang 167 pp. €29.80. 3-631-392-11-7.

6027 *Marczewski, Marek* Świeccy w kościołach nowotestamentalnych [I laici nelle chiese nei scritti del Nuovo Testamento]. Vox Patrum 22 (2002) 31-51 Sum. 50s. **P.**

6028 *Meeks, Wayne A.* Reflections on an era;
6029 Afterword. In search. 2002 ⇒208. xi-xxviii/254-261.

6030 *Öhler, Markus* Römisches Vereinsrecht und christliche Gemeinden. Zwischen den Reichen. TANZ 36: 2002 ⇒568. 51-71.

6031 (*a*) **Rowland, Christopher** Christian origins: an account of the setting and character of the most important Messianic sect of Judaism. L [²]2002, SPCK xxvi; 451 pp. $32. 0-281-05366-9. Bibl. 381-429.
(*b*) *Schwank, Benedikt* Syrien im Januar 2002. EuA 78 (2002) 233-236.

6032 **Theissen, Gerd** La religion des premiers chrétiens: une théorie du christianisme primitif. [T]*Hoffmann, Joseph*: Initiations au christianisme ancien: P 2002, Cerf 528 pp. €38. 2-204-06866-7. Bibl. 487-504. [R]Brotéria 155/1 (2002) 93-94 (*Silva, I. Ribeiro da*); RHPhR 82 (2002) 223-225 (*Grappe, Ch.*); FV 101/5 (2002) 87-89 (*Flichy, Odile*); REJ 161 (2002) 483-489 (*Mimouni, Simon C.*);

6033 La religión de los primeros cristianos: una teoría del cristianismo primitivo. BEB 108: S 2002, Sígueme 408 pp. 84-301-1465-3. [R]EstAg 37 (2002) 595-596 (*Cineira, D.A.*).

6034 **Trocmé, Étienne** L'enfance du christianisme. 1997 ⇒13,5552; 15, 5661. [R]EstB 60 (2002) 425-427 (*Guijarro, Santiago*).

6035 *Van Houwelingen, Pieter H.* Vlucht naar voren: het vertrek van de christenen uit Jeruzalem naar Pella. ThRef 45 (2002) 339-361.

6036 *Wilson, Stephen G.* Dissidents and defectors: the limits of pluralism. [F]RÄISÄNEN, H.: NT.S 103: 2002 ⇒97. 441-456.

F8.5 **Ascensio, Pentecostes; ministerium Petri**—*Act 1...*

6037 *Deneken, Michel* La résurrection de Jésus ou la détermination pascale de la foi chrétienne. LV(L) 253 (2002) 67-83.
6038 *Galot, Jean* Il mistero della pentecoste. CivCatt 153/2 (2002) 315-327.
6039 *Ignatius, Jesudasan* Pentecost: the birthday of the church. Third Millennium 5/4 (2002) 96-99.
6040 *Pilhofer, Peter* LIVIUS, Lukas und LUKIAN: drei Himmelfahrten. Die frühen Christen. WUNT 145: 2002 ⇒225.166-182.

6041 *Poythress, Vern Sheridan* Translating λέγων in Acts 1:3. WThJ 64 (2002) 273-278.
6042 *Gilbert, Gary* The list of nations in Acts 2: Roman propaganda and the Lukan response. JBL 121 (2002) 497-529;
6043 From eschatology to imperialism: mapping the territory of Acts 2. Gospels according to Goulder. 2002 ⇒594. 84-110.
6044 *Kilgallen, John J.* 'With many other words' (Acts 2,40): theological assumptions in Peter's Pentecost speech. Bib. 83 (2002) 71-87.
6045 *Schreiber, Stefan* Aktualisierung göttlichen Handelns am Pfingsttag: das frühjüdische Fest in Apg 2,1. ZNW 93 (2002) 58-77.
6046 *Hennig, Gerhard* Wenn der Geist in euch wohnt ...: Predigt zu Pfingsten (Apostelgeschichte 2,1-18). ThBeitr 33 (2002) 176-178.
6047 *Genuyt, François* Écritures et résurrection de Jésus: une lecture du premier discours de Pierre (Ac 2,14-36). LV(L) 253 (2002) 55-66.
6048 *Demandt, Johannes* Gott hat Jesus zum Herrn und Christus gemacht: Predigt zu Christi Himmelfahrt (Apostelgeschichte 2,29-36). ThBeitr 33 (2002) 57-61.
6049 *Kilgallen, John J.* What the apostles proclaimed at Acts 4,2. [F]LAMBRECHT, J.: BEThL 165: 2002 ⇒72. 233-248.
6050 **Soosai Fernando, Nazarene** 'Salvation in no one else': a contemporary theological reading of Acts 4:12. [D]*O'Collins, Gerald*: 2002, 151 pp. Extr. Diss. Gregorian [RTL 34,601].
6051 *Rosik, Mariusz* Duch Święty—śródło odwagi w głoszeniu słowa zbawievia (Dz 4,23-31) [The Holy Spirit—source of courage in preaching the words of salvation (Acts 4,23-31). Verbum Vitae 2 (2002) 151-164 Som. 163. **P**.
6052 *Marconi, Gilberto* Anania e Saffira (At 5,1-11): la guida dello Spirito e la presenza storica di Satana nella comunità. San Luca evangelista. FRSEP 28: 2002 ⇒5731. 477-492.
6053 *Reid, Barbara E.* Puzzling passages: Acts 6:1. BiTod 40 (2002) 253-254.
6054 *Walter, Nikolaus* Nikolaos, Proselyt aus Antiochien, und die Nikolaiten in Ephesus und Pergamon. ZNW 93 (2002) 200-226 [Acts 6,1-7; Rev 2,6; 2,14-16].
6055 *Curkpatrick, Stephen* The spectre of Stephen and the haunting of Acts. JHiC 9/1 (2002) 16-30 [Acts 6,8-7,60].
6056 *Trainor, Michael* A footstool or a throne?: Luke's attitude to earth (*ge*) in Acts 7. Earth story. 2002 ⇒322. 122-136.
6057 *Ngugi, J. Njoroge wa* Stephen's speech in Acts 7:1-53 as a challenge for enculturation in catechesis. African Christian Studies 18/1 (2002) 34-66.

6058 **Jeska, Joachim** Die Geschichte Israels in der Sicht des Lukas: Apg 7,2b-53 und 13,17-25 im Kontext antik-jüdischer Summarien der Geschichte Israels. FRLANT 195: 2001 ⇒17,5636. [R]RHPhR 82 (2002) 238-239 (*Grappe, Ch.*).

6059 *Siffer-Wiederhold, Nathalie* La figure de Joseph dans le discours d'Étienne en Ac 7,9-16: amorce d'une typologie christologique. Typologie biblique. LeDiv: 2002 ⇒341. 141-163.

6060 **Matthews, Christopher R.** Philip, apostle and evangelist: configurations of a tradition. NT.S 105: Lei 2002, Brill xv; 257 pp. €79. 90-04-12054-8. Diss. Harvard 1993; Bibl. 219-238 [Acts 8].

6061 *Ferreiro, Alberto* Typological portraits of Simon Magus in anti-Gnostic sources. [F]TREVIJANO ETCHEVERRÍA, R. 2002 ⇒122. 363-378 [Acts 8,9-24].

6062 *Tuzlak, Ayse* The magician and the heretic: the case of Simon Magus. Magic and ritual. RGRW 141: 2002 ⇒505. 416-426 [Acts 8,9-24].

6063 *Burfeind, Carsten* Wen hörte Philippus?: leises Lesen und lautes Vorlesen in der Antike. ZNW 93 (2002) 138-145 [Acts 8,28-30].

6064 *Pilch, John J.* Paul's ecstatic trance experience near Damascus in Acts of the Apostles. HTS 58 (2002) 690-707 [NTAb 47,260] [Acts 9,1-19].

6065 **Peace, Richard V.** Conversion in the New Testament: Paul and the Twelve. 1999 ⇒15,5688...17,5644. [R]EvQ 74 (2002) 179-180 (*Proctor, John*) [Acts 9,1-22].

6066 *Schnelle, Udo* Vom Verfolger zum Verkündiger: Inhalt und Tragweite des Damaskusgeschehens. [F]FUCHS, A.: 2002 ⇒41. 299-323 [Acts 9,3-19; 22,6-16; 26,12-18; 1 Cor 9,1; Gal 1,12-16].

6067 *Scholz, Daniel J.* 'Rise, Peter, kill and eat': eating unclean food and dining with unclean people in Acts 10:1-11:18. ProcGLM 22 (2002) 47-61.

6068 *Arterbury, Andrew E.* The ancient custom of hospitality, the Greek novels, and Acts 10:1-11:18. PRSt 29/1 (2002) 53-72.

6069 *Barbi, Augusto* La fatica di una chiesa che si apre ad accogliere i pagani: l'episodio di Cornelio (At 10,1-11,18). Ad Gentes 6/1 (2002) 36-48.

6070 *Miller, Chris A.* Did Peter's vision in Acts 10 pertain to men or the menu?. BS 159 (2002) 302-317.

6071 *Wilson, Walter T.* Urban legends: Acts 10:1-11:18 and the strategies of Greco-Roman foundation narratives. JBL 120 (2001) 77-99.

6072 *Henze, Dagmar* Peter: a transgressor in his own time. [F]SCHOTTROFF, L. 2002 ⇒111. 47-51 [Acts 10,1-34].

6073 *Marguerat, Daniel* Un jeu d'échos intertextuels: l'évasion de Pierre et la mort du tyran (Actes 12). Quand la bible se raconte. 2002 ⇒ 355. 163-188.

F8.7 Act 13...*Itinera Pauli*; Paul's journeys

6074 *Bianchi, Francesco* Un amico ricorda il maestro: la testimonianza di Luca in Atti. PaVi 47/6 (2002) 34-39.

6075 **Omerzu, Heike** Der Prozeß des Paulus: eine exegetische und rechtshistorische Untersuchung der Apostelgeschichte. [D]*Horn, Friedrich W.*: BZNW 115: B 2002, De Gruyter xiii; 615 pp. €138. 3-11-01751-2-6. Diss. Mainz; Bibl. 509-565.

6076 *Patitucci, Stella; Uggeri, Giovanni* Aspetti archeologici del primo
      viaggio missionario di San Paolo in Anatolia. VII Simposio di Tarso.
      2002 ⇒587. 345-374.
6077 *Rakocy, Waldemar* Problem datacji i kolokacji w misji Pawła tzw.
      Soboru Jerozolimskiego. CoTh 72/2 (2002) 31-44 [Acts 9,26-30;
      11,29-30; 15; Gal 2,1-10]. **P.**
6078 **Reichardt, Michael** Psychologische Erklärung der paulinischen Da-
      maskusvision?: ein Beitrag zum   interdisziplinären Gespräch zwi-
      schen Exegese und Psychologie seit dem 18. Jahrhundert. SBB 42:
      1999 ⇒15,5695; 17,5657. ᴿRBLit 4 (2002) 412-415 (*Stenschke,
      Christoph W.*).
6079 *Ricci, Maria Cristina* I viaggi di San Paolo in Grecia: aspetti archeo-
      logici VII. Simposio di Tarso. 2002 ⇒587. 375-412.
6080 *Wedderburn, Alexander J. M.* Paul and Barnabas: the anatomy and
      chronology of a parting of the ways. ᶠRÄISÄNEN, H.: NT.S 103: 2002
      ⇒97. 291-310.

6081 *Back, Peter* Exegesis of some key passages relating to mission, part
      1: Acts 13,1-4. Evangel 20 (2002) 15-20.
6082 **Deutschmann, Anton** Synagoge und Gemeindebildung: christliche
      Gemeinde und Israel in der Apostelgeschichte des Lukas untersucht
      am Beispiel von Apg 13,42-52. 2001 ⇒17,5660. ᴿActBib 39 (2002)
      188-190 (*Boada, J.*); SNTU.A 27 (2002) 244-246 (*Fuchs, Albert*).
6083 **Béchard, Dean Philip** Paul outside the walls: a study of Luke's
      socio-geographical universalism in Acts 14:8-20. AnBib 143: 2000
      ⇒16,5711; 17,5663. ᴿRivBib 50 (2002) 103-105 (*Rossé, Gérard*);
      ATG 65 (2002) 308-309 (*Rodríguez Carmona, A.*); ABR 50 (2002)
      90 (*Palmer, Darryl W.*); ThLZ 127 (2002) 514-517 (*Reinbold, Wolf-
      gang*); Bib. 83 (2002) 284-288 (*Scott, James M.*); RBLit 4 (2002)
      401-403 = JBL 121 (2002) 570-573 (*Spencer, F. Scott*).
6084 *Back, Peter* Exegesis of some key passages relating to mission, part
      2: Acts 14:21-28, Acts 15:36-41 and Acts 16:2. Evangel 20 (2002)
      20-22.
6085 **Okoronkwo, Michael Enyinwa** The Jerusalem compromise as a
      conflict-resolution model: a rhetoric-communicative analysis of Acts
      15 in the light of modern linguistics. 2001 ⇒17,5664. ᴿJThS 53
      (2002) 229-230 (*Ellingworth, Paul*); CBQ 64 (2002) 385-387
      (*Topel, John*).
6086 *Ponsot, Hervé* Peut-on encore parler de 'concile' de Jérusalem?: à
      propos d'Ac 15 et de la chronologie paulinienne. RB 109 (2002) 556-
      586.
6087 *Malcolm, Lois* Conversion, conversation and Acts 15. WaW 22
      (2002) 246-254.
6088 *Amphoux, Christian-B.* Les variantes et l'histoire du "décret aposto-
      lique": Actes 15,20.29; 21,25. ᶠDELOBEL, J.: BEThL 161: 2002
      ⇒24. 209-226.
6089 *MacIntosh, John* "For it seemed good to the Holy Spirit" Acts 15:28:
      how did the members of the Jerusalem Council know this?. RTR 61/3
      (2002) 131-147.

6090 *Iovino, Paolo* Paolo a Filippi. Ho Theológos 20 (2002) 3-19 [Acts
      16,9-40].

6091 *Brenk, Frederick E.* The exorcism at Philippoi in Acts 16.11-40: divine possession or diabolic inspiration?. Πρακτικα, ιαδιεθνους συνεδριου κλασσικων σπουδων φιες [Acts of the XI congrès de la Féderation international des associations d'études classiques, 2, Kavala, Greece, Aug. 1999. ^E**Manaphes, K.A.**: Athens 2002 <2000>. 172-183.

6092 *Fiedrowicz, Michael* Die Rezeption und Interpretation der paulinischen Areopag-Rede in der patristischen Theologie. TThZ 111 (2002) 85-105 [Acts 17].

6093 *Gourgues, Michel* La littérature profane dans le discours d'Athènes (Ac 17,16-31): un dossier fermé?. RB 109 (2002) 241-269.

6094 *Flemming, Dean* Contextualizing the gospel in Athens: Paul's Areopagus address as a paradigm for missionary communication. Miss. 30/2 (2002) 199-214 [Acts 17,16-34].

6095 *Reis, David M.* The Areopagus as echo chamber: "mimesis" and intertextuality in Acts 17. JHiC 9/2 (2002) 259-277 [Acts 17,22-31].

6096 *Mundhenk, Norman A.* A note on Acts 17.24. BiTr 53 (2002) 441-2.

6097 *Van Tilborg, S.* Acts 17:27—'that they might feel after him and find ...'. HTS 57 (2001) 86-104 [NTAb 46,479].

6098 *Troiani, Lucio* Lucio Giunio Gallione e le comunità ebraiche. Materia giudaica. 2002 ⇒727. 47-54 [Acts 18].

6099 **Bunine, Alexis** Une légende tenace: le retour de Paul à Antioche: après sa mission en Macédoine et en Grèce (Actes 18,18-19,1). CRB 52: P 2002, Gabalda 142 pp. €21. 2-85021-136-9. Bibl. 132-140.

6100 *Court, John M.* Rivals in the mission field. ET 113 (2002) 399-403 [Acts 20].

6101 *Garuti, Paolo* Manus iniecerunt—II: At 21,27: l'arresto di San Paolo a Gerusalemme, i processi a Cesarea, il ricorso a Cesare: un'ipotesi. Ang. 79 (2002) 769-801.

6102 *Morgan Gillman, Florence* Berenice as Paul's witness to the resurrection (Acts 25-26). ^FLAMBRECHT, J.: BEThL 165: 2002 ⇒72. 249-64.

6103 *Meijer, Fik* Paulus' zeereis naar Rome. Phoenix 48/1 2002 14-24 [Acts 27-28].

6104 *White, R.W.* A meteorological appraisal of Acts 27:5-26. ET 113 (2002) 403-407.

6105 *Gempf, Conrad* Luke's story of Paul's reception in Rome. Rome in the bible. 2002 ⇒363. 42-66 [Acts 28].

X. Johannes

G1.1 *Corpus johanneum*: John and his community

6106 **Arockiam, Michaelsami** The concept of joy in the Johannine literature. ^D*Von Wahlde, Urban C.*: Delhi 2002, ISPCK xiv; 254 pp. Rs125. 81-7214-678-7. Diss. Loyola, Chicago.

6107 **Bartolomé, Juan José** Cuarto Evangelio; cartas de Juan: introducción y comentario. Claves Cristianas 13: M 2002, CCS 455 pp. €19.50. 84-8316-464-7. Bibl. 443-449. ^RSal. 64 (2002) 652-653 (*Buzzetti, Carlo*).

6108   **Brown, Raymond E.** Para que tengáis vida: a solas con Juan Evangelista. [T]*Tosaus Abadía, José Pedro*: El pozo de Siquem 132: Sdr 2002, Sal Terrae 142 pp. 84-293-1427-X.

6109   **Bull, Klaus-Michael** Gemeinde zwischen Integration und Abgrenzung: ein Beitrag zur Frage nach dem Ort der joh Gemeinde(n) in der Geschichte des Urchristentums. BET 24: 1992 ⇒9,5406. [R]ThR 67 (2002) 445-447 (*Haldimann, Konrad; Weder, Hans*).

6110   *Cazelles, Henri* Johannes, ein Sohn des Zebedäus, 'Priester' und Apostel. IKaZ 31 (2002) 479-484.

6111   [E]**Dube, Musa W.; Staley, Jeffrey Lloyd** John and postcolonialism: travel, space and power. The Bible and postcolonialism 7: L 2002, Sheffield A. x; 254 pp. $18. 1-84127-312-0. Bibl. 225-242. [R]StWC 8/1 (2002) 164-165 (*Middleton, Paul*).

6112   **Ferraro, Giuseppe** La gioia di Cristo: nel quarto vangelo, nelle lettere giovannee e nell'Apocalisse. 2000 ⇒16,5750; 17,5692. [R]Mar. 64 (2002) 679-680 (*Masini, Mario*).

6113   [E]**Fortna, Robert Tomson; Thatcher, Tom** Jesus in Johannine tradition. 2001 ⇒17,5694. [R]Theol. 105 (2002) 451-452 (*Harvey, A.E.*).

6114   **Frey, Jörg** Die johanneische Eschatologie, 3: die eschatologische Verkündigung in den johanneischen Texten. WUNT 117: 2000 ⇒16, 5751; 17,5695. [R]WThJ 63 (2002) 211-214 (*Gamble, Richard C.*); ThLZ 127 (2002) 44-45 (*Wengst, Klaus*); SNTU.A 27 (2002) 233-235 (*Oberforcher, R.*).

6115   *Helou, Clémence* Le conflit des ténèbres et de la lumière dans les écrits johanniques: une approche symbolique. Symbolisme et expérience. 2002 ⇒666. 159-173.

6116   *Hill, C.E.* A notice of corrections in standard editions of two Johannine manuscripts. TC: a journal of biblical textual criticism [http://purl.org/TC] 7 (2002) pars. 1-4 [NTAb 47,473] [Jn 19,5; 2 Jn 2; 8].

6117   *Hoffmann, R.J.* Love for love: conceptual unity and idiomatic difference in the Johannine tradition. ThRev 23/2 (2002) 67-94.

6118   [E]**Kaestli, Jean-Daniel; Poffet, Jean-Michel; Zumstein, Jean** La communauté johannique et son histoire. 1990 ⇒6,538*... 10,5203. [R]ThR 67 (2002) 341-344 (*Haldimann, Konrad; Weder, Hans*).

6119   **Lindars, Barnabas; Edwards, Ruth B.; Court, John M.** The Johannine literature. 2000 ⇒16,5733. [R]RBLit 4 (2002) 399-400 (*Koester, Craig R.*).

6120   **Lingad, Celestino G.** The problems of Jewish christians in the Johannine community. TGr.T 73: 2001 ⇒17,5698. [R]RivBib 50 (2002) 488-492 (*Belli, Filippo*).

6121   *Meeks, Wayne A.* The man from heaven in Johannine sectarianism. In search. 2002 ⇒208. 55-90.

6122   *Michaels, J. Ramsey* By water and blood: sin and purification in John and First John. Dimensions of baptism. JSNT.S 234: 2002 ⇒434. 149-162.

6123   **Nguyen Manh Thu, Raymond** The Christ-Lamb in the Johannine writings. [D]*Marcato, G.*: 2002 Diss. Angelicum [RTL 34,600].

6124   *Panimolle, Salvatore A.* Grazia divina e divinizzazione dell'uomo negli scritti giovannei. DSBP 30 (2002) 145-194.

6125   **Pasquetto, Virgilio** In comunione con Cristo e con i fratelli: lessico antropologico del vangelo e delle lettere di Giovanni. 2001 ⇒17, 5706. [R]MF 102 (2002) 405-409 (*Uricchio, Francesco*); Ter. 53 (2002) 567-572 (*Rosso, Armando*); REsp 61 (2002) 485-487 (*Castro, Secundino*).

6126 *Reiser, Marius* "Und das Licht leuchtet in der Finsternis": das johanneische Weltbild. Religion und Weltbild. Marburger Religionsgeschichtliche Beiträge 2: 2002 ⇒443. 73-89.

6127 **Schmithals, Walter** Johannesevangelium und Johannesbriefe: Forschungsgeschichte und Analyse. BZNW 64: 1992 ⇒8,5694... 11/1, 4017. ᴿThR 67 (2002) 438-440 (*Haldimann, Konrad; Weder, Hans*).

6128 **Scholtissek, Klaus** In ihm sein und bleiben: die Sprache der Immanenz in den Johanneischen Schriften. Herders bibl. Studien 21: 2000 ⇒16,5757; 17,5710. ᴿBiLi 75 (2002) 147 (*Kühschelm, Roman*); TThZ 111 (2002) 241-243 (*Schwindt, Rainer*); StPhiloA 14 (2002) 217-219 (*Sellin, Gerhard*); StBob 2 (2002) 173-177 (*Sieg, Franciszek*); CBQ 64 (2002) 394-395 (*Moloney, Francis J.*); LebZeug 57 (2002) 307-308 (*Hieke, Thomas*); ThLZ 127 (2002) 48-51 (*Metzner, Rainer*); ThZ 58 (2002) 370-372 (*Zimmermann, Ruben*); Bib. 83 (2002) 125-131 (*Tuñí, Josep Oriol*) [Jn 13,31-14,31; 6; 15-17; 10].

6129 **Smith, D. Moody** Johannine christianity. 1987 <1984> ⇒65,4745... 6,5629 ᴿThR 67 (2002) 337-339 (*Haldimann, Konrad; Weder, Hans*).

6130 *Vargas, Niceta M.* Roles of men and woman in the Johannine community: paradigms for discipleship roles in the 21st century. The roles. 2002 ⇒540. 28-69.

6131 **Volfing, Annette** John the Evangelist and medieval German writing: imitating the inimitable. Oxf 2002, OUP 284 pp. £45. 0-19-924684-X. ᴿMAe 71 (2002) 364-366 (*Hamburger, Jeffrey*).

G1.2 **Evangelium Johannis**: *textus, commentarii*

6132 **Barrett, Charles K.** Das Evangelium nach Johannes. KEK Sonderband: 1990 ⇒6,5637... 8,5635. ᴿThR 67 (2002) 333-334 (*Haldimann, Konrad; Weder, Hans*).

6133 **Bréchet, R.** L'évangile de Jean aujourd'hui. Saint-Benoît-du Sault 2002, Bénédictines 152 pp. €13. 2-910972-84-4.

6134 *Burton, Philip* Johannes. BVLI 46 (2002) 33-36.

6135 **Castro Sánchez, Secundino** Evangelio de Juan: comprensión exegético-existencial. 2001 ⇒17,5721. ᴿTer. 53 (2002) 288-289 (*Pasquetto,Virgilio*); RevAg 43 (2002) 716-717 (*Sánchez Navarro, Luis*).

6136 **Fausti, S.** Una comunità legge il vangelo di Giovanni, 1, Bo 2002, EDB 318 pp. €23.50.

6137 ᴱ**Feld, Helmut** Ioannis CALVINI opera exegetica 11/1-2. In evangelium secundum Johannem commentarius. 1997-1998 ⇒13,5636... 15, 5747. ᴿCTJ 37 (2002) 371-373 (*Blacketer, Raymond A.*).

6138 **Gangel, Kenneth O.; Anders, Max** John Holman NT Commentary: Nv 2000, Broadman & H. 496 pp. $20. 0-8054-0204-7. ᴿRBLit (2002)* (*Brown, H. Stephen*).

6139 **Georgeot, J.-M.** Évangile de Saint-Jean: v.1, (Jn XVIII-1 à XXI-fin) De Saint-Marc jusqu'à Tertullien 19,1: n.p. 2002 n.p.

6140 **Hofrichter, Peter Leander** Modell und Vorlage der Synoptiker: das vorredaktionelle "Johannesevangelium". Theologische Texte und Studien 6: Hildesheim ²2002, Olms 250 pp. €24.80. 3-487-10371-0. Bibl. 245-250.

6141 **Keddie, Gordon J.** John: volume 1—chapters 1-12; volume 2— chapters 13-21. Darlington 2001, Evangelical 511 + 445 pp. £18 + 18. 0-85234-454-6/79-1.

6142   **Mateos, J.; Barreto, J.** Juan: texto y comentario. Córdoba 2002, El
       Almendro 429 pp [BiFe 29,155—Salas, A.].
6143   **Matson, Mark A.** John. Interpretation Bible Studies: LVL 2002,
       Westminster vi; 140 pp. $8. 0-664-22580-2. Bibl. 129.
6144   *Milewski, Douglas* Augustine's 124 tractates on the gospel of John:
       the *status quaestionis* and the state of neglect. AugSt 33 (2002) 61-
       77.
6145   **Moloney, Francis J.** The gospel of John. Sacra Pagina 4: 1998 ⇒14,
       5273; 15,5750. ᴿVJTR 66 (2002) 463-465 (*Meagher, Patrick M.*).
6146   **Osculati, Roberto** L'evangelo di Giovanni: commento. 2000 ⇒16,
       5778. ᴿPaVi 47/4 (2002) 61-62 (*Minissale, Antonino*).
6147   *Rico, Christophe* La linguistique peut-elle définir l'acte de traduc-
       tion?: à propos d'une version du quatrième évangile. L'autorité de
       l'Écriture. LeDiv: 2002 ⇒588. 193-226.
6148   *Rius-Camps, Josep* The spelling of Jerusalem in the gospel of John:
       the significance of two forms in Codex Bezae. NTS 48 (2002) 84-94.
6149   **Schenke, Ludger** Das Johannesevangelium. UB 446: 1992 ⇒8,5663
       ...10,5239. ᴿThR 67 (2002) 345-347 (*Haldimann, Konrad; Weder,
       Hans*).
6150   **Schneiders, Sandra M.** Written that you may believe: encountering
       Jesus in the fourth gospel. 1999 ⇒15,5756...17,5726. ᴿThRv 98
       (2002) 110-113 (*Scholtissek, Klaus*).
6151   **Wengst, Klaus** Das Johannesevangelium, 1. Teilband: Kapitel 1-10.
       TKNT 4/1: 2000 ⇒16,5787; 17,5732. ᴿBZ 46 (2002) 137-140 (*Frey,
       Jörg*);
6152   1-2. TKNT 4/1-2: 2000-2001 ⇒16,5787; 17,5730/1. ᴿSNTU.A 27
       (2002) 226-227 (*Fuchs, Albert*).
6153   **Wilckens, Ulrich** Il vangelo secondo Giovanni. NT 4: Brescia 2002,
       Paideia 441 pp. €36.80. 88-394-0649-1/2.
6154   **Wright, Tom** John for everyone: part 1: chapters 1-10; part 2: chap-
       ters 11-21. L 2002, SPCK 2 vols; xii; 180; xii; 188 pp. 0-281-05302-
       2/520-3.

G1.3 **Introductio** *in Evangelium Johannis*

6155   *Anderson, Paul N.* "Interfluential, formative, and dialectical"—a
       theory of John's relation to the synoptics. Priorität. Theologische
       Texte und Studien: 2002 ⇒561. 19-58.
6156   *Athikalam, James* The gospel of life: an introduction to the fourth
       gospel. JJSS 2 (2002) 44-66.
6157   *Berger, Klaus* Neue Argumente für die Frühdatierung des Johannes-
       evangeliums. Priorität. 2002 ⇒561. 59-72.
6158   *Charlesworth, James H.* The priority of John?: reflections on the Es-
       senes and the first edition of John. Priorität. 2002 ⇒561. 73-114.
6159   **Fuchs, Albert** Das Verhältnis der synoptischen agreements zur jo-
       hanneischen Tradition, untersucht anhand der messianischen Periko-
       pe Mk 6,32-44 par Mt 14,13-21 par Lk 9,10-17; Joh 6,1-15. Priorität.
       2002 ⇒561. 115-138 = ᶠAICHERN, M. 2002 ⇒2. 27-54; SNTU.A 27
       (2002) 85-115.
6160   *Hainz, Josef* Das Johannesevangelium in der Sicht der neueren Re-
       daktionskritik unter besonderer Berücksichtigung seines Verhältnis-
       ses zu den Synoptikern. Priorität. 2002 ⇒561. 139-150.

6161 *Haldimann, Konrad; Weder, Hans* Aus der Literatur zum Johannesevangelium 1985-1994: erster Teil: historische Situierung und diachrone Analysen. ThR 67 2002 328-348, 425-456.

6162 **Hengel, Martin** Die johanneische Frage: ein Lösungsversuch mit einem Beitrag zur Apokalypse von Jörg Frey. WUNT 2/67: 1993 ⇒ 9,5477... 15,5768. [R]ThR 67 (2002) 330-333 (*Haldimann, Konrad; Weder, Hans*).

6163 **Kealy, John Seán P.** John's gospel and the history of biblical interpretation. Mellen Biblical Press 60a-b: Lewiston, NY 2002 Mellen 2 vols; xiv; 417 + vii; 473-971 pp. $130 + 140. 0-7734-6980/2-6.

6164 **Kysar, Robert** Preaching John. Fortress Resources for Preaching: Mp 2002, Fortress 252 pp. $18. 0-8006-3226-5. Bibl. 240-243. [R]Kerux 17/2 (2002) 73-75 (*Dennison, James T.*).

6165 *MacRae, George W.* Invitation to John. Invitation to the gospels. [E]*Harrington, Daniel J.*: 2002 ⇒4694. 325-406.

6166 [E]**Marchadour, Alain** ORIGINE et postérité de l'évangile de Jean. 1990 ⇒6,545*... 9,5471. [R]ThR 67 (2002) 339-341 (*Haldimann, Konrad; Weder, Hans*).

6167 *Matson, Mark A.* The influence of John on Luke's passion: toward a theory of intergospel dialogue [Lk 22-23; Jn 18-19];

6168 *Morgan, Robert* The priority of John—over Luke. Priorität. 2002 ⇒ 561. 183-194/195-211.

6169 **Nagel, Titus** Die Rezeption des Johannesevangeliums im 2. Jahrhundert: Studien zur vorirenäischen Aneignung und Auslegung des vierten Evangeliums in christlicher und christlich-gnostischer Literatur. ABiG 2: 2000 ⇒16,5799; 17,5738. [R]ThRv 98 (2002) 488-489 (*Scholtissek, Klaus*).

6170 **Philippe, Marie-Dominique** Seguir al cordero: retiro sobre el evangelio de san Juan (1). M 2002, Cuadernos Palabra 490 pp.

6171 **Prigent, Pierre** Ainsi parlait l'apôtre Jean. LiBi 122: P 2001, Cerf 174 pp. €14.48. 2-204-06672-9. [R]EeV 50 (2002) 24 (*Trimaille, Michel*); RTL 33 (2002) 263-265 (*Gérard, J.-P.*).

6172 **Robinson, John A.T.** The priority of John. [E]*Coakley, J.F.*: 1985 ⇒ 1,5234... 5,5403. [R]ThR 67 (2002) 334-336 (*Haldimann, Konrad; Weder, Hans*).

6173 **Ruckstuhl, Eugen; Dschulnigg, Peter** Stilkritik und Verfasserfrage: die johanneischen Sprachmerkmale. NOrb 17: 1991 ⇒7,4790... 12, 5371. [R]ThR 67 (2002) 426-428 (*Veijola, Timo*).

6174 *Scholtissek, Klaus* Johannes auslegen III: ein Forschungsbericht. SNTU.A 27 (2002) 117-153.

6175 *Shellard, Barbara* The relationship of Luke and John: a fresh look at an old problem. Priorität. 2002 ⇒561. 255-280.

6176 *Söding, Thomas* Johanneische Fragen, Einleitungswissenschaft: Traditionsgeschichte—Theologie. Priorität. 2002 ⇒561. 213-239.

6177 *Untergaßmair, Franz G.* Das Verhältnis des *Evanglium Veritatis* zum Johannesevangelium—Indiz gegen eine kanonisch-johanneische Priorität?. Priorität. 2002 ⇒561. 241-252.

G1.4 *Themata de evangelio Johannis*—**John's Gospel, topics**

6178 **Asiedu-Peprah, Martin** Johannine sabbath conflicts as juridical controversy. WUNT 2/132: 2001 ⇒17,5751. [R]ETR 77 2002) 127-

128 (*Gloor, Daniel*); JThS 53 (2002) 223-224 (*Harvey, A.E.*); JSNT 85 (2002) 127-128 (*Lieu, Judith*); RHPhR 82 (2002) 235-236 (*Grappe, Ch.*); ThLZ 127 (2002) 905-906 (*Labahn, Michael*); RBLit (2002)* (*Sheppard, Beth M.*).

6179 Attridge, Harold W. Genre bending in the fourth gospel. JBL 121 (2002) 3-21.

6180 Basset, Lytta La crédibilité du 'moi je suis' dans l'évangile de Jean. ETR 77 (2002) 329-341.

6181 Becker, Jürgen Das vierte Evangelium und die Frage nach seinen externen und internen Quellen. ᶠRÄISÄNEN, H.: NT.S 103: 2002 ⇒97. 203-241.

6182 Belli, Filippo "I giudei" nel vangelo secondo Giovanni: come affrontare il problema. RivBib 50 (2002) 63-75.

6183 Bennema, Cornelis The giving of the Spirit in John's gospel—a new proposal?. EvQ 74 (2002) 195-213 [Jn 20,22].

6184 **Bennema, Cornelis** The power of saving wisdom: an investigation of spirit and wisdom in relation to the soteriology of the fourth gospel. WUNT 2/148: Tü 2002, Mohr S. xii; 318 pp. $59. 3-16-147746-4. Bibl. 264-281.

6185 Beutler, Johannes Jésus en conflit—histoire et théologie en Jean 5-12. SIDIC 34/3 (2002) 3-11;

6186 Faith and confession: the purpose of John. ᶠKYSAR, R.: 2002 ⇒70. 19-31.

6187 ᴱ**Bieringer, Reimund; Pollefeyt, D.; Vandecasteele-Vanneuville, F.** Anti-Judaism and the fourth gospel: papers of the Leuven Colloquium, 2000. 2001 ⇒17,5747. ᴿTheol. 105 (2002) 139-140 (*Smalley, Stephen*) BiblInterp 10 (2002) 436-438 (*Ashton, John*) ET 113 (2002) 233-235 (*Edwards, Ruth*); CBQ 64 (2002) 796-799 (*Danker, Frederick W.*); HBT 24/2 (2002) 118-119 (*Baker, Murray*); RBLit (2002)* (*Kysar, Robert*).

6188 **Bjerkelund, Carl J.** Tauta egeneto: die Präzisierungssätze im Johannesevangelium. WUNT 40: 1987 ⇒3,5275... 7,4766. ᴿThR 67 (2002) 431-432 (*Veijola, Timo*).

6189 **Blomberg, Craig L.** The historical reliability of John's gospel. 2001 ⇒17,5759. ᴿTheol. 105 (2002) 452-453 (*Smalley, Stephen*).

6190 Borgonovo, Giantonio Incarnazione del Logos: il Logos giovanneo alla luce della tradizione giudaica. ScC 130 (2002) 43-75.

6191 Bowe, Barbara E. The portrait of Jesus in the gospel of John. BiTod 40 (2002) 80-85.

6192 Bowen, John P. Coming to faith in the gospel of John. Anvil 19/4 (2002) 277-283.

6193 Boyarin, Daniel The Ioudaioi in John and the prehistory of 'Judaism'. ᶠROETZEL, C.: JSNT.S 221: 2002 ⇒104. 216-239.

6194 Brändle, Francisco 'El Enviado del Padre': teología de la 'misión' nel evangelio de Juan. REsp 61 (2002) 391-402.

6195 **Busse, Ulrich** Das Johannesevangelium: Bildlichkeit, Diskurs und Ritual: mit einer Bibliographie über den Zeitraum 1986-1998. BEThL 162: Lv 2002, Peeters xiii; 572 pp. 90-429-1100-X.

6196 Caballero, José Antonio El discípulo amado en el evangelio de Juan. EstB 60 (2002) 311-336.

6197 Casalegno, Alberto Tempo e momento escatologico nel vangelo di Giovanni. Tempo ed eternità. 2002 ⇒545. 165-194.

6198 **Cebulj, Christian** Ich bin es:Studien zur Identitätsbildung im Johannesevangelium. SBB 44: 2000 ⇒16,5826; 17,5772. ᴿFrRu 9 (2002) 212-214 (*Renker, Alwin*).

6199 **Chatelion Counet, Patrick** John, a postmodern gospel: introduction to deconstructive exegesis applied to the fourth gospel. Bibl.Interp. 44: 2000 ⇒16,5828; 17,5775. ᴿCBQ 64 (2002) 372-373 (*Adam, A.K.M.*) [John 6; 17; 21,24-25].

6200 **Coloe, Mary L.** God dwells with us: temple symbolism in the fourth gospel. 2001 ⇒17,5778. ᴿPacifica 15 (2002) 88-90 (*Elvey, Anne*); CBQ 64 (2002) 371-372 (*Lozada, Francisco*); RBLit (2002)* (*Kealy, Sean P.*).

6201 *Conway, Colleen M.* The production of the Johannine community: a new historicist perspective. JBL 121 (2002) 479-495;

6202 Speaking through ambiguity: minor characters in the fourth gospel. BiblInterp 10 (2002) 324-341.

6203 **Corsini, Eugenio** Apocalisse di Gesù: Cristo secondo Giovanni. T 2002, Sei xxi; 454 pp. €19.50. 88-05-05885-8.

6204 *Culpepper, R. Alan* Inclusivism and exclusivism in the fourth gospel. ᶠKYSAR, R.: 2002 ⇒70. 85-108.

6205 **Daly-Denton, Margaret** David in the fourth gospel: the Johannine reception of the Psalms. AGJU 47: 2000 ⇒16,5835; 17,5783. ᴿRBLit 4 (2002) 391-395 (*Labahn, Michael*).

6206 *Danna, Elizabeth* Intertextuality, verbal echoes and characterisation in the gospel of John. RB 109 (2002) 210-216.

6207 *Davis, Basil S.* The identity of the disciple whom Jesus loved. ET 113 (2002) 230-231.

6208 **DeConick, April D.** Voices of the mystics: early christian discourse in the gospels of John and Thomas and other ancient christian literature. JSNT.S 157: 2001 ⇒17,5787. ᴿThRv 98 (2002) 307-308 (*Scholtissek, Klaus*); ThLZ 127 (2002) 641-642 (*Schenke, Hans-Martin*).

6209 ᴱ**Denaux, Adelbert** John and the synoptics. BEThL 101: 1992 ⇒8, 465...10,5248. ᴿThR 67 (2002) 453-5 (*Haldimann, Konrad; Weder, Hans*).

6210 **Destro, A.; Pesce, M.** Cómo nació el cristianismo joánico: antropología y exégesis del evangelio de Juan. Sdr 2002, Sal Terrae 245 pp. €16. 84-293-1446-6. ᴿRF 246 (2002) 375-376 (*Vallarino, Jesús María*); REsp 61 (2002) 647-648 (*Castro, Secundino*).

6211 **Diefenbach, Manfred** Der Konflikt Jesu mit den "Juden": ein Versuch zur Lösung der johanneischen Antijudaismus-Diskussion mit Hilfe des antiken Handlungsverständnisses. NTA 41: Müns 2002, Aschendorff viii; 360 pp. €47. 3-402-04789-6. Diss.-Habil. Innsbruck 2001. Bibl. 283-327.

6212 **Dschulnigg, Peter** Jesus begegnen: Personen und ihre Bedeutung im Johannesevangelium. Theologie 30: 2000 ⇒16,5841. ᴿThLZ 127 (2002) 642-645 (*Zimmermann, Ruben*).

6213 **Dumm, Demetrius R.** A mystical portrait of Jesus: new perspectives on John's gospel. 2001 ⇒17,5794. ᴿScrB 32 (2002) 114-115 (*Turner, Geoffrey*); RBLit (2002)* (*Dennis, John*).

6214 *Dunderberg, Ismo* The beloved disciple in John: ideal figure in an early christian controversy. ᶠRÄISÄNEN, H.: NT.S 103: 2002 ⇒97. 243-269.

6215 *Dupont, Véronique* Le disciple, chez Jean et chez BENOÎT. CCist 64 (2002) 56-64.

6216 *Du Rand, Jan A.* The Johannine Jesus in Africa?. [F]KYSAR, R. 2002 ⇒70. 211-228.

6217 *Edwards, Ruth* John and the Jews. ET 113 (2002) 233-235.

6218 *Ekenberg, Anders* The fourth gospel and the history of Jesus. CV 44 (2002) 182-191.

6219 **Ensor, Peter W.** Jesus and his 'works': the Johannine sayings in historical perspective. WUNT 2/85: 1996 ⇒12,5403... 16,5846. [R]RB 109 (2002) 143-145 (*Devillers, Luc*).

6220 **Fortna, Robert T.** The fourth gospel and its predecessor: from narrative source to present gospel. 1989 ⇒4,5454... 9,5470. [R]ThR 67 (2002) 437-438 (*Haldimann, Konrad; Weder, Hans*).

6221 **Frey, Jörg** Die johanneische Eschatologie I: ihre Probleme im Spiegel der Forschung seit REIMARUS. WUNT 96: 1997 ⇒13,5702... 16,5851. [R]ASEs 19 (2002) 287-288 (*Pesce, Mauro*);

6222 II: das johanneische Zeitverständnis. WUNT 110: 1998 ⇒14,5330... 17,5806. [R]WThJ 63 (2002) 210-211 (*Gamble, Richard C.*).

6223 *Frey, Jörg* Die "theologia crucifixi" des Johannesevangeliums. Kreuzestheologie. WUNT 151: 2002 ⇒298. 169-238.

6224 **Fuglseth, Kåre Sigvald** A sectarian John?: a sociological-critical, historical and comparative analysis of the gospel of John, PHILO and Qumran. 2002 Diss. Trondheim [StTh 57,80].

6225 **García Moreno, Antonio** Temi teologici del vangelo di Giovanni, 3: i sacramenti. 2001 ⇒17,5810. [R]StPat 49 (2002) 255-257 (*Tura, Ermanno Roberto*);

6226 Jesús el nazareno, el rey de los judíos: estudio de cristología joánica. 2001 ⇒17,5809. [R]Cart. 18 (2002) 562-564 (*Álvarez Barredo, M.*); CDios 215 (2002) 674 (*Gutiérrez, J.*); LASBF 51 (2001) 432-434 (*Manns, F.*).

6227 *Ghiberti, Giuseppe* Giustizia e giudizio di fronte al mondo nel quarto vangelo. RStB 14/1-2 (2002) 235-244.

6228 *González García, José Antonio* El discípulo amado, o el maestro sin rostro. ResB 36 (2002) 29-36.

6229 **Guérillot, Cl.** La lumière incréée: chercher Dieu aujourd'hui. P 2001, Dervy 288 pp. €19. 2-84454-082-1 [NRTh 126,477—Radermakers, Jean].

6230 **Hamid-Khani, Saeed** Revelation and concealment of Christ: a theological inquiry into the elusive language of the fourth gospel. WUNT 2/120: 2000 ⇒16,5859. [R]ThGl 92 (2002) 123-125 (*Meyer, Annegret*).

6231 **Harstine, Stan** Moses as a character in the fourth gospel: a study of ancient reading techniques. JSNT.S 229: L 2002, Sheffield A. viii; 194 pp. £50. 0-8264-6026-7. Bibl. 173-184.

6232 **Hinrichs, Boy** 'Ich bin': die Konsistenz des Johannes-Evangeliums in der Konzentration auf das Wort Jesu. SBS 133: 1988 ⇒4,5456... 6,5672. [R]ThR 67 (2002) 450-452 (*Haldimann, Konrad; Weder, Hans*).

6233 *Howard-Brook, Wes* John's gospel's call to be reborn of God. NT: introducing. 2002 ⇒332. 80-102.

6234 *Igirukwayo, Antoine M.Z.* Elévation du Christ en croix dans l'évangile selon saint Jean et vie filiale. AETSC 7 (2002) 365-378 .

6235 **Jerumanis, Pascal-Marie** Réaliser la communion avec Dieu: croire, vivre et demeurer dans l'évangile selon Saint Jean. 1996 ⇒12,5423 ... 15,5838. [R]RivBib 50 (2002) 244-245 (*Fabris, Rinaldo*).

6236 **Kerber, Daniel** "No me eligieron ustedes a mí, sino que yo los elegí a ustedes": estudio exegético teológico sobre el verbo eklégomai en el cuarto evangelio. Montevideo 2002, Facultad de Teología del Uruguay 246 pp. Bibl. 223-237.

6237 **Kerr, Alan R.** The temple of Jesus' body: the temple theme in the gospel of John. JSNT.S 220: Shf 2002, Sheffield A. xii; 416 pp. £60/ $115. 1-8412-7262-0.

6238 *Koester, Craig R.* Comedy, humor, and the gospel of John. [F]KYSAR, R.: 2002 ⇒70. 123-141.

6239 **Kotila, Markku** Umstrittener Zeuge: Studien zur Stellung des Gesetzes in der johanneischen Theologiegeschichte. AASF.DHL 48: 1988 ⇒4,5496. [R]ThR 67 (2002) 447-8 (*Haldimann, Konrad; Weder, Hans*).

6240 **Krecidlo, Janusz** Funkcja pneumatologii w chrystologicznej strukturze czwartej ewangelii [La fonction de la pneumatologie dans la structure christologique du quatrième évangile]. [D]MEDALA, S.: 2002 417 pp. Diss. Warsaw [RTL 34,598].

6241 **Kügler, Joachim** Der Jünger, den Jesus liebte. SBB 16: 1988 ⇒5, 5399; 6,5673. [R]ThR 67 (2002) 336-37 (*Haldimann, Konrad; Weder, Hans*).

6242 *Kügler, Joachim* 'Denen aber, die ihn aufnahmen ...' (Joh 1,12): die Würde der Gotteskinder in der johanneischen Theologie. JBTh 17 (2002) 163-179.

6243 *Kyungu, Rigobert* L'heure et la gloire dans le quatrième évangile. Hekima Review 28 (2002) 50-61,

6244 L'évangile de Jean: conflits et controverses. SIDIC 34/3-35/1 (2001-2002) 1-38.

6245 *Labahn, Michael* 'Heiland der Welt': der gesandte Gottessohn und der römische Kaiser—ein Thema johanneischer Christologie?. Zwischen den Reichen. TANZ 36: 2002 ⇒568. 147-173 [Jn 4,42; 20, 28].

6246 **Larsson, Tord** God in the fourth gospel: a hermeneutical study of the history of interpretations. CB.NT 35: 2001 ⇒17,5838. [R]BZ 46 (2002) 140-141 (*Frey, Jörg*).

6247 **Lee, Dorothy A.** Flesh and glory: symbol, gender, and theology in the gospel of John. NY 2002, Crossroad viii; 296 pp. $27.50. 0-824-5-1981-7. Bibl. 274-287.

6248 **Leijgraaf, Monique** Brood en wijn binnen de spanning van Gods verkiezing: een bijbels-theologische interpretatie van het brood des levens (Johannes 6), de wijn van de bruiloft van Kana (Johannes 2:1-12) en de betrouwbare wijnstok (Johannes 15:1-8). 2001 ⇒17,5839. [R]ITBT 10/7 (2002) 33-34 (*Landman, G.M.*).

6249 *Leinhäupl-Wilke, Andreas* Rettet ein Buch?: Spurensuche in den Rahmenteilen des Johannesevangeliums. Rettendes Wissen. AOAT 300: 2002 ⇒352. 269-315 [John 1,12-2,12; 20-21].

6250 *Létourneau, Pierre* Dieu qui se fait connaître. Dieu, vingt-six portraits. 2002 ⇒312. 311-322.

6251 *Liew, Tat-siong Benny* Ambiguous admittance: consent and descent in John's community of 'upward' mobility. John and postcolonialism. 2002 ⇒6111. 193-224;

6252 Endless friends?: problematizing John's paradoxical politics of friendship. [F]PATTE, D.: 2002 ⇒89. 292-310.

6253 *Lincoln, Andrew T.* The beloved disciple as eyewitness and the fourth gospel as witness. JSNT 85 (2002) 3-26;

6254 *Lincoln, Andrew T.* Power, judgement and possession: John's gospel in political perspective. ^FO'DONOVAN, O.: 2002 ⇒272. 147-169.

6255 *Maceri, Francesco* Dalla presunzione all'amore: la sequela di Pietro nel vangelo di Giovanni. Asp. 49/4 (2002) 519-534.

6256 **Maia, Francisco Helton Reis** O acontecer da fé no evangelho de João: estudo a partir de uma obra de Xavier LÉON-DUFOUR, SJ. ^D*Konings, Johan*: RBBras 19/3 (2002) 181-321. Diss. Mestrado Belo Horizonte 2001.

6257 **Maillard, Anne** Dieu à la croisée de nos questions: l'évangile de Jean témoigne. Poliez-le-Grand 2002, Moulin 91 pp. €11.

6258 *Marrow, Stanley B.* Κόσμος in John. CBQ 64 (2002) 90-102.

6259 **Martín-Moreno, Juan Manuel** Personajes del cuarto evangelio. Biblioteca de Teología Comillas 7: M 2002, Universidad Pontificia Comillas 394 pp. €18. 84-330-1684-9.

6260 **McGrath, James Frank** John's apologetic christology: legitimation and development in Johannine christology. MSSNTS 111: 2001 ⇒17,5849. ^RJSNT 86 (2002) 115-116 (*Lieu, Judith*).

6261 **Metzner, Rainer** Das Verständnis der Sünde im Johannesevangelium. WUNT 122: 2000 ⇒16,5878; 17,5852. ^RBiLi 75 (2002) 311-312 (*Scholtissek, Klaus*); ThLZ 127 (2002) 46-48 (*Knöppler, Thomas*); ThG 45 (2002) 296-298 (*Giesen, Heinz*).

6262 *Moloney, Francis J.* John and the lectionary. BiTod 40 (2002) 72-79;

6263 "The Jews" in the fourth gospel: another perspective. Pacifica 15/1 (2002) 16-36;

6264 Telling God's story: the fourth gospel. ^FACHTEMEIER, P. 2002 ⇒1. 107-122.

6265 *Morgan Gillman, Florence* The women of John's gospel. BiTod 40 (2002) 91-98.

6266 *Nagel, Titus* Das "Unbekannte Berliner Evangelium" und das Johannesevangelium. ZNW 93 (2002) 251-267.

6267 *Navone, John* The compassion of Jesus in John. BiTod 40 (2002) 86-90.

6268 **Newheart, Michael Willett** Word and soul: a psychological, literary, and cultural reading of the fourth gospel. 2001 ⇒17,5859. ^RPacifica 15 (2002) 219-221 (*Patiner, John*); RBLit (2002)* (*Jonaitis, Dorothy*).

6269 *Neyrey, Jerome H.* Spaces and places, whence and whither, homes and rooms: 'territoriality' in the fourth gospel. BTB 32 (2002) 60-74;

6270 Spaced out: 'territoriality' in the fourth gospel. HTS 58 (2002) 632-663 [NTAb 47,254].

6271 **Ng, Wai-yee** Water symbolism in John: an eschatological interpretation. Studies in Biblical Literature 15: 2001 ⇒17,5860. ^RRBLit (2002)* (*Brant, Jo-Ann A.*).

6272 **Nicklas, Tobias** Ablösung und Verstrickung: "Juden" und Jüngergestalten als Charaktere der erzählten Welt des Johannesevangeliums und ihre Wirkung auf den impliziten Leser. RSTh 60: 2001 ⇒17, 5861. ^RThLZ 127 (2002) 1190-1192 (*Meiser, Martin*).

6273 *O'Day, Gail R.* 'I have said these things to you...': the unsettled place of Jesus' discourses in literary approaches to the fourth gospel. ^FKYSAR, R. 2002 ⇒70. 143-154.

6274 *O'Donovan, Oliver* Response to Andrew Lincoln. ^FO'DONOVAN, O. 2002 ⇒272. 170-172.

6275 *Painter, John* Earth made whole: John's rereading of Genesis. ^FKYSAR, R.: 2002 ⇒70. 65-84.

6276 *Petterson, Christina* Johannesevangeliets identitetskonstruktion. DTT 65 (2002) 184-195.
6277 *Potgieter, S.T.* 'n Johannese ekklesiologie?. VeE 23 (2002) 502-515.
6278 **Ray, Stephen K.** St. John's gospel: a bible study guide and commentary. SF 2002, Ignatius 461 pp. $18. 0-89870-821-4. Bibl. 403-416.
6279 **Rebell, Walter** Gemeinde als Gegenwelt: zur soziologischen und didaktischen Funktion des Johannesevangeliums. BET 20: 1987 ⟹3, 5234; 4,5398. ᴿThR 67 (2002) 347-48 (*Haldimann, Konrad; Weder, Hans*).
6280 **Reinhartz, Adele** Befriending the beloved disciple: a Jewish reading of the gospel of John. 2001 ⟹17,5874. ᴿThTo 59 (2002) 323-324, 326 (*Smith, D. Moody*); SR 31 (2002) 479-480 (*Smith, Mahlon H.*); JBL 121 (2002) 568-570 (*Tovey, Derek M.H.*).
6281 *Reinhartz, Adele* The gospel of John: how the 'Jews' became part of the plot. Jesus, Judaism. 2002 ⟹308. 99-116;
6282 The colonizer as colonized: intertextual dialogue between the gospel of John and Canadian identity. John and postcolonialism. 2002 ⟹ 6111. 170-192.
6283 *Rensberger, David* Spirituality and christology in Johannine sectarianism. ᶠKʏSAR, R. 2002 ⟹70. 173-188.
6284 **Riesner, Rainer** Bethanien jenseits des Jordans: Topographie und Theologie im Johannes-Evangelium. Biblische Archäologie und Zeitgeschichte 12: Giessen 2002, Brunnen 200 pp. 3-7655-9812-7 [John 1,28].
6285 *Román H., Carlos Eduardo* Implicaciones morales de la justicia en el Nuevo Testamento desde el evangelio de Juan. ThX 52 (2002) 615-640.
6286 **Ruschmann, Susanne** Maria von Magdala im Johannesevangelium: Jüngerin—Zeugin—Lebensbotin. ᴰOBERLINNER, L.: NTA 40: Müns 2002, Aschendorff ix; 269 pp. €35.80. 3-402-04788-8. Diss. Freiburg 2001; Bibl. 255-266. ᴿBib. 83 (2002) 589-592 (*Lieu, Judith*) [John 19,25; 20].
6287 **Sasse, Markus** Der Menschensohn im Evangelium nach Johannes. TANZ 35: 2000 ⟹16,5900. ᴿJThS 53 (2002) 210-215 (*Moloney, Francis J.*); SNTU.A 27 (2002) 235-238 (*Giesen, H.*).
6288 **Schnelle, Udo** Antidoketische Christologie im Johannesevangelium. FRLANT 144: 1987 ⟹3,5237... 6,5628. ᴿThR 67 (2002) 428-431 (*Haldimann, Konrad; Weder, Hans*).
6289 **Schroeder, Edward H.** Mosaic and christian ethos in the gospel of John. CThMi 29 (2002) 189-196.
6290 *Simoens, Yves* Le quatrième évangile—au service de la louange. SIDIC 34/3-35/1 (2002) 11-17.
6291 *Smith, D. Moody* Ethics and the interpretation of the fourth gospel. ᶠKʏSAR, R. 2002 ⟹70. 109-122.
6292 *Söding, Thomas* "Ich und der Vater sind eins" (Joh 10,30): die johanneische Christologie vor dem Anspruch des Hauptgebotes (Dtn 6,4f). ZNW 93 (2002) 177-199.
6293 *Dube, Musa W.* Descending from and ascending into heaven: a postcolonial analysis of travel, space and power in John. John and postcolonialism. 2002 ⟹6111. 1-10.
6294 *Straub, Esther* Der Irdische als der Auferstandene: kritische Theologie bei Johannes ohne ein Wort vom Kreuz. Kreuzestheologie. WUNT 151: 2002 ⟹298. 239-264.

6295　*Swanson, Tod D.* To prepare a place: Johannine christianity and the collapse of ethnic territory. John and postcolonialism. 2002 ⇒6111. 11-31.

6296　*Tanzer, Sarah J.* Jewish-christian relations and the gospel of John. BiTod 40 (2002) 99-105.

6297　**Tapel, René Oliver** Joy and sorrow in the gospel of Saint John. ^D*Aranda, G.* 2002, 316 pp. Diss. Pampelune [RTL 34,601].

6298　**Thatcher, Tom** The riddles of Jesus in John: a study in tradition and folklore. SBL.MS 53: 2000 ⇒16,5908; 17,5896. ^RBiblInterp 10 (2002) 96-99 (*Painter, John*); JSSt 47 (2002) 362-363 (*North, Wendy Sproston*); CBQ 64 (2002) 591-593 (*Segovia, Fernando F.*).

6299　*Theobald, Michael* Ansätze einer biblischen Spiritualität: Impulse aus dem Johannesevangelium. GuL 75 (2002) 166-182.

6300　**Theobald, Michael** Herrenworte im Johannesevangelium. Herders Biblische Studien 34: FrB 2002, Herder xiv; 663 pp. €70 3-451-274-94-9. Bibl. 626-646.

6301　**Thompson, Marianne Meye** The God of the gospel of John. 2001 ⇒17,5898. ^RScrB 32 (2002) 39-40 (*Docherty, Susan*); SNTU.A 27 (2002) 238-240 (*Labahn, M.*); LASBF 51 (2001) 430-432 (*Manns, F.*); VJTR 66 (2002) 228-232 (*Mlakuzhyil, George*); Third Millennium 5/2 (2002) 110-111 (*Mattam, J.*); EThL 78 (2002) 209-212 (*Van Belle, G.*); Theol. 105 (2002) 298-299 (*Smalley, Stephen*); EstTrin 36 (2002) 365-366 (*Pikaza, Xabier*); Horizons 29 (2002) 363-364 (*Koenig, John*); CTJ 37 (2002) 355-356 (*Brouwer, Wayne*); CBQ 64 (2002) 779-780 (*Koester, Craig R.*).

6302　*Tiedemann, Holger* Jesus und der Lieblingsjünger: zur Rezeption einer figuralen Leerstelle des Johannesevangeliums. Paare. 2002 ⇒ 489. 163-194.

6303　**Trumbower, Jeffrey A.** Born from above: the anthropology of the gospel of John. HUTh 29: 1992 ⇒8,5741... 12,5484. ^RThR 67 (2002) 344-345 (*Haldimann, Konrad; Weder, Hans*).

6304　**Urban, Christina** Das Menschenbild nach dem Johannesevangelium: Grundlagen johanneischer Anthropologie. WUNT 137: 2001 ⇒ 17,5905. ^ROrdKor 43 (2002) 489-490 (*Giesen, Heinz*).

6305　*Van den Heever, Gerhard* 'From the pragmatics of textures to a christian utopia': the case of the gospel of John. Rhetorical criticism. JSNT.S 195: 2002 ⇒369. 297-334.

6306　*Van der Merwe, Dirk G.* Hora, a possible theological setting for understanding Johannine eschatology. APB 13 (2002) 255-287.

6307　*Van der Watt, Jan Gabriël* The presence of Jesus through the gospel of John. Neotest. 36 (2002) 89-95.

6308　**Van der Watt, Jan Gabriel** Family of the King: dynamics of metaphor in the gospel according to John. BiblInterp 47: 2000 ⇒16,5911. ^RBZ 46 (2002) 280-282 (*Zimmermann, Ruben*).

6309　**Vaz, Joe** Bible quiz: John's gospel. Indore 2002, Akhand Vani 129 pp. Rs15 [VJTR 67,736—Meagher, P.M.].

6310　*Wehr, Lothar* Das Eucharistieverständnis an der Wende vom ersten zum zweiten Jahrhundert: Johannesevangelium und außerbiblische Traditionen. BiKi 57 (2002) 22-27 [John 6,22-59; 13].

6311　**Westermann, Claus** The gospel of John: in the light of the Old Testament. 1998 ⇒14,5411... 17,5916. ^RRB 109 (2002) 472-473 (*Viviano, Benedict T.*).

6312 **Wróbel, Miroslaw** Synagoga a Rodzacy sie Kosciól: studium egzegetyczno-teologiczne czwartej ewangelii (J 9,22; 12,42; 16,2). Studia Biblica (Kielce) 3: Kielce 2002, Verbum 276 pp. 83-915855-4-9. Bibl. 14-56. **P.**

6313 **Yamaguchi, Satoko** Mary and Martha: women in the world of Jesus. Mkn 2002, Orbis xi; 204 pp. $24. 1-57075-401-2. Diss. Episcopal Divinity School, CM; Bibl. 179-196. [R]America 187/1 (2002) 18-20 (*Hawkins, Nancy*).

6314 **Zangenberg, Jürgen** Frühes Christentum in Samarien: topographische und traditionsgeschichtliche Studien zu den Samarientexten im Johannesevangelium. TANZ 27: 1998 ⇒14,5413. [R]ThLZ 127 (2002) 302-304 (*Scholtissek, Klaus*) [John 8,48; 10,16; 11,54; 3,22-30; 4,1-43].

6315 *Zumstein, Jean* Lectura narratológica del ciclo pascual en el cuarto evangelio. SelTeol 41 (2002) 244-250 <ETR 76 (2001) 1-15.

6316 **Zumstein, Jean** Kreative Erinnerung: Relecture und Auslegung im Johannesevangelium. [T]*Straub, Esther*: 1999 ⇒15,5740; 16,5919. [R]ThLZ 127 (2002) 58-59 (*Wengst, Klaus*).

G1.5 Johannis Prologus 1,1...

6317 *Balabanski, Vicky* John 1—the earth bible challenge: an intra-textual approach to reading John 1. Earth story. 2002 ⇒322. 89-94.

6318 *Blanchard, Yves-Marie* Le regard d'un bibliste [Incarnation]. RICP 81 (2002) 29-42. Réponses de *Michel Henry* 94-104.

6319 *Borgonovo, Gianantonio* Incarnazione del Logos: il Logos giovanneo alla luce della tradizione giudaica. ScC 130/1 (2002) 43-75.

6320 *Cozzi, Alberto* Il Logos e Gesù: alla ricerca di un nuovo spazio di pensabilità dell'incarnazione. ScC 130/1 (2002) 77-116.

6321 **Denker, Jochen** Das Wort wurde messianischer Mensch: die Theologie Karl BARTHs und die Theologie des Johannesprologs. [D]*Klappert, Bertold*: Neuk 2002, Neuk'er 348 pp. €39.90. 3-7887-1925-7. Diss. Wuppertal [EuA 79,75—Schwank, Benedikt].

6322 *Du Rand, J.A.* Die Johannese Logos kom opnuut tuis in Afrika. VeE 23 (2002) 80-91.

6323 **Endo, Masanobu** Creation and christology: a study on the Johannine Prologue in the light of early Jewish creation accounts. WUNT 2/149: Tü 2002, Mohr S. xx; 292 pp. €54. 31614-77898. Bibl. 254-64.

6324 *Ford, David F.* Jesus Christ in scripture, community and mission: the wisdom of John 1:1-18. [F]NILES, D. 2002 ⇒82. 292-303.

6325 *Habel, Norman C.* An ecojustice challenge: is earth valued in John 1?. Earth story. 2002 ⇒322. 76-82.

6326 **Hofrichter, Peter Leander** Im Anfang was der 'Johannesprolog': das urchristliche Logosbekenntnis—die Basis neutestamentlicher und gnostischer Theologie. BU 17: 1986 ⇒2,4217... 6,5767. [R]ThR 67 (2002) 444-445 (*Haldimann, Konrad; Weder, Hans*).

6327 *Kurz, William* Beyond historical criticism: reading John's prologue as catholics. The future of Catholic biblical scholarship. 2002 ⇒337. 159-181.

6328 *Segovia, Fernando F.* John 1:1-18 as entrée into Johannine reality: representation and ramifications. [F]KYSAR, R. 2002 ⇒70. 33-64.

6329 *Tovey, Derek* Narrative strategies in the prologue and the metaphor of ὁ λόγος in John's gospel. Pacifica 15/2 (2002) 138-153.

6330 *Voorwinde, Stephen* John's Prologue: beyond some impasses of twentieth-century scholarship. WThJ 64 (2002) 15-44.
6331 *Wainwright, Elizabeth* Which intertext?: a response to an ecojustice challenge: is earth valued in John 1. Earth story. 2002 ⇒322. 83-88.

6332 *Blocher, Henri* Mise au point johannique (Jn 1.3-4). ThEv(VS) 1/1 (2002) 77-80.
6333 *Vanoni, Gottfried* Blinde Flecke bei christlicher Wahrnehmung?: Versuch über Johannes 1,14-17. ᶠTHOMA, C.: JudChr 20: 2002 ⇒ 119. 307-320.
6334 *Kurianal, James* Theological significance of the phrase χαρις αντι χαριτος in John 1,16. ETJ 6 (2002) 128-141.
6335 *Segalla, Giuseppe* "In Betania ... aldilà del Giordano" (Gv 1,28). StPat 49 (2002) 201-206.
6336 *Kelsey, Catherine* Calling disciples: SCHLEIERMACHER's application of his hermeneutics to John 1:35-51. TJT 18 (2002) 33-42.
6337 **Kuhn, Hans-Jürgen** Christologie und Wunder: Untersuchungen zu Joh 1,35-51. BU 18: 1988 ⇒4,5547... 7,4869. ᴿThR 67 (2002) 433-434 (*Haldimann, Konrad; Weder, Hans*).

6338 *Joosse, N. Peter* An introduction to the so-called Persian Diatessaron of Iwannis 'IZZ AL-DIN of Tabriz: the testimony of John 2:1-11 (the wedding at Cana). OrChr 86 (2002) 13-45.
6339 **Lütgehetmann, Walter** Die Hochzeit von Kana. 1990 ⇒6,5796... 12,5517. ᴿThR 67 (2002) 434-435 (*Veijola, Timo*) [John 2,1-11].
6340 *Israel, Nilva D.* Maria, minha mãe ... nasci mulher, é suficiente!: algumas reflexões mergulhando em Jo 2,1-12. Estudos bíblicos 75 (2002) 11-21.
6341 *Chacón, Luis* Principales líneas de interpretación de Jn 2,3c-4 en la historia de la exégesis. EE 77 (2002) 385-460.
6342 *Stramare, Tarcisio* La risposta di Gesù a Maria alle nozze di Cana: il test della ragionevolezza. BeO 44 (2002) 179-192 [John 2,4].
6343 **López Rosas, Ricardo** La señal del templo: Jn 2,13-22: redefinición cristológica de lo sacro. 2001 ⇒17,5955. ᴿQol 28 (2002) 107-115 (*Noguez, Ma. Eugenia*); Qol 28 (2002) 117-122 (*Figueroa Jácome, Leonor*); Ang. 79 (2002) 990-992 (*Jurič, Stipe*).

G1.6 Jn 3ss... Nicodemus, Samaritana

6344 **Cimbumba Ndayango, Antoine Cilumba** Wunder, Glaube und Leben bei Johannes: eine exegetisch-hermeneutische Studie am Beispiel von Joh 3 im Hinblick auf die Inkulturationsaufgabe. Arbeiten zur Interkulturalität 3: 2001 ⇒17,5958. ᴿNZM 58 (2002) 229 (*Schelbert, Georg*); CrSt 23 (2002) 823-25 (*Segalla, Giuseppe*).
6345 **Popp, Thomas** Grammatik des Geistes: literarische Kunst und theologische Konzeption in Johannes 3 und 6. Arbeiten zur Bibel und ihrer Geschichte 3: 2001 ⇒17,5960. ᴿThLZ 127 (2002) 764-767 (*Scholtissek, Klaus*).
6346 *Canales, Arthur D.* A rebirth of being "born again": theological, sacramental and pastoral reflections from a Roman Catholic perspective. JPentec 11/1 (2002) 98-119 [John 3,1-15].

6347 *Theißen, Gerd* Liebe und Wiedergeburt: eine Zusammenfassung der Botschaft des Johannesevangeliums (Joh 3,1-16). Erlösungsbilder. 2002 ⇒1460. 97-103.

6348 *Górka, Bogusław* Zstąpienie i wstąpienie Syna Człowieczego (J 3, 13) [The descent and the ascent of the Son of Man (John 3,13)]. StBob 2 (2002) 45-52 Sum. 52. **P.**

6349 *Reynolds, E.E.* Another look at the serpent on the pole. Asia Adventist Seminary Studies [Silang, Cavite, Philippines] 4 (2001) 35-47 [NTAb 47,52] [Num 21,4-9; John 3,14-16].

6350 *Nicklas, Tobias* Literarkritik und Leserrezeption: ein Beitrag zur Methodendiskussion am Beispiel Joh 3,22-4,3. Bib. 83 (2002) 175-192.

6351 *Crüsemann, Marlene* Living water: elements of a feminist proclamation according to John 4. ᶠSCHOTTROFF, L.: 2002 ⇒111. 39-46.

6352 *Vanhoozer, Kevin J.* Worship at the well: from dogmatics to doxology (and back again). TrinJ 23 (2002) 3-16 [John 4].

6353 *Van Belle, Gilbert* Κύριος or Ἰησοῦς in John 4,1?. ᶠDELOBEL, J.: BEThL 161: 2002 ⇒24. 159-174.

6354 **Day, Janeth Norfleete** The woman at the well: interpretation of John 4:1-42 in retrospect and prospect. BiblInterp 61 Lei 2002 Brill xi; 203 pp €70 90-04-12482-9 Bibl. 183-197 {John}04,01-42.

6355 *Dube, Musa W.* Reading for decolonization (John 4.1-42). John and postcolonialism. 2002 ⇒6111. 51-75.

6356 **Link, Andrea Hildegard** Was redest du mit ihr?:...Joh 4,1-42. 1992 ⇒8,5794... 13,5808. ᴿThR 67 (2002) 442-443 (*Haldimann, Konrad; Weder, Hans*).

6357 **Schapdick, Stefan** Auf dem Weg in den Konflikt: exegetische Studien zum theologischen Profil der Erzählung vom Aufenthalt Jesu in Samarien (Joh 4, 1-42). BBB 126: 2000 ⇒16,5951; 17,5972. ᴿBiLi 75 (2002) 313-315 (*Scholtissek, Klaus*).

6358 *Mulzac, K.D.* The church's mission: Jesus' example in John 4:4-42 as a model. Asia Adventist Seminary Studies [Silang, Cavite, Philippines] 4 (2001) 101-112 [NTAb 47,52].

6359 *Croatto, J. Severino* Nazaret en el evangelio de Juan (interpretación de Jn 4,44). RevBib 64 (2002) 53-60.

6360 *Attridge, Harold W.* Argumentation in John 5. Rhetorical argumentation. 2002 ⇒553. 188-199.

6361 *Lozada, Francisco* Contesting an interpretation of John 5: moving beyond colonial evangelism. John and postcolonialism. 2002 ⇒6111. 76-93.

6362 *Spijkerboer, Anne M.* Een toegevoegde engel. KeTh 53 (2002) 275-277 [John 5,1-18].

6363 *Huie-Jolly, Mary* Maori 'Jews' and a resistant reading of John 5.10-47. John and postcolonialism. 2002 ⇒6111. 94-110.

6364 **Kammler, Hans-Christian** Christologie und Eschatologie: Joh 5,17-30 als Schlüsseltext johanneischer Theologie. WUNT 126: 2000 ⇒16,5962; 17,5980. ᴿBiLi 75 (2002) 148-149 (*Scholtissek, Klaus*); StPat 49 (2002) 257-259 (*Segalla, Giuseppe*); BZ 46 (2002) 283-286 (*Popkes, Enno Edzard*).

6365 *Meeks, Wayne A.* Equal to God. In search. 2002 ⇒208. 91-105 [John 5,18].

G1.7 **Panis Vitae**—*Jn 6...*

6366   *Castellano, Antonio* Juan 6 en la interpretación de ORÍGENES (1a parte). TyV 43 (2002) 138-166.
6367   *Kurz, William* Bread of life in John 6: intertextuality and the unity of scripture;
6368   Feeding the 5000 in John 6 and the eucharist: spiritual senses and actualization. The future of Catholic biblical scholarship. 2002 ⇒ 337. 203-218/219-236.
6369   *Lembke, Matti* Biblische Besinnung: Ich bin das Brot des Lebens. ZMiss 28 (2002) 203-205 [John 6].
6370   *Need, Stephen W.* Jesus the bread of God: the eucharist as metaphor in John 6. Theol. 105 (2002) 194-200.
6371   *Chung, Meehyun* A meditation on John 6:1-14. VFTW 25/1 (2002) 28-31.
6372   **Labahn, Michael** Offenbarung in Zeichen und Wort: Untersuchungen zur Vorgeschichte von Joh. 6,1-25 a und seiner Rezeption in der Brotrede. WUNT 2/117: 2000 ⇒16,5966; 17,5982. ᴿJThS 53 (2002) 215-23 (*Borgen, Peder*); SNTU.A 27 (2002) 227-33 (*Fuchs, Albert*).
6373   *Billy, Dennis J.* Eucharistic faith: Jesus' bread-of-life discourse. RfR 61 (2002) 640-648 [John 6,22-71].
6374   *Ashby, Godfrey W.* Body and blood in John 6:41-65. Neotest. 36 (2002) 57-61.

6375   *Moloney, Francis J.* Narrative and discourse at the feast of Tabernacles: John 7:1-8:59. ᶠKYSAR, R.: 2002 ⇒70. 155-172.
6376   **Devillers, Luc** La fête de l'Envoyé: la section johannique de la Fête des Tentes (Jean 7,1-10,21) et la christologie. ÉtB 49: P 2002, Gabalda 589 pp. €75. 2-85021-144-3. Bibl. 519-558.
6377   *Buscemi, Maria S.* "De corpos, pavores e utopias ...": uma hermenêutica feminista de Jo 7,53-8,11. Estudos bíblicos 75 (2002) 85-96.
6378   *Guardiola-Sáenz, Leticia A.* Border-crossing and its redemptive power in John 7.53-8.11: a cultural reading of Jesus and the accused. John and postcolonialism. 2002 ⇒6111. 129-152.
6379   *Kim, Jean K.* Adultery or hybridity?: reading John 7.53-8.11 from a postcolonial context. John and postcolonialism. 2002 ⇒6111. 111-128.
6380   ᴱ**Kreitzer, Larry Joseph; Rooke, Deborah W.** Ciphers in the sand: interpretations of the woman taken in adultery (John 7.53-8.11). BiSe 74: 2000 ⇒16,285. ᴿCBQ 64 (2002) 200-202 (*McGinn, Sheila E.*); HeyJ 43 (2002) 358-359 (*Webster, Jane S.*); RBLit (2002)* (*Harstine, Stan*).
6381   *Sánchez, Eduardo* El comentario de AMBROSIO y AGUSTÍN sobre la perícopa de la adúltera (Jn 7,53-8,11): parte segunda: análisis comparativo. Augustinus 47 (2002) 155-184.
6382   *Jacobs, Stevens Leonard* Aux prises avec Dieu et le diable: une lecture post-Holocauste/Shoa de Jean 8. SIDIC 34/3-35/1 (2002) 27-30.
6383   *Knight, Henry F.* Face au saint: lire Jean 8 avec un regard devenu plus sage. SIDIC 34/3-35/1 (2002) 30-32.
6384   *Philippe, Marie D.* Commentaire de l'évangile de saint Jean : sur les traditions religieuses et la foi (ch.8). Aletheia 22 (2002) 161-168.

6385 *Wasserman, T.* The Patmos family of New Testament MSS and its allies in the pericope of the adulteress and beyond. TC: a journal of biblical textual criticism [http://purl.org/TC] 7 (2002) pars. 1-59 [NTAb 47,472] [John 8,8-9].

6386 *Philippe, Marie D.* Commentaire de l'évangile de saint Jean : "Je suis la lumière du monde"—"Je suis" (2). Aletheia 21 (2002) 155-163 [John 8,12].

6387 **Vanneuville, Frederique** Jesus and 'the Jews' in John 8:31-59: an interdisciplinary investigation into the problem of Anti-Judaism in the gospel of John. *DBieringer, R.*: 2002, xxviii; 223 pp. Diss. Leuven 2002 [EThL 79,238].

6388 *Gnadt, Martina S.* 'What we will be has not yet been revealed': an archaeology of seeing in John 9. *FSCHOTTROFF, L.*: 2002 ⇒111. 127-136.

6389 *Maldamé, Jean-Michel* Quand Jésus guérit: une lecture théologique de la guérison de l'aveugle-né (Jn 9). EeV 50 (2002) 9-15.

6390 *Schneiders, Sandra M.* To see or not to see: John 9 as a synthesis of the theology and spirituality of discipleship. *FKYSAR, R.*: 2002 ⇒70. 189-209.

6391 *Olajubu, Oyeronke* Reconnecting with the waters: John 9.1-11. Earth story. 2002 ⇒322. 108-121.

6392 *Neyrey, Jerome H.* The 'noble shepherd' in John 10: cultural and rhetorical background. JBL 120 (2001) 267-291.

6393 *Köstenberger, Andreas J.* Jesus the Good Shepherd who will also bring other sheep (John 10:16): the Old Testament background of a familiar metaphor. BBR 12 (2002) 67-96.

6394 *Combes, Alain* Mise en scène de la résurrection de Lazare dans Jean 11. ThEv(VS) 1/2 (2002) 79-86.

6395 **Sproston North, Wendy E.** The Lazarus story within the Johannine tradition. JSNT.S 212: 2001 ⇒17,6004. RBZ 46 (2002) 286-287 (*Frey, Jörg*).

6396 **Wagner, Josef** Auferstehung und Leben: Joh 11,1-12,19 als Spiegel johanneischer Redaktions- und Theologiegeschichte. BU 19: 1988 ⇒ 4,5588b... 11/1,4210. RThR 67 (2002) 440-442 (*Haldimann, Konrad; Weder, Hans*).

6397 *Theißen, Gerd* Der Tod als Schattenriss Gottes: Gott und Nichts als schwarze Löcher in unserer Wirklichkeit (Joh 11,1.3.17-26). Erlösungsbilder. 2002 ⇒1460. 104-113.

6398 *Luzarraga, Jesús* El nardo y la Sulamita en la unción de Maryam (Jn 12,1-8). Gr. 83 (2002) 679-715.

6399 *Balz, Heinrich* "Die Stunde ist gekommen": welche denn?: Predigt über Joh 12,20-26, gehalten in der Kirche des Makumira University College (Tanzania) am 25.3.2001. ZMiss 28 (2002) 2-6.

6400 *Ensor, Peter W.* The authenticity of John 12.24. EvQ 74 (2002) 99-107.

6401 *Boismard, Marie-Émile* Le prince de ce monde sera jeté en bas: Jn 12,31. FDELOBEL, J.: BEThL 161: 2002 ⇒24. 175-181.

G1.8 Jn 13... Sermo sacerdotalis et Passio

6402 **Brouns-Wewerinke, Door** In verhalen krijgt geschiedenis betekenis: verbeelding van Jezus' lijden en dood in het Johannesevangelie

[Stories lend significance to history: the depiction of the passion and death of Jesus in the gospel according to John]. ᴰ*Weren, W.J.C.*: Boekencentrum 2002, 288 pp. €24.90. 90-239-0974-7. Diss. Tilburg 2002. ᴿEThL 78 (2002) 212-217 (*Van Belle, G.*).

6403 *Nolan, Brian* "In the very temple of delight": a study of John 13-21. PIBA 25 (2002) 97-115.

6404 *Patella, Michael* Seers' corner: triduum topography according to John. BiTod 40 (2002) 106-110.

6405 *Rathinam, Selva* The Old Testament in John's passion narrative. VJTR 66 (2002) 405-418.

6406 **Neri, Umberto** L'addio di Gesù ai discepoli: il discorso della grande consolazione (Gv 13-16). Sussidi biblici 75: Reggio Emilia 2002, San Lorenzo 183 pp. 88-8071-127-X.

6407 **Brouwer, Wayne** The literary development of John 13-17:a chiastic reading. SBL.DS 182: 2000 ⇒17,6006. ᴿCBQ 64 (2002) 153-154 (*Just, Felix*).

6408 **Parsenios, George** Departure and consolation: the polyphony of genres in John 13-17. ᴰ*Attridge, H.*: 2002, 247 pp. Diss. Yale [RTL 34,600].

6409 *Veerkamp, Ton* Der Abschied des Messias: Johannes 13-17. TeKo 25/3 (2002) 1-95.

6410 **Winter, Martin** Das Vermächtnis Jesu und die Abschiedsworte der Väter: gattungsgeschichtliche Untersuchung der Vermächtnisrede im Blick auf Joh. 13-17. FRLANT 161: 1994 ⇒10,5410... 13,5871. ᴿThR 67 (2002) 449-450 (*Haldimann, Konrad; Weder, Hans*).

6411 **Tolmie, D.F.** Jesus' farewell to the disciples: John 13:1-17:26 in narratological perspective. Bibl.Interp. 12: 1995 ⇒11/1,4235... 14, 5490. ᴿRBLit (2002)* (*Brownson, James V.; Van der Watt, Jan G.*).

6412 **Oyer, Linda** Dieu à nos pieds... une étude sur le lavement des pieds. Les dossiers de Christ seul 4/2002: Montbéliard 2002, Mennonites 75 pp [ThEv(VS) 2,92—Marie Claude Saoût] [John 13,1-20].

6413 **Gangemi, Attilio** Signore, Tu a me lavi i piedi ?: Pietro e il mistero dell'amore di Gesù: studio esegetico teologico di Gv 13,6-11. 1999 ⇒15,6044. ᴿItin. 10 (2002) 215-216 (*Costa, Giuseppe*).

6414 *Staley, Jeffrey L.* 'Dis place, man': a postcolonial critique of the vine (the mountain and the temple) in the gospel of John. John and post-colonialism. 2002 ⇒6111. 32-50 [John 15].

6415 **Haldimann, Konrad** Rekonstruktion und Entfaltung: exegetische Untersuchungen zu Joh 15 und 16. BZNW 104: 2000 ⇒16,6018; 17, 6023. ᴿThLZ 127 (2002) 1298-1301 (*Zimmermann, Ruben*); RBLit 4 (2002) 397-399 (*Köstenberger, Andreas J.*).

6416 *Glass, Zipporah G.* Building toward 'nation-ness' in the vine: a post-colonial critique of John 15.1-8. John and postcolonialism. 2002 ⇒ 6111. 153-169.

6417 *Bieringer, Reimund* The spirit's guidance into all the truth: the text-critical problems of John 16,13. ᶠDELOBEL, J.: BEThL 161: 2002 ⇒ 24. 183-207.

6418 *Counet, Patrick Chatelion* Paroimiai (John 16:25): a post-hermeneutical model. Philosophical hermeneutics. WUNT 153: 2002 ⇒367. 252-269.

6419 *Zumstein, Jean* Le passé transfiguré: l'histoire sub specie aeternitatis selon Jean 17. ᶠHAMMANN, G.: 2002 ⇒57. 431-440 [BuBB 38,126].

6420 *Van der Merwe, D.G.* The glory-motif in John 17:1-5: an exercise in biblical semantics. VeE 23 (2002) 226-249;

6421 The character of unity expected among the disciples of Jesus, according to John 17:20-23. APB 13 (2002) 224-254.

6422 *Bourdeau, Gilles* 'Un comme nous sommes un': communion, unité et témoignage selon Jean 17,20-26. Oecumenisme 147 (2002) 22-26.

6423 **Sprecher, Marie-Therese** Einheitsdenken aus der Perspektive von Joh 17: eine exegetische und bibeltheologisiche Untersuchung von John 17,20-26. EHS.T 495: 1993 ⇒9,5626. [R]ZKTh 124 (2002) 100-103 (*Lies, Lothar*).

6424 [E]**Bienert, Wolfgang A.** Einheit als Gabe und Verpflichtung: eine Studie des Deutschen Ökumenischen Studienausschusses (DÖSTA) zu Johannes 17 Vers 21. Fra 2002, Lembeck 183 pp. 3-87476-404-4.

6425 Einheit als Gabe und Verpflichtung: eine Studie des Deutschen Ökumenischen Studienausschusses (DÖSTA) zu Johannes 17,21. Einheit als Gabe. 2002 ⇒6424. 15-26.

6426 *Geldbach, Erich* "Ut unum sint": der Gebrauch von Joh 17,21 im 19. Jahrhundert: ein Werkstattbericht. Einheit als Gabe. 2002 ⇒6424. 61-78.

6427 *Oeyen, Christian* Joh 17,21 und die Auslegung der Kirchenväter. Einheit als Gabe. 2002 ⇒6424. 39-59.

6428 *Wanke, Joachim* Skizze einer Studie zu Joh 17,21. Einheit als Gabe. 2002 ⇒6424. 13-14.

6429 *Hill, Charles E.* Did the scribe of P52 use the nomina sacra?: another look. NTS 48 (2002) 587-592 [John 18].

6430 *Cunningham, Philip* 'Traduire le récit de la passion selon saint Jean ou en faire des citations pour la proclamation liturgique'. SIDIC 34/3-35/1 (2002) 17-27 [John 18-19].

6431 *Hasitschka, Martin* Beobachtungen zur Chronologie und Topographie der Passionsgeschichte nach Johannes. Priorität. 2002 ⇒561. 151-159 [John 18-19].

6432 *Bladh, Elisabeth Le jardinier* or *le gardien*?: who did Mary think she met in the garden?: lexical comparison of nouns in modern French translations of John 18:1-20:31. Bible and computer. 2002 ⇒548. 463-474.

6433 *Seeanner, Paulus* Jesus, rei e testemunha da verdade (II): pesquisa exegética-teológica de *Jo* 18,33-38a. Sapientia Crucis 3/3 (2002) 5-30 [BuBB 38,129].

6434 *Theißen, Gerd* Die Frage nach der Wahrheit: SOKRATES und Jesus vor ihren Richtern (Joh 18,33-38). Erlösungsbilder. 2002 ⇒1460. 114-121.

6435 *Steinlein, Heinz* 'Seht, das ist der Mensch' (Joh 19,5): eine bibeltheologische Meditation im Anschluss an die Betrachtung des Bildes 'Menschenschöpfung' von Nika Bakhia. [F]HAAG, E.: 2002 ⇒55. 387-393.

6436 **Kollmann, Hanjo-Christoph** Die Kreuzigung Jesu nach John 19,16-22: ein Beitrag zur Kreuzestheologie des Johannes im Vergleich mit den Synoptikern. EHS.T 710: 2000 ⇒16,6035. [R]ThLZ 127 (2002) 290-291 (*Lang, Manfred*).

6437 **Corbin, Michel** Résurrection et nativité: lecture théologique de Jean 20,1-31. Théologies: P 2002, Cerf 362 pp. €28. [R]REsp 61 (2002)

487-490 (*Castro, Secundino*); LTP 58 (2002) 613-614 (*Cazelais, Serge*).

6438 *Kurz, William* Test case: "whose sins you shall forgive" in John 20: applying scripture with the catechism. The future of Catholic biblical scholarship. 2002 ⇒337. 237-248.

6439 *Panier, Louis* De corps manquant à l'écriture à lire. [F]PATTE, D. 2002 ⇒89. 37-48 [John 20].

6440 **George, Larry Darnell** Reading the tapestry: a literary-rhetorical analysis of the Johannine resurrection narrative (John 20-21). Studies in Biblical Literature 14: 2000 ⇒16,6039. [R]RBLit 4 (2002) 395-396 (*Conway, Colleen M.*).

6441 *Menken, Maarten J.J.* Interpretation of the Old Testament and the resurrection of Jesus in John's gospel. [F]LAMBRECHT, J.: BEThL 165: 2002 ⇒72. 189-205 [John 20-21].

6442 *Zumstein, Jean* Le cycle pascal du quatrième évangile (Jean 20-21). Quand la bible se raconte. 2002 ⇒355. 143-161.

6443 *López Rosas, Ricardo* La nueva era: pascua de Jesús: lectura meditativa de Jn 20,1-18. Qol 29 (2002) 105-110.

6444 *Draper, Jonathan A.* What did Isaiah see?: angelic theophany in the tomb in John 20:11-18. Neotest. 36 (2002) 63-76 [Isa 6; John 1,51].

6445 *Still, E. Coye* Sent to be scarred: John 20:19-23. ET 113 (2002) 190-191.

6446 *Moreno García, Abdón* Manos y dedos: hacia la comprensión de los merismos en la perícopa Tomasiana de Jn 20,19-31. EstB 60 (2002) 523-542.

6447 **Bonney, William** Caused to believe: the doubting Thomas story at the climax of John's christological narrative. BiblInterp 62: Lei 2002, Brill vi; 192 pp. 90-04-12660-0. Bibl. 175-182 [John 20,24-29].

6448 **Arnold, Kenneth** Night fishing in Galilee: the journey toward spiritual wisdom. CM 2002, Cowley xvi; 143 pp. $13. 1-56101-195-9 [John 21].

6449 *Söding, Thomas* Erscheinung, Vergebung und Sendung: Joh 21 als Zeugnis entwickelten Osterglaubens. [F]LAMBRECHT, J. BEThL 165: 2002 ⇒72. 207-232.

6450 *Bauckham, Richard* The 153 fish and the unity of the fourth gospel. Neotest. 36 (2002) 77-88 [Ezek 47,10; John 21,11].

G2.1 Epistulae Johannis

6451 **Akin, Daniel L.** 1,2,3 John. NAC 38: 2001 ⇒17,6046. [R]RBLit (2002)* (*Johnson, Thomas F.*).

6452 **Beutler, Johannes** Die Johannesbriefe. Regensburger NT: 2000 ⇒ 16,6049; 17,6047. [R]BZ 46 (2002) 156-157 (*Frey, Jörg*).

6453 **Kruse, Colin G.** The letters of John. 2000 ⇒16,6052; 17,6050. [R]RBLit 4 (2002) 446-448 (*Batten, Alicia*).

6454 [E]**Mills, Watson Early** The letters of John. Bibliographies for biblical research, NT 18: Lewiston, NY 2002, Mellen xviii; 96 pp. 0-7734-2471-7.

6455 **Painter, John** 1, 2, and 3 John. Sacra Pagina 18: ColMn 2002, Liturgical xvii; 411 pp. $40. 0-8146-5812-1.

6456 **Tidball, Dianne** John's letters. Crossway Bible Guide: Leicester 2002, Crossway 154 pp. 1-85684-211-8. Bibl. 154.

6457 **Uebele, Wolfram** "Viele Verführer sind in die Welt ausgegangen": die Gegner in den Briefen des IGNATIUS von Antiochien und in den Johannesbriefen. BWANT 151: 2001 ⇒17,6053. ᴿThLZ 127 (2002) 1056-1058 (*Nagel, Titus*).

6458 **Barfield, Virginia** 1 John: a social-scientific interpretation. ᴰ*Smith, D.M.*: 2002, 241 pp. Diss. Duke [RTL 34,596]..

6459 **Giurisato, Giorgio** Struttura e teologia della prima lettera di Giovanni: analisi letteraria e retorica, contenuto teologico. AnBib 138: 1998 ⇒14,5528...17,6054. ᴿEstB 60 (2002) 418-422 (*Urbán, Á.*); EThL 78 (2002) 228-230 (*Verheyden, J.*).

6460 **Griffith, Terry** Keep yourselves from idols: a new look at 1 John. JSNT.S 233: L 2002, Sheffield A. xvi; 247 pp. £50. 0-8264-6051-8. Bibl. 213-225.

6461 *Manns, Frédéric* The christology of the first letter of John. ᶠTUDDA, F. 2002 ⇒123. 51-84.

6462 **Schmid, Hans-Jörg** Gegner im 1. Johannesbrief?: zur Konstruktion und Selbstreferenz im johanneischen Sinnsystem. ᴰ*Oberlinner, Lorenz*: BWANT 159: Stu 2002, Kohlhammer 335 pp. €35. 3-17-0175-99-8. Diss. Feiburg/Br. Bibl. 306-327.

6463 *Studer, Basil* Gesù Cristo, nostra propiziazione, in Giovanni e Paolo: osservazioni sull'esegesi patristica della prima lettera di Giovanni. VII Simposio di Tarso. 2002 ⇒587. 191-201.

6464 *Von Wahlde, Urban C.* The stereotyped structure and the puzzling pronouns of 1 John 2:28-3:10. CBQ 64 (2002) 319-338.

6465 *Morgen, Michèle* La figure du frère dans 1 Jn 3,12: l'audace de la typologie et ses clins d'oeil au lecteur. Typologie biblique. LeDiv: 2002 ⇒341. 203-221.

6466 *Tacelli, Ronald* "Wir sollen einander lieben" (vgl. 1 Joh 4,7): vom Problem der "Nächstenliebe". EuA 78 (2002) 236-237.

6467 *Theißen, Gerd* Gott auf Partnersuche: Kontaktanzeigen des Himmels für einen schwierigen Partner (1 Joh 4,7-19). Erlösungsbilder. 2002 ⇒1460. 184-190.

6468 *Landrus, Heather L.* Hearing 3 John 2 in the voices of history;
6469 *Roberts, Mark E.* A hermeneutic of charity: response to Heather Landrus. JPentec 11/1 (2002) 70-88/89-97.

G2.3 *Apocalypsis Johannis*—Revelation: text, commentaries

6470 ᴱ**Acinas, Blanca** En torno al Apocalipsis. BAC, Teologia 14: 2001 ⇒17,6059. ᴿEfMex 20 (2002) 275-276 (*López Rosas, Ricardo*).

6471 ᴱ**Backhaus, Knut** Theologie als Vision: Studien zur Johannes-Offenbarung. SBS 191: 2001 ⇒17,6062. ᴿBZ 46 (2002) 292-293 (*Frey, Jörg*); ThPQ 150 (2002) 423-425 (*Niemand, Christoph*).

6472 **Beale, Gregory K.** The book of Revelation: a commentary on the Greek text. NIGTC: 1999 ⇒16,6072; 17,6063. ᴿHBT 24/2 (2002) 124-125 (*Aune, David E.*).

6473 *Bettencourt, Estêvão* O Apocalipse. RCB 43 (2002) 141-156.

6474 **Boxall, Ian** Revelation: vision and insight: an introduction to the Apocalypse. L 2002, SPCK x; 166 pp. £13. 0-281-05362-6. Bibl. 159-162. ᴿTheol. 105 (2002) 359-360 (*Smalley, Stephen*).

6475 **Dawn, Marva J.** Joy in our weakness. GR 2002, Eerdmans xiv; 220 pp. $16 [BiTod 40,400—Senior, Donald].
6476 **Giesen, Heinz** Studien zur Johannesapokalypse. SBAB 29: 2000 ⇒ 16,6085. RThRv 98 (2002) 310-311 (*Scholtissek, Klaus*); ThG 45 (2002) 152-153 (*Böcher, Otto*); RBLit 4 (2002) 448-450 (*Oegema, Gerbern S.*).
6477 *Gryson, Roger* Apocalypsis Johannis. BVLI 46 (2002) 38-43.
6478 **ᴱGryson, Roger** Apocalypsis Johannis: 1. & 2. Lief., Einleitung, Einleitung (Fortsetzung und Schluss) Apc 1,1-2,7. VL 26/2: 2000 ⇒ 16,6087 ᴿREAug 48 (2002) 195-196 (*Milhau, Marc*);
6479 4 : Apc 4,1-6,12. 241-316 pp. 3-451-00204-3;
6480 5: Apc 6,12-9,19. 321-400 pp. 3-451-00205-1;
6481 6: Apc 9,19-13,1. VL 26/2: FrB 2002, Herder. 401-480 pp. 3-451-00206-X;
6482 BEDA Venerabilis: expositio Apocalypseos. CChr.SL 121 A; Bedae Opera 2/5: 2001 ⇒17,6069. ᴿRBen 112 (2002) 173-174 (*Bogaert, P.-M.*).
6483 **Kistemaker, Simon J.** New Testament commentary: exposition of the book of Revelation. 2001 ⇒17,6073. ᴿWThJ 63 (2002) 201-202 (*Poythress, Vern Sheridan*).
6484 **Koester, Craig R.** Revelation and the end of all things. 2001 ⇒17, 6075. ᴿNewTR 15/4 (2002) 87-88 (*Moloney, Francis J.*).
6485 ᵀ**Milizia, Pietro** L'Apucalessa 'd Zvàn: volgarizzata in dialetto bolognese. Bo 2000, Dehoniana 117 pp. Pres. *Giuseppe Stanzani*; Ill. *Albrecht Dürer*; Bibl. 113.
6486 **Osborne, Grant R.** Revelation. Baker exegetical commentary on the NT: GR 2002, Baker xx; 869 pp. $50. 0-8010-2299-1 [ThD 50,85—Heiser, W. Charles].
6487 **Prigent, Pierre** L'Apocalypse de Saint Jean. CNT 14: ²2000 ⇒16, 6097; 17,6085. ᴿLV(L) 254 (2002) 90-91 (*Lémonon, Jean-Pierre*); CrSt 23 (2002) 496-499 (*Garuti, Paolo*);
6488 Les secrets de l'Apocalypse: mystique, ésotérisme et apocalypse. LiBi 124: P 2002, Cerf 104 pp. €15. 2204-06965-5 [RHPhR 82,381].
6489 **Roloff, Jürgen** Die Offenbarung des Johannes. ZBK.AT 18: Z ³2001, Theol. Verl. 219 pp. 3-290-14735-5.
6490 **Stefanovic, Ranko** Revelation of Jesus Christ: commentary on the book of Revelation. Berrien Springs, Michigan 2002, Andrews University Pr. xvi; 654 pp. 1-883925-32-0. Bibl. 615-626.
6491 ᴱ**Suckale-Redlefsen, Gude; Schemmel, Bernhard** Die Bamberger Apokalypse: Kommentar zur Faksimile-Ausgabe der Handschrift Msc.Bibl.140 der Staatsbibliothek Bamberg. Luzern 2000, Faksimile 219 pp. Ill. [RBen 114,208—P.-M. Bogaert].
6492 *Vogt, Ernesto* †1984 Apocalipse: evangelho de Cristo glorificado. RCB 43 (2002) 113-140.
6493 **Wenig, Laurin J.** The challenge of the Apocalypse: embracing the book of Revelation with hope and faith. Mahwah, NJ 2002, Paulist xv; 160 pp. $13. 0-8081-4064-0 [ThD 50,94—Heiser, W. Charles].

G2.4 *Apocalypsis, themata*—Revelation, topics

6494 **Adamsen, Georg S.** Parousia and paraenesis: the parousia motif and its paraenetic use in the book of Revelation. 2002 Diss. Oslo: Norwegian Lutheran School of Theology [StTh 57,80].

6495 **Adinolfi, Marco** Apocalisse: testo, simboli e visioni. 2001 ⇒17, 6098. [R]LASBF 51 (2001) 440-441 (*Bottini, G.C.*).

6496 *Alegre, Xavier* Resistencia cristiana y esperanza profética: lectura del Apocalipsis de Juan desde las víctimas. RLAT 19 (2002) 3-24.

6497 **Ammannati, Renato** Apocalisse: le cose che stanno per accadere : linearità e reversibilità del tempo nell'Apocalisse di Giovanni. R 2001, Armando 254 pp. 88-8358-193-8. Bibl. 151-254. [R]CivCatt 153/3 (2002) 96-98 (*Scaiola, D.*).

6498 *Arcari, Luca* Apocalisse di Giovanni e apocalittica "danielico-storica" del I sec. e.v.: prospettive per una 'nuova' ipotesi. VetChr 39 (2002) 115-132.

6499 *Arens K., Eduardo* El Apocalipsis de Juan: ¿una teologia politica?. RevBib 63 (2001) 195-220.

6500 *Aune, David E.* God and time in the Apocalypse of John. [F]ACHTE-MEIER, P. 2002 ⇒1. 229-248.

6501 **Backus, Irena Dorota** Reformation readings of the Apocalypse: Geneva, Zurich, and Wittenberg. 2000 ⇒16,6104. [R]SCJ 33 (2002) 548-549 (*Dipple, Geoffrey*); Reformation 7 (2002) 234-236 (*Ryrie, Alec*); CHR 88 (2002) 588-589 (*Barnes, Robin B.*).

6502 **Barker, Margaret** The revelation of Jesus Christ, which God gave to him to show to his servants what must soon take place (Revelation 1.1). 2000 ⇒16,6108; 17,6104. [R]CBQ 64 (2002) 367-368 (*Mathews, Susan F.*); SJTh 55 (2002) 242-244 (*Court, John M.*).

6503 *Biguzzi, Giancarlo* L'Apocalisse e lo Spirito di vendetta. ED 55 (2002) 45-61;

6504 Spirito e profezia nell'Apocalisse di Giovanni. EstB 60 (2002) 503-522.

6505 *Boxall, Ian* Reclaiming the Apocalypse. PrPe 16 (2002) 327-331.

6506 *Böcher, Otto* Die Apokalypse des Johannes—jüdisch oder christlich?. [F]ASCHOFF, D. 2002 ⇒3. 89-97.

6507 *Brutti, Maria* Popoli e nazioni nel libro dell'Apocalisse (seconda parte). Convivium Assisiense 4/1 (2002) 277-298.

6508 *Campbell, Gordon* Un procédé de composition négligé de l'Apocalypse de Jean: repérage, caractéristiques et cas témoin d'une approche parodique. ETR 77 (2002) 491-516.

6509 **Campbell, William Gordon** Parody in the Apocalypse: a literary-theological study of convergent antithetical themes in John's Revelation. [D]McCullough, J.C. 2002, 382 pp. Diss. Belfast [RTL 34,596].

6510 *Carvalho, José Carlos* A simbologia nupcial da νύμφη e do αρνίον na escatologia do Apocalipse. HumTeo 23/1 (2002) 57-98.

6511 *Charry, Ellen T.* 'A sharp two-edged sword': pastoral implications of apocalyptic. Character and scripture. 2002 ⇒283. 344-360.

6512 **Cunningham, Andrew; Grell, Ole Peter** The four horsemen of the Apocalypse: religion, war, famine, and death in Reformation Europe. 2000 ⇒16,6130. [R]TS 63 (2002) 174-175 (*Hudon, William V.*); ChH 71 (2002) 411-412 (*Karant-Nunn, Susan C.*); International History Review 24 (2002) 401-403 (*Parker, Geoffrey*).

6513 **D'Souza, Jerome** Power violence and suffering in the book of Revelation: a contextual reading. [D]Beutler, Johannes: 2002, 113 pp. Exc. Diss. Gregoriana 2002. Bibl. 53-110

6514 **Dąbrowa, Wiesław** Idea wierności Chrystusowi w Apokalipsie św. Jana [L'idée de la fidélité au Christ dans l'Apocalypse de saint Jean]. [D]Paciorek, A.: 2002, 260 pp. Diss. Lublin [RTL 34,597]..

6515 *De Groote, Marc* Apokalyptik und die eigene Art der Johannesapokalypse. BZ 46 (2002) 103-106.

6516 *DeVilliers, Pieter G.* Rome in the historical interpretation of Revelation. APB 13 (2002) 120-142.

6517 **Doglio, Claudio** La risurrezione di Cristo e dei cristiani nell'Apocalisse di Giovanni. ᴰ*Vanni, Ugo*: 2002 Diss. Gregorian [RTL 34,597].

6518 **Duff, Paul Brooks** Who rides the beast?: prophetic rivalry and the rhetoric of crisis in the churches of the Apocalypse. 2001 ⇒17,6123. ᴿRRT 9 (2002) 218-221 (*Court, John M.*); Theol. 105 (2002) 301-302 (*Boxall, Ian*); CBQ 64 (2002) 569-570 (*Sullivan, Kevin*); JBL 121 (2002) 386-388 (*Carey, Greg*).

6519 **Edinger, Edward F.** Archetype of the Apocalypse: divine vengeance, terrorism, and the end of the world. ᴱ*Elder, George R.*: Ch 2002, Open Court xx; 222 pp. 0-8126-9516-X.

6520 *Filho, José Adriano* The Apocalypse of John as an account of a visionary experience: notes on the book's structure. JSNT 25 (2002) 213-234.

6521 **Friesen, Steven J.** Imperial cults and the Apocalypse of John: reading Revelation in the ruins. 2001 ⇒17,6127. ᴿCBQ 64 (2002) 756-758 (*Thompson, Leonard L.*); JBL 121 (2002) 575-578 (*Frilingos, Chris*).

6522 *Guadagno, Francesca* L'Apocalisse: un libro misterioso nella genesi e nei riflessi storici. Studi Etno-Antropologici e Sociologici 30 (2002) 79-83.

6523 **Herghelegiu, Monica-Elena** Studien zur Christologie der Johannesoffenbarung. ᴰ*Stuhlmacher, P.*: 2002, Diss. Tübingen]ThRv 99/2,x].

6524 *Hoff, Johannes* Fundamentaltheologische Implikationen der Apokalyptik: Annäherung an den Begriff der Offenbarung, ausgehend von DERRIDAs dekonstruktiver Lektüre der Apokalypse des Johannes. ThG 45 (2002) 42-51, 107-120.

6525 *Howard-Brook, Wes* Revelation: claiming the victory Jesus won over empire. NT: introducing. 2002 ⇒332. 188-206.

6526 *Jang, Y.* Narrative function of the Apocalypse. Scriptura 80 (2002) 186-196 [NTAb 47,500].

6527 *Jonge, Henk Jan de* The Apocalypse of John and the imperial cult. ᶠVERSNEL, H.: 2002 ⇒126, 127-141.

6528 *Kowalski, Beate* "Lichtfrau, Drache, Zornesschalen...": zur Bedeutung eschatalogischer Zeichen in der Offenbarung des Johannes. EThL 78 (2002) 358-384;

6529 Vrouwenfiguren in de Openbaring van Johannes. TTh 42 (2002) 378-389.

6530 **Lee, Dal** The narrative asides in the book of Revelation. Lanham, MD 2002, Univ. Pr. of America 186 pp. $30. 0-7618-2357-3. Diss. Chicago Theol. Sem.; Bibl. 165-183.

6531 *Lietaert Peerbolte, Bert Jan* To worship the beast: the Revelation of John and the imperial cult in Asia Minor. Zwischen den Reichen. TANZ 36: 2002 ⇒568. 239-259.

6532 *Locker, Markus E.* The lamb of Revelation in the light of Peircean semiotics. Landas 16 (2002) 65-81.

6533 *Lupieri, Edmondo* Apocalisse, sacerdozio e Yom Kippur. ASEs 19 (2002) 11-21.

6534 *Luter, A. Boyd; Hunter, Emily K.* The 'earth dwellers' and the 'heaven dwellers': an overlooked interpretive key to the Apocalypse. Faith & Mission 19/1 (2002) 3-18.

6535 *Maier, Harry O.* There's a new world coming!: reading the Apocalypse in the shadow of the Canadian Rockies. Earth story. 2002 ⇒ 322. 166-179.

6536 **Maier, Harry O.** Apocalypse recalled: the book of Revelation after christendom. Mp 2002, Fortress xvi; 271 pp. $18. 0-8006-3492-6 [ThD 50,82—Heiser, W. Charles].

6537 **Malina, Bruce J.** The New Jerusalem in the Revelation of John: the city as symbol of life with God. 2000 ⇒16,6171; 17,6147. ᴿRivBib 50 (2002) 116-119 (*Biguzzi, Giancarlo*); RBLit 4 (2002) 454-456 (*Neufeld, Dietmar*);

6538 Die Offenbarung des Johannes: Sternvisionen und Himmelsreisen. Stu 2002, Kohlhammer 300 pp. €25. 3-17-014241-0. Bibl. 275-287.

6539 *Marcato, Giorgio* Carisma profetico e autorità apostolica nell'Apocalisse. Ang. 79 (2002) 5-18.

6540 **Marino, Marcello** Il verbo τηρειν nell'Apocalisse alla luce della tradizione giovannea: ricerca biblico teologica. ᴰ*Vanni, Ugo*: 2002, 212 pp. Exc. Diss. Gregoriana, Roma 2002.

6541 *Mayhue, R.L.* Why a pretribulational rapture?. MastJ 13/2 (2002) 241-253 [NTAb 47,299].

6542 *McGuckin, John A.* The book of Revelation and Orthodox eschatology: the theodrama of judgment. The last things. 2002 ⇒279. 113-134.

6543 *Moyise, Steve* Does the author of Revelation misappropriate the scriptures?. AUSS 40 (2002) 3-21.

6544 *Mueller, E.* The end time remnant in Revelation. JATS 11/1-2 (2000) 188-204 [NTAb 47,80] [Rev 12,17];

6545 Jesus and his second coming in the Apocalypse. JATS 11/1-2 (2000) 205-215 [NTAb 47,81];

6546 Introduction to the ecclesiology of the book of Revelation. JATS 12/2 (2001) 199-215 [NTAb 47,81].

6547 *Munoa, Phillip B.* Jesus, the merkavah, and martyrdom in early christian tradition. JBL 121 (2002) 303-325 [Acts 7,54-60; Rev 4-5].

6548 *Neufeld, D.* Sumptuous clothing and ornamentation in the Apcalypse. HTS 58 (2002) 664-689 [NTAb 47,286].

6549 **Newport, Kenneth G.C.** Apocalypse and millennium: studies in biblical eisegesis. 2000 ⇒16,6184. ᴿThTo 58 (2002) 626-628 (*Towner, W. Sibley*).

6550 *Nogueira, Paulo Augusto de Souza* Introduction;

6551 Celestial worship and ecstatic-visionary experience. JSNT 25 (2002) 123-126/165-184.

6552 *O'Donovan, Oliver* Response to Christopher Rowland. ᶠO'DONOVAN, O. 2002 ⇒272. 255-258.

6553 **Olutola, Peter** The mandate of the church in the Apocalypse of John. ᴰ*Westerholm, S.* 2002, 207 pp. Diss. McMaster [RTL 34,600].

6554 *Panattoni, Riccardo* Apocalisse e rivoluzione: il potere e il male. DT(P) 105 (2002) 93-103.

6555 *Pattemore, Stephen* Repetition in Revelation: implications for translation. BiTr 53 (2002) 425-441 .

6556 *Peters, Tiemo R.* Gott und das Ende der Zeit: vom Nutzen und Nachteil der Apokaliptik für die Theologie. WuA(M) 43/3 (2002) 112-16.

6557 *Pieris, Aloysius* El *corazón* de la espiritualidad jesuita y la misión profética en *favor de los pobres*: una meditación bíblica. RLAT 19 2002 47-59.

6558   *Pippin, Tina* The never-ending Apocalypse: evil and antichrists in a postmodern world. ^FPATTE, D.: 2002 ⇒89. 49-65.

6559   **Pisano, Ombretta** La radice e la stirpe di David: salmi davidici nel libro dell'Apocalisse. TGr.T 85: R 2002, E.P.U.G. 487 pp. €27. 88-7652-921-7. Bibl. 445-475.

6560   *Poucouta, Paulin* Violence et religion selon l'Apocalypse johannique. JKTh 10 (2002) 53-69.

6561   **Puthussery, Johnson** Days of man and God's day: an exegetico-theological study of hemèra in the book of Revelation. TGr.T 82: R 2002, E.P.U.G. 325 pp. €20. 88-7652-913-6. Bibl. 279-301.

6562   *Ravasi, Gianfranco* Chiesa e stato nell'Apocalisse. Com(I) 185 (2002) 9-20.

6563   *Reinbold, Wolfgang* Christentum und Esoterik aus neutestamentlicher Perspektive. Deutsches Pfarrerblatt 102/8 (2002) 383-386.

6564   *Reynolds, E.* Ten keys for interpreting the book of Revelation. JATS 11/1-2 (2000) 261-276 [NTAb 47,81].

6565   **Rogers, Randolph R.** An exegetical analysis of John's use of Zechariah in the book of Revelation: the impact and transformation of Zechariah's themes in the Apocalypse. ^D*Crutchley, D.*: 2002. 201 pp. Diss. Fort Worth [RTL 34,601].

6566   **Roose, Hanna** Das Zeugnis Jesu: seine Bedeutung für die Christologie, Eschatologie und Prophetie in der Offenbarung des Johannes. TANZ 32: 2000 ⇒16,6195; 17,6174. ^RZKTh 124 (2002) 235-236 (*Huber, Konrad*).

6567   *Rowland, Christopher* Afterword. JSNT 25 (2002) 255-262;

6568   The Apocalypse in history: the place of the book of Revelation in christian theology and life. Apocalyptic. JSPE.S 43: 2002 ⇒373. 151-171;

6569   The Apocalypse and political theology. ^FO'DONOVAN, O. 2002 ⇒ 272. 241-254.

6570   **Saoût, Yves** ₁No escribí el Apocalipsis para asustaros!. ^T*Aguirre Setas, José Antonio*: Bilbao 2002, Mensajero 223 pp. €13.25. 84-271-2432-5.

6571   *Schnabel, Eckhard J.* John and the future of the nations. BBR 12 (2002) 243-271.

6572   *Shea, W.H.* The controversy over the commandments in the central chiasm of Revelation [NTAb 47,81] [Rev 12-14];

6573   The cultic calendar for the introductory sanctuary scenes of Revelation [NTAb 47,82]..JATS 11/1-2 (2000) 216-231/120-147

6574   *Smith, Ian* A rational choice model of the book of Revelation. JSNT 85 (2002) 97-116.

6575   **Soeting, A.G.** Auditieve aspecten van het boek Openbaring van Johannes. 2001 ⇒17,6177. ^RKeTh 53 (2002) 260 (*Spijkerboer, Anne Marijke*).

6576   *Sperry-White, Grant* The imagery of angelic praise and heavenly topography in the Testament of our Lord. EO 19 (2002) 315-332.

6577   *Stefanovic, R.* Finding meaning in the literary patterns of Revelation. JATS 13/1 (2002) 27-43 [NTAb 47,82].

6578   *Stitzinger, J.F.* The rapture in twenty centuries of biblical interpretation. MastJ 13/2 (2002) 149-171 [NTAb 47,302].

6579   *Tavo, Felise* The ecclesial notions of the Apocalypse in recent studies. CuBR 1/1 (2002) 112-136.

6580 *Toenges, Elke* 'See, I am making all things new': new creation in the book of Revelation. Creation in Jewish and christian tradition. JSOT. S 319: 2002 ⇒593. 138-152.

6581 *Ulfgard, Håkan* In quest of the elevated Jesus: reflections on the angelomorphic christology of the book of Revelation within its Jewish setting. NT as reception. JSNT.S 230: 2002 ⇒360. 120-130.

6582 *Vanni, Ugo* La grazia nell'Apocalisse. DSBP 30 (2002) 195-223;

6583 Guerra e pace nell'Apocalisse. DSBP 32 (2002) 179-220;

6584 Da Paolo all'Apocalisse: il cammino religioso dei Giudei. VII Simposio di Tarso. 2002 ⇒587. 57-84;

6585 Tempo ed eternità nell'Apocalisse: traccia per una riflessione teologico-biblica. Tempo ed eternità. 2002 ⇒545. 25-71.

6586 *Vasconcellos, Pedro Lima* Apocalypses in the history of Brazil. JSNT 25/2 (2002) 235-254.

6587 *Viljoen, D.A.; Van Aarde, A.G.* Die boek Openbaring—brandpunte in die teologiese debat. HTS 57 (2001) 1288-1311 [NTAb 46,494].

6588 *Viljoen, F.P.* Die betekenis en funksie van die himnes in Openbaring 12-22. VeE 23 (2002) 558-574.

6589 *Villiers, Pieter G.R. de* Persecution in the book of Revelation. AcTh(B) 22/2 (2002) 47-70.

6590 *Vollenweider, Samuel* Die Beschwörung der Mächte: Überlegungen zur Botschaft der Johannesapokalypse. Horizonte. WUNT 144: 2002 <1993> ⇒257. 309-326.

6591 *Whidden, W.W.* Trinitarian evidences in the Apocalypse. JATS 11/1-2 (2000) 248-260 [NTAb 47,82].

6592 *Woodruff, Archibald M.* Thirty years of near neglect: apocalyptic in Brazil. JSNT 25 (2002) 127-139.

G2.5 *Apocalypsis*, **Revelation 1,1...**

6593 **Faragau, Ilie Beniamin** New purchases on large meanings in the light of John's conscious and contextual interlocking of Revelation 1. 1-2.7 with its Old Testament background. *DMoore, H.*: 2002, 360 pp. Diss. Belfast [RTL 34,597] [Rev 1,1-2,7].

6594 **Hemer, Colin J.** The letters to the seven churches of Asia in their local setting. 2001 <1986> ⇒17,6194. *RRBLit* 4 (2002) 451-453 (*Litwak, Kenneth D.*) [Rev 2-3].

6595 **Tkacz, Roman** Listy do siedmiu Kościołów (Ap 2.1-3.22): studium historyczno-egsegetyczne [Lettres aux sept Églises]. *DChrostowski, W.*: 2002, 403 pp. Diss. Warsaw [RTL 34,601]. **P.**

6596 *Iwamura, Jane N.* The "hidden manna" that sustains: reading Revelation 2:17 in Joy Kogawa's Obasan. Semeia 90/91 (2002) 161-179.

6597 *Friedrich, Nestor Paulo* Adapt or resist?: a socio-political reading of Revelation 2.18-29. JSNT 25/2 (2002) 185-211.

6598 *Essex, K.H.* The rapture and the book of Revelation. MastJ 13/2 (2002) 215-239 [NTAb 47,285] [Rev 3,10-11].

6599 **Schimanowski, Gottfried** Die himmlische Liturgie in der Apokalypse des Johannes: die frühjüdischen Traditionen in Offenbarung 4-5 unter Einschluß der Hekhalotliteratur. WUNT 2/154: Tü 2002, Mohr S. xii; 367 pp. €69. 3-16-147777-4. Bibl. 295-338.

6600 *Douglass, H.* Why God holds the winds. JATS 11/1-2 (2000) 287-294 [NTAb 47,82] [Rev 7,1-3].

6601 *Hall, Mark Seaborn* The hook interlocking structure of Revelation: the most important verses in the book and how they may unify its structure. NT 44 (2002) 278-296 [Rev 10,11-11,1].

6602 *Müller, E.* The two witnesses of Revelation 11. JATS 13/2 (2002) 30-45 [NTAb 47,287].

6603 *Friedrich, Nestor P.* A besta (therion) no Apocalipse : uma descrição. Estudos bíblicos 74 (2002) 96-106 [Rev 11-12].

6604 *Jauhiainen, Marko* The measuring of the sanctuary reconsidered (Rev 11,1-2). Bib. 83 (2002) 507-526.

6605 *Rossing, Barbara R.* Alas for earth!: lament and resistance in Revelation 12. Earth story. 2002 ⇒322. 180-192.

6606 *Alcácer Orts, José Manuel* La historia de la salvación celebrada como Pascua: Apocalipsis 12,10-12. EsVe 32 (2002) 7-79.

6607 *Doglio, Claudio* Le due bestie dell'Apocalisse: un invito simbolico a discernere l'idolatria 'Guardatevi dagli idoli'. PSV 46 (2002) 137-148 [Rev 13].

6608 *Pezzoli-Olgiati, Daria* Between fascination and destruction: considerations on the power of the beast in Rev 13:1-10. Zwischen den Reichen. TANZ 36: 2002 ⇒568. 229-237.

6609 **López, Javier** La figura de la bestia entre historia y profecía: investigación teológico-bíblica de Apocalipsis 13,1-18. TGr.T 39: 1998 ⇒ 14,5687; 15,6296. ^REstB 60 (2002) 543-545 (*Urbán, Á.*).

6610 *Lambrecht, Jan* Rev 13,9-10 and exhortation in the Apocalypse;

6611 *Birdsall, J. Neville* IRENAEUS and the number of the beast: Revelation 13,18. ^FDELOBEL, J.: BEThL 161: 2002 ⇒24. 331-347/349-359.

6612 *Marucci, Corrado* Gematrie und Isopsephie im Neuen Testament— eine wirkliche Hilfe zum Verständnis?. SNTU.A 27 (2002) 179-197 [Rev 13,18].

6613 *Schmidt, Josef* Die Rätselzahl 666 in Offb 13:18: ein Lösungsvergleich auf der Basis lateinischer Gematrie. NT 44 (2002) 35-54.

6614 *Shea, W.H.* Literary and theological parallels between Revelation 14-15 and Exodus 19-24. JATS 12/2 (2001) 164-179 [NTAb 47,82].

6615 *Douglass, H.E.* What is the 'everlasting gospel'?. JATS 12/2 (2001) 145-151 [NTAb 47,83] [Rev 14,6].

6616 *Mazzeo, Michele* 'Beati i morti che muoiono nel Signore: sì, dice lo Spirito, riposeranno dalle loro fatiche...' (Ap 14,13). ^FTUDDA, F. 2002 ⇒123. 85-95.

6617 *DeSilva, David A.* Final topics: the rhetorical functions of intertexture in Revelation 14:14-16:21. Intertexture. SBL.Symposium 14: 2002 ⇒385. 215-241.

6618 *Marquardt, Friedrich W.* Predigt über Offenbarung 15,2-4. TeKo 25/1 (2002) 4-15.

6619 *DeVilliers, Pieter G.* The composition of Revelation 17 and its place in the book as a whole. APB 13 (2002) 97-119.

6620 *Cheung, Paul W.* The mystery of Revelation 17:5 & 7: a typological entrance. Jian Dao 18 (2002) 1-19. Sum. 18, 19.

G2.7 **Millenniarismus**, *Apc 20...*

6621 ^E**Amanat, Abbas; Bernhardsson, Magnus** Imagining the end: visions of apocalypse from the ancient Middle East to modern America. L 2002, Tauris xi; 416 pp. 1-86064-724-3. Bibl. 393-405.

6622 *Biguzzi, Giancarlo* Giustizia di Dio e millennio nell'Apocalisse. RStB 14/1-2 (2002) 295-311.

6623 ᴱ**Bock, Darrell L.** Three views on the millennium and beyond. 1999 ⇒16,6255. ᴿSWJT 45/1 (2002) 70-71 (*Garrett, James Leo*).

6624 **Fanlo, Jean-Raymond; Tournon, André** Formes de millénarisme en Europe à l'aube des temps moderne. 2001 ⇒17,6230. ᴿSCJ 33 (2002) 841-843 (*Rollo-Koster, Joëlle*).

6625 *Groenewald, J.; Van Aarde, A.G.* Apokaliptiek en millennialisme: die relevansie van die begrip 'duisendjarige vredesryk' vir vandag. HTS 57 (2001) 676-704 [NTAb 46,495].

6626 **Lerner, Robert E.** The feast of Saint Abraham: medieval millenarians and the Jews. Ph 2001, Univ. of Pennsylvania Pr. 186 pp. $35.

6627 *Remy, Gérard* Millénarisme historique et espérance eschatologique: à propos de La Venue de Dieu de J. MOLTMANN. RSR 90 (2002) 187-201.

6628 ᴱ**Ruiz Sánchez, José-Leonardo** Milenarismos: mesianismo y apocalipsis desde la historia y la religión. 2001 ⇒17,543. ᴿIsidorianum 21 (2002) 487-488 (*Martín Riego, Manuel*).

6629 ᴱ**Stone, Jon R.** Expecting Armageddon: essential readings in failed prophecy. 2000 ⇒16,336. ᴿStWC 8/1 (2002) 182-184 (*Thompson, T. Jack*).

6630 *Wilson, Bryan* Millennialism and sect formation in the nineteenth and twentieth centuries. Apocalyptic. JSPE.S 43: 2002 ⇒373. 212-232.

6631 *Synnes, Martin* Kommer det et tusenårsrike?: Joh åp 20,4-6 som akilleshael i bibeltolkningen. TTK 73/1 (2002) 3-17.

6632 *Böcher, Otto* Das himmlische Jerusalem—zur Wirkungsgeschichte. Edelsteine. 2002 ⇒538. 71-77 [Rev 21].

6633 **Lee, Pilchan** The New Jerusalem in the book of Revelation: a study of Revelation 21-22 in the light of its background in Jewish tradition. WUNT 2/129: 2001 ⇒17,6255. ᴿJR 82 (2002) 276-277 (*Duff, Paul*); CDios 215 (2002) 676-677 (*Gutiérrez, J.*); Sal. 64 (2002) 578-579 (*Vicent, R.*); CBQ 64 (2002) 768-769 (*Morton, Russell*).

6634 *Hasitschka, Martin* Vision vom kommenden Jerusalem (Offb 21,1-22, 5): die Offenbarung des Johannes als Beispiel für literarische Rezeption innerhalb der Bibel. Religion—Literatur—Künste II. Im Kontext 14: 2002 ⇒530. 547-555.

6635 **Höck, Andreas** The descent of the New Jerusalem: a discourse analysis of Rev 21:1-22:5. ᴰ*Vanni, Ugo*: Denver 2002, Andreas Höck 107 pp. Diss. Extr. Pontificio Istituto Biblico 2001; Bibl. 49-102.

6636 *Mathewson, Dave* The destiny of the nations in Revelation 21:1-22:5: a reconsideration. TynB 53 (2002) 121-142.

6637 *Moriconi, Bruno* 'E vidi un cielo nuovo e una terra nuova' (Ap 21,1-22,5): visione delle ultime realtà o dichiarazione ultima sulla storia?. La speranza. 2002 ⇒277. 279-297.

6638 *Biguzzi, Giancarlo* The chaos of Rev 22,6-21 and prophecy in Asia. Bib. 83 (2002) 193-210 [1 Cor 14].

XII. Paulus

G3.1 Pauli biographia

6639 **Ashton, John** The religion of Paul the apostle. 2000 ⇒16,6284; 17, 6258. ᴿJThS 53 (2002) 253-255 (*Hickling, C.J.A.*); RB 109 (2002) 295-297 (*Murphy-O'Connor, Jerome*): HeyJ 43 (2002) 225-226 (*Edmonds, Peter*); JBL 121 (2002) 774-777 (*Ellington, Dustin W.*).

6640 *Bauckham, Richard* Paul and the other Jews with Latin names in the New Testament. ᶠWEDDERBURN, A.: JSNT.S 217: 2002 ⇒132. 202-220.

6641 **Berger, Klaus** Paulus. Wissen 2197: Mü 2002, Beck 128 pp. 3-406-47997-9.

6642 **Cassidy, Richard J.** Paul in chains: Roman imprisonment and the letters of St. Paul. 2001 ⇒17,6260. ᴿScrB 32 (2002) 40-42 (*Clarke, Fern*); CrSt 23 (2002) 494-495 (*Pitta, Antonio*); CBQ 64 (2002) 752-3 (*Kealy, Seán P.*); TJT 18 (2002) 260-1 (*Crook, Zeba Antonin*).

6643 *Compton, Michael* From Saul to Paul: patristic interpretation of the names of the apostle. ᶠWILKEN, R.: 2002 ⇒136. 50-68.

6644 **Dreyfus, Paul** Święty Paweł: reporter na tropach apostoła. ᵀ*Wojciechowski, M.*: Czestochowa 2002, Święty Paweł 432 pp. **P.**

6645 *Engberg-Pedersen, Troels* Hvad er det vaerd at vide om Paulus lige nu?. DTT 65 (2002) 241-254.

6646 **Glover, Terrot R.** Paul of Tarsus. Peabody, MA 2002 <1925>, Hendrickson xi; 256 pp. $20. 1-56563-728-3. Introd. *Donald Hagner* [ThD 50,170—Heiser, W. Charles].

6647 *Gnuse, Robert* Vita apologetica: the lives of JOSEPHUS and Paul in apologetic historiography. JSPE 13 (2002) 151-169.

6648 *Haacker, Klaus* Paulus unter den Zeloten?. Versöhnung mit Israel. VKHW 5: 2002 <1989> ⇒174. 147-152.

6649 *Hengel, Martin* Paul in Arabia. BBR 12 (2002) 47-66;

6650 Der vorchristliche Paulus <1991>;

6651 Paulus in Arabien <2000>. Paulus und Jakobus. WUNT 141: 2002 ⇒178. 68-192/193-212.

6652 **Hengel, Martin; Schwemer, Anna Maria** Paulus zwischen Damaskus und Antiochien: die unbekannten Jahre des Apostels. WUNT 108: 1998 ⇒14,5732...17,6265. ᴿNZM 58 (2002) 61-65 (*Schelbert, Georg*).

6653 *Hollander, Harm W.* De bekering van Paulus. NedThT 56/1 (2002) 27-38.

6654 ᴱ**Horn, Friedrich Wilhelm** Das Ende des Paulus: historische, theologische und literaturgeschichtliche Aspekte. BZNW 106: 2001 ⇒ 17,281. ᴿThLZ 127 (2002) 909-912 (*Schwemer, Anna Maria*); SNTU.A 27 (2002) 241-244 (*Fuchs, Albert*).

6655 *Horrell, David G.* Paul. Biblical world, 2: 2002 ⇒273. 258-283.

6656 *Kieffer, René* Juden Paulus. SEÅ 67 (2002) 79-87.

6657 *Kim, Seyoon* Paul's conversion/call, James D.G. DUNN, and the new perspective on Paul;

6658 Isaiah 42 and Paul's call. Paul and the new perspective. WUNT 140: 2002 ⇒190. 1-84/101-127 [Gal 1,15-16].

6659 **Légasse, Simon** Paul apôtre. P [2]2000 <1991> ⇒16,6292. [R]LV(L) 254 (2002) 253-254 (*Lémonon, Jean-Pierre*).

6660 **Luibhéid, Colm** A scholarly reconstruction of St. Paul and his times: the historical evidence. Studies in classics 18: Lewiston, NY 2002, Mellen ix; 136 pp. 0-7734-7279-7. Bibl. 129-132.

6661 **Lüdemann, Gerd** Paul: the founder of christianity. Amherst, NY 2002, Prometheus 292 pp. 1-59102-021-2. Bibl. 283-286.

6662 *Overman, J. Andrew Kata nomon pharisaios*: a short history of Paul's pharisaism. [F]ROETZEL, C.: JSNT.S 221: 2002 ⇒104. 180-193.

6663 *Suhl, Alfred* Zur paulinischen Chronologie: Vorstellung einer Website und ihrer Hauptergebnisse. ITE 11 (2002) 281-301.

6664 **Tajra, Harry W.** The martyrdom of St Paul. WUNT 2/67: 1994 ⇒ 11/1,4499... 13,6092. [R]Ist. 47 (2002) 407-409 (*Dupuy, B.*).

6665 *Taylor, Nicholas H.* Conflicting bases of identity in early christianity: the example of Paul. Handbook of early christianity. 2002 ⇒275. 577-597.

    Verdoodt, A. The gospels in comparison with the Pauline letters 2002 ⇒4881;

    Jesus und Paulus 2002 ⇒4880.

6666 *Wedderburn, A.J.M.* Paul's collection: chronology and history. NTS 48 (2002) 95-110.

6667 **Witherington III, Ben** The Paul quest: the renewed search for the Jew of Tarsus. 1999 ⇒15,6387; 16,6310. [R]SBET 20 (2002) 237-239 (*Chester, Stephen*).

G3.2 Corpus paulinum; *generalia, technica epistularis*

6668 [E]**Nanos, Mark** The Galatians debate: contemporary issues in rhetorical and historical interpretation. Peabody 2002, Hendrickson 517 pp. $35. 1-56563-468-3. Bibl. 441-490.

6669 **Adams, Edward** Constructing the world: a study in Paul's cosmological language. 2000 ⇒16,6313; 17,6290. [R]JR 82 (2002) 103-104 (*Badley, Jo-Ann*); EvQ 74 (2002) 75-77 (*Proctor, John*).

6670 **Akenson, Donald Harman** Saint Saul: a skeleton key to the historical Jesus. 2000 ⇒16,6315; 17,6291. [R]RB 109 (2002) 300-303 (*Murphy-O'Connor, Jerome*); SR 31 (2002) 400-402 (*Megivern, James J.*); RBLit (2002)* (*Mitchell, Matthew W.*).

6671 [E]**Aland, Barbara; Juckel, Andreas** Das Neue Testament in syrischer Überlieferung, 2. die paulinischen Briefe, Teil 3: 1./2. Thessalonicherbrief, 1./2. Timotheusbrief, Titusbrief, Philemonbrief und Hebräerbrief. ANTT 32: B 2002, De Gruyter viii; 551 pp. 3-11-01-7387-5. [R]LASBF 51 (2001) 452-453 (*Pazzini, M.*).

6672 **Bailey, Robert Arthur** The structure of Paul's letters. Fairfax, VA 2002, Xulon 163 pp. $13. 15916-00081 [ThD 49,158: Heiser, W.C.].

6673 *Barr, George K.* The impact of scalometry on New Testament letters. ET 114 (2002) 3-9.

6674 **Bortolini, José** Introdução a Paulo e suas cartas. Como ler a Biblia: 2001 ⇒17,6296. [R]PerTeol 34 (2002) 397-398 (*Marques, Valdir*).

6675 *Classen, C. Joachim* St. Paul's epistles and ancient Greek and Roman rhetoric. The Galatians debate. 2002 <2000> ⇒6668. 95-113.

6676 *Dunn, James D.G.* The narrative approach to Paul: whose story?. Narrative dynamics. 2002 ⇒351. 217-230.

6677 *Ehrensperger, Kathy* '...Let everyone be convinced in his/her own mind': DERRIDA and the deconstruction of Paulinism. SBL.SP 2002. SBL.SPS 41: 2002 ⇒598. 53-73.

6678 **ᴱEngberg-Pedersen, Troels** Paul beyond the Judaism/Hellenism divide. 2001 ⇒17,262. ᴿCThMi 29 (2002) 470-471 (*Pickett, Ray*); CBQ 64 (2002) 799-801 (*Marrow, Stanley B.*); ET 114 (2002) 26-27 (*McDonald, J. Ian*).

6679 *Eriksson, Anders* Contrary arguments in Paul's letters. Rhetorical criticism. JSNT.S 195: 2002 ⇒369. 336-354.

6680 *Gamble, Harry* Letters in the New Testament and in the Greco-Roman world. Biblical world, 1. 2002 ⇒273. 188-204.

6681 *Gignac, Alain* TAUBES, BADIOU, AGAMBEN: reception of Paul by non-christian philosophers today. SBL.SP 2002. SBL.SPS 41: 2002 ⇒598. 74-110.

6682 *Gooder, Paula* Interpreting Paul. PrPe 16 (2002) 332-336.

6683 **Harvey, John D.** Listening to the text: oral patterning in Paul's letters. ETS Studies 1: 1998 ⇒14,5756...17,6306. ᴿEThL 78 (2002) 219-220 (*Verheyden, J.*).

6684 **Heil, Johannes** Kompilation oder Konstruktion?: die Juden in den Pauluskommentaren des 9. Jahrhunderts. 1998 ⇒14,5757; 16,6337. ᴿFrRu 9 (2002) 215-217 (*Kampling, Rainer*).

6685 *Janssen, Claudia* Paul: walking the line between traditions and ages. ᶠSCHOTTROFF, L.: 2002 ⇒111. 31-38.

6686 **ᴱJanssen, Claudia; Schottroff, Luise; Wehn, Beate** Paulus: umstrittene Traditionen—lebendige Theologie: eine feministische Lektüre. 2001 <2000> ⇒17,6308. ᴿYESW 10 (2002) 239-241 (*Tönges, Elke*).

6687 **Kim, Byung-Mo** Die paulinische Kollekte. Tü 2002, Francke vii; 199 pp. 3-7720-2830-6. Bibl. 187-199.

6688 **Lee, Jae Won** Paul and the politics of difference: a contextual study of the Jewish-Gentile difference in Galatians and Romans. ᴰ*Kahl, B.*: 2002 Diss. New York, Union [RTL 34,598].

6689 *Lim, Timothy H.* Studying the Qumran scrolls and Paul in their historical context. Dead Sea scrolls as background. StTDJ 46: 2002 ⇒732. 135-156.

6690 **Lim, Timothy H.** Holy Scripture in the Qumran commentaries and Pauline letters. 1997 ⇒13,6111... 16,9242. ᴿJQR 92 (2001) 261-264 (*Weidmann, Fred*).

6691 *Longenecker, Bruce W.* Narrative interest in the study of Paul: retrospective and prospective. Narrative dynamics. 2002 ⇒351. 3-16.

6692 *Maleparampil, Joseph* The letters of St. Paul: the first New Testament writings. JJSS 1 (2001) 153-175.

6693 *Matlock, R. Barry* The arrow and the web: critical reflecrions on a narrative approach to Paul. Narrative dynamics. 2002 ⇒351. 44-57.

6694 *Mikhael, Mary* St. Paul and the place of women in the church. ThRev 23/2 (2002) 125-142.

6695 *Pacomio, Luciano* Le parenesi / paraclesi delle lettere paoline e di tutto il Nuovo Testamento. ATT 8 (2002) 12-16.

6696 *Padovese, Luigi* L'antipaulinisme chrétien au IIe siècle. RSR 90 (2002) 399-422.

6697 *Penna, Romano* Paolo scrittore. PaVi 47/4 (2002) 4-9.

6698 *Poster, Carol* The economy of letter writing in Graeco-Roman antiquity. Rhetorical argumentation. 2002 ⇒553. 112-124.

6699 **Poucouta, Paulin** Paul, notre ancêtre, introduction au corpus paulinien. 2001 ⇒17,6319. ᴿHekima Review 28 (2002) 85-86 (*Folilack, Aurélien*).

6700 *Puigdollers i Noblom, Rodolf* Classificació i datació de les glosses en les colleccions de cartes paulines (cont.). RCatT 27/1 (2002) 43-66 Sum. 66.

6701 **Quesnel, Michel** Paul et les commencements du christianisme. 2001 ⇒17,6321. ᴿRICP 84 (2002) 233-235 (*Tassin, Claude*); EeV 50 (2002) 23-24 (*Cothenet, Edouard*).

6702 *Reuter, Rainer* Introduction to synoptic work on the New Testament epistles. JHiC 9/2 (2002) 246-258.

6703 **Rosenmeyer, P.A.** Ancient epistolary fictions: the letter in Greek literature. 2001 ⇒17,6324. ᴿClR 52 (2002) 32-34 (*Barbantani, Silvia*); BZ 46 (2002) 274-275 (*Klauck, Hans-Josef*); AnCl 71 (2002) 302-303 (*Donnet, Daniel*); Gn. 75 (2003) 160-162 (*Holzberg, Niklas*).

6704 *Scroggs, Robin* Paul: myth remaker: the refashioning of early ecclesial traditions. ᶠROETZEL, C.: JSNT.S 221: 2002 ⇒104. 87-101.

6705 **Seifrid, Mark A.; Tan, Randall K.J.** The Pauline writings: an annotated bibliography. Bibliographies 9: GR 2002, Baker 245 pp. $25. 0-8010-2482-X.

6706 *Smith, Craig A.* The consequences of the increase in and the changed role of letter-writing for the early church. IBSt 24 (2002) 146-174.

6707 *Stuhl, Alfred* Zur paulinischen Chronologie: Vorstellung einer Website und ihrer Hauptergebnisse. ITE 11 (2002) 281-301.

6708 **Tellbe, Mikael** Med framtiden i ryggen: en guide til Paulus brev och budskap. Libris guideserie till Nya testamentet: Örebro 2002, Libris 271 pp [TTK 74,124—Røsoeg, Nils Aksel];

6709 Paul between synagogue and state: christians, Jews, and civic authorities in 1 Thessalonians, Romans, and Philippians. CB.NT 34: 2001 ⇒17,6332. ᴿCBQ 64 (2002) 395-396 (*Smiga, George M.*).

6710 *Van den Bergh van Eysinga, Gustaaf A.* Early christianity's letters. JHiC 9/2 (2002) 294-317.

6711 *Vos, Johan S.* Die Kunst, recht zu behalten, 2: Paulus und die Kunst, recht zu behalten. Die Kunst der Argumentation. 2002 ⇒6712. 24-8.

6712 **Vos, Johan S.** Die Kunst der Argumentation bei Paulus: Studien zur antiken Rhetorik. WUNT 149: Tü 2002, Mohr S. xii; 220 pp. €59. 3-16-147849-5. Bibl. 173-198.

6713 *Watson, Francis* Is there a story in these texts?. Narrative dynamics. 2002 ⇒351. 231-239.

6714 *Zelzer, Klaus; Zelzer, Michaela* 'Retractationes" zu Brief und Briefgenos bei PLINIUS, AMBROSIUS und SIDONIUS Appolinaris. ᶠGNILKA, C.: JAC.E 33: 2002 ⇒48. 393-405.

G3.3 Pauli theologia

6715 *Aletti, Jean-Noël* Le statut de l'église dans les lettres pauliniennes: réflexion sur quelques paradoxes. Bib. 83 (2002) 153-174 [Rom 9, 25-26; 2 Cor 6,16-18].

6716 **Alkier, Stefan** Wunder und Wirklichkeit in den Briefen des Apostels Paulus. WUNT 134: 2001 ⇒17,6342. ᴿBZ 46 (2002) 288-290 (*Pellegrini, Silvia*).

6717 **Ashton, John** La religione dell'apostolo Paolo. ᴱ*Ianovitz, Oscar*: StBi 136: Brescia 2002, Paideia 340 pp. €30. 8839406468 [⇒6639].

6718 *Bachmann, Michael* Verus Israel: ein Vorschlag zu einer 'mengentheoretischen' Neubeschreibung der betreffenden paulinischen Terminologie. NTS 48 (2002) 500-512.

6719 **Badiou, Alain** Paulus: die Begründung des Universalismus. [T]*Jatho, Heinz*: Mü 2002, Sequenzia 204 pp. €19. 3-936488-00-2.

6720 **Baldanza, Giuseppe** La metafora sponsale in S. Paolo e nella tradizione liturgica siriaca: studi. BEL.S 114: 2001 ⇒17,6344. [R]RivBib 50 (2002) 369-371 (*Pitta, Antonio*); VivH 13/1 (2002) 195-197 (*Cirignano, Giulio*).

6721 *Bell, Richard H.* Sacrifice and christology in Paul. JThS 53 (2002) 1-27 [Rom 3,23-26; 8,3; 2 Cor 5,14-21].

6722 *Boer, Martinus C. de* Paul, theologian of God's apocalypse. Interp. 56 (2002) 21-33.

6723 **Buscemi, A.M.** Gli inni di Paolo: una sinfonia a Christo Signore. SBFA 48: 2000 ⇒16,6374; 17,6351. [R]RivBib 50 (2002) 249-52 (*Romanello, Stefano*) [Phil 2,6-11; Eph 1,3-14; 2,14-18; Col 1,15-20].

6724 **Carter, Timothy Leonard** Paul and the power of sin: redefining 'beyond the pale'. MSSNTS 115: C 2002, CUP xiv; 241 pp. $60. 0-521-81041-8. Diss. Oxford 1998, Bibl. 210-226.

6725 **Cho, Young-Mo** Spirit and kingdom in the writings of Luke and Paul. [D]*Clarke, A.D.* 2002 Diss. Aberdeen [RTL 34,596].

6726 *Curkpatrick, Stephen* Apostrophic desire and parousia in the apostle Paul's epistles: a Derridean proposal for textual interpretation. BiblInterp 10 (2002) 175-193.

6727 **Dernowski, Piotr** Modele parenezy chrzcielnej w listach świętego Pawła [Les modèles d'enseignement baptismal dans les lettres de saint Paul]. [D]*Langkammer, H.*: 2002, 297 pp. Diss. Lublin [RTL 34, 597]. **P**.

6728 *Dugandzic, Ivan* Krstenje i (nova) evangelizacija: Krstenje kao temelj i obveza krscanske egzistencije prema sv. Pavlu. BoSm 72 (2002) 499-520. **Croatian**.

6729 *Dunn, James D.G.* Noch einmal "works of the law": the dialogue continues. [F]RÄISÄNEN, H.: NT.S 103: 2002 ⇒97. 273-290.

6730 **Dunn, James D.G.** The theology of Paul the apostle. 1998 ⇒14, 5800...17,6357. [R]EvQ 74 (2002) 187-188 (*Watson, Francis*);

6731 La teologia dell'apostolo Paolo. 1999 ⇒15,6445...17,6358. [R]Asp. 49 (2002) 107-110 (*Di Palma, Gaetano*).

6732 *Engberg-Pedersen, Troels* Response to Martyn. JSNT 86 (2002) 103-114.

6733 *Eskola, Timo* Paul et le Judaïsme du second temple: la sotériologie de Paul avant et après E.P. Sanders. RSR 90 (2002) 377-398.

6734 **Eskola, Timo** Theodicy and predestination in Pauline soteriology. WUNT 2/100: 1998 ⇒14,5803...17,6363. [R]RdQ 20 (2002) 492-493 (*Maurer, Alexander*).

6735 *Fee, Gordon D.* St. Paul and the Incarnation: a reassessment of the data. The incarnation. 2002 ⇒624. 62-92.

6736 *Forbes, Chris* Pauline demonology and/or cosmology?: principalities, powers and the elements of the world in their Hellenistic context. JSNT 85 (2002) 51-73.

6737 *Frey, Jörg* Flesh and spirit in the Palestinian Jewish sapiential tradition and in the Qumran texts: an inquiry into the background of Pauline usage. Wisdom texts. BEThL 159: 2002 ⇒482. 367-404.

6738 *Furnish, Victor Paul* Inside looking out: some Pauline views of the unbelieving public. [F]ROETZEL, C.: JSNT.S 221: 2002 ⇒104. 104-24.

6739 **Gager, John G.** Reinventing Paul. 2000 ⇒16,6391; 17,6368. ^RAUSS 40 (2002) 146-148 (*Choi, P. Richard*); RB 109 (2002) 435-438 (*Taylor, Justin*).

6740 *Georgi, Dieter* Aeneas und Abraham: Paulus unter dem Aspekt der Latinität?. ZNT 10 (2002) 37-43.

6741 **Gräbe, Petrus J.** The power of God in Paul's letters. WUNT 2/123: 2000 ⇒16,6400. ^RZMR 86 (2002) 73-74 (*Viviano, Benedict T.*); ThLZ 127 (2002) 520-522 (*Klumbies, Paul-Gerhard*); CBQ 64 (2002) 761-762 (*Asher, Jeffrey R.*).

6742 *Hay, David M.* All the fullnesss of God: concepts of deity in Colossians and Ephesians. ^FACHTEMEIER, P. 2002 ⇒1. 163-179.

6743 *Hays, Richard B.* The God of mercy who rescues us from the present evil age: Romans and Galatians. ^FACHTEMEIER, P. 2002 ⇒1. 123-43.

Heckel, T. Der Gekreuzigte bei Paulus... 2002 ⇒5587.

6744 *Hengel, Martin* Paulus und die frühchristliche Apokalyptik;

6745 Paulus, Israel und die Kirche;

6746 Paulus und die Frage einer vorchristlichen Gnosis;

6747 Erwägungen zum Sprachgebrauch von Χριστός bei Paulus und in der "vorpaulinischen" Überlieferung <1982>;

6748 Präexistenz bei Paulus <1997>. Paulus und Jakobus. WUNT 141: 2002 ⇒178. 302-417/418-472/473-510/240-261/262-301.

6749 **Hillert, Sven** Limited and universal salvation: a text-oriented and hermeneutical study of two perspectives in Paul. CB.NT 31: 1999 ⇒15,6455; 17,6370. ^RThRv 98 (2002) 35-36 (*Dormeyer, Detlev*); EThL 78 (2002) 220-221 (*Verheyden, J.*).

6750 *Hofius, Otfried* "Die Wahrheit des Evangeliums": exegetische und theologische Erwägungen zum Wahrheitsanspruch der paulinischen Verkündigung. Paulusstudien II. WUNT 143: 2002 <2001> ⇒180. 17-37.

6751 **Hubbard, Moyer V.** New creation in Paul's letters and thought. MSSNTS 119: C 2002, CUP xiii; 293 pp. £45. 0-521-81485-5. Bibl. 242-267 [Rom 6,1-11; 7,1-6; 2 Cor 5,17; 2,19-20; Gal 6,15].

6752 **Julius, Christiane-Barbara** Die ausgeführten Schrifttypologien bei Paulus. EHS.T. 668: 1999 ⇒15,6463; 16,6408. ^RRivBib 50 (2002) 112-113 (*Penna, Romano*).

6753 **Kim, Byoung Chan** Spirit language in second temple Jewish literature as a possible source for the eschatological role of the Holy Spirit in the Pauline writings. ^DSchatzmann, S.: 2002, 282 pp. Diss. Fort Worth [RTL 34,598].

6754 *Kim, Seyoon* Paul, the spirit, and the law [Gal 3,10-14];

6755 Christ, the image of God and the last Adam;

6756 The Jesus tradition in Paul. Paul and the new perspective. WUNT 140: 2002 ⇒190. 128-164/165-213/259-292.

6757 *Klein, Hans* Craftsmanship assumptions in Pauline theology. ^FWEDDERBURN, A.: JSNT.S 217: 2002 ⇒132. 94-101.

6758 *Koperski, Veronica* Resurrection terminology in Paul. ^FLAMBRECHT, J.: BEThL 165: 2002 ⇒72. 265-281.

6759 **Koperski, Veronica** What are they saying about Paul and the law?. NY 2001, Paulist xi; 148 pp. 0-8091-3965-0. ^RStCan 36 (2002) 557-560 (*Lewis, Scott M.*).

6760 *Kraftchick, Steven J.* Death's passing: experience as a mode of theology in Paul. ^FROETZEL, C.: JSNT.S 221: 2002 ⇒104. 144-166 [2 Cor 1,8-10].

6761 *Loubser, J.A.* The mystery of the missing core in Pauline theology: the case for a multi-dimensional interpretation with reference to J H Roberts and J C Beker. HTS 57 (2001) 344-378 [NTAb 46,481].

6762 *Martyn, J. Louis* De-apocalypticizing Paul: an essay focused on Paul and the stoics by Troels Engberg-Pedersen. JSNT 86 (2002) 61-102.

6763 **Mathlin, Teijo** The fall and rise of God's people: the Golden Calf pericope in Paul's thought. ^D*Clarke, A.D.*: 2002 Diss. Aberdeen [RTL 34,599].

6764 *Matlock, R. Barry* "Even the demons believe": Paul and πίστις Χριστοῦ. CBQ 64 (2002) 300-318.

6765 *McDonald, Ian* Paul beyond the Judaism/Hellenism divide. ET 114 (2002) 26-27.

6766 *Meiser, Martin* Die paulinischen Adamaussagen im Kontext frühjüdischer und frühchristlicher Literatur. Jüdische Schriften. 2002 ⇒345. 376-401.

6767 **Melczewski, Paweł** La 'vita' in San Paolo: un'indagine biblico-teologica. ^D*Vanni, Ugo*: 2002, 186 pp. Exc. Diss. Gregoriana, R 2002.

6768 **Moore, Richard Kingsley** Rectification ('justification') in Paul, in historical perspective and in the English Bible: God's gift of right relationship, 1: Paul's doctrine of rectification. SBEC 50a: Lewiston, NY 2002, Mellen 21*; 336 pp. Bibl. 293-321.

6769 *Morgan, Robert C.* The letters of Paul in the context of a New Testament theology. ^FROETZEL, C.: JSNT.S 221: 2002 ⇒104. 240-261.

6770 *Mosetto, Francesco* La chiesa nelle lettere di Paolo. PaVi 47/3 (2002) 35-38.

6771 *Natoli, Salvatore* Il tempo della fine, il presente e l'*escaton* nella teologia di Paolo. Il libro sacro. 2002 ⇒356. 121-135.

6772 *Nebe, Gottfried* Creation in Paul's theology. Creation in Jewish and christian tradition. JSOT.S 319: 2002 ⇒593. 111-137.

6773 *Neuhaus, David M.* À la rencontre de Paul: connaître Paul aujourd' hui—un changement de paradigme?. RSR 90 (2002) 353-376.

6774 *Nobile, Marco* Le citazioni veterotestamentarie di Paolo. VII Simposio di Tarso. 2002 ⇒587. 21-27.

6775 *Nürnberger, Klaus* Paul's concept of salvation—culmination of an evolutionary process. Scriptura 80 (2002) 226-258 [NTAb 47,481].

6776 **Oegema, Gerbern S.** Für Israel und die Völker: Studien zum alttestamentlich-jüdischen Hintergrund der paulinischen Theologie. NT.S 95: 1999 ⇒15,6483. ^RNT 44 (2002) 397-400 (*Schnabel, E.J.*).

6777 *Oropeza, B.J.* Echoes of Isaiah in the rhetoric of Paul: new exodus, wisdom, and the humility of the cross in utopian-apocalyptic expectations. Intertexture. SBL.Symposium 14: 2002 ⇒385. 87-112.

6778 **Pao, David W.** Thanksgiving: an investigation of a Pauline theme. New Studies in Biblical Theology 13: Leicester 2002, Apollos 212 pp. £13. 0-85111-272-2. Bibl. 174-196.

6779 *Pascuzzi, Maria* Paul the enforcer: using rhetoric to deconstruct an image and to reconstruct theology. Theology and sacred scripture. 2002 ⇒549. 69-82.

6780 *Penna, Romano* La dialettica paolina tra possibilità e impossibilità di conoscere Dio. RdT 43 (2002) 659-670;

6781 La chiesa come corpo di Cristo secondo S. Paolo: metafora sociale-comunitaria o individuale-cristologica?. Lat. 68 (2002) 243-278.

6782 *Pitta, Antonio* L'escatologia paolina. PaVi 47/4 (2002) 35-39;

6783 Lo "scandalo della croce" nel pensiero di Paolo. Asp. 49/1 (2002) 5-32.

6784 *Punt, Jeremy* Paul, hermeneutics and character: implications for scripture and identity. Scriptura 79 (2002) 122-142;

6785 Towards a postcolonial reading of freedom in Paul. Reading the Bible in the global village. 2002 ⇒607. 125-149.

6786 *Plummer, Robert L.* A theological basis for the church's mission in Paul. WThJ 64 (2002) 253-271.

6787 *Rand, J.A. du* Die verhouding tussen kerk en ἀγάπη in Pauliniese perspektief. AcTh(B) 22/1 (2002) 31-41.

6788 *Räisänen, Heikki* Did Paul expect an earthly kingdom.? [F]WEDDERBURN, A.: JSNT.S 217: 2002 ⇒132. 2-20.

6789 *Rossano, Pietro* La communication de l'évangile selon Saint Paul. Teologia cristiana. DMis 27: 2002 <1979> ⇒232. 363-376.

6790 **Sandnes, Karl Olav** Belly and body in the Pauline epistles. MSSNTS 120: C 2002, CUP xiv; 318 pp. $60. 0-521-81535-5. Bibl. 275-291.

6791 *Schnelle, Udo* Gerechtigkeit in den Psalmen Salomos und bei Paulus. Jüdische Schriften. 2002 ⇒345. 365-375.

6792 **Schrage, Wolfgang** Unterwegs zur Einzigkeit und Einheit Gottes: zum "Monotheismus" des Paulus und seiner alttestamentlich-frühjüdischen Tradition. BThSt 48: Neuk 2002, Neuk ix; 195 pp. €24.90. 3-7887-1862-5. Bibl. 187-195. [R]OrdKor 43 (2002) 491-492 (*Giesen, Heinz*).

6793 *Sherman, Hazel* 'Getting in and staying in': unexpected connections between E.P. Sanders on Paul and expectations of baptism today. Dimensions of baptism. JSNT.S 234: 2002 ⇒434. 110-119.

6794 **Smith, Barry D.** Paul's seven explanations of the suffering of the righteous. Studies in biblical literature 47: NY 2002, Lang viii; 251 pp. $57. 0-8204-5689-6.

6795 **Söding, Thomas** Das Wort vom Kreuz: Studien zur paulinischen Theologie. WUNT 93: 1997 ⇒13,6185; 14,5842. [R]Anton. 77 (2002) 174 (*Nobile, Marco*).

6796 *Stuhlmacher, Peter* Eschatologie und Hoffnung bei Paulus. Biblische Theologie. WUNT 146: 2002 ⇒245. 66-87.

6797 *Támez, Elsa* Die Sünde der Ungerechtigkeit und die Rechtfertigung durch den Glauben. BiKi 57 (2002) 145-151.

6798 **Thurén, Lauri** Derhetorizing Paul: a dynamic perspective on Pauline theology and the law. Harrisburg [2]2002 <2000>, Trinity ix; 213 pp. $20;

6799 Derhetorizing Paul. WUNT 124: 2000 ⇒16,6434; 17,6413. [R]ThG 45 (2002) 227-229 (*Giesen, Heinz*); TJT 18 (2002) 269-271 (*Damm, Alex*).

6800 *Tonstad, Sigve* πιστις Χριστου: reading Paul in a new paradigm. AUSS 40 (2002) 37-59.

6801 *Trevijano Etcheverría, Ramón* La evolución de la escatología paulina. Estudios paulinos. 2002 <1996> ⇒248. 417-448.

6802 *Vadakkedom, Jose* 'According to the grace of God given to me' (1 Cor 3,10): St. Paul's understanding of grace. BiBh 27 (2002) 374-90.

6803 *Van Aarde, A.G.* Die "evangelie" van Paulus. VeE 23 (2002) 516-32.

6804 **Van Spanje, Teunis Erik** Inconsistency in Paul?: a critique of the work of Heikki RÄISÄNEN. WUNT 2/110: 1999 ⇒15,6499; 17,6415. [R]AcTh(B) 22/2 (2002) 278-279 (*Tolmie, D.F.*).

6805 *Vassiliadis, Petros* Paul's *theologia crucis* as an intermediate state of the trajectory from Q to Mark. VII Simposio di Tarso. 2002 ⇒587. 47-55.

6806 *Vollenweider, Samuel* Zeit und Gesetz: Erwägungen zur Bedeutung apokalyptischer Denkformen bei Paulus <1988>;
6807 Grosser Tod und grosses Leben: ein Beitrag zum buddhistisch-christlichen Gespräch im Blick auf die Mystik des Paulus <1991>;
6808 Der Geist als Selbst der Glaubenden: Überlegungen zu einem ontologischen Problem in der paulinischen Anthropologie <1996>. Horizonte. WUNT 144: 2002 ⇒257. 143-162/215-235/163-192.
6809 **Walter, Matthias** Gemeinde als Leib Christi: Untersuchungen zum Corpus Paulinum und zu den "apostolischen Vätern". NTOA 49: 2001 ⇒17,6418. ᴿEstAg 37 (2002) 594-595 (*Luis, P. de*).
6810 **Wenham, David** Paul and Jesus: the true story. GR 2002, Eerdmans xii; 195 pp. $20. 0-8028-3983-5.
6811 **Wiles, Virginia** Making sense of Paul: a basic introduction to Pauline theology. 2000 ⇒16,6442. ᴿRBLit 4 (2002) 417-419 (*Rogers, Patrick*); RBLit (2002)* (*Rogers, Patrick*).
6812 **Williams, David John** Paul's metaphors: their context and character 1999 ⇒15,6504; 16,6443. ᴿNRTh 124 (2002) 284-285 (*Rouwez, J.*); BBR 12 (2002) 142-144 (*Trites, Allison A.*).
6813 *Williams, Drake* 'Let God be proved true': Paul's view of scripture and the faithfulness of God. The trustworthiness of God. 2002 ⇒410. 96-117.
6814 *Wischmeyer, Oda* Paul's religion: a review of the problem. ᶠWEDDERBURN, A.: JSNT.S 217: 2002 ⇒132. 74-93.
6815 **Young, Brad H.** Paul the Jewish theologian: a pharisee among christians. 1997 ⇒13,6192; 14,5852. ᴿSBET 20 (2002) 118-119 (*Carson, Marion L.S.*).
6816 *Zahl, Paul F.M.* Mistakes of the new perspective on Paul. Themelios 27/1 (2001) 5-11.
6817 *Zumstein, Jean* Das Wort vom Kreuz als Mitte der paulinischen Theologie. Kreuzestheologie. WUNT 151: 2002 ⇒298. 27-41.
6818 **Zumstein, Jean** Le protestantisme et les premiers chrétiens: entre Jésus et Paul. Genève 2002, Labor et F. 136 pp. €11.35. 2-8309-1034-6. ᴿIst. 47 (2002) 411-413 (*Couteau, Elisabeth*).

G3.4 *Pauli stylus et modus operandi*—**Paul's image**

6819 *Dunn, James D.* The Jew Paul and his meaning for Israel. A shadow of glory. 2002 ⇒347. 201-215.
6820 **Légasse, Simon** L'antipaulinisme sectaire au temps des pères de l'église. CRB 47: 2000 ⇒16,6450; 17,6425. ᴿApocrypha 13 (2002) 295-296 (*Jones, F. Stanley*).
6821 *Renker, Alwin* Wandlungen im heutigen Paulusbild. ᶠTHOMA, C.: JudChr 20: 2002 ⇒119. 209-228.
6822 *Rubenstein, Richard L.* The apostle and the seed of Abraham. A shadow of glory. 2002 ⇒347. 68-88.
6823 *Strijdom, J.* A model *NOT* to be imitated?: recent criticisms of Paul. HTS 57 (2001) 412-422 [NTAb 46,482].
6824 **Walton, Steve** Leadership and lifestyle: the portrait of Paul in the Miletus speech and 1 Thessalonians. MSSNTS 108: 2000 ⇒16,6454; 17,6429. ᴿJR 82 (2002) 100-101 (*Mount, Christopher*); RBLit 4 (2002) 416-417 (*Fox, Kenneth A.*) [Acts 20,17-38].

G3.5 **Apostolus Gentium** [⇒G4.6, Israel et Lex/Jews & Law]

6825 **Alvarez Cineira, David** Die Religionspolitik des Kaisers Claudius und die paulinische Mission. Herders Biblische Studien 19: 1999 ⇒ 15,6515...17,6430. ᴿNZM 58 (2002) 58-61 (*Schelbert, Georg*).

6826 *Dhavamony, Mariasusai* St Paul offers five ways of dialogue and mission: reflection on interreligious dialogue in honour of Bp Rossano. Teologia cristiana. DMis 27: 2002 <2001> ⇒232. i-vi.

6827 *Gager, John G.* Paul, the apostle of Judaism. Jesus, Judaism. 2002 ⇒ 308. 56-76.

6828 *Hofius, Otfried* Paulus—Missionar und Theologe. Paulusstudien II. WUNT 143: 2002 <1997> ⇒180. 1-16.

6829 **Kraus, Wolfgang** Zwischen Jerusalem und Antiochia: die 'Hellenisten', Paulus und die Aufnahme der Heiden in das endzeitliche Gottesvolk. SBS 179: 1999 ⇒15,6526...17,6438. ᴿSNTU.A 27 (2002) 253-256 (*Scholtissek, K.*).

6830 **Krug, Johannes** Die Kraft des Schwachen: ein Beitrag zur paulinischen Apostolatstheologie. TANZ 37: 2001 ⇒17,6439. ᴿFZThPh 49 (2002) 282-284 (*Venetz, Hermann-Josef*); ThLZ 127 (2002) 1305-1306 (*Sandnes, Karl O.*).

6831 *Landgrave G., Daniel R.* Pablo, agente-modelo de pastoral. Medellín 28 (2002) 63-77.

6832 **Legrand, Lucien** L'apôtre des nations?: Paul et la stratégie missionnaire des églises apostoliques. LeDiv 184: 2001 ⇒17,6440. ᴿLV(L) 254 (2002) 91-93 (*Lémonon, Jean-Pierre*).

6833 *Roure, Damià* L'esperit de dolcesa en les cartes de Pau. QVC 208 (2002) 19-30.

6834 *Söding, Thomas* Charisma und Amt des Apostels: paulinische Impulse. LebZeug 57 (2002) 5-13.

G3.6 *Pauli fundamentum* **philosophicum** [⇒G4.3] *et* **morale**

6835 *Aasgaard, Reidar* 'Role ethics' in Paul: the significance of the sibling role for Paul's ethical thinking. NTS 48 (2002) 513-530.

6836 **Alvarez Verdes, Lorenzo** Caminar en el Espíritu: el pensamiento ético de S. Pablo. Quaestiones Morales 12: 2000 ⇒16,6485; 17,6446. ᴿTer. 53 (2002) 572-575 (*Igirukwayo, Antoine M.Z.*); EstB 60 (2002) 274-275 (*Pastor-Ramos, F.*); CDios 215 (2002) 675-676 (*Gutiérrez, J.*).

6837 *Brown, Alexandra R.* Character formation or character transformation?: the challenge of cruciform exegesis for character ethics in Paul. Character and scripture. 2002 ⇒283. 264-289.

6838 *Elliott, Neil* Paul's letters: God's justice against empire. NT: introducing. 2002 ⇒332. 122-147.

6839 **Engberg-Pedersen, Troels** Paul and the Stoics. 2000 ⇒16,6491; 17, 6452. ᴿBZ 46 (2002) 141-143 (*Hoegen-Rohls, Christina*); AThR 84 (2002) 150-151 (*Scroggs, Robin*); JSNT 86 (2002) 61-102 [Resp. 103-14] (*Martyn, J. Louis*); SNTU.A 27 (2002) 259-60 (*Scholtissek, K.*); HBT 24/2 (2002) 120-121 (*Denova, Rebecca I.*); RBLit (2002)* (*Engberg-Pedersen, Troels; Stowers, Stanley K.; Attridge, Harold W.; Fitzgerald, John T.; Gaca, Kathy L.; Furnish, Victor Paul*).

6840   *Fabris, Rinaldo* La coscienza nella riflessione di san Paolo. CredOg 128 (2002) 47-56.

6841   *Faßnacht, Martin* Das paulinische Wissenskonzept und seine soteriologische Relevanz. Rettendes Wissen. AOAT 300: 2002 ⇒352. 185-227.

6842   **Given, Mark Douglas** Paul's true rhetoric: ambiguity, cunning, and deception in Greece and Rome. Emory Studies in Early Christianity 7: 2001 ⇒17,6453. ᴿJBL 121 (2002) 573-575 (*Byrskog, Samuel*).

6843   *Henley, John A.* The patience of Paul. TJT 18 (2002) 43-48.

6844   **Hjort, Birgitte Graakjaer** The irreversible sequence: Paul's ethics: their foundation and present relevance. 2000 ⇒16,6494. ᴿRBLit (2002)* (*Seim, Turid K.*).

6845   *Kudilil, George* 'Remember the poor' (Gal 2,10): Paul, the apostle of globalization. BiBh 27 (2002) 391-415.

6846   *Meeks, Wayne A.* The circle of reference in Pauline morality;

6847   The polyphonic ethics of the apostle Paul. In search. 2002 ⇒208. 167-182/196-209.

6848   *Moore, Stephen D.* Radical orthodox sex?: Francis Watson's Pauline sexual ethic. JSNT 25/1 (2002) 97-107.

6849   *Murphy-O'Connor, Jerome* Paul challenges the Celtic tiger. DoLi 52 (2002) 517-524.

6850   *Phipps, William E.* Paul on 'unnatural' sex. CThMi 29 (2002) 128-135.

6851   *Prasad, Jacob* 'Walking in newness of life' (Rom 6:4): foundations of Pauline ethics. Jeevadhara 32 (2002) 476-489.

6852   **Repole, Renato** Eschatology and ethics in the letters of St. Paul. ᴰ*Aletti, Jean-Noël*: R 2002, 1v; 125 pp. Extr. Diss. Gregoriana.

6853   *Rizzi, Armido* Destino e libertà nell'ottica paolina. Servitium 36 (2002) 436-440.

6854   *Stolle, Volker* Das jüdische Selbstverständnis des Paulus und LUTHERs 'eigenwillige' Interpretation. ᶠASCHOFF, D. 2002 ⇒3. 75-87.

6855   *Tambasco, Anthony J.* Paul's universal gospel and social ethic. BiTod 40 (2002) 154-158.

6856   **Van Kooten, G.H.** Paulus en de kosmos: het vroege christendom te midden van de andere Grieks-Romeinse filosofieën: essay. Zoetermeer 2002, Boekencentrum 266 pp. €24.90. 90-239-0877-5.

6857   **Zakopoulos, Athenagoras Ch.** PLATO and Saint Paul on man: a psychological, philosophical and theological study. Thessalonica 2002, Melissa 246 pp. 960-7298-969 [Theol(A) 74,404ss: Pharantos, M.].

G3.7 *Pauli* communitates *et* spiritualitas

6858   **Adarkwa, Kennedy Ahenkora** Selected aspects of spiritual warfare in the New Testament and their implications for evangelism. ᴰ*McDow, M.*: 2002, 272 pp. Diss. Forth Worth [RTL 34,641].

6859   *Bellia, Giuseppe* Aggregazioni socio-religiose nelle comunità paoline: l'apporto della lettura storico-antropologica. Ho Theológos 20 (2002) 437-444.

6860   *Bieberstein, Sabine* Die Freiheit, die Tora und die Gemeinden des Messias Jesus: Anfragen an das Konzept des "gesetzesfreien Heidenchristentums". BiKi 57 (2002) 139-144.

6861   *Biguzzi, Giancarlo* Ritratto interiore di Paolo. PaVi 47/6 (2002) 4-8.

6862 *Bommas, Martin* Apostel Paulus und die ägyptischen Heiligtümer Makedoniens. Ägyptische Mysterien?. 2002 ⇒389. 127-141.

6863 **Cipriani, Settimio** Il messaggio spirituale di San Paolo. 2001 ⇒17, 6465. [R]RivBib 50 (2002) 113-114 (*Rolla, Armando*).

6864 **De Genaro, Giuseppe; Salzer, Elisabetta C.** Literatura mistica: San Pablo místico. Burgos 2002, Monte Carmelo 555 pp. 84-7239-645-2.

6865 **Fusco, Vittorio** Les premières communautés chrétiennes: traditions et tendances dans le christianisme des origines. [T]*Lucas, Noël*: LeDiv 188: 2001 ⇒17,6468. [R]CEv 119 (2002) 64-65; Brot. 154 (2002) 408-409 (*Silva, I. Ribeiro da*).

6866 *Garland, David E.* The absence of an ordained ministry in the churches of Paul. PRSt 29/2 (2002) 183-195.

6867 *Gielen, Marlis* Frauen in den Gemeinden des Paulus: von den Anfängen bis zum Ende des 1. Jahrhunderts. SaThZ 6 (2002) 182-191.

6868 **Gorman, Michael J.** Cruciformity: Paul's narrative spirituality of the cross. 2001 ⇒17,6470. [R]Theol. 105 (2002) 366-367 (*Hooker, Morna D.*); Worship 76 (2002) 567-569 (*Sloyan, Gerard S.*); CBQ 64 (2002) 573-5 (*Miller, James C.*); ET 113 (2002) 192-95 (*McDonald, J. Ian*).

6869 *Grieb, A. Katherine* Deutero-Pauline letters: Colossians, Ephesians, and the Pastoral Epistles. NT: introducing. 2002 ⇒332. 148-167.

6870 *Günther, Matthias* Paulus von Tarsus: eine lebensstilorientierte Annäherung. ThZ 58 (2002) 31-45.

6871 *Helewa, Giovanni* La fede nel messaggio di Paolo apostolo. RVS 56 (2002) 244-271.

6872 *Hofius, Otfried* "De waarheid van het evangelie": exegetische en theologische overwegingen bij de waarheidsclaim van de paulinische prediking. ThRef 45/3 (2002) 198-218.

6873 *Horrell, David G.* From ἀδελφοί to οἶκος θεοῦ: social transformation in Pauline christianity. JBL 120 (2001) 293-311.

6874 *Jennings, Theodore W.* Community with the poor: Pauline reflections. QR 22/1 (2002) 73-84.

6875 *Jervis, L. Ann* Accepting affliction: Paul's preaching on suffering. Character and scripture. 2002 ⇒283. 290-316.

6876 *Kelhoffer, James A.* The struggle to define *Heilsgeschichte*: Paul on the origins of the christian tradition. BR 47 (2002) 19-39.

6877 *Kippenberg, Hans G.* Christliche Gemeinden im Römischen Reich: collegium licitum oder illicitum?. [F]HOHEISEL, K.: JAC.E 34: 2002 ⇒ 59. 172-183.

6878 *Longenecker, Richard N.* Paul's vision of the church and community formation in his major missionary letters. Community formation. 2002 ⇒644. 73-88.

6879 *Murphy-O'Connor, Jerome* Paul and stewardship. BiTod 40 (2002) 285-289.

6880 *Ostmeyer, Karl-Heinrich* Das immerwährende Gebet bei Paulus. ThBeitr 33 (2002) 274-289.

6881 **Pieri, Fabrizio** Paolo e IGNAZIO: testimoni e maestri del discernimento spirituale. Bibbia e Preghiera 43: R 2002, ADP 184 pp. 88-73-57-267-7.

6882 *Pilhofer, Peter* Die ökonomische Attraktivität christlicher Gemeinden der Frühzeit. Die frühen Christen. WUNT 145: 2002 <2001> ⇒225. 194-218.

6883 **Pinckaers, S.** Das geistliche Leben des Christen: Theologie und Spiritualität nach Paulus und THOMAS von Aquin. AMATECA 17/2: 1999 ⇒15,6563. ᴿThG 45 (2002) 309-311 (*Fuchs, Gotthard*).
6884 *Rossano, Pietro* Paul en dialogue avec Corinthe et Éphèse. Teologia cristiana. DMis 27: 2002 <1971> ⇒232. 11-18.
6885 *Still, Todd D.* Historical anachronism and ministerial ordination: a response to David E. Garland. PRSt 29/2 (2002) 197-203.
6886 **Sumney, Jerry L.** 'Servants of Satan', 'false brothers' and other opponents of Paul. JSNT.S 188: 1999 ⇒15,6565; 17,6482. ᴿCBQ 64 (2002) 179-180 (*Pattee, Stephen*); ThLZ 127 (2002) 51-54 (*Lindemann, Andreas*).
6887 **Thomas, Carolyn** Reading the letters of Saint Paul: study, reflection and prayer. NY 2002, Paulist ix; 194 pp. 0-8091-4065-9.
6888 *Trevijano Etcheverría, Ramón* El misterio de Dios en las comunidades paulinas. Estudios paulinos. 2002 <1987> ⇒248. 233-256.
6889 **Umbach, Helmut** In Christus getauft—von der Sünde befreit: die Gemeinde als sündenfreier Raum bei Paulus. FRLANT 181: 1999 ⇒ 15,6568; 17,6530. ᴿBBR 12 (2002) 309-311 (*Yinger, Kent L.*).
6890 *Venetz, Hermann-Josef* Frauen von Rang und Namen: ein anderer Blick in paulinische Gemeinden. BiKi 57 (2002) 127-133 [Rom 16].
6891 **Viagulamuthu, Xavier Paul B.** Offering our bodies as a living sacrifice to God: a study in Pauline spirituality based on Romans 12, 1. ᴰ*Martinez, E.*: TGr.Spiritualità 7: R 2002, E.P.U.G. 526 pp. $30. 88-7652-948-9. Diss. Gregoriana; Bibl. 477-510.

G3.8 *Pauli receptio*, history of research

6892 *Aletti, Jean-Noël* Où en sont les études sur Saint Paul?: enjeux et propositions. RSR 90 (2002) 329-351.
6893 *Campbell, William S.* Significant nuances in contemporary Pauline interpretation. IBSt 24 (2002) 184-200.
6894 *Fuller, Reginald H.* Justification in recent Pauline studies. AThR 84 (2002) 411-416.
6895 **Lannon, Joseph** A critical analysis of the new perspective on Paul, with particular reference to the methodology of E.P. Sanders. ᴰ*Moore, H.*: 2002, 260 pp. Diss. Belfast [RTL 34,598].
6896 *Longenecker, Bruce W.* The narrative approach to Paul: an early retrospective. CuBR 1/1 (2002) 88-111.
6897 ᴱ**Mara, Maria Grazia,** *al.*, Paolo di Tarso nell'esegesi cristiana antica. La bibbia nelle comunità antiche. 2002 ⇒286. 65-73.
6898 *Pani, Giancarlo* Il ritorno a Paolo nel secolo XVI: 700 titoli. VII Simposio di Tarso. 2002 ⇒587. 271-305.
6899 *Sutter Rehmann, Luzia* Die Durchbrechung des Bannkreises oder: wenn Frauen Paulus lesen: eine kleine Forschungsgeschichte. BiKi 57 (2002) 122-126.

G3.9 *Themata particularia de Paulo*, details

6900 **Dobraczynski, Jan** La spada santa: la storia di Paolo. Mi 2002, Gribaudi 302 pp. Romanzo..
6901 *Holloway, Paul A.* The enthymeme as an element of style in Paul. JBL 120 (2001) 329-343.

6902 *Mara, Maria Grazia* Prefigurazioni paoline nel cristianesimo antico;
6903 *Nazzaro, Antonio V.* La figura di Paolo nella *Historia apostolica* di
ARATORE. VII Simposio di Tarso. 2002 ⇒587. 163-172/227-251.
6904 **Payne, G. Andrew** A textual analysis, critical reconstruction and
evaluation of the superscriptions and subscriptions to the corpus paulinum. ᴰ*Schatzmann, S.*: 2002, 219 pp. Diss. Fort Worth [RTL 34,
600].
6905 *Porter, Stanley E.* Did Paul baptize himself?: a problem of the Greek
voice system. Dimensions of baptism. JSNT.S 234: 2002 ⇒434. 91-
109 [Acts 22,16].
6906 *Rotar, Janez* Jezikovni nauk apostola Pavla in skrb Primoža Trubarja
za avtonomnost knjižne slovenščine [Language teachings of apostle
Paul and Primoža Trubarja's care for the independence of the Slovenian written language]. Bogoslovni vestnik 62 (2002) 463-475. Sum.
475. S.

G4.1 **Ad Romanos** *Textus, commentarii*

6907 ᴱ**Bammel, Caroline P. Hammond** Der Römerbriefkommentar des
ORIGINES: kritische Ausgabe der Übersetzung RUFINs: Buch 7-10.
AGLB 34: 1998 ⇒14,5923; 15,6579. Aus dem Nachlass hrsg. von
H. Frede u. *H. Stanjek.* ᴿLatomus 61 (2002) 188-189 (*Savon, Hervé*).
6908 **Barth, Karl** L'epistola ai Romani. ᵀ*Miegge, G.*: Mi 2002, Feltrinelli
523 pp. €13.50. ᴿOecumenica Civitas 2/1 (2002) 111-112 (*Litrico,
Lorenza*).
6909 ᴱ**Bray, Gerald** Romanos. La Biblia comentada por los Padres de la
Iglesia, NT 6: 2000 ⇒16,6545. ᴿEstB 60 (2002) 133-134 (*Pastor-
Ramos, F.*).
6910 **Bryan, Christopher** A preface to Romans: notes on the epistle in its
literary and cultural setting. 2000 ⇒16,6547; 17,6492. ᴿJR 82 (2002)
104-105 (*Reasoner, Mark*).
6911 **Cantalamessa, Raniero** Life in Christ: the spiritual message of the
letter to the Romans. ᵀ*Villa, Frances Lonergan*: ColMn 2002,
Liturgical 221 pp. $15. 0-8146-2799-4 [ThD 49,263—W.C. Heiser].
6912 ᴱ**Díaz Rodelas, Juan Miguel** La carta a los Romanos. ResB 34
(2002) 1-64.
6913 **Grieb, A. Katherine** The story of Romans: a narrative defense of
God's righteousness. LVL 2002, Westminster xxiv; 167 pp. $20. 0-
664-22525-X. Bibl. 151-156 [BiTod 41,331—Senior, Donald].
6914 **Kroll, Woodrow** The book of Romans: righteousness in Christ.
Chattanooga 2002, AMG xviii; 267 pp. $20 [BS 160,502–Witmer,
John A.].
6915 **Légasse, Simon** L'épître de Paul aux Romains. LeDiv 10: P 2002,
Cerf 992 pp. €76. 2-204-06896-9. Bibl. 21-28. ᴿBrot. 155 (2002)
523-524 (*Silva, I. Ribeiro da*).
6916 **Moo, Douglas J.** The epistle to the Romans. NIC: 1996 ⇒12,6043
... 15,6591. ᴿVJTR 66 (2002) 545-547 (*Meagher, P.M.*);
6917 Encountering the book of Romans: a theological survey. Encountering biblical studies: GR 2002, Baker 230 pp. $25. 0-8010-2546-X.
6918 **Orsatti, Mauro** Il capolavoro di Paolo: lettura pastorale della lettera
ai Romani. Lettura pastorale della bibbia, bibbia e spiritualità 16: Bo
2002, EDB 208 pp. €13. 88-10-20158-2. Bibl. 201-203.

6919 **Pitta, Antonio** Lettera ai Romani. I libri biblici, NT 6: [2]2001 ⇒17,
      6501. [R]StPat 49 (2002) 249-250 (*Segalla, Giuseppe*); Annales Theo-
      logici 16 (2002) 507-509 (*Estrada, B.*); CivCatt 153/2 (2002) 207-
      208 (*Scaiola, D.*).
6920 **Prigent, Pierre** L'épître aux Romains. Bible en face: P 2002, Bayard
      190 pp. €18.90. 2-227-47096-8 [RHPhR 82,380].
6921 [T]**Scheck, Thomas P.** ORIGEN: commentary on the epistle to the Ro-
      mans: books 1-5, 6-10. FaCh 103-104: 2001 ⇒17,6502-3. [R]JECS 10
      (2002) 526-527 (*Moser, Maureen Beyer*); LTP 58 (2002) 637-638
      (*Kaler, Michael*).
6922 **Stuhlmacher, Peter** La lettera ai Romani. NT 6: Brescia 2002,
      Paideia 313 pp. €27. 88-394-0630-1. Bibl. 305-309.
6923 **Theobald, Michael** Der Römerbrief. EdF 294: 2000 ⇒16,6558; 17,
      6508. [R]ThRv 98 (2002) 113-114 (*Zeller, Dieter*); OLZ 97 (2002)
      271-273 (*Bull, Klaus-M.*); ThLZ 127 (2002) 189-192 (*Horn, Fried-
      rich Wilhelm*).
6924 **Wright, N. Thomas** NIntB 10: The letter to the Romans: introduc-
      tion, commentary, and reflections. 2002 ⇒4655. 393-770 pp.

G4.2 *Ad Romans: themata*, topics

6925 *Adams, Edward* Paul's story of God and creation: the story of how
      God fulfils his purposes in creation. Narrative dynamics. 2002 ⇒
      351. 19-43.
6926 *Brindle, Wayne A.* "To the Jew first": rhetoric, strategy, history, or
      theology?. BS 159 (2002) 221-233.
6927 **Burnett, Gary** Paul and the salvation of the individual. BiblInterp
      57: 2001 ⇒17,6510. [R]JBL 121 (2002) 777-780 (*Keay, Robert*) [Rom
      1-8].
6928 *Curkpatrick, Stephen* Paul's epistle to the Romans: a dialogue. ET
      114 (2002) 11-17.
6929 *Díaz Rodelas, Juan Miguel* La justicia de Dios revelada en Cristo.
      ResB 34 (2002) 5-12.
      [F]FEE, G. Romans and the people of God 1999 ⇒37.
6930 *Fernández, Victor M.* Le meilleur de la Lettre aux Romains procède
      du judaïsme de Paul. NRTh 124 (2002) 403-414.
6931 *Gaston, Lloyd* Romans in context: the conversation revisited. [F]ROET-
      ZEL, C.: JSNT.S 221: 2002 ⇒104. 125-141.
6932 *Gignac, Alain* Dieu juge et avocat. Dieu, vingt-six portraits. 2002 ⇒
      312. 183-192.
6933 *Haacker, Klaus* Der Römerbrief als Friedensmemorandum;
6934 Das Evangelium Gottes und die Erwählung Israels: zum Beitrag des
      Römerbriefs zur Erneuerung des Verhältnisses zwischen Christen und
      Juden <1982>;
6935 Bibelübersetzung nach dem Holocaust: ein Beispiel aus dem Römer-
      brief <2000>. Versöhnung mit Israel. VKHW 5: 2002 ⇒174. 111-
      126/95-109/209-216.
6936 *Hofius, Otfried* Der Psalter als Zeuge des Evangeliums: die Ver-
      wendung der Septuaginta-Psalmen in den ersten beiden Hauptteilen
      des Römerbriefes. Paulusstudien II. WUNT 143: 2002 <1997> ⇒
      180. 38-57.

6937 Lohse, Eduard Der Wandel der Christen im Zeichen der Aufer-
      stehung: zur Begründung christlicher Ethik im Römerbrief. [F]LAM-
      BRECHT, J.: BEThL 165: 2002 ⇒72. 315-322.
6938 **Mainville, Odette** Un plaidoyer en faveur de l'unité: la lettre aux
      Romains. 1999 ⇒15,6612...17,6519. [R]RBLit 4 (2002) 419-420
      (Miller, James C.).
6939 Malina, B.J. We and they in Romans. HTS 58 (2002) 608-631
      [NTAb 47,266].
6940 **Martens, Dominique** 'Désormais, il n'y a plus de différences': en-
      jeux théologiques et christologiques de la manifestation de la justice
      de Dieu en Rm 3,21-26 et 9,30-10,21. [D]Focant, C.: 2002, 345 pp.
      Diss. Louvain-la-Neuve 2002 [EThL 79,239].
6941 **Miller, James C.** The obedience of faith, the eschatological people
      of God, and the purpose of Romans. SBL.DS 177: 2000 ⇒16,6575.
      [R]CBQ 64 (2002) 384-385 (Lodge, John G.).
6942 Noordegraaf, Albert Paulus' spreken over rechtvaardiging: tendensen
      in het nieuwere onderzoek. ThRef 45/1 (2002) 4-26.
6943 O'Donovan, Oliver Response to N.T. Wright. [F]O'DONOVAN, O. 2002
      ⇒272. 194-195.
6944 Otero Lázaro, Tomás La descendencia de Abrahán. ResB 34 (2002)
      13-24.
6945 Penna, Romano Da Adamo a Isaia: prosopografia biblica nella lettera
      ai Romani. VII Simposio di Tarso. 2002 ⇒587. 7-20.
6946 Porter, Stanley E. The rhetorical scribe: textual variants in Romans
      and their possible rhetorical purpose. Rhetorical criticism. JSNT.S
      195: 2002 ⇒369. 403-419.
6947 Rakotoharintsifa, Andrianjatovo Peace in the epistle to the Romans
      and in the Malagasy culture. SBL.SP 2002. SBL.SPS 41: 2002 ⇒
      598. 33-52.
6948 **Reichert, Angelika** Der Römerbrief als Gratwanderung: eine Unter-
      suchung zur Abfassungsproblematik. FRLANT 194. 2001 ⇒17,
      6523. [R]OrdKor 43 (2002) 114-115 (Giesen, Heinz).
6949 **Shum, Shiu-Lun** Paul's use of Isaiah in Romans: a comparative
      study of Paul's letter to the Romans and the Sibylline and Qumran
      sectarian texts. [D]Barclay, J.: WUNT 2/156: Tü 2002, Mohr S. xii;
      321 pp. €59. 3-16-147925-4. Diss. Glasgow 1999. Bibl. 277-294.
6950 Sider, Robert D. Early commentators in ERASMUS's Annotations on
      Romans. [F]WILKEN, R. 2002 ⇒136. 118-143.
6951 **Stendahl, Krister** Das Vermächtnis des Paulus: eine neue Sicht auf
      den Römerbrief. Z 2001, Theol. Verl. 98 pp. 3-290-17275-9.
6952 Swearingen, C. Jan The tongues of men: understanding Greek rhetor-
      ical sources for Paul's letters to the Romans and 1 Corinthians. Rhe-
      torical argumentation. 2002 ⇒553. 232-242.
6953 Vidal, Enrique Benavent Para una lectura teológica de la carta a los
      Romanos. ResB 34 (2002) 47-55.
6954 Vos, Johan S. 'To make the weaker argument defeat the stronger':
      sophistical argumentation in Paul's letter to the Romans. Rhetorical
      argumentation. 2002 ⇒553. 217-231;
6955 Sophistische Argumentation im Römerbrief. Die Kunst der Argumen-
      tation. 2002 <1990; 2001> ⇒6712. 65-86.
6956 **Wagner, J. Ross** Heralds of the good news: Isaiah and Paul "in con-
      cert" in the letter to the Romans. NT.S 101: Lei 2002, Brill xxii; 437
      pp. 90-04-11691-5. Bibl. 365-397.

6957 Wright, N.T. Coming home to St Paul?: reading Romans a hundred years after Charles GORE. SJTh 55 (2002) 392-407;
6958 Paul and Caesar: A new reading of Romans. ᶠO'DONOVAN, O. 2002 ⇒272. 173-193.

G4.3 Naturalis cognitio Dei, Rom 1-4

6959 Malina, B.J. The New Testament and homosexuality?, 1: the social system behind Romans 1. VeE 23 (2002) 141-150;
6960 The New Testament and homosexuality?, 2: the traditions influencing Paul's thinking in Romans 1. VeE 23 (2002) 393-407.
6961 Gathercole, Simon J. Where is boasting?: early Jewish soteriology and Paul's response in Romans 1-5. ᴰDunn, James: GR 2002, Eerdmans xii; 311 pp. $32. 0-8028-3991-6. Diss.; Bibl. 267-289.
6962 Snyman, A.H. De-automatisation in Romans 1-5. AcTh(B) 22/1 (2002) 135-145.
6963 Thorsteinsson, Runar M. Paul's missionary duty towards gentiles in Rome: a note on the punctuation and syntax of Rom 1.13-15. NTS 48 (2002) 531-547.
6964 Romanello, Stefano Jakie jest oredzie ewangeliczne w Rz 1,16-3,20? [What is the gospel proclamation in Rom 1,16-3,20?]. Verbum Vitae 2 (2002) 165-182. Sum. 182. P.;
6965 La giustizia di Dio in Rm 1,16-4,25: concezioni in conflitto?. RStB 14/1-2 (2002) 245-294.
6966 Penna, Romano Prospettiva evangelica su idolatria e degrado umano (Rm 1,18-32). PSV 46 (2002) 97-111.
6967 Botha, P.J.J. Die drange van hulle hart ...(Rom 1:24-27). VeE 23 (2002) 18-51.
6968 Gathercole, Simon J. A law unto themselves: the gentiles in Romans 2.14-15 revisited. JSNT 85 (2002) 27-49.
6969 Berkley, Timothy W. From a broken covenant to circumcision of the heart: Pauline intertextual exegesis in Romans 2:17-29. SBL.DS 175: 2000 ⇒16,6599; 17,6545. ᴿRBLit (2002)* (Morrison, Gregg).
6970 Lambrecht, Jan Zondigen tot meerdere eer en glorie van God?: Paulus' gedachtegang in Romeinen 3,1-9. Coll. 32/2 (2002) 199-206.
6971 Belli, Filippo 'Testimoniada por la ley y los profetas': Rom 3,21: Pablo y las escrituras. RevAg 43 (2002) 413-426.
6972 Campbell, Douglas A. Towards a new, rhetorical assisted reading of Romans 3.27-4.25. Rhetorical criticism. JSNT.S 195: 2002 ⇒369. 355-402.
6973 Kreuzer, Siegfried "Der den Gottlosen rechtfertigt" (Röm 4,5): die frühjüdische Einordnung von Gen 15 als Hintergrund für das Abrahambild und die Rechtfertigungslehre des Paulus. ThBeitr 33 (2002) 208-219.
6974 Neubrand, Maria Abraham—Vater von Juden und Nichtjuden: eine exegetische Studie zu Röm 4. FzB 85: 1997 ⇒14,5989; 16,6603. ᴿFrRu 9 (2002) 63-64 (Vonach, Andreas).
6975 Hofius, Otfried Die Gottesprädikationen Röm 4,17b. Paulusstudien II. WUNT 143: 2002 <1971/72> ⇒180. 58-61.
6976 Hooker, Morna D. Raised for our acquittal (Rom 4,25.). ᶠLAMBRECHT, J.: BEThL 165: 2002 ⇒72. 323-341.

G4.4 *Redemptio cosmica*: **Rom 5-8**

6977 **Gargano, Innocenzo** Lectio divina sulla lettera ai Romani, 2. Conversazioni bibliche: Bo 2002, EDB 128 pp. 88-10-70980-2.

6978 *Theißen, Gerd* Zugang zu Gott ohne Türhüter: eine Variante zur Parabel "Vor dem Gesetz" (Röm 5,1-5). Erlösungsbilder. 2002 ⇒1460. 122-128.

6979 *Manicardi, Ermenegildo* 'La speranza non delude' (Rm 5,5). CoSe.S 51/3 (2002) 26-34.

6980 *Martin, Troy W.* The Good as God (Romans 5.7). JSNT 25/1 (2002) 55-70.

6981 *Bell, Richard H.* The myth of Adam and the myth of Christ in Romans 5.12-21. [F]WEDDERBURN, A.: JSNT.S 217: 2002 ⇒132. 21-36.

6982 *Hofius, Otfried* Die Adam—Christus—Antithese und das Gesetz: Erwägungen zu Röm 5,12-21. Paulusstudien II. WUNT 143: 2002 <1996> ⇒180. 62-103.

6983 *Bell, Richard H.* Rom 5.18-19 and universal salvation. NTS 48 (2002) 417-432.

6984 *Patrzynski, Jean-Frédéric* 'L'homme devant Dieu': une lecture 'méditative' de Romains 6. Unité chrétienne 146 (2002) 15-18.

6985 *Viard, Jean-Sébastien* Obéissance ou liberté?: redécouverte structurelle de Rm 6,15-23. ScEs 54 (2002) 351-366.

6986 *Crüsemann, Marlene* Sklaverei in Freiheit: Römer 6,19-23. JK 63/3 (2002) 59-61.

6987 **Middendorf, Michael Paul** The "I" in the storm: a study of Romans 7. 1997 ⇒13,6342b. [R]RBLit 4 (2002) 421-423 (*Das, A. Andrew*).

6988 *Thurén, Lauri* Romans 7 derhetorized. Rhetorical criticism. JSNT.S 195: 2002 ⇒369. 420-440.

6989 *Baldanza, Giuseppe* La rilevanza del linguaggio sponsale nella lettera ai Romani: Rm 7,1-6. Sal. 64 (2002) 411-429.

6990 **Burton, Keith Augustus** Rhetoric, law, and the mystery of salvation in Romans 7:1-6. 2001 ⇒17,6560. [R]AUSS 40 (2002) 309-311 (*Westerholm, Stephen*).

6991 *Anderson, Valérie Nicolet* Can KIERKEGAARD help us understand the role of the law in Romans 7:7-12?: tools for a Kierkegaardian reading of Paul. SBL.SP 2002. SBL.SPS 41: 2002 ⇒598. 111-135.

6992 *Aletti, Jean-Noël* Rm 7.7-25 encore une fois: enjeux et propositions. NTS 48 (2002) 358-376.

6993 *Engberg-Pedersen, Troels* The reception of Graeco-Roman culture in the New Testament: the case of Romans 7.7-25. NT as reception. JSNT.S 230: 2002 ⇒360. 32-57.

6994 *Hofius, Otfried* Der Mensch im Schatten Adams: Römer 7,7-25a. Paulusstudien II. WUNT 143: 2002 ⇒180. 104-154.

6995 *Napier, Daniel* Paul's analysis of sin and Torah in Romans 7:7-25. RestQ 44/1 (2002) 15-32.

6996 *Grappe, Christian* Qui me délivrera de ce corps de mort?: l'Esprit de vie!: Romains 7,24 et 8,2 comme éléments de typologie adamique. Bib. 83 (2002) 472-492.

6997 **Martin, Thomas Frank** Rhetoric and exegesis in AUGUSTINE's interpretation of Romans 7:24-25a. SBEC 47: 2001 ⇒17,6564. [R]Augustinus 47 (2002) 458-459 (*Oldfield, John*).

6998 *Aletti, Jean-Noël* Romans 8: the Incarnation and its redemptive impact. The incarnation. 2002 ⇒624. 93-115.

6999 *Lemoine, Laurent Charnels* et *spirituels:* des chrétiens irréconciliables?: libre commentaire de Romains 8. VS 156 (2002) 783-788.
7000 *Janssen, Claudia* Leben ist möglich: Römer 8,1-11. JK 63/2 (2002) 55-58.
7001 *Moreno García, Abdón* La sabiduría del Espíritu es biógena: hacia una sintaxis de la alteridad (Rm 8,6 y Flp 2,2). EstB 60 (2002) 3-30.
7002 *Bray, Gerald* The love of God (Romans 8:18-39). Evangel 20 (2002) 5-8.
7003 *Eastman, Susan* Whose apocalypse?: the identity of the sons of God in Romans 8:19. JBL 121 (2002) 263-277.
7004 *Gieniusz, Andrea* La paziente attesa della creazione è in ansia per la rivelazione dei figli di Dio (Rm 8,19-22). La speranza. 2002 ⇒277. 299-333.
7005 *Belli, Filippo* Un'allusione a Is 50,8-9 in Rm 8,31-34. RivBib 50 (2002) 153-184.
7006 *Jewett, Robert* Impeaching God's elect: Romans 8.33-37 in its rhetorical situation. ᶠWEDDERBURN, A.: JSNT.S 217: 2002 ⇒132. 37-58.

G4.6 *Israel et Lex*; **The Law and the Jews**, *Rom 9-11*

7007 *Buch-Hansen, Gitte* Dobbeltperspektivet i Romerbrevet kap. 9-11: et forsøg på med udgangspunkt i receptionshistorien at komme med et aktuelt bud på en eksegese af Rom 9-11. DTT 65 (2002) 81-106.
7008 *Burgos Núñez, Miguel de* La salvación de los paganos y de Israel, misterio de la fidelidad de Dios: Rom 9-11. ResB 34 (2002) 25-34.
7009 **Davis, Stephan K.** The antithesis of the ages: Paul's reconfiguration of torah. CBQ.MS 33: Wsh 2002, The Catholic Biblical Association of America x; 259 pp. $11. 0-915170-32-9. Bibl. 219-243. ᴿRExp 99 (2002) 623-624 *(Biddle, Mark E.)*.
7010 ᴱ**Dunn, James D.G.** Paul and the Mosaic law. 2001 ⇒17,462. ᴿCThMi 29 (2002) 145-146 *(Linss, Wilhelm C.)*; AUSS 40 (2002) 140-143 *(Burton, Keith Augustus)*; RBLit (2002)* *(Nanos, Mark D.)*.
7011 *Fernández, Victor M.* 2. Reacción: lo mejor de la carta a los Romanos procede del pensamiento judío de Pablo. RevBib 63 (2001) 184-193.
7012 *Haacker, Klaus* Der "Antinomismus" des Paulus im Kontext antiker Gesetzestheorie. Versöhnung mit Israel. VKHW 5: 2002 <1996> ⇒ 174. 171-188.
7013 *Hengel, Martin* Die Stellung des Apostels Paulus zum Gesetz in den unbekannten Jahren zwischen Damaskus und Antiochien. Paulus und Jakobus. WUNT 141: 2002 <1996> ⇒178. 213-239.
7014 **Kim, Johann D.** God, Israel, and the gentiles: rhetoric and situation in Romans 9-11. SBL.DS 176: 2000 ⇒16,6628; 17,6578. ᴿJSSt 47 (2002) 365-366 *(Campbell, W.S.)*.
7015 *Kot, Silvia* 1. Provocación: el enigma de Pablo y la pretendida 'conversión' de los judíos. RevBib 63 (2001) 169-183.
7016 *Martin, François* Romains 9-11: Israël et la mystère du vouloir de Dieu. SémBib 106 (2002) 12-25.
7017 *Meeks, Wayne A.* On trusting an unpredictable God: a hermeneutical meditation on Romans 9-11. In search. 2002 ⇒208. 210-229.
7018 *Mußner, Franz* Die "Geschichtstheologie" von Röm 9-11. ᶠTHOMA, C.: JudChr 20: 2002 ⇒119. 181-194.

7019 *Pedersen, Sigfred* Paul's understanding of the biblical law. NT 44 (2002) 1-34.

7020 *Renker, Alwin* Das Mysterium Israels: Karl THIEMES Paulusexegese (Röm 9-11). FrRu 9 (2002) 126-135.

7021 *Theißen, Gerd* Röm 9-11—eine Auseinandersetzung des Paulus mit Israel und mit sich selbst: Versuch einer psychologischen Auslegung. ^FRÄISÄNEN, H.: NT.S 103: 2002 ⇒97. 311-341.

7022 **Thielman, Frank** The law and the New Testament: the question of continuity. 1999 ⇒15,6672; 16,6637. ^RCBQ 64 (2002) 396-398 (*Viviano, Benedict T.*); RBLit 4 (2002) 325-326 (*Orr, Mary C.*).

7023 *Tomson, Peter* Glaubensgerechtigkeit und Gesetzeswerke: zu David FLUSSERs Paulusrezeption. ^FTHOMA, C.: JudChr 20: 2002 ⇒119. 285-305.

7024 *Vahanian, Gabriel* God as Israel's problem. ^FPATTE, D. 2002 ⇒89. 251-257.

7025 *Vig Skoven, Anne* Romerbrevet kap. 9-11 som eksegetisk spejl og gåde. DTT 65 (2002) 15-39.

7026 **Yinger, Kent L.** Paul, Judaism and judgment according to deeds. MSSNTS 105: 1999 ⇒15,6675...17,6584. ^RBBR 12 (2002) 311-314 (*Abegg, Martin G.*).

7027 *Heil, John Paul* From remnant to seed of hope for Israel: Romans 9:27-29. CBQ 64 (2002) 703-720.

7028 *Hofius, Otfried* Zur Auslegung von Römer 9,30-33. Paulusstudien II. WUNT 143: 2002 <1993> ⇒180. 155-166.

7029 *Smiles, Vincent M.* The concept of "zeal" in second-temple Judaism and Paul's critique of it in Romans 10:2. CBQ 64 (2002) 282-299.

7030 *Mußner, Franz* "Wenn sie nicht im Unglauben verharren": Bemerkungen zu Römer 11,23. TThZ 111 (2002) 62-67.

7031 *Kim, Seyoon* The "mystery" of Romans 11:25-26 once more. Paul and the new perspective. WUNT 140: 2002 ⇒190. 239-257.

G4.8 **Rom 12...**

7032 *Ramírez Fueyo, Francisco* Comensales del reino y ciudadanos de Roma: el reino de Dios en Rom 12-15. ResB 34 (2002) 35-46.

7033 *Winter, Bruce* Roman law and society in Romans 12-15. Rome in the bible. 2002 ⇒363. 67-102.

7034 *Wannenwetsch, Bernd* 'Members of one another': charis, ministry and representation: a politico-ecclesial reading of Romans 12;

7035 *O'Donovan, Oliver* Response to Bernd Wannenwetsch. ^FO'DONOVAN, O. 2002 ⇒272. 196-220/221-224.

7036 *Richard, Daniel* El "sacrificio vivo" del cristiano: un estudio de Romanos 12:1-2. Theologika 17 (2002) 224-246.-02.

7037 *Kruijf, Gerrit de* The function of Romans 13 in christian ethics;

7038 *O'Donovan, Oliver* Response to Gerrit de Kruijf. ^FO'DONOVAN, O. 2002 ⇒272. 225-237/238-240.

7039 **Lloyd-Jones, David Martyn** Romans: an exposition of chapter 13: life in two kingdoms. E 2002, Banner of Truth Trust x; 323 pp. 0-85151-824-9.

7040 *Destro, Adriana; Pesce, Mauro* I 'corpi' sacrificali: smembramento e
      rimembramento: i presupposti culturali di Rom 13,1-2. VII Simposio
      di Tarso. 2002 ⇒587. 85-113.
7041 **MacKenzie, Edward E.M.** The state and the community of God:
      political motifs in Romans and the occasion for Romans 13:1-7.
      ᴰ*Hurtado, L.W.*: 2001, 337 pp. Diss. Edinburgh [RTL 34,599].
7042 **Monera, Arnold** Paul and 'the powers that be': an exegesis of Ro-
      mans 13,1-7. ᴰ*Delobel, J.*: 2002, lxvi; 494 pp. Diss. Leuven 2002
      [EThL 79,237].
7043 *Theißen, Gerd* Respekt vor der Verfassung: Gegenlektüre eines
      staatstragenden Textes (Röm 13,1-7). Erlösungsbilder. 2002 ⇒1460.
      129-133.
7044 *Lo, Lung-kwong* Identity crisis reflected in Romans 14:1-15:13 and
      the implications for the Chinese christians' controversy on ancestral
      worship. Ching Feng 3 (2002) 23-59 = SBL.SP 2002 ⇒598. 1-32.
7045 *Meeks, Wayne A.* Judgement and the brother: Romans 14:1-15:13. In
      search. 2002 ⇒208. 153-166.
7046 *Pitta, Antonio* I forti e i deboli nelle comunità di Roma (Rm 14,1-
      15,13). RivBib 50 (2002) 401-420.
7047 *Theißen, Gerd* Macht korrumpiert und die Notwendigkeit von Anti-
      korruptionsräumen (Röm 15,1-13). Erlösungsbilder. 2002 ⇒1460.
      134-141.
7048 *Heil, John Paul* The voices of Scripture and Paul's rhetorical strategy
      of hope in Romans 15:7-13. Theoforum 33 (2002) 187-211.
7049 *Lambrecht, Jan* The confirmation of the promises: a critical note on
      Romans 15,8. EThL 78 (2002) 156-160.
7050 *Mongillo, Dalmazio* La familiarità dei rapporti tra Paolo e i fedeli
      della chiesa di Roma: note su Rm 15,14-16,1-27 in dialogo con la
      lectura di Tᴏᴍᴍᴀsᴏ d'Aquino. VII Simposio di Tarso. 2002 ⇒587.
      259-269.
7051 *Clarke, Andrew D.* Jew and Greek, slave and free, male and female:
      Paul's theology of ethnic, social and gender inclusiveness in Romans
      16. Rome in the bible. 2002 ⇒363. 103-125 [Gal 3,28].
7052 *Epp, Eldon Jay* Text-critical, exegetical, and socio-cultural factors
      affecting the Junia/Junias variation in Romans 16,7;
7053 *Collins, Raymond F.* The case of a wandering doxology: Rom 16,25-
      27. ᶠDᴇʟᴏʙᴇʟ, J.: BEThL 161: 2002 ⇒24. 227-291/293-303.

G5.1 **Epistulae ad Corinthios I** (vel I-II), *textus, commentarii*

7054 ᴱ**Bray, Gerald** La biblia comentada por los Padres de la iglesia...
      Nuevo Testamento 7: 1-2 Corintios. ᴱ*Merino, Marcelo*: 2001 ⇒17,
      6609. ᴿCTom 129 (2002) 199-200 (*Huarte, Juan*).
7055 *Doglio, Claudio* Corinto. PaVi 47/1 (2002) 4-11;
7056 La religione di Corinto. PaVi 47/2 (2002) 4-9.
7057 *Pitta, Antonio* Le due lettere ai Corinzi: per una chiesa in maturazio-
      ne. PaVi 47/1 (2002) 14-20.

7058 **Collins, Raymond F.** First Corinthians. 1999 ⇒15,6705... 17,6614.
      ᴿThemelios 27/3 (2002) 23-27 (*Fox, K.A.*).
7059 **Grasso, Santi** Prima lettera ai Corinzi Nuovo Testamento—com-
      mento esegetico e spirituale. R 2002, Città N. 193 pp. 88-311-3775-
      1. Bibl. 189-190.

7060 **Kapkin, David** 1 Corintios: una iglesia inquieta. Medellín 2002, Escuela Bíblica 427 pp. €27.50.
7061 **Lindemann, Andreas** Der erste Korintherbrief. HNT 9/1: 2000 ⇒ 16,6683; 17,6616. ᴿBZ 46 (2002) 143-148 (*Dautzenberg, Gerhard*); ThRv 98 (2002) 312-313 (*Eckert, Jost*); SNTU.A 27 (2002) 247-248 (*Repschinski, Boris*).
7062 **Lockwood, Gregory L.** 1 Corinthians. Concordia commentary: 2000 ⇒16,6684. ᴿRBLit 4 (2002) 423-426 (*Wanamaker, Charles A.*).
7063 **Sampley, J. Paul** The first letter to the Corinthians: introduction, commentary, and reflections. NIntB 10. 2002 ⇒4655. 771-1003.
7064 **Somerville, Robert** La première épître de Paul aux Corinthiens, 1. Vaux-sur-Seine 2002, Edifac 254 pp. €22. 2-904407-30-8.
7065 **Thiselton, Anthony C.** The first epistle to the Corinthians: a commentary on the Greek text. NIGTC: 2000 ⇒16,6689; 17,6621. ᴿEvangel 20/1 (2002) 26 (*Wilson, Alistair I.*); ThLZ 127 (2002) 399-401 (*Bull, Klaus-Michael*); Bib. 83 (2002) 288-292 (*Schrage, Wolfgang*); Themelios 27/3 (2002) 23-27 (*Fox, K.A.*); BZ 46 (2002) 143-148 (*Dautzenberg, Gerhard*); JBL 121 (2002) 183-186 (*Horrell, David G.*); TS 63 (2002) 164-165 (*Byron, John*); JThS 53 (2002) 231-235 (*Jones, Ivor H.*); NT 44 (2002) 186-189 (*Elliott, J.K.*); RRT 9 (2002) 216-218 (*Seddon, Philip*); JR 82 (2002) 431-433 (*Furnish, Victor Paul*); RivBib 50 (2002) 486-488 (*Barbaglio, Giuseppe*); HBT 24 (2002) 141-143 (*Williams, H.H. Drake*).

G5.2 1 & 1-2 ad Corinthios—themata, topics

7066 *Aejmelaeus, Lars* The question of salary in the conflict between Paul and the "super apostles" in Corinth. ᶠRÄISÄNEN, H.: NT.S 103: 2002 ⇒97. 343-376.
7067 *Becker, Eve-Marie* MARCION und die Korintherbriefe nach TERTULLIAN, Adversus Marcionem V. Marcion. 2002 ⇒578. 95-109.
7068 *Blomberg, Craig L.* Applying 1 Corinthians in the early twenty-first century. SWJT 45/1 (2002) 19-38.
7069 *Botha, P.H.; Van Rensburg, F.J.* Seksuele reinheid voor die huwelik in Korinte in die eerste eeu nC. VeE 23 (2002) 52-66.
7070 *Brooke, George J.* Between Qumran and Corinth: embroidered allusions to women's authority. Dead Sea scrolls as background. StTDJ 46: 2002 ⇒732. 157-176.
7071 *De Virgilio, Giuseppe* L'Etica della libertà e dell'amore (1Cor 5-10). PaVi 47/2 (2002) 37-44.
7072 *Díaz Rodelas, Juan Miguel* Corinto. ResB 35 (2002) 27-36.
7073 *Eriksson, Anders* Enthymemes in Pauline argumentation: reading between the lines in 1 Corinthians. Rhetorical argumentation. 2002 ⇒553. 243-259.
7074 *Fabris, Rinaldo* Paolo rilegge l'Antico Testamento. PaVi 47/4 (2002) 30-34.
7075 *Hyldahl, Niels* Corinthian Gnosis?. The Nag Hammadi texts. DVSS. HF 26: 2002 ⇒740. 183-188.
7076 **Johnson, Lee Ann** The epistolary apostle: Paul's response to the challenge of the Corinthian congregation. ᴰVaag, L. 2002, 269 pp. Diss. Toronto, St Michael [RTL 34,598].

7077 *Joubert, S.J.* Shifting styles of church leadership: Paul's pragmatic leadership style in 1 and 2 Corinthians during the organization of the collection for Jerusalem. VeE 23 (2002) 678-688.

7078 *Kovacs, Judith L.* Servant of Christ and steward of the mysteries of God: the purpose of a Pauline letter according to ORIGEN's *Homilies on 1 Corinthians.* [F]WILKEN, R. 2002 ⇒136. 147-171.

7079 *Montagnini, Felice* 'Uomo carnale' e 'uomo spirituale'. PaVi 47/1 (2002) 38-42.

7080 *Noethlichs, Karl Leo* Korinth—ein "Aussenposten Roms"?: zur kirchengeschichtlichen Bedeutung des Bischofs DIONYSIUS von Korinth. [F]HOHEISEL, K.: JAC.E 34: 2002 ⇒59. 232-247.

7081 *Perkins, Pheme* God's power in human weakness: Paul teaches the Corinthians about God. [F]ACHTEMEIER, P. 2002 ⇒1. 145-162.

7082 **Reichert, Andreas** Das Verständnis der Taufe im 1. Korintherbrief. [D]*Schrage, Wolfgang:* 2002 Diss. Bonn [ThRv 99/2,v].

7083 *Richardson, Peter* Judaism and christianity in Corinth after Paul: texts and material evidence. [F]ROETZEL, C.: JSNT.S 221: 2002 ⇒104. 42-66.

7084 *Schrage, Wolfgang* Die Bedeutung der "Schriften" im 1. Korintherbrief. [F]SMEND, R. 2002 ⇒113. 412-432.
            Swearingen, C. J. The tongues of men: understanding Greek rhetorical sources for Paul's letters to...1 Corinthians 2002 ⇒6952.

7085 *Tarocchi, Stefano* Paolo e la comunità di Corinto. PaVi 47/3 (2002) 4-8.

7086 *Thrall, Margaret E.* The initial attraction of Paul's mission in Corinth and of the church he founded there. [F]WEDDERBURN, A.: JSNT.S 217: 2002 ⇒132. 59-73.

7087 *Vollenweider, Samuel* Viele Welten und ein Geist: Überlegungen zum theologischen Umgang mit dem neuzeitlichen Pluralismus im Blick auf den 1. Korintherbrief. Horizonte. WUNT 144: 2002 <1995> ⇒257. 193-213.

7088 *Vos, Johan S.* Die erste und die zweite Schöpfung im ersten Korintherbrief des Paulus und in PSEUDO-JUSTINs 'De Resurrectione'. [F]LEENE, H. 2002 ⇒73. 247-252.

7089 **Voss, Florian** Das Wort vom Kreuz und die menschliche Vernunft: eine Untersuchung zur Soteriologie des 1. Korintherbriefes. [D]*Weder, Hans:* FRLANT 199: Gö 2002, Vandenhoeck & R. 320 pp. €64. 3-525-53883-9. Diss. Zürich. Bibl. 297-314.

7090 *Welborn, L.L.* 'Take up the epistle of the blessed Paul the Apostle': the contrasting fates of Paul's letters to Corinth in the patristic period. [F]PATTE, D.: 2002 ⇒89. 345-357.

7091 **Winter, Bruce W.** After Paul left Corinth: the influence of secular ethics and social change. 2001 ⇒17,6635. [R]Pacifica 15 (2002) 94-96 (*Guy, Laurie*); SNTU.A 27 (2002) 250-251 (*Repschinski, Boris*); RBLit (2002)* (*Engels, Donald*); BiblInterp 10 (2002) 208-210 (*Taylor, N.H.*); JR 82 (2002) 437-438 (*Deming, Will*); Evangel 20 (2002) 90-91 (*Marshall, Howard*); LouvSt 27 (2002) 178-180 (*Koperski, Veronica*); ThLZ 127 (2002) 767-770 (*Schrage, Wolfgang*); CBQ 64 (2002) 594-595 (*Braun, Willi*); AUSS 40 (2002) 346-348 (*Brown, Ian R.*); TJT 18 (2002) 271-273 (*Donaldson, Terence L.*).

7092 *Wong, Eric K.C.* The deradicalization of Jesus' ethical sayings in 1 Corinthians. NTS 48 (2002) 181-194.

G5.3 **1 Cor 1-7**: *sapientia crucis... abusus matrimonii*

7093 *Haldimann, Konrad* Kreuz—Wort vom Kreuz—Kreuzestheologie: zu einer Begriffsdifferenzierung in der Paulusinterpretation. Kreuzestheologie. WUNT 151: 2002 ⇒298. 1-25.

7094 **Pate, C. Marvin** The reverse of the curse: Paul, wisdom, and the law. WUNT 2/114: 2000 ⇒16,6713; 17,6643. ^RCBQ 64 (2002) 588-590 (*McDonald, Patricia M.*); ThLZ 127 (2002) 180-181 (*Horn, Friedrich Wilhelm*); RBLit 4 (2002) 409-412 (*Finlan, Stephen*).

7095 **Ruggiero, Fabio** La follia dei cristiani: la reazione pagana al cristianesimo nei secoli I-V. I volti della storia: R 2002, Città N 260 pp. Pref. *Manlio Simonetti*.

7096 **Yang, David Sunghyon** The impact of the Damascus Road encounter on Paul's theology of the cross. ^D*Schatzmann, S.*: 2002, 282 pp. Diss. Fort Worth [RTL 34,602.

7097 *Klostergaard Petersen, A.* Wisdom as cognition: creating the others in the Book of mysteries and 1 Cor 1-2. Wisdom texts. BEThL 159: 2002 ⇒482. 405-432.

7098 *Vollenweider, Samuel* Weisheit am Kreuzweg: zum theologischen Programm von 1 Kor 1 und 2. Kreuzestheologie. WUNT 151: 2002 ⇒298. 43-58.

7099 **Stott, John** Calling christian leaders: biblical models of church, gospel and ministry. Nottingham 2002, Inter-Varsity Pr. 150 pp. £8. 085-111-257-9. Bibl. 139-140 [1 Cor 1-4].

7100 *Welborn, Laurence L.* μωρὸς γενέσθω: Paul's appropriation of the role of the fool in 1 Corinthians 1-4. BiblInterp 10 (2002) 420-435.

7101 *Stamps, Dennis L.* The christological premise in Pauline theological rhetoric: 1 Corinthians 1.4-2.5 as an example. Rhetorical criticism. JSNT.S 195: 2002 ⇒369. 441-457.

7102 **Kammler, Hans-Christian** Kreuz und Weisheit: eine exegetische Untersuchung zu 1 Kor 1,10-3,4. ^D*Hofius, O.*: 2002 Diss.-Habil. Tübingen [ThRv 99/2,xiii].

7103 *Vos, Johan S.* Weltliche und geistliche Rhetorik (1Kor 1,10-3,4). Die Kunst der Argumentation. 2002 <1995> ⇒6712. 29-64.

7104 *Smit, Joop F.M.* "What is Apollos? What is Paul?": in search for the coherence of First Corinthians 1:10-4:21. NT 44 (2002) 231-251.

7105 *Romanello, Stefano* Una chiesa divisa (1Cor 1,10-17). PaVi 47/1 (2002) 21-27.

7106 *Trevijano Etcheverría, Ramón* El contraste de sabidurías (1 Cor 1, 17-4,20). Estudios paulinos. 2002 <1987> ⇒248. 147-170.

7107 *Barbaglio, Giuseppe* La sapiente stoltezza della croce (1Cor 1,17-25 e 2,6-16). PaVi 47/1 (2002) 28-32.

7108 *Koperski, Veronica* "Mystery of God" or "testimony of God" in 1 Cor 2,1: textual and exegetical considerations. ^FDELOBEL, J.: BEThL 161: 2002 ⇒24. 305-315.

7109 *Burnett, Fred W.* The place of 'the wisdom of God' in Paul's proclamation of salvation (1 Cor 2:6-16). ^FPATTE, D. 2002 ⇒89. 324-340.

7110 *Grindheim, Sigurd* Wisdom for the perfect: Paul's challenge to the Corinthian church (1 Corinthians 2:6-16). JBL 121 (2002) 689-709.

7111 *Stuhlmacher, Peter* Zur hermeneutischen Bedeutung von 1Kor 2,6-16. Biblische Theologie. WUNT 146: 2002 <1987> ⇒245. 143-166.

7112 *Lorusso, Giacomo* I ministri del Cristo crocifisso (1Cor 3-4). PaVi 47/1 (2002) 33-37.
7113 *Ostmeyer, Karl-Heinrich* Satan und Passa in 1. Korinther 5. ZNT 9 (2002) 38-45.
7114 *Trevijano Etcheverría, Ramón* A propósito del incestuoso (1 Cor 5-7). Estudios paulinos. 2002 <1991> ⇒248. 355-384.
7115 *Cramarossa, Lydia* Togliete il malvagio di mezzo a voi (1Cor 5,1-13). PaVi 47/2 (2002) 10-16.
7116 *Ciccarelli, Michele* Il corpo del cristiano, tempio dello Spirito (1Cor 6,12-20). PaVi 47/2 (2002) 17-23.
7117 *Ellis, J.E.* Controlled burn: the romantic note in I Corinthians 7. PRSt 29/1 (2002) 89-98.
7118 *Valentini, Alberto* Continenza e matrimonio (1Cor 7,1-40). PaVi 47/2 (2002) 24-29.
7119 *Gillihan, Yonder Moynihan* Jewish laws on illicit marriage, the defilement of offspring,and the holiness of the temple: a new halakic interpretation of 1 Corinthians 7:14. JBL 121 (2002) 711-744.
7120 **Braxton, Brad Ronnell** The tyranny of resolution: 1 Corinthians 7: 17-24. SBL.DS 181: 2000 ⇒16,6727. [R]BiblInterp 10 (2002) 210-212 (*Horrell, David G.*); JBL 121 (2002) 373-376 (*Byron, John*); JR 82 (2002) 273-274 (*Frilingos, Chris*).
7121 *Adinolfi, Marco* Gli ὡς μή di 1 Cor 7,29-31 secondo PORFIRIO. VII Simposio di Tarso. 2002 ⇒587. 253-257.
7122 *Guenther, Allen R.* One woman or two?: 1 Corinthians 7:34a. BBR 12 (2002) 33-45.

G5.4 *Idolothyta... Eucharistia*: **1 Cor 8-11**

7123 *Berger, Teresa* Das Brot des Lebens im Land des Fast Food. BiKi 57 (2002) 36-39.
7124 **McGowan, Andrew Brian** Ascetic eucharists: food and drink in early christian ritual meals. 1999 ⇒ 15,6775...17,6663. [R]Worship 76 (2002) 561-562 (*Johnson, Luke Timothy*).
7125 **Smith, Dennis E.** From symposium to eucharist: the banquet in the early christian world. Mp 2002, Fortress xi; 411 pp. 0-8006-3489-6. Bibl. 361-387.

7126 *Mosetto, Francesco* Il pericolo della idolatria (1Cor 8,1-11,1). PaVi 47/2 (2002) 30-36.
7127 *Still, E. Coye* Paul's aims regarding εἰδωλόθυτα: a new proposal for interpreting 1 Corinthians 8:1-11:1. NT 44 (2002) 333-343.
7128 *Barbaglio, Giuseppe* 'C'è una quantità di dèi e signori, ma per noi...' (1Cor 8,5-6). PSV 46 (2002) 113-120.
7129 *Hofius, Otfried* "Einer ist Gott—einer ist Herr": Erwägungen zu Struktur und Aussage des Bekenntnisses 1Kor 8,6 <1997>;
7130 Christus als Schöpfungsmittler und Erlösungsmittler: das Bekenntnis 1Kor 8,6 im Kontext der paulinischen Theologie <2000>. Paulusstudien II. WUNT 143: 2002 ⇒180. 167-180/181-192.
7131 *Instone-Brewer, David* Paul's literal interpretation of 'Do not muzzle the ox'. The trustworthiness of God. 2002 ⇒410. 139-153 [1 Cor 9, 9-11].

7132 *Theißen, Gerd* Leben auf Konkurrenz und die Rechtfertigung des Wettkämpfers (1 Kor 9,24-27). Erlösungsbilder. 2002 ⇒1460. 142-147.

7133 **Oropeza, B.J.** Paul and apostasy: eschatology, perseverance, and falling away in the Corinthian congregation. WUNT 2/115: 2000 ⇒ 16,6750. [R]BBR 12 (2002) 306-309 (*Webb, William J.*) [1 Cor 10].

7134 **Ostmeyer, Karl-Heinrich** Taufe und Typos: Elemente und Theologie der Tauftypologien in 1. Korinther 10 und 1. Petrus 3. WUNT 2/118: 2000 ⇒16,6751; 17,6671. [R]CBQ 64 (2002) 388-389 (*Thompson, Leonard L.*).

7135 *May, George* The Lord's Supper: ritual or relationship?: making a meal of it in Corinth, part 2: meals at Corinth. RTR 61/1 (2002) 1-18 [1 Cor 10-11].

7136 *Klauck, Hans-Josef* "Leib Christi"—das Mahl des Herrn in 1 Kor 10-12. BiKi 57 (2002) 15-21.

7137 **Inostroza Lanas, Juan Carlos** Moisés e Israel en el desierto: el midrás paulino de 1Cor 10,1-13. 2000 ⇒16,6752; 17,6673. [R]CTom 129 (2002) 197-199 (*Huarte, Juan*); CBQ 64 (2002) 378-380 (*Lampe, Stephen J.*).

7138 *Meeks, Wayne A.* "And rose up to play": midrash and parenesis in 1 Corinthians 10:1-22. In search. 2002 ⇒208. 139-152.

7139 *Buitendag, J.* 'Saam een liggaam' (1 Kor 10:17)—deelname van kinders aan die nagmaal. HTS 57 (2001) 531-562 [NTAb 46,485] [1 Cor 11,28-29].

7140 *Maeland, Bård* Unntaksteologi og normalteologi: relevansen av 1 Kor 10,20f for religionsteologien. TTK 73/1 (2002) 19-39.

7141 **Taiwo, Moses Oladele** Paul's apparent reversal of concern for the weak brother in 1 Corinthians 10:29b-30: an examination of the text in light of Greco-Roman rhetoric. [D]*Richards, W. Larry*: Diss. Andrews 2002 [AUSS 41,293s].

7142 *Franco, Ettore* Uguali sì, ma diversi: uomini e donne nell'assemblea liturgica (1Cor 11,2-16). PaVi 47/3 (2002) 9-14.

7143 *Gielen, Marlis* "Gehört es sich, dass eine Frau unverhüllt zu Gott betet?": der Streit um Kopfbedeckung oder Frisur in 1 Kor 11,2-16. BiKi 57 (2002) 134-138.

7144 **Biguzzi, Giancarlo** Velo e silenzio: Paolo e la donna in 1Cor 11,2-16 e 14,33b-36. SRivBib 37: 2001 ⇒17,6678. [R]Annales Theologici 16 (2002) 210-212 (*Estrada, B.*); LASBF 51 (2001) 434-437 (*Chrupcała, L.D.*).

7145 *Ligo, Arche L.* Paul, woman and midrash. The roles. 2002 ⇒540. 107-117 [1 Cor 11,3-16].

7146 *Cramarossa, Lydia* La cena del Signore (1Cor 11,17-33). PaVi 47/3 (2002) 15-22.

7147 *Kremer, Jacob* Eucharistie und Abendmahl: Überprüfung einer Neuinterpretation an 1 Kor 11,17-34. StZ 220 (2002) 767-780.

7148 *Schottroff, Luise* Damals in Korinth: "wer auf unsolidarische Weise das Brot isst ..." (1 Kor 11,17-34). WuA(M) 43/2 (2002) 91-93.

7149 *Watts Henderson, Suzanne* 'If anyone hungers ...': an integrated reading of 1 Cor 11.17-34. NTS 48 (2002) 195-208.

7150 *Kuhn, Heinz-Wolfgang* The Qumran meal and the Lord's supper in Paul in the context of the Graeco-Roman world. [F]WEDDERBURN, A.: JSNT.S 217: 2002 ⇒132. 221-248 [1 Cor 11,23-25].

7151 *Hofius, Otfried* τὸ σῶμα τὸ ὑπὲρ ὑμῶν 1Kor 11,24. Paulusstudien II. WUNT 143: 2002 <1989> ⇒180. 193-201.

7152 *O'Neill, John C.* "This is my body..." (1 Corinthians 11.24). IBSt 24 (2002) 32-43.

G5.5 1 Cor 12s... Glossolalia, charismata

7153 **Baumert, Norbert** Charisma—Taufe—Geisttaufe, 1: Entflechtung einer semantischen Verwirrung; 2: Normativität und persönliche Berufung. 2001 ⇒17,6685. ᴿThLZ 127 (2002) 751-754 (*Klaiber, Walter*); LASBF 52 (2002) 579-585 (*Casalini, Nello*).
7154 *Doldán, Felipe L.* Consideraciones bíblicas sobre los carismas. RevBib 64 (2002) 61-67.
7155 ᴱ**Donnelly, Doris** Retrieving charisms for the twenty-first century. 1999 ⇒15,6782. ᴿPacifica 15 (2002) 242-243 (*Edwards, Denis*).
7156 **Hovenden, Gerald** Speaking in tongues: the New Testament evidence in context. JPentec.S 22: L 2002, Sheffield Academic x; 181 pp. 1-84127-316-3. Bibl. 169-173.
7157 **Levison, J.** Of two minds: ecstasy and inspired interpretation in the New Testament world. 1999 ⇒15,6787; 17,6689. ᴿStPhiloA 14 (2002) 216-217 (*Fox, Kenneth A.*).
7158 **Nasrallah, Laura S.** Rhetorical strategies in early christian debates over prophecy. Diss. Harvard 2002 [HThR 95,345].
7159 **Ndubuisi, Luke** Paul's concept of χάρισμα in 1 Corinthians: with emphasis on Nigerian charismatic movement. ᴰ*Klauck, Hans-Josef*: 2002, 294 pp. Diss. München [ThRv 99/2,x].
7160 *Romerowski, Sylvain* Les '*charismata*' du Nouveau Testament: aptitudes ou ministères?. ThEv(VS) 1/1 (2002) 15-38.
7161 *Schatzmann, Siegfried S.* Purpose and function of gifts in 1 Corinthians. SWJT 45/1 (2002) 53-68.

7162 *Kosch, Daniel* Nur nicht abheben!: das Zusammenspiel von Geist und Leib bei Paulus (1 Kor 12). BiHe 38 (2002) 72-75;
7163 Geistes Gaben: 1 Kor 12: Juni—Pfingsten. zwölfmal bibel. 2002 ⇒ 1087. 60-69.
7164 *Murre-van den Berg, Hendrike L.* Bible study I Corinthians 12: mission relationships and partnership: new models of partnership?. IRM 91 (2002) 583-588.
7165 *Lorusso, Giacomo* Carismi e ministeri (1Cor 12-14). PaVi 47/3 (2002) 23-28.
7166 **Njiru, Paul Kariuki** Charisms and the Holy Spirit's activity in the body of Christ: an exegetical-theological study of 1 Corinthians 12,4-11 and Romans 12,6-8. TGr.T 86: R 2002, E.P.U.G. 368 pp. €22. 88-7652-926-8. Bibl. 347-359. ᴿITS 39 (2002) 379-381 (*Francis, B. Joseph*).
7167 *Cross, Anthony R.* Spirit- and water-baptism in 1 Corinthians 12.13. Dimensions of baptism. JSNT.S 234: 2002 ⇒434. 120-148.
7168 *Nason, Luigi* La via per eccellenza, l'amore (1Cor 12,31b-14,1). PaVi 47/3 (2002) 29-34.
7169 *Badewien, Jan* Liebe macht nicht blind: eine Paulus-Auslegung zum Kampf der Kulturen. Evangelische Aspekte 12/2 (2002) 37-38 [1 Cor 13].
7170 *Combet-Galland, Corina* L'intrigue amoureuse d'une ode à l'amour (1 Corinthiens 13). Quand la bible se raconte. 2002 ⇒355. 189-208.

7171 *Hietanen, Mika* Profetian är primärt inte för de otrogna—en argumentationsanalys av 1 Kor 14:22b. SEÅ 67 (2002) 89-104 [1 Cor 14, 22].

7172 *Pokorný, Petr* Christliche Verkündigung als Modell des hermeneutischen Prozesses nach 1Kor 14,23-25. Philosophical hermeneutics. WUNT 153: 2002 ⇒367. 245-251.

7173 *Gourgues, Michel* Quién es misógino: Pablo o algunos Corintios?. AnáMnesis 12/1 (2002) 17-24 [1 Cor 14,33-36].

7174 *Paige, Terence* The social matrix of women's speech at Corinth: the context and meaning of the command to silence in 1 Corinthians 14: 33b-36. BBR 12 (2002) 217-242.

7175 *Toit, A. du* Die swyggebod van 1 Korintiërs 14:34-35 weer eens onder die loep. HTS 57 (2001) 172-186 [NTAb 46,486].

G5.6 **Resurrectio**; *1 Cor 15*...[⇒F5.6]

Crüsemann, F. Schrift und Auferstehung 2002 ⇒5931.

7176 *Fabris, Rinaldo* "Noi annunziamo che Cristo Gesù è Signore". RSEc 20 (2002) 239-249..

7177 *Gaffin, Richard B.* Redemption and resurrection: an exercise in biblical-systematic theology. Themelios 27/2 (2002) 16-31.

7178 **Gerhardsson, Birger** Kristi uppståndelse. Lund 2001, Novapress 158 pp. SEK175. 9171-37009-9.

7179 *Hauger, Martin* Die Deutung der Auferweckung Jesu Christi durch Paulus. Die Wirklichkeit. 2002 ⇒302. 31-58.

7180 *Lang, Bernhard* Der politische und der mystische Himmel in der jüdisch-christlichen Tradition. Tod, Jenseits. 2002 ⇒390. 680-700.

7181 **Park, Joseph S.** Conceptions of afterlife in Jewish inscriptions: with special reference to Pauline literature. WUNT 2/121: 2000 ⇒16, 6787. [R]Sal. 64 (2002) 152-153 (*Vicent, R.*); JThS 53 (2002) 261-263 (*Noy, David*); Anton. 77 (2002) 360-362 (*Volgger, David*).

7182 **Schrage, Wolfgang** Der erste Brief an die Korinther, 4. Teilband 1Kor 15,1-16,24. EKK 7/4: 2001 ⇒17,6619. [R]Bib. 83 (2002) 422-426 (*Aletti, Jean-Noël*).

7183 *Thrall, Margaret E.* Paul's understanding of continuity between the present life and the life of the resurrection. [F]LAMBRECHT, J.: BEThL 165: 2002 ⇒72. 283-300.

7184 *Trevijano Etcheverría, Ramón* Los que dicen que no hay resurrección (1 Cor 15,12). Estudios paulinos. 2002 <1986> ⇒248. 385-415.

7185 *Vos, Johan S.* Die Schattenseite der Auferstehung im Evangelium des Paulus. [F]LAMBRECHT, J.: BEThL 165: 2002 ⇒72. 301-313.

7186 **Asher, Jeffrey R.** Polarity and change in 1 Corinthians 15: a study of metaphysics, rhetoric, and resurrection. HUTh 42: 2000 ⇒16,6790. [R]RB 109 (2002) 297-298 (*Murphy-O'Connor, Jerome*); JR 82 (2002) 433-434 (*Tuckett, Christopher*); CBQ 64 (2002) 366-367 (*Gillman, John*); ThLZ 127 (2002) 1296-1298 (*Back, Frances*).

7187 *Delobel, Joël* The Corinthians' (un-)belief in the resurrection. [F]LAMBRECHT, J.: BEThL 165: 2002 ⇒72. 343-355 [1 Cor 15].

7188 *Dunn, James D.* How are the dead raised?: with what body do they come?: reflections on 1 Corinthians 15. SWJT 45/1 (2002) 4-18.

7189 **García Pérez, José Miguel** La catequesis más consoladora de San
Pablo: las luminosas oscuridades de 1Cor 15. Studia Semitica NT 10:
M 2002, Encuentro 189 pp. 84-7490-660-1. Bibl. 19-30. [R]VyV 60
(2002) 624-626 (*Álvarez Barredo, Miguel*).

7190 **Schneider, Sebastian** Auferstehen: eine neue Deutung von 1 Kor 15.
[D]*Müller*: 2002 Diss.-Habil. Vallendar.

7191 *Tomson, Peter J.* "Death, where is thy victory?": Paul's theology in
the twinkling of an eye. [F]LAMBRECHT, J.: BEThL 165: 2002 ⇒72.
357-386 [1 Cor 15].

7192 *Romanello, Stefano* Cristo è risorto (1Cor 15,1-34). PaVi 47/4
(2002) 10-16.

7193 *Vos, Johan S.* Logik und Rhetorik in 1Kor 15,12-20. Die Kunst der
Argumentation. 2002 <1999> ⇒6712. 158-171.

7194 *English, Adam C.* Mediated, mediation, unmediated: 1 Corinthians
15:29: the history of interpretation, and the current state of biblical
studies. RExp 99 (2002) 419-428.

7195 *Taylor, N.H.* Baptism for the dead (1 Cor 15:29)?. Neotest. 36 (2002)
111-120.

7196 *Charpilloz, Hugues* 1 Corinthiens 15,35-49: promesse d'une réalité
tout autre. Lire et Dire 51 (2002) 39-51 [BuBB 39,72].

7197 *Casale, Cesare Marcheselli* Risorgeremo, ma come?: dal noto all'
ignoto (1Cor 15,35-53). PaVi 47/4 (2002) 17-24.

7198 *Padgett, Alan G.* The body in resurrection: science and scripture on
the "spiritual body" (1 Cor 15:35-58). WaW 22 (2002) 155-163.

7199 *Asher, Jeffrey R.* σπείρεται: Paul's anthropogenic metaphor in 1
Corinthians 15:42-44. JBL 120 (2001) 101-122.

7200 *Abernathy, David* Christ as life-giving spirit in 1 Corinthians 15:45.
IBSt 24 (2002) 2-13.

7201 **Schneider, Sebastian** Vollendung des Auferstehens: eine exegetische Untersuchung von 1 Kor 15,51-52 und 1 Thess 4,13-18. FzB
97: 2000 ⇒16,6798; 17,6720. [R]ThRv 98 (2002) 313-316 (*Oberlinner, Lorenz*); ThPh 77 (2002) 246-248 (*Frankemölle, H.*).

7202 *García Pérez, J.M.* 1Co 15,56: ¿una polémica contra la ley judía?.
EstB 60 (2002) 405-414.

7203 *Fallica di Vertemate, Luca* L'evangelo si fa saluto (1Cor 16,5-24).
PaVi 47/4 (2002) 25-29.

G5.9 Secunda epistula ad Corinthios

7204 *Álvarez Cineira, David* Los adversarios paulinos en 2 Corintios.
EstAg 37 (2002) 249-274.

7205 **Becker, Eve-Marie** Schreiben und Verstehen: paulinische Brief-
hermeneutik im zweiten Korintherbrief. [D]*Wischmeyer, Oda*: Diss. Erlangen 2001 [ThRv 99/2,vi].

7206 **Corsani, Bruno** La seconda lettera ai Corinzi: guida alla lettura.
2000 ⇒16,6801; 17,6725. [R]TeFi 16/1 (2002) 173-174 (*Spera, Salvatore*).

7207 *Doglio, Claudio* L'apostolo, gli avversari e le lettere;

7208 *Giavini, Giovanni* Gesù Cristo immagine di Dio in 2Cor. PaVi 47/5
(2002) 4-9/36-40.

7209 **Gräßer, Erich** Der zweite Brief an die Korinther, 1: Kapitel 1,1-7,
16. Ökumenischer Taschenbuchkommentar zum NT 8/1; GTBS 513:
Gü 2002, Gü'er 280 pp. €26. 3-579-00513-8. Bibl. 13-22.

7210   *Hester, J. David* Re-reading 2 Corinthians: a rhetorical approach.
       Rhetorical argumentation. 2002 ⇒553. 276-295.
7211   *Humphrey, Edith M.* Ambivalent apocalypse: apocalyptic rhetoric
       and intertextuality in 2 Corinthians. Intertexture. SBL.Symposium
       14: 2002 ⇒385. 113-135.
7212   **Lambrecht, Jan** Second Corinthians. Sacra pagina 8: 1999 ⇒15,
       6826…17,6729. [R]VJTR 66 (2002) 787-789 (*Meagher, P.M.*).
7213   *Manzi, Franco* Il vanto della coscienza apostolica di Paolo: la struttu-
       ra letteraria e il messaggio della seconda lettera ai Corinzi. ScC 130/4
       (2002) 671-749.
7214   **Manzi, Franco** Seconda lettera ai Corinzi: nuova versione, introdu-
       zione e commento. I libri biblici, NT 9: Mi 2002, Paoline 462 pp.
       €27.50. 883152383X [Riv. di Scienze religiose 17,413: Lorusso, G.].
7215   **Naylor, Peter** 2 Corinthians: volume 1—chapters 1-7; volume 2—
       chapters 8-13. Darlington 2002, Evangelical 368 + 304 pp. £17 + 14.
       0-85234-502-X/16-X.
7216   **Thrall, Margaret E.** A critical and exegetical commentary on the
       second epistle to the Corinthians, 1-2. ICC: 1994-2000. ⇒10,5953…
       17,6734. [R]BiTr 53 (2002) 155-156 (*Ellingworth, Paul*); ThLZ 127
       (2002) 401-403 (*Bull, Klaus-Michael*); JThS 53 (2002) 235-238 [vol.
       2 only] (*Hickling, C.J.A.*).
7217   **Wan, Sze-kar** Power in weakness: conflict and rhetoric in Paul's
       second letter to the Corinthians. 2000 ⇒16,6812; 17,6735. [R]CBQ 64
       (2002) 181-183 (*Gillman, Florence Morgan*).

7218   **Lorusso, Giacomo** Il ministero pasquale di Paolo in 2Cor 1-7: le
       implicazioni del soffrire e gioire per il vangelo. Intellectus fidei 11: R
       2001, Vivere In 312 pp. €11.88. 88-7263-182-3. Bibl. 273-287.
       [R]Asprenas 49 (2002) 452 (*Castello, Gaetano*); EstB 60 (2002) 550-
       552 (*Moreno García, Abdón*); CivCatt 153/4 (2002) 92-93 (*Scaiola,
       D.*); CredOg 123 (2001) 139 (*Lorenzin, Tiziano*).
7219   **Kleine, Werner** Zwischen Furcht und Hoffnung: eine textlinguisti-
       sche Untersuchung des Briefes 2 Kor 1-9 zur wechselseitigen Be-
       deutsamkeit der Beziehung von Apostel und Gemeinde. [D]*Hoppe, Ru-
       dolf:* BBB 141: B 2002, Philo 474 pp. 3-8257-0323-1. Diss. Bonn.
       Bibl. 452-473.
7220   *Manzi, Franco* Il padre della consolazione (2Cor 1,1-11). PaVi 47/5
       (2002) 10-16.
7221   *Trevijano Etcheverría, Ramón* Estudio sobre la eulogía paulina (2
       Cor 1,3, y Ef 1,3). Estudios paulinos. 2002 <1969> ⇒248. 325-353.
7222   *Theißen, Gerd* Trost ohne Vertröstung: vom einzigen Trost im Leben
       und im Sterben (2 Kor 1,3-7). Erlösungsbilder. 2002 ⇒1460. 148-51.
7223   *Carrón, Julián* Los adversarios de 2 Corintios: el difícil griego de
       1,11 y 2,17. RET 62 (2002) 419-436.
7224   *Scalabrini, Patrizio Rota* Le sofferenze di un apostolo (2Cor 1,12 - 2,
       17). PaVi 47/5 (2002) 17-23.
7225   *Frankemölle, Hubert* Die paulinische Theologie im Kontext der heili-
       gen Schriften Israels: 'So viele Verheißungen Gottes, in ihm das Ja' (2
       Kor 1.20). NTS 48 (2002) 332-357.
7226   *Valentini, Alberto* Tutte le promesse di Dio in lui sono divenute *sì*
       (2Cor 1,20a). La speranza. 2002 ⇒277. 107-128.
7227   *Làconi, Mauro* Ministero apostolico: dramma e splendore (2Cor 2-
       3). PaVi 47/5 (2002) 24-29.

7228 **Kuschnerus, Bernd** Die Gemeinde als Brief Christi: die kommunikative Funktion der Metapher bei Paulus am Beispiel von 2 Kor 2-5. FRLANT 197: Gö 2002, Vandenhoeck & R. 398 pp. €79. 3-525538-81-2. Bibl. 368-398.

7229 **Back, Frances** Verwandlung durch Offenbarung bei Paulus: eine religionsgeschichtlich-exegetische Untersuchung zu 2 Kor 2,14-4,6. ^D*Lichtenberger, H.*: WUNT 2/153: Tü 2002, Mohr S. xi; 250 pp. €49. 3-16-147880-0. Diss. Tübingen; Bibl. 205-226.

7230 *Trevijano Etcheverría, Ramón* La idoneidad del apóstol (2 Cor 2,14-4,6). Estudios paulinos. 2002 <1990> ⇒248. 171-201.

7231 *Burgos Núñez, Miguel de* La comunidad cristiana, carta del Espíritu, escrita por el apóstol: lectura de 2Cor 2,14-7,4. Isidorianum 21 (2002) 119-151.

7232 *Dumbrell, William J.* The newness of the new covenant: the logic of the argument in 2 Corinthians 3. RTR 61/2 (2002) 61-84.

7233 *Manns, Frederic* De la réalité au symbole: 2 Cor 3,7-18 à la lumière de la tradition juive. VII Simposio di Tarso. 2002 ⇒587. 29-46.

7234 *Nayak, Ignatius* The meaning of "*katoptrizomenoi*" in 2 Cor 3,18. ED 55 (2002) 33-44.

7235 *Matera, Frank J.* Apostolic suffering and resurrection faith: distinguishing between appearance and reality (2 Cor 4,7-5,10). ^FLAMBRECHT, J.: BEThL 165: 2002 ⇒72. 387-405.

7236 *Kaithakottil, Joyce* 'Death in us, life in you': ministry and suffering: a study of 2 Cor 4,7-15. BiBh 28/2 (2002) 433-460.

7237 *Kleemann, Jürg* Responsabilità e fragilità della parola: "ho creduto perciò ho parlato" (2 Cor 4,13). RSEc 20 (2002) 309-321.

7238 *Eckert, Jost* Wenn auch unser äußerer Mensch vernichtet wird, unser innerer aber wird erneuert Tag um Tag (2 Kor 4,16). ^FHAAG, E.: 2002 ⇒55. 61-85.

7239 *Cipriani, Settimio* Il ministero della riconciliazione (2Cor 5,1-6,2). PaVi 47/5 (2002) 30-35.

7240 *Aune, David E.* The judgement seat of Christ (2 Cor. 5.10). ^FROETZEL, C.: JSNT.S 221: 2002 ⇒104. 68-86.

7241 *Kim, Seyoon* 2 Corinthians 5:11-21 and the origin of Paul's concept of reconciliation. Paul and the new perspective. WUNT 140: 2002 ⇒ 190. 214-238.

7242 *Boers, Hendrikus* 2 Corinthians 5:14-6:2: a fragment of Pauline christology. CBQ 64 (2002) 527-547.

7243 *Catchpole, David* Q's thesis and Paul's antithesis: a study of 2 Corinthians 5,16. ^FFUCHS, A.: 2002 ⇒41. 347-366.

7244 *Koperski, Veronica* Paul's ministry of reconciliation. BiTod 40 (2002) 25-31 [2 Cor 5,17-21].

7245 *Heller, Karin* 'Fateci posto nei vostri cuori': 2Cor 6-7. PaVi 47/6 (2002) 9-15.

7246 *Theißen, Gerd* Zwischen Glück und Klage: Paulus—ein Mensch im Widerspruch (2 Kor 6,1-10). Erlösungsbilder. 2002 ⇒1460. 152-56.

7247 *Walker, William O.* 2 Cor 6.14-7.1 and the chiastic structure of 6.11-13; 7.2-3. NTS 48 (2002) 142-144.

7248 *Orsatti, Mauro* La colletta per i poveri di Gerusalemme: 2Cor 8-9. PaVi 47/6 (2002) 16-21.

7249 **Angstenberger, Pius** Der reiche und der arme Christus: die Rezeptionsgeschichte von 2 Kor 8,9 zwischen dem zweiten und dem sechsten Jahrhundert. Hereditas 12: 1997 ⇒13,6548... 15,6855. ^REstB 60 (2002) 134-136 (*Rodríguez Ruiz, M.*).

7250 *Bruehler, Bart B.* Proverbs, persuasion and people: a three-dimensional investigation of 2 Cor 9.6-15. NTS 48 (2002) 209-224.

7251 *Watson, Duane F.* Paul's boasting in 2 Corinthians 10-13 as defense of his honor: a socio-rhetorical analysis. Rhetorical argumentation. 2002 ⇒553. 260-275.

7252 **Walker, Donald Dale** Paul's offer of leniency (2 Cor 10:1): populist ideology and rhetoric in a Pauline letter fragment. [D]*Betz, Hans Dieter*: WUNT 2/152: Tü 2002, Mohr S. xvi; 443 pp. €69. 3-16-147891-6. Diss. Chicago. Bibl. 379-417.

7253 *De Virgilio, Giuseppe* 'Chi si vanta si vanti nel Signore': 2Cor 10,12-11,6. PaVi 47/6 (2002) 22-27.

7254 *Campbell, Douglas A.* An anchor for Pauline chronology: Paul's flight from "the ethnarch of King Aretas" (2 Corinthians 11:32-33). JBL 121 (2002) 279-302.

7255 *Segal, Alan F.* Transformation and afterlife. Gospels according to Goulder. 2002 ⇒594. 111-130 [2 Cor 12]..

7256 *Trevijano Etcheverría, Ramón* El 'apocalipsis' de Pablo (2 Cor 12,1-4) y sus primeras interpretaciones. Estudios paulinos. 2002 <1998> ⇒248. 475-506.

7257 *Grasso, Santi* 'Ti basta la mia grazia': 2Cor 12,1-13. PaVi 47/6 (2002) 28-33.

G6.1 Ad Galatas

7258 **Jervis, L. Ann** Galatians. NIBC.NT: 1999 ⇒15,6868; 17,6770. [R]TJT 18 (2002) 267-268 (*Buck, Erwin*).

7259 **Légasse, Simon** L'Épître de Paul aux Galates. LeDiv Commentaires 9: 2000 ⇒16,6834. [R]EstB 60 (2002) 273 (*Ibarzábal, S.*); Bib. 83 (2002) 133-135 (*Pastor Ramos, Federico*).

7260 **Martyn, J. Louis** Galatians. AncB 33a: 1997 ⇒13,6561... 17,6771. [R]AsbTJ 56/2-57/1 (2001-2002) 151-152 (*Watson, Duane*).

7261 [T]**Ring, T.G.** AUGUSTINUS: Schriften über die Gnade, Schriften gegen die Pelagianer, 2: die Auslegung des Briefes an die Galater—die angefangene Auslegung des Briefes an die Römer—über dreiundachtzig verschiedene Fragen: Fragen 66-68. 1999 ⇒13,6564... 16,6838. [R]AugSt 33 (2002) 134-138 (*Martin, Thomas F.*).

7262 **Witherington III, Ben** Grace in Galatia: a commentary on St. Paul's letter to the Galatians. 1998 ⇒14,6197... 16,6843. [R]SNTU.A 27 (2002) 251-253 (*Fuchs, Albert*).

7263 **Wright, Tom** Paul for everyone: Galatians and Thessalonians. L 2002, SPCK xi; 177 pp. 0-281-05304-9.

7264 *Barclay, John M.G.* Mirror-reading a polemical letter: Galatians as a test case. The Galatians debate. 2002 <1987> ⇒6668. 367-382;

7265 Paul's story: theology as testimony. Narrative dynamics. 2002 ⇒351. 133-156.

7266 *Betz, Hans Dieter* The literary composition and function of Paul's letter to the Galatians. The Galatians debate. 2002 <1975> ⇒6668. 3-28.

7267 *Boer, Martinus C. de* Second Isaiah and Paul's eschatology in the letter to the Galatians. [F]LEENE, H.: 2002 ⇒73. 35-43.

7268 *Brawley, Robert L.* Contextuality, intertextuality, and the hendiadic relationship of promise and law in Galatians. ZNW 93 (2002) 99-119.

7269 **Braxton, Brad Ronnell** No longer slaves: Galatians and African American experience. ColMn 2002, Liturgical xiv; 142 pp. $16. 0-8146-5948-9. Bibl. 127-137.

7270 *Campbell, Douglas A.* The story of Jesus in Romans and Galatians. Narrative dynamics. 2002 ⇒351. 97-124.

7271 *Cook, Richard B.* Paul and the victims of his persecution: the opponents in Galatia. BTB 32 (2002) 182-191.

7272 *Cosby, Michael R.* Galatians: red-hot rhetoric. Rhetorical argumentation. 2002 ⇒553. 296-309.

7273 *Dahl, Nils A.* Paul's letter to the Galatians: epistolary genre, content, and structure. ᴱ*Nanos, Mark D.*: The Galatians debate. 2002 ⇒6668. 117-142.

7274 *Haacker, Klaus* Paulus und das Judentum im Galaterbrief. Versöhnung mit Israel. VKHW 5: 2002 <1986> ⇒174. 127-145.

7275 *Hall, Robert G.* The rhetorical outline for Galatians: a reconsideration. The Galatians debate. 2002 <1987> ⇒6668. 29-38.

7276 *Hansen, G. Walter* A paradigm of the Apocalypse: the gospel in the light of epistolary analysis <1994>;

7277 *Harvey, A.E.* The opposition to Paul <1968>. The Galatians debate. 2002 ⇒6668. 143-154/321-333.

7278 *Hooker, Morna D.* 'Heirs of Abraham': the gentiles' role in Israel's story. Narrative dynamics. 2002 ⇒351. 85-96.

7279 *Horrell, David G.* Paul's narratives or narrative substructure: the significance of 'Paul's story'. Narrative dynamics. 2002 ⇒351. 157-71.

7280 *Jewett, Robert* The agitators and the Galatian congregation. The Galatians debate. 2002 <1970-71> ⇒6668. 334-347.

7281 **Kremendahl, Dieter** Die Botschaft der Form: zum Verhältnis von antiker Epistolographie und Rhetorik im Galaterbrief. NTOA 46: 2000 ⇒16,6856; 17,6781. ᴿJThS 53 (2002) 238-241 (*Betz, Hans Dieter*); CBQ 64 (2002) 581-583 (*Muller, Earl C.*).

7282 *Lategan, B.C.* The argumentative situation of Galatians. The Galatians debate. 2002 <1992> ⇒6668. 383-395;

7283 Paul's use of history in Galatians: some remarks on his style of theological argumentation. Neotest. 36 (2002) 121-130.

7284 *Lincoln, Andrew T.* The stories of predecessors and inheritors in Galatians and Romans. Narrative dynamics. 2002 ⇒351. 172-203.

7285 *Longenecker, Bruce W.* Sharing in their spiritual blessings?: the stories of Israel in Galatians and Romans. Narrative dynamics. 2002 ⇒351. 58-84.

7286 *Manzi, Franco* L'annullamento della maledizione di Dt. 21,23 in Galati e nel Dialogo con Trifone. Aug. 42 (2002) 5-34.

7287 *Marshall, I. Howard* Response to A.T. Lincoln: the stories of predecessors and inheritors in Galatians and Romans. Narrative dynamics. 2002 ⇒351. 204-214.

7288 *Martin, Troy* Apostasy to paganism: the rhetorical stasis of the Galatian controversy. The Galatians debate. 2002 <1995> ⇒6668. 73-94;

7289 The brother body: addressing and describing the Galatians and the agitators as ἀδελφοί. BR 47 (2002) 5-18.

7290 *Martyn, J. Louis* A law-observant mission to gentiles. The Galatians debate 2002 <1997> ⇒6668. 348-361.

7291 *Mitternacht, Dieter* Foolish Galatians—a recipient-oriented assessment of Paul's letter. The Galatians debate. 2002 ⇒6668. 408-433.

7292 **Mitternacht, Dieter** Forum für Sprachlose: eine kommunikationspsychologische und epistolärrhetorische Untersuchung des Galaterbriefs. CB.NT 30: 1999 ⇒15,6901; 16,6864. ᴿRBLit 4 (2002) 426-430 (*Schröter, Jens*).

7293 *Nanos, Mark D.* Introduction;

7294 The inter- and intra-Jewish political context of Paul's letter to the Galatians. Galatians debate. 2002 <2000> ⇒6668. xi-xli./396-407.

7295 **Nanos, Mark D.** The irony of Galatians: Paul's letter in first-century context. 2001 ⇒17,6787. ᴿJR 82 (2002) 621-622 (*Duff, Paul B.*); HBT 24/2 (2002) 122-123 (*Keay, Robert D.*); JBL 121 (2002) 376-378 (*Heen, Erik M.*).

7296 *Sanborn, Scott* Paul and the law. Kerux 17/2 (2002) 24-53.

7297 *Sänger, Dieter* 'Vergeblich bemüht' (Gal 4.11)?: zur paulinischen Argumentationsstrategie im Galaterbrief. NTS 48 (2002) 377-399.

7298 **Silva, Moisés** Interpreting Galatians: explorations in exegetical method. 2001 ⇒17,6795. ᴿRBLit (2002)* (*Lindsay, Dennis R.*).

7299 *Smit, Joop* The letter of Paul to the Galatians: a deliberative speech. The Galatians debate. 2002 <1989> ⇒6668. 39-59.

7300 *Stanton, Graham N.* 'I think, when I read that sweet story of old': a response to Douglas Campbell. Narrative dynamics. 2002 ⇒351. 125-132.

7301 *Varickasseril, Jose* Strengthening a backsliding community: a study of Paul's letter to the Galatians. MissTod 4 (2002) 140-147.

7302 *Walter, Nikolaus* Paul and the opponents of the Christ-gospel in Galatia. The Galatians debate. 2002 <1986> ⇒6668. 362-366.

7303 *Winger, Michael* Act one: Paul arrives in Galatia. NTS 48 (2002) 548-567.

7304 **Witulski, Thomas** Die Adressaten des Galaterbriefes: Untersuchungen zur Gemeinde von Antiochia ad Pisidiam. FRLANT 193: 2000 ⇒16,6874; 17,6799. ᴿThLZ 127 (2002) 403-407 (*Bachmann, Michael*).

7305 **Cummins, Stephen Anthony** Paul and the crucified Christ in Antioch: Maccabean martyrdom and Galatians 1 and 2. MSSNTS 114: 2001 ⇒17,6801. ᴿCBQ 64 (2002) 754-755 (*Paffenroth, Kim*).

7306 *Fredriksen, Paula* Judaism, the circumcision of gentiles, and apocalyptic hope: another look at Galatians 1 and 2 <1991>;

7307 *Hester, James D.* Epideictic rhetoric and persona in Galatians 1 and 2. The Galatians debate. 2002 ⇒6668. 235-260/181-196.

7308 *Rakocy, Waldemar* Lata wizyt Pawła w Jerozolimie po nawróceniu i rok ucieczki z Damaszku. CoTh 72/1 (2002) 89-98 [2 Cor 11; Gal 1-2]. **P.**

7309 *Trevijano Etcheverría, Ramón* Los primeros viajes de San Pablo a Jerusalén (Gal 1,18-20 y 2,1-10) <1995>;

7310 Il contrapunto lucano (Hch 9,26-30; 11,27-30; 12,25 y 15,1-35) a Gal 1,18-20 y 2,1-10 <1997>. Estudios paulinos 2002 ⇒248. 31-69/71-112.

7311 *Vos, Johan S.* Paul's argumentation in Galatians 1-2. The Galatians debate. 2002 <1994> ⇒6668. 169-180;

7312 Offenbarungsrhetorik (Gal 1,1-2,11). Die Kunst der Argumentation. 2002 <1993; 2001> ⇒6712. 87-114.

7313 *Berchman, Robert M.* Galatians (1:1-5): Paul and Greco-Roman rhetoric. The Galatians debate 2002 <1987> ⇒6668. 60-72.
7314 *Trevijano Etcheverría, Ramón* Gal 1,15[! 1]-5 en ORÍGENES. Estudios paulinos. 2002 <1999> ⇒248. 507-529.
7315 *Vanhoye, Albert* La définition de l'"autre évangile" en Ga 1,6-7. Bib. 83 (2002) 392-398.
7316 *Koptak, Paul E.* Rhetorical identification in Paul's autobiographical narrative: Galatians 1:13-2:14. The Galatians debate. 2002 <1990> ⇒6668. 157-168.
7317 *Oegema, Gerbern S.* Zum jüdischen Hintergrund des Apostels Paulus nach Gal 1,13-14. [F]ASCHOFF, D.: 2002 ⇒3. 61-74.
7318 *Seland, Torrey* Saul of Tarsus and early Zealotism: reading Gal 1,13-14 in light of PHILO's writings. Bib. 83 (2002) 449-471.
7319 *Rossé, Gérard* La questione della legge all'assemblea di Gerusalemme nella prospettiva di Paolo (Gal 2) e di Luca (At 15). San Luca evangelista. FRSEP 28: 2002 ⇒5731. 521-534.
7320 *Silberman, Lou H.* Paul, dogmatist or argufier?. [F]PATTE, D.: 2002 ⇒89. 341-344 [Gal 2-3].
7321 *Iori, Renato* La colletta come carità in Galati 2,10. [F]POMPEDDA, M. 2002 ⇒90. 27-32.
7322 *Joubert, S.* Die leierskap van die Jerusalem-kerk as weldoeners tydens die ontmoeting met Paulus: Galasiërs 2:10 en antieke Joodse resiprositeit. HTS 57 (2001) 1213-1228 [NTAb 46,486].
7323 *MacGuire, Frank* The posthumous clash between Peter and Paul. JHiC 9/2 (2002) 161-174 [Gal 2,11-12]..
7324 *Dunn, James D.G.* The incident at Antioch (Gal 2:11-18). The Galatians debate. 2002 <1983> ⇒6668. 199-234.
7325 *Böttrich, Christfried* Petrus und Paulus in Antiochien (Gal 2,11-21). BThZ 19 (2002) 224-239.
7326 *Nanos, Mark D.* What was at stake in Peter's 'eating with gentiles' at Antioch [Gal 2,11-21]?;
7327 *Esler, Philip F.* Making and breaking an agreement Mediteranean style: a new reading of Galatians 2:1-14 <1995>. The Galatians debate. 2002 ⇒6668. 292-318/261-281.
7328 *Koehne, Mark* Saint THOMAS Aquinas: on 'works of the law' and 'faith of Christ' in Galatians 2:15-16. ScrB 32 (2002) 9-20.
7329 **Núñez Regodón, Jacinto** El evangelio en Antioquía: Gál 2,15-21 entre el incidente Antioqueno y la crisis Gálata. Plenitudo Temporis 7: S 2002, Publicaciones Universidad Pontificia 324 pp. €14. 84-72-99-522-4. Bibl. 263-302.
7330 *Barth, Hans-Martin* "Ich lebe, aber nicht mehr ich ...": christlicher Glaube und personale Identität. NZSTh 44 (2002) 174-88 [Gal 2,20].
7331 *Nüssel, Friederike* "Ich lebe, doch nun nicht ich, sondern Christus lebt in mir" (Gal 2,20a): dogmatische Überlegungen zur Rede vom 'Sein in Christus'. ZThK 99 (2002) 480-502.
7332 **Hays, Richard B.** The faith of Jesus Christ: the narrative substructure of Galatians 3:1-4:11. Biblical Resource: GR [2]2002 <1983>, Eerdmans lii; 308 pp. $25. 0-8028-4957-1.
7333 **Davis, Basil S.** Christ as devotio: the argument of Galatians 3:1-14. Lanham 2002, University Press of America (4) 270 pp. 0-7618-2428-6. Bibl. 251-265.
7334 *Tolmie, D.F.* Paulus se retoriese strategie in Galasiërs 3:1-14. VeE 23 (2002) 209-225.

7335 **Wisdom, Jeffrey R.** Blessing for the nations and the curse of the law: Paul's citation of Genesis and Deuteronomy in Gal 3.8-10. WUNT 2/133: 2001 ⇒17,6815. ᴿSal. 64 (2002) 584-585 (*Vicent, R.*); CBQ 64 (2002) 784-785 (*Gillman, Florence Morgan*).

7336 *Vos, Johan S.* Juristische Rhetorik (Gal 3,11-12; Röm 10,5-10). Die Kunst der Argumentation. 2002 <1991; 1992> ⇒6712. 115-134.

7337 *Harrill, J. Albert* Coming of age and putting on Christ: the Toga Virilis ceremony, its paraenesis, and Paul's interpretation of baptism in Galatians. NT 44 (2002) 252-277 [Gal 3,27].

7338 *D'Angelo, Mary Rose* Gender refusers in the early christian mission: Gal 3:28 as an interpretation of Gen 1:27b. ᶠGREER, R.: 2002 ⇒51. 149-173.

7339 *Miller, Ed.L.* Is Galatians 3:28 the great egalitarian text?. ET 114 (2002) 9-11.

7340 *Standhartinger, Angela* "Zur Freiheit ... befreit"?: Hagar im Galaterbrief. EvTh 62 (2002) [Gal 4].

7341 *Trevijano, Ramon* La plenitudo temporis (Gál 4,4): interpretaciones de ORÍGENES: TyV 43 (2002) 377-396 = Estudios paulinos 2002 ⇒ 248. 531-557.

7342 *Tolmie, D.F.* Allegorie as argument: Galasiërs 4:21-5:1 in retoriese perspektief. AcTh(B) 22/2 (2002) 163-178.

7343 *Gerber, Daniel* Ga 4,21-31 ou l'indéfinissable méthode?. Typologie biblique. LeDiv: 2002 ⇒341. 165-176.

7344 *Rondez, Pascale* Ein Zentrum paulinischer Theologie?: eine pneumatologische Erschließung des Zusammenhangs von Soteriologie und Christologie anhand von Gal 5,25. Kreuzestheologie. WUNT 151: 2002 ⇒298. 59-79.

G6.2 Ad Ephesios

7345 **Aletti, Jean-Noël** Saint Paul: épitre aux Éphésiens. EtB 42: 2001 ⇒ 17,6835. ᴿGr. 83 (2002) 176-177 (*Galot, Jean*); CBQ 64 (2002) 563-564 (*Gormley, Joan F.*).

7346 **Best, Ernest** A critical and exegetical commentary on Ephesians. ICC: 1998 ⇒14,6245...17,6837. ᴿAt. 90 (2002) 278-286 (*Zoroddu, Donatella*).

7347 **Dahl, Nils Alstrup** Studies in Ephesians. WUNT 131: 2000 ⇒16, 147; 17,6840. ᴿTS 63 (2002) 165-167 (*Soards, Marion L.*); JR 82 (2002) 274-275 (*Betz, Hans Dieter*); SEÅ 67 (2002) 176-179 (*Hartman, Lars*).

7348 ᵀ**Heine, Ronald E.** The commentaries of ORIGEN and JEROME on St. Paul's epistle to the Ephesians. Oxford Early Christian Studies: Oxf 2002, OUP xii; 297 pp. £50. 0-19-924551-7. Bibl. 282-286.

7349 **Hoehner, Harold W.** Ephesians: an exegetical commentary. GR 2002 Baker xxix; 930 pp $55 0-8010-2614-8 ThD 50,76—Heiser, W. Charles.

7350 **MacDonald, Margaret Y.** Colossians and Ephesians. Sacra Pagina 17: 2000 ⇒16,6924; 17,6841. ᴿSR 30 (2002) 248-250 (*Reinhartz, Adele*); LouvSt 27 (2002) 180-182 (*Koperski, Veronica*).

7351 **Muddiman, John** The epistle to the Ephesians. Black's NT commentaries: 2001 ⇒17,6842. ᴿTheol. 105 (2002) 140-141 (*Turner, Max*); JR 82 (2002) 436-437 (*Harrill, J. Albert*).

7352 **O'Brien, Peter Thomas** The letter to the Ephesians. Pillar NT Commentary: 1999 ⇒15,6943...17,6844. [R]Evangel 20 (2002) 88 (*Van Neste, Ray*); Orpheus 23 (2002) 280-282 (*Osculati, Roberto*).

7353 **Yoder Neufeld, Thomas R.** Ephesians. Believers Church Bible Commentary: Waterloo, Ontario 2002, Herald 400 pp. $25. 0-8361-9167-6. Bibl. 366-384.

7354 *Adamczewski, Bartosz* Ewangelizacja Izraela w liście do Efezjan [The preaching of the gospel to Israel in the letter to the Ephesians]. Verbum Vitae 2 (2002) 183-199. Sum. 198. **P.**

7355 **Boismard, Marie-Émile** L'énigme de la lettre aux Éphésiens. EtB 39: 1999 ⇒15,6945; 17,6847. [R]EThL 78 (2002) 224-225 (*Verheyden, J.*).

7356 **Cabras, Anna** La lettera agli Efesini e il quarto vangelo: uno studio sulla tradizione cristiana nella comunità efesina. [D]*Vanni, Ugo*: R 2002, 146 pp. Extr. Diss. Gregoriana; Bibl.

7357 *Fredrickson, David E.* Ephesians and Stoic physics. WaW 22 (2002) 144-154.

7358 *Jeal, Roy R.* Rhetorical argumentation in the letter to the Ephesians. Rhetorical argumentation. 2002 ⇒553. 310-324.

7359 **Kohlgraf, Peter** Die Ekklesiologie des Epheserbriefes in der Auslegung durch Johannes CHRYSOSTOMUS: eine Untersuchung zur Wirkungsgeschichte paulinischer Theologie. Hereditas 19: 2001 ⇒17, 6850. [R]FKTh 18 (2002) 156-157 (*Lochbrunner, Manfred*); RSPhTh 86 (2002) 521-523 (*Meunier, Bernard*); ThPh 77 (2002) 565-567 (*Sieben, H.-J.*).

7360 *Lemmer, Richard* Rhetoric and metaphor, and the metaphysical in the letter to the Ephesians. Rhetorical criticism. JSNT.S 195: 2002 ⇒ 369. 458-480.

7361 **Los Santos, Edmundo de** La novedad de la metáfora κεφαλή—σῶμα en la carta a los Efesios. TGr.T 59: 2000 ⇒16,6945. [R]RivBib 50 (2002) 371-374 (*Romanello, Stefano*).

7362 *Manzi, Franco* 'Si prostrino davanti a lui tutti gli angeli di Dio': le potenze angeliche e demoniache in Efesini, Colossesi ed Ebrei. PSV 46 (2002) 121-135.

7363 **Mayer, Annemarie C.** Sprache der Einheit im Epheserbrief und in der Ökumene. [D]*Hiberath, B.J.* WUNT 2/150: Tü 2002, Mohr xv; 394 pp. €49. 3-16-147865-7. Diss. Tübingen; Bibl. 342-368.

7364 **Mouton, Elna** Reading a New Testament document ethically. Academia biblica 1: Lei 2002, Brill xiv; 290 pp. $38. 90-04-12658-9. Bibl. 261-285.

7365 *Schwindt, Rainer* Die Bitte um Gottes Gaben als Mitte christlicher Existenz: zur Theologie des Epheserbriefes. TThZ 111 (2002) 42-61.

7366 **Schwindt, Rainer** Das Weltbild des Epheserbriefes: eine religionsgeschichtlich-exegetische Studie. [D]*Eckert, J.*: WUNT 2/148: Tü 2002, Mohr xiii; 649 pp. €119. 3-16-147848-7. Diss. Trier 2001. Bibl. 525-613.

7367 **Theobald, Michael** Mit den Augen des Herzens sehen: der Epheserbrief als Leitfaden für Spiritualität und Kirche. 2000 ⇒16,6949. [R]OrdKor 43 (2002) 359-360 (*Giesen, Heinz*).

7368 *Flor, Elmer* The cosmic Christ and ecojustice in the new cosmos (Ephesians 1). Earth story. 2002 ⇒322. 137-147.

7369 *Romanello, Stefano* Ef 1,3-14: una pericope discussa. RivBib 50 (2002) 31-62.
7370 *Hofius, Otfried* "Erwählt vor Grundlegung der Welt" (Eph 1,4). Paulusstudien II. WUNT 143: 2002 <1971> ⇒180. 234-246.
7371 *Leyrer, D.P.* Ephesians 1:23—the 'fullness' of Ascension comfort. WLQ 99/2 (2002) 135-137 [NTAb 47,72].
7372 *Sisack, Viviana* 'Él es nuestra paz' (Ef 2,14). RevBib 64 (2002) 205-215.
7373 *Ruthven, Jon* The "foundational gifts" of Ephesians 2.20. JPentec 10/2 (2002) 28-43.
7374 *Foster, Paul* The first contribution to the πίστις Χριστοῦ debate: a study of Ephesians 3.12. JSNT 85 (2002) 75-96.
7375 *Müller, Christoph Gregor* Wider die Geschwätzigkeit!: Mahnungen zur Zügelung der Zunge in frühchristlicher Tradition. BZ 46 (2002) 164-189 [Eph 4,29; James 1,26].
7376 *Gombis, Timothy G.* Being the fullness of God in Christ by the Spirit: Ephesians 5:18 in its epistolary setting. TynB 53 (2002) 259-271.
7377 **Dawes, Gregory W.** The body in question: metaphor and meaning in the interpretation of Ephesians 5:21-33. BiblInterp. 30: 1998 ⇒14, 6268...17,6858. ᴿJBL 121 (2002) 378-380 (*Yorke, Gosnell L.O.R.*).
7378 *Pokorný, Petr* Das Geheimnis ist groß: Eph 5,21-33: theologische Voraussetzungen und hermeneutische Folgen einer paränetischen Aussage: ein Beitrag zur Begründung der christlichen Ethik. BThZ 19 (2002) 175-182.
7379 *Osiek, Carolyn* The bride of Christ (Ephesians 5:22-33): a problematic wedding. BTB 32 (2002) 29-39.

G6.3 Ad Philippenses

7380 **Barth, Karl** Epistle to the Philippians: 40th anniversary edition. LVL 2002 <1962>, Westminster 128 pp. $15. 0-664-22420-2. Introd. *Bruce L. McCormack; Francis B. Watson.*
7381 **Behler, Gebhard-Maria** Afferrati da Gesù Cristo: commento spirituale alla *Lettera di S. Paolo ai Filippesi.* ᵀ*Palazzi, Claudia*: SacDoc 47/6: Bo 2002, Studio Domenicano 162 pp. €16. 88-7094-476-X.
7382 **Penna, Romano** Lettera ai Filippesi—lettera a Filemone. Nuovo Testamento—commento esegetico e spirituale: R 2002, Città Nuova 198 pp. €15. 88-311-3776-X. Bibl. 195-196.

7383 *Bolay, Bernard* Jalons pour une anthropologie paulinienne. Ḥokhma 80 (2002) 32-49.
7384 *Debanné, Marc J.* An enthymematic reading of Philippians: towards a typology of Pauline arguments. Rhetorical criticism. JSNT.S 195: 2002 ⇒369. 481-503.
7385 **Edart, Jean-Baptiste** L'Épître aux Philippiens, rhétorique et composition stylistique. ÉtB 45: P 2002, Gabalda 394 pp. €57. 2-85021-13-8-2. Bibl. 353-378. ᴿAng. 79 (2002) 981-984 (*Garuti, Paolo*).
7386 *Fowl, Stephen E.* Believing forms seeing: formation for martyrdom in Philippians. Character and scripture. 2002 ⇒283. 317-330.
7387 *Hooker, Morna D.* Philippians: phantom opponents and the real source of conflict. ᶠRÄISÄNEN, H.: NT.S 103: 2002 ⇒97. 377-395.
7388 *Iovino, Paolo* Paolo ai Filippesi: struttura della lettera ai Filippesi. Ho Theológos 20 (2002) 185-203.

7389 *Meeks, Wayne A.* The man from heaven in Paul's letter to the Philippians. In search. 2002 ⇒208. 106-114.
7390 *Oakes, Peter* God's sovereignty over Roman authorities: a theme in Philippians. Rome in the bible. 2002 ⇒363. 126-141.
7391 **Oakes, Peter** Philippians: from people to letter. MSSNTS 110: 2001 ⇒17,6871. ᴿBZ 46 (2002) 151-152 (*Vollenweider, Samuel*); JR 82 (2002) 434-436 (*Holloway, Paul A.*).
7392 *Ramsaran, Rollin A.* Living and dying, living is dying (Philippians 1:21): Paul's maxim and exemplary argumentation in Philippians. Rhetorical argumentation. 2002 ⇒553. 325-338.
7393 *Reumann, John* Resurrection in Philippi and Paul's letter(s) to the Philippians. ᶠLAMBRECHT, J.: BEThL 165: 2002 ⇒72. 407-422.

7394 *Vos, Johan S.* Die Rhetorik des Erfolges (Phil 1,12-26). Die Kunst der Argumentation. 2002 ⇒6712. 135-157.
7395 *Vollenweider, Samuel* Die Waagschalen von Leben und Tod: Phil 1, 21-26 vor dem Hintergrund der antiken Rhetorik. Horizonte. WUNT 144: 2002 <1994> ⇒257. 237-261.
7396 ᴱ**Dodd, Brian J.; Martin, Ralph Philip** Where christology began: essays on Philippians 2. 1998 ⇒14,6297; 15,6985. ᴿSBET 20 (2002) 115-116 (*Wilson, Alistair I.*).
7397 **Williams, Demetrius** Enemies of the cross of Christ: a rhetorical analysis of the terminology of the cross and conflict in Philippians. JSNT.S 223: Shf 2002, Sheffield Academic xv; 278 pp. $105/£55. 0-8264-6052-6 [Phil 2-3].
7398 *Trevijano Etcheverría, Ramón* Flp 2,5-11: un λόγος σοφίας paulino sobre Cristo. Estudios paulinos. 2002 <1995> ⇒248. 257-290.
7399 *Vollenweider, Samuel* Die Metamorphose des Gottessohns: zum epiphanialen Motivfeld in Phil 2,6-8. Horizonte. WUNT 144: 2002 <1999> ⇒257. 285-306.
7400 *Bellia, Giuseppe; Iovino, Paolo* La croce: kenosi del Servo: la cristologia cosmica di *Fil* 2,6-11. Il crocifisso. 2002 ⇒620. 29-47.
7401 *Vollenweider, Samuel* Der "Raub" der Gottgleichheit: ein religionsgeschichtlicher Vorschlag zu Phil 2,6(-11). Horizonte. WUNT 144: 2002 <1999> ⇒257. 263-284.
7402 *Junginger, Jens* Gemeinde Jesu Christi—eine gelebte Kontrastgesellschaft! Philipper 2,12-13. JK 63/5 (2002) 48-51.
7403 *Poythress, Vern Sheridan* "Hold fast" versus "hold out" in Philippians 2:16. WThJ 64 (2002) 45-53.
7404 *Metzner, Rainer* In aller Freundschaft: ein frühchristlicher Fall freundschaftlicher Gemeinschaft (Phil 2.25-30). NTS 48 (2002) 111-131.
7405 *Theißen, Gerd* Die Verwandlung des Paulus und die Bekehrungskultur der modernen Welt (Phil 3,1-16). Erlösungsbilder. 2002 ⇒1460. 157-164.
7406 *Doble, Peter* 'Vile bodies' or transformed persons?: Philippians 3.21 in context. JSNT 86 (2002) 3-27.
7407 *Fowl, Stephen* Know your context: giving and receiving money in Philippians. Interp. 56 (2002) 45-58 [Phil 4,10-20].

G6.4 Ad Colossenses

7408 **Bentley, Michael** The guide—Colossians and Philemon. Darlington 2002, Evangelical 205 pp. £6. 0-85234-489-9.

7409   **Dunn, James D.G.** The epistles to the Colossians and to Philemon.
NIGTC: 1996 ⇒12,6450...17,6892. ᴿHeyJ 43 (2002) 223-225
(*McNamara, Martin*); VJTR 66 (2002) 465-7 (*Meagher, Patrick M.*).
7410   **Gaukroger, Stephen; Wood, Derek** Colossians and Philemon.
Crossway Bible Guide: Wheaton, IL 2002, Crossway 119 pp. 1-856-
84-208-8. Bibl. 119.
MacDonald, M. Colossians and Ephesians 2000 ⇒7350.
7411   **Reuter, Rainer** Textvergleichende und synoptische Arbeit an den
Briefen des Neuen Testaments: Geschichte—Methodik—Praxis:
Textvergleich Kolosser- und Philemonbrief. ᴰ*Schaller, B.*: 2002 Diss.
Göttingen [ThRv 99/2,viii].

7412   *Dettwiler, Andreas* Das Verständnis des Kreuzes Jesu im Kolosser-
brief. Kreuzestheologie. WUNT 151: 2002 ⇒298. 81-105.
7413   *Renard, Helmut; Tauchner, Cristian* Something in the air. IRM 91
(2002) 52-61.
7414   *Royalty, Robert M.* Dwelling on visions: on the nature of the so-
called 'Colossians heresy'. Bib. 83 (2002) 329-357.
7415   *Sumney, Jerry L.* The argument of Colossians. Rhetorical argumentation. 2002 ⇒553. 339-352.
7416   *Tosaus Abadía, José Pedro* Colosenses 1,9-23: estructura y reflexiones teológicas sobre su contenido. ᶠTREVIJANO ETCHEVERRÍA, R.
2002 ⇒122. 233-248.

7417   *Roberts, J.H.* Die sintaktiese binding van μετὰ χαρᾶς in Kolossense
1:11: 'n strukturele motivering. HTS 57 (2001) 187-209 [NTAb 46,
490].
7418   *Hofius, Otfried* "Erstgeborener vor aller Schöpfung"—"Erstgeborener aus den Toten": Erwägungen zu Struktur und Aussage des Chri-
stushymnus Kol 1,15-20. Paulusstudien II. WUNT 143: 2002
<2001> ⇒180. 215-233.
7419   *Okure, Teresa* "In him all things hold together": a missiological reading of Colossians 1:15-20. IRM 91 (2002) 62-72.
7420   **Stettler, Christian** Der Kolosserhymnus: Untersuchungen zu Form,
traditionsgeschichtlichem Hintergrund und Aussage von Kol 1,15-20.
WUNT 2/131: 2000 ⇒16,6999. ᴿJThS 53 (2002) 247-250 (*Hurtado,
L.W.*); RB 109 (2002) 299-300 (*Murphy-O'Connor, Jerome*); ZKTh
124 (2002) 243 (*Hasitschka, Martin*).
7421   *Garuti, Paolo* L'eresia di Colossi, l'antanaclasi e la storia della redazione: qualche considerazione a proposito di Col 2,6-23. Ang. 79
(2002) 303-326.
7422   *Cueni, R. Robert* Sending forth this servant of God: Colossians 3:12-
17. LexTQ 37/1-2 (2002) 85-91 [BuBB 40,120].
7423   *Sweeney, James P.* The priority of prayer in Colossians 4:2-4;
7424   Guidelines on christian witness in Colossians 4:5-6. BS 159 (2002)
318-333/449-461.

G6.6 Ad Thessalonicenses

7425   **Brocke, Christoph vom** Thessaloniki—Stadt des Kassander und Gemeinde des Paulus: eine frühe christliche Gemeinde in ihrer heidnischen Umwelt. WUNT 2/125: 2001 ⇒17,6903. ᴿJThS 53 (2002)
244-247 (*Oakes, Peter*); JAC 45 (2002) 211-215 (*Elliger, Winfried*).

7426 **Cenci, Anna Maria** Egli abita una luce inaccessibile: prima e seconda lettera di san Paolo ai Tessalonicesi, prima e seconda lettera a Timoteo, lettera a Tito. Mi 2001, Gribaudi 122 pp. 88-7152-611-2.

7427 **Donfried, Karl Paul** Paul, Thessalonica, and early christianity. GR 2002, Eerdmans xxxviii; 347 pp. $26. 0-8028-0509-4. Bibl. 305-331.

7428 **Green, Gene L.** The letters to the Thessalonians. The Pillar New Testament Commentary: GR 2002, Eerdmans xl; 400 pp. $42. 0-8028-3738-7. Bibl. xix-xl.

7429 *Harrison, J.R.* Paul and the imperial gospel at Thessaloniki. JSNT 25/1 (2002) 71-96.

7430 *Holtz, Traugott* Thessalonicherbriefe. TRE 33. 2002 ⇒799. 412-421.

7431 **Malherbe, Abraham Johannes** The letters to the Thessalonians. AncB 32B: 2000 ⇒16,7006. ᴿETR 77 (2002) 436-439 (*Redalié, Yann*); Prudentia 34/1 (2002) 98-100 (*Gilmour, Calum*); CBQ 64 (2002) 382-384 (*Bauer, David R.*); NT 44 (2002) 395-397 (*Fox, Kenneth A.*); ThLZ 127 (2002) 176-179 (*Holtz, Traugott*); RExp 99 (2002) 281-282 (*Vinson, Richard B.*); Bib. 83 (2002) 135-138 (*Lambrecht, Jan*); JBL 121 (2002) 380-383 (*Cousland, J.R.C.*).

7432 **Müller, Paul-Gerhard** Der erste und zweite Brief an die Thessalonicher. RNT: 2001 ⇒17,6909. ᴿTThZ 111 (2002) 79-80 (*Mußner, Franz*); OrdKor 43 (2002) 361 (*Giesen, Heinz*).

7433 *Taylor, N.H.* Who persecuted the Thessalonian christians?. HTS 58 (2002) 784-801 [NTAb 47,279].

       Wright, T. Paul for everyone: Gal. & Thess. 2002 ⇒7263.

7434 **Yeo, Khiok-Khing** Chairman Mao meets the apostle Paul: christianity, communism, and the hope of China. GR 2002, Brazos 302 pp. $30. 1-58743-034-7 [ThD 50,96—Heiser, W. Charles].

7435 *Cipriani, Settimio* Un confronto fra Paolo (1 Ts) e Luca (At 20,17-38) sul tema della 'missione'. San Luca evangelista. FRSEP 28: 2002 ⇒5731. 507-519.

7436 *Cornelius, E.M.* The purpose of 1 Thessalonians. HTS 57 (2001) 435-446 [NTAb 46,490].

7437 *Hester, James D.* A fantasy theme analysis of 1 Thessalonians. Rhetorical criticism. JSNT.S 195: 2002 ⇒369. 504-525;

7438 Apocalyptic discourse in 1 Thessalonians. Intertexture. SBL.Symposium 14: 2002 ⇒385. 137-163.

7439 *Kim, Seyoon* Justification by grace and through faith in 1 Thessalonians. Paul and the new perspective. WUNT 140: 2002 ⇒190. 85-100.

7440 *O'Mahony, Kieran J.* The rhetorical dispositio of 1 Thessalonians. PIBA 25 (2002) 81-96.

7441 *Wanamaker, Charles A.* Apocalyptic discourse, paraenesis and identity maintenance in 1 Thessalonians. Neotest. 36 (2002) 131-145.

7442 *Yeo, K.K.* The rhetoric of election and calling language in 1 Thessalonians. Rhetorical criticism. JSNT.S 195: 2002 ⇒369. 526-547.

7443 *Trevijano Etcheverría, Ramón* La misión en Tesalónica (1 Tes 1,1-2,16). Estudios paulinos. 2002 <1985> ⇒248. 113-146.

7444 *Rodríguez Plaza, Braulio* La acción de gracias y la imitación en 1 Tes 1,5-2,14. ᶠTREVIJANO ETCHEVERRÍA, R. 2002 ⇒122. 207-217.

7445 *Weima, Jeffrey A.* Infants, nursing mother, and father: Paul's portrayal of a pastor. CTJ 37 (2002) 209-229 [1 Thess 2,1-12].

7446 *Hoppe, Rudolf* Verkündiger—Botschaft—Gemeinde: Überlegungen zu 1 Thess 2,1-12.13-16. ᶠFUCHS, A.: 2002 ⇒41. 325-345.

7447 *Kampling, Rainer* Eine auslegungsgeschichtliche Skizze zu 1 Thess 2,14-16. Im Angesicht. SBB 47: 2002 <1993> ⇒189. 153-181.

7448 *Córdova González, Eduardo* La tradicion y la redaccion en 1Tes 4, 13-5,11. EfMex 20 (2002) 155-182.

7449 *Kim, Seyoon* The Jesus tradition in 1 Thess 4.13-5.11. NTS 48 (2002) 225-242.

7450 *Pilhofer, Peter* Περὶ δὲ τῆς φιλαδελφίας ... (1Thess 4,9): ekklesiologische Überlegungen zu einem Proprium früher christlicher Gemeinden. Die frühen Christen. WUNT 145: 2002 ⇒225. 139-153.

7451 *Ntumba Kapambu, Valentin* La prière comme "âme" de l'apostolat en 2 Th. 3:1-2. Ter. 53 (2002) 375-389.

G7.0 Epistulae pastorales

7452 *Bassler, Jouette M.* Epiphany christology in the Pastoral Letters: another look. ᶠROETZEL, C.: JSNT.S 221: 2002 ⇒104. 194-214.

7453 *Blecker, Iris Maria* Die παραθήκη rettenden Wissens nach den Pastoralbriefen. Rettendes Wissen. AOAT 300: 2002 ⇒352. 229-267 [2 Tim 1,12-14].

Cenci, A. Egli abita una luce inaccessibile 2001 ⇒7426.

7454 *Collins, Raymond F.* Timothy and Titus: on reading the Pastoral Epistles. ᶠFUCHS, A.: 2002 ⇒41. 367-381;

7455 What happened to Jesus' resurrection from the dead?: a reflection on Paul and the Pastoral Epistles. ᶠLAMBRECHT, J.: BEThL 165: 2002 ⇒72. 423-440;

7456 The origins of church law. Jurist [Wsh] 61/1 (2001) 134-156 [NTAb 47,495].

7457 **Collins, Raymond F.** 1 & 2 Timothy and Titus: a commentary. NTLi: LVL 2002, Westminster xxiv; 408 pp. $35. 0-664-22247-1. Bibl. xviii-xxiv.

7458 **Fairbairn, Patrick** A commentary on 1 & 2 Timothy and Titus. GSC: E 2002, Banner of Truth Trust ix; (2) 451 pp. 0-85151-820-6.

7459 *Fitzmyer, Joseph A.* The Savior God: the Pastoral Epistles. ᶠACHTEMEIER, P. 2002 ⇒1. 181-196.

7460 **Häfner, Gerd** "Nützlich zur Belehrung" (2 Tim 3,16):die Rolle der Schrift in den Pastoralbriefen im Rahmen der Paulusrezeption. Herders Biblische Studien 25: 2000 ⇒16,7055. ᴿBZ 46 (2002) 290-292 *(Backhaus, Knut).*

7461 **Looks, Carsten** Das Anvertraute bewahren: die Rezeption der Pastoralbriefe im 2. Jahrhundert. Münchner Theologische Beiträge: 1999 ⇒15,7079; 17,6940. ᴿBZ 46 (2002) 154-155 *(Häfner, Gerd).*

7462 *Marshall, I. Howard* Congregation and ministry in the Pastoral Letters. Community formation. 2002 ⇒644. 105-125.

7463 **Mounce, William D.** Pastoral epistles. WBC 46: 2000 ⇒16,7065. ᴿBS 159 (2002) 378-379 *(Constable, Thomas L.).*

7464 *Ortega Orcajo, Rafael* El "obispo" en las Cartas Pastorales. Labor Theologicus 29 (2002) 127-149.

7465 *Poidlouë, Joëlle* Le vocabulaire de l'exhortation dans les épîtres pastorales. AnBru 7 (2002) 198-209.

7466 **Richards, William A.** Difference and distance in post-Pauline christianity: an epistolary analysis of the Pastorals. Studies in Biblical Lit-

erature 44: NY 2002, Lang xiv; 282 pp. $60. 0-8204-5599-7. Bibl.
255-266.

7467   *Trebilco, Paul R.* What shall we call each other?: part 1: the issue of
self-designation in the Pastoral Epistles. TynB 53 (2002) 239-258.

7468   **Van Neste, Ray** Cohesion and structure in the Pastoral Epistles.
ᴰMarshall, I.H.: 2002 Diss. Aberdeen [RTL 34,602].

G7.2 1-2 ad Timotheum, ad Titum

7469   **Johnson, Luke Timothy** The First and Second Letters to Timothy.
AncB 35A: 2001 ⇒17,6948. ᴿBiblInterp 10 (2002) 100-102
(*Marshall, I. Howard*); AUSS 40 (2002) 335-337 (*Cosaert, Carl P.*);
HBT 24 (2002) 135-136 (*Sumney, Jerry L.*); TrinJ 23 (2002) 263-
266 (*Yarbrough, Robert W.*); JBL 121 (2002) 186-189 (*Towner,
Philip H.*).

7470   **Quinn, Jerome D.; Wacker, William C.** The first and second letters
to Timothy. 2000 ⇒16,7073; 17,6949. ᴿInterp. 56 (2002) 94-95
(*Krause, Deborah*); RBLit 4 (2002) 432-435 (*Seesengood, Robert
Paul*).

7471   *Trevijano Etcheverría, Ramón* Los viajes de Timoteo y la secuencia
de las paulinas. Estudios paulinos. 2002 <1999> ⇒248. 203-229.

7472   *Mitchell, Margaret M.* PTebt 703 and the genre of 1 Timothy: the
curious career of a Ptolemaic papyrus in Pauline scholarship. NT 44
(2002) 344-370.

7473   *Petit, Olivier* Une figure de la piété selon 1 Timothée. SémBib 108
(2002) 47-59.

7474   *Price, Robert M.* SCHLEIERMACHER's dormant discovery. JHiC 9/2
(2002) 203-216.

7475   *Tamez, Elsa 1 Timoteo* e *Giacomo* di fronte ai ricchi, alle donne e
alle dispute teologiche. Conc(I) 38/1 (2002) 66-78; Conc(E) 294,57-
66; Conc(D) 38/1,41-50; Conc(P) 294, 51-60.

7476   **Taniguchi, Yuko** To lead quiet and peaceable lives: rhetorical analysis of the first letter to Timothy. Diss. Harvard 2002 [HThR 95,347].

7477   *Heininger, Bernhard* Die "mystische" Eva: 1 Tim 2,8-15 und die Folgen des Sündenfalls in der Apokalypsis Mosis. BZ 46 (2002) 205-
221.

7478   **Holmes, J.M.** Text in a whirlwind: a critique of four exegetical
devices at 1 Timothy 2.9-15. JSNT.S 196; Studies in New Testament
Greek 7: 2000 ⇒16,7079. ᴿRBLit 4 (2002) 430-432 (*Köstenberger,
Andreas J.*).

7479   *Valleskey, D.* The victory of Christ for the pastor and his own personal warfare in the light of 1 Timothy 3:1-7. WLQ 99/1 (2002) 37-
54 [NTAb 46,490].

7480   *Petit, Olivier* 1 Timothée 4: où la piété se découvre une pratique sa-
lutaire. SémBib 105 (2002) 29-39;

7481   1 Timothée 5: des anciens, des veuves et un corps où le désir
s'incarne. SémBib 106 (2002) 26-40;

7482   1 Timothée 6: où Paul invite Timothée au combat de la foi. SémBib
107 (2002) 51-62.

7483 *Helm, Paul* John CALVIN on "before all ages". TynB 53 (2002) 143-
      148 [2 Tim 1,9; Titus 1,2].
7484 *Blocher, Henri* Les vases séparés (2 Timothée 2.19-21). ThEv(VS)
      1/2 (2002) 87-89.
7485 *Torres, Milton L.* Pauline vicissitudes and 2 Tim 3:11. Hermenêutíca
      2 (2002) 45-59 [BuBB 40,124].
7486 *Poythress, Vern Sheridan* The meaning of μάλιστα in 2 Timothy 4:13
      and related verses. JThS 53 (2002) 523-532.

7487 *Clark, David J.* Discourse structure in Titus. BiTr 53 (2002) 101-17.
7488 *Manicardi, Luciano* 'Si è manifestata la grazia di Dio... che ci
      insegna a vivere' (Tt 2,11-12). PSV 45 (2002) 111-128.
7489 *Van Neste, Ray* Structure and cohesion in Titus: problems and
      method. BiTr 53 (2002) 118-133.

G7.3 Ad Philemonem

7490 **Barth, Markus; Blanke, Helmut** The letter to Philemon: a new
      translation with notes and commentary. 2000 ⇒16,7088; 17,6971.
      [R]HeyJ 43 (2002) 360 (*Taylor, N.H.*); VJTR 66 (2002) 467-468
      (*Meagher, Patrick M.*); Bib. 83 (2002) 293-296 (*Osiek, Carolyn*);
      RBLit 4 (2002) 435-438 = JBL 121 (2002) 383-386 (*Byron, John*).
      Bentley, M. The guide—Coloss. and Philemon 2002 ⇒7408.
7491 **Burtchaell, James Tunstead** Philemon's problem: a theology of
      grace. [2]1998 ⇒14,6385; 15,7114. [R]EvQ 74 (2002) 184-186
      (*Stenschke, Christoph W.*).
7492 *Dana, H.E.* Philemon. SWJT 44/3 (2002) 60-69.
7493 **Fitzmyer, Joseph A.** The letter to Philemon. AncB 34C: 2000 ⇒16,
      7093; 17,6976. [R]IThQ 67 (2002) 177-178 (*O'Neill, J.C.*); ACR 79
      (2002) 501-502 (*Woods, Laurie*).
      Gaukroger, S.; Wood, D. Coloss. & Philemon 2002 ⇒7410.
7494 *Genre, Gianni* Filemone: un biglietto di accompagnamento. Protest.
      57/4 (2002) 267-274.
      Penna, R. Filippesi—Filemone 2002 ⇒7382.
      Reuter, R. Textvergleichende... Arbeit an den Briefen des NT:
      Kolosser- und Philemonbrief 2002 ⇒7411.

G8 Epistula ad Hebraeos

7495 **Attridge, Harold W.** La lettera agli Ebrei: commento storico esege-
      tico. 1999 ⇒15,7123...17,6982. [R]Asp. 49 (2002) 261-263 (*Di Pal-
      ma, Gaetano*); LASBF 51 (2001) 438-440 (*Bissoli, G.*).
7496 **deSilva, David A.** Perseverance in gratitude: a socio-rhetorical com-
      mentary on the epistle to the Hebrews. 2000 ⇒16,7100; 17,6983.
      [R]AThR 84 (2002) 417-418 (*Eisenbaum, Pamela M.*); EvQ 74 (2002)
      77-78 (*Ellingworth, Paul*).
7497 **Hagner, Donald Alfred** Encountering the book of Hebrews: an
      exposition. Encountering biblical studies: GR 2002, Baker 213 pp.
      $22. 0-8010-2580-X. Bibl. 197-200.
7498 **Karrer, Martin** Der Brief an die Hebräer: Kapitel 1,1-5,10. ÖTBK
      20/1: Gü 2002, Gü'er 278 pp. €29.90. 3-579-00520-0. Bibl. 13-23.

7499 **Koester, Craig R.** Hebrews. AncB 36: 2001 ⇒17,6985. [R]JThS 53 (2002) 263-266 (*Browne, Arnold S.*).
7500 **Lightfoot, Neil R.** Everyone's guide to Hebrews. GR 2002, Baker 184 pp. $13. 0-8010-6420-1 [ThD 50,81—Heiser, W. Charles].
7501 **Rouiller, Grégoire** "une voie nouvelle et vivante": l'épître aux Hébreux: textes et théologie. Cahier de l'ABC 9: FrS 2002, Association Biblique Catholique (Suisse Romande) 210 pp.
7502 **Schunack, Gerd** Der Hebräerbrief. ZBK 14: Z 2002, Theol. Verl. 247 pp. €30. 3-290-14747-9. Bibl. 241.

7503 **Anderson, David R.** The king-priest of Psalm 110 in Hebrews. Studies in Biblical Literature 21: 2001 ⇒17,6991. [R]RBLit (2002)* (*Goutzioudis, Moschos; Johnson, Richard W.*).
7504 *Attridge, Harold W.* God in Hebrews: urging children to heavenly glory. [F]ACHTEMEIER, P.: 2002 ⇒1. 197-209.
7505 *Corley, Bruce* We see Jesus: biblical vision for a new millennium. SWJT 44/3 (2002) 14-27.
7506 **deSilva, David A.** Bearing Christ's reproach. 1999 ⇒15,7135. [R]RBLit 4 (2002) 438-440 (*Goutzioudis, Moschos*);
7507 **Di Giovambattista, Fulvio** Il giorno dell'espiazione nella lettera agli Ebrei. TGr.T 61: 2000 ⇒16,7110; 17,6994. [R]RivBib 50 (2002) 106-111 (*Manzi, Franco*).
7508 *Emmrich, Martin* Pneuma in Hebrews: prophet and interpreter. WThJ 64 (2002) 55-71.
7509 *Finney, T.J.* Computer-oriented transcription, collation and analysis of the New Testament manuscript tradition (starting with Hebrews). Bible and computer. 2002 ⇒548. 435-461.
7510 *Garuti, Paolo* San Luca e la lettera agli Ebrei: un'antica teoria da riconsiderare?. San Luca evangelista. FRSEP 28: 2002 ⇒5731. 535-547.
7511 *Grieb, A. Katherine* Catholic Epistles: Hebrews, James, 1 Peter, 2 Peter, Jude. NT: introducing. 2002 ⇒332. 168-187.
7512 **Hoppin, Ruth** Priscilla's letter: finding the author of the epistle to the Hebrews. 2000 <1997> ⇒16,7115. [R]RBLit 4 (2002) 441-443 (*Johnson, Richard W.*).
7513 *Isaacs, Marie E.* Why bother with Hebrews?. HeyJ 43 (2002) 60-72.
7514 **Jones, Hywel R.** Let's study Hebrews. E 2002, Banner of Truth xxii; 169 pp. £6.
7515 *Kasiłowski, Piotr* Nowość kapłaństwa Chrystusa [The novelty of Christ's priesthood]. StBob 2 (2002) 5-24. Sum. 24. **P.**
7516 *Koester, Craig R.* Hebrews, rhetoric, and the future of humanity. CBQ 64 (2002) 103-123.
7517 *Koosed, Jennifer L.* Double bind: sacrifice in the epistle to the Hebrews. A shadow of glory. 2002 ⇒347. 89-101.
7518 *Linnemann, Eta* A call for a retrial in the case of the epsitle to the Hebrews. Faith & Mission 19/2 (2002) 19-59.
7519 *Manzi, Franco* Una recente ricerca su Melchisedek e l'angelologia nell'Epistola agli Ebrei e a Qumran. ATT 8 (2002) 301-324;
7520 L'"affidabilità" di Gesu nell'epistola agli Ebrei: in margine a un libro recente sulla "progettualità di Dio" e la "risposta del Cristo". RivBib 50 (2002) 311-327.
7521 *März, Claus-Peter* Das "Wort vom Kult" und der "Kult des Wortes": der Hebräerbrief und die rechte Feier des Gottesdienstes. Wie das Wort Gottes feiern?. QD 194: 2002 ⇒417. 82-98.

7522	**Molinaro, Italo** "Ha parlato nel Figlio": progettualità di Dio e risposta del Cristo nella lettera agli Ebrei. SBFA 55: 2001 ⇒17,7001. ^REL 116 (2002) 126-128 (*Manzi, Franco*); StFr 99 (2002) 174-177 (*Giovannetti, Ottaviano*); CDios 215 (2002) 320-321 (*Gutiérrez, J.*).
7523	*Olbricht, Thomas H.* Anticipating and presenting the case for Christ as high priest in Hebrews. Rhetorical argumentation. 2002 ⇒553. 355-372.
7524	*Peterson, David* God and scripture in Hebrews. The trustworthiness of God. 2002 ⇒410. 118-138.
7525	*Pilhofer, Peter* κρείττονος διαθήκης ἔγγυος: die Bedeutung der Präexistenzchristologie für die Theologie des Hebräerbriefs. Die frühen Christen. WUNT 145: 2002 <1996> ⇒225. 58-72.
7526	*Riesner, Rainer* Der Hebräer-Brief nach altkirchlichen Zeugnissen. EurJT 11 (2002) 15-29.
7527	**Salevao, Lutisone** Legitimation in the letter to the Hebrews: the construction and maintenance of a symbolic universe. JSNT.S 219: L 2002, Continuum viii; 448 pp. $145. 1-84127-261-2.
7528	*Schenck, Kenneth L.* PHILO and the epistle to the Hebrews: Ronald Williamson's study after thirty years. StPhiloA 14 (2002) 112-135.
7529	*Schunack, Gerd* Der Brief an die Hebräer: exegetische und theologische Bemerkungen. PTh 91 (2002) 124-131.
7530	**Vanhoye, Albert** La lettre aux Hébreux: Jésus-Christ, médiateur d'une nouvelle alliance. CJJC 84: P 2002, Desclée 235 pp. 2-7189-0963-3.
7531	*Vanhoye, Albert* L'ancora della speranza nell'epistola agli Ebrei. La speranza. 2002 ⇒277. 231-256.
7532	**Winter, Aloysius** Die überzeitliche Einmaligkeit des Heils im "Heute": zur Theologie des Hebräerbriefes. Neuried 2002, Ars Una ix; 299 pp. 3-89391-459-5. Bibl. 229-276.

7533	*Musvosvi, J.N.* Jesus as the model for the new humanity in Heb 2. Asia Adventist Seminary Studies [Silang, Cavite, Philippines] 4 (2001) 49-55 [NTAb 47,76].
7534	*McCruden, Kevin* Christ's perfection in Hebrews: divine beneficence as an exegetical key to Hebrews 2:10. BR 47 (2002) 40-62.
7535	*Theißen, Gerd* Der ferne und der nahe Gott: theologische Fragen einer Juristin (Hebr 4,14-5,9). Erlösungsbilder. 2002 ⇒1460. 165-172.
7536	**Kurianal, James** Jesus our high priest: Ps 110,4 as the substructure of Heb 5,1-7,28. EHS.T 693: 2000 ⇒16,7137. ^REL 116 (2002) 506-508 (*Manzi, Franco*); JJSS 1 (2001) 253-254 (*Kudiyiruppil, John*).
7537	*Cross, Anthony R.* The meaning of 'baptism' in Hebrews 6.2. Dimensions of baptism. JSNT.S 234: 2002 ⇒434. 163-186.
7538	*Nicole, Roger* Some comments on Hebrews 6:4-6, and the doctrine of the perseverance of God with the saints. Standing forth. 2002 <1975> ⇒215. 437-451.
7539	*Davidson, Richard M.* Inauguration or Day of Atonement?: a response to Norman Young's 'Old Testament background to Hebrews 6:19-20 revisited'. AUSS 40 (2002) 69-88.
7540	*Young, Norman H.* The Day of Dedication or the Day of Atonement?: the Old Testament background to Hebrews 6:19-20 revisited. AUSS 40 (2002) 61-68.
7541	*Steyn, Gert J.* The Vorlage of the Melchizedek phrases in Heb 7.1-4. APB 13 (2002) 207-223.

7542 *Bogacz, Roman* Kapłaństwo Chrystusa na wzór Melchizedeka (Hbr 7,1-28) [Il sacerdozio di Christo secondo l'ordine di Melchisedek]. ACra 34 (2002) 121-130.
7543 *Emmrich, Martin* 'Amtscharisma': through the eternal Spirit (Hebrews 9:14). BBR 12 (2002) 17-32.
7544 *Gleason, Randall C.* The eschatology of the warning in Hebrews 10:26-31. TynB 53 (2002) 97-120.
7545 **Rose, Christian** Die Wolke der Zeugen: eine exegetisch-traditions-geschichtliche Untersuchung zu Hebräer 10,32-12,3. WUNT 2/60: 1994 ⇒10,6253; 13,6784. [R]RB 109 (2002) 273-275 (*Garuti, Paolo*).
7546 *Cadwallader, Alan H.* Earth as host or stranger?: reading Hebrews 11 from diasporan experience. Earth story. 2002 ⇒322. 148-165.
7547 *Theißen, Gerd* Du liebst mich, also bin ich: Vertrauen als Lebenselement (Hebr 11,1). Erlösungsbilder. 2002 ⇒1460. 173-178.
7548 *Hetzel, Isabelle; Fritsch, Catherine* Hébreux 13,7-21: foi et sacrifice. Lire et Dire 53 (2002) 41-52 [BuBB 39,73].
7549 *Young, Norman H.* 'Bearing his reproach' (Heb 13.9-14). NTS 48 (2002) 243-261.
7550 *O'Neill, John C.* Who killed whom (4Q285) without the camp (Heb 13:12-13)?. JHiC 9/1 (2002) 125-139.

G9.1 **1 Petri** (vel I-II)

7551 **Elliott, John H.** 1 Peter. AncB 37B: 2000 ⇒16,7175; 17,7028. [R]BTB 32 (2002) 150-153 (*Achtemeier, Paul J.*).
7552 **Mazzeo, Michele** Lettere di Pietro; lettera di Giuda. Libri Biblici.NT 18: Mi 2002, Paoline 490 pp. 88-315-2256-6. Bibl. 429-450.
7553 *Novum Testamentum Graecum: editio critica maior,* 4: die Katholischen Briefe, Teil 1: Text, 2. Lfg.: die Petrusbriefe. [E]**Aland, B.,** *al.,* 2000 ⇒16,7156. [R]ThLZ 127 (2002) 297-300 (*Parker, David C.*).
7554 *Thiede, Carsten-Peter* The apostle Peter and the Jewish scriptures in 1 and 2 Peter. AnBru 7 (2002) 145-155.
7555 **Thiede, C.P.** Simone Pietro dalla Galilea a Roma. [T]*Scarabelli, R.; Vacca, V.*: 1999 ⇒15,7191. [R]ATT 8 (2002) 228-230 (*Ghiberti, Giuseppe*).

7556 *Cervantes Gabarrón, José* La ética de la disponibilidad en la primera carta de Pedro. [F]TREVIJANO ETCHEVERRÍA, R. 2002 ⇒122. 249-267.
7557 *Horrell, David G.* The product of a Petrine circle?: a reassessment of the origin and character of 1 Peter. JSNT 86 (2002) 29-60.
7558 *Marconi, Gilberto* La speranza nella prima lettera di Pietro. La speranza. 2002 ⇒277. 205-229.
7559 *Moy, Russell G.* Resident aliens of the diaspora: 1 Peter and Chinese Protestants in San Francisco. Semeia 90/91 (2002) 51-67.
7560 *Schlosser, Jacques* La résurrection de Jésus d'après la Prima Petri. [F]LAMBRECHT, J.: BEThL 165: 2002 ⇒72. 441-456.
7561 *Thurén, Lauri* Jeremiah 27 and civil obedience in 1 Peter. Zwischen den Reichen. TANZ 36: 2002 ⇒568. 215-228.

7562 *Dubuis, Francine* 1 Pierre 1,3-12: une même grâce pour tous. Lire et Dire 52 (2002) 3-12 [BuBB 40,132].
7563 *Beckman, John C.* Live a fear-of-God lifestyle, ransomed ones: 1 Peter 1:17-21. Stulos theological journal 10/1 (2002) 77-98.

7564 *Jobes, Karen H.* Got milk?: Septuagint Psalm 33 and the interpretation of 1 Peter 2:1-3. WThJ 64 (2002) 1-14.
7565 *Bornand, Eric; Subilia, Marc* Les pierres vivantes de 1 Pierre 2,1-10: une espérance en chantier. Lire et Dire 52 (2002) 13-24 [BuBB 40, 132].
7566 *Dunant, Sylvie; Allisson, David; Kahlil, Samuel* 1 Pierre 2,18-25: patience, le ver est dans le fruit. Lire et Dire 52 (2002) 27-37 [BuBB 40,132].
7567 *Van Rensburg, F.J.; Moyise, S.* Isaiah in 1 Peter 3:13-17: applying intertextuality to the study of the Old Testament in the New. Scriptura 80 (2002) 275-286 [NTAb 47,498].
7568 *McGowan, Mike* La structure en chiasme de 1 Pierre 3.17-4.2. ThEv(VS) 1/2 (2002) 47-73.
7569 *Schlosser, Jacques* Déluge et typologie dans 1 P 3,19-21. Typologie biblique. LeDiv (2002) 177-202.
7570 **Dubis, Mark** Messianic woes in First Peter: suffering and eschatology in 1 Peter 4:12-19. Studies in Biblical Literature 33: NY 2002, Lang xviii; 234 pp. $57. 0-8204-5186-X. Bibl. 192-210.
7571 *Holloway, Paul A.* Nihil inopinati accidisse—'nothing unexpected has happened': a Cyrenaic consolatory topos in 1 Pet 4.12ff. NTS 48 (2002) 433-448.

G9.2 **2 Petri**

7572 *Charles, J. Daryl* The function of moral typology in 2 Peter. Character and scripture. 2002 ⇒283. 331-343.
7573 **Gerdmar, Anders** Rethinking the Judaism-Hellenism dichotomy: a historiographical case study of Second Peter and Jude. CB.NT 36: 2001 ⇒17,7052. [R]TrinJ 23 (2002) 266-269 (*Yarbrough, Robert W.*).
7574 **Gilmour, Michael J.** The significance of parallels between 2 Peter and other early christian literature. Academia biblica 10: Atlanta, GA 2002, SBL xiii; 176 pp. $30. 1-58983-049-0. Bibl. 161-171. [R]SR 31 (2002) 432-433 (*Batten, Alicia*).
7575 **Kraftchick, Steven John** Jude, 2 Peter. Abingdon NT Commentaries: Nv 2002, Abingdon 190 pp. $20. 0-687-05762-0. Bibl. 181-186.
7576 **Kraus, Thomas J.** Sprache, Stil und historischer Ort des zweiten Petrusbriefes. WUNT 2/136 2001 ⇒17,7055. [R]ThLZ 127 (2002) 1303-1305 (*Fornberg, Tord*); SEÅ 67 (2002) 180-181 (*Gerdmar, Anders*); SNTU.A 27 (2002) 262-263 (*Kieffer, R.*).

7577 **Charles, J. Daryl** Virtue amidst vice: the catalog of virtues in 2 Peter 1. JSNT.S 150: 1997 ⇒13,6821; 15,7200. [R]Sal. 64 (2002) 389-391 (*Abbà, Giuseppe*).
7578 **Starr, James M.** Sharers in divine nature: 2 Peter 1:4 in its Hellenistic context. CB.NT 33: 2000 ⇒16,7198; 17,7059. [R]JThS 53 (2002) 278-281 (*Bauckham, Richard*).
7579 *Breed, D.G.; Van Rensburg, F.J.* Paraatmaking teen immoraliteit in 'n postmodenistiese samelewing: 'n hermeneuse van 2 Petrus 1:12-15. HTS 57 (2001) 408-434 [NTAb 46,493].
7580 *Kuske, D.P.* Exegetical brief: conveyed from heaven—2 Peter 1:17, 18, 21. WLQ 99/1 (2002) 55-57 [NTAb 46,493].

G9.4 **Epistula Jacobi**..data on both apostles James

7581 **Bottini, Giovanni Claudio** Giacomo e la sua lettera: una introduzione. SBFA 50: 2000 ⇒16,7200; 17,7064. ᴿCBQ 64 (2002) 151-153
(*Fiore, Benjamin*).
7582 **Burchard, Christoph** Der Jakobusbrief. HNT 15/1: 2000 ⇒16,
7202. ᴿThRv 98 (2002) 209-211 (*Frankemölle, Hubert*).
7583 ᵀ**Karsten, Matthias** BEDA Venerabilis: Kommentar zum Jakobusbrief. FC 40: 2000 ⇒16,7203. ᴿThLZ 127 (2002) 116-117 (*Haendler, Gert*).
7584 **Moo, Douglas J.** The letter of James. Pillar NT Commentary: 2000
⇒16,7204; 17,7077. ᴿBBR 12 (2002) 141-142 (*Davids, Peter H.*);
Orpheus 23 (2002) 269-270 (*Osculati, Roberto*).
7585 **Sleeper, Charles Freeman** James. Abingdon NT Commentaries:
1998 ⇒14,6465. ᴿRBLit 4 (2002) 444-446 (*Jackson-McCabe, Matt*).

7586 *Baker, William R.* Christology in the epistle of James. EvQ 74 (2002)
47-57.
7587 **Bauckham, Richard J.** James: wisdom of James, disciple of Jesus
the Sage. 1999 ⇒15,7222; 16,7209. ᴿJThS 53 (2002) 266-272
(*Carleton Paget, James*).
7588 *Casalini, Nello* Giacomo e la sua lettera. RivBib 50 (2002) 329-351.
7589 *Hengel, Martin* Jakobus der Herrenbruder—der erste "Papst"?. Paulus und Jakobus. WUNT 141: 2002 <1985> ⇒178. 549-582;
7590 Der Jakobusbrief als antipaulinische Polemik. Paulus und Jakobus.
WUNT 141: 2002 <1987> ⇒178. 511-548.
7591 **Jackson-McCabe, Matt A.** Logos & law in the letter of James. NT.
S 100: 2001 ⇒17,7075. ᴿCBQ 64 (2002) 577-579 (*Marcus, Joel*);
RBLit (2002)* (*Green, Joel B.*).
7592 **Kot, Tomasz** La fede, via della vita: composizione e interpretazione
della lettera di Giacomo. Retorica biblica 6: Bo 2002, EDB 299 pp.
€22. 88-10-25104-0. Bibl. 291-295.
7593 *Lambers-Petry, Doris* How to become a christian martyr: reflections
on the death of James as described by JOSEPHUS and in early christian literature. Studies on the Antiquities of Josephus. ᴱSiegert, Folker; Kalms, Jürgen U.: Münsteraner judaistische Studien 12: Müns
2002, Lit. 101-124.
7594 *Parker, David C.* The developmnet of the critical text of the epistle
of James: from LACHMANN to the Editio Critica Major. ᶠDELOBEL, J.:
BEThL 161: 2002 ⇒24. 317-330.
7595 *Syreeni, Kari* James and the Pauline legacy: power play in Corinth?.
ᶠRÄISÄNEN, H.: NT.S 103: 2002 ⇒97. 397-437.
    Tamez, E. 1 Timoteo e Giacomo 2002 ⇒7475.
7596 *Theissen, Gerd* Éthique et communauté dans l'épître de Jacques.
ETR 77 (2002) 157-176.
7597 *Wachob, Wesley Hiram* The apocalyptic intertexture of the epistle of
James. Intertexture. SBL.Symposium 14: 2002 ⇒385. 165-185.

7598 *Theißen, Gerd* Zwischen Wasser und Dürre: die Bilderwelt des Jako-
busbriefs (Jak 1,2-21). Erlösungsbilder. 2002 ⇒1460. 179-183.
7599 *Wilson, Walter T.* Sin as sex and sex with sin: the anthropology of
James 1:12-15. HThR 95 (2002) 147-168.

7600 *Van der Watt, J.* Sit u hier maar gaan staan jy daar': kantaantekeninge by Jakobus 2:1-4. HTS 57 (2001) 210-229 [NTAb 46,492].
7601 **Wachob, Wesley Hiram** The voice of Jesus in the social rhetoric of James. MSSNTS 106: 2000 ⇒16,7224; 17,7089. [R]JThS 53 (2002) 272-278 (*Painter, John*) [James 2,1-13].
7602 *Croatto, J. Severino* La fe che llega a su *teléiosis* o perfección (Santiago 2,22b): retórica, estructura literaria y teología de Santiago 2,14-26. RevBib 62 (2000) 101-119.
7603 *Yates, Jonathan* The epistle of James in AUGUSTINE and his Pelagian adversaries: some preliminary observations. Aug(L) 52 (2002) 273-290 [James 2,14-26].
7604 *Albl, Martin C.* "Are any among you sick?": the health care system in the letter of James. JBL 121 (2002) 123-143 [James 5,14-16].

G9.6 Epistula Judae

Gerdmar, A. The Judaism-Hellenism dichotomy 2001 ⇒7573.
7605 *Joubert, S.J.* When the dead are alive!: the influence of the living dead in the letter of Jude. HTS 58 (2002) 576-592 [NTAb 47,284].
Kraftchick, S. Jude, 2 Peter 2002 ⇒7575.
Mazzeo, M. Lettere di Pietro; lettera di Giuda 2002 ⇒7552.
7606 [E]**McGrath, A.; Packer, J.I.** Jude by Thomas MANTON. Leicester 1999, Crossway xi; 223 pp. £10. 1-58134-120-2 [NRTh 126,483—Radermakers, Jean].
7607 **Wilson, William Renay, II** Jude: apocalyptic eschatology as theological exclusivism. [D]*Carley, B.*: 2002, 292 pp. Diss. Fort Worth [RTL 34,602].

XIII. Theologia Biblica

H1.1 Biblical Theology [OT] God

7608 **Babut, Étienne** Le Dieu puissamment faible de la bible. LiBi 118: 1999 ⇒15,7258. [R]Brot. 154 (2002) 303-304 (*Silva, I. Ribeiro da*).
7609 **Barbiero, Gianguerrino** Dio di misericordia e di grazia: la rivelazione del volto di Dio in Esodo 32-34. CasM 2002, Portalupi 199 pp. 88-8441-015-0. Bibl. 193-196.
7610 *Baudler, Georg* "Ich lasse dich nicht los, bis dass du mich segnest": Befreiung von einem Gott der Gewalt. Evangelische Aspekte 12/3 (2002) 44-46.
7611 *Beyers, J.* 'n Ou-Testamentiese perspektief op sinkretisme: die aanbidding van die 'God van die voorvaders' as gevalle-studie. HTS 58 (2002) 1154-1173 [OTA 26,514].
7612 *Boulnois, Olivier* Unser Gottesbild und die Vorsehung. IKaZ 31 (2002) 303-323.
7613 **Bottéro, J.; Ouaknin, M.A.; Moingt, J.** La historia más bella de Dios: ?*quién es el Dios de la biblia?. [T]*Molina, O.C.*: 1998 ⇒14, 6506. [R]RelCult 48/1 (2002) 183-184 (*Moral, Alejandro*).

7614 **Charamsa, Krzysztof Olaf** L'immutabilità di Dio: l'insegnamento di San TOMMASO d'Aquino nei suoi sviluppi presso i commentatori scolastici. TGr.T 91: R 2002, E.P.U.G. 514 pp. €29. 88-7652-943-8.
7615 *Crüsemann, Frank* Gott als Anwalt der Kinder!?: zur Frage von Kinderrechten in der Bibel. JBTh 17 (2002) 183-197.
7616 *Debergé, Pierre* Dieu tout-puissant. Dieu, vingt-six portraits. 2002 ⇒ 312. 147-157.
7617 *Deiana, Giovanni* Bibbia e culture: fondamenti biblici per una teologia dell'inculturazione. ED 55 (2002) 19-40.
7618 **Dietrich, Walter; Link, Christian** Die dunklen Seiten Gottes, 1: Willkür und Gewalt. Neuk. ³2000 Neuk. 233 pp. 3-7887-1524-3. ᴿZNT 5 (2002) 67-69 (*Erlemann, Kurt*).
7619 *Dietrich, Walter* Gott als König: zur Frage nach der theologischen und politischen Legitimität religiöser Begriffsbildung <1980>;
7620 Gott der Rache versus Gott der Liebe?: wider die Verzerrung biblischer Gottesbilder <1999>;
7621 Grenzen göttlicher Macht nach dem Alten Testament <1999>. Theopolitik. 2002 ⇒159. 58-70/29-42/43-57.
7622 *Dolzani, Michael* The ashes of the stars: Northrop FRYE and the trickster-god. Semeia 89 (2002) 59-73.
7623 *Ebach, Jürgen; Frettlöh, Magdalene L.* Jabboq 2: zur Einführung. Gretchenfrage. 2002 ⇒399. 7-23.
7624 *Faessler, Marc* Dieu qui se tait;
7625 *Ferry, Joëlle* Dieu que l'on questionne. Dieu, vingt-six portraits. 2002 ⇒312. 279-295/263-277.
7626 *Fretheim, Terence E.* Theological reflections on the wrath of God in the Old Testament. HBT 24/2 (2002) 1-26.
7627 *Fullerton, J. Andrew* God by any other name?. MoTh 18 (2002) 171-181.
7628 *Gibert, Pierre* Dieu sage;
7629 *Gomez-Géraud, Marie-Christine* Dieu qui voit tout;
7630 *Grappe, Christian* Dieu qui se manifeste. Dieu, vingt-six portraits. 2002 ⇒312. 159-172/203-212/237-246.
7631 *Harg, Joseph* "Der in den Himmeln wohnt, er lacht ...": biblische Spurensuche nach dem Humor Gottes, Teil 1. CPB 115 (2002) 90-4.
7632 *Highfield, Ron* Divine self-limitation in the theology of Jürgen MOLTMANN: a critical appraisal. CScR 32 (2002) 49-71.
7633 **Hunziker-Rodewald, Regine** Hirt und Herde: ein Beitrag zum alttestamentlichen Gottesverständnis. BWANT 155: 2001 ⇒17,7122. ᴿThZ 58 (2002) 363-364 (*Weber, Beat*).
7634 *Kal, Victor* Der Barmherzige (Ha-Rachaman) und die Freiheit des Menschen. Gretchenfrage. Jabboq 2: 2002 ⇒399. 111-126.
7635 *Kearney, Richard* God who may be: a phenomenological study. MoTh 18 (2002) 75-85.
7636 *Klein, Stephanie* Das männliche Gottesbild und die Religiosität von Frauen und Männern. Die zwei Geschlechter. 2002 ⇒7637. 9-27.
7637 ᴱ*Klinger, Elmar; Böhm, Stephanie; Franz, Thomas* Die zwei Geschlechter und der eine Gott. Wü 2002, Echter 125 pp. 3-429-02517-6.
7638 *L'Hour, Jean* Dieu perd la parole. Dieu, vingt-six portraits. 2002 ⇒ 312. 247-262.
7639 *Lang, Bernhard* Der Gott der Bibel. Die Bibel: Geschichte und Gegenwart. 2002 ⇒971. 34-43, 46-48.

7640 **Lang, Bernhard** The Hebrew God: portrait of an ancient deity. NHv 2002, Yale University Press x: 246 pp. £25. 0-300-09025-0. Bibl. 230-239. [R]BTB 32 (2002) 192-193 (*Gnuse, Robert*);

7641 *Jahwe der biblische Gott: ein Portrait*. Mü 2002, Beck 320 pp. €22. 90. 3-406-48713-0. [R]LuThK 26 (2002) 204-205 (*Kandler, Karl-Hermann*).

7642 *Lavoie, Jean-Jacques* Dieu créateur. Dieu, vingt-six portraits. 2002 ⇒312. 135-145.

7643 **Magnani, Giovanni** Religione e religioni, 1: dalla monolatria al monoteismo profetico. 2001 ⇒17,7132. [R]CivCatt 153/1 (2002) 614-615 (*Salatiello, G.*).

7644 *Manoussakis, John P.* From exodus to eschaton: on the God who may be. MoTh 18 (2002) 95-107.

7645 *Marguerat, Daniel* La pudeur de Dieu;

7646 *Marx, Alfred* Dieu de l'univers, Dieu des marginaux. Dieu, vingt-six portraits. 2002 ⇒312. 77-84/27-35.

7647 *Meurer, Thomas* Aggressiver Monotheismus im Alten Testament?. rhs 45 (2002) 351-358.

7648 **Miggelbrink, Ralf** Der zornige Gott: die Bedeutung einer anstößigen biblischen Tradition. Da:Wiss 2002, 168 pp. €19.90. 3-534-15582-3. [R]ZNT 5 (2002) 70-72 (*Erlemann, Kurt*).

7649 *Nodet, Étienne* Dieu dans l'histoire ou Dieu hors de l'histoire;

7650 *Pelletier, Anne-Marie* Dieu qui vient juger. Dieu, vingt-six portraits. 2002 ⇒312. 47-54/173-182.

7651 *Pérez Fernández, Miguel* Experienca y manifestación de Dios en la literatura y la liturgia del Judaísmo Clásico. EstTrin 36 (2002) 205-230.

7652 **Phillips, Graham** The Moses legacy: in search of the origins of God. L 2002, Sidgwick & J. xi; 327 pp. 0-283-07315-2. Bibl. 311-320.

7653 *Pilch, John J.* God and the lying spirits. BiTod 40 (2002) 112-116.

7654 *Pixley, Jorge* Dio, pomo della discordia nella bibbia ebraica. Conc(I) 38/1 (2002) 15-24; Conc(E) 294,11-18; Conc(D) 38/1,3-10; Conc(P) 294, 9-16.

7655 *Prévost, Jean-Pierre* Dieu qui se ravise. Dieu, vingt-six portraits. 2002 ⇒312. 87-99.

7656 *Rizzuto, Ana-María* One God, two genders: psychoanalytic reflections. Die zwei Geschlechter. 2002 ⇒7637. 29-45.

7657 *Roukema, Riemer* La transcendance et la proximité de Dieu dans le christianisme ancien. RHPhR 82/1 (2002) 15-31.

7658 *Römer, Thomas* Dieu guerrier. Dieu, vingt-six portraits. 2002 ⇒312. 125-134;

7659 La violence de Dieu dans l'Ancien Testament. Variations Herméneutiques 16 (2002) 3-19 [BuBB 37,13].

7660 *Sans, Isidro M.* Dios fuego. EE 77 (2002) 73-97.

7661 *Schmidt, N.F.; Nel, P.J.* Theophany as type-scene in the Hebrew Bible. JSem 11/2 (2002) 256-281.

7662 *Speyer, Wolfgang* Zur Grundstruktur und Geschichte des Gottesgedankens. [F]HOHEISEL, K.: JAC.E 34: 2002 ⇒59. 456-463.

7663 *Steffensky, Fulbert* Was meine ich eigentlich, wenn ich Gott sage?. Gretchenfrage. Jabboq 2: 2002 ⇒399. 24-35.

7664 *Tamani, Giuliano* Dio, Israele e la legge nel mondo ebraico dei secoli VI-IV a.C. CredOg 129 (2002) 143-154.

7665 **Thabut, Marie-Noëlle** A la découverte du Dieu inattendu. P 2002, Desclée de B. 144 pp. €14.

7666   *Van de Beek, A.* God's omnipotence and human freedom. [F]POTGIE-
       TER, P.: AcTh(B).S 3: 2002 ⇒92. 169-186.
7667   *Vanoni, Gottfried* Gott als oberste und letzte Gewalt: Abwägungen
       aus bibeltheologischer Sicht. Diak. 33 (2002) 320-325.
7668   *Van Oyen, Geert* De godsbeelden in Israël en Jezus: verbanden tus-
       sen verbonden. KeTh 53 (2002) 224-236.
7669   *Van Wolde, Ellen* Prospettive diverse sulla fede e la giustizia: il Dio
       di Giacobbe e il Dio di Giobbe. Conc(I) 38/1 (2002) 25-33; Conc(E)
       294,19-26; Conc(D) 38/1,10-17; Conc(P) 294,17-24.
7670   *Voorwinde, Stephen* Does God have real feelings?. VR 67 (2002) 24-
       51.
7671   **Wackenheim, Charles** Quand Dieu se tait. P 2002, Cerf 190 pp.
       €22. 2-204-06919-1.
7672   *Weinrich, Michael* Wir sind aber Menschen: von der möglichen Un-
       möglichkeit, von Gott zu reden. Gretchenfrage. Jabboq 2: 2002 ⇒
       399. 36-99.
7673   *Wénin, André* Dieu jaloux. Dieu, vingt-six portraits. 2002 ⇒312. 67-
       76.
7674   *Wilke, Annette* Aktuelles zur Gretchenfrage: "Wiederkehr des Religi-
       ösen" und mediale Inszenierung des "Kampfes der Kulturen". Gret-
       chenfrage. Jabboq 2: 2002 ⇒399. 137-171.
7675   *Yekutieli, Yuval* Divine royal power. [F]GOPHNA, R.: 2002 ⇒49. 243-
       253.
7676   *Zeeb, Frank* Jahwe und der Sonnengott. [F]DIETRICH, M.: 2002 ⇒28.
       899-917.

H1.3 *Immutabilitas*—God's suffering; process theology

7677   **Gnuse, Robert K.** The Old Testament and process theology. 2000
       ⇒16,7293; 17,7154 [R]RBLit 4 (2002) 151-154 (*Heard, R. Christoph-
       er*); CBQ 64 (2002) 348-349 (*Penchansky, David*).

H1.4 *Femininum in Deo*—God as father and mother

7678   *Ballabio, Fabio* Cura passione e tenerezza: il volto materno di Dio
       nella tradizione ebraica. Studi Fatti Ricerche 100 (2002) 7-10.
7679   **Böckler, Annette** Gott als Vater im Alten Testament: traditionsge-
       schichtliche Untersuchungen zur Entstehung und Entwicklung eines
       Gottesbildes, Jes 63,16. 2000 ⇒16,7298; 17,7155. [R]OrdKor 43
       (2002) 111 (*Heinemann, Franz Karl*); YESW 10 (2002) 233-234
       (*Baumann, Gerlinde*).
7680   *Cazelles, Henri* Maternité et bible. Com(F) 37/2 (2002) 91-101.
7681   *Graesslé, Isabelle* Dieu masculin. Dieu, vingt-six portraits. 2002 ⇒
       312. 113-122.
7682   *Lasine, Stuart* Divine narcissism and Yahweh's parenting style.
       BiblInterp 10 (2002) 36-56.
7683   *Nel, Philip* Does changing the metaphor liberate?: on the 'fatherhood'
       of God. OTEs 15 (2002) 131-148.
7684   *Nieuviarts, Jacques* Dieu père ou mère?. Dieu, vingt-six portraits.
       2002 ⇒312. 297-310.

7685 **Ravasi, Gianfranco** La paternité de Dieu dans la bible: cycle de conférences bibliques. [T]*Rouers, Simone*: Saint-Maurice 2002, Saint-Augustin 132 pp. €16. 2-88011-261-3.

7686 **Schäfer, Peter** Mirror of His beauty: feminine images of God from the bible to the early kabbalah. Jews, Christians and Muslims from the ancient to the modern world: Princeton, NJ 2002, Princeton Univ. Pr. xv (2); 306 pp. $30. 0-691-09068-8. Bibl. 289-300.

7687 *Strotmann, Angelika* Die Vaterschaft Gottes in der Bibel. Biblisches Forum 1 (2002)*.

7688 **Tasker, David R.** The fatherhood of God: an exegetical study from the Hebrew scriptures. [D]*Doukhan, J.B.*: 2002, 332 pp. Diss. Andrews [RTL 34,594].

7689 *Thanner, Natanael* 'Pai nosso que estais Déus': por que Deus pai e não 'Deusa Mãe'?. Sapientia Crucis 3/3 (2002) 61-87 [BuBB 38,95].

7690 *Vermeylen, Jacques* Dieu féminin. Dieu, vingt-six portraits. 2002 ⇒ 312. 101-111.

7691 **Widdicombe, Peter** The fatherhood of God from ORIGEN to ATHANASIUS. 2000 ⇒16,7312. [R]ThTo 59 (2002) 160, 162 (*Rusch, William G.*); RSPhTh 86 (2002) 511-513 (*Meunier, Bernard*).

H1.7 Revelatio

7692 *Abraham, William J.* The offense of divine revelation. HThR 95 (2002) 251-264.

7693 *Bernhardt, Reinhold* Offenbarung als Erschliessungsgeschehen. ThZ 58 (2002) 61-80.

7694 *Bordoni, Marcello* Riflessione teologica sulla verità della rivelazione cristiana. Path 1 (2002) 251-266.

7695 *Bultmann, Rudolf* Der Begriff des Wortes Gottes im Neuen Testament <1933>;

7696 Die Frage der natürlichen Offenbarung <1941>. NT und christliche Existenz. UTB 2316: 2002 ⇒152. 122-147/181-206.

7697 *Castaño Félix, Angel* La revelación como testimonio en el Nuevo Testamento. Teología y Catequesis 81 (2002) 17-34.

7698 **Dotolo, Carmelo** La rivelazione cristiana: parola evento mistero. Mi 2002, Paoline 205 pp. €11.36. [R]CivCatt 153/4 (2002) 623-624 (*Mazzolini, S.*).

7699 **Fisichella Rino** La rivelazione: evento e credibilità. Corso di teologia sistematica 2: Bo [8]2002, Dehoniane 618 pp. 88-10-50352-X. [R]Path 1 (2002) 386-387 (*Amato, Angelo*).

7700 *Gäde, Gerhard* Der Zumutungscharakter der christlichen Botschaft: seine Bedeutung für eine Theologie der Religionen. FZPhTh 49 (2002) 166-188.

7701 **Gracia, Jorge J.E.** How can we know what God means?: the interpretation of revelation. 2001 ⇒17,7178. [R]CBQ 64 (2002) 762-763 (*Bergant, Dianne*).

7702 **Greco, Carlo** La rivelazione: fenomenologia, dottrina e credibilità. Intellectus fidei: 2000 ⇒16,7325; 17,7179. [R]RdT 43 (2002) 292-294 (*Ardusso, Franco*).

7703 **Halivni, David Weiss** Revelation restored: divine writ and critical responses. 2001 ⇒17,9541. [R]Theol. 105 (2002) 358-359 (*Clements, Ronald E.*).

7704 **Jensen, Peter** The revelation of God. Contours of Christian Theology: DG 2002, IVP 304 pp.
7705 *Lamberth, David* Discernment and practice: questions for a logic of revelation–response to William Abraham. HThR 95 (2002) 273-276.
7706 **Maggioni, Bruno** La difficile fede: figure dell'Antico Testamento, 1: dai patriarchi all'esilio. In cammino: Mi 2002, Àncora 153 pp. 88-51-4-0030-X.
7707 *Mello, Alberto* Quando Dio si nasconde: una metafora della rivelazione biblica. LASBF 52 (2002) 9-28.
7708 **Moingt, Joseph** Dieu qui vient à l'homme: du deuil au dévoilement de Dieu. CFi 222: P 2002, Cerf 560 pp. €45. 2-204-06909-4 [RB 109,638].
7709 **Moran, Gabriel** Both sides: the story of revelation. Mahwah 2002, Paulist ix; 275 pp. $23. 0-8091-4105-1 [ThD 50,176—Heiser, W.C.].
7710 *Pratas, Maria Helena da Guerra* Harmonia de acções e palavras na economia da revelação. Theologica 37 (2002) 305-314.
7711 *Rehnman, Sebastian* A realist conception of revelation. The trustworthiness of God. 2002 ⇒410. 253-272.
7712 *Rossano, Pietro* Rivelazione e storia della salvezza <1967>;
7713 La rivelazione come dialogo di Dio con l'uomo <1968>. Teologia cristiana. DMis 27: 2002 ⇒232. 229-236/201-213.
7714 **Samuelson, Norbert Max** Revelation and the God of Israel. C 2002, CUP x; 259 pp. $60. 0-521-81202-X. Bibl. 242-247.
7715 *Schüssler Fiorenza, Francis* A Roman Catholic perspective on the offense of revelation—response to William Abraham. HThR 95 (2002) 265-271.
7716 **Sell, Alan P.F.** Confessing and commending the faith: historic witness and apologetic method. Cardiff 2002, Univ. of Wales Pr. 500 pp.
7717 **Theobald, Christoph** La révélation... tout simplement. 2001 ⇒17, 7188. [R]RevSR 76 (2002) 110-111 (*Deneken, Michel*).
7718 *Van der Toorn, Karel* Sources in heaven: revelation as a scholarly construct in second temple Judaism. [F]WEIPPERT, M.: OBO 186: 2002 ⇒133. 265-277.

H1.8 Theologia fundamentalis

7719 **Dola, Tadeusz** Teologia misteriów życia Jezusa [Theologie der Mysterien des Lebens Jesu]. Opole 2002, Świętego Krzyża 312 pp. 83-88939-24-6. P.
7720 **Hasenhütl, Gotthold** Glaube ohne Mythos, 1: Offenbarung, Jesus Christus, Gott, 2: Mensch, Glaubensgemeinschaft, Symbolhandlungen, Zukunft. 2001 ⇒17,7196. [R]Conc(D) 38/1 (2002) 109-111 (*Dankert, Jürgen*).
7721 **Körtner, Ulrich H.J.** Theologie des Wortes Gottes: Positionen—Probleme—Perspektiven. 2001 ⇒17,7198. [R]ÖR 51 (2002) 397-399 (*Werbick, Jürgen*).
7722 *Lemieux, Raymond* Théologie de l'écriture et écriture théologique: l'invention de l'autre. LTP 58 (2002) 221-241.
7723 **Patrick, Dale A.** The rhetoric of revelation in the Hebrew Bible. 1999 ⇒15,7382...17,7200. [R]HBT 24 (2002) 129-31 (*Watts, James*).

7724 **Pié-Ninot, S.** La teologia fondamentale: 'rendere ragione della speranza' (1Pt 3,15). BTC 121: Brescia 2002, Queriniana 688 pp. €48.50.

7725 **Westra, Liuwe H.** The Apostles' Creed: origin, history, and some early commentaries. IP 43: Turnhout 2002, Brepols (6); 603 pp. 2-503-51395-6. Bibl. 565-584.

H2.1 Anthropologia theologica—VT & NT

7726 **Apfelbacher, Karl-Ernst** Selig die Trauernden: kulturgeschichtliche Aspekte des Christentums. Rg 2002, Pustet 464 pp. €40. 3-7917-179-7-9.

7727 *Arx, Urs von* The gender aspects of creation from a theological, christological, and soteriological perspective: an exegetical contribution. AThR 84 (2002) 519-554.

7728 *Baker, D.W.* The wind and the waves: biblical theology in protology and eschatology. AThJ 34 (2002) 13-37 [NTAb 47,293].

7729 *Bakon, Shimon* Suffering: three biblical views. JBQ 30 (2002) 183-190.

7730 **Bar, Shaul** A letter that has not been read: dreams in the Hebrew Bible. [T]*Schramm, Lenn J.*: MHUC 25: 2001 ⇒17,7205. [R]RBLit (2002)* (*Gnuse, Robert*); JBL 121 (2002) 536-537 (*Flannery-Dailey, Frances*).

7731 *Bartolini, Elena* Dio ci chiederà conto dei beni di cui non abbiamo goduto. PSV 45 (2002) 55-68.

7732 **Basset, Lytta** Sainte colère: Jacob, Job, Jésus. Genève 2002, Labor et F. 328 pp. [Choisir 520,41—Desthieux, Monique].

7733 *Bauckham, Richard* Freedom in the bible: Exodus and service. God and the crisis. 2002 <1989> ⇒142. 7-25.

7734 **Báez Ortega, Silvio José** Tiempo de callar y tiempo de hablar: el silencio en la biblia hebrea. 2000 ⇒16,7345. [R]RivBib 50 (2002) 362-364 (*Strola, Germana*).

7735 *Báez, Silvio José* 'Siate santi, perché io, il Signore, Dio vostro, sono santo' (Lev 19,2): la santità nella bibbia: attributo divino e vocazione umana. RVS 56 (2002) 364-386.

7736 **Berquist, Jon L.** Controlling corporeality: the body and the household in ancient Israel. New Brunswick, NJ 2002, Rutgers University Pr. xiii; 238 pp. $22. 0-8135-3015-6. Bibl. 217-229.

7737 *Bertuletti, Angelo* Tra l'esegesi e la teologia: l'antropologia. Teol(Br) 27 (2002) 11-19.

7738 **Bénétreau, Samuel** Bonheur des hommes, bonheur de Dieu: spécificité et paradoxe de la joie chrétienne. 2001 ⇒17,7210. [R]EvTh(VS) 1/2 (2002) 106-108 (*Carrez, Maurice*).

7739 **Bordreuil, Pierre; Briquel-Chatonnet, Françoise** Le temps de la bible. P 2002, Gallimard 461 pp [FV 102/5,105—Gabriel Vahanian].

7740 *Bosch ı Veciana, Antoni* Perdonar. Perdó i reconciliació. 2002 ⇒ 591. 11-37.

7741 *Botero Giraldo, J. Silvio* La verdad y el amor: presencia de un binomio en la S. Escritura y en el magisterio. StMor 40 (2002) 425-465.

7742 *Bowald, Béatrice; Halter, Hans* "Preist Gott mit eurem Leib!" (1 Kor 6,20): Leiblichkeit aus biblisch-ethischer Perspektive. Diak. 33 (2002) 235-241.

7743 *Buell, Denise Kimber* Race and universalism in early christianity. JECS 10 (2002) 429-468.
7744 *Bultmann, Rudolf* Welchen Sinn hat es, von Gott zu reden? <1925>; .
7745 Der Gedanke der Freiheit nach antikem und christlichem Verständnis <1959>. NT und christliche Existenz. 2002 ⇒152. 1-12/274-283.
7746 *Burggraeve, Roger* De bijbel als denkwijze en de eigenzinnige wijsheid van de liefde. Coll. 32/1 (2002) 47-80.
7747 *Cannuyer, Christian* Lebt Gott im Himmel?: Himmel und Licht in religiösen Bildern und Texten. WUB 26 (2002) 5-9.
7748 *Carrière, Jean-Marie* Le respect dans la bible. Christus 195 (2002) 284-293.
7749 *Chartrand, Martin; Duhaime, Jean* L'homme et l'animal: sélection bibliographique. Théologiques 10/1 (2002) 179-205.
7750 *Colombo, Giuseppe* Il cristiano e la croce. PSV 45 (2002) 129-133.
7751 *Davis, Stephen J.* Crossed texts, crossed sex: intertextuality and gender in early christian legends of holy women disguised as men. JECS 10 (2002) 1-36.
7752 **Debergé, Pierre** Amore e sessualità nella bibbia. CinB 2002, San Paolo 140 pp.;
7753 L'amour et la sexualité dans la bible. 2001 ⇒17,7225. [R]RCatT 27/1 (2002) 242-244 (*Salvat, Ignasi*); ActBib 39 (2002) 173-175 (*Salvat, Ignasi*).
7754 **DeSilva, David Arthur** Honor, patronage, kinship & purity: unlocking New Testament culture. 2000 ⇒16,7356. [R]CBQ 64 (2002) 156-157 (*Osiek, Carolyn*); RBLit 4 (2002) 322-324 (*Litwak, Ken*).
7755 *Dickson, Charles* Response: does the Hebrew Bible have anything to say about homosexuality?. OTEs 15 (2002) 350-367.
7756 *Edgar, Brian* Biblical anthropology and the intermediate state. EvQ 74 (2002) 27-45, 109-121.
7757 **Elliott, Matthew** Emotion and the New Testament: a critique of emotion in New Testament studies and analysis of emotion in the New Testament. 2002 Diss. Aberdeen [RTL 34,597].
7758 **Estrada-Barbier, Bernardo** "Lieti nella speranza": la gioia nel Nuovo Testamento. Studi di teologia 8: 2001 ⇒17,7229. [R]Annales Theologici 16 (2002) 233-237 (*De Virgilio, G.*); EstB 60 (2002) 429-431 (*Moreno García, Abdón*).
7759 **Falque, Emmanuel** Le Passeur de Gethsémani: angoisse, souffrance et mort: lecture existentielle et phénoménologique. 1999 ⇒15,7405. [R]RSR 90 (2002) 466-467 (*Olivier, Paul*).
7760 **Felder, Cain Hope** Race, racism, and the biblical narratives. Facets: Mp 2002, Fortress (6) 54 pp. 0-8006-3578-7.
7761 *Fernández-Martos, José María* 'Locos de alegría, abandonar a toda prisa los sepulcros' (Mt 28,8): trabajándose el optimismo y acogiendo la alegría verdadera. SalTer 90 (2002) 835-847.
7762 *Fischer, Irmtraud* Über Lust und Last, Kinder zu haben: soziale, genealogische und theologische Aspekte in der Literatur Alt-Israels. JBTh 17 (2002) 55-82.
7763 **Fisher, Loren** Who hears the cries of the innocent?. Willits, Calif. 2002, Fisher 124 pp. 1-4010-4025-X; 1-4010-4026-8.
7764 *Frame, John* Uomo e donna ad immagine di Dio. Studi di teologia 14 (2002) 151-166.
7765 *Frenschkowski, Marco; Morgenthaler, Christoph* Traum. TRE 34. 2002 ⇒800. 28-50.

7766 *Furnish, Victor Paul* La bibbia e l'omosessualità: i testi letti nel loro contesto. Bibbia e omosessualità. 2002 <1994> ⇒310. 9-36.

7767 *Gagnon, Robert A.J.* Are there universally valid sex precepts?: a critique of Walter Wink's views on the bible and homosexuality. HBT 24/1 (2002) 72-125.

7768 *Gangemi, Attilio* La morte e il dono della vita nelle scritture. Synaxis 20/1 (2002) 7-32.

7769 **García Trapiello, Jesús** El hombre según la biblia. S 2002, San Esteban 306 pp. ᴿCommunio 35 (2002) 495-497 (*Garzón, F. Javier*).

7770 *Giokarines, Konstantinos M.* A patristic basis for a theological anthropology of women in their distinctive humanity. AThR 84 (2002) 585-608.

7771 *Gordon, J.D.* Where to lay their heads?: gender, anthropology and New Testament interpretation. TJT 18 (2002) 115-128.

7772 *Grenz, Stanley J.* The social God and the relational self: toward a theology of the Imago Dei in the postmodern context. HBT 24/1 (2002) 33-57.

7773 *Gubler, Marie-Louise* Segen und Fluch in der Bibel. Diak. 33 (2002) 11-17.

7774 **Hahn, Udo** Grundbegriffe Christentum: Segen. GTBS 688: Gü 2002, Gü 62 pp. 3-579-00688-6.

7775 *Hasenfratz, Hans-Peter, al.,* Tod. TRE 33. 2002 ⇒799. 579-638.

7776 **Heckel, Ulrich** Der Segen im Neuen Testament: Begriff, Formeln, Gesten: mit einem praktisch-theologischen Ausblick. ᴰ*Lichtenberger, E.*: WUNT 150: Tü 2002, Mohr S. x; 431 pp. €39/79. 3-16-147855-X. Diss.-Habil. Tübingen [Bibl. 374-400].

7777 *Hieke, Thomas* "Schon zähle ich zu denen, die in die Grube fahren ..." (Ps 88,5): einige Sichtweisen des Todes im Alten Testament. LebZeug 57 (2002) 164-177.

7778 *Hohnjec, Nikola* Tri biblijske filozofije života: život kao ispraznost (Prop), trpljenje (Job) i ljubav (Pj) [Three biblical philosophies of life: the life as vanity (Eccl), the life as suffering (Job) and the life as love (Song)]. Obnovljeni Život 57 (2002) 333-351 Sum. 351. **Croatian.**

7779 *Janecko, Benedict* Friendship in the bible. Spiritual Life 48 (2002) 170-179.

7780 *Kaiser, Otto* Freiheit im Alten Testament. ꟳDIETRICH, M.: 2002 ⇒28. 177-190.

7781 *Kalluveettil, Paul* 'Rest' as celebrative mission—biblical foundations. Third Millennium 5/4 (2002) 100-104.

7782 *Kähler, Christoph* Was tun wir, wenn wir segnen?. ThBeitr 33 (2002) 260-273.

7783 *Kealy, Seán* Humour and Jesus. DoLi 52 (2002) 132-137.

7784 *Kirchschläger, Walter* Marriage as convenant [!]: a biblical approach to a familiar notion. INTAMS Review 8 (2002) 153-163. Rés. 163.

7785 **Klawans, Jonathan** Impurity and sin in ancient Judaism. 2000 ⇒16, 7384; 17,7252. ᴿJJS 53 (2002) 173-174 (*Satlow, Michael L.*).

7786 *Knoche, Hansjürgen* Mensch und Tier in der neuen Schöpfung. US 57 (2002) 292-303.

7787 *Koerrenz, Ralf* 'Vom Kinde aus'—Nachdenken über einen Anspruch. JBTh 17 (2002) 369-387.

7788 **Kosmider, Boguslaw Wieslaw** Studio teologico del dramma dello spirito ribelle: interpretazione sulla base della teologia della persona. R 2002, Pontificia Universitas Sanctae Crucis 332 pp. Bibl. 305-332.

7789   **Lasine, Stuart** Knowing kings: knowledge, power, and narcissism in the Hebrew Bible. SBL Semeia Studies 40: 2001 ⇒17,7256. ᴿCBQ 64 (2002) 355-357 (*Moore, Michael S.*); RBLit (2002)* (*Cohn, Robert L.*).

7790   *Lefebvre, Philippe* Appel pour une enquête biblique sur les termes 'frères' et 'soeurs'. Cahiers de l'Atelier 498 (2002) 47-60.

7791   *Lewis, Robert P.* "No more male and female": bodiliness and eucharist in Andre Dubus's stories. Religion and the arts 6/1 (2002) 36-51.

7792   *López, Mariola* 'Entra en el gozo de tu Señor': la alegría en la tradición bíblica. SalTer 90 (2002) 813-834.

7793   *Lutterbach, Hubertus* 'Was ihr einem dieser Kleinen getan habt, das habt ihr mir getan ...': der historische Beitrag des Christentums zum 'Jahrhundert des Kindes'. JBTh 17 (2002) 199-223.

7794   **Malina, Bruce J.** The New Testament world: insights from cultural anthropology. ³2001 ⇒17,7262. ᴿNBl 83 (2002) 99-101 (*Ferguson, Neil*).

7795   *Marucci, Corrado* Tempo ed eternità nel Nuovo Testamento: un tentativo di sintesi. Tempo ed eternità. 2002 ⇒545. 141-163.

7796   *Masenya, Madipoane* '... but you shall let every girl live': reading Exodus 1:1-2:10 the Bosadi (womanhood) way. OTEs 15 (2002) 99-112.

7797   *McCabe, R.V.* The Old Testament foundation for separation. Detroit Baptist Seminary Journal [Allen Park, MI] 7 (2002) 3-22 [NTAb 47, 292].

7798   *Mead, James K.* "All our griefs to bear": a biblical and theological reflection. RefR(H) 56/1 (2002) 5-18.

7799   *Meeks, Wayne A.* The image of the androgyne: some uses of a symbol in earliest christianity. In search. 2002 ⇒208. 3-54.

7800   *Meinhold, Arndt* Menschsein in der Welt vor Gott: alttestamentliche Perspektiven. Zur weisheitlichen Sicht. 2002 ⇒209. 13-34 [BuBB 39,103];

7801   Bewertung und Beginn des Greisenalters. Zur weisheitlichen Sicht. 2002 ⇒209. 99-116 [BuBB 39,111].

7802   **Miggelbrink, Ralf** Der Zorn Gottes: Geschichte und Aktualität einer ungeliebten biblischen Tradition. 2000 ⇒16,7407; 17,7266. ᴿFZPhTh 49 (2002) 515-517 (*Schenker, Adrian*).

7803   **Moore, Stephen D.** God's beauty parlor and other queer spaces in and around the bible. Contraversions: Jews and other differences. Stanford 2001, Standord Univ. Pr. xv; 244 pp. 0-8047-4332-0.

7804   *Müller, Peter* Gottes Kinder: zur Metaphorik der Gotteskindschaft im Neuen Testament. JBTh 17 (2002) 141-161.

7805   *Nadeau, Jean-Guy* Dicotomia o unione dell'anima e del corpo?: le origini dell'ambivalenza del cristianesimo nei confronti del corpo. Conc(I) 38 (2002) 244-255.

7806   *Noratto G., José Alfredo* El ser humano en la cultura semita: breve acercamiento narrativo. ThX 52 (2002) 599-614.

7807   *Núñez, José Miguel* Luchando con el angel una metáfora para no-velar el acontecer de la existencia. Isidorianum 21 (2002) 223-233 [Gen 32,25].

7808   *Oelkers, Jürgen* Die Zukunft der Kindheit angesichts der heutigen Lebenssituation von Kindern. JBTh 17 (2002) 21-53.

7809   *Ortkemper, Franz-Josef* Glück—biblische Aspekte. KatBl 127 (2002) 169-170.

7810 *Parmentier, Martien F.* Greek patristic foundations for a theological anthropology of women in their distinctiveness as human beings. AThR 84 (2002) 555-583.

7811 *Pelletier, Anne-Marie* Lectures culturelles de la bible. CEv 119 (2002) 60-63.

7812 *Pereira, Nancy Cardoso* La danza immobile: corpo e bibbia in America Latina. Conc(I) 38 (2002) 269-279; Conc(GB) 2002/2, 76-83; Conc(E) 295,97-105; Conc(D) 38,178-186.

7813 *Perrone, Lorenzo* "Eunuchi per il regno dei cieli"?: amore e sessualità dal Nuovo Testamento al primo cristianesimo. CrSt 23 (2002) 281-305.

7814 *Pilch, John* Marriage. BiTod 40 (2002) 315-319;

7815 No thank you!. BiTod 40 (2002) 49-53.

7816 *Piper, John* La visione biblica della complementarità. Studi di teologia 14 (2002) 123-150.

7817 **Ravasi, Gianfranco** L'uomo della bibbia. Bologna 2002, EDB 88 pp [Eccl(R) 17,626s].

7818 *Retief, F.P.; Riekert, S.J.P.K.; Cilliers, J.F.G.* Eunugs in die bybel. AcTh(B) 22/2 (2002) 114-125.

7819 **Riches, John K.** Conflicting mythologies: identity formation in the gospels of Mark and Matthew. 2000 ⇒16,7433; 17,7277. [R]Theol. 105 (2002) 55-56 (*Morgan, Robert*); JThS 53 (2002) 185-191 (*Foster, Paul*); CBQ 64 (2002) 774-776 (*Pilch, John J.*); StWC 8/1 (2002) 162-164 (*Hurtado, Larry W.*).

7820 **Ridder, A.W.** Vreugde als aanzet tot geloof: over geloofservaring, vreugde en angst, toegespitst op het Oude Testament. [D]*Vroom, H.M.*: Zoetermeer 2002, Boekencentrum 231 pp. €24.90. 90-239-1157-1. Diss. Amsterdam 2002 [ITBT 10/7,31s—Schelling, Piet].

7821 *Rossano, Pietro* A imagen y semejanza de Dios. Teologia cristiana. DMis 27: 2002 <1985> ⇒232. 189-199.

7822 **Röhser, Günter** Stellvertretung im Neuen Testament. SBS 195: Stu 2002, Verlag Katholisches Bibelwerk 163 pp. €22. 3-460-04951-0. Bibl. 147-156.

7823 **Samellas, Antigone** Death in the eastern Mediterranean (50-600 A. D.): the christianization of the East: an interpretation. Studien und Texte zu Antike und Christentum 12: Tü 2002, Mohr x; 378 pp. €64. 3-16-147668-9. Bibl. 301-338.

7824 **Sawyer, Deborah F.** God, gender and the bible. L 2002, Routledge vii; 184 pp. £17.

7825 *Scanu, Maria Pina* L'uomo nel mondo creato da Dio. PSV 45 (2002) 11-26. Ripubblicata in PSV 46.

7826 *Schmidt, Werner H.* "Was ist der Mensch?": alttestamentliche Einsichten. ITE 11 (2002) 185-193.

7827 **Schroer, Silvia; Staubli, Thomas** Body symbolism in the bible. [T]*Maloney, Linda M.*: 2001 ⇒17,7281. [R]Pacifica 15 (2002) 339-340 (*Reid, Duncan*); CBQ 64 (2002) 749-50 (*Benjamin, Don C.*); LASBF 51 (2001) 416-8 (*Chrupcała, L.D.*); RBLit (2002)* (*Power, Bruce*).

7828 *Schröer, Henning* Lachend ins gelobte Land: auf dem Weg zu einer Theologie des Komischen. PTh 91 (2002) 2-11.

7829 *Scoralick, Ruth* Freundschaft in der Bibel: Ansatzpunkte zum Weiterdenken. Diak. 33 (2002) 393-399.

7830 **Screech, M.A.** Le rire au pied de la croix: de la bible à RABELAIS. [T]*Dauzat, Pierre-Emmanuel*: P 2002, Bayard 458 pp. €29.50. 2-227-31730-2.

7831	*Seijas de los Ríos-Zarzosa, Guadalupe* Desarrollos apocalípticos y místicos de algunas expresiones bíblicas. Sef. 62 (2002) 169-183.
7832	*Seow, Choon-Leong* Orientamento testuale. Bibbia e omosessualità. 2002 <1996> ⇒310. 37-64.
7833	*Sesboué, Bernard* Dieu et le concept de personne. RTL 33 (2002) 321-350.
7834	*Shaw, Perry W.* Education as hospitality: a christian approach to teaching and learning. ThRev 23/2 (2002) 95-124.
7835	*Siegwalt, Gérard* Y a-t-il un "élémentaire humain", et qu'est-il?. RHPhR 82/2 (2002) 169-186.
7836	**Ska, Jean-Louis** L'argila, la dansa i el jardí: assaig d'antropologia bíblica. Glossa 13: Barc 2001, Claret 85 pp. 84-8297-708-3. Bibl. 77-80;
7837	L'argille, la danse e le jardin: essais d'anthropologie biblique. [T]*Escaffre, Bernadette*: ConBib 27: Bru 2002, Lumen Vitae 77 pp. 2-873-24-173-X. Bibl. 71-72.
7838	*Smend, Rudolf* Essen und Trinken—ein Stück Weltlichkeit des Alten Testaments. Mitte des A.T. 2002 <1977> ⇒244. 250-61 [Gen 6,13].
7839	*Staubli, Thomas* Biblische Anthropologie und Gesundheitspräventi-on. ThPQ 150 (2002) 361-368.
7840	*Van Zyl, H.C.* Die Nuwe Testament en seksualiteit. AcTh(B) 22/2 (2002) 234-261.
7841	*Vogels, Walter* Hospitality in biblical perspective. Liturgical ministry 11/4 (2002) 161-173.
7842	*Waetjen, Herman C.* Rapporti omosessuali nell'antichità: sessualità e identità sessuale nella società americana contemporanea. Bibbia e omosessualità. 2002 <1996> ⇒310. 91-112.
7843	**Whybray, Roger N.** The good life in the Old Testament. E 2002, Clark x; 294 pp. 0-567-08721-2/09855-X. Bibl. 293-294.
7844	**Wolff, Hans** Anthropologie des Alten Testaments. Gü [7]2002, Gü'er 368 pp. 3-579-05091-5.
7845	*Yagi, Seiichi* "Bashology" in the New Testament and implication a-nalysis. AJBI 28 (2002) 33-53.
7846	*Yaron, Shlomith* The politics of sex—woman's body as an instrument of achieving man's aims. OTEs 15 (2002) 269-292.
7847	*Yates, John* Comment Dieu nous parle-t-il aujourd'hui?: anthropolo-gie biblique et témoignage du Saint-Esprit. Ḥokhma 79 (2002) 1-32.
7848	**Zimmermann, Ruben** Geschlechtermetaphorik und Gottesverhält-nis: Traditionsgeschichte und Theologie eines Bildfelds in Urchri-stentum und antiker Umwelt. WUNT 2/122: 2001 ⇒17,7306. [R]BZ 46 (2002) 152-153 (*Theobald, Michael*).

H2.8 Œcologia VT & NT—*saecularitas*

7849	**Barros, Marcelo** O Espírito vem pelas águas: bíblia, espiritualidade ecumênica e a questão da água. São Leopoldo 2002, Goiás 175 pp.
7850	*Bauckham, Richard* Human authority in creation. God and the crisis. 2002 ⇒142. 128-177.
7851	*Ceresko, Anthony R.* Ecology and Genesis 1:26-28: an interpretative strategy. Prophets and proverbs. 2002 <1998>⇒154. 97-113.
7852	Ecojustice hermeneutics: reflections and challenges. Earth story in the NT. 2002 ⇒322. 1-14. The Earth Bible team.

7853 *Eisenberg, Evan* The ecology of Eden. Judaism and ecology. 2002 ⇒ 528. 27-51.
7854 *Meloni, Pietro* La salvaguardia della natura: una riflessione sui fondamenti biblici e patristici. ᶠPOMPEDDA, M.: 2002 ⇒90. 171-191.
7855 *Rasmussen, Larry L.* Sightings of primal visions: community and ecology. Character and scripture. 2002 ⇒283. 389-409.
7856 *Schilson, Arno* Die Wiederentdeckung der Natur durch die Physikotheologie: Aspekte "natürlicher Religion" in nachkopernikanischer Zeit. Religion und Weltbild. 2002 ⇒443. 91-115.

H3.1 *Foedus*—The Covenant; *the Chosen People, Providence*

7857 **Berger, Klaus** Wer bestimmt unser Leben?: Schicksal—Zufall—Fügung. Gü 2002, Quell 205 pp. 3-579-03311-5.
7858 **Bergjan, Silke-Petra** Der fürsorgende Gott: der Begriff ΠΡΟΝΟΙΑ in der apologetischen Literatur der Alten Kirche. AKG 81: B 2002, De Gruyter xiii; 422 pp. €118. 3-11-017062-0.
7859 *Capper, Brian J.* The church as the new covenant of effective economics: the social origins of mutually supportive christian community. IJSCC 2/1 (2002) 83-102;
7860 The new covenant in southern Palestine at the arrest of Jesus. Dead Sea scrolls as background. StTDJ 46: 2002 ⇒732. 90-116.
7861 ᴱ**Cartledge, Mark J.; Mills, David** Covenant theology: contemporary approaches. Carlisle 2001, Paternoster 128 pp. £15. 1-84227-00-79.
7862 *Doubell, F.B.* Voorsienigheid, persoonlikheid en spiritualiteit—'n vier-kantige voorsienigheidsleer. ᶠPOTGIETER, P.: AcTh(B).S 3: 2002 ⇒92. 48-65.
7863 **Gräbe, Petrus J.** Der neue Bund in der frühchristlichen Literatur: unter Berücksichtigung der alttestamentlich-jüdischen Voraussetzungen. FzB 96: 2001 ⇒17,7320. ᴿThLZ 127 (2002) 518-520 (*Gräßer, Erich*).
7864 **Greenslade, Philip** A passion for God's story: discovering your place in God's strategic plan. Carlisle 2002, Paternoster xi; 274 pp. 1-8422-7-094-X. Bibl. 264-274.
7865 *Gribben, Crawford* Wrongly dividing the word of truth: the uncertain soteriology of the Scofield Reference Bible. EvQ 74 (2002) 3-25.
7866 *Grosby, Steven* The chosen people of ancient Israel and the occident: why does nationality exist and survive?. Biblical ideas. 2002 <1999> ⇒172. 92-119.
7867 *Horton, Michael* Law, gospel, and covenant: reassessing some emerging antitheses. WThJ 64 (2002) 279-287.
7868 **Horton, Michael S.** Covenant and eschatology: the divine drama. LVL 2002, Westminster vii; 351 pp. $26. 0-664-22501-2.
7869 *Köckert, Matthias, al.*, Verheißung. TRE 34. 2002 ⇒800. 697-714.
7870 *Kreuzer, Siegfried* Die Botschaft von der Rechtfertigung im Alten Testament. Gerechtigkeit glauben. VKHW 7: 2002 ⇒419. 120-144.
7871 *Levin, Christoph* Verheißung und Rechtfertigung. ᶠSMEND, R. 2002 ⇒113. 327-344.
7872 *Mazzinghi, Luca* Libertà di Dio e libertà ell'uomo: note sull'approccio dell'*Antico Testamento* al problema del destino. Servitium 36 (2002) 420-435.

7873 **Novak, David** L'elezione d'Israele: l'idea di popolo eletto. [E]*Bassani,
Franco*: BCR 64 2001 ⇒17,7326. [R]Anton. 77 (2002) 172-173 (*Nobile, Marco*); RivBib 50 (2002) 236-240 (*Prato, Gain [!] Luigi*); Sal.
64 (2002) 657-658 (*Vicent, R.*); CivCatt 153/2 (2002) 200-202 (*Prato, G.L.*).

7874 *Pomplun, Robert T.* Israel and the Eucharist: a Scotist perspective.
ProEc 11/3 (2002) 272-294.

7875 **Wells, Jo Bailey** God's holy people: a theme in biblical theology.
JSOT.S 305: 2000 ⇒16,7489; 17,7334. [R]BiblInterp 10 (2002) 199-
201 (*Seitz, Christopher R.*).

7876 **Wells, Tom; Zaspel, Fred** New covenant theology, Frederick, MD
2002, New Covenant Media 324 pp.

H3.5 *Liturgia, spiritualitas VT*—OT prayer

7877 **Berger, Klaus** ¿Qué es la espiritualidad bíblica?: fuentes de la místi-
ca cristiana. [T]*Tosaus Abadía, José Pedro*: El pozo de Siquem 127:
2001 ⇒17,7335. [R]ActBib 38/1 (2002) 77-78 (*Melloni, J.*).

7878 **Crainshaw, Jill Y.** Wise and discerning hearts: an introduction to
wisdom liturgical theology. 2000 ⇒16,7494; 17,7338. [R]Worship 76
(2002) 91-92 (*Nowell, Irene*).

7879 [E]**Franz, Ansgar** Streit am Tisch des Wortes?: zur Deutung und Bedeutung des Alten Testaments und seiner Verwendung in der Liturgie. PiLi 8: 1997 ⇒13,7034... 17,7341. [R]ALW 43-44 (2001-2002)
128-132 (*Klöckener, Martin*).

7880 *Fuchs, Werner* Espiritualidade de travessia. Estudos bíblicos 75
(2002) 48-51.

7881 *Gathercole, Simon J.* Devotional books on the Old Testament: some
recommended reading. Themelios 27/3 (2002) 5-18.

7882 **Helewa, Giovanni** 'Ascolta, popolo mio'—la fede nella religiosità
d'Israele. RVS 56 (2002) 11-36.

7883 **Ligo, Vivian** Sing the Lord's song in a foreign land: reclaiming faith
in a new culture. Toronto 2002, Novalis 168 pp. $15.

7884 **Newman, Judith Hood** Praying by the book: the scripturalization of
prayer in Second Temple Judaism. 1999 ⇒15,7505...17,7345.
[R]RBLit (2002)* (*De Troyer, Kristin*).

7885 **Ro, Johannes Un-Sok** Die sogenannte "Armenfrömmigkeit" im
nachexilischen Israel. [D]*Pohlmann, Karl-Friedrich*: BZAW 322: B
2002, De Gruyter xi; 238 pp. €68. 3-11-017471-5. Diss. Münster.
Bibl. 207-231.

7886 *Vallin, Philippe* La sagesse de l'Ancien Testament: éléments pour la
lectio divina. Carmel 103 (2002) 87-99.

7887 **Werline, Rodney Alan** Penitential prayer in second temple Judaism:
the development of a religious institution. SBL Early Judaism and Its
Literature 13: 1998 ⇒14,6742; 17,7350. [R]JQR 92 (2001) 265-268
(*Werman, Cana*).

H3.7 *Theologia moralis*—OT moral theology

7888 **Barton, John** Ethics and the Old Testament. L [2]2002 <1998>, SCM
112 pp. £10. 0-334-02894-9.

7889 *Bovati, Pietro* "Quando le fondamenta sono demolite, che cosa fa il giusto?" (Sal 11,3): la giustizia in situazione di ingiustizia. RStB 14/1-2 (2002) 9-38.

7890 *Dietrich, Walter* Der rote Faden im Alten Testament. Theopolitik. 2002 <1989> ⇒159. 13-28.

7891 *Levin, Christopher* The poor in the Old Testament: some observations. R&T 8 (2001) 253-273 [OTA 25,314].

7892 **Malul, Meir** Knowledge, control and sex: studies in biblical thought, culture and worldview. TA 2002, Archaeological Center xiii; 582 pp. 965-7162-03-3. Bibl. 499-520.

7893 **Mills, Mary E.** Biblical morality: moral perspectives in Old Testament narratives. 2001 ⇒17,7364. ᴿScrB 32 (2002) 104-106 (*Jenkins, Allan K.*); Theol. 105 (2002) 450-451 (*Ingram, Doug*).

7894 **Mol, Juniën** Collectieve en individuele verantwoordelijkheid: een beschrijving van 'corporate personality' naar Ezechiël 18 en 20 (Collective and individual responsibility: a description of corporate personality according to Ezekiel 18 and 20]. ᴰ*Becking, B.*: 2002, 306 pp. Diss. Utrecht [RTL 34,592].

7895 **Nachson, Amichai** God's requirements in historiographic and prophetic bible literature. ᴰ*Kasher, R.*: 2002, 300 pp. Diss. Bar Ilan [RTL 34,593].

7896 *Phillips, Anthony* Old Testament and moral tradition. Essays on biblical law. JSOT.S 344: 2002 <1997> ⇒223. 264-268.

7897 **Rodd, Cyril S.** Glimpses of a strange land: studies in Old Testament ethics. 2001 ⇒17,7370. ᴿPrPe 16 (2002) 38-39 (*Robinson, Bernard*); Theol. 105 (2002) 216-217 (*Clements, Ronald E.*); RRT 9 (2002) 349-350 (*Brummit, Mark*); OLZ 97 (2002) 550-554 (*Delkurt, Holger*); ET 113 (2002) 339-341 (*Auld, Graeme*).

7898 **Schenker, Adrian** Percorsi biblici della riconciliazione. ᵀ*Barchi, Alessandro; Borghi, Ernesto*: 1999 ⇒15,7535. ᴿPaVi 47/2 (2002) 60-61 (*Cappelletto, Gianni*).

7899 **Schroeder, Christoph O.** History, justice, and the agency of God: a hermeneutical and exegetical investigation on Isaiah and Psalms. BiblInterp 52: 2001 ⇒17,7374. ᴿBZ 46 (2002) 107-109 (*Zenger, Erich*); CBQ 64 (2002) 146-147 (*Creach, Jerome F.D.*); ThLZ 127 (2002) 901-902 (*Schöpflin, Karin*); ThZ 58 (2002) 365-366 (*Weber, Beat*); RBLit (2002)* (*Bellinger, W.H.*).

7900 *Shemesh, Yael* Lies by the prophets and other lies in the Hebrew Bible. JANES 29 (2002) 81-95.

7901 **Sicker, Martin** Reading Genesis politically: an introduction to Mosaic political philosophy. Westport, CONN 2002, Praeger xviii; 152 pp. 0-275-97493-6. Bibl. 145-149.

7902 *Snyman, Gerrie* Narravite rationality, morality and reader's identification. OTEs 15 (2002) 179-199 [Esther 9].

7903 *Utzschneider, Helmut* Der Beginn des Lebens: die gegenwärtige Diskussion um die Bioethik und das Alte Testament. ZEE 46 (2002) 135-143.

7904 **Wenham, Gordon J.** Story as torah: reading the Old Testament ethically. Old Testament Studies: 2000 ⇒16,7534; 17,7379. ᴿNBl 83 (2002) 200-202 (*Hibbert, Giles*); OLZ 97 (2002) 376-386 (*Scherer, Andreas*); ThLZ 127 (2002) 510-512 (*Otto, Eckart*).

7905 **Wold, Donald J.** Out of order: homosexuality in the bible and the ancient Near East. 1998 ⇒14,6788; 16,7535. ᴿ JPsT 30 (2002) 170-171 (*Burkett, Lori A.*).

7906 *Zimmermann, Ruben* Theologisierung der Ethik: Relikt oder Richtmaß?: die implizite Ethik der alttestamentlichen Weisheit und ihre Impulse für die gegenwärtige Diskussion. BThZ 19 (2002) 99-124.

H3.8 *Bellum et pax VT-NT*—War and peace in the whole Bible

7907 *Alonso Vicente, Pablo* La paz en la biblia y la paz de Jesús de Nazaret. SalTer 90 (2002) 341-350.
7908 *Barth, Heinz-Lothar* Das Verhältnis des frühen Christentums zum Militär. ᶠGNILKA, C.: JAC.E 33: 2002 ⇒48. 1-25.
7909 *Bovon, François* L'enfant et la bête: combattre la violence dans le christianisme ancien. BCPE 54/6-7 (2002) 3-32.
7910 *Breytenbach, A.P.B.* Monoteïsme en geweld: 'n perspektief op die standpunt van J Assmann. HTS 57 (2001) 447-457 [NTAb 46,502].
7911 *Callaghan, Denise Marie* Justice and peace: a biblical view. Spiritual Life 48 (2002) 139-141.
7912 **Cazeaux, Jacques** La guerre sainte n'aura pas lieu. LeDiv 185: 2001 ⇒17,7385. ᴿCBQ 64 (2002) 125-126 (*Morschauser, Scott N.*); Cart. 18 (2002) 555-556 (*Sanz Valdivieso, R.*).
7913 *Colzani, Gianni* La parola opera giustizia e pace: un'antropologia a servizio della pace. RCI 83 (2002) 165-177.
7914 *Cox, Harvey* Violenza e nonviolenza nel Nuovo Testamento. Pace e guerra. 2002 ⇒600. 65-78.
7915 *Dietrich, Walter* Ungesicherter Friede?: das Ringen um ein neues Sicherheitsdenken im Alten Testament. Theopolitik. 2002 <1987> ⇒ 159. 98-116.
7916 *Di Segni, Riccardo* Pace e guerra nella storia e nel diritto di Israele. Pace e guerra. 2002 ⇒600. 29-40.
7917 **Dousse, Michel** Dieu en guerre: la violence au coeur des trois monothéismes. P 2002, Michel 254 pp. ᴿIslChr 28 (2002) 290 (*Stäger, Roman*).
7918 *Eichler, Ulrike* Die Körper Gottes oder Gott in Zeiten des Krieges. Gretchenfrage. Jabboq 2: 2002 ⇒399. 127-136.
7919 *Filoramo, Giovanni* Il Dio violento: monoteismo e violenza divina. Pace e guerra. 2002 ⇒600. 17-28.
7920 **Gibert, Pierre** L'espérance de Caïn: la bible et la violence. P 2002, Bayard 252 pp. €21. 2-227-47061-5.
7921 **Jenson, Philip** The problem of war in the Old Testament. C 2002, Grove 28 pp. £2.50. 1-85174-509-2.
7922 *Kalluveettil, Paul* The warrior God and the prince of peace: biblical perspectives on war and peace. JDh 27 (2002) 291-308.
7923 **Krieger, Klaus-Stefan** Gewalt in der Bibel: eine Überprüfung unseres Gottesbildes. Münsterschwarzacher Kleinschriften 134: Münsterschwarzach 2002, Vier Türme 108 pp. 3-87868-634-X.
7924 *Lage, Francisco* Las religiones del libro, ¿escuela de violencia?. Moralia 25/1 (2002) 5-26.
7925 *Landman, C.* Reference to the Old Testament in women's stories of suffering. OTEs 15 (2002) 85-98.
7926 **Maier, Johann** Kriegsrecht und Friedensordnung in jüdischer Tradition. ThFr 14: 2000 ⇒16,7550. ᴿAnton. 77 (2002) 171-172 (*Nobile, Marco*).
7927 *Manns, Frédéric* Guerra e pace nella tradizione giudaica;

7928 Guerra e pace nel Nuovo Testamento. DSBP 32 (2002) 98-133/134-178.
7929 *Mejía, Jorge M.* Quale pace?: testi biblici e patristici a confronto. Asp. 49/4 (2002) 483-492.
7930 *Menestrina, Giovanni* Antologia di testi: pace e guerra nel mondo biblico. Pace e guerra. 2002 ⇒600. 223-244.
7931 *Nannini, Damián* La guerra santa en el Antiguo Testamento. RevBib 64 (2002) 161-174.
7932 **Otto, Eckart** Krieg und Frieden in der Hebräischen Bibel und im Alten Orient: Aspekte für eine Friedensordnung in der Moderne. 1999 ⇒15,7557; 17,7396. [R]RBLit (2002)* (*Moore, Michael S.*).
7933 *Palaver, Wolfgang* Die antike Polis im Lichte biblischer Gewaltanschauung: die mimetische Theorie René GIRARDs zum Problem des Politischen. Aktualität der Antike. BThZ.B 19: 2002 ⇒406. 65-85.
7934 *Panimolle, Salvatore A.* 'Da pacem, Domine!' DSBP 32 (2002) 7-16;
7935 Beati gli operatori di pace!. DSBP 33 (2002) 7-21.
7936 *Peretto, Elio* Il fattore guerra-pace nell'Antico Testamento. DSBP 32 (2002) 17-97.
7937 *Punt, J.* Empire, messiah and violence: a contemporary view. Scriptura 80 (2002) 259-274 [NTAb 47,444].
7938 *Ravasi, Gianfranco* La bibbia e le guerre di Dio. Filosofia Politica 16 (2002) 359-374.
7939 **Römer, Th.** I lati oscuri di Dio: crudeltà e violenza nell'Antico Testamento. T 2002, Claudiana 100 pp. €8.50.
7940 *Sicre Díaz, José Luis* La violencia en el Antiguo Testamento. RevBib 64 (2002) 137-160.
7941 *Soggin, Alberto J.* Guerra 'santa' o 'guerra di JHWH' nella bibbia ebraica. Pace e guerra. 2002 ⇒600. 41-46.

H4.1 Messianismus

7942 *Auffarth, Christoph, al.*, Messias/Messianismus. RGG 5. 2002 ⇒796. 1143-1162.
7943 *Boschi, Bernardo Gianluigi* Messianismo e bibbia: ebraismo e cristianesimo. DT(P) 105 (2002) 241-281.
7944 **Cohn-Sherbok, Dan** Messianic Judaism. 2000 ⇒16,7565; 17,7403. [R]TJT 18 (2002) 276-277 (*Serroul, Leo*).
7945 **Condra, Ed** Salvation for the righteous revealed: Jesus amid covenantal and messianic expectations in second temple Judaism. AGJU 51: Lei 2002, Brill xvii; 391 pp. €102/$122. 90-04-12617-1. Bibl. 331-362.
7946 **Fabry, Heinz-Josef; Scholtissek, Klaus** Der Messias: Perspektiven des Alten und Neuen Testaments. Die Neue Echter-Bibel, Themen 5: Wü 2002, Echter 124 pp. €14.40. 3-429-02171-5.
7947 *Kurian, Aji Maria* Setting the eyes on the eternal: Old Testament vision of a new king and a new rule. God of big dreams. 2002 ⇒359. 106-132.
7948 *Lichtenberger, Hermann* Messiasvorstellungen in Qumran und die neutestamentliche Christologie. CV 44 (2002) 139-160.
7949 *Philonenko, Marc* Adonaï, le Messie et le Saoshyant: observations nouvelles sur 4Q521. RHPhR 82/3 (2002) 259-266.
7950 *Roberts, J.J.M.* The Old Testament's contribution to Messianic expectations. The bible and the ANE. 2002 <1992> ⇒230. 376-389.

7951 **Rose, Wolter H.** Zemah and Zerubbabel: Messianic expectations in the early postexilic period. JSOT.S 304: 2000 ⇒16,7592; 17,7420. [R]RSR 90 (2002) 246-247 (*Abadie, Philippe*); HebStud 43 (2002) 265-267 (*Bowley, James E.*); TEuph 24 (2002) 167-171 (*Gosse, B.*).

7952 **Schochet, I.** Il messia: il concetto di messia e di era messianica nelle regole e nella tradizione ebraica. [2]2000 <1986> ⇒16,7595. [R]Annales Theologici 16 (2002) 282-283 (*Tábet, M.*).

7953 **Schreiber, Stefan** Gesalbter und König: Titel und Konzeptionen der königlichen Gesalbtenerwartung in frühjüdischen und urchristlichen Schriften. BZNT 105: 2000 ⇒16,7596; 17,7424. [R]ZKTh 124 (2002) 242-243 (*Hasitschka, Martin*).

7954 **Wise, Michael Owen** The first messiah: investigating the savior before Jesus. 1999 ⇒15,7601. [R]CV 44 (2002) 208-210 (*Segert, Stanislav*).

H4.3 *Eschatologia VT*—OT hope of future life

7955 *Ausín, S.* La esperanza escatológica en el Antiguo Testamento. Escatología y vida cristiana. 2002 ⇒641. 217-247.

7956 *Bronner, Leila Leah* The resurrection motif in the Hebrew Bible: allusions or illusions?. JBQ 30 (2002) 143-154.

7957 *Collins, John J.* Death and afterlife. Biblical world, 2. 2002 ⇒273. 357-377.

7958 *Diebner, Bernd Jørg* Genesis 23: 'Auferstehung' für Sadduzäer 'lesbar' formuliert?—die Torah als Koexistenz-Basis für konträre Meinungen im antiken Judentum. HBO 34 (2002) 129-148.

7959 *Dietrich, Walter* Leben beiderseits der Todesgrenze: Israels Ringen um den Auferstehungglauben als Chance für uns. Theopolitik. 2002 <1987> ⇒159. 84-97.

7960 **Johnston, Philip S.** Shades of Sheol: death and afterlife in the Old Testament. Leicester 2002, Apollos 288 pp. £15. 0-85111-266-8. Bibl. 243-272.

7961 *Lang, Bernhard* Verwandlung im Jenseits: zur Anthropologie einer privilegierten Reise: mit einer Notiz zur jüdischen Jenseitstopographie. Tod, Jenseits. 2002 ⇒390. 657-679.

7962 *Levenson, Jon D.* The resurrection of the dead and the construction of personal identity in ancient Israel. Congress volume Basel 2001. VT.S 92: 2002 ⇒570. 305-322.

7963 *Podella, Thomas* Totenrituale und Jenseitsbeschreibungen: zur anamnetischen Struktur der Religionsgeschichte Israels. Tod, Jenseits. 2002 ⇒390. 530-561.

7964 *Puech, E.* La escatología del Antiguo Testamento y en el Judaísmo antiguo. Escatología y vida cristiana. 2002 ⇒641. 249-270.

7965 *Tantlevskij, Igor R.* Monotheism of the pentateuch and polemics with the cult of the ancestors' spirits: biblical and Canaanite views of the immortality of the soul and the world beyond the grave. [M]DIAKONOFF, I. 2002 ⇒27. 280-298.

7966 *Van der Kooij, Arie* 'Coming' things and 'last' things: Isaianic terminology as understood in the Wisdom of Ben Sira and in the Septuagint of Isaiah. [F]LEENE, H.: 2002 ⇒73. 135-140.

7967 **Vos, Geerhardus** The eschatology of the Old Testament. [E]*Dennison, James T.*: 2001 ⇒17,7446. [R]Kerux 17/1 (2002) 66-71 (*Olinger, Danny*); Faith & Mission 19/1 (2002) 67-69 (*Rooker, Mark*).

H4.5 *Theologia totius VT*—General Old Testament theology

7968 **Barr, James** The concept of biblical theology: an Old Testament perspective. 1999 ⇒15,7611...17,7449. [R]EvQ 74 (2002) 71-72 (*Job, John B.*).

7969 *Brueggemann, Walter* The ABC's of Old Testament theology in the US. ZAW 114 (2002) 412-432.

7970 **Brueggemann, Walter** Theology of the Old Testament: testimony, dispute, advocacy. 1997 ⇒13,7170... 17,7451. [R]WThJ 63 (2002) 202-207 (*Enns, Peter*); OTEs 15 (2002) 821-825 (*Wessels, W.J.*);

7971 Teologia dell'AnticoTestamento: testimonianza, dibattito, perorazione. Biblioteca Teologica 27: Brescia 2002, Queriniana 1016 pp. €82.

7972 *Dempster, Stephen G.* Geography and genealogy, dominion and dynasty: a theology of the Hebrew Bible. Biblical theology. 2002 ⇒ 558. 66-82.

7973 **Dumbrell, William J.** The faith of Israel: a theological survey of the Old Testament. GR [2]2002, Baker 347 pp. $26. 0-8010-2532-X.

7974 *Ebach, Jürgen* Hören auf das, was Israel gesagt ist—hören auf das, was in Israel gesagt ist: Perspektiven einer "Theologie des Alten Testaments" im Angesicht Israels. EvTh 62 (2002) 37-53.

7975 *Friedlander, Albert* Die hebräische Bibel: ihre grossen Gestalten. Die Bibel: Geschichte und Gegenwart. 2002 ⇒971. 64-69, 72-79.

7976 **Gerstenberger, Erhard S.** Theologies of the Old Testament. [T]*Bowden, John*: Mp 2002, Fortress 358 pp. $30. 0-8006-3465-9. Bibl. 327-337. [R]BTB 32 (2002) 163-167 (*Murphy, Roland E.*);

7977 Theologien im Alten Testament: Pluralität und Synkretismus alttestamentlichen Gottesglaubens. 2001 ⇒17, 7455. [K]ThQ 182 (2002) 50-52 (*Groß, Walter*); BiLi 75 (2002) 145-6 (*Hubmann, Franz D.*); BiKi 57 (2002) 228-229 (*Bechmann, Ulrike*).

7978 **House, Paul R.** Old Testament theology. 1998 ⇒14,6877... 16, 7631. [R]WThJ 63 (2002) 202-207 (*Enns, Peter*).

7979 *Janowski, Bernd* Theologie des Alten Testaments: Plädoyer für eine integrative Perspektive. Congress volume Basel 2001. VT.S 92: 2002 ⇒570. 241-276.

7980 *Kratz, Reinhard G.* Noch einmal: Theologie im Alten Testament. [F]SMEND, R.: 2002 ⇒113. 310-326.

7981 *Lang, Bernhard* Die Erfindung des Himmels: das Zeugnis des Alten Testaments. WUB 26 (2002) 11-15.

7982 **Melanchthon, Monica J.** Rejection by God: the history and significance of the rejection motif in the Hebrew Bible. Studies in Biblical Literature 22: 2001 ⇒17,7460. [R]OTEs 15 (2002) 834-6 (*Branch, R.G.*).

7983 **Nobile, Marco** Teologia dell'Antico Testamento. 1998 ⇒15,7620... 17,7462. [R]RTL 33 (2002) 426-428 (*Wénin, A.*).

7984 **Rendtorff, Rolf** Theologie des Alten Testaments: ein kanonischer Entwurf: v.1, kanonische Grundlegung. 1999 ⇒15,7625...17,7466. [R]FrRu 9 (2002) 147-148 (*Vonach, Andreas*);

7985 v.2: thematische Entfaltung. 2001 ⇒17,7467. [R]KuI 17 (2002) 111-112 (*Ebach, Jürgen*); RBBras 19 (2002) 395-397 (*Minette de Tillesse, Gaëtan*);

7986 v.1-2: [R]ThLZ 127 (2002) 1045-1047 (*Waschke, Ernst-Joachim*);

7987   Teologia dell'Antico Testamento: v.1, sviluppo canonico. ᵀ*Di Pasquale, Marco*: Strumenti 5: 2001 ⇒17,7468. ᴿProtest. 57 (2002) 244-246 (*Spanu, Alessandro*); PaVi 47/5 (2002) 59-60 (*Ferrari, Pier Luigi*); CivCatt 153/3 (2002) 542-543 (*Scaiola, D.*).
7988   *Roberts, J.J.M.* In defense of the monarchy: the contribution of Israelite kingship to biblical theology. The bible and the ANE. 2002 <1987> ⇒230. 358-375.
7989   *Sailhamer, John H.* Biblical theology and the composition of the Hebrew Bible. Biblical theology. 2002 ⇒558. 25-37.
7990   *Schmidt, Werner H.* Zur Theologie und Hermeneutik des Alten Testaments: Erinnerungen und Erwägungen zur Exegese. EvTh 62 (2002) 11-25.
7991   *Smend, Rudolf* Die Mitte des Alten Testaments <1970>;
7992   Theologie im Alten Testament <1982>. Die Mitte des A.T. 2002 ⇒ 244. 30-74/75-88.
7993   **Smith-Christopher, Daniel L.** A biblical theology of exile. Overtures to Biblical Theology: Mp 2002, Fortress xiv; 209 pp. $20. 080-06-3224-9.
7994   *Toews, Brian G.* Genesis 1-4: the genesis of Old Testament instruction. Biblical theology. 2002 ⇒558. 38-52.
7995   **Westermann, Claus** Théologie de l'Ancien Testament. ᵀ*Jeanneret, Lore*: Genève 2002, Labor et F. 328 pp. €30. 2-8309-1061-3.

H5.1 *Deus*—NT—God [as Father ⇒H1.4]

7996   **Bachmann, Michael** Göttliche Allmacht und theologische Vorsicht: zu Rezeption, Funktion und Konnotationen des biblisch-frühchristlichen Gottesepithetons pantokrator. SBS 188: Stu 2002, Kathol. Bibelwerk 256 pp. €24.60. 3-460-04881-6. Bibl. 210-233.
7997   *Cuvillier, Élian* Dieu qui conteste le monde. .
7998   *Gignac, Alain* Dieu juge et avocat. Dieu, vingt-six portraits. 2002 ⇒ 312. 15-26/183-192.
7999   *Gladigow, Burkhard* Polytheismus und Monotheismus: zur historischen Dynamik einer europäischen Alternative. Polytheismus. AOAT 298: 2002 ⇒418. 3-20.
8000   *Lehnert, Volker A.* Wenn der liebe Gott "böse" wird—Überlegungen zum Zorn Gottes im Neuen Testament. ZNT 9 (2002) 15-25.
8001   *Létourneau, Pierre* Dieu qui se fait connaître. Dieu, vingt-six portraits. 2002 ⇒312. 311-322.
8002   *Markschies, Christoph Heis Theos*—ein Gott?: der Monotheismus und das antike Christentum. Polytheismus. AOAT 298: 2002 ⇒418. 209-234.
8003   *Morreall, John* Is God in heaven?. JHiC 9/2 (2002) 217-233.
8004   *Myre, André* Dieu des riches, Dieu des pauvres. Dieu, vingt-six portraits. 2002 ⇒312. 37-45 [Mt 6,3-18].
8005   *Naro, Massimo* Il Dio di Gesù Cristo e i monoteismi. RdT 43 (2002) 754-758.
8006   *Schlosser, Jacques* Dieu déconcertant. Dieu, vingt-six portraits. 2002 ⇒312. 55-63.
8007   *Schoberth, Ingrid* Kein bloß "lieber Gott": die Verharmlosung der Gottesrede als Problem der Praktischen Theologie. ZNT 9 (2002) 60-66.

H5.2 Christologia ipsius NT

8008 **Bauckham, Richard** God crucified: monotheism and christology in the New Testament. 1998 ⇒15,7643...17,7484. [R]ProEc 11 (2002) 106-107 (*Wilson, Jonathan R.*).

8009 *Biffi, Giacomo* Cristocentrismo: presupposti e problemi. Cristocentrismo. 2002 ⇒437. 7-21.

8010 *Bille, Florian* Christologie et violence. Variations Herméneutiques 16 (2002) 31-43 [BuBB 38,57].

8011 **Brown, Raymond E.** An introduction to New Testament christology. 1994 ⇒10,7410...12,6911. [R]VJTR 66 (2002) 145-46 (*Lesser, R.H.*);

8012 Introducción a la cristología del Nuevo Testamento. Biblioteca de Estudios Bíblicos 97: 2001 ⇒17,7487. [R]RevAg 43 (2002) 712-714 (*Sánchez Navarro, Luis*).

8013 *Bultmann, Rudolf* Die Christologie des Neuen Testaments. NT und christliche Existenz. UTB 2316: 2002 <1933> ⇒152. 99-121.

8014 *Canobbio, Giacomo* La fede di Gesù. RCI 83 (2002) 255-268.

8015 *Cañizares, Antonio* Cristo, ieri, oggi e sempre. Cristocentrismo. 2002 ⇒437. 243-245.

8016 *Dearman, J. Andrew* Theophany: anthropomorphism, and the *Imago Dei*: some observations about the Incarnation in the light of the Old Testament. The incarnation. 2002 ⇒624. 31-46.

8017 *Dewey, Arthur J.* Some ragged lines: from christology to christopoetics. FORUM n.s. 3 (2002) 307-319.

8018 *Frenschkowski, Marco* Kyrios in context: Q 6:46, the emperor as "Lord", and political implications of christology in Q. Zwischen den Reichen. TANZ 36: 2002 ⇒568. 95-118.

8019 **Gagliardi, Mauro** La cristologia adamitica: tentativo di recupero del suo significato originario. Ment. *Irenaeus*: TGr.T 90: R 2002, E.P.U. G. 617 pp. €32. 88-7652-942-X. Bibl. 569-601 [Rom 5; 1 Cor 15].

8020 *Hofius, Otfried* "Am dritten Tage auferstanden von den Toten": Erwägungen zum Passiv ἐγείρεσθαι in christologischen Aussagen des Neuen Testaments. Paulusstudien II. WUNT 143: 2002 ⇒180. 202-214.

8021 **Hogan, Maurice Patrick** Seeking Jesus of Nazareth: an introduction to the christology of the four gospels. 2001 ⇒17,7498. [R]Furrow 53 (2002) 514-515 (*Greehy, J.J.*); IThQ 67 (2002) 176-177 (*Mullins, Michael*); DoLi 52 (2002) 638-640 (*Norris, Thomas*).

8022 *Karlic, Ivan* Temeljne odrednice implicitne kristologije. BoSm 72 (2002) 557-571. **Croatian.**

8023 *Karrer, Martin* Jesus, der Retter (Sôtêr): zur Aufnahme eines hellenistischen Prädikats im Neuen Testament. ZNW 93 (2002) 153-176.

8024 **Karrer, Martin** Jesucristo en el Nuevo Testamento. Biblioteca de estudios bíblicos 105: S 2002, Sígueme 556 pp. €29.50. 84-301-145-7-2. Bibl. 517-519. [R]CTom 129 (2002) 659-660 (*González Blanco, Rafael*).

8025 *Keefe, Donald J.* "The word was made flesh and dwelt among us" (John 1.14). StMiss 51 (2002) 23-52.

8026 **Knight, George A.F.** Christ the centre. 1999 ⇒15,7673. [R]ProEc 11 (2002) 105-105 (*Wilson, Jonathan R.*).

8027 *Lindemann, Andreas* Jesus als der Christus bei Paulus und Lukas: Erwägungen zum Verhältnis von Bekenntnis und historischer Erkennt-

nis in der neutestamentlichen Christologie. Der historische Jesus.
BZNW 114: 2002 ⇒4859. 429-461.

8028 **Magnani, Giovanni** "Tu sei il Cristo": cristologia storica. R 2002,
E.P.U.G. 478 pp. 88-7652-923-3.

8029 **Mußner, Franz** Was hat Jesus Neues in die Welt gebracht?. 2001 ⇒
17,7513. ᴿFrRu 9 (2002) 146-147 (*Renker, Alwin*).

8030 **Parkinson, William** In the name of Jesus: the ritual use and christological significance of the name of Jesus in early christianity. ᴰ*Hurtado, L.*: 2002 Diss. Edinburgh [RTL 34,600].

8031 *Petersen, Silke* Die Weiblichkeit Jesu Christi. Die zwei Geschlechter.
2002 ⇒7637. 97-123.

8032 *Pilhofer, Peter* Dionysos und Christus: zwei Erlöser im Vergleich.
Die frühen Christen. WUNT 145: 2002 ⇒225. 73-91.

8033 *Pratscher, Wilhelm* Die Sündlosigkeit Jesu im Neuen Testament.
BThZ 19 (2002) 159-174.

8034 *Prete, Benedetto* Il titolo cristologico ἀρχηγός: suo significato e origine. DT(P) 105 (2002) 177-202.

8035 **Riley, Gregory J.** Un Jésus, plusieurs Christs: essai sur les origines
plurielles de la foi chrétienne. ᵀ*Rebeaud, Jean-François*: Genève
2002, Labor & F. 224 pp. €24. 2-8309-1020-6.

8036 *Roukema, Riemer* Le Fils du Très-Haut sur les anges et la christologie. ETR 77 (2002) 343-357.

8037 *Rusconi, Carlo* Mediatore-mediazione. DT(P) 105 (2002) 59-63.

8038 *Scaturchio, Vincenzo* La centralità di Cristo nella rivelazione biblica.
ᶠTUDDA, F. 2002 ⇒123. 153-182.

8039 **Schröter, Jens** Jesus und die Anfänge der Christologie: methodolo-
gische und exegetische Studien zu den Ursprüngen des christlichen
Glaubens. BThSt 47: 2001 ⇒17,7520. ᴿOrdKor 43 (2002) 492-494
(*Giesen, Heinz*).

8040 *Segalla, Giuseppe* La memoria di Gesù come struttura di base del
Nuovo Testamento. Cristocentrismo. 2002 ⇒437. 23-42.

8041 **Skierkowski, Marek** Jezus historii i wiary: chrystologia fundamen-
talna Geralda O'COLLINSA. Wsz 2002, Wydawnictwa Uniwersytetu
Kardynała Stefana Wyszynkiego 316 pp. 83-7072-221-0.

8042 *Smith, Mahlon H.* Doing and undoing the word: Jesus and the dialec-
tics of christology. FORUM n.s. 3 (2002) 321-356.

8043 *Tilley, Terrence W.* "O Caesarea Philippi": on starting christology in
the right place. Theology and sacred scripture. 2002 ⇒549. 135-161
[Mk 8,29].

8044 *Vasconcellos, Pedro L.* O profeta assassinado e a recriação de um en-
redo. Estudos bíblicos 73 (2002) 76-81.

8045 *Voigt, Simão* Jesus Cristo no Novo Testamento. REB 62 (2002) 771-
792.

8046 *Vollenweider, Samuel* Christus als Weisheit: Gedanken zu einer be-
deutsamen Weichenstellung in der frühchristlichen Theologiegeschichte. Horizonte. WUNT 144: 2002 <1993> ⇒257. 29-51;

8047 Der Menschgewordene als Ebenbild Gottes: zum frühchristlichen
Verständnis der Imago Dei <1998>;

8048 Zwischen Monotheismus und Engelchristologie: Überlegungen zur
Frühgeschichte des Christusglaubens. Horizonte. WUNT 144: 2002
⇒257. 53-70/3-27.

8049 *Walter, Nikolaus* Der Mose-Roman des ARTAPANOS und die Frage
nach einer Theios-Anēr-Vorstellung im hellenistischen Judentum so-

wie nach "paganen" Einflüssen auf die neutestamentliche Christologie. Jüdische Schriften. 2002 ⇒345. 284-303.

8050 *Wright, N.T.* Jesus' self-understanding. The incarnation. 2002 ⇒624. 47-61.

8051 *Zimmermann, Ruben* Jenseits von Historie und Kerygma: zum Ansatz einer wirkungsästhetischen Christologie des Neuen Testaments. Jesus im 21. Jahrhundert. 2002 ⇒1380. 153-188.

H5.3 *Christologia praemoderna*—Patristic to Reformation

8052 **Behr, John** The way to Nicaea. Formation of Christian Theology 1: 2001 ⇒17,7529. ^RArchaeus 6 (2002) 437-443 (*Neamțu, Mihail*).

8053 **Casula, Lucio** La cristologia di san LEONE Magno: il fondamento dottrinale e soteriologico. 2000 ⇒16,7699. ^RAng. 79 (2002) 459-461 (*Degórski, Bazyli*); CrSt 23 (2002) 504-508 (*Studer, Basil*).

8054 *Dell'Osso, Carlo* Il concilio di Calcedonia e il neocalcedonismo. Cristocentrismo. 2002 ⇒437. 43-62.

8055 **Ghattas, Michael** Die Christologie DIDYMUS des Blinden von Alexandria in den Schriften von Tura: zur Entwicklung der antiochenischen Theologie des 4. Jahrhunderts. ^D*Bienert, Wolfgang*: Studien zur orientalischen Kirchengeschichte 7: Münster 2002, Lit 371 pp. 3-8258-3904-4. Diss. Marburg.

8056 **Gondreau, Paul** The passions of Christ's soul in the theology of St. THOMAS Aquinas. BGPhMA 61: Müns 2002, Aschendorff 516 pp. €62.

8057 **Grillmeier, Alois** Jesus der Christus im Glauben der Kirche, 2/3: die Kirchen von Jerusalem und Antiochien. ^E*Hainthaler, Theresia*: FrB 2002, Herder xxv; 694 pp. €58. 3-451-22026-1;

8058 Gesù il Cristo nella fede della chiesa, 2/4: la chiesa di Alessandria, la Nubia e l'Etiopia doppo il 451. Biblioteca teologica 26: 2001 ⇒17, 7538. ^RSal. 64 (2002) 666-667 (*Amato, Angelo*).

8059 ^E**Malek, Roman** The Chinese face of Jesus Christ, 1. Monograph 50/1: Sankt Augustin 2002, Institut Monumenta Serica 391 pp. €40. 3-8050-0476-1 ^RBgMiss 66 (2002) 337-339 (*Müller, Wilhelm K.*).

8060 *Moreno Martínez, José Luis* Cristo en el lagar: pervivencia de una alegoría patrística. ^FTREVIJANO ETCHEVERRÍA, R. 2002 ⇒122. 541-560.

8061 **Nardin, Roberto** Il *Cur Deus homo* di ANSELMO d'Aosta: indagine storico-ermeneutica e orizzonte triprospettico di una cristologia. Cor-Lat 17: R 2002, Lateran Univ. Pr. 416 pp. 88-465-0222-1. Diss.

8062 **Panicker, Mathunny John** The person of Jesus Christ in the writings of Juhanon Gregorius Abu'l Faraj commonly called BAR EBRA-YA. Studien zur orientalischen Kirchengeschichte 4: Münster 2002, Lit 239 pp. 3-8258-3390-9. Diss. Pontificio Istituto Orientale.

8063 ^E**Pouthier, Jean-Luc** Querelles sur la divinité de Jésus. MoBi 147 (2002) 10-51.

8064 *Sousa, Pio G. Alves de* Elementos de mariologia nos autores da literatura patrística galaico-lusitana. ^FTREVIJANO ETCHEVERRÍA, R. 2002 ⇒122. 527-539.

8065 *Trocmé, Étienne* Le Jésus de LUTHER, de CALVIN... et de quelques autres Protestants. ETR 77 (2002) 177-186.

H5.4 *(Commentationes de) Christologia* **moderna**

8066 **Bergami, Augusto** Cristo parola del Padre nella storia. Credere: Bo 2002, Dehoniane 160 pp.
8067 **Biser, Eugen** Das Antlitz: eine Christologie von innen. Dü 1999, Patmos 358 pp. 3-491-70308-5.
8068 **Bombonatto, Vera Ivanise** Seguimento de Jesus: uma abordagem segundo a cristologia de Jon SOBRINO. Ensaios Teológicos: São Paulo 2002, Paulinas 486 pp. 85-356-0673-7.
8069 *Bordoni, Marcello* Identità di Cristo alla luce della sua missione. Cristocentrismo. 2002 ⇒437. 63-87.
8070 **Botella Cubells,V.** Dios escribe y se escribe con trazo humano: cristología fundamental. S 2002, San Esteban 225 pp. ᴿAugustinus 47 (2002) 465-467 (*Gómez, Enrique*).
8071 **Burns, Charlene P.E.** Divine becoming: rethinking Jesus and incarnation. Mp 2002, Fortress ix; 197 pp. $18. 0-8006-3278-8 [ThD 49, 162—Heiser, W. Charles]..
8072 **Chan, Mark L.Y.** Christology from within and ahead: hermeneutics, contingency and the quest for transcontextual criteria. BiblInterp 49: 2001 ⇒17,7554. ᴿExchange 33 (2002) 203-204 (*Nissen, Johannes*).
8073 **Coll, Niall** Christ in eternity and time—modern Anglican perspectives. 2001 ⇒17,7555. ᴿIThQ 67 (2002) 70-72 (*Norris, Thomas*).
8074 *Cozzi, Alberto* Il Logos e Gesù: alla ricerca di un nuovo spazio di pensabilità dell'Incarnazione. ScC 130 (2002) 77-116.
8075 *Daecke, Sigurd Martin* Jesus Christus und das Christentum als Gegenstände der Wissenschaft. Jesus von Nazareth und das Christentum. 2000 ⇒293. 209-223.
8076 **Duquoc, Christian** L'unique Christ: la symphonie différée. P 2002, Cerf 259 pp. 2-204-06971-X.
8077 *Egbulefu, John* Cristo: la ricerca sull'identità storica di Gesù Cristo e sulla sua attività salvifica in tutte e tre le epoche del cristiaiesimo. Cristocentrismo. 2002 ⇒437. 251-280.
8078 *Elenga, Yvon C.* African christologies: naming Jesus. ThD 49 (2002) 229-232 <VJTR 65 (2001) 667-676.
8079 **Espeja Pardo, Jesús** Jesucristo: ampliación del horizonte humano. S 2002, San Esteban 136 pp. 84-8360-105-9. ᴿSalTer 90 (2002) 806-807 (*Alcaraz Moreno, Juan Pedro*).
8080 *Gamberini, Paolo* Cristologia per il terzo millennio;
8081 *García, Javier* L'umanità di Cristo, strumento della nostra salvezza, oggi. Cristocentrismo. 2002 ⇒437. 393-401/89-113.
8082 *Gardocki, Dariusz* Chrystologia historyczna w ujęciu Jon Sobrino. [The historical christology of Jon Sobrino]. StBob 2 (2002) 75-98. Sum. 98. P.
8083 **Gesché, A.** Jesucristo. Dios para pensar VI: ᵀ*Bernal, J.M.*: Verdad e Imagen 150: S 2002, Sígueme 270 pp [EstAg 37,604—Sala, R.];
8084 Le Christ. Dieu pour penser 6: 2001 ⇒17,7563. ᴿAugustinus 47 (2002) 483-484 (*Oldfield, John J.*).
8085 **González de Cardedal, Olegario** Cristología. 2001 ⇒17,7564. ᴿVyV 60 (2002) 187-189 (*Sanz Valdivieso, Rafael*).
8086 **Haight, Roger** Jesus, symbol of God. 1999 ⇒15,4472...17,7565. ᴿSJTh 55 (2002) 250-252 (*McFarland, Ian A.*); ChiSt 41 (2002) 80-91 & NewTR 15 (2002) 50-66 (*Pramuk, Christopher*).

8087 ^E**Kabasélé, F.; Doré, J.; Luneau, R.** Chemins de la christologie africaine. CJJC 25: 2001 <1986> ⇒17,7570. ^RGr. 83 (2002) 787-788 (*Wolanin, Adam*).

8088 **Kessler, Hans** Cristologia. 2001 ⇒17,7571. ^RHumTeo 23/1 (2002) 128-129 (*Meneses, Ramiro Délio Borges de*).
     König, A. Die helfte is my nooit oor Jesus vertel nie: 'n nuwe kyk op Een wat jou lewe verander. 2001 ⇒4980.

8089 **Küster, Volker** The many faces of Jesus Christ: intercultural christology. ^T*Bowden, John*: 2001 ⇒17,7576. ^RNewTR 15 (2002) 93-94 (*Loewe, William P.*).

8090 **La Due, William J.** Jesus among the theologians: contemporary interpretations of Christ. 2001 ⇒17,7577. ^RAThR 84 (2002) 1039-1040 (*Anderson, Derek*).

8091 **Lorenzo Salas, G.** El hombre de Nazaret o Jesulogía: verdad y mito. Gijón 2002, Gumersindo Lorenzo Salas 331 pp. €20. 84-93-0539-88.

8092 **Magnani, Giovanni** Origini del cristianesimo, 1: Gesù il fondatore e i filosofi: critica delle critiche, 2: Gesù costruttore e maestro l'ambiente: nuove prospettive. 1997 ⇒15,7737. ^RGr. 83 (2002) 397-400;

8093 "Tu sei il Cristo": cristologia storica. R 2002, E.P.U.G. 478 pp. €25. 88-7652-923-3.

8094 **Moloney, Raymond** The knowledge of Christ. Problems in theology: 1999 ⇒15,7742. ^RIThQ 67 (2002) 69-70 (*Madden, Nicholas*).

8095 **Moly, Thomas** A christology of christian witnessing: kenotic christology reconsidered. ^D*Haers, J.*: 2002 lxx; 323 pp. Diss. Leuven 2002 [EThL 79,238].

8096 **Neville, Robert C.** Symbols of Jesus: a christology of symbolic engagement. 2001 ⇒17,7583. ^RRRT 9 (2002) 351-353 (*Marsh, Clive*).

8097 *Pavlou, Telesphora* Il cristocentrismo nella teologia ortodossa contemporanea. Cristocentrismo. 2002 ⇒437. 115-148.

8098 **Porro, Carlo** Io sono la via. 2000 ⇒16,7733. ^RED 55/1 (2002) 182-183 (*Mondin, Battista*).

8099 *Pozo Abejón, Gerardo del* La encarnación del Hijo de Dios. Dios para pensar. 2002 ⇒432. 135-162.

8100 *Renwart, Léon* L'unique médiateur (1 Tim 2,5): chronique de christologie. NRTh 124 (2002) 269-273.

8101 *Rossano, Pietro* Christ's lordship and religious pluralism in Roman Catholic perspective <1981>;

8102 Unicité du Christ et rencontre des religions <1990>. Teologia cristiana. DMis 27: 2002 ⇒232. 237-273/275-285.

8103 **Ruberti, Andrea** Per una cristologia dell'agire di Gesù in ascolto di H. SCHÜRMANN, C. DUQUOC ed E. SCHILLEBEECKX. ^D*Rosato, Philip J.*: R 2002, 359 pp. Diss. Gregoriana 2002.

8104 *Scarafoni, Paolo* Il concetto di 'persona' nella cristologia e nella teologia trinitaria contemporanea. Cristocentrismo. 2002 ⇒437. 149-77.

8105 *Schillebeeckx, Edward* De vroeg-christelijke receptie van Jezus bezien vanuit het heden: een kritisch model voor christelijk geloven nu. TTh 42 (2002) 390-400.

8106 **Schillebeeckx, Edward** Jesús: la historia de un viviente. M 2002, Trotta 700 pp.

8107 *Schnakenberg, Jürgen* Führt der Weg zu Gott allein über Jesus?: Grenzüberschreitungen aus den empirischen Naturwissenschaften. Jesus von Nazareth und das Christentum. 2000 ⇒293. 37-50.

8108 **Schönborn, Christoph** Gott sandte seinen Sohn: Christologie. AMATECA 7: Pd 2002, Bonifatius 372 pp. €34.90. 3-89710-202-1. Mitarbeit v. *Michael Konrad* u. *Hubert Philipp Weber.*

8109 **Stott, John** The incomparable Christ. DG 2002, InterVarsity 250 pp. $20 [Miss. 31,114—Smith, A. Christopher].

8110 **Tilliette, Xavier** Jésus romantique. CJJC 85: P 2002, Desclée 348 pp. €23. 2-7189-0970-6. Préf. *Joseph Doré.*

8111 *Van de Beek, A.* Theologen van de twintigste eeuw en de christologie. AcTh(B) 22/1 (2002) 165-194.

8112 **Van de Beek, Abraham** Jesus Kyrios: christology as heart of theology. Zoetermeer 2002, Meinema 344 pp. €30. 90-211-3898-0.

8113 **Vasel, Stephan** Philosophisch verantwortete Christologie und christlich-jüdischer Dialog: Schritte zu einer doppelt apologetischen Christologie. 2001 ⇒17,7599. [R]SaThZ 6 (2002) 81-86 (*Winkler, Ulrich*).

8114 *Waetjen, H.C.* The dichotomization of the christological paradox in the history of christian thought and critical biblical scholarship. HTS 57 (2001) 105-147 [NTAb 46,498].

8115 **Wilson, Jonathan R.** God so loved the world: a christology for disciples. 2001 ⇒17,7601. [R]CTJ 37 (2002) 164-165 (*Brouwer, Wayne*).

8116 **Yoder, John H.** Preface to theology: christology and theological method. GR 2002, Brazos. $35. Intro. *Stanley Hauerwas; Alex Sider.*

H5.5 *Spiritus Sanctus: pneumatologia*—The Holy Spirit

8117 *Alvarez Valdés, Ariel* Quando desceu o Espírito Santo sobre os apóstolos?. REB 62 (2002) 913-918.

8118 **Brown, Paul E.** The Holy Spirit and the bible. Fearn 2002, Mentor 271 pp.

8119 **Dünzl, Franz** Pneuma: Funktionen des theologischen Begriffs in frühchristlicher Literatur. JAC.E 30: 2000 ⇒16,7745; 17,7605. [R]ThLZ 127 (2002) 773-776 (*Drecoll, Volker Henning*).

8120 *Guijarro Oporto, Santiago* El Espíritu Santo en la vida de Jesús y de los primeros cristianos. CuesTF 29 (2002) 295-318.

8121 *Hahn, Sylvia* Wie kommt der Geist zur Taube?: Darstellungen des Heiligen Geistes in der bildenden Kunst. BiHe 38 (2002) 86-88.

8122 *Kim, Dongsoo* The Paraclete: the Spirit of the Church. AJPS 5/2 (2002) 255-270.

8123 *Matthiae, Gisela* Geistesverwirrung: wie Ruach unsere Gottesvorstellungen verändert. BiHe 38 (2002) 80-83.

8124 *Nürnberger, Klaus* The spirit of God: a soteriological metaphor in biblical history and its significance for us today. Scriptura 79 (2002) 55-80.

8125 *Pathrapankal, Joseph* Spirit: divine and human biblical perspectives. [F]HAAG, E. 2002 ⇒55. 175-193.

8126 **Skrzyp, Benita** Misja Ducha Świetego w królestwie bożym Nowego Testamentu [The mission of the Holy Spirit in the kingdom of God's new covenant]. 2001 ⇒17,7616. [R]Verbum Vitae 2 (2002) 313-318 (*Kudasiewicz, Józef*).

8127 *Theron, P.F.* Die oudheid van die letter en die nuutheid van die gees: enkele omperkings oor die skrif as lewende woord. [F]POTGIETER, P.: AcTh(B).S 3: 2000 ⇒92. 150-168.

8128 *Trevijano Etcheverría, Ramón* Don del espíritu (Gal 3,5) y vida cristiana. Estudios paulinos. 2002 ⇒248. 291-323.

8129 *Wellmann, Bettina* Wie redet die Bibel vom Geist?. BiHe 38 (2002) 66.

H5.6 *Spiritus et Filius*; 'Spirit-Christology'

8130 *Brambilla, Franco Giulio* Il Gesù dello Spirito e lo Spirito di Gesù. ScC 130/1 (2002) 161-210.
8131 **Preß, Michael** Jesus und der Geist: Grundlagen einer Geist-Christologie. 2001 ⇒17,7620. [R]ThGl 92 (2002) 462-463 (*Fuchs, Gotthard*).

H5.7 *Ssma Trinitas*—The Holy Trinity

8132 *Bitter, Gottfried* Auf den Spuren des dreieinen Gottes: Bibel lesen. LS 53 (2002) 47-52.
8133 **Faraone, J. Mario** La inhabitación trinitaria según San JUAN de la Cruz. AnGr 284: R 2002, E.P.U.G. 490 pp. €33. 88-7652-903-9.
8134 *Jenson, Robert W.* The bible and the Trinity. ProEc 11/3 (2002) 329-339.
8135 *Klappert, Bertold* Die Trinitätslehre als Auslegung des NAMENs des Gottes Israels: die Bedeutung des Alten Testaments und des Judentums für die Trinitätslehre. EvTh 62 (2002) 54-72.
8136 *Ladaria, Luis F.* La Trinidad y la misíon ad gentes. StMiss 51 (2002) 63-83.
8137 *Maggiali, Luigi* Gesù di Nazaret nella sua identità filiale. Cristocentrismo. 2002 ⇒437. 327-338.
8138 *Molnar, Paul D.* Deus Trinitas: some dogmatic implications of David Coffey's biblical approach to the Trinity. IThQ 67 (2002) 33-54.
8139 *Müller, Gerhard-Ludwig* El monoteísmo trinitario. Dios para pensar. 2002 ⇒432. 163-176.
8140 *Rowe, C.K.* Biblical pressure and trinitarian hermeneutics. ProEc 11/3 (2002) 295-312.
8141 *Schaab, Gloria L.* Of models and metaphors: the trinitarian proposals of Sallie McFague and Elizabeth A. Johnson. Theoforum 33 (2002) 213-234.
8142 *Signer, Michael A.* Trinity, unity, idolatry?: medieval and modern perspectives on Shittuf. [F]THOMA, C.: 2002 ⇒119. 275-284.
8143 *Terra, João Evangelista Martins* A fé trinitária do Oriente Cristão. RCB 43 (2002) 15-47.
8144 **Toon, Peter** Our triune God: a biblical portrayal of the Trinity. 1996 ⇒12,7065. [R]SBET 20 (2002) 251-252 (*Kearsley, Roy*).
8145 **Witherington, Ben; Ice, Laura Michaels** The Shadow of the Almighty: Father, Son and Spirit in biblical perspective. GR 2002, Eerdmans xii; 156 pp. $14. 0-8028-3948-7. [R]Theol. 105 (2002) 459-460 (*Beaton, Richard*).
8146 *Wunder, Bernhard* Die Trinitätslehre und der 'jüdische Traditionshorizont': Anmerkungen zur christlich-jüdischen Beziehung in der Gottesfrage. ThGl 92 (2002) 508-517.

H5.8 *Regnum messianicum, Filius hominis—*
Messianic kingdom Son of Man

8147 *Buchhold, Jacques* Jésus ou l'énigme du Fils de l'homme. ThEv(VS)
1/2-3 (2002) 21-46, 3-24.
8148 **Burkett, Delbert R.** The Son of Man debate: a history and evaluation. MSSNTS 107: 1999 ⇒15,7787; 17,7634. ᴿSNTU.A 27 (2002)
267-269 (*Fuchs, Albert*).
8149 *Cahill, Michael* Did Jesus refer to himself in the third person?: a contribution to the Son of Man debate. PIBA 25 (2002) 58-68.
8150 *Casey, Maurice* Aramaic idiom and the Son of Man problem: a
response to Owen and Shepherd. JSNT 25/1 (2002) 3-32.
8151 *Goulder, Michael* Psalm 8 and the Son of Man. NTS 48 (2002) 18-
29 [Heb 2,8-9].
8152 **Grappe, Ch.** Le royaume de Dieu: avant et après Jésus. MoBi 42:
2001 ⇒17,7636. ᴿASEs 19 (2002) 265-267 (*Pesce, Mauro*); BBR 12
(2002) 287-290 (*Chilton, Bruce*).
8153 **Hengel, Martin; Schwemer, Anna Maria** Der messianische Anspruch Jesu und die Anfänge der Christologie: vier Studien. WUNT
138: 2001 ⇒17,276. ᴿRHPhR 82 (2002) 232-233 (*Grappe, Ch.*);
ThLZ 127 (2002) 1050-1051 (*Becker, Jürgen*); SNTU.A 27 (2002)
263-267 (*Fuchs, Albert*).
8154 *Heyer, Cees den* Het koninkrijk van God is nabijgekomen: een complex vraagstuk. ITBT 10/2 (2002) 4-6.
8155 *Nel, G.C.J.; Van Aarde, Andries G.* Die koninkryk van God by Jesus:
'n apokalipties-eskatologiese of eties-eskatologiese begrip?. HTS 58
(2002) 1113-1133 [NTAb 47,444].
8156 *O'Conaill, Seán* What do we mean by the Kingdom of God?. DoLi
52 (2002) 241-247.
8157 El reino de Dios: horizonte y realización de la misión. MisEx(M) 189
(2002) 323-326.
8158 *Uemura, Shizuka* The origin of the 'Son of Man' as a messianic title:
a philological and tradition-historical study. AJBI 28 (2002) 3-32.
8159 **Vanoni, Gottfried; Heininger, Bernhard** Das Reich Gottes: Perspektiven des Alten und Neuen Testaments. Die neue Echter-Bibel,
Themen 4: Wü 2002, Echter 136 pp. €14.40. 3-429-02170-7.
8160 **Wink, Walter P.** The human being: Jesus and the enigma of the Son
of the man. Mp 2002, Fortress xvi; 356 pp. $26. 0-8006-3262-1.
ᴿCBQ 64 (2002) 782-784 (*Ringe, Sharon H.*); AThR 84 (2002)
1057-1058 (*Weidmann, Frederick W.*).

H6.1 *Creatio, sabbatum NT;* **The Creation** [⇒E1.6]

8161 **Bacchiocchi, Samuele** Divine rest for human restlessness: a theological investigation of the good news of the sabbath for today. Biblical
Perspectives 2: Berrien Springs, MI 2002, Biblical Perspectives 319
pp. Bibl. 313-316.
8162 *Beale, G.K.* The New Testament and new creation. Biblical theology.
2002 ⇒558. 159-173.
8163 *Cairus, A.E.* Gnostic roots of Sunday-keeping. JATS 13/1 (2002) 67-
80 [NTAb 47,137].

8164 **Doering, Lutz** Schabbat: Sabbathalacha und -praxis im antiken Judentum und Urchristentum. TSAJ 78: 1999 ⇒15,7806...17,7654. [R]JSSt 47 (2002) 355-357 (*Niessen, F.*); StPhiloA 14 (2002) 200-204 (*Weiss, Herold*).
8165 *Harg, Joseph* Sonntags-Frust und Sonntags-Freude: biblische und sozialethische Betrachtungen zur Sonntagsarbeit. CPB 115 (2002) 218-222.
8166 *Link, Christian* Providence: an unsolved problem of the doctrine of creation;
8167 *Reventlow, Henning Graf* Creation as a topic in biblical theology. Creation in Jewish and christian tradition. JSOT.S 319: 2002 ⇒593. 266-276/153-171.
8168 *Rossano, Pietro* La creazione nel Nuovo Testamento. Teologia cristiana. DMis 27: 2002 <1969> ⇒232. 175-187.
8169 *Velasco Arias, Javier* El día del sábado. ResB 36 (2002) 55-61.
8170 *Zager, Werner* Biblischer Schöpfungsglaube: Entwicklung und Wandlung. Deutsches Pfarrerblatt 102/6 (2002) 279-282.

H6.3 *Fides, veritas in NT*—Faith and truth

8171 *Bultmann, Rudolf* Die Geschichtlichkeit des Daseins und der Glaube: Antwort an Gerhardt Kuhlmann <1930>;
8172 Anknüpfung und Widerspruch <1946>. NT und christliche Existenz. UTB 2316: 2002 ⇒152. 59-83/207-222.
8173 *Helm, Paul* The perfect trustworthiness of God. The trustworthiness of God. 2002 ⇒410. 237-252.
8174 *Jenkins, C.R.* Faith and works in Paul and James. BS 159 (2002) 62-78 [Rom 4,1-8; James 2,14-26].
8175 **Landmesser, Christof** Wahrheit als Grundbegriff neutestamentlicher Wissenschaft. WUNT 113: 1999 ⇒15,7815...17,7672. [R]ThG 45 (2002) 294-296 (*Giesen, Heinz*).
8176 **Longenecker, Richard N.** New wine into fresh wineskins: contextualizing the early christian confessions. 1999 ⇒15,7817. [R]TJT 18 (2002) 268-269 (*Trites, Allison A.*).
8177 *Lüdemann, Gerd* Glaube und Wissen: ein Vortrag für solche, die dem Christentum entwachsen sind und trotzdem weiter nach seiner Wahrheit suchen. [F]RÄISÄNEN, H.: NT.S 103: 2002 ⇒97. 553-564.
8178 *Nicole, Roger* The biblical concept of truth. Standing forth. 2002 <1983> ⇒215. 133-149.
8179 *Penna, Romano* Il concetto biblico di 'verità': alcuni aspetti semantici. Path 1 (2002) 203-219.
8180 *Rossano, Pietro* Fede e cultura. Teologia cristiana. DMis 27: 2002 <1987> ⇒232. 391-398.
8181 *Snoeberger, M.A.* The logical priority of regeneration to saving faith in a theological *ordo salutis*. Detroit Baptist Seminary Journal [Allen Park, MI] 7 (2002) 40-93 [NTAb 47,302].
8182 *Sorg, Theo* "Bewahre, was dir anvertraut ist ...". ThBeitr 33 (2002) 242-244.
8183 *Tavares, Sinivaldo S.* O mistério do Verbo Encarnado funda uma peculiar relação entre história e fé. REB 62 (2002) 793-822.
8184 **Theissen, Gerd** La fe bíblica: una perspectiva evolucionista. Estella 2002, Verbo Divino 270 pp. €18. 84-8169-554-8.

8185 **Yeung, Maureen W.** Faith in Jesus and Paul: a comparison with special reference to 'Faith that can remove mountains' and 'Your faith has healed/saved you'. WUNT 2/147: Tü 2002, Mohr S. xv; 341 pp. €59. 3-16-147737-5. Bibl. 299-321.

H6.6 *Peccatum NT*—Sin, evil [⇒E1.9]

8186 **Girard, René** Veo a Satan caer como un relámpago. [T]*Díez del Corral, Francisco.* Barc 2002, Anagrama 248 pp. €13.80;

8187 Ich sah den Satan vom Himmel fallen wie einen Blitz: eine kritische Apologie des Christentums. [T]*Mainberger-Ruh, Elisabeth*: Mü 2002, 256 pp. €21.50. Nachwort *Peter Sloterdijk*;

8188 I see Satan fall like lightning. [T]*Williams, James G.*: 2001 ⇒17,7682. [R]AThR 84 (2002) 458-459 (*Baker, Anthony D.*); RRT 9 (2002) 64-66 (*Winn, Christian T.C.*).

8189 **Hermanni, Friedrich** Das Böse und die Theodizee: eine philosophisch-theologische Grundlegung. Gü 2002, Kaiser 361 pp. 3-579-05391-4.

8190 **Kelly, Joseph Francis** The problem of evil in the western tradition: from the book of Job to modern genetics. ColMn 2002, Liturgical viii; 245 pp. $18. 0-8146-5104-6. Bibl. 235-241 [ThD 49,272—W. Charles Heiser].

8191 *Marshall, Ian H.* "Sins" and "sin". BS 159 (2002) 3-20.

H7.0 Soteriologia NT

8192 **Anikuzhikattil, Thomas** Jesus Christ the Saviour: soteriology according to East Syriac tradition. Satna 2002, Ephrem ix; 392 pp. 81-88065-01-3. Diss. Paurastya Vidyapitham.

8193 *Arens, Eduardo* La reconciliación desde una perspectiva bíblica. Páginas 178 (2002) 24-33.

8194 **Baudler, Georg** Die Befreiung von einem Gott der Gewalt: Erlösung in der Religionsgeschichte von Judentum, Christentum und Islam. 1999 ⇒15,7830. [R]ZMR 86 (2002) 63-65 (*Ott, Martin*).

8195 *Chester, Andrew* Salvation in christian thought. Biblical world, 2. 2002 ⇒273. 317-331.

8196 *Destro, Adriana; Pesce, Mauro* Forgiveness of sins without a victim: Jesus and the Levitical jubilee. Sacrifice in religious experience. 2002 ⇒612. 151-173.

8197 **Fischer, Georg; Backhaus, Knut** Espiazione e riconciliazione: prospettive dell'Antico e del Nuovo Testamento. Collana biblica; I temi della Bibbia 7: B 2002, Dehoniane 190 pp. 88-10-22109-5. Bibl. 185-186.

8198 *Gardocki, Dariusz* Solidarność i reprezentacja: współczesne modele soteriologiczne [Solidarity and representation: contemporary soteriological models]. Ment. *Sobrino, J.; Galot, J.*: StBob 2 (2002) 53-77. Sum. 77. P.

8199 *Hahn, Ferdinand* Observations on the soteriology of the letters to the Colossians and Ephesians. [F]WEDDERBURN, A.: JSNT.S 217: 2002 ⇒ 132. 123-135.

8200 **Jüngel, Eberhard** Das Evangelium von der Rechtfertigung des Gottlosen als Zentrum des christlichen Glaubens: eine theologische Studie in ökumenischer Absicht. [3]1999 ⇒16,7810. [R]WThJ 63 (2002) 214-217 (*Gamble, Richard C.*);

8201 Il vangelo della giustificazione come centro della fede cristiana: uno studio teologico in prospettiva ecumenica. BTCon 112: 2000 ⇒16, 7810; 17,7692. [R]Studi di teologia 14 (2002) 212-213 (*De Chirico, Leonardo*).

8202 **Kamanzi, Speratus** Soteriological models in their historical contexts: with special reference to René GIRARD's contribution and his reception in contemporary theology. [D]*De Schrijver, G.*: 2002, xxxiv; 418 pp. Diss. Leuven.

8203 *Karrer, Martin* Rechtfertigung, Kirche und Israel: Thesen im Gespräch mit Klaus Haacker. ThBeitr 33 (2002) 232-241.

8204 *Lange, Ulrich-Paul* Die notwendige Bekehrung: "Bekehret euch und glaubt an das Evangelium!". Theologisches 32 (2002) 533-549.

8205 *Lang, Walter* Die Botschaft vom Reich Gottes und vom Heil. Theologisches 32 (2002) 119-126.

8206 *Löning, Karl* Die Konfrontation des Menschen mit der Weisheit Gottes: Elemente einer sapientialen Soteriologie. Rettendes Wissen. AOAT 300: 2002 ⇒352. 1-41.

8207 *Nersinger, Ulrich* Christentum. Was ist der Sinn. GTBS 1170: 2002 ⇒438. 59-78.

8208 *Nicole, Roger* The nature of redemption. Standing forth. 2002 <1964> ⇒215. 245-282.

8209 *Noordegraaf, Albert* De heilsbetekenis van Jezus' dood in het Nieuwe Testament. ThRef 45/3 (2002) 256-260.

8210 *Núñez Regodón, Jacinto* La idea prepaulina y paulina de justificación (a propósito de 1Cor 1,30; 6,11). [F]TREVIJANO ETCHEVERRÍA, R. 2002 ⇒122. 219-231.

8211 **Nwachukwu, Mary Sylvia Chinyere** Creation-covenant scheme and justification by faith: a canonical study of the God-human drama in the pentateuch and the letter to the Romans. [D]*Swetnam, James*: TGr.T 89: R 2002, E.P.U.G. 372 pp. €23/$22. 88-7652-941-1. Diss. Gregoriana. Bibl. 335-361.

8212 *Pitta, Antonio* La giustificazione nella sacra scrittura. CredOg 130 (2002) 39-50.

8213 **Rieger, Hans-Martin** Adolf SCHLATTERs Rechtfertigungslehre und die Möglichkeit ökumenischer Verständigung. 2000 ⇒16,7820. [R]ÖR 51(2002) 387-388 (*Nüssel, Friederike*).

8214 **Roberts, Richard Owen** Repentance: the first word of the gospel. Wheaton, IL 2002, Crossway 368 pp. $20. 1-58134-400-7 [ThD 50, 88—Heiser, W. Charles].

8215 *Rossano, Pietro* Le religioni non cristiane nella storia della salvezza: rassegna delle posizioni teologiche attuali. Teologia cristiana. DMis 27: 2002 <1965> ⇒232. 215-227.

8216 *Schenker, Adrian, al.,* Vergebung der Sünden. TRE 34. 2002 ⇒800. 663-690.

8217 *Schwikart, Georg* Einführung. Was ist der Sinn. GTBS 1170: 2002 ⇒438. 9-38.

8218 *Stuhlmacher, Peter* Zum Thema Rechtfertigung. Biblische Theologie. WUNT 146: 2002 ⇒245. 23-65.

8219 **Sungenis, Robert A.** Not by faith alone: the biblical evidence for the catholic doctrine of justification. 1997 ⇒15,7853. ᴿBS 159 (2002) 370-371 (*Powell, Charles E.*).

8220 **Weaver, J. Denny** The nonviolent atonement. 2001 ⇒17,7703. ᴿWThJ 63 (2002) 217-220 (*McWilliams, David B.*).

8221 **Work, Telford** Living and active: scripture in the economy of salvation. Sacra Doctrina: Christian Theology for a Postmodern Age: GR 2002, Eerdmans xx; 343 pp. $35. 0-8028-4724-2. Bibl. 329-337. ᴿTheol. 105 (2002) 460-462 (*Fowl, Stephen*).

8222 *Zerafa, Pietro Paolo* La giustificazione nella bibbia. Ang. 79 (2002) 19-50 [Dt 6,25; Hos 14,5; Rom 3,20-31; 11,5-6; Gal 2,16].

H7.2 *Crux, sacrificium*; The Cross, the nature of sacrifice [⇒E3.4]

8223 *Barth, Gerhard* L'interpretazione della morte di Gesù nel Nuovo Testamento. Colpa. 2002 ⇒401. 93-102.

8224 **Bille, Florian; Dettwiler, Andreas; Rose, Martin** 'Maudit quiconque est pendu au bois': la crucifixion dans la loi et dans la foi. Lausanne 2002, Zèbre 150 pp. €20/FS30. 2-9700-2358-X.

8225 **Brandt, Sigrid** Opfer als Gedächtnis: auf dem Weg zu einer befreienden theologischen Rede von Opfer. Altes Testament und Moderne 2: Müns 2002, LIT xii; 505 pp. €40.90 [BiLi 76,149–Steins, Georg.].

8226 *Bühler, Pierre* Kreuzestheologie und Soteriologie zwischen Neuem Testament und systematischer Theologie;

8227 Kreuzestheologie und die Frage nach dem Kanon: einige hermeneutische Thesen—im Gespräch mit François Vouga. Kreuzestheologie. WUNT 151: 2002 ⇒298. 265-281/327-332.

8228 *Chirassi Colombo, Ileana* Sacrificio divino. Colpa. 2002 ⇒401. 21-38.

8229 *Collange, Jean F.* La mort du Christ sur la croix a-t-elle encore un sens?. PosLuth 50/1 (2002) 5-17.

8230 *Collu, Mario* Il vocabolario della croce nel NuovoTestamento e la teologia della croce di 1Cor 1-4 in alcuni autori moderni. LSDC 17 (2002) 263-285. Sum. 285.

8231 *Colombo, Adele* Il 'capro espiatorio' nell'ipotesi scientifica di René GIRARD. Colpa. 2002 ⇒401. 39-54.

8232 **Deiana, Giovanni** Dai sacrifici dell'Antico Testamento al sacrificio di Cristo. Spiritualità 5: Città del Vaticano 2002, Urbaniana University Pr. 120 pp. 88-401-2068-8. Bibl. 115-120.

8233 ᴱ**Dreyer, Elizabeth A.** The cross in christian tradition: from Paul to BONAVENTURE. 2000 ⇒16,506; 17,522. ᴿScEs 54 (2002) 115-7 (*Bigaouette, Francine*); IThQ 67 (2002) 180-182 (*Cunningham, Enda*).

8234 ᵀᴱ**Drijvers, Han Jan Willem** The finding of the true cross: the Judas Kyriakos legend in Syriac. CSCO 565; CSCO.Sub 93: 1997 ⇒13, 7490. ᴿRHE 97 (2002) 580-582 (*Kohlbacher, Michael*).

8235 *Fabris, Rinaldo* La morte di Gesù 'sacrificio di espiazione'?;

8236 *Fiorensoli, Dario* Il sacrificio vicario e la rilettura delle interpretazioni. Colpa. 2002 ⇒401. 103-117/137-155.

8237 **Forano, Luca** La libertà del Golgotha. Aosta 2002, Le Château 138 pp [Eccl(R) 17,284].

8238 *Galot, Jean* Il 'perché' della croce. CivCatt 153/2 (2002) 12-25.

8239 ᴱGerhards, Albert; Richter, Klemens Das Opfer—biblischer Anspruch und liturgische Gestalt. QD 186: 2000 ⇒16,365. ᴿThLZ 127 (2002) 553-554 (Hallensleben, Barbara).

8240 Green, Joel B.; Baker, Mark D. Recovering the scandal of the cross. 2000 ⇒16,7837. ᴿBS 159 (2002) 118-121 (Horrell, J. Scott).

8241 Grottanelli, Cristiano Il sacrificio. 1999 ⇒16,7838. ᴿASEs 19 (2002) 288-291 (Pesce, Mauro).

8242 Heid, Stefan Das Kreuz als Religions-, Missions- und Imperialsymbol in der frühen Kirche. RivAC 78 (2002) 191-259;

8243 Die frühkirchliche Beurteilung der Häretiker als "Feinde des Kreuzes". ᶠHOHEISEL, K.: JAC.E 34: 2002 ⇒59. 107-139.

8244 Johnson, Luke Timothy Sacrifice is the body language of love. PrPe 16 (2002) 87-91.

8245 Lang, Bernhard This is my body: sacrificial presentation and the origins of christian ritual. Sacrifice in religious experience. 2002 ⇒ 612. 189-205.

8246 McDade, John The sacrifice of Christ. PrPe 16 (2002) 92-96.

8247 Menke, Karl-Heinz Opfer und Martyrium—die Antwort Christi. IKaZ 31 (2002) 143-164.

8248 Moltmann, Jürgen Der gekreuzigte Gott: das Kreuz Christi als Grund und Kritik christlicher Theologie. Gü 2002, Gü'er 320 pp. €40. ᴿRBBras 19 (2002) 437-438 (Minette de Tillesse, Gaëtan).

8249 Ouro, R. Daniel 9:27a: a key for understanding the law's end in the New Testament. JATS 12/2 (2001) 180-198 [NTAb 47,94].

8250 Paupert, Catherine Un apocryphe sans texte: le chemin de croix. ᶠGEOLTRAIN, P.: BEHE.R 113: 2002 ⇒45. 277-283 [BuBB 38,105] [Sirach 50,1-21].

8251 Pfüller, Wolfgang Der Tod Jesu—Manifestation der göttlichen Heilsmacht, nicht Grund des menschlichen Heils. MThZ 53 (2002) 236-250.

8252 Reinders, Franz Il 'sacrificio vicario' in Eugen DREWERMANN;

8253 Rostagno, Sergio Il significato della passione di Gesù. Colpa. 2002 ⇒401. 157-185/119-136.

8254 Stott, John La croce di Cristo. 2001 ⇒17,7728. ᴿStudi di teologia 14 (2002) 210-211 (Dalla Pozza, Luigi).

8255 Stuhlmacher, Peter Jesus Christus—für uns gekreuzigt und auferweckt. Biblische Theologie. WUNT 146: 2002 <1998> ⇒245. 302-316.

8256 Thiede, Carsen Peter; D'Ancona, Matthew The quest for the true cross. 2000 ⇒16,7858; 17,7730. ᴿEvangel 20/1 (2002) 29-30 (Lalleman, Pieter J.).

8257 Vollenweider, Samuel Diesseits von Golgatha: zum Verständnis des Kreuzestodes Jesu als Sühnopfer. Horizonte. WUNT 144: 2002 <1996> ⇒257. 89-103.

8258 Vouga, François Ist die Kreuzestheologie das hermeneutische Zentrum des Neuen Testament?;

8259 Crux probat omnia": der oder ein Prüfstein neutestamentlicher Hermeneutik?: Dialog und Konsens mit Pierre Bühler. Kreuzestheologie. WUNT 151: 2002 ⇒298. 283-326/333-339.

8260 Wanke, Daniel Das Kreuz Christi bei IRENÄUS von Lyon. BZNW 99: 2000 ⇒16,7862; 17,7732. ᴿRevSR 76 (2002) 103-104 (Fantino, Jacques); RSR 90 (2002) 256-258 (Sesboüé, Bernard).

8261 *Witczyk, Henryk* Od ewangelii o Jezusie pełnym mocy do ewangelii krzyża [From the gospel of Jesus full of power to the gospel of the cross]. Verbum Vitae 2 (2002) 201-222. Sum. 221. **P.**

H7.4 *Sacramenta, gratia*

8262 **Alule, Cosmas** Baptism and faith: their relationship in our salvific encounter with God today in the light of the New Testament baptismal theology and Vatican II sacramental theology. EHS.T 100: 2000 ⇒16,7863; 17,7734. [R]TS 63 (2002) 416-417 (*Kelly, Gerard*).
8263 **Barth, Gerhard** Die Taufe in frühchristlicher Zeit. Neuk [2]2002, <1981> Neuk'er 144 pp. €19.90. 3-7887-1840-4.
8264 **Boismard, Marie-Émile** Le baptême chrétien selon le Nouveau Testament. Théologies: 2001 ⇒17,7735. [R]EeV 60 (2002) 33-34 (*Jay, Pierre*); LASBF 52 (2002) 585-587 (*Casalini, Nello*).
8265 *Böhm, Uwe; Buschmann, Gerd* The "Matrix" und Röm 6—christliche Taufvorstellung in popkulturellem Science-Fiction-Ambiente. ZNT 10 (2002) 69-77.
8266 *Chilton, Bruce* Eucharist: surrogate, metaphor, sacrament of sacrifice. Sacrifice in religious experience. 2002 ⇒612. 175-188.
8267 *Cimosa, Mario* La rivelazione della 'grazia divina' nell'Antico Testamento. DSBP 30 (2002) 14-65.
8268 *Ellis, Christopher J.* The baptism of disciples and the nature of the church. Dimensions of baptism. JSNT.S 234: 2002 ⇒434. 333-353.
8269 *Ferguson, Everett* Christian and Jewish baptism according to the epistle of Barnabas;
8270 The doctrine of baptism in GREGORY of Nyssa's *Oratio catechetica*;
8271 *Fiddes, Paul S.* Baptism and the process of christian initiation. Dimensions of baptism. JSNT.S 234: 2002 ⇒434. 207-223/224-234/280-303.
8272 *Foley, Edward* Being a people of word and deed. BiTod 40 (2002) 179-183.
8273 *Haymes, Brian* The moral miracle of faith;
8274 *Holmes, Stephen R.* Baptism: patristic resources for ecumenical dialogue;
8275 *Kearsley, Roy* Baptism then and now: does MOLTMANN bury TERTULLIAN or praise him?. Dimensions of baptism. JSNT.S 234: 2002 ⇒434. 325-332/253-267/236-252.
8276 *Maggioni, Bruno* La grazia divina nel Nuovo Testamento. DSBP 30 (2002) 83-101.
8277 *McCarron, Richard E.* Biblical motifs in the liturgy of baptism. BiTod 40 (2002) 308-313.
8278 *Nicole, Roger* A tale of two marriages. Standing forth. 2002 <2000> ⇒215. 453-475.
8279 *Panimolle, Salvatore A.* Canterò per sempre la grazia del Signore!. DSBP 30 (2002) 7-13;
8280 Ci preceda e ci accompagni sempre la tua grazia, Signore!. DSBP 31 (2002) 7-26.
8281 *Porter, Stanley E.; Cross, Anthony R.* Introduction: baptism—an ongoing debate. Dimensions of baptism. JSNT.S 234: 2002 ⇒434. 1-6.
8282 *Ramshaw, Gail* In the name: towards alternative baptismal idioms. ER 54 (2002) 343-352.

8283 **Rochetta, Carlos** Los sacramentos de la fe: sacramentología bíblica fundamental (vol. 1); sacramentología bíblica especial (vol. 2). Ágape 28: S 2002, Trinitario 282; 376 pp.

8284 *Thompson, Philip E.* Memorial dimensions of baptism. Dimensions of baptism. JSNT.S 234: 2002 ⇒434. 304-324.

8285 *Tragan, Pius-Ramon* Gesù di Nazareth intendeva fondare un nuovo culto?. FilTeo 16 (2002) 309-329 Sum. 309.

8286 *Turner, Paul* Biblical roots of confirmation. BiTod 40 (2002) 380-385.

8287 *Vibert, S.* The *telos* or 'chief end' of marriage. Churchman 116/4 (2002) 353-369 [NTAb 47,303] [Gen 2,24; Eph 5,31-32].

8288 *Wade, L.* Marriage and covenant: reflections on the theology of marriage. JATS 13/2 (2002) 73-93 [NTAb 47,304].

8289 *Watts, Graham* Baptism and the hiddenness of God. Dimensions of baptism. JSNT.S 234: 2002 ⇒434. 268-279.

8290 **Winstanley, Michael T.** Scripture, sacraments, spirituality. Great Wakering 2002, McCrimmons 141 pp. £7.

8291 *Wright, David F.* Out, in, out: Jesus' blessing for the children and infant baptism. Dimensions of baptism. JSNT.S 234: 2002 ⇒434. 188-206 [Mt 19,13-15; Mk 10,13-16; Lk 18,15-17].

H7.6 *Ecclesiologia, Theologia missionis, laici*—The Church

8292 *Bardski, Krzysztof* 'Daj mi usłyszeć twój głos!'wezwanie do zwiastowania ewangelii w wybranych alegoriach Pieśni nad Pieśniami ['Let me hear your voice!']. Verbum Vitae 2 (2002) 225-41 Riass. 241. **P.**

8293 *Buitendag, J.* Die belydenis van die kerk. [F]POTGIETER, P.: AcTh(B).S 3: 2002 ⇒92. 17-34.

8294 **Caputa, Giovanni** Il sacerdozio dei fedeli secondo San BEDA: un itinerario di maturità cristiana. Monumenta Studia Instrumenta Liturgica 16: Città del Vaticano 2002, Libreria Editrice Vaticana vii; 326 pp. 88-209-7268-9. Pres. *Achille Maria Triacca*. Bibl. 297-318.

8295 *Collani, Claudia von* Verbotene Riten: das tragische Scheitern der Chinamission in der frühen Neuzeit. WUB Sonderheft (2002) 58-60.

8296 **Comblin, José** O povo de Deus. São Paulo 2002, Paulus 412 pp. R$27. [R]RBBras 19 (2002) 451-454 (*Furtado, Marco Antonio Tourinho*).

8297 *Dreyer, D.J.* 'n Kerk wat getuig is 'n kerk wat leef (I): 'n bybels-teologiese perspektief op die missionêre karakter van die kerk. VeE 23 (2002) 319-332.

8298 *Duncan, G.A.* A place in the sun?: the role of the church in moral renewal and social transformation. VeE 23 (2002) 333-342.

8299 *Galot, Jean* A la ressemblance du Christ l'Eglise est missionaire. StMiss 51 (2002) 107-156.

8300 **Gnilka, Joachim** I primi cristiani: origini e inizio della chiesa. Commentario teologico del Nuovo Testamento, Supplementi 9: 2000 ⇒ 16,7891; 17,7759. [R]ATT 8 (2002) 230-233 (*Ghiberti, Giuseppe*).

8301 **Goldsmith, Martin** Good news for all nations: mission at the heart of the New Testament. L 2002, Hodder & Stoughton ix; 166 pp. £7.

8302 *Guggenheim, Antoine* Mission, dialogue interreligieux et salut: pour une lecture historique et spirituelle de l'Écriture. NRTh 124 (2002) 415-434.

8303 *Guijarro, Santiago* La misión de los discípulos de Jesús. Seminarios
      48 (2002) 333-355.
8304 **Harrington, Daniel J.** The church according to the New Testament.
      2001 ⇒17,7760. ᴿNewTR 15/4 (2002) 81-82 (*Matera, Frank J.*).
8305 **Hellerman, Joseph H.** The ancient church as family. 2001 ⇒17,
      7762. ᴿASEs 19 (2002) 283-286 (*Balch, David*); JR 82 (2002) 626-
      626 (*Osiek, Carolyn*); CBQ 64 (2002) 764-765 (*Rawson, Beryl*);
      AThR 84 (2002) 1034-1035 (*Garland, Diana*).
8306 *Hintzen, Georg* Die Einheit der Kirche in katholischer Sicht. Einheit
      als Gabe. 2002 ⇒6424. 97-111.
8307 **Howard-Brook, Wes** The church before christianity. 2001 ⇒17,
      7763. ᴿNewTR 15/4 (2002) 84-85 (*Gittins, Anthony J.*).
8308 *Hultgren, Arland J.* The church as the body of Christ: engaging an
      image in the New Testament. WaW 22 (2002) 124-132.
8309 *Johnson, Luke Timothy* The church as God's household. BiTod 40
      (2002) 224-228.
8310 **Kaiser, Walter C.** Mission in the Old Testament: Israel as a light to
      the nations. 2000 ⇒16,7897; 17,7767. ᴿBS 159 (2002) 255-256
      (*Young, Mark*).
8311 **Kizhakkeyil, Sebastian** Liberative prophetic roles. Ujjain 2002,
      Ruhalaya 160 pp. ᴿJJSS 2 (2002) 256 (*Vedikunnel, Joseph*).
8312 *Köhler, Joachim* Von der Tatmission zur Wortmission;
8313 Zeugnisse des Glaubens in den Missionsgebieten. Die Bibel: Ge-
      schichte und Gegenwart. 2002 ⇒971. 148-161/162-163.
8314 **Köstenberger, Andreas J.; O'Brien, Peter Thomas** Salvation to
      the ends of the earth: a biblical theology of mission. New Studies in
      Biblical Theology 11: 2001 ⇒17,7771. ᴿTrinJ 23 (2002) 270-272
      (*Schnabel, Eckhard J.*); HBT 24/2 (2002) 126-7 (*Sunquist, Scott W.*).
8315 *Kritzinger, J.N.J.* The function of the bible in Protestant mission.
      ᶠNILES, D.: 2002 ⇒82. 18-43.
8316 *Legrand, L.* Trinitarian mission: universal mission: a biblical ap-
      proach. ITS 39 (2002) 109-115.
8317 *Lenchak, Timothy A.* The function of the bible in Roman Catholic
      mission. ᶠNILES, D. 2002 ⇒82. 1-17.
8318 *Lienemann-Perrin, Christine* Frauen zwischen "Missionsbefehl" und
      Männermacht. US 57 (2002) 103-121 [Mt 28].
8319 **Loerbroks, Matthias** Weisung vom Zion: biblisch-theologische Ori-
      entierungen für eine Kirche neben Israel. SKI 19: 2000 ⇒16,7902.
      ᴿThR 67 (2002) 389-390 (*Lindemann, Andreas*).
8320 **Lohfink, Gerhard** Braucht Gott die Kirche?: zur Theologie des Vol-
      kes Gottes. 1998 ⇒14,7162... 16,7903. ᴿThPQ 150 (2002) 204-205
      (*Gmainer-Pranzl, Franz*).
8321 *Löser, Werner* Das Volk Gottes und die Kirche aus Juden und Hei-
      den: Anmerkungen zur Katholizität und zur Apostolizität der Kirche.
      Cath(M) 56/3 (2002) 212-225 [Rom 9-11].
8322 *Manjaly, Thomas* Evangelisation through bible study groups.
      MissTod 4 (2002) 148-152.
8323 **Martuccelli, Paolo** Origine e natura della chiesa: la prospettiva
      storico-dommatica di Joseph RATZINGER. RSTh: 2001 ⇒17,7781.
      ᴿRdT 43 (2002) 295-297 (*Barruffo, Antonio*).
8324 *Mehedintu, Viorel* Die Einheit der Kirche aus orthodoxer Sicht nach
      Johannes 17,21. Einheit als Gabe. 2002 ⇒6424. 79-96.
8325 *Mueller, Celeste DeSchryver* People of God, hear God who calls.
      BiTod 40 (2002) 211-217.

8326 *Naumowicz, Józef* Orzech i laska Aarona czyli zgłebianie i głoszenie słowa bożego w ujeciu ojców kościoła [The almonds and the staff of Aaron—the deepening and proclaiming of the word of God according to the Church Fathers]. Verbum Vitae 2 (2002) 243-251. **P.**

8327 **Nissen, Johannes** New Testament and mission: historical and hermeneutical perspectives. 1999 ⇒15,7952...17,7785. [R]NT 44 (2002) 401-404 *(Schnabel, E.J.).*

8328 *Pelser, G.M.M.* Kerkvorming en -ontwikkeling in die Nuwe-Testamentiese tydvak. HTS 58 (2002) 1459-1485 [NTAb 47,507].

8329 *Raguin, Yves* Mission im Dialog: die erste Evangelisierung Chinas durch "nestorianische" Mönche. WUB Sonderheft (2002) 51-55.

8330 **Reinbold, Wolfgang** Propaganda und Mission im ältesten Christentum: eine Untersuchung zu den Modalitäten der Ausbreitung der frühen Kirche. FRLANT 188: 2000 ⇒16,7917; 17,7792. [R]ThLZ 127 (2002) 187-189 *(Niebuhr, Karl-Wilhelm)*.

8331 *Roloff, Jürgen* La diversidad de imágines de iglesia en el cristianismo primitivo. SelTeol 41 (2002) 244-250 <BiKi 56 (2001) 203-211.

8332 *Rossano, Pietro* Dialogue and mission;

8333 Teologia della missione <1972>;

8334 Missione e dialogo <1973>;

8335 L'annuncio cristiano di fronte alle sife della cultura contemporanea <1978>;

8336 Il dialogo nella missione della chiesa ad gentes <1990>. Teologia cristiana. DMis 27: 2002 ⇒232. 423-436/327-362/399-408/377-389/409-421.

8337 *Sattler, Dorothea* Von der als bestehend behaupteten zu der von Gott erflehten Einheit: Römisch-katholische Besinnung auf Joh 17,21. Einheit als Gabe. 2002 ⇒6424. 113-130.

8338 *Scheffczyk, Leo* Die Mission der Kirche: Verwirklichung des Königtums Christi im Reiche Christi. StMiss 51 (2002) 85-105.

8339 **Schnabel, Eckhard J.** Urchristliche Mission. Wu 2002, Brockhaus xxxii; 1806 pp. €59. 3-417-29475-4. Bibl. 1569-1679 [EuA 79,77—Schwank, Benedikt].

8340 **Senft, Christophe** Jésus et Paul: qui fut l'inventeur du christianisme?. Intersections: Genève 2002, Labor et F. 135 pp. €16.65. 2-8309-1037-0.

8341 *Sklba, Richard J.* Body of Christ. BiTod 40 (2002) 219-223.

8342 *Stuhlmacher, Peter* Kirche nach dem Neuen Testament <1995>;

8343 Der Zeugnisauftrag der Gemeinde Jesu Christi <2000>. Biblische Theologie. WUNT 146: 2002 ⇒245. 253-278/279-291.

8344 *Sultana, Joseph M.* Church government in the first century. Emmaus 3 (2002) 81-99.

8345 *Sundermeier, Theo* Matthäus 28 und die Frage nach dem Sinn der Mission. US 57 (2002) 98-102.

8346 *Ternynck, Marie J.* De Jérusalem à Rome : jalons historiques et bibliques pour une théologie de l'économie divine dans le cadre du christianisme naissant. Aletheia 21 (2002) 111-118.

8347 *Vos, C.J.A.* God's household and the poor in contextual ecclesiology. HTS 57 (2001) 49-69 [NTAb 46,501].

8348 *Vouga, François* Urchristentum. TRE 34. 2002 ⇒800. 411-436.

8349 *Wickeri, Philip L.* Toward a kenosis of mission: emptying and empowerment for the church and for the world. [F]NILES, D. 2002 ⇒82. 332-356.

8350 *Witczyk, H.* Dlaczego ewangelia? [Why the gospel?]. Verbum Vitae 2 (2002) 9-16. **P.**

H7.7 *Œcumenismus*—The ecumenical movement

8351 *Brueggemann, Walter* Ecumenism as the shared practice of a peculiar identity. Character and scripture. 2002 ⇒283. 231-247.
8352 *Edelmann, Helmut* Einträchtige Verschiedenheit: Beschreibung zwischenkirchlicher Erfahrungen im Hinblick auf Einheitsbemühungen. Einheit als Gabe. 2002 ⇒6424. 131-150.
      ᴱ**Innocenti, M.** La bibbia lacerata 2002 ⇒333.
8353 *Kähler, Christoph* Einheit, die ich meine: exegetische Anmerkungen zu einem ökumenischen Thema von Joh 17,21 her;
8354 *Kindt-Siegwalt, Irmgard* "Einheit in versöhnter Verschiedenheit"?: anders an die Einheit glauben und den Gegensatz erlauben. Einheit als Gabe. 2002 ⇒6424. 27-37/151-159.
8355 *Neuner, Peter* Mahlgemeinschaft: konfessionelle und ökumenische Erfahrungen, mögliche Schritte und Stolpersteine. BiKi 57 (2002) 31-35.
8356 *Nicole, Roger* Polemic theology—how to deal with those who differ from us. Standing forth. 2002 <1998> ⇒215. 9-25.
8357 *Norris, Thomas J.* A pioneering catholic ecumenist: Igino Giordani. IBSt 24 (2002) 118-133.
8358 *Rossano, Pietro* Identity and openness of religions: a catholic approach. Teologia cristiana. DMis 27: 2002 <1978> ⇒232. 305-316;
8359 Teologia e religioni: un problema contemporaneo. Teologia cristiana. DMis 27: 2002 <1980> ⇒232. 135-158.
8360 *Stobbe, Heinz-Günther* Konfessionelle Identität und Hermeneutik. US 57 (2002) 227-233.
8361 *Stuhlmacher, Peter* Biblisch-theologische Erwägungen zur Ökumene. Biblische Theologie. WUNT 146: 2002 ⇒245. 292-301.
8362 *Weyer, Michel* "... damit die Welt glaube": Joh 17,21 aus evangelisch-methodistischer Sicht. Einheit als Gabe. 2002 ⇒6424. 161-183 {John}17,21.

H7.8 **Amt**—*Ministerium ecclesiasticum*

8363 *Abir, Peter Antonysamy* Bible in the life of the priest. ITS 39 (2002) 257-279.
8364 ᴱ**Bellia, Giuseppe** Il diaconato: percorsi teologici. Reggio Emilia 2001, San Lorenzo 119 pp. 88-8071-109-1.
8365 *Bray, G.* Bishops, presbyters and women. ChM 116/1 (2002) 7-20 [NTAb 46,499].
8366 **Brent, Allen** The imperial cult and the development of church order: concepts and images of authority in paganism and early christianity before the age of CYPRIAN. SVigChr 45: 1999 ⇒15,7977...17,7817. ᴿChH 71 (2002) 867-870 (*Holt, Laura*).
8367 *Cornelius, Elma M.* Patriarchy and the New Testament. APB 13 (2002) 50-65.
8368 *Crawford, Sidnie White* Mothers, sisters, and elders: titles for women in second temple Jewish and early christian communities. Dead Sea scrolls as background. StTDJ 46: 2002 ⇒732. 177-191.

8369 *Creech, Richard R.* A response to "'Ordination' in Acts and the Pastoral Epistles" by Sharyn Dowd .PRSt 29/2 (2002) 219-221.

8370 *Dowd, Sharyn* "Ordination" in Acts and the Pastoral Epistles. PRSt 29/2 (2002) 205-217.

8371 **Eisen, Ute E.** Women officeholders in early christianity: epigraphical and literary studies. ᵀ*Maloney, Linda M.*: 2000 ⇒16,7946; 17,7820. ᴿJECS 10 (2002) 135-138 (*Jensen, Robin M.*); JEH 53 (2002) 118-119 (*Clark, Elizabeth A.*); CBQ 64 (2002) 571-572 (*Osiek, Carolyn*).

8372 *Espinosa, E.* The principle of authority and the criteria of orthodoxy in the early church. Asia Adventist Seminary Studies [Silang, Cavite, Philippines] 4 (2001) 77-88 [NTAb 47,86].

8373 *Ferguson, Everett* The 'congregationalism' of the early church. The Free Church. 2002 ⇒441. 129-140.

8374 *Grossman, Maxine* Priesthood and authority: interpretive competition in first-century Judaism and christianity. Dead Sea scrolls as background. StTDJ 46: 2002 ⇒732. 117-131.

8375 **Haag, Herbert** Da Gesù al sacerdozio. ᴱ*Tognina, Paolo*: 2001 ⇒17,7822. ᴿATT 8 (2002) 226-228 (*Piola, Alberto*).

8376 *Kasper, Card. Walter* Apostolic succession in the office of bishop as an ecumenical problem. ThD 47 (2002) 203-210.

8377 **Monari, Luciano; Gianotti, Daniele; Lombardini, Daniele** Gesù Servo, tipo della diaconia della chiesa. Sussidi biblici 76: Reggio Emilia 2002, San Lorenzo 107 pp. 88-8071-133-4.

8378 **Müller, Gerhard Ludwig** Priesthood and the diaconate: the recipient of the sacrament of holy orders from the perspective of creation theology and christology. ᵀ*Miller, Michael J.*: SF 2002, Ignatius 246 pp. 0-89870-892-3.

8379 *Nel, M.* Predikante opleiding: roeping, keuring en legitimering. VeE 23 (2002) 151-167.

8380 *Overath, Joseph* Zehn Bemerkungen zu einer Apologie der "Frauenordination" vom 29. Juni 2002. Theologisches 32 (2002) 463-474.

8381 **Perrot, Charles** Après Jésus: le ministère chez les premiers chrétiens. 2000 ⇒16,7956; 17,7829. ᴿLTP 58 (2002) 381-383 (*Poirier, Paul-Hubert*).

8382 *Pietras, Henryk* From presbyter to priest: the evolution of the concept of ministry. StBob 3 (2002) 5-17 Sum. 16. **P.**

8383 *Pigott, Susan M.* A response to "The Old Testament antecedents for ordination" by Thomas Brisco. PRSt 29/2 (2002) 177-182.

8384 *Robinson, Bernard P.* Patterns of ministry in the New Testament church. NBl 83 (2002) 73-85.

8385 *Rodríguez Souquet, Carlos* El obispo y la palabra. Labor Theologicus 29 (2002) 111-125.

8386 *Roloff, Jürgen* Eucharist and ministry in the NT. ThD 49 (2002) 128-138.

8387 **Schmelz, Georg** Kirchliche Amtsträger im spätantiken Ägypten: nach den Aussagen der griechischen und koptischen Papyri und Ostraka. APF.B 13: Mü 2002, Saur ix (2); 411 pp. 3-598-77548-2. Bibl. 330-367.

8388 **Schöllgen, Georg** Die Anfänge der Professionalisierung des Klerus und das kirchliche Amt in der syrischen Didaskalie. JAC.E 26: 1998 ⇒14,7208. ᴿGn. 74 (2002) 559-561 (*Gizewski, Christian*).

8389 *Sporcic, Ivan* Biblijsko poimanje sluzenja i crkvenosti sluzbâ. BoSm 72 (2002) 277-308.

8390   *Sumney, Jerry L.* New Testament perspectives on ministry. LexTQ
       37/1-2 (2002) 27-41 [BuBB 38,97].
8391   *Tchape, Jean Bosco* Le ministère de l'alliance nouvelle: lecture afri-
       caine des sources bibliques. AETSC 10 (2002) 31-46.
8392   *Varó, Francisco* Santidad y sacerdocio: del Antiguo al Nuevo Testa-
       mento. ScrTh 34 (2002) 13-43.
8393   *Warford, Malcolm L.* The hope of our calling: thinking about minis-
       try in the context of Ephesians 1-4:16. LexTQ 37/1-2 (2002) 43-59
       [BuBB 38,97].
8394   **Wijngaards, John** No women in holy orders?: the women deacons
       of the early church. Norwich 2002, Canterbury vii (2) 222 pp. 1-853-
       11-507-X. Bibl. 211-214.

H8.0 **Oratio**, *spiritualitas personalis NT*

       Abir, Peter A. Bible in the life of the priest 2002 ⇒8363.
8395   **Baudoz, Jean-François** Avec le Christ, l'évangile à l'école de saint
       BENOÎT. P 2002, Desclée de B. 116 pp. €14.5. ᴿRICP 82 (2002) 203-
       204 (*Quesnel, Michel*).
8396   *Bellia, Giuseppe* Parola di Dio e discernimento. CredOg 127 (2002)
       21-36.
8397   **Bernard-Marie, Frère** Prier le rosaire avec la bible. Versailles
       ⁶2002, Saint-Paul 112 pp. €8.50.
8398   **Bissoli, C.** Maestro, dove abiti: itinerari giovanile con il vangelo.
       Leumann 2002, Elledici 144 pp. €7.50.
8399   **Boada ı Rafí, Jaume** Fijos los ojos en Jesús: la parábola del agua. M
       2002, Narcea 171 pp. €9.10. 84-277-1393-2 [EstJos 56,287—Jesús
       María, José de].
8400   ᵀ**Boenig, Robert** Anglo-Saxon spirituality: selected writings. Clas-
       sics of western spirituality: 2000 ⇒16,7969. ᴿTheoforum 33 (2002)
       255-256 (*Russell, Kenneth C.*).
8401   *Böke, Hubert* Die Bibel im seelsorgerlichen Gespräch mit Kranken.
       Die Bibel neu ins Spiel bringen. 2002 ⇒994. 103-117.
8402   **Bunge, Gabriel** Earthen vessels: the practice of personal prayer ac-
       cording to the patristic tradition. ᵀ*Miller, Michael J.*: SF 2002, Igna-
       tius 222 pp. $15. 0-89870-837-0. Drawings by *Francesco Riganti*
       [ThD 49,365—Heiser, W. Charles].
8403   *Cariou-Charton, Sylvain* Le Dieu qui tient parole. Christus 49/193
       (2002) 17-25.
8404   **Castronovo, Filippa** 'Alzo gli occhi verso i monti' (Sal 121,1). CoSe
       51/11 (2002) 11-19.
8405   **Cavalcoli, Giovanni** Il silenzio della parola: le mistiche a confronto.
       SacDo.Mon. 47/3-4: Bo 2002, Studio Domenicano 357 pp. 88-7094-
       461-1.
8406   **Collins, Pat** Prayer in practice: a biblical approach. 2000 ⇒17,7851.
       ᴿIThQ 67 (2002) 92-93 (*Cunningham, Enda*); Horizons 29 (2002)
       181-182 (*Reiser, William*).
8407   **Cones, Bryan M.** Daily prayer 2002. Ch 2002, Liturgical Training
       390 pp. $15 [BiTod 39,380—Bergant, Dianne].
8408   **De Luca, Erri** Nocciolo d'oliva. Terra & cielo 8: Padova 2002, Mes-
       saggero 130 pp. 88-250-1020-6.

8409 **Dunne, John S.** Reading the gospel. 2000 ⇒16,7979. [R]ABenR 53 (2002) 219-221 (*Kodell, Jerome*); NewTR 15/2 (2002) 87-88 (*Tambasco, Anthony J.*).

8410 *Fenske, Wolfgang* Gebetserhörung. MThZ 53 (2002) 265-274.

8411 *Fortin, Pierre* 'Rabbi, ubi habitas?'. Contacts 54 (2002) 311-322 [Jn 1,35-39].

8412 **García, Pablo** Las siete palabras de Jesús en la cruz. Nueva Alianza Minor 7: S 2002, Sígueme 126 pp [LSDC 18/1,98–Quintero, J.L.].

8413 **Giallanza, Joel** Questions Jesus asked. Staten Island 2002, Alba 106 pp. $6 [BiTod 41,132—Senior, Donald].

8414 **Giorgianni, Giovanni** Pane per un giorno: meditazioni evangeliche. Bibbia e Preghiera 44: R 2002, ADP 92 pp. 88-7357-271-5.

8415 **Gittins, Anthony J.** Encountering Jesus. Liguori 2002, Liguori xii; 132 pp. $15 [BiTod 41,65—Senior, Donald.].

8416 **Goldingay, John** Walk on: life, loss, trust, and other realities. GR 2002, Baker 200 pp. $17.

8417 *Grayston, John* The bible and spirituality: the decline in biblical literacy among evangelicals and the future of the quiet time. Anvil 19/2 (2002) 99-107.

8418 **Guardini, Romano** El Señor: meditaciones sobre la persona y la vida de Jesucristo. M 2002, Cristiandad 706 pp. 84-7057-461-2.

8419 **Harrington, Wilfrid J.** Seeking spiritual growth through the bible. Robert J. Wicks Spirituality Selection: NY 2002, Paulist v; 143 pp. $15. 0-8091-3999-5.

8420 *Hughes, Peter* Monizioni e preghiere per la liturgia delle ore durante il colloquio. VM 56/222 (2002) 75-79.

8421 **Hurtado, Larry W.** At the origins of christian worship: the context and character of earliest christian devotion. 2000 ⇒16,7985; 17,7865. [R]AThR 84 (2002) 173-174 (*McGowan, Andrew*); TJT 18 (2002) 265-266 (*Knowles, Michael*); RBLit 4 (2002) 301-303 (*Luper, Michael*).

8422 **Ibáñez Ramos, Miguel-Antonio** Al ayuno en el Nuevo Testamento, a la luz de la tradición veterotestamentaria y los apócrifos del Antiguo Testamento. Pamplona 2002, 85 pp. Extr. Diss. Navarra 2002.

8423 **Karris, Robert J.** Prayer and the New Testament. 2000 ⇒16,7987. [R]CBQ 64 (2002) 165-167 (*Kiley, Mark*); LASBF 51 (2001) 441-444 (*Chrupcała, L.D.*).

8424 **Keating, Thomas** Open mind, open heart: the contemplative dimension of the gospel. NY 2002, Continuum vi; 148 pp. 0-8264-1420-6.

8425 **Larsen, David L.** Biblical spirituality: discovering the real connection between the bible and life. 2001 ⇒17,7871. [R]CTJ 37 (2002) 184-185 (*Schwanda, Tom*).

8426 [E]**Longenecker, Richard N.** Into God's presence: prayer in the New Testament. 2001 ⇒17,294. [R]RTR 61 (2002) 106-107 (*Oakes, Barry*); ScrB 32 (2002) 108-110 (*Corley, Jeremy*); Worship 76 (2002) 475-476 (*Dumm, Demetrius R.*); Theol. 105 (2002) 456-457 (*Fenton, John*); CBQ 64 (2002) 801-802 (*Clabeaux, John J.*); RExp 99 (2002) 278-279 (*Brachlow, Stephen*).

8427 *Maier, Bernhard* Ex oriente lux: ein altirisches Gebet und seine Parallelen. [F]HOHEISEL, K.: JAC.E 34: 2002 ⇒59. 423-426.

8428 *Martínez de Pisón Liébanas, Ramón* Del templo en piedras al verdadero templo de Dios: el itinerario de la vida en el Espíritu. Communio 35/1 (2002) 63-78.

8429   **Masini, Mario** Spiritualità biblica: temi e percorsi. 2000 ⇒16,7993; 17,7877. ᴿTer. 53 (2002) 286-288 (*Pasquetto,Virgilio*); Annales Theologici 16 (2002) 251-253 (*Tábet, M.*).

8430   **McKenna, Megan** Christ, all merciful. Ment. Mkn 2002, Orbis 168 pp. $20. 1-57075-449-7. Icons by *McNichols, William H.* [ThD 50, 174—Heiser, W. Charles].

8431   *Melo, Luís Rochae* Die Mysterien des Lebens Jesu in den geistlichen Schulen vor und während des 16. Jahrhunderts. IKaZ 31 (2002) 34-49; Communio 24,191-205.

8432   **Metzger, Marcel** Les sources de la prière. Vivre, croire, célèbrer: P 2002, L'Atelier 141 pp. €13.50. 2-7082-3602-4.

8433   *Monzio Compagnoni, Giordano* "Avete ascoltato la scrittura? Fa al caso vostro" : proclamazione, lectio divina e meditazione. Ambrosius 78/4 (2002) 469-512.

8434   **O'Donnell, Desmond; Mohen, Maureen** Praying the New Testament as psalms. Ch 2002, ACTA 216 pp. $13. 0-87946-233-7 [BiTod 40,332—Senior, Donald].

8435   **Pasquetto, Virgilio** Chiamati a vita nuova: temi di spiritualità biblica, 1: Antico Testamento, 2: Nuovo Testamento. R 2002, Libreria Editrice Vaticana 277 + 375 pp. €17+21.50. 88-209-7355-3/6-1 [REsp 61,656—Castro, Secundino].

8436   *Petey-Girard, Bruno* Bible et tradition liturgique dans les prières françaises de la fin du XVIᵉ siècle. BHR 64 (2002) 353-368.

8437   **Pérez Prieto, Victorino** Con cuerdas de ternura: para un encuentro con el Dios de Jesús de Nazaret. M 2002, Narcea 179 pp.

8438   ᴱ**Pricoco, Salvatore; Simonetti, Manlio** La preghiera dei cristiani. Scritti greci e latini: 2000 ⇒16,7997. ᴿRSLR 38 (2002) 153-156 (*Lucca, Claudia; Parrinello, Rosa Maria*).

8439   **Quéré, France** Au fil de la foi, 1: le chemin d l'écriture, 2: le pas à pas de la vie. 2000 ⇒16,7998. ᴿNRTh 124 (2002) 455-457 (*Rader-makers, J.*).

8440   *Richerd, Joël* Atelier sur l'efficacité de la prière. ThEv(VS) 1/1 (2002) 81-89 [James 5,16-18].

8441   *Schneiders, Sandra M.* Biblical spirituality. Interp. 56 (2002) 133-42.

8442   *Schreiter, Robert J.* Gebet und Gottesdienst. Die Bibel: Geschichte und Gegenwart. 2002 ⇒971. 92-93.

8443   *Schütz, Christian* Die Mysterien des Lebens Jesu als Prisma des Glaubens. IKaZ 31 (2002) 8-21; Communio 24,158-170.

8444   *Sokołowski, Marek* Biblijno-duchowe wymiary kultu Serca Bożego [The biblical and spiritual dimensions of devotion to the Sacred Heart]. StBob 2 (2002) 117-130 Sum. 129. **P**.

8445   *Tosato, Angelo* Vangelo e libertà. Vangelo e ricchezza. 2002 <2000> ⇒246. 189-251.

8446   **Uciecha, Andrzej** Ascetyczna Nauka w "Mowach" Afrahata. Studia i Materialy Wydzialu Teologicznego Univ. Slaskiego w Katowicach 3: Katowice 2002, Sw. Jacka 192 pp. 83-7030-386-2. Bibl. 181-185.

8447   *Van Zyl, H.C.* Die probleemareas in gebed: 'n perspektief vanuit die Nuewe Testament. HTS 57 (2001) 379-396 [NTAb 46,510].

8448   *Vanhoye, Albert* La lettera uccide, lo Spirito vivifica. Potenza divina d'amore 11/6 (2002) 5 col. (senza paginazione) [AcBib 10,915];

8449   Cristo ci ha liberati perché restassimo liberi. Vita consacrata in Lombardia 16/61 (2002) 7-30 [AcBib 10,1032].

8450   **Vanhoye, Albert** Cristo sommo sacerdote della nuova alleanza. Spiritualità e Vita 2: Treviso 2002, San Liberale 136 pp.

8451 **Verlinde, Joseph-Marie** Initiation à la lectio divina. P 2002, Parole et Silence: 237 pp. €17. 2845731280 [RTL 33,603: Houdart, M.-A.].
8452 **Weber, Hans-Ruedi** Walking on the way: biblical signposts. Risk Book 97: Geneva 2002, WCC x; 99 pp. $11/£7. 2-8254-1357-7.
8453 **Welborn, Amy** Prayer. Prove it!: Huntington, IN 2002, Our Sunday Visitor 109 pp. $7. 0-87973-544-9 [ThD 50,94: Heiser, W. Charles].

H8.1 *Spiritualitas publica*: Liturgia, Via communitatis, Sancti

8454 *Antoniou, Spyridon* Les lectures psalmodiées dans la tradition liturgique orthodoxe. Contacts 54 (2002) 299-310.
8455 *Bäumer, Regina* Mitteilung statt Wiedergabe: zum Sinn sprecherischer Inszenierung biblischer Texte im Gottesdienst. HlD 56 (2002) 287-291.
8456 *Black, C. Clifton* Journeying through scripture with the lectionary's map. Interp. 56 (2002) 59-72.
8457 *Blanchard, Yves-Marie* Ancien et Nouveau Testament dans le cycle liturgique. La liturgie, interprète. BEL.P 119: 2002 ⇒606. 221-233.
8458 *Blaza, Marek* Proklamacja słowa Bożego w bizantyjskiej tradycji liturgicznej [The proclamation of the word of God in the Byzantine liturgical tradition]. StBob 2 (2002) 131-155 Sum. 155. **P**.
8459 *Bobrinskoy, Boris* Les formes rituelles des lectures bibliques: les rites accompagnant les lectures évangéliques et leur sens dans la tradition liturgique byzantine orthodoxe. Contacts 54 (2002) 292-298;
8460 Formes rituelles des lectures bibliques. La liturgie, interprète. BEL.P 119: 2002 ⇒606. 123-128.
8461 *Boisclair, Regina A.* Conflicting messages?: the sunday lectionaries and official church teachings. Theology and sacred scripture. 2002 ⇒ 549. 165-183.
8462 **Bolchi, Elena Lucia** La consacrazione nell'Ordo Virginum: forma di vita e disciplina canonica. TGr.Diritto Canonico 56: R 2002, E.P.U.G. 446 pp. €26. 88-7652-937-3.
8463 **Bongartz, Heinz-Günter; Steins, Georg** Österliche Lichtspuren: alttestamentliche Wege in die Osternacht. Mü 2002, Bernward 144 pp. €15.30 [BiLi 75,66—Wellmann, Bettina].
8464 **Bradshaw, Paul** Early christian worship: a basic introduction. 2000 ⇒16,8015. [R]SVTQ 46/1 (2002) 98-99 (*Stewart-Sykes, Alistair*);
8465 The search for the origins of christian worship: sources and methods for the study of early liturgy. NY [2]2002 <1992>, OUP xi; 244 pp. $20. 0-1952-1732-2.
8466 **Butcher, John Beverley** An uncommon lectionary: a companion to common lectionaries. Santa Rosa, CA 2002, Polebridge viii; 255 pp. 0-944344-91-7.
8467 **Cantalamessa, Raniero** Gettate le reti: riflessioni sui vangeli: Anno B. Piemme Religione: CasM 2002, Piemme 408 pp. 88-384-6440-5.
8468 *Carbonnier-Burkard, Marianne* La tradition des lectures bibliques dans le culte réformé. La liturgie, interprète. BEL.P 119: 2002 ⇒ 606. 83-96.
8469 *Carmassi, Patrizia* Die Bearbeitung des ambrosianischen Lektionars in karolingischer Zeit: Kontinuität trotz Reform. Liturgiereformen. 2002 ⇒416. 295-303.

8470 *Carmassi, Patrizia* ...qualiter beatus AMBROSIUS libros Veteris Testamenti et Novi ad legendum ecclesiae suae disposuisset: il lezionario della chiesa milanese tra età tardo antica e medioevale. ScC 130 (2002) 837-879.

8471 *Casciaro, José María* La "lectura" de la biblia en los escritos y en la predicación del Beato Josemaria ESCRIVÁ de Balaguer. ScrTh 34 (2002) 133-167.

8472 **Casel, Odo** Fede, gnosi e mistero: saggio di teologia del culto cristiano. 2001 ⇒17,7908. ᴿRdT 43 (2002) 294-295 (*Cattaneo, Enrico*).

8473 *Cernokrak, Nicolas* La narratologie liturgique byzantine selon les péricopes dominicales du Grand Carême de l'évangile de Saint Marc. La liturgie, interprète. BEL.P 119: 2002 ⇒606. 183-200.

8474 **Chiaroni, Angelo** Alzo gli occhi verso i monti: commenti alle letture della liturgia: ciclo B e feste. Studi e ricerche di liturgia: Bo 2002, EDB 236 pp. €14.98.

8475 *Chilton, Bruce* Festivals and lectionaries: correspondence and distinctions .Gospels according to Goulder. 2002 ⇒594. 12-28.

8476 *Crainshaw, Jill Y.* Embodied remembering: wisdom, character, and worship. Character and scripture. 2002 ⇒283. 363-388.

8477 **Davis, Stephen J.** The cult of St. THECLA: a tradition of women's piety in late antiquity. Oxf 2002, OUP xiv; 288 pp. £45. 0-1982-7019-4. ᴿJBL 121 (2002) 582-585 (*Burrus, Virginia*).

8478 **De Virgilio, Giuseppe** Il tesoro e il cuore: un itinerario biblico in prospettiva vocazionale. R 2002, Rogate 198 pp. 88-8075-111-5. Bibl. 193-194.

8479 *Doeker, Andrea* Identität durch Gebet?: zur gemeinschaftsbildenden Funktion institutionalisierten Betens in Judentum und Christentum. LJ 52 (2002) 116-121.

8480 **Donahue, John R.** Hearing the word of God: reflections on the Sunday readings—year B. ColMn 2002, Liturgical x; 169 pp. 0-8146-27-83-8.

8481 *Donohue, James M.* The choice and function of biblical texts in the post-conciliar rites for the commendation of the dying. Theology and sacred scripture. 2002 ⇒549. 184-207.

8482 **Dunn, James D.G.** La llamada de Jesús al seguimiento. 2001 ⇒17, 7919. ᴿSalTer 90/1 (2002) 81 (*Alcaraz, Juan Pedro*).

8483 *Earey, Mark* This is the word of the Lord: the bible and worship. Anvil 19/2 (2002) 89-97.

8484 **Federici, T.** Cristo Signore risorto amato e celebrato: commento al lezionario domenicale cicli A,B,C. Quaderni di 'Oriente cristiano' 11: 2001 ⇒17,7922. ᴿRivLi 89 (2002) 747-756 (*Falcone, Antonio*).

8485 *Ferris, Susanne Sartor* The bible on sterioids: the effect of androcentrism on the lectionary. NewTR 15/1 (2002) 21-31.

8486 *Fiedler, Peter* Kultkritik im Neuen Testament?. Liturgiereformen. 2002 ⇒416. 68-94.

8487 *Fleinert-Jensen, Flemming* Les lectures bibliques du culte dans la tradition luthérienne. La liturgie, interprète. BEL.P 119: 2002 ⇒606. 75-82.

8488 **Förster, Hans** Die Feier der Geburt Christi in der Alten Kirche: Beiträge zur Erforschung der Anfänge des Epiphanie- und des Weihnachtsfests. STAC 4: 2000 ⇒16,8024. ᴷZKG 113 (2002) 97-99 (*Baumeister, Theofried*).

8489 **Fumagalli, Edoardo** San FRANCESCO, il Cantico, il Pater Noster. Biblioteca di Cultura Medievale/Di fronte e attraverso 576: Mi 2002, Jaca 112 pp.

8490 *Gagnebin, Laurent* Y a-t-il un rite reformé de la lecture biblique dans le culte?. La liturgie, interprète. BEL.P 119: 2002 ⇒606. 135-144.

8491 *Garnier, Sébastien* Les leçons scripturaires de la Mi-Pentecôte. La liturgie, interprète. BEL.P 119: 2002 ⇒606. 213-220.

8492 *Gerhards, Albert* Dem Wort Gottes Gestalt geben: heutige Anfragen an tradierte Formen des Wortgottesdienstes. Wie das Wort Gottes feiern?. QD 194: 2002 ⇒417. 146-165.

8493 *Getcha, Job* Le système des lectures bibliques du rite byzantin. La liturgie, interprète. BEL.P 119: 2002 ⇒606. 25-56.

8494 **Glen, Genevieve** Take with your words: hymn texts with biblical reflections. Portland 2002, OCP 184 pp. $20.

8495 ᴱ**Gruson, Philippe** Paroles de vie: 59 textes bibliques pour les funérailles. CEv 120: P 2002, Cerf 66 pp. €5.79. 0222-9714.

8496 **Gutiérrez, Guillermo** Hablaré de ti a mis hermanos: la palabra de Dios de los domingos y fiestas: ciclo B. Alcalá 2002, CCS 340 pp [Eccl(R) 17,409—Yajure, Roger].

8497 *Haroutiounian-Thomas, Gohar* Les lectures eucharistiques des dimanches du Grand Carême d'après le rite arménien. La liturgie, interprète. BEL.P 119: 2002 ⇒606. 173-182.

8498 *Hauser-Borel, Sylvie* Profetisas, mártires, testigos de Cristo en la historia : una "martyría" enraizada en la tradición neotestamentaria y patrística. AnáMnesis 12/2 (2002) 5-36.

8499 **Hoagland, Victor** Saints of the New Testament. ᴱ*Bence, Evelyn*: NY 2002, Regina 147 pp. $20 [BiTod 41,134—Senior, Donald].

8500 *Houlden, James L.* Why were the disciples ever called disciples?. Theol. 105 (2002) 411-417.

8501 ᴱ**Houlden, Leslie; Rogerson, John** The common worship lectionary: a scripture commentary, year A. 2001 ⇒17,7939. ᴿAThR 84 (2002) 775-776 (*Thompson, H.L.*).

8502 *Janeras, Sebastià* 'Testament' et 'talent', deux péricopes évangéliques de la liturgie de Jérusalem [Mt 24,1-26,2; Jn 13,16-18,1];

8503 *Jeanlin, Françoise* Lecture liturgique de Proverbes 9,1-11 pour les fêtes mariales byzantines. La liturgie, interprète. BEL.P 119: 2002 ⇒ 606. 163-171/201-209.

8504 *Kijas, Zdzisław J.* La donna che calpesta la testa del serpente, "ossia ... il fuoco dell'apostolato in P. KOLBE". EphMar 52/2 (2002) 245-65 [Gen 3,15].

8505 *Klein, Wassilios* Liturgisches in der Barlaam-Legende im Dienst der Katechese. ᶠHOHEISEL, K.: JAC.E 34: 2002 ⇒59. 295-302.

8506 **Kranemann, Daniela** Israelitica dignitas?: Studien zur Israeltheologie Eucharistischer Hochgebete. MThA 66: 2001 ⇒17,7946. ᴿLJ 52 (2002) 279-280 (*Leonhard, Clemens*).

8507 *Kreier, Johannes* "... wächst eine Kette ins Ostern: Elemente zur Einheit der österlichen Drei-Tage-Feier. BiLi 75 (2002) 167-173.

8508 *Lang, Walter* Unsere Christusnachfolge. Theologisches 32 (2002) 266-274.

8509 ᴱᵀ**Laurence, Patrick** Gerontius: la vie latine de Sainte MÉLANIE. SBF.CMi 41: J 2002, Franciscan Printing Press 352 pp. $30. 965-51-6049-1. Bibl. 10-27. ᴿLASBF 52 (2002) 591-595 (*Guazzelli, Giuseppe Antonio*).

8510 **Lewis, Alan E.** Between cross and resurrection: a theology of Holy Saturday. 2001 ⇒17,7951. [R]IBSt 24 (2002) 134-144 (*Russell, R. Alan*); TrinJ 23 (2002) 277-280 (*Pegler, Stephen*).

8511 *Longeat, Jean-Pierre* Cantillation, chant ou lecture de la parole de Dieu dans la liturgie. La liturgie, interprète. 2002 ⇒606. 129-133.

8512 *Lossky, André* Péricopes johanniques lues en temps pascal: récits de guérison et résurrection. La liturgie, interprète. BEL.P 119: 2002 ⇒ 606. 147-161 [Jn 5,1-15; 9,1-38].

8513 *Manzi, Franco* Tradizione e traduzione della sacra scrittura in 'Liturgiam authenticam'. Not. 38 (2002) 602-635.

8514 *Marshall, I. Howard* Worshipping biblically. SBET 20 (2002) 146-161.

8515 **Masini, Mario** La "lectio divina": teologia, spiritualità, metodo. CinB 2002, San Paolo 509 pp. 88-215-3126-0. Bibl. 469-472.

8516 **Matura, Th.** E lasciato tutto lo seguirono: fondamenti biblici della vita religiosa. 1999 ⇒16,8042. Comunità di Bose. [R]Asp. 49 (2002) 142-143 (*Rega, Stefano*).

8517 *McRaith, John* The disciple of Christ as steward. BiTod 40 (2002) 291-295.

8518 *Meggitt, Justin J.* The first churches: relegous life. Biblical world, 2. 2002 ⇒273. 157-172.

8519 **Meissner, W.W.** The cultic origins of christianity: the dynamics of religious development. 2000 ⇒16,8044; 17,7964. [R]NewTR 15/2 (2002) 76-77 (*Duffy, Regis A.*); RBLit 4 (2002) 460-465 (*Swartley, Willard M.*).

8520 *Mesters, Carlos* Formati alla scuola del vangelo. VitaCon 38 (2002) 451-462.

8521 *Metropolit Pitirim* Die orthodoxe Liturgie. Die Bibel: Geschichte und Gegenwart. 2002 ⇒971. 146-147.

8522 *Metzger, Marcel* De la synagogue à l'église: fonction ecclésiale des lectures bibliques dans la liturgie. La liturgie, interprète. BEL.P 119: 2002 ⇒606. 235-250.

8523 *Mohr, Johannes* 'Lobpreis seiner Herrlichkeit': Leben als Ebenbild Gottes—das Beispiel der seligen ELISABETH von Dijon. [F]HAAG, E. 2002 ⇒55. 361-381 [Gen 1,26-27].

8524 *Morales, José* La vocación en los evangelios. ScrTh 34 (2002) 785-825.

8525 **Mulloor, Augustine** Called to be special: salvation-historical vistas on consecrated life. Theological Series 13: Kerala 2002, Jyothir Dhara viii; 203 pp.

8526 **Murphy, Roland E.** Experiencing our biblical heritage. 2001 ⇒17, 7966. [R]Spiritual Life 48 (2002) 180-182 (*Bergant, Dianne*); HPR 103/2 (2002) 78-79 (*Miller, Michael J.*); IThQ 67 (2002) 300-301 & 68 (2003) 85-87 (*Maher, Michael*).

8527 **Müllner, Ilse; Dschulnigg, Peter** Jüdische und christliche Feste: Perspektiven des Alten und Neuen Testaments. Die neue Echter-Bibel, Themen 9: Wü 2002, Echter 136 pp. €14.40. 3-429-02175-8.

8528 **Old, Hughes Oliphant** Worship: Reformed according to scripture. LVL 2002, Westminster 195 pp. $20. 0-664-22579-9.

8529 *Padovese, Luigi* Cercatori di Dio: sulle tracce dell'ascetismo pagano, ebraico e cristiano dei primi secoli. Uomini e religioni, Saggi: Mi 2002, Mondadori 366 pp. 88-04-49019-5.

8530 **Pardilla, A.** La forma di vita di Cristo al centro della formazione alla vita religiosa: il quadro biblico e teologico della formazione. 2001 ⇒ 17,7969. ᴿClar. 42 (2002) 357-358 (*Cabra, Pier Giordano*).

8531 **Pilch, John J.** The cultural world of the Apostles: the second reading, Sunday by Sunday, year B. ColMn 2002, Liturgical xvi; 124 pp. $12. 0-8146-2726-9. Bibl. 123-124;

8532 The cultural world of the prophets: the first reading and responsorial psalm: Sunday by Sunday, Year B. ColMn 2002, Liturgical xiv; 127 pp. 0-8146-2787-0. Bibl. 126-127.

8533 *Polfliet, Joris* Les lectures bibliques liturgiques pour les dimanches et les fêtes, dans l'usage romain actuel. La liturgie, interprète. BEL.P 119: 2002 ⇒606. 57-73.

8534 **Power, David Noel** "The Word of the Lord": liturgy's use of scripture. 2001 ⇒17,7971. ᴿRRT 9 (2002) 337-339 (*Burdon, Adrian*); Horizons 29 (2002) 366-367 (*Morrill, Bruce T.*).

8535 ᴱ**Pryce, Mark** Literary companion to the lectionary: readings throughout the year. Mp 2002, Fortress xiii; 143 pp. $17. 0-8006-34-64-0 [CThMi 30/1,55—Carlson, Paula J.].

8536 **Ramshaw, Gail** Treasures old and new: images in the lectionary. Mp 2002, Fortress 477 pp. $45. 0-8006-3189-7 [CThMi 30/1,54—Dentry, Ann].

8537 *Renoux, Charles* Les premiers systèmes de lecture dans l'Orient chrétien, Jérusalem, Édesse, Antioche, et la synagogue. La liturgie, interprète. BEL.P 119: 2002 ⇒606. 99-121.

8538 *Repschinski, Boris* Anmerkungen zu einigen Thesen von Liturgiam Authenticam. PzB 11 (2002) 71-76.

8539 *Rolheiser, Ronald* Vocations: the cultural, ecclesial, and biblical moment. Seminarium 42 (2002) 137-144.

8540 *Rouwhorst, Gerard A.M.* The reading of scripture in early christian liturgy. ᶠFOERSTER, G. 2002 ⇒39. 305-331.

8541 **Sacino, G.** Verso la pasqua in compagnia dei profeti. Terlizzi 2002, Insieme 193 pp. ᴿMiles Immaculatae 38/1 (2002) 221-222 (*Pagano, Dario*).

8542 *Sattler, Dorothea* Gegenwart Gottes im Wort: systematisch-theologische Aspekte. Wie das Wort Gottes feiern?. QD 194: 2002 ⇒417. 123-143.

8543 **Saxer, Victor** Saint VINCENT diacre et martyr: culte et légendes avant l'An Mil. SHG 83: Bru 2002, Société des Bollandistes vii; 372 pp. 2-87365-011-7.

8544 *Schilson, Arno* Liturgie als Ort der Gegenwart und Wirksamkeit der Geheimnisse des Lebens Jesu. IKaZ 31 (2002) 22-33; Communio 24, 179-190.

8545 *Senior, Donald* Come, follow me: foundations for the christian vocations of ordained ministry and consecrated life. Seminarium 42/1 (2002) 95-111.

8546 *Sloyan, Gerard S.* 'Thus faith comes from what is heard' (Romans 10:17): how much of the bible do people hear?. BTB 32 (2002) 100-106.

8547 *Söding, Thomas* Wort des lebendigen Gottes?: die neutestamentlichen Briefe im Wortgottesdienst der Eucharistiefeier. Wie das Wort Gottes feiern?. QD 194: 2002 ⇒417. 41-81.

8548 **Spicer, J.E.** Preparing for Sunday: exploring the readings for Year B. Toronto 2002, Novalis 139 pp. $10 [BiTod 41,271—Senior, D.].

8549   **Staubli, Thomas** Erinnerung stiftet Leben: Begleiter zu den Sonn-
       tagslesungen aus dem Ersten Testament: Lesejahr B. Luzern 2002,
       Exodus 256 pp. €24. 3-905577-58-5. 88 ill. [EuA 79,351].

8550   **Stock, Klemens** La liturgia della parola: spiegazione dei vangeli do-
       menicali e festivi: Anno B (Marco). Bibbia e Preghiera 45: R 2002,
       ADP 385 pp. 88-7357-274-X.

8551   **Terrinoni, U.** Parola di Dio e voti religiosi: icone bibliche, 1: obbe-
       dienza. Bo 2002, EDB 143 pp [Clar. 43,428s—García Castro, F.].

8552   **Theissen, Gerd** De godsdienst van de eerste christenen—een theorie
       van het oerchristendom. 2001 ⇒17,7991. [R]Coll. 113-114 (2002)
       217-218 (*Hoet, Hendrik*).

8553   *Towner, W. Sibley* The inner self, the word of God, and the cause that
       matters. Interp. 56 (2002) 192-195.

8554   *Tucker, Karen B. Westerfield* The lectionary our common table?: a
       Protestant view. OiC 37/4 (2002) 55-62.

8555   **Van Henten, Jan Willem; Avemarie, Friedrich** Martyrdom and
       noble death: selected texts from Graeco-Roman, Jewish and Chris-
       tian antiquity. The context of early Christianity: L 2002, Routledge
       xvi; 200 pp. £15. 0-415-13890-6/1-4. Bibl. 177-191.

8556   **Vanni, Ugo** Con Gesù verso il Padre: per una spiritualità della seque-
       la. Bibbia e Preghiera 41: R 2002, ADP 316 pp. €10.33. 88-7357-25-
       6-1.

8557   **Weiner, Eugene; Weiner, Anita** The martyr's conviction: a socio-
       logical analysis, Studies in Judaism: Lanham 2002, Univ. Pr. of
       America x; 159 pp. 0-7618-2283-6.

8558   **Wick, Peter** Die urchristlichen Gottesdienste: Entstehung und Ent-
       wicklung im Rahmen der frühjüdischen Tempel-, Synagogen- und
       Hausfrömmigkeit. BWANT 150: Stu 2002, Kohlhammer 423 pp.
       €40.80. 3-17-016692-1. Bibl. 394-415. [R]RHPhR 82 (2002) 220-221
       (*Grappe, Ch.*).

8559   *Winkler, Gabriele* Zur Bedeutung alttestamentlicher Schriftzitate im
       ante Sanctus und ihre liturgiewissenschaftliche Deutung. OrChr 86
       (2002) 192-205.

8560   **Winkler, Gabriele** Das Sanctus: über den Ursprung und die Anfänge
       des Sanctus und sein Fortwirken. OCA 267: R 2002, E.P.I.O xlii; 281
       pp. 88-7210-334-7. Bibl. xviii-xxxix.

8561   *Wright, N.T.* Freedom and framework, spirit and truth: recovering
       biblical worship. StLi 32 (2002) 176-195.

8562   **Zevini, Giorgio** La lectio divina nella comunità cristiana: spiritualità
       —metodo—prassi. Interpretare la Bibbia oggi, 1/2: Brescia [2]2001,
       Queriniana 157 pp. 88-399-2452-3.;

8563   [E]**Zevini, Giorgio; Cabra, Pier Giordano** Ferias del tiempo ordina-
       rio (semanas 1-8, años pares). Lectio divina para cada día del año 5:
       Estella (Navarra) 2002, Verbo Divino 381 pp. 84-8169-489-4;

8564   Lectio divina 7: ferias del tiempo ordinario, semanas 18-25, años pa-
       res. Estella 2002, Verbo Divino 384 pp. €14. 84-8169-491-6;

8565   Lectio divina 8: ferias del tiempo ordinario, semanas 26-34, años pa-
       res. Estella 2002, Verbo Divino 432 pp. €15.60. 84-8169-492-4;

8566   Lectio divina 13: domingos del tiempo ordinario (ciclo A). Estella
       2002, Verbo Divino 372 pp. €14. 84-8169-497-5.

H8.2 Theologia moralis NT

8567 *Anderson, J.K.* Cloning, stem-cell research, and the bible. BS 159 (2002) 462-472.

8568 ^E**Balch, David L.** Homosexuality, science, and the 'plain sense' of scripture. 2000 ⇒16,231; 17,8005. ^RHeyJ 43 (2002) 245-247 (*Hardy, Richard P.*); RBLit (2002)* (*Hester, J. David*).

8569 *Bartholomew, Craig G.* Introduction. ^FO'DONOVAN, O. 2002 ⇒272. 1-45 [Ex 19,3-6].

8570 *Bauckham, Richard* Authority and scripture. God and the crisis. 2002 ⇒142. 50-77.

8571 **Bellis, Alice Ogden; Hufford, Terry L.** Science, scripture, and homosexuality. Cleveland 2002, Pilgrim 128 pp. 0-8298-1485-X.

8572 **Bockmuehl, Markus** Jewish law in Gentile churches: halakhah and the beginning of christian public ethics. 2000 ⇒16,8074; 17,8008. ^RJThS 53 (2002) 282-288 (*Tomson, P.J.*); HeyJ 43 (2002) 363-364 (*Taylor, N.H.*); CBQ 64 (2002) 369-371 (*Matera, Frank J.*).

8573 *Botha, P.J.J.* Young bodies and religion: exploring the role of religion in child abuse. R&T 9/1-2 (2002) 42-62 [NTAb 47,294].

8574 *Bowe, Barbara E.; Nairn,Thomas A.* The bible and moral theology: pitfalls and possibilities. NewTR 15/1 (2002) 32-43.

8575 *Brawley, Robert L.* Il potere di Dio all'opera nei figli di Dio. Bibbia e omosessualità. 2002 <1996> ⇒310. 65-90.

8576 *Cahill, Lisa Sowle* Christian character, biblical community, and human values. Character and scripture. 2002 ⇒283. 3-17.

8577 **Catherwood, Fred** The creation of wealth: recovering a christian understanding of money, work, and ethics. Wheaton, Ill 2002, Good News 208 pp. 1-58134-352-3.

8578 **Collins, Raymond F.** Sexual ethics and the New Testament. 2000 ⇒ 16,8081; 17,8015. ^RINTAMS Review 8/1 (2002) 119-120 (*Bourg, Florence C.*).

8579 **Coninck, Frédéric de** La justice et la puissance: dire et vivre sa foi dans la société d'aujourd'hui (II). 1998 ⇒17,8017. ^REvTh(VS) 1/1 (2002) 90-92 (*Blough, Neal*).

8580 **Cosgrove, Charles H.** Appealing to scripture in moral debate: five hermeneutical rules. GR 2002, Eerdmans viii; 224 pp. $22. 0-8028-4942-3. Bibl. 202-215.

8581 **Culver, Robert D.** Civil government: a biblical view. Edmonton 2000, Canadian Institute for Law 308 pp. $28. ^RRBLit 4 (2002) 93-96 (*MacCammon, Linda M.*).

8582 *De Mingo Kaminouchi, Alberto* La vida moral y el misterio trinitario en el Nuevo Testamento. EstTrin 36 (2002) 231-251.

8583 **Desečar, Alexander** Die Bibel und Homosexualität: Kritik der revisionistischen Exegese. Schriften des Initiativkreises Katholischer Laien und Priester der Diözese 43: Augsburg 2002, 30 pp. ^RBoSm 72 (2002) 684-686 (*Hohnjec, Nikola*).

8584 **Di Sante, Carmine** Lo straniero nella bibbia: saggio sull'ospitalità. Saggi: Troina 2002, Città Aperta 236 pp. €13.

8585 **Elsbernd, Mary; Bieringer, Reimund** When love is not enough: a theo-ethic of justice. ColMn 2002, Liturgical xxi; 225 pp. $25 [BiTod 40,264—Senior, Donald].

8586 **Essex, Barbara Jean** Bad boys of the bible: exploring men of questionable virtue. Cleveland 2002, Pilgrim xx; 122 pp. 0-8298-1466-3. Bibl. 121-122.
8587 *Francis, Leslie J.* The relationship between bible reading and attitude toward substance use among 13-15 year olds. RelEd 97/1 (2002) 44-60.
8588 **Gauthier, André-Pierre** Paul RICOEUR et l'agir ensemble: les figures bibliques du prophète et du témoin. 2001 ⇒17,8031. ᴿRTL 33 (2002) 436-437 (*Étienne, J.*).
8589 *Geyser, P.A.* Bybelse getuienis oor homoseksualiteit—met ander oë gesien. HTS 58 (2002) 1655-1677 [NTAb 47,510].
8590 *Haacker, Klaus* Christliche Ethik und reformatorisches Prinzip. ThBeitr 33 (2002) 46-48.
8591 **Hanks, Gardner C.** Capital punishment and the bible. Scottdale, PA 2002, Herald 288 pp. $17. 08361-91951 [ThD 50,171–Heiser, W.].
8592 *Harrington, Daniel; Keenan, James F.* Jesus and virtue ethics: building bridges between New Testament ethics and moral theology. Catholic International 13/3 (2002) 60-65.
8593 **Harrington, Daniel J.; Keenan, James F.** Jesus and virtue ethics: building bridges between New Testament studies and moral theology. Ch 2002, Sheed & W. xv; 216 pp. $28. 0-58051-125-2 [ThD 50,171 —Heiser, W. Charles].
8594 *Ihne, Hartmut* Menschenwürde und Kinderrechte in der Einen Welt. JBTh 17 (2002) 3-20.
8595 **Jersild, Paul T.** Spirit ethics: scripture and the moral life. 2000 ⇒ 16,8098. ᴿNewTR 15/1 (2002) 89-90 (*Ginter, Mark E.*); RExp 99 (2002) 299-300 (*Marshall, Molly T.*).
8596 **Köhler, Josef** Einsamkeit und gelingendes Leben: eine biblisch-moraltheologische Auseinandersetzung. Rg 2002, Pustet 366 pp. €39.90. 3-7017-1798-7 [EuA 79,346].
8597 *Kunnunkal, Thomas V.* Human rights and the gospel paradigm. VJTR 66 (2002) 325-336.
8598 *Lebacqz, Karen* Who "owns" cells and tissues?. StTh 56 (2002) 118-131.
8599 **Léon-Dufour, Xavier** Agir selon l'évangile. Parole de Dieu: P 2002, Seuil 186 pp. €19. 2-02-0541-10-6. ᴿBrot. 155 (2002) 535-536 (*Silva, I. Ribeiro da*).
8600 *Lombard, J.A.; Schoeman, N.J.* Leadership towards a just economic society. VeE 23 (2002) 689-706.
8601 **Lugo Rodríguez, Raúl H.** Flor que nace de la muerte: los derechos humanos y la palabra de Dios. México 2002, Univ. Pont. de México. ᴿQol 30 (2002) 119-126 (*Miranda Flores, Teresa; Noguez de Gómez, Aurora*).
8602 *Mądel, Krzysztof* Biblijne i etyczne motywy pomocy prostytutkom [Les motifs bibliques et éthiques du secours aux prostituées]. PrzPow 5 (2002) 215-226. P.
8603 **Marshall, Christopher D.** Beyond retribution: a New Testament vision for justice, crime, and punishment. 2001 ⇒17,8051. ᴿRRT 9 (2002) 1-2 (*Wollaston, Isabel*); Theol. 105 (2002) 454-455 (*Willmer, Haddon*).
8604 *Meilaender, Gilbert* Ethics and exegesis: a great gulf?. ᶠO'DONOVAN, O. 2002 ⇒272. 259-264.

8605 **Noichl, Franz** Ethische Schriftauslegung: biblische Weisung und moral-theologische Argumentation. FrB 2002, Herder 294 pp. €39. 3-451-27861-8. Diss.-Habil. FrB.

8606 *Noratto G., José Alfredo* La justicia occidental es cristiana, pero ¿se inspira en el evangelio?. ThX 52/1 (2002) 61-80.

8607 *Oakman, Douglas E.* Die Rolle des Geldes im moralischen Universum des Neuen Testaments. Jesus in neuen Kontexten. 2002 ⇒602. 158-166;

8608 Money in the moral universe of the New Testament. The social setting. 2002 ⇒601. 335-348.

8609 **Pfeiffer, Matthias** Einweisung in das neue Sein: neutestamentliche Erwägungen zur Grundlegung der Ethik. BEvTh 119: 2001 ⇒17, 8061. ᴿThLZ 127 (2002) 914-918 (*Schrage, Wolfgang*); SNTU.A 27 (2002) 272-273 (*Repschinski, Boris*).

8610 *Porter, Jean* Natural law as a scriptural concept: theological reflections on a medieval theme. ThTo 59 (2002) 226-243.

8611 *Pratscher, Wilhelm* Grundlinien der Begründung der Ethik im Neuen Testament. ᶠFUCHS, A. 2002 ⇒41. 383-401.

8612 *Prieur, Jean-Marc* L'éthique sexuelle et conjugale des chrétiens des premiers siècles et ses justifications. RHPhR 82/3 (2002) 267-282.

8613 *Redalié, Yann* Nuovo Testamento ed etica: quale prospettiva?. Protest. 57/1 (2002) 19-34.

8614 *Richter Reimer, Ivoni* Life calls for triumph and celebration. ᶠSCHOTTROFF, L.: 2002 ⇒111. 87-95.

8615 **Roy, Louis** Self-actualization and the radical gospel. Michael Glazier: ColMn 2002, Liturgical viii; 72 pp. $10. 0-8146-5107-0 [ThD 49, 389—Heiser, W. Charles].

8616 **Schmidt, Thomas E.** L'homosexualité: perspectives bibliques et réalités contemporaines. Terre Nouvelle: Cléon d'Andran 2002, Excelsis 256 pp.

8617 *Schmidt, Ulla* Euthanasia, autonomy and beneficence. StTh 56 (2002) 132-151.

8618 *Schwantes, Milton* Es fließe das Recht der Armen: die Armen und die Bibel. Ordensnachrichten 41/5 (2002) 3-10.

8619 *Schweiker, William* Images of scripture and contemporary theological ethics. Character and scripture. 2002 ⇒283. 34-52.

8620 *Siker, Jeffrey S.* I gentili 'buon seme' e i cristiani omosessuali: direttive del Nuovo Testamento per la chiesa eterosessuale. Bibbia e omosessualità. 2002 <1996> ⇒310. 145-169.

8621 **Spohn, William C.** Go and do likewise: Jesus and ethics. 1999 ⇒15, 8136; 17,8075. ᴿThTo 58 (2002) 633-635 (*Hays, Richard B.*); RBLit 4 (2002) 351-353 (*Lewis, Scott M.*); JAAR 70 (2002) 678-681 (*Cartwright, Michael G.*).

8622 *Stegemann, Wolfgang* Kontingenz und Kontextualität der moralischen Aussagen Jesu: Plädoyer für eine Neubesinnung auf die sogenannte Ethik Jesu. Jesus in neuen Kontexten. 2002 ⇒602. 167-184;

8623 The contextual ethics of Jesus. Social setting. 2002 ⇒601. 45-61.

8624 **Stemm, Sönke von** Der betende Sünder vor Gott: Studien zu Vergebungsvorstellungen in urchristlichen und frühjüdischen Texten. AGJU 45: 1999 ⇒15,8138; 17,8078. ᴿBib. 83 (2002) 139-142 (*Aranda Pérez, Gonzalo*); RBLit (2002)* (*Hamilton, Mark Wade*).

8625 *Stone, Ken* Che cosa accade quando i *gay* leggono la bibbia?. Conc(I) 38/1 2002 102-112; Conc(E) 294,89-98; Conc(D) 38/1,68-75; Conc(P) 294, 82-91.

8626 *Thumma, Lucas* Human person, human dignity and human society: biblical foundations and theological perspectives in the church. ITS 39 (2002) 219-256.

8627 *Tosato, Angelo* Cristianesimo e mercato (criticando l'esegesi di Ludwig von Mieses) <1994>;

8628 Il vangelo e la ricchezza (per la fuoriuscita dai luoghi comuni) <1997>. Vangelo e ricchezza. 2002 ⇒246. 253-305/307-422;

8629 Cristianesimo e capitalismo (il problema esegetico di alcuni passi evangelici). Vangelo e ricchezza. 2002 <1994> ⇒246. 423-457;

8630 Presentazione del libro di Michael Novak 'Lo spirito del capitalismo democratico e il cristianesimo' <1987>;

8631 Dall'economismo ad una economia per l'uomo <1996>;

8632 Solidarietà e profitto: il ruolo degli imprenditori <1996>. Vangelo e ricchezza <1996>. 2002 ⇒246. 459-490/491-526/527-549.

8633 **Trompf, G.W.** Early christian historiography: narratives of retributive justice. 2000 ⇒16,7123. [R]JRH 26 (2002) 315-316 (*Wilson, Stephen G.*).

8634 **Verhey, Allen** Remembering Jesus: christian community, scripture, and the moral life. GR 2002, Eerdmans xii; 526 pp. $35. 0-8028-032-37.

8635 *Villiers, E. de* Euthanasia and assisted suicide: a christian ethical perspective. [F]POTGIETER, P.: AcTh(B).S 3: 2002 ⇒92. 35-47.

8636 *Vincent, John J.* Outworkings: gospel practice today. ET 113 (2002) 367-371.

8637 *Watson, Francis* Spaces sacred and profane: Stephen Moore, sex and the bible. JSNT 25/1 (2002) 109-117.

8638 **Whallon, William** The Jesus rule. East Lansing, Michigan 2002, Bennett & K. xiii; 271 pp. $15. 2-002111-30-2. Bibl. 258-264.

8639 *Wolbert, Werner* Medical ethics and the prohibition of killing. StTh 56 (2002) 106-117.

8640 **Woyke, Johannes** Die neutestamentlichen Haustafeln: ein kritischer und konstruktiver Forschungsüberblick. SBS 184: 2000 ⇒16,8123; 17,8089. [R]INTAMS Review 8 (2002) 277-278 (*Feldmeier, Reinhard*); SNTU.A 27 (2002) 261-262 (*Scholtissek, Klaus*).

8641 *Zuccaro, Cataldo* In relazione al disabile: i paradigmi del vangelo e l'interpretazione teologica. RTM 34 (2002) 547-561.

H8.4 *NT de reformatione sociali*—Political action in Scripture

8642 *Ahrens, Matthias* "... aber um dein Wort zu tun". JK 63/2 (2002) 49-54.

8643 *Chaplin, Jonathan* Political eschatology and responsible government: Oliver O'Donovan's 'Christian Liberalism';

8644 *Greene, Colin J.D.* Revisiting christendom: a crisis of legitimization. [F]O'DONOVAN, O. 2002 ⇒ 272. 265-308/314-340.

8645 *Horn, Friedrich Wilhelm* Die politische Umkehr in der Verkündigung Jesu. [F]FUCHS, A. 2002 ⇒41. 53-70.

8646 *Lockwood O'Donovan, Joan* A timely conversation with *The desire of the nations on civil society, nation and state*. [F]O'Donovan, O. 2002 ⇒272. 377-394.

8647 *Mattioli, Umberto* "Non resistere al male", ma porgere l'altra guancia" (Mt. 5, 39; Lc. 6,29): aspetti politici dell'esegesi antica. [F]GNILKA, C.: JAC.E 33: 2002 ⇒48. 253-272.

8648 *O'Donovan, Oliver* Response to Jonathan Chaplin;
8649 Response to Colin Greene;
8650 Response to Joan Lockwood O'Donovan;
8651 Response to James W. Skillen. FO'DONOVAN, O. 2002 ⇒ 272. 309-313/341-343/395-397/418-420.
8652 **Pilgrim, Walter** Uneasy neighbors: church and state in the New Testament. 1999 ⇒15,8145...17,8092. RHBT 24/2 (2002) 128-129 (*Rowe, C. Kavin*).
8653 *Skillen, James W.* Acting politically in biblical obedience?. FO'DONOVAN, O. 2002 ⇒272. 398-417.

H8.5 Theologia liberationis latino-americana...

8654 *Guardiola-Sáenz, Leticia* Minoranze in una società opulenta. Conc(I) 38/1 (2002) 113-122; Conc(E) 294,99-106; Conc(D) 38/1,76-82; Conc(P) 294, 92-99.
8655 **Hanks, Thomas** The subversive gospel: a New Testament commentary of liberation. TDoner, John P. 2000 ⇒16,8133. RRBLit (2002)* (*Carter, Warren*).
8656 *Lamb, Regene* Entdecken, wie sich die Texte des Lebens und der Bibel berühren. JK 63/2 (2002) 40-43.
8657 *Santa Ana, Julio de* Scripture, community and mission in the framework of Latin American liberation theology. FNILES, D.: 2002 ⇒82. 315-331.
8658 **Sobrino, Jon** Jesucristo liberador: lectura histórico-teológica de Jesús de Nazaret. 42001 ⇒17,8099. RNZM 58 (2002) 309-310 (*Heiniger, Ernstpeter*).
8659 **Tavares, Sinivaldo S.** A cruz de Jesus e o sofrimento no mundo. TAlves, Ephraim F.: Petrópolis 2002, Vozes 293 pp [REB 248, 999].

H8.6 *Theologiae emergentes*—Theologies of emergent groups

8660 *Alumkal, Antony W.* The scandal of the "model minority" mind?: the bible and second-generation Asian American evangelicals. Semeia 90/91 (2002) 237-250.
8661 *Baldwin, Lewis V.* 'Deliverance to the captives': images of Jesus Christ in the slave community. FPATTE, D.: 2002 ⇒89. 235-248.
8662 *Bundang, Rachel A.R.* Home as memory, metaphor, and promise in Asian/Pacific American religious experience;
8663 *Cheng, Patrick S.* Multiplicity and Judges 19: constructing a queer Asian Pacific American biblical hermeneutic;
8664 *Clark, Peter Yuichi* Biblical themes for pastoral care revisited: an Asian American rereading of a classic pastoral care text. Semeia 90/91 (2002) 87-104/119-133./291-314.
8665 *Fernandez, Eleazar S.* From Babel to Pentecost: finding a home in the belly of the empire. Semeia 90/91 (2002) 29-50.
8666 *Foskett, Mary F.* The accidents of being and the politics of identity: biblical images of adoption and Asian adoptees in America. Semeia 90/91 (2002) 135-144.
8667 **Fugmann, Haringke** Unsere Ahnen konnten Berge versetzen: Mt 17,14-21 und Gal 5,2-6 in der Auslegung papua-neuguineischer Pa-

storen und die Bedeutung der melanesischen Perspektive für die wissenschaftlich-exegetische Auslegung neutestamentlicher Texte. *Wischmeyer, O.*: 2002, 341 pp. Diss. Erlangen [RTL 34,597].

8668   *Jeung, Russell* Evangelical and mainline teachings on Asian American identity. Semeia 90/91 (2002) 211-236.

8669   *Kim, Jung Ha* At the tables of an Asian American banquet;

8670   *Kim, Uriah Yong-Hwan* Uriah the Hittite: a (con)text of struggle for identity [2 Sam 11]. Semeia 90/91 (2002) 325-337/69-85.

8671   *Liew, Tat-siong Benny* Introduction: whose bible?: which (Asian) America?. Semeia 90/91 (2002) 1-26.

8672   *Lim, Leng Leroy* "The bible tells me to hate myself": the crisis in Asian American spiritual leadership. Semeia 90/91 (2002) 315-322.

8673   *Manus, Ukachukwu Chris* Inculturating New Testament christologies in Africa: a case study of the Yoruba and Igbo grassroots christians in Ile-Ife, Nigeria. ZMR 86 (2002) 116-143.

8674   *Melanchthon, Monica Jyotsna* A Dalit reading of Genesis 10-11:9;

8675   *Míguez, Néstor O.* A comparative bible study of Genesis 10-11:9: an approach from the Argentine. ᶠNILES, D. 2002 ⇒82. 161-76/147-60.

8676   *Mojola, Aloo Osotsi* How the bible is received in communities: a brief overview with particular reference to East Africa;

8677   *Niles, Damayanthi M.A.* Whose text is it anyway?: how text functions to build identity and community;

8678   *Pui-Lan, Kwok* Postcolonialism, feminism and biblical interpretation. ᶠNILES, D.: 2002 ⇒82. 44-69/304-314/261-276.

8679   *Rietz, Henry W.* My father has no children: reflections on a Hapa identity toward a hermeneutic of particularity. Semeia 90/91 (2002) 145-157.

8680   *Roper, Garnett* Out of Egypt have I called my son. ᶠNILES, D. 2002 ⇒82. 223-228.

8681   *Sanneh, Lamin* Domesticating the transcendent: the African transformation of christianity: comparative reflections on ethnicity and religous mobilization in Africa. Bible translation. JSOT.S 353: 2002 ⇒2136. 70-85.

8682   *Sano, Roy I.* Shifts in reading the bible: hermeneutical moves among Asian Americans. Semeia 90/91 (2002) 105-118.

8683   *Smith, Abraham* 'It seems to me we do agree' said Booker T. and W.E.B.: 'structures of oppression in the hermeneutics of *Up from slavery* and *The souls of black folk*. ᶠPATTE, D.: 2002 ⇒89. 163-183.

8684   **Sugirtharajah, Rasiah S.** The bible and the third world: precolonial, colonial and postcolonial encounters. 2001 ⇒17,8111. ᴿTheol. 105 (2002) 214-215 (*Wingate, Andrew*); BiblInterp 10 (2002) 450-452 (*Taylor, N.H.*); RStT 21/2 (2002) 79-82 (*Jacobs, Mignon R.*).

8685   *Tseng, Timothy* Second-generation Chinese evangelical use of the bible in identity discourse in North America. Semeia 90/91 (2002) 251-267.

8686   **West, Gerald O.** Biblical hermeneutics of liberation: modes of reading the bible in the South African context. 1995 <1991> ⇒7,8713... 9,9233. ᴿScriptura 78 (2001) 467-478 (*Lombaard, Christo J.S.*).

8687   *Witvliet, Theo* Response to Lamin Sanneh, 'Domesticating the transcendent: the African transformation of christianity'. Bible translation. JSOT.S 353: 2002 ⇒2136. 86-93.

8688   *Yong-Bock, Kim* The bible among the Minjung of Korea: kairotic listening and reading of the bible. ᶠNILES, D. 2002 ⇒82. 70-91.

H8.7 *Mariologia*—The mother of Jesus in the NT

8689 **Adinolfi, Marco** Maria: la docile figlia di Sion. CasM 2001, Portalupi 222 pp. [R]LASBF 51 (2001) 447-448 (*Bottini, G.C.*).

8690 **Becker, Jürgen** Maria: Mutter Jesu und erwählte Jungfrau. Biblische Gestalten 4: 2001 ⇒17,8113. [R]ThLZ 127 (2002) 1180-1183 (*Müller, Paul-Gerhard*).

8691 **Bertalot, Renzo** Ecco la serva del Signore: una voce protestante. SPFTM 56: R 2002, Marianum 176 pp. €15.50. 88-87016-60-7.

8692 **Biestro, Carlos** Jardín cerrado: la Virgen en la escritura y los santos padres. Mendoza 2002, Deus in te 444 pp.

8693 **Calì, Rosa** I testi antimariologici nell'esegesi dei Padri: da Nicea a Calcedonia: per una mariologia in prospettiva ecclesiale. 1999 ⇒15, 8172; 17,8118. [R]Itinerarium(Messina) 10 (2002) 264-266 (*Stelladoro, Gabriella*).

8694 [E]**Castelli, Ferdinando** Testi mariani del secondo millennio, 8: poesia e prosa letteraria. R 2002, Città Nuova 1182 pp. 88-311-9266-3.

8695 *Clark, Anne L.* The priesthood of the virgin Mary: gender trouble in the twelfth century. JFSR 18/1 (2002) 5-24.

8696 **Cuvillier, Elian** Maria chi sei veramente?: i diversi volti della madre di Gesù nel Nuovo Testamento. [T]*Comba, Fernanda Jourdan*: Piccola collana moderna, serie biblica 95: T 2002, Claudiana 82 pp. 88-70-16-437-3.

8697 **Flecha, José María; Stock, Klemens; Martínez Puche, José A.** María en la biblia y en los Santos Padres. Biblioteca Mariana 1: M 2002, Edibesa 391 pp [EstJos 56,274—Llamas, Román].

8698 **Foskett, Mary F.** A virgin conceived: Mary and classical representations of virginity. Bloomington 2002, Indiana Univ. Pr. 238 pp. $35. 0-253-34055-1. Bibl. 209-229 [BiTod 40,401—Senior, Donald].

8699 *Freitas Faria, Jacir de* Maria segundo os evangelhos apócrifos. Convergência 37 (2002) 217-221.

8700 *Garcia, Hugues* Remarques critiques sur la promotion de la mère de Jésus dans le christianisme ancien et sur son traitement oecuménique récent. ETR 77 (2002) 193-216.

8701 **Hahn, Scott** Hail, Holy Queen: the mother of God in the word of God. 2001 ⇒17,8128. [R]Faith 34/3 (2002) 39-40 (*Findlay-Wilson, Chris*);

8702 Dios te salve, reina y madre: la madre de Dios en la palabra de Dios. M 2002, Rialp 219 pp [Augustinus 48,340—Campo, A.].

8703 **Herranz Marco, Mariano** La virginidad perpetua de María. Studia Semitica NT 9: M 2002, Encuentro 148 pp. 84-7490-644-X. Bibl. 17-20.

8704 **Jordan, Michael** Mary, the unauthorised biography. L 2002, Weidenfeld & N 338 pp. £15. [R]Tablet (10 Aug. 2002) 16 (*Maunder, Chris*).

8705 **Karlsen Seim, Turid** The virgin mother: Mary and ascetic discipleship in Luke. A feminist companion to Luke. FCNT: 2002 ⇒5732. 89-105.

8706 **Kottackal, Joseph** Mariological studies. 1999 ⇒16,8179. [R]VJTR 66 (2002) 948-949, 935 (*Kumar, J. Raj*).

8707 *Lange, Günter* Lukas, Porträtmaler der Gottesmutter. KatBl 127 (2002) 196-201.

8708 **Masciarelli, Michele Giulio** La discepola: Maria di Nazaret beata perché ha creduto. 2001 ⇒17,8132. [R]Mar. 64 (2002) 669-671 (*Maggioni, Corrado*).

8709 **Menke, Karl-Heinz** Incarnato nel seno della vergine Maria: Maria nella storia di Israele e della chiesa. CinB 2002, S. Paolo 237 pp. €17. [R]RTLu 7 (2002) 295-297 (*Schulz, Michael*).

8710 *Muñoz Iglesias, Salvador* La maternidad divina de María en los evangelios de la infancia. EstMar 68 (2002) 9-24.

8711 *Nyk, Adam* Immagine evangelica di Maria madre di Gesù nei primi tre secoli. Vox Patrum 22 (2002) 391-401.

8712 **Parravicini, Giovanna** Vida de María en iconos. M 2002, San Pablo 149 pp [EstJos 57,135—Rey, José Ignacio].

8713 *Pedico, Maria Marcellina* Maria di Nazaret figlia del Padre e sorella nostra. CoSe 51/5 (2002) 30-38.

8714 **Ponce Cuéllar, Miguel** María, madre del Redentor y madre de la iglesia. [2]2001 ⇒17,8136. [R]Mar. 64 (2002) 637-641 (*García-Murga, José-Ramón*).

8715 **Ronchi, Ermes Maria** Bibbia e pietà mariana: presenze di Maria nella scrittura. Interpretare la Bibbia oggi, 1/8: Brescia 2002, Queriniana 136 pp. €9. 88-399-2458-2. Bibl. 133-134.

8716 *Santoro, Maria M.* Maria, una persona da narrare. EphMar 52/2 (2002) 177-190.

8717 **Stramare, Tarcisio** Il matrimonio della Madre de Dio: i santi sposi. 2001 ⇒17,8143. [R]BeO 44 (2002) 61-63 (*Sardini, Davide*).

8718 **Wolf, Peter** Christsein mit Maria. Vallendar-Schönstatt 2002, Schönstatt 192 pp. 3-935396-02-3. Bibl. 189.

H8.8 *Feminae NT*—Women in the NT and church history

8719 [E]**Jones, Stanley F.** Which Mary?: the Marys of early christian tradition. Symposium series 19: Atlanta 2002, SBL x; 141 pp. $30. 1-589-83-043-1. [R]SR 31 (2002) 444-446 (*Piovanelli, Pierluigi*).

8720 Ricerche Teologiche. Ricerche Teologiche 13,1: Bo 2002, Dehoniane 263 pp. Società Italiana per la Ricerca Teologica.

8721 *Agurides, Sabbas C.* Women in the work of the church: an exegetical contribution to the New Testament. AThR 84 (2002) 507-517.

8722 *Alexandre Parra, Dolores* Otros discípulos de Jesús. ResB 36 (2002) 37-44.

8723 *Alvarez Valdés, Ariel* ¿Era María Magdalena una prostituta?. RevBib 62 (2000) 121-126.

8724 **Bauckham, Richard J.** Gospel women: studies of the named women in the gospels. GR 2002, Eerdmans xxi; 343 pp. $22. 0-8028-4999-7.

8725 *Bernabé Ubieta, Carmen* María Magadalena: de discípula y apóstol a prostituta. ResB 36 (2002) 21-28.

8726 *Billon, Gérard* Marie-Madeleine, femme et apôtre. DosB 92 (2002) 7-30.

8727 *Boer, Esther A. de* The Lukan Mary Magdalene and the other women following Jesus. A feminist companion to Luke. FCNT: 2002 ⇒ 5732. 140-160.

8728 *Bovon, François* Mary Magdalene in the Acts of Philip;

8729 *Brock, Ann Graham* Setting the record straight: the politics of identification: Mary Magdalene and Mary the mother in Pistis Sophia. Which Mary?. SBL.Symposium 19: 2002 ⇒8719. 75-89/43-52.

8730 **Corley, Kathleen E.** Women and the historical Jesus: feminist myths of christian origins. Santa Rosa, CA 2002, Polebridge (10); 254 pp. $20. 0-944344-93-3. Bibl. 205-239.

8731 *Dobrovolny, Mary K.* Mary Magdalene: an icon for women religious. RfR 61 (2002) 602-614.

8732 *Dreyer, Y.* Vroue in di sinoptiese evangelies—méér as dekoratiewe karakters. HTS 58 (2002) 1679-1706 [NTAb 47,448].

8733 **Getty-Sullivan, Mary Ann** Women in the New Testament. 2001 ⇒ 17,8155. ᴿPacifica 15 (2002) 221-223 (*Dowling, Elizabeth*).

8734 *Giorgi, Tilde* Ascesi ed esegesi nella Roma imperiale del IV secolo. Ricerche teologiche 13 (2002) 89-97.

8735 **Jansen, Katherine Ludwig** The making of the Magdalen: preaching and popular devotion in the later Middle Ages. 2000 ⇒16,8221; 17, 8158. ᴿRSPhTh 86 (2002) 154-156 (*Bataillon, Louis-Jacques*).

8736 *Jensen, Anne* Gottes selbstbewusste Töchter: Selbstverständnis und Rolle der Frauen im frühen Christentum. SaThZ 6 (2002) 192-203.

8737 **Jensen, Anne** Femmes des premiers siècles chrétiens. ᵀ*Poupon, G.*: TC 11: Bern 2002, Lang lxxii; 316 pp. €63.20. 3-906767-67-1. Avec *L. Neureiter* [NRTh 126,147s—Hausman, N.];

8738 Frauen im frühen Christentum. TC 11: Bern 2002, Lang lxxx; 319 pp. Collab. *Livia Neureiter*.

8739 *King, Karen L.* Why all the controversy?: Mary in the gospel of Mary. Which Mary?. SBL.Symposium 19: 2002 ⇒8719. 53-74.

8740 *Knight, Jonathan* The portrait of Mary in the Ascension of Isaiah. Which Mary?. SBL.Symposium 19: 2002 ⇒8719. 91-105.

8741 *Kwasniewski, Clarissa* The meaning of the veil. HPR 102/10 (2002) 47-54.

8742 **Malone, Mary T.** Women & christianity, 1: the first thousand years. 2001 ⇒17,8160. ᴿJRH 26 (2002) 220-221 (*West, Janet*).

8743 *Marjanen, Antti* The mother of Jesus or the Magdalene?: the identity of Mary in the so-called gnostic christian texts. Which Mary?. SBL. Symposium 19: 2002 ⇒8719. 31-41.

8744 **Moltmann-Wendel, Elisabeth** Ein eigener Mensch werden: Frauen um Jesus. GTBS 531: Gü ⁹2002, Gü'er 150 pp. 3-579-00531-6.

8745 **Pinto-Mathieu, Elisabeth** Marie-Madeleine dans la littérature du moyen âge. 1997 ⇒13,7845. ᴿSpec. 77 (2002) 624-5 (*Vitz, Evelyn*).

8746 ᴱ**Pouthier, Jean-Luc** Les visages de Marie-Madeleine. MoBi 143 (2002) 12-51.

8747 *Rigato, Maria Luisa* Presenza viva e marginalizzazione della donna nella chiesa romana delle origini. Ricerche teologiche 13 (2002) 31-87.

8748 *Ruiz Pérez, Maria Dolores* Mujer de evangelio para un mundo nuevo. Isidorianum 21 (2002) 153-172.

8749 *Schaberg, Jane* The resurrection of Mary Magdalene: legends, apocrypha, and the christian testament. CrossCur 52 (2002) 81-89.

8750 **Schaberg, Jane** The resurrection of Mary Magdalene: legends, apocrypha, and the christian Testament. NY 2002, Continuum 379 pp. $35. 0-8264-1383-8. ᴿRBLit (2002)* (*Hearon, Holly*).

8751 **Schnabl, Beatrix** Umgang mit Übergang: Konzeption der Frauenrollen in Mk 15,40f. 47; 16,1-8 und Lk 23,49.55f.; 24,1-12 im Spannungsfeld von Kontinuität, Liminalität und Lebenswelt. *DLaub, Franz* 2002 Diss. München [ThRv 99/2,x].

8752 *Shoemaker, Stephen J.* A case of mistaken identity?: naming the gnostic Mary. Which Mary?. 2002 ⇒8719. 5-30.

8753 *Wehn, Beate* 'I am a handmaid of the living God!': the apostle Thecla and the consequences of transgression. *F*SCHOTTROFF, L. 2002 ⇒ 111. 19-30.

8754 *Winkett, Lucy* Go tell!: thinking about Mary Magdalene. Feminist Theology 29 (2002) 19-31.

8755 *Zervos, George T.* Seeking the source of the Marian myth: have we found the missing link?. Which Mary?. 2002 ⇒8719. 107-120.

H8.9 *Theologia feminae*—Feminist theology

8756 *Aigner, Maria-Elisabeth* Schwarze Buchstaben, weißes Feuer und die Farbe Lila: Bibliodrama und feministische Theologie. SaThZ 6 (2002) 307-314.

8757 **Beattie, Tina** Eve's pilgrimage: a woman's quest for the city of God. L 2002, Burns & O. xi; (2) 224 pp. 0-8601-2323-5. Bibl. 217-224;

8758 The Last Supper according to Mary and Martha. 2001 ⇒17,8173. *R*RRT 9 (2002) 128-130 (*Guest, Deryn*).

8759 *Beavis, Mary Ann* Introduction: seeking the 'lost coin' of parables about women. The lost coin. BiSe 86: 2002 ⇒5282. 17-32;

8760 Joy in heaven, sorrow on earth: Luke 15.10. The lost coin. BiSe 86: 2002 ⇒5282. 39-45.

8761 *Braun, W.* Body, character and the problem of femaleness in early christian discourse. R&T 9/1-2 (2002) 108-117 [NTAb 47,343].

8762 *Brenner, Athalya* Gendering in/by the Hebrew Bible—ten years later. OTEs 15 (2002) 42-51.

8763 **Clifford, Anne M.** Introducing feminist theology. 2001 ⇒17,8176. *R*TS 63 (2002) 403-405 (*Zagang, Phyllis*); Horizons 29 (2002) 135-154 (*Procario-Foley, Elena; Gentry-Akin, David; Murray, Ellen; Hammond, David; Clifford, Anne M.*).

8764 *Daly, Mary* The qualitative leap beyond patriarchal religion. Arc 30 (2002) 35-57.

8765 *Demers, Patricia* Early modern women's words with power: absence and presence. Ment. *Frye, N.:* Semeia 89 (2002) 89-102.

8766 **Dube, Musa W.** Postcolonial feminist interpretation of the bible. 2000 ⇒16,8251; 17,8179. *R*JAAR 70 (2002) 409-412 (*Antonio, Edward P.*).

8767 *Elvey, Anne* The birth of the mother: a reading of Luke 2:1-20 in conversation with some recent feminist theory on pregnancy and birth. Pacifica 15/1 (2002) 1-15.

8768 **Fiorenza, Elisabeth Schüssler** Rhetoric and ethic: the politics of biblical studies. 1999 ⇒15,8249...17,8180. *R*NewTR 15/1 (2002) 80-81 (*Bowe, Barbara E.*);

8769 Jesus and the politics of interpretation. 2000 ⇒17,4325. *R*MoTh 18/1 (2002) 419-422 (*Adam, A.K.M.*); HeyJ 43 (2002) 508-509 (*Taylor, N.H.*); CBQ 64 (2002) 777-779 (*McGinn, Sheila E.*);

8770 Wisdom ways: introducing feminist biblical interpretation. 2001 ⇒ 17,8182. *R*Third Millennium 5 (2002) 125-126 (*Mattam, Joseph*).

8771 *Fischer, Irmtraud* Ein Blick auf den BK und seine Hermeneutik von der "anderen" Seite: andere Generation—weiblich—katholisch. EvTh 62 (2002) 26-36.

8772 **Fuchs, Esther** Sexual politics in the biblical narrative: reading the Hebrew Bible as a woman. JSOT.S 310: 2000 ⇒16,8261; 17,8183. [R]YESW 10 (2002) 238-239 (*McKay, Heather A.*).

8773 [E]**Gößmann , Elisabeth** Wörterbuch der feministischen Theologie. Gü [2]2002, Gü'er 640 pp. €69. 3-579-00285-6. Ill..

8774 *Gudmundsdóttir, Arnfrídur* Female Christ-figures in films: a feminist critical analysis of Breaking the Waves and Dead Man Walking. StTh 56 (2002) 27-43.

8775 *Guillemin, Elaine* Jesus/holy mother wisdom (Mt. 23.37-39);

8776 *Hearon, Holly; Clark Wire, Antoinette* Women's work in the realm of God (Mt. 13.33; Lk. 13.20,21; Gos. Thom. 96; Mt 6.28-30; Lk. 12.27-28; Gos. Thom. 36). The lost coin. BiSe 86: 2002 ⇒5282. 244-267/136-157.

8777 *Ilan, Tal* Jewish women's studies in Israel. JFSR 18/2 (2002) 91-95.

8778 *Jackson, Melissa* Lot's daughters and Tamar as tricksters and the patriarchal narratives as feminist theology. JSOT 98 (2002) 29-46 [Gen 19,30-38; 38].

8779 *Jacobs, M..M.* The 'sense' of feminist biblical scholarship for church and society. Scriptura 80 (2002) 173-185 [NTAb 47,422].

8780 **Jobling, J'annine** Feminist biblical interpretation in theological context: restless readings. Ashgate new critical thinking in theology and biblical studies: Aldershot 2002, Ashgate 180 pp. £40. 0-7546-0791-7. Bibl. 165-178.

8781 **Johnson, E.A.** La que es: el misterio de Dios en el discurso teológico feminista. [T]*Morla, Víctor*: Barc 2002, Herder 368 pp. [R]EstTrin 36 (2002) 148-150 (*Pikaza, X.*);

8782 Dieu au-delà du masculin et du féminin: celui/celle qui est. [T]*Lambert, Pierrot*: CFi 214: 1999 ⇒15,8262...17,8190. [R]SR 30 (2002) 245-247 (*Melançon, Louise*).

8783 **Lee, Yeong Mee** Zion in prophetic traditions with special attention to Isaiah 62:1-5 and 66:7-14 and the implications for Asian feminist theologies. [D]*Trible, P.*: 2001-2002 Diss. New York, Union [RTL 34, 592].

8784 *Maloney, Linda* 'Swept under the rug': feminist homiletical reflections on the parable of the lost coin (Lk. 15.8-9). The lost coin. BiSe 86: 2002 ⇒5282. 34-38.

8785 *Mattison, Robin* The (Patte)r(n) of timely feet. [F]PATTE, D. 2002 ⇒ 89. 218-234.

8786 *Militello, Cettina* Scrittura, tradizione, chiesa: la prospettiva della laicità. Ricerche teologiche 13 (2002) 161-181.

8787 *Nadar, Sarojini* Gender, power, sexuality and suffering bodies in the book of Esther: reading the characters of Esther and Vashti for the purpose of social transformation. OTEs 15 (2002) 113-130.

8788 *Økland, Jorunn* Feminist reception of the New Testament: a critical reception. NT as reception. JSNT.S 230: 2002 ⇒360. 131-156.

8789 *Pereira, Nancy C.* Leitlinien für eine feministische Hermeneutik der Befreiung. JK 63/2 (2002) 44-48.

8790 *Perkins, Pheme* Patched garments and ruined wine: whose folly? (Mk 2.21-22; Mt. 9.16-17; Lk. 5.36-39). The lost coin. BiSe 86: 2002 ⇒ 5282. 124-135.

8791 *Rapp, Ursula* Befreien und Begehren: feministische Exegese am Ende des Patriarchats. SaThZ 6 (2002) 297-306.
8792 *Reid, Barbara E.* Wisdom's children justified (Mt. 11.16-19; Lk. 7. 31-35). The lost coin. BiSe 86: 2002 ⇒5282. 287-305.
8793 *Reinhartz, Adele* The 'bride' in John 3.29: a feminist rereading. The lost coin. BiSe 86: 2002 ⇒5282. 230-241.
8794 *Rogers, Sara* Journeys out of the victim role: male violence and the Hebrew Scriptures. Feminist Theology 11/2 (2002) 190-196.
8795 *Rushton, Kathleen* The (pro)creative parables of labour and childbirth (Jn 3.1-10 and 16.21-22). The lost coin. BiSe 86: 2002 ⇒5282. 206-229.
8796 *Schaberg, Jane; Mitchem, Stephanie* An interview with Jane D. Schaberg, CrossCur 52 (2002) 72-80.
8797 **Shepherd, Loraine MacKenzie** Feminist theologies for a postmodern church: diversity, community, and scripture. AmUSt.TR 219: NY 2002, Lang ix; 252 pp. $30. 0-8204-5572-5. Bibl. 239-245. RSR 31 (2002) 491-493 (*Faber, Alyda*).
8798 **Smith, Elizabeth J.** Bearing fruit in due season: feminist hermeneutics and the bible in worship. 1999 ⇒15,8285; 17,8211. RAThR 84 (2002) 174-175 (*Procter-Smith, Marjorie*).
8799 *Stenström, Hanna* Grandma, RÄISÄNEN, and the global village: a feminist approach to ethical criticism. FRÄISÄNEN, H.: NT.S 103: 2002 ⇒97. 521-540.
8800 **Strube, Sonja Angelika** "Wegen dieses Wortes ...": feministische und nichtfeministische Exegese im Vergleich am Beispiel der Auslegung zu Mk 7.24-30. 2000 ⇒16,8287. RRTL 33 (2002) 92-95 (*Dermience, Alice*); YESW 10 (2002) 242-244 (*Stenström, Hanna*).
8801 *Taddei Ferretti, Cloe* Hulda, ovvero "il coraggio della rilettura". Ricerche teologiche 13 (2002) 247-262.
8802 *Valerio, Adriana* Per una storia dell'esegesi femminile. La bibbia nell'interpretazione. 2002 ⇒572. 3-21 [BuBB 39,33].
8803 *Vélez C., Consuelo* Biblia y feminismo: caminos trazados por la hermenéutica bíblica feminista. ThX 52 (2002) 663-681.
8804 *Wacker, Marie-Theres* Zwischen Monotheismusdebatte und Geschlechtergerechtigkeit: aus dem Seminar für Theologische Frauenforschung. ThRv 98 (2002) 433-440.
8805 *Wetzlaugk, Sigrun* 'Do justice for me!'. FSCHOTTROFF, L. 2002 ⇒ 111. 77-85.

H9.0 Eschatologia NT, *spes*, hope

8806 *Alkier, Stefan* Das "letzte Gericht"—ein abständiges Mythologumenon?—eine Einführung zur Kontroverse Kurt Erlemann versus Lukas Bormann. ZNT 9 (2002) 46.
8807 *Andresen, Gisela; Andresen, Dieter* Das kommende Reich. Die Bibel: Geschichte und Gegenwart. 2002 ⇒971. 94-97, 101-108.
8808 **Berger, Klaus** Wie kommt das Ende der Welt?. Gütersloher Taschenbücher 1455: Gü 2002, Gü'er 231 pp. €9.90. 3-579-01455-2 [OrdKor 44,113—Giesen, Heinz].
8809 *Berner, Knut* Vorzeitiges Begräbnis: fängt das Leben mit dem Tode an?. BThZ 19 (2002) 240-256.

8810 **Blank, Renold J.** Escatologia do mundo: o projeto cósmico de Deus (Escatologia II). 2001 ⇒17,8217. [R]REB 248 (2002) 982-986 (*Fonseca, Fabiano José*).

8811 *Bormann, Lukas* Das "letzte Gericht"—ein abständiges Mythologumenon? ZNT 9 (2002) 54-59.

8812 *Boshoff, P.B.* Apokaliptiek en eskatologie: die verband en onderskeid volgens Walter Schmithals. HTS 57 (2001) 563-575 [NTAb 46,502].

8813 *Bosman, Hendrik Jan* Eschaton. [F]LEENE, H.: 2002 ⇒73. 45-47.

8814 *Braaten, Carl E.* The recovery of apocalyptic imagination. The last things. 2002 ⇒279. 14-32.

8815 **Bryan, Steven M.** Jesus and Israel's tradition of judgement and restoration. [D]*Chester, Andrew*: MSSNTS 117: C 2002, CUP xv; 278 pp. $60. 0-521-81183-X. Diss. Cambridge. Bibl. 246-264.

8816 *Bultmann, Rudolf* Die christliche Hoffnung und das Problem der Entmythologisierung. NT und christliche Existenz. UTB 2316: 2002 <1954> ⇒152. 248-257.

8817 *Carroll R., M. Daniel* The power of the future in the present: eschatology and ethics in O'Donovan and beyond. [F]O'DONOVAN, O. 2002 ⇒272. 116-143.

8818 *Christian, E.* Annihilation and biblical inspiration: do words mean what they say?. JATS 12/2 (2001) 219-224 [NTAb 47,90].

8819 *Derrett, J. Duncan M.* He descended into hell. JHiC 9/2 (2002) 234-245.

8820 **Ellis, E. Earle** Christ and the future in New Testament history. NT.S 97: 2000 ⇒16,8301; 17,8223. [R]EvQ 74 (2002) 269-271 (*Moritz, Thorsten*).

8821 *Erlemann, Kurt* Das "letzte Gericht"—ein erledigtes Mythologumenon?. ZNT 9 (2002) 47-53.

8822 *Hagene, Sylvia* Der Weg in die eschatologische Sabbatruhe (Mt 11, 28-30; Hebr 3,7-4,13 und "Evangelium Veritatis"). Rettendes Wissen. AOAT 300: 2002 ⇒352. 317-344.

8823 *Harrington, Wilfrid J.* Biblical spirituality—hope. PIBA 25 (2002) 133-149.

8824 **Hill, Craig C.** In God's time: the bible and the future. GR 2002, Eerdmans viii; 229 pp. $16. 0-8028-6090-7. Bibl. 210-213 [BiTod 41,133—Senior, Donald].

8825 *Hultgren, Arland J.* Eschatology in the New Testament: the current debate. The last things. 2002 ⇒279. 67-89.

8826 *Janowski, J. Christine* 'Was wird aus den Kindern ...?': einige Anfragen an die klassische Theologie in Zuspitzung auf die eschatologische Perspektive. JBTh 17 (2002) 337-367.

8827 *Jarick, John* The fall of the house (of cards) of Ussher: why the world as we know it did not end at sunset on 22 October 1997. Apocalyptic. JSPE.S 43: 2002 ⇒373. 233-252.

8828 *Jenson, Robert W.* The great transformation. The last things. 2002 ⇒ 279. 33-42.

8829 *Kee, James M.* Introduction. Ment. *Frye, N.*: Semeia 89 (2002) 1-6.

8830 **Klaine, Roger** Le devenir du monde et la bible, 1-2. 2000 ⇒16, 8309; 17,8231. [R]NRTh 124 (2002) 279-280 (*Radermakers, J.*); RSPhT 86 (2002) 116-120.

8831 *Le Bon, Pierre* Sleep, death and resurrection in Hebrew, Greek and Latin. ET 113 (2002) 223-225.

8832 *Marucci, Corrado* La vigilanza nel Nuovo Testamento. La speranza. 2002 ⇒277. 71-105.

8833   *Murphy, George L.* Hints from science for eschatology—and vice versa. The last things. 2002 ⇒279. 146-168.
8834   *Novak, David* Law and eschatology: a Jewish-christian intersection. The last things. 2002 ⇒279. 90-112.
8835   *O'Donovan, Oliver* Response to Daniel Carroll R. ᶠO'DONOVAN, O. 2002 ⇒272. 144-146.
8836   **Oegema, Gerbern S.** Zwischen Hoffnung und Gericht: Untersuchungen zur Rezeption der Apokalyptik im frühen Christentum und Judentum. ᴰ*Lichtenberger, H.*: WMANT 82: Neukirchen-Vluyn 1999, Neukirchener xxxiii; 453 pp. 3-7887-1719-X. Diss.-Habil. Tübingen 1996/97. Bibl. 363-420. ᴿThLZ 127 (2002) 647-650 (*Sänger, Peter*); ITBT 7/6 (1999) 33-34 (*Heer, Jos de*); JSJ 31 (2000) 343-347 (*Tigchelaar, Eibert*); JJS 52 (2001) 373-374 (*Joynes, Christine*); RBLit 3 (2001) 481-483 (*Marshall, John W.*).
8837   *Pannenberg, Wolfhart* The task of christian eschatology. The last things. 2002 ⇒279. 1-13.
8838   **Polkinghorn, John** The God of hope and the end of the world. NHv 2002, Yale Univ. Pr. 154 pp. $20.
8839   **Powys, David** 'Hell': a hard look at a hard question: the fate of the unrighteous in New Testament thought. 1998 ⇒15,8333. ᴿEvangel 20/1 (2002) 23-25 (*Stenschke, Christoph W.*).
8840   *Reiser, Marius* Eschatologie in der Verkündigung Jesu. SNTU.A 27 (2002) 155-177.
8841   *Richard, Pablo* El pensamiento apocalíptico en el movimiento de Jesús. Qol 30 (2002) 55-76.
8842   *Riniker, Christian* Jesus als Gerichtsprediger?: Auseinandersetzung mit einem wieder aktuell gewordenen Thema. ZNT 9 (2002) 2-14.
8843   *Robinson, Bernard P.* Hell and damnation: biblical concepts of hell. ScrB 32 (2002) 21-32.
8844   *Rodriguez, A.M.* The heavenly books of life and of human deeds. JATS 13/1 (2002) 10-26 [NTAb 47,95].
8845   **Roose, Hanna** Heil als Machtausübung: zur Traditionsgeschichte, den Ausprägungen und Funktionen eines eschatologischen Motivkomplexes. ᴰ*Theissen, G.*: Diss.-Habil. Heidelberg 2002 [ThLZ 128, 693].
8846   *Röhser, Günter* Hat Jesus die Hölle gepredigt?: Gericht, Vorherbestimmung und Weltende im frühen Christentum. ZNT 9 (2002) 26-37.
8847   *Saunders, Stanley P.* "Learning Christ": eschatology and spiritual formation in New Testament christianity. Interp. 56 (2002) 155-167.
8848   **Scognamiglio, Edoardo** Ecco, io faccio nuove tutte le cose: avvento di Dio, futuro dell'uomo e destino del mondo. Padova 2002, Messagero 832 pp. €45.
8849   *Sherwood, Yvonne* 'Not with a bang but a whimper': shrunken eschatologies of the twentieth century—and the bible. Apocalyptic. JSPE.S 43: 2002 ⇒373. 94-116.
8850   *Shippee, Arthur Bradford* Paradoxes of now and not yet: the separation between the church and the kingdom in John CHRYSOSTOM, THEODORE, and AUGUSTINE. ᶠGREER, R. 2002 ⇒51. 106-123.
8851   *Stone, Bryan* Hope and happy endings. RExp 99 (2002) 37-50.
8852   **Twelftree, Graham H.** Life after death. Thinking clearly: L 2002, Monarch 224 pp. $12. 1-85424-525-2 [ThD 50,390—W.C. Heiser].
8853   *Vignolo, Roberto* Speranza della scrittura, speranza cristologica: risorsa per tempi postmoderni, 1-2. RCI 83 (2002) 106-120, 212-221.

8854 *Vollenweider, Samuel* Reinkarnation—ein abendländisches Erbstück. Horizonte. WUNT 144: 2002 <1995> ⇒257. 327-346.
8855 *Ward, Keith* Cosmology and religious ideas about the end of the world. The far-future universe. 2002 ⇒631. 235-248.
8856 *Watson, Duane F.* Introduction;
8857 The oral-scribal and cultural intertexture of apocalyptic discourse in Jude and 2 Peter. Intertexture. SBL.Symposium 14: 2002 ⇒385. 1-9/ 187-213.

H9.5 *Theologia totius [VT-]NT*—General [OT-]NT theology

8858 **Balla, Peter** Challenges to New Testament theology: an attempt to justify the enterprise. WUNT 2/95: 1997 ⇒13,7955... 17,8249. [R]RevBib 61 (1999) 268-272 (*Levoratti, A.J.*).
8859 *Böcher, Otto* Das Weltbild des Neuen Testaments. Religion und Weltbild. 2002 ⇒443. 65-71.
8860 *Bultmann, Rudolf* Die Aufgabe der Theologie in der gegenwärtigen Situation. NT und christliche Existenz. UTB 2316: 2002 <1933> ⇒ 152. 172-180.
8861 **Casalini, Nello** Teologia dei vangeli: lezioni e ricerche. SBFA 57: J 2002, Franciscan Printing Press 455 pp. $35. 965-516-032-7.
8862 **Childs, Brevard S.** Biblical theology: a proposal. Facets: Mp 2002, Fortress (6) 90 pp. $6. 0-8006-3481-0. Bibl. 83-90;
8863 Die Theologie der einen Bible, 1: Grundstrukturen, 2: Hauptthemen. [T]*Oeming, Christiane; Oeming, Manfred*: FrB 2002, Herder 411+495 pp. €38. 3-451-27899-5 [OrdKor 45,110s—Giesen, Heinz].
8864 *Das, A. Andrew; Matera, Frank J.* Introduction: introducing the forgotten God. [F]ACHTEMEIER, P. 2002 ⇒1. 1-10.
8865 *De Menezes, Rui* Functions of the word in the bible. VJTR 66 (2002) 873-883.
8866 **Diprose, R.** La teologia del nuovo patto: elementi fondamentali della teologia del Nuovo Testamento. R 2002, I.B.E.I. xi; 308 pp.
8867 *Dorman, Ted M.* The future of biblical theology. Biblical theology. 2002 ⇒558. 250-263.
8868 *Dulk, Maarten den* De strategische functie van de bijbelse theologie. KeTh 53 (2002) 181-187.
8869 *Fowl, Stephen E.* The conceptual structure of New Testament theology. Biblical theology. 2002 ⇒558. 225-236.
8870 *Frankemölle, Hubert* "Biblische" Theologie: semantisch-historische Anmerkungen und Thesen. ThGl 92 (2002) 157-176.
8871 *Gaston, Lloyd* New Testament theology after the Holocaust. A shadow of glory. 2002 ⇒347. 128-139.
8872 *Goldsworthy, Graeme L.* Biblical theology as the heartbeat of effective ministry. Biblical theology. 2002 ⇒558. 280-286.
8873 *Hafemann, Scott J.* Biblical theology: retrospect and prospect. Biblical theology. 2002 ⇒558. 15-21.
8874 *Hahn, Ferdinand* Das Zeugnis des Neuen Testaments in seiner Vielfalt und Einheit: zu den Grundproblemen einer neutestamentlichen Theologie. KuD 48/4 (2002) 240-260.
8875 **Hahn, Ferdinand** Theologie des Neuen Testaments, 1: Die Vielfalt des Neuen Testaments: Theologiegeschichte des Urchristentums; 2: Die Einheit des Neuen Testaments: thematische Darstellung. Tü

2002, Mohr S. 2 vols. €49+49. 3-16-147952-1. Bibl. v.1,772-834, v.2,808-844.
    [E]Hossfeld, F. Wieviel Systematik erlaubt die Schrift? 2001 ⇒ 331.
8876 House, Paul R. Biblical theology and the wholeness of scripture: steps toward a program for the future. Biblical theology. 2002 ⇒558. 267-279.
8877 **Hübner, Hans** Teologia biblica del Nuovo Testamento, 3: lettera agli Ebrei, vangeli e Apocalisse: epilegomeni. [E]*Tomasoni, Francesco*: CTNT.S 8: 2000 ⇒16,8334; 17,8259. [R]Protest. 57 (2002) 80-81 (*Noffke, Eric*); Hum(B) 57/1 (2002) 159-60 (*Menestrina, Giovanni*).
8878 *Jeremias, Joachim* The central message of the New Testament. Jesus and the message. 2002 <1965> ⇒184. 63-110.
8879 *Johnson, Luke Timothy* God ever new, ever the same: the witness of James and Peter. [F]ACHTEMEIER, P. 2002 ⇒1. 211-227.
8880 *Lehnardt, Andreas* Der Geburtstag in den jüdischen Schriften aus hellenistisch-römischer Zeit, im Neuen Testament und in der rabbinischen Literatur. Jüdische Schriften. 2002 ⇒345. 402-428.
8881 *Lindemann, Andreas* Zur "Religion" des Urchristentums. ThR 67 (2002) 238-261.
8882 *Maris, Johannes W.* De Schrift, het dogma en de dogmatiek—een pleidooi voor gelovige theologie: (co-referaat naast *J. Muis*, contio predikanten Gereformeerde Bond, 4 januari 2002). ThRef 45 (2002) 333-338.
8883 *Moberly, R.W.* How may we speak of God?: a reconsideration of the nature of biblical theology. TynB 53 (2002) 177-202 [Hag 2,7].
8884 *Muis, Jan* De Schrift, het dogma en de dogmatiek. ThRef 45 (2002) 320-332.
8885 *Niebuhr, Karl-Wilhelm* Jesu Wirken, Weg und Geschick: zum Ansatz einer Theologie des Neuen Testaments in ökumenischer Perspektive. ThLZ 127 (2002) 3-22.
8886 **Räisänen, Heikki** Neutestamentliche Theologie?: eine religionswissenschaftliche Alternative. SBS 186: 2000 ⇒16,8346. [R]ThR 67 (2002) 238-246 (*Lindemann, Andreas*); RBLit 4 (2002) 316-319 (*Balla, Peter*).
8887 *Rogerson, John W.* What is religion?: the challenge of Wilhelm VATKE's *Biblische Theologie*. [F]SMEND, R. 2002 ⇒113. 272-284.
8888 **Sacchi, Alessandro** Fede di Israele e messaggio cristiano: alle radici del cristianesimo. 2001 ⇒17,8271. [R]Protest. 57 (2002) 77-79 (*Corsani, Bruno*); PaVi 47/2 (2002) 62-63 (*De Virgilio, Giuseppe*); LASBF 51 (2001) 455-456 (*Bottini, G.C.*).
8889 *Sayão, Luiz A.* A importância da teologia bíblica. VoxScr 11/1 (2002) 23-27.
8890 *Scholtissek, Klaus* Mystik im Neuen Testament?: exegetisch-theologische Bausteine. GuL 75 (2002) 281-292, 363-382.
8891 *Scott, James M.* Jesus' vision for the restoration of Israel as the basis for a biblical theology of the New Testament. Biblical theology. 2002 ⇒558. 129-143.
8892 **Strecker, Georg** Theology of the New Testament. [T]*Boring, M. Eugene*; [E]*Horn, Friedrich Wilhelm*: 2000 ⇒16,8356; 17,8274. [R]RRT 9 (2002) 89-90 (*Moyise, Steve*).
8893 *Stuhlmacher, Peter* Erfahrungen mit der Biblischen Theologie. Biblische Theologie. WUNT 146: ⇒245. 2002. 3-22;

8894 My experience with biblical theology. Biblical theology. 2002 ⇒558. 174-191.
8895 **Stuhlmacher, Peter** Biblische Theologie des Neuen Testaments. 1992-1999 ⇒15,8373...17,8275. [R]EvTh 62 (2002) 153-162 (*Hahn, Ferdinand*).
8896 *Talstra, Eep* Actuele basisposities in de bijbelse theologie: wijzen van lezen. KeTh 53 (2002) 188-201.
8897 **Terrien, Samuel** The elusive presence: toward a new biblical theology. 2000 <1978> ⇒16,8358. [R]StMon 44 (2002) 185-186 (*Pou, A.*).
8898 **Theißen, Gerd** Die Religion der ersten Christen: eine Theorie des Urchristentums. 2000 ⇒16,8359; 17,8276. [R]TThZ 111 (2002) 77-78 (*Reiser, Marius*); ThR 67 (2002) 246-261 (*Lindemann, Andreas*); Orien. 66 (2002) 193-196 (*Reinl, Peter; Venetz, Hermann-Josef*).
8899 **Via, Dan Otto** What is New Testament theology?. Guides to Biblical Scholarship, OT: Mp 2002, Fortress v; 148 pp. $15. 0-8806-3263-X. Bibl. 133-144.
8900 *Vollenweider, Samuel* Zwischen Monotheismus und Engelchristologie: Überlegungen zur Frühgeschichte des Christusglaubens. ZThK 99 (2002) 21-44.
8901 **Vouga, François** Una teología del Nuevo Testamento. [T]*Barrado, Pedro; Pilar Salas, M. del*: Αγορα 12: Estella 2002, Verbo Divino 504 pp. €29.12. 84-8169-509-2. Pról. *A. Gounelle*;
8902 Une théologie du Nouveau Testament. MoBi 43: 2001 ⇒17,8278. [R]Teol(Br) 27 (2002) 194-204 (*Segalla, Giuseppe*); LV(L) 255 (2002) 125-126 (*Lémonon, Jean-Pierre*); ETR 77 (2002) 597-598 (*Singer, Christophe*).

XIV. Philologia biblica

J1.1 Hebraica *grammatica*

8903 [E]**Kaltner, John; McKenzie, Steven L.** Beyond Babel: a handbook for Biblical Hebrew and related languages. SBL.Resources for Biblical Study 42: Atlanta 2002, SBL xiii; 241 pp. $30. 1-58983-035-0.
8904 [E]**Ouhalla, Jamal; Shlonsky, Ur** Themes in Arabic and Hebrew syntax. Studies in natural languages and linguistic theory 53: Dordrecht 2002, Kluwer ix; 324 pp. 1-4020-0536-9.

8905 *Andersen, F.I.; Forbes, A.D.* Attachment preferences in the Primary History. Bible and computer. 2002 ⇒548. 167-186 [Gen 1-11].
8906 *Arad, Maya* Hebrew lexical causatives. Themes in Arabic and Hebrew syntax. 2002 ⇒8904. 241-266.
8907 **Bartelt, Andrew H.** Fundamental Biblical Hebrew. St. Louis 2000, Concordia xii; 276 pp. $27. [R]RBLit 4 (2002) 133-5 (*Branch, Robin*).
8908 **Brettler, Marc Zvi** Biblical Hebrew for students of modern Israeli Hebrew. 2001 ⇒17,8288. [R]HebStud 43 (2002) 235-238 (*Raizen, Esther*).
8909 *Charlap, Luba* The ellipsis in the biblical text and the exegetical completions: between style and syntax. BetM 172 (2002) 19-34 Sum. 95. H.

8910 **Coetzee, Andries W.** Tiberian Hebrew phonology: focussing on consonant clusters. SSN 38: 1999 ⇒15,8393. ᴿJSSt 47 (2002) 317-318 (*De Caen, Vincent*).

8911 **De Claissé-Walford, Nancy L.** Biblical Hebrew: an introductory textbook. St. Louis 2002, Chalice 280 pp. $40 [BiTod 41,263—Bergant, Dianne].

8912 *Décoppet, Alain* Méthode d'hébreu biblique: une méthode pour apprendre l'hébreu biblique au moyen d'un CD-ROM multimédia. Hokhma 80 (2002) 75-77.

8913 **Disse, Andreas** Informationsstruktur im Biblischen Hebräisch... Korpusuntersuchung zu den Büchern Deut., Richter und 2 Könige. ATSAT 56/1-2: 1998 ⇒14,7597; 16,8372. ᴿThLZ 127 (2002) 742-745 (*Bartelmus, Rüdiger*) [Dt 12; Judg 4; 2 Kgs 22-23].

8914 **Driver, Samuel Rolles** A treatise on the use of the tenses in Hebrew and some other syntactical questions 1998 <1892 [3rd ed.]> ⇒14, 7598; 16,8375. ᴿJNES 61 (2002) 223-225 (*Miller, Cynthia*).

8915 **Durand, Olivier** La lingua ebraica: profilo storico-strutturale. 2001 ⇒17,8298. ᴿAnnales Theologici 16 (2002) 275-276 (*Tábet, M.*); CivCatt 153/1 (2002) 622-624 (*Prato, G.L.*).

8916 **Ehrensvärd, Martin Gustaf** Studies in the syntax and dating of Biblical Hebrew. Aarhus 2002, Diss. Aarhus [StTh 57,76].

8917 *Ephratt, Michal* Hebrew morphology by itself (part 1). JNSL 28/2 (2002) 83-99.

8918 **Garrett, Duane** A modern grammar for classical Hebrew. Nv 2002, Broadman & H. vii; 395 pp. $35. 0-8054-2159-9. ᴿRBLit (2002)* (*Van der Merwe, Christo H.J.*).

8919 *Gaß, Erasmus* w-compaginis als ursprünglich proleptisches Personalpronomen mit abhängiger Appositionsverbindung. BN 113 (2002) 51-60.

8920 *Greenberg, Yael* The manifestation of genericity in the tense aspect system of Hebrew nominal sentences. Themes in Arabic and Hebrew syntax. 2002 ⇒8904. 267-298.

8921 **Gross, Walter** Doppelt besetztes Vorfeld... Studien zum althebräischen Verbalsatz. BZAW 305: 2001 ⇒17,8303. ᴿATG 65 (2002) 311-313 (*Torres, A.*).

8922 *Hackett, Jo Ann* Hebrew (biblical and epigraphic). Beyond Babel. 2002 ⇒8903. 139-156.

8923 **Hostetter, Edwin C.** An elementary grammar of Biblical Hebrew. Biblical Languages: Hebrew 1. 2000 ⇒16,8384. ᴿJSSt 47 (2002) 314-315 (*Stec, David M.*).

8924 *Huehnergard, John; Hackett, Jo Ann* The Hebrew and Aramaic languages. Biblical world, 2. 2002 ⇒273. 3-24.

8925 *Huehnergard, John* Introduction. Beyond Babel. 2002 ⇒8903. 1-18.

8926 *Jenni, Ernst* Höfliche Bitte im Alten Testament. Congress volume Basel 2001. VT.S 92: 2002 ⇒570. 1-16.

8927 **Jenni, Ernst** Die hebräischen Präpositionen, 3: die Präposition Lamed. 2000 ⇒16,8388; 17,8311. ᴿJSSt 47 (2002) 315-317 (*Malessa, Michael*).

8928 *Joosten, Jan* Do the finite verbal forms in Biblical Hebrew express aspect?. JANES 29 (2002) 49-70.

8929 *Keown, Elaine Renée* Hebrew alphabets, symbols and computer codes: history and preliminary tabulation. REJ 161 (2002) 235-240 .

8930 *Khan, Geoffrey* The notion of transitive and intransitive actions in the early Karaite grammatical tradition. JStAI 27 (2002) 363-368.

8931 *Kizhakkeyil, S.* A further look at Biblical Hebrew (עברית). JJSS 2 (2002) 119-122.

8932 *Kogut, Simḥa* The status of adjectives and adverbs in Biblical Hebrew: morphological and syntactic studies and exegetical implications. Shnaton 13 (2002) 111-137. **H.**

8933 *Kotjatko, Jens* Infinitive und Verbalnomina bei den hebräischen Grammatikern des Mittelalters und das Problem der Terminologie: die Bedeutung der Termini *hpwʿl ṣm, mqwr* sowie *maṣdar* und *ism alfiʿl.* KUSATU 3 (2002) 5-54.

8934 *Kroeze, Jan H.* The Hofʿal in Biblical Hebrew: simple passives, single passives and double passives—and reflexives?. JNSL 28/1 (2002) 39-55.

8935 *Kvalvaag, Robert W.* Nesjama: vind, pust, ånd, ikke enten-eller, men b[a- Kreis]de-og. Ung teologi 35/2 (2002) 75-84.

8936 *Lee, Noah S.* The use of the definite article in the development of some biblical toponyms. VT 52 (2002) 334-349.

8937 **Lehmann, Winfred; Raizen, Winfred; Jakusz Hewitt, Helen-Jo** Biblical Hebrew: an analytical introduction. 1999 ⇒15,8417. ᴿRBLit 4 (2002) 140-143 (*Good, Roger*).

Ljungberg, B. Verbal meaning...Ruth 2001 ⇒3073.

8938 **Long, Gary Aland** Grammatical concepts 101 for Biblical Hebrew: learning Biblical Hebrew grammatical concepts through English grammar. Peabody, MASS 2002, Hendrickson xvii; 189 pp. $20. 1-56563-713-5. Bibl. 177-178.

8939 ᴱ**Miller, Cynthia Lynn** The verbless clause in Biblical Hebrew: linguistic approaches. 1999 ⇒15,371; 16,8397. ᴿJNES 61 (2002) 225-227 (*Rollston, Christopher A.*).

8940 *Niclós Albarracín, José-V; Rauret Domènech, Marta* Aspectos gramaticales en el evangelio en Hebreo de "la piedra de toque" de IBN ŠAPRUT. LASBF 51 (2001) 145-182.

8941 *O'Connor, M.* Discourse linguistics and the study of Biblical Hebrew. Congress volume Basel 2001. VT.S 92: 2002 ⇒570. 17-42.

8942 *Pereltsvaig, Asya* Cognate objects in Modern and Biblical Hebrew. Themes in Arabic and Hebrew syntax. 2002 ⇒8904. 107-136.

8943 *Rendsburg, Gary A.* Hebrew philological notes (III). HebStud 43 (2002) 21-30 [1 Kgs 20,15; Ps 22,17; Zech 3,7];

8944 Some false leads in the identification of late Biblical Hebrew texts: the cases of Genesis 24 and 1 Samuel 2:27-36. JBL 121 (2002) 23-46.

8945 *Revell, E.J.* Logic of concord with collectives in biblical narrative. Maarav 9 (2002) 61-91.

8946 *Richter, Wolfgang; Rechenmacher, Hans; Riepl, Christian* Materialien einer althebräischen Datenbank–Verbalformen. ᶠSTEINGRIMSSON, S.: ATSAT 72: 2002 ⇒117. 305-332.

8947 **Ross, Allen P.** Introducing Biblical Hebrew. 2001 ⇒17,8324. ᴿThZ 58 (2002) 369-370 (*Jenni, Hanna*); OTEs 15 (2002) 572-574 (*Naudé, J.A.*).

8948 **Schorch, Stefan** Euphemismen in der Hebräischen Bibel. Orientalia biblica et christiana 12: 2000 ⇒16,8410. ᴿThLZ 127 (2002) 626-629 (*Krispenz, Jutta*).

8949 **Shimasaki, Katsuomi** Focus structure in Biblical Hebrew: a study of word order and information structure. Bethesda, MD 2002, CDL xvi; 314 pp. $35. 1-883053-62-5. Bibl. 291-301. ᴿLASBF 52 (2002) 523-534 (*Niccacci, Alviero*).

8950 *Siloni, Tal* Adjectival constructs and inalienable constructions. Themes in Arabic and Hebrew syntax. 2002 ⇒8904. 161-187.
8951 *Talstra, Eep* Computer-assisted linguistic analysis: the Hebrew database used in Quest.2. Bible and computer. 2002 ⇒548. 3-22.
8952 *Tropper, Josef* Kasusflexion westsemitischer Personennamen in den Amarnabriefen. AltOrF 29 (2002) 150-165.
8953 **Valle Rodríguez, Carlos del** Historia de la gramática hebrea en España, 1: los orígenes (MENAHEM, DUNAS y los discípulos). España Judia, gramática hebrea: M 2002, Aben Ezra. 665 pp. 8488-32415-4.
8954 *Van der Merwe, Christo H.J.* Biblical Hebrew instruction: a programme benefitting from second-language learning and computer-assisted language learning. Bible and computer. 2002 ⇒548. 615-639.
8955 *Verheij, Arian J.C.* Striking exceptions?: some remarks on imperative forms of Hof'al verbs. ᶠLEENE, H.: 2002 ⇒73. 243-246 [Jer 49,8; Ezek 32,19].
8956 **Wagner, Andreas** Sprechakte und Sprechaktanalyse im Alten Testament. BZAW 253: 1997 ⇒13,8073; 15,8451. ᴿZAR 8 (2002) 343-356 (*Otto, Eckart*).
8957 *Wagner, Andreas* Die Stellung der Sprechakttheorie in Hebraistik und Exegese. Congress volume Basel 2001. VT.S 92: 2002 ⇒570. 55-83 [Ps 2].
8958 *Willi-Plein, Ina* Heilige Schrift oder Heilige Übersetzung—zur theologischen Relevanz hebraistischer Forschung und Lehre. Sprache als Schlüssel. 2002 <1991> ⇒261. 1-10.

J1.2 Lexica et inscriptiones hebraicae; *later Hebrew*

8959 ᴱ**Streck, Michael P.; Weninger, Stefan** Altorientalische und semitische Onomastik. AOAT 296: Müns 2002, Ugarit-Verlag vii; 241 pp. €68. 3-934628-25-7.
8960 **Azar, Moshe** The syntax of Mishnaic Hebrew. J 1995, Academy of the Hebrew Language xx; 336 pp. ᴿLeš. 64 (2002) 315-319 (*Kaddari, Menah*em Zevi*).
8961 **Babut, Jean-Marc** Idiomatic expressions of the Hebrew Bible: their meaning and translation through componential analysis. ᵀ*Lind, Sarah E.*: BIBAL Dissertation Series 5: North Richland Hills, TX 1999, BIBAL xv; 369 pp. 0-94-103750-9. Bibl. 307-327.
8962 ᴱ**Bar-Asher, M.** Le commentaire biblique 'Leshon limmudim' de Rabbi Raphaël BERDUGO. 2000 ⇒16,8434. ᴿLeš. 64 (2002) 331-338 (*Avishur, Yitzhak*).
8963 *Bar-Asher, Moshe* On several linguistic features of Qumran Hebrew. Leš. 64/1-2 (2002) 7-31 Sum. I. H.
8964 **Ben-Hayyim, Ze'ev; Tal, Abraham** A grammar of Samaritan Hebrew: based on the recitation of the law in comparison with the Tiberian and other Jewish traditions. 2000 ⇒16,8437. ᴿHebStud 43 (2002) 240-244 (*Hendel, Ronald*).
8965 *Berge, Kåre* Hebraisk sannhet. Ung teologi 35/1 (2002) 49-61.
8966 *Blois, Reinier de* Semantic domains for Biblical Hebrew. Bible and computer. 2002 ⇒548. 209-229.
8967 *Cross, Frank Moore* The Hebrew inscriptions from Sardis. HThR 95 (2002) 3-19.

8968 *Davies, Graham I.* Hebrew inscriptions. Biblical world, 1. 2002 ⇒ 273. 270-286.
8969 *Dogniez, Cécile* The Greek renderings of Hebrew idiomatic expressions and their treatment in the Septuaginta lexica. JNSL 28/1 (2002) 1-17.
8970 *Fingernagel, Andreas; Haidinger, Alois* Neue Zeugen des Niederösterreichischen Randleistenstils in hebräischen, deutschen und lateinischen Handschriften. Codices Manuscripti 39740 (2002) 15-44.
8971 **Garbini, Giovanni** Note di lessicografia ebraica. StBi 118: 1998 ⇒ 14,7663. ᴿRivBib 50 (2002) 79-82 (*Deiana, Giovanni*).
8972 *Hagelia, Hallvard* Debatten om Siloa-innskriften. TTK 73 (2002) 261-280.
8973 *Heide, Martin* Wheat and wine: a new ostracon from the Shlomo Moussaieff collection. BN 114/115 (2002) 40-46;
8974 Die theophoren Personennamen der Kuntillet-ʿAğrud Inschriften. WO 32 (2002) 110-120.
8975 **Heller, Jan** Vocabularium biblicum septem linguarum (hebraico-graeco-latino-anglico-germanico-hungarico-bohemicum). ⁴2000 <1955> ⇒16,8460; 17,8358. ᴿAUSS 40 (2002) 151-152 (*Moskala, Jiří*).
8976 **Hempel, Charlotte** The laws of the Damascus document: sources, tradition and redaction. StTDJ 29: 1998 ⇒14,7664...17,8360. ᴿDSD 9 (2002) 411-414 (*Grossman, Maxine*).
8977 **Ilan, Tal** Lexicon of Jewish names in late antiquity, 1: Palestine 330 BCE - 200 CE. TSAJ 91: Tü 2002, Mohr S. xxvi; 484 pp. €159. 3-16-147646-8.
8978 **Jaroš, Karl** Inschriften des Heiligen Landes aus vier Jahrtausenden. 2001 ⇒17,8363. CD-ROM. ᴿWZKM 92 (2002) 238-239 (*Selz, Gebhard J.*).
8979 **Karni, Shlomo** Dictionary of basic Biblical Hebrew. J 2002, Carta 190 pp. 965-220-498-6.
8980 ᴱ**Koehler, Ludwig; Baumgartner, Walter** The Hebrew and Aramaic lexicon of the Old Testament, 4. ᵀᴱ*Richardson, M.E.J.*: 1999 ⇒15, 8487 ...17,8365. ᴿRBLit 4 (2002) 138-140 (*Vaughn, Andrew G.*);
8981 The Hebr. and Aram. lexicon of the OT: CD-ROM. ᵀ*Richardson, M. E.J.*: 2000. ᴿRBLit 4 (2002) 135-138 (*Tucker, Gene M.*).
8982 *Läufer, Erich* 'Jakob, Sohn des Josef, Bruder des Jesus'—zum wem gehörte der Jerusalemer Steinsarg?: eine Inschrift sorgt für Aufregung, Neugier und Vermutungen. HlL 134/3 (2002) 3-4.
8983 *Lemaire, André* Das achamenidische Juda und seine Nachbarn im Lichte der Epigraphie. Religion und Religionskontakte. 2002 ⇒492. 210-230.
8984 *Levine, Baruch A.* Hebrew (postbiblical). Beyond Babel. 2002 ⇒ 8903. 157-182.
8985 *Lübbe, J.C.* Idioms in the Old Testament. JSem 11/1 (2002) 45-63;
8986 Semantic domains and the difficulties of a paradigm shift in Old Testament lexicography. JSem 11/2 (2002) 245-255.
8987 **Mankowski, Paul V.** Akkadian loanwords in Biblical Hebrew. HSS 47: 2000 ⇒16,8477; 17,8369. ᴿOLZ 97 (2002) 283-6 (*Streck, Michael P.*); BSOAS 65 (2002) 567-569 (*Richardson, M.E.J.*); RBLit (2002)* (*Byrne, Ryan*).
8988 *Naʾaman, Nadav* Ostracon no. 7 from Arad—testimony to a prohibition of work on the new moon day?. Tarbiz 71 (2002) 565-568. Sum. xi. **H**.

8989 *Naudé, J.A.* Verbless clauses containing personal pronouns in Qumran Hebrew. JSem 11/1 (2002) 126-168. Errata rectified pp. 285-292;
8990 Words in a cultural context: the case of Biblical Hebrew lexicography. OTEs 15 (2002) 417-434.
8991 *Naveh, Joseph* Epigraphic miscellanea. IEJ 52 (2002) 240-253.
8992 **Nissim, Ute** Die Bedeutung des Ergehens: ein Beitrag zu einem biblisch-hebräischen Valenzlexikon am Beispiel von Ergehensverben. ATSAT 65: 2000 ⇒16,8486. ᴿCBQ 64 (2002) 744-745 (*Winther-Nielsen, Nicolai*).
8993 *O'Connor, M.* Semitic lexicography: European dictionaries of Biblical Hebrew in the twentieth century. IOS 20 (2002) 173-212.
8994 *Pazzini, Massimo* Grammatiche e dizionari di ebraico-aramaico in italiano: catalogo ragionato—aggiornamento (dicembre 2001). LASBF 51 (2001) 183-190.
8995 *Podolsky, Baruch* A selected list of dictionaries of Semitic languages. IOS 20 (2002) 213-221.
8996 **Rabin, Chaim** The development of the syntax of post-Biblical Hebrew. SStLL 29: 2000 ⇒16,8490. ᴿJSSt 47 (2002) 318-320 (*Fassberg, Steven E.*).
8997 *Rainey, Anson F.* The new inscription from Khirbet el-Mudeiyineh. IEJ 52 (2002) 81-86.
8998 **Raizen, Esther** Modern Hebrew for intermediate students: a multimedia program. Austin 2002, Univ. of Texas x; 174 pp. $19. ᴿHebStud 43 (2002) 323-326 (*Etzion, Giore*).
8999 *Rechenmacher, Hans* Eigennamen in einer Datenbank: methodische Überlegungen am Beispiel des althebräischen Korpus. Onomastik. AOAT 296: 2002 ⇒8959. 185-193.
9000 *Reich, Ronny; Greenhut, Zvi* Another 'boundary of Gezer' inscription found recently. IEJ 52 (2002) 58-63.
9001 *Rosenhouse, Judith* Personal names in Hebrew and Arabic: modern trends compared to the past. JSSt 47 (2002) 97-114.
9002 ᴱ**Sermoneta, Hillel M.; Fumagalli, Pier Francesco** Manoscritti ebraici nell'Archivio di Stato di Pesaro: catalogo con riproduzione del Mahazor francese di Pesaro. Quaderni della rassegna degli Archivi di Stato 102: R 2002, Ministero per i Beni Culturali e Ambientali 122 pp. 88-7125-237-3. Introd. *Gianfranco Ravasi*; 114 pl..
9003 *Shanks, Hershel* Scrolls, scripts & stelae: a Norwegian collector shows BAR his rare inscriptions. BArR 28/5 (2002) 25-34, 68.
9004 *Shemesh, Rivka* About 'speaking' that is not 'saying': a survey of verbs of speech production in Mishnaic Hebrew. JQR 93 (2002) 201-215.
9005 **Sirat, Colette** Hebrew manuscripts of the Middle Ages. ᴱᵀ*De Lange, Nicholas Robert Michael*: C 2002, CUP xvi; 349 pp. £65. 0-521-770-79-3. Bibl. 320-335.
9006 **Sirat, Colette; Glatzer, Mordechai; Beit-Arié, Malachi** Monumenta palaeographica medii aevi, series hebraica: codices hebraicis litteris exarati quo tempore scripti fuerint exhibentes, t. III, de 1085 à 1140. Turnhout 2002, Brepols 119 pp. Ill..
9007 *Tawil, Hayim* Two biblical and Akkadian comparative lexical notes VIII. JSSt 47 (2002) 209-214.
9008 *Van Steenbergen, Gerrit* Componential analysis of meaning and cognitive linguistics: some prospects for Biblical Hebrew lexicology. JNSL 28/1, 2 (2002) 19-37, 109-126.

9009 **Vázquez Allegue, Jaime** Diccionario bíblico hebreo-español, español-hebreo. Estella 2002, Verbo Divino 342 pp. €24. 84-8169-513-0.

9010 **Wodziński, Marcin** Hebrajskie inskrypcje na Śląsku XIII-XVIII wieku [Hebrew inscriptions in Silesia in the 13th through 18th centuries]. Wrocław 1996, Towarzystwo Przyjaciół Polonistyki Wrocławskie 561 pp. ^RJQR 92 (2001) 255-257 (*Rosman, Moshe*). **P**.

9011 ^E**Yadin (Sukenik), Yigael; Greenfield, Jonas C.**, *al.*, The documents from the Bar Kokhba period in the Cave of Letters: Hebrew, Aramaic and Nabatean-Aramaic papyri. Judean Desert Studies: J 2002, Israel Exploration Society 2 vols. $132. 965-221-046-3. Additional contrib. *Hannah M. Cotton; Joseph Naveh*. Bibl. v.1, 411-422.

9012 **Zemach-Tendler, Shulamit** Lehrbuch der neuhebräischen Sprache. 1999 ⇒15,8521. ^RREJ 161 (2002) 338-340 (*Schattner-Rieser, Ursula*).

9013 **Zilkha, Avraham** Modern English-Hebrew dictionary. Yale Language series: NHv 2002, Yale University Press vi; 457 pp. 0-300-09-005-6.

J1.3 Voces *ordine alphabetico consonantium* hebraicarum

9014 ^E**Steele, John M.; Imhausen, Annette** Under one sky: astronomy and mathematics in the ancient Near East. AOAT 297: Müns 2002, Ugarit-Verlag vii; 496 pp. 3-934628-26-5.

Akkadian

9015 *g: Kogan, Leonid* Additions and corrections to '*ǧ in Akkadian' (UF 33). UF 34 (2002) 315-317.

9016 *izuzzum; itūlum: Huehnergard, John izuzzum* and *itūlum*;

9017 *lugalbanda: Vanstiphout, H.L.J. Sanctus* Lugalbanda. ^MJACOBSEN, T. 2002 ⇒62. 161-185/259-289.

9018 *r'm: Mazzini, Giovanni* Akkadian *r'm* as a West Semitic lexical trait. UF 34 (2002) 577-584.

Aramaic

9019 קרבן: *Benovitz, Moshe* The *korban* vow and the ossuary inscriptions from the Arnona neighborhood in Jerusalem. Cathedra 104 (2002) 177-179. **H**.

Hebrew

9020 אב: *Loretz, Oswald* Ugaritisch ʾap (III) und syllabisch-keilschriftlich abi/apu als Vorläufer von hebräisch ʾb/ʾôb ʿ(Kult/Nekromantie-)Grube': ein Beitrag zu Nekromantie und Magie in Ugarit, Emar und Israel. UF 34 (2002) 481-519.

9021 אהב: *Ackerman, Susan* The personal is political: covenantal and affectionate love (ʾāheb, ʾahăbâ) in the Hebrew Bible. VT 52 (2002) 437-458.

9022 אמה: *Kessler, Rainer* Die Sklavin als Ehefrau: zur Stellung der ʾāmāh. VT 52 (2002) 501-512 [Ex 21,7-11].

9023 במה: *Kogan, Leonid; Tishchenko, Serguei* Lexicographic notes on Hebrew bamah. UF 34 (2002) 319-352.

9024 ברית: *Linington, Silvia* The term בְּרִית in the Old Testament, part I: an enquiry into the meaning and use of the word in the contexts of the covenants between God and humans in the pentateuch. OTEs 15 (2002) 687-714.

9025 גר: *Barbiero, Gianni* Der Fremde im Bundesbuch und im Heiligkeits-gesetz: zwischen Absonderung und Annahme. Studien. SBAB 34: 2002 <1996> ⇒139. 221-254;

9026 **Ramírez Kidd, José E.** Alterity and identity in Israel: the "ger" in the Old Testament. BZAW 283: 1999 ⇒15,8530; 16,8523. ᴿThR 67 (2002) 316-317 (*Veijola, Timo*).

9027 דבורה: *Kagerer, Bernhard* Die Biene in der Bibel: ein Beitrag zur Exegese der דְּבוֹרָה-Stellen. BN 114/115 (2002) 71-88.

9028 האמין: *Smend, Rudolf* Zur Geschichte von האמין. Die Mitte des A.T. 2002 <1967> ⇒244. 244-249 [Gen 6,13].

9029 הנה: *Tropper, Josef* Die hebräische Partikel *hinneh* 'siehe!': morpholo-gische und syntaktische Probleme. KUSATU 3 (2002) 81-121.

9030 חטאת: *Dennis, John* The function of the חטאת sacrifice in the priestly literature: an evaluation of the view of Jacob Milgrom. EThL 78 (2002) 108-129.

9031 חלק: *Depuydt, Leo* History of the ḥeleq. Under one sky. AOAT 297: 2002 ⇒9014. 79-107.

9032 יד: *Roberts, J.J.M.* The hand of Yahweh. The bible and the ANE. 2002 <1971> ⇒230. 95-101.

9033 ישע: *Gosse, Bernard* Le salut et le messie en 1 Sam 2,1-10, et Yavé juge, à oeuvre sur la terre et dans l'histoire, dans la tradition des Can-tiques et du Psautier. BN 111 (2002) 18-22 [Ps 75; 113].

9034 לקח: *Yadin, Azzan* A Greek witness to the semantic shift לקח—'buy'. HebStud 43 (2002) 31-37.

9035 מחיר: *Heltzer, M.; Avishur, Y.* The term *sōfēr māhir* as designating a courtier in the Old Testament and the Aḥiqar story. UF 34 (2002) 217-221.

9036 פלט; מלט: *Williams, Peter J.* Difference between the roots *mlṭ* and *plṭ*. ZAW 114 (2002) 438-442.

9037 מלך: *Fassberg, Steven E.* Why doesn't *melex* appear as *ma:lex* in pause in Tiberian Hebrew?. Leš. 64/3-4 (2002) 207-219 Sum. II. **H.**

9038 משא: *Floyd, Michael H.* The מַשָּׂא (maśśā᾿) as a type of prophetic book. JBL 121 (2002) 401-422.

9039 משל: *Schöpflin, Karin* mašal—ein eigentümlicher Begriff der hebräi-schen Literatur. BZ 46 (2002) 1-24.

9040 נבלה: *Phillips, Anthony* nebalah: a term for serious disorderly and un-ruly conduct. Essays on biblical law. JSOT.S 344: 2002 <1975> ⇒ 223. 239-244.

9041 נח: *Schwartz, Martin* Qumran, Turfan, Arabic magic, and Noah's name. Charmes et sortilèges. 2002 ⇒477. 231-238.

9042 נחם: *Willi-Plein, Ina* Hiobs Widerruf?—eine Untersuchung der Wur-zel *nhm* und ihrer erzählerischen Funktion im Hiobbuch. Sprache als Schlüssel. 2002 <1983> ⇒261. 130-145.

9043 נכר: *Caero Bustillos, Bernardeth Carmen* Liebt Gott den *nkr*?. BN 111 (2002) 48-65.

9044 סד: *Görg, Manfred* Ein etymologischer Versuch zu hebr. *sōd*. BN 111 (2002) 12-15.

9045 סריס: *Everhart, Janet* Hidden eunuchs of the Hebrew Bible. SBL.SP 2002. SBL.SPS 41: 2002 ⇒598. 137-155.

9046 עֶבֶד: *Lipschits, Oded* On the titles 'bd hmlk and 'bd yhwh. Shnaton 13 (2002) 157-171. **H.**

9047 עוֹל: *Ruwe, Andreas; Weise, Uwe* Das Joch Assurs und Jhwhs Joch: ein Realienbegriff und seine Metaphorisierung in neuassyrischen und alttestamentlichen Texten. ZAR 8 (2002) 274-307 [Isa 9,3; Hos 11,4].

9048 עַלְמָנָה: *Leeb, Carolyn S.* The widow: homeless and post-menopausal. BTB 32 (2002) 160-162.

9049 עָנָה: *Van Wolde, Ellen* Does *'innâ* denote rape?: a semantic analysis of a controversial word. VT 52 (2002) 528-544 [Gen 34,2].

9050 עָרַךְ: **Suarez Codorniu, Carlos Luis** Construyendo la vida: la raiz 'rk en el Antiguo Testamento. ᴰ*Breton, S.* 2002 105 pp. Diss. Gregorian [RTL 34,594].

9051 שׁוּב: *Willi-Plein, Ina* שְׁבוּת שׁוּב—eine Wiedererwägung. Sprache als Schlüssel 2002 <1991> ⇒261. 189-208.

9052 שָׂטָן: *Gershenson, Daniel E.* The name Satan. ZAW 114 (2002) 443-445.

9053 שָׁלוֹם: *Schelling, Piet* Sjalom, veelkleurig bijbels sleutelwoord. ITBT 10/4 (2002) 15-17.

9054 שָׁמַר: *Muraoka, T.; Malessa, M.* A Deuteronomistic formula <שָׁמַר + עָשָׂה>. VT 52 (2002) 548-551.

9055 שֶׁמֶשׁ; שׁפשׁ: *Heltzer, M.* The West Semtic word for 'sun' (*šmš* and *špš*). Sex and gender. 2002 ⇒712. 235-238.

Phoenician

9056 *dl*: *Schmitz, Philip C.* The vocalization of the Phoenician-Punic word *dl*. StEeL 19 (2002) 87-88.

Ugaritic

'*ap* (III) ⇒9020.

9057 ʿ*ḏ/db Dietrich, Manfried; Loretz, Oswald* Die Wurzel ʿ*ḏ/db* und ihre Ableitungen im Ugaritischen. UF 34 (2002) 75-108.

9058 *ǵzr*: *Xella, Paolo* *ǵzr in Ugaritico: analisi contestuale e ricerca etimologica. ᶠDIETRICH, M. 2002 ⇒28. 857-869.

9059 *m't*: *Pardee, Dennis* Un 'nouveau' mot ougaritique. AuOr 20 (2002) 163-182.

9060 *sākinu*: *Van Soldt, Wilfred* Studies on the *sākinu*-official (2): the functions of the *sākinu* of Ugarit. UF 34 (2002) 805-828.

9061 *ṣśǵr*: *Watson, Wilfred G.E.* The meaning of Ugaritic *ṣśǵr*. JSSt 47 (2002) 203-207.

9062 *ṯbr*; *ṯbrn Dietrich, Manfried; Loretz, Oswald* Der ugaritische Parallelismus p//ṯbrn qn (KTU 1.4 VIII 17-20; 1.6 II 22-23): lexikographische Ergebnisse in Zusammenhang mit *ṯbr* und *ṯbrn*. UF 34 (2002) 109-118.

J1.5 Phoenicia, ugaritica—Northwest Semitic [⇒T5.4]

9063 *Altschuler, Eric L.* Gloss of one of the Wadi el-Hol inscriptions. ANESt 39 (2002) 201-204.

9064 *Archi, Alfonso* Prepositions at Ebla. Eblaitica 4. 2002 ⇒474. 1-21.

9065 **Avishur, Yitzhak** Phoenician inscriptions and the bible: select inscriptions and studies in stylistic and literary devices common to the Phoenician inscriptions and the bible. 2000 ⇒16,8551. ᴿOLZ 97 (2002) 277-282 (*Heltzer, Michael*).

9066 *Bonnet, Corinne; Xella, Paolo* Les inscriptions phéniciennes de Bo-dashtart roi de Sidon. ᴹCIASCA, A.: 2002 ⇒15. 93-104. 3 pl.

9067 *Bordreuil, Pierre* Ugaritisch: dem Alphabet auf der Spur. WUB 23 (2002) 22;

9068 Un scribe étranger et/ou dur d'oreille. ᶠDIETRICH, M.: 2002 ⇒28. 67-71.

9069 *Byrne, Ryan* Philistine semitics and dynastic history at Ekron. UF 34 (2002) 1-23.

9070 *Day, Peggy L.* Dies diem docet: the decipherment of Ugaritic. StEeL 19 (2002) 37-57;

9071 Ugaritic. Beyond Babel. 2002 ⇒8903. 223-241.

9072 ᴱ**Donner, Herbert; Röllig, Wolfgang** Kanaanäische und aramäische Inschriften. Wsb ⁵2002, Harrassowitz xviii; 79 pp. 3-447-04587-6.

9073 *Easterly, Ellis* "Tower" or "towers" in the Mesha inscription?. Maarav 9 (2002) 9-18.

9074 *Emerton, J.A.* The value of the Moabite stone as an historical source. VT 52 (2002) 483-492.

9075 *Firmage, Edwin* The definite article in Phoenician. Maarav 9 (2002) 33-53.

9076 *Ford, J.N.* The new Ugaritic incantation against sorcery RS 1992. 2014. UF 34 (2002) 119-152;

9077 The Ugaritic incantation against sorcery RIH 78/20 (KTU² 1.169). UF 34 (2002) 153-211.

9078 *Frendo, Anthony J.* Two long-lost Phoenician inscriptions and the emergence of ancient Israel. PEQ 134 (2002) 37-43.

9079 **Friedrich, Johannes; Röllig, Wolfgang** Phönizisch-punische Grammatik. ᴱ*Amadasi Guzzo, Maria Giulia; Mayer, Werner R.*: AnOr 55: ³1999 ⇒15,8580. ᴿOLZ 97 (2002) 63-68 (*Streck, Michael P.*); IEJ 52 (2002) 100-102 (*Naveh, Joseph*).

9080 *Garbini, Giovanni* Terminologia finanziaria in Punico (a proposito di KAI 119). ᴹCIASCA, A.: 2002 ⇒15. 245-251.

9081 *Jongeling, K.; Kerr, R.* A personal Phoenico-Punic dictionary. Or. 71 (2002) 173-181.

9082 *Kottsieper, Ingo* Zur Inschrift auf der Flasche vom Tell Sīrān und ihrem historischen Hintergrund. UF 34 (2002) 353-362.

9083 *Krahmalkov, Charles R.* Phoenician. Beyond Babel. 2002 ⇒8903. 207-222.

9084 **Krahmalkov, Charles R.** Phoenician-Punic dictionary. OLA 90; Studia Phoenicia 15: 2000 ⇒16,8568; 17,8477. ᴿAUSS 40 (2002) 341-343 (*Li, Tarsee*).

9085 *Lemaire, André* Inscription phénicienne sur oeuf d'autruche décoré. ᴹCIASCA, A. 2002 ⇒15. 287-288. 1 pl.

9086 *Mazzini, Giovanni* A new suggestion to KTU 1.14 I 15. UF 34 (2002) 569-575.

9087 *Mittmann, Siegfried* Zwei "Rätsel" der Mešaʿ-Inschrift: mit einem Beitrag zur aramäischen Steleninschrift von Dan (Tell el-Qaḍi). ZDPV 118 (2002) 33-65.

9088 *Olmo Lete, G. del; Sanmartín, J.* Drei ugaritische Briefe: KTU 2.70, 2.71, 2.72. ᶠDIETRICH, M. 2002 ⇒28. 547-558.

9089 *Pardee, Dennis* RIH 77/27, RIH 77/12, RIH 78/26 et le principe de l'écriture cunéiforme alphabétique. Syria 79 (2002) 51-63.

9090 *Parker, Simon B.* Ammonite, Edomite, and Moabite. Beyond Babel. 2002 ⇒8903. 43-60.

9091 *Puech, Émile* Notes sur quatre inscriptions protosinaïtiques. RB 109 (2002) 5-39. Planches I-II.

9092 *Rendsburg, Gary A.* Eblaite and some Northwest Semitic lexical links. Eblaitica 4. 2002 ⇒474. 199-208.

9093 *Röllig, Wolfgang* Eine punische Weihinschrift für Ešmun. ᴹCIASCA, A. 2002 ⇒15. 447-454. 1 pl..

9094 *Ruiz Cabrero, Luis A.; Mederos Martín, Alfredo* Comercio de ánaforas, escritura y presencia fenicia en la Península Ibérica. StEeL 19 (2002) 89-120.

9095 *Tropper, Josef* Zur Rekonstruktion von KTU 1.4 VII 19. UF 34 (2002) 799-803;

9096 Schlange, Hund und Götter: neue Überlegungen zu KTU 1.100:6 und 1.114:4-6. AuOr 20 (2002) 221-230;

9097 **Tropper, Josef** Ugaritisch: kurzgefasste Grammatik mit Übungstexten und Glossar. Elementa Linguarum Orientis. ELO 1: Müns 2002, Ugarit-Verlag xii; 168 pp. €28. 3-934628-12-5. Bibl. 164-168.

9098 *Van Soldt, Wilfred* The orthography of Ugaritic words in texts written by the Assyrian scribe Naḫuš-šalmu. ᶠDIETRICH, M.: 2002 ⇒28. 685-697.

9099 *Wagenaar, Jan A.* In the sixth month: the day of the new moon of Ḫiyaru: text and interpretation of KTU 1.78: a new proposal. UF 34 (2002) 913-919.

9100 *Watson, Wilfred G.E.* Ugaritic onomastics (6). AuOr 20 (2002) 231-238;

9101 Tools of the trade (KTU 4.127 and 4.385). UF 34 (2002) 921-930;

9102 Terms for 'rain' in Ugaritic. ᶠDIETRICH, M. 2002 ⇒28. 795-801.

9103 **Westenholz, Joan Goodnick** Cuneiform inscriptions in the collection of the Bible Lands Museum Jerusalem: the Emar tablets. Cuneiform monographs 13: 2000 ⇒16,8593; 17,8498. ᴿOLZ 97 (2002) 519-527 (*d'Alfonso, Lorenzo*); JESHO 45 (2002) 365-376 (*Fleming, Daniel E.*).

9104 *Wyatt, N.* Ilimilku the theologian: the ideological roles of Athtar and Baal in KTU 1.1 and 1.6. ᶠDIETRICH, M. 2002 ⇒28. 845-856.

9105 *Younger, K. Lawson Jr.* The 'contextual method': some West Semitic reflections. Context of scripture. 2002 ⇒326. xxxv-xlii.

J1.6 Aramaica

9106 **Beyer, Klaus** Die aramäischen Inschriften aus Assur, Hatra und dem übrigen Ostmesopotamien (datiert 44 v.Chr. bis 238 n. Chr.). 1998 ⇒14,7796...17,8503. ᴿWO 32 (2002) 209-211 (*Röllig, Wolfgang*); ThLZ 127 (2002) 618-619 (*Müller, Hans-Peter*).

9107 **Brock, Sebastian P.; Taylor, David G.K.,** *al.*, The hidden pearl: the Syrian Orthodox Church and its ancient Aramaic heritage. 2001 ⇒ 17,8504. ᴿCBQ 64 (2002) 740-741 (*Owens, Robert J., Jr.*).

9108 *Cussini, Eleonora* Additions to *Palmyrene Aramaic texts*. StEeL 19 (2002) 131-135.

9109 *Dombrowski, Bruno W.* A note on Eisenman's paper "The James ossuary—is it authentic?". PJBR 2/1 (2002) 25-29.

9110 *Fassberg, Steven E.* Qumran Aramaic. Maarav 9 (2002) 19-31.
9111 **Fitzmyer, Joseph A.; Harrington, Daniel J.** A manual of Palestinian Aramaic texts (second century B.C.-second century A.D.). BibOr 34: R ³2002, E.P.I.B. xx; 373 pp. €30. 88-7653-334-6.
9112 *Ford, J.N.* Another look at the Mandaic incantation bowl BM 91715. JANES 29 (2002) 31-47.
9113 *Gmirkin, Russel* Tool slippage and the Tel Dan incription. SJOT 16 (2002) 293-302.
9114 *Görg, Manfred* Zu einem Lehnwort in Achiqar IX (53) 5. BN 114/115 (2002) 38-39.
9115 **Greenspahn, Frederick E.** An introduction to Aramaic. SBL, Resources for Biblical Study 38: 1999 ⇒15,8605; 16,8611. ᴿHebStud 43 (2002) 238-240 (*Creason, Stuart*); RBLit (2002)* (*Goodfriend, Elaine Adler*).
9116 *Greenspahn, Frederick E.* Aramaic. Beyond Babel. 2002 ⇒8903. 93-108.
9117 *Hayajneh, Hani* Zwei beschriftete Stelen aus dem Museum der Yarmouk-Universität. WO 32 (2002) 102-109.
9118 **Hvidberg-Hansen, Finn Ove** The Palmyrene Inscriptions. 1998 ⇒ 14,7811. ᴿJNES 61 (2002) 127-128 (*Briquel Chatonnet, Françoise*).
9119 **Juusola, Hannu** Linguistic peculiarities in the Aramaic magic bowl texts. StOr 86: 1999 ⇒15,8610; 16,8615. ᴿJJS 53 (2002) 392-3 (*Salvesen, Alison*); ZDMG 152 (2002) 397-9 (*Müller-Kessler, Christa*).
9120 *Kapera, Zdzisław Jan* Preliminary discussion concerning the so-called ossuary of Jacob from a Tel Aviv collection. PJBR 2/1 (2002) 31-66.
9121 *Kaufman, Stephen A.* Recent contributions of Aramaic studies to Biblical Hebrew philology and the exegesis of the Hebrew Bible. Congress volume Basel 2001. VT.S 92: 2002 ⇒570. 43-54.
9122 **Khan, Geoffrey** The Neo-Aramaic dialect of Qaraqosh. SStLL 36: Lei 2002, Brill xxiv; 750 pp. €179. 90-04-12863-8.
9123 **Kombi, Ngwese** Concordance et lexique d'Araméen biblique—Swahili / Concordance and Biblical Aramaic—Swahili lexicon / Itifaki na kamusi ya kiaramu cha Biblia. Kinshasa 2002, Baobab 39 pp.
9124 *Kottsieper, Ingo* Zum aramäischen Text der 'Trilingue' von Xanthos und ihrem historischen Hintergrund. ᶠDIETRICH, M. 2002 ⇒28. 209-243.
9125 *Kwasman, Theodore; Lemaire, André* An Aramaic inscription from Kemaliye (Lydian Philadelpheia). Epigraphica Anatolica 34 (2002) 185-187.
9126 *Leibner, Uzi* The 23rd day of Heshvan in *Megillat Taʿanit*. Tarb. 71 (2002) 5-17 Sum. v. **H.**
9127 *Lemaire, A.* Syrie—Phénicie—Palestine: épigraphie. TEuph 24 (2002) 137-141;
9128 Nouvelle inscription araméenne d'époque achéménide provenant de Kenger (Lydie). Epigraphica Anatolica 34 (2002) 179-184;
9129 Burial box of James the brother of Jesus. BArR 28/6 (2002) 25-33, 70.
9130 **Lemaire, André** Nouvelles tablettes araméennes. 2001 ⇒17,8566. ᴿOLZ 97 (2002) 407-412 (*Tropper, Josef*); TEuph 24 (2002) 146-148 (*Elayi, J.*);
9131 Nouvelles inscriptions araméennes d'Idumée, 2: collections Moussaïeff, Jeselsohn, Welch et divers. TEuph.S 9: P 2002, Gabalda 285 pp. €77. 69 pl..

9132 *Lieu, J.M.* A Jewish deed of marriage. [F]BARNETT, P. 2002 ⇒4. 82-5.
9133 *Llewelyn, S.R.* A Jewish deed of marriage: some further observations. [F]BARNETT, P. 2002 ⇒4. 86-98.
9134 *Milikowsky, Chaim Vayyiqra Rabba*, chapter 28, sections 1-3: questions of text redaction and affinity to *Pesiqta d'Rav Kahana*. Tarb. 71 (2002) 19-65 Sum. v. H.
9135 *Morenz, Ludwig D.* Ein tiefgreifender interkultureller Kontakt: die ägyptische Unschuldserklärung im aramäischen Text der Stele von Carpentras (KAI 269). WZKM 92 (2002) 81-90.
9136 **Nosek, Bedřich** Aramejština babylónského talmudu: praktická gramatika [Das Aramäisch des babylonischen Talmuds: eine praktische Grammatik]. 2001 ⇒17,8573. [R]ArOr 70 (2002) 239-240 (*Oliverius, Jaroslav*). **Czech.**
9137 [ET]**Porten, Bezalel; Yardeni, Ada** אוסף תעודות ארמיות ממצרם העתיקה Textbook of Aramaic documents from ancient Egypt. חרסים ושונות 1999 ⇒15,8626...17,8574. [R]TEuph 24 (2002) 160-63 (*Lemaire, A.*).
9138 **Porten, Bezalel; Lund, Jerome A.** Aramaic documents from Egypt: a key-word-in-context concordance. The Comprehensive Aramaic Lexicon project, texts and studies 1: WL 2002, Eisenbrauns xvi; 495 pp. 1-57506-068-X. Bibl. 491-495.
9139 *Puech, Émile* A propos de l'ossuaire de Jacques, le frère de Jésus. PJBR 2/1 (2002) 7-23.
9140 **Puech, Émile** Qumrân Grotte 4 XXII: textes araméens première partie 4Q529-549. DJD 31: 2001 ⇒17,8576. [R]RB 109 (2002) 428-434 (*Grelot, Pierre*).
9141 **Sabar, Yona** A Jewish Neo-Aramaic dictionary: dialects of Amidya, Dihok, Nerwa and Zakho, Northwestern Iraq. Wsb 2002, Harrassowitz xiii; 337 pp. €33. 3-447-04557-4.
9142 **Segal, J.B.** Catalogue of the Aramaic and Mandaic Incantation bowls in the British Museum. 2000 ⇒16,8638. [R]JStAI 26 (2002) 237-272 (*Ford, James Nathan*).
9143 **Sokoloff, Michael** A dictionary of Jewish Babylonian Aramaic of the Talmudic and Geonic periods. Ramat-Gan 2002, Johns Hopkins University 1582 pp. $160. 965-226-260-9.
9144 **Sokoloff, Michael; Yahalom, Joseph** Jewish Palestinian Aramaic poetry from late antiquity: critical edition with introduction and commentary. 1999 ⇒15,8632... 17,8579. [R]JQR 92 (2002) 293-298 (*Hazan, Ephraim*).
9145 **Tal, Abraham** A dictionary of Samaritan Aramaic. HO 1,50/1-2: 2000 ⇒16,8643; 17,8581. [R]ZDMG 152 (2002) 399-400 (*Arnold, Werner*).
9146 *Young, Ian* The languages of ancient Sam'al. Maarav 9 (2002) 93-105.

J1.7 Syriaca

9147 *Becker, Adam H.* Anti-Judaism and care for the poor in Aphrahat's Demonstration 20. JECS 10 (2002) 305-327.
9148 [ET]**Drijvers, Hendrik Jan Willem; Healey, John F.** The Old Syriac inscriptions of Edessa and Osrhoene: text, translations and commentary. HO 42: 1999 ⇒15,8639; 17,8590. [R]Muséon 115/1-2 (2002) 221 (*Haelewyck, J.-C.*); AfO 48-49 (2001-2002) 278-280 (*Sima, Alexander*).

9149 **Kiraz, George Anton** Lexical tools to the Syriac New Testament.
       Gorgias Reprint 26: Piscataway NJ ²2002 <1994>, Gorgias 136 pp.
9150 **Muraoka, Takamitsu** Classical Syriac: a basic grammar with a chre-
       stomathy. PLO 19: 1997 ⇒13,8264... 17,8597. ᴿOrChr 86 (2002)
       248-250 (*Kropp, Manfred*).
9151 **Nöldeke, Theodor** Compendious Syriac grammar. ᵀ*Crichton, James
       A.*: WL 2001 <1904>, Eisenbrauns xxxiv; 336 pp. $45/€22. 1-57506-
       050-7.
9152 *Reinink, Gerrit J.* The lamb on the tree: Syriac exegesis and anti-Is-
       lamic apologetics. Aqedah. 2002 ⇒2524. 109-124 [Gen 22].
9153 **Robinson, Theodore H.** Robinson's paradigms and exercises in Syri-
       ac grammar. ᴱ*Coakley, J.F.*: Oxf ⁵2002, OUP viii; 181 pp. 0-19-92-
       6129-6.
9154 *Wertheimer, Ada* Syriac nominal sentences. JSSt 47 (2002) 1-21.
9155 **Wright, William** Catalogue of the Syriac manuscripts in the British
       Museum. Piscataway 2002 <1870>, Gorgias 3 vols; c.1500 pp. $350.
       1-931-956-29-4.
9156 **Wright, William; Cook, Stanley Arthur** A catalogue of the Syriac
       manuscripts preserved in the library of the University of Cambridge,
       I-II. Piscataway 2002 <1901>, Gorgias 2 vols; 1290 pp. $250. 1-931-
       956-27-8.

J1.8 Akkadica (sumerica)

9157 *Aaboe, Asger* On columns H and J in Babylonian lunar theory of sys-
       tem B. Under one sky. AOAT 297: 2002 ⇒9014. 1-4.
9158 *Alster, Bendt* Relative clause and case relations in Sumerian. WZKM
       92 (2002) 7-31.
9159 *André-Salvini, Béatrice; Salvini, Mirjo* Eine dreisprachige Wortliste:
       Sumerisch-Akkadisch-Hurritisch. WUB 23 (2002) 24.
9160 *Baker, Heather D.* Approaches to Akkadian name-giving in first-mil-
       lennium BC Mesopotamia. ᶠWALKER, C. 2002 ⇒130. 1-24.
9161 *Becking, Bob* West Semites at Tell Šeḫ Ḥamad: evidence for the Isra-
       elite exile?. ᶠWEIPPERT, M.: OBO 186: 2002 ⇒133. 153-166.
9162 ᴱ**Black, J.A.; George, A.R.; Postgate, N.** A concise dictionary of
       Akkadian. 1999 ⇒15,8648; 16,8657. ᴿZDMG 152 (2002) 396-397
       (*Röllig, Wolfgang*); AfO 48-49 (2001-2) 181-82 (*Streck, Michael P.*);
9163 2000 ⇒16,8658. 2° (corrected) printing. ᴿOLZ 97 (2002) 223-225
       (*Kämmerer, Th.R.*).
9164 **Black, Jeremy A.** Reading Sumerian poetry. 1998 ⇒14,7853... 17,
       8603. ᴿJNES 61 (2002) 285-287 (*Ferrara, A.J.*).
9165 **Borger, Rykele** Beiträge zum Inschriftenwerk Assurbanipals: die
       Prismenklassen A, B, C = K, D, E, F, G, H, J, T sowie andere In-
       schriften. 1996 ⇒14,7854. ᴿJNES 61 (2002) 315-317 (*Farber,
       Walter*); JSSt 47 (2002) 310-311 (*Livingstone, A.*).
9166 *Brack-Bernsen, Lis* Predictions of lunar phenomena in Babylonian
       astronomy. Under one sky. AOAT 297: 2002 ⇒9014. 5-19.
9167 *Britton, John P.* Treatment of annual phenomena in cuneiform
       sources. Under one sky. AOAT 297: 2002 ⇒9014. 21-78.
9168 **Caplice, Richard** Introduction to Akkadian. StP.SM 9: R ⁴2002, E.
       P.I.B. ix; 108 pp. €16. 88-7653-566-7. Collaboration of *Daniel Snell*.

9169 **Carreira, José Nunes** Literaturas da Mesopotâmia. Centro de Historía da Universidade de Lisboa, Cadernos Clio 3: Lisboa 2002, Centro de Historia 207 pp. 972-98766-2.

9170 *Cassidy, Kyle* Scholars build internet dictionary to unravel Sumerian language. NEA (BA) 65 (2002) 284-285.

9171 *Civil, Miguel* The forerunners of *marû* and *ḫamṭu* in Old Babylonian. ᴹJACOBSEN, T.: 2002 ⇒62. 63-71.

9172 *Coghill, Eleanor; Deutscher, Guy* The origin of ergativity in Sumerian, and the 'inversion' in pronominal agreement: a historical explanation based on neo-Aramaic parallels. Or. 71 (2002) 267-290.

9173 ᴱ**Cole, Steven William; Machinist, Peter B.** Letters from priests to the kings Esarhaddon and Assurbanipal. 1998 ⇒14,7861; 16,8661. ᴿAfO 48-49 (2001-2002) 216-219 (*Dalley, Stephanie*).

9174 ᴱ**D'Agostino, Franco** Testi umoristici babilonesi e assiri. Testi del Vicino Oriente ant. 2, Lett. mesopotamiche 4: 2000 ⇒16,8663; 17, 8607. ᴿAnton. 77 (2002) 383-385 (*Stamm, Heinz-Meinolf*).

9175 **D'Agostino, Franco; Pomponio, Francesco** Umma messenger texts in the British Museum: part one: (UMTBM 1). Nisaba 1: Messina 2002, Di.Sc.A.M. 286 pp.

9176 *Dassow, Eva von* Lists of people from the Alalaḫ IV administrative archives. UF 34 (2002) 835-911.

9177 *Deuel, David C.* Apprehending kidnappers by correspondence at provincial Arrapḫa. Mesopotamia and the bible. JSOT.S 341: 2002 ⇒ 458. 191-208.

9178 **Deutscher, Guy** Syntactic change in Akkadian. 2000 ⇒16,8664. ᴿBiOr 59 (2002) 348-351 (*Kouwenberg, N.J.C.*); BSOAS 65 (2002) 564-567 (*Geller, M.J.*).

9179 **Ellermeier, Friedrich; Studt, Margret** Gudea, Stadtfürst von Lagas, Inschrift der Statue "I": Gesetz mit Gudea-Keilschrifttype Lagash 1/2.ttf sowie mit der neuassyrischen... Theologische und orientalistische Arbeiten aus Göttingen 4; Sumerische Glossar 1: Gö 2002, Selbstverlag Dr. Friedrich Ellermeier 75 pp. 3921747317. Bibl. 67-8.

9180 **Freedman, Sally M.** If a city is set on a height: the Akkadian omen series Summa Alu ina Melê Sakin. 1998 ⇒15,8660. v.1: Tablets 1-21. ᴿBiOr 59 (2002) 355-361 (*Böck, B.*).

9181 *George, A.R.; Bongenaar, A.C.V.M.* Tablets from Sippar: supplementary bibliography etc. for Leichty, catalogues VI-VIII, up to the end of 2000. Or. 71 (2002) 55-156.

9182 **Hämeen-Anttilla, Jaakko** A sketch of Neo-Assyrian grammar. SAA.S 13: 2000 ⇒16,8670. ᴿBSOAS 65 (2002) 562-564 (*Geller, M.J.*).

9183 **Hilgert, Markus** Akkadisch in der Ur III-Zeit. IMGITA 5: Müns 2002, Rhema xlvii; 768 pp. 3-930454-32-7. Bibl. xxx-xlvii.

9184 *Horowitz, Wayne; Oshima, Takayoshi* Two more cuneiform finds from Hazor. IEJ 52 (2002) 179-186.

9185 *Hunger, Hermann* Über die Bedeutungslosigkeit der Finsternisse in *Enūma Anu Enlil* für die Chronologie. ᶠDIETRICH, M. 2002 ⇒28. 171-176.

9186 *Jean, Cynthia* Berceuses et chansons en Mésopotamie. ᶠDUCHESNE-GUILLEMIN, J. 2002 ⇒32. 115-122.

9187 *Jong, Teije de* Early Babylonian observations of Saturn: astronomical considerations. Under one sky. AOAT 297: 2002 ⇒9014. 175-192.

9188 *Kaplan, G.C.* On the aspect-tense verbal system in Akkadian. ᴹDIAKONOFF, I. 2002 ⇒27. 133-139.

9189 *Krebernik, Manfred* Zur Struktur und Geschichte des älteren sumerischen Onomastikons. Onomastik. AOAT 296: 2002 ⇒8959. 1-74.

9190 **Larsen, Mogens Trolle** The Assur-nada archive. Old Assyrian Archives 1; Uitgaven van het Nederlands Instituut voor het Nabijie Oosten te Leiden 96: Lei 2002, Nederlands Instituut voor het Nabije Oosten xlvi; 248 pp. 90-6258-097-1. Bibl. xliii-xlvi.

9191 *Marcus, David* Akkadian. Beyond Babel. 2002 ⇒8903. 19-41.

9192 **Metzler, Kai Alexander** Tempora in altbabylonischen literarischen Texten. AOAT 279: Müns 2002, Ugarit-Verlag xvii; 964 pp. 3-9346-28-03-6. Bibl. 909-945.

9193 *Nemet-Nejat, Karen R.* Square tablet in the Yale Babylonian collection. Under one sky. AOAT 297: 2002 ⇒9014. 253-281.

9194 **Novotny, Jamie R.** The standard Babylonian Etana epic: cuneiform text, transliteration, score, glossary, indices and sign list. SAA.Cuneiform Texts II: 2001 ⇒17,8622. ᴿBiOr 59 (2002) 566-572 (*Haul, Michael*).

9195 **Pentiuc, Eugen J.** West Semitic vocabulary in the Akkadian texts from Emar. Harvard Semitic Studies 49: 2001 ⇒17,8623. ᴿJJS 53 (2002) 380-381 (*Bhayro, Siam*); RBLit (2002)* (*Zewi, Tamar*).

9196 *Pruzsinszky, Regine* Beobachtungen zur geschlechtsspezifischen Namensgebung anhand des Emar-Onomastikons. Onomastik. AOAT 296: 2002 ⇒8959. 171-183.

9197 *Roughton, Norbert A.* A study of Babylonian normal-star almanacs and observational texts. Under one sky. AOAT 297: 2002 ⇒9014. 367-378.

9198 *Sanmartín, Joaquín* Universales semánticos y su lexificación en acádico. AuOr 20 (2002) 183-219.

9199 *Sasson, Jack M.* The burden of scribes. ᴹJACOBSEN, T.: 2002 ⇒62. 211-228.

9200 *Schaudig, Hanspeter* Die Keilschrifttexte des Archäologischen Museums der Westfälischen Wilhelms-Universität Münster. WZKM 92 (2002) 111-128.

9201 ᴱ**Sefati, Yitschak** Love songs in Sumerian literature: critical edition of the Dumuzi-Inanna songs. 1998 ⇒14,9759; 16,10677. ᴿJNES 61 (2002) 131-134 (*Ferrara, A.J.*).

9202 *Selz, Gebhard J.* Bemerkungen zum sumerischen Genitiv nebst einigen Beobachtungen zur sumerischen Wortbildung. WZKM 92 (2002) 129-153;

9203 *Steele, John M.* A simple function for the length of the Saros in Babylonian astronomy. Under one sky. AOAT 297: 2002 ⇒9014. 405-420;

9204 Some lunar ephemerides and related texts from Babylon. ᶠWALKER, C.: 2002 ⇒130. 293-318.

9205 *Stephenson, F. Richard; Willis, David, M.* The earliest datable observation of the Aurora Borealis. Under one sky. AOAT 297: 2002 ⇒ 9014. 421-428.

9206 *Streck, Michael P.* Die Prologe der sumerischen Epen. Or. 71 (2002) 189-266;

9207 Sprachliche Innovationen und Archaismen in den akkadischen Personennamen. Onomastik. AOAT 296: 2002 ⇒8959. 109-122.

9208 **Streck, Michael P.** Die Bildersprache der akkadischen Epik. AOAT 264: 1999 ⇒15,11037. ᴿAfO 48-49 (2001-2002) 225-226 (*Dalley, Stephanie*).

Tawil, H. Two biblical and akkadian lexical notes 2002 ⇒9007.

9209 **Thomsen, Marie-Louise** The Sumerian language: an introduction to its history and grammatical structure. Mes.(C) 10 K: 2001 Akademisk 376 pp. 87-500-3654-8. Bibl. 332-348. Supp. Bibl. 364-376.

9210 *Vanderhooft, David; Horowitz, Wayne* The cuneiform incription from Tell en-Naṣbeh: the demise of an unknown king. TelAv 29 (2002) 318-327.

9211 *Verderame, Lorenzo* Enuma Anu Enlil tablet 1-13. Under one sky. AOAT 297: 2002 ⇒9014. 447-457.

9212 **Verderame, Lorenzo** Le Tavole I-VI della serie astrologica. Enuma Anu Enlil Nisaba 2: Messina 2002, Di.Sc.A.M. x; 268 pp. 88-8268-009-6. Bibl. 260-263.

9213 *Vermaak, P.S.* Characteristics of the non-literary Ur III documents. JSem 11/2 (2002) 175-210.

9214 *Vita, Juan-Pablo* Textos republicados de Emar. UF 34 (2002) 829-833.

9215 **Volk, Konrad** A Sumerian reader. StP.SM 18: ²1999 <1997> ⇒15, 8689. ᴿRBLit 4 (2002) 80-81 *(Hunt, Joel H.)*.

9216 *Yamada, Keiko* The names of seas in the Assyrian royal inscriptions. Bulletin of the Society for Near Eastern Studies in Japan 45/2 (2002) 1-25 Sum. 1.

9217 *Younger, K. Lawson* Yahweh at Ashkelon and Calaḫ?: Yahwistic names in Neo-Assyrian. VT 52 (2002) 207-218.

J2.7 Arabica

9218 **Arbach, Mounir** Les noms propres du Corpus Inscriptionum Semiticarum: Pars IV: Inscriptiones Himyariticas et Sabaeas continens. Inventaire des inscriptions sudarabiques 7: P 2002, De Boccard 463 pp. 2-87754-126-6. Bibl. 93-113. ᴿAfO 48-49 (2001-2002) 280-282 *(Sima, Alexander)*.

9219 *Bikai, Pierre M.* A Thamudic E text from Madaba. ADAJ 46 (2002) 215-224.

9220 *Bordreuil, Pierre* Das südarabische Alphabet: ein aufregender Fund. WUB 23 (2002) 23.

9221 **Fischer, Wolfdietrich** A grammar of classical Arabic. ᵀRodgers, Jonathan: Yale Language series: NHv ³2002, Yale University Press xiv; 338 pp. 0-300-08437-4. Bibl. 259-318.

9222 *Harahsheh, Rafe M.* Religious life of the ancient Arabs (the Safaitics) through their inscriptions. ADAJ 46 (2002) 119*-126*. **A**.

9223 *Kaltner, John* Arabic. Beyond Babel. 2002 ⇒8903. 61-92.

9224 *Kropp, Manfred* Iatromagie und der Beginn der arabischen Schriftsprache: die nabatäisch-arabische Inschrift von ʿAyn ʿAbada. MUSJ 55 (1997-1998) 89-117.

9225 *Maʾani, Sultan A.; Sadaqah, Ibrahim S.* New Safaitic inscriptions from the Mafraq Office Department of Archeology of Jordan. Syria 79 (2002) 249-269.

ᴱ**Ouhalla, J.** Themes in Arabic & Hebrew syntax 2002 ⇒8904.

9226 *Rosenhouse, Judith* Personal names in Hebrew and Arabic: modern trends compared to the past. JSSt 47 (2002) 97-114.

9227 *Ryckmans, Jacques* Een nieuwe uitdaging in de semitische epigrafie: oudzuidarabische inscripties op hout. Phoenix 48 (2002) 141-156.

9228 **Schimmel, Annemarie** Morgenland und Abendland: mein west-östliches Leben. Mü 2002, Beck 352 pp. 3-406-49564-8.

9229 *Shatnawi, Ma'en Ali* Die Personennamen in den tamudischen Inschriften: eine lexikalisch-grammatische Analyse im Rahmen der gemeinsemitischen Namengebung. UF 34 (2002) 619-784.

9230 *Sima, Alexander* Neue Möglichkeiten der altsüdarabischen Namensforschung. Onomastik. AOÄT 296: 2002 ⇒8959. 195-207.

9231 **Sima, Alexander** Tiere, Pflanzen, Steine und Metalle in den altsüdarabischen Inschriften: eine lexikalische und realienkundliche Untersuchung. VOK 46: 2000 ⇒16,8706. [R]Or. 71 (2002) 468-471 (*Bron, François*).

9232 **Stein, Peter** Zur Morphologie des sabäischen Infinitivs. Or. 71 (2002) 393-414.

9233 Urwolke und Welt: mystische Texte des Größten Meisters. Neue Orientalische Bibliothek: Mü 2002, Beck 351 pp. 3-406-48055-1.

9234 **Weipert, Reinhard** Classical Arabic philology and poetry: a bibliographical handbook of important editions from 1960 to 2000. HO 1/63: Lei 2002, Brill xiv; 274 pp. 90-04-12342-3.

9235 *Weninger, Stefan* Arabische Imperfektnamen. Onomastik. AOAT 296: 2002 ⇒8959. 209-226.

J3.0 **Aegyptia**

9236 [E]**Abd el-Raziq, Mahmud,** *al.*, Les inscriptions d'Ayn Soukhna. MIFAO 122: Le Caire 2002, Institut Français d'Archéologie Orientale. 135 pp. 2-7247-0322-7. Plan topographique: *Nicolas Passsera et al.* Bibl. 127-130.

9237 **Ali, Mohamed Sherif** Hieratische Ritzinschriften aus Theben: Paläographie der Graffiti und Steinbruchinschriften. GOF.Ä 34: Wsb 2002, Harrassowitz xiv; 154 pp. €86. 3-447-03854-3. Bibl. 149-154.

9238 **Beylage, Peter** Aufbau der königlichen Stelentexte: vom Beginn der 18. Dynastie bis zur Amarnazeit: v.1, Transkription und Übersetzung der Texte; v.2, Methodik und Analyse der Texte. ÄAT 54,1-2: Wsb 2002, Harrassowitz 2 vols. €108. 3-447-04520-5. Bibl. 791-819.

9239 **Bresciani, Edda; Menchetti, Angiolo** Nozioni elementari di grammatica demotica: con liste grafiche e letture demotiche di *Angiolo Menchett*i. Biblioteca di studi egittologici 2: Pisa 2002, ETS 161 pp. 88-467-0581-5. Bibl. 155-159.

9240 *Clackson, Sarah J.* Fish and chits: the Synodontis schall. ZÄS 129/1 (2002) 6-11.

9241 *Clarysse, Willy* A Jewish family in Ptolemaic Thebes. JJP 32 (2002) 7-9.

9242 [E]**Collier, Mark; Quirke, Stephen** The UCL Lahun papyri: letters. BAR Internat. Ser. 1083: Oxf 2002, Archaeopress xiv; 203 pp. £34. 1-84171-462-3 with CD.

9243 **Darnell, John Coleman** Theban desert road survey in the Egyptian Western desert: vol. 1: Gebel Tjauti rock inscriptions 1-45 and Wadi el-Hôl rock inscriptions 1-45. UCOIP 119: Ch 2002, The Oriental Institute of the University of Chicago lvi; 175 pp. 1-885923-17-1. Collab. *Darnell, Deborah*; *al.*; 126 pl. Bibl. xxi-lvi.

9244 **David, Arlette** De l'infériorité à la perturbation: l'oiseau du "mal" et la catégorisation en Egypte ancienne. Classification and Categorization in Ancient Egypt 1; GOF.Ä 38: 2000 ⇒16,8715. ᴿDiscEg 53 (2002) 135-152 (*Warburton, David*); BiOr 59 (2002) 269-271 (*Roccati, Alessandro*).

9245 *Depauw, Mark; Clarysse, Willy* When a pharaoh becomes magic. CÉg 153-154 (2002) 55-64.

9246 *Felber, Heinz* Die Demotische Chronik. Apokalyptik und Ägypten. OLA 107: 2002 ⇒451. 65-111.

9247 *Gauger, Jörg-Dieter* Der "Traum des Nektanebos": die griechische Fassung. Apokalyptik und Ägypten. OLA 107: 2002 ⇒451. 189-219.

9248 *Gierlich, Gabriele* Bilderwelten: einführende Bemerkungen zur altägyptischen Hieroglyphenschrift anhand ausgewählter Beispiele. Symb. 15 (2002) 131-156.

9249 *Goedicke, Hans* The building inscription from Tell el-DAbʿa of the time of Sesostris III. Ä&L 12 (2002) 187-190;

9250 Merikare E 106-115. ZÄS 129/2 (2002) 115-121.

9251 **Goldwasser, Orly** Prophets, lovers and giraffes: wor(l)d classification in Ancient Egypt. GOF.Ä 38; Classification and Categorisation in Ancient Egypt 3: Wsb 2002, Harrassowitz pag. varia €54. 3-447-04590-6. Bibl. 133-144.

9252 *Görg, Manfred* Eine ramessidische Prinzessin in Aschdod. BN 111 (2002) 16-17.

9253 **Gutgesell, Manfred** Die Datierung der Ostraka und Papyri aus Deir el Medineh: Teil II: die Ostraka der 19. Dynastie. HÄB 44: Hildesheim 2002, Gerstenberg xv; 207 pp. €39. 38067-81389. Bibl. xiii-xv.

9254 **Hannig, Rainer** Die Sprache der Pharaonen: großes Handwörterbuch Deutsch-Ägyptisch (2800 - 950 v.Chr.). Hannig-Lexica 3: 2000 ⇒16,8720. ᴿOLZ 97 (2002) 212-214 (*Quack, Friedrich*).

9255 **Helck, Hans Wolfgang** Die datierten und datierbaren Ostraka, Papyri und Graffiti von Deir el-Medineh. ᴱ*Schlott, Adelheid*: ÄA 63: Wsb 2002, Harrassowitz 573 pp. €150. 3-447-03586-2. Bibl. 15-16.

9256 *Hjelm, Ingrid; Thompson, Thomas L.* The victory song of Merneptah, Israel and the people of Palestine. JSOT 27 (2002) 3-18.

9257 **Hoch, James E.** Semitic words in Egyptian texts of the New Kingdom and third intermediate period. 1994 ⇒10,9205... 15,8718. ᴿOLZ 97 (2002) 29-43 (*Müller, Matthias*).

9258 *Hutto, David* Ancient Egyptian rhetoric in the Old and Middle Kingdoms. Rhetorica 20 (2002) 213-233.

9259 *Imhausen, Annette* The algorithmic structure of the Egyptian mathematical problem texts. Under one sky. AOAT 297: 2002 ⇒9014. 147-166.

9260 *Jasnow, Richard* Recent trends and advances in the study of late period Egyptian literature. JARCE 39 (2002) 207-216.

9261 *Jones, Alexander* Babylonian lunar theory in Roman Egypt: two new texts. Under one sky. AOAT 297: 2002 ⇒9014. 167-174.

9262 **Junge, Friedrich** Late Egyptian grammar: an introduction. ᵀ*Warburton, David*: 2001 ⇒17,8667. ᴿBiOr 59 (2002) 260-269 (*Neveu, François*).

9263 *Kaplony, Peter* The Bet Yerah jar inscription and the annals of King Dewen—Dewen as 'King Narmer Redivivus'. Egypt and the Levant. 2002 ⇒497. 464-486.

9264 **Kloth, Nicole** Die (auto-)biographischen Inschriften des ägyptischen Alten Reiches: Untersuchungen zu Phraseologie und Entwicklung. SAÄK.B 8: Ha 2002, Buske xii; 335 pp. €86. 3-87548-310-3. Bibl. 287-317. ᴿArOr 70 (2002) 442-445 (*Landgráfová, Renata*).

9265 **Klug, Andrea** Königliche Stelen in der Zeit von Ahmose bis Amenophis III. MonAeg 8: Turnhout 2002, Brepols xi; 580 pp. 2-503-9912-3-8. Bibl. 499-536.

9266 *Koenen, Ludwig; Blasius, Andreas* Die Apologie des Töpfers an König Amenophis oder das Töpferorakel. Apokalyptik und Ägypten. OLA 107: 2002 ⇒451. 139-187. Tafel I-III.

9267 *Kogan, Leonid* Addenda et corrigenda to the Hamito-Semitic Etymological Dictionary (HSED) by V. OREL and O. STOLBOVA (II). JSSt 47 (2002) 183-202.

9268 *Krauss, Rolf* The eye of Horus and the planet Venus: astronomical and mythological references. Under one sky. AOAT 297: 2002 ⇒ 9014. 193-208.

9269 *Kyriakidis, Evangelos* Indications on the nature of the language on the Keftiew from Egyptian sources. Ä&L 12 (2002) 211-219.

9270 [E]**Leclant, Jean** Les textes de la Pyramide de Pépy Ier. Mémoires de l'Institut Français d'Archéologie Orientale du Caire 118,1-2: 2001 ⇒17,8670. [R]CRAI (2002/1) 30-33 (*Leclant, Jean*).

9271 [E]**Leitz, Christian**, *al.*, Kurzbibliographie zu den übersetzten Tempeltexten der griechisch-römischen Zeit. Bibliothèque d'étude 136: Le Caire 2002, Institut Français d'Archéologie Orientale vi; 172 pp. 2-7247-0328-6.

9272 *Migahid, Abd-El-Gawad* Zwei spätdemotische Zahlungsquittungen aus der Zeit des AUGUSTUS. ZÄS 129/1 (2002) 61-74;

9273 Eine neue spätdemotische Zahlungsquittung aus Soknopaiu Nesos. ZÄS 129/2 (2002) 122-129.

9274 *Morenz, Ludwig D.* Die Phonetisierung des Bildes und ihre Folgen: ein Modell für die Entstehung der ägyptischen Schrift. Saec. 53 (2002) 175-192;

9275 Zu Formen, Gründen und Wegen der Textüberlieferung in der ägyptischen Kultur (Teil 1). ZÄS 129/2 (2002) 130-141.

9276 **Mosher, M.** The papyrus of Hor. L 2002, British Museum Pr. xvi; 108 pp. £50. 0-7141-1949-0. 30 pl. [R]BiOr 59 (2002) 491-493 (*Meulenaere, H.J.A. de*).

9277 **Ockinga, Boyo** G. Mittelägyptische Grundgrammatik: Abriss der mittelägyptischen Grammatik. [E]*Brunner, Hellmut:* 1998 ⇒14,7962. [R]CEg 153-154 (2002) 131-135 (*Malaise, Michel*).

9278 **Parkinson, Richard B.** Poetry and culture in Middle Kingdom Egypt: a dark side to perfection. Athlone Publications in Egyptology and Ancient Near Eastern Studies: L 2002, Continuum xxii; 393 pp. £75. 0-8264-5637-5. Bibl. 328-383.

9279 **Peden, Alexander J.** The graffiti of Pharaonic Egypt: scope and roles of informal writings (c. 3100-332 B.C.). PÄ 17: 2001 ⇒17, 8674. [R]BiOr 59 (2002) 489-491 (*Müller-Wollermann, Renate*).

9280 *Quack, Joachim Friedrich* Zu einer angeblich apokalyptischen Passage in den Ostraka des Hor. Apokalyptik und Ägypten. OLA 107: 2002 ⇒451. 243-252.

9281 *Redford, Donald B.* Egyptian. Beyond Babel. 2002 ⇒8903. 109-137.

9282 *Ritter, Jim* Closing the eye of Horus: the rise and fall of 'Horus-eye fractions". Under one sky. AOAT 297: 2002 ⇒9014. 297-323.

9283 **Roccati, Alessandro** Elementi di lingua egizia. T 2002, Théléme 136 pp. 88-87419-21-3. Bibl. 117.

9284 *Rossi, Corinna; Ikram, Salima* Petroglyphs and incriptions along the Darb Ayn Amur, Kharga Oasis. ZÄS 129/2 (2002) 142-151.

9285 **Ryholt, K.** The story of Petese son of Petetum: and seventy other good and bad stories (P. Petese). 1999 ⇒16,8732. ^{R}CEg 153-154 (2002) 141-149 (*Widmer, Ghislaine*).

9286 *Ryholt, Kim* Nectanebo's dream or the prophecy of Petesis. Apokalyptik und Ägypten. OLA 107: 2002 ⇒451. 221-241. Tafel IV-VIII.

9287 *Sass, Benjamin* Wenamun and his Levant—1075 BC or 925 BC?. Ä&L 12 (2002) 247-255.

9288 **Spalinger, Anthony John** The private feast lists of ancient Egypt. ÄA 57: 1996 ⇒12,7884; 14,7971. ^{R}BiOr 59 (2002) 486-489 (*Van Walsem, René*);

9289 The transformation of an ancient Egyptian narrative: P. Sallier III and the battle of Kadesh. GOF.Ä 40: Wsb 2002, Harrassowitz xiii; 389 pp. 3-447-04355-5. Bibl. 367-372.

9290 **Takács, Gábor** Etymological dictionary of Egyptian, 1: a phonological introduction. HO 1/48: 1999 ⇒15,8737; 17,8681. ^{R}AuOr 20/1-2 (2002) 294-297 (*Kogan, L.*).

9291 *Thissen, Heinz-Josef* Das Lamm des Bokchoris. Apokalyptik und Ägypten. OLA 107: 2002 ⇒451. 113-138.

9292 **Topmann, Doris** Die "Abscheu"-Sprüche der altägyptischen Sargtexte: Untersuchungen zu Textemen und Dialogstrukturen. GOF.Ä 39: Wsb 2002, Harrassowitz xiii; 236 pp. 3447043032. Bibl. 209-28.

9293 *Trapani, Marcella* Une nouvelle enquête sur la stèle d'Ahmès-Néfertari. ZÄS 129/2 (2002) 152-165.

9294 *Vernus, Pascal* Les premières attestations de l'écriture hiéroglyphique. Aeg. 81 (2001) 13-35.

9295 *Vittmann, Günther* Ägyptische Onomastik der Spätzeit im Spiegel der nordwestsemitischen und karischen Nebenüberlieferung. Onomastik AOAT 296 2002 ⇒8959. 85-107.

9296 *Wells, Ronald A.* The role of astronomical techniques in Ancient Egyptian chronology: the use of lunar month lengths in absolute dating. Under one sky. AOAT 297: 2002 ⇒9014. 459-472.

J3.4 Coptica

9297 *Bethge, Hans-Gebhard; Kaiser, Ursula Ulrike; Plisch, Uwe-Karsten* Bericht über Editionen von koptischen Texten und Publikationen von Hilfsmitteln. ZAC 6 (2002) 232-252.

9298 **Biedenkopf-Ziehner, Anneliese** Koptische Ostraka: v.1, Ostraka aus dem Britischen Museum in London, mit Einführung...; v.2, Ostraka aus dem Ashmolean Museum in Oxford, mit Einführung... 2000 ⇒ 16,8742. ^{R}BiOr 59 (2002) 331-333 (*Delattre, Alain*).

9299 *Feder, Frank* Koptische Bibelfragmente der Berliner Papyrussammlung I: Fragmente von Proverbien (31,26-31) und Sirach (Prol., 4,2-6,4) aus einem Codex mit Weisheitsbüchern. APF 48 (2002) 159-174. Mit Tafeln XI-XXI.

9300 *Förster, Hans* 'Erhebt euch und betet': Fragment einer Erzählung über die Gefangennahme Jesu: Edition von Cambridge MS Add. 1876 (10). Aeg. 81 (2001) 323-331.

9301 ^{E}**Förster, Hans** Wörterbuch der griechischen Wörter in den koptischen dokumentarischen Texten. TU 148: B 2002, De Gruyter lx; 914 pp. €198. 3-11-017403-0. Bibl. li-lx.

9302 *Hansen, Nicole B.* Ancient execration magic in Coptic and Islamic Egypt. Magic and ritual. RGRW 141: 2002 ⇒505. 427-445.

9302 *Hansen, Nicole B.* Ancient execration magic in Coptic and Islamic Egypt. Magic and ritual. RGRW 141: 2002 ⇒505. 427-445.

9303 *Hedrick, Charles W.* Newly identified fragments of Coptic Acts and the Apocalypse. Journal of Coptic Studies 4 (2002) 127-132 [Acts 10,35-38; 11,3-6; Rev 5,13-6,1; 6,5-7].

9304 *Kasser, Rodolphe* Le lyco-diospolitain en sa complexité, vestiges régionaux, altérés, devenus polymorphes, de la langue véhiculaire précopte utilisée en Haute-Égypte?. ᶠSCHENKE, H.: NHS 54: 2002 ⇒ 108. 341-351.

9305 ᴱ**Kuhn, K.H.; Tait, W.J.** Thirteen Coptic acrostic hymns. Oxf 1996, Griffith Institute ix; 162 pp. Pierpont Morgan Library. Ms. M574. ᴿEnchoria 28 (2002-2003) 201-202 (*Luft, Ulrich; Hasznos, Andrea*).

9306 **Layton, Bentley** A Coptic grammar: with chrestomathy and glossary, Sahidic dialect. PLO 20: 2000 ⇒16,8745; 17,8692. ᴿOLZ 97 (2002) 214-223 (*Peust, Carsten*); BiOr 59 (2002) 322-331 (*Biedenkopf-Ziehner, Anneliese*); WZKM 92 (2002) 224-228 (*Satzinger, Helmut*).

9307 *Lucchesi, Enzo* D'"une étrange recension de l'Apocalypse'. Aeg. 81 (2001) 333-336.

9308 *Meyer, Marvin* The prayer of Mary who dissolves chains in Coptic magic and religion;

9309 *Mirecki, Paul* A seventh-century Coptic limestone in the Ashmolean museum, Oxford (Bodl. Copt. Inscr. 426). Magic and ritual. RGRW 141: 2002 ⇒505. 407-415/47-69.

9310 **Plisch, Uwe-Karsten** Einführung in die koptische Sprache: Sahidischer Dialekt. Sprachen und Kulturen des Christlichen Orients 5: 1999 ⇒15,8746; 17,8694. ᴿEnchoria 28 (2002-2003) 205-211 (*Satzinger, Helmut*).

9311 *Schüssler, Karlheinz* Analyse der Lektionarhandschrift sa 530ᴸ. Journal of Coptic Studies 4 (2002) 133-166.

9312 *Schwendner, Gregg* Under Homer's spell: bilingualism, oracular magic, and the Michigan excavation at Dimê. Magic and divination. Ancient magic and divination 2: 2002 ⇒729. 107-118.

9313 *Shisha-Halevy, Ariel* An emerging new dialect of Coptic;

9314 A definite Sahidic Coptic grammar. Or. 71 (2002) 298-308/424-459;

9315 The focalizing conversion: structural preliminaries to a chapter in the grammar of oxyrhynchite Coptic. ᶠSCHENKE, H.: NHS 54: 2002 ⇒ 108. 309-340.

9316 **Störk, L.** Koptische Handschriften, 4. VOHD 21/4: Stu 2002, Steiner 334 pp. €68. 3-515-07360-4.

9317 **Witte, Bernd** Die Sünden der Priester und Mönche: koptische Eschatologie des 8. Jahrhunderts nach Kodex M 602 ppp 104-154 (ps. Athanasius) der Pierpont Morgan Library, 1: Textausgabe. Arbeiten zum spätantiken und koptischen Ägypten 12: Altenberge 2002, Oros 302 pp. 3-89375-208-0. Bibl. 276-296.

J3.8 Aethiopica

9318 ᴱᵀ**Colin, Gérard** La version éthiopienne de L'histoire de Bsoy. PO 49/3 (N. 219): Turnhout 2002, Brepols 289-363 pp.

9319 ᵀ**Colin, Gérard** La gloire des rois (Kebra Nagast): épopée nationale de l'Éthiopie. COr 23: Genève 2002, Cramer 117 pp.

9320 *Fellman, Jack* Lines on the Kebra Nagast. ANESt 39 (2002) 205-6;

9322 **Leslau, Wolf** Introductory grammar of Amharic. PLO 21: 2000 ⇒ 16,8748. [R]OrChr 86 (2002) 274-279 (*Meyer, Ronny*).

9323 [E]**Raineri, Osvaldo** Introduzione alla lingua ge'ez: (etiopico classico). R 2002, "Orientalia Christiana" 231 pp. 88-7210-335-5. Bibl. 231.

9324 .**Tropper, Josef** Altäthiopisch: Grammatik des Ge'ez mit Übungstexten und Glossar. Elementa Linguarum Orientis 2: Müns 2002, Ugarit-Verlag xiii; 309 pp. $42. 3-934628-29-X. Bibl. 255-257.

9325 **Weninger, Stefan** Das Verbalsystem des Altäthiopischen: eine Untersuchung seiner Verwendung und Funktion unter Berücksichtigung des Interferenzproblems. VOK 47: 2001 ⇒17,8700. [R]OrChr 86 (2002) 267-269 (*Kropp, Manfred*); Vox Patrum 22 (2002) 628-629 (*Woźniak, Jerzy*).

J4.0 Anatolica

9326 *Adiego, Ignasi-Xavier* Cario de Cauno punoΩ. AuOr 20 (2002) 13-20.

9327 **Boley, Jacqueline** Dynamics of transformation in Hittite: the Hittite particles -kan, -asta and -san. Innsbruck 2000, Institut für Sprachwissenschaft der Universität Innsbruck 488 pp. 3-85124-676-4. Bibl. 480-488.

9328 *Dardano, Paola* 'La main est coupable', 'le sang devient abondant': sur quelques expressions avec de noms de parties et d'éléments du corps humain dans la littérature juridoco-politique de l'Ancien et du Moyen Royaume hittite. Or. 71 (2002) 333-392.

9329 **Francia, Rita** Le funzioni sintattiche degli elementi avverbiali di luogo ittiti: anda(n), appa(n), katta(n), katti-, peran, para, ser, sara. Studia Asiana 1: R 2002, Herder x; 245 pp. 88-85876-66-8. Bibl. 222-230.

9330 *Gibbal, Christian* Zum hattischen Lexikon. AltOrF 29 (2002) 249-287.

9331 **Groddek, Detlev** Hethitische Texte in Transkription. KBo 30; Dresdner Beiträge zur Hethitologie 2 (Philologica): Dresden 2002, Verlag der TU xiv; 275 pp. 3-86005-309-4. Bibl. xiii-xiv;

9332 Hethitische Texte in Transkription. KUB 55: Dresdner Beiträge zur Hethitologie 4 (Philologica): Dresden 2002, Verlag der TU viii; 139 pp. 3-86005-320-5. Bibl. vii-viii;

9333 Konkordanz zu den Grabungsnummern. Dresdner Beiträge zur Hethitologie 5 (Instrumenta): Dresden 2002, Verlag der TU x; 248 pp. 3-86005-343-4. Bibl. v-x.

9334 **Groddek, Detlev; Hagenbuchner, Albertine; Hoffmann, Inge** Hethitische Texte in Transkription. VS NF 12: Dresdner Beiträge zur Hethitologie 6 (Philologica): Dresden 2002, Verlag der TU xii; 221 pp. 3-86005-344-2. Bibl. ix-xi.

9335 [E]**Güterbock, Hans G.; Hoffner, Harry A.; Van den Hout, Theo P.J.** The Hittite Dictionary: Š, 1: ša- to šaptamenzu. Ch 2002, Oriental Institute of the Univ. of Ch. viii; 208 pp. 1-885923-20-1.

9336 *Hoffner, Harry A., Jr.* New directions in the study of early Anatolian texts. [M]GÜTERBOCK, H. 2002 ⇒54. 193-206;

9337 Hittite. Beyond Babel. 2002 ⇒8903. 183-206.

9338 *Hoffner, Harry; Melchert, Craig* A practical approach to verbal aspect in Hittite. [M]IMPARATI, F. 2002 ⇒61. 377-390.

9339   **Hrozny, Friedrich** Die Sprache der Hethiter: ihr Bau und ihre Zuge-
hörigheit zum indogermanischen Sprachstamm: die Lösung des hethitischen Problems: ein vorläufiger Bericht. Dresdner Beiträge zur Hethitologie 3 (Analecta): Dresden 2002 <1917>, Verlag der TU xv;
245 pp. 3-86005-319-1. Anhang aus: Mitteilungen der Deutschen
Orient-Gesellschaft zu Berlin Nr. 56, Dezember 1915, S. 17-50.

9340   *Karasu, Cem* The great sea according to the Hittite texts. ^FPOPKO, M.
2002 ⇒91. 197-203.

9341   *Karasu, Cem* Some observations on the women in the Hittite texts.
^MIMPARATI, F. 2002 ⇒61. 419-424.

9342   *Miller, Jared L.* Hittite notes. JCS 54 (2002) 87-92.

9343   *Neu, Erich* Zur Morphologie und Syntax einer mythologischen Erzählung aus althethitischer Zeit. ^FNEUMANN, G. 2002 ⇒80. 315-331.

9344   *Oettinger, Norbert* Indogermanische Sprachträger lebten schon im 3.
Jahrtausend v. Chr. in Kleinasien: die Ausbildung der anatolischen
Sprachen. Die Hethiter. 2002 ⇒535. 50-55.

9345   **Oettinger, Norbert** Die Stammbildung des hethitischen Verbums:
Nachdruck mit einer kurzen Revision der hethitischen Verbalklassen.
Dresdner Beiträge zur Hethitologie 7 (Linguistica): Dresden 2002,
Verlag der TU xxx; 636 pp. 3-86005-345-0.

9346   *Puhvel, Jaan* Nomen proprium in Hittite. ^MIMPARATI, F. 2002 ⇒61.
671-675;

9347   The fate of Hittite dictionaries. Epilecta. 2002 <2001> ⇒226. 235-
243.

9348   **Schuster, Hans-Siegfried** Die hattisch-hethitischen Bilinguen, 2:
Textbearbeitungen. T.2/3 DMOA 17: Lei 2002, Brill xxiv; 152-649
pp. €99. 90-04-11637-0.

9349   *Stefanini, Ruggero* Toward a diachronic reconstruction of the linguistic map of ancient Anatolia. ^MIMPARATI, F. 2002 ⇒61. 783-806.

9350   (*a*) *Tischler, Johann* Zur Morphologie und Semantik der hethitischen
Personen- und Götternamen. Onomastik. AOAT 296: 2002 ⇒8959.
75-84.

(*b*) **Tischler, Johann** Hethitisches Handwörterbuch. ²2001 <1982>
⇒17,8709. ^ROLZ 97 (2002) 499-511 (*Haas, Volkert*).

9351   *Van den Hout, Theo* Self, soul and portrait in hieroglyphic Luwian.
^FPOPKO, M. 2002 ⇒91. 171-186;

9352   Another view of Hittite literature. ^MIMPARATI, F. 2002 ⇒61. 857-78.

9353   **Wegner, Ilse** Einführung in die hurritische Sprache. 2000 ⇒16,
8760. ^RBiOr 59 (2002) 589-592 (*Prechel, Doris*);

9354   ·Hurritische Opferlisten aus hethitischen Festbeschreibungen, Teil 2:
Texte für Teššub, Ḫebat und weitere Gottheiten Corpus der hurriti-
schen Sprachdenkmäler, 1. Abteilung: die Texte aus Boğazköy, 3-2.
R 2002, CNR xxii; 345 pp. 88-87345-07-4.

9355   *Wilhelm, Gernot* Die Sprache des Hethiterreiches. Die Hethiter. 2002
⇒535. 46-49.

J4.8 Armena, georgica

9356   *Tandašvili, Manana* Zum Kasussystem des Udischen (auf der Grundlage der udischen Evangelien). Georgica 25 (2002) 98-112.

9357   *Vaux, Bert* The Armenian dialects of Jerusalem. Armenians in Jerusalem. Hebrew University Armenian studies 4: 2002 ⇒771. 231-254.

J5.1 Graeca grammatica

9358 ·**Bauer, Walter** A Greek-English lexicon of the New Testament and other early christian literature. [E]*Danker, Frederick William*: ³2000 ⇒ 16,8764; 17,8713. [R]RBLit 4 (2002) 33-59 (*Fitzgerald, John T.; Roberts, Terry; Malherbe, Abraham J.; Klauck, Hans-Josef; Attridge, Harold W.*); CThMi 29 (2002) 132-135 (*Krentz, Edgar*).

9359 **Black, David Alan** Linguistics for students of New Testament Greek. GR ²2000 Baker xviii; 216 pp. $17. [R]RBLit 4 (2002) 143-145 (*Lukaszewski, A.*); RBLit (2002)* (*Percer, Leo*).

9360 [E]**Christidis, Anastasios-Phoibos** Histoire de la langue grecque: des origines à l'antiquité tardive. 2001 ⇒17,8718. [R]BSL 97/2 (2002) 147-157 (*Tsamadou-Jacoberger, Irini*).

9361 *Dienhart, Johannes* Lexikographische Lesefrüchte III: weitere Bemerkungen zu 'LIDDELL-SCOTT', 'Revised supplement' 1996 und G. W.H. LAMPE, A patristic Greek lexicon. APF 48 (2002) 147-155.

9362 **Friberg, Timothy; Friberg, Barbara; Miller, Neva F.** Analytical lexicon of the Greek New Testament. 2000 ⇒16,8773. [R]NT 44 (2002) 192-195 (*Black, David Alan*).

9363 **García Santos, Amador-Ángel** Introducción al griego bíblico. Estella 2002, Verbo Divino 252 pp. €23.92. 84-8169-514-9.

9364 **Ghinatti, Franco** Alfabeti greci. 1999 ⇒15,8774. [R]Aevum 76 (2002) 201.203 (*Iodice, Mario*).

9365 **Godart, Louis; Sacconi, Anna; Aravantinos, Vassilis L.** Thèbes: fouilles de la cadmée, 3: corpus des documents d'archives en linéaire B de Thèbes (1-433). Biblioteca di "Pasiphae" 3: Pisa 2002, Istituti Editoriali e Poligrafici Internazionali 327 pp. 88-8147-354-2.

9366 A Greek Anthology. Joint Association of Classical Teachers' Greek Course: C 2002, CUP xxi; 179 pp. 0-521-00026-2.

9367 **Guidi, Michele** Problémata: dizionario grammaticale del greco antico. Mi 2002, Hoepli x; 214 pp. 88-203-2555-1.

9368 *Kraft, Robert A.* Exploring early Jewish Greek literary practices. Bible and computer. 2002 ⇒548. 673-676.

9369 [E]**Kramer, Johannes** Glossaria bilinguia altera: (C. Gloss. Biling. II). APF.B 8: 2001 ⇒17,8726. [R]BiOr 59 (2002) 312-316 (*Rochette, Bruno*).

9370 *Muddiman, John* The Greek language. Biblical world, 2. 2002 ⇒ 273. 25-32.

9371 [E]**Porter, Stanley E.; Reed, Jeffrey T.** Discourse analysis and the New Testament: approaches and results. JSNT.S 170: 1999 ⇒15, 270; 16,8792. [R]EvQ 74 (2002) 272-274 (*Van Neste, Ray*).

9372 [E]**Porter, Stanley E.** Diglossia and other topics in New Testament linguistics. JSNT.S 193; Studies in NT Greek 6: 2000 ⇒16,313. [R]RBLit 4 (2002) 145-147 (*Adam, A.K.M.*).

9373 **Rijksbaron, Albert** The syntax and semantics of the verb in classical Greek. Amst ³2002, Gieben xv; 214 pp. €33. 90-5063-338-2.

9374 **Rocci, Lorenzo** Vocabolario greco-italiano. R ⁴⁰2002, Societá ·Editrice Dante Alighieri xx; 2074 pp.

9375 **Santana Henríquez, Germán** Semántica y lingüística: aplicaciones del método de la Sprachinhaltsforschung al griego antiguo. Las Palmas 2000, Universidad 157 pp. 84-95286-66-1.

9376 **Simmons, Tracy Lee** Climbing Parnassus: a new apologia for Greek and Latin. Wilmington, DEL 2002, ISI xvii; 268 pp. 1-882926-62-5. Bibl. 249-255.
9377 **Swetnam, James** Gramática do Grego do Novo Testamento: parte 1 morfologia. ᵀ*Murachco, Henrique; Maria, Juvino A.; Bazaglia, Paulo*: São Paulo 2002, Paulus 2 vols; 451 + 334 pp. 85-349-2001-X.
9378 **Webb, Joseph M.; Kysar, Robert** Greek for preachers. St. Louis 2002, Chalice 195 pp. $25. 0-8272-1244-5.
ᴱ**Worthington, I.** Epea and grammata 2002 ⇒537.

J5.2 Voces ordine alphabetico consonantium **graecarum**

9379 ἅγιος: *Chepey, Stuart D.* Samson the 'Holy One': a suggestion regarding the reviser's use of ἅγιος in Judg 13,7; 16,17 LXX Vaticanus. Bib. 83 (2002) 97-99.
9380 ἀδελφός: *Arzt-Grabner, Peter* "Brothers" and "sisters" in documentary papyri and early christianity. RivBib 50 (2002) 185-204.
9381 ἀδολεσχέω: *Lazarenco, Oleg* Does ἀδολεσχέω mean 'to meditate' in the LXX?. BIOSCS 35 (2002) 110-120.
9382 ἀποκᾰραδοκία: *Chang, Hae-Kyung* (ἀπο)κᾰραδοκία bei Paulus und ˙Aquila. ZNW 93 (2002) 268-278 [Rom 8,19; Phil 1,20].
9383 ἀρσενοκοίτης; μαλᾰκός: *Martin, Dale B. Arsenokoitês* e *malakos*: significati e conseguenze. Bibbia e omosessualità. 2002 <1996> ⇒ 310. 113-144.
9384 βαπτίζω: *Marshall, Howard* The meaning of the word 'baptize'. Dimensions of baptism. JSNT.S 234: 2002 ⇒434. 8-24.
9385 γαμῶ: *Van Tilborg, S.* The meaning of the word γαμῶ in Lk 14:20; 17,27; Mk 12:25 and in a number of early Jewish and christian authors. HTS 58 (2002) 802-810 [NTAb 47,251].
9386 διακονία: *Puthenveettil, Jos* Ministry or 'diakonia': a biblical reinterpretation. BiBh 28/2 (2002) 461-488, 565-589.
9387 δύναμις: *Metternich, Ulrike* 'Dynamis and womanpower': an investigation of the concept of *dynamis* in the gospels and Paul. ᶠSCHOTTROFF, L. 2002 ⇒111. 121-126.
9388 ἐγείρεσθαι: *Hofius, Otfried* "Am dritten Tage auferstanden von den Toten": Erwägungen zum Passiv ἐγείρεσθαι in christologischen Aussagen des Neuen Testaments. ᶠLAMBRECHT, J.: BEThL 165: 2002 ⇒ 72. 93-106.
9389 εἴδωλον: *Griffith, Terry* εἴδωλον as 'idol' in non-Jewish and non-Christian Greek. JThS 53 (2002) 95-101.
9390 ἐκπορεύομαι: *Patfoort, Albert* Emplois bibliques et patristiques du verbe ἐκπορεύομαι: une enquête. RThom 102 (2002) 63-72.
9391 εὐαγγελιστής: *Combs, W.W.* The biblical role of the evangelist. Detroit Baptist Seminary Journal [Allen Park, MI] 7 (2002) 23-48 [NTAb 47,291] [Acts 21,8; Eph 4,11; 2 Tim 4,5].
9392 κλέπτης: *Stanley, Christopher D.* Who's afraid of a thief in the night?. NTS 48 (2002) 468-486.
9393 κόσμος: *Ellingworth, Paul* Translating *kosmos* 'world', in Paul. BiTr 53 (2002) 414-421.
9394 κτίσις: *Hoegen-Rohls, Christina* κτίσις and καινὴ κτίσις in Paul's letters. ᶠWEDDERBURN, A.: JSNT.S 217: 2002 ⇒132. 102-122.
9395 λόγος: *Peppel, Matthias; Slenczka, Notger; Figal, Günter* Logos. RGG 5. 2002 ⇒796. 494-500.

9396 λόγος; σάρξ: *Galloway, Allan D.* Logos and Sarx. TJT 18 (2002) 49-54.

9397 μαρτυρία: *Collu, Mario* Aspetti biblici della *martyría* cristiana. LSDC 17 (2002) 413-427.

9398 ὁμοούσιος: *Beatrice, Pier Franco* The word "homoousios" from Hellenism to Christianity. ChH 71 (2002) 243-272.

9399 ὄνομα: *Tolmie, D.F.* Die vertaling van ὄνομα-uitdrukkings in die Nuwe Testament. HTS 58 (2002) 901-918 [NTAb 47,430].

9400 ὀπίσω: *Balode, Sanita; Blomqvist, Jerker* ὀπίσω with genitive im extra-Biblical Greek. Er. 100 (2002) 101-108.

9401 παιδαγωγός: *Markschies, Christoph* Lehrer, Schüler, Schule: zur Bedeutung einer Institution für das antike Christentum. Religiöse Vereine. STAC 13: 2002 ⇒468. 97-120.

9402 παρθένος: *Pilch, John J.* Who is a virgin?. BiTod 40 (2002) 248-252.

9403 πίστις: *Rusam, Dietrich* Was versteht Paulus unter der πίστις (Ἰησοῦ) Χριστοῦ (Röm 3,22.26; Gal 2,16.20; 3,22; Phil 3,9)?. PzB 11 (2002) 47-70.

9404 πνεῦμα: *Paige, Terence* Who believes in "Spirit"?: πνεῦμα in pagan usage and implications for the gentile Christian mission. HThR 95 (2002) 417-436.

9405 συνεργος: **Manjaly, Thomas** Collaborative ministry: an exegetical and theological study of synergos in Paul. 2001 ⇒17,8760. ᴿMissTod 4/1-2 (2002) 168-169 (*Orvan, Etwa*).

9406 σῶμα: *Bracchi, Remo* Sôma-corpus-corpo: una parola con numerosi significati. RivLi 89 (2002) 93-104.

9407 σωτηρ: **Jung, Franz** Σωτηρ: Studien zur Rezeption eines hellenistischen Ehrentitels im Neuen Testament. ᴰ*Gnilka, J.*: NTA 39: Müns 2002, Aschendorff xii; 404 pp. €59. 3-402-04787-X. Diss. München 2001. Bibl. 355-388.

9408 ὑπόκρῐσις: *Marshall, Ian H.* Who is a hypocrite?. BS 159 (2002) 131-150.

9409 χάρις: *Pachas, José Antonio* Significado teológico del término χάρις en el *In Inscriptiones Psalmorum* de GREGORIO de Nisa. TyV 43 (2002) 310-318.

J5.4 *Papyri et inscriptiones graecae*—Greek epigraphy

9410 *Agosti, Gianfranco* Considerazioni preliminari sui generi letterari dei poemi del Codice Bodmer. Aeg. 81 (2001) 185-217.

9411 *Augier, Yannis; Sartre, Maurice* Le dieu de Rabbos, maître du "temple périptère" de Canatha. DaM 13 (2002) 125-130.

9412 **Bernard, Etienne** Inscriptions grecques d'Alexandrie ptolémaïque. BEt 133: 2001 ⇒17,8766. ᴿCEg 153-154 (2002) 345-346 (*Bingen, Jean*).

9413 Bulletin épigraphique. REG 115 (2002) 622-777.

9414 **Cavallo, Guglielmo** Dalla parte del libro: storie di trasmissione dei classici. Ludus philologiae 10: Urbino 2002, QuattroVenti 315 pp. 88-392-0623-X.

9415 *Chiron, Pierre* L'épître dédicatoire de la *Rhétorique à Alexandre*: un faux si impudent?. ᶠGEOLTRAIN, P.: BEHE.R 113: 2002 ⇒45. 51-76 [BuBB 38,32] [Sir 50,1-21].

9416   ᴱᵀ**Chiron, Pierre** PSEUDO-ARISTOTE: rhétorique à Alexandre. CUFr. Association Guillaume Budé: P 2002, Belles Lettres clxxiv; 269 pp. 2-251-00498-X.

9417   **Citati, Pietro** La mente colorata: Ulisse e l'Odissea. Letteratura contemporanea: Mi 2002, Mondadori 322 pp. 88-04-50275-4 Con uno scritto di *Marcel Detienne*.

9418   Corpus dei papiri filosofici greci e latini (CPF): testi e lessico nei papiri di cultura greca e latina, parte IV/2: tavole (I, 1 e III). F 2002, Olschki xlii pp. €22+375. 88-222-5104-0/5060-5. 310 fig. Accademia toscana di scienze e lettere 'La Colombaria'; Union académique internationale [AnCl 72,511—Martin, Alain].

9419   Corpus e papiri filosofici greci e latini: testi e lessico nei papiri di cultura greca e latina, I: autori noti, 1. (NICOLAUS Damascenus - ZENO Tarsensis). 1999 ⇒15,8826; 17,8772. ᴿAeg. 81 (2001) 353-359 (*Agus, Alessandro*).

9420   **Cribiore, Raffaella** Gymnastics of the mind: Greek education in Hellenistic and Roman Egypt. 2001 ⇒17,8774. ᴿREG 115 (2002) 426-427 (*Blanchard, Alain*); Prudentia 34 (2002) 235-237 (*Pomeroy, Arthur J.*).

9421   **Dupont, Florence** Le plaisir et la loi: du Banquet de PLATON au Satiricon. [Re]découverte, Sciences humaines et sociales: P 2002, La Découverte 202 pp. 2-7071-3687-5. Bibl. 189-199.

9422   ᴱ**Duttenhöfer, Ruth** Griechische Urkunden der Papyrussammlung zu Leipzig (P. Lips. II). APF.B 10: Mü 2002, Saur xxii; 263 pp. 3-598-77544-X. Beitrag *Reinhold Scholl*; Bibl. xiii-xxii.

9423   *Ertel, Christine; Freyberger, Klaus Stefan* Zwischen Hellenisierung und Romanisierung: ein Friesblock mit Weihinschrift aus dem Vorgängerbau des 'Peripteraltempels' in Kanatha. DaM 13 (2002) 131-169.

9424   **Fantuzzi, M.; Hunter, R.** Muse e modelli: la poesia ellenistica da ALESSANDRO Magno ad AUGUSTO. R 2002, Laterza 600 pp. 88-420-6537-4.

9425   ᴱ**Frösén, Jaakko; Arjava, Antti; Lehtinen, Marjo** The Petra papyri, I Publications 4: Amman 2002, American Center of Oriental Research xix; 142 pp. $80. 0-90956-54-3. 22 fig.; 26 pl.

9426   *Gatier, Pierre-Louis* Inscriptions du Iᵉʳ siècle à Gérasa. Syria 79 (2002) 271-283.

9427   ᴱ**Gentili, Bruno; Prato, Carlo** Poetae elegiaci testimonia et fragmenta: pars altera. BSGRT: Monachii ²2002, Saur xxiii; 233 pp. 3-598-71702-4. Editio altera novis Simonidis fragmentis aucta.

9428   *Gnoli, Tommaso* A Byzantine Greek inscription from Qaṣr ar-Rabba (Karak district). ADAJ 46 (2002) 499-502.

9429   **Gonis, N.**, *al.*, The Oxyrhynchus papyri, 66 [nos 4494-4544]. PEES. GR 86: 1999 ⇒15,8834; 17,8784. ᴿGn. 74 (2002) 485-470 (*Lappe, Wolfgang*).

9430   **Gregg, Robert C.; Urman, Dan** Jews, pagans, and christians in the Golan Heights: Greek and other inscriptions of the Roman and Byzantine eras. SFSHJ 140: 1996 ⇒12,7963; 14,8091. ᴿSCI 21 (2002) 327-330 (*Eck, Werner*).

9431   *Hays, Harold M.* The historicity of Papyrus Westcar. ZÄS 129/1 (2002) 20-30.

9432   ᵀᴱ**Hock, Ronald F.; O'Neil, Edward N.** The Chreia and ancient rhetoric: classroom exercises. Writings from the Greco-Roman world 2: Atlanta 2002, SBL xiv; 411 pp. $50. 15898-3018-0. Bibl. 361-73.

9433 *Johnston, Sarah Iles* Sacrifice in the Greek magical papyri. Magic and ritual. RGRW 141: 2002 ⇒505. 344-358.

9434 [E]**Jones, Alexander** Astronomical papyri from Oxyrhynchus (P. Oxy. 4133-4300a). 1999 ⇒15,8839; 17,8789. [R]Gn. 74 (2002) 357-359 (*Wenskus, Otta*).

9435 *Jordan, David* Une prière de vengeance sur une tablette de plomb à Delos. RAr 1 (2002) 55-60;

9436 Two papyri with formulae for divination. Magic and ritual. RGRW 141: 2002 ⇒505. 25-36.

9437 ·*Judge, E.A.* Jews, proselytes and God-fearers club together. [F]BARNETT, P. 2002 ⇒4. 73-80.

9438 [E]**Kaltsas, D.** Dokumentarische Papyri des 2. Jh. v. Chr. aus dem Herakleopolites (P.Heid. VIII). 2001 ⇒17,8791. [R]BiOr 59 (2002) 540-541 (*Sarischouli, Panagiota*).

9439 *Kruger, Michael J.* P. Oxy. 840: amulet or miniature codex?. JThS 53 (2002) 81-94.

9440 **Legras, Bernard** Lire en Égypte, D'ALEXANDRE à l'Islam. Antiqua 6: P 2002, Picard 192 pp. 2-7084-0674-4. 116 fig.. Bibl. 175-181.

9441 **Lehmann, Clayton Miles; Holum, Kenneth G.** The Greek and Latin inscriptions of Caesarea Maritima. 2000 ⇒16,8828. [R]SCI 21 (2002) 323-327 (*Haensch, Rudolf*); ThLZ 127 (2002) 24-27 (*Pilhofer, Peter*); CBQ 64 (2002) 169-171 (*Brink, Laurie*).

9442 *Lehtinen, Marjo* The Petra papyri. NEA (BA) 65 (2002) 277-278.

9443 [E]**Llewelyn, S.R.** A review of the Greek inscriptions and papyri published in 1984-85. New documents illustrating early Christianity 8: 1998 ⇒14,8103... 16,8830. [R]LASBF 51 (2001) 456-459 (*Pierri, R.*);

9444 published in 1986-1987. New documents illustrating early christianity, 9: GR 2002, Eerdmans xvi; 136 pp. $35. 0-8028-4519-3.

9445 *Llewelyn, S.R.* The elders and rulers (archons) of the Jews;

9446 *Llewelyn, S.R.; Nobbs, A.M.* The earliest dated reference to Sunday in the papyri. [F]BARNETT, P. 2002 ⇒4. 69-72/106-118.

9447 *Macris, Constantinos* Jamblique et la littérature pseudo-pythagoricienne. [F]GEOLTRAIN, P.: BEHE.R 113: 2002 ⇒45. 77-129 [BuBB 38,32] [[Sir 50,1-21].

9448 [ET]**Maisano, Riccardo** ROMANO il Melodo: Cantici. Classici greci: T 2002, Utet 648+668 pp. €109. 14 pl..

9449 *Martin, Matthew J.* Interpreting the Theodotos inscription: some reflections on a first century Jerusalem synagogue inscription and E.P. Sanders' 'common Judaism'. ANESt 39 (2002) 160-181.

9450 **McLean, B.H.** Regional epigraphic catalogues of Asia Minor, 4: Greek and Latin inscriptions in the Konya Archaeological Museum. British Inst. of Archaeology at Ankara Mon. 29: L 2002, British Inst. of Archaeology at Ankara xvi; 134 pp. $72. 1-8982-49-148. 282 fig.;

9451 An introduction to Greek epigraphy of the Hellenistic and Roman periods from ALEXANDER the Great down to the reign of CONSTANTINE (323 B.C.-A.D. 337). AA 2002, Univ. of Michigan Pr. xx; 516 pp. £46. 0-472-11238-4.

9452 [E]**Merkelbach, Reinhold** Steinepigramme aus dem griechischen Osten, 4: die Südküste Kleinasiens, Syrien und Palästina. Mü 2002, Saur xvi; 471 pp. 3-598-73007-1.

9453 *Messeri, Gabriella: Pintaudi, Rosario* Corrigenda ad OGN I. Aeg. 81 (2001) 253-282.

9454 EMitthof, Fritz Ein spätantikes Wirtschaftsbuch aus Diospolis Parva: der Erlanger Papyruskodex und die Texte aus seinem Umfeld (P. Erl. Diosp.). APF.B 12: Mü 2002, Saur xviii; 105 pp. 3-598-77547-4. Bibl. xiii-xvi.

9455 Morton, Andrew Q. Codex Sinaiticus revisited. IBSt 24 (2002) 14-31.

9456 Napolitano, Maria Luisa PHILOKTETES e l'arco: dalla Magnesia all'Oeta. AANL.M 9/15,2: R 2002, Accademia Nazionale dei Lincei 97-217 pp. 88-218-0875-0. Bibl. 195-215.

9457 Natoli, Salvatore Libertà e destino nella tragedia greca. ECaramore, Gabriella: Uomini e profeti 10: Brescia 2002, Morcelliana 143 pp. 88-372-1883-4.

9458 Oates, John F., al., Checklist of editions of Greek and Latin papyri, ostraca and tablets. BASPap.S 9: ⁵2001 ⇒17,8805. RCEg 153-154 (2002) 334-335 (Nachtergael, Georges).

9459 Otranto, Rosa Antiche liste di libri su papiro. SusEr 49: 2000 ⇒16, 8834. RCEg 153-154 (2002) 340-342 (Lenaerts, Jean).

9460 EPapapolychroniou, E. Greek papyri in the Benaki Museum. 2000 ⇒16,8835. RBiOr 59 (2002) 86-87 (Husson, Geneviève).

9461 Perceau, Sylvie La parole vive: communiquer en catalogue dans l'épopée homérique. Bibliothèque d'Études Classiques 30: Lv 2002, Peeters viii; 331 pp. 90-429-1164-6. Bibl. 299-317.

9462 Petrucci, Armando Prima lezione di paleografia. Universale Laterza 811: R 2002, Laterza viii; 137 pp. 88-420-6643-5. Bibl. 127-137.

9463 Pilhofer, Peter Philippi, Bd. II: Katalog der Inschriften von Philippi. WUNT 119: 2000 ⇒16,8836; 17,8810. RRB 109 (2002) 145-147 (Murphy-O'Connor, J.); BZ 46 (2002) 149-50 (Vollenweider, Samuel); JThS 53 (2002) 241-4 (Bockmuehl, M.); ThLZ 127 (2002) 621-3 (Zahrnt, Michael); CBQ 64 (2002) 590-91 (Thompson, Leonard L.).

9464 EPontani, Filippo Maria Angelo POLIZIANO: Liber epigrammatum Graecorum. Edizione nazionale dei testi umanistici 5: R 2002, Edizioni di Storia e Letteratura cxl; 295 pp. 88-8498-053-4.

9465 Pryor, J.W. Awaiting the trumpet of God. FBARNETT, P. 2002 ⇒4. 102-105.

9466 Quack, Joachim Friedrich Ein neuer prophetischer Text aus Tebtynis (Papyrus Carlsberg 399 + Papyrus Psi Inv D.17 + Papyrus Tebtunis Tait 13 Vs.). Apokalyptik und Ägypten. OLA 107: 2002 ⇒451. 253-274; Tafel IX-XVI.

9467 Rémy, Bernard; Kayser, François Initiation à l'épigraphie grecque et latine. Universités, histoire: P 1999, Ellipses 192 pp. 2-7298-9933-2. Ill.

9468 Rodríguez Adrados, Francisco History of the Graeco-Latin fable, 2: the fable during the Roman Empire and in the Middle Ages. TRay, Leslie A.: Mn.S 207: Lei 2000, Brill xviii; 756 pp. 90-04-11583-8. Revised and updated by the author and Gert-Jan van Dijk.

9469 ERupprecht, H.-A. Berichtigungsliste der griechischen Papyrusurkunden aus Ägypten, 11. Lei 2002, Brill x; 354 pp. 90-04-12141-2;

9470 Wörterbuch der griechischen Papyrusurkunden, supplement 3 (1977-1988). 2000 ⇒16,8840. RAnCl 71 (2002) 407-408 (Martin, Alain); ThLZ 127 (2002) 1275-1278 (Papathomas, Amphilochios);

9471 Sammelbuch griechischer Urkunden aus Ägypten, 22 (Nr. 15205-15874). 2001 ⇒17,8815. RCEg 153-154 (2002) 337-340 (Nachtergael, Georges); Aeg. 81 (2001) 360-362 (Montevecchi, O.);

9472 23 (Index zu Band 22). Wsb 2002, Harrassowitz 162 pp. 3-447-045-30-2. Mitarbeit von *Joachim Hengstl; Andrea Jördens*.

9473 **Russo, Simona** I gioielli nei papiri di età greco-romana. 1999 ⇒15, 8849; 17,8816. ᴿBiOr 59 (2002) 318-322 (*Schenke, Gesa*).

9474 *Sabek, Yasser* Der hieratische Papyrus Berlin P 10497. ZÄS 129/1 (2002) 75-84.

9475 *Schlesier, Renate* Heimliche Liebe im Zeichen der Mysterien: Verschleierung und Enthüllung in EURIPIDES' *Hippolytos*. Paare. 2002 ⇒ 489. 51-91.

9476 **Usher, Stephen** Greek oratory: tradition and originality. 1999 ⇒15, 8857. ᴿGn. 74 (2002) 398-402 (*Schmitz, Thomas A.*).

9477 ·*Van der Horst, Pieter W.* Greek in Jewish Palestine in the light of Jewish epigraphy. Japheth. CBET 32: 2002 <2001> ⇒251. 9-26;

9478 De synagoge van Sardis en haar inscripties. NedThT 56/1 (2002) 16-26.

9479 *Van Elderen, Bastiaan* Early christian libraries. The bible as book. 2002 ⇒364. 45-59.

9480 **Visilis, I. Anastasiadis; Souris, George A.** An index to Roman imperial constitutions from Greek inscriptions and papyri 27 BC to 284 AD. 2000 ⇒16,8847. ᴿHZ 275 (2002) 713-714 (*Bartels, Jens*).

9481 **Wagner, G.** Les ostraca grecs de Douch, 5. Cairo 2001, Institut Français x; 94 pp. 2-7247-0307-3. 20 pl.;

9482 Elephantine XIII: les papyrus et les ostraca grecs d'Elephantine. Deutsches Archäologisches Institut, Abt. Kairo, Archäologische Veröffentlichungen 70: 1998 ⇒15,8858. ᴿJNES 61 (2002) 128-129 (*Wilfong, Terry G.*).

9483 **Worman, Nancy** The cast of character: style in Greek literature. Austin 2002, Univ. of Texas Pr. xiv; 274 pp. $45.

9484 **Zambarbieri, Mario** L'Odissea com'è: lettura critica. Studi e ricerche: Mi 2002, LED 903 pp. 88-7916-189-X. Bibl. 19-38.

J6.0 Iranian

9485 ·*Jullien, Christelle; Jullien, Florence* Aux frontières de l'iranité: "naṣraye" et "kristyone" des inscriptions du mobad Kirdir: enquête littéraire et historique. Numen 49 (2002) 282-335.

9486 *Kellens, Jean* L'idéologie religieuse des inscriptions achéménides. JA 290 (2002) 417-464.

9487 **Lecoq, Pierre** Recherches sur les dialectes kermaniens (Iran Central): grammaire, textes, traductions et glossaires. Acta Iranica 39: Lv 2002, Peeters ix; 686 pp. 90-429-1173-5. Bibl. 8.

J6.5 Latina

9488 *Alföldy, Géza* Nochmals: Pontius PILATUS und das Tiberieum von Caesarea Maritima. SCI 21 (2002) 133-148.

9489 ᴱ**Alföldy, Géza; Panciera, Silvio** Corpus inscriptionum latinarum: volumen sextum: inscriptiones urbis Romae latinae: pars octava: fasciculus tertius: titulos magistratuum populi Romani ordinum senatorii equestrisque. 2000 ⇒16,8854. ᴿAnCl 71 (2002) 392-395 (*Raepsaet-Charlier, Marie-Thérèse*).

9490   ^T**Bartels, Klaus** Roms sprechende Steine: Inschriften aus zwei Jahr-
       tausenden. 2000 ⇒16,8855. ^RAnCl 71 (2002) 405-407 (*Deman,
       Albert*).
9491   **Brown, Michelle P.** A guide to western historical scripts from antiq-
       uity to 1600. L 2002, British Library (6) 138 pp. 0-7123-0307-3.
       Bibl. 9-11.
9492   *Cugusi, Paolo* Note esegetiche, linguistiche e testuali su papiri latini.
       Aeg. 81 (2001) 307-321.
9493   **Donati, Angela** Epigrafia romana: la comunicazione nell'antichità.
       Itinerari: Bo 2002, Mulino 111 pp. €9.50. 88-15-08636-6. 11 fig.
9494   Handbuch der lateinischen Literatur der Antike, 1. die archaische Li-
       teratur: von den Anfängen bis SULLAsTod: die vorliterarische Peri-
       ode und die Zeit von 240 bis 78 v.Chr. ^E**Herzog, Reinhard;
       Schmidt, Peter Lebrecht; Suerbaum, Werner**, *al.*, Mü 2002, Beck
       xlviii; 611 pp. €118.
9495   ^E**Jakobi, Rainer** GRILLIUS: commentum in CICERONIS rhetorica.
       BSGRT: Monachii 2002, Saur x; 102 pp. 3-598-81230-8.
9496   **Kennedy, Duncan F.** Rethinking reality: LUCRETIUS and the tex-
       tualization of nature. Studies in literature and science: AA 2002, Uni-
       versity of Michigan Press ix; 145 pp. 0-472-11288-0. Bibl. 133-139.
9497   ^E**Lanham, Carol Dana** Latin grammar and rhetoric: from classical
       theory and medieval practice. L 2002, Continuum xiii (2) 304 pp. 0-
       8264-5708-8.
       Lehmann, C. The Greek and Latin inscriptions of Caesarea
       Maritima 2000 ⇒9441.
9498   **Masselli, Grazia Maria** Il rancore dell'esule: OVIDIO, l'Ibis e i modi
       di un'invettiva. Scrinia 20: Bari 2002, Edipuglia 193 pp. 88-7228-
       341-8. Bibl. 161-180.
       McLean, B.H. Greek and Latin inscriptions in the Konya
       Archaeological Museum 2002 ⇒9450.
9499   **Novak, Ralph Martin** Christianity and the Roman Empire: back-
       ground texts. 2001 ⇒17,8834. ^RRBLit 4 (2002) 465-467 (*Miller,
       John B. Faulkenberry*).
9500   ^{ET}**Patillon, Michel** Pseudo-Aelius ARISTIDE: arts rhétoriques, 1: livre
       I: le discours politique, 2: livre II: le discours simple. CUFr Associa-
       tion Guillaume Budé: P 2002, Belles Lettres 2 vols. €32+28. 2-251-
       0050-56/64.
9501   **Pernot, Laurent** La rhétorique dans l'Antiquité. 2000 ⇒16,8868.
       ^RLatomus 61 (2002) 230-231 (*Achard, Guy*).
9502   **Pinotti, Paola** L'elegia latina: storia di una forma poetica. Università,
       Lettere classiche 419: R 2002, Carocci 256 pp. 88-430-2364-0.
9503   **Ramelli, Ilaria** I romanzi antichi e il cristianesimo: contesto e contat-
       ti Graeco-Romanae. Religionis Electa Collectio 6: 2001 ⇒17,8838.
       ^RAevum 76 (2002) 221-222 (*Sordi, Marta*).
9504   Thesavrus lingvae latinae, X/2, Fasc. XIII: pronuntiatus-propositio.
       ^E**Beikircher, Hugo**, *al.*, Lp 2002, Saur 1921-2080 Sp. 35987-70502.
9505   **Thomas, Jean-François** Gloria et laus: étude sémantique. Biblio-
       thèque d'Études Classiques 31: LvN 2002, Peeters (4); 460 pp. €65.
       90-429-1176-X. Bibl. 439-443.
9506   **Totola, Giorgia** Donne e follia nell'epica romana: VIRGILIO, OVIDIO,
       LUCANO, STAZIO. Mi 2002, Mimesis 85 pp. 88-8483-083-4. Contiene
       un CD. Bibl. 75-82.

9507 *Vos, Johan S.* Die Kunst, recht zu behalten, 1: die Kunst, recht zu behalten, in der klassischen rhetorischen Tradition. Die Kunst der Argumentation. 2002 ⇒6712. 1-24.

9508 **Wright, Roger** A sociophilological study of late Latin. Utrecht studies in medieval literacy 10: Turnhout 2002, Brepols viii; 389 pp. 2-503-51338-7. Bibl. 361-381.

J8.1 General philology and linguistics

9509 ^E**Barbiers, Sjef; Beukema, Frits; Van der Wurff, Wim** Modality and its interaction with the verbal system. Linguistics today 47: Amst 2002, Benjamins x; 288 pp. $98. 1-5881-1167-9 [Lg. 79,828s—Javier Gutiérrez-Rexach].

9510 *Bevir, Mark* What is a text?: a pragmatic theory. IPQ 42 (2002) 493-508.

9511 **Catford, J.C.** A practical introduction to phonetics. NY ²2001, OUP xiii; 229 pp. $24. 0-1992-4635-1.

9512 **Chomsky, Noam Avram** On nature and language: with an essay on "The secular priesthood and the perils of democracy". ^E*Belletti, Adriana; Rizzi, Luigi*: C 2002, CUP x; 206 pp. 0521-815487. Bibl. 191-9.

9513 **Graffi, Giorgio; Scalise, Sergio** Le lingue e il linguaggio: introduzione alla linguistica. Manuali, linguistica: Bo 2002, Il Mulino 270 pp. 88-15-08495-9. Bibl. 259-262.

9514 **Hagège, Claude** Morte e rinascita delle lingue: diversità linguistica come patrimonio dell'umanità. ^T*Cortese, Luisa*: Campi del sapere: Mi 2002, Feltrinelli 279 pp. 88-07-10328-1. Bibl. 255-264.

9515 **Haspelmath, Martin** Understanding morphology. Understanding Language: L 2002, Arnold xiii; 290 pp. 0-340-76025-7. Bibl. 253-64.

9516 **Johansen, Jørgen Dines; Larsen, Svend Erik** Signs in use: an introduction to semiotics. ^T*Gorlée, Dinda L.; Irons, John*: L 2002, Routledge 246 pp. $26. 0-4152-6204-6 [Lg. 80,348—Jan Holeš].

9517 **Korenjak, M.** Publikum und Redner: ihre Interaktion in der sophistischen Rhetorik der Kaiserzeit. Zetemata 104: 2000 ⇒16,8893; 17, 8859. ^RLatomus 61 (2002) 233-234 *(Billault, Alain)*.

9518 **Lee, David** Cognitive linguistics: an introduction. Oxf 2002, OUP 223 pp. $25. 0-1955-1424-6 [Lg. 80,351—Laura & Radu Daniliuc].

9519 ^E**Litosseliti, Lia; Sunderland, Jane** Gender identity and discourse analysis. Amst 2002, Benjamins vii; 335 pp. $99. 1-588-1121-36 [Lg. 80,351s—Eve Chuen Ng].

9520 **Löbner, Sebastian** Understanding semantics. Understanding Language: L 2002, Arnold xii; 260 pp. 0-340-73197-4. Bibl. 251-253.

9521 **Lycan, William G.** Philosophy of language: contemporary introduction. L 2002, Routledge xv; 243 pp. 0-415-17116-4. Bibl. 229-238.

9522 **McCarthy, Timothy** Radical interpretation and indeterminacy. Oxf 2002, OUP xiv (2); 253 pp. 0-19-514506-2.

9523 **Obler, Loraine K.; Gjerlow, Kris** Language and the brain. Approaches to Linguistics: C 2002, CUP xviii; 206 pp. 0-521-46641-5. Bibl. 183-196.

9524 **Palmer, Frank Robert** Mood and modality. C ²2001, CUP xxi; 236 pp. 0-521-80035-8. Bibl. 222-230.

9525 *Perrot, Jean-Charles* Qu'est-ce qu'un système verbal?. CRAI 1 (2002) 333-352.

9526 .^E**Ravin, Yael; Leacock, Claudia** Polysemy: theoretical and compu-
tational approaches. Oxf 2000, OUP xi; 227 pp. $25.
9527 **Romaniello, Giuseppe** Dalla tenebra alla luce semantica: nei segreti
della glottologia. Saggi: R 2002, Sovera 175 pp. 88-8124-300-8.
9528 **Van Valin, Robert D., Jr.** An introduction to syntax. C 2001, CUP
xvi; 239 pp. $65 [Lg. 79,225—Edward J. Vajda].

J8.2 **Comparative grammar**

9529 **Androutsopoulos, Ion** Exploring time, tense and aspect in natural
language database interfaces. Natural language processing 6: Amst
2002, Benjamins ix; 306 pp. $116. 1-5881-1269-1. Diss. Edinburgh
[Lg. 80,334s—Filiouchkina, Maria].
9530 *Belova, A.G.* Towards the problem of the Semitic root-structure. ^MDI-
AKONOFF, I. 2002 ⇒27. 29-36.
9531 **Bennett, Patrick R.** Comparative Semitic linguistics: a manual.
1998 ⇒14,8135...17,8844. ^RHebStud 43 (2002) 521-525 (*Izre'el,
Shlomo*); BiOr 59 (2002) 597-599 (*Muraoka, T.*).
9532 **Bhat, S. Darbhe Narayana** Adverbial: the prominence of tense,
aspect and mood. Studies in language companion: 1999 ⇒16,8874.
^RAGI 87 (2002) 125-129 (*Bertinetto, Pier Marco*).
9533 **Edzard, Lutz** Polygenesis, convergence and entropy: an alternative
·model of linguistic evolution applied to Semitic linguistics. 1998 ⇒
14,8142; 17,8849. ^ROLZ 97 (2002) 5-26 (*Voigt, Rainer*).
9534 ^E**Gerlach, Birgit; Grijzenhout, Janet** Clitics in phonology, morphology, and syntax. Linguistics today 36: Amst 2000, Benjamins xi;
441 pp. $114. 1-55619-799-3 [Lg. 79,653s—Joseph F. Eska].
9535 **Huang, Yan** Anaphora: a cross-linguistic study. Oxf 2000, OUP 396
pp. $35. 0-19-8235-283.
9536 *Huehnergard, John* Comparative Semitic linguistics. IOS 20 (2002)
119-150.
9537 *Jansen-Winkeln, Karl* Zur Bildung der Personalpronomina im Altägyptischen und Semitischen. WO 32 (2002) 7-19.
9538 *Kaufman, Stephen A.* Languages in contact: the ancient Near East.
IOS 20 (2002) 297-306.
9539 *Khan, Geoffrey* The study of Semitic syntax. IOS 20 (2002) 151-172.
9540 **Levin, Saul** Semitic and Indo-European II: comparative morphology,
syntax and phonetics. Current Issues in Linguistic Theory 226: Amst
2002, Benjamins xvii; 592 pp. 90-272-4734-X.
9541 **Lipiński, Edouard** Semitic languages: outline of a comparative
grammar. OLA 80: 1997 ⇒13,8492... 17,8860. ^RIOS 20 (2002) 511-
520 (*Testen, David*).
9542 *Nemirovskaya, A.V.* Once again on Semitic verbal innovations. ^MDIA-
KONOFF, I. 2002 ⇒27. 226-231.
9543 *Olmo Lete, Gregorio del* Notes on Semitic lexicography (II): the pro-
·to-Semitic base (/dal-/). AuOr 20 (2002) 99-113.
9544 **Saari, Rami** The Maltese prepositions. J 2002, Carmel 24; 271 pp.
965-407-422-2.
9545 *Steiner, Gerd* Grammatisches Geschlecht und nominale Bedeutungs-
klassen in den Sprachen des Alten Orients. Sex and gender. 2002 ⇒
712. 589-602.
9546 *Waltisberg, Michael* Zur Ergativitätshypothese im Semitischen.
ZDMG 152 (2002) 11-62.

J8.4 The origin of writing

9547 **Casson, Lionel** Libraries in the ancient world. 2001 ⇒17,8847. ᴿSCI 21 (2002) 278-280 (*Wasserstein, David J.*); AnCl 71 (2002) 383-384 (*Isaac, Marie-Thérèse*).
9548 ᴱ**Christin, Anne-Marie** A history of writing: from hieroglyph to multimedia. P 2002, Flammarion 403 pp. €75. 2-0801-0887-5.
9549 *Hamilton, Gordon J.* W.F. ALBRIGHT and early alphabetic epigraphy. NEA (BA) 65 (2002) 35-42.
9550 *MacGinnis, John* The use of writing boards in the neo-Babylonian ·temple administration at Sippar. Iraq 64 (2002) 217-236.
9551 **Parkinson, Richard B.** Cracking codes: the Rosetta Stone and decipherment. 1999 ⇒15,8904; 17,8902. ᴿAJA 106 (2002) 602-604 (*Possehl, Gregory L.*).
9552 **Powell, Barry B.** Writing and the origins of Greek literature. C 2002, CUP xvi; 210 pp. $55/£40. 0-521-78206-6 57. Ill.
9553 **Robinson, Andrew** Lost languages: the enigma of the world's undeciphered scripts. NY 2002, McGraw-Hill 352 pp. $34.95. 0-071357-43-2. 258 fig.
9554 **Visicato, Giuseppe** The power and the writing: the early scribes of Mesopotamia. 2000 ⇒16,8914. ᴿOLZ 97 (2002) 68-74 (*Maaijer, Remco de*); WZKM 92 (2002) 231-234 (*Hruška, Blahoslav*).
9555 **Yardeni, Ada** The book of Hebrew script: history, palaeography, script styles, calligraphy & design. L 2002 <1997>, British Library 355 pp. $70. 0-7123-4793-3.

J9 Computers and linguistic research; structural linguistics

9556 *Andersen, F.I.; Forbes, A.D.* What kind of taxonomy is best for feeding into [sic] computer-assisted research into the syntax of a natural language?. Bible and computer. 2002 ⇒548. 23-42.
9557 *Bosman, H.J.; Sikkel, C.J.* Reading authors and reading documents. ·Bible and computer. 2002 ⇒548. 113-133.
9558 *Maldamé, Jean-Michel* Contingence et providence: histoire du salut et nouveau paradigme scientifique. Bogoslovni Vestnik 62/1 (2002) 27-45.
9559 **Matthews, Peter** A short history of structural linguistics. C 2001, CUP ix; 163 pp. $60/22.

XV. Postbiblica

K1.1 Pseudepigrapha [=catholicis 'Apocrypha'] VT generalis

9560 *Adler, William* The pseudepigrapha in the early church. Canon debate. 2002 ⇒1551. 211-228.
9561 **Atkinson, Kenneth** An intertextual study of the Psalms of Solomon: Pseudepigrapha. Studies in the bible and early Christianity 49: 2001 ⇒17,8872. ᴿRHPhR 82 (2002) 210-211 (*Grappe, Ch.*).

9562 *Baynes, Leslie* Christ as text: Odes of Solomon 23 and the letter shot from heaven. BR 47 (2002) 63-72.
9563 *Bianchi, Francesco* La grazia nella letteratura giudaica apocrifa e nei testi di Qumran. DSBP 30 (2002) 66-82.
9564 *Büllesbach, Claudia, al.*, Die Erschließung der JSHRZ durch ein Register: Gesamtkonzeption und ausgewählte Beispiele. Jüdische Schriften. 2002 ⇒345. 134-159.
9565 *Charlesworth, James H.* The JSHRZ and the OTP: a celebration. Jüdische Schriften. 2002 ⇒345. 11-34;
9566 The Odes of Solomon and the Jewish wisdom texts. Wisdom texts. BEThL 159: 2002 ⇒482. 323-349.
9567 **Delamarter, Steve** A scripture index to Charlesworth's the Old Testament Pseudepigrapha. L 2002, Sheffield A. viii; 99 pp. £16. 0-82-64-6431-9. Contribution by *James H. Charlesworth*.
9568 **DeSilva, David Arthur** Introducing the Apocrypha: message, context, and significance. GR 2002, Baker 428 pp. $30. 0-8010-2319-X. Bibl. 381-395.
9569 **Díez Macho, A.; Piñero Sáenz, A.** Apócrifos del Antiguo Testamento, 3. M ²2002, Cristiandad 612 pp. €33. 84-7057-323-3 [EstAg 38,156—Mielgo, C.].
9570 *Embry, Brad* The Psalms of Solomon and the New Testament: intertextuality and the need for a re-evaluation. JSPE 13 (2002) 99-136.
9571 **Harrington, Daniel J.** Invitation to the Apocrypha. 1999 ⇒15,8936 ...17,8883. ᴿCDios 215 (2002) 322-323 (*Gutiérrez, J.*).
9572 *Harrington, Daniel J.* The Old Testament apocrypha in the early church and today. Canon debate. 2002 ⇒1551. 196-210.
9573 **Helyer, Larry R.** Exploring Jewish literature of the second temple period: a guide for New Testament students. DG 2002, InterVarsity 528 pp. $30. 0-8308-2678-5.
9574 *Kaiser, Otto* Politische und persönliche Freiheit im jüdisch-hellenistischen Schrifttum des 2. Jh.s v. Chr. Jüdische Schriften. 2002 ⇒345. 43-58.
9575 **Kaiser, Otto** Die alttestamentlichen Apokryphen: eine Einleitung in Grundzügen. 2000 ⇒16,767. ᴿThLZ 127 (2002) 1165-7 (*Schmitt, Armin*).
9576 *Lattke, Michael* Titel, Überschriften und Unterschriften der sogenannten Oden und Psalmen Salomos. ꟳSCHENKE, H.: NHS 54: 2002 ⇒108. 439-447.
9577 **Lattke, Michael** Oden Salomos: Text, Übersetzung, Kommentar, 1: Oden 1 und 3-14. NTOA 41: 1999 ⇒15,8939; 17,8885. ᴿRTL 33 (2002) 572-573 (*Haelewyck, J.-Cl.*);
9578 NTOA 41/1-2: 1999-2001 ⇒17,8885/6. V.1: Oden 1 und 3-14; v.2: Oden 15-28. ᴿThLZ 127 (2002) 1052-1054 (*Frey, Jörg*).
9579 *Liebes, Yehuda* A Greek contribution to the faith of Abraham: a response to B. Bar-Kochva (Tarb. 70,327-352). Tarb. 71 (2002) 249-264 Sum. ix. H.
9580 *Martin, Annick* L'historienne et les apocryphes. Apocrypha 13 (2002) 9-27.
9581 *Mendels, Doron* Jewish historical writings between Judaism and Hellenism: new methods of research;
9582 *Mittmann-Richert, Ulrike* Theologie als Schlüssel zur Historie: neue Wege zur Datierung frühjüdischer Schriften. Jüdische Schriften. 2002 ⇒345. 35-42/75-101.

9583 **Oegema, Gerbern S.** Poetische Schriften. Jüdische Schriften aus hellenistisch-römischer Zeit 6, Suppl. 1/4: Gü 2002, Gü'er ix; 101 pp. €59. 3-579-04275-0.

9584 **Pietersma, Albert** The Apocryphon of Jannes and Jambres the magicians: P. Chester Beatty XVI. RGRW 119: 1994 ⇒10,9643*... 12,8155. ᴿSR 31 (2002) 471-472 (*Noegel, Scott B.*).

9585 **Porter, J.R.** The lost bible: forgotten scriptures revealed. 2001 ⇒17, 8889. ᴿPrPe 16 (2002) 350-351 (*Barker, Margaret*).

9586 *Reinhartz, Adele* The Apocrypha. Biblical world, 1. 2002 ⇒273. 15-27.

9587 *Ribera-Florit, Josep* El perdó i la reconciliació en el període intertestamentari i en el targum dels profetes. Perdó i reconciliació. 2002 ⇒ 591. 197-207.

9588 ᴱ**Sacchi, Paolo** Apocrifi dell'Antico Testamento, 4. Biblica 8: 2000 ⇒16,8937. ᴿApocrypha 13 (2002) 285-288 (*Norelli, E.*).

9589 **Satran, David** Biblical prophets in Byzantine Palestine: reassessing the Lives of the Prophets. SVTP 11: 1995 ⇒11/2,6745... 14,8203. ᴿREJ 161 (2002) 241-244 (*Ayoun, Richard*).

9590 *Schaller, Berndt* Zur Methodologie der Datierung und Lokalisierung pseud- und anonymer Schriften dargestellt an Beispielen vornehmlich aus dem Bereich der JSHRZ. Jüdische Schriften. 2002 ⇒345. 59-74.

9591 *Stone, Michael E.* Aramaic Levi in its contexts. JSQ 9 (2002) 307-26.

9592 ᴱ**Stone, Michael E.; Wright, Benjamin G.; Satran, David** The Apocryphal Ezechiel. SBL Early Judaism and its Literature 18: 2000 ⇒16, 8918. ᴿHebStud 43 (2002) 306-308 (*Grabbe, Lester L.*).

9593 *Van der Horst, Pieter Willem* Antediluvian knowledge: Jewish speculations about wisdom from before the flood in their ancient context. Jüdische Schriften. 2002 ⇒345. 163-181.

9594 *Winninge, Mikael* The New Testament reception of Judaism in the second temple period. NT as reception. JSNT.S 230: 2002 ⇒360. 15-31.

K1.2 Henoch

9595 (*a*) *Alexander, Philip S.* Enoch and the beginnings of Jewish interest in natural science. Wisdom texts. BEThL 159: 2002 ⇒482. 223-243; (*b*) The Enochic literature and the bible: intertextuality and its implications. The bible as book: the Hebrew Bible. 2002 ⇒9817. 57-69.

9596 *Bedenbender, Andreas* Traces of Enochic Judaism within the Hebrew Bible. Henoch 24 (2002) 39-48.

9597 *Böttrich, Christfried* Frühjüdische Weisheitstraditionen im slavischen Henochbuch und in Qumran. Wisdom texts. BEThL 159: 2002 ⇒ ·482. 297-321.

9598 *Charlesworth, James H.* A rare consensus among Enoch specialists: the date of the earliest Enoch books. Henoch 24 (2002) 225-234.

9599 **Chialà, Sabino** Libro delle parabole di Enoc: testo e commento. StBi 117: 1997 ⇒13,8536... 16,8949. ᴿVivH 13/1 (2002) 188-191 (*Mazzinghi, Luca*).

9600 **Coblentz Bautch, Kelley** 'No one has seen what I have seen': a study of the geography of 1 Enoch 17-19. ᴰ*VanderKam, J.*: 2002, 421 pp. Diss. Notre Dame [RTL 34,595].

9601   *Collins, Adela Yarbro* The theology of early Enoch literature. Henoch 24 (2002) 107-112.

9602   *Collins, John J.* Theology and identity in the early Enoch literature. Henoch 24 (2002) 57-62.

9603   *Dimant, Devorah 1* Enoch 6-11: a fragment of a parabiblical work. JJS 53 (2002) 223-237.

9604   *Ellens, J. Harold* Enochians and Zadokites;

9605   Bibliography. Henoch 24 (2002) 147-153/235-254.

9606   *Elliott, Mark* Covenant and cosmology in the book of the Watchers and the astronomical book. Henoch 24 (2002) 23-38;

9607   Origins and functions of the Watchers theodicy. Henoch 24 (2002) 63-75.

9608   *Eshel, Esther; Eshel, Hanan* Toponymic midrash in 1 Enoch and in other second temple Jewish literature. Henoch 24 (2002) 115-130.

9609   *Felber, Anneliese* Die Henochgestalt in der Patristik. PzB 11 (2002) 21-32.

9610   *Gruenwald, Ithamar* The cultural setting of Enoch-apocalypticism: new reflections. Henoch 24 (2002) 213-223.

9611   *Himmelfarb, Martha* The book of the Watchers and the priests of Jerusalem. Henoch 24 (2002) 131-135.

9612   *Knibb, Michael A.* Enoch literature and wisdom literature;

9613   *Kvanvig, Helge S.* The Watchers story, Genesis and *Atra-Ḥasīs*, a triangular reading. Henoch 24 (2002) 197-203/17-21;

9614   Origin and identity of the Enoch group. Henoch 24 (2002) 207-212.

9615   *Nickelsburg, George W.E.* From roots to branches: 1 Enoch in its Jewish and christian contexts. Jüdische Schriften. 2002 ⇒345. 335-346.

9616   **Nickelsburg, George W.E.** 1 Enoch 1: a commentary on the book of 1 Enoch, chapters 1-36; 81-108. Hermeneia 2001 ⇒17,8901. ᴿDSD 9 (2002) 265-268 (*Collins, John J.*); CTJ 37 (2002) 352-354 (*Ellens, J. Harold*); JSJ 33 (2002) 437-450 (*Knibb, Michael A.*).

9617   *Pearson, Birger A.* The Munier Enoch fragments, revisited. ᶠSCHENKE, H.: NHS 54: 2002 ⇒108. 375-383.

9618   *Piovanelli, Pierluigi* A theology of the supernatural in the *Book of the Watchers*?: an African perspective. Henoch 24 (2002) 87-98.

9619   *Repschinski, Boris* Ausmaß und Funktion der Henochfragmente in Qumran. PzB 11 (2002) 3-20.

9620   *Sacchi, Paolo* The theology of early Enochism and apocalyptic: the problem of the relation between form and content of the apocalypses: the worldview of apocalypses. Henoch 24 (2002) 77-85.

9621   *Schmidt, Brian* The origins of Enoch traditions: the view from outside. Henoch 24 (2002) 49-53.

9622   *Suter, David W.* Revisiting 'fallen angel, fallen priest'. Henoch 24 (2002) 137-142.

9623   *Tigchelaar, Eibert J.C.* Some remarks on the book of the Watchers, the priests, Enoch and Genesis, and 4Q208. Henoch 24 (2002) 143-5.

9624   *Venter, P.M.* Die makrososiale ruimte van die boek van die Wagte (1 Henog 1-36). HTS 58 (2002) 1513-1536 [OTA 26,532].

9625   *Wacker, Marie-Theres* "Rettendes Wissen" im äthiopischen Henochbuch. Rettendes Wissen. AOAT 300: 2002 ⇒352. 115-154.

K1.3 Testamenta

9626 ET**Heide, Martin** Die Testamente Isaaks und Jakobs: Edition und Übersetzung der arabischen und äthiopischen Versionen. ÄthF 56: 2000 ⇒16,8972. ROLZ 97 (2002) 586-90 (*Burtea, Bogdan*); WZKM 92 (2002) 278-281 (*Wagner, Ewald*).

9627 *Johnston, Sarah Iles* The Testament of Solomon from late antiquity to the Renaissance. Metamorphosis. 2002 ⇒394. 35-49.

9628 *Jonge, M. de* The two great commandments in the Testaments of the Twelve Patriarchs. NT 44 (2002) 371-392;

9629 Testamente der XII Patriarchen. TRE 33. 2002 ⇒799. 107-110;

9630 Testamentenliteratur. TRE 33 (2002) ⇒799. 110-113.

9631 **Latorre i Castillo, Jordi** La teologia sacerdotal del Testament de Leví en el conjunt de la literatura bíblica i parabíblica de finals del segon temple. D*Cortés, Enric*: 2001, 141 pp. Extr. Diss. Barcelona. RResB 33 (2002) 69-70 (*Cervantes Gabarrón, José*).

9632 *Ludlow, Jared W.* The Testament of Abraham: which came first—recension A or recension B?. JSPE 13 (2002) 3-15.

9633 **Ludlow, Jared W.** Abraham meets death: narrative humor in the Testament of Abraham. JSPE.S 41: L 2002, Sheffield Academic x; 209 pp. 0-8264-6204-9. Bibl. 195-201.

9634 *Puech, Émile* Le Testament de Lévi en araméen de la Geniza du Caire. RdQ 20 (2002) 511-556.

9635 *Vázquez Allegue, Jaime* 4Q215: 'Testamento de Neftalí': edición española anotada. FTREVIJANO ETCHEVERRÍA, R. 2002 ⇒122. 81-101.

K1.6 Adam, Jubilaea, Asenet

9636 *Anderson, Gary A.* The resurrection of Adam and Eve. FWILKEN, R. 2002 ⇒136. 3-34.

9637 **Anderson, Gary A.** The Genesis of perfection: Adam and Eve in Jewish and christian imagination. 2001 ⇒17,8915. RTheol. 105 (2002) 449-450 (*Charles-Murray, Mary*); HDB 31/1 (2002) 10-16 (*Sullivan, L.; Clifford, R.; Stone, M.; Fredriksen, P.; Levenson, J.*).

9638 *Assmann, Aleida* Die Träume von Adam und Eva im Paradies. Paare. 2002 ⇒489. 195-209.

9639 *Dochhorn, Jan* Warum der Dämon Eva verführte: über eine Variante in Apc Mos 26,2-mit einem Seitenblick auf Narr Zos (gr) 18-23. Jüdische Schriften. 2002 ⇒345. 347-364.

9640 **Eldridge, Michael D.** Dying Adam with his multiethnic family: understanding the Greek Life of Adam and Eve. SVTP 16: Lei 2001, Brill xv; 313 pp. €91. 90-04-12325-3. Bibl. 285-300. RArOr 70 (2002) 86-88 (*Pečirková, Jana*).

9641 *Isaacs, Ronald* Adam and Eve;

9642 Cain and Abel. Legends of biblical heroes. 2002 ⇒334. 1-9/11-17.

9643 **Knittel, Thomas** Das griechische 'Leben Adams und Evas': Studien zu einer narrativen Anthropologie im frühen Judentum. TSAJ 88: Tü 2002, Mohr S. xiv; 349 pp. €99. 3-16-147712-X. Bibl. 307-326. RJud. 58 (2002) 218-219 (*Avemarie, Friedrich*).

9644 **Levison, John R.** Texts in transition: the Greek Life of Adam and Eve. SBL Early Judaism and its Literature 16: 2000 ⇒16,9004. RCBQ 64 (2002) 381-382 (*Tobin, Thomas H.*).

9645 ᵀ**Monferrer Sala, Juan Pedro** Historia de Adán y Eva: apócrifo en versión árabe. 1998 ⇒14,8230; 15,8997. ᴿEstB 60 (2002) 128-131 (*Urbán, A.*).

9646 ᴱ**Murdoch, Brian; Tasioulas, J.A.** The apocryphal Lives of Adam and Eve, edited from the Auchinleck manuscript and fromTrinity College. Oxford, MS 57. Exeter Medieval English Texts and Studies: Exeter 2002, Univ. of Exeter Pr. viii; 158 pp. £17/$30. 085989-6986.

9647 *Painchaud, Louis; Wees, Jennifer* Connaître la différence entre les hommes mauvais et les bons: le charisme de clairvoyance d'Adam et Ève à PACHÔME et THÉODORE. ᶠSCHENKE, H: NHS 54: 2002 ⇒108. 139-155.

9648 .*Pettorelli, J.-P.* Deux témoins latins singuliers de la Vie d'Adam et Ève Paris, BNF, Lat. 3832 & Milan, B. Ambrosiana, O 35 Sup. JSJ 33 (2002) 1-27.

9649 *Philonenko, Marc* "Les cieux et la terre obéiront à son messie" (4Q521, 2, II, 1 et Vie latine d'Adam et Ève, 29,8). RHPhR 82/2 (2002) 115-122.

9650 **Stone, Michael Edward** Adam's contract with Satan: the legend of the cheirograph of Adam. Bloomington, IND 2002, Indiana University Press xv (2); 194 pp. $40. 0-253-33902-2. Bibl. 178-184. ᴿRBLit (2002)* (*Nielsen, Kirsten*);

9651 A concordance of the Armenian Apocryphal Adam books. 2001 ⇒ 17,8916. ᴿApocrypha 13 (2002) 317-318 (*Outtier, B.*).

9652 *Tromp, Johannes* The textual history of the Life of Adam and Eve in the light of a newly discovered Latin text-form. JSJ 33 (2002) 28-41.

9653 *Zarzecny, Rafał* Żywot Adama i Ewy według synaksariów etiopskich [La vie d'Adam et Eve selon les synaxaires ethiopiens]. PrzPow 4 (2002) 9-13. **P.**

9654 *Doering, Lutz* Jub 50:6-13 als Schlussabschnitt des Jubiläenbuchs— Nachtrag aus Qumran oder ursprünglicher Bestandteil des Werks?. RdQ 20 (2002) 359-387.

9655 **Halpern-Amaru, Betsy** The empowerment of women in the book of Jubilees. JSJ.S 60: 1999 ⇒15,8983; 17,8923. ᴿCBQ 64 (2002) 160-·61 (*Timbie, Janet*); JQR 92 (2002) 623-627 (*Reed, Annette Yoshiko*).

9656 *Huizenga, Leroy Andrew* The battle for Isaac: exploring the composition and function of the Aqedah in the book of Jubilees. JSPE 13 (2002) 33-59 [Gen 22].

9657 *Muñoz León, Domingo* Derás en el libro de los Jubileos. ᶠTREVIJANO ETCHEVERRÍA, R. 2002 ⇒122. 67-79.

9658 *Ravid, Liora* Purity and impurity in the book of Jubilees. JSPE 13 (2002) 61-86.

9659 **Scott, James M.** Geography in early Judaism and Christianity: the book of Jubilees. MSSNTS 113: C 2002, CUP viii; 337 pp. £45. 0-5-21-80812-X. Bibl. 259-304 [Gen 10].

9660 *VanderKam, James C.* Viewed from another angle: purity and impurity in the book of Jubilees. JSPE 13 (2002) 209-215.

9661 **Van Ruiten, Jacobus T.A.G.M.** Primaeval history interpreted: the rewriting of Genesis 1-11 in the book of Jubilees. JSJ.S 66: 2000 ⇒ 16,8982. ᴿJSJ 33 (2002) 339-342 (*Bedenbender, Andreas*); REJ 161 (2002) 497 (*Lemaire, André*).

9662 *Werman, Cana* "The תורה and the יתעודה" engraved on the tablets. DSD 9 (2002) 75-103.

9663 **Humphrey, Edith M.** Joseph and Aseneth. Guides to apocrypha and pseudepigrapha. 2000 ⇒16,9107. [R]SR 31 (2002) 225-226 (*Pietersma, Albert*).

9664 **Inowlocki, Sabrina** Des idoles mortes et muettes au Dieu vivant: Joseph, Aséneth et le fils de Pharaon dans un roman du judaïsme hellénisé. Monothéismes et philosophie: Turnhout 2002, Brepols 210 pp. 2-503-51039-6.

9665 *Penn, Michael* Identity transformation and authorial identification in Joseph and Aseneth. JSPE 13 (2002) 171-183.

K1.7 Apocalypses, ascensiones

9666 *Arcari, Luca* Il simbolismo e la metafora in alcuni testi apocalittici del I sec. e.v. analisi per una riconsiderazione. RdT 43 (2002) 843-866.

9667 **Henze, Matthias** The Syriac Apocalypse of Daniel. 2001 ⇒17,8928. [R]RHPhR 82 (2002) 348 (*Grappe, Ch.*).

9668 [E]**Kappler, C.** Apocalypses et voyages dans l'au-delà. 1987 ⇒3, 3625... 6,9977. [R]AuOr 20/1-2 (2002) 289-291 (*Olmo Lete, Gregorio del*).

9669 *Kulik, Alexander* Interpretation and reconstruction: retroverting the Apocalypse of Abraham. Apocrypha 13 (2002) 203-226.

9670 **Martin de Viviés, Pierre de** Apocalypses et cosmologie du salut. LeDiv 191: P 2002, Cerf 416 pp. €37. 2-204-07008-4. Bibl. 401-404.

9671 *Whealey, Alice* The apocryphal Apocalypse of John: a Byzantine apocalypse from the early Islamic period. JThS 53 (2002) 533-540.

K2.1 Philo judaeus alexandrinus

9672 *Baynes, Leslie* Philo, personification, and the transformation of grammatical gender. StPhiloA 14 (2002) 31-47.

9673 *Berthelot, Katell* Philo and kindness towards animals (*De virtutibus* 125-147). StPhiloA 14 (2002) 48-65;

9674 La mise en cause et la défense de la 'philanthropie' des lois juives au Ier et au XVIIIe siècles de notre ère. REJ 161 (2002) 41-82 [Prov 31,1-9.

9675 **Borgen, Peder** Philo of Alexandria: an exegete for his time. NT.S 86: 1997 ⇒13,8586... 15,9037. [R]VigChr 56 (2002) 200-202 (*Geljon, A.C.*).

9676 **Calabi, Francesca** The language and the law of God: interpretation and politics in Philo of Alexandria. SFSHJ 188: 1998 ⇒14,8269. [R]RPFE 127 (2002) 231-232 (*Pradeau, Jean-François*).

9677 .*Cavadini, John C.* Exegetical transformations: the sacrifice of Isaac in Philo, ORIGEN, and AMBROSE. [F]WILKEN, R. 2002 ⇒136. 35-49 [Gen 22,1-19].

9678 *Cohen, Naomi G.* Context and connotation: Greek words for Jewish concepts in Philo. Shem. JSJ.S 74: 2002 ⇒755. 31-61.

9679 *Davidzon, Irith* Il deserto nel *De vita Mosis* di Filone Alessandrino: possibilità di un'ascesa etica e conoscitiva attraverso i prodigi. Materia giudaica. 2002 ⇒727. 67-73.

9680 *Dyck, Jonathan* Philo, Alexandria and empire: the politics of allegorical interpretation. Jews in... cities. 2002 ⇒719. 149-174.

9681   *Feldman, Louis H.* Philo's view of Moses' birth and upbringing. CBQ
       64 (2002) 258-281;
9682   The death of Moses, according to Philo. EstB 60 (2002) 225-254;
9683   Philo's version of the biblical episode of the spies. HUCA 73 (2002)
       29-48 [Num 13-14];
9684   The portrayal of Sihon and Og in Philo, Pseudo-Philo and Josephus.
       JJS 53 (2002) 264-272;
9685   The portrayal of Phinehas by Philo, Pseudo-Philo, and Josephus. JQR
       92 (2002) 315-345.
9686   **Fisk, Bruce Norman** Do you not remember?: scripture, story and ex-
       egesis in the rewritten bible of Pseudo-Philo. JSPE.S 37: 2001 ⇒17,
       8941. ᴿSal. 64 (2002) 655-656 (*Vicent, R.*).
9687   *Frazier, Françoise* Les visages de Joseph dans le *De Josepho*.
       StPhiloA 14 (2002) 1-30 [Gen 37-50].
9688   **Frick, Peter** Divine Providence in Philo of Alexandria. TSAJ 77:
       1999 ⇒15,9042...17,8942. ᴿRSR 90 (2002) 453-455 (*Paul, André*);
       CBQ 64 (2002) 755-756 (*Sheridan, Mark*); StPhiloA 14 (2002) 182-
       185 (*Terian, Abraham*).
9689   *Gillet-Didier, Véronique* Passé généalogique et passé électif: usage
       comparé des généalogies dans les livres des *Chroniques* et le *Livre
       des antiquités bibliques* du Pseudo-Philon. REJ 161 (2002) 357-392.
9690   **Leonhardt, Jutta** Jewish worship in Philo of Alexandria. TSAJ 84:
       2001 ⇒17,8945. ᴿJud 58 (2002) 53-54 (*Avemarie, Friedrich*);
       RHPhR 82 (2002) 213-214 (*Grappe, Ch.*); RSR 90 (2002) 455-456
       (*Paul, André*).
9691   ᴱLévy, **Carlos** Philon d'Alexandrie et le langage de la philosophie.
       1998 ⇒14,433...17,8946. ᴿRPFE 127 (2002) 245-246 (*Lassègue,
       Monique*); RSR 90 (2002) 452-453 (*Paul, André*).
9692   **Niehoff, Maren R.** Philo on Jewish identity and culture. TSAJ 86:
       2001 ⇒17,8949. ᴿSCI 21 (2002) 314-318 (*Feldman, Louis H.*); FJB
       29 (2002) 155-157 (*Van der Horst, Pieter W.*); StPhiloA 14 (2002)
       186-193 (*Birnbaum, Ellen*).
9693   **Noack, Christian** Gottesbewußtsein: exegetische Studien zur Soteri-
       ologie und Mystik bei Philo von Alexandria. WUNT 2/116: 2000 ⇒
       16,9054; 17,8950. ᴿJThS 53 (2002) 165-173 (*Borgen, Peder*); JR 82
       (2002) 318-319 (*Hilgert, Earle*); JAC 45 (2002) 206-209 (*Runia,
       David T.*).
9694   *Olbricht, Thomas H.* Greek rhetoric and the allegorical rhetoric of
       Philo and CLEMENT of Alexandria. Rhetorical criticism. JSNT.S 195:
       2002 ⇒369. 24-47.
9695   *Reinmuth, Eckart* Zwischen Investitur und Testament: Beobachtun-
       gen zur Rezeption des Josuabuches im Liber Antiquitatum Biblica-
       rum. SJOT 16 (2002) 24-43.
9696   *Reynard, Jean* La notion d'athéisme dans l'oeuvre de Philon d'Ale-
       xandrie. Nier les dieux. 2002 ⇒626. 211-221.
9697   *Runia, David T.* One of us or one of them?: christian reception of
       Philo the Jew in Egypt. Shem. JSJ.S 74: 2002 ⇒755. 203-222;
9698   Philo of Alexandria: an annotated bibliography 1999. StPhiloA 14
       (2002) 141-169; al. auct.;
9699   Supplement: a provisional bibliography 2000-2002. StPhiloA 14
       (2002) 170-179; al. auct.
9700   **Runia, David T.** Philo of Alexandria: an annotated bibliography
       1987-1996 with addenda for 1937-1986. SVigChr 57: 2000 ⇒16,

9060. [R]NT 44 (2002) 196-197 (*Fox, Kenneth A.*); StPhiloA 14 (2002) 193-200 (*Royse, James R.*);

9701 [T]**Runia, David T.** Philo of Alexandria: on the creation of the cosmos according to Moses. Philo of Alexandria Commentary Series 1: 2001 ⇒17,8958. [R]StPhiloA 14 (2002) 180-182 (*Hilgert, Earle*).

9702 *Schimanowski, Gottfried* Philo als Prophet, Philo als Christ, Philo als Bischof. [F]ASCHOFF, D. 2002 ⇒3. 37-49.

9703 *Scott, Ian W.* Is Philo's Moses a divine man?. StPhiloA 14 (2002) 87-111.

9704 *Veltri, Giuseppe* Azaria de' ROSSIs Kritik an Philo von Alexandrien. Gegenwart der Tradition. 2002 <1995> ⇒255. 282-304.

9705 .**Winter, Bruce W.** Philo and Paul among the Sophists: Alexandrian and Corinthian responses to a Julio-Claudian movement. GR [2]2002 <1997>, Eerdmans xix; 302 pp. $32/€23. 0-8028-3977-0. Bibl. 261-282.

9706 *Zatsepin,Victor* Russian scholarship on Philo. StPhiloA 14 (2002) 136-140.

K2.4 *Evangelia apocrypha*—Apocryphal gospels

9707 *Albrile, Ezio* La maculazione redentrice: uno studio sull'*Evangelium Aegyptiorum*. Muséon 115/1-2 (2002) 57-68.

9708 **Andrisani, M.** Fabrizio DE ANDRÉ e la buona novella: evangeli apocrifi e leggende popolari. Mercator 46: F 2002, Atheneum 101 pp. €8.50.

9709 *Beatrice, Pier Franco* Forgery, propaganda and power in christian antiquity: some methodological remarks. [F]GNILKA, C.: JAC.E 33: 2002 ⇒48. 39-51.

9710 *Blackhirst, Rod* Herbs and wild fruit: Judas Maccabee and reflections of Rechabitism in the medieval gospel of Barnabas. JHiC 9/2 (2002) 278-292.

9711 **Boer, E.A. de** The gospel of Mary: beyond a Gnostic and a biblical Mary Magdalene. [D]*Roukema, R.*: 2002, 236 pp. Diss. Kampen [RTL .34,597].

9712 *Colpe, Carsten* "Vertraulich-verborgen-verboten-verraten": zur Psychologie der Geheimhaltung und der Erforschung "apokrypher" Schriften. [F]SCHENKE, H.: NHS 54: 2002 ⇒108. 27-46.

9713 *Dewey, Arthur J.* The Gospel of the Savior: a gem of a jigsaw puzzle. ProcGLM 22 (2002) 1-15.

9714 *Emmel, Stephen* The recently published Gospel of the Saviour ("Unbekanntes Berliner Evangelium"): righting the order of pages and events. HThR 95 (2002) 45-72;

9715 Unbekanntes Berliner Evangelium = The Strasbourg Coptic Gospel: prolegomena to a new edition of the Strasbourg fragments. [F]SCHENKE, H.: NHS 54: 2002 ⇒108. 353-374.

9716 *Gijsel, J.* Nouveaux témoins du pseudo-Matthieu. SE 41 (2002) 273-300.

9717 **Hedrick, Charles W.; Mirecki, Paul A.** Gospel of the Savior: a new ancient gospel. 1999 ⇒15,9079. [R]Apocrypha 13 (2002) 319-321 (*Dubois, J.-D.*).

9718 *Joosten, Jan* The Gospel of Barnabas and the Diatesseron. HThR 95 (2002) 73-96.

9719 **Karavidopoulos, John** Ἀπόκρυφα Χριστιανικά Κείμενα, Α΄, Ἀπό-
·κρυφα Εὐαγγέλια [Christian apocryphal texts: A': Apocryphal gos-
pels]. Βιβλική Βιβλιοθήκη 13: 1999 ⇒15,9080; 16,9085. ᴿNT 44
(2002) 307 (*Bovon, François*); OrthFor 16 (2002) 52-55 (*Nikolakopoulos, Konstantin*); Apocrypha 13 (2002) 309-310 (*Bouvier, B.*).

9720 **Klauck, Hans-Josef** Apokryphe Evangelien: eine Einführung. Stu
2002, Katholisches Bibelwerk 297 pp. €23.90. 3-460-33022-8.

9721 *Leirvik, Oddbjørn* History as a literary weapon: the gospel of Barnabas in Muslim-Christian polemics. StTh 56 (2002) 4-26.

9722 *Logan, Alastair H.B.* The gnostic gospels. Biblical world, 1. 2002 ⇒
273. 305-322.

9723 ᴱᵀ**Lührmann, Dieter H.; Schlarb, Egbert** Fragmente apokryph ge-
wordener Evangelien in griechischer und lateinischer Sprache.
MThSt 59: 2000 ⇒16,9088; 17,8986. ᴿNT 44 (2002) 97-99 (*Elliott,
J.K.*); EThL 78 (2002) 231-235 (*Verheyden, J.*).

9724 ᵀ**Mara, Maria Grazia** Il vangelo di Pietro: introduzione, versione,
commento. SOCr 30: Bo 2002, Dehoniane 140 pp. 88-10-20620-7.

9725 **Morrice, William** Dichos desconocidos de Jesús: palabras atribuidas
de Jesús fuera de los cuatro evangelios. Sdr 2002, Sal Terrae 271 pp.
€18.50. 84-293-1464-4 [BiFe 29,156—Salas, A.].

9726 *Mourad, Suleiman A.* From Hellenism to Christianity and Islam: the
origin of the palm tree story concerning Mary and Jesus in the gospel
of Pseudo-Matthew and the Qur'an. OrChr 86 (2002) 206-216.

9727 *Nicklas, Tobias* Ein "neutestamentliches Apokryphon"?: zum umstrit-
·tenen Kanonbezug des sog. "Petrusevangeliums". VigChr 56 (2002)
260-272.

9728 *Økland, Jorunn* I vangeli esclusi e i loro lettori: ovvero come dire
che un bacio è solo un bacio. Conc(I) 38 1 (2002) 90-101; Conc(E)
294,77-86; Conc(D) 38/1,59-67; Conc(P) 294, 71-81.

9729 *Pryor, J.W.* Fragment from the unknown gospel (Papyrus Egerton 2).
ᶠBARNETT, P. 2002 ⇒4. 99-101.

9730 **Santos Otero, A. de** Los evangelios apócrifos. 2001 ⇒17,8996.
ᴿAugustinus 47 (2002) 202-203 (*Pérez Catalán, Tomás*).

9731 *Verheyden, Joseph* Silent witnesses: Mary Magdalene and the women
at the tomb in the gospel of Peter. ᶠLAMBRECHT, J.: BEThL 165:
2002 ⇒72. 457-482.

K2.7 *Alia apocrypha NT*—**Apocryphal acts of apostles**

9732 ᵀᴱ**Amsler, Frédéric; Bovon, François; Bouvier, Bertrand** Acta
Philippi: textus. CChr.SA 11: 1999 ⇒15,9111. ᴿNT 44 (2002) 198
(*Elliott, J.K.*); JAC 45 (2002) 239-240 (*Schenke, Hans-Martin*).

9733 ᴱ**Amsler, Frédéric; Frey, Albert** Concordantia Actorum Philippi.
CChr.SA Instrumenta 1: Turnhout 2002, Brepols 845 pp. 2-503-509-
91-6.

9734 .**Amsler, Frédéric** Acta Philippi: commentarius. CChr.SA 12: 1999
⇒15,9112; 17,8999. ᴿNT 44 (2002) 198-199 (*Elliott, J.K.*); JAC 45
(2002) 242-247 (*Schenke, Hans-Martin*).

9735 ᴱ**Aranda Pérez, Gonzalo;** ᵀᴱ**García Lázaro, Concepción** Hechos de
Andrés y Mateo en la ciudad de los antropófagos; Martirio del apóstol San Mateo. Apócrifos cristianos 4: 2001 ⇒17,9000. ᴿAugustinus
47 (2002) 462-3 (*Flores, Miguel*); RevAg 43 (2002) 721-723 (*Sánchez Navarro, Luis*); RelCult 48 (2002) 792-793 (*Langa, Pedro*).

9736 **Baldwin, Matthew** 'Whose Acts of Peter?': text and historical context of the 'Actus Vercellenses'. 2002 Diss. Chicago [RTL 34,596].

9737 *Begrich, Gerhard* "Lasst das Himmelreich nicht welken!" Jes 52,16 und EpJac 7,22. [F]SCHENKE, H.: NHS 54: 2002 ⇒108. 175-180.

9738 *Beretta, Chiara* La visione di Dinocrate nella *Passio Perpetuae* come ermeneutica di 1Cor 15,29. AnScR 7 (2002) 195-223.

9739 [E]**Bovon, François; Graham Brock, Ann; Matthews, Christopher R.** The apocryphal acts of the Apostles. 1999 ⇒15,200...17,9003. [R]JR 82 (2002) 272-273 (*Baldwin, Matthew C.*); RBLit 4 (2002) 458-460 (*Schroeder, Caroline T.*).

9740 *Bremmer, Jan N.* Magic in the Apocryphal *Acts of the Apostles*. Metamorphosis. 2002 ⇒394. 51-70.

9741 [E]**Bremmer, Jan N.** Studies on the apocryphal acts of the apostles, 5: the apocryphal Acts of Andrew. 2000 ⇒16,9101; 17,9005. [R]NT 44 (2002) 199-200 (*Elliott, J.K.*).

9742 *Burnet, Régis* Pourquoi avoir écrit l'insipide épître aux Laodicéens?. NTS 48 (2002) 132-141.

9743 **Hartenstein, Judith** Die zweite Lehre: Erscheinungen des Auferstandenen als Rahmenerzählungen frühchristlicher Dialoge. TU 146: 2000 ⇒16,9099. [R]OLZ 97 (2002) 398-403 (*Nagel, Titus*); GGA 254(2002) 161-178 (*Schenke, Hans-Martin*).

9744 **Hovhanessian, Vahan** Third Corinthians: reclaiming Paul for christian orthodoxy. 2000 ⇒16,9126; 17,9014. [R]JR 82 (2002) 101-103 (*Pervo, Richard I.*); CBQ 64 (2002) 164-165 (*Sheridan, Mark*); ThR 67 (2002) 494-496 (*Lindemann, Andreas*).

9745 **Hvalvik, Reidar** The struggle for scripture and covenant: the purpose of the epistle of Barnabas and Jewish-Christian competition in the second century. WUNT 2/82: 1996 ⇒12,10844... 17,9015. [R]RB 109 (2002) 630-631 (*Nodet, Étienne*).

9746 [T]**Jullien, Christelle; Jullien, Florence** Les Actes de Mar Mari: l'apôtre de la Mésopotamie. Apocryphes, (L'Aelac) 11: 2001 ⇒17, 9018. [R]CRAI (2002) 1170-1171 (*Gignoux, Philippe*).

9747 *Karaulashvili, Irma* The date of the Epistula Abgari. Apocrypha 13 (2002) 85-111.

9748 ·*Lalleman, Pieter J.* The Acts of John as a gnostic text. Evangel 20 (2002) 9-15.

9749 *Lanchantin, Éve* Une homélie sur le Martyre de Pilate, attribuée à CYRIAQUE de Behnessa. Apocrypha 13 (2002) 135-202.

9750 *Lanzillotta, L. Roig* Vaticanus Graecus 808 revisited: a re-evaluation of the oldest fragment of *Acta Andreae*. Scr. 56 (2002) 126-140 [Ps 54-55].

9751 *Lusini, Gianfrancesco* Les Actes de Marc en éthiopien: remarques philologiques et histoire de la tradition. Apocrypha 13 (2002) 123-134.

9752 *Luttikhuizen, Gerard P.* Traces of Aristotelian thought in the Apocryphon of John. [F]SCHENKE, H.: NHS 54: 2002 ⇒108. 181-202.

9753 *Marshall, John W.* Revelation and romance: genre bending in the Shepherd of Hermas and the Acts of Peter. Rhetorical argumentation. 2002 ⇒553. 375-388.

9754 **Molinari, Andrea Lorenzo** The Acts of Peter and the Twelve Apostles (NHC 6.1): allegory, ascent, and ministry in the wake of the Decian persecution. SBL.DS 174: 2000 ⇒16,9132. [R]CBQ 64 (2002) 174-175 (*Bergren, Theodore A.*);

9755 I never knew the man: the Coptic Acts of Peter (Papyrus Berolinensis 8502.4): its independence from the Apocryphal Acts of Peter: genre and legendary origins. Bibliothèque copte de Nag Hammadi, Etudes 5: 2000 ⇒17,9025. ᴿJAC 45 (2002) 247-53 (*Schenke, Hans-Martin*).

9756 *Morolli, Danilo Ceccarelli* Alcune riflessioni intorno ad una importante collezione canonica delle origini: 'Gli 85 canoni degli apostoli'. Studi sull'Oriente Cristiano 6/1 (2002) 151-175.

9757 *Nagel, Peter* Beiträge zur Gleichnisauslegung in der Epistula Jacobi apocrypha (NHC I,2). ᶠSCHENKE, H.: NHS 54: 2002 ⇒108. 157-173.

9758 *Orselli, Alba Maria* Tecla, la santa discepola: itinerari della costruzione di una memoria agiografica. VII Simposio di Tarso. 2002 ⇒587. 173-190.

9759 *Palmer, Andrew* Les actes de Thaddée. Apocrypha 13 (2002) 63-84.

9760 *Pérès, Jacques-Noel* Un élément de christologie quartodécimane dans l'Épître des apôtres: l'agape pascale comme occurrence de solidarité. Apocrypha 13 (2002) 113-121 [Mt 25,1-13].

9761 *Prostmeier, Ferdinand R.* Antijudaismus im Rahmen christlicher Hermeneutik: zum Streit über christliche Identität in der Alten Kirche: Notizen zum Barnabasbrief. ZAC 6 (2002) 38-58.

9762 **Shoemaker, Stephen J.** The ancient traditions of the Virgin Mary's Dormition and Assumption. Oxford early christian studies: Oxf 2002, OUP xvi; 460 pp. $140. 0-19-925075-8.

9763 *Smith, Mitzi Jane* Understand ye a parable!: the Acts of Peter and the twelve apostles as parable narrative. Apocrypha 13 (2002) 29-52.

9764 *Van der Horst, Pieter W.* The Greek synagogue prayers in the *Apostolic Constitutions*, book VII. Japheth. CBET 32: 2002 <1999> ⇒ 251. 83-108.

9765 *White, Grant S.* The imagery of angelic praise and heavenly topography in the *Testament of our Lord*. EO 19 (2002) 315-332.

9766 *Zieme, Peter* Paulus und Thekla in der türkischen Überlieferung. Apocrypha 13 (2002) 53-62.

K3.1 **Qumran**—*generalia*

9767 ᴱ**Tov, Emanuel**, *al.*, The texts from the Judaean desert: indices and introduction to the Discoveries in the Judaean Desert series. DJD 39: Oxf 2002, Clarendon x; 452 pp. 0-19-924924-5.

9768 *Abusch, Raʿanan* Sevenfold hymns in the Songs of the Sabbath Sacrifice and the hekhalot literature: formalism, hierarchy and the limits of human participation. Dead Sea scrolls as background. StTDJ 46: 2002 ⇒732. 220-247.

9769 *Barstad, Hans M.* Nyere Qumranforskning i Skandinavia. NTT 103 (2002) 41-44.

9770 *Behringer, A.* Synopsis of fragment numbers employed in the editions of sapiential manuscripts from Qumran. Wisdom texts. BEThL 159: 2002 ⇒482. 435-442.

9771 *Brooke, George J.* The Dead Sea scrolls. Biblical world, 1. 2002 ⇒ 273. 250-269.

9772 *Crawford, Sidnie White* The Dead Sea scrolls: retrospective and prospective. Ment. *Albright, W.:* NEA (BA) 65 (2002) 81-86.

9773 **Davies, Philip R.; Brooke, George J.; Callaway, Phillip R.** The complete world of the Dead Sea scrolls. L 2002, Thames and H. 216 pp. £25. 0-500-05111-9. Bibl. 208-210;

9774 Qumran: die Schriftrollen vom Toten Meer. Da:Wiss 2002, 216 pp.;

9775 Los rollos del Mar Muerto y su mundo. M 2002, Alianza 216 pp [Salm. 50,537];

9776 De wereld van de Dode Zeerollen. Abcoude 2002, Fontaine 216 pp. 90-5956-019-1.

9777 *Donceel, Robert* Synthèse des observations faites en fouillant les tombes des nécropoles de Khirbet Qumrân et des environs = The Khirbet Qumran cemeteries: a synthesis of the archaeological data. Qumran Chronicle 10 (2002) 11-114 [BuBB 38,10].

9778 *Elgvin, Torleif; Pfann, Stephen J.* An incense altar from Qumran?. DSD 9 (2002) 20-33.

9779 *Emanuel, David* Orion Center bibliography of the Dead Sea scrolls (November 2001-May 2002). RdQ 20 (2002) 495-508;

9780 (May 2002-October 2002). RdQ 20 (2002) 599-623.

9781 *Eshel, Hanan, al.*, New data on the cemetery east of Khirbet Qumran. DSD 9 (2002) 135-165;

9782 Qumran studies in light of archeological excavations between 1967 and 1997. JRH 26/2 (2002) 179-188.

9783 **Fitzmyer, Joseph A.** 101 pytan o Qumran [Responses to 101 questions on the Dead Sea scrolls]. [T]*Fizia, Teresa*: 1997 ⇒14,8377. [R]CV 44 (2002) 213-215 (*Segert, Stanislav*). **P.**

9784 [E]**García Martínez, Florentino; Tigchelaar, Eibert J.C.** The Dead Sea scrolls: study edition. [2]2000 <1997> ⇒16,9163. [R]DSD 9 (2002) 114-124 (*Stuckenbruck, Loren*).

9785 *Ghiberti, Giuseppe* Qumran al giro di boa del 2000. ATT 8 (2002) 512-526.

9786 **Hanson, Kenneth** Qumran: the untold story. 1997 ⇒13,8758. [R]DSD 9 (2002) 408-411 (*Harding, James E.*).

9787 *Harding, Mark* Introduction 2: recent history of Dead Sea Scrolls scholarship. JRH 26/2 (2002) 145-156.

9788 *Hirschfeld, Yizhar* Qumran in the second temple period: reassessing the archaeological evidence. LASBF 52 (2002) 247-296. 8 pl.. [M]KLAWEK, A. Mogilany 1995. 1998 ⇒67.

9789 *Lange, A.; Mittmann-Richert, U.* Annotated list of the texts from the Judaean Desert classified by content and genre. Texts from the Judaean Desert. DJD 39: 2002 ⇒9767. 115-164.

9790 *Lemonon, Jean-Pierre* Qumran: où en est-on?. Etudes 5 (2002) 499-511.

9791 *Lim, Timothy H.* Intellectual property and the Dead Sea scrolls. DSD 9 (2002) 187-198.

9792 [E]**Lim, Timothy H.** The Dead Sea scrolls in their historical context. 2000 ⇒16,419; 17,9054. [R]RSR 90 (2002) 448-450 (*Paul, André*); SJTh 55 (2002) 121-113 (*Gathercole, Simon*).

9793 **Lönnqvist, Mina; Lönnqvist, Kenneth** Archaeology of the hidden Qumran: a new paradigm. Helsinki 2002, Helsinki Univ. Pr. 377 pp. €35. 952-91-4958-1. 145 fig. [JJS 54,153s—Broshi, Magen].

9794 *Magness, Jodi* Women at Qumran?. [F]FOERSTER, G. 2002 ⇒39. 89-123;

9795 **Magness, Jodi** The archaeology of Qumran and the Dead Sea scrolls. GR 2002, Eerdmans x; (36) 238 pp. $26/£19. 0-8028-4589-4.

9796 **Milik, Józef** Tadeusz Dziesiec odkryc na Pustyni Judzkiej. [T]*Kubiak, Zygmunt*: 1999 <1968> ⇒15,9188. [R]CV 44 (2002) 211-213 (*Segert, Stanislav*). **P.**

9797 *Netzer, E.* A proposal concerning the utilization of the ritual baths at Qumran. Qad. 35 (2002) 116-117. **H.**

9798 **Nimmer, David** Copyright in the Dead Sea Scrolls: authorship and originality. Houston Law Review 38/1 (2001) 217 pp ⇒17,9057. [R]CV 44 (2002) 215-216 (*Segert, Stanislav*).

9799 **Puech, Émile** Qumrân Grotte 4 XXII: textes araméens première partie 4Q529-549. DJD 31: 2001 ⇒17,8576. [R]RB 109 (2002) 428-434 (*Grelot, Pierre*).

9800 *Rasmussen, K.L.*, *al.*, The effects of possible contamination on the radiocarbon dating of the Dead Sea Scrolls 1: castor oil. Radiocarbon [Tucson, AZ] 43/1 (2001) 127-132 [NTAb 47,106].

9801 *Schiffman, Lawrence H.* The many battles of the Scrolls. JRH 26/2 (2002) 157-178.

9802 [E]**Schiffman, Lawrence H.; VanderKam, James C.** The Encyclope-dia of the Dead Sea Scrolls. 2000 ⇒16,9193; 17,9066. [R]CV 44 (2002) 117-122 (*Segert, Stanislav*).

9803 *Segert, Stanislav* Access to the Dead Sea Scrolls, 5, 6. CV 44 (2002) 69-125, 192-219.

9804 *Shanks, Hershel* Chief scroll editor opens up: an interview with Emanuel Tov. BArR 28/3 (2002) 32-35, 62.

9805 *Sheridan, Susan Guise* Scholars, soldiers, craftsmen, elites?: analysis of French collection of human remains from Qumran. DSD 9 (2002) 199-248.

9806 *Taylor, Joan E.* Khirbet Qumran in the nineteenth century and the name of the site. PEQ 134 (2002) 144-164.

9807 *Tov, Emanuel* Scribal practices and physical aspects of the Dead Sea scrolls. The bible as book. 2002 ⇒364. 9-33;

9808 The *Discoveries in the Judaean Desert* series: history and system of presentation;

9809 Lists of specific groups of texts from the Judaean Desert;

9810 Scribal notations in the texts from the Judaean Desert. Texts from the Judaean Desert. DJD 39: 2002 ⇒9767. 1-25/203-228/323-349.

9811 *Tov, Emanuel; Pfann, S.J.* Lists of the texts from the Judaean Desert. Texts from the Judaean Desert. DJD 39: 2002 ⇒9767. 27-114.

9812 *Trompf, Garry W.* Introduction 1: the long history of Dead Sea Scrolls scholarship. JRH 26/2 (2002) 123-144.

9813 **Washburn, David L.** A catalog of biblical passages in the Dead Sea scrolls. Text-Critical Studies 2: Atlanta, GA 2002, SBL ix; 161 pp. $30. 1-58983-040-7. Bibl. 157-161.

9814 *Webster, B.* Chronological index of the texts from the Judaean Des-ert: introduction. Texts from the Judaean Desert. DJD 39: 2002 ⇒ 9767. 351-446.

9815 [T]**Wise, Michael Owen; Abegg, Martin G., Jr.; Cook, Edward M.** The Dead Sea Scrolls: a new translation. 1996 ⇒12,8230... 16,9215. [R]JSSt 47 (2002) 342-343 (*Campbell, Jonathan*).

K3.4 *Qumran*, **libri biblici et parabiblici**

9816 [E]**Charlesworth, James H.** The Dead Sea scrolls: Hebrew, Aramaic, and Greek texts with English translations: 6B, Pesharim, other commentaries, and related documents: songs of the Sabbath sacrifices. The Princeton Theological Seminary Dead Sea Scrolls Project: Tü 2002, Mohr xxv; 384 pp. €109. 3-16-147426-0.

9817 ᴱHerbert, Edward D.; Tov, Emmanuel The bible as book: the Hebrew Bible and the Judean Desert discoveries. The Bible as Book 4: L 2002, British Library 360 pp. 0-7123-4726-7. Bibl. 305-326.

9818 ᵀAbegg, Martin; Flint, Peter; Ulrich, Eugene The Dead Sea scrolls bible. 1999 ⇒15,9227...17,9081. ᴿHeyJ 43 (2002) 361-362 (King, Nicholas); SWJT 45/1 (2002) 79-80 (Johnson, Rick).

9819 Abegg, Martin G., Jr. 1QIsaᴬ and 1QIsaᴮ: a rematch;

9820 Brooke, George J. The rewritten law, prophets and psalms: issues for understanding the text of the bible. The bible as book: the Hebrew Bible. 2002 ⇒9817. 221-228/31-40;

9821 Biblical interpretation in the wisdom texts from Qumran. Wisdom texts. BEThL 159: 2002 ⇒482. 201-220;

9822 Commentary on Genesis B (4Q253=4QCommGen B);

9823 Commentary on Genesis C (4Q254=4QCommGen C) [Gen 6-8; 9,24-25; 16; 22; 49,15-17; Gen 49,24-26];

9824 Commentary on Genesis D (4Q254a=4QCommGen D) [Gen 6,15];

9825 Commentary on Malachi B (4Q253a) [Mal 3,6-18]. The Dead Sea scrolls: texts. 2002 ⇒9816. 220-223/224-233/235-239/244-247.

9826 Charlesworth, James H. Commentary on Malachi A (5Q10). The Dead Sea scrolls: texts. 2002 ⇒9816. 240-243 [Mal 1,14].

9827 Charlesworth, James H.; Elledge, Casey D. Unidentified pesharim fragments (4Q172=4QpUnid);

9828 Midwives to Pharaoh fragment (4Q464a);

9829 Pesher-like fragment (4Q183=4QPesher-like Fragment);.

9830 Exposition on the patriarchs (4Q464=4QExposition on the Patriarchs=4QExpPat) The Dead Sea scrolls: texts. 2002 ⇒9816. 195-201/351-353/358-361/274-285.

9831 Charlesworth, James Hamilton The pesharim and Qumran history: chaos or consensus?. GR 2002, Eerdmans xiv; 171 pp. $28. 0-8028-3988-6. With appendixes by Lidija Novakovic. Bibl. 159-160.

9832 Crawford, Sidnie White 4QTales of the Persian court (4Q550ᴬ⁻ᴱ) and its relation to biblical royal courtier tales, especially Esther, Daniel and Joseph. The bible as book: Hebrew Bible. 2002 ⇒9817. 121-37.

9833 Cross, Frank Moore Testimonia (4Q175=4QTestimonia=4QTestim). The Dead Sea scrolls: texts. 2002 ⇒9816. 308-327 [Ex 20,22; Num 24,15-17; Dt 5,28-29; 18,18-19; 33,8-11].

9834 Dahmen, Ulrich New identifications and re-groupings of psalms fragments from Qumran cave I and IV. RdQ 20 (2002) 479-485.

9835 Daley, Stephen C. Textual influence of the Qumran scrolls on English Bible versions. The bible as book: the Hebrew Bible. 2002 ⇒9817. 253-287.

9836 De Troyer, Kristin Qumran research and textual studies: a different approach. RStR 28 (2002) 115-122;

9837 4Q550 in the context of the Darius traditions: the need for integration of different tools. Bible and computer. 2002 ⇒548. 573-581.

9838 Dimant, Devorah Qumran Cave 4 XXI: parabiblical texts, part 4: pseudo-prophetic texts [4Q383-391]. DJD 30: 2001 ⇒17,9088. ᴿDSD 9 (2002) 249-253 (Wright, Benjamin G.).

9839   *Dochhorn, J.* "Sie wird dir nicht ihre Kraft geben": Adam, Kain und der Ackerbau in 4Q423 2 3 und Apc Mos 24. Wisdom texts. BEThL 159: 2002 ⇒482. 351-364.

9840   **Doudna, Gregory L.** 4Q pesher Nahum: a critical edition. JSPE.S 35: Shf 2002, Sheffield A. 813 pp. $175. 1-841-27156X. Diss. Copenhagen.

9841   *Fernández Marcos, Natalio* Rhetorical expansions of biblical traditions in the Hellenistic period. OTEs 15 (2002) 766-779.

9842   **Fincke, Andrew** The Samuel Scroll from Qumran: 4QSam^a restored and compared to the Septuagint and 4QSam^c. StTDJ 43: 2001 ⇒17, 9092. ^RDSD 9 (2002) 404-408 (*Herbert, Edward D.*); RSO 76 (2002) 267-275 (*Catastini, Alessandro*).

9843   *Flint, Peter W.* The book of Isaiah in the Dead Sea scrolls. The bible as book: the Hebrew Bible. 2002 ⇒9817. 229-251;

9844   The bible and the Dead Sea scrolls. Bible and computer. 2002 ⇒548. 323-336.

9845   *Friedman, Shamma* Lexicographic enigmas in the Dead Sea scrolls [Ps-Ezek 4Q386]. Leš. 64/1-2 (2002) 167-174 Sum. VII. **H.**

9846   *García Martínez, Florentino* The sacrifice of Isaac in 4Q225. Aqedah. 2002 ⇒2624. 44-57 [Gen 22].

9847   *Green, Dennis* 4QIs^c: a rabbinic production of Isaiah found at Qumran?. JJS 53 (2002) 120-145.

9848   *Hamidović, David* 4Q279, 4QFour Lots, une interprétation du Psaume 135 appartenant à 4Q421, 4QWays of Righteousness. DSD 9 (2002) 166-186.

9849   *Herbert, Edward D.; Tov, Emanuel* Introduction;

9850   *Herbert, Edward D.* The kaige recension of Samuel: light from 4QSam^A. The bible as book: Hebr. Bible. 2002 ⇒9817. 1-3/197-208.

9851   *Horgan, Maurya P.* Habakkuk Pesher (1QpHab). The Dead Sea scrolls: texts. 2002 ⇒9816. 157-185 [Hab 1,1-17; 2,1-20]:

9852   Hosea Pesher 1 (4Q166=4QpHos^a) ⇒9816. 113-117 [Hos 2,8-14];

9853   Hosea Pesher 2 (4Q167=4QpHos^b) ⇒9816. 119-131 [Hos 5,13-15; 6,4; 6,7; 6,9-11; 8,6-8; 8,13-14];

9854   House of Stumbling fragment (4Q173a=4Q173 frg. 5 *olim*) ⇒9816. 363-365 [Ps 118,20];

9855   Isaiah Pesher 1 (3Q4=3QpIsa) ⇒9816. 35-37 [Isa 1,1-2];

9856   Isaiah Pesher 2 (4Q162=4QpIsa^b) ⇒9816. 39-45 [Isa 5];

9857   Isaiah Pesher 30 (4Q163=4QpIsa^c) ⇒9816. 47-81 [8,7-8; 9,11; 9,13-16; 10,12-13; 10,19; 10,20-26; 14,8; 14,26-30; 19,9-12; 29; 30,1-5; 30,23; 30,15-21; 31,1; Hos 6,9; Zech 11,11];

9858   Isaiah Pesher 4 (4Q161=4QpIsa^a) ⇒9816. 83-97 [Isa 10,22-11,5];

9859   Isaiah Pesher 5 (4Q165=4QpIsa^e) ⇒9816. 99-107 [Isa 11; 14; 15; 21; 32; 40];

9860   Isaiah Pesher 6 (4Q164=4QpIsa^d) ⇒9816. 109-111 [Isa 54,11-12];

9861   Micah Pesher 1 (1Q14=1QpMic) ⇒9816. 133-139 [Mic 1,2-6; 1,9; 6,15-16];

9862   Micah Pesher 2 (4Q168=1QpMic) ⇒9816. 141-143 [Mic 4,8-12];

9863   Nahum Pesher 2 (4Q169=4QpNah) ⇒9816. 144-155 [Nah 1,3-6; 2,12-14; 3,1-14];

9864   Psalm Pesher 1 (4Q171=4QpPs^a=4QpPs37 and 45) ⇒9816. 6-23;

9865   Psalm Pesher 2 (1Q16=1QpPs=1QpPs68) ⇒9816. 25-29;

9866   Psalm Pesher 3 (4Q173=4QpPs^b=4QpPs 118,127,129) ⇒9816. 31-3;

9867   Zephaniah Pesher 1 (4Q170=4QpZeph) ⇒9816. 187-189 [1,12-13];

9868 Zephaniah Pesher 2 (1Q15=1QpZeph) ⇒9816. 191-193 [1,18-22].
9869 .Høgenhaven, Jesper Biblical quotations and allusions in 4Qapocry-
      phal Lamentations. The bible as book: the Hebrew Bible. 2002 ⇒
      9817. 113-120.
9870 Jain, Eva Die materielle Rekonstruktion von 1 QJesb (1Q8) und eini-
      ge bisher nicht edierte Fragmente dieser Handschrift. RdQ 20 (2002)
      389-409.
9871 Kim, Angela Y. The textual alignment of the tabernacle sections of
      4Q365 (fragments 8a-b, 9a-b i, 9b ii, 12a i, 12b iii). Textus 21 (2002)
      45-69 [Ex 25-40].
9872 Lange, Armin The status of the biblical texts in the Qumran corpus
      and the canonical process. The bible as book: the Hebrew Bible.
      2002 ⇒9817. 21-30.
9873 Lichtenberger, Hermann Consolations (4Q176=4QTanh). The Dead
      Sea scrolls: texts. 2002 ⇒9816. 329-349 [Isa 40,1-5; 41,8-9; 43,1-2;
      43,4-6; 49,7; 49,13-17; 51,22-23; 51,8; 52,1-3; 54,4-10; Zech 13,9;
      Ps 79,2-3].
9874 Lim, Timothy H. Biblical quotations in the pesharim and the text of
      the bible—methodological considerations. The bible as book: the
      Hebrew Bible. 2002 ⇒9817. 71-79.
9875 Lim, Timothy H. Pesharim. Companion to the Qumran Scrolls 3: L
      2002, Sheffield A. x; 106 pp. £15. 1-84127-273-6. Bibl. 86-97;
          Holy Scripture in the Qumran commentaries 1997 ⇒6690.
9876 Lukaszewski, Albert "This" or "that": the far demonstrative pronoun
      in 1QapGen II,6. RdQ 20 (2002) 589-592.
9877 Luzarraga, Jesús El cilantro en 4QCant^b 4,16b. EstB 60 (2002) 107-
      123.
9878 Metso, Sarianna Biblical quotations in the Community Rule. The
      bible as book: the Hebrew Bible. 2002 ⇒9817. 81-92.
9879 Milgrom, Jacob; Novakovic, Lidija Catena A (4Q177=4QCat^a). The
      Dead Sea scrolls: texts. 2002 ⇒9816. 286-303 [Dt 7,15; Ps 16,3;
      17,1; 11,1-2; 12,1; 12,7; 13,5; 6,2-5; Isa 37,30; 32,7; 22,13; 35,10;
      Jer 18,18; Ezek 25,8; Hos 5,8; Nah 2,11; Zech 3,9];
9880 Catena B (4Q182=4QCat^b). The Dead Sea scrolls: texts. 2002 ⇒
      9816. 305-307 [Jer 5,7].
9881 Niehr, Herbert Die Weisheit des Achikar und der Musar Lammebin
      im Vergleich. Wisdom texts. BEThL 159: 2002 ⇒482. 173-186.
9882 Parry, Donald W. Unique readings in 4QSam^A. The bible as book:
      the Hebrew Bible. 2002 ⇒9817. 209-219.
9883 Pulikottil, Paulson Transmission of biblical texts in Qumran: the
      case of the large Isaiah scroll 1QIsa^a. JSPE.S 34: 2001 ⇒17,9123.
      ^RRSR 90 (2002) 439-441 (Paul, André); ThLZ 127 (2002) 1153-56
      (Nebe, G. Wilhelm); JBL 121 (2002) 556-559 (Vasholz, Robert).
9884 Qimron, Elisha Dismissing דמֶּה. Leš. 64/1-2 (2002) 165-166 [Ps-
      Ezek 4Q386]. Sum. VII. H.
9885 Rofé, Alexander Moses' mother and her slave-girl according to
      4QExod^b. DSD 9 (2002) 38-43.
9886 Scanlin, Harold P. Text, truth and tradition: the public's view of the
      bible in the light of the Dead Sea scrolls. The bible as book: the He-
      brew Bible. 2002 ⇒9817. 289-299.
9887 Schoors, Antoon The language of the Qumran sapiential works. Wis-
      dom texts. BEThL 159: 2002 ⇒482. 61-95.

9888   TESteudel, Annette Die Texte aus Qumran II: Hebräisch/Aramäisch
       und Deutsch. 2001 ⇒17,9128. Var. collab. RZRGG 54 (2002) 282-
       283 (Herr, Bertram).
9889   ETStuckenbruck, Loren T. The book of Giants from Qumran: text,
       translation, and commentary [1Q23-24]. TSAJ 63: 1997 ⇒13,8829;
       15,9249. RFrRu 9 (2002) 150-152 (Rapp, Hans A.); DSD 9 (2002)
       271-273 (Schiffman, Lawrence H.).
9890   Talmon, Shemaryahu The crystallization of the 'Canon of Hebrew
       Scriptures' in the light of biblical scrolls from Qumran;
9891   Tigchelaar, Eibert The Cave 4 Damascus document manuscripts and
       the text of the bible;
9892   Tov, Emanuel The biblical texts from the Judean Desert—an over-
       view and analysis of the published texts. The bible as book: the He-
       brew Bible. 2002 ⇒9817. 5-20/93-111/139-166;
9893   The biblical texts from the Judaean Desert, 1: categorized list of the
       'biblical texts'. Texts from the Judaean Desert. DJD 39: 2002 ⇒
       9767. 165-183.
9894   Trafton, Joseph L. Commentary on Genesis A (4Q252=4QCommGen
       A=4QPBless). The Dead Sea scrolls: texts. 2002 ⇒9816. 203-219
       [Gen 6,3; 8,13; 7-9; 11,31-32; 12,4; 15; 18; 22,10-12; 24,3-4; 36,12;
       49].
9895   Ulrich, Eugene The absence of 'sectarian variants' in the Jewish
       scriptural scrolls found at Qumran. The bible as book: the Hebrew
       Bible. 2002 ⇒9817. 179-195;
9896   ·The biblical texts from the Judaean Desert, 2: index of passages in
       the 'biblical texts'. Texts from the Judaean Desert. DJD 39: 2002 ⇒
       9767. 185-201.
9897   EUlrich, Eugene; Cross, Frank Moore Qumran Cave 4 VII: Gene-
       sis to Numbers. DJD 12: 1994 ⇒11/2,6966a... 14,8486. RCV 44
       (2002) 78-80 (Segert, Stanislav).
9898   EUlrich, Eugene Charles Qumran Cave 4, X: the Prophets. DJD 15:
       1997 ⇒13,8835...15,9256. RCV 44 (2002) 82-83 (Segert, Stanislav);
9899   Qumran Cave 4 IX: Deut., Joshua, Judges, Kings. DJD 12: 1995
       ⇒11/2,6967...15,9257. RCV 44 (2002) 80-82 (Segert, Stanislav).
9900   Ulrich, Eugene Charles, al., Qumran Cave 4, XI: Psalms to Chroni-
       cles. DJD 16: 2000 ⇒16,9218. RJThS 53 (2002) 159-161 (Davila,
       James R.); CV 44 (2002) 84-85 (Segert, Stanislav); DSD 9 (2002)
       278-280 (Seybold, Klaus); HebStud 43 (2002) 304-306 (Bowley,
       James E.); JBL 121 (2002) 162-164 (Abegg, Martin G.).
9901   Van der Kooij, Arie The textual criticism of the Hebrew Bible before
       and after the Qumran discoveries. The bible as book: the Hebrew
       Bible. 2002 ⇒9817. 167-177.
9902   Van Rooy, Harry F. The headings of the Psalms in the Dead Sea
       scrolls. JNSL 28/2 (2002) 127-141.
9903   VanderKam, James C. The wording of biblical citations in some re-
       written scriptural works. The bible as book: the Hebrew Bible. 2002
       ⇒9817. 41-56.
9904   Venturini, Simone Alcune caratteristiche editoriali di 4QSamᵃ. R
       2002, Extr. Diss. Pont. Ist. Biblico.
9905   Wacholder, Ben Zion The righteous teacher in the Pesherite com-
       mentaries. HUCA 73 (2002) 1-27.

к3.5 *Qumran*—varii rotuli et fragmenta

9906 EBrooke, George J.; Davies, Philip R. Copper Scroll studies. JSPE. S 40: Shf 2002, Sheffield A. xvi; 344 pp. £95. 0-82646-055-0.

9907 *Abegg, M.G., Jr.* Concordance of proper nouns in the non-biblical texts from Qumran: introduction. Texts from the Judaean Desert. DJD 39: 2002 ⇒9767. 229-284.

9908 *Bar-Ilan, Meir* The process of writing the Copper Scroll. Copper Scroll studies. JSPE.S 40: 2002 ⇒9906. 198-209.

9909 EBaumgarten, Joseph Qumrân Grotte 4 Halakhic texts. DJD 25: 1999 ⇒15,9270; 17,9141. RJSSt 47 (2002) 339-341 (*Campbell, Jonathan*).

9910 *Bertholon, Regis; Lacoudre, Noel; Vasquez, Jorge* The conservation and restoration of the Copper Scroll from Qumran. Copper Scroll studies. JSPE.S 40: 2002 ⇒9906. 12-24.

9911 *Bro Larsen, Kasper* Visdom og apokalyptik i "Musar leMevin" (1Q/4QInstruction). DTT 65 (2002) 1-14.

9912 *Brooke, George J.* Introduction. Copper Scroll studies. JSPE.S 40: 2002 ⇒9906. 1-9.

9913 ECharlesworth, James H. The Dead Sea Scrolls: Hebrew, Aramaic, and Greek texts with English translations, 2: Damascus Document, War Scroll... Princeton Theological Seminary Dead Sea Scrolls Project 2: 1994 ⇒12,8286... 14,8496. RFrRu 4 (2002) 289-291 (*Rapp, Hans A.*); RdQ 80 (2002) 593-597 (*Puech, Émile*);

9914 *Angelic liturgy: songs of the sabbath sacrifice.* 1999 ⇒15,9278; 17, 9147. RCV 44 (2002) 192-194 (*Segert, Stanislav*).

9915 *Charlesworth, James H.; Elledge, Casey D.* Unidentified fragments (4Q464b=4QUnidentified Fragments). The Dead Sea scrolls: texts. 2002 ⇒9816. 355-357.

9916 *Davies, Philip R.* John ALLEGRO and the Copper Scroll. Copper Scroll studies. JSPE.S 40: 2002 ⇒9906. 25-36.

9917 Davila, James R. Liturgical works. Eerdmans Commentaries on the Dead Sea Scrolls 6: 2000 ⇒16,9298; 17,9151. RScEs 54 (2002) 234-236 (*Duhaime, Jean*); HebStud 43 (2002) 311-313 (*Kugler, Robert A.*); DSD 9 (2002) 399-402 (*Fletcher-Louis, Crispin*); JBL 121 (2002) 160-162 (*Rietz, Henry W.L.*).

9918 *Elwolde, John F.* 3Q15: its linguistic affiliation, with lexicographical comments. Copper Scroll studies. JSPE.S 40: 2002 ⇒9906. 108-121.

9919 EEshel, Esther Qumrân Grotte 4: Poetical and liturgical texts, part 2. DJD 20: 1999 ⇒15,9264; 17,9153. RJSSt 47 (2002) 336-8 (*Hempel, Charlotte*).

9920 *Eshel, Hanan* Aqueducts in the copper sroll. Copper Scroll studies. JSPE.S 40: 2002 ⇒9906. 92-107.

9921 *Eshel, Hanan; Safrai, Zeev* The Copper Scroll: a sectarian composition documenting where the treasures of the first temple were hidden. Cathedra 103 (2002) 7-20 Sum. 189. H.

9922 *Fidler, Ruth* Inclusio and symbolic geography in the Copper Scroll. Copper Scroll studies. JSPE.S 40: 2002 ⇒9906. 210-225.

9923 *Fraade, Steven D.* The torah of the king (Deut 17:14-20) in the Temple Scroll and early rabbinic law. Dead Sea scrolls as background. StTDJ 46: 2002 ⇒732. 25-60.

9924 ^E**Garcia Martinez, Florentino** Qumran Cave 11, 2: 11Q2-18, 11Q20-31. DJD 23: 1998 ⇒14,8505...17,9159. ^RCV 44 (2002) 75-78 (*Segert, Stanislav*).

9925 *García Martínez, Florentino* Old texts and modern mirages: the "I" of two Qumran hymns. EThL 78 (2002) 321-339;

9926 ¿Ángel, hombre, mesías, maestro de justicia?: el problemático 'yo' de un poema qumránico. ^FTREVIJANO ETCHEVERRÍA, R. 2002 ⇒122. 103-131.

9927 *Goranson, Stephen* Further reflections on the Copper Scroll. Copper Scroll studies. JSPE.S 40: 2002 ⇒9906. 226-232.

9928 **Grossman, Maxine L.** Reading for history in the Damascus document: a methodological method. StTDJ 45: Lei 2002, Brill xiii; 255 pp. €68/$79. 90-04-12252-4. Bibl. 229-241.

9929 *Hurowitz, Victor Avigdor rwqmh* in Damascus Document 4QDe (4Q270) 7 i 14. DSD 9 (2002) 34-37.

9930 **Jacobs, Steven Leonard** The biblical masorah and the Temple Scroll: an orthographical inquiry. Lanham 2002, University Press of America xv; 136 pp. 0-7618-2306-9. Bibl. 111-124.

9931 **Jiménez Bedman, Francisco** El misterio del Rollo de Cobre de Qumrán: análisis lingüístico. Estella 2002, Verbo Divino 272 pp. €20.80. 84-8169-507-6.

9932 *Johnson, William* Professor Henry Wright BAKER: the Copper Scroll and his career. Copper Scroll studies. JSPE.S 40: 2002 ⇒9906. 37-44.

9933 ·*Knohl, Israel* The date and innovation of the messianic hymns. RdQ 20 (2002) 487-489;

9934 New light on the Copper Scroll and 4QMMT;

9935 *Lange, Armin* The meaning of *dema'* in the Copper Scroll and ancient Jewish literature. Copper Scroll studies. JSPE.S 40: 2002 ⇒9906. 233-256/122-138.

9936 *Lefkovits, Judah K.* The Copper Scroll treasure: fact or fiction?: the abbreviation כך versus ככרין. Copper Scroll studies. JSPE.S 40: 2002 ⇒9906. 139-154.

9937 **Lefkovits, Judah K.** The Copper Scroll—3Q15: a reevaluation: a new reading, translation, and commentary. StTDJ 25: 2000 ⇒16, 9322; 17,9165. ^RRBLit 4 (2002) 280-283 (*Jordan, David J.*).

9938 *Levinson, Bernard M.; Zahn, Molly M.* Revelation regained: the hermeneutics of כי and אם in the Temple Scroll. DSD 9 (2002) 295-346.

9939 *Lichtenberger, Hermann* Der Weisheitstext 4Q185: eine neue Edition. Wisdom texts. BEThL 159: 2002 ⇒482. 127-150.

9940 *Lundberg, Marilyn J.; Zuckerman, Bruce* When images meet: the potential of photographic and computer imaging technology for the study of the Copper Scroll. Copper Scroll studies. JSPE.S 40: 2002 ⇒9906. 45-57.

9941 *Lübbe, John* The Copper Scroll and language issues. Copper Scroll studies. JSPE.S 40: 2002 ⇒9906. 155-162.

9942 *Marenco Bovone, Maria R.* La colonna XI della "Regola della comunità": un inno che racchiude un'economia di salvezza. ATT 8 (2002) 271-300.

9943 *Metso, Sarianna* Biblical quotations in the Community Rule. The bible as book: the Hebrew Bible. 2002 ⇒9817. 81-92.

9944 *Muchowski, Piotr* The origin of 3Q15: forty years of discussion. Copper Scroll studies. JSPE.S 40: 2002 ⇒9906. 257-270.

9945 *Penner, Ken* Realized or future salvation in the Hodayot. Journal of Biblical Studies 2/1 (2002)*.
9946 *Pfann, Stephen J.* Kelei Dema‘: tithe jars, scroll jars and cookie jars. Copper Scroll studies. JSPE.S 40: 2002 ⇒9906. 163-179.
9947 *Poirier, John C.* 4Q464: not eschatological. RdQ 20 (2002) 583-587.
9948 **Puech, Émile** Qumrân Grotte 4.XVIII: textes hébreux (4Q521-4Q528, 4Q576-4Q579). DJD 25: 1998 ⇒14,8530... 17,9171. [R]JNES 61 (2002) 143-144 (*Pardee, Dennis*);
9949 Littérature quamranienne et épigraphie sémitique: déchiffrement et interprétation: le rouleau de cuivre de la Grotte 3 de Qumrân. [D]*Kuntzmann*: 2002 Diss.-Habil. Strasbourg.
9950 *Puech, Émile* Some results of a new examination of the Copper Scroll (3Q15). Copper Scroll studies. JSPE.S 40: 2002 ⇒9906. 58-89.
9951 **Riska, Magnus** The Temple Scroll and the biblical text tradtions: a study of columns 2-13:9. [D]*Veijola, T.*: SESJ 81: Helsinki 2001, Finnish Exegetical Society 213 pp. 951-9217-36-3. Diss. Helsinki. Bibl. 208-213.
9952 *Schiffman, Lawrence H.* The architectural vocabulary of the Copper Scroll and the Temple Scroll;
9953 *Segal, Brenda Lesley* The Copper Scroll: novel approaches. Copper Scroll studies. JSPE.S 40: 2002 ⇒9906. 180-195/271-275.
9954 *Shemesh, Aharon* Expulsion and exclusion in the Community Rule and the Damascus Document. DSD 9 (2002) 44-74.
9955 *Strugnell, John* The smaller Hebrew wisdom texts found at Qumran: variations, resemblances, and lines of development. Wisdom texts. BEThL 159: 2002 ⇒482. 31-60.
9956 [E]**Strugnell, John; Harrington, Daniel J.; Elgvin, Torleif** Qumrân Grotte 4 Sapiential texts, Pt. 2, 4Q Instruction: 4Q415ff. DJD 24: 1999 ⇒15,9265; 17,9176. [R]DSD 9 (2002) 127-132 (*Harding, James; Davies, Philip*).
9957 *Stuckenbruck, Loren T.* 4QInstruction and the possible influence of early Enochic traditions: an evaluation. Wisdom texts. BEThL 159: 2002 ⇒482. 245-261.
9958 *Thiering, Barbara* The Copper Scroll: King Herod's bank account?. Copper Scroll studies. JSPE.S 40: 2002 ⇒9906. 276-287.
9959 *Tigchelaar, Eibert J.C.* Towards a reconstruction of the beginning of 4QInstruction (4Q416 Fragment 1 and parallels). Wisdom texts. BEThL 159: 2002 ⇒482. 99-126;
9960 The Cave 4 Damascus document manuscripts and the text of the bible. The bible as book: the Hebrew Bible. 2002 ⇒9817. 93-111;
9961 Annotated lists of overlaps and parallels in the non-biblical texts from Qumran and Masada. Texts from the Judaean Desert. DJD 39: 2002 ⇒9767. 285-322.
9962 *Tov, Lika* Some palaeographical observations regarding the cover art;
9963 *Wise, Michael O.* David J. WILMOT and the Copper Scroll;
9964 *Wolters, Al* Palaeography and literary structure as guides to reading the Copper Scroll. Copper Scroll studies. JSPE.S 40: 2002 ⇒9906. 288-290/291-310/311-333.

K3.6 Qumran et Novum Testamentum

9965 ^E**Allison, Dale C.** Scriptural allusions in the New Testament: light
from the Dead Sea scrolls. 2000 ⇒16,9356. ^RDSD 9 (2002) 391-393
(*Brooke, George J.*).

9966 *Bissoli, Giovanni* Il vangelo di Marco a Qumran?. CredOg 131-132
(2002) 199-204.

9967 **Fitzmyer, Joseph A.** The Dead Sea scrolls and christian origins.
2000 ⇒16,156; 17,146. ^RDSD 9 (2002) 111-112 (*Hempel, Charlotte*); HeyJ 43 (2002) 362-363 (*King, Nicholas*); RBLit 4 (2002)
275-280 (*Lukaszewski, Albert L.*); LTP 58 (2002) 369-371 (*Poirier,
Paul-Hubert*).

9968 **Flusser, David** Entdeckungen im Neuen Testament, 2: Jesus—Qumran—Urchristentum. ^E*Majer, Martin*: 1999 ⇒15,9363. ^RRBLit 4
(2002) 288-290 (*Evans, Craig A.*).

9969 *Kuhn, Heinz-Wolfgang* Jesus vor dem Hintergrund der Qumrange-
meinde. ^FASCHOFF, D. 2002 ⇒3. 50-60.

9970 **Paul, André** I manoscritti del Mar Morto: possono davero sconvol-
gere tutto quello che sappiamo sulla bibbia?: che cosa dicono questi
testi scoperti 55 anni fa?: chi li ha scritti e perché?. BCR 1: Leumann
(TO) 2002, LDC 328 pp. €18. 88-01-02377-4.

9971 *Ruzer, Serge* The double love precept in the New Testament and in
the Rule of the Congregation. Tarbiz 71 (2002) 353-370 Sum. v. H.

9972 ·**Stegemann, Hartmut** Esseńczycy z Qumran, Jan Chrzciciel i Jezus.
^T*Małecki, Zdzisław; Tronina, Antoni*: Biblioteka Zwojów, NT 9:
Kraków 2002, Enigma 336 pp. **P.**

9973 **Thiede, Carsten Peter** Die Messias-Sucher: die Schriftrollen vom
Toten Meer und die jüdischen Ursprünge des Christentums. Stu
2002, Kreuz 288 pp. €19.90. 3-7831-2150-7.

9974 **Ulrich, Eugene Charles** The Dead Sea scrolls and the origins of the
bible. Studies in the Dea Sea Scrolls and related literature: 1999 ⇒
15,9378...17,9196. ^RCV 44 (2002) 202-205 (*Segert, Stanislav*); RSR
90 (2002) 438-39 (*Paul, André*); RBLit (2002)* (*Kugler, Robert A.*).

9975 **VanderKam, James C.; Flint, Peter W.** The meaning of the Dead
Sea scrolls: their significance for understanding the bible, Judaism,
Jesus, and christianity. SF 2002, Harper Collins xii; 467 pp. 0-06-06-
8464-X.

9976 *Vermes, Geza* Significance of the scrolls for understanding christianity. JRH 26/2 (2002) 210-219.

K3.8 Historia et doctrinae Qumran

9977 *Caquot, André* Malédictions et bénédictions qoumrâniennes. RHPhR
82 (2002) 3-14.

9978 ^E**Collins, John Joseph; Kugler, Robert A.** Religion in the Dead Sea
scrolls. 2000 ⇒16,393; 17,9200. ^RJSJ 33 (2002) 330-331
(*Tigchelaar, Eibert*); BiOr 59 (2002) 392-395 (*Cansdale, Lena*);
HebStud 43 (2002) 300-302 (*Jastram, Nathan*); OTEs 15 (2002)
558-560 (*Naudé, J.A.*).

9979 *Davies, Philip R.* Space and sects in the Qumran scrolls. ^FFLANAGAN,
J.: JSOT.S 359: 2002 ⇒38. 81-98.

9980 *Davila, James R.* The macrocosmic temple, scriptural exegesis, and the songs of the sabbath sacrifice. DSD 9 (2002) 1-19.

9981 **DiTommaso, Lorenzo** The Qumran New Jerusalem texts: contents and contexts. ᴰ*Schuller, E.*: 2001 354 pp. Diss. McMaster [RTL 34, 595].

9982 *Fabry, Heinz-Josef* Qumran und die Essener: vom Beginn frühjüdischer Gruppenbildung bis zur Vielfalt der 'Häresien'. Ethos und Identität. 2002 ⇒490. 123-147.

9983 **Fletcher-Louis, Crispin H.T.** All the glory of Adam: liturgical anthropology in the Dead Sea scrolls. StTDJ 42: Lei 2002, Brill xii; 546 pp. €140/$163. 90-04-12326-1. Bibl. 481-497.

9984 *García Martínez, Florentino* Magic in the Dead Sea scrolls. Metamorphosis. 2002 ⇒394. 13-33.

9985 *Gilbert, Maurice* La lumière dans les textes de Qumrân. Symbolisme et expérience. 2002 ⇒666. 149-158.

9986 *Golitzin, Alexander* Recovering the "glory of Adam": "divine light" traditions in the Dead Sea scrolls and the christian ascetical literature of fourth-century Syro-Mesopotamia. Dead Sea scrolls as background. StTDJ 46: 2002 ⇒732. 275-308.

9987 *Hempel, Charlotte* The Qumran sapiential texts and the rule books. Wisdom texts. BEThL 159: 2002 ⇒482. 277-295.

9988 **Ibba, Giovanni** La teologia di Qumran. CSB 40: Bo 2002, EDB 87 pp. €8. 88-10-40740-7. Pres. di *Paolo Sacchi.*

9989 *Kugler, Rob* Making all experience religious: the hegemony of ritual at Qumran. JSJ 33 (2002) 131-152.

9990 *Lange, Armin* Die Weisheitstexte aus Qumran: eine Einleitung. Wisdom texts. BEThL 159: 2002 ⇒482. 3-30.

9991 *Marenco, Maria R.* "Giustizia" e "Maestro di giustizia" nei testi di Qumran. RStB 14/1-2 (2002) 147-167.

9992 *Metso, Sarianna* Qumran community structure and terminology as theological statement. RdQ 20 (2002) 429-444.

9993 **Murphy, Catherine M.** Wealth in the Dead Sea scrolls and in the Qumran community. StTDJ 40: Lei 2002, Brill xxi; 672 pp. €150. 90-04-11934-5. Diss. Notre Dame [Bibl. 543-571].

9994 *Nakman, David* When were the 'daily prayers' (4Q503) said in Qumran?. Shnaton 13 (2002) 177-183. **H.**

9995 *Nitzan, Bilha* The idea of creation and its implications in Qumran literature. Creation in Jewish and christian tradition. JSOT.S 319: 2002 ⇒593. 240-264;

9996 The Dead Sea scrolls and the Jewish liturgy;

9997 *Schiffman, Lawrence H.* The Dead Sea scrolls and rabbinic Halakhah. Dead Sea scrolls as background. StTDJ 46: 2002 ⇒732. 195-219/3-24.

9998 **Swarup, Paul N.W.** An eternal planting, a house of holiness: the self-understanding of the Dead Sea scrolls community. ᴰ*Gordon, R. P.*: Diss. Cambridge 2002 [Sum. TynB 54,151-156].

9999 *Tassin, Claude* Qumrân: disparition et découvertes: un renouveau de la mémoire judéo-chrétienne. RICP 83 (2002) 33-49.

10000 *Young, Ian* The stabilization of the biblical text in the light of Qumran and Masada: a challenge for conventional Qumran chronology?. DSD 9 (2002) 364-390.

10001 *Zurli, Emanuela* La giustificazione "solo per grazia" in 1QS X,9-XI e 1QHa. RdQ 20 (2002) 445-477.

K4.1 **Sectae iam extra Qumran notae: Esseni, Zelotae**

10002 **Boccaccini, Gabriele** Beyond the Essene hypothesis: the parting of the ways between Qumran and Enochic Judaism. 1998 ⇒14,8607... 17,9227. [R]HeyJ 43 (2002) 90-92 (*McNamara, Martin*); JThS 53 (2002) 161-165 (*Hempel, Charlotte*); CV 44 (2002) 205-208 (*Segert, Stanislav*); ASEs 19 (2002) 503-506 (*Collins, John J.*).

10003 *Dillon, John* The Essenes in Greek sources: some reflections. Jews in ... cities. 2002 ⇒719. 117-128.

10004 *Grappe, Christian* L'apport de l'essénisme à la compréhension du christianisme naissant: une perspective historique. ETR 77 (2002) 517-536.

10005 *Philonenko, Marc* "Faire la vérité": contribution à l'étude du socio-lecte esséno-qumrânien. Jüdische Schriften. 2002 ⇒345. 251-257.

10006 *Shanks, Hershel* Searching for Essenes: at Ein Gedi, not Qumran. BArR 28/4 (2002) 18-27, 60.

K4.3 **Samaritani**

10007 **Anderson, Robert; Giles, Terry** The keepers: an introduction to the history and culture of the Samaritans. Peabody 2002, Hendrickson xvi; 165 pp. $30. 15656-35191 [BiTod 40,262—Senior, D.].

10008 *Baudy, Gerhard* Die brennende Terebinthe von Sichem: ein multi-kulturelles Epiphaniefest auf dem Garizim im Spiegel lokaler Land-verheißungsmythen und apokalyptischer Heilserwartungen;

10009 *Böhm, Martina* 'Und sie nahmen ihn nicht auf, weil sein Gesicht nach Jerusalem zu ging' (Lk 9,53): Samaritaner und Juden zwischen dem 4. Jh. v. und 1. Jh. n. Chr. HBO 34 (2002) 5-97/113-27.

10010 **Crown, Alan David** Samaritan scribes and manuscripts. TSAJ 80: 2001 ⇒17,9236. [R]Sal. 64 (2002) 568-569 (*Vicent, R.*).

10011 *Grabbe, Lester L.* Betwixt and between: the Samaritans in the Hasmonean period. Second temple studies III. JSOT.S 340: 2002 ⇒ 296. 202-217.

10012 **Hjelm, Ingrid** The Samaritans and early Judaism: a literary analysis. JSOT.S 303 ; Copenhagen International Seminar 7: 2000 ⇒16, 9450; 17,9240. [R]RSR 90 (2002) 425-427 (*Paul, André*).

10013 *Lehnardt, Andreas* The Samaritans (Kutim) in the Talmud Yerushalmi: constructs of 'rabbinnic mind' or reflections of social reality?. Talmud Yerushalmi, 3. TSAJ 93: 2002 ⇒767. 139-160.

10014 *Lerner, Berel Dov* Samaritans, Jews and philosophers. ET 113 (2002) 152-156.

10015 *Niessen, Friedrich* A Judaeo-Arabic fragment of a Samaritan chronicle from the Cairo geniza. JSSt 47 (2002) 215-236.

10016 *Pilch, John* Jesus and the Samaritans. BiTod 40 (2002) 172-177.

10017 **Pummer, Reinhard** Early christian authors on Samaritans and Samaritanism: texts, translations and commentary. TSAJ 92: Tü 2002, Mohr xiv; 518 pp. €129. 3-16-147831-2. Bibl. 445-477.

10018 *Stern, Ephraim; Magen, Yitzhak* Archaeological evidence for the first stage of the Samaritan temple on Mount Gerizim. IEJ 52 (2002) 49-57.

10019 *Van der Horst, Pieter W.* The Samaritan language in the pre-Islamic period. Japheth. CBET 32: 2002 <2001> ⇒251. 235-249;
10020 Samaritans at Rome. Japheth. CBET 32: 2002 ⇒251. 251-260.

K4.5 *Sadoqitae, Qaraitae–*Cairo Genizah; Zadokites, Karaites

10021 **Baker, F. Colin; Polliack, Meira** Arabic and Judaeo-Arabic manuscripts in the Cambridge Genizah Collections: Arabic Old Series (T-S Ar. 1a-54). CULGS 12: 2001 ⇒17,9244. [R]RStT 21/2 (2002) 82-84 (*Hughes, Aaron*).
10022 *Brin, Gershon* The issue of editing the scriptures according to Karaite exegetes. BetM 171 (2002) 305-321 Sum. 383. **H.**
10023 *Coulot, Claude* La nouvelle alliance au pays de Damas. Typologie biblique. LeDiv: 2002 ⇒341. 103-118.
10024 **Faü, Jean-François** Les Caraïtes. 2000 ⇒16,9471. [R]SR 30 (2002) 244-245 (*Lavoie, Jean-Jacques*).
10025 **Khan, Geoffrey** Early Karaite grammatical texts. SBL Masoretic studies 9: 2000 ⇒16,9475. [R]CBQ 64 (2002) 552-554 (*Greenspahn, Frederick E.*).
10026 *Lasker, Daniel J.* The Dead Sea scrolls in the historiography and self-image of contemporary Karaites. DSD 9 (2002) 281-294.
10027 *Reif, Stefan C.* The Cairo Genizah. Biblical world, 1. 2002 ⇒273. 287-304.
10028 **Reif, Stefan C.** A Jewish archive from Old Cairo: the history of Cambridge University's Genizah collection. 2000 ⇒16,9479; 17, 9256. [R]JSSt 47 (2002) 358-361 (*Shivtiel, Avihai*).
10029 [E]**Reif, Stefan C.** The Cambridge Genizah collections: their contents and significance. Genizah series 1: C 2002, CUP xiv, 241 pp. 0-521-81361-1. Assist. *Shulamit Reif.* Conf. Cambridge 1994.
10030 *Veltri, Giuseppe* Das *Mētra*-Motiv in den PGM und in den Fragmenten der Kairoer Geniza. Gegenwart der Tradition. 2002 <1996> ⇒255. 153-171.

K5 **Judaismus prior vel totus**

10031 **Anderson, Jeff S.** The internal diversification of second temple Judaism: an introduction to the second temple period. Lanham 2002, Univ. Pr. of America xii; 211 pp. 0-7618-23271. Bibl. 203-4.
10032 **Avemarie, Friedrich** Tora und Leben: Untersuchungen zur Heilsbedeutung der Tora in der frühen rabbinischen Literatur. TSAJ 55: 1996 ⇒12,8398...14,8638. [R]JQR 92 (2001) 258-260 (*Thoma, Clemens*).
10033 *Barclay, John* Apologetics in the Jewish diaspora. Jews in... cities 2002 ⇒719. 129-148.
10034 *Bar-Kochva, Bezalel* Everyone has his Gedaliahu Alon. JewSt 41 (2002) 95-106.
10035. **Bar-Kochva, Bezalel** PSEUDO-HECATAEUS: on the Jews: legitimizing the Jewish diaspora. Hellenistic Culture and Society 21: 1996 ⇒12,8400. [R]JAC 45 (2002) 203-206 (*Walter, Nikolaus*).
10036 **Basser, Herbert W.** Perush—Studies in exegesis: christian critiques of Jewish law and rabbinic responses 70-300 C.E. 2000 ⇒16, 9487. [R]VigChr 56 (2002) 319-321 (*Van der Horst, P.W.*).

10037 *Becking, Bob* Joods syncretisme in Elefantine?. NedThT 56/3 (2002) 216-232.

10038 *Berger, Paul-Richard* Rabbi JEHOSCHUA ben Chananja: Weltbürger zwischen babylonischer Astrologie und biblischer Theologie. ^FASCHOFF, D. 2002 ⇒3. 98-116.

10039 *Bergson, Steven M.* Internet resources for 'hot topics' in Judaica. JRTI 5/2 (2002) 33-41.

10040 **Bloch, René** Antike Vorstellungen vom Judentum: der Judenexkurs des TACITUS im Rahmen der griechisch-römischen Ethnographie. Stu 2002, Steiner 260 pp. €44. 3-515-07664-6.

10041 **Boccaccini, Gabriele** Roots of rabbinic Judaism: an intellectual history from Ezekiel to Daniel. GR 2002, Eerdmans xvii; 230 pp. $24/£17. 0-8028-4361-1. Bibl. 211-226. ^RJSJ 33 (2002) 320-322 (*Van Bekkum, Wout*); HebStud 43 (2002) 289-292 (*Kaminsky, Joel S.*); OTEs 15 (2002) 293-294 (*Venter, P.M.*); RBLit (2002)* (*Goff, Matthew*).

10042 *Bohak, Gideon* Ethnic continuity in the Jewish diaspora in antiquity. Jews in... cities 2002 ⇒719. 175-192.

10043 **Bohrmann, Monette** Valeurs du judaïsme du début de notre ère. 2000 ⇒16,9493. ^ROLZ 97 (2002) 87-88 (*Wächter, Ludwig*); Journal of Ancient History 242 (2002) 233-235 (*Lurie, V.M.*).

10044 *Breuer, Mordechai* Über die Bibelkritik. Jud. 58 (2002) 18-29.

10045 **Buxbaum, Yitzhak** Jewish tales of holy women. SF 2002, Jossey-Bass xxv; 301 pp. 0-7879-6271-6.

10046 **Castaldini, Alberto** L'ipotesi mimetica: contributo a una antropologia dell'ebraismo. 2001 ⇒17,9269. ^RRivista di scienze religiose 16 (2002) 499-500 (*Lorusso, Giacomo*); Studi, fatti, ricerche 101 (2002) 13-14 (*Menestrina, Giovanni*).

10047 **Chouraqui, André** Histoire du judaïsme. QSJ: P ¹³2002 <1957>, PUF 127 pp. [SR 32,365s—Diane Steigerwald].

10048 **Cohen, Shaye J.D.** The beginnings of Jewishness: boundaries, varieties, uncertainties. 1999 ⇒15,9473... 17,9271. ^RJQR 92 (2002) 594-597 (*Gruen, Erich S.*).

10049 *Cohn-Sherbok, Dan* Salvation in Jewish thought. Biblical world, 2. 2002 ⇒273. 287-316.

10050 *Cotton, Hannah M.* Jewish jurisdiction under Roman rule: prolegomena. Zwischen den Reichen. TANZ 36: 2002 ⇒568. 13-28.

10051 *Davies, Philip R.* The origin of evil in ancient Judaism. ABR 50 (2002) 43-54.

10052 *Dubin, Lois C.* Who's blessing whom?: transcendence, agency, and gender in Jewish prayer. CrossCur 52 (2002) 165-177.

10053 **Elliott, Mark Adam** The survivors of Israel: a reconsideration of the theology of pre-christian Judaism. 2000 ⇒16,9505; 17,9278. ^RThTo 59 (2002) 302, 304 (*Charlesworth, James H.*); CBQ 64 (2002) 572-573 (*Chartrand-Burke, Tony*); EvQ 74 (2002) 257-266 (*Gathercole, Simon J.*).

10054 *Elliott, Neil* The 'patience of the Jews': strategies of resistance and accommodation to imperial cultures. ^FROETZEL, C.: JSNT.S 221: 2002 ⇒104. 32-41.

10055 *Felder, Stephen* What is the fifth Sibylline Oracle?. JSJ 33 (2002) 363-385.

10056 *Fitzpatrick-McKinley, Anne* Synagogue communities in the Graeco-Roman cities. Jews in... cities 2002 ⇒719. 55-87.

10057 **Fonrobert, Charlotte Elisheva** Menstrual purity: rabbinic and christian reconstructions of biblical gender. 2000 ⇒16,9509. ᴿJJS 53 (2002) 172-173 (*Satlow, Michael L.*); TS 63 (2002) 843-844 (*Malina, Bruce J.*); JQR 92 (2002) 312-313 (*Levitt, Laura*).

10058 *Fossum, Jarl* Judaism at the turn of the era. Biblical world, 2. 2002 ⇒273. 125-136.

10059 *Freyne, Seán* Introduction: studying the Jewish diaspora in antiquity. Jews in... cities 2002 ⇒719. 1-5.

10060 **Gilbert, Martin** Letters to Auntie Fori: the 5000-year history of the Jewish people and their faith. L 2002, Weidenfeld xvii; (2) 460 pp. 0-297-60740-5. Bibl. 377-379.

10061 **Gruen, Erich S.** Diaspora: Jews amidst Greeks and Romans. CM 2002, Harvard Univ. Pr. ix; 386 pp. $40. 0-674-00750-6. ᴿEtCl 70 (2002) 294-295 (*Rochette, Br.*).

10062 **Hayes, Christine Elizabeth** Gentile impurities and Jewish identities: intermarriage and conversion from the Bible to the Talmud. Oxf 2002, OUP xiii; 309 pp. 0-19-515120-8. Bibl. 285-291.

10063 **Hezser, Catherine** Jewish literacy in Roman Palestine. TSAJ 81: 2001 ⇒17,9291. ᴿThLZ 127 (2002) 1174-1177 (*Avemarie, Friedrich*); Sal. 64 (2002) 656-657 (*Vicent, R.*); JBL 121 (2002) 559-562 (*Snyder, Harlow Gregory*).

10064 **Hoffman, Lawrence A.** The journey home: discovering the deep spritual wisdom of the Jewish tradition. Boston 2002, Beacon 233 pp. $25. 0-8070-3620-X.

10065 *Jaffé, Dan* Les 'mei-ha-areṣ durant la IIᵉ et le IIIᵉ siècle: état des sources et des recherches. REJ 161 (2002) 1-40 Rés., sum. 1.

10066· *Janzen, David* Politics, settlement, and temple community in Persian-period Yehud. CBQ 64 (2002) 490-510.

10067 **Kalimi, Isaac** Early Jewish exegesis and theological controversy: studies in scriptures in the shadow of internal and external controversies. Jewish and Christian Heritage 2: Assen 2002, Van Gorcum xvi; 209 pp. €59. 90-232-3713-7 [RB 110,156].

10068 ᴱ**Katsumata, Naoya** The liturgical poetry of NEHEMIAH ben Shelomoh ben Heiman HaNasi: a critical edition. Hebrew Language and Literature 2: Lei 2002, Brill (10) 325 pp. 90-04-12390-3.

10069 **Kieweler, Hans Volker** Erziehung zum guten Verhalten und zur rechten Frömmigkeit: die hiskianische Sammlung, ein hebräischer und ein griechischer Schultext. BEAT 49: 2001 ⇒17,9295. ᴿThZ 58 (2002) 366-367 (*Lauchsinger, Jürg*).

10070 *Kister, Menahem* From PHILOTAS to HILLEL: 'betrothal' contracts and their violation. SCI 21 (2002) 57-60.

10071 *Knauf, Ernst Axel* Elephantine und das vor-biblische Judentum. Religion und Religionskontakte. 2002 ⇒492. 179-188.

10072 *Kopciowski, Elia* Giustizia e misericordia secondo la voce dei profeti e dei maestri d'Israele. Studi Fatti Ricerche 99 (2002) 3-7.

10073 *Koskenniemi, Erkki* Greeks, Egyptians and Jews in the fragments of ARTAPANUS. JSPE 13 (2002) 17-31.

10074 *Kottsieper, Ingo* Die Religionspolitik der Achameniden und die Juden von Elephantine. Religion und Religionskontakte. 2002 ⇒492. 150-178.

10075 *Kugel, James L.* Biblical authority in Judaism: problems of an "aging text". L'autorité de l'Écriture. LeDiv: 2002 ⇒588. 139-151.

10076 **Lange, Nicholas de** An introduction to Judaism. 2000 ⇒16,9525; 17,9298. ᴿSal. 64 (2002) 382 (*Vicent, R.*).

10077 **Levine, Lee I.** Judaism and Hellenism in antiquity: conflict or con-
fluence?. 1998 ⇒14,8698...16,9528. ᴿTheoforum 33 (2002) 241-
242 (*Vogels, Walter*);

10078 The ancient synagogue: the first thousand years. 2000 ⇒16,9529;
17,9301. ᴿJJS 53 (2002) 161-162 (*Beall, Christopher*); TrinJ 23
(2002) 118-120 (*Schnabel, Eckhard J.*); Medieval Encounters 8
(2002) 228-235 (*Holum, Kenneth G.*).

10079 *Lichtenberger, Hermann* Einleitung. Jüdische Schriften. 2002
⇒345. 1-8.

10080 *Luke, K.* Ancient Jewish exegesis. ITS 39 (2002) 126-149.

10081 *Maier, Johann* Der monotheistische Anspruch in der rabbinisch-jü-
dischen Tradition. Polytheismus. AOAT 298: 2002 ⇒418. 137-74;

10082 Systeme ritueller Reinheit im Rahmen sozialer Bindungen und
Gruppenbildungen im Judentum des zweiten Tempels. Ethos und
Identität. 2002 ⇒490. 67-121.

10083 *McGing, Brian* Population and proselytism: how many Jews were
there in the ancient world?. Jews in... cities 2002 ⇒719. 88-106.

10084 *Miller, Robert D.* Popular, ideological, and textual dimensions of
postexilic Judean culture. EstB 60 (2002) 337-350.

10085 **Morrison, Martha A.; Brown, Stephen F.** Judaism. World Religions: NY ²2002 <1991>, Brown 144 pp. 0-8160-4766-9.

10086 **Murphy, Frederick James** Early Judaism: the exile to the time of
Jesus. Peabody, MASS 2002, Hendrickson xviii; 474 pp. $35. 1-
56563-087-4.

10087 *Müller, Stefanie* Living with the torah: a conversation with Rabbi
Beruriah. ᶠSCHOTTROFF, L. 2002 ⇒111. 9-17.

10088 **Neusner, J.; Chilton, B.** Jewish and christian doctrines: the classics compared. 1999 ⇒16,9934; 17,9677. ᴿJSSt 47 (2002) 363-365
(*Kessler, Edward*).

10089 **Neusner, Jacob** Judaism: an introduction. L 2002, Penguin vi; 307
pp. 0-141-00849-0. Bibl. 292-294;

10090 Three questions of formative Judaism: history, literature, and religion. Boston 2002, Brill xxii; 264 pp. 0391-0413-8X. Bibl. 233-64.

10091 ᴱ**Neusner, Jacob; Avery-Peck, Alan J.** Judaism in late antiquity,
3: Death, life-after-death, resurrection and the world-to-come in
the Judaisms of antiquity. HO 1/49,4: 2000 ⇒16,348; 17,337.
ᴿJBL 121 (2002) 164-168 (*Suter, David W.*).

10092 ᴱ**Neusner, Jacob; Avery-Peck, Alan J.; Green, William S.** The
encyclopaedia of judaism, 4: Suppl. 1. Lei 2002, Brill xix; 1594-
2029 pp. €129/$150. 90-04-12222-2.

10093 ᴱ**Neusner, Jacob** Dictionary of Judaism in the biblical period, 450
B.C.E. to 600 C.E. ᴱ*Green, William S.*: ²1999 <1996> ⇒15,9532...
17,9319. ᴿJThS 53 (2002) 175-176 (*Hayward, C.T.R.*).

10094 *Novak, David* The doctrine of creation and the idea of nature. Judaism and ecology. 2002 ⇒528. 155-175.

10095 *Otto, Eckart* Die Pharisäer: eine werkbiographische Interpretation
der gleichnamigen Studie Max WEBERs einschließlich des unveröf-
fentlichten SCHÜRER-Exzerptes. BSB Ana 446: ZAR 8 (2002) 1-
87.

10096 *Paul, André* Bulletin du judaïsme ancien (première partie). RSR 90
(2002) 423-460.

10097 **Pearl, Chaim** Theology in rabbinic stories. 1997 ⇒14,8715; 15,
9537. ᴿSBET 20 (2002) 126-127 (*Bond, Helen K.*).

10098 *Rajak, Tessa* Synagogue and community in the Graeco-Roman diaspora. Jews in... cities 2002 ⇒719. 22-38.

10099 **Rodríguez Carmona, A.** La religión judía: historia y teología. 2001 ⇒17,9329. ᴿComp 46 (2002) 303-304 (*Precede Lafuente, M.J.*); ActBib 38/1 (2002) 112-113 (*Boada, J.*).

10100· *Rosenberg, Shalom* Concepts of torah and nature in Jewish thought. Judaism and ecology. 2002 ⇒528. 189-225.

10101 *Runesson, Anders* Från integration till marginalisering: arkeologi som text i analysen av tidig diasporajudendom. SEÅ 67 (2002) 121-144.

10102 **Runesson, Anders** The origins of the synagogue: a socio-historical study. CB.NT 37: 2001 ⇒17,9330. ᴿSvTK 78 (2002) 188-189 (*Bilde, Per*); CBQ 64 (2002) 776-777 (*Hoppe, Leslie J.*).

10103 *Ruzer, Serge* From 'love your neighbour' to 'love your enemy': trajectories in early Jewish exegesis. RB 109 2002 371-389 [Lev 19, 18; Sir 27,33-28,9].

10104 *Salvesen, Alison* Early Jewish biblical interpretation. Biblical world, 1. 2002 ⇒273. 323-332.

10105 **Satlow, Michael L.** Jewish marriage in antiquity. 2001 ⇒17,9334. ᴿJRS 92 (2002) 207 (*Tropper, Amram*).

10106 **Schall, Ute** Die Juden im römischen Reich. Rg 2002, Pustet 365 pp. €29.90. 3-7917-1786-3 [EuA 78,343].

10107 **Schmidt, Francis** How the temple thinks: identity and social cohesion in ancient Judaism. ᵀ*Crowley, J. Edward*: BiSe 78: 2001 ⇒17, 9336. ᴿRBLit (2002)* (*Matthews, Victor H.*).

10108 ᴱ**Schoeps, Julius H.; Wallenborn, Hiltrud** Juden in Europa: ihre Geschichte in Quellen, 1: von den Anfängen bis zum späten Mittelalter. 2001 ⇒17,9337. ᴿHZ 274 (2002) 398-400 (*Botermann, Helga*).

10109 **Schwartz, Seth** Imperialism and Jewish society, 200 BCE to 640. CE 2001 ⇒17,9340. ᴿIHR 24 (2002) 864-865 (*Rives, J.B.*).

10110 *Stefani, Piero* Il perdono nella tradizione ebraica. Studi Fatti Ricerche 100 (2002) 3-6.

10111 *Stemberger, G.* Was there a 'mainstream Judaism' in the late second temple period?. Review of Rabbinic Judaism [Lei] 4 (2001) 189-208 [NTAb 47,533].

10112 **Stemberger, Günter** Einführung in die Judaistik. Mü 2002, Beck 207 pp. €18.90. 3-406-49333-5. Bibl. 189-199.

10113 *Stern, Sacha* Jewish calendar reckoning in the Graeco-Roman cities. Jews in... cities 2002 ⇒719. 107-116.

10114 *Swartz, Michael D.* Sacrifical themes in Jewish magic. Magic and ritual. RGRW 141: 2002 ⇒505. 303-315.

10115 *Van der Horst, Pieter W.* Celibato en el judaísmo antiguo. Sef. 62 (2002) 85-98;

10116 Celibacy in early Judaism. RB 109 (2002) 390-402;

10117 = Japheth. CBET 32: 2002 <2001> ⇒251. 191-201;

10118 Maria ALCHEMISTA, the first female Jewish author <2001>;

10119 Neglected Greek evidence for early Jewish liturgical prayer <1998>. Japheth. CBET 32: 2002 ⇒251. 203-205/37-54;

10120 Sortes: sacred books as instant oracles in late antiquity <1998>;

10121 Was the synagogue a place of sabbath worship before 70 CE? <1999>. Japheth. CBET 32: 2002 ⇒251. 159-189/55-82;

10122 Joden en hooligans in de late oudheid. NedThT 56/4 (2002) 273-9.

10123   **VanderKam, James C.** An introduction to early Judaism. 2000 ⇒
        16,9567; 17,9352. ᴿDSD 9 (2002) 132-134 (*Roo, Jacqueline C.R.
        de*); Anton. 77 (2002) 354-356 (*Volgger, David*); BASOR 326
        (2002) 98-100 (*Wright, Benjamin G.*); BiOr 59 (2002) 385-386
        (*Tromp, Johannes*); HebStud 43 (2002) 298-300 (*Wassen, Cecilia*);
        CBQ 64 (2002) 781-782 (*McLaren, James S.*); RRT 9 (2002) 35-
        37 (*Campbell, Jonathan*); OTEs 15 (2002) 298-300 (*Naudé, J.A.*).
10124   *Veltri, Giuseppe* Konzept des 'Glücks' im antiken Judentum. Ge-
        genwart der Tradition. 2002 <1994> ⇒255. 212-233.
10125   *Wenham, Gordon* Purity. Biblical world, 2. 2002 ⇒273. 378-394.
10126   *Willi, Thomas* 'Wie geschrieben steht'—Schriftbezug und Schrift:
        Überlegungen zur frühjüdischen Literaturwerdung im persischen
        Kontext. Religion und Religionskontakte. 2002 ⇒492. 257-277.
10127   *Wills, Lawrence M.* The Jewish novel. Biblical world, 1. 2002 ⇒
        273. 149-161.
10128   ᵀᴱ**Wills, Lawrence M.** Ancient Jewish novels: an anthology. Oxf
        2002, OUP x; 298 pp. £40.50/20. 0-19-515141-0/2-9.
10129   **Wire, Antoinette Clark** Holy lives, holy deaths: a close hearing of
        early Jewish storytellers. Studies in Biblical Literature 1: Atlanta
        2002, SBL x; 420 pp. $50. 1-58983-022-9.
10130   *Yamauchi, Edwin* The eastern Jewish diaspora under the Babyloni-
        ans. Mesopotamia and the bible. JSOT.S 341: 2002 ⇒458. 356-77.

к6.0 Mišna, *tosepta: Tannaim*

10131   ᴱ**Avery-Peck, Alan Jeffery; Neusner, Jacob** The Mishnah in con-
        temporary perspective. HO 1/65: Lei 2002, Brill xv; 270 pp. 90-04-
        12515-9.
10132   **Basser, Herbert W.** Studies in exegesis: christian critiques of Jew-
        ish law and rabbinic responses, 70-300 C.E. Lei 2002, Brill 148 pp.
10133   **Becker, Michael** Wunder und Wundertäter im frührabbinischen
        Judentum: Studien zum Phänomen und seiner Überlieferung im
        Horizont von Magie und Dämonismus. WUNT 2/144: Tü 2002,
        Mohr S. xviii; 534 pp. €74. 3-16-147666-2. Diss. München
        1999/20. Bibl. 443-492.
10134   ᴱ**Cohen, Shaye J.D.** The synoptic problem in rabbinic literature.
        BJSt 326: 2000 ⇒16,9578; 17,9362. ᴿJJS 53 (2002) 170-172
        (*Stern, Sacha*); JSJ 33 (2002) 324-325 (*Stemberger, Günter*).
10135   ᴱ**Di Segni, David Gianfranco** Mishnà: testo ebraico, introduzione,
        traduzione e note in italiano. R 1999-2002, Lamed. ᴿRasIsr 68/2
        (2002) 139-142 (*Guetta, Alessandro*).
10136   **Houtman, Alberdina** Mishnah and Tosefta: a synoptic comparison
        of the tractates Berakhot and Shebiit. TSAJ 59: 1996 ⇒12,8487...
        16,9583. ᴿASEs 19 (2002) 297-299 (*Pesce, Mauro*).
10137   *Kadari, Tamar* 'Within it was decked with love': the torah as the
        bride in tannaitic exegesis on Song of Songs. Tarbiz 71 (2002) 391-
        404 Sum. vii. H.
10138   **Krieg, Carola** Megilla: Text, textkritischer Apparat, Übersetzung
        und Kommentar des Toseftatraktats Megilla. ᴰ*Mayer, Günter*: 2002
        Diss. Mainz [ThRv 99/2,ix].
10139   **Lightstone, Jack N.** Mishnah and the social formation of the early
        rabbinic guild: a socio-rhetorical approach. Studies in Christianity

and Judaism 1: Waterloo, Ont. 2002, Wilfrid Laurier Univ. Pr. xi; 200 + 16 pp. $30.

10140 ᵀ**Mayer, Günter** Die Tosefta: Seder II: Moëd, 4: Taanijjot-Megilla. Rabbinische Texte, Reihe 1: Stu 2002, Kohlhammer 185 pp. 3-17-017592-0.

10141 *Noam, Vered* From textual criticism to historical reconstruction. Cathedra 104 (2002) 7-30 Sum. 189. **H.**

10142 **Samely, Alexander** Rabbinic interpretation of scripture in the mishnah. Oxf 2002, OUP xi; 481 pp. £55. 0-19-827031-3. Bibl. 436-456.

10143 **Schiff, Avraham** The relation between passages in the Tosefta Sukka and their parallels in the Mishna. ᴰ*Friedman, S.*: 2002, 265 pp. Diss. Bar Ilan [RTL 34,595].

10144 *Steinmetz, Devora* Distancing and bringing near: a new look at Mishnah Tractates 'Edyyot and 'Abot. HUCA 73 (2002) 49-96.

10145 *Sutter Rehmann, Luzia* The *agunah*, the bound wife: a transgressive woman in Jewish law and her significance for early christian communities. ᶠSCHOTTROFF, L. 2002 ⇒111. 67-76.

10146 *Tilly, Michael* Tosefta. TRE 33. 2002 ⇒799. 680-683.

10147 *Zellentin, Holger M.* Mishna. RGG 5. 2002 ⇒796. 1263-1266.

K6.5 Talmud; midraš

10148 **Agus, Aharon R.E.** Das Judentum in seiner Entstehung: Grundzüge rabbinisch-biblischer Religiosität. Judentum und Christentum 4: 2001 ⇒17,9381. ᴿStZ 220 (2002) 718-719 (*Oberforcher, Robert*).

10149 **Akenson, Donald Harman** Surpassing wonder: the invention of the bible and the talmuds. 1998 ⇒14,596...17,9382. ᴿSR 31 (2002) 109-110 (*Gaston, LLoyd*).

10150 **Albeck, Shalom** Introduction to Jewish law in talmudic times. 1999 ⇒15,9587; 17,9383. ᴿJQR 92 (2002) 280-285 (*Friedell, Steven F.*). **H.**

10151 *Amit, Aaron* The place of the Yemenite manuscripts in the transmission-history of b.Pesah1im. HUCA 73 (2002) *31-*77. **H.**

10152 *Baharier, Haim H.* Il Dio e il popolo che scaturiscono dalle scritture. Il libro sacro. 2002 ⇒356. 79-94 [Num 10,35-36].

10153 *Bar-Levav, Liora Elias* Talmudic redaction, transmission, and exegesis: the example of the columnar or creeping fire. Tarbiz 71 (2002) 371-389 Sum. vi. **H.**

10154 **Becker, Hans-Jürgen** Die grossen rabbinischen Sammelwerke Palästinas: zur literarischen Genese von Talmud Yerushalmi und Midrash Bereshit Rabba. TSAJ 70: 1999 ⇒15,9593... 17,9386. ᴿJQR 92 (2002) 521-567 (*Milikowsky, Chaim*).

10155 *Bohak, Gideon* The Hellenization of biblical history in rabbinic literature. The Talmud Yerushalmi, 3. TSAJ 93: 2002 ⇒767. 3-16.

10156 *Börner-Klein, Dagmar* Rabbinische Kommentare zu Genesis 6,2-7. Der Kommentar. 2002 ⇒472. 151-162.

10157 ᵀ**Börner-Klein, Dagmar; Hollender, Elisabeth** Rabbinische Kommentare zum Buch Ester: Band 1, der Traktat Megilla; Band 2, die Midraschim zu Ester. 2000 ⇒17,9600. ᴿJud 58 (2002) 52-53 (*Ego, Beate*); FJB 29 (2002) 157-162 (*Lehnardt, Andreas*).

10158   ^E**Börner-Klein, Dagmar** Tannaitische Midraschim: Übersetzung und Erklärung, 3 A: der Midrasch Sifre Zuta. Stu 2002, Kohlhammer 347 pp. €197. 3-17-017367-7. Neuausgabe.

10159   *Braiterman, Zachary* Elu ve-elu: textual difference and sublime judgement in *Eruvin* and Lyotard. Textual reasonings. 2002 ⇒ 2680. 206-213.

10160   *Breslauer, S. Daniel* Secrecy and magic, publicity and torah: unpacking a talmudic tale. Magic and ritual. RGRW 141: 2002 ⇒ 505. 263-282.

10161   **Buber, Martin** Die Geschichten des Rabbi NACHMAN. GTBS 1217: Gü 2002, Gü 127 pp. 3-579-01217-7.

10162   *Cohen, Aryeh* Response to 'Revelation revealed'. Textual reasonings. 2002 ⇒2680. 82-88 [Ex 20,15-18; Dt 5].

10163   *De Benedetti, Paolo* Gli idoli. PSV 46 (2002) 151-154.

10164   *Dohrmann, Natalie B.* Analogy, empire and political conflict in a rabbinic midrash. JJS 53 (2002) 273-297 [Ex 21].

10165   *Dov, Herman* The different approaches of the rabbis in Yavneh, Lod, and Galilee regarding the ninth of Av as reflected in the laws of the day. HUCA 73 (2002) *1-*29. **H.**

10166   **Egger, Peter** Verdienste vor Gott?:der Begriff der *zekhut* im arabischen Genesiskommentar *Bereshit Rabba*. NTOA 43: 2000 ⇒16, 9606; 17,9394. ^RCBQ 64 (2002) 157-158 (*Teugels, Lieve M.*).

10167   *Eliav, Yaron Z.* Realia, daily life, and the transmission of local stories during the talmudic period. ^FFOERSTER, G. 2002 ⇒39. 235-65.

10168   *Feldman, Louis H.* The plague of the first-born Egyptians in rabbinic tradition, PHILO, PSEUDO-PHILO, and JOSEPHUS. RB 109 (2002) 403-421 [Ex 11,5; 12,29].

10169· *Fishbane, Michael* Anthological midrash and cultural paideia: the case of *Songs Rabba* 1.2. Textual reasonings. 2002 ⇒2680. 32-51 [Cant 1,2].

10170   *Fontana, Raniero* Omaggio al talmud. Studi Fatti Ricerche 99 (2002) 9-13.

10171   *Fox, Harry* Biography, stories, tall tales: fishing for gullibility. JewSt 41 (2002) 105*-141*.

10172   *Fraade, Steven D.* 'The kisses of his mouth': intimacy and intermediacy as performative aspectrs of a midrash commentary. Textual reasonings. 2002 ⇒2680. 52-56 [Cant 1,2].

10173   *Gafni, Isaiah* Babylonian rabbinic culture. Cultures. 2002 ⇒448. 223-265.

10174   *Gafni, Yeshayahu* On Gedaliahu ALON and his role in the study of rabbinic historiography. JewSt 41 (2002) 75-83. **H.**

10175   *Gamoran, Hillel* How the rabbis interpreted Halakhah to meet the needs of the people: a study of mortgages during the period of the Rishonim. HUCA 73 (2002) 227-247.

10176   *Gibbs, Robert* Why talmud: renewing response;

10177   **Gibbs, Robert; Ochs, Peter** Gold and silver: philosophical talmud. Textual reasonings. 2002 ⇒2680. 113-118/90-102.

10178   *Gillman, Neil* Creation in the bible and in the liturgy. Judaism and ecology. 2002 ⇒528. 133-154.

10179   *Goldsmith, Simcha* The role of the Tanya Nami Hakhi Baraita. HUCA 73 (2002) 133-156.

10180   *Goodman, Lenn E.* Respect for nature in the Jewish tradition. Judaism and ecology. 2002 ⇒528. 227-259.

10181 **Goshen-Gottstein, Alon** The sinner and the amnesiac: the rabbinic invention of Elisha ben Abuya and Eleazar ben Arach. 2000 ⇒16, 9617; 17,9399. ᴿRBLit (2002)* (*Teugels, Lieve M.*).

10182 **Grohmann, Marianne** Aneignung der Schrift: Wege einer christlichen Rezeption jüdischer Hermeneutik. 2000 ⇒16,9618; 17,9400. ᴿThRv 98 (2002) 346-348 (*Stemberger, Günter*); ThR 67 (2002) 386-389 (*Dörrfuß, Ernst Michael*).

10183 ᴱᵀ**Guggenheimer, Heinrich W.** The Jerusalem Talmud: first order: Zeraïm: tractates Peah and Demay. SJ 19: 2000 ⇒16, 9619. ᴿThLZ 127 (2002) 1172-1174 (*Lehnardt, Andreas*); JAC 45 (2002) 209-211 (*Maier, Johann*);

10184 Zeraïm: Tractates Terumot and Ma'serot. SJ 21: B 2002, De Gruyter xii; 584 pp. €148. 3-11-017436-7;

10185 Zeraïm: tractates Kilaim and Seviit. SJ 147: 2001 ⇒17,9401. ᴿThLZ 127 (2002) 1172-1174 (*Lehnardt, Andreas*); JAC 45 (2002) 209-211 (*Maier, Johann*).

10186 *Haas, Peter J.* Where there is a rabbinic will there is an halachic way: authority and the rabbinic reading of scripture. ᶠPATTE, D. 2002 ⇒89. 184-193.

10187 *Haddad, Philippe* L'autre dans la tradition juive. Spiritus 168 (2002) 294-298.

10188 *Halivni, David Weiss* Response to 'Talmudic scholarship as textual reasoning'. Textual reasonings. 2002 ⇒2680. 144-151.

10189 *Hansberger, Therese* "Mose segnete Israel mit אשרי, und David segnete Israel mit אשרי (MTeh 1,2): Psalm 1 und der Psalter im rabbinischen Midrash zu den Psalmen (MTeh). BZ 46 (2002) 25-47.

10190 **Hedner Zetterholm, Karin** Portrait of a villain: Laban the Aramean in rabbinic literature. Interdisciplinary Studies in Ancient Culture and Religion 2: Lv 2002, Peeters x; 214 pp. €34. 90-429-1033-X. Bibl. 191-204 [Gen 24-31].

10191 *Hezser, Catherine* Einheit und Vielfalt in der rabbinischen Halakhah. Ethos und Identität. 2002 ⇒490. 149-163.

10192 *Isaacs, Ronald* Aaron. Legends of biblical heroes. 2002 ⇒334. 121-132:

10193 Abraham ⇒334. 29-39;
10194 David ⇒334. 155-162;
10195 Deborah ⇒334. 133-137;
10196 Esther ⇒334. 139-147;
10197 Isaac ⇒334. 51-59;
10198 Jacob ⇒334. 67-77;
10199 Joseph ⇒334. 93-102;
10200 Leah ⇒334. 87-92;
10201 Moses ⇒334. 103-119;
10202 Noah ⇒334. 19-27;
10203 Rachel ⇒334. 79-86;
10204 Rebekah ⇒334. 51-66;
10205 Ruth ⇒334. 149-154;
10206 Sarah ⇒334. 41-49;
10207 Solomon ⇒334. 163-169.

10208 *Kalimi, Isaac* ...und Josef verleumdete seine Brüder: Josefs Verrat in den Midraschim als Beitrag zur zeitgenössischen jüdisch-christlichen Kontroverse. ZRGG 54 (2002) 23-31;

10209   Die Bibel und die klassisch-jüdische Bibelauslegung: eine interpre-
        tations- und religionsgeschichtliche Studie. ZAW 114 (2002) 594-
        610;
10210   "He was born circumcised": some midrashic sources, their concept,
        roots and presumably historical context. ZNW 93 (2002) 1-12.
10211   *Kalmin, Richard* Jewish sources of the second temple period in rab-
        binic compilations of late antiquity. The Talmud Yerushalmi, 3.
        TSAJ 93: 2002 ⇒767. 17-53.
10212   ᵀ**Kapstein, Israel James; Braude, William Gordon** Pesikta de-
        Rab Kahana: R. Kahana's compilation of discourses for Sabbaths
        and festal days. Ph 2002, Jewish Publication Society of America
        795 pp. 0-8276-0679-6.
10213   *Kavka, Martin* Textual reasoning and cultural memory: a response
        ot Jacob Meskin. Textual reasonings. 2002 ⇒2680. 175-190.
10214   *Käppeli, Silvia* 'Alles ist ein Gleichnis': Verdeutlichungen der Tora
        durch rabbinische Gleichnisse. FrRu 9 (2002) 34-40.
10215   *Kepnes, Steven* Fishbane's commentary to *Song of Songs Rabba* as
        analytic textual reasoning. Textual reasonings. 2002 ⇒2680. 57-66
        [Cant 1,2].
10216   *Koch, Anne* Sühne oder Unversöhnlichkeit?: religionsphilosophi-
        sche Überlegungen zu einer Talmudlektüre von E. LEVINAS. MThZ
        53 (2002) 353-367.
10217   *Koet, Bart J.* "Sag lieber, dass er diesen Traum positiv deuten soll":
        über die Traumdeutung nach einem rabbinischen Traumbuch
        (Babylonischer Talmud Berachot 55-57). KuI 17 (2002) 133-149.
10218   *Kosman, Admiel* The story of a giant story: the winding way of Og
        king of Bashan in the Jewish haggadic tradition. HUCA 73 (2002)
        157-190 [Num 21,33-35; Dt 3].
10219   **Kosovski, Mosheh** Concordance to the Talmud Yerushalmi
        (Palestinian Talmud), volume eight. J 2002, Israel Acad. of
        Sciences and Humanities 739 pp. 965-208-009-9. **H.**
10220   *Lachs, Nicky* Isaac: a spychological perspective. JBQ 30 (2002)
        266-271.
10221   ᵀ**Lehnardt, Andreas** Rosh ha-Shana—Neujahr. Übersetzung des
        Talmud Yerushalmi 2/7: 2000 ⇒16,9632; 17,9408. ᴿSal. 64 (2002)
        143-144 (*Vicent, R.*).
10222   **Lehnardt, Andreas** Qaddish: Untersuchungen zur Entstehung und
        Rezeption eines rabbinischen Gebetes. TSAJ 87: Tü 2002, Mohr
        xiv; 386 pp. €89. 3-16-147723-5. Bibl. 321-354.
10223   **Lenhard, Doris** Die rabbinische Homilie: ein formanalytischer In-
        dex. FJS 10: 1998 ⇒14,8791. ᴿJJS 53 (2002) 371-379 (*Samely,
        Alexander*).
10224   *Levine, Nachman* Reading crowned letters and semiotic silences in
        Menachot 29b. JJS 53 (2002) 35-48;
10225   R. Elazar b. Arach: the "overflowing spring", the Emmaus hot
        spring, and intertextual irony. JSJ 33 (2002) 278-289.
10226   ᴱ**Lieber, Moshe M.; Scherman, Nosson** The Pirkei Avos treasury:
        ethics of the fathers; the sages' guide to living. Brooklyn, NY 2002,
        Mesorah 3 vols. 0-89906-641-0.
10227   *Magid, Shaul* Rabbis of gold and sages of silver: a response to
        'Philosophical talmud'. Textual reasonings. 2002 ⇒2680. 103-112.
10228   *Manns, Frédéric* Rabbinic literature as a historical source for the
        study of the gospels' background. LASBF 52 (2002) 217-246.

10229 *Martín Contreras, Elvira* Noticias masoréticas en el midrás *Lamentaciones Rabbâ.* Sef. 62 (2002) 125-141.

10230 **Martín Contreras, Elvira** La interpretación de la creación: técnicas exegéticas en 'Génesis Rabbah'. Biblioteca Midrásica 24: Estella 2002, Verbo Divino 244 pp.

10231 [ET]**Mello, A.** Commenti rabbinici allo Shema' Jisra'el. Spiritualità ebraica: Magnano 2002, Qiqajon 114 pp. €8. 88-8227-112-9 [Dt 6, 4-6].

10232 **Menirav, Joseph** The marking system in the Jewish community in Palestine during the Mishna and Talmud era. [D]*Rosefeld, B.-Z.*: 2002, 343 pp. Diss. Bar Ilan [RTL 34,595].

10233 *Menn, Esther Marie* Praying king and sanctuary of prayer, part II: David's deferment and the temple's dedication in rabbinic psalms commentary (midrash Tehillim). JJS 53 (2002) 298-323.

10234 *Meskin, Jacob* Textual reasoning, modernity and the limits of history. Textual reasonings. 2002 ⇒2680. 162-174.

10235 *Milgrom, Jacob* Florilegium: a midrash on 2 Samuel and Psalms 1-2. The Dead Sea scrolls: texts. 2002 ⇒9816. 248-263 [Dt 33,8-12; 33,20-21; 2 Sam 7,10-11; Ps 1,1; 2,1-2; Isa 8,11; 65,22-23; Ezek 37,23; Dan 11,32; Amos 9,11].

10236 *Milikowsky, Chaim* Seder olam as a first or second century composition. Shem. JSJ.S 74: 2002 ⇒755. 198-200.

10237 *Morfino, Mauro Maria* "Metti in pratica più de quello che hai studiato" (Pirqé Abot 6,4): alcuni tratti esistenziali caratteristici del maestro della parola nel trattato Pirqé Abot e nel Midrash Abot de Rabbi NATAN e in alcuni commenti posteriori. RivBib 50 (2002) 257-310;

10238 'Rimirala, invecchia e consumatici sopra!' (Pirqé Abot 5,24): il dono e lo studio della torah e le sue implicanze esistenziali in alcuni testi rabbinici. [F]POMPEDDA, M. 2002 ⇒90. 3-26 .

10239 *Morgenstern, Matthias; Schreiner, Stefan* Exegese für den Alltag: der Midrasch Teman: ein Kapitel Schriftauslegung aus dem Jemen. Jud. 58 (2002) 202-217.

10240 **Moscovitz, Leib** Talmudic reasoning: from casuistics to conceptualization. TSAJ 89: Tü 2002, Mohr S. xiii; 403 pp. €94. 3-16-1477-26-X. Bibl. 367-373.

10241 **Neudecker, Reinhard** The voice of God on Mount Sinai: rabbinic commentaries on Exodus 20:1 in the light of Sufi and Zen-Buddhist texts. SubBi 23: R 2002, E.P.I.B. xvi (2); 157 pp. €15. 88-7653-619-1. Bibl. 147-157. [R]AJBI 28 (2002) 87-94 (*Teshima, Isaiah*).

10242 *Neusner, Jacob* The formation of rabbinic Judaism: from the mishnah's philosophy to the talmud's religion. CV 44 (2002) 19-43.

10243 **Neusner, Jacob** The Halakhah: religious and historical perspectives. Brill Reference Library of Ancient Judaism 8: Lei 2002, Brill ix; 247 pp. 90-04-12219-2;

10244 Handbook of rabbinic theology: language, system, structure. Boston 2002, Brill xxii; 611 pp. 0-391-04139-8. Bibl. xxi-xxii;

10245 How the talmud works. Brill Reference Library of Ancient Judaism 9: Lei 2002, Brill xix; 240 pp. €139/$162. 90-04-12796-8 [RB 110, 314];

10246 Religion, comparisons, history, recent reviews. Lanham 2002, Univ. Pr. of America ix; 281 pp. 0-7618-2375-1;

10247 The halakhah and the aggadah: theological perspectives. 2001 ⇒ 17,9420. [R]RRT 9 (2002) 131-133 (*Gruber, Mayer I.*);

10248　The aggadic role in halakhic discourse. 2001 ⇒17,9421. [R]RRT 9 (2002) 37-44 (*Gruber, Mayer I.*);

10249　Dual discourse, single judaism: the category-formation of the hala-khah and the aggadah defined, compared, and contrasted. Studies in Ancient Judaism: 2001 ⇒17,9422. [R]RRT 9 (2002) 209-212 (*Gruber, Mayer I.*).

10250　*Noam, Vered* The miracle of the cruse of oil: questioning its use as a source for assessing the sages' attitude towards the Hasmoneans. Zion 67 (2002) 381-400. **H.**;

10251　The miracle of the cruse of oil: the metamorphosis of a legend. HUCA 73 (2002) 191-226;

10252　Beit Shammai and the sectarian Halakha. JewSt 41 (2002) 45-67. **H.**

10253　**Oberhänsli-Widmer, Gabrielle** Biblische Figuren in der rabbinischen Literatur: Gleichnisse und Bilder zu Adam, Noah und Abraham im Midrasch Bereschit Rabba. JudChr 17: 1998 ⇒14, 8803... 17,9423. [R]KuI 17 (2002) 105-106 (*Kirchberg, Julie*).

10254　*Ochs, Peter* Talmudic scholarship as textual reasoning: Halivni's pragmatic historiography. Textual reasonings. 2002 ⇒2680. 120-143.

10255　**Petuchowski, Jakob J.** Das große Buch der rabbinischen Weisheit: Geschichten der Meister. [E]*Petuchowski, Elizabeth*: 2001 ⇒17, 9425. [R]FrRu 9 (2002) 226-227 (*Franz-Klauser, Olivia*).

10256　*Pérez Fernández, Miguel* Tradiciones rabínicas en el Nuevo Testamento. EstB 60 (2002) 493-502.

10257　*Porten, Bezalel* The ideology of totality—frontality: the literary and contextual continuity from P'sukei d'Zimra through Aleinu. JJS 53 (2002) 324-338.

10258　*Raurell, Frederic* Jàfet, un grec a l'escola de Sem. RCatT 27/1 (2002) 1-21 Sum. 21 [Gen 9,27].

10259　*Reiss, Moshe* Ishmael, son of Abraham. JBQ 30 (2002) 253-256.

10260·　**Rosen, Jonathan** The talmud and the internet: a journey between worlds. NY 2000, Picador 144 pp. 0-31242017-X;

10261　Il talmud e internet: un viaggio tra mondi. [T]*Maglioni, S.*: T 2001, Einaudi 150 pp. 88-0615571-7. [R]Materia giudaica 7/1 (2002) 163-168 (*Capelli, Piero*).

10262　[T]**Rubenstein, Jeffrey L.** Rabbinic stories. Classics of Western Spirituality: Mahwah 2002, Paulist xxi; 315 pp. $40/25. 0-8091-05-33-0/4024-1 [ThD 49,387—Heiser, W. Charles].

10263　*Safrai, Chana* Abraham und Sara—Spender des Lebens. EvTh 62 (2002) 348-362.

　　　　[E]**Schäfer, P.** The Talmud Yerushalmi and Graeco-Roman culture, 3. 2002 ⇒767.

10264　*Seidel, Jonathan* Neocromatic praxis in the midrash on the seance at En Dor. Magic and divination. 2002 ⇒729. 97-106 [1 Sam 28].

10265　*Shalem, Avinoam* The Midrash Rabbah: evidence for the material culture of the Jews in Palestine in the pre- and early Islamic periods. ZDMG 152 (2002) 253-267.

10266　*Shanks Alexander, Elizabeth* Art, argument, and ambiguity in the talmud: conflicting conceptions of the evil impulse in b.Sukkah 51b-52a. HUCA 73 (2002) 97-132.

10267　*Singer, Aaron M.* And God sat "siva": biblical tracings of a midrashic text. TJT 18 (2002) 199-212 [Gen 6,5-7].

10268 *Sirat, René Samuel* Introduzione al *midrash*. Il libro sacro. 2002 ⇒ 356. 95-120.

10269 *Stemberger, Günter* Kinder lernen Tora: rabbinische Perspektiven. JBTh 17 (2002) 121-137;

10270 Einführung in die Tora: Pflichten eines Vaters aus Sicht der Rabbinen. ᶠHAAG, E. 2002 ⇒55. 299-317;

10271 Reaktionen auf die Tempelzerstörung in der rabbinischen Literatur. Zerstörungen. WUNT 147: 2002 ⇒559. 207-236.

10272 ᴱ**Sussmann, Yaacov** Talmud Yerushalmi: according to Ms. Or. 4720 (Scal. 3) of the Leiden University Library. 2001 ⇒17,9436. ᴿTarbiz 71 (2002) 569-603 (*Naeh, Shlomo*).

10273 *Sussmann, Ya'akov* The Yerushalmi in the literature of the Rishonim: 100 years after "Ahavat Zion ViYerushalaim". JewSt 41 (2002) 17-28. H.

10274 ᵀᴱ**Thoma, Clemens; Ernst, Hanspeter** Die Gleichnisse der Rabbinen, 4: vom Lied des Mose bis zum Bundesbuch: ShemR 23-30. 2000 ⇒16,9664. ᴿJud 58 (2002) 55-56 (*Eißler, Friedmann*).

10275 **Valler, Shulamit** Women and womanhood in the talmud. BJSt 321: Atlanta 1999, Scholars xx; 139 pp.

10276 *Veltri, Giuseppe* Greek loanwords in the Palestinian Talmud: some new suggestions. JSSt 47 (2002) 237-240;

10277· Platonische Mythen und rabbinische exegetische Entwicklungen. Gegenwart der Tradition. 2002 <1991/1992> ⇒255. 195-211;

10278 Zur jüdischen und christlichen Wertung der Aggada. Gegenwart der Tradition. 2002 <1995> ⇒255. 264-281.

10279 *Yadin, Azzan* Shnei Ketuvim and rabbinic intermediation. JSJ 33 (2002) 386-410.

10280 *Yuval, Israel J.* Rabbinical perspectives on the bearing of weapons by the Jews. JewSt 41 (2002) 51*-55*.

10281 *Zimmermann, Heidy* "... und Mirjam sang ihnen vor": die narrative Entfaltung einer biblischen Frauenfigur im Midrasch. KuI 17 (2002) 4-19.

K7.1 Judaismus mediaevalis, *generalia*

10282 *Amit, David; Stone, Michael E.* Report of the survey of a medieval Jewish cemetery in Eghegis, Vayots Dzor Region, Armenia. JJS 53 (2002) 66-106.

10283 **Breslauer, Richard I.** Weltgericht und Martyrium in der jüdischen Neujahrsliturgie: 'Heiligkeit des Tages' im Gebet Unetanneh Tokkef. Judaica et christiana 19: Bern 2002, Lang 241 pp. FS74/€51. 3-9067-6920-8. Diss. Hochschule Luzern.

10284 *Dodi, Amos* The vocalization of the Barcelona Haggadah. JJS 53 (2002) 339-353.

10285 *Elizur, Shulamit* Between Joseph and Joseph: the author of an early *yotser*. Tarb. 71 (2002) 67-86 Sum. vi. H.

10286 *Firestone, Reuven* Jewish culture in the formative period of Islam. Cultures. 2002 ⇒448. 267-302.

10287 *Gruber, Samuel* Archaeological remains of Ashkenazic Jewry in Europe: a new source of pride and history. ᶠFOERSTER, G. 2002 ⇒ 39. 267-301.

10288   *Hollender, Elisabeth* Hebräische Kommentare hebräischer liturgi-
scher Poesie: eine Taxonomie der wichtigsten Kommentarelemente.
Der Kommentar. 2002 ⇒472. 163-182.

10289   **Hyman, Arthur** Eschatological themes in medieval Jewish philosophy. The Aquinas Lecture 2002: Milwaukee, WI 2002, Marquette Univ. Pr. 135 pp. 0-87462-169-0.

10290   *Loewe, Raphael* A 13th-century *piyyut* set to French music. REJ
161 (2002) 83-96.

10291   *Magin, Christine* Armed Jews in legal sources from the high and
late middle ages. JewSt 41 (2002) 67*-81*.

10292   *Mentgen, Gerd* Alltagsgeschichte und Geschichte der Juden: die Juden und das Glücksspiel im Mittelalter. HZ 274 (2002) 25-60.

10293   **Romero, Elena** Andanzas y prodigios de Ben-Sirá: edición del
texto judeoespañol y traducción del texto hebreo. 2001 ⇒17,9459.
[R]Sef. 62 (2002) 442-444 (*Berenguer Amador, A.*).

10294   *Sáenz-Badillos, Ángel* El contacto intelectual de musulmanes y judíos: gramática y exégesis. Judíos y musulmanes. 2002 ⇒710. 29-
58.

10295   *Scheindlin, Raymond P.* Merchants and intellectuals, rabbis and
poets: Judeo-Arabic culture in the golden age of Islam. Cultures.
2002 ⇒448. 313-386.

10296   *Schwartz, Dov* Giosuè fermò veramente il sole?: aspetti della concezione del miracolo nella filosofia ebraica medievale. RasIsr 68/3
(2002 <1999>) 1-24 [Josh 10,12-14].

10297   *Ta-Shma, Israel* Prof. E.E. Urbach "Baalei Ha-Tosafot"—50 years
after its appearance. JewSt 41 (2002) 37-43. **H**.

10298   *Veltri, Giuseppe* Das Ordal der ehebruchsverdächtigen Frau im jüdischen Mittelalter <1993>;

10299   Mittelalterliche Nachahmung weisheitlicher Texte <1993/1994>.
Gegenwart der Tradition. 2002 ⇒255. 172-191/234-263.

10300   *Wenninger, Markus J.* Bearing and use of weapons by Jews in the
(late) middle ages. JewSt 41 (2002) 83*-92*.

K7.2 Maimonides

10301   *Bicknell, Jeanette* Self-scrutiny in Maimonides' ethical and religious thought. LTP 58 (2002) 531-543.

10302   **Diamond, James Arthur** Maimonides and the hermeneutics of
concealment: deciphering scripture and midrash in *The guide of the
perplexed.* SUNY Series in Jewish Philosophy: Albany 2002, State
Univ. of New York viii; 235 pp. $21. 0-7914-5247-6. [R]SR 31
(2002) 423-424 (*Lockshin, Martin I.*).

10303   *Hasselhoff, Görge K.* Maimonides in the Latin Middle Ages: an introductory survey. JSQ 9 (2002) 1-20;

10304   Anmerkungen zur Rezeption des Maimonides in den Schriften des
THOMAS von Aquino. Judentum und Christentum. Judentum und
Christentum 11: 2002 ⇒415. 55-73.

10305   **Hayoun, Maurice-Ruben** Maimonides: Arzt und Philosoph im
Mittelalter. [T]*Wildermann, Ansgar:* 1999 ⇒15,9701; 16,9708.
[R]ZRGG 54 (2002) 86-89 (*Hasselhoff, Görge K.*).

10306   **Lerner, Ralph** Maimonides' empire of light: popular enlightenment in an age of belief. 2000 ⇒16,9709. [R]JQR 92 (2002) 613-614
(*Kellner, Menachem*).

10307 *Lorberboim, Yair* 'The men of knowledge and the sages are drawn, as it were, toward this purpose by the divine will' (*The guide of the perplexe*d, introduction): on Maimonides' conception of parables. Tarb. 71 (2002) 87-132 Sum. vi. **H**.

10308 *Oberhänsli-Widmer, Gabrielle* Ist auch Hiob unter den Philosophen?: Maimonides' Interpretation des Hiob. KuI 17 (2002) 62-75.

10309 ᵀ**Powels-Niami, Sylvia** Moses Maimondies: der Brief in den Jemen: Texte zum Messias. B 2002, Parerga 117 pp. €15. 3-930-450-74-7. Vorwort *Friedrich Niewöhner*; Mitwirkung *Helen Thein* [Jud. 60,257—Stefan Schreiner].

10310 **Stern, Josef** Problems and parables of law: Maimonides and NAH-MANIDES on reasons for the commandments (Ta'amei Ha-Mitzvot). 1998 ⇒14,8836. ᴿSpec. 77 (2002) 250-251 (*Eisen, Robert*).

K7.3 Alteri magistri Judaismi mediaevalis

10311 **Davidovitz, Tmima** Menachem Ben SIMON's exegetic method according to his commentary to Ezekiel. ᴰ*Kasher, R.*: 2002, 380 pp. Diss. Bar Ilan [RTL 34,595].

10312 **Fenton, Paul** Philosophie et exégèse dans le Jardin de la métaphore de Moïse IBN 'EZRA. Lei 1997, Brill xiii; 459 pp.

10313 *Gómez-Aranda, Mariano; Ortega-Monasterio, María-Teresa* Critical editions of medieval biblical commentaries and masorahs: the cases of Abraham IBN EZRA and the masorah of Spanish manuscripts. Bible and computer. 2002 ⇒548. 231-243.

10314 *Halbertal, Moshe* NACHMANIDES' conception of death, sin, law and redemption. Tarb. 71 (2002) 133-162 Sum. vii. **H**.

10315 ᴱᵀ**Jiménez Patón, Lorenzo** Abraham IBN 'EZRA': Sefer moznayim: libro de la balanza. ᴱᴰ*Sáenz-Badillos, Ángel*: Autores Hebreos de Al-Andalus. Córdoba 2002, El Almendro 224 + 132* pp. €30. 84-8005-054-3. Diss.

10316 ᴱ**Linetsky, Michael** Rabbi SAADIA Gaon's commentary on the book of creation. Northvale, NJ 2002, Aronson xvi; 374 pp. 0-7657-6087-8 [Gen 1,1-27,47].

10317 ᵀ**Lockshin, Martin I.** RASHBAM's commentary on Leviticus and Numbers: an annotated translation. BJSt 330: 2001 ⇒17,9476. ᴿRBLit (2002)* (*Gruber, Mayer I.*).

10318 *Maori, Yeshayahu* The meaning of the term דברי יחיד in the commentary of IBN EZRA on the Torah: on Ibn Ezra's attitude towards rabbinic midrash. Shnaton 13 (2002) 201-246. **H**.

10319 **Sela, Solomon** Astrology and biblical exegesis in Abraham IBN-EZRA's thought. 1999 ⇒15,9715; 16,9722. ᴿREJ 161 (2002) 304-305 (*Rothschild, Jean-Pierre*); JQR 92 (2002) 579-580 (*Freudenthal, Gad*).

Stern, J. Problems... parables... NAHMANIDES 2002 ⇒10310.

10320 *Urvoy, Dominique* IBN ḪALDUN et la notion d'altération des textes bibliques. Judíos y musulmanes. 2002 ⇒710. 165-178.

10321 *Van Uchelen, N.A.* Where are the prophecies of olden times?: unrealized eschatology. ᶠLEENE, H. 2002 ⇒73. 237-241.

K7.4 *Qabbalâ, Zohar, Merkabā*—Jewish mysticism

10322 *Davila, James R.* Shamanic initiatory death and resurrection in the Hekhalot literature. Magic and ritual. 2002 ⇒505. 283-302.

10323 **Giller, Pinchas** Reading the Zohar: the sacred text of the kabbalah. 2001 ⇒17,9487. ᴿHebStud 43 (2002) 320-23 (*Bland, Kalman P.*).

10324 *Green, Arthur* A kabbalah for the environmental age. Judaism and ecology. 2002 ⇒528. 3-15.

10325 **Hallamish, Moshe** Kabbalah in liturgy, halakhah and customs. 2000 ⇒16,9733. ᴿREJ 161 (2002) 324-325 (*Rothschild, Jean-Pierre*).

10326 *Henry, Martin* The kabbalah, Paul Celan, and a view of redemption. IThQ 67 (2002) 152.

10327 **Idel, Moshe** Absorbing perfections: Kabbalah and interpretation. NHv 2002, Yale University Press xvii; 668 pp. 0-300-08379-3. Bibl. 619-645.

10328 **Laenen, J.H.** Jewish mysticism: an introduction. ᵀ*Orton, D.E.*: 2001 ⇒17,9494. ᴿThLZ 127 (2002) 1177-1179 (*Veltri, Giuseppe*).

10329 *Meroz, Ronit* 'And I was not there': the complaints of Rabbi SIME-ON Bar Yoḥai according to an unknown Zoharic story. Tarb. 71 (2002) 163-193 Sum. vii. **H.**

10330 **Morray-Jones, Christopher R.A.** A transparent illusion: the dangerous vision of water in Hekhalot mysticism: a source-critical and tradition-historical inquiry. JSJ.S 59: Lei 2002, Brill xiii;, 322 pp. €89/$104. 90-04-11337-1. Bibl. 290-305. ᴿJBL 121 (2002) 585-588 (*Davila, James R.*).

10331 **Shokek, Shimon** Kabbalah and the art of being: the Smithsonian lectures. ᴱ*Leavitt, Michael*: L 2001, Routledge xiii; 176 pp. $80/24. 0-415-24044-1/5-X.

10332 **Steinsaltz, A.** La rose aux treize pétales: introduction à la cabbale et au judaïsme. Spiritualités vivantes: P 2002, Michel 196 pp. €7. 2-226-13326-7 [NRTh 125,454s—Radermakers, J.].

10333 **Vajda, Georges** Le commentaire sur le "Livre de la création" de DUNAS ben Tamim de Kairouan (Xe siècle). ᴱ*Fenton, Paul B.*: Coll. REJ 24: Lv 2002, Peeters (8) 248 pp. 90-429-1092-5. Bibl. 187-200.

10334 **Vidas, Elijah ben Moses de** The beginning of wisdom. ᵀ*Benyosef, Simcha H.*: Hoboken, NJ 2002, KTAV lx; 458 pp. 0-88125-696-X.

10335 *Vollmer, Ulrich* Pico della MIRANDOLAs Deutung der Kabbala und die Verurteilung als Häresie. ᶠHOHEISEL, K.: 2002 ⇒59. 437-455.

10336 **Wexelman, David M.** Kabbalah: the Splendor of Judaism. North-vale, NJ 2000, Aronson xxvi; 258 pp. 0-7657-6108-4.

10337 *Wolfson, Elliot R.* Assaulting the border: kabbalistic traces in the margins of DERRIDA. JAAR 70 (2002) 475-514.

K7.5 **Judaismus saec. 14-18**

10338 ᴱ**Bar-Asher, Moshé** Le commentaire biblique: *Leshon limmudim* de Rabbi Raphaël BERDUGO, I-III. J 2001, Centre des langues, Univ. hebraïque 3 vols.

10339 *Bertrams, Oliver* Der "innere Jude" als "verbesserter Jude"?: Moses MENDELSSOHN und die rechtliche Stellung der Juden in der Sicht der Neologie. Judentum und Christentum. 2002 ⇒415. 117-143.

10340 *Burnett, Stephen G.* Johannes BUXTORF Westphalus und die Erforschung des Judentums in der Neuzeit. Jud. 58 (2002) 30-43.

10341 *Díaz-Mas, Paloma* Una edición crítica de la quiná sefardí de *La destrucción del Templo.* Sef. 62 (2002) 275-308.

10342· *Epelbaum, Dina* Die Wandmalereien im Haus 'Zum Brunnenhof', Zürich: ein Beispiel jüdischer Kunst aus dem 14. Jahrhundert im Spannungsfeld zwischen Adaption und Abgrenzung. Jud. 58 (2002) 261-280.

10343 *Facchini, Cristiana* Una insinuante modernità: note su LEONE Modena e l'ebraismo nel Seicento: rassegna bibliografica. ASEs 19 (2002) 467-497.

10344 *Gries, Zeev* A bibliographer and a librarian as an agent of culture: the contribution of Abraham YA'ARI to the study of Jewish print in eastern Europe. JewSt 41 (2002) 109-130. H.

10345 *Mark, Tzvi* On laughter and foolishness as the worship of God: reading "The story of the humble king" of R. NAHMAN of Bratslav. JewSt 41 (2002) 131-168. H.

10346 **Rauschenbach, Sina** Josef ALBO (um 1380-1444): jüdische Philosophie und christliche Kontroverstheologie in der frühen Neuzeit. Studies in European Judaism 3: Lei 2002, Brill xvii; 312 pp. 90-04-12485-3. Bibl. 289-304.

10347 ᴱ**Somekh, Alberto Moshe** Kal Le-Rosh: il Seder di Rosh haShanah secondo il Minhag della comunità di Cuneo: una testimonianza dell' antico rito provenzale da manoscritti. T 2002, Zamorani 33; xiii pp. €10. 88-7158-105-9.

10348 *Willi, Thomas; Willi-Plein, Ina* Das Christentum im Lichte der Tora—Jakob EMDENs Sendschreiben: theologische und philologische Beobachtungen zu einem unbekannten hebräischen Dokument der Lessingzeit. ᶠSMEND, R. 2002 ⇒113. 257-271.

K7.7 Hasidismus et Judaismus saeculi XIX

10349 **Benamozegh, Elia** L'origine dei dogmi cristiani. ᴱ*Morselli, Marco*: Genova 2002, Marietti xiv; 253 pp. €31.

10350 **Buber, Martin** The way of man: according to the teaching of Hasidism. Routledge classics: L 2002, Routledge xi; 33 pp. 0-415-27828-7. Introd. *Julia Neuberger*;

10351 Ten rungs: collected Hasidic sayings. ᵀ*Marx, Olga*: L 2002, Routledge 96 pp. 0-415-28268-3;

10352 The legend of the Baal-Shem. ᵀ*Friedman, M.*: L 2002, Routledge 223 pp. 0-415-28264-0.

10353 *Cohen, Richard I.* Urban visibility and biblical visions: Jewish culture in western and central Europe in the modern age. Cultures. 2002 ⇒448. 731-796.

10354 **Jacobs, Louis** La preghiera chassidica. ᵀ*Romagnoli, Gloria*: 2001 ⇒17,9508. ᴿCivCatt 153/3 (2002) 547-549 (*Prato, G.L.*).

10355 **Kajon, Irene** Il pensiero ebraico del novecento: una introduzione. R 2002, Donzelli viii; 228 pp. €18. 88-7989-736-5.

10356   *Liss, Hanna* Jewish bible scholars in the 19th and early 20th
        centuries and the debate on the Hebrew Bible. LexTQ 37/3 (2002)
        129-144 [BuBB 37,3].
10357   ᴱ**Magid, Shaul** God's voice from the void: old and new studies in
        Bratslav Hasidism. SUNY Judaica: Hermeneutics, Mysticism and
        Religion: Albany 2002, State University of New York Pr. xi; 298
        pp. 0-7914-5175-5.
10358   *Rabello, Alfredo Mordechai* Su alcune interpretazioni dei primi ca-
        pitoli di Genesi nel pensiero di Rav Elia BENAMOZEGH. RasIsr 68/3
        (2002) 25-57.
10359   *Vargon, Shmuel* LUZZATTO's attitude towards higher criticism of
        the Torah. Shnaton 13 (2002) 271-304. **H.**

к7.8 Judaismus contemporaneus

10360   *Albertini, Francesca* Die Dialektik Eros / Thanatos als phänomeno-
        logische Aufgeschlossenheit zum Anderen in Franz ROSENZWEIGS
        Der Stern der Erlösung.Jud. 58 (2002) 44-51.
10361   *Astell, Ann W.* Reading the bible with Holocaust survivors and res-
        cuers: a new biblical spirituality. Interp. 56 (2002) 181-191.
10362   *Banse, Holger* Il patto, Israele, i popoli: sfide pronunciate da Leo
        BAECK. Studi Fatti Ricerche 97, 98 (2002) 3-9, 3-8.
10363   *Belkin, Dmitrij* Ein Jude zwischen jüdischer und russischer Kultur:
        Anmerkungen zur Neuausgabe der Werke Michail GERŠENZONs.
        Jud. 58 (2002) 129-133.
10364   **Ben-Rafael, Eliezer** Jewish identities: fifty intellectuals answer
        BEN GURION. Lei 2002, Brill xxvi; 394 pp. 90-04-12535-3. Bibl.
        364-379.
10365   *Bloch, Rolf* Die jüdische Gemeinschaft der Schweiz und ihr Umfeld
        im Wandel der letzten Jahrzehnte. ᶠTHOMA, C.: JudChr 20: 2002
        ⇒119. 33-39.
10366   *Bollag, Michel* Einheit und Vielfalt des Judentums an der Schwelle
        zum 21. Jahrhundert. Ethos und Identität. 2002 ⇒490. 179-190.
10367   **Bonder, Nilton; Sorj, Bernardo** Judaísmo para o século XXI: o
        rabino e o sociólogo. Rio de Janeiro 2001, Zahar 111 pp.
10368   **Borowitz, Eugene B.** Studies in the meaning of Judaism. Ph 2002,
        Jewish Publication Society xvii; 473 pp. 0-8276-0721-0. Bibl. 443-
        465.
10369   **Cardozo, Nathan Lopes** Thoughts to ponder: daring observations
        about the Jewish tradition. NY 2002, Urim 198 pp. 965-7108-40-3.
        Bibl. 195-198.
10370   *Comeau, Geneviève* Un regard sur le statut du livre dans le juda-
        ïsme. LV(L) 255 (2002) 71-79.
10371   *Dober, Hans Martin* Die Religion bedarf der Ethik und die Ethik
        der Religion: zur philosophischen Bedeutung des jüdischen Ver-
        söhnungsgedankens bei Hermann COHEN. Jud. 58 (2002) 297-302.
10372   **Dresner, Samuel H.** HESCHEL, Hasidism and Halakha. NY 2002,
        Fordham University Pr. xiii; 133 pp. $35. 0-8232-2115-6. Bibl.
        125-130.
10373   *Dubois, Marcel* Ce qu'un chrétien peut attendre d'une lecture juive
        de la bible. SIDIC 35/2-3 (2002 <1977>) 39-41.
10374   **Ellis, Marc H.** Toward a Jewish theology of liberation. L 2002,
        SCM xiv; 146 pp. 0-334-02899-X. Bibl. 141-142.

10375 **Fackenheim, Emil L.** La presencia de Dios en la historia. S 2002, Sígueme 142 pp. ᴿCTom 129 (2002) 421-423 (*González Blanco, Rafael*).

10376 *Fiorato, Pierfrancesco* "Hier Hermann COHEN und dort Gritli": Bemerkungen über ROSENZWEIGs Verhältnis zu H. Cohen im Licht der "Gritli"-Briefe. Jud. 58 (2002) 93-105.

10377 **Fishbane, Michael** Haftarot: the traditional Hebrew text with the new JPS translation: commentary. JPS Bible commentary: Ph 2002, Jewish Publication Soc. xxxix; 593 pp. 0-8276-0691-5.

10378 **Fishman, Aryei** Judaism and collective life: self and community in the religious kibbutz. Routledge Studies in religion 1: L 2002, Routledge viii; 148 pp. 0-415-28966-1.

10379 *Frankel, Jonah* The study of the Ashkenazi Siddur: 200 years after the Heidenheim Siddur. JewSt 41 (2002) 29-36. H.

10380 *Green, Yosef* Universalism and/or particularism. JBQ 30 (2002) 3-9.

10381 *Greenberg, Gershon* The holocaust apocalypse of Yaʻakov Moshe Harlap. JewSt 41 (2002) 5*-14*.

10382 *Haussig, Hans-Michael* Judentum. Was ist der Sinn. GTBS 1170: 2002 ⇒438. 39-58.

10383 **Heilman, Samuel C.** The people of the book: drama, fellowship, & religion. New Brunswick, NJ 2002, Transaction xiv (2) 337 pp. 0-7658-0747-5. New preface by the author. Bibl. 323-332.

10384 **Hirsch, Ammiel; Reinman, Yosef** One people, two worlds: a reform rabbi and an orthodox rabbi explore the issues that divide them. NY 2002, Schocken xi; 322 pp. 0-8052-4191-4.

10385 ᴱ**Hoffman, Lawrence** My people's prayer book: traditional prayers, modern commentaries. Tachanun and concluding prayers 6: Woodstock, VT 2002, Jewish Lights vii; 214 pp. 1-879045-84-2.

10386 *Jacobson, Howard* Shoes and Jews. REJ 161 (2002) 233.

10387 *Katz, Stephen* To be as the others: E.E. Lisitzky's re-presentation of native-Americans. HUCA 73 (2002) 249-297.

10388 *Kessler, Colette* L'idée de révélation dans le judaïsme contemporain. LV(L) 255 (2002) 55-69.

10389 ᴱ**Knigge, Volkhard** Verbrechen erinnern: die Auseinandersetzung mit Holocaust und Völkermord. Neue Orientalische Bibliothek: Mü 2002, Beck xii; 446 pp. 3-406-48204-X.

10390 **Langton, Daniel R.** Claude MONTEFIORE: his life and thought. Parkes-Wiener series on Jewish studies: L 2002, Mitchell xii; 347 pp. 0-85303-369-2. Bibl. 325-337.

10391 **Lau, Benjamin** To return the crown to its former splendor: an examination of the halachic thought of Rav Ovadia JOSEF. ᴰ*Sperber, D.*: 2002, 369 pp. Diss. Bar Ilan [RTL 34,595].

10392 *Levenson, Jon D.* Response: natural and supernatural justice. Judaism and ecology. 2002 ⇒528. 177-185.

10393 ᴱ**Lieber, Moshe M.** The Torah treasury: an anthology of insights, commentary and anecdotes on the weekly Torah readings. ᴱ*Scherman, Nosson*: The Artscroll Mesorah Series: Brooklyn, NY 2002, Mesorah (16) 560 pp. 0-57819-720-1.

10394 *Luzzatto, Amos* L'ebraismo in Italia : intervista a un protagonista: Amos Luzzatto. Ambrosius 78/4 (2002) 733-737.

10395 *Mendels, Doron* The Graeco-Roman background in Gedaliahu Alon's scholarship. JewSt 41 (2002) 85-94. H.

10396   **Moreen, Vera Basch** In Queen Esther's garden: an anthology of Judeo-Persian literature. YJS 30: 2000 ⇒16,9799. [R]RBLit 4 (2002) 260-261 (*Garber, Zev*).

10397   *Morgenstern, Matthias* Die Bibel im zeitgenössischen hebräischen Theater: Formen des "nicht-religiösen" Umgangs mit theologischen Motiven und Begriffen im zeitgenössischen Judentum. BThZ 19 (2002) 125-141.

10398   [E]**Neuhaus, Richard John** The chosen people in an almost chosen nation: Jews and Judaism in America. GR 2002, Eerdmans xii; 218 pp. 0-8028-4929-6.

10399   **Neusner, Jacob** Talmud Torah: ways to God's presence through learning: an exercise in practical theology. Studies in Ancient Judaism: Lanham 2002, University Press of America xiii; 127 pp. 0-76-18-2176-7.

[E]**Ochs, P.** Textual reasonings 2002 ⇒2680.

10400   *Oldenhage, Tania* Reading the cross at Auschwitz: Holocaust memories and passion narratives. A shadow of glory. 2002 ⇒347. 140-154.

10401·   **Ouaknin, Marc-Alain; Rotnemer, Dory** Mein Rabbi ist der Beste!: jüdischer Humor. GTBS 1215: Gü 2002, Gü 95 pp. 3-579-01-215-0.

10402   **Parfitt, Tudor; Semi, Emanuela Trevisan** Judaising movements: studies in the margins of Judaism. L 2002, RoutledgeCurzon xv; 159 pp. £45. SOAS Centre for Near and Middle East Studies.

10403   *Peskowitz, Miriam* A letter to Elizabeth. CrossCur 51 (2002) 489-494.

10404   *Plietzsch, Susanne* Das Böse ist außer Kontrolle. KuI 17 (2002) 115-132.

10405   *Rashkover, Randi* Exegesis, redemption and the maculate torah. Textual reasonings. 2002 ⇒2680. 191-205.

10406   *Rivlin, Yosef* A unique introductory formula in the Jewish bill. HUCA 73 (2002) *79-*96. **H**.

10407   **Romm, Diane** The Jewish guide to the internet. Northvale, NJ 2002, Aronson xvi; 359 pp. 0-7657-6187-4.

10408   **Rosenzweig, Franz** On Jewish learning. [E]*Glatzer, Nahum Norbert*: Modern Jewish philosophy and religion. Madison, WI 2002, Univ. of Wisconsin Pr. 128 pp. 0-299-18234-7.

10409   **Rutishauser, Christian Michael** Halachische Existenz: philosophisch-theologische Deutung des jüdisch-orthodoxen Daseinsvollzugs in den Schriften von Josef Dov Halevi SOLOVEITCHIK (1903-1993). [D]*Thoma, Clemens*: 2002 Diss. Lucerne [RTL 34,595].

10410·   **Sacks, Jonathan** The dignity of difference: how to avoid the clash of civilizations. L 2002, Continuum 216 pp. £9.50. 0-826-41443-5.

10411   **Sadun, Manuela Paggi** Dialogo guarigione del mondo: sorgenti ebraiche. Bo 2002, Missionaria Italiana 156 pp. Pres. di *Brunetto Salvarani* [Studi Fatti Ricerche 99,14—Paolo De Benedetti].

10412   *Safrai, Shmuel* Gedaliahu Alon the teacher. JewSt 41 (2002) 71-73. **H**.

10413   *Samuelson, Norbert M.* "Revenge and forgiveness in Jewish virtue ethics". [F]THOMA, C.: JudChr 20: 2002 ⇒119. 229-244.

10414   *Schäfer, Peter* The triumph of pure spirituality: Sigmund FREUD's *Moses and monotheism*. JSQ 9 (2002) 381-406.

10415 **Scholem, Gershom Gerhard** A life in letters, 1914-1982. ETSkinner, *Anthony David*: CM 2002, Harvard University Pr. vii; (4) 547 pp. 0-674-00642-9. Bibl. 533-534.

10416 **Solomon, Lewis D.** The Jewish tradition, sexuality and procreation. Lanham 2002, Univ. Pr. of America (12); 235 pp. 0-7618-22-27-5. Bibl. 225.

10417 **Viorst, Milton** What shall I do with this people?: Jews and the fractious politics of Judaism. NY 2002, The Free Press (14) 287 pp. 0-684-86289-1. Bibl. 265-272.

10418 *Weingarten, Ralph* Schweizerische Gesellschaft für Judaistische Forschung (SGJF): Société Suisse des Etudes Juives (SSEJ): Jahresbericht. Bulletin der Schweizerischen Gesellschaft für Judaistische Forschung 11 (2002) 1-2.

10419 *Wojnowska, Bozena* Nahe Begegnungen: KORCAK, BUBER, MICKIEWICZ. Jud. 58 (2002) 82-92.

10420 *Yudkin, Leon I.* Hebrew, Yiddish and other modern Jewish literatures. JJS 53 (2002) 152-156.

10421 **Zimet, Ben** Cuentos del pueblo judío. S 2002, Sígueme 222 pp. €12.20 [Proyección 50,183—Sicre, J.L.].

10422 *Zimmermann, Moshe* Das neue Judentum zwischen Nation und Shoah. Judentum und Christentum. 2002 ⇒415. 197-210.

10423 *Zoloth, Laurie* Seeing the doubting judge: Jewish ethics and the postmodern project. Textual reasonings. 2002 ⇒2680. 214-228.

K8 *Philosemitismus*—Jewish Christian relations

10424 *Aerne, Peter* "Wehe der Christenheit ..., Wehe der Judenschaft ...": der Weihnachtsbrief an die Juden in der Schweiz von 1942 (Teil 1). Jud. 58 (2002) 234-260.

10425 *Altermatt, Urs* Die Hochhuth-Debatte in der katholischen Schweiz 1963. FTHOMA, C.: JudChr 20: 2002 ⇒119. 19-32.

10426 *Assel, Heinrich* Worüber man (noch) nicht reden kann: die Grenze jüdischer und christlicher Gottesrede und die Aporie ihrer theopolitischen Verwandtschaft. Judentum und Christentum. 2002 ⇒415. 181-195.

10427 *Aulisa, Immacolata* La polemica antiguidaica agli inizi del V secolo in due scritti anonimi. VetChr 39 (2002) 69-100.

10428 *Bachmann, Michael* Zur Entstehung (und zur Überwindung) des christlichen Antijudaismus. ZNT 10 (2002) 44-52.

10429 *Banse, Holger* Chiesa e Israele: un contributo delle chiese d'Europa della riforma al rapporto tra cristiani ed ebrei. Studi Fatti Ricerche 97 (2002) 9.

10430 **Beckmann, Klaus** Die fremde Wurzel: Altes Testament und Judentum in der evangelischen Theologie des 19. Jahrhunderts. FKDG 85: Gö 2002, Vandenhoeck & R. 400 pp. €64. 3-525-55193-2.

10431 EBellis, Alice Ogden; Kaminsky, Joel S. Jews, christians, and the theology of Hebrew scriptures. SBL Symposium 8: 2000 ⇒16,237; 17,9588. RBiblInterp 10 (2002) 212-215 (*Mendenhall, George E.*); RBLit 4 (2002) 148-151 (*Moore, Michael S.*).

10432 **Ben-Chorin, Schalom** Ein Leben für den Dialog. EHomolka, Walter: 1999 ⇒15,9802. RZMR 86 (2002) 67 (*Kreiml, Josef*).

10433 *Bergler, Siegfried* Von Hillel zu Jesus: jüdische und christliche Hillel-Bilder. FASCHOFF, D. 2002 ⇒3. 12-35.

10434   **Bergmann, Werner** Geschichte des Antisemitismus. Mü 2002,
         Beck 143 pp. €7.90.
10435   **Blanchetière, François** Enquête sur les racines juives du mouve-
         ment chrétien (30-135). 2001 ⇒17,9592. [R]RSPhTh 86 (2002) 127-
         129 (*Cerbelaud, Dominique*); REJ 161 (2002) 294-295 (*Maraval,
         Pierre*); Brot. 155 (2002) 521-522 (*Silva, I. Ribeiro da*); RThom
         102 (2002) 663-669 (*Grelot, Pierre*); EeV 53 (2002) 15-18
         (*Rastoin, Cécile*); LTP 58 (2002) 371-373 (*Côté, Dominique*).
10436   *Blet, Pierre* Pio XII, il Terzo "Reich" e gli ebrei. CivCatt 153/3
         (2002) 117-131.
10437   *Bohlen, Reinhold* Zum Stand des christlich-jüdischen Dialogs in
         Deutschland. TThZ 111 (2002) 169-175.
10438   **Boyarin, Daniel** Dying for God: martyrdom and the making of
         christianity and Judaism. 1999 ⇒15,9806…17,9597. [R]ChH 71
         (2002) 865-867 (*Burns, J. Patout*); HR 42 (2002) 175-180 (*Droge,
         A.J.*); JQR 92 (2002) 586-588 (*Goldenberg, Robert*).
10439   **Boys, Mary C.** Has God only one blessing?:Judaism as a source
         for christian self-understanding. 2000 ⇒16,9832; 17,9598. [R]JThS
         53 (2002) 307-309 (*Kessler, Edward*); RSPhTh 86 (2002) 132-134
         (*Cerbelaud, Dominique*); Horizons 29 (2002) 164-166 (*Sloyan,
         Gerard S.*); MoTh 18/1 (2002) 417-419 (*Bader-Saye, Scott*); RStT
         20/2 (2002) 87-91 (*Oosterhuis, Tom*); IThQ 66 (2002) 393-394
         (*Niland, Carmel*).
10440   *Brasser, Martin* Der Ton macht das Gespräch: zu Franz ROSEN-
         ZWEIGs Bestimmung des Christentums im Stern der Erlösung.
         [F]THOMA, C.: JudChr 20: 2002 ⇒119. 41-53.
10441   *Breuning, Wilhelm* Die Juden—unsere älteren Geschwister im
         Bund Gottes. FrRu 9 (2002) 95-105.
10442   *Brocke, Edna* Dreißig Jahre in Folge: Erfahrungen einer Jüdin bei
         Kirchentagen. KuI 17 (2002) 86-100.
10443   *Brueggemann, Walter* Signification et exigences de la Déclaration
         Dabru emet pour les chrétiens. Ist. 47 (2002) 284-286.
10444   **Cabaud, Judith** Il rabbino che si arrese a Cristo: la storia di Euge-
         nio ZOLLI, rabbino capo a Roma durante la seconda guerra mondia-
         le. Attualità e Storia 31: CinB 2002, San Paolo 120 pp. 88-215-46-
         29-2. Pref. *Vittorio Messori*.
10445   **Caron, Gérald** L'antisémitisme chrétien: un défi pour les églises.
         Sciences bibliques, études 12: Montréal 2002, Médiaspaul 309 pp.
         CAN$28. 2-89420-519-8 [NRTh 125,449—Radermakers, J.].
10446   *Cerbelaud, Dominique* Bulletin d'études juives et judéo-chréti-
         ennes: judéo-christianisme antique dialogue judéo-chrétien actuel.
         RSPhTh 86 (2002) 123-144.
10447   **Chalier, Catherine; Faessler, Marc** Judaïsme et christianisme:
         l'écoute en partage. Patrimoines: 2001 ⇒17,9606. [R]RSPhTh 86
         (2002) 142-143 (*Cerbelaud, Dominique*); SIDIC 35/2-3 (2002) 58-
         59 (*Derousseaux, Louis*); ETR 77 (2002) 608-609 (*Causse, Jean-
         Daniel*).
10448   **Chilton, Bruce; Neusner, Jacob** Comparing spiritualities. 2000 ⇒
         16,9838. [R]AThR 84 (2002) 1020-1022 (*Radner, Ephraim*).
10449   **Cohen, Jeremy** Living letters of the law: ideas of the Jew in medi-
         eval christianity. 1999 ⇒15,9816. [R]JAAR 70 (2002) 406-409
         (*Chazan, Robert*).

10450 **Cunningham, Philip A.** A story of shalom: the calling of Christians and Jews by a covenanting God. 2001 ⇒17,9616. ᴿRRT 9 (2002) 177-178 (*Scholefield, Lynne*); DoLi 52 (2002) 254-255 (*Troy, Mary*); Pacifica 15 (2002) 344-346 (*Watson, Patricia*).

10451 *Detmers, Achim* Vom "Judaismus" zum "Antijudaismus": Anmerkungen zum Verhältnis von Christen und Juden in der Reformationszeit. Judentum und Christentum. 2002 ⇒415. 75-95.

10452 ᴱ**Dietrich, Walter** Antijudaismus—christliche Erblast. 1999 ⇒15, 349. ᴿFrRu 9 (2002) 214-215 (*Maisch, Ingrid*); ZKG 113 (2002) 91-93 (*Bitter, Stephan*).

10453 **Doukhan, Jacques B.** Israel and the church: two voices for the same God. Peabody, MASS 2002, Hendrickson x; 108 pp. 1-5656-3-616-3.

10454 *Eisenbaum, Pamela* The christian canon and the problem of antisemitism. A shadow of glory. 2002 ⇒347. 3-17.

10455˙ *Frankemölle, Hubert* Die Bedeutung der Christologie im christlich-jüdischen Dialog: bibeltheologische und (päpstliche) Impulse. Diak. 33 (2002) 105-113.

10456 ᴱ**Frankemölle, Hubert** Christen und Juden gemeinsam ins dritte Jahrtausend: das Geheimnis der Erlösung heißt Erinnerung. 2000 ⇒16,362; 17,352. ᴿFrRu 9 (2002) 59 (*Thouet, Julian*).

10457 *Frassetto, Michael* Heretics and Jews in the writings of ADEMAR of Chabannes and the origins of medieval anti-semitism. ChH 71 (2002) 1-15.

10458 *Fredriksen, Paula* The birth of christianity and the origins of christian anti-Judaism. Jesus, Judaism. 2002 ⇒308. 8-30.

10459 *Friedrich, Martin* Jesus Christus zwischen Juden und Heiden: das Christusbild in der Germanenmission dargestellt am "Heliand". ZKG 113 (2002) 313-328.

10460 ᴱ**Frymer-Kensky, Tikva Simone; Novak, David** Christianity in Jewish terms. 2000 ⇒16,9859. ᴿOiC 37 (2002) 96-99 (*Gorsky, Jonathan*).

10461 **Gadecki, Stanislaw** Kto spotyka Jezusa, spotyka judaizm: dialog chrzescijansko-zydowski w Polsce [Qui rencontre Jésus rencontre le judaïsme: le dialogue judéo-chrétien en Pologne]. Gniezno 2002, Prymasowskie Wydawnictwo Gaudentinum 254 pp. 838-7965-752.

10462 **Gardenal, Gianna** L'antigiudaismo nella letteratura cristiana antica e medievale. Shalom 2001 ⇒17,9634. ᴿOecumenica Civitas 2/1 (2002) 125-127 (*Barile, Nino*); Materia giudaica 7/1 (2002) 193-196 (*Troiani, Lucio*).

10463 *Garder, Zev* Tora et témoignage: échange au niveau de l'étude de textes. SIDIC 34/3-35/1 (2002) 32-38.

10464 *George, Mark K.* Shoah consciousness and the silence of American christian biblical scholarship. A shadow of glory. 2002 ⇒347. 42-54.

10465 **Giniewski, Paul** L'antijudaïsme chrétien: la mutation. 2000 ⇒16, 9863. ᴿRSPhTh 86 (2002) 139-140 (*Cerbelaud, Dominique*).

10466 **González Salinero, Raúl** El antijudaísmo cristiano occidental (siglos IV y V). 2000 ⇒16,9866. ᴿSef. 62 (2002) 208-210 (*Torallas Tovar, S.*).

10467 *Goshen-Gottstein, Alon* Judaisms and incarnational theologies: mapping out the parameters of dialogue. JES 39 (2002) 219-247.

10468 *Grappe, Christian* Antijudaïsme et Nouveau Testament. PosLuth 50/2 (2002) 103-119.

10469   **Greenberg, I.** La nuée et le feu—le judaïsme, le christianisme et la
        modernité après l'Holocauste. 2000 ⇒16,9868. ᴿRSPhTh 86
        (2002) 140-141 (*Cerbelaud, Dominique*).
10470   *Haacker, Klaus* Der Holocaust als Datum der Theologiegeschichte.
        Versöhnung mit Israel. VKHW 5: 2002 <1986> ⇒174. 11-20;
10471   Elemente des heidnischen Antijudaismus im Neuen Testament.
        Versöhnung mit Israel. VKHW 5: 2002 <1988> ⇒174. 153-169;
10472   Feindesliebe kontra Nächstenliebe?: Bemerkungen zu einer ver-
        breiteten Gegenüberstellung von Christentum und Judentum. Ver-
        söhnung mit Israel. VKHW 5: 2002 <1992> ⇒174. 23-27;
10473   Umkehr zu Israel und "Heimholung ins Judentum": Schritte zur
        Versöhnung zwischen Christen und Juden. Versöhnung mit Israel.
        VKHW 5: 2002 <2000> ⇒174. 191-208.
10474   *Halpérin, Jean* Le dialogue comme pédagogie. ꟳTHOMA, C.:
        JudChr 20: 2002 ⇒119. 65-71.
10475   *Haynes, Stephen R.* Who needs enemies?: Jews and Judaism in
        anti-Nazi religious discourse. ChH 71 (2002) 341-367.
10476   *Hecquet-Noti, Nicole* Le corbeau nécrophage, figure du juif, dans le
        De diluuio mundi d'Aᴠɪᴛ de Vienne: à propos de l'interprétation de
        Gn 8,6-7 dans carm. 4,544-584. REAug 48 (2002) 297-320.
10477   *Heep, Stefan* Der Nationalsozialismus—eine jüdisch-christliche
        Häresie?. ꟳHOHEISEL, K.: JAC.E 34: 2002 ⇒59. 487-510.
10478   *Heilbronner, Oded* Vom protestantischen Antisemitismus zum pro-
        testantischen Fundamentalismus: Antisemiten und Antisemitismus
        in Deutschland und Palästina vom späten 19. Jahrhundert bis in die
        frühen 1940er Jahre. Judentum und Christentum. 2002 ⇒415. 145-
        164.
10479   *Henrix, Hans Hermann* Krisenerprobt und doch störanfällig: das
        aktuelle jüdisch-christliche Verhältnis. HerKorr 56 (2002) 336-342;
10480   Christliches Plus in der Nächstenliebe?: zum rabbinischen und phi-
        losophischen Verständnis der Hauptsache der Tora. ꟳTHOMA, C.:
        JudChr 20: 2002 ⇒119. 73-89.
10481   ᴱ**Henrix, Hans Hermann; Kraus, Wolfgang** Die Kirchen und das
        Judentum, 2: Dokumente von 1986 bis 2000. 2001 ⇒17,9643.
        ᴿBiLi 75 (2002) 209-211 (*Schubert, Kurt*).
10482   *Heschel, Susannah* Reading Jesus as a Nazi. A shadow of glory.
        2002 ⇒347. 27-41.
10483   *Hubmann, Franz* "Im Angesicht der Synagoge ...". ꟳAICHERN, M.:
        2002 ⇒2. 111-129.
10484   **Huguet, Marie-Thérèse** Un peuple unique pour le Dieu unique:
        'Israël'. 2001 ⇒17,9648. ᴿRSPhTh 86 (2002) 134-137 (*Cerbelaud,
        Dominique*).
10485   **Israël, Gérard** La question chrétienne—une pensée juive du chri-
        stianisme. 1999 ⇒15,9848; 16,9880. ᴿRB 109 (2002) 109-119
        (*Grelot, Pierre*).
        Kalimi, I. ...und Josef verleumdete seine Brüder: Josefs Verrat
        in den Midraschim...jüdisch-christliche Kontroverse 2002 ⇒10208.
10486   *Kampling, Rainer* Eine offene Frage—theologische und historische
        Implikationen der Antijudaismusforschung. ThRv 98 (2002) 179-
        196;
10487   "... zumal nur eine Synagoge angezündet wurde ..." (Ambrosius von
        Mailand): die Judenfeindschaft der Alten Kirche und ihre Rezep-
        tion. Im Angesicht Israels. SBB 47: 2002 ⇒189. 183-194;

10488 Zu einem Motiv deutschsprachiger mittelalterlicher Judeneide;
10489 "... eine Erfahrung, die ich heute noch in mir trage ...": die Israeltheologie des Papstes JOHANNES PAUL II: ein Versuch;
10490 Die Darstellung der Juden und des Judentums in den Predigten des
ZENO von Verona <1984>;
10491 Neutestamentliche Texte als Bausteine der späten Adversus-Judae-
os-Literatur <1990>;
10492 Antijudaismus von Anfang an?: zur Diskussion um den neutestamentlichen Ursprung des christlichen Antijudaismus <1997>;
10493 Ist das Christentum die humanere Religion?: antijudaistische Implikationen einer konstruierten Wahrnehmung <2000>. Im Angesicht.
2002 ⇒189. 213-217/261-272/139-152/123-137/85-100/221-237.
10494 *Kinzig, Wolfram* Nähe und Distanz: auf dem Weg zu einer neuen
Beschreibung der jüdisch-christlichen Beziehungen. Judentum und
Christentum. 2002 ⇒415. 9-27.
10495 Kirche und Israel: ein Beitrag der reformatorischen Kirchen Europas zum Verhältnis von Christen und Juden. [E]**Schwier, H.** 2001 ⇒
17,9660. Leuenberger Kirchengemeinschaft. [R]ThLZ 127 (2002)
1319-1321 (*Schüle, Andreas*).
10496 *Klappert, Bertold* Israel und die Kirche—Zeugen Gottes vor der
Welt und voreinander;
10497 *Klenicki, Leon* A hopeful reflection on the future of the interfaith
dialogue relationship;
10498 *Koch, Kurt* Die Wirklichkeit Gottes als Herz des jüdisch-christlichen Dialogs. [F]THOMA, C.: JudChr 20: 2002 ⇒119. 97-107/109-
126/127-145.
10499 *Kraft, Sigisbert* Das jüdische Erbe in der christlichen Liturgie
wieder entdecken. US 57 (2002) 262-272.
10500 **Krapf, Martin** Kein Stein bleibt auf dem anderen: die christliche
Schuld am Antisemitismus. 1999 ⇒15,9857; 16,9901. [R]FrRu 9
(2002) 218-220 (*Gollinger, Hildegard*).
10501 **Külzer, Andreas** Disputationes graecae contra judaeos: Untersuchungen zur byzantinischen antijüdischen Dialogliteratur und ihrem
Judenbild. 1999 ⇒15,9860. [R]ZRGG 54 (2002) 81-82 (*Beltz,
Walter*).
10502 *Lacerenza, Giancarlo* Jewish magicians and christian clients in late
antiquity: the testimony of amulets and inscriptions. [F]FOERSTER, G.:
2002 ⇒39. 393-419.
10503 *Lauer, Simon* Gedanken zu einer jüdischen Theologie (des Christentums). [F]THOMA, C.: JudChr 20: 2002 ⇒119. 147-155.
10504 *Lehnardt, Andreas* Christlicher Einfluss auf das Jahrzeit-Kad-
disch?. Jud. 58 (2002) 281-296.
10505 *Lenzen, Verena* Erinnerung und Hoffnung: das deutsch-jüdische
Verhältnis und der christlich-jüdische Dialog. Bulletin der Schweizerischen Gesellschaft für Judaistische Forschung 11 (2002) 3-16;
10506 Keine Zukunft ohne Vergangenheit. [F]THOMA, C.: JudChr 20: 2002
⇒119. 157-170.
10507 *Levenson, Alan* Missionary Protestants as defenders and detractors
of Judaism: Franz DELITZSCH and Hermann STRACK. JQR 92
(2002) 383-420.
10508 *Levenson, Jon D.* Wie man den jüdisch-christlichen Dialog nicht
führen soll. KuI 17 (2002) 163-174.

10509   *Lieu, Judith* 'Impregnable ramparts and walls of iron': boundary and identity in early 'Judaism' and 'Christianity'. NTS 48 (2002) 297-313.

10510   **Lieu, Judith M.** Image and reality: the Jews in the world of the christians in the second century. 1996 ⇒12,8673... 15,9868. [R]Vox Patrum 22 (2002) 581-584 (*Misiarczyk, Leszek*).

10511   *Lustiger, J.-M.* Juifs et chrétiens: que doivent-ils espérer de leur rencontre?. NRTh 124 (2002) 353-362.

10512   **Manns, Frédéric** Le Judéo-christianisme: mémoire ou prophétie?. ThH 112: 2000 ⇒16,9924; 17,9672. [R]RSPhTh 86 (2002) 123-125 (*Cerbelaud, Dominique*);

10513   Les enfants de Rébecca: Judaïsme et christianisme aux premiers siècles de notre ère. "Vivre la Parole": Saint-Germanin-lès-Arpajon 2002, Médiaspaul 320 pp €29.90. 2-7122-0837-4. [R]MoBi 144 (2002) 71 (*Boyer, Frédéric*).

10514   *Martini, Carlo Maria* Profonda consonanza di radici. Il libro sacro. 2002 ⇒356. xi-xxiii [Lev 19,18; Dt 6,4-5; Mk 12,28-34].

10515   *Meeks, Wayne A.* Breaking away: three New Testament pictures of christianity's separation from the Jewish communities. In search. 2002 ⇒208. 115-138.

10516   *Mejia, Jorge Maria* The theological dimension of Jewish-Christian dialogue. [F]THOMA, C.: JudChr 20: 2002 ⇒119. 171-180.

10517   *Mendels, Doron* The relationship of christians and Jews during the years 300-450: a preliminary report of the christian point of view. Judentum und Christentum. 2002 ⇒415. 45-54.

10518   **Mimouni, Simon Claude** Le judéo-christianisme ancien: essais historiques. 1998 ⇒14,9002... 17,9674. [R]RSPhTh 86 (2002) 125-127 (*Cerbelaud, Dominique*); VigChr 56 (2002) 326-328 (*Rouwhorst, Gerard*); Apocrypha 13 (2002) 291-293 (*Dubois, J.-D.*).

10519   **Neusner, Jacob** Judaism when christianity began: a survey of belief and practice. LVL 2002, Westminster 202 pp. $20. 0-664-225-27-6.

10520   *Oechslen, Rainer* Kirche und Israel—ein Beitrag der reformatorischen Kirchen Europas zum Verhältnis von Christen und Juden. EvTh 62 (2002) 252-254.

10521   [E]**Osten-Sacken, Peter von der** Das missbrauchte Evangelium: Studien zur Theologie und Praxis der Thüringer Deutschen Christen. B 2002, Institut Kirche und Judentum 432 pp.

10522   *Panayotov, Alexander* The synagogue in the copper market of Constantinople: a note on the christian attitudes towards Jews in the fifth century. OCP 68 (2002) 319-334.

10523   *Pangritz, Andreas* "Auf dem Schul-Weg": zu Friedrich-Wilhelm Marquardts Arbeit an der Erneuerung des christlich-jüdischen Verhältnisses. KuI 17 (2002) 175-181.

10524   *Pastis, Jacqueline Z.* Dating the Dialogue of Timothy and Aquila: revisiting the earlier vorlage hypothesis. HThR 95 (2002) 169-195.

10525   *Pawlikowski, John T.* Reimaging the Christian-Jewish relationship: an evaluation of contemporary perspectives. [F]THOMA, C.: JudChr 20: 2002 ⇒119. 197-208.

10526   **Perry, Marvin; Schweitzer, Frederick M.** Antisemitism: myth and hate from antiquity to the present. NY 2002, Palgrave x; 309 pp. $35. 0-312-16561-7.

10527   *Phillips, Anthony* The place of law in contemporary society. Essays on biblical law. JSOT.S 344: 2002 <1981> ⇒223. 221-230.

10528 *Pikaza Ibarrondo, Xabier* Confesión de fe y mandamiento de amor: trasfondo judío del credo cristiano. ^FTREVIJANO ETCHEVERRÍA, R. 2002 ⇒122. 281-296.

10529 Il popolo ebraico e le sue sacre scritture nella bibbia cristiana. 2001 ⇒17,9682. Pontificia Commissio Biblica. ^RPath 1 (2002) 385-386 (*Farina, Marcella*).

10530 ^E**Porter, Stanley E.; Pearson, Brook W.R.** Christian-Jewish relations through the centuries. JSNT.S 192: 2000 ⇒16,433; 17,9683. ^RCBQ 64 (2002) 802-804 (*Broadhurst, Laurence*); BBR 12 (2002) 144-147 (*VanEpps, Cameron*); BgMiss 66 (2002) 345-347 (*Lopez-Gay, Jesús*); RBLit 4 (2002) 479-481 (*Chilton, Bruce*).

10531 **Qalimi, Yishaq** Early Jewish exegesis and theological controversy: studies on scriptures in the shadow of internal and external controversies. Jewish and Christian heritage series 2: Assen 2002, Van Gorcum xvi; 209 pp. 90-232-3713-7.

10532 **Ragacs, Ursula** "Mit Zaum und Zügel muss man ihr Ungestüm bändigen": Ps 32,9: ein Beitrag zur christlichen Hebraistik und antijüdischen Polemik im Mittelalter. JudUm 65: 1997 ⇒13,9258. ^RFJB 29 (2002) 162-166 (*Hasselhoff, Görge K.*).

10533 *Rausell Guillot, Helena* Antijudaïsme et exégèse chrétienne dans la monarchie hispanique: les "Annotationes decem ad Sacram Scripturam" de Pedro Antonio BEUTER. PosLuth 50/2 (2002) 167-179.

10534 Reflections on covenant and mission. Wsh 2002, USCCB Consultation of the National Council of Synagogues and the Bishops' Committee for Ecumenical and Interreligious Affairs—August 12, 2002.

10535 *Reif, Stefan C.* Jews, Hebraists and 'Old Testament' studies. ^MCARROLL, R.: JSOT.S 348: 2002 ⇒13. 224-245.

10536 **Remaud, Michel** Chrétiens et juifs entre le passé et l'avenir. 2000 ⇒16,9945; 17,9690. ^RRSPhTh 86 (2002) 137-138 (*Cerbelaud, Dominique*); SR 31 (2002) 480-482 (*Lavoie, Jean-Jacques*).

10537 *Rendtorff, Rolf* Did christianity die at Auschwitz?. A shadow of glory. 2002 ⇒347. 155-168.

10538 *Risse, Siegfried* Die Juden in deutschsprachigen katholischen Psalmenerklärungen des 16. Jahrhunderts. FrRu 9 (2002) 105-113.

10539 *Rosenkranz-Verhelst, Simone* Juden, Christen, Muslime und die Erwähnung der Ka'ba bei Daniel al-Qumisi. Jud. 58 (2002) 106-118.

10540 *Rossano, Pietro* Lo stato attuale del dialogo tra ebrei, cristiani e musulmani. Teologia cristiana. DMis 27: 2002 <1983> ⇒232. 19-31.

10541 *Ruppert, Lothar* Das jüdische Volk und seine heiligen Schriften in der christlichen Bibel: zum neuesten Dokument der Päpstlichen Bibelkommission. FrRu 9 (2002) 19-29.

10542 **Sadun Paggi, Manuela** Dialogo guarigione del mondo: sorgenti ebraiche. Religioni in dialogo. Bo 2002, EMI 155 pp. 88-307-11-46-2.

10543 *Sale, Giovanni* Antigiudaismo o antisemitismo?: le accuse contro la chiesa e la "Civiltà Cattolica". CivCatt 153/2 (2002) 419-431.

10544 **Santogrossi, A.** L'évangile prêché à Israël: à propos du dialogue judéo-chrétien. Etampes 2002, Clovis 78 pp. €10.50. 2-912642-87-6 [NRTh 125,451s—Radermakers, J.].

10545 ^E**Sapir Abulafia, Anna** Religious violence between Christians and Jews: medieval roots, modern perspectives. L 2002, Palgrave xviii; 205 pp. 0-333-92187-9. Bibl. 193-195.

10546   *Schmid, Rudolf* In Gottes Treue gehalten: jüdisch-christliche For-
        schung als Aufgabe katholischer Theologie. ^FTHOMA, C.: JudChr
        20: 2002 ⇒119. 245-256.

10547   *Schmidt, Matthias* Staat Israel und Heiliges Land: der Papstbesuch
        als Testfall eines christlich-jüdischen Dialogs. Judentum und
        Christentum. 2002 ⇒415. 165-179.

10548   **Schreckenberg, Heinz** Die christlichen Adversus-Judaeos-Texte/
        Bilder. EHS.T 172, 335, 497, 650: 1991-1999 ⇒7,a221... 17,
        10970. ^RCCMéd 45 (2002) 307-309 (*Knoch-Mund, Gaby*).

10549   *Schreiner, Stefan R.* Gamli'els Antwort und das Gespräch zwischen
        den Religionen: Isaak TROKIs Auslegung von Apg 5,38-39. ^FTHO-
        MA, C.: JudChr 20: 2002 ⇒119. 259-274.

10550   *Siegert, Folker* Das Judenchristentum in der Antike: ein neuer An-
        satz zu seiner Erforschung. ^FASCHOFF, D. 2002 ⇒3. 117-128.

10551   **Skarsaune, Oskar** In the shadow of the temple: Jewish influences
        on early christianity. DG 2002, InterVarsity 455 pp. $30. 0-8308-
        2670-X.

10552· *Stein, Hannes* 'Alttestamentarisch': über eine Spielart des Antise-
        mitismus. Merkur 56 (2002) 353-356.

10553   *Stuckrad, Kocku von* "Christen" und "Nichtchristen" in der Antike:
        von religiös konstruierten Grenzen zur diskursorientierten Religi-
        onswissenschaft. ^FHOHEISEL, K.: JAC.E 34: 2002 ⇒59. 184-202.

10554   **Thiede, Carsten Peter; Stingelin, Urs** Die Wurzeln des Antisemi-
        tismus: Judenfeindschaft in der Antike, im frühen Christentum und
        im Koran. Ba 2002, Brunnen 176 pp. FS19.80. 3-7655-1264-8.

10555   *Thoma, Clemens* Die Bibel im jüdisch-christlichen Verständnis.
        Die Bibel: Geschichte und Gegenwart. 2002 ⇒971. 202-212.

10556   *Van der Horst, Pieter W.* Jews and christians in Antioch at the end
        of the fourth century. Japheth. 2002 <2000> ⇒251. 109-118.

10557   *Veltri, Giuseppe* Vom Nutzen und Nachteil der jüdischen Existenz
        in der Diaspora: Streiflichter auf Simone LUZZATTO. Judentum und
        Christentum. 2002 ⇒415. 97-115.

10558   *Vollenweider, Samuel* Antijudaismus im Neuen Testament: der An-
        fang einer unseligen Tradition. Horizonte. WUNT 144: 2002
        <1999> ⇒257. 125-140.

10559   *Weksler-Waszkinel, Romuald Jakub* Les "rencontres" de JEAN-
        PAUL II avec Emmanuel LEVINAS. Ist. 47 (2002) 228-242.

10560   *Wyschogrod, Michael* Democracy, Judaism and the church. ^FTHO-
        MA, C.: JudChr 20: 2002 ⇒119. 343-350.

10561   *Zenger, Erich* Die Bibel Israels—Wurzel der Gemeinsamkeit für
        Juden und Christen. FrRu 9 (2002) 81-94;

10562   Exegese des Alten Testaments im Spannungsfeld von Judentum
        und Christentum. ThRv 98 (2002) 357-366.

XVI. Religiones parabiblicae

M1.1 Gnosticismus classicus

10563   *Abd el-Saheed, Samiha* Tensions between Gnosticism and early
        Egyptian christianity reflected in christian Copto-Arabic manu-
        scripts. The Nag Hammadi texts. DVSS.HF 26: 2002 ⇒740. 211-4.

10564 *Aland, Barbara* Gnostischer Polytheismus oder gnostischer Monotheismus?: zum Problem von polytheistischen Ausdrucksformen in
der Gnosis. Polytheismus. AOAT 298: 2002 ⇒418. 195-208;

10565 Gnosis und Christentum: die Geschichte einer Konkurrenz?. Rettendes Wissen. AOAT 300: 2002 ⇒352. 345-361.

10566 *Aranda Pérez, Gonzalo* El origen de la autoridad apostólica perma-
nente entre los gnósticos. ᶠTREVIJANO ETCHEVERRÍA, R. 2002 ⇒
122. 347-361.

10567 *Beltz, Walter* Wie gnostisch sind die Gnostiker (gewesen)?.
ᶠSCHENKE, H.: NHS 54: 2002 ⇒108. 231-245.

10568 *Bermejo Rubio, Fernando* La relevancia de las soteriologías gnósticas y maniquea para una crítica de la pseudociencia de la religión.
ᶠTREVIJANO ETCHEVERRÍA, R. 2002 ⇒122. 333-346.

10569 *Brakke, David* The seed of Seth at the Flood: biblical interpretation
and Gnostic theological reflection. ᶠGREER, R. 2002 ⇒51. 41-62.

10570 *Emmel, Stephen* The Gnostic tradition in relation to Greek philosophy. The Nag Hammadi texts. DVSS.HF 26: 2002 ⇒740. 125-136.

10571 *Filoramo, Giovanni* 'Nier les dieux, nier Dieu' dans les textes gnostiques. Nier les dieux. 2002 ⇒626. 253-262.

10572 *King, Karen L.* Introduction. ᶠSCHENKE, H.: NHS 54: 2002 ⇒108.
1-12.

10573 ᴱ**King, Karen L.** Images of the feminine in gnosticism. Studies in
antiquity and christianity: Harrisburg, Pa. 2000 <1988>, Trinity v;
455 pp. ᴿRBLit 4 (2002) 467-469 (*Wallace, Donna K.*).

10574 *Kirchner, Dankwart* Das Recht des Geschöpfs: wie sind gnostische
Auseinandersetzungen mit dem Demiurgen zu beurteilen?. ᶠSCHEN-
KE, H.: NHS 54: 2002 ⇒108. 255-290.

10575 **Lancellotti, Maria Grazia** The Naassenes: a Gnostic identity
among Judaism, christianity, classical and ancient Near Eastern traditions. FARG 35: 2000 ⇒16,10003; 17,9726. ᴿNumen 49 (2002)
344-6 (*Gilhus, Ingvild Saelid*); UF 34 (2002) 960-2 (*Grypeou, E.*).

10576 ᵀ**Layton, Bentley** As escrituras gnósticas. ᵀ*Oliva, Margarida*: São
Paulo 2002, Loyola xlii; 584 pp. 85-15-02532-9 [PerTeol 36,148—
Johan Konings].

10577 *Lieven, Alexandra von* Gnosis and astrology: 'Book IV' of the Pistis
Sophia. Under one sky. AOAT 297: 2002 ⇒9014. 223-236.

10578 **Magris, Aldo** La logica del pensiero gnostico. Scienze delle religioni: 1997 ⇒13,9314. ᴿLTP 58 (2002) 385-7 (*Painchaud, Louis*).

10579 *Mastrocinque, Attilio* Studies in gnostic gems: the gem of Judah.
JSJ 33 (2002) 164-170.

10580 *Pearson, Birger* From Jewish apocalypticism to Gnosis. The Nag
Hammadi texts. DVSS.HF 26: 2002 ⇒740. 146-163.

10581 **Rudolph, Kurt** La gnosi: natura e storia di una religione tardoantica. 2000 ⇒16,10011; 17,9732. ᴿStPat 49 (2002) 253-254 (*Corsato, Celestino*).

10582 *Schneemelcher, Wilhelm-Peter* Zur Gestalt der Eva in der Gnosis.
ᶠHOHEISEL, K.: JAC.E 34: 2002 ⇒59. 48-63.

10583 *Scholer, David M.* Bibliographia gnostica: supplementum II/5. NT
44 (2002) 55-94.

10584 *Scibona, Concetta Giuffrè* Nature of the divine and types of Gnostic systems. Nag Hammadi texts. DVSS.HF 26: 2002 ⇒740. 54-
60.

10585 *Scopello, Madeleine* Les penseurs gnostiques face à la vision. Voir
les dieux. 2002 ⇒629. 95-108.

10586   **Segal, Alan F.** Two powers in heaven: early rabbinic reports about christianity and gnosticism. Boston, Mass. 2002, Brill xxiv; 313 pp. 0-391-04172-X.
10587   *Sfameni Gasparro, Giulia* Grazia divina e divinizzazione dell'uomo nello Gnosticismo. DSBP 31 (2002) 48-84;
10588   La notion greque du destin et la sotériologie gnostique;
10589   *Sørensen, Jørgen Podemann* COOYN̄—The Late Egyptian background of *gnosis*. The Nag Hammadi texts. DVSS.HF 26: 2002 ⇒740. 105-124/137-145.
10590   *Turner, John D.* Time and history in Sethian gnosticism. [F]SCHENKE, H.: NHS 54: 2002 ⇒108. 203-214.
10591   *Vollenweider, Samuel* Gnosis in der Moderne?: Überlegungen zu einem spannungsvollen Verhältnis. Horizonte. WUNT 144: 2002 <2000> ⇒257. 347-361.
10592   *Wisse, Frederik* Indirect textual evidence for the history of early christianity and gnosticism. [F]SCHENKE, H.: NHS 54: 2002 ⇒108. 215-230.
10593   *Zmorzanka, Anna Z.* Kobieta—uczennica i nauczycielka w przekazach gnostyckich [A woman: a student and teacher in imparting gnostic messaages]. Vox Patrum 22 (2002) 89-100 Sum 99s. P.

M1.3 Valentinus; Corpus hermeticum; Orphismus

10594   *Betz, Hans Dieter* Hermetism and Gnosticism: the question of the 'Poimandres'. Nag Hammadi texts. DVSS.HF 26: 2002 ⇒740. 84-94.
10595   [E]**Camplani, A.** Scritti ermetici in copto: l'ogdoade e l'enneade, preghiera di ringraziamento, frammento del discorso perfetto. 2000 ⇒16,10025. [R]Muséon 115/1-2 (2002) 219-220 (*Brankaer, J.*).
10596   *Cirillo, Luigi* CMC 97,9 S.: 'Cette terre est la chair et le sang de mon Seigneur': les trois niveaux du logion d'ALCHASAÏOS: judéo-chrétien, gnostique et manichéen. The Nag Hammadi texts. DVSS. HF 26: 2002 ⇒740. 215-225.
10597   *Holzhausen, Jens* HERMES und PTOLEMAIOS: zu einem Silberteller im Getty-Museum. [F]SCHENKE, H.: NHS 54: 2002 ⇒108. 291-305.
10598   *Krause, Martin* Die hermetischen Nag Hammadi Texte. The Nag Hammadi texts. DVSS.HF 26: 2002 ⇒740. 61-72.
10599   *Lenski, Noel* Were VALENTINIAN, VALENS and JOVIAN confessors before JULIAN the Apostate?. ZAC 6 (2002) 253-276.
10600   **Löw, Andreas** HERMES Trismegistos als Zeuge der Wahrheit: die christliche Hermetikrezeption von ATHENAGORAS bis LAKTANZ. Theophaneia 36: B 2002, Philo xii; 293 pp. 3-8257-0322-3. Bibl. 261-284.
10601   *Markschies, Christoph* VALENTIN/Valentinianer. TRE 34. 2002 ⇒ 800. 495-500.
10602   *Petersen, Tage* Hermetic dualism?: CH. VI. against the background of Nag Hammadi dualistic Gnosticism. The Nag Hammadi texts. DVSS.HF 26: 2002 ⇒740. 95-102.

M1.5 **Mani**, *dualismus*; **Mandaei**

10603 **BeDuhn, Jason David** The Manichaean body: in discipline and ritual. 2000 ⇒16,10030; 17,9749. [R]BSOAS 65 (2002) 173-175 (*Durkin-Meisterernst, Desmond*); CHR 88 (2002) 564-567 (*Lieu, Samuel N.C.*).

10604 **Biedenkopf-Ziehner, Anneliese** MANI und ARISTOTELES: das sechste Kapitel der koptischen Kephalaia: Textanalyse und Interpretation. GOF.Ä 42: Wsb 2002, Harrassowitz vi; 368 pp. 3-447-04613-9. Bibl. 365-368.

10605 *Cerutti, Maria Vittoria* Il mito manicheo tra universalismo e particolarismi regionali: la testimonianza di ALESSANDRO di Licopoli. AnScR 7 (2002) 225-258.

10606 [E]**Clackson, Sarah** Dictionary of Manichaean texts, 1: texts from the Roman Empire. Corpus Fontium Manichaeorum: 1999 ⇒15, 9942. [R]Apocrypha 13 (2002) 300-302 (*Van den Kerchove, A.*).

10607 *Franzmann, Majella* Mandäismus. RGG 5. 2002 ⇒796. 725-728.

10608 *Heil, Uta* "... bloß nicht wie die Manichäer!": ein Vorschlag zu den Hintergründen des arianischen Streits. ZAC 6 (2002) 299-319.

10609 *Hutter, Manfred* Der Manichäismu: eine spätantike Alternative zum Christentum. WUB Sonderheft (2002) 17-19.

10610 **Lieu, Samuel N.C.** Manichaeism in Central Asia and China. NHMS 45: 1998 ⇒14,9106. [R]Ist. 47 (2002) 413-415 (*Dupuy, B.*).

10611 **Lupieri, Edmondo F.** The Mandaeans: the last Gnostics. [T]*Hindley, Charles*: Italian Texts & Studies on Religion & Society: GR 2002, Eerdmans xix; 273 pp. $25. 0-8028-3924-X.

10612 *Müller-Kessler, Christa* Die aramäische Beschwörung und ihre Rezeption in den mandäisch-magischen Texten am Beispiel ausgewählter aramäischer Beschwörungsformulare. Charmes et sortilèges. 2002 ⇒477. 193-208.

10613 *Pedersen, Nils Arne* Über einen manichäisch-koptischen Hymnus von der Erlösung der Seele (das *manichäische Psalmenbuch*, teil [!] I: Faksimileausgabe Band III, Tafel 127-128). The Nag Hammadi texts. DVSS.HF 26: 2002 ⇒740. 199-210.

10614 **Richter, Siegfried G.** The Manichaean Coptic papyri in the Chester Beatty Library: Psalm Book II, Fasc. 2: die Herakleides-Psalmen. Corpus Fontium Manichaeorum, Series Coptica, I/2/2: 1998 ⇒16,10041; 17,9768. [R]Apocrypha 13 (2002) 304-306 (*Van den Kerchove, A.*).

10615 *Ries, Julien* Symbolisme de la lumière et illumination gnostique selon les textes manichéens coptes. Symbolisme et expérience. 2002 ⇒666. 177-188.

10616 [ET]**Schipper, Hendrik Gerhard; Van Oort, Johannes** LEO I: Sermons and letters against the Manichaeans: selected fragments. Corpus Fontium Manichaeorum, Series Latina 1: 2000 ⇒16,10043. [R]Apocrypha 13 (2002) 306-308 (*Gounelle, R.*).

10617 *Van Oort, Johannes* Manichäismus. RGG 5. 2002 ⇒796. 732-741.

M2.1 **Nag Hammadi**, *generalia*

10618 **Funk, Wolf-Peter; Poirier, Paul-Hubert** Concordance des textes de Nag Hammadi, les codices XIB, XII, XIII. Bibliothèque copte

de Nag Hammadi, Concordances 7: Lv 2002, Peeters xxxiii; 359 pp. 90-429-1095-X.
10619 **Funk, Wolf-Peter** Concordance des textes de Nag Hammadi, les codices X et XI. Bibliothèque copte de Nag Hammadi, Concordances 6: 2000 ⇒16,10049. ^ROLZ 97 (2002) 468-471 (*Behlmer, Heike*); Apocrypha 13 (2002) 296-297 (*Van den Kerchove, A.*).
10620 **Reeves, John C.** Heralds of that good realm: Syro-Mesopotamian Gnosis and Jewish traditions. NHMS 41: 1996 ⇒12,8787... 16, 10050. ^RVigChr 56 (2002) 310-313 (*Lieu, Samuel N.C.*).
10621 *Rudolph, Kurt* Stand und Aufgaben der Gnosisforschung aufgrund der Nag Hammadi-Texte. The Nag Hammadi texts. DVSS.HF 26: 2002 ⇒740. 11-23.
10622 ^E**Schenke, Hans-Martin; Bethge, Hans-Gebhard; Kaiser, Ursula Ulrike** Nag Hammadi deutsch, 1: NHC I,1-V,1. Die griechischen christlichen Schriftsteller der ersten Jahrhunderte 8: 2001. ⇒17, 9783. ^RArOr 70 (2002) 95-96 (*Pokorný, Petr*); JBL 121 (2002) 579-582 (*Robinson, James M.*).
10623 *Van Lindt, Paul* The religious terminology in the Nag Hammadi texts and in Manichaean literature. The Nag Hammadi texts. DVSS.HF 26: 2002 ⇒740. 191-198.

M2.2 *Evangelium etc. Thomae*—The Gospel of Thomas

10624. *Anikuzhikattil, Thomas* Syriac soteriology in the "Acts of Judas Thomas". ETJ 6 (2002) 33-57.
10625 *Arnold, Kenneth* The circle of the way: reading the gospel of Thomas as a ChristZen text. CrossCur 51 (2002) 459-469.
10626 *Athikalam, James* St. Thomas the Apostle and Thomas christians. StMiss 51 (2002) 333-351.
10627 *Blessing, Kamila* The women carrying a jar of meal (Gos. Thom. 97). The lost coin. BiSe 86: 2002 ⇒5282. 158-173.
10628 ^E**Bremmer, Jan Nicolaas** The Apocryphal Acts of Thomas. Studies in Early Christian Apocrypha 6: 2001 ⇒17,9785. ^RLTP 58 (2002) 626-627 (*Kaler, Michael*).
10629 **Dart, John; Riegert, Ray** The gospel of Thomas: unearthing the lost words of Jesus. 2000 ⇒16,10056. ^RJECS 10 (2002) 389-390 (*Bingham, D. Jeffrey*).
10630 ^T**Davies, Stevan L.** The gospel of Thomas: annotated & explained. SkyLight Illuminations Series: Woodstock, VT 2002, Skylight Paths xxxviii; 141 pp 1-893361-45-4. Foreword *Andrew Harvey*.
10631 *DeConick, April D.* The original gospel of Thomas. VigChr 56 (2002) 167-199.
10632 *Frid, Bo; Svartvik, Jesper* Thomasevangeliet med Jesusorden från Oxyrhynchus. Lund 2002, Arcus 320 pp.
10633 *Funk, Wolf-Peter* "Einer aus tausend, zwei aus zehntausend": Zitate aus dem Thomasevangelium in den koptischen Manichaica;
10634. *Hedrick, Charles W.* An anecdotal argument for the independence of the gospel of Thomas from the synoptic gospels. ^FSCHENKE, H.: NHS 54: 2002 ⇒108. 67-94/113-126.
10635 *Johnson, Steven R.* The hidden/revealed saying in the Greek and Coptic versions of Gos. Thom. 5 & 6. NT 44 (2002) 176-185.

10636   **Kurikilamkatt, James** The Apostle Thomas at Taxila: historical investigation of the mission of Thomas to North India with special reference to the *Acts of Thomas*. [D]*Shelke, Christopher*: 135 pp. Exc. Diss. Gregoriana 2002.

10637   *Liebenberg, J.* To know what is before one's face: group-specific metaphors and the composition of the gospel of Thomas. HTS 58 (2002) 593-607 [NTAb 47,348];

10638   Going places with bodies that can seek and find, eyes that can see, and ears that can hear: some remarks on the body and understanding in the gospel of Thomas. HTS 58 (2002) 1747-1759 [NTAb 47, 549].

10639   *Meyer, Marvin W.* Gospel of Thomas logion 114 revisited. [F]SCHENKE, H.: NHS 54: 2002 ⇒108. 101-111.

10640   *Nash, Kathleen* The language of mother work in the gospel of Thomas: keeping momma out of the kingdom (Gos. Thom. 22). The lost coin. BiSe 86: 2002 ⇒5282. 174-195.

10641   **Patterson, Stephen J.; Robinson, James McConkey** The fifth gospel: the gospel of Thomas comes of age. [T]*Bethge, Hans-Gebhard*: 1998 ⇒14,9128; 17,9801. [R]Apocrypha 13 (2002) 322-324 (*Gianotto, C.*).

10642   **Perrin, Nicholas** Thomas and TATIAN: the relationship between the gospel of Thomas and the Diatessaron. Academia Biblica 5: Atlanta, GA 2002, SBL xii; 216 pp. $30. 1-58983-045-8. Bibl. 197-216.

10643   *Poirier, Paul-Hubert* Un parallèle grec partiel au logion 24 de l'évangile selon Thomas. [F]SCHENKE, H. 2002 ⇒108. 95-100.

10644   *Uro, Risto* "Who will be our leader?": authority and autonomy in the Gospel of Thomas. [F]RÄISÄNEN, H.: 2002 ⇒97. 457-485.

10645   **Vadakkekara, Benedict** Origin of India's St. Thomas christians: a historiographical critique. Delhi 1995, Media xii; 511 pp. [R]ETJ 6 (2002) 105-106 (*Emprayil, Thomas*).

10646   **Zöckler, Thomas** Jesu Lehren im Thomasevangelium. NHMS 47: 1999 ⇒15,9988...17,9807. [R]JECS 10 (2002) 390-392 (*Bingham, D. Jeffrey*); RBLit (2002)* (*Franzmann, Majella*).

M2.3 *Singula scripta*—Various titles [⇒K3.4]

10647   *Charron, Régine* Le dieu "Semeur" dans le Dialogue du Sauveur. (NHC III,5). FSchenke, H.: NHS 54: 2002 ⇒108. 127-137.

10648   *Fernández Sangrador, Jorge Juan* El origen alejandrino de Enseñanzas de Silvano. [F]TREVIJANO ETCHEVERRÍA, R. 2002 ⇒122. 393-401.

10649   *García Bazán, Francisco* La literatura gnóstica en copto y el alegato antignóstico de PLOTINO: aportes del *Códice de Bruce* y del *Zostriano*. [F]TREVIJANO ETCHEVERRÍA, R. 2002 ⇒122. 379-392.

10650   *Khosroyev, Alexandr L.* Zur Frage nach *Eugnostos* in Codex III von Nag Hammadi;

10651   *Leopold, Anita Maria* Syncretism and transformation in the *Gospel of truth*;

10652   *Mahé, Jean-Pierre* Mental faculties and cosmic levels in *The eighth and the ninth* (NH VI,6) and related hermetic writings. The Nag Hammadi texts. DVSS.HF 26: 2002 ⇒740. 24-34./46-53/73-83.

10653 *Marjanen, Antti* The suffering of one who is a stranger to suffering: the crucifixion of Jesus in the letter of Peter to Philip. [F]RÄISÄNEN, H.: NT.S 103: 2002 ⇒97. 487-498.

10654 [R]**Roberge, Michel** La Paraphrase de Sem (NH VII,1). BCNH.T 25: 2000 ⇒16,10071; 17,9811. [R]OLZ 97 (2002) 471-475 (*Schenke, Hans-Martin*).

10655 *Thomassen, Einar* Revelation as book and book as revelation: reflections on the *Gospel of truth*. The Nag Hammadi texts. DVSS. HF 26: 2002 ⇒740. 35-45.

10656 *Trevijano Etcheverría, Ramón* El apocalipsis de Pablo (NHC V 2: 27[! 17],29[! 19]-24,9): traducción y comentario. Estudios paulinos. 2002 <1981> 451-473 [2 Cor 12,1-4].

M3.2 **Religio comparativa**

10657 *Becker, Michael* Die 'Magie'-Problematik der Antike: genügt eine sozialwissenschaftliche Erfassung?. ZRGG 54 (2002) 1-22.

10658 **Cunningham, Graham** Religion and magic: approaches and theories. 1999 ⇒16,10075. [R]AfO 48-49 (2001-2002) 226-228 (*Veldhuis, Nick*).

10659 **Diez de Velasco, Francisco** Introducción a la historia de las religiones. M [3]2002 <1995, 1998>, Trotta 637 pp. 84-8164-564-8.

10660 [E]**Gisel, P.; Tétaz, J.-M.** Théories de la religion: diversité des pratiques de recherche, changements des contextes socio-culturels, requêtes réflexives. Religions en perspective: Genève 2002, Labor et F. 414 pp. €32. 2-8309-1021-6.

10661 *Gladigow, Burkhard* Mediterrane Religionsgeschichte, römische Religionsgeschichte, europäische Religionsgeschichte: zur Genese eines Fachkonzepts. [F]VERSNEL, H.: 2002 ⇒126. 49-67.

10662 **Halbmayr, Alois** Lob der Vielheit: zur Kritik Odo Marquards am Monotheismus. 2000 ⇒16,10079. [R]TThZ 111 (2002) 161-162 (*Scheuer, Manfred*).

10663 **Lüddeckens, Dorothea** Das Weltparlament der Religionen von 1893: Strukturen interreligiöser Begegnung im 19. Jahrhundert. RVV 48: B 2002, De Gruyter xii; 349 pp. 3-11-017256-9. Bibl. 321-336.

10664 *Wilhelm, Gernot* Monotheistische Tendenzen und Genusdualität in altorientalischen Religionen. Die zwei Geschlechter. 2002 ⇒7637. 47-63.

M3.5 **Religiones mundi cum christianismo comparatae**

10665 [E]**Becchio, Ambrose J.** Sacred books of the world. NY 2002, Nova Science vii; 241 pp. 1-59033-253-9.

10666 **Dal Ferro, Giuseppe** Nel segno di Abramo: Ebraismo e Islam a confronto con il Cristianesimo. Strumenti di Scienze Religiose: Padova 2002, Messaggero 366 pp. 88-250-1099-0. Bibl. 343-358.

10667 **Edwards, Douglas R.** Religion & power: pagans, Jews, and christians in the Greek East. 1996 ⇒12,8806. [R]JThS 53 (2002) 309-311 (*Lieu, Judith*).

10668 **Favaro, Gaetano** Letture della Bibbia nel contesto religioso e so-
cioculturale dell'India contemporanea. Interpretare la Bibbia oggi
53: 2001 ⇒17,9825. [R]Salm. 49 (2002) 207-211 (*Sánchez Caro,
J.M.*).

10669 **Ferrari, Silvio** Lo spirito dei diritti religiosi: Ebraismo, Cristianesimo e Islam a confronto. Saggi 560: Bo 2002, Il Mulino 300 pp. 88-
15-08670-6.

10670 **Filoramo, Giovanni; Prandi, Carlo** Le scienze delle religioni.
Brescia [3]2002, Morcelliana 330 pp. 88-372-1661-0.

10671 **Küng, Hans** Tracing the way: spiritual dimensions of the world
religions. [T]*Bowden, John*: L 2002, Continuum xv; 280 pp. 0-8264-
5683-9.

10672 **Neusner, Jacob; Chilton, Bruce D.; Graham, William A.** Three
faiths, one God: the formative faith and practice of Judaism, Christianity, and Islam. Boston 2002, Brill xiii; 329 pp. 0-391-04146-0.

10673 [E]**Palmer, Martin** The Times world religions. L 2002, Times Books
256 pp. 0-0071-3140-2. Bibl. 242-247.

10674 *Rossano, Pietro* Teologia dei non cristiani <1966>;

10675 What the II Vatican Council has taught regarding non-christians
<1967>;

10676 La chiesa e le religioni <1969>;

10677 La teologia delle religioni dopo il Concilio Vaticano II <1970>;

10678 L'insidia del sincretismo e del relativismo nel dialogo con le religioni di cultura <1975>;

10679 Problème théologique du dialogue entre le christianisme et les religions non-chrétiennes <1978>;

10680 Un cristiano di fronte alle religioni del mondo <1980>;

10681 Tâche et responsabilité de la théologie <1990>. Teologia cristiana.
DMis 27: 2002 ⇒232. 101-113/87-99/287-304/115-124/317-
324/125-133/159-174/77-86.

M3.6 *Sectae*—Cults

10682 [E]**Assmann, Jan; Stroumsa, Guy G.** Transformations of the inner
self in ancient religions. SHR 83: 1999 ⇒15,2930. [R]ThLZ 127
(2002) 616-618 (*Koch, Klaus*).

10683 *Bingham, D. Jeffrey* Evangelicals, IRENAEUS, and the bible. The
Free Church. 2002 ⇒441. 27-46.

10684 *Bultmann, Rudolf* Die protestantische Theologie und der Atheis-
mus. NT und christliche Existenz. UTB 2316: 2002 <1971> ⇒152.
294-298.

10685 *FitzGerald, Kyriaki A.* The Eve-Mary typology and women in the
Orthodox Church: reconsidering Rhodes. AThR 84 (2002) 627-44.

10686 *Fuller, Daniel P.* Progressive dispensationalism and the law/gospel
contrast: a case study in biblical theology. Biblical theology. 2002
⇒558. 237-249.

10687 **Gundry, Robert Horton** Jesus the Word according to John the
Sectarian: a paleofundamentalist manifesto for contemporary evan-
gelicalism, especially its elites, in North America. GR 2002, Eerdmans xvii; 137 pp. $14. 0-8028-4980-6. Bibl. 115-137. [R]Third Mil-
lennium 5/2 (2002) 112-113 (*Mattam, J.*); CTJ 37 (2002) 374-377
(*Brouwer, Wayne*).

10688   **Kamil, Jill** Christianity in the land of the pharaohs: the Coptic
orthodox church. L 2002, Routledge xxii; 311 pp. $55. 0-415-242-
53-2. 135 fig.
10689   *Loth, Heinz-Jürgen* Bibel und Afrikanizität: Revivalism und
Rastafari in Jamaika. HBO 34 (2002) 231-256 .
10690   **McKim, Donald K.** Introducing the Reformed faith: biblical
revelation, christian tradition, contemporary significance. 2001
⇒17,9839. ᴿRRT 9 (2002) 144-147 (*Otto, Randall E.*); CTJ 37
(2002) 146-147 (*Hoezee, Scott*).
10691   **Newport, John P.** The New Age movement and the biblical worldview: conflict and dialogue. 1998 ⇒14,9185... 16,10093. ᴿSJTh 55
(2002) 488-490 (*Macpherson, Judith*).
10692   *Partee, C.* The reformed doctrine of irresistible sanctification;
10693   *Smit, D.* "Christ transforming culture"?: nagedink oor die aard van
die gereformeerde geloof. FPotgieter, P.: AcTh(B).S 3: 2002 ⇒92.
107-124/125-149.
10694   *Steyn, H.C.* South African New Age prophets: past and present. R
& T 9/3 (2002) 282-296.
10695   *Van Lieburg, Frederik A.* Het piëtisme en de bijbel: vroeger en nu.
ThRef 45/2 (2002) 145-158.

M3.8 **Mythologia**

10696   **Ackerman, Robert** The myth and ritual school: J.G. FRAZER and
the Cambridge ritualists. L ²2002 <1991>, Routledge 234 pp. £19.
0-415-93963-1.
10697   **Block, Daniel I.** The gods of the nations: studies in ancient Near
Eastern national theology. ²2000 ⇒16,10105. ᴿAUSS 40 (2002)
136-137 (*Souza, Elias Brazil de*); Pacifica 15 (2002) 211-213 (*Collins, Antoinette*).
10698   **Bradley, Richard** The past in prehistoric societies. L 2002, Routledge xiii; 171 pp. 0-415-27627-6. Bibl. 158-167.
10699   *Buddruss, Georg* Vom mythischen Weltbild eines Hochgebirgsvol-
kes im Hindukusch. Religion und Weltbild. 2002 ⇒443. 117-134.
10700   *Burkert, Walter* 'Mythos und Ritual' im Wechselwind der Moderne. ᶠVERSNEL, H. 2002 ⇒126. 1-22.
10701   *Callatay, Godefroid de* Die astrologische Geographie in der Antike.
Religiöse Landschaften. AOAT 301: 2002 ⇒408. 85-104.
10702   **Carandini, Andrea** Archeologia del mito: emozione e ragione fra
primitivi e moderni. Saggi 849: T 2002, Einaudi xiv; (2) 400 pp.
88-06-16253-5. Con un contributo iconografico di *Marco Paccia-
relli* e uno scambio di lettere con *Giancarlo G.M. Scoditti*.
10703   **Deutsch, Nathaniel** Guardians of the gate: angelic vice regency in
late antiquity. Jewish Studies 22: 1999 ⇒15,10029; 16,10108.
ᴿJQR 92 (2002) 628-631 (*Reeves, John C.*).
10704   *Funk, Robert W.* The mythical matrix and God as metaphor.
FORUM n.s. 3 (2002) 381-399.
10705   *Gangloff, Anne* Mythes, fables et rhétorique à l'époque impériale.
Rhetorica 20/1 (2002) 25-56.
10706   ᴱ**Goodison, Lucy; Morris, Christine** Ancient goddesses: the
myths and the evidence. 1998 ⇒14,9200; 15,10036. ᴿJAAR 70
(2002) 198-200 (*Gudorf, Christine E.*).

10707 ^E**Harris, Roy** The language myth in Western culture. Communication and linguistic theory: L 2002, Curzon vii; 228 pp. 0-7007-14-53-7.

10708 **Izre'el, Shlomo** Adapa and the south wind: language has the power of life and death. Mesopotamian Civilizations 10: 2001 ⇒17,9853. ^RArOr 70 (2002) 231-238 (*Hruška, Blahoslav*).

10709 **Keul, István** Hanuman, der Gott in Affengestalt: Entwicklung und Erscheinungsformen seiner Verehrung. RVV 47: B 2002, De Gruyter x; 350 pp. 3-11-017187-2. Bibl. 312-322.

10710 **Mander, Pietro; Durand, Jean-Marie** Mitología y religión del Oriente Antiguo: Semitas occidentales (Ebla, Mari). Estudios Orientales 8/2.1: 1995 ⇒12,8832; 15,10040. ^RSef. 62 (2002) 210-213 (*Such Gutiérrez, M.*).

10711 *Müller, Hans-Peter* Die Kunst der Selbstverwandlung in imaginären Landschaften—zur Vorgeschichte von Vergils "Arkadien"—. Religiöse Landschaften. AOAT 301: 2002 ⇒408. 69-84.

10712 *Scherb, Victor I.* Assimilating giants: the appropriation of Gog and Magog in medieval and early modern England. JMEMS 32 (2002) 59-84.

10713 *Segal, Robert Alan, al.*, Mythos/Mythologie. RGG 5. 2002 ⇒796. 1682-1704.

10714 **Sermonti, Giuseppe** Il mito della grande madre: dalle amigdale a Çatal Hüyük. Airesis: Mi 2002, Mimesis 151 pp. 88-8483-082-6.

10715 *Zeller, Dieter* Halt und Bedrohung im Weltall: zum Astralglauben der Antike. Religion und Weltbild. 2002 ⇒443. 49-63.

M4.0 Religio romana

10716 **Bakhouche, Béatrice** L'astrologie à Rome. Bibliothèque d'études classiques 29: Lv 2002, Peeters 241 pp. €55. 90-42'/-1127-1. Bibl. 215-233.

10717 *Brelich, Angelo* Tre note (sul concetto di magia). Mitologia. 2002 <1976> ⇒148. 129-137.

10718 **Brown, John Pairman** Israel and Hellas, 2: sacred institutions with Roman counterparts. BZAW 276: 2000 ⇒16,10119; 17,9862. ^RRB 109 (2002) 270-273 (*Taylor, Justin*).

10719 **Clauss, Manfred** Kaiser und Gott: Herrscherkult im römischen Reich. 1999 ⇒15,10046...17,9865. ^RAt. 90 (2002) 625-632 (*Letta, Cesare*); ClR 52 (2002) 319-321 (*Fears, J. Rufus*).

10720 *DeMaris, Richard E.* Cults and the imperial cult in early Roman Corinth: literary versus material record. Zwischen den Reichen. TANZ 36: 2002 ⇒568. 73-91.

10721 *Dittmann-Schöne, Imogen* Götterverehrung bei den Berufsvereinen im kaiserlichen Kleinasien. Religiöse Vereine. STAC 13: 2002 ⇒ 468. 81-96.

10722 *Ebner, Martin* Mensch wird Gott: der Kaiserkult und die christlichen Gemeinden. WUB 25 (2002) 36-45.

10723 ^E**Edwards, Mark; Goodman, Martin; Price, Simon R.F.** Apologetics in the Roman Empire: pagans, Jews, and christians. 1999 ⇒ 15,10047...17,9868. ^RCThMi 29 (2002) 47-48 (*Pickett, Ray*); ClR 52 (2002) 138-140 (*Noy, David*).

10724 **Egelhaaf-Gaiser, Ulrike** Kulträume im römischen Alltag: das Isis-buch des APULEIUS und der Ort von Religion im kaiserzeitlichen Rom. 2000 ⇒16,10125. [R]Latomus 61 (2002) 219-220 (*Turcan, Robert*); JRS 92 (2002) 258-259 (*May, Regine*).

10725 *Faraone, Christopher A.* The ethnic origins of a Roman-era Phil-trokatadesmos (PGM IV 296-434). Magic and ritual. RGRW 141: 2002 ⇒505. 319-343.

10726 **Fishwick, Duncan** The imperial cult in the Latin West: studies in the ruler cult of the western provinces of the Roman Empire: vol. III: provincial cult, part 1: institution and evolution; part 2: the pro-vincial priesthood. RGRW 145-146: Lei 2002, Brill 2 vols. €96 + 101. 90-04-12536-1/9-6.

10727 *Friedheim, Emmanuel* Quelques remarques sur l'introduction du culte de Jupiter héliopolitain à Emmaüs-Nicopolis à l'époque ro-maine. RB 109 (2002) 101-108.

10728 **Gradel, Ittai** Emperor worship and Roman religion. Oxford Classi-cal Monographs: Oxf 2002, Clarendon xvii; 398 pp. £55. 0-19-815-275-2.

10729 *Graf, Fritz* Roman festivals in Syria Palaestina. The Talmud Yeru-shalmi, 3. TSAJ 93: 2002 ⇒767. 435-451.

10730 *Hoffman, C.A.* Fiat magia. Magic and ritual. RGRW 141: 2002 ⇒ 505. 179-194.

10731 **Hopkins, Keith** A world full of gods: pagans, Jews and christians in the Roman Empire. 1999 ⇒15,10050...17,9871. [R]Gn. 74 (2002) 153-157 (*Leppin, Hartmut*); Journal of Interdisciplinary History 33/1 (2002) 102-103 (*Temin, Peter*).

10732 **Janes, Dominic** Romans and christians. Stroud, Gloucestershire 2002, Tempus 159 pp. 0-7524-1954-4. Bibl. 147-155.

10733 **Lichocka, Barbara** L'iconographie de Fortuna dans l'empire ro-main (Ier siècle avant n.è.-IVe siècle de n.è.). 1997 ⇒15,10051. [R]Gn. 74 (2002) 165-170 (*Winkler-Horacék, Lorenz*).

10734 *Rosenberger, Veit* Antike Lebenshilfe: die Orakel der griechisch-römischen Welt. WUB 25 (2002) 54-60.

10735 *Röwekamp, Georg* Die Sonnenanbeter: Heidnisches im Kirchen-jahr. WUB 25 (2002) 47-48.

10736 *Rüpke, Jörg* Collegia sacerdotum: religiöse Vereine in der Ober-schicht. Religiöse Vereine. STAC 13: 2002 ⇒468. 41-67.

10737 **Rüpke, Jörg** Die Religion der Römer: eine Einführung. 2001 ⇒17, 9880. [R]Latomus 61 (2002) 480-481 (*Turcan, Robert*); ThLZ 127 (2002) 1264-1266 (*Auffarth, Christoph*).

10738 *Santi, Claudia* L'idea romana di *sanctitas*. SMSR 68 (2002) 239-264.

10739 **Staples, Ariadne** From good goddess to vestal virgins: sex and category in Roman religion. 1998 ⇒14,9224. [R]RHR 219 (2002) 358-363 (*Sternbenc-Erker, Darja*).

10740 *Stähler, Klaus* Saturnia terra: Bilder heiliger Landschaften. Religiö-se Landschaften. AOAT 301: 2002 ⇒408. 105-139.

10741 *Sventsitskaya, I.S.* The imperial cult in the cities of Asia Minor in the first century A.D. [M]DIAKONOFF, I. 2002 ⇒27. 259-267.

10742 **Tripolitis, Antonia** Religions of the Hellenistic-Roman age. L 2002, Eerdmans 165 pp. $16. 0-8028-4913-X. Bibl. 150-158. [R]Pacifica 15 (2002) 342-344 (*Gaden, Timothy*); JECS 10 (2002) 540-541 (*Jefford, Clayton N.*); OTEs 15 (2002) 576-578 (*Nel, M.*).

10743 *Vernole, Vittorio Emanuele* Mos maiorum: problemi storico-religiosi. SMSR 68 (2002) 265-274.
10744 **Viola, L.M.A.** Sacra privata: introduzione generale ai fondamenti del culto privato. Forlì 2002, Victrix 83 pp. 88-88646-02-7.
10745 *Zerbini, Maurizio* Consumo di cereali e consumo di carne: aspetti del sacrificio romano. ASEs 19 (2002) 225-235.

M4.5 **Mithraismus**

10746 **Arcella, Stefano** I misteri del sole: il culto di Mithra nell'Italia antica. N 2002, Controcorrente 239 pp.
10747 *Betz, Hans Dieter* Mithrasreligion. RGG 5. 2002 ⇒796. 1344-47.
10748 *Dumermuth, Carlo F.* Rivalling with incipient christianism. AJTh 16/2 (2002) 409-414.
10749 *Mitescu, Adriana* Sull'ipotesi del "monoteismo pagano": Mithra e la preghiera pre-cristiana. Ter. 53 (2002) 453-476.
10750 *Sanzi, Ennio* Mithras: a *deus invictus* among Persia, stars, oriental cults and magical gems. Charmes et sortilèges. 2002 ⇒477. 209-229.
10751 *Turcan, Robert* Mithras: ein Gott der Soldaten, der Piraten und der Männerfreundschaft. WUB 25 (2002) 23-27.

M5.1 *Divinitates Graeciae*—**Greek gods and goddesses**

10752 [E]**Blundell, Sue; Williamson, Margaret** The sacred and the feminine in Ancient Greece. 1998 ⇒14,9235. [R]Numen 49 (2002) 348-349 (*Baudy, Dorothea*).
10753 *Bodinger, Martin* Deux problèmes d'histoire des religions au monde antique: 1, le dieu Sabazios et le judaïsme. Archaeus 6 (2002) 121-139.
10754 **Bremmer, Jan N.** La religione greca. [T]*Rosetti, Marcello*: Biblioteca di studi religiosi 4: Cosenza 2002, Giordano 190 pp.
10755 [ET]**Brodersen, Kai** Die Wahrheit über die griechischen Mythen: PALAIPHATOS' unglaubliche Geschichten. Universal-Bibliothek 18200: Stu 2002, Reclam 150 pp. €4.10. 3-15-018200-X.
10756 **Bruit Zaidman, Louise** Le commerce des dieux: *eusebeia*, essai sur la piété en Grèce ancienne. 2000 ⇒16,10150. [R]Kernos 15 (2002) 489-495 (*Motte, André*).
10757 *Busine, Aude* HERMÈS trismégiste, Moïse et APOLLONIUS de Tyane dans un oracle d'Apollon. Apocrypha 13 (2002) 227-243.
10758 **Calame, Claude** Mythe et histoire dans l'Antiquité grecque: la création symbolique d'une colonie. 1996 ⇒12,8863... 14,9242. [R]REG 115 (2002) 421-422 (*Perceau, Sylvie*).
10759 *Cursaru, Gabriela* Le dixième régal des κερνοφοροι. Archaeus 6 (2002) 409-423.
10760 *Dickie, M.W.* Who were privileged to see the gods?. Er. 100 (2002) 109-127.
10761 **Dickie, M.W.** Magic and magicians in the Greco-Roman world. 2001 ⇒17,9897. [R]ClR 52 (2002) 129-132 (*Ogden, Daniel*).
10762 **Dillon, Matthew** Girls and women in classical Greek religion. L 2002, Routledge x; 435 pp. £60. 0-415-20272-8. Bibl. 380-401.

10763   **Ekroth, Gunnel** The sacrificial rituals of Greek hero-cults in the archaic to the early Hellenistic periods. Kernos.S 12: Liège 2002, Centre International d'Etudes de la religion grecque antique 429 pp. 0776-3824. 12 fig..

10764   **Fowler, R.L.** Early Greek mythography, 1: text and introduction. 2001 ⇒17,9899. [R]CIR 52 (2002) 236-237 (*Liapis, Vayos J.*).

10765   **Furley, William D.; Bremer, Jan Maarten** Greek hymns: selected cult songs from the archaic to the Hellenistic period.. STAC 9-10: 2001 ⇒17,9900. [R]RHPhR 82 (2002) 217-218 (*Grappe, Ch.*).

10766·   *Gočeva, Zlatozara* Le culte des grands dieux de Samothrace à la période hellénistique. Kernos 15 (2002) 309-315.

10767   *Graf, Fritz* What is new about Greek sacrifice?. [F]VERSNEL, H. 2002 ⇒126. 113-125.

10768   **Johnston, Sarah Iles** Restless dead: encounters between the living and the dead in ancient Greece. 1999 ⇒15,10072...17,9904. [R]Prudentia 34/1 (2002) 88-91 (*Cropp, Martin*).

10769   *Keuls, Eva C.* Pair-bonding in classical Athens. Paare. 2002 ⇒489. 29-38.

10770   *Kollmann, Bernd* Halbgott in Weiß: Asklepioskult und Christentum. WUB 25 (2002) 29-34.

10771   **Le Bris, Anne** La mort et les conceptions de l'au-delà en Grèce ancienne à travers les épigrammes funéraires. 2001 ⇒17,9906. [R]REG 115 (2002) 433-435 (*Pouderon, Bernard*).

10772   *Mangin, Pascaline* Les manifestations divines dans les romans grecs: le cas du roman de Leucippe et Clitophon d'Achille TATIUS. Voir les dieux. 2002 ⇒629. 39-53.

10773   *Mezzadri, Bernard* Arès: dieu niais, dieu nié. Nier les dieux. 2002 ⇒626. 29-36.

10774   *Miccoli, Paolo* Lo spirito festivo della religione greco-romana. Ment. *Keréni, K.*: ED 55 (2002) 125-127.

10775   *Moutsopoulos, Evanghelos* De quelques thématiques déterminantes de la religion grecque. Kernos 15 (2002) 13-17.

10776·   **Muñoz Llamosas, Virginia** La intervención divina en el hombre a través de la literatura griega de época arcaica y clásica. Amst 2002, Hakkert xi; 726 pp.

10777   **Murray, Gilbert** Five stages of Greek religion. Mineola, NY [3]2002 <1951>, Dover xv, 221 pp. $13. 0-486-42500-2 [ThD 50, 379—W. Charles Heiser].

10778   [E]**Nissim, Liana** "La cruelle douceur d'Artémis": il mito di Artemide-Diana nelle lettere francesi. Quaderni di ACME 53: Mi 2002, Cisalpino 488 pp. 88-323-4613-3. Convegno Internazionale di Studi, Gargnano, Palazzo Feltrinelli: 13-16 giugno 2001.

10779   **Parisinou, Eva** The light of the gods: the role of light in archaic and classical Greek cult. 2000 ⇒16,10167. [R]Prudentia 34 (2002) 262-265 (*Salapata, Gina*).

10780   *Parker, Robert* The cult of Aphrodite Pandamos and Pontia on Cos. [F]VERSNEL, H.: 2002 ⇒126. 143-160.

10781   **Price, Simon** Religions of the ancient Greeks. 1999 ⇒15,10078; 17,9911. [R]JR 82 (2002) 329-331 (*Alderink, Larry J.*).

10782   **Scheer, T.S.** Die Gottheit und ihr Bild: Untersuchungen zur Funktion griechischer Kultbilder in Religion und Politik. Zetemata 105: 2000 ⇒16,10171. [R]CIR 52 (2002) 111-113 (*Parker, Robert*).

10783   *Schlesier, Renate* Der Fuß des Dionysos: zu *PMG* 871. [F]VERSNEL, H.: 2002 ⇒126. 161-191.

10784 *Schroer, Silvia* Griechische Heiligtümer im Spiegel alttestamentlicher Kosmologien und Theologien. Gottesstadt. QD 191: 2002 ⇒ 567. 231-288.

10785 *Sfameni, Carla* Ὁ βωμὸς μαντεῖος: altari 'di cenere' e prassi oracolare nei santuari greci. SMSR 68 (2002) 5-41.

10786 *Ternes, Charles Marie* Apollon chez Dionysos. Symbolisme et expérience. 2002 ⇒666. 75-89.

10787 *Zeitlin, Froma I.* Apollo und Dionysos: starting from birth. ᶠVERS-NEL, H. 2002 ⇒126. 193-218.

10788 *Zeller, Dieter* So wahr mir Hercules helfe!: die griechisch-römischen Götter und ihre Gläubigen am Beispiel von Korinth. WUB 25 (2002) 5-13.

M5.2 *Philosophorum critica religionis*—Greek philosopher religion

10789 **Baltes, Matthias** Die philosophische Lehre des Platonismus; von der 'Seele' als der Ursache aller sinnvollen Abläufe. Der Platonismus in der Antike 6,1-2: Stu 2002, Frommann xxiii; 437 + ix; 454 pp. €710. 3-7728-1158-2.

10790 ᴱᵀ**Bompaire, Jacques** LUCIEN: Oeuvres, 2: Opuscules 11-20. P 1998, Les Belles Lettres xii; 350 pp. 2-251-00463-7.

10791 **Boys-Stones, G.R.** Post-Hellenistic philosophy: a study of its development from the Stoics to ORIGEN. 2001 ⇒17,9921. ᴿStPhiloA 14 (2002) 236-238 (*Dillon, John*).

10792 *Brenk, Frederick E.* In the image, reflection and reason of Osiris: PLUTARCH and the Egyptian cults. Estudios sobre Plutarco. 2002 ⇒ 696. 83-98;

10793 Social and unsocial memory: the liberation of Thebes in PLUTARCH's *The Daimonion of Sokrates*. Scritti in onore di Italo Gallo. ᴱTorraca, L.: N 2002, Ed. Scientifiche Italiane. 97-114 [AcBib 10, 911];

10794 Religion under TRAJAN: PLUTARCH's resurrection of Osiris. Sage and emperor. 2002 ⇒701. 73-92 [AcBib 10,1029].

10795 **Busine, Aude** Les Sept sages de la Grèce antique: transmission et utilisation d'un patrimoine légendaire d'HÉRODOTE à PLUTARQUE. Culture et cité 1: P 2002, De Boccard 144 pp. 2-7018-0148-6 [Kernos 16,373s—Pirenne-Delforge, Vinciane].

10796 *Camplani, Alberto; Zambon, Marco* Il sacrificio come problema in alcune correnti filosofiche di età imperiale. ASEs 19 (2002) 59-99.

10797 **Harris, William Vernon** Restraining rage: the ideology of anger control in classical antiquity. CM 2002, Harvard University Press xii; 468 pp. $50. 0-674-00618-6. Bibl. 421-456. ᴿRBLit (2002)* (*Ruprecht, Louis A.*).

10798 **Hirsch-Luipold, Rainer** PLUTARCHs Denken in Bildern: Studien zur literarischen, philosophischen und religiösen Funktion des Bildhaften. STAC 14: Tü 2002, Mohr S. xii; 324 pp. 3-16-147752-9. Bibl. 291-312.

10799 **Lloyd, Geoffrey E.R.** The ambitions of curiosity: understanding the world in Ancient Greece and China. Ideas in context: C 2002, CUP xvi; 175 pp. 0-521-89461-1. Bibl. 154-169.

10800 **Long, A.A.** EPICTETUS—A Stoic and Socratic guide to life. Oxf 2002, Clarendon xiv; 310 pp. 0-19-924556-8. Bibl. 281-290.

10801   **Ludwig, Paul Walter** Eros and polis: desire and community in Greek political theory. C 2002, CUP xiii; 398 pp. 0-521-81065-5. Bibl. 381-392.

10802   ᵀ**Maclean, Jennifer K.B.; Aitken, Ellen B.** FLAVIUS PHILOSTRA-TUS: on heroes. Writings from the Greco-Roman World 3: Atlanta, GA 2002, SBL lxxxv; 187 pp. 1-58983-037-7. Preliminary essay by *Casey Dué* and *Gregory Nagy*. Bibl. 151-160.

10803   ᴱᵀ**Ramelli, Ilaria** MUSONIO RUFO: Diatribe, frammenti e testimonianze. Bompiani Testi a Fronte 31: Mi 2001, Bompiani 357 pp. 88-452-9099-9. Bibl. 339-345.

10804   *Simmons, Michael B.* PORPHYRY of Tyre's biblical criticism: a historical and theological appraisal. ᶠGREER, R.: 2002 ⇒51. 90-105.

10805   *Töchterle, Karlheinz* Gottessohn im Intertext: APOLLONIUS von Tyana. Religion—Literatur—Kunst II. Im Kontext 14: 2002 ⇒530. 295-304.

M5.3 *Mysteria eleusinia; Hellenistica*—**Mysteries; Hellenistic cults**

10806   **Acker, Clara** Dionysos en transe: la voix des femmes. Histoire Ancienne et Anthropologie: P 2002, L'Harmattan 384 pp. 2-7475-20-95-1. Bibl. 353-381.

10807   **Adinolfi, Marco** Scintille del verbo: ellenismo e bibbia a confronto. 2001 ⇒17,9926. ᴿRivBib 50 (2002) 471-473 (*Rolla, Armando*); LASBF 51 (2001) 448-449 (*Bottini, G.C.*).

10808   *Assmann, Jan* PYTHAGORAS und LUCIUS: zwei Formen 'ägyptischer Mysterien'. Ägyptische Mysterien?. 2002 ⇒389. 59-75.

10809   *Avram, Alexandru* Der dionysische thiasos in Kallatis: Organisation, Repräsentation, Funktion. Religiöse Vereine. STAC 13: 2002 ⇒468. 69-80.

10810   *Beal, Richard H.* Dividing a god;

10811   *Brashear, William M.; Kotansky, Roy* A new magical formulary. Magic and ritual. RGRW 141: 2002 ⇒505. 197-208/3-24.

10812   *Burkert, Walter* Mysterien der Ägypter in griechischer Sicht: Projektionen im Kulturkontakt;

10813   *DuQuesne, Terence* 'Effective in heaven and on earth': interpreting Egyptian religious practice for both worlds. Ägyptische Mysterien?. Kulte, Kulturen: 2002 ⇒389. 9-26/37-46.

10814   *Evans, Nancy A.* Sanctuaries, sacrifices, and the Eleusinian Mysteries. Numen 49 (2002) 227-254.

10815   ᴱᵀ**Fayant, Marie-Christine** NONNOS de Panopolis: les dionysiaques, 17: chant XLVII. CUFr: 2000 ⇒16,10190. ᴿAnCl 71 (2002) 311-312 (*Somville, Pierre*); ClR 52 (2002) 282-283 (*Whitby, Mary*); REA 104 (2002) 586-587 (*Cusset, Christophe*).

10816   *Fischer-Elfert, H.-W.* Das verschwiegene Wissen der Irtisen (Stele Louvre C 14): zwischen Arcanum und Preisgabe. Ägyptische Mysterien?. Kulte, Kulturen: 2002 ⇒389. 27-35.

10817   *Frankfurter, David* Dynamics of ritual expertise in antiquity and beyond: towards a new taxonomy of "magicians". Magic and ritual. RGRW 141: 2002 ⇒505. 159-178.

10818   *Frenschkowski, Marco* Religion auf dem Markt: Schlangenbeschwörer, Traumdeuter, inspirierte Bauchredner als Träger "abgesunkener" Religion in paganer und christlicher Antike: ein Beitrag zur Sozialgeschichte religiöser Berufe. [F]HOHEISEL, K.: JAC.E 34: 2002 ⇒59. 140-158 [Acts 16,16-22].

10819 *Giebel, Marion* Nur für Eingeweihte!: die Mysterienkulte in der griechisch-römischen Welt. WUB 25 (2002) 15-21.

10820 *Gordon, Richard L.*, *al.*, Mysterienreligion. RGG 5. 2002 ⇒796. 1638-1645.

10821 *Graf, Fritz* Theories of magic in antiquity. Magic and ritual. RGRW 141: 2002 ⇒505. 93-104.

10822 **Janowitz, Naomi** Icons of power: ritual practices in late antiquity. Magic in history: University Park, PA 2002, Pennsylvania State Univ. Pr. xxvii; 161 pp. 0-271-02147-0. Bibl. 129-143.

10823 *Klauck, Hans-Josef* Die antiken Mysterienkulte und das Urchristentum: Anknüpfung und Widerspruch. ZMR 86 (2002) 3-25.

10824 **Klauck, Hans-Josef** The religious context of early christianity: a guide to Graeco-Roman religions. [T]*McNeil, Brian*: Studies of the NT and its world: 2000 ⇒16,10191; 17,9931. [R]JR 82 (2002) 439-440 (*Frankfurter, David*); EvQ 74 (2002) 366-368 (*Gill, David W.J.*); HTS 57 (2001) 397-407 (*Thom, J.C.*).

10825 *LiDonnici, Lynn R.* Beans, fleawort, and the blood of a hamadryas baboon: recipe ingredients in Greco-Roman magical materials. Magic and ritual. RGRW 141: 2002 ⇒505. 359-377.

10826 *Lieven, Alexandra von* Mysterien des Kosmos: Kosmographie und Priesterwissenschaft. Ägyptische Mysterien?. 2002 ⇒389. 47-58.

10827 *Mazza, Enrico* Il tema del sacrificio nelle mistagogie della fine del quarto secolo. ASEs 19 (2002) 167-199.

10828 *Morenz, Ludwig D.* Schrift-Mysterium: Gottes-Schau in der visuellen Poesie von Esna—insbesondere zu den omnipotenten Widder-Zeichen zwischen Symbolik und Lesbarkeit. Ägyptische Mysterien?. Kulte, Kulturen: 2002 ⇒389. 77-94.

10829 *Motte, André* Nuit et lumière dans les mystères d'Éleusis. Symbolisme et expérience. 2002 ⇒666. 91-104.

10830 **Ogden, Daniel** Magic, witchcraft, and ghosts in the Greek and Roman worlds: a sourcebook. Oxf 2002, OUP x; 353 pp. 0-19-513-575-X. Bibl. 301-337.

10831 *Phillips, Oliver* The witches' thessaly. Magic and ritual. RGRW 141: 2002 ⇒505. 378-386.

10832 *Pilhofer, Peter* Ein andres Volk ohne Tempel: die θιασοι der Dionysos-Verehrer. Die frühen Christen. WUNT 145: 2002 ⇒225. 123-138.

10833 *Quack, Joachim Friedrich* Königsweihe, Priesterweihe, Isisweihe;
10834 *Rebrik, Victor* Confessio Cypriani und ägyptische Mysterien. Ägyptische Mysterien?. Kulte, Kulturen: 2002 ⇒389. 95-108/143-147.

10835 [E]**Scarpi, Paolo** Le religioni dei misteri, 1: Eleusi, Dionisismo, Orfismo; 2: Samotracia, Andania, Iside, Cibele e Attis, Mitraismo. Scrittori greci e latini: Mi 2002, Mondadori xlvii; 616 + lxxxii; 692 pp. €27. 88-04-50667/317-3.

10836 *Scibilia, Anna* Supernatural assistance in the Greek magical papyri: the figure of the Parhedros. Metamorphosis. 2002 ⇒394. 71-86.

10837 **Sfameni Gasparro, Giulia** Oracoli, profeti, sibille: rivelazione e salvezza nel mondo antico. BSRel 171: R 2002, LAS 489 pp. €31. 88-213-0482-5. Bibl. 377-472. [R]Ang. 79 (2002) 725-728 (*Garuti, Paolo*); Annales Theologici 16 (2002) 546-548 (*Tábet, M.*); VetChr 39 (2002) 408-410 (*Bettocchi, Silvia*).

10838   ᴱᵀSimon, Bernadette NONNOS de Panopolis: les dionysiaques, 14: chants xxxviii-xl. 1999 ⇒15,10096; 17,9936. ᴿOrpheus 23 (2002) 279-280 (*White, Heather*).

10839   *Smith, Jonathan* Great Scott!: thought and action one more time. Magic and ritual. RGRW 141: 2002 ⇒505. 73-91.

10840   *Stadler, Martin Andreas* Isis, das göttliche Kind und die Weltord-nung: Prolegomena zur Deutung des unpublizierten Papyrus Wien D.12006 Recto. Ägyptische Mysterien?. 2002 ⇒389. 109-125.

10841   *Struck, Peter T.* Speech acts and the stakes of Hellenism in late antiquity. Magic and ritual. RGRW 141: 2002 ⇒505. 387-403.

10842   **Tripolitis, Antonia** Religions of the Hellenistic-Roman age. 2001 ⇒17,9938. ᴿKerux 17/2 (2002) 79-80 (*Dennison, James T.*).

10843   *Versnel, H.S.* The poetics of the magical charm: an essay in the power of words. Magic and ritual. RGRW 141: 2002 ⇒505. 105-158.

10844   ᵀᴱVian, Francis NONNOS de Panopolis: les dionysiaques: Tome V, chants XI-XIII. 1995 ⇒13,9501. ᴿOrpheus 23 (2002) 277-279 (*White, Heather*).

M5.5 Religiones anatolicae

10845   *Alexander, Robert L.* The storm-god at ʿAin Dara;
10846   *Archi, Alfonso* Formation of the West Hurrian pantheon: the case of Išḫara. ᴹGÜTERBOCK, H. 2002 ⇒54. 11-19/21-33;
10847   Ea and the beast: a song related to the Kumarpi cycle. ᶠPOPKO, M. 2002 ⇒91. 1-10;
10848   Kizzuwatna amid Anatolian and Syrian cults. ᴹIMPARATI, F. 2002 ⇒61. 47-53.
10849   *Beal, Richard H.* Hittite oracles. Magic and divination. Ancient magic and divination 2: 2002 ⇒729. 57-81;
10850   Gleanings from Hittite oracle questions on religion, society, psychology and decision making. ᶠPOPKO, M. 2002 ⇒91. 11-37.
10851   *Beckman, Gary* Babylonica hethitica: the '*babilili*-ritual' from Boğazköy (CTH 718). ᴹGÜTERBOCK, H. 2002 ⇒54. 35-41.
10852   *Biga, Maria Giovanna* Marginal considerations on the Hittite ki.lam festival, ᴹIMPARATI, F. 2002 ⇒61. 101-108.
10853   **Cohen, Yoram** Taboos and prohibitions in Hittite society: a study of the Hittite expression natta ara ('not permitted'). Texte der Hethi-ter 24: Heid 2002, Winter xv; 198 pp. €49. 3-8253-1309-3. Bibl. 181-198.
10854   *Collins, Billie Jean* Necromancy, fertility and the dark earth: the use of ritual pits in Hittite cult. Magic and ritual. RGRW 141: 2002 ⇒505. 224-241.
10855   *Del Monte, Giuseppe* Sui rituali di Mallidunna di Turmita. ᶠPOPKO, M. 2002 ⇒91. 63-75.
10856   **Dignas, Beate** Economy of the sacred in Hellenistic and Roman Asia Minor. Oxford Classical Monographs: Oxf, 2002, OUP xiv; 364 pp. £55. 0-19-925408-7. Bibl. 300-340.
10857   ᴱᵀGarcía Trabazo, J.V. Textos religiosos hititas: mitos, plegarias, rituales. M 2002, Trotta 685 pp. €35.50. 84-8164-522-2.
10858   *Giorgieri, Mauro* Birra, acqua ed olio: paralleli siriani e neo-assiri ad un giuramento ittita. ᴹIMPARATI, F. 2002 ⇒61. 299-320.

10859 *Goedegebuure, Petra M.* Rituele reinheid bij de Hettieten. Phoenix 48 (2002) 93-102;

10860 KBo 17.17+: remarks on an Old Hittite royal substitution ritual. JANER 2 (2002) 61-73.

10861 *Groddek, Detlev* Die rituelle Behandlung des verschwundenen Sonnengottes (CTH 323). ᶠPOPKO, M. 2002 ⇒91. 119-131.

10862 *Haas, Volkert* Die hethitische Religion. Die Hethiter. 2002 ⇒535. 102-111;

10863 Die Göttin Ḫapantali(ja) und die Schafe. ᶠPOPKO, M. 2002 ⇒91. 143-146.

10864 *Hutter, Manfred* Das Ḫijara-Fest in Ḫattuša: Transformation und Funktion eines syrischen Festes. ᶠPOPKO, M. 2002 ⇒91. 186-196.

10865 *Klinger, Jörg* Reinigungsriten und Abwehrzauber: Funktion und Rolle magischer Rituale bei den Hethitern. Die Hethiter. 2002 ⇒ 535. 146-149.

10866 **Lancellotti, Maria Grazia** Attis: between myth and history: king, priest and god. RGRW 149: Lei 2002, Brill xiii; 207 pp. 90-04-12-851-4. Bibl. 175-198.

10867 *Lebrun, René* Divinités solaires d'Anatolie au second millénaire avant Jésus-Christ. Symbolisme et expérience. 2002 ⇒666. 67-73.

10868 *Lombardi, Alessandra* Sfondo storico e analisi strutturale della preghiera di Tudḫaliya IV alla dea Sole di Arinna (CTH 385,9). ᴹIMPARATI, F. 2002 ⇒61. 497-506.

10869 *Martino, Stefano de* Kult- und Festliturgie im hethitischen Reich: öffentlicher Ausdruck staatlich-religiöser Interdependenz. Die Hethiter. 2002 ⇒535. 118-121.

10870 *McMahon, Gregory* Comparative observations on Hittite rituals. ᴹGÜTERBOCK, H. 2002 ⇒54. 127-135.

10871 *Melchert, H. Craig* The god Sanda in Lycia?. ᶠPOPKO, M. 2002 ⇒ 91. 241-251.

10872 *Murphy, Susana B.* The practice of power in the ancient Near East: sorceresses and serpents in Hittite myths. Sex and gender. 2002 ⇒ 712. 433-442.

10873 **Nakamura, Mitsuo** Das hethitische nuntarriyasha-Fest. UNHAII 94: Lei 2002, Nederlands Instituut voor het Nabije Oosten: xi; 439 pp. 90-6258-095-5.

10874 *Özgüç, Tahsin* Opfer und Libation. Die Hethiter. 2002 ⇒535. 122-127.

10875 *Petzl, Georg* Zum religiösen Leben im westlichen Kleinasien: Einflüsse und Wechselwirkungen. Brückenland Anatolien?. 2002 ⇒ 453. 381-391.

10876 *Polvani, Anna Maria* Il dio Šanta nell'Anatolia del II millennio. ᴹIMPARATI, F. 2002 ⇒61. 645-652.

10877 *Prechel, Doris* Betrachtungen zum Ritual der Pupuwanni. ᶠPOPKO, M. 2002 ⇒91. 277-288.

10878 **Roller, Lynn E.** In search of god the mother: the cult of Anatolian Cybele. 1999 ⇒15,10103...17,9946. ᴿGn. 74 (2002) 473-475 (*Naumann-Steckner, Friederike*); JAAR 70 (2002) 201-202 (*Gudorf, Christine E.*).

10879 *Schwemer, Daniel* Leberschau, Losorakel, Vogelflug und Traumgesicht: Formen und Funktionen der Vorzeichendeutung. Die Hethiter. 2002 ⇒535. 140-145.

10880 *Singer, Itamar* Kantuzili the priest and the birth of Hittite personal prayer. ᶠPOPKO, M. 2002 ⇒91. 301-313.

10881   **Singer, Itamar** Hittite prayers. [E]*Hoffner, Harry Angier*: Writings from the ancient world 11: Atlanta, GA 2002, SBL xv; 141 pp. $25. 1-58983-032-6. Bibl. 119-132.

10882   *Strauss, Rita* Elemente mesopotamischer Ritualistik in hethitischen Texten: das "Šamuḫa-Ritual" CTH 480. Brückenland Anatolien?. 2002 ⇒453. 323-338.

10883   *Taggar-Cohen, Ada* The Ezen *pulaš*—'a Hittite installation rite of a new priest': in light of the installation of the [d]IM priestess in Emar;

10884   The casting of lots among the Hittites in light of ancient Near Eastern parallels. JANES 29 (2002) 127-159/97-103.

10885   *Taracha, Piotr* Another Hittite fragment of a substitution ritual;

10886   *Trémouille, Marie-Claude* Une cérémonie pour Ḫuwaššanna à Kuliwišna. [F]POPKO, M. 2002 ⇒91. 339-344/351-369.

10887   **Van Gessel, Ben H.L.** Onomasticon of the Hittite pantheon, 3. HO I/33,3: 2001 ⇒17,9951. [R]BiOr 59 (2002) 117-18 (*Popko, Maciej*).

10888   *Wilhelm, Gernot* 'Gleichsetzungstheologie', 'Synkretismus' und 'Gottesspaltungen' im Polytheismus Altanatoliens. Polytheismus. AOAT 298: 2002 ⇒418. 53-70.

10889   *Ziegler, Ruprecht* Aspekte der Entwicklung tarsischer Kulte in hellenistischer und römischer Zeit. Brückenland Anatolien?. 2002 ⇒ 453. 363-379.

M6.0 Religio canaanaea, syra

10890   *Albertz, Rainer* Religion in pre-exilic Israel;

10891   Religion in Israel during and after the exile. Biblical world, 2. 2002 ⇒273. 90-100/101-124.

10892   *Archi, Alfonso* Šeš-II-IB: a religious confraternity. Eblaitica 4. 2002 ⇒474. 23-55.

10893   *Barker, Margaret* Wisdom: the queen of heaven. SJTh 55 (2002) 141-159.

10894   *Beckman, Gary* The pantheon of Emar. [F]POPKO, M. 2002 ⇒91. 39-54.

10895   **Belayche, Nicole** Iudaea-Palaestina: the pagan cults in Roman Palestine. Religion der Römischen Provinzen 1: 2001 ⇒17,9957. [R]RHPhR 82 (2002) 216-217 (*Grappe, Ch.*); EtCl 70 (2002) 295-96 (*Bonnet, Corinne*).

10896   *Blanchetière, François* 'Tu n'auras pas d'autre dieu devant ma face': du Dieu des pères au Maître du monde. Nier les dieux. 2002 ⇒626. 111-117.

10897   *Bloch-Smith, Elizabeth* Death in the life of Israel. Sacred time. 2002 ⇒2679. 139-143.

10898   *Breitner, Georg; Seepe-Breitner, Anja* Das Quellheiligtum von Qanawat: ein Arbeitsbericht. DaM 13 (2002) 227-243.

10899   *Brelich, Angelo* Osservazioni storico-religiose sulle antiche divinità semitiche. Mitologia. 2002 <1958> ⇒148. 25-28.

10900   *Břeňová, Klára* The reminiscences of the deities of death in the Old Testament. ArOr 70 (2002) 481-488.

10901   **Brody, Aaron Jed** "Each man cried out to his God": the specialized religion of Canaanite and Phoenician seafarers. HSM 58: 1998 ⇒14,9292. [R]OLZ 97 (2002) 369-372 (*Márquez Rowe, Ignacio*).

10902   *Caquot, André* An den Wurzeln der Bibel. WUB 23 (2002) 37-41.

10903 *Daviau, P.M. Michèle; Dion, Paul-Eugène* Moab comes to life. BArR 28/1 (2002) 38-49; 63.

10904 *Davis, David* Divination in the bible. JBQ 30 (2002) 121-126.

10905 **Day, John** Yahweh and the gods and goddesses of Canaan. JSOT.S 265: 2000 ⇒16,10217; 17,9963. ᴿBiblInterp 10 (2002) 79-81 (*Edelman, Diana*); CBQ 64 (2002) 128-129 (*Rollston, Christopher A.*); BS 159 (2002) 490-491 (*Chisholm, Robert B.*); OLZ 97 (2002) 464-468 (*Scherer, Andreas*).

10906 *Dever, William G.* Theology, philology, and archaeology: in the pursuit of Ancient Israelite religion. Sacred time. 2002 ⇒2679. 11-33.

10907 *Dijkstra, Meindert* Schone handen: reinheid in de culturen van de Levant. Phoenix 48 (2002) 73-92.

10908 *Dion, Paul-Eugène* La religion des papyrus d'Éléphantine: un reflet du Juda d'avant l'exil. ᶠWEIPPERT, M.: ÖBO 186: 2002 ⇒133. 243-254.

10909 *Edelman, Diana* The disappearance of Mrs. God. BAIAS 19-20 (2001-2002) 184-185.

10910 *Fleming, Daniel E.* Emar: on the road from Harran to Hebron. Mesopotamia and the bible. JSOT.S 341: 2002 ⇒458. 222-250.

10911 **Goldstein, Jonathan A.** Peoples of an Almighty God: competing religions in the ancient world. AncB Reference Library: NY 2002, Doubleday xiv; 575 pp. $37. 0-385-42347-0. Bibl. 493-512. ᴿRBLit (2002)* (*Goff, Matthew*).

10912 **Grabbe, Lester L.** Judaic religion in the second temple period: belief and practice from the exile to Yavneh. 2000 ⇒16,10227; 17, 9970. ᴿStPhiloA 14 (2002) 206-216 (*Feldman, Louis H.*).

10913· *Grosby, Steven* 'Aram Kulloh and the worship of Hadad: a nation of Aram?. Biblical ideas. 2002 <1995> ⇒172. 150-165.

10914 **Hadley, Judith M.** The cult of Asherah in ancient Israel and Judah: evidence for a Hebrew goddess. UCOP 57: 2000 ⇒16, 10228; 17,9976. ᴿScEs 54 (2002) 120-121 (*Hentrich, Thomas*).

10915 **Haettner Blomquist, Tina** Gates and gods: cults in the city gates of Iron Age Palestine: an investigation of the archaeological and biblical sources. CB.OT 46: 1999 ⇒15,10137. ᴿJBL 121 (2002) 343-346 (*Roddy, Nicolae*).

10916 *Hahn, Johannes* "Die Tempel sind die Augen der Städte"—religiö-se Landschaft und Christianisierung in Nordsyrien. Religiöse Land-schaften. AOAT 301: 2002 ⇒408. 141-179.

10917 *Harl, Marguerite* L'exclusion des négateurs de Dieu dans la bible. Nier les dieux. 2002 ⇒626. 119-127.

10918 **Healey, John F.** The religion of the Nabataeans: a conspectus. RGRW 136 2001 ⇒17,9978. ᴿBiOr 59 (2002) 609-615 (*Dirven, Lucinda*).

10919 **Kaizer, Ted** The religious life of Palmyra: a study of social pat-terns of worship in the Roman period. Oriens et Occidens 4: Stu 2002, Steiner 305 pp. €64. 3-515-08027-9. Diss. Oxford. Bibl. 265-293.

10920 **Keel, Othmar; Uehlinger, Christoph** Gods, goddesses, and im-ages of God in Ancient Israel. ᵀ*Trapp, Thomas H.*: 1998 ⇒15, 10143; 16,10233. ᴿOLZ 97 (2002) 82-83 (*Hübner, Ulrich*).

10921 *Kinet, Dirk* "Baal ließ seine heilige Stimme erschallen ...": der theo-logische Ertrag der religiösen Texte aus Ugarit. WUB 23 (2002) 43-48.

10922 *Koch, Klaus* Der König als Sohn Gottes in Ägypten und Israel. 'Mein Sohn bist du'. SBS 192: 2002 ⇒366. 1-32 [Ps 2,7].

10923 *Lang, Bernhard* Israels Göttin: vom semitischen Mythos zum mythischen Rest. Die zwei Geschlechter. 2002 ⇒7637. 83-95.

10924 *Lewis, Theodore J.* How far can texts take us?: evaluating textual sources for reconstructing Ancient Israelite beliefs about the dead. Sacred time. 2002 ⇒2679. 169-217.

10925 *Lightfoot, Jane L.* On Greek ethnography of the Near East: the case of LUCIAN's *De dea syria*. StEeL 19 (2002) 137-148.

10926 *Loretz, Oswald* Die Einzigkeit eines Gottes im Polytheismus von Ugarit: zur Levante als Ursprungsort des biblischen Monotheismus. Polytheismus. AOAT 298: 2002 ⇒418. 71-89.

10927 **Lundager Jensen, Hans J.** Gammeltestamentlig religion: en indføring. 1998 ⇒14,9306; 16,10235. ᴿSEÅ 67 (2002) 166-167 (*Oredsson, Dag*).

10928 *Menezes, Rui de* Pluralismo religioso en el Antiguo Testamento. ᵀ*Hernández, Manuel*: SelTeol 41 (2002) 177-183 <VJTR 64 (2000) 834-844.

10929 **Merlo, Paolo** La dea Asratum—Atiratu—Asera: un contributo alla storia della religione semitica del nord. 1998 ⇒14,9309... 17,9986. ᴿJNES 61 (2002) 117-123 (*Pardee, Dennis*); RBLit (2002)* (*Holm, Tawny L.*).

10930 **Mettinger, Tryggve N.D.** The riddle of resurrection: "Dying and rising Gods" in the ancient Near East. CB.OT 50: 2001 ⇒17,9987. ᴿSEÅ 67 (2002) 172-173 (*Norin, Stig*).

10931 *Meyers, Carol* From household to house of Yahweh: women's religious culture in ancient Israel. Congress volume Basel 2001. VT.S 92: 2002 ⇒570. 277-303.

10932 **Miller, Patrick D.** The religion of ancient Israel. 2000 ⇒16, 10238; 17,9988. ᴿJThS 53 (2002) 126-129 (*Bray, Jason*); AsbTJ 56/2-57/1 (2001-2002) 143-145 (*Choi, John H.*); SWJT 45/1 (2002) 72-74 (*Johnson, Rick*); BS 159 (2002) 489-490 (*Chisholm, Robert B.*); JBL 121 (2002) 147-150 (*Burns, John Barclay*).

10933 *Müller, Hans-Peter* Anthropoide Sarkophage und phönizisch-punische Jenseitsvorstellungen. Die phönizischen anthropoiden Sarkophage, 2. 2002 ⇒471. 183-189.

10934 *Niehr, Herbert* Religiöse Wechselbeziehungen zwischen Syrien und Anatolien im 1. Jahrtausend v. Chr. Brückenland Anatolien?. 2002 ⇒453. 339-362.

10935 **Niehr, Herbert** Il contesto religioso dell'Israele antico: introduzione alle religioni della Siria-Palestina. Introduzione allo studio della Bibbia, Suppl. 7: Brescia 2002, Paideia 263 pp. €29. 88-394-0636-0. ᴱ*Merlo, Paolo*. ᴿCivCatt 153/4 (2002) 631-633 (*Prato, G.L.*).

10936 *Norin, Stig* Baal, Kinderopfer und 'über die Schwelle springen': Propheten und israelitische Religion im siebten Jahrhundert v. Chr. ᶠSTEINGRIMSSON, S.: ATSAT 72: 2002 ⇒117. 75-100 [Zeph 1,4].

10937 *Otto, Adelheid* Ein Wettergott auf dem Stier: Rekonstruktion eines spätbronzezeitlichen Kultgefäßes. DaM 13 (2002) 53-64.

10938 *Pardee, Dennis* Kulte, Orakel und Opferungen. WUB 23 (2002) 54-57.

10939 *Pitard, Wayne T.* Tombs and offerings: archaeological data and comparative methodology in the study of death in Israel. Sacred time. 2002 ⇒2679. 145-167.

10940 *Roberts, J.J.M.* Divine freedom and cultic manipulation in Israel and Mesopotamia <1975>;

10941 The Davidic origin of the Zion tradition <1973>;

10942 Zion in the theology of the Davidic-Solomonic empire<1982>. The bible and the ANE. 2002 ⇒230. 72-82/313-330/331-347.

10943 *Roche, M.-J.* La religion nabatéenne archaïque (résumé). TEuph 23 (2002) 155.

10944 *Rouault, Olivier* Religion et cultures locales dans le Moyen-Euphrate syrien au Bronze Moyen. Hethitica XV. 2002 ⇒683. 217-232.

10945 *Römer, T.; Sapin, J.* Conclusion. TEuph 23 (2002) 157-173.

10946 *Schmidt, Brian* Der unheimliche Tod. WUB 23 (2002) 58-60.

10947 **Simbanduku, Célestin** YHWH, les dieux et les anges: permanence du polythéisme dans la religion de la bible. ᴰ*Schenker, Adrian*: 2002 Diss. Fribourg [ThRv 99/2,vii].

10948 *Smith, Jonathan Z.* Religion up and down, out and in. Sacred time. 2002 ⇒2679. 3-10.

10949 *Smith, Mark S.* Remembering God: collective memory in Israelite religion. CBQ 64 (2002) 631-651;

10950 Ugaritic studies and Israelite religion: a retrospective view. Ment. *Albright, W.* NEA (BA) 65 (2002) 17-29.

10951 **Smith, Mark S.** The early history of God: Yahweh and the other deities in Ancient Israel. Biblical Resource: GR ²2002 <1990>, Eerdmans xlvi; 243 pp $25. 0-8028-3972-X. Foreword by *Patrick D. Miller*;

10952 The origins of biblical monotheism: Israel's polytheistic background and the Ugaritic texts. 2001 ⇒17,10001. ᴿJQR 92 (2002) 276-279 (*Freedman, David Noel*).

10953 **Smith, William Robertson** Religion of the Semites. New Brunswick, NJ ²2002, Transaction xlix; 507 pp. $40. 0-7658-0936-2. Introd. *Robert A. Segal*.

10954 **Stark, Rodney** One true God: historical consequences of monotheism. 2001 ⇒17,10002. ᴿAnton. 77 (2002) 593-595 (*Oviedo, Lluís*); RRelRes 44/1 (2002) 98-99 (*Robbins, Thomas*); CHR 88 (2002) 554-555 (*Fisher, Eugene J.*).

10955 *Stern, Ephraim* Goddesses and cults at Tel Dor. Qad. 35 (2002) 108-112. **H.**

10956 *Stuckey, Johanna H.* The great goddesses of the Levant. JSSEA 29 (2002) 28-57.

10957 *Swartz, Michael D.* The semiotics of the priestly vestments in ancient Judaism. Sacrifice in religious experience. 2002 ⇒612. 57-80.

10958 *Sweek, Joel* Inquiring for the state in the ancient Near East: delineating political location. Magic and divination. Ancient magic and divination 2: 2002 ⇒729. 41-56.

10959 **Thasiho Mahiniro, Jean-Pierre** Du 'Dieu des pères' ʾEl à YHWH (Ex 3,6.15), modèle hiistorico-évolutif pour une inculturation du 'Dieu des ancêtres' négro-africain dans le christianisme: le cas des Bantu *Nande*. ᴰ*Deiana, Giovanni*: R 2002, x; 201 pp. Extr. Diss. Urbaniana 2002.

10960 **Thelle, Rannfrid I.** Ask God: divine consultation in the literature of the Hebrew Bible. ᴰ*Barstad, Hans*: BET 30: Fra 2002, Lang 284 pp. 3-631-37161-6. Diss. Oslo 1999 Bibl. 247-264].

10961 *Theuer, Gabriele* Göttinnen in Ugarit-und im Alten Testament?. WUB 23 (2002) 50-53.
10962 **Tigay, Jeffrey H.** You shall have no other gods: Israelite religion in the light of Hebrew inscriptions. Harvard Semitic Studies 31: 1986 ⇒3,b276... 7,a764. [R]Maarav 9 (2002) 113-118 (*Lewis, Theodore J.*).
10963 *Van der Toorn, Karel* Israelite figurines: a view from the texts. Sacred time. 2002 ⇒2679. 45-62;
10964 Recent trends in the study of Israelite religion. [F]LEERTOUWER, L. 2002 ⇒74. 223-243.
10965 *Verhoeven, Marc* Transformations of society: the changing role of ritual and symbolism in the PPNB and the PN in the Levant, Syria and south-east Anatolia. Paléorient 28 (2002) 5-13 [BuBB 39,56].
10966 *Wiggermann, F.A.M., al.,* Magie. RGG 5. 2002 ⇒796. 661-679.
10967 *Wright, J. Edward* W.F. ALBRIGHT's vision of Israelite religion. NEA (BA) 65 (2002) 63-68;
10968 Wisdom: the queen of heaven. SJTh 55 (2002) 141-159.
10969 *Zevit, Ziony* Philology and archaeology: imagining new questions, begetting new ideas. Sacred time. 2002 ⇒2679. 35-42.

M6.5 **Religio aegyptia**

10970 **Antonelli, Stefano** Osiride: aspetti magici ed esoterici dell'antico Egitto. Patti (ME) 2002, Nicola Calabria 54 pp. 88-88010-27-0. Bibl. 53-54.
10971 *Assmann, Jan* L'immortalité dans l'Egypte ancienne. MoBi 145 (2002) 12-17.
10972 **Assmann, Jan** Ma'at: Gerechtigkeit und Unsterblichkeit im alten Ägypten. Mü 2001 <1990, 1995>, Beck 319 pp. €16.50. 3-406-45-943-9.
10973 *Assmann, Jan* Isis und Osiris: Geschlechterdifferenz im altägyptischen Totenritual. Paare. 2002 ⇒489. 9-28;
10974 Todesbefallenheit im alten Ägypten;
10975 Die Nacht vor der Beisetzung: der rituelle Kontext des Totengerichts im alten Ägypten. Tod, Jenseits. 2002 ⇒390. 230-51/420-36.
10976 **Assmann, Jan** Ägyptische Hymnen und Gebete. OBO: [2]1999 <1975> ⇒15,10177. [R]WO 32 (2002) 165-168 (*Quack, Joachim Friedrich*);
10977 Images et rites de la mort dans l'Égypte ancienne: l'apport des liturgies funéraires. 2000 ⇒16,10274. [R]MSR 59/2 (2002) 87-88 (*Cannuyer, Christian*);
10978 La morte come tema culturale. T 2002, Einaudi 95 pp.;
10979 The search for God in ancient Egypt. [T]*Lorton, David*: 2001 ⇒17, 10017. [R]CamArchJ 12 (2002) 283-285 (*Hare, Tom*); JARCE 39 (2002) 257-258 (*Hollis, Susan Tower*).
10980 *Bartel, Hans-Georg* Funktionale Aspekte des Täglichen Rituals im Tempel Sethos' I. in Abydos. Ägyptologische Tempeltagung. ÄAT 33,3: 2002 ⇒721. 1-16.
10981 **Bedier, Shafia** Die Rolle des Gottes Geb in den ägyptischen Tempelinschriften der griechisch-römischen Zeit. HÄB 41: 1995 ⇒ 11/2,8742; 16,10279. [R]OLZ 97 (2002) 351-353 (*Hallof, Jochen*).

10982 **Beinlich, Horst** Das Buch vom Ba. Studien zum altägyptischen Totenbuch 4: 2000 ⇒16,10280; 17,10025. [R]BiOr 59 (2002) 45-48 (*Goyon, Jean-Claude*); ZDMG 152 (2002) 192-194 (*Gutschmidt, Holger*).

10983 *Bell, Lanny* Divine kingship and the theology of the obelisk cult in the temples of Thebes. Ägyptologische Tempeltagung. ÄAT 33,3: 2002 ⇒721. 17-46.

10984 *Bickel, Susanne* Aspects et fonctions de la déification d'Amenhotep III. BIFAO 102 (2002) 63-90.

10985 **Bricault, Laurent** Atlas de la diffusion des cultes isiaques: (IVe S. AV. J.-C. - IVe S. Apr. J.-C.). Mémoires de l'Académie des inscriptions et Belles-Lettres 23: 2001 ⇒17,10029. [R]CEg 153-154 (2002) 351-352 (*Malaise, Michel*).

10986 *Browne, Gerald M.* The government of "heaven" in Old Nubian. Or. 71 (2002) 296-297.

10987 *Cannuyer, Christian* Questions sur la religion d'Akhénaton et son prétendu "monothéisme". MSR 59/2 (2002) 23-82;

10988 L'illumination du défunt comme hiérophanie de sa divinisation dans l'Égypte ancienne. Symbolisme et expérience. 2002 ⇒666. 45-66.

10989 *Cimmino, Franco* Interpreti e comunicatori del sacro e del religioso nell'antico Egitto. La Critica Sociologica 140 (2001-2002) 40-43.

10990. **David, Rosalie** Religion and magic in Ancient Egypt. L 2002, Penguin xvii; 488 pp. 0-14-026252-0. Bibl. 434-453.

10991 **Demichelis, Sara** Il calendario delle feste di Montu: papiro ieratico CGT 54021, verso. Catalogo del Museo Egizio di Torino 1, Monumenti e testi 10: T 2002, Ministero per i beni...culturali, Soprintendenza al Museo delle antichità egizie 124 pp. Bibl. 111-124.

10992 **Depuydt, Leo** Civil calendar and lunar calendar in ancient Egypt. OLA 77: 1997 ⇒13,9590; 16,10287. [R]JARCE 39 (2002) 241-250 (*Spalinger, Anthony*).

10993 *Dieleman, Jacco* Rituele reinheid in het oude Egypte. Phoenix 48 (2002) 63-72.

10994 *Donnat, Sylvie* Des lettres pour les morts. MoBi 145 (2002) 30-31.

10995 *Dunand, Françoise* Le désir de connaître Dieu: une vision de Mandoulis au temple de Kalabscha. Voir les dieux. 2002 ⇒629. 23-38.

10996 *Ernst, Herbert* Der Opferkult in den Vorhöfen der Tempel in Edfu, Medamud und Kom Ombo. ZÄS 129/1 (2002) 12-19.

10997 *Fabbian, Tiziano* La seconda nascita o rinascita animale: un rito di iniziazione nell'antico Egitto. CredOg 129 (2002) 79-102.

10998 *Forgeau, Annie* Horus enfant, quel nom, quel champ d'action?. BSFE 153 (2002) 6-23.

10999 **Frankfurter, David** Religion in Roman Egypt: assimilation and resistance. 2000 <1998> ⇒14,9358...17,10039. [R]Numen 49 (2002) 350-351 (*Haase, Mareile*); OCP 68 (2002) 499-503 (*Luisier, Ph.*); HR 42 (2002) 188-191 (*Sørensen, Jørgen Podemann*); JARCE 39 (2002) 256-257 (*Bianchi, Robert Steven*).

11000 *Gee, John* Oracle by image: Coffin text 103 in context. Magic and divination. Ancient magic and divination 2: 2002 ⇒729. 83-88.

11001 *Gestoso, Graciela N.* Atonismo e imperialismo. DavarLogos 1/2 (2002) 163-187.

11002 *Goebs, Katja* A functional approach to Egyptian myth and mythemes. JANER 2 (2002) 27-59.

11003   *Gordon, Richard* Shaping the text: innovation and authority in Graeco-Egyptian malign magic. [F]VERSNEL, H. 2002 ⇒126. 69-111.

11004   *Görg, Manfred* Zweigeschlechtlichkeit bei ägyptischen Göttern. Die zwei Geschlechter. 2002 ⇒7637. 65-81.

11005   *Gubel, Eric* The anthroponym ḥr: new light on the iconography of the god Horon?. [M]CIASCA, A. 2002 ⇒15. 269-279. 2 pl.

11006   *Gundlach, Rolf* Weltschöpfung versus Welterklärung: zum mythischen Bild der Pharaonen. Religion und Weltbild. Marburger religionsgeschichtliche Beiträge 2: 2002 ⇒443. 13-29.

11007   **Haring, B.J.J.** Divine households: administrative and economic aspects of the New Kingdom memorial temples in western Thebes. Egyptologische Uitgaven 11: 1997 ⇒13,9601... 17,10043. [R]CEg 153-154 (2002) 108-127 (*Grandel, Pierre*).

11008   *Hasenfratz, Hans-Peter* Patterns of creation in ancient Egypt. Creation in Jewish... tradition. JSOT.S 319: 2002 ⇒593. 174-178.

11009   *Hornung, Erik* Das Denken des Einen im alten Ägypten. Polytheismus. AOAT 298: 2002 ⇒418. 21-32;

11010   Pharaos Reise in den 'Weltinnenraum'. Tod, Jenseits. 2002 ⇒390. 613-629.

11011   **Hornung, Erik** Spiritualità nell'antico Egitto. [E]*Amenta, Alessia*: Egitto antico 1: R 2002, "L'Erma" di Bretschneider 206 pp. 88-826-5-132-0. Bibl. 191-197.

11012   *Kettel, Jeannot* Schriften der Brüder CHAMPOLLION in deutschen Sammlungen, I: <...les Brames de l'Hindoustan et les docteurs de Thèbes et de Memphis...>: ein unveröffentlichter Brief Champollions an Joseph von Hammer-Purgstall. ZÄS 129/1 (2002) 49-60.

11013   *Kormyscheva, Eleonora* Riten des Amun in den nubischen Tempeln von Ramses II. Ägyptologische Tempeltagung. ÄAT 33,3: 2002 ⇒721. 109-135.

11014   **Krauss, Rolf** Astronomische Konzepte und Jenseitsvorstellungen in den Pyramidentexten. ÄA 59: 1998 ⇒14,9376...16,10303. [R]JNES 61 (2002) 62-68 (*Allen, James P.*).

11015   **Lichtheim, Miriam** Moral values in ancient Egypt. OBO 155: 1997 ⇒13,9611...16,10306. [R]IEJ 52 (2002) 111-17 (*Shupak, Nili*).

11016   *Lieven, Alexandra von* Wissen, was die Welt im Innersten zusammenhält *oder* Faust in Ägypten. JANER 2 (2002) 75-89.

11017   **Lieven, Alexandra von** Der Himmel über Esna: eine Fallstudie zur religiösen Astronomie in Ägypten am Beispiel der kosmologischen Decken- und Architravinschriften im Tempel von Esna. ÄA 64: 2000 ⇒16,10308. [R]BiOr 59 (2002) 272-275 (*Hallof, Jochen*); JANER 2 (2002) 161-164 (*Jasnow, Richard*).

11018   **Lüscher, Barbara** Das Totenbuch pBerlin P.10477 aus Achmim (mit Photographien des verwandten pHildesheim 5248). Handschriften des altägyptischen Totenbuches 6: 2000 ⇒16,10310. [R]BiOr 59 (2002) 48-50 (*Laan, G.P.*); OLZ 97 (2002) 477-481 (*Lieven, Alexandra von*).

11019   *Manniche, Lise* Goddess and woman in ancient Egypt. BCSMS 37 (2002) 7-11;

11020   JSSEA 29 (2002) 1-8.

11021   *McCarthy, Heather Lee* The Osiris Nefertari: a case study of decorum, gender, and regeneration. JARCE 39 (2002) 173-195.

11022   *Meeks, Dimitri* Nier, mésestimer ou ignorer les dieux?: le cas de l'Égypte ancienne. Nier les dieux. 2002 ⇒626. 15-27.

11023 **Meurer, Georg** Die Feinde des Königs in den Pyramidentexten. OBO 189: Gö 2002, Vandenhoeck & R. ix; 404 pp. FS120. 3-525-53046-3. Bibl. 341-365.

11024 *Miosi, Frank T.* Some aspects of geb in the coffin texts. JSSEA 29 (2002) 100-107.

11025 *Morenz, Ludwig D.* (Unrechtmäßiges) Erwerben von Schlachtopfer-Fleisch(?): eine Metapher für Hungersnot aus der Zeit der Regionen (Erste Zwischenzeit). BN 114/115 (2002) 47-52;

11026 Mytho-Geographie der vier Himmelsrichtungen: drei bzw. vier Fabelwesen in zwei Gräbern des ägyptischen Mittleren Reiches und ägyptisch-altorientalische Kulturkontakte. WO 32 (2002) 20-32.

11027 **Munro, Irmtraut** Spruchvorkommen auf Totenbuch-Textzeugen der Dritten Zwischenzeit. Studien zum altägyptischen Totenbuch 5: 2001 ⇒17,10055. ᴿJANER 2 (2002) 165-68 (*Verhoeven, Ursula*);

11028 Das Totenbuch des Pa-en-nesti-taui aus der Regierungszeit des Amenemope (pLondon BM 10064). Handschriften des altägyptischen Totenbuches 7: 2001 ⇒17,10054. ᴿJANER 2 (2002) 168-172 (*Verhoeven, Ursula*).

11029 **Négrier, Patrick** La bible et l'Égypte: introduction à l'ésotérisme biblique. Les Architectes de la Connaissance: Bagnolet (Seine—Saint-Denis) 2002, Ivoire-Clair 126 pp. 2-913882-13-7. Bibl. 124.

11030 *Pernigotti, Sergio* La concezione di Dio e degli dèi nella religione egizia. CredOg 129 (2002) 69-78.

11031 *Peters, Ulrike* Xolotl und Anubis: die Hund-Mensch-Beziehung als religionsgeschichtliches Phänomen in Amerika und Afrika. ᶠHOHEISEL, K.: JAC.E 34: 2002 ⇒59. 361-380.

11032 *Preys, René* Hathor au sceptre-*ouas*: images et textes au service de la théologie. Revue d'Égyptologie 53 (2002) 197-211.

11033 *Quack, Joachim Friedrich* Die Dienstanweisungen des Oberlehrers aus dem Buch vom Tempel. Ägyptologische Tempeltagung. ÄAT 33,3: 2002 ⇒721. 159-171.

11034 ᴱ**Redford, Donald B.** The ancient gods speak: a guide to Egyptian religion. Oxf 2002, OUP 405 pp. $30. 0-19-515401-0.

11035 **Rhodes, Michael D.** The Hor Book of Breathings: a translation and commentary. Studies in the Book of Abraham 2: Provo 2002, Young Univ. 97 pp. 0-934893-63-2. ᴿArOr 70 (2002) 568-569 (*Janák, Jiří*).

11036 *Ritner, Robert K.* Necromancy in ancient Egypt. Magic and divination. Ancient magic and divination 2: 2002 ⇒729. 89-96.

11037 **Rochholz, Matthias** Schöpfung, Feindvernichtung, Regeneration: Untersuchung zum Symbolgehalt der machtgeladenen Zahl 7 im alten Ägypten. ÄAT 56: Wsb 2002, Harrassowitz xlii; 279 pp. 3-447-04604-X. Bibl. xi-xl.

11038 *Spalinger, Anthony* Egyptian festival dating and the moon. Under one sky. AOAT 297: 2002 ⇒9014. 379-403.

11039 **Spieser, Cathie** Les noms du Pharaon: comme êtres autonomes au Nouvel Empire. OBO 174: 2000 ⇒16,10327; 17,10064. ᴿJSSEA 29 (2002) 118-121 (*Lurson, Benoit*).

11040 **Sternberg-El Hotabi, Heike** Untersuchungen zur Überlieferungsgeschichte der Horusstelen: ein Beitrag zur Religionsgeschichte Ägyptens im 1. Jahrtausend v. Chr. ÄA 62: 1999 ⇒15,10227; 17, 10065. ᴿArOr 70 (2002) 240-242 (*Bareš, Ladislav*); OLZ 97 (2002) 713-729 (*Quack, Joachim Friedrich*).

11041 *Symons, Sarah* The 'transit star clock' from the book of Nut. Under one sky. AOAT 297: 2002 ⇒9014. 429-446.
11042 **Taylor, John Hammond** Death and the afterlife in Ancient Egypt. 2001 ⇒17,10066. [R]DiscEg 52 (2002) 115-128 (*Warburton, David*); ArOr 70 (2002) 427-429 (*Bareš, Ladislav*).
11043 **Ullmann, Martina** König für die Ewigkeit: die Häuser der Millionen von Jahren: eine Untersuchung zu Königskult und Tempeltypologie in Ägypten. ÄAT 51: Wsb 2002, Harrassowitz xxii; 702 pp. 3-447-04521-3. 14 pl.
11044 *Velde, Herman te* De symboliek van apen en bavianen in de oudegyptische cultuur en religie. Phoenix 48/1 (2002) 25-45.
11045 *Verhoeven, Ursula* Der Himmel über Ägypten: Götter, Mythen und Rituale im Reich der Pharaonen. WUB 26 (2002) 16-19.
11046 *Volokhine, Youri* Le dieu Thot au Qasr el-Agoûz Dd-ḥr-p'-hb, Dḥwty-stm. BIFAO 102 (2002) 405-423.
11047 *Welvaert, Eric* The fossils of Qau el Kebir and their role in the mythology of the 10th nome of Upper-Egypt. ZÄS 129/2 (2002) 166-183.

M7.0 Religio mesopotamica

11048 *Abusch, Tzvi* The socio-religious framework of the Babylonian witchcraft ceremony *maqlû*: some observations on the introductory section of the text, part I. [M]JACOBSEN, T. 2002 ⇒62. 1-34;
11049 Sacrifice in Mesopotamia. Sacrifice in religious experience. 2002 ⇒612. 39-48.
11050 **Abusch, Tzvi** Mesopotamian witchcraft: towards a history and understanding of Babylonian witchcraft beliefs and literature. Ancient Magic and Divination 5: Lei 2002, Brill xvi; 314 pp. $87. 90-04-12387-3. Bibl. 293-305.
11051 **Annus, Amar** The god Ninurta in the mythology and royal ideology of ancient Mesopotamia. SAAS 14: Helsinki 2002, The Neo-Assyrian Text Corpus Project: xvi; 242 pp. 971-45-9057-0. Bibl. 215-229. [R]UF 34 (2002) 932-934 (*Dietrich, Manfried*).
11052 **Bidmead, Julye** The Akitu festival: religious continuity and royal legitimation in Mesopotamia. Gorgias Dissertations, Near Eastern Studies 2: Piscataway, NJ 2002, Gorgias 220 pp. 1-931956-34-0. Bibl. 175-211.
11053 *Böck, Barbara* Physiognomie und Schicksal?: oder wie der altmesopotamische Mensch mit einem durch ein physiognomisches Omen angekündigtes Unheil umgegangen sein mag. Sef. 62 (2002) 241-257.
11054 *Charlier, Pascal* Intempéries et magie en Mésopotamie ancienne. Charmes et sortilèges. 2002 ⇒477. 37-49.
11055 **Chiodi, Silvia Maria** Offerte "funebri" nella Lagas presargonica. Materiali per il vocabolario sumerico 5,1-2: 1997 ⇒13,2026... 17, 10076. [R]AfO 48-49 (2001-2002) 175-180 (*Foxvog, Daniel A.*).
11056 *Cussini, Eleonora* La concezione di dio e gli dèi nel mondo mesopotamico. CredOg 129 (2002) 31-50.
11057 *Da Riva, Rocío* Schafe, die 'aus den Häusern' herbeigeführt wurden: BM 78910 und die Rolle des privaten Spenders (*kāribu*) im neubabylonischen Sippar. [F]WALKER, C. 2002 ⇒130. 57-64.

11058 *Dalley, Stephanie* Near Eastern myths and legends. Biblical world, 1. 2002 ⇒273. 41-64.

11059 **Dijkstra, Klaas** Life & loyalty: a study in the socio-religious culture of Syria and Mesopotamia in the Graeco-Roman period based on epigraphical evidence. RGRW 128: 1995 ⇒11/2,8834... 15, 10239. ^RJNES 61 (2002) 156-157 (*Briquel Chatonnet, Françoise*).

11060 *Edzard, D.O.* Eas doppelzüngiger Rat an Adapa: ein Lösungsvorschlag. Or. 71 (2002) 415-416.

11061 *Fischer, Claudia* Twilight of the sun-god. Iraq 64 (2002) 125-134.

11062 *Frahm, Eckart* Zwischen Tradition und Neuerung: babylonische Priestergelehrte im achamenidenzeitlichen Uruk. Religion und Religionskontakte. 2002 ⇒492. 74-108.

11063 *Geller, M.J.* The Free Library Inanna Prism reconsidered. ^MJACOBSEN, T. 2002 ⇒62. 87-100.

11064 **Haul, Michael** Das Etana-Epos: ein Mythos von der Himmelfahrt des Königs von Kiš. 2000 ⇒16,10347. ^RBiOr 59 (2002) 352-354 (*Novotny, Jamie R.*).

11065 *Heimpel, Wolfgang* The lady of Girsu. ^MJACOBSEN, T. 2002 ⇒62. 155-160.

11066 **Holloway, Steven W.** Aššur is King! Assur is King!: religion in the exercise of power in the Neo-Assyrian Empire. Culture & history of the Ancient Near East 10: Lei 2002, Brill xxxiv; 559 pp. 9004-12-328-8. Bibl. 445-501. ^RArOr 70 (2002) 569-571 (*Pečirková, Jana*).

11067 **Hunger, Hermann; Pingree, David** Astral sciences in Mesopotamia. HO 1/44 1999 ⇒15,10244; 17,10083. ^RAfO 48-49 (2001-2002) 244-247 (*Brack-Bernsen, Lis*).

11068 *Jean, Cynthia* Male and female supernatural assistants in Mesopotamian magic. Sex and gender. 2002 ⇒712. 255-261.

11069 *Kämmerer, Th.R.* Archetypen in sumerischen, babylonischen und assyrischen Traumschilderungen. ^FDIETRICH, M. 2002 ⇒28. 191-207.

11070 *Kessler Guinan, Ann* A severed head laughed: stories of divinatory interpretation. Magic and divination. 2002 ⇒729. 7-40.

11071 *Koch-Westenholz, Ulla* Old Babylonian extispicy reports. ^FWALKER, C. 2002 ⇒130. 131-145.

11072 **Koch-Westenholz, Ulla** Babylonian liver omens: the chapters Manzazu, Padanu and Pan takalti of the Babylonian extispicy series mainly from Assurbanipal's library. 2000 ⇒16,10349. ^RBSOAS 65 (2002) 379-380 (*George, A.R.*).

11073 *Krebernik, Manfred* Vielzahl und Einheit im altmesopotamischen Pantheon. Polytheismus. AOAT 298: 2002 ⇒418. 33-51;

11074 Geschlachtete Gottheiten und ihre Namen. ^FDIETRICH, M. 2002 ⇒ 28. 289-298.

11075 *Lambert, W.G.* A rare exorcistic fragment. ^MJACOBSEN, T. 2002 ⇒62. 203-210;

11076 Units of time as cosmic powers in Sumero-Babylonian texts. ^FWALKER, C. 2002 ⇒130. 189;

11077 The background of the neo-Assyrian sacred tree. Sex and gender. 2002 ⇒712. 321-326.

11078 *Lapinkivi, Pirjo* The adorning of the bride: providing her with wisdom. Sex and gender. 2002 ⇒712. 327-335.

11079 *Lehoux, Daryn* The historicity question in Mesopotamian divination. Under one sky. AOAT 297: 2002 ⇒9014. 209-222.

11080   *Maier, John* Gender differences in the first millennium: additions to
        a canonical lamentation. Sex and gender. 2002 ⇒712. 345-354.
11081   *Marchesi, Gianni* On the divine Name dBA.Ú. Or. 71 (2002) 161-
        172.
11082   *Michalowski, Piotr* 'Round about Nidaba: on the early goddesses of
        Sumer'. Sex and gender. 2002 ⇒712. 413-422.
11083   *Müller-Kessler, Christa* A charm against demons of time. ᶠWALK-
        ER, C. 2002 ⇒130. 183-188.
11084   *Porter, Barbara Nevling* Beds, sex, and politics: the return of Mar-
        duk's bed to Babylon. Sex and gender. 2002 ⇒712. 523-535.
11085   *Reynolds, Frances S.* Describing the body of a god;
11086   *Richardson, Seth* Ewe should be so lucky: extispicy reports and
        everyday life. ᶠWALKER, C. 2002 ⇒130. 215-227/229-244.
11087   **Sahrhage, Dietrich** Fischfang und Fischkult im alten Mesopotami-
        en. Fra 1999, Lang 241 pp. 3-631-34815-0. Bibl. 213-231.
11088   *Schaudig, Hanspeter* Nabonid, der 'Gelehrte auf dem Königs-
        thron': Omina, Synkretismen und die Ausdeutung von Tempel- und
        Götternamen als Mittel zur Wahrheitsfindung spätbabylonischer
        Religionspolitik. ᶠDIETRICH, M. 2002 ⇒28. 619-645.
11089   **Schwemer, Daniel** Die Wettergottgestalten Mesopotamiens und
        Nordsyriens im Zeitalter der Keilschriftkulturen. 2001 ⇒17,10106.
        ᴿOLZ 97 (2002) 752-754 (*Klengel, Horst*).
11090   *Scurlock, JoAnn* Translating transfers in ancient Mesopotamia.
        Magic and ritual. RGRW 141: 2002 ⇒505. 209-223.
11091   *Sefati, Yitschak; Klein, Jacob* The role of women in Mesopotamian
        witchcraft. Sex and gender. 2002 ⇒712. 569-587.
11092   *Sommerfeld, Walter* Der Stadtgott von Ešnunna und der Prozeß des
        frühen sumerisch-akkadischen Synkretismus. ᶠDIETRICH, M. 2002
        ⇒28. 699-706.
11093   *Stol, Marten* Reinheid in Mesopotamië. Phoenix 48 (2002) 103-7.
11094   **Vanstiphout, Herman** Helden en goden van Sumer. 1998 ⇒14,
        9452; 17,10108. ᴿMuséon 115/1-2 (2002) 215-216 (*Lebrun, R.*).
11095   *Vázquez Hoys, A.M.* Diosas de occidente, diosas de oriente (résu-
        mé). TEuph 23 (2002) 156.
11096   *Veldhuis, Niek* The solution of the dream: a new interpretation of
        Bilgames' death. JCS 53 (2001) 133-148.
11097   **Vera Chamaza, Galo W.** Die Omnipotenz Assurs: Entwicklungen
        in der Assur-Theologie unter den Sargoniden Sargon II., Sanherib
        und Asarhaddon. AOAT 295: Müns 2002, Ugarit-Verlag 586 pp. 3-
        934628-24-9. Bibl. 515-533.
11098   *Weippert, Manfred* 'König, fürchte dich nicht!': assyrische Prophe-
        tie im 7. Jahrhundert v. Chr. Or. 71 (2002) 1-54.
11099   *Westenholz, Joan Goodnick* Great goddesses in Mesopotamia: the
        female aspect of divinity. BCSMS 37 (2002) 13-26;
11100   JSSEA 29 (2002) 9-27.
11101   *Wiesehöfer, Josef* Kontinuität oder Zäsur?: Babylonien unter den
        Achameniden. Religion und Religionskontakte. 2002 ⇒492. 29-48.
11102   *Wilcke, Claus* Der Tod im Leben der Babylonier. Tod, Jenseits.
        2002 ⇒390. 252-266.
11103   *Williams, Clemency* Signs from the sky, signs from the earth: the
        diviner's manual revisited. Under one sky. AOAT 297: 2002 ⇒
        9014. 473-485.
11104   *Zgoll, Annette* Auf Adlerschwingen zu den Göttern: Entdeckungen
        im Mythos von Etana. WUB 26 (2002) 20-25;

11105 Die Welt im Schlaf sehen—Inkubation von Träumen im antiken Mesopotamien. WO 32 (2002) 74-101.

M7.5 Religio persiana

11106 *Ahn, Gregor* 'Toleranz' und Reglement: die Signifikanz achameni-discher Religionspolitik für den jüdisch-persischen Kulturkontakt. Religion und Religionskontakte. 2002 ⇒492. 191-209.
11107 **Choksy, Jamsheed Kairshasp** Evil, good, and gender: facets of the feminine in Zoroastrian religious history. TStR 28: NY 2002, Lang xii; 166 pp. $50. 0-8204-5664-0. Bibl. 133-160.
11108 *Durkin-Meisterernst, Desmond* Form und Datierung des Zand i Wahman Yasn: mit einem Anhang von Karl Löning. Rettendes Wissen. AOAT 300: 2002 ⇒352. 155-183.
11109 *Gignoux, Philippe* Die Magier und die Christen: religiöse Ausei-nandersetzungen im Persien der Sassaniden. WUB Sonderheft (2002) 12-15.
11110 **Gignoux, Philippe** Man and cosmos in ancient Iran. Serie orientale Roma 91: 2001 ⇒17,10113. [R]CRAI (2002/1) 390-392 (*Gignoux, Philippe*).
11111 *Herrenschmidt, C.* Présentation hypothétique du mazdéisme officiel à la période achéménide (résumé). TEuph 23 (2002) 154-155.
11112 *Koch, Heidemarie* Iranische Religion im achämenidischen Zeital-ter. Religion und Religionskontakte. 2002 ⇒492. 11-26.
11113 *Koch, Klaus* Persisch-hellenistischer Synkretismus am Beispiel Kommagene: mit einem Seitenblick auf Israel. Religion und Religi-onskontakte. 2002 ⇒492. 281-301.
11114 **Kriwaczek, Paul** In search of Zarathustra. L 2002, Weidenfeld & N. xi; 244 pp. 0-297-64622-2.
11115 *Panaino, Antonio* La concezione di Dio e degli altri dèi nella cultu-ra religiosa dell'Iran antico. CredOg 129 (2002) 51-68.
11116 *Römer, Thomas Chr.* Tendances dualistes dans quelques écrits bib-liques de l'époque perse. TEuph 23 (2002) 45-58 [1 Chr 21; Job 1; Isa 45,7].
11117 *Stausberg, Michael* Monotheismus, Polytheismus und Dualismus im Alten Iran. Polytheismus. AOAT 298: 2002 ⇒418. 91-111.
11118 **Stausberg, Michael** Die Religion Zarathustras: Geschichte—Ge-genwart—Rituale, 1. Stu 2002, Kohlhammer xiv; 480 pp. 3-17-01-7118-6. Bibl. 461-469.
11119 **Vahman, Fereydun; Asatrian, Garnik** Notes on the language and ethnography of the Zoroastrians of Yazd. DVS.HF Meddelelser 85: K 2002, Reitzel 115 pp. 87-7876-292-8. Bibl. 91-94.

M8.2 *Muḥammad et asseclae*—Qur'an and early diffusion of Islam

11120 **Alawi, Yahya; Hadidi, Javad** Le Coran, voilà le livre: traduction annotée accompagnée d'études, de concordances et de lexiques, 1. Qom 2000, Centre pour la traduction du Saint Coran 624 pp. [R]Studia Islamica 94 (2002) 188-190 (*Chodkiewicz, Michel*).
11121 *Bar-Asher, Meir M.* La formation du Coran et son autorité. L'autorité de l'Écriture. LeDiv: 2002 ⇒588. 153-174.

11122   **Basetti Sani, Giulio** Gesù nascosto nel Corano. San Pietro in Cariano 2002, Gabrielli 166 pp.

11123   ᵀ**Bewley, Abdalhaqq; Bewley, Aisha** The noble Qur'an: a new rendering of its meaning in English. 1999 ⇒16,10371. ᴿJSSt 47 (2002) 372-374 (*Christmann, Andreas*).

11124   *Branca, Paolo* Il Corano in italiano: le molte versioni di un testo intraducibile. AnScR 7 (2002) 85-105.

11125· **Cuende Plaza, María** María, la mujer y la virgen del Corán. M 2002, Letrúmero 267 pp.

11126   ᴱ**Haarmann, Maria** Der Islam: ein Lesebuch. Beck'sche Reihe 479: Mü 2002, Beck 310 pp. 3-406-47640-6.

11127   **Jomier, Jacques** The Bible and the Qur'an. ᵀ*Arbez, Edward P.*: SF 2002, Ignatius xiii; 130 pp. $11. 0-89870-928-8. Bibl. 127-130.

11128   *Khalife, Ignace Abdo; Nwyia, Paul* Catalogue raisonné des manuscrits de la Bibliothèque Orientale de Beyrouth, Coran et commentaires, partie II. MUSJ 55 (1997-1998) 11-33.

11129   *Khoury, Adel Theodor* Bibel und Koran: der Eingottglaube in der modernen Welt;

11130   Gebete aus dem Koran. Die Bibel: Geschichte und Gegenwart. 2002 ⇒ 971. 216-227/228-229.

11131   *Kropp, Manfred* Den Koran neu lesen: über Versuche einer Vereinbarung des koranischen mit dem modernen Weltbild. Religion und Weltbild. 2002 ⇒443. 151-178.

11132   *Kuschel, Karl J.* Die "Weihnachtsgeschichte" im Koran als Modell eines Dialogs. JK 63/6 (2002) 29-34.

11133   *Leemhuis, F.* Ibrahim's sacrifice of his son in the early post-Koranic tradition. Aqedah. 2002 ⇒2624. 125-139 [Gen 22].

11134   *McAuliffe, Jane Dammen* Is there a connection between the bible and the Qur'an?. ThD 49 (2002) 303-317.

11135   *Müller, Walter W.* Religion und Kult im antiken Südarabien. Polytheismus. AOAT 298: 2002 ⇒418. 175-194.

11136   *Renfer, Marc* Gott ist Kalligraph—im Islam ist die arabische Schrift heilig. BiKi 57 (2002) 215-219.

11137   ᴱ**Rippin, Andrew** The Qur'an: formative interpretation. 1999 ⇒16, 10392; 17,10130. ᴿIslam 79 (2002) 343-344 (*Görke, Andreas*).

11138   **Rubin, Uri** Between Bible and Qur'an: the children of Israel and the Islamic self-imag.e 1999 ⇒17,10132. ᴿJRAS 12/1 (2002) 91-92 (*Platti, Emilio*); BSOAS 65 (2002) 140-142 (*Berg, Herbert*); BiOr 59 (2002) 410-412 (*Wessels, A.*).

11139   *Samir, Samir Khalil* La crocifissione di Cristo nel Corano. Il crocifisso. 2002 ⇒620. 49-82.

11140   **Seddik, Youssef** Le Coran, autre lecture. P 2002, Barzakh 254 pp. €18 [MoBi 149,69—Boyer, Frédéric].

11141   *Seidensticker, Tilman* Der Islam: vom 'Hochgottglauben' zum Monotheismus?. Polytheismus. AOAT 298: 2002 ⇒418. 235-244.

11142   *Tottoli, Roberto* Pace e guerra nel Corano. Pace e guerra. 2002 ⇒ 600. 245-250.

11143   **Tottoli, Roberto** Biblical prophets in the Qur'an and Muslim literature. Richmond 2002, Curzon 213 pp. 0-7007-1394-8.

11144   *Tröger, Karl-Wolfgang* MUHAMMAD, SALMAN al-Farisi und die islamische Gnosis. FSchenke, H.: NHS 54: 2002 ⇒108. 247-254.

11145   *Voderholzer, Rudolf* Bibel und Koran: christliches und islamisches Offenbarungsverständnis im Vergleich. RTLu 7 (2002) 313-322.

11146   ᴱᵀWarraq, Muhammad ibn Harun What the Koran really says: language, text, and commentary. Amherst, NY, 2002 Prometheus 782 pp. $36. 1-57392-945-X.
11147   *Wenzel, Catherina* Abraham-Ibrahim: Ähnlichkeit statt Verwandtschaft. EvTh 62 (2002) 362-384;
11148   "Und als Ibrahim und Isma'il die Fundamente des Hauses (der Ka'ba) legten ..." (Sure 2,127): Abrahahmsrezeption und Legitimität im Koran. ZRGG 54 (2002) 193-209.
11149   **Wessels, Anton** Understanding the Qur'an. ᵀ*Bowden, John*: 2000 ⇒16,10398. ᴿCTJ 37 (2002) 385-388 (*Chacko, Mohan*).
11150   **Wheeler, Brannon M.** Moses in the Quran and Islamic exegesis. RoutledgeCurzon Studies in the Quran: NY 2002, Routledge viii; 228 pp. $75. 0-7007-1603-3. Bibl. 186-210.
11151   ᵀ**Wheeler, Brannon M.** Prophets in the Quran: an introduction to the Quran and Muslim exegesis. Comparative Islamic Studies: L 2002, Continuum viii; 391 pp. $105/25. 0-8264-4957-3. Selected by Brannon Wheeler. Bibl. 372-374.
11152   **Zilio-Grandi, I.** Il Corano e il male. T 2002, Einaudi 233 pp. €16.

M8.3 Islam, *evolutio recentior*—later theory and practice

11153   **Adang, Camilla** Muslim writers on Judaism and the Hebrew Bible from iBN RABBAN to IBN HAZM. Lei 1996, Brill 321 pp.
11154   ᵀ**Fyzee, Asaf A.A.; Poonawala, Ismail K.** Nu'm an IBN MUHAMMAD Ab u Han ifah: The pillars of Islam volume I: Acts of devotion and religious observances. Oxf 2002, OUP xxxiii; 558 pp. 0-19-565-5354. Revised, annotated by I.K.H. Poonawala; Bibl. 504-519.
11155   **Meri, Josef W.** The cult of saints among Muslims and Jews in medieval Syria. Oxford oriental monographs: Oxf 2002, OUP xiv; 327 pp. 0-19-925078-2. Bibl. 289-316.
11156   *Miehl, Melanie* Islam. Was ist der Sinn. 2002 ⇒438. 79-96.
11157   **Samir, Samir Khalil** Cento domande sull'islam: intervista a Samir Khalil Samir. ᴱ*Paolucci, Giorgio; Eid, Camille*: Genova 2002, Marietti xii (2); 223 pp. 88-211-6462-4. Bibl. 219-221.

M8.4 Islamic-Christian relations

11158   **Bauschke, Martin** Jesus—Stein des Anstosses: die Christologie des Korans und die deutsch-sprachige Theologie. 2000 ⇒16, 10400. ᴿIslChr 28 (2002) 276-277 (*Hirsch, Marie-Thérèse*).
11159   *Fisher, Humphrey J.* Booty taken in holy war: a cross-cultural perspective: the bible and the history of Muslim Black Africa. Theol. 105 (2002) 273-283.
11160   **Khalidi, Tarif** Der muslimische Jesus: Aussprüche Jesu in der arabischen Literatur. Dü 2002, Patmos 230 pp. €19.90. 3-491-70355-7 [OrdKor 45,118—Hugoth, Matthias].
11161   **Maqsood, Ruqaiyyah Waris** What every christian should know about Islam. 2000 ⇒16,10403. ᴿIslam and Christian-Muslim Relations 13 (2002) 488-489 (*Buaben, Jabal M.*).
11162   **Nitoglia, Stefano** L'Islam com'è: un confronto con il cristianesimo. Identità e cultura: R 2002, Il minotauro 139 pp. 88-8073-067-3. Pref. di *Gianni Baget Bozzo*.

11163   *Räisänen, Heikki* Vad kristendom och islam kunde lära sig av va-
        randra: ett exegetiskt perspektiv på en mödosam religionsdialog.
        SvTK 78/4 (2002) 154-163.
11164   *Rizzardi, Giuseppe* Cristo e l'islam: condivisione o sfida. RTLu 7
        (2002) 375-391.
11165   *Rossano, Pietro* Les grands documents de l'église catholique au
        sujet des Musulmans <1982>;
11166· Chiesa e Islam prima e dopo il concilio <1989>. Teologia cristiana.
        DMis 27: 2002 ⇒232. 33-45/47-61.
11167   *Saeed, Abdullah* The charge of distortion of Jewish and christian
        scriptures. MW 92 (2002) 419-436.
11168   *Schulz, Michael* Rivelazione e Trinità nel dialogo fra islam e cristi-
        anesimo con uno sguardo all'ebraismo. RTLu 7 (2002) 341-357.
11169   **Schumann, Olaf** Jesus the Messiah in Muslim thought. New Delhi
        2002, ISPCK xxxvi; 272 pp. Rs130. 81-7214-522-5 Diss. Tübin-
        gen, German 1975, 1988 [VJTR 67,393s—Pinto, Desiderio].
11170   ^{ET}**Thomas, David Richard** Early Muslim polemic against chris-
        tianity: ABU 'ISA al-Warraq's "Against the Incarnation". UCOP 59:
        C 2002, CUP x; 314 pp. 0-521-81132-5. Bibl. 305-310.

M8.5 **Religiones Indiae**, *Extremi Orientis, Africae*

11171   *Baumann, Christoph Peter* Buddhismus. Was ist der Sinn. GTBS
        1170: 2002 ⇒438. 123-137.
11172   *Derrett, J.D.M.* Christ, the Messiah, and Bodhisattvas descend into
        hell. ArOr 70 (2002) 489-504 [1 Pet 3:19].
11173   *Ducoeur, Guillaume* Indien in den Augen der Kirchenväter. WUB
        Sonderheft (2002) 76-77.
11174   **Krasser, Helmut** Sankaranandanas Isvarapakaranasanksepa: mit
        einem anonymen Kommentar und weiteren Materialien zur buddhi-
        stischen Gottespolemik. Österr. Ak.. d. Wiss. Ph..-Hi. Kl. Sitzungs-
        berichte 689; Beiträge... Geistesgeschichte Asiens 39: W 2002, Öst.
        Ak. d. Wiss. 2 vols. 370-0130-244. Bibl. v.I, 88-92; v.II, 289-309.
11175   *Magnone, Paolo* La parola inafferrabile: problematiche della tradu-
        zione delle scritture indiane. AnScR 7 (2002) 107-126.
11176   ^E**Oberhammer, Gerhard; Rastelli, Marion** Studies in Hinduism
        III: Pancaratra and Visistadvaitavedanta. SÖAW.PH 694; BKGA
        40: W 2002, Verlag der Österreichischen Akademie der Wissen-
        schaften 152 pp. 3-7001-3065-1.
11177   *Rossano, Pietro* Dio nelle culture orientali. Teologia cristiana.
        DMis 27: 2002 <1989> ⇒232. 63-73.
11178   *Schneider, Horst* Ein antiker Reisender: Kosmas der Indienfahrer;
11179   *Stein, Jürgen* Eine traditionsreiche Gemeinschaft: die Geschichte
        der Christen in Indien. WUB Sonderheft (2002) 75-76/68-73;
11180   Christen in Indien heute;
11181   *Tamcke, Martin* Der heilige Thomas—Apostel Indiens?. WUB
        Sonderheft (2002) 80-81/66-67.
11182   *Willers, Christiane* Hinduismus. Was ist der Sinn. GTBS 1170:
        2002 ⇒438. 97-122

11183   *Dash, Michael I.N.; Rasor, Stephen C.* African American spirituali-
        ty: some biblical and historical resources for reflection. ExAu 18
        (2002) 120-136.

M8.7 *Interactio cum religione orientali*: **Christian dialogue with the East**

11184 EAronson, Martin Jesus und Lao-Tse: eine Botschaft zwei Stimmen: parallele Aussagen der zwei großen Weisheitslehrer der Menschheit. Mü 2002, Kösel 256 pp.

11185 *Ceresko, Anthony R.* Reading and teaching the bible in India. Prophets and proverbs. 2002 <1996> ⇒154. 47-51.

11186 *D'Sa, Francis X.* How is it that we hear, each of us, in our own native language?: a tentative cross-cultural reading of the incarnation (John 1) and Avatara (Bhagavadgita 4). FNILES, D. 2002 ⇒82. 123-146.

11187 *Gálik, Marian* Soirée davidienne: more musings over the necessity of the third covenant. Studia Orientalia Slovaca 1 (2002) 5-16 [Comenius Univ. Bratislava].

11188 EGross, Rita M.; Muck, Terry C. Buddhists talk about Jesus: christians talk about the Buddha. 2000 ⇒16,10421. RPacifica 15 (2002) 223-225 (*Johnston, William M.*).

11189 Kadowaki, Kakichi Zen and the bible. TRieck, J.: Mkn 2002, Orbis x; 182 pp. $17. 1-57075-444-6 [ThD 50,79—Heiser, W.C.].

11190· *Klein, Wassilios* Die Erzählung von Barlaam und Joasaph: Motive aus der Buddha-Vita in einem christlichen Bestseller. WUB Sonderheft (2002) 78-79.

11191 Luz, Ulrich; Michaels, Axel Jesus oder Buddha: Leben und Lehre im Vergleich. Mü 2002, Beck 225 pp. €12.90. 3-406-47602-3 [BiKi 58,186].

11192 *Mudathotty, Paul* The word and word of God: an analytical study of the scriptural understanding. JJSS 1 (2002) 231-244.

11193 *Pieris, Aloysius* Cross-scripture reading in Buddhist-Christian dialogue: a search for the right method. FNILES, D. 2002 ⇒82. 229-50.

11194 *Raguin, Yves* Die Stele von Xi'an. WUB Sonderheft (2002) 56-57.

11195 *Raja, A. Maria Arul* Breaking hegemonic boundaries: an intertextual reading of the Madurai Veeran legend and Mark's story of Jesus. FNILES, D. 2002 ⇒82. 251-260.

11196 *Sonnemans, Heino M.* Christus—Krishna—Buddha: zur pluralistischen Religionstheologie. Jesus von Nazareth und das Christentum. 2000 ⇒293. 51-79.

11197 *Swarup, Paul* The bible in the context of multi-textual communities: a study of Pandita RAMABAI's response (1858-1922). FNILES, D. 2002 ⇒82. 204-222.

11198 Wai, Maurice Nyunt PANCASILA and catholic moral teaching: moral principles as expression of spiritual experience in Theravada Buddhism and christianity. Interreligious and intercultural investigations 6: R 2002, E.P.U.G. 334 pp. €25. 88-7652-920-9.

11199 *Wenzel-Teuber, Katharina* Wie leben Christen in China heute?;

11200 *Yaldiz, Marianne* Die Seidenstraße: Spiegel kultureller Kontakte. WUB Sonderheft (2002) 60-61/40-41.

XVII. Historia Medii Orientis Biblici

Q1 *Syria prae-Islamica, Canaan* Israel Veteris Testamenti

11201 **Ahlström, Gösta W.** Ancient Palestine: a historical introduction. Facets: Mp 2002, Fortress 90 pp. $6 [BiTod 41,125—Bergant, D.].

11202 **Albertz, Rainer** Die Exilzeit: 6. Jahrhundert v. Chr. Biblische Enzyklopädie 7: 2001 ⇒17,10163. REstAg 37 (2002) 391-393 (*Mielgo, C.*).

11203 *Ben-Tor, Amnon* Hazor—a city state between the major powers. SJOT 16 (2002) 303-308 [Josh 11; Judg 4].

11204 *Blenkinsopp, Joseph* The bible, archaeology and politics; or the empty land revisited. JSOT 27 (2002) 169-187;

11205 The Babylonian gap revisited: there was no gap. BArR 28/3 (2002) 36-38, 59;

11206 The age of the exile. Biblical world, 1. 2002 ⇒273. 416-439.

11207 *Boer, Roland* Introduction: on re-reading 'The tribes of Yahweh'. Tracking the tribes. JSOT.S 351: 2002 ⇒455. 1-9.

11208 **Bright, John** A history of Israel. 42000 ⇒16,10443; 17,10167. REfMex 20 (2002) 277-279 (*López Rosas, Ricardo*);

11209 Storia dell'antico Israele: dagli albori del popolo ebraico alla rivolta dei Maccabei. R 2002, Newon & C. 559 pp [SdT 15,224s—Frediani, Agostino].

11210 *Carter, Charles E.* Powerful ideologies, challenging models and lasting changes: continuing the journey of tribes. Tracking the tribes. JSOT.S 351: 2002 ⇒455. 46-58.

11211 **Carter, E. Charles** The emergence of Yehud in the Persian period: a social and demographic study. JSOT.S 294: 1999 ⇒15,10325; 17,10170. RJSJ 33 (2002) 322-323 (*Xeravits, Géza*); RSR 90 (2002) 242-243; BiOr 59 (2002) 373-377 (*Labahn, Antje*); Bib. 83 (2002) 427-432 (*Kreuzer, Siegfried*); TEuph 23 (2002) 194-198 (*Heltzer, M.*).

11212 *Čech, Pavel* Königslisten und ihre (Ir)relevanz für die Geschichtsforschung. UF 34 (2002) 39-44.

11213 *Charpin, Dominique* Le voyage d'un roi de Mari. MoBi 146 (2002) 24-29.

11214 *Chavalas, Mark W.* Syria and northern Mesopotamia to the end of the third millennium BCE. Mesopotamia and the bible. JSOT.S 341: 2002 ⇒458. 126-148

11215 La civiltà dei Hurriti. La parola del passato 55: 2000 ⇒16,10445. RAfO 48-49 (2001-2002) 201-205 (*Pruzsinszky, Regine*).

11216 **Cohen, Susan L.** Canaanites, chronologies, and connections: the relationship of Middle Bronze IIA Canaan to Middle Kingdom Egypt. Studies in the Archaeology and History of the Levant 3: WL 2002, Eisenbrauns ix; 168 pp. $40. 1-57506-908-3. Diss. Harvard. Bibl. 143-156.

11217 **Dever, William G.** What did the biblical writers know and when did they know it?: what archaeology can tell us about the reality of Ancient Israel. 2001 ⇒17,10177. RCBQ 64 (2002) 129-130 (*Hoppe, Leslie J.*); RRT 9 (2002) 30-32 (*Moberly, Walter*); Sal. 64

(2002) 572-573 (*Vicent, R.*); HebStud 43 (2002) 247-250 (*Hoffmeier, James K.*); SEÅ 67 (2002) 170-171 (*Norin, Stig*).

11218 **Dietrich, Walter** Die frühe Königszeit in Israel: 10. Jahrhundert v. Chr. Biblische Enzyklopädie 3: 1997 ⇒13,9735... 16,10449. [R]ThR 67 (2002) 406-410 (*Veijola, Timo*).

11219 **Dion, Paul Eugène** Les araméens à l'Âge du fer: histoire politique et structures sociales. ÉtB 34: 1997 ⇒13,9736... 17,10178. [R]JNES 61 (2002) 125-127 (*Briquel Chatonnet, Françoise*).

11220 *Fales, Frederick Mario* Central Syria in the letters to Sargon II. [F]WEIPPERT, M.: OBO 186: 2002 ⇒133. 134-152.

11221 *Finkelstein, Israel* The Philistines in the bible: a late-monarchic perspective. JSOT 27 (2002) 131-167;

11222 Chronology rejoinders. PEQ 134 (2002) 118-129.

11223 **Fox, Nili Sacher** In the service of the king: officialdom in ancient Israel and Judah. MHUC 23: 2000 ⇒16,10455; 17,10179. [R]Zion 67 (2002) 213-218 H. (*Na'aman, Nadav*); CBQ 64 (2002) 345-347 (*White, Marsha C.*); IEJ 52 (2002) 99-100 (*Cogan, Mordechai*); AUSS 40 (2002) 327-329 (*Shea, William H.*).

11224 *Fritz, Volkmar* Israelites & Canaanites: you can tell them apart. BArR 28/4 (2002) 28-31, 63.

11225 *Fugitt, Stephen M.* Some thoughts on Philistine identity, movements, and settlement. OTEs 15 (2002) 368-380.

11226 **Gallagher, William R.** Sennacherib's campaign to Judah: new studies. 1999 ⇒15,10337; 17,10181. [R]ThRv 98 (2002) 478-481 (*Uehlinger, Christoph*).

11227 *Garbini, Giovanni* I Fenici nel Mare Eritreo. AANL.R 13 (2002) 45-49.

11228 **Garbini, Giovanni** Il ritorno dall'esilio babilonese. StBi 129: 2001 ⇒17,10183. [R]RivBib 50 (2002) 223-226 (*Boschi, G. Bernardo*).

11229 *Gottwald, Norman K.* Rethinking the origins of ancient Israel. [F]FLANAGAN, J.: JSOT.S 359: 2002 ⇒38. 190-201.

11230 *Grabbe, Lester L.* Israel under Persia and Greece. Biblical world, 1. 2002 ⇒273. 440-457.

11231 [E]**Guidotti, Maria Cristina; Pecchioli Daddi, Franca** La battaglia di Qadesh: Ramesse II contro gli Ittiti per la conquista della Siria. Livorno 2002, Sillabe 223 pp. 88-8347-134-2. Bibl. 222-223.

11232 **Heinz, Marlies** Altsyrien und Libanon: Geschichte, Wirtschaft, Kultur vom Neolithikum bis Nebukadnezar. Da:Wiss 2002, xi; 286 pp. €35. 3-534-13280-7.

11233 *Herrmann, Siegfried* Israels Frühgeschichte im Spannungsfeld neuer Hypothesen <1988>;

11234 Zwischen Stamm und Staat: gestaltende Kräfte altorientalischer Geschichte in gewandelter Sicht <1980>. Geschichte und Prophetie. BWANT 157: 2002 ⇒179. 11-65/67-88.

11235 *Hjelm, Ingrid; Thompson, Thomas L.* The victory song of Merneptah, Israel and the people of Palestine. JSOT 27 (2002) 3-18.

11236 **Hoglund, Kenneth G.** Achaemenid imperial administration in Syria-Palestine and the missions of Ezra and Nehemiah. SBL.DS 125: 1992 ⇒8,3044... 12,9128. [R]ThR 67 (2002) 102-103 (*Willi, Thomas*).

11237 **Isserlin, B.S.J.** The Israelites, 2001 ⇒17,10190. [R]JBL 121 (2002) 347-348 (*Raney, Donald C., II*).

11238 *Jobling, David* Specters of tribes: on the 'revenance' of a classic. Tracking the tribes. JSOT.S 351: 2002 ⇒455. 10-16.

11239   *Joffe, Alexander H.* The rise of secondary states in the Iron Age Levant. JESHO 45 (2002) 425-467.
11240   *Kelle, Brad E.* What's in a name?: neo-Assyrian designations for the Northern Kingdom and their implications for Israelite history and biblical interpretation. JBL 121 (2002) 639-666.
11241   **Kinet, Dirk** Geschichte Israels. NEB.E 2 z. AT: 2001 ⇒17,10192. ᴿRivBib 50 (2002) 353-357 (*Boschi, B.G.*); Cart. 18 (2002) 550-552 (*Álvarez Barredo, M.*).
11242   *Knauf, Ernst Axel* Low or lower?: new data on early Iron Age chronology from Beth Shean, Tel Rehov and Dor. BN 112 (2002) 21-27.
11243   **Kofoed, Jens Bruun** Text and history: the Old Testament texts as a source for the history of Ancient Israel. Aarhus 2002, Diss. Aarhus [StTh 57,76].
11244   *Lemaire, André* Le siècle disparu de David et Salomon. MoBi 146 (2002) 35-39.
11245   *Lemche, Niels Peter* Chronology and archives—when does the history of Israel and Judah begin?. ᶠFLANAGAN, J.: JSOT.S 359: 2002 ⇒38. 264-276.
11246·   **Lemche, Niels Peter** The Israelites in history and tradition. 1998 ⇒14,9550...17,10197. ᴿJQR 92 (2001) 250-54 (*Rainey, Anson F.*).
11247   **Lipinski, Edouard** The Aramaeans: their ancient history, culture, religion. OLA 100: 2000 ⇒16,10473. ᴿBASOR 327 (2002) 55-61 (*Dion, Paul E.*).
11248   *Long, V. Philips* How reliable are biblical reports?: repeating Lester Grabbe's comparative experiment. VT 52 (2002) 367-384;
11249   Introduction to Windows into Old Testament history: evidence, argument, and the crisis of "biblical Israel". Windows. 2002 ⇒500. 1-22.
11250   **Markoe, Glenn** Phoenicians. 2000 ⇒16,10475. ᴿGn. 74 (2002) 373-375 (*Niemeyer, Hans Georg*).
11251   *Matthews, Victor H.* Syria to the early second millennium. Mesopotamia and the bible. JSOT.S 341: 2002 ⇒458. 168-190.
11252   **Matthews, Victor H.** A brief history of ancient Israel. LVL 2002, Westminster 171 pp. $17. 0-664-22436-9. Bibl. 140-156 [BiTod 41,264—Bergant, Dianne].
11253   *McDonagh, John* Foreskins, foreigners and foes: the Philistines and the creation of the colonial other. ScrB 32 (2002) 80-92.
11254   *Meyers, Carol* Tribes and tribulations: retheorizing earliest 'Israel'. Tracking the tribes. JSOT.S 351: 2002 ⇒455. 35-45.
11255   *Nápole, Gabriel M.* La historia del 'Israel bíblico': cuestiones disputadas. RevBib 64 (2002) 69-87.
11256·   *Niemann, Hermann Michael* Nachbarn und Gegner, Konkurrenten und Verwandte Judas: die Philister zwischen Geographie und Ökonomie, Geschichte und Theologie. ᶠWEIPPERT, M.: OBO 186: 2002 ⇒133. 70-91.
11257   *Noël, Damien* Histoire d'Israël, 3: aux temps des empires: de l'exil à Antiochos Epiphane (587-175). CEv 121 (2002) 5-57.
11258   *Oded, Bustenay* Israel's neighbours. Biblical world, 1. 2002 ⇒273. 492-525.
11259   *Ortiz, Steven M.* Methodological comments on the low chronology: a reply to Ernst Axel Knauf. BN 111 (2002) 34-39.

11260 *Richter, Thomas* Der 'einjährige Feldzug' Šuppiluliumas I. von Ḫatti in Syrien nach Textfunden des Jahres 2002 in Mišrife/Qaṭna. UF 34 (2002) 603-618.

11261 **Sacchi, Paolo** The history of the second temple period. JSOT.S 285: 2000 ⇒16,10485; 17,10215. [R]ThLZ 127 (2002) 748-751 (*Kessler, Rainer*); RBLit 4 (2002) 265-67 (*Stenstrup, Kenneth G.*);

11262 Storia del secondo tempio: Israele tra VI secolo a.C. e I secolo d.C. T 2002, SEI 529 pp.

11263 **Schams, Christine** Jewish scribes in the Second-Temple period. JSOT.S 291: 1998 ⇒14,9570; 17,10216. [R]RSR 90 (2002) 427-429 (*Paul, André*).

11264 **Schipper, Bernd Ulrich** Israel und Ägypten in der Königszeit: die kulturellen Kontakte von Salomo bis zum Fall Jerusalems. OBO 170: 1999 ⇒15,10372; 17,10219. [R]OLZ 97 (2002) 248-254 (*Dietrich, Walter*).

11265 *Schloen, J. David* W.F. ALBRIGHT and the origins of Israel. NEA (BA) 65 (2002) 56-62.

11266 *Schniedewind, William M.* The rise of the Aramean states. Mesopotamia and the bible. JSOT.S 341: 2002 ⇒458. 276-287.

11267 *Shanks, Hershel* A 'centrist' at the center of controversy: BAR interviews Israel Finkelstein. BArR 28/6 (2002) 38-49, 64-68.

11268 **Soggin, J. Alberto** Storia d'Israele: introduzione alla storia d'Israele e Giuda dalle origini alla rivolta di Bar Kochbà. BCR 44: Brescia [2]2002, Paideia 525 pp. €37. 88-394-0637-9. Bibl. 431-508.

11269 *Soggin, Jan Alberto* Storiografia nel Vicino Oriente antico e in Israele: a proposito della seconda edizione della mia *Storia d'Israele*. Materia giudaica. 2002 ⇒727. 5-6.

11270 **Sommer, Michael** Europas Ahnen: Ursprünge des Politischen bei den Phönikern. 2000 ⇒16,10490. [R]HZ 275 (2002) 710-712 (*Flaig, Egon*).

11271 *Stern, Ephraim* The Babylonian gap revisited: yes there was. BArR 28/3 (2002) 39, 55.

11272 *Tetley, M. Christine* The date of Samaria's fall as a reason for rejecting the hypothesis of two conquests. CBQ 64 (2002) 59-77.

11273 *Tzirkin, Yu.B.* The 'Phoenician History' of Sanchuniaton. Journal of Ancient History 241 (2002) 121-133 Sum. 132. **R**.

11274 *Whitelam, Keith* The poetics of the history of Israel: shaping Palestinian history. [F]FLANAGAN, J.: JSOT.S 359: 2002 ⇒38. 277-296;

11275 Palestine during the Iron Age. Biblical world, 1. 2002 ⇒273. 391-415.

11276 *Zertal, Adam* Philistine kin found in early Israel. BArR 28/3 (2002) 18-31, 60-61.

Q2 Historiographia—*theologia historiae*

11277 **Alonso-Núñez, José Miguel** The idea of universal history in Greece: from HERODOTUS to the age of AUGUSTUS. Amsterdam Classical Monographs 4: Amst 2002, Gieben 153 pp. 90-5063-398-X. Bibl. 141-142.

11278 **Amit, Yairah** History and ideology: introduction to historiography in the Hebrew Bible. BiSe 60: 1999 ⇒15,10387; 17,10230. [R]JJS 53 (2002) 382-383 (*Nahkola, Aulikki*); JQR 92 (2002) 602-603 (*Holtz, Shalom E.*).

11279   ^E**Bakker, Egbert J.; Jong, Irene J.F. de; Van Wees, Hans** Brill's Companion to HERODOTUS. Lei 2002, Brill xx; 652 pp. 90-04-120-60-2. Bibl. 591-627.

11280   *Barstad, Hans M.* "Fact" versus "fiction" and other issues in the history debate, and their relevance for the study of the Old Testament. ^FSMEND, R. 2002 ⇒113. 433-447.

11281   **Bordreuil, Pierre; Briquel-Chatonnet, Françoise** Le temps de la bible. 2000 ⇒16,10507; 17,10234. ^RRB 109 (2002) 602-604 (*Tarragon, J.-M. de*) TEuph 23 (2002) 185-186 (*Lemaire, A.*).

11282   *Bultmann, Christoph* Bibliotheken der Geschichte: DIODORUS Siculus und das Alte Testament. ^FSMEND, R. 2002 ⇒113. 242-256.

11283   ^E**Enenkel, Karl A.; Jong, Jan L. de; Landtsheer, Jeanine de** Re-creating ancient history: episodes from the Greek and Roman past in the arts and literature of the early modern period. Boston 2002, Brill xiii; 371 pp. 0-391-04129-0. Collab. *Alicia Montoya.*

11284. *Finkelstein, Israel* Archaeology and text in the third millennium: a view from the center. Congress volume Basel 2001. VT.S 92: 2002 ⇒570. 323-342.

11285   *Grosby, Steven* Kinship, territory, and the nation in the historiography of ancient Israel. Biblical ideas. 2002 <1991> ⇒172. 52-68.

11286   ^E**Hallbäck, Geert; Strange, John** Bibel og historieskrivning. 1999 ⇒16,10524. ^RSEÅ 67 (2002) 169-170 (*Ericsson, Bengt*).

11287   **Harrison, Thomas** Divinity and history: the religion of HERODOTUS. Oxford Classical Monographs: Oxf 2002, Clarendon xii; 320 pp. 0-19-815291-4. Bibl. 265-293.

11288   *Herrmann, Siegfried* Die Abwertung des Alten Testaments als Geschichtsquelle: Anmerkungen zu einem geistesgeschichtlichen Problem. Geschichte und Prophetie. BWANT 157: 2002 <1991> ⇒179. 1-10.

11289   **Ishida, Tomoo** History and historical writing in ancient Israel: studies in biblical historiography. 1999 ⇒15,10408. ^RThLZ 127 (2002) 23-24 (*Timm, Stefan*).

11290   *Kalliath, Antony* 'Revisiting' the Hebrew historiography. Jeevadhara 32 (2002) 406-424.

11291   *Kofoed, Jens Bruun* Epistemology, historiographical method, and the "Copenhagen school". Windows. 2002 ⇒500. 23-43.

11292   *Laurant, Sophie* La bible entre mythe, histoire et théologie.MoBi 142 (2002) 51-55. Entretien avec *Israël Finkelstein.*

11293· *Loader, James Alfred* Das Alte Testament—ein Geschichtsbuch?. OTEs 15 (2002) 398-410.

11294   *López Rosas, Ricardo* Biblia, memoria histórica y encrucijada de culturas. EfMex 20 (2002) 397-412.

11295   *Mayes, A.D.H.* Historiography in the Old Testament. Biblical world, 1. 2002 ⇒273. 65-87.

11296   **Minear, Paul Sevier** The bible and the historian: breaking the silence about God in biblical studies. Nv 2002, Abingdon 280 pp. $30. 0-687-03043-9.

11297   **Morley, Neville** Writing ancient history. 1999 ⇒15,10429. ^RGn. 74 (2002) 552-553 (*Walter, Uwe*).

11298   *Mundadan, A.M.* History as revelation. Jeevadhara 32 (2002) 384-405.

11299   **Na'aman, N.** The past that shapes the present: the creation of biblical historiography in the late first temple period and after the downfall: 'Yeriot', in memoriam Yitzhak (Izik) HESS. Essays and papers in the Jewish studies bearing on the humanities and the social sciences: J 2002, 128 pp. ᴿUF 33 (2001) 734-738 (*Heltzer, M.*).

11300 **Pani, Mario** Le ragioni della storiografia in Grecia e a Roma: una introduzione. Documenti e Studi 28: 2001 ⇒17,10265. ᴿAnCl 71 (2002) 244-245 (*Desy, Philippe*).

11301 **Pasquale, Gianluigi** La storia della salvezza: Dio Signore del tempo e della storia. Diaconia alla verità 11: Mi 2002, Paoline 178 pp. 88-315-2378-3. Bibl. 167-174.

11302 *Patterson, Stephen J.* History and theology: a reflection on the work of the Jesus Seminar. FORUM n.s. 3 (2002) 357-379.

11303 **Porciani, Leone** Prime forme della storiografia greca: prospettiva locale e generale nella narrazione storica. 2001 ⇒17,10267. ᴿAt. 90 (2002) 521-524 (*Gabba, Emilio*).

11304 *Provan, Iain W.* In the stable with the dwarves: testimony, interpretation, faith, and the history of Israel. Windows. 2002 ⇒500. 161-197 [2 Kgs 18,13-16].

11305 **Ska, Jean-Louis** Les énigmes du passé: histoire d'Israël et récit biblique. ᵀ*Di Pede, Elena*: Le livre et le rouleau 14: 2001 ⇒17, 10269. ᴿCEv 120 (2002) 62 (*Gruson, Philippe*); MoBi 144 (2002) 59 (*Brossier, François*); LV(L) 256 (2002) 109-112 (*Abadie, Philippe*); RTL 33 (2002) 569-570 (*Wénin, A.*).

11306 *Smend, Rudolf* Elemente alttestamentlichen Geschichtsdenkens. Die Mitte des A.T. 2002 <1968> ⇒244. 89-114.

11307 **Sommer, Andreas Urs** Geschichte als Trost: Isaak ISELINs Geschichtsphilosophie. Schwabe 2002, Basel 124 pp. 3-7965-1940-7.

11308 **Van de Mieroop, Marc** Cuneiform texts and the writing of history. 1999 ⇒15,10452; 17,10680. ᴿBASOR 327 (2002) 78-80 (*Cooper, J.S.*).

11309 *Van Seters, John* Is there any historiography in the Hebrew Bible?: a Hebrew-Greek comparison. JNSL 28/2 (2002) 1-25.

11310 *Weeks, Stuart D.E.* Biblical literature and the emergence of ancient Jewish nationalism. BiblInterp 10 (2002) 144-157.

11311 **Wesselius, Jan-Wim** The origin of the history of Israel: HERODOTUS's Histories as blueprint for the first books of the bible. JSOT.S 345: Shf 2002, Sheffield A. xi; 175 pp. $95. 1-84127-267-1. Bibl. 164-168.

11312 *Whitelam, Keith W.* Representing minimalism: the rhetoric and reality of revisionism. ᴹCARROLL, R. JSOT.S 348: 2002 ⇒13. 194-223.

11313 *Willi-Plein, Ina* Am Anfang einer Geschichte der Zeit. Sprache als Schlüssel. 2002 <1997> ⇒261. 11-23.

Q3 Historia Ægypti—Egypt

11314 **Assmann, Jan** Weisheit und Mysterium: das Bild der Griechen von Ägypten. 1999 ⇒15,10457. ᴿPrudentia 34/1 (2002) 62-64 (*Spalinger, Anthony*);

11315 Herrschaft und Heil: politische Theologie in Altägypten, Israel und Europa. 2000 ⇒16,10562; 17,10277. ᴿOLZ 97 (2002) 27-29 (*Twardella, Johannes*);

11316   The mind of Egypt: history and meaning in the time of the Phara-
        ohs. ᵀ*Jenkins, Andrew*: NY 2002, Metropolitan Books xi; (2) 514
        pp. 0-8050-5462-6.
11317   *Balconi, Carla* La donna in Egitto: in margine a una recente pub-
        blicazione. Aeg. 81 (2001) 243-251.
11318   *Beckerath, Jürgen von* Nochmals die Eroberung Ägyptens durch
        Kambyses. ZÄS 129/1 (2002) 1-5.
11319   **Beckerath, Jürgen von** Handbuch der ägyptischen Königsnamen.
        MÄSt 49: ²1999 <1984> ⇒15,10461; 17,10282. ᴿOLZ 97 (2002)
        190-212 (*Schneider, Thomas*).
11320   *Bennett, Chris* A genealogical chronology of the seventeenth dy-
        nasty. JARCE 39 (2002) 123-155.
11321   **Betrò, Marilina** Armant dal I Periodo Intermedio alla fine del
        Nuovo Regno: prosopografia. Biblioteca di studi egittologici 1: Pi-
        sa 2002, ETS 123 pp. 88-467-0498-3. Bibl. 103-113.
11322   **Doherty, Paul** The mysterious death of Tutankhamun. L 2002,
        Constable xii; 260 pp. 1-84119-595-2. Bibl. 247-252.
11323   **Eichler, Selke Susan** Die Verwaltung des "Hauses des Amun" in
        der 18. Dynastie. SAÄK.B 7: 2000 ⇒16,10577. ᴿBiOr 59 (2002)
        50-53 (*Hüttner, Michaela*); OLZ 97 (2002) 55-63 (*Haring, Ben*);
        JESHO 45 (2002) 288-291 (*Römer, Malte*).
11324. *Finkelstein, Israel* The campaign of Shoshenq I to Palestine: a
        guide to the 10th century BCE polity. ZDPV 118 (2002) 109-135
        [1 Kgs 14,25-28; 2 Chr 12,1-2].
11325   *Gabolde, Marc* La parenté de Toutânkhamon. BSFE 155 (2002)
        32-48.
11326   *Görg, Manfred* Weiteres zum Hyksoskönig Jannas. BN 112 (2002)
        16-20.
11327   **Grajetzki, W.** Two treasurers of the Middle Kingdom. BAR
        S1007: Oxf 2001, Archaeopress iv; 103 pp. £25. 1841712868. 8 pl.
11328   *Greenberg, Gary* Manetho's twelfth dynasty and the standard
        chronology. JSSEA 29 (2002) 58-73.
111329 **Gundlach, Rolf** Der Pharao und sein Staat: die Grundlegung der
        ägyptischen Königsideologie im 4. und 3. Jahrtausend. 1998 ⇒14,
        9649; 16,10585. ᴷJJP 32 (2002) 266-267 (*Hengstl, Joachim*).
11330   **Higginbotham, Carolyn R.** Egyptianization and elite emulation in
        Ramesside Palestine: governance and accommodation on the impe-
        rial periphery. 2000 ⇒16,10587; 17,10299. ᴿBiOr 59 (2002) 53-58
        (*Aston, D.A.*); JESHO 45 (2002) 128-129 (*Tyson Smith, Stuart*);
        ArOr 70 (2002) 434-436 (*Mynářová-Kořínková, Jana*); ZDPV 118
        (2002) 176-179 (*Quack, Joachim Friedrich*); JSSEA 29 (2002)
        112-115 (*Sagrillo, Troy Leiland*).
11331   **Huss, Werner** Ägypten in hellenistischer Zeit, 332-30 v. Chr. 2001
        ⇒17,10301. ᴿBiOr 59 (2002) 531-534 (*Rochette, Bruno*); CEg
        153-154 (2002) 343-344 (*Bingen, Jean*).
11332   **Jiménez Serrano, A.** Royal festivals in the late pre-dynastic period
        and the first dynasty. BAR Internat. Ser. 1076: Oxf 2002, Archaeo-
        press viii; 116 pp. £25. 1-84171-455-0.
11333   **Jones, Dilwyn** An index of Ancient Egyptian titles, epithets and
        phrases of the Old Kingdom. BAR Intern. Ser. 866: 2000 ⇒16,
        10593. ᴿDiscEg 52 (2002) 97-100 (*DuQuesne, Terence*); JESHO
        45 (2002) 387-398 (*Andrássy, Petra*).
11334   *Kahl, Jochem* Zu den Namen spätzeitlicher Usurpatoren, Fremd-
        herrscher, Gegen- und Lokalkönige. ZÄS 129/1 (2002) 31-42.

11335 **Kamrin, Janice** The cosmos of Khnumhotep II at Beni Hasan. 1999 ⇒15,10491. ᴿBiOr 59 (2002) 298-299 (*Doxey, Denise M.*).

11336 **Kanawati, Naguib** Conspiracies in the Egyptian palace: Unis to Pepy I. L 2002, Routledge 208 pp. £50. 0-415-27107-X.

11337 **Kessler, Rainer** Die Ägyptenbilder der Hebräischen Bibel: ein Beitrag zur neueren Monotheismusdebatte. SBS 197: Stu 2002, Verlag Katholisches Bibelwerk 176 pp. €21.90. 3-460-04971-5. Bibl. 162-170.

11338· *Kitchen, Kenneth A.* Hazor and Egypt: an egyptological & ancient Near-Eastern perspective. SJOT 16 (2002) 309-313.

11339 *Klengel, Horst* From war to eternal peace: Ramesses II and Khattushili III. BCSMS 37 (2002) 49-56.

11340 **Kruse, Thomas** Der königliche Schreiber und die Gauverwaltung: Untersuchungen zur Verwaltungsgeschichte Ägyptens in der Zeit von Augustus bis Philippus Arabs (30 v. Chr. - 245 n. Chr.). APF.B 11/1-2: Mü 2002, Saur 2 vols. Bibl. v.1, xiv-xxxix.

11341 **La'da, Csaba A.** Foreign ethnics in Hellenistic Egypt. ᴱ*Clarysse, W., al.*, Prosopographia Ptolemaica 10; StHell 38: Lv 2002, Peeters 384 pp. €94. 90-429-1195-6.

11342 **Lampela, Anssi** Rome and the Ptolemies of Egypt: the development of their political relations, 273-80 B.C. 1998 ⇒14,9660; 15, 10493. ᴿGn. 74 (2002) 464-466 (*Gruen, Erich S.*).

11343 *Legras, Bernard* Les experts égyptiens à la cour des Ptolémées. RH 307 (2002) 963-991.

11344 **Menu, Bernadette** Recherches sur l'histoire juridique, économique et sociale de l'ancienne Égypte II. BEt 122: 1998 ⇒14,9662. ᴿWO 32 (2002) 168-179 (*Trapani, Marcella*).

11345 **Minas, Martina** Die hieroglyphischen Ahnenreihen der ptolemäischen Könige: ein Vergleich mit den Titeln der eponymen Priester in den demotischen und griechischen Papyri. Aegyptiaca Treverensia 9: 2000 ⇒16,10599. ᴿGn. 74 (2002) 516-520 (*Chauveau, Michel*).

11346 **Mysliwiec, Karol** The twilight of Ancient Egypt: first millennium B.C.E. ᵀ*Lorton, David*: 2000 ⇒16,10603. ᴿAJA 106 (2002) 613-614 (*Wilfong, T.G.*); JSSEA 29 (2002) 115-116 (*Chadwick, Robert*).

11347 ᴱ**O'Connor, David; Cline, Eric H.** Amenhotep III: perspectives on his reign. 1997 ⇒16,10604. ᴿBiOr 59 (2002) 494-500 (*Pamminger, Peter*); CEg 153-154 (2002) 153-156 (*Vandersleyen, Claude*); JSSEA 29 (2002) 116-118 (*Hellum, Jennifer*).

11348 *Perdu, Olivier* De Stéphinatès a Néchao ou les débuts de la XXVIe dynastie. CRAI 4 (2002) 1215-1243.

11349 **Pfrommer, M.** Königinnen vom Nil. Mainz 2002, Von Zabern 126 pp. €25.80. 3-8053-2916-4.

11350 **Ray, John** Reflections of Osiris: lives from Ancient Egypt. L 2002, Profile xv; 176 pp. 1-86197-490-6. Bibl. 160-164.

11351 **Redford, Susan** The harem conspiracy: the murder of Ramesses III. DeKalb 2002, Northern Illinois Univ. Pr. xxvi; 148 pp. 0-8758-0-29508. 28 ill.

11352 **Reeves, Nicholas** Echnaton: Ägyptens falscher Prophet. ᵀ*Jaroš-Deckert, Brigitte*: Mainz 2002, Von Zabern 238 pp. Num. ill.

11353 **Rice, Michael** Egypt's legacy: archetypes of western civilization 3000-30 BC. 1997 ⇒13,9909. ᴿCEg 153-154 (2002) 180-184 (*Héral, Suzanne*).

11354   *Roccati, Alessandro* L'Egitto e il Levante nel II millennio a.C. [M]CIASCA, A. 2002 ⇒15. 441-446.
11355   **Rose, Lynn E.** Sun, moon, and Sothis: a study of calendars and calendar reforms in ancient Egypt. Osiris 2: 1999 ⇒15,10510; 17, 10321. [R]JNES 61 (2002) 311-315 (*Wells, Ronald A.*).
11356   **Roth, Silke** Gebieterin alle Länder: die Rolle der königlichen Frauen in der fiktiven und realen Aussenpolitik des ägyptischen Neuen Reiches. OBO 185: Gö 2002, Vandenhoeck & R. xii; 168 pp. FS 55. 3-525-53042-0. Bibl. 145-154;
11357   Die Königsmütter des Alten Ägypten: von der Frühzeit bis zum Ende der 12. Dynastie. ÄAT 46: 2001 ⇒17,10322. [R]DiscEg 54 (2002) 109-113 (*Grajetzki, Wolfram*).
11358   [E]**Rowlandson, Jane** Women and society in Greek and Roman Egypt: a sourcebook. 1998 ⇒14,9678... 17,435. [R]Latomus 61 (2002) 470-471 (*Straus, Jean A.*).
11359   *Schneider, Thomas* Sinuhes Notiz über die Könige: syrisch-anatolische Herrschertitel in ägyptischer Überlieferung. [E]*Bietak, Manfred*: Ä&L 12 (2002) 257-272.
11360   *Spieser, Cathie* Les cartouches divins. ZÄS 129/1 (2002) 85-95.
11361   *Sternberg-el Hotabi, Heike* Die persische Herrschaft in Ägypten. Religion und Religionskontakte. 2002 ⇒492. 111-149.
11362   *Vandersleyen, Claude* Les étrangers dans le delta égyptien. [F]*Duchesne-Guillemin, J.* 2002 ⇒32. 23-29.
11363   [E]**Walker, Susan; Higgs, Peter** Cleopatra of Egypt: from history to myth. 2001 ⇒17,10333. [R]ArOr 70 (2002) 436-437 (*Smoláriková, Květa*).
11364   **Welsby, D.A.** The kingdom of Kush: the Napatan and Meroitic empires. L 2002 <1996>, British Museum Pr. 240 pp. £16. 0-7141-1951-2.
11365· **Wilkinson, T.A.H.** Early dynastic Egypt. [2]2001 <1999> ⇒17, 10335. [R]DiscEg 53 (2002) 83-86 (*Ciałowicz, Krzysztof M.*);
11366   1999 ⇒15,10518... 17,10335. [R]CEg 153-154 (2002) 151-153 (*Trigger, Bruce G.*); JARCE 39 (2002) 263-264 (*Bard, Kathryn*);
11367   Royal annals of ancient Egypt: the Palermo Stone and its associated fragments. 2000 ⇒16,10631; 17,10336. [R]ArOr 70 (2002) 441-442 (*Navrátilová, Hana*).
11368   *Wilkinson, Toby* Reality versus ideology: the evidence for 'Asiatics' in predynastic and early dynastic Egypt. Egypt and the Levant. 2002 ⇒497. 512-520.
11369   *Yoyotte, Jean* En Égypte, le faux mystère des dynasties hyksos. MoBi 146 (2002) 40-45.
11370   [E]**Ziegler, Christiane** I Faraoni. Mi 2002, Bompiani 511 pp. 88-74-23-020-6.

Q4.0 Historia Mesopotamiae

11371   *Achenbach, Reinhard* Jabâ und Atalja—zwei jüdische Königstöchter am assyrischen Königshof?: zu einer These von Stephanie Dalley. BN 113 (2002) 29-38.
11372   *Anbar, Moshe* Hammu-rabi in the Mari letters. BetM 172 (2002) 35-41 Sum. 95. **H.**

11373 [E]**Baker, Heather D.; Parpola, Simo** The prosopography of the Neo-Assyrian empire, 2: Parts 1 (Ḫ - K) and II (L-N). Helsinki 2000, The Neo-Assyrian Text Corpus Project x; 212 + x; 238 pp. $50 + 60. 951-45-9045-7/55-4.

11374 **Bauer, Josef; Englund, Robert K.; Krebernik, Manfred** Mesopotamien: Späturuk-Zeit und frühdynastische Zeit. OBO 160,1: 1998 ⇒14,9706...16,10634. [R]JNES 61 (2002) 134-136 (*Biggs, Robert D.*).

11375 *Beaulieu, Paul-Alain* Ea-dayān, governor of the sealand, and other dignitaries of the Neo-Babylonian Empire. JCS 54 (2002) 99-123.

11376 *Black, Jeremy* The Sumerians in their landscape. [M]JACOBSEN, T. 2002 ⇒62. 41-61.

11377 **Bottéro, Jean** Everyday life in ancient Mesopotamia. [T]*Nevill, Antonia*: 2001 ⇒17,10344. [R]BCSMS 37 (2002) 64 (*Chadwick, Robert*).

11378 *Charpin, Dominique* Chroniques du Moyen-Euphrate, 1: le 'royaume de Hana': textes et histoire. RA 96 (2002) 61-92.

11379 *Dietrich, Walter* Ninive in der Bibel. [F]DIETRICH, M. 2002 ⇒28. 115-131.

11380 **Fales, Frederick Mario** L'impero assiro: storia e amministrazione (IX-VII secolo a.C.). Bari 2001, Laterza xiii; 423 pp. Bibl. 359-96.

11381 **Fuchs, Andreas** Die Annalen des Jahres 711 v. Chr.: nach Prismenfragmenten aus Ninive und Assur. 1998 ⇒15,10532; 16,10647. [R]Or. 71 (2002) 313-314 (*Schramm, Wolfgang*).

11382 **Fuchs, Andreas; Parpola, Simo** The correspondence of Sargon II Part III: letters from Babylonia and the eastern provinces. State Archives of Assyria 15: 2001 ⇒17,10352. [R]ArOr 70 (2002) 85-86 (*Pečírková, Jana*).

11383 *Galil, Gershon* Shalmaneser III in the west. RB 109 (2002) 40-56.

11384 *Görg, Manfred* Zu einer weiteren Königsschrift Tukulti-Ninurtas I. BN 114/115 (2002) 31-33.

11385 *Götzelt, Thomas* Descent, private and public: social environments in early Mesopotamia (Od Babylonian period). AltOrF 29 (2002) 339-354.

11386 **Grayson, Albert Kirk** Assyrian rulers of the early first millennium BC II (858-745 BC). 1996 ⇒12,9226... 17,10362. [R]AfO 44-45 (1997-98) 393-396; 48-49 (2001-2002) 207-208 (*Schramm, Wolfgang*).

11387 *Hämeen-Anttila, Jaakko* Mesopotamian national identity in early Arabic sources. WZKM 92 (2002) 53-79.

11388 *Hecker, Karl* Mesopotamien. RGG 5. 2002 ⇒796. 1114-1127.

11389 *Holloway, Steven W.* The quest for Sargon, Pul and Tiglath-Pileser in the nineteenth century Mesopotamia and the bible. JSOT.S 341: 2002 ⇒458. 68-87.

11390 *Kalla, Gábor* Namensgebung und verwandtschaftliche Beziehungen in der altbabylonischen Zeit. Onomastik. AOAT 296: 2002 ⇒ 8959. 123-169.

11391 *Lacambre, Denis* Études sur le règne de Zimrî-Lîm de Mari. RA 96 (2002) 1-21.

11392 *Lanfranchi, Giovanni B.* Chronology in the inscriptions of Shalmaneser III and in the eponym chronicle: the number of the campaigns against Que. [M]IMPARATI, F. 2002 ⇒61. 453-469.

11393 *Limet, Henri* Repères identitaires d'un Sumérien. [F]DUCHESNE-GUILLEMIN, J. 2002 ⇒32. 3-22.

11394 *Llop, Jaume; George, A.R.* Die babylonisch-assyrischen Beziehungen und die innere Lage Assyriens in der Zeit der Auseinandersetzung zwischen Ninurta-tukulti-Aššur und Mutakkil-Nusku nach
neuen keilschriftlichen Quellen. AfO 48-49 (2001-2002) 1-23.

11395 **Luukko, Mikko; Van Buylaere, Greta** The political correspondence of Esarhaddon. State Archives of Assyria 16: Helsinki 2002,
University Pr. lv; 221 pp 951-570-538-X. Contrib. *Simo Parpola*;
illustrations edited by *Julian Reade*.

11396 *Malbran-Labat, Florence* La civilisation des cunéiformes: oubli
mythique et historicité. RICP 83 (2002) 15-31.

11397 *Massmann, Ludwig* Sanheribs Politik in Juda: Beobachtungen und
Erwägungen zum Ausgang der Konfrontation Hiskias mit den Assyrern. [F]WEIPPERT, M.: OBO 186: 2002 ⇒133. 167-180.

11398 **Matthiae, Paolo** Gli stati territoriali: 2100-1600 a.C. Mi 2000,
Electa 291 pp. 88-435-5348-8. Bibl. 269-290.

11399 **Mattila, Raija** Legal transactions of the royal court of Nineveh,
part II: Assurbanipal through Sin-sarru-iskun. SAA 14: Helsinki
2002, University Press xxix; 381 pp. 951-570-483-9. Illustrations
edited by *Dominique Collon.*

11400 **Melville, Sarah C.** The role of Naqia/Zakutu in Sargonid politics.
SAAS 9: 1999 ⇒15,10545; 16,10663. [R]BiOr 59 (2002) 369-372
(*Macgregor, Sherry Lou*); OLZ 97 (2002) 534-537 (*Vogel, Helga*).

11401 *Meyer, Jan-Waalke* Sargon II. als Scheibenschütze. DaM 13 (2002)
113-118.

11402 *Millard, Alan R.* History and legend in early Babylonia. Windows.
2002 ⇒500. 103-110.

11403 *Mitsuma, Yasuyuki* Offices of generals in Seleucid and Aršakid
Babylonia. Bulletin of the Society for Near Eastern Studies in
Japan 45/2 (2002) 26-55 Sum. 26. **J.**

11404 *Na'aman, Nadav* Aribua and the Patina-Hamath border. Or. 71
(2002) 291-295.

11405 *Oelsner, Joachim* Babylonische Kultur nach dem Ende des babylonischen Staates. Religion und Religionskontakte. 2002 ⇒492. 49-
73.

11406 **Parpola, Simo; Radner, Karen; Whiting, Robert M.** The prosopography of the Neo-Assyrian Empire,1/1: A; 1/2: B-G. 1998-1999
⇒15,10550. [R]BiOr 59 (2002) 110-113 (*Stol, M.*); Or. 71 (2002)
315-320 (*Guzzo, Maria Giulia Amadasi*); AfO 48-49 (2001-2002)
219-221 (*Streck, Michael P.*).

11407 **Podany, Amanda H.** The land of Hana: Kings, chronology, and
scribal tradition. Bethesda, MD 2002, CDL xiv; 305 pp. 1-883053-
48X. Bibl. 253-271. [R]UF 33 (2001) 641-656 (*Dietrich, Manfried*).

11408 *Roberts, J.J.M.* Nebuchadnezzar I's Elamite crisis in theological
perspective. The bible and the ANE. 2002 <1977> ⇒230. 83-92.

11409 *Sallaberger, Walther* Stillstellung von Geschichte in den Texten
des Herrschers im Frühen Mesopotamien. ArOr 70 (2002) 117-124.

11410 **Sallaberger, Walther; Westenholz, Aage** Mesopotamien: Akka-
de-Zeit und Ur-III-Zeit. OBO 160/3: 1999 ⇒15,10556...17,10399.
[R]AfO 48-49 (2001-2002) 180-181 (*Liverani, Mario*).

11411 **Saporetti, Claudio** La rivale di Babilonia: storia di Esnunna, un
potente regno che sfidò Hammurapi. I volti della storia 118: R
2002, Newton Compton 476 pp. 88-8289-728-1. Bibl. 429-453.

11412 **Sassmannshausen, Leonhard** Beiträge zur Verwaltung und Gesellschaft Babyloniens in der Kassitenzeit. 2001 ⇒17,10402. ^RBiOr 59 (2002) 575-579 (*Deheselle, Danielle*).

11413 **Schuol, Monika** Die Charakene: ein mesopotamisches Königreich in hellenistisch-parthischer Zeit. Oriens et Occidens 1: 2000 ⇒16,10676; 17,10403. ^RHZ 274 (2002) 157-158 (*Heller, André*); WO 32 (2002) 260-264 (*Kettenhofen, Erich*); AfO 48-49 (2001-2002) 248-250 (*Kessler, Karlheinz*).

11414 *Steinkeller, Piotr* Archaic city seals and the question of Early Babylonian unity. ^MJACOBSEN, T. 2002 ⇒62. 249-257.

11415 *Streck, Michael P.* Der Wiederaufbau Babylons unter Asarhaddon und Assurbanipal in Briefen aus Ninive. AltOrF 29 (2002) 205-33.

11416 Sumer. DBS 73. 2000 ⇒783. 257-359 col. Various authors; cont. from Fasc. 72.

11417 *Tadmor, Hayim* The role of the chief eunuch and the place of eunuchs in the Assyrian Empire. Sex and gender. 2002 ⇒712. 603-611.

11418 **Waters, Matthew W.** A survey of Neo-Elamite history. SAA.S 12: 2000 ⇒16,10682. ^ROLZ 97 (2002) 372-376 (*Vallat, François*); Or 71 (2002) 465-467 (*Koch, Heidemarie*).

11419 **Yamada, Shigeo** The construction of the Assyrian Empire: a historical study of the inscriptions of Shalmanesar III (859-824 B.C.) relating to his campaigns to the west. Culture and history of the Ancient Near East 3: 2000 ⇒16,10683; 17,10411. ^RArOr 70 (2002) 245-246 (*Pečirková, Jana*); BASOR 327 (2002) 96-99 (*Na'aman, Nadav*); UF 34 (2002) 989-992 (*Dietrich, M.*).

11420 *Younger, K. Lawson Jr.* Recent study on Sargon II, king of Assyria: implications for biblical studies. Mesopotamia and the bible. JSOT. S 341: 2002 ⇒458. 288-329.

11421 *Zaccagnini, Carlo* Guerra, carestie e povertà nel Vicino Oriente antico: la sorte dei bambini. AcBib 10 (2002) 991-1003.

11422 **Zadok, Ran** The earliest diaspora: Israelites and Judeans in pre-Hellenistic Mesopotamia. TA 2002, Diaspora Research Institute, Tel Aviv Univ. 93 pp.

Q4.5 *Historia Persiae*—Iran

11423 **Briant, Pierre** From Cyrus to Alexander: a history of the Persian Empire. ^T*Daniels, Peter T.*: WL 2002, Eisenbrauns xx; 1196 pp. $69.50. 1-57506-031-0. Bibl. 1059-1124;

11424 Bulletin d'histoire achéménide II (=BHAch II, 1997-2000). Persika 1: 2001 ⇒17,10413. ^ROr. 71 (2002) 467-468 (*Koch, Heidemarie*).

11425 **Brown, John Pairman** Israel and Hellas, 3: the legacy of Iranian imperialism and the individual, with cumulative indexes to vols. I-III. BZAW 299: 2001 ⇒17,10414. ^RCBQ 64 (2002) 342-343 (*Hawk, L. Daniel*); OTEs 15 (2002) 556-558 (*Muntingh, L.M.*).

11426 **Grewe, Christian** Die Entstehung regionaler staatlicher Siedlungsstrukturen im Bereich des prähistorischen Zagros-Gebirges: eine Analyse von Siedlungsverteilungen in der Susiana und im Kur-Flussbecken. Altertumskunde des Vorderen Orients 11: Müns 2002, Ugarit-Verlag ix; 580 pp. 3-9346-2804-4. Bibl. 271-283.

11427 **Jullien, Christelle; Jullien, Florence** Apôtres des confins: processus missionnaires chrétiens dans l'empire iranien. Res Orientales 15: Bures-sur-Yvette 2002, Groupe pour l'Étude de la Civilisation du Moyen-Orient. 2-9508266-9-5 [RB 110,156].

11428 *Kuhrt, Amélie* New light on the Persian empire. BAIAS 19-20 (2001-2002) 185-186.

11429 *Medvedskaya, I.N.* The rise and fall of Media. ᴹDIAKONOFF, I. 2002 ⇒27. 212-225.

11430 **Potts, Daniel T.** The archaeology of Elam: formation and transformation of an ancient Iranian state. 1999 ⇒16,10693; 17,10422. ᴿAJA 106 (2002) 126-127 (*Amiet, Pierre*).

11431 *Puhvel, Jaan* Constraints on historicity in the Book of kings. Epilecta. 2002 ⇒226. 289-292.

11432 *Steve, M.J.; Vallat, F.; Gasche, H.* Suse. DBS 73. 2002 ⇒783. 359-512 col.

11433 **Zadok, Ran** The ethno-linguistic character of northwestern Iran and Kurdistan in the Neo-Assyrian period. Old City of Jaffa 2002, Archaeological Center 164 pp. 965-7162-08-4. Bibl. 114-125.

Q5 *Historia Anatoliae*—Asia Minor, Hittites [⇒T8.2]

11434 *Beal, Richard H.* The Hurrian dynasty and the double names of Hittite kings. ᴹIMPARATI, F. 2002 ⇒61. 55-70.

11435 ᴱ**Bernabé, Alberto; Alvarez-Pedrosa, Juan Antonio** Historia y leyes de los hittitas: textos del imperio antiguo: el código. Akal/Oriente 3 Indoeuropeo: M 2000, Akal 255 pp. ᴿAuOr 20/1-2 (2002) 267-271 (*González Salazar, J.M.*).

11436 **Bryce, Trevor** Life and society in the Hittite world. Oxf 2002, OUP xiv; 312 pp. £45. 0-19-924170-8. Bibl. 293-301.

11437 *Cancik, Hubert* "Das ganze Land Het": "Hethiter" und die luwischen Staaten in der Bibel. Die Hethiter. 2002 ⇒535. 30-33;

11438 Die hethitische Historiographie. Die Hethiter. 2002 ⇒535. 74-77;

11439 Die luwische Historiographie: Geschichtsschreibung vor den Griechen II. Die Hethiter. 2002. ⇒535. 78-81.

11440 *Cancik-Kirschbaum, Eva* Konfrontation und Koexistenz: Ḫattusa und die nordmesopotamischen Staaten Mittanni und Assyrien. Die Hethiter. 2002 ⇒535. 282-287.

11441 *Daddi, Franca Pecchioli* A 'new' instruction from Arnuwanda I;

11442 *De Martino, Stefano* The military exploits of the Hittite king Ḫattušili I in lands situated between the Upper Euphrates and the Upper Tigris. ᶠPOPKO, M. 2002 ⇒91. 261-268/77-85.

11443 *Dinçol, Ali; Dincol, Belkis* Große, Prinzen, Herren: die Spitze der Reichsadministration im Spiegel ihrer Siegel. Die Hethiter. 2002 ⇒ 535. 82-87.

11444 *Freu, Jacques* La chronologie du règne de Suppiluliuma: essai de mise au point. ᶠPOPKO, M. 2002 ⇒91. 87-107.

11445 *Fuscagni, Francesco* Walanni e due nuove possibili sequenze di regine ittite. ᴹIMPARATI, F. 2002 ⇒61. 289-297.

11446 *Groddek, Detlev* Muršili II., die großen Feste und die 'Pest': Überlegungen zur Anordnung der Fragmente der späteren Jahre seiner Regierung in den AM. ᴹIMPARATI, F. 2002 ⇒61. 329-338.

11447 *Gurney, Oliver* The authorship of the Ulmi-Tešub treaty . ᴹIMPARATI, F. 2002 ⇒61. 339-344.

11448 *Haroutunian, Hripsime* Bearded or beardless?: some speculations on the function of the beard among the Hittites. ^MGÜTERBOCK, H. 2002 ⇒54. 43-52.

11449 *Hawkins, J.D.* Eunuchs among the Hittites. Sex and gender. 2002 ⇒712. 217-233;

11450 Die Erben des Großreiches I: die Geschichte der späthethitischen Kleinkönigreiche Anatoliens und Nordsyriens im Überblick (ca. 1180-700 v. Chr.). Die Hethiter. 2002 ⇒535. 56-59.

11451 *Hoffner, Harry A., Jr.* The treatment and long-term use of persons captured in battle according to the Maşat texts;

11452 *Imparati, Fiorella* Palaces and local communities in some Hittite provincial seats. ^MGÜTERBOCK, H. 2002 ⇒54. 61-72/93-100.

11453 **Keen, Anthony G.** Dynastic Lycia: a political history of the Lycians and their relations with foreign powers. Mn.S 178: 1998 ⇒15, 10592. ^RJNES 61 (2002) 158 (*Melchert, H. Craig*).

11454 *Khazaradze, Nana* The 'western Muski' in central Anatolia. ^MDIAKONOFF, I. 2002 ⇒27. 307-313.

11455 *Klengel, Horst* Die Geschichte des hethitischen Reiches. Die Hethiter. 2002 ⇒535. 62-73;

11456 Problems in Hittite history, solved and unsolved. ^MGÜTERBOCK, H. 2002 ⇒54. 101-109;

11457 Prolegomena zu einer hethitischen Wirtschaftsgeschichte. ^MIMPARATI, F. 2002 ⇒61. 425-436.

11458 **Klengel, Horst** Hattuschili und Ramses: Hethiter und Ägypter—ihr langer Weg zum Frieden. Kulturgeschichte der antiken Welt 95: Mainz 2002, Von Zabern 179 pp. €39.80. 3-8053-2917-2. 78 ill.

11459 *Klinger, Jörg* Die hethitisch-kaškäische Geschichte bis zum Beginn der Großreichszeit. ^MIMPARATI, F. 2002 ⇒61. 437-451.

11460 *Klinkott, Hilmar* Zur politischen Akkulturation unter den Achaimeniden: der Testfall Karien. Brückenland Anatolien?. 2002 ⇒453. 173-204.

11461 *Kossian, A.V.* Luwians, Phrigians and Mushkians. ^MDIAKONOFF, I. 2002 ⇒27. 187-196. **R.**

11462 *Mahé, Jean-Pierre* Christen im Kaukasus: die Evangelisierung von Armenien und Georgien. WUB Sonderheft (2002) 20-25.

11463 *Quack, Joachim Friedrich* Da wurden diese zwei großen Länder zu einem Land: die Beziehung zwischen Ḫattusa und Ägypten im Lichte ihrer diplomatischen Korrespondenz. Die Hethiter. 2002 ⇒ 535. 288-293.

11464 *Roos, Johan de* Vows concerning military campaigns of Ḫattušiliš III and Tutḫaliaš IV. ^MIMPARATI, F. 2002 ⇒61. 181-188.

11465 *Roszkowska-Mutschler, Hanna* Zu den Mannestaten der hethischen Könige und ihrem Sitz im Leben. ^FPOPKO, M. 2002 ⇒91. 289-300.

11466 **Schweyer, Anne-Valérie** Les Lyciens et la mort: une étude d'histoire sociale. Varia anatolica 14: P 2002, De Boccard (4) 319 pp. 2-906053-67-8. Bibl. 277-291.

11467 *Starke, Frank* Die Verfassung des hethitischen Reiches. Die Hethiter. 2002 ⇒535. 316-317.

11468 *Strobel, Karl* Die Staatenbildung bei den kleinasiatischen Galatern: politisch-historische und kulturelle Prozesse im hellenistischen Zentralanatolien. Brückenland Anatolien?. 2002 ⇒453. 231-293.

11469 *Yakar, Jak* Towards an absolute chronology for Middle and Late Bronze Age Anatolia. AnaAra 16 (2002) 557-570.

11470   *Yiğit, Turgut* Hititçe çivi yazılı belgelere göre çoban [Herdsmen in the Hittite cuneiform texts]. BTTK 66 (2002) 765-787. **Turkish**.

Q6.1 Historia Graeciae classicae

11471   **Camp, John; Fisher, Elizabeth** Exploring the world of the ancient Greeks. L 2002, Thames and H. 224 pp. 0-500-05112-7. 376 ill., 107 col..
11472   **Doblhofer, Georg** Vergewaltigung in der Antike. 1994 ⇒12,9316; 14,9816. [R]JJP 32 (2002) 291-295 (*Hengstl, Joachim*).
11473   **Legras, Bernard** Education et culture dans le monde grec (VIIIᵉ siècle av. J.-C.-IVᵉ siècle ap. J.-C.). Cursus: P 2002, Colin 160 pp. €14. 2-200-26287-6 [AnCl 72,483s—Rochette, Bruno].
11474   **McGlew, James F.** Citizens on stage: comedy and political culture in the Athenian democracy. AA 2002, Univ. of Michigan Pr. vii; 239 pp. 0-472-11285-6. Bibl. 223-231.
11475   **Nevett, Lisa C.** House and society in the ancient Greek world. New Studies in Archaeology: 1999 ⇒15,10607; 17,10448. [R]Antiquity 76 (2002) 583-584 (*Parisinou, Eva*).
11476   *Rawlins, Dennis* ARISTARCHOS and the 'Babylonian' month. Under one sky. AOAT 297: 2002 ⇒9014. 295-296.
11477   *Schmid, Wilhelm* Aspasia und Perikles: Philosophie der Erotik und Erziehung zur Selbstsorge. Paare. 2002 ⇒489. 39-50.
11478   **Schnapp-Gourbeillon, Annie** Aux origines de la Grèce, XIIIe-VIIIe siècles avant notre ère: la genèse du politique. P 2002, Belles Lettres 426 pp. 2-251-38059-0. Bibl. 379-405.
11479   **Wohl, Victoria** Love among the ruins: the erotics of democracy in classical Athens. Princeton, NJ 2002, Princeton Univ. Pr. xii (2); 329 pp. 0-691-09522-1. Bibl. 285-312.

Q6.5 Alexander, Seleucidae; historia Hellenismi

11480   [E]**Algra, Keimpe**, *al.*, The Cambridge history of Hellenistic philosophy. 1999 ⇒15,10612; 17,10459. [R]AGPh 84 (2002) 102-105 (*Cooper, John M.*); Phron. 47 (2002) 264-286 (*Lévy, Carlos*); Ancient Philosophy 22 (2002) 458-479 (*Glidden, David*); PhRev 111 (2002) 101-105 (*Sharples, R.W.*); StPhiloA 14 (2002) 228-235 (*Winston, David*).
11481   **Barc, Bernard** Les arpenteurs du temps: essai sur l'histoire religieuse de la Judée à la période hellénistique. Histoire du texte biblique 5: 2000 ⇒16,10721. [R]RThPh 134 (2002) 101-103 (*Nihan, Christophe*); Apocrypha 13 (2002) 283-284 (*Naef, Th.*); LTP 58 (2002) 367-369 (*Poirier, Paul-Hubert*).
11482   *Barclay, John M.G.* Using and refusing: Jewish identity strategies under the hegemony of Hellenism. Ethos und Identität. 2002 ⇒490. 13-25.
11483   *Baumgarten, Albert I.* Were the Greeks different?: if so, how and why?. Shem. JSJ.S 74: 2002 ⇒755. 1-10.
11484   **Bielman, Anne** Femmes en public dans le monde hellénistique: IVe-Ier s. av. J.-C. P 2002, Sedes 330 pp. 2-7181-9604-1. Bibl. 329-330.

11485 *Bivar, A.D.H.* Beyond the Tigris. Ancient West & East 1/1 (2002) 59-65.

11486 *Blasius, Andreas* Zur Frage des geistigen Widerstandes im griechisch-römischen Ägypten: die historische Situation. Apokalyptik und Ägypten. OLA 107: 2002 ⇒451. 41-62.

11487 **Boardman, John; Griffin, Jasper; Murray, Oswyn** The Oxford illustrated history of Greece and the Hellenistic world. 2001 <1986> ⇒17,10458. [R]Prudentia 34/1 (2002) 77-78 (*Young, Gary*).

11488 *Boiy, Tom* Early Hellenistic chronography in cueniform tradition. ZPE 138 (2002) 249-255;

11489 Dating methods during the early Hellenistic period. JCS 52 (2000) 115-121;

11490 The 'accession year' in the late Achaemenid and early Hellenistic period. [F]WALKER, C. 2002 ⇒130. 25-33.

11491 *Bos, Abraham P.* 'Aristotelian' and 'Platonic' dualism in Hellenistic and early christian philosophy and in gnosticism. VigChr 56 (2002) 273-291.

11492 **Bosworth, A.B.** The legacy of Alexander: politics, warfare, and propaganda under the successors. Oxf 2002, OUP 307 pp. CDN$127.50.

11493 [E]**Bosworth, A.B.; Baynham, Elizabeth** ALEXANDER the Great in fact and fiction. 2000 ⇒16,10727. [R]ClR 52 (2002) 103-105 (*Stoneman, Richard*).

11494 *Buitenwerf, Rieuwerd* Sibyllijnse orakels III: joodse identiteit in Klein-Azië. NedThT 56/1 (2002) 1-15.

11495 **Clarke, Katherine** Between geography and history: Hellenistic constructions of the Roman world. 1999 ⇒15,10621; 17,10461. [R]SCI 21 (2002) 289-294 (*Eich, Peter*); JRS 92 (2002) 198-199 (*Beagon, Mary*);

11496 Oxf 2002, Clarendon xi; 407 pp. 0-19-924003-5. Bibl. 379-393.

11497 **Claußen, Carsten** Versammlung, Gemeinde, Synagoge: das hellenistisch-jüdische Umfeld der frühchristlichen Gemeinden. StUNT 27: Gö 2002, Vandenhoeck & R. 368 pp. €82. 3-525-53381-0. Bibl. 315-351. [R]OrdKor 43 (2002) 494-495 (*Giesen, Heinz*).

11498 **Collins, John Joseph** Between Athens and Jerusalem: Jewish identity in the Hellenistic Diaspora. Biblical Resource: [2]2000 ⇒16, 10729; 17,10464. [R]REJ 161 (2002) 501-503 (*Mimouni, Simon C.*); RBLit 4 (2002) 267-269 (*Valeta, David M.*).

11499 *Feldman, Louis H.* How much Hellenism in the land of Israel?. JSJ 33 (2002) 290-313.

11500 **Goldhill, Simon** Who needs Greek?: contests in the cultural history of Hellenism. C 2002, CUP viii; 326 pp. £45/16. 0-521-81228-3. Bibl. 300-321.

11501 *Grabbe, Lester L.* The Jews and Hellenization: Hengel and his critics. Second temple studies III. JSOT.S 340: 2002 ⇒296. 52-66.

11502 *Gruen, Erich S.* Hellenistic Judaism. Cultures. 2002 ⇒448. 77-132.

11503. *Gygax, Marc Domingo* Zum Mitregenten des Ptolemaios II. Philadelphos. Hist. 51 (2002) 49-56.

11504 *Halligan, John M.* Conflicting ideologies concerning the second temple. Second temple studies III. JSOT.S 340: 2002 ⇒296. 108-115.

11505 **Hall, Jonathan M.** Hellenicity: between ethnicity and culture. Ch 2002, Univ. of Chicago Pr. xxii; 312 pp. $50.

11506 *Held, Winfried* Die Residenzstädte der Seleukiden: Babylon, Seleukeia am Tigris, Ai Khanum, Seleukeia in Pieria, Antiocheia am
Orontes. JdI 117 (2002) 217-249.
11507 **Hengel, Martin** Giudaismo ed ellenismo: studi sul loro incontro,
con particolare riguardo per la Palestina fino alla metà del II secolo
a.C. ᴱ*Monaco, Sergio*: BSSTB 14: 2001 ⇒17,10476. ᴿRivBib 50
(2002) 376-382 (*Troiani, Lucio*); CivCatt 153/4 (2002) 304-306
(*Prato, G.L.*).
11508 *Hoglund, Kenneth* The material culture of the Seleucid period in
Palestine: social and economic observations. Second temple studies
III. JSOT.S 340: 2002 ⇒296. 67-73.
11509 *Holladay, Carl R.* Hellenism in the fragmentary Hellenistic Jewish
authors: resonance and resistance. Shem. JSJ.S 74: 2002 ⇒755. 65-
91.
11510 *Johnson, Carl Garth OGIS* 98 and the divinization of the Ptolemies. Hist. 51 (2002) 112-116.
11511 *Laras, Giuseppe* Ebraismo ed ellenismo. Il monoteismo. 2002 ⇒
435. 123-137.
11512 *Mathys, Hans-Peter* Das Alte Testament—ein hellenistisches Buch.
ᶠWEIPPERT, M.: OBO 186: 2002 ⇒133. 278-293.
11513 **Mendels, Doron** Identity, religion and historiography: studies in
Hellenistic history. JSPE.S 24: 1998 ⇒14,174; 15,10638. ᴿDSD 9
(2002) 263-264 (*Aitken, James K.*).
11514 *Meyers, Eric M.* Jewish culture in Greco-Roman Palestine. Cultures. 2002 ⇒448. 135-179.
11515 *Niebuhr, Karl-Wilhelm* Hellenistisch-jüdisches Ethos im Spannungsfeld von Weisheit und Tora. Ethos und Identität. 2002 ⇒490.
27-50.
11516 *Nissinen, Martti* A prophetic riot in Seleucid Babylonia. ᶠSTEIN-
GRIMSSON, S.: ATSAT 72: 2002 ⇒117. 63-74.
11517 ᴱ**Oppenheimer, Aharon** Jüdische Geschichte in hellenistisch-römischer Zeit: Wege der Forschung: vom alten zum neuen SCHÜ-
RER. 1999 ⇒15,376. ᴿHZ 274 (2002) 421-423 (*Botermann,
Helga*).
11518 ᴱ**Runia, David; Sterling, Gregory** The Studia Philonica annual:
studies in Hellenistic Judaism. 1999 ⇒15,10646; 17,10756. ᴿRBLit
4 (2002) 272-273 (*Fox, Kenneth A.*).
11519 *Runia, David T.* Eudaimonism in Hellenistic-Jewish literature.
Shem. JSJ.S 74: 2002 ⇒755. 131-157.
11520 **Sartre, Maurice** D'ALEXANDRE à ZÉNOBIE: histoire du Levant antique, IVᵉ siècle avant J.-C.-IIIᵉ siècle après J.-C. 2001 ⇒17,10492.
ᴿPOC 52 (2002) 441-442 (*Merceron, Roger*).
11521 **Spinelli, Miguel** Helenização e recriação de sentidos: a filosofia na
época da expansão do cristianismo—séculos II, III e IV. Porto Alegre 2002, EDIPUCRS 392 pp.
11522 **Tcherikover, Victor** Hellenistic civilization and the Jews. 1999
<1959> ⇒15,10651. Pref. *John J. Collins.* ᴿRSR 90 (2002) 434-
435 (*Paul, André*).
11523 **Weber, Reinhard** Das Gesetz im hellenistischen Judentum: Studi-
en zum Verständnis und zur Funktion der Thora von DEMETRIOS
bis PSEUDO-PHOKYLIDES. ARGU 10: 2000 ⇒16,10761. ᴿAnton. 77
(2002) 356-360 (*Volgger, David*); REJ 161 (2002) 475-478 (*Lévy,
Carlos*).

11524   *Wiemer, Hans-Ulrich* Ökonomie und Politik im hellenistischen
         Rhodos. HZ 275 (2002) 561-591.

Q7 Josephus Flavius

11525   ^ESiegert, Folker; Kalms, Jürgen U. Internationales Josephus-Kol-
         loquium Paris 2001: studies on the Antiquities of Josephus: études
         sur les Antiquités de Josèphe. Münsteraner judaistische Studien 12:
         Müns 2002, LIT 220 pp. 3-8258-5859-6.

11526   Bardet, Serge Le Testimonium Flavianum: examen historique,
         considérations historiographiques. Josèphe et son temps 5: P 2002,
         Cerf 280 pp. €25. 2-204-07002-5. Postface de *Pierre Geoltrain*.
         Bibl. 25-45.
11527   Begg, Christopher T. Josephus' story of the later monarchy (AJ
         9,1-10, 185). BEThL 145: 2000 ⇒16,10767; 17,10508. ^RJJS 53
         (2002) 165-166 (*Taverner, Steve*); RivBib 50 (2002) 473-475
         (*Sievers, Joseph*); ThLZ 127 (2002) 881-884 (*Deines, Roland*);
         JSSt 47 (2002) 349-352 (*Bilde, Per*); Materia giudaica 7/1 (2002)
         196-199 (*Ceriani, Silvia*).
11528   *Ben Zeev, Miriam* Five Jewish delegations to MARCUS ANTONIUS
         (44-41 BCE) and Josephus' apologetic purposes. Materia giudaica.
         2002 ⇒727. 24-27.
11529   *Bernat, David* Josephus's portrayal of Phinehas. JSPE 13 (2002)
         137-149.
11530   Bohrmann, Monette La version vieux russe de la Guerre Juive de
         Flavius Josèphe. Ment. *Mescerskij, N.A.*: P 2002, Presses Universi-
         taires Franc-Comtoises 115 pp. €17. 2-84627-056-2. Bibl. 113-114.
11531   *Carvalho, José Carlos* O palácio norte de Massada e os ecos de
         Flávio Josefo. HumTeo 23 (2002) 227-245 Sum. 424.
11532   Castelli, Silvia Il terzo libro delle Antichità giudaiche di Flavio
         Giuseppe e la bibbia: problemi storici e letterari: traduzioni e com-
         mento. Biblioteca di Athenaeum 48: Como 2002, New Press 363
         pp. €40. Bibl. 319-333.
11533   *Colautti, Federico M.* The celebration of Passover in Josephus: a
         means of strengthening Jewish identity?. SBL.SP 2002. SBL.SPS
         41: 2002 ⇒598. 285-305.
11534   Colautti, Federico M. Passover in the works of Josephus. JSJ.S
         75: Lei 2002, Brill xii; 277 pp. €90/$99. 90-04-12372-5. Bibl. 245-
         257.
11535   *Eberhardt, Barbara* Zwischen Toleranz und Kritik: Josephus' Ein-
         stellung gegenüber anderen Religionen in A 4:126-155; 8:335-343;
         9:132-139. Studies...Antiquities of Josephus. 2002 ⇒11525. 9-21.
11536   *Feldman, Louis H.* Josephus's view of the Amalekites. BBR 12
         (2002) 161-186;
11537   Josephus on the spies (Num 13-14). Studies...Antiquities of Jose-
         phus. 2002 ⇒11525. 22-41;
         The portrayal of Phinehas by... Josephus 2002 ⇒9685.
         The portrayal of Sihon and Og in...Josephus 2002 ⇒9684.
11538   ^TFeldman, Louis H. Josephus Flavius: translation and commentary
         3: Judean Antiquities 1-4. 2000 ⇒16,10805. ^RStPhiloA 14 (2002)
         219-223 (*Runia, David T.*).

11539 **Feldman, Louis H.** Josephus's interpretation of the bible. 1998 ⇒ 14,9909...17,10522. ᴿHeyJ 43 (2002) 219-220 (*McNamara, Martin*); RSR 90 (2002) 457-458 (*Paul, André*).

11540 ᴱ**Feldman, Louis H.; Levison, John R.** Josephus' Contra Apionem: studies in its character and context with a Latin concordance to the portion missing in Greek. AGJU 34: 1996 ⇒12,9384... 16, 10800. ᴿStPhiloA 14 (2002) 223-226 (*Sterling, Gregory E.*).

11541 *Feliks, Yehuda* Josephus' botanical description of the high priestly headdress. Leš. 64/1-2 (2002) 51-57 Sum. II. H.

11542 *Fuks, Gideon* Josephus on Herod's attitude towards Jewish religion: the darker side. JJS 53 (2002) 238-245.

11543 *Gnuse, Robert* Vita apologetica: the lives of Josephus and Paul in apologetic historiography. JSPE 13 (2002) 151-169.

11544 **Grünenfelder, Regula** Frauen an den Krisenherden: eine rhetorisch-politische Deutung des Bellum Judaicum. Exegese in unserer Zeit 10: Müns 2002, Lit 316 pp. 3-8258-5978-9.

11545 *Haaland, Gunnar* Addressing the Romans on behalf of the Jews: a rhetorical analysis of Antiquitates 16:31-57. Studies...Antiquities of Josephus. 2002 ⇒11525. 42-58.

11546 *Hadas-Lebel, Mireille* Alexandre Jannée a-t-il crucifié ses opposants pharisiens?: ètude de σταυρος, ἀνασταυροω chez Flavius Josèphe. Studies...Antiquities of Josephus. 2002 ⇒11525. 59-71.

11547 *Höffken, Peter* Zur Rolle der Davidsverheißung bei Josephus Flavius. ZAW 114 (2002) 577-593 [2 Sam 7,13].

11548 *Jones, Christopher P.* Towards a chronology of Josephus. SCI 21 (2002) 113-121.

11549 *Jonquière, Tessel M.* Two prayers by King Solomon in Josephus' Antiquities 8 and the bible. Studies...Antiquities of Josephus. 2002 ⇒11525. 72-89.

11550 **Krieger, Klaus-Stefan** Geschichtsschreibung als Apologetik bei Flavius Josephus. 1994 ⇒11/2,9694... 14,9920. ᴿRB 109 (2002) 303-305 (*Nodet, Étienne*).

11551 *Krieger, Klaus-Stefan* A synoptic approach to B 2:117-283 and A 18-20. Studies...Antiquities of Josephus. 2002 ⇒11525. 90-100.

11552 *Lanfranchi, Pierluigi* Le motif de μετανοια dans les Antiquités juives. Studies...Antiquities of Josephus. 2002 ⇒11525. 125-137.

11553 *Lemaire, André* L'expérience essénienne de Flavius Josèphe. Studies...Antiquities of Josephus. 2002 ⇒11525. 138-151.

11554 *Levison, John R.* The Roman character of funerals in the writings of Josephus. JSJ 33 (2002) 245-277.
  Lieu, J. Not Hellenes... Maccabees & Josephus 2002 ⇒3411.

11555 *Lindner, Helgo* Der Bau des größeren Tempels (A 15:380-390): herodianische Propaganda und Josephus' Auffassung der jüdischen Geschichte. Studies...Antiquities of Josephus. 2002 ⇒11525. 152-160.

11556 *Mason, Steve* Josephus and his twenty-two book canon. Canon debate. 2002 ⇒1551. 110-127.

11557 **Mason, Steve** Understanding Josephus: seven perspectives. JSEP.S 32: 1998 ⇒14,9889... 16,10814. ᴿDSD 9 (2002) 124-126 (*Brooke, George J.*);

11558 Flavius Josephus on the pharisees: a composition-critical study. 2001 <1991> ⇒17,10545. ᴿAng. 79 (2002) 986-989 (*Jurič, Stipe*).

11559 ᵀ**Mason, Steve** Life of Josephus: translation and commentary. 2001 ⇒17,10547. ᴿJSJ 33 (2002) 335-336 (*Spottorno, Ma. Victoria*); CBQ 64 (2002) 766-767 (*Attridge, Harold W.*).

11560 *Mendels, Doron* Josephus' Antiquities and the centrality of the land of Israel in international politics from the 4th to the 1st century BCE. Studies...Antiquities of Josephus. 2002 ⇒11525. 161-171.

11561 *Milikowsky, Chaim* Josephus between rabbinic culture and Hellenistic historiography. Shem. JSJ.S 74: 2002 ⇒755. 159-190;

11562 The chronology of Israel from the Exodus until the building of the temple according to Josephus. Shem. 2002 ⇒755. 191-197.

11563 *Parente, Fausto* L'oeuvre de Flavius Josèphe comme source pour l'histoire de l'eschatologie juive de Ier siècle ap. J.-C. Studies... Antiquities of Josephus. 2002 ⇒11525. 172-188.

11564 **Rajak, Tessa** Josephus: the historian and his society. L ²2002, Duckworth xv; 261 pp. £15. 0-7156-3170-5.

11565 *Regev, Eyal; Nakman, David* Josephus and the halakhah of the pharisees, the sadducees and Qumran. Zion 67 (2002) 401-433. **H.**

11566 ᴱ**Rengstorf, Karl Heinrich** A complete concordance to Flavius Josephus: study edition: vol. 1: A-K; vol. 2: Λ-Ω: including supplement 1: Namenwörterbuch zu Flavius Josephus von Abraham Schalit. Lei 2002 <1983>, Brill xxxii; 1095; viii; 1097-2235 pp. €299/$299. 90-04-12829-8.

11567 *Schwartz, Daniel R.* Rome and the Jews: Josephus on 'freedom' and 'autonomy'. ᶠMILLAR, F. 2002 ⇒79. 65-81;

11568 Should Josephus have ignored the christians?. Ethos und Identität. 2002 ⇒490. 165-178;

11569 Once again on Tobiad chronology: should we let a stated anomaly be anomalous?: a response to Gideon Fuks. JJS 53 (2002) 146-151.

11570 ᵀ**Simonetti, Manlio** Josephus, Flavius: Storia dei Giudei: da ALESSANDRO Magno a NERONE. I Meridiani; Classici dello spirito: Mi 2002, Mondadori clvii; 884 pp. 88-04-50314-9. "Antichità Giudaiche", Libri XII-XX; introd., note.

11571˙ *Spilsbury, Paul* Josephus on the burning of the temple, the Flavian triumph, and the providence of God. SBL.SP 2002. SBL.SPS 41: 2002 ⇒598. 306-327.

11572 *Strickert, Fred* Josephus' reference to Julia, Caesar's daughter: Jewish Antiquities 18.27-28. JJS 53 (2002) 27-34.

11573 **Thackeray, Henry St. John** Flavius Josèphe: l'homme et l'historien. ᵀ*Nodet, Etienne*: Josèphe et son temps 3: 2000 ⇒16,10828; 17, 10576. ᴿRTL 33 (2002) 573-574 (*Auwers, J.-M.*).

11574 *Tomson, Peter* Les systèmes de halakha, du Contre Apion et des Antiquités. Studies...Antiquities of Josephus. 2002 ⇒11525. 189-220.

11575 *Udoh, Fabian E.* Jewish Antiquities XIV. 205, 207-08 and 'The great plain'. PEQ 134 (2002) 130-143.

11576 *Ullmann, Lisa; Price, Jonathan J.* Drama and history in Josephus' *Bellum Judaicum*. SCI 21 (2002) 97-111.

11577 *Van der Horst, Pieter W.* Who was Apion?;

11578 The distinctive vocabulary of Josephus' *Contra Apionem* <1996>. Japheth. CBET 32: 2002 ⇒251. 207-221/223-233.

Q8.1 *Roma Pompeii et Caesaris*—**Hyrcanus to Herod**

11579 *Bar-Kochva, Bezalel* The conquest of Samaria by John Hyrcanus: the pretext for the siege, Jewish settlement in the ʿAkraba district, and the destruction of the city of Samaria. Cathedra 106 (2002) 7-34 Sum. 205. **H.**

11580 *Horsley, Richard A.* The expansion of Hasmonean rule in Idumea and Gallilee: toward a historical sociology. Second temple studies III. JSOT.S 340: 2002 ⇒296. 134-165.

11581 *Jacobson, David* Placing Herod the Great and his works in context. PEQ 134 (2002) 84-91.

11582 *Kokkinos, Nikos* Herod's horrid death. BArR 28/2 (2002) 29-35, 62.

11583 **Lichtenberger, Achim** Die Baupolitik Herodes des Großen. ADPV 26: 1999 ⇒15,10711...17,10584. ^RAJA 106 (2002) 484-485 (*Schmid, Stephan G.*); RSR 90 (2002) 430 (*Paul, André*).

11584 *Pasto, James* The origin, expansion and impact of the Hasmoneans in light of comparative ethnographic studies (and outside of its nineteenth-century context). Second temple studies III. JSOT.S 340: 2002 ⇒296. 166-201.

11585 **Vogel, Manuel** Herodes: König der Juden, Freund der Römer. Biblische Gestalten 5: Lp 2002, Evangelische Verlagsanstalt 375 pp. €16.50. 3-374-01945-5. Bibl. 365-373. ^RThLZ 127 (2002) 1306-1308 (*Ebner, Martin*).

Q8.4 **Zeitalter Jesu Christi**: *particular/general*

11586 **Crossan, John Dominic** El nacimiento del cristianismo: qué sucedió en los años immediatamente posteriores a la ejecución de Jesús. Sdr 2002, Sal Terrae 653 pp. €54. 84-293-1454-7. ^RRF 246 (2002) 369-370 (*Irazabal, Juan Antonio*);

11587 The birth of christianity: discovering what happened in the years immediately after the execution of Jesus. 1998 ⇒14,8303...17, 10601. ^RASEs 19 (2002) 272-277 (*Bovon, François*); EThL 78 (2002) 199-203 (*Verheyden, J.*).

11588 **Declercq, Georges** Anno Domini: the origins of the christian era. 2000 ⇒16,10842. ^RHZ 274 (2002) 393-395 (*Demandt, Alexander*).

11589 *Dundas, Gregory S.* AUGUSTUS and the kingship of Egypt. Hist. 51 (2002) 433-448.

11590 **Hanson, K.C.; Oakman, Douglas E.** Palestine in the time of Jesus: social structures and social conflicts. Mp 2002, Fortress 235 pp. $23. 0-8006-3470-5.

11591 **Kienast, Dietmar** AUGUSTUS: Prinzeps und Monarch. ³1999 ⇒15, 10726. ^RHZ 274 (2002) 164-166 (*Strothmann, Meret*).

11592 *Lindner, Ruth* Frau und Beruf in der frühen römischen Kaiserzeit. BiKi 57 (2002) 153-157.

11593 **Miano, Peter J.** The word of God and the world of the bible: an introduction to the cultural backgrounds of the New Testament. 2001 ⇒17,10611. ^ROCP 68 (2002) 521-522 (*Farrugia, E.G.*).

11594 **Millard, Alan R.** Pergament und Papyrus, Tafeln und Ton: Lesen und Schreiben zur Zeit Jesu. Biblische Archäologie und Zeitgeschichte 9: 2000 ⇒16,10850. ᴿThLZ 127 (2002) 27-30 (*Pellegrini, Silvia*);

11595 Reading and writing in the time of Jesus. BiSe 69: 2000 ⇒16, 10851; 17,8862. ᴿThLZ 127 (2002) 27-30 (*Pellegrini, Silvia*); CBQ 64 (2002) 773-774 (*Chesnutt, Randall D.*); EvQ 74 (2002) 356-359 (*Head, Peter M.*).

11596 Pearce, Sarah Judea under Roman rule: 63 BCE-135 CE. Biblical world, 1. 2002 ⇒273. 458-491.

11597 ᴱPietri, Luce Histoire du christianisme, 1: le nouveau peuple: des origines à 250. 2001 ⇒17,10614. ᴿRHE 97 (2002) 916-919 (*Gain, Benoît*).

11598 ᴱPouthier, Jean-Luc Les apôtres de Jésus en route vers l'Asie. MoBi 141 (2002) 14-50.

11599 Segal, Alan F. The Jewish experience: temple, synagogue, home and fraternal groups. Community formation. 2002 ⇒644. 20-35.

11600 Tilly, Michael Der Fuchs auf dem Herrscherthron: Herodes Antipas, Tetrarch von Galiläa und Peräa. WUB 24 (2002) 15-20.

11601 Turpin, Joanne The world of Jesus: culture, history, religion, politics, geography. Mystic 2002, Twenty-Third $15. 1-58595-186-2 [BiTod 41,203—Senior, Donald].

11602 Witherington, Ben New Testament history: a narrative account. 2001 ⇒17,10624. ᴿRExp 99 (2002) 283-284 (*Vinson, Richard B.*).

Q8.7 *Roma et Oriens*, prima decennia post Christum

11603 Andrei, Osvalda M. Acilio Glabrione ed il leone: DOMIZIANO tra ebraismo e cristianesimo. Quaderni di Henoch 12: T 2002, Zamorani 119 pp. €24. 88-7158-104-0 [JSJ 35,76s—B. Dehandschutter].

11604 Baltrusch, Ernst Die Juden und das römische Reich: Geschichte einer konfliktreichen Beziehung. Da:Wiss 2002, 223 pp. €34.90 3-534-15585-8. Bibl. 201-217. ᴿJud. 58 (2002) 219-220 (*Avemarie, Friedrich*).

11605 Blanchetière, François Les premiers chrétiens étaient-ils missionnaires?: (30-135). Initiations: P 2002, Cerf 225 pp. €26. 2-204-070-10-6.

11606 Bodinger, Martin Deux problèmes d'histoire des religions au monde antique: 2, TACITE et la 'persécution néronienne'. Archaeus 6 (2002) 261-281.

11607 ᴱBowman, Alan K.; Garnsey, Peter; Rathbone, Dominic The High Empire, A.D. 70-192 CAH 11 ²2000 ⇒17,654. ᴿAnCl 71 (2002) 455-456 (*Raepsaet-Charlier, Marie-Thérèse*) Latomus 61 (2002) 1003-1004 (*Gascou, Jacques*) [⇒781].

11608 Cassidy, Richard J. Christians and Roman rule in the New Testament: new perspectives. 2001 ⇒17,10630. ᴿScrB 32 (2002) 36-37 (*Docherty, Susan*).

11609 Cotton, Hannah M.; Eck, Werner P. Murabbaʿat 114 und die Anwesenheit römischer Truppen in den Höhlen des Wadi Murabbaʿat nach dem Bar Kochba Aufstand. ZPE 138 (2002) 173-183.

11610 Eck, Werner Die Inschriften Iudäas im 1. und frühen 2. Jh. n. Chr. als Zeugnisse der römischen Herrschaft. Zwischen den Reichen. TANZ 36: 2002 ⇒568. 29-50.

11611 **Faulkner, Neil** Apocalypse: the great Jewish revolt against Rome AD 66-73. Stroud 2002, Tempus 416 pp. 0-7524-2573-0. Bibl. 400-405.
11612 *Firpo, Giulio* La distruzione di Gerusalemme e del secondo tempio nel 70. d.C. RSIt 114 (2002) 774-802.
11613 **Firpo, Giulio** Le rivolte giudaiche. 1999 ⇒15,10751. [R]At. 90 (2002) 642-644 (*Troiani, Lucio*).
11614 *Horsley, Richard A.* The new world order: the historical context of New Testament history and literature. NT: introducing. 2002 ⇒ 332. 1-15.
11615 **Levick, Barbara** VESPASIAN. 1999 ⇒15,10757...17,10635. [R]AnCl 71 (2002) 457-459 (*Benoist, Stéphane*).
11616 **Lovano, Michael** The age of CINNA: crucible of late Republican Rome. Historia, Einzelschriften 158: Stu 2002, Steiner 188 pp. 3-515-07948-3. Bibl. 161-173.
11617 **Montero, Santiago** TRAJANO y la adivinación: prodigios, oráculos y apocalíptica en el imperio romano (98-117 d.C.). Gerión, Anejos 4: 2000 ⇒16,10875. [R]Aevum 76 (2002) 231-233 (*Ramelli, Ilaria*); Latomus 61 (2002) 509-510 (*Blázquez, José M*).
11618 **Perea Yébenes, Sabino** Berenice: reina y concubina. 2000 ⇒16, 10638. [R]Aevum 76 (2002) 214-217 (*Ramelli, Ilaria*).
11619 *Reichert, Angelika* Durchdachte Konfusion: PLINIUS, TRAJAN und das Christentum. ZNW 93 (2002) 227-250.

Q9.1 *Historia Romae generalis et* **post-christiana**

11620 **Aldrete, Gregory** Gestures and acclamations in ancient Rome. 1999 ⇒15,10761; 17,10643. [R]Semiotica 139 (2002) 327-330 (*McNiven, Timothy*); Latomus 61 (2002) 471-3 (*Bradley, Keith R.*).
11621 **Ando, Clifford** Imperial ideology and provincial loyalty in the Roman Empire. 2000 ⇒16,10883. [R]Prudentia 34/1 (2002) 58-61 (*Schubert, Alexander*).
11622 *Ascough, Richard S.* Greco-Roman philosophic, religious, and voluntary associations. Community formation. 2002 ⇒644. 3-19.
11623 **Bauman, Richard A.** Human rights in ancient Rome. 2000 ⇒15, 10763; 17,10644. [R]Gn. 74 (2002) 420-423 (*Hölkeskamp, Karl-Joachim*).
11624 [E]**Blagg, Thomas; Millett, Martin** The early Roman Empire in the west. Oxf 2002, Oxbow (6) 250 pp. 1-84217-069-4.
11625 *Bowen, Alan C.* The art of the commander and the emergence of predictive astronomy. Science and mathematics. 2002 ⇒532. 76-111.
11626 **Brancato, Nicolò Giuseppe** Nuclei familiari e variazioni gentilizie nell'antica Roma: probleme connesse (a proposito di una epigrafe inedita). 1999 ⇒15,10766. [R]HZ 275 (2002) 440-442 (*Linke, Bernhard*).
11627 **Bringmann, Klaus** Geschichte der römischen Republik: von den Anfängen bis AUGUSTUS. Mü 2002, Beck 463 pp. 3-406-49292-4.
11628 **Chadwick, Henry** The Church in ancient society: from Galilee to GREGORY the Great. Oxford history of the Christian church: 2001 ⇒17,10647. [R]EHR 117 (2002) 895-897 (*Frend, W.H.C.*).

11629. **Dalby, Andrew** Empire of pleasures: luxury and indulgence in the Roman world. 2000 ⇒16,10889. [R]Gn. 74 (2002) 520-523 (*Stein-Hölkeskamp, Elke*).

11630   *Derrett, J. Duncan M.* Law and administration in the New Testament world. Biblical world, 2. 2002 ⇒273. 75-89.

11631   [E]**Dixon, Suzanne** Childhood, class and kin in the Roman world. 2001 ⇒17,10649. [R]HZ 275 (2002) 438-440 (*Linke, Bernhard*); JRS 92 (2002) 205-206 (*Hope, Valerie*).

11632   **Dixon, Suzanne** Reading Roman women. 2001 ⇒17,10650. [R]Prudentia 34 (2002) 238-239 (*Bligh, Lisa*).

11633   [E]**Eck, Werner** Lokale Autonomie und römische Ordnungsmacht in den kaiserzeitlichen Provinzen vom 1.-3. Jahrhundert. 1999 ⇒15, 10769. [R]Gn. 74 (2002) 523-527 (*Alpers, Michael*); AnCl 71 (2002) 471-472 (*Raepsaet-Charlier, Marie-Thérèse*).

11634   EUSÉBIO de Cesaréia: História eclesiástica. [E]**Frangiotti, R.**: Patrística 15: 2000 ⇒16,10892. [R]REB 62 (2002) 461-468 (*Pereira, Ney Brasil*).

11635   **Evans-Grubbs, Judith** Women and the law in the Roman Empire: a sourcebook on marriage, divorce, and widowhood. L 2002, Routledge xxiv; 349 pp. £55/18. 0-415-1524-0-2/1-0.

11636   [E]**Freyburger-Galland, Marie-Laure** DION CASSIUS: histoire romaine: livres 41 & 42. CUF; Association Guillaume Budé: P 2002, Les Belles Lettres lxxxiii; 151 pp. 2-251-00504-8. Texte établi par *Marie-Laure Freyburger-Galland*; traduit et annoté par *François Hinard* et *Pierre Cordier*.

11637   [E]**Goldhill, Simon** Being Greek under Rome: cultural identity, the second Sophistic and the development of Empire. 2001 ⇒17, 10655. [R]JRS 92 (2002) 256-257 (*Harrison, S.J.*); AJP 123 (2002) 637-641 (*Perkins, Judith*).

11638   *Gregory, Andrew* Disturbing trajectories: 1 Clement, the Shepherd of Hermas and the development of early Roman christianity. Rome in the bible. 2002 ⇒363. 142-166.

11639   *Hekster, O.* COMMODUS: an emperor at the crossroads. Dutch Monographs on Ancient History and Archaeology 23: Amst 2002, Gieben vi; 250 pp. 90-506-3238-6. 19 fig.

11640   *Hezser, Catherine* The social status of slaves in the Talmud Yerushalmi and in Graeco-Roman society. The Talmud Yerushalmi, 3. TSAJ 93: 2002 ⇒767. 91-137.

11641   *Hutter, Manfred* Die Texte von Turfan—einmalige Zeugnisse verschwundener Religionsgemeinschaften. WUB Sonderheft (2002) 47-49.

11642   **Jackson, Robert B.** At empire's edge: exploring Rome's Egyptian frontier. NHv 2002, Yale Univ. Pr. xxvi; 350 pp. £26/$37.50. 0-300-08856-6. Bibl. 301-335.

11643   *Labahn, Michael; Zangenberg, Jürgen* "Zwischen den Reichen": zur komplexen Interaktion von frühem Christentum und römischer Herrschaft. Zwischen den Reichen. TANZ 36: 2002 ⇒568. 3-9.

11644   **Lapin, Hayim** Economy, geography, and provincial history in later Roman Palestine. TSAJ 10: 2001 ⇒17,10665. [R]REJ 161 (2002) 293 (*Mimouni, Simon*); RBLit (2002)* (*Hagith, Sivan*).

11645   **MacMullen, Ramsay** Romanization in the time of AUGUSTUS. 2000 ⇒16,10902; 17,10667. [R]TS 63 (2002) 169-170 (*Bakewell, Geoffrey*).

11646 **McKechnie, Paul** The first christian centuries: perspectives on the early church. DG 2002, InterVarsity Pr. 270 pp. $18. 0-8308-2677-7 [ThD 49,276—W. Charles Heiser].

11647 **Meyer-Zwiffelhoffer, E.** Πολιτικῶς ἄρχειν: zum Regierungsstil der senatorischen Statthalter in den kaiserzeitlichen griechischen Provinzen. Historia Einzelschriften 165: Stu 2002, Steiner 369 pp. 3-515-07648-4.

11648 **Mommsen, Theodor** A history of Rome under the emperors. [E]*De-mandt, Barbara; Demandt, Alexandre*: 1996 ⇒14,10007; 16, 10904. [R]EtCl 70 (2002) 317-318 (*Devillers, O.*).

11649 **Moreau, Philippe** Incestus et prohibitae nuptiae: conception ro-main de l'inceste et histoire des prohibitions matrimoniales pour cause de parenté dans la Rome antique. CEA.Série latine 62: P 2002, Belles Lettres 451 pp. 2-251-32653-7. Bibl. 419-432.

11650 **Poma, Gabriella** Le istituzioni politiche del mondo romano. Bo 2002, Il Mulino 247 pp. €14. 88-15-08815-6.

11651 *Ramelli, Ilaria L.E.* Note sulla presenza giudaica e cristiana a Pom-pei, Ercolano e Pozzuoli nel I secolo d.C. RSCI 56 (2002) 3-16.

11652 **Roller, Matthew B.** Constructing autocracy: aristocrats and emper-ors in Julio-Claudian Rome. 2001 ⇒17,10676. [R]Prudentia 34/1 (2002) 109-114 (*Stevenson, Tom*).

11653 **Rousseau, Philip** The early christian centuries. L 2002, Longman viii; 333 pp. 0-582-25653-4.

11654 [E]**Rowe, Christopher; Schofield, Malcolm** The Cambridge History of Greek and Roman political thought. 2000 ⇒16,10911; 17, 10678. [R]AnCl 71 (2002) 412-413 (*Duplouy, Alain*).

11655 **Salzman, Michele Renee** The making of a christian aristocracy: social and religious change in the western Roman Empire. CM 2002, Harvard University Press xiv; 354 pp. 0-674-00641-0. Bibl. 265-268.

11656 *Schöllgen, Georg* De ultima plebe: die soziale Niedrigkeit der Chri-sten als Vorwurf ihrer Gegner. [F]HOHEISEL, K.: JAC.E 34: 2002 ⇒ 59. 159-171.

11657 **Schuller, Wolfgang; Schreiner, Peter; Wirth, Gerhard** Das Rö-mische Weltreich: von der Entstehung der Republik bis zum Aus-gang der Antike. Illustrierte Weltgeschichte: DaWiss 2002, 257 pp.

11658 **Schumacher, Leonhard** Sklaverei in der Antike: Alltag und Schicksal der Unfreien. 2001 ⇒17,10680. [R]HZ 275 (2002) 706-707 (*Herz, Peter*).

11659 *Speckman, MacGlory T.* "Bread and circuses" in antiquity: the obli-gation of a public figure to his/her social constituency. APB 13 (2002) 187-206.

11660 **Stahlmann, Ines** Der gefesselte Sexus: weibliche Keuschheit und Askese im Westen des Römischen Reiches. 1997 ⇒15,10787. [R]Gn. 74 (2002) 372-373 (*Frank, K. Suso*).

11661 *Tamcke, Martin* Zwischen Ost und West: Syrien als Drehscheibe des frühen Christentums. WUB Sonderheft (2002) 5-11.

11662 **Treggiari, Susan** Roman social history. Classical Foundations: L 2002, Routledge xiii; 170 pp. £10. 0-415-19522-5. Bibl. 139-154.

Q9.5 Constantine, Julian, Byzantine Empire

11663 **Ball, Warwick** Rome in the east: the transformation of an empire. 2000 ⇒16,10920. [R]Latomus 61 (2002) 475-476 (*Lipiński, Edward*); ZDPV 118 (2002) 183-186 (*Lichtenberger, Achim*); AnCl 71 (2002) 514-516 (*Sartre, Maurice*).

11664 **Dauphin, Claudine** La Palestine byzantine: peuplement et population, 1: Texte, 2: Texte et illustrations, 3: Catalogue. BAR International Series 726: Oxf 1998, Archaeopress 1042 pp. [R]LASBF 52 (2002) 595-598 (*Piccirillo, Michele*).

11665 **Gil, Moshe** A history of Palestine, 634-1099. [T]*Broido, Ethel*: 1997 <1992> ⇒13,9691; 14,9469. [R]Islam 79 (2002) 148-150 (*Havemann, Axel*).

11666 *Irshai, Oded* Confronting a christian empire: Jewish culture in the world of Byzantium. Cultures. 2002 ⇒448. 181-221.

11667 [E]**Mango, Cyril** The Oxford history of Byzantium. Oxf 2002, OUP xviii; 334 pp. 0-19-814098-3. Bibl. 313-318.

11668 *Saggioro, Alessandro* Il sacrificio pagano nella reazione al cristianesimo: GIULIANO e MACROBIO. ASEs 19 (2002) 237-254.

11669 **Sivertsev, Alexei** Private households and public politics in 3rd-5th century Jewish Palestine. TSAJ 90: Tü 2002, Mohr S. viii; 279 pp. €79. 3-16-147780-4. Bibl. 259-267.

11670 *Stemberger, Günter* Die Verbindung von Juden mit Häretikern in der spätantiken römischen Gesetzgebung. [F]HOHEISEL, K.: JAC.E 34: 2002 ⇒59. 203-214.

11671 *Veltri, Giuseppe* Justinians Novelle 146 *Peri hebraiōn*. Gegenwart der Tradition 2002 <1994> ⇒255. 104-119.

11672 *Zinser, Hartmut* Religio, secta, haeresis in den Haeresiegesetzen des Codex Theodosianus (16,5,1/66) von 438. [F]HOHEISEL, K.: JAC.E 34: 2002 ⇒59. 215-219.

XVIII. Archaeologia terrae biblicae

T1.1 General biblical-area archaeologies

11673 *Boardman, John* Archaeology beyond the classical world. Ancient West & East 1/1 (2002) 7-12.

11674 **Braudel, F.** The Mediterranean in the ancient world. [E]*De Ayala, R.; Braudel, P.*; [T]*Reynolds, S.* 2001 ⇒17,10703. [R]JRS 92 (2002) 195 (*Nixon, Lucia*).

11675 *Briend, Jacques; Sapin, J.* Syrie—Phénicie—Palestine: archéologie. TEuph 24 (2002) 113-135.

11676 *Brody, Aaron* From the hills of Adonis through the pillars of Hercules: recent advances in the archaeology of Canaan and Phoenicia. Ment. *Albright, W.*: NEA (BA) 65 (2002) 69-80.

11677 *Cobbing, Felicity J.* Biblical archaeology. Biblical world, 1. 2002 ⇒273. 345-362.

11678 **Deist, Ferdinand E.** The material culture of the bible: an introduction. [E]*Carroll, Robert P.*: BiSe 70: 2000 ⇒16,10933; 17,10706. [R]JBL 121 (2002) 145-147 (*Strange, James F.*).

11679 Dig now 2002. BArR 28/1 (2002) 18-33.
11680 **Elliott, Mark** Biblical interpretation using archaeological evidence, 1900-1930. SBEC 51: Lewiston, NY 2002, Mellen (8) iii; 300 pp. 0-7734-7146-4. Bibl. 273-290.
11681 **Finkelstein, I.; Silberman, N.A.** La bible dévoilée: les nouvelles révélations de l'archéologie. P 2002, Bayard 432 pp. €24. [R]CEv 121 (2002) 66-67 (*Artus, Olivier*); LV(L) 256 (2002) 106-109 (*Abadie, Philippe*);
11682 Keine Posaunen vor Jericho: die archäologische Wahrheit über die Bibel. Mü 2002, Beck 381 pp. €26.90. 3-406-49321-1 [EuA 79,75s —Schwank, Benedikt].
11683 *Finkelstein, Israel; Silberman, Neil Asher* The bible unearthed: a rejoinder. BASOR 327 (2002) 63-73.
11684 *Gibert, Pierre; Villeneuve, François* Exégètes et archéologues face à la bible. MoBi 146 (2002) 14-17.
11685 *Hoppe, Leslie J.* Biblical archaeology today. NewTR 15/4 (2002) 70-73.
11686 **Hölscher, Tonio** Klassische Archäologie: Grundwissen. 2002, Da: Wiss 360 pp. Bibl. 337-347.
11687 *Keel, Othmar* Die biblische Archäologie;
11688 Schätze der Vergangenheit. Die Bibel: Geschichte und Gegenwart. 2002 ⇒971. 50-55, 58-63/56-57.
11689 **King, Philip J.; Stager, Lawrence E.** Life in biblical Israel. Library of Ancient Israel: 2001 ⇒17,10711. [R]RExp 99 (2002) 282-283 (*Eddinger, Terry*).
11690 *Knauf, Ernst Axel* Introduction. [F]WEIPPERT, M.: OBO 186: 2002 ⇒ 133. 1-3.
11691 **Laughlin, John C.H.** Archaeology and the bible. 2000 ⇒16, 10942; 17,10712. [R]BASOR 325 (2002) 94-96 (*Clark, Douglas R.*).
11692 **Marchiori, Antonio** Antiche civiltà viste dal cielo. Rimini 2002, Idea libri 255 pp. 88-7082-777-1. Bibl. 254.
11693 **Mazar, Amihai** Archaeology of the land of the bible: 10,000-586 B.C.E. 1990 ⇒6,b927... 9,12925. [R]CTJ 37 (2002) 128-129 (*Bierling, Neal*); ThLZ 127 (2002) 1271-1273 (*Fritz, Volkmar*).
11694 *Meyers, Eric M.* Aspects of everyday life in Roman Palestine with special reference to private domiciles and ritual baths. Jews in... cities 2002 ⇒719. 193-220.
11695 *Miller, J. Maxwell* Palestine during the Bronze Age. Biblical world, 1. 2002 ⇒273. 363-390.
11696 *Schipper, Friedrich* Zum Geleit: Bibel und Archäologie im Heiligen Land. PzB 11 (2002) 81-86.
11697 **Stern, Ephraim** Archaeology of the land of the bible, 2: the Assyrian, Babylonian & Persian periods (732-332 B.C.E.). 2001 ⇒17, 10717. [R]RivBib 50 (2002) 82-84 (*Rolla, Armando*); CTJ 37 (2002) 129-130 (*Bierling, Neal*); AsbTJ 56/2-57/1 (2001-2002) 145-146 (*Arnold, Bill T.*); BiblInterp 10 (2002) 447-450 (*Edelman, Diana*); TrinJ 23 (2002) 255-257 (*Younger, K. Lawson*); CBQ 64 (2002) 557-558 (*Betlyon, John W.*).
11698 **Wright, G. Ernest** Arqueología bíblica. [T]*Valiente Malla, J.*: M [2]2002 <1975>, Cristiandad 568 pp. €26.92. 84-70857-453-1. 200 ill.; introd. *Carolina Aznar Sánchez*. [R]SalTer 90 (2002) 982-983 (*Sanz Giménez-Rico, Enrique*).
11699 *Zevit, Ziony* Three debates about bible and archaeology. Bib. 83 (2002) 1-27.

11700. **Zwickel, Wolfgang** Die Welt des Alten und Neuen Testaments: ein Sach- und Arbeitsbuch. 1997 ⇒13,10156. [R]ThGl 92 (2002) 147-148 (*Herr, Bertram*).

T1.2 Musea, organismi, *displays*

11701 *Ajaj, Ahmad* The computerisation of the Jordan archaeological museum collections (Phase 1). ADAJ 46 (2002) 153*-159*. A.

11702 **Arnold, Dorothea** When the pyramids were built: Egyptian art of the Old Kingdom. 2000 ⇒16,10951. Exhib. Paris, NY, Toronto 1999-2000. [R]OLZ 97 (2002) 475-477 (*Malek, Jaromir*).

11703 [E]**Borriello, Mariarosaria; Giove, Teresa** La collezione epigrafica del museo archeologico nazionale di Napoli: guida alla collezione. N 2002, Electa 47 pp. 88-435-8515-0. Bibl. 47.

11704 *Dohmen, Christoph* Atemmaschinen: Dialog zwischen Bibel und Kunst: eine Ausstellungseröffnung. BiHe 38 (2002) 70-71.

11705 **Fildes, Alan; Fletcher, Joann** ALEXANDER the Great: son of the gods. LA 2002, J. Paul Getty Museum 176 pp. 0-89236-678-8. Bibl. 169.

11706 **Foster, Jennifer** Life and death in the Iron Age. Oxf 2002, Ashmolean Museum (6) 49 pp. 1-85444-179-5. Bibl. 48.

11707 **Grenier, Jean-Claude** Les bronzes du Museo Gregoriano Egizio. Museo Gregoriano Egizio Aegyptiaca Gregoriana 5: Città del Vaticano 2002 Monumenti, Musei e Gallerie Pontificie 377 pp. 81 pl.

11708 [E]**Hanebutt-Benz, Eva** Sprachen des Nahen Ostens und die Druckrevolution: eine interkulturelle Begegnung: Katalog und Begleitband zur Ausstellung = Middle Eastern languages and the print revolution [Gutenberg-Museum, Mainz]. Westhofen 2002, Skulima xxiv; 555 pp. 3-936136-02-5.

11709 The Holy Land: David Roberts, Dead Sea scrolls, house of David inscription. 2001 ⇒17,10728. [R]AmA 104 (2002) 953-956 (*Kelly, Marjorie*).

11710 **Muscarella, O.W.** The lie became great: the forgery of ancient eastern cultures. 2000 ⇒16,10969. [R]BiOr 59 (2002) 148-150 (*Bivar, A.D.H.*).

11711 [E]**Roccati, Alessandro; Capriotti Vittozzi, Giuseppina** Tra le palme del Piceno: Egitto terra del Nilo. Poggibonsi (SI) 2002, Nencini 223 (5) pp. San Benedetto del Tronto, Palacongressi, 13 luglio - 30 ottobre 2002, esposizione organizzata dal Consorzio Turistico "Riviera delle Palme".

11712 [E]**Simpson, St John** Queen of Sheba: treasures from ancient Yemen. L 2002, British Museum 224 pp. $45. 0-7141-1151-1. Bibl. 210-215. [R]BAIAS 19-20 (2001-2002) 177-180 (*Dauphin, Claudine*).

11713 *Staubli, Thomas* Das Projekt BIBEL+ORIENT Museum. WUB 24 (2002) 70-75.

11714˙ *Tamari, Ittai Joseph* Zu den hebräisch-schriftlichen Drucken vom 15. bis 19. Jahrhundert: notes of the printing in Hebrew typefaces from the 15th to the 19th centuries. Sprachen des Nahen Ostens. 2002 ⇒11708. 33-52

11715 In Terrasanta: dalla crociata alla custodia dei luoghi santi. 2000 ⇒ 16,10974. Mostra, Palazza Reale, 2000. [R]CFr 72 (2002) 480-481 (*Gieben, Servus*).

11716 ᴱUlianich, B., *al.*, La croce: dalle origini agli inizi del secolo XVI. N 1999, Electa 150 pp. Mostra Napoli, 25.3-14.5.2000.

11717 ᴱWildung, D. Ägypten 2000 v. Chr. 2000 ⇒16,10975. Exhib. B, Wü. ᴿBiOr 59 (2002) 277-294 (*Marée, Marcel*).

11718 ᴱZettler, Richard L.; Horne, Lee Treasures from the royal tombs of Ur. 1998 ⇒15,10858. ᴿJNES 61 (2002) 291-292 (*Bahrani, Zainab*).

T1.3 *Methodi*—Science in archaeology

11719· *Alpi, Frédéric* Aux origines de l'archéologie aérienne: A. Poidebard: (1878-1955). MUSJ 55 (1997-1998) 327-355.

11720 **Atkinson, Austen** Lost civilizations: rediscovering ancient sites through new technology. L 2002, Pavilion 192 pp. 1-86205-522-X. Bibl. 190.

11721 **Banning, E.B.** The archaeologist's laboratory: the analysis of archaeological data. 2000 ⇒16,10979. ᴿBASOR 328 (2002) 99-100 (*Younker, Randall W.*).

11722 ᴱCastellano, Alfredo; Martini, Marco; Sibilia, Emanuela Elementi di archeometria: metodi fisici per i Beni Culturali: Mi 2002, EGEA 371 pp. 88-238-2009-X.

11723 **Felici, Enrico** Archeologia subacquea: metodi, tecniche e strumenti. R 2002, Istituto Poligrafico...dello Stato 359 pp. 88-240-3556-6.

11724 **Gabucci, Ada** Archeologia. Guide cultura: Mi 2002, Mondadori 191 pp. 88-435-8217-8. Bibl. 190-191.

11725 ᴱHodder, Ian Towards reflexive method in archaeology: the example of Çatalhöyük. 2000 ⇒16,10986. ᴿAJA 106 (2002) 320-321 (*Strasser, Thomas F.*).

11726 *Krafeld-Daugherty, Maria* Archäologie, Philologie und Anthropologie: eine Synthese. ᶠDIETRICH, M. 2002 ⇒28. 245-287.

11727 *Manuelian, Peter Der* An approach to archaeological information management: the Giza archives project. ArOr 70 (2002) 319-328.

11728. **Pearson, James L.** Shamanism and the ancient mind: a cognitive approach to archaeology. Archaeology of religion 2: Walnut Creek, CA 2002, Alta Mira ix; 195 pp. 0-7591-0155-8. Bibl. 169-187.

T1.4 *Exploratores*—Excavators, pioneers

11729 **Bongard-Levin, Grigorij M.; Lardinois, Roland; Vigasin, Aleksej A.** Correspondances orientalistes: entre Paris et Saint-Pétersbourg (1887-1935). MAIBL 26: P 2002, De Boccard 303 pp. 2-87754-129-0.

11730 *Bonnet, Corinne* La découverte archéologique de la Syro-Phénicie dans les années '20 et '30 d'après quelques témoinages épistolaires. ᶠDIETRICH, M.: 2002 ⇒28. 55-66.

11731 **Chevalier, Nicole** La recherche archéologique française au Moyen-Orient, 1842-1947. P 2002, Recherches sur les Civilisations 630 pp. €51. Préf. *Jean-Louis Huot*.

11732 ALBRIGHT, W.: *Dessel, J.P.* Reading between the lines: W.F. Albright 'in' the field and 'on' the field. NEA (BA) 65 (2002) 43-50;

11733. *Gitin, Seymour* The house that Albright built. NEA (BA) 65 (2002) 5-10.
11734 BANKES, William John: **Usick, Patricia** Adventures in Egypt and Nubia: the travels of William John Bankes (1786-1855). L 2002, British Museum 224 pp. £25. 0-07141-1803-6. Bibl. 212-217.
11735 EVANS, Arthur John: **MacGillivray, Joseph A.** Minotaur: Sir Arthur Evans and the archaeology of the Minoan myth. 2000 ⇒16, 10996; 17,10752. ᴿAJA 106 (2002) 601-602 (*Allen, Susan Heuck*).
11736 FREER, C.; **Gunter, Ann C.** A collector's journey: Charles Lang Freer and Egypt. San Diego 2002, Scala 160 pp. £20. 1-85759-297-2 [EgArch 23,43—Usick, Patricia].
11737 GARROD, D.: ᴱ**Davies, William; Charles, Ruth** Dorothy Garrod and the progress of the palaeolithic: studies in the prehistoric archaeology of the Near East and Europe. 1999 ⇒15,10876. ᴿBASOR 326 (2002) 81-83 (*Clark, Geoffrey A.*).
11738 OPPENHEIM, M. von: *Cholidis, Nadja; Stern, Tom* 'I would enjoy immensely...': der Ausgräber Max Freiherr von Oppenheim vor der Filmkamera. UF 34 (2002) 25-38.
11739 SCHLIEMANN, H.: **Runnels, Curtis** The archaeology of Heinrich Schliemann: an annotated bibliographic handlist. Boston 2002, Archaeological Institute of America vii; 83 pp. 1-931909-00-8. Bibl. 61-81.

T1.5 *Materiae primae*—metals, glass

11740 ᴱ**Bianchi, R.S.** Reflections on ancient glass from the Borowski Collection. Mainz 2002, Von Zabern 379 pp. €76.80. 3-8053-2791-1.
11741 *Chanut, Claude; Dardaillon, Ella* Die Metallkunst. WUB 23 (2002) 32-33.
11742 *Golden, Jonathan* The origins of the metals trade in the eastern Mediterranean: social organization of production in the early copper industries. Egypt and the Levant. 2002 ⇒497. 225-238.
11743 *Hauptmann, Andreas; Maddin, Robert; Prange, Michael* On the structure and composition of copper and tin ingots excavated from the shipwreck of Uluburun. BASOR 328 (2002) 1-30.
11744 *Jennings, Sarah; Abdallah, Joanna* Roman and later blown glass from the Aub excavations in Beirut (sites Bey 006, 007 and 045). Aram 13 (2001-2002) 237-264.
11745 *Levy, Thomas E., al.,* Early Bronze Age metallurgy: a newly discovered copper manufactory in southern Jordan. Antiquity 76 (2002) 425-437.
11746 *Noguez, M.E., al.,* Los metales en la biblia, 1: introducción, antecedentes y el oro. Qol 28 (2002) 1-24;
11747 Los metales en la biblia, 2: plata, cobre y bronce, hierro, estaño, antimonio y plomo. Qol 29 (2002) 25-56.
11748 **Spaer, Maud** Ancient glass in the Israel Museum: beads and other small objects. J 2001, Israel Museum 384 pp. 965-278-260-2. 51 pl.; num. fig.
11749 *Tadmor, Miriam* The Kfar Monash hoard again: a view from Egypt and Nubia. Egypt and the Levant. 2002 ⇒497. 239-251.
11750 *Watai, Yoko* Types of silver circulated in Babylonia during the reign of Darius I. Bulletin of the Society for Near Eastern Studies in Japan 45/1 (2002) 1-17 Sum. 1. J.

11751   **Yener, K. Aslihan** The domestication of metals: the rise of complex metal industries in Anatolia. 2000 ⇒16,11009; 17,10764. [R]BiOr 59 (2002) 140-145 (*Siegelová, Jana*).

T1.7 Technologia antiqua

11752   *Gazit, Dan* The translation from the Chalcolithic period to the early Bronze Age: an analogy to a known historical situation. [F]GOPHNA, R. 2002 ⇒49. 155-158.
11753   **Meissner, Burkhard** Die technologische Fachliteratur der Antike: Struktur, Überlieferung und Wirkung technischen Wissens in der Antike (ca. 400 v.Chr. - ca. 500 n.Chr.). 1999 ⇒15,10894. [R]Gn. 74 (2002) 355-357 (*Fögen, Thorsten*).
11754   *Nader, Moheb; Saz, Chaneh* Water powered olive press in Lebanon: the 'maṭrūf': a comparative field study in cultural technology. Aram 13-14 (2001-2002) 599-671.
11755   *Pappalardo, Carmelo* Il cortile a sud della chiesa di S. Paolo ad Umm al-Rasas—Kastron Mefaa in Giordania. LASBF 52 (2002) 385-440.
11756   *Shanks, Hershel* The puzzling channels in ancient latrines. BArR 28/5 (2002) 48-51, 70.
11757   *Wagner, Clarence H.* Metalworking in the bible: turning spears into pruning hooks. JBQ 30 (2002) 262-265.
11758   *Webb, Jennifer M.* New evidence for the origins of textile production in Bronze Age Cyprus. Antiquity 76 (2002) 364-371.

T1.8 Architectura

11759   **Arnold, Dieter** The encyclopaedia of ancient Egyptian architecture. [T]*Gardiner, Sabine H.; Strudwick, Helen*: L 2002, Tauris 304 pp. £30 1-86064-465-1.
11760   *Aubert, Catherine* Architecture et décor de la maison hellénistique à Beyrouth. Aram 13 (2001-2002) 73-85.
11761   *Baffi Guardata, Francesca* Osservazioni sull'architettura domestica lungo il corso del medio Eufrate nell'età del Bronzo Tardo: il caso di Tell Fray. [M]CIASCA, A. 2002 ⇒15. 41-55. 5 pl.
11762   **Barletta, Barbara A.** The origins of the Greek architectural orders. 2001 ⇒17,10769. [R]AJA 106 (2002) 620-2 (*Klein, Nancy L.*).
11763   *Bier, Lionel* Sarvistan reconsidered. [F]HANSEN, D. 2002 ⇒58. 43-51.
11764   *Bunimovitz, Shlomo; Faust, Avraham* Ideology in stone: understanding the four-room house. BArR 28/4 (2002) 32-41, 59-60.
11765   *Callot, Olivier* 3000 Jahre zurück: Besuch in einem spätbronzezeitlichen Wohnhaus. WUB 23 (2002) 61-63.
11766   *Cannuyer, Christian* Die altorientalischen Kirchen: ein Christentum mit eigenständigen Traditionen. WUB Sonderheft (2002) 26-28.
11767   *Egelhaaf-Gaiser, Ulrike* Religionsästhetik und Raumordnung am Beispiel der Vereinsgebäude von Ostia. Religiöse Vereine. STAC 13: 2002 ⇒468. 123-172.
11768   **Ellis, Simon P.** Roman housing. L 2002, Duckworth viii; 224 pp. $27. 0-7156-3196-9. 30 fig.; 21 pl..

11769 *Faust, Avraham* Accessibility, defence and town planning in Iron Age Israel. TelAv 29 (2002) 297-317.

11770 *Gillingham, Susan* The arts: architecture, music, poetry, psalmody. Biblical world, 2. 2002 ⇒273. 53-74.

11771 **Grossmann, Peter** Christliche Architektur in Ägypten. HO 1/62: Lei 2002, Brill xxxi; 605 pp. €125. 90-04-12128-5. Bibl. 571-584.

11772 **Hellman, Marie-Christine** L'architecture grecque, 1: les principles de la construction. P 2002, Picard 351 pp. €83. 2-7084-0606-X. 450 ill.; 38 pl.

11773 [E]*Hellmann, M.-Ch.* Bulletin analytique d'architecture du monde grec. RAr 2 (2002) 291-406.

11774 **Ito, Juko** Theory and practice of site planning in classical sanctuaries. Fukuoka 2002, Kyushu Univ. Pr. vii; 160 pp. ¥6.500. 4-87378-717-3. 43 fig.; 16 pl.

11775 **Japp, Sarah** Die Baupolitik Herodes' des Grossen: die Bedeutung der Architektur für die Herrschaftslegitimation eines römischen Klientelkönigs. 2000 ⇒16,11028. [R]AJA 106 (2002) 108-109 (*Burrell, Barbara*).

11776 **Jones, Mark Wilson** Principles of Roman architecture. 2000 ⇒16, 11029; 17,10778. [R]AJA 106 (2002) 344-345 (*Packer, James E.*).

11777 *Kafafi, Zeidan A.* Egyptian governors' residencies in Jordan and Palestine: new lights. [F]WEIPPERT, M.: OBO 186: 2002 ⇒133. 20-30.

11778 *Kahera, Akel I.* Gardens of the righteous: sacred space in Judaism, Christianity and Islam. CrossCur 52 (2002) 328-341.

11779 *La Torre, Martino* Bauforschung am Nymphäum in Qanawat. DaM 13 (2002) 205-226.

11780 **Miglus, Peter A.** Städtische Wohnarchitektur in Babylonien und Assyrien. Baghdader Forschungen 22: 1999 ⇒15,10919...17, 10784. [R]WO 32 (2002) 249-256 (*Nasrabadi, Behzad Mofidi*).

11781 **Netzer, Ehud** Die Paläste der Hasmonäer und Herodes' des Großen. 1999 ⇒15,10923; 16,11038. [R]AJA 106 (2002) 107-108 (*Burrell, Barbara*); RAr (2002/1) 151-54 (*Donceel, Robert*); JNES 61 (2002) 305-306 (*Magness, Jodi*).

11782 **Oredsson, Dag** Moats in ancient Palestine. CB.OT 48: 2000 ⇒16, 11043; 17,10787. [R]AJA 106 (2002) 616-617 (*Herzog, Ze'ev*).

11783 **Pfälzner, Peter** Haus und Haushalt: Wohnformen des dritten Jahrtausends vor Christus in Nordmesopotamien. Damaszener Forschungen 9: 2001 ⇒17,10788. [R]BiOr 59 (2002) 623-627 (*Wright, G.R.H.*).

11784 *Pitta, Antonio* Der frühe Kirchenbau und die Bibel. Die Bibel: Geschichte und Gegenwart. 2002 ⇒971. 128-129.

11785 *Richardson, Peter* Building an association (*synodos*)... and a place of their own. Community formation. 2002 ⇒644. 36-56.

11786 **Richardson, Peter** City and sanctuary: religion and architecture in the Roman Near East. L 2002, SCM xiv; 209 pp. £13. 0-334-02884-1 [RRT 10,323s—Casiday, Augustine].

11787 *Roche, Bonnie* The mishkan as metaphor—form and anti-form: on the transformation of urban space. CrossCur 52 (2002) 342-352.

11788 *Schäfer, Alfred* Raumnutzung und Raumwahrnehmung im Vereinslokal der Iobakchen von Athen. Religiöse Vereine. STAC 13: 2002 ⇒468. 173-220.

11789 *Schirmer, Wulf* Stadt, Palast, Tempel: Charakteristika hethitischer Architektur im 2. und 1. Jahrhundert v. Chr. Die Hethiter. 2002 ⇒ 535. 204-217.

11790 **Segal, Arthur** Theatres in Roman Palestine and Provincia Arabia. Mn.S 140: 1995 ⇒11/2,a287; 12,9584. ᴿZion 67/1 (2002) 72-77 (*Amit, David*).

11791 *Sharp Joukowsky, Martha* The Petra great temple: a Nabataean architectural miracle. NEA (BA) 65 (2002) 235-248.

11792 *Sievertsen, Uwe* Private space, public space and connected architectural developments throughout the early periods of Mesopotamian history. AltOrF 29 (2002) 307-329.

11793 *Sion, Ofer; Said, Abed Al Slam* A mansion house from the late Byzantine-Umayyad period in Beth Shean-Scythopolis. LASBF 52 (2002) 353-366.

11794 *Verstegen, Ute* Gemeinschaftserlebnis in Ritual und Raum: zur Raumdisposition in frühchristlichen Basiliken des vierten und fünften Jahrhunderts. Religiöse Vereine. 2002 ⇒468. 261-297.

11795 *Viviani R., María Teresa* Comunidades cristianas al este del Jordán: un análisis arquitectónico (S. I-VI D.C.). TyV 43 (2002) 403-435.

11796 **Wright, George R.H.** Ancient building technology. 2000 ⇒16, 11060. ᴿCEg 153-154 (2002) 156-158 (*Tunca, Önhan*).

T2.1 *Res militaris*—military matters

11797 **Berman, Joshua** The battle report as narrative analogy in biblical literature. ᴰ*Greenstein, E.*: 2002, 310 pp. Diss. Bar Ilan [RTL 34, 590].

11798 *Bolin, Thomas M.* Warfare. Biblical world, 2. 2002 ⇒273. 33-52.

11799 ᴱ**Chaniotis, A.; Ducrey, P.** Army and power in the ancient world. Heidelberger althistorische Beiträge und epigraphische Studien 37: Stu 2002, Steiner viii; 204 pp. €44. 3-515-08197-6.

11800 **Chapman, Cynthia Ruth** The gendered language of warfare in the Israelite/Assyrian encounter. Diss. Harvard 2002 [HTHR 95,458].

11801 **Cline, Eric H.** The battles of Armageddon: Megiddo and the Jezreel Valley from the Bronze Age to the Nuclear Age. 2000 ⇒16, 11065. ᴿBASOR 327 (2002) 89-90 (*Nakhal, Beth Alpert*).

11802 **Debidour, Michel** Les Grecs et la guerre, Ve-IVe siècles: de la guerre rituelle à la guerre totale. L'Art de la Guerre: Monaco 2002, Rocher 217 pp. 2-268-04277-4. Bibl. 211-213.

11803 *Elgavish, David* The division of the spoils of war in the bible and in the ancient Near East. ZAR 8 (2002) 242-273.

11804 *Hoffmeier, James K.* Understanding Hebrew and Egyptian military texts: a contextual approach. Context of scripture. 2002 ⇒326. xxi-xxvii.

11805 *Lewin, Ariel* Kastron Mefaa, the *equites promoti indigenae* and the creation of a late Roman frontier. LASBF 51 (2001) 293-304.

11806 **Malamat, A.** Weapons deposited in a sanctuary by Zimri-Lim of Mari and David and Saul of Israel. ᶠDIETRICH, M. 2002 ⇒28. 325-327 [1 Sam 21,9; 31,9-10].

11807 *Marazzi, Massimiliano* Esercitazioni di carri da guerra: revisione di un passaggio della Cronaca di Palazzo. ᴹIMPARATI, F. 2002 ⇒61. 507-518.

11808 *Niemeier, Wolf-Dietrich* Greek mercenaries at Tel Kabri and other sites in the Levant. TelAv 29 (2002) 328-331.

11809 *Olmo Lete, Gregorio del* Glosas ugaríticas II: ¿Se organizaba el ejército de Ugarit en 'cinco' cuerpos?. AuOr 20 (2002) 252-256.

11810 **Partridge, Robert B.** Fighting Pharaohs: weapons and warfare in ancient Egypt. Manchester 2002, Peartree 336 pp. £17.80. 0-9543-497-3-3/2-5. 418 ill. Bibl. 307-314.

11811 **Pollard, Nigel** Soldiers, cities, and civilians in Roman Syria. 2000 ⇒16,11070. ᴿAnCl 71 (2002) 473-474 (*Sartre, Maurice*).

T2.2 *Vehicula, nautica*—**transport, navigation**

11812 **Bollweg, Jutta** Vorderasiatische Wagentypen: im Spiegel der Terracottaplastk bis zur Altbabylonischen Zeit. OBO 167: 1999 ⇒15, 10945; 17,10803. ᴿWO 32 (2002) 247-249 (*Genz, Hermann*).

11813 *Gündüz, Serhan* M.Ö.I. Binyılın ilk yarisinda önasya kralliklarinda araba tekerleklerinin özellikleri ve yapim teknikleri ([Characteristics and manufacturing techniques of wheels in the kingdoms of Asia Minor in the first half of the first millennium B.C.]. BTTK 66 (2002) 789-817 98 fig. **Turkish.**

11814 **Littauer, M.A.; Crouwel, J.H.** Selected writings on chariots and other early vehicles, riding and harness. ᴱ*Raulwing, Peter*: Culture and history of the Ancient Near East 6: Lei 2002, Brill xlvi; 609 pp. 90-04-11799-7. 234 pl. Bibl. xxxvii-xlvi.

11815 **Raepsaet, Georges** Attelages et techniques de transport dans le monde gréco-romain. Bru 2002, Laboratoire d'Archéologie classique de l'Univ. Libre 316 pp. €38. 90-71868-62-1. 155 fig. Préf. *Marie-Claire Amouretti*. ᴿREG 115 (2002) 809-810 (*Chandezon, Christophe*).

11816 *Ballard, Robert D.*, al., Iron Age shipwrecks in deep water off Ashkelon, Israel. AJA 106 (2002) 151-168.

11817 *Gophna, Ram* Elusive anchorage points along the Israel littoral and the Egyptian-Canaanite maritime route during the Early Bronze Age I. Egypt and the Levant. 2002 ⇒497. 418-421.

11818 *Marcus, Ezra* Early seafaring and maritime activity in the southern Levant from prehistory through the third millennium BCE. Egypt and the Levant. 2002 ⇒497. 403-417.

11819 **Nibbi, Alessandra** Ancient Egyptian anchors and the sea. DiscEg Sp. No. 4: Oxf 2002, DE vii; 120 pp. £15. 0-9510-7048-7 [RB 110, 477].

11820 *Sharvit, Jacob* Predynastic maritime traffic along the Carmel coast of Israel: a submerged find from North Atlit Bay. ᶠGOPHNA, R. 2002 ⇒49. 159-166.

T2.4 *Athletica*—**sport, games**

11821 **Beacham, Richard C.** Spectacle entertainments of early imperial Rome. 1999 ⇒15,10951; 17,10809. ᴿLatomus 61 (2002) 473-475 (*Fear, A.T.*); AnCl 71 (2002) 466-468 (*Benoist, Stéphane*).

11822 **Decker, Wolfgang, Föster, Frank** Annotierte Bibliographie zum Sport im Alten Ägypten II: 1978-2000: nebst Nachträgen aus früheren Jahren und unter Einbeziehung des Sports der Nachbarkulturen. Nikephoros, Beihefte—Beitraege zu Sport und Kultur im Altertum 8: Hildesheim 2002, Weidmann 307 pp. €51. 3-615-10013-1.

11823 **Kyle, Donald G.** Spectacles of death in ancient Rome. 1998 ⇒14, 10156...17,10812. [R]RH 307 (2002) 1013-15 (*Benoist, Stéphane*).

11824 *Limet, Henri* Les jeux dans les mythes et dans les rituels de Mésopotamie. [F]DUCHESNE-GUILLEMIN, J. 2002 ⇒32. 95-114.

11825 *Patrich, Joseph* Herod's hippodrome-stadium at Caesarea and the games conducted therein. [F]FOERSTER, G. 2002 ⇒39. 29-68.

11826 **Scanlon, Thomas F.** Eros and Greek athletics. Oxf 2002, OUP 466 pp. $74/35. 0-19-513889-9/514985-8. 55 fig.

11827 *Van Reeth, Jan M.F.* L'hippodrome et l'aurige de Tyr. [F]DUCHESNE-GUILLEMIN, J. 2002 ⇒32. 143-154.

T2.5 *Musica, drama, saltario*—music, drama, dance

11828 *Anwar Rashid, Subhi* Bedeutung und Ursprung der Laute. DaM 13 (2002) 119-123.

11829 **Bermond, Cristina** La danza negli scritti di FILONE, CLEMENTE Alessandrino e ORIGENE: storia e simbologia. 2001 ⇒17,10818. [R]StPat 49 (2002) 499-501 (*Corsato, Celestino*).

11830 **Braun, Joachim** Die Musikkultur Altisraels/Palästinas: Studien zu archäologischen, schriftlichen und vergleichenden Quellen. OBO 164: 1999 ⇒15,339; 17,10820. [R]WO 32 (2002) 238-240 (*Eichmann, Ricardo*);

11831 Music in ancient Israel/Palestine: archaeological, written, and comparative sources. [T]*Stott, Douglas W.*: The Bible in its world: GR 2002, Eerdmans xxxvi; 368 pp. $30/£22. 0-8028-4477-4. Bibl. 321-354.

11832 *Emerit, Sibylle* À propos de l'origine des interdits musicaux dans l'Égypte ancienne. BIFAO 102 (2002) 189-210.

11833 *Fittler, Katalin* Die Bibel und die zeitgenössische ungarische Musik. Religion—Literatur—Kunst II. 2002 ⇒530. 436-444.

11834 **Flynn, William T.** Medieval music as medieval exegesis. 1999 ⇒ 15,10966...17,10826. [R]CCMéd 45 (2002) 373-74 (*Huglo, Michel*).

11835 *Giuliani, Massimo* Parsifal contra Moses: WAGNER, SCHOENBERG e il dramma musicale della redenzione. StPat 49 (2002) 113-156.

11836 *González Valle, José V.* J.S. BACH: técnica de composición como *explicatio textus*. AMus 57 (2002) 157-174.

11837 **Montagu, Jeremy** Musical instruments of the bible. Lanham 2002, Scarecrow xiv; 177 pp. 0-8108-4282-3. Bibl. 151-156.

11838 *Nadeau, Jean G.* La bible coulée dans le rock: fragmentation et reconstruction du texte biblique dans la musique rock. Religiologiques 26 (2002) 87-99.

11839 *Porter, Wendy J.* The composer of sacred music as an interpreter of the bible. Borders. JSOT.S 313: 2002 ⇒585. 126-153 [Ps 93,3-4; 1 Tim 3,16].

11840 [E]**Pöhlmann, Egert; West, Martin L.** Documents of ancient Greek music: the extant melodies and fragments. Oxf 2001, Clarendon 225 pp.

11841 **Schauensee, Maude de** Two lyres from Ur. Ph 2002, University of Pennsylvania Pr. xix (2); 125 pp. 0-924171-88-X. Bibl. 115-121.

11842 **Teja, Valentina** La "satura" drammatica e i suoi rapporti con la "satura" letteraria e con il teatro latino. AANL.M 9/15,1: R 2002, Accademia Nazionale dei Lincei 85 pp. 88-218-0872-6.

11843 **Todisco, Luigi** Teatro e spettacolo in Magna Grecia e in Sicilia: testi, immagini, architettura. Biblioteca di archeologia 32: Mi 2002, Longanesi 267 pp. 88-304-1587-1. 86 fig., 64 pl.

11844 *Tschuggnall, Peter* Ein musikalisches Opfer wider die Resignation: zu einer Theologie der Träne im Anschluss an J.S. BACH. Religion —Literatur—Kunst II. Im Kontext 14: 2002 ⇒530. 358-369.

11845 *Viljoen, Francois P.* Song and music in the early christian communities: Paul's utilisation of Jewish, Roman and Greek musical traditions to encourage the early christian communities to praise God and to explain his arguments. Zwischen den Reichen. TANZ 36: 2002 ⇒568. 195-213.

11846 *Wright, David P.* Music and dance in 2 Samuel 6. JBL 121 (2002) 201-225.

T2.6 *Vestis*, clothing; *ornamenta*, jewellry

11847 *Atkins, Peter* More than outward appearances: the importance of 'clothing' in some New Testament passages. ET 113 (2002) 363-67.

11848 *Eger, Christoph* Gürtelschnallen des 6. bis 8. Jahrhunderts aus der Sammlung des Studium Biblicum Franciscanum. LASBF 51 (2001) 337-350.

11849 ^E**Fluck, Cäcilia, Linscheid, Petra; Merz, Susanne** Textilien aus Ägypten, 1. 2000 ⇒16,11113. ^ROLZ 97 (2002) 481-485 (*Nauerth, C.*).

11850 *Hershkovitz, M.* A carved bone plaque from Tel Dan. Qad. 35 (2002) 113-115. **H.**

11851 **Szarzynska, Krystyna** Sheep husbandry and production of wool, garments and cloths in archaic Sumer. Wsz 2002, Agade iv; 60 pp. 83-87111-22-8.
^FWILD, J. The Roman textile industry 2002 ⇒135.

T2.8 Utensilia

11852 **Bignasca, Andrea M.** I kernoi circolari in Oriente e in Occidente: strumenti di culto e immagini cosmiche. OBO.A 19: 2000 ⇒16, 11122. ^RBASOR 328 (2002) 92-94 (*Smith, Joanna S.*).

11853 *Engemann, Josef* Palästinische frühchristliche Pilgerampullen: Erstveröffentlichungen und Berichtigungen. JAC 45 (2002) 153-169.

11854 *Garlan, Yvon* Bulletin archéologique: amphores et timbres amphoriques (1997-2001). REG 115 (2002) 149-215.

11855 *Loretz, O.* Die Gefäße *Rdmns* für ein Marziḫu-Gelage zu Ehren Baals und der Nestorbecher der Ilias: zu mykenisch-ugaritischen Beziehungen nach KTU 1.3 I 10-15a. ^FDIETRICH, M.: 2002 ⇒28. 299-323.

11856 **Lüdorf, Gundula** Die Lekane: Typologie und Chronologie einer Leitform der attischen Gebrauchskeramik des 6.-1. Jahrhunderts v.Chr. Internationale Archäologie 61: Rahden 2000, Leidorf 199 pp. €76.59. 3-89646-333-0. 21 fig.; 195 pl..

11857 *Matoïan, Valérie* Die Kunst der glasierten Gegenstände. WUB 23 (2002) 30-31.

11858 *Özgüç, Tahsin* Karum—zeitliche Kulturgefäße;

11859 Die Keramik der althethitischen Zeit: Kultgefäße. Die Hethiter. 2002 ⇒535. 128-133/248-255.

11860 *Yaylali, Serap* Observations on the teapots from Bakla Tepe, Western Anatolia. ANESt 39 (2002) 113-140.

T2.9 *Pondera et mensurae*—weights and measures

11861 *Ascalone, E.; Peyronel, L.* Two weights from temple N at Tell Mardkih-Ebla, Syria: a link between metrology and cultic activities in the second millennium BC?. JCS 53 (2001) 1-12.

11862 *Bodega Barahona, Fernando* Sistemas de masas en la India. AuOr 20 (2002) 49-59.

11863 **Elalyi, J.; Elayi, A.G.** Recherches sur les poids phéniciens. TEuph. S 5: P 1997, Gabalda 398 pp. 45 pl. [R]AuOr 20/1-2 (2002) 276-278 (*Olmo Lete, Gregorio del*).

11864 **Hagenbuchner-Dresel, Albertine** Massangaben bei hethitischen Backwaren. Dresdner Beiträge zur Hethitologie 1 (Philologica): Dresden 2002, Verl. der TU xii; 197 pp. 38600-53051. Bibl. vi-xi.

11865 *Kushnir-Stein, Alla* New Hellenistic lead weights from Palestine and Phoenicia. IEJ 52 (2002) 225-230.

11866 *Melville, Duncan J.* Ration computations at Fara: multiplication or repeated addition?;

11867 *Quack, Joachim Friedrich* A goddess rising 10,000 cubit into the air ... or only one cubit, one finger?;

11868 *Robson, Eleanor* More than metrology: mathematics education in an Old Babylonian scribal school. Under one sky. AOAT 297: 2002 ⇒9014. 237-252/283-294/325-365.

11869 **Schärlig, Alain** Compter avec des cailloux: le calcul elementaire sur l'abaque chez les anciens Grecs. Lausanne 2001, Presses polytechniques et universitaires romandes 339 pp. €39.70. 2-88074-45-3-9 228 fig..

11870 **Stuckrad, Kocku von** Das Ringen um die Astrologie: jüdische und christliche Beiträge zum antiken Zeitverständnis. RVV 49: 2000 ⇒ 16,11145. [R]ZRGG 54 (2002) 83-86 (*Horn, Friedrich Wilhelm*); Numen 49 (2002) 343-344 (*Maier, Johann*); JAC 45 (2002) 215-219 (*Frenschkowski, Marco*).

11871 *Thiering, Barbara* The Qumran sundial as an odometer using fixed lengths of hours. DSD 9 (2002) 347-363.

11872 *Wolters, Al* Meterological PRS-terms from Ebla to Mishna. Eblaitica 4. 2002 ⇒474. 223-241.

T3.0 **Ars antiqua**, *motiva, picturae* [icones T3.1 infra]

11873 **Altenmüller, Hartwig** Die Wanddarstellungen im Grab des Mehu in Saqqara. 1998 ⇒14,10196; 16,11148. [R]WO 32 (2002) 179-186 (*Guglielmi, Waltraud*).

11874 *Aruz, Joan* Power and protection: a little proto-Elamite silver bull pendant. [F]HANSEN, D. 2002 ⇒58. 1-14.

11875 *Aslanidou, Katherina* Der minoische Spiralfries aus dem Grabungsareal H/IV in Tell el-Dab'a: Malvorgang und Rekonstruktion. Ä&L 12 (2002) 13-27.

11876 *Assante, Julia* Style and replication in 'Old Babylonian' terracotta plaques: strategies for entrapping the power of images. [F]DIETRICH, M. 2002 ⇒28. 1-26.

11877 *Azize, Joseph* Wrestling as a symbol for maintaining the order of nature in ancient Mesopotamia. JANER 2 (2002) 1-26.

11878 **Bahrani, Zainab** Women of Babylon: gender and representation in Mesopotamia. 2001 ⇒17,10863. [R]BiOr 59 (2002) 103-6 (*Stol, M.*).

11879 **Beard, Mary; Henderson, John** Classical art: from Greece to Rome. 2001 ⇒17,10866. [R]Prudentia 34/1 (2002) 65-68 (*Rankin, Elizabeth*).

11880 *Berger, Pamela* Archaeology, iconography, and the recreation of the past in Iron Age Holy Lands. Religion and the arts 6/4 (2002) 499-506.

11881 **Berlejung, Angelika** Die Theologie der Bilder: Herstellung und Einweihung von Kultbildern in Mesopotamien und die alttestamentliche Bilderpolemik. OBO 162: 1998 ⇒14,10201. [R]OLZ 97 (2002) 254-269 (*Bär, Jürgen; Prechel, Doris*).

11882 *Blakolmer, Fritz* Afrikaner in der minoischen Ikonographie?: zum Fremdenbild in der bronzezeitlichen Ägäis. Ä&L 12 (2002) 71-94.

11883 **Boardman, John** Die Perser und der Westen: eine archäologische Untersuchung zur Entwicklung der achämenidischen Kunst. [T]*Jaroš-Deckert, Brigitte*: Kulturgeschichte der A.W. 96: Mainz 2002, Von Zabern 311 pp. €39.80. 3-8053-2919-9. Ill. [RB 110,474].

11884 *Brysbaert, Ann* Common craftsmanship in the Aegean and east Mediterranean Bronze Age: preliminary technological evidence with emphasis on the painted plaster from Tell el-Dab'a, Egypt. Ä&L 12 (2002) 95-107.

11885 [E]**Chappaz, Jean-Luc; Vuilleumier, Sandrine** "Sortir au jour": art égyptien de la Fondation Martin Bodmer. Cahiers de la Société d'Égyptologie 7: 2001 ⇒17,10870. [R]BiOr 59 (2002) 500-504 (*Bochi, Patricia A.*).

11886 *Cholidis, Nadja* Kyros und die kriegerische Ištar?: kritische Anmerkungen zu einer 'altorientalischen' Steintafel. [F]DIETRICH, M. 2002 ⇒28. 105-113.

11887 [E]**Davies, W.V.** Colour and painting in Ancient Egypt. 2001 ⇒17, 10872. [R]JARCE 39 (2002) 265-268 (*Hartwig, Melinda K.*).

11888 *Ehrenberg, Erica* The Kassite cross revisited. [F]WALKER, C. 2002 ⇒130. 65-74.

11889 *Eschweiler, Peter* Glaubten die Ägypter an die Heilkraft ihrer Bilder?: Medizin, Magie und Mythos-und die altägyptische Bildkunst. Symb. 15 (2002) 157-176.

11890 **Ewald, Björn Christian** Der Philosoph als Leitbild: ikonographische Untersuchungen an römischen Sarkophagreliefs. MDAI.RE 34: 1999 ⇒15,11016; 17,10873. [R]Gn. 74 (2002) 62-66 (*Raeck, Wulf*).

11891 *Fleischer, Robert* True ancestors and false ancestors in Hellenistic rulers' portraiture. Images of ancestors. 2002 ⇒488. 59-74.

11892 **Garfinkel, Yosef; Miller, Michele A.**, *al.*, Sha'ar Hagolan: v.1, Neolithic art in context. Oxf 2002, Oxbow x; 262 pp. 18421-70570.

11893 **Holliday, Peter James** The origins of Roman historical commemoration in the visual arts. C 2002, CUP xxv; 283 pp. 0-521-81-
013-2. Bibl. 259-278.

11894 *Jacobs, Bruno* Die Galerie der Ahnen des Königs Antiochos I. von
Kommagene auf dem Nemrud Daği. Images of ancestors. 2002 ⇒
488. 75-88.

11895 *Köhler, E. Christiana* History or ideology?: new reflections on the
Narmer palette and the nature of foreign relations in pre- and early
dynastic Egypt. Egypt and the Levant. 2002 ⇒497. 499-513.

11896 **Leitz, Christian** Die Aussenwand des Sanktuars in Dendara: Untersuchungen zur Dekorationssystematik. MÄSt 50: 2001 ⇒17,
10889. [R]BiOr 59 (2002) 70-73 (*Cauville, S.*).

11897 **Lewis, Sian** The Athenian woman: an iconographic handbook. L
2002, Routledge xii; 261 pp. £55/19. 0-415-23234-1/5-X. 153 fig.

11898 *Lurson, Benoît* Le façonnage des images divines par le roi à travers
les textes et les représentations de la chapelle méridionale d'Abou
Simbel: une contrepartie à son engendrement par les dieux. [F]Du-
CHESNE-GUILLEMIN, J. 2002 ⇒32. 189-204.

11899 *Mayer-Opificius, Ruth* Götterreisen im Alten Orient. [F]DIETRICH, M.
2002 ⇒28. 369-387.

11900 *Mazzoni, Stefania* Percorsi figurativi tra Oriente e Occidente: immagini di donne dell'arte siro-ittita. 6 pl.;

11901 *Michelini-Tocci, Franco* Simbolismo del serpente in area siro-feni-
cia. [M]CIASCA, A. 2002 ⇒15. 343-362/363-366.

11902 *Novák, Mirko* Akkulturation von Aramäern und Luwiern und der
Austausch von ikonographischen Konzepten in der späthethitischen
Kunst. Brückenland Anatolien?. 2002 ⇒453. 147-171.

11903 *Nunn, A.* Images et croyances au Levant du VIe au IVe siècle av.J.-
C. TEuph 23 (2002) 9-25. Pls I-III.

11904 **Nunn, Astrid** Der figürliche Motivschatz Phöniziens, Syriens und
Transjordaniens vom 6. bis zum 4. Jahrhundert v. Chr. OBO.A 18:
2000 ⇒16,11186; 17,10892. [R]TEuph 24 (2002) 153-56 (*Elayi, J.*).

11905 *Ornan, Tallay* The queen in public: royal women in neo-Assyrian
art. Sex and gender. 2002 ⇒712. 461-477.

11906 *Orthmann, Winfried* Kontinuität und neue Einflüsse: die Entwicklung der späthethitischen Kunst zwischen 1200 und 700 v. Chr.;

11907 *Özgüç, Nimet* Erlesene Werke der Kleinkunst: anatolische Elfen-
beinschnitzereien. Die Hethiter. 2002 ⇒535. 274-279/244-247.

11908 *Peck, Elsie Holmes* A decorated bronze belt in the Detroit Institute
of Arts. [F]HANSEN, D. 2002 ⇒58. 183-202.

11909 *Pinnock, Frances* Note sull'iconografia di Melqart. [M]CIASCA, A.
2002 ⇒15. 379-389. 8 pl.

11910 *Schmidt, Brian B.* The Iron Age *pithoi* drawings from Horvat
Teman or Kuntillet 'Ajrud: some new proposals. JANER 2 (2002)
91-125.

11911 *Sole, L.* L'iconografia religiosa fenicia nelle emissioni puniche della
Sicilia: il caso di Cossura. TEuph 23 (2002) 77-87. Pls IV-VIII.

11912 *Strommenger, Eva* Ein altvorderasiatischer Standartenaufsatz. DaM
13 (2002) 101-103.

11913 **Turnheim, Yehudit; Ovadiah, Asher** Art in the public and private
spheres in Roman Caesarea Maritima: temples, architectural
decoration and tesserae. Rivista di archeologia.S 27: R 2002,
Bretschneider 80 pp. 116 ill.

11914 **Vickers, Michael** Scythian and Thracian antiquities in Oxford. Oxf 2002, Ashmolean Museum 80 pp. 1-85444-181-7. Bibl. 76-80.

11915 **Volokhine, Youri** La frontalité dans l'iconographie de l'Égypte Ancienne. 2000 ⇒16,11200; 17,10904. [R]BiOr 59 (2002) 58-63 (*Müller-Hazenbos, Christiane*); OLZ 97 (2002) 485-490 (*Verbovsek, Alexandra*); JSSEA 29 (2002) 121-123 (*Brand, Peter J.*).

T3.1 *Icones*—ars postbiblica

11916 **Anania, Valeriu** Bilder vom Reich Gottes: Ikonen und Fresken rumänischer Klöster. [T]*Maurer, Ute*: Metzingen 2002, Sternberg 92 pp. €24.50. 3-87785-027-8. [R]COst 57 (2002) 280-282 (*Müller, A.*).

11917 *Aston, Margaret* Cross and crucifix in the English reformation. Macht und Ohnmacht. HZ.B 33: 2002 ⇒392. 253-272.

11918 *Baert, Barbara* Imagining the mystery: the resurrection and the visual medium in the Middle Ages. [F]LAMBRECHT, J.: BEThL 165: 2002 ⇒72. 483-506.

11919 **Barber, Charles** Figure and likeness: on the limits of representation of Byzantine iconoclasm. Princeton 2002, Princeton Univ. Pr. 207 pp. $40. 0-691-09177-3.

11920 *Bätschmann, Oskar* Kunstgenuß statt Bilderkult: Wirkung und Rezeption des Gemäldes nach Leon Battista Alberti;

11921 *Belting, Hans* Macht und Ohnmacht der Bilder. Macht und Ohnmacht. HZ.B 33: 2002 ⇒392. 359-375/11-32.

11922 **Belting, Hans** Il culto delle immagini: storia dell'icona dall'età imperiale al tardo Medioevo. 2001 ⇒17,10908. [R]LRI 54/631-634 (2002) 81-84 (*Colombo, Giorgio*).

11923 **Bisconti, Fabrizio** Temi di iconografia paleocristiana. Sussidi allo studio delle antichità cristiane 13: 2000 ⇒16,11206; 17,10910. [R]Aug. 42 (2002) 506-507 (*Ghilardi, Massimiliano*); CaSa 33/1-2 (2002) 270-273 (*Lentino, Francesco*).

11924 *Blickle, Peter* Bilder und ihr gesellschaftlicher Rahmen: zur Einführung. Macht und Ohnmacht. HZ.B 33: 2002 ⇒392. 1-7.

11925 **Boespflug, F.**, *al.*, Le Christ dans l'art: des catacombes au XXe siècle. 2000 ⇒16,11207. [R]CrSt 23 (2002) 215-217 (*Menozzi, Daniele*).

11926 *Boespflug, François* Sur la transfiguration dans l'art médiéval d'Occident (IXe-XIVe siècle). Symbolisme et expérience. 2002 ⇒ 666. 199-223 Ill.

11927 **Boespflug, François** ARCABAS: et incarnatus est: polyptiek van Jezus' geboorte en kindertijd en andere werken. Antwerpen 2002, Halewijn 116 pp.

11928 Bollettino d'arte 119. R 2002, Istituto Poligrafico dello Stato, Libreria dello Stato (4); 117 pp. Ministero per i Beni Culturali.

11929 *Burg, Christian von* 'Das bildt vnsers Herrn ab dem esel geschlagen': der Palmesel in den Riten der Zerstörung;

11930 *Burkart, Lucas* 'Das crutzsyfix, so im munster uff dem letner stund': Bildersturm als Mediengeschichte. Macht und Ohnmacht. HZ.B 33: 2002 ⇒392. 117-141/177-193.

11931 **Burnham, Renée K.** Le vetrate del Duomo di Pisa. ASNSP 4/13: Pisa 2002, Scuola Normale Superiore di Pisa xv; 297 pp. Bibl. 289-292.

11932 **Cappelletti, Lorenzo** Gli affreschi della cripta anagnina, iconolo-
gia. R 2002, E.P.U.G. xxxii; 384 pp. €35/$35. 88-7652-910-1.

11933 **Cartlidge, David R.; Elliott, J. Keith** Art and the christian apocrypha. 2001 ⇒17,10917. ᴿRRT 9 (2002) 221-223 (*Spira, Andrew*).

11934 *Cempari, Mario* La Passione di Cristo negli affreschi della Scala
Santa. LSDC 17 (2002) 471-496.

11935 **Cerbellaud, D.**, *al.*, Ce que nos yeux ont vu: richesse et limites
d'une théologie chrétienne de l'image. Lyon 2000, Profac 170 pp.
€16.77. 2-85317-082-9 [NRTh 126,466—Radermakers, Jean].

11936 *Christensen, Carl C.* The reformation of bible illustration: Genesis
woodcuts in Wittenberg, 1523-1534. ᵀ*Skocir, Joan*: Luther Digest
10 (2002) 11-14 <ARG 90 (1999) 103-129.

11937 **Cocke, Richard Paolo** VERONESE: piety and display in an age of
religious reform. 2001 ⇒17,10923. ᴿScEs 54 (2002) 101-103
(*O'Kane, Martin*).

11938 **Collins, Gregory** The Glenstal book of icons: praying with the
Glenstal icons. Dublin 2002, Columba 138 pp. £15. 18560-7362-9.

11939 **Debray, Régis** L'Ancien Testament à travers 100 chefs d'oeuvre
de la peinture; Le Nouveau Testament à travers 100 chefs d'oeuvre
de la peinture. P 2002, Renaissance 224 + 224 pp. €29 + 29 [DosB
99,34—Pierre, Dominique].

11940 *Enss, Elisabet* Eine geschnitzte Apostelhuldigung: zwei Fragmente
eines Friesbretts aus Ägypten in Berlin und Athen. ꟳHOHEISEL, K.:
JAC.E 34: 2002 ⇒59. 220-225.

11941 *Fortunati, Maria Cristina* La Cappella Sistina e l'eredità del tempio di Salomone: per una nuova ipotesi interpretativa circa gli archi
costantiniani negli affreschi sistini. Hum(B) 57 (2002) 620-641.

11942 *García Domene, Juan Carlos* Biblia y bellas artes: 1, pintura.
Ment. *Van Eyck, J.*: ResB 34 (2002) 65-69;

11943 Biblia y bellas artes, 3: escultura: Juan, Pedro y Judas en la obra de
Francisco SALZILLO. ResB 36 (2002) 63-69.

11944 *Gisi, Lucas Marco* Niklaus MANUEL und der Berner Bildersturm
1528. Macht und Ohnmacht. HZ.B 33: 2002 ⇒392. 143-163.

11945 *Goertz, Hans-Jürgen* Bildersturm im Täufertum. Macht und Ohnmacht. HZ.B 33: 2002 ⇒392. 239-252.

11946 **Gulácsi, Zsuzsanna** Manichaean art in Berlin collections. Corpus
Fontium Manichaeorum, Series Archaeologica et Iconographica 1:
2001 ⇒17,10935. ᴿApocrypha 13 (2002) 302-304 (*Dubois, J.-D.*).

11947 *Gunn, David M.* Covering David: MICHELANGELO's David from the
Piazza della Signoria to my refrigerator door. ꟳFLANAGAN, J.:
JSOT.S 359: 2002 ⇒38. 139-170.

11948 **Hamburger, Jeffrey F.** St. John the Divine: the deified evangelist
in medieval art and theology. Berkeley 2002, Univ. of California
Pr. 323 pp. $60. 0-520-22877-4.

11949 ᴱHari, Albert Cantique des cantiques et Qohélet. 2001 ⇒17,
10937. ᴿSR 31 (2002) 440-441 (*Lavoie, Jean-Jacques*).

11950 ᴱHeller, Ena Giurescu Icons or portraits?: images of Jesus and
Mary from the collection of Michael Hall. NY 2002, American
Bible Society 283 pp. $45. 1-585-16682-0. ᴿAmerica 187/21
(2002) 13-14 (*Dempsey, Terrence E.*).

11951 *Hersche, Peter* Die Allmacht der Bilder: zum Fortleben ihres Kults
im nachtridentinischen Katholizismus. Macht und Ohnmacht. HZ.B
33: 2002 ⇒392. 391-405.

11952 *Hoekema, Alle* Kunst als sacrament en gebed in azië. ITBT 10/3 (2002) 7-9.
11953 *Holenstein, André; Schmidt, Heinrich R.* Bilder als Objekte —Bilder in Relationen: auf dem Weg zu einer wahrnehmungs- und handlungsgeschichtlichen Deutung von Bilderverehrung und Bilderzerstörung. Macht und Ohnmacht. HZ.B 33: 2002 ⇒392. 511-527.
11954 **Honour, Hugh; Fleming, John** A world history of art. L 2002, King 960 pp. 1-85669-314-7. Bibl. 933-941.
11955 ᴱ**Hourihane, Colum** King David: in the index of christian art. Index of christian art resources 2: Princeton 2002, Princeton Univ. Pr. 438 pp. 0-691-09547-7. 110 photos. Bibl. 405-414.
11956 **Jensen, Robin Margaret** Understanding early christian art. 2000 ⇒16,11233; 17,10943. ᴿJECS 10 (2002) 143-144 (*Ferguson, Everett*).
11957 *Johnstone, William* Interpictoriality: the lives of Moses and Jesus in the murals of the Sistine Chapel. ᴹCARROLL, R.: JSOT.S 348: 2002 ⇒13. 416-455.
11958 *Jong, Jan L. De* Three Italian sacrifices: Lorenzo GHIBERTI, Andrea DEL SARTO, Michelangelo Merisi da CARAVAGGIO. Aqedah. 2002 ⇒2523. 152-165 [Gen 22].
11959 *Kakovkin, A.Y.* The first miracle of Jesus in Coptic art. ᴹDIAKONOFF, I. 2002 ⇒27. 119-124 [Jn 2,1-12].
11960 *Kampling, Rainer* Zur Polemik der Bilder: Motive des kirchlichen Antijudaismus und ihre Rezeption in der bildenden Kunst des Mittelalters. Im Angesicht. SBB 47: 2002 <1998> ⇒189. 195-212.
11961 *Kapsová, Eva* Intertextuality in visual interpretation of biblical motifs in contemporary Slovak fine art. Philosophical hermeneutics. WUNT 153: 2002 ⇒367. 352-363.
11962 *Kaufmann, Thomas* Die Bilderfrage im frühneuzeitlichen Luthertum. Macht und Ohnmacht. HZ.B 33: 2002 ⇒392. 407-454.
11963 *Kirchgessner, Bernhard* Ausstellungsprojekt "Auferstehung": ein Dialogversuch zwischen Kunst und Kirche im Bistum Passau. AnzSS 111/7-8 (2002) 11-13.
11964 **Knipp, Philip David Ezra** 'Christus Medicus' in der frühchristlichen Sarkophagskulptur: ikonographische Studien zur Sepulkralkunst des späten vierten Jahrhunderts. SVigChr 37: 1998 ⇒14, 10290. ᴿThLZ 127 (2002) 667-669 (*Nauerth, Claudia*).
11965 *Krafft, Fritz* Der Heiland als Apotheker in der Himmelsapotheke. CistC 109 (2002) 225-240.
11966 *Kramiszewska, Aneta* Wybrane zagadnienia ikonografii tak zwanej Wielkiej Świętej Rodziny [Ausgewählte Probleme der Ikonographie von der Heiligen Sippe]. ACra 34 (2002) 353-369. **P**.
11967 *Kreitzer, Larry J.* Hans HOLBEIN's The ambassadors: biblical reflections on a Renaissance masterpiece. Borders. JSOT.S 313: 2002 ⇒585. 217-228 [2 Cor 5,18-20; Col 1,15-20].
11968 ᵀ**Labriola, Albert C.; Smeltz, John W.** The mirror of salvation [Speculum humanae salvationis]. Pittsburgh 2002, Duquesne Univ. Pr. viii; 194 pp. $65. 0-8207-0323-0. Edition of British Library Blockbook G. 11784 [ThD 49,191—Heiser, W. Charles].
11969 *Lepage, Claude* A propos d'une image éthiopienne inspirée d'Hénoch. CRAI 1 (2002) 363-386.
11970 *Litz, Gudrun* Die Problematik der reformatorischen Bilderfrage in den schwäbischen Reichsstädten. Macht und Ohnmacht. HZ.B 33: 2002 ⇒392. 99-116.

11971 **Lowden, John** The making of the bibles moralisées, 1: the manuscripts; 2: the book of Ruth. 2000 ⇒16,2705; 17,2737. [R]HeyJ 43 (2002) 250-252 (*Tanner, Norman*); Spec. 77 (2002) 586-588 (*Rouse, Mary A.*); JR 82 (2002) 281-282 (*McGinn, Bernard*); CCMéd 45 (2002) 190-195 (*Skubiszewski, Piotr*); RMab 13 (2002) 362-364 (*Heck, Christian*).

11972 **Lüken, Sven** Die Verkündigung an Maria im 15. und frühen 16. Jahrhundert: historische und kunsthistorische Untersuchungen. 2000 ⇒16,11239. [R]CrSt 23 (2002) 536-537 (*Boespflug, François*).

11973 *Maier, Hans* Die politischen Religionen und die Bibel;

11974 *Marchal, Guy P.* Das vieldeutige Heiligenbild: Bildersturm im Mittelalter. Macht und Ohnmacht. 2002 ⇒392. 485-507/307-332.

11975 **Martin, Linette** Sacred doorways: a beginner's guide to icons. Brewster, MA 2002, Paraclete xvii; 258 pp. $24. 1-55725-307-2 [ThD 50,175—Heiser, W. Charles].

11976 **Martin, Pierre** La résurrection en images: le cheminement des symboles de la résurrection. 2001 ⇒17,10952. [R]FV 101/3 (2002) 106-107 (*Vahanian, Gabriel*).

11977 Matthaeus MERIAN: great scenes from the bible. Mineola, NY 2002, Dover vi; 116 pp. $13. 0-486-42043-4 230. 17th cent. engravings [ThD 49,382—Heiser, W. Charles].

11978 *Mayr-Harting, Henry* Apocalyptic book illustration in the early Middle Ages. Apocalyptic. JSPE.S 43: 2002 ⇒373. 172-211.

11979 *Metzler, Dieter* Zwischen Kythera und Thebais: Antike in Gartenparadiesen der Neuzeit. Religiöse Landschaften. AOAT 301: 2002 ⇒408. 181-216.

11980 [E]**Metzsch, Friedrich-A. von** Bild und Botschaft: biblische Geschichten auf Bildern der Alten Pinakothek München. Rg 2002, Schnell & S. 115 pp. 3-7954-1451-2. 39 ill. [LuThK 26,209s— Stolle, Volker].

11981 **Meyer zu Capellen, Jürg** RAPHAEL, a critical catalogue of his paintings, 1. [ET]*Polter, Stefan B.*: 2001 ⇒17,10955. [R]SCJ 33 (2002) 1075-1077 (*Joost-Gaugier, Christiane L.*).

11982 *Michalski, Sergiusz* Bilderstürme im Ostseeraum. Macht und Ohnmacht. HZ.B 33: 2002 ⇒392. 223-237.

11983 *Muller, Elianne* 'Van gheenen man en had si confuys': apocriefe kerstmotieven in tekst en beeld. Streven 69 (2002) 963-977.

11984 *Mundhenk, Norman A.* Translating bible comics. BiTr 53 (2002) 402-413.

11985 **Nagel, Alexander** MICHELANGELO and the reform of art. 2000 ⇒ 16,11251. [R]SCJ 33 (2002) 832-833 (*McIver, Katherine*).

11986 *Navone, John* Il valore dell'arte cristiana. CivCatt 153/2 (2002) 255-264.

11987 [E]**O'Grady, Ron** Christ for all people. 2001 ⇒17,10958. [R]VJTR 66 (2002) 693-694 (*Meagher, P.M.*).

11988 *O'Kane, Martin* The flight into Egypt: icon of refuge for the h(a)unted. Borders. JSOT.S 313: 2002 ⇒585. 15-60 [Mt 2,13-23].

11989 *Palmer Wandel, Lee* Bildersturm im Elsaß. Macht und Ohnmacht. HZ.B 33: 2002 ⇒392. 165-175.

11990 *Parravicini, Giovanna* La Terra Santa nell'arte russa. La Nuova Europa 3 (2002) 66-76.

11991 [E]**Paupert, Catherine** Aux frontières du Nouveau Testament: répertoire des artistes, voyages des Valsésians, glossaire et varia: motifs apocryphes en Maurienne et en Tarentaise (Savoie), 4: vies et morts des apôtres, de saint Joseph et de saint Jean-Baptiste. Grenoble 2002, Alzieu 152 pp. 29107-17550 [RHEF 89,551: J.-L. Lemaitre].

11992 **Quenot, Michel** L'icône, fenêtre sur le royaume. P 2002, Cerf 197 pp. €23 [EeV 59,26—Pousseur, Robert].

11993 *Ritmeyer, Kathleen; Ritmeyer, Leen* Backward glance: divergent visions of the Holy Land. BArR 28/4 (2002) 52-55.

11994 *Roeck, Bernd* Macht und Ohnmacht der Bilder: die historische Perspektive. Macht und Ohnmacht. HZ.B 33: 2002 ⇒392. 33-63.

11995 *Rümelin, Christian* Bilderverwendung im Spannungsfeld der Reformation: Aspekte oberrheinischer Buchillustration. Macht und Ohnmacht. HZ.B 33: 2002 ⇒392. 195-222.

11996 *Ryan, Thomas; Rubin, Lawrence* By the numbers: material spirituality and the Last Supper. Spiritus 2 (2002) 147-162.

11997 **Sala, Giuseppe** Il libro delle origini: l'annuncio biblico nello splendore dell'arte. Bo 2002, EDB vi; 76 pp. 88-10-60718-X. Ill.

11998 *Saracino, Francesco* 'In the east to illustrate scripture with historical truth': William Holman HUNT e l'ombra del Carpentiere. ACr 90 (2002) 449-464;

11999 Il più forte: RUBENS e la persuasione del risorto. Vivens Homo 13 (2002) 313-333.

12000 *Schnitzler, Norbert* Der Vorwurf des 'Judaisierens' in den Bilderkontroversen des späten Mittelalters und der frühen Neuzeit. Macht und Ohnmacht. HZ.B 33: 2002 ⇒392. 333-358.

12001 **Schreckenberg, Heinz** Christliche Adversus-Judaeos-Bilder: das Alte und Neue Testament im Spiegel der christlichen Kunst. EHS.T 650: 1999 ⇒15,11098...17,10970. ᴿThRv 98 (2002) 540-542 (*Hoeps, Reinhard*); CrSt 23 (2002) 487-489 (*Boespflug, François*).

12002 *Schrenk, Sabine* Die "topographischen" Friese auf den Behangfragmenten mit Danielszene und Petrusszene in Berlin. ᶠHOHEISEL, K.: JAC.E 34: 2002 ⇒59. 72-83.

12003 *Shani, Raya Y.* Noah's ark and the ship of faith in Persian painting: from the fourteenth to the sixteenth-century. JStAI 27 (2002) 127-203.

12004 *Sladeczek, Franz-Josef* 'das wir entlichs verderbens und des bettelstabs sind': Künstlerschicksale zur Zeit der Reformation. Macht und Ohnmacht. HZ.B 33: 2002 ⇒392. 273-304.

12005 *Spijkerboer, Anne Marijke* Over geweld en armoede: de tempelreiniging vanuit het beeld gelezen. Ment. *Rembrandt.* ITBT 10/4 (2002) 21-23 [Mt 10,5-42];

12006 Over dronkenschap en dienstbaarheid: de bruiloft in Kana vanuit het beeld gelezen. ITBT 10/3 (2002) 10-12 [Jn 2,1-11];

12007 Over een put en een emmer: de Samaritaanse vrouw vanuit het beeld gelezen. ITBT 10/6 2002 19-21 [Jn 4].

12008 *Spronk, Klaas* Samson as the suffering servant: some remarks on a painting by Lovis Corinth. ᶠLEENE, H. 2002 ⇒73. 219-224 [Judg 13-16].

12009 **Steinberg, Leo** LEONARDO's incessant Last Supper. 2001 ⇒17, 10977. ᴿFirst Things 123 (2002) 43-46 (*Wolfe, Gregory*).

12010 *Stein, Markus* Die Inschriften auf dem Daniel- und dem Petrus-Stoff in Berlin. ᶠHOHEISEL, K.: JAC.E 34: 2002 ⇒59. 84-98.

12011 *Thomke, Hellmut* Der Bildersturm in schweizerischen Dramen der Reformationszeit. Macht und Ohnmacht. HZ.B 33: 2002 ⇒392. 379-390.

12012   A treasury of wisdom: the words of Jesus. SF 2002, Ignatius 77 pp.
        $16. 0-89870-912-1. 40 pl. [ThD 49,393—Heiser, W. Charles].
12013   *Trivellone, Alessia* L'iconographie de deux bas-reliefs de Saint-
        Jean-in-Tumba à Monte Sant'Angelo (Pouilles): narration de la
        passion et liturgie de l'eucharistie. CCMéd 45 (2002) 141-164.
12014   *Štrukelj, Anton* La beauté spirituelle des icônes. Com(F) 37/2
        (2002) 81-89; IKaZ 31, 50-57; Communio 24,171-178.
12015   *Van den Brink, Eddy* Abraham's sacrifice in early Jewish and early
        christian art. Aqedah. 2002 ⇒2523. 140-151 [Gen 22].
12016   **Van Loon, Gertrud J.M.** The gate of heaven: wall paintings with
        Old Testament scenes in the altar room and the Hûrus of Coptic
        churches. UNHAII 85: 1999 ⇒15,11115. [R]BiOr 59 (2002) 94-98
        (*Rutschowscaya, M.H.*).
12017   **Van Moorsel, Paul** Les peintures du Monastère de Saint-Paul près
        de la Mer Rouge. MIFAO 120: Le Caire 2002, Institut Français
        d'Archéologie Orientale viii; 133 pp. 2-7247-0317-0. Contributions
        de *Peter Grossmann* et *Pierre-Henry Laferrière*; Bibl. 125-126.
12018   [E]**Velmans, Tania** Le grand livre des icônes: des origines à la chute
        de Byzance. Mi 2002 Hazan 238 pp. €60.25. 2-85025-841-5.
12019   **Verdon, Timothy** L'arte sacra in Italia: dai mosaici paleocristani
        alle espressioni contemporanee. 2001 ⇒17,10987. [R]ACr 90 (2002)
        157-158 (*Vigorelli, Valerio*); Teol (Br) 27 (2002) 79-81 (*Sequeri,
        Pierangelo*).
12020   *Villeneuve, Estelle* Die Auferstehung der Fresken von Emmaus.
        WUB 25 (2002) 61-62.
12021   **Wiesemann, Falk** 'kommt heraus und schaut'—jüdische und
        christliche Illustrationen zur Bibel in alter Zeit. Essen 2002, Klar-
        text 148 pp. €24.90. Beiträge *Marion Aptroot; William L. Gross*.
12022   [E]**Williams, John** Imaging the early medieval bible. 1999 ⇒15,
        11120. [R]Spec. 77 (2002) 654-657 (*Cahn, Walter*).
12023   *Wirth, Jean* Aspects modernes et contemporains de l'iconoclasme.
        Macht und Ohnmacht. HZ.B 33: 2002 ⇒392. 455-481.
12024   **Zlatohlávek, Martin; Rätsch, Christian; Müller-Ebeling, Clau-
        dia** Das Jüngste Gericht: Fresken, Bilder und Gemälde. Dü 2001,
        Benziger 234 pp. €34.90. 3-545-34160-7 [ThRv 100,255—Harald
        Wagner].

T3.2 Sculptura

12025   **Albersmeier, Sabine** Untersuchungen zu den Frauenstatuen des
        ptolemäischen Ägypten. Aegyptiaca Treverensia 10: Mainz 2002,
        Von Zabern xii; 457 pp. 3-8053-2976-8. 86 pl.
12026   **Angelicoussis, Elizabeth** The Holkham collection of classical
        sculptures. CSIR: Great Britain 3/10; Monumenta Artis Romanae
        30: Mainz 2001, Von Zabern 189 pp. €76.69. 3-8053-2697-1. 43
        fig.; 101 pl.
12027   **Attula, R.** Griechisch-Römische Terrakotten aus Ägypten. Rostock
        2001, Univ. Rostock 294 pp. 3-86009-219-7.
12028   *Basile, Joseph John* Recently discovered relief sculptures from the
        great temple at Petra, Jordan. ADAJ 46 (2002) 331-346.
12029   *Bleibtreu, Erika* Zum Schema der Kriegsdarstellungen auf neuassy-
        rischen Wandreliefs des 9.-7. Jahrhunderts v. Chr. Krieg und Sieg.
        2002 ⇒723. 69-79.

12030 ^E**Bol, Peter C.**, *al.*, Die Geschichte der antiken Bildhauerkunst, 1: frühgriechische Plastik. Schriften des Liebieghauses: Mainz 2002, Von Zabern ix; 342 pp. €75.80. 3-8053-2869-9. Num. ill.

12031 *Börker-Klähn, Jutta* Götterkämpfe? Historie!. ^MIMPARATI, F. 2002 ⇒61. 109-140.

12032 **Brand, Peter James** The monuments of Seti I: epigraphic, historical and art historical analysis. PÄ 16: 2000 ⇒16,11284; 17,10994. ^RJSSEA 29 (2002) 108-110 (*Delia, Robert D.*).

12033 **Brugger, Laurence** La façade occidentale de Saint-Étienne de Bourges: le midrash comme fondement du message chrétien. Civilisation Médiévale 9: Poitiers 2000, C.E.S.C.M. 7-295 pp. 92 ill..

12034 **Bühler, Andreas** Kontrapost und Kanon: Studien zur Entwicklung der Skulptur in Antike und Renaissance. Kunstwissenschaftliche Studien 85: Mü 2002, Deutscher Kunstverlag 450 pp. €68. 3-422-06293-9. 220 ill.

12035 **Damaskos, Dimitris** Untersuchungen zu hellenistischen Kultbildern. 1999 ⇒15,11125; 17,10997. ^RAJA 106 (2002) 491-492 (*Barringer, Judith M.*).

12036 **Dorman, Peter F.** Faces in clay: technique, imagery, and allusion in a corpus of ceramic sculpture from ancient Egypt. MÄSt 52; MU.PF: Mainz 2002, Von Zabern xx; 202, 38 pp. €65.50. 3-8053-2992-X. Bibl. 171-197.

12037 *Emre, Kutlu* Felsreliefs, Stelen, Orthostaten: Großplastik als monumentale Form staatlicher und religiöser Repräsentation. Die Hethiter. 2002 ⇒535. 218-233.

12038 *Eule, J. Cordelia* Die statuarische Darstellung von Frauen in Athen im 4. und frühen 3.Jh. v.Chr. Brückenland Anatolien?. 2002 ⇒453. 205-229.

12039 **Ferris, I.M.** Enemies of Rome: barbarians through Roman eyes. 2000 ⇒16,11285. ^RJRS 92 (2002) 214-215 (*Milnor, Kristina*).

12040 *Fittschen, Klaus* Zur Panzerstatue aus Samaria Sebaste. ^FFOERSTER, G. 2002 ⇒39. 9-17.

12041 *Forstner-Müller, Irene; Müller, Wolfgang; Radner, Karen* Statuen in Verbannung: ägyptischer Statuenexport in den Vorderen Orient unter Amenophis III. und IV. Ä&L 12 (2002) 155-166.

12042 *Freed, Rita E.* Defending connoisseurship: a thrice re-inscribed sphinx of Dynasty XII. ^FHANSEN, D. 2002 ⇒58. 77-88.

12043 **Fuchs, Michaela** Römische Reliefwerke. Glyptothek München, Katalog der Skulpturen 7: Mü, 2002 Beck 158 pp.

12044 ^E**Grummond, Nancy T. de; Ridgway, Brunilde S.** From Pergamon to Sperlonga: sculpture and context. 2000 ⇒16,11289. ^RAJA 106 (2002) 489-491 (*Kosmetatou, Elizabeth*).

12045 *Gubalnick, Eleanor* New drawings of Khorsabad sculptures by Paul Émile Botta. RA 96 (2002) 23-56.

12046 **Gubel, E.** La sculpture de tradition phénicienne. P 2002, Musée du Louvre 172 pp. €57. Ill.

12047 *Hazenbos, Joost* Zum İmamkulu-Relief. ^FPOPKO, M. 2002 ⇒91. 147-161.

12048 **Hermary, Antoine** Les figurines en terre cuite archaïques et classiques: les sculptures en pierre. Amathonte 5; Etudes chypriotes 15: 2000 ⇒16,11290. ^RRAr (2002/2) 421-422 (*Queyrel, Anne*).

12049 *Hoffmann, Friedhelm* Measuring Egyptian statues. Under one sky. AOAT 297: 2002 ⇒9014. 109-119.

12050 **Hölzl, Regina** Reliefs und Inschriftensteine des Alten Reiches I.
CAA Wien 18: 1999 ⇒16,11292. [R]CEg 153-154 (2002) 158-161
(*Baud, Michel*);
12051 II. CAA Wien 21: 2000 ⇒16,11293. [R]BiOr 59 (2002) 64-66 (*Der Manuelian, Peter*); CEg 153-154 (2002) 162-164 (*Baud, Michel*).
12052 *Ivantchik, Askold I.* On the problem of the Near Eastern portrayals of Eurasian nomads. [M]DIAKONOFF, I. 2002 ⇒27. 102-118.
12053 **Jenkins, Ian** Cleaning and controversy: the Parthenon sculptures 1911-1939. British Museum Occasional Papers 146: L 2002, British Museum 84 pp. £25. 0-861-1591-46-1. 21 pl.; 13 fig.
12054 *Kletter, R.* Asherah and the Judean pillar figurines engendered?. Sex and gender. 2002 ⇒712. 289-300.
12055 *Kopanias, Konstantinos* Akkulturation am Beispiel einer arkadischen Statue des 7.Jh.v.Chr. Brückenland Anatolien?. 2002 ⇒453. 85-98.
12056 **Kosmopoulou, Angeliki** The iconography of sculptured statue bases in the archaic and classical periods. Madison 2002, Univ. of Wisconsin Pr. xxxi; 259 pp. $50. 0-299-176-40-1. 107 fig.
12057 **Kourou, Nota,** *al.*, Limestone statuettes of Cypriote type found in the Aegean: provenance studies. Nicosia 2002, Leventis xiv; 118 pp. Cyp£12. 13 fig.; 19 pl.; 4 tables.
12058 *Kreppner, Florian Janoscha* Public space in nature: the case of Neo-Assyrian rock reliefs. AltOrF 29 (2002) 367-383.
12059 *Lancellotti, M.G.* La statuetta leontocefala di Tharros: contributo allo studio delle rappresentazioni del *Kosmokrator* mitriaco e gnostico. RSFen 30 (2002) 19-39.
12060 **Lapatin, Kenneth** Mysteries of the snake goddess: art, desire, and the forging of history. Boston 2002, Houghton M. 274 pp. $24. 0-618-14475-7. 113 fig.
12061 **Martinez-Sève, Laurianne** Les figurines de Suse: de l'époque néo-élamite à l'époque sassanide. P 2002, Réunion des musées nationaux 2 vols; 848 pp. €145. 2-7118-4324-6. [R]Akkadica 123 (2002) 197-199 (*Caubet, Annie*).
12062 *Milevski, Ianir* A new fertility figurine and new animal motifs from the chalcolithic in the southern Levant: finds from Cave K-1 at Quleh, Israel. Paléorient 28/2 (2002) 133-141.
12063 *Mitchell, T.C.; Middleton, A.P.* The stones used in the Assyrian sculptures. JCS 54 (2002) 93-98.
12064 [E]**Muller-Dufeu, Marion** La sculpture grecque: sources littéraires et épigraphiques. P 2002, Ecole Nationale Supérieure des Beaux-Arts xv; 1080 pp. €35. 2-84056-115-8.
12065 *Osten-Sacken, Elisabeth von der* Überlegungen zur Göttin auf dem Burneyrelief. Sex and gender. 2002 ⇒712. 479-487.
12066 *Özgüç, Tahsin* Frühe Zeugnisse religiöser Volkskunst: Bleistatuetten und ihre steinernen Gußformen im 20.-18. Jahrhundert v. Chr. Die Hethiter. 2002 ⇒535. 240-243.
12067 *Peck, William H.* An Egyptian goddess in Detroit. [F]HANSEN, D.: 2002 ⇒58 . 203-209.
12068 **Ridgway, Brunilde Sismondo** Hellenistic sculpture III: the styles of ca. 100-31 B.C. Wisconsin Studies in Classics: Madison, WI 2002, Univ. of Wisconsin Pr. xxii; 313 pp. $45. 0-299-17710-6. Bibl. 283-302.
12069 *Rolley, Claude* Les bronzes grecs et romains: recherches récentes. RAr 2 (2002) 269-289.

12070 **Rolley, Claude** La sculpture grecque, 1: des origines au milieu du Ve siècle. 1994 ⇒10,11943*; 14,10363. ^RRAr (2002/1) 94-95 (*Holtzmann, Bernard*);

12071 La sculpture grecque, 2: la période classique. 1999 ⇒15,11143; 16, 11305. ^RRAr (2002/1) 95-96 (*Holtzmann, Bernard*).

12072 **Rose, Charles Brian** Dynastic commemoration and imperial portraiture in the Julio-Claudian period. Cambridge Studies in Classical Art and Iconography: 1997 ⇒13,10297. ^RAnCl 71 (2002) 501-504 (*Balty, Jean Ch.*).

12073 **Russell, John Malcolm** From Nineveh to New York: the strange story of the Assyrian reliefs in the Metropolitan Museum and the hidden masterpiece at Canford School. 1997 ⇒14,10364. ^RBCSMS 37 (2002) 59-60 (*Bedal, Leigh-Ann*).

12074 **Steiner, Deborah Tarn** Images in mind: statues in archaic and classical Greek literature and thought. 2001 ⇒17,11021. ^RAJA 106 (2002) 331-332 (*Pollitt, J.J.*); AJP 123 (2002) 513-516 (*Rehak, Paul*).

12075 *Thiers, Christophe* Deux statues des dieux Philométors à Karnak (Karnak Caracol R177 + Cheikh Labib 94CL1421 et Caire JE 41218). BIFAO 102 (2002) 389-404.

12076 *Uehlinger, Christoph* Hanun von Gaza und seine Gottheiten auf Orthostatenreliefs Tiglatpilesers III. ^FWEIPPERT, M.: OBO 186: 2002 ⇒133. 92-125.

12077 **Vlizos, Stavros** Der thronende Zeus: eine Untersuchung zur statuarischen Ikonographie des Gottes in der spätklassischen und hellenistischen Kunst. 1999 ⇒15,11148. ^RAJA 106 (2002) 134-135 (*Waywell, Geoffrey*).

12078 *Winter, Irene J.* How tall was Naram-Sîn's victory stele?: speculation on the broken bottom. ^FHANSEN, D. 2002 ⇒58. 301-311.

12079 **Zivie-Coche, Christiane M.** Sphinx: history of a monument. ^T*Lorton, David*: Ithaca, NY 2002, Cornell Univ. Pr. xvi; 122 pp. $25. 0-8014-3962-0. Bibl. 111-116.

T3.3 *Glyptica*; **stamp and cylinder seals**; *scarabs, amulets*

12080 **Amorai-Stark, Shua** Wolfe family collection of Near Eastern prehistoric stamp seals. OBO.A 16: 1997 ⇒13,10409; 15,11152. ^RJNES 61 (2002) 130-131 (*Suter, Claudia E.*).

12081 *Boehmer, Rainer Michael* Eine in Uruk gefundene Abrollung aus dem frühdynastischen Ur. DaM 13 (2002) 1-2.

12082 *Brandl, Baruch* A dagger pommel, two scarabs and a seal from tomb 65 at Khirbet Nisya. 'Atiqot 43 (2002) 37-48.

12083 *Cecchini, Serena Maria* Il re e la dea con il disco su un sigillo a stampo di Tell Afis. ^MCIASCA, A. 2002 ⇒15. 153-161. 2 pl..

12084 *Dalix, Anne-Sophie Dlq* et le sphinx: le cachet RS 25.188. UF 34 (2002) 45-52.

12085 *Deutsch, Robert* Lasting impressions: new bullae reveal Egyptian-style emblems on Judah's royal seals. BArR 28/4 (2002) 42-51, 60-62.

12086 **Deutsch, Robert** Messages from the past: Hebrew bullae from the time of Isaiah through the destruction of the first temple. 1999 ⇒ 15,11163; 16,11317. ^RRBLit (2002)* (*Vaughn, Andrew C.*).

12087 **Deutsch, Robert; Lemaire, André** Biblical period personal seals in the Shlomo Moussaieff collection. 2000 ⇒16,11318. ᴿRB 109 (2002) 426-428 (*Puech, Émile*); ZDMG 152 (2002) 395-396 (*Röllig, Wolfgang*); JBL 121 (2002) 339-343 (*Vaughn, Andrew G.*).

12088 **Dickers, Aurelia** Die spätmykenischen Siegel aus weichem Stein: Untersuchungen zur spätbronzezeitlichen Glyptik auf dem griechischen Festland und in der Ägäis. Internationale Archäologie 33: 2001 ⇒17,11035. ᴿAJA 106 (2002) 483-4 (*Krzyszkowska, Olga*).

12089 *Dinçol, Ali* "Tabarna"- und "Ädikula"-Siegel: die Siegel hethitischer Größkönige und Großköniginnen. Die Hethiter. 2002 ⇒535. 88-93.

12090 *Elayi, Josette* Uno de los primeros sellos fenicios. AuOr 20 (2002) 257-262.

12091 *Garbini, Giovanni* Il sigillo di Aliya Regina di Gerusalemme. AANL.R 13 (2002) 589-600. Contrib. *Guido Devoto.*

12092 **Garlan, Yvon** Amphores et timbres amphoriques grecs: entre érudition et idéologie. 2000 ⇒16,11320. ᴿREG 115 (2002) 803-804 (*Sève, Michel*).

12093 **Gill, Margaret A.V.; Müller, Walter; Pini, Ingo** Corpus der minoischen und mykenischen Siegel, II: Iraklion. Archäologisches Museum, 8: die Siegelabdrücke von Knossos Mainz 2002 Von Zabern 2 vols; xxv; 859 pp. €230. 3-8053-3107-X. 1855 fig.

12094 *Goldwasser, Orly* A 'Kirgipa' commemorative scarab of Amenhotep III from Beit-Shean. Ä&L 12 (2002) 191-193.

12095 *Göhde, Hildegard* Zwei altbabylonische Siegelabrollungen aus Tell ed-Dēr: Identifizierung von zwei weiblichen Gottheiten. ᶠDIETRICH, M. 2002 ⇒28. 159-168.

12096 ᴱ**Gyselen, Rika** Sceaux d'Orient et leur emploi. 1997 ⇒13,10421 ...15,11167. ᴿJNES 61 (2002) 280-282 (*Suter, Claudia E.*).

12097 *Herbordt, Suzanne* Hittite seals and sealings from the Nişantepe archive, Boğazköy: a prosopographical study. ᴹGÜTERBOCK, H. 2002 ⇒54. 53-60.

12098 **Herrmann, Christian** Ägyptische Amulette aus Palästina/Israel II. OBO 184: Gö 2002, Vandenhoeck & R. (12) 194 pp. FS65/€44. 3-525-53040-4. Bibl. 157-159.

12099 *Kaplony, Peter* The 'En Besor seal impressions—revised. Egypt and the Levant. 2002 ⇒497. 487-498.

12100 **Kaptan, D.** The Daskyleion bullae: seal images from the western Achaemenid Empire. Achaemenid History 12: Lei 2002, Nederlands Institut voor het Nabije Oosten 2 vols; xxii; 486 pp. €130. 90-6258-41-28. Num. ill; 473 fig.

12101 *Karaca, Özgen; Akdeniz, Engin* Stamp seals from the early levels at Pirot Höyük. ANESt 39 (2002) 152-159.

12102 *Klengel, Horst* '*An der Hand der Gottheit*': Bemerkungen zur 'Umarmungsszene' in der hethitischen Tradition;

12103 *Koliński, Rafal* Bulls from Tell Arbid. ᶠPOPKO, M. 2002 ⇒91. 205-210/211-224.

12104 **Leith, M.J. Winn** Wadi Daliyeh I: the Wadi Daliyeh seal impressions. DJD 24: 1997 ⇒13,10432; 15,11174. ᴿDSD 9 (2002) 258-262 (*Mędala, Stanisław*).

12105 *Mallet, Joël; Lebrun, René* Document sous sceau hittite, écriture et langue à déchiffrer. UF 34 (2002) 551-567.

12106 *Mayr, R.* The depiction of ordinary men and women on the seals of the Ur III kingdom. Sex and gender. 2002 ⇒712. 359-366.

12107 *McCarter, P. Kyle Jr.* Biblical detective work identifies the eunuch [אמריהו]. BArR 28/2 (2002) 46-48, 61 [2 Chr 31,15].

12108 **Müller, Walter; Olivier, Jean-Pierre; Pini, Ingo** Die Tonplomben aus dem Nestorpalast von Pylos. Mainz 1997, Von Zabern xii; 123 pp. €81.81. 3-8053-1981-9. 46 fig.

12109 **Müller, Walter; Pini, Ingo** Corpus der minoischen und mykenischen Siegel, II: Iraklion Archäologisches Museum, 6: die Siegelabdrücke von Aj. Triada und anderen zentral- und ostkretischen Fundorten. B 1999, Mann xlvii; 519 pp. €181. 3-7861-2292-2. 1024 fig.;

12110 Iraklion Archäologisches Museum, 7: die Siegelabdrücke von Kato Zakros. B 1998, Mann xxxv; 277 pp. €118. 3-7861-19600. 755 fig.

12111 *Naveh, Joseph* Some new Jewish Palestinian Aramaic amulets. JStAI 26 (2002) 231-236.

12112 *Nikulina, N.M.* The Aegean glyptics. Journal of Ancient History 242 (2002) 104-115 Sum. 115. **R**.

12113 **Nunn, Astrid** Stamp seals from the collections of the Aleppo Museum, Syrian Arab Republic BAR international series 804: 1999 ⇒ 15,11182. ᴿOLZ 97 (2002) 366-369 (*Osten-Sacken, Elisabeth von der*).

12114 *Özgüç, Nimet* Götterprozessionen, Kriegs- und Jagdszenen: ein Überblick über den Motivreichtum anatolischer Roll- und Stempelsiegel des 20.-18. Jahrhunderts v. Chr. Die Hethiter. 2002 ⇒535. 234-239.

12115 *Pittman, Holly* The 'jeweler's' seal from Susa and art of Awan. ᶠHANSEN, D. 2002 ⇒58. 211-235.

12116 *Poetto, Massimo* Nuovi sigilli in luvio geroglifico V. ᶠPOPKO, M. 2002 ⇒91. 273-276.

12117 *Reichel, Clemens* Administrative complexity in Syria during the 4th millennium B.C.—the seals and sealings from Tell Hamoukar. Akkadica 123 (2002) 35-56.

12118 *Seidl, Ursula* Der Mond, der vom Himmel fällt. DaM 13 (2002) 105-111.

12119 *Uehlinger, C.* L'apport de la glyptique à l'histoire culturelle et religieuse de la Palestine à l'époque perse (résumé). TEuph 23 (2002) 156.

12120 *Van Koppen, Frans* Redeeming a father's seal. ᶠWALKER, C. 2002 ⇒130. 147-176.

12121 *Wimmer, Stefan Jakob* Sichimitica Varia II: ein Skarabäus vom Tell Balaṭa. BN 112 (2002) 33-37.

T3.4 **Mosaica**

12122 *Abadie-Reynal, Catherine* Les maisons aux décors mosaïqués de Zeugma. CRAI 2 (2002) 743-771.

12123 *Andreopoulos, A.* The mosaic of the transfiguration in St Catherine's Monastery on Mount Sinai: a discussion of its origins. Byz. 72 (2002) 9-41.

12124 **Balmelle, C.**, *al.*, Le décor géométrique de la mosaïque romaine, 2: répertoire graphique et descriptif des décors centrés. P 2002, Picard 264 pp. 1000 dessins de *M.-P. Raynaud.*

12125 *Baumann, Peter* Mythological heroes in the service of private representation: a case study on some late antique mosaics in the Holy Land. [F]FOERSTER, G. 2002 ⇒39. 69-85.

12126 *Bloedhorn, Hanswulf; Strohmaier-Wiederwanders, Gerlinde* Mosaik-Kunst. RGG 5. 2002 ⇒796. 1514-1522.

12127 *Brands, Gunnar* Anmerkungen zu spätantiken Bodenmosaiken aus Nordsyrien. JAC 45 (2002) 122-136.

12128 *Briend, Jacques* Surprenantes mosaïques de Sepphoris. MoBi 146 (2002) 47-51.

12129 **Ennaïfer, M.; Rebourg, A.** La mosaïque gréco-romaine VII/1-2: VIIe colloque... pour l'étude de la mosaïque antique, 1994. 1999. ⇒15,11203; 17,11082. [R]AnCl 71 (2002) 483-484 *(Balty, Janine)*.

12130 *Haddad, Riham* Procedures of mosaic floor conservation and restoration in Jordan. ADAJ 46 (2002) 113*-118*. **A.**

12131 **Jolly, Penny Howell** Made in God's image?: Eve and Adam in the Genesis mosaics at San Marco, Venice. 1997 ⇒13,10443. [R]StMed 43 (2002) 475-476 *(Tampieri, Roberta)*.

12132 *Meeks, Wayne A.* Vision of God and scripture interpretation in a fifth-century mosaic. In search. 2002 ⇒208. 230-253.

12133 *Meeks, Wayne A.; Meeks, Martha F.* Vision of God and scripture interpretation in a fifth-century mosaic. [F]GREER, R. 2002 ⇒51. 124-145.

12134 *Stone, Michael E.* A reassessment of the bird and the Eustathius mosaic. Armenians in Jerusalem. 2002 ⇒771. 203-219.

12135 *Van den Brink, Eddy* Christus in Ravenna: gekleed in *battledress*. ITBT 10/6 (2002) 4-7.

12136 *Wisskirchen, Rotraut* Der bekleidete Adam thront inmitten der Tiere: zum Bodenmosaik des Mittelschiffs der Nordkirche von Huarte/ Syrien. JAC 45 (2002) 137-152.

T3.5 *Ceramica,* **pottery**

12137 [E]**Al-Maqdissi, Michel; Matoian, Valérie; Nicolle, Christophe** Céramique de l'âge du Bronze en Syrie, 1: la Syrie du Sud et la vallée de l'Oronte. BAH Beyr. 161: Beyrouth 2002, n.p. vi; 170 pp. €25. 2-912738-16-4. Ill.

12138 *Amiran, Ruth; Van den Brink, Edwin C.M.* The ceramic assemblage from Tel Ma'ahaz, stratum I (seasons 1975-1976). Egypt and the Levant. 2002 ⇒497. 273-279.

12139 *Bader, Bettina* A concise guide to Marl C-pottery. Ä&L 12 (2002) 29-54.

12140 *Bahrani, Zainab* Performativity and the image: narrative, representation, and the Uruk vase. [F]HANSEN, D. 2002 ⇒58. 15-22.

12141 *Banning, Edward B.* Consensus and debate on the late neolithic and chalcolithic of the southern Levant. Paléorient 28/2 (2002) 148-55.

12142 [E]**Bentz, M.; Zanker, P.** Corpus vasorum antiquorum Deutschland, Beiheft 1: Vasenforschung und corpus vasorum antiquorum— Standortbestimmung und Perspektiven. Mü 2002, Beck 144 pp. €49.90. 3-406-49043-3. 126 fig.

12143 *Bergoffen, Celia J.* Early Late Cypriot ceramic exports to Canaan: White Slip I. [F]HANSEN, D. 2002 ⇒58. 23-41.

12144 **Bourriau, J.D.; Smith, L.M.V.; Nicholson, P.T.** New Kingdom pottery fabrics: Nile clay and mixed Nile/Marl clay fabrics from Memphis and Amarna. 2000 ⇒16,11349. [R]Or. 71 (2002) 309-311 (*Guidotti, M. Cristina*); AJA 106 (2002) 608-609 (*Shaw, Ian*); BiOr 59 (2002) 305-308 (*Hope, Colin A.*).

12145 **Coldstream, J.N.; Eiring, L.J.; Forster, G.** Knossos pottery handbook, Greek and Roman. ABSA Studies 7: 2001 ⇒17,11097. [R]RAr (2002/2) 423-424 (*Boardman, John*).

12146 *Dupont, P., al.*, Bulletin archéologique: céramique. REG 115 (2002) 216-404.

12147 **Ferrari, Gloria** Figures of speech: men and maidens in ancient Greece. Ch 2002, Univ. of Chicago Pr. viii; 352 pp. $60. 0-226-22-436-9. Bibl. 313-338.

12148 *Fuscaldo, Perla* The Nubian pottery from the palace district of Avaris at ʿEzbet Helmi, Areas H/III and H/IV, part I: the 'classic' Kerma pottery from the 18th dynasty. Ä&L 12 (2002) 167-186.

12149 [E]**Glascock, Michael D.** Geochemical evidence for long-distance exchange. Scientific archaeology for the Third Millennium: West-port, CONN 2002, Bergin and G viii (2) 282 pp. 0-89789-869-9.

12150 *Goren, Yuval* Appendix 2: provenance study of the eulogia tokens. [F]FOERSTER, G. 2002 ⇒39. 513-533.

12151 *Gschwind, Markus* Hellenistische Tradition contra italische Mode: ein frühkaiserzeitlicher Keramikkomplex aus den türkischen Rettungsgrabungen in Zeugma am mittleren Euphrat. DaM 13 (2002) 321-359.

12152 *Hartung, Ulrich* Imported jars from cemetery U at Abydos and the relations between Egypt and Canaan in predynastic times. Egypt and the Levant. 2002 ⇒497. 437-449.

12153 [E]**Hausleiter, A.; Reiche, A.** Iron Age pottery in northern Mesopotamia, northern Syria and south-eastern Anatolia. Altertumskunde des Vorderen Orients 10: 1999 ⇒17,614. [R]BASOR 325 (2002) 81-83 (*Lehmann, Gunnar*).

12154 *Henrich, Peter* Studien zur römischen Keramik im Hauran—Untersuchungen am Beispiel eines Fundkomplexes aus Qanawat/Südsyrien. DaM 13 (2002) 245-315.

12155 [E]**Herfort-Koch, Marlene; Mandel, Ursula; Schädler, Ulrich** Hellenistische und kaiserzeitliche Keramik des östlichen Mittelmeergebietes. 1996 ⇒12,312. [R]AJA 106 (2002) 340-341 (*Rosenthal-Heginbottom, Renate*).

12156 *Herr, Larry G.* W.F. ALBRIGHT and the history of pottery in Palestine. NEA (BA) 65 (2002) 51-55.

12157 *Ivantchik, A.I.* Who were the 'Scythian' archers on archaic Attic vases?, 1. Journal of Ancient History 242 (2002) 33-55. R.

12158 **Jorgensen, John** Typology of the Late Bronze II and Early Iron Age: pottery from Tel ʿEin Zippori, Galilee: persistence and chance across an archeological horizon. [D]*Meyers, E.M.*: 2002, 640 pp. Diss. Duke [RTL 34,592].

12159 *Kansa, Eric, al.*, Nahal Tillah reed decorated pottery: aspect of early Bronze Age IB ceramic production and Egyptian counterparts. [F]GOPHNA, R. 2002 ⇒49. 193-218.

12160 *Kopcke, Günter* 1000 B.C.E.? 900 B.C.E.?: a Greek vase from Lake Galilee. [F]HANSEN, D. 2002 ⇒58. 109-117.

12161 *Kuijt, I.; Chesson, M.S.* Excavations at 'Ain Waida', Jordan: new insights into pottery neolithic lifeways in the southern Levant. Palé-orient 28/2 (2002) 109-122.
12162 *Landgraf, John E.* The thrown closed base. BAIAS 19-20 (2001-2002) 29-37.
12163 *Lilyquist, Christine* Pithoi of Hatshepsut's time. [F]HANSEN, D. 2002 ⇒58. 119-124.
12164 **Lissarrague, François** Greek vases: the Athenians and their images. [T]*Allen, Kim*: 2001 ⇒17,11108. [R]AJA 106 (2002) 334-335 (*Spivey, Nigel*).
12165 **Loffreda, Stanislao** Ceramica del tempo di Gesù: vasi della Terra Santa nel periodo romano antico 63 a.C. - 70 d.C. Studium Biblicum Franciscanum.Museum 14: 2000 ⇒16,11370; 17,11110. [R]RivBib 50 (2002) 85-86 (*Rolla, Armando*);
12166 Holy Land pottery at the time of Jesus: early Roman period 63 BC-70 AD. Studium Biblicum Franciscanum, Museum 15: J 2002, Franciscan Printing Press 118 pp. 965-516-054-8.
12167 **McGovern, Patrick E.** The foreign relations of the "Hyksos": a neutron activation study of Middle Bronze Age pottery from the Eastern Mediterranean. BAR international series 888: 2000 ⇒16, 11372. [R]BASOR 326 (2002) 90-94 (*Bourke, Stephen J.*); DiscEg 53 (2002) 115-122 (*Hulin, Linda*).
12168 *Merrillees, Robert S.* The relative and absolute chronology of the Cypriote white painted pendent line style. BASOR 326 (2002) 1-9.
12169 *Müller-Karpe, Andreas* Die Keramik des Mittleren und Jüngeren hethitischen Reiches: die Entwicklung der anatolischen Keramik—ihre Formen und Funktionen. Die Hethiter. 2002 ⇒535. 256-263.
12170 *Özfirat, Aynur* Kahbur ware from Hakkâri. ANESt 39 (2002) 141-151.
12171 *Pavúk, Peter* Das Aufkommen und die Verbreitung der Grauminy-schen Ware in Westanatolien. Brückenland Anatolien?. 2002 ⇒ 453. 99-115.
12172 *Paz, Yitzhak* Early Bronze Age III 'corrugated Rim Pithoi' from the southern Golan. [F]GOPHNA, R. 2002 ⇒49. 237-241.
12173 *Porat, Naomi; Goren, Yuval* Petrography of the Naqada IIIa Canaanite pottery from tomb U-j in Abydos. Egypt and the Levant. 2002 ⇒497. 252-270.
12174 *Singer-Avitz, Lily* Arad: the Iron Age pottery assemblages. TelAv 29/1 (2002) 110-214.
12175 **Tempesta, Alessandra** Le raffigurazioni mitologiche sulla cerami-ca greco-orientale arcaica. 1998 ⇒15,11243. [R]AJA 106 (2002) 332-333 (*Carpenter, T.H.*).
12176 **Vaag, Leif Erik; Nørskov, Vinnie; Lund, John** The Maussolleion at Halikarnassos: reports of the Danish Archaeological Expedition to Bodrum, 7: the pottery: ceramic material and other finds from selected contexts. Jutland Archaeological Society Publications 15/7: Moesgaard 2002, Jutland Archaeological Society 243 pp. $92. 87-88415-17-1. 85 pl.
12177 *Van den Brink, Edwin C.M.; Braun, Eliot* Wine jars with serekhs from early Bronze Lod: appelation vallée du Nil contrôlée, but for whom?. [F]GOPHNA, R. 2002 ⇒49. 167-192.
12178 **Van Wijngaarden, Gert Jan** Use and appreciation of Mycenaean pottery in the Levant, Cyprus and Italy (1600-1200 BC). Amster-

dam archaeological studies 8: Amst 2002, Amsterdam University Press vii; 441 pp. 90-5356-482-9. Bibl. 397-429.

12179 *Vogt, Christine, al.*, Notes on some of the Abbasid amphorae of Istabl 'Antar-Fustat (Egypt). BASOR 326 (2002) 65-80.

12180 *Watrin, Luc* Tributes and the rise of a predatory power: unraveling the intrigue of EB I Palestinian jars found by E. Amélineau at Abydos. Egypt and the Levant. 2002 ⇒497. 450-463.

T3.6 *Lampas*, lamps

12181 **Hadad, S.** The oil lamps from the Hebrew University excavations at Bet Shean Excavations at Beth Shean 1; Qedem Reports 4: J 2002, Hebr. Univ. ix; 176 pp. 0793-4289 [Byz. 73,586s—Yannopoulos, P.].

12182 *Hammond, Philip C.* A note on a zodiac lamp from Petra. PEQ 134 (2002) 165-168.

12183 *Mikati, Rima* Chronological, functional and spatial aspects in lamp studies: the Roman bath lamps, Bey 045;

12184 *Mulder-Hymans, Noor* The 'egg shell-thin' oil lamps from the souk of Beirut. Aram 13 (2001-2002) 281-292/265-280.

T3.7 *Cultica*—cultic remains

12185 **Arnold, Dieter** Temples of the last pharaohs. 1999 ⇒15,11247; 17,11129. [R]ClR 52 (2002) 337-338 (*Adams, Colin*).

12186 *Aviam, M.* The ancient synagogues of Baram. Qad. 35 (2002) 118-125.

12187 *Bernhauer, Edith* Hathorkapitelle in Zypern—eine eigenständige Variante?. Ägyptologische Tempeltagung. ÄAT 33,3: 2002 ⇒721. 47-56.

12188 **Binder, Donald D.** Into the temple courts: the place of the synagogues in the Second Temple period. SBL.DS 169: 1999 ⇒ 15,11250...17,11130. [R]JJS 53 (2002) 162-164 (*Beall, Christopher*); SvTK 78 (2002) 85-86 (*Runesson, Anders*).

12189 *Bordreuil, Pierre* À propos des temples dédiés à Echmoun par les rois Echmounazor et Bodachtart. [M]CIASCA, A. 2002 ⇒15. 105-108.

12190 **Cauville, Sylvie** Dendara: les fêtes d'Hathor. OLA 105: Lv 2002, Peeters (6) 186 pp. €60. 90-429-1097-6. Composition hiéroglyphique: *J. Hallof* et *H. van den Berg*. Photographies: *A. Lecler*. [R]ArOr 70 (2002) 567-568 (*Coppens, Filip*).

12191 *Coppens, Filip* A variety of designations: some terms for wabet and court in Graeco-Roman temples. ArOr 70 (2002) 13-26.

12192 **Da Riva, Rocío** Der Ebabbar-Tempel von Sippar: in frühneubabylonischer Zeit (640-580 v. Chr.). AOAT 291: Müns 2002, Ugarit-Verlag xxxi; 487 pp. 3-934628-20-6. Bibl. xiii-xxxi.

12193 *Daviau, P. M. Michèle; Dion, Paul-Eugène; Laurier, Wilfrid* Erster moabitischer Tempel entdeckt!. WUB 25 (2002) 66-67.

12194 *Derchain-Urtel, Maria-Theresia* Text- und Bildkongruenz: die Kronen der Götter als Objekt der Forschung. Ägyptologische Tempeltagung. ÄAT 33,3: 2002 ⇒721. 57-69.

12195 *Dothan, Trude* Bronze and iron objects with cultic connotations from Philistine temple building 350 at Ekron. IEJ 52 (2002) 1-27.

12196 **Du Bourguet, Pierre Marie** Le temple de Deir al-Médîna. ^{E}*Gabolde, Luc*: MIFAO 121: Le Caire 2002, Institut Français d'Archéologie Orientale xiv; 365 pp. 2-7247-0321-9. Dessins de *Leïla Ménassa*. Bibl. xiii-xiv.

12197 **Eder, Christian** Die Barkenkapelle des Königs Sobekhotep III in Elkab: Beiträge zur Bautätigkeit der 13. und 17. Dynastie an den Göttertempeln Ägyptens. Elkab 7: Turnhout 2002, Brepols ix; 266 pp. 2-503-51313-1. Bibl. 169-196.

12198 *Egberts, Arno* Substanz und Symbolik: Überlegungen zur Darstellung und Verwendung des Halskragens im Tempel von Edfu. Ägyptologische Tempeltagung. ÄAT 33,3: 2002 ⇒721. 71-81.

12199 *Elgvin, Torleif* Rare incense altar raises burning questions. BArR 28/5 (2002) 35-39, 68-69.

12200 *Ertel, Christine* Ornamentik und Rekonstruktion des jüngeren 'Peripteraltempels' in Qanawat. DaM 13 (2002) 171-203.

12201 *Fazzini, Richard A.* Some aspects of the precinct of the goddess Mut in the New Kingdom. ^{F}HANSEN, D. 2002 ⇒58. 63-76.

12202 *Ferrari, Gloria* The ancient temple on the Acropolis at Athens. AJA 106 (2002) 11-35.

12203 *Gitin, Seymour* The four-horned altar and sacred space: an archaeological perspective. Sacred time. 2002 ⇒2679. 95-123.

12204 *Gorzalczany, Amir* A baptismal font at Nir Gallim. ʿAtiqot 43 (2002) 115-126.

12205 *Graindorge, Catherine* Der Tempel des Amun-Re von Karnak zu Beginn der 18. Dynastie. Ägyptologische Tempeltagung. ÄAT 33, 3: 2002 ⇒721. 83-90.

12206 *Grossmann, Peter* Frühchristliche Kirchen im Gebiet des Ammon-Tempels von Luqsur. RQ 97 (2002) 17-39.

12207 *Gundlach, Rolf* 'Ich gebe dir das Königreich der Beiden Länder'—der ägyptische Tempel als politsches Zentrum. Ägyptologische Tempeltagung. ÄAT 33,3: 2002 ⇒721. 91-108.

12208 **Hawass, Zahi** The mysteries of Abu Simbel: Ramesses II and the temples of the Rising Sun. 2000 ⇒16,11409. ^{R}JARCE 39 (2002) 252-253 (*Routledge, Carolyn*).

12209 **Held, Winfried** Milesische Forschungen, 2: das Heiligtum der Athena in Milet. 2000 ⇒16,11410. ^{R}AJA 106 (2002) 487-488 (*Carstens, Anne Marie*).

12210 *Hitchcock, Louise A.* Levantine horned altars: an Aegean perspective on the transformation of socio-religous reproduction. ^{F}FLANAGAN, J. JSOT.S 359: 2002 ⇒38. 233-249.

12211 **Hölzl, Regina** Ägyptische Opfertafeln und Kultbecken: eine Form- und Funktionsanalyse für das Alte, Mittlere und Neue Reich. HÄB 45: Hildesheim 2002, Gerstenberg xli; 221 pp. €45. 3-8067-8139-7. 17 pl. Bibl. xxi-xli. ^{R}BiOr 59 (2002) 504-509 (*Ernst, Herbert*).

12212 **Hurst, Henry** The sanctuary of Tanit at Carthage in the Roman period: a re-interpretation. 1999 ⇒15,11261. ^{R}Latomus 61 (2002) 264-265 (*Debergh, Jacques*).

12213 **Kockelmann, Holger** Die Toponymen- und Kultnamenlisten zur Tempelanlage von Dendera nach den hieroglyphischen Inschriften von Edfu und Dendera. ^{E}*Kurth, Dieter*: Inschriften des Tempels von Edfu, Begleithefte 3: Wsb 2002, Harrassowitz xiii (2); 299 pp. €96. 3-447-04580-9. Bibl. 281-299.

12214 *Lumsden, Stephen* Gavurkalesi: Investigations at a Hittite sacred place. ^{M}Güterbock, H. 2002 ⇒54. 111-125.

12215 *Magen, Yitzhak* The Crusader church of St. Mary in el-Bira. LASBF 51 (2001) 257-266.

12216 **Mari, Manuela** Al di là dell'Olimpo: Macedoni e grandi santuari della Grecia dall'età arcaica al primo ellenismo. Meletêmata 34: Athens 2002, Centro di ricerca sull'antichità greca e romana 391 pp. 960-7905-14-8. Bibl. 341-359 [RB 110,313].

12217 *May, Natalie Naomi; Stark, Stas Itzhak* Reconstruction of the architectural decor of the major synagogue at Korazim. ʿAtiqot 43 (2002) 207-252.

12218 *Mazzoni, Stefania* Temples in the city and the countryside: new trends in Iron Age Syria. DaM 13 (2002) 89-99.

12219 *McKenzie, Judith S.; Gibson, Sheila; Reyes, A.T.* Reconstruction of the Nabataean temple complex at Khirbet et-Tannur. PEQ 134 (2002) 44-83.

12220 *Milevski, I.* A new fertility figurine and new animal motifs from the chalcolithic in the southern Levant: finds from cave K-1 at Quleh, Israel. Paléorient 28/2 (2002) 133-142.

12221 *Mofidi-Nasrabadi, Behzad* Bemerkungen zum Aufbau der Ziqqurrat Etemenanki in Babylon. WO 32 (2002) 151-164.

12222 *Morenz, Ludwig D.* Die Götter und ihr Redetext: die ältestbelegte Sakral-Monumentalisierung von Textlichkeit auf Fragmenten der Zeit des Djoser aus Heliopolis. Ägyptologische Tempeltagung. ÄAT 33,3: 2002 ⇒721. 137-158.

12223 *Naʾaman, Nadav* The abandonment of cult places in the Kingdoms of Israel and Judah as acts of cult reform. UF 34 (2002) 585-602.

12224 **Nielsen, Inge** Cultic theatres and ritual drama, a study in regional development and religious interchange between east and west in antiquity. Aarhus studies in Mediterranean antiquity 4: Aarhus 2002, Aarhus Univ. Pr. 396 pp. 128 fig.

12225 **Ognibene, S.** La chiesa di Santo Stefano ad Umm al-Rasas: il problema iconofobico. Studia archaeologica 114: R 2002, Bretschneider 519 pp. €259. Ill.

12226 *Orthmann, Winfried* Ein neuer Antentempel in Tell Chuera. DaM 13 (2002) 3-9.

12227 *Piccirillo, Michele* La chiesa del vescovo Giovanni a Zizia. LASBF 52 (2002) 367-384.

12228 *Pierallini, Sibilla* Luoghi di culto sulla cittadella di Ḫattuša;

12229 *Popko, Maciej* Zu einigen Kultstätten zwischen Ḫattuša und Arinna. ᴹIMPARATI, F. 2002 ⇒61. 627-635/665-670.

12230 **Preys, René** Les complexes de la demeure du Sistre et du trône de Rê: théologie et décoration dans le temple d'Hathor à Dendera. OLA 106: Lv 2002, Peeters xxxiii; 635 pp. 90-429-1099-2. Bibl. 593-610.

12231 *Reade, J.E.* The ziggurrat and temples of Nimrud. Iraq 64 (2002) 135-216.

12232 *Ribichini, Sergio* Il sacello nel 'tofet'. ᴹCIASCA, A. 2002 ⇒15. 425-439.

12233 *Rosenberg, Stephen* Two Jewish temples in antiquity in Egypt. BAIAS 19-20 (2001-2002) 182-184.

12234 *Runesson, Anders* A monumental synagogue from the first century: the case of Ostia. JSJ 33 (2002) 171-220.

12235 *Scandone Matthiae, Gabriella* Un recipiente cultuale siriano del Bronzo Medio II. ᴹCIASCA, A. 2002 ⇒15. 481-488. 4 pl..

12236 **Schiff Giorgini, Michela** Soleb V: le temple: bas-reliefs et inscriptions. ᴱ*Beaux, Nathalie*: Bibliothèque générale 19: Le Caire 1998, Institut Français d'Archéologie Orientale. pag. var. 2-7247-0223-9. Collab. *Clément Robichon* et *Jean Leclant*; 335 ill.;

12237 Soleb III: le temple: description. ᴱ*Beaux, Nathalie*: Bibliothèque générale 23: Le Caire 2002, Institut Français d'Archéologie Orientale vi; 446 pp. 2-7247-0323-5. Collab. *Clément Robichon* et *Jean Leclant*.

12238 *Seeher, Jürgen* Ein Einblick in das Reichspantheon: das Felsenheiligtum vom Yazilikaya. Die Hethiter. 2002 ⇒535. 112-117;

12239 Heiligtümer-Kultstätten und multifunktionale Wirtschaftsbetriebe: der Große Tempel und das Tempelviertel der hethitischen Hauptstadt Ḫattusa. Die Hethiter. 2002 ⇒535. 134-139.

12240 *Stucky, Rolf A.* Das Heiligtum des Ešmun bei Sidon in vorhellenistischer Zeit. ZDPV 118 (2002) 66-86.

12241 *Taha, Hamdan* The sanctuary of Sheikh el-Qatrawani. LASBF 52 (2002) 441-456.

12242 *Thiem, Andrea-Christina* Anmerkungen zur Analyse der architektonischen und ikonographischen Konzeption des Speos von Gebel es-Silsileh. Ägyptologische Tempeltagung. ÄAT 33,3: 2002 ⇒721. 173-178.

12243 *Timm, Stefan* Ein assyrisch bezeugter Tempel in Samaria?. ᶠWEIPPERT, M.: OBO 186: 2002 ⇒133. 126-133.

12244 *Ullmann, Martina* Der Tempel Ramses' II. in Abydos als 'Haus der Millionen an Jahren'. Ägyptologische Tempeltagung. ÄAT 33,3: 2002 ⇒721. 179-200.

12245 *Van den Hout, Theo* Tombs and memorials: the (divine) stonehouse and Ḫegur reconsidered. ᴹGÜTERBOCK, H. 2002 ⇒54. 73-91.

12246 *Vella, Nicholas C.* The lie of the land: Ptolemy's temple of Hercules in Malta. ANESt 39 (2002) 83-112.

12247 *Vörös, Gyozo* Hungarian excavations on Thot Hill at the Temple of Pharao Montuhotep Sankhkara in Thebes (1995-1998). Ägyptologische Tempeltagung. ÄAT 33,3: 2002 ⇒721. 201-211.

12248 *Wilson, Karen* The temple mound at Bismaya. ᶠHANSEN, D.: 2002 ⇒58. 279-299.

12249 *Wimmer, Stefan* Y a-t-il eu des temples égyptiens en Israël/Palestine?. MSR 59/2 (2002) 7-22.

12250 *Zäh, Alexander* Die Basilika von Misti: eine unbekannte Kirche des 19. Jhs. im südlichen Kappadokien. WZKM 92 (2002) 205-216.

12251 *Zimansky, Paul* The 'Hittites' at 'Ain Dara. ᴹGÜTERBOCK, H. 2002 ⇒54. 177-191.

T3.8 **Funeraria;** *Sindon,* **the Shroud**

12252 *Altenmüller, Hartwig* Funerary boats and boat pits of the Old Kingdom. ArOr 70 (2002) 269-290.

12253 *Aviam, Mordechai; Syon, Danny* Jewish ossilegium in Galilee. ᶠFOERSTER, G. 2002 ⇒39. 151-187.

12254 *Barag, D.* New developments in the research of the tombs of the sons of Ḥezir and Zecharias. Qad. 35/1 (2002) 38-47. H.

12255 *Bareš, Ladislav* The shaft tomb of Iufaa at Abusir in 2001. ZÄS 129/2 (2002) 97-108.

12256   *Bar-Levav, Avriel* We are where we are not: the cemetery in Jewish culture. JewSt 41 (2002) 15*-46*.

12257   *Bárta, Miroslav* Sociology of the minor cemeteries during the Old Kingdom: a view from Abusir South. ArOr 70 (2002) 291-300.

12258   **Bárta, Miroslav** Memories of 4500 years ago. Praha 2002, Czech Institute of Egyptology 46 pp. 80-238-8726-2. 47 fig.; Photo: *Kamil Vodera*; Bibl. 46.

12259   *Buckley, Stephen* Les momies livrent leurs secrets. MoBi 145 (2002) 32-35.

12260   *Callender, Vivienne G.* A contribution to the burial of women in the Old Kingdom. ArOr 70 (2002) 301-308.

12261   *Clauss, Pascale* Les tours funéraires du Djebel Baghoûz dans l'histoire de la tour funéraire syrienne. Syria 79 (2002) 155-194.

12262   *Coppens, Filip* The wabet: an Old Kingdom mortuary workshop in a Graeco-Roman temple?. ArOr 70 (2002) 309-318.

12263   *Coulon, Laurent; Leclère, François* Les catacombes d'Osiris. MoBi 145 (2002) 46-49.

12264   **David, Rosalie; Rick, Archbold** Conversations with mummies: new light on the ancient Egyptians. 2000 ⇒16,11448. [R]ArOr 70 (2002) 82-84 (*Strouhal, Eugen*).

12265   **Davies, Penelope J.E.** Death and the emperor: Roman imperial funerary monuments, from AUGUSTUS to MARCUS AURELIUS. 2000 ⇒16,11449; 17,11167. [R]JRS 92 (2002) 237-238 (*Peña, J. Theodore*); CIR 52 (2002) 340-341 (*Newby, Zahra*).

12266   **Dayagi-Mendels, Michal** The Akhziv cemeteries: the Ben-Dor excavations, 1941-1944. IAA Reports 15: J 2002, Israel Antiquities Authority vi; 176 pp. 965-406-144-9.

12267   *De Cesari, Chiara* Graves as public space?: some questions about possible 'public' aspects of graves and cemeteries in ancient Mesopotamia. AltOrF 29 (2002) 355-366.

12268   *Demarée, Robert Johannes O.* Heidelberg Inv. Nr. 567: fragment of a necropolis journal. ZÄS 129/2 (2002) 109-114.

12269   *Dodson, Aidan* Duke Alexander's sarcophagi. ArOr 70 (2002) 329-336.

12270   *Dunand, Françoise; Lichtenberg, Roger* Découverte d'une nécropole d'animaux. MoBi 145 (2002) 50-53.

12271   *Dunan, Françoise* De la cendre à la myrrhe: les usages du corps mort en Égypte tardive. Religions méditerranéennes. 2002 ⇒756. 101-119.

12272   *Edelstein, Gershon* A section of the Hellenistic-Roman cemetery at Berit Aḥim, north of 'Akko (Acre). Sum. 257. **H.**;

12273   Two burial caves from the Roman period near Tel Qedesh. Sum. 259. 'Atiqot 43 (2002) 75*-98*/99*-105*. **H.**

12274   **El-Shohoumi, Nadia; Schwarz, Mario** Der Tod im Leben: eine vergleichende Analyse altägyptischer und rezenter ägyptischer Totenbräuche, eine phänomenologische Studie. DÖAW 27; Untersuchungen der Zweigstelle Kairo des Österreichischen Archäologischen Institutes 22: W 2002, Verl. d. Österr. Akad. d. Wiss. 352 pp. €98. 3-7001-3151-8.

12275   [E]**Empereur, Jean-Yves; Nenna, Marie-Dominique** Nécropolis 1. Études alexandrines 5: 2001 ⇒17,11170. [R]REG 115 (2002) 417-418 (*Sève, Michel*).

12276   *Filer, Joyce M.* Ancient bodies, but modern techniques: the utilisation of CT scanning in the study of ancient Egyptian mummies. The archaeology of medicine. [E]**Arnott, Robert**: Oxf 2002, Archaeopress. 33-40.
12277   **Ghiberti, Giuseppe** Sindone, le immagini, 2002. T 2002, ODPF 18 pp. 88-88441-06-9. 37 pl.
12278   Goldsarg des Echnaton nun komplett in Kairo. WUB 24 (2002) 78.
12279   **Gomaà, Farouk; Hegazy, El Sayed Aly** Die neuentdeckte Nekropole von Athribis. ÄAT 48: 2001 ⇒17,11176. [R]BiOr 59 (2002) 304-305 (*Meulenaere, H.J.A. de*).
12280   *Grévin, Gilles; Bailet, Paul* La crémation à l'époque ptolémaïque. MoBi 145 (2002) 36-39.
12281   **Guerrera,Vittorio** The Shroud of Turin: a case for authenticity. 2000 ⇒16,11454. [R]HPR 102/7 (2002) 76, 78-79 (*Allen, Michael*).
12282   *Hauptmann, A., al.*, Chemical compostion and lead isotopy of metal objects from the 'royal' tomb and other related finds at Arslantepe, eastern Anatolia. Paléorient 28/2 (2002) 43-70.
12283   *Hendrickx, Stan; Bavay, Laurent* The relative chronological position of Egyptian predynastic and early dynastic tombs with objects imported from the Near East and the nature of interregional contacts. Egypt and the Levant. 2002 ⇒497. 58-80.
12284   **Janot, Francis** Les instruments d'embaumement de l'Égypte ancienne. 2000 ⇒16,11460. [R]BiOr 59 (2002) 77-80 (*Filer, Joyce M.*).
12285   *Janßen, Ursula* Die frühbronzezeitlichen Gräberfelder von Halawa, Shamseddin, Djerniye, Tawi und Wreide am mittleren Euphrat: Versuch einer Datierung und Deutung sozialer Strukturen anhand multivariater statistischer Verfahren (Korrespondenzanalyse und Seriation). UF 34 (2002) 223-313.
12286   *Jánosi, Peter* Aspects of mastaba development: the position of shafts and the identification of tomb owners. ArOr 70 (2002) 337-350.
12287   [E]**Jenni, Hanna** Das Grab Ramses' X. (KV 18). Aegyptiaca Helvetica 16: 2000 ⇒16,11461. [R]BiOr 59 (2002) 68-70 (*Dodson, Aidan*).
12288   **Jeppesen, Christian** The Maussolleion at Halikarnassos: reports of the Danish Archaeological Expedition to Bodrum, 5: the superstructure: a comparative analysis of the architectural, sculptural, and literary evidence. Jutland Archaeological Society Publications 15/5: Höjbjerg 2002, Jutland Archaeological Society 265 pp. €34. 87-88415-15-5. 176 fig.
12289   *Jong, Lidewijde de* Aspects of Roman burial practices in Beirut: on Romanization and cultural exchange. Aram 13 (2001-2002) 293-312.
12290   **Jørgensen, Morgens** Catalogue Egypt 3: coffins, mummy adornments and mummies form the third Intermediate, Late, Ptolemaic and the Roman periods (1080 BC-AD 400). 2001 ⇒17,11186. [R]ArOr 70 (2002) 439-441 (*Janák, Jiří*).
12291   **Kanawati, Naguib; Abdel-Raziq, Mahmud**, *al.*, The Teti cemetery at Saqqara VI: the tomb of Nikauisesi. 2000 ⇒16,11462. [R]OLZ 97 (2002) 494-497 (*Grunert, Stefan*); BiOr 59 (2002) 509-520 (*Moreno Garcia, Juan Carlos*).
12292   **Kanawati, Naguib** The tomb and beyond: burial customs of Egyptian officials. 2001 ⇒17,11187. [R]DiscEg 53 (2002) 89-92 (*DuQuesne, Terence*); Prudentia 34/1 (2002) 92-93 (*Spalinger, Anthony*).

12293   *Kletter, Raz* An intermediate Bronze Age tomb at Shoham. 'Atiqot 43 (2002) 25*-28* Sum. 254. **H**.
12294   *Kloner, Amos* Iron Age burial caves in Jerusalem and its vicinity. BAIAS 19-20 (2001-2002) 95-118.
12295   *Koch, Guntram* Jüdische Sarkophage der Kaiserzeit und der Spätantike. [F]FOERSTER, G. 2002 ⇒39. 189-210.
12296   **Koch, Guntram** Frühchristliche Sarkophage. Handbuch der Archäologie. 2000 ⇒16,11464. [R]GGA 254 (2002) 28-46 (*Dresken-Weiland, Jutta*).
12297   [E]**Koch, Guntram** Akten des Symposiums 'Frühchristliche Sarkophage'. Sarkophag-Studien 2: Mainz 2002, Von Zabern viii; 258 pp. €92.50. 3-8053-2880-X. Marburg, 30.6.-4.7.1999. 88 pl..
12298   **Korolëv, Andrej; Sidel'tsev, Andrej** Hittite funerary ritual: sallis wastais. AOAT 288: Müns 2002, Ugarit-Verlag ix; 973 pp. 3-9346-28-16-8. Bibl. 1-8.
12299   *Kuraszkiewicz, Kamil Omar* Inscribed objects from the Old Kingdom necropolis west of the Step Pyramid (with remarks on their white coating). ArOr 70 (2002) 351-376.
12300   **Labrousse, Audran; Moussa, Ahmed M.** La chaussée du complexe funéraire du roi Ounas. Bibliothèque d'étude 134: Le Caire 2002, Institut Français d'Archéologie Orientale (4); 216 pp. 2-724-7-0311-1. Bibl. 201-204.
12301   *Laurant, Sophie* Exposition d'Arles: pratiques funéraires d'ALEXANDRE à CLÉOPÂTRE. MoBi 145 (2002) 40-45.
12302   **Lembke, K.** Phönizische anthropoide Sarkophage. Damaszener Forschungen 10: 2001 ⇒17,11188. [R]BiOr 59 (2002) 405-408 (*Bonatz, Dominik*).
12303   *Livingston, David* A Middle Bronze Age II and Iron Age I tomb (no. 65) at Khirbet Nisya. 'Atiqot 43 (2002) 17-35.
12304   **Lull, J.** Las tumbas reales egipcias del Tercer Periodo Intermedio (dinastías XXI-XXV). BAR International Series 1045: Oxf 2002, Archaeopress 326 pp. £42. 1-84171-426-7.
12305   *Magen, Y.* Tombs decorated in Jerusalem style in Samaria and the Hebron hills. Qad. 35/1 (2002) 28-37. **H**.
12306   *Martinez, Philippe* La fabrique du mort. MoBi 145 (2002) 18-23.
12307   **Málek, J.**, *al.*, Saqqara No. 60 (D 22): le mastaba de Ti Tombes et Mastabas de l'Egypte ancienne. P 2002, Livet 25 pp. 69 slides.
12308   **McFarlane, Ann** The Unis cemetery at Saqqara 1: the tomb of Irukaptah. 2000 ⇒16,11473. [R]BiOr 59 (2002) 295-397 (*Baud, M.*); OLZ 97 (2002) 494-497 (*Grunert, Stefan*).
12309   [E]**Minor, Michael; Adler, Alan D.; Piczek, Isabel** The Shroud of Turin: unraveling the mystery: proceedings of the 1998 Dallas Symposium. Alexander, NC 2002, Alexander 368 pp. 1-57090-16-8-6.
12310   *Mojsov, Bojana* Sacred pathways. [F]HANSEN, D. 2002 ⇒58. 139-43.
12311   *Monchot, H.; Horwitz, L.K.* Représentation squelettique au paléolithique inférieur, le site d'Holon (Israël). Paléorient 28/2 (2002) 71-86.
12312   *Morales, Antonio J.* El ritual funerario en el Reino Antiguo: los oficiantes. AuOr 20 (2002) 123-146.
12313   *Nahshoni, Pirhiya, al.*, A rock-cut burial cave from the second temple period at Ḥorbat Żefiyya, Judean Shephelah. 'Atiqot 43 (2002) 49-71.

12314 *Netzer, Ehud* The search for Herod's tomb. BAIAS 19-20 (2001-2002) 186-187.

12315 ᴱ**Pearce, John; Millett, Martin; Struck, Manuela** Burial, society and context in the Roman world. 2000 ⇒16,11477. ᴿCIR 52 (2002) 348-349 (*Hope, Valerie*).

12316 *Peleg, Yifat* Gender and ossuaries: ideology and meaning. BASOR 325 (2002) 65-73.

12317 *Perry, Megan A.* Life and death in Nabataea: the north ridge tombs and Nabataean burial practices. NEA (BA) 65 (2002) 265-270.

12318 *Porter, Anne* The dynamics of death: ancestors, pastoralism, and the origins of a third-millennium city in Syria. BASOR 325 (2002) 1-36.

12319 ᴱ**Pouthier, Jean-Luc** Tombeaux et momies d'Egypte. MoBi 145 (2002) 10-53.

12320 *Raven, Maarten J.* Les fouilles de Leyde dans la tombe de Méryneith à Saqqara campagnes 2001-2002. BSFE 155 (2002) 11-31.

12321 *Regev, Eyal* Family burial in Herodianic Jerusalem and its environs and the social organization of immigrants and sectarians. Cathedra 106 (2002) 35-60 Sum. 204. **H**.

12322 *Riggs, Christian* Facing the dead: recent research on the funerary art of Ptolemaic and Roman Egypt. AJA 106 (2002) 85-101.

12323 **Rose, John** Tomb KV39 in the Valley of the Kings: a double archaeological enigma. 2000 ⇒16,11483. ᴿBiOr 59 (2002) 299-301 (*Wilkinson, Richard H.*).

12324 *Roth, Ann Macy* The meaning of menial labor: 'servant statues' in Old Kingdom serdabs. JARCE 39 (2002) 103-121.

12325 *Rzeuska, Teodozja Izabela* The necropolis at West Saqqara: the late Old Kingdom shafts with no burial chamber: were they false, dummy, unfinished or intentional?. ArOr 70 (2002) 377-402.

12326 **Sartre-Fauriat, Annie** Des tombeaux et des morts. 2001 ⇒17, 11215. ᴿBiOr 59 (2002) 638-644 (*Wright, G.R.H.*).

12327 *Scurlock, JoAnn* Soul emplacements in ancient Mesopotamian funerary rituals. Magic and divination. 2002 ⇒729. 1-6.

12328 **Sowada, K.; Callaghan, T.; Bentley, P.** Minor burials and other material. Teti Cemetery at Saqqara 4: 1999 ⇒16,11491. ᴿOLZ 97 (2002) 490-494 (*Forstner-Müller, Irene*).

12329 *Strouhal, Eugen* The relation of Iufaa to persons found beside his shaft-tomb at Abusir. ArOr 70 (2002) 403-414.

12330 **Strudwick, N.; Strudwick, H.M.** The tombs of Amenhotep, Khnumose, and Amenmose at Thebes. 1996 ⇒12,9981... 15, 11359. ᴿCEg 153-154 (2002) 170-172 (*Spieser, Cathie*).

12331 *Stuart, Barbara* Cemeteries in Beirut. Aram 13 (2001-2002) 87-112.

12332 *Sussman, Varda* An IAA sarcophagus adorned with personal objects. IEJ 52 (2002) 64-80.

12333 **Thomas, Thelma K.** Late antique Egyptian funerary sculpture. 2000 ⇒16,11494; 17,11220. ᴿByZ 95 (2002) 152-155 (*Grossmann, Peter*).

12334 *Van der Horst, Pieter W.* The tombs of the prophets in early Judaism. Japheth. CBET 32: 2002 <2001> ⇒251. 119-137.

12335 *Webb, S.G.; Edwards, P.C.* The Natufian human skeletal remains from Wadi Hammeh 27 (Jordan). Paléorient 28/1 (2002) 103-123.

12336 ᴱ**Weeks, Kent R.** KV 5:a preliminary report on the excavation of the tomb of the sons of Rameses II in the Valley of the Kings. 2000 ⇒16,11497. ᴿJARCE 39 (2002) 251-252 (*Wilkinson, Richard H.*); JSSEA 29 (2002) 123-126 (*Brand, Peter J.*).

12337 *Winkes, Rolf* A dionysiac sarcophagus at Roger William Park. ᶠFOERSTER, G. 2002 ⇒39. 19-27.

12338 **Worschech, Udo** Cromlechs, Dolmen und Menhire: Beiträge zur Erforschung der antiken Moabitis (Ard El-Kerak), 2: vergleichende Studien zu vor- und frühgeschichtlichen Grabanlagen in Jordanien. Fra 2002, Lang 130 pp. 37 ill.; 10 photos. ᴿADAJ 46 (2002) 629-631 (*Kafafi, Zeidan A.*).

12339 *Yannai, Eli* Imported finds from the ʿEin Assawir tombs (Israel) and their significance in understanding the chronological synchronization between Israel, Egypt, and eastern Anatolia. Egypt and the Levant. 2002 ⇒497. 334-345;

12340 An Iron Age burial cave at Et-Ṭaiyiba. ʿAtiqot 43 (2002) 29*-55* Sum. 255. **H.**

12341 *Yezerski, Irit; Lender, Yeshaʿyahu* An Iron Age II burial cave at Lower Ḥorbat ʿAnim. ʿAtiqot 43 (2002) 57*-73* Sum. 256. **H.**

T3.9 *Numismatica,* coins

12342 *Abramzon, M.G.* Astral symbols in Roman coinage: origin and development of coin types. Journal of Ancient History 240 (2002) 122-142 Sum. 142. **R.**

12343 *Berman, Ariel; Bijovsky, Gabriela* The coins from Nevé Ur. ʿAtiqot 43 (2002) 177-184.

12344 *Bijovsky, Gabriela* Appendix 1: the coins. ᶠFOERSTER, G. 2002 ⇒ 39. 507-512.

12345 *Butcher, Kevin* The coin assemblages from Bey 006 and Bey 045. Aram 13 (2001-2002) 227-236.

12346 *Butcher, Kevin, al.,* Small change in ancient Beirut: the coin finds from BEY 006 and BEY 045: Persian, Hellenistic, Roman, and Byzantine periods. Archaeology of the Beirut Souks AUB and ACRE excavations in Beirut, 1994-1996, 1. Ber. 45-46 (2001-2002) 7-304. 23 pl.

12347 **Depeyrot, Georges** La numismatique antique et médiévale en occident: problèmes et méthodes. P 2002, Errance 126 pp. 2-87772-23-8-4. Bibl. 115-118.

12348 *Frolova, N.A.* The corpus of Sindian coins (first half - end of the V C. BC). Journal of Ancient History 242 (2002) 71-84 Sum. 84. **R.**

12349 **Howgego, Christopher** La storia antica attraverso le monete. ᵀ*Bolis, Alessia*: R 2002, Quasar xviii; 216 pp.

12350 *Kool, Robert* Coins at Vadum Jacob: new evidence on the circulation of money in the Latin Kingdom of Jerusalem during the second half of the twelfth century. Crusades 1 (2002) 73-88.

12351 *Kool, Robert; Ariel, Donald T.* Coins from the salvage excavations at Meron. ʿAtiqot 43 (2002) 109-114.

12352 *Kushnir-Stein, Alla* The coinage of Agrippa II. SCI 21 (2002) 123-131.

12353 **Le Rider, G.** La naissance de la monnaie: pratiques monétaires de l'Orient ancien. P 2001, Presses Universitaires de France 286 pp 8 pl. ᴿTEuph 24 (2002) 148-151 (*Elayi, J.*).

12354 **Meshorer, Ya'akov; Qedar, Shraga** Samarian coinage. 1999 ⇒ 15,11377. [R]TEuph 24 (2002) 152-153 (*Lemaire, A.*).

12355 *Mildenberg, L.* On some coin images of 4th century Persian Transeuphratesia: fact and conjecture (résumé). TEuph 23 (2002) 155.

12356 *Naghaway, Aida; Ajaj, Ahmad* A statistical study of the Jordan archaeological museum numismatic collections. ADAJ 46 (2002) 133*-152*. **A.**

12357 **Nicolet-Pierre, Hélène** Numismatique grecque. 'U', histoire: P 2002, Colin 302 pp.

12358 **Noeske, H.-Chr.** Die Münzen der Ptolemäer. 2000 ⇒16,11520; 17,11242. [R]HZ 274 (2002) 158-159 (*Huß, Werner*).

12359 *Radner, Karen* Zu den frühesten lydischen Münzprägungen aus der Sicht Assyriens. Brückenland Anatolien?. 2002 ⇒453. 45-57.

12360 *Schaper, Joachim* Numismatik, Epigraphie, alttestamentliche Exegese und die Frage nach der politischen Verfassung des achämedischen Juda. ZDPV 118 (2002) 150-168.

12361 **Sear, D.R.** Roman coins and their values, 1: the Republic and the twelve Caesars 280 BC - AD 96. [5]2000 ⇒16,11525. [R]JRS 92 (2002) 217-218 (*Sugden, Keith*).

12362 *Strickert, Fred* The first woman to be portrayed on a Jewish coin: Julia Sebaste. JSJ 33 (2002) 65-91.

12363 *Tietz, Werner* Der westlykische Münzstandard zwischen Athen und Persien. Brückenland Anatolien?. 2002 ⇒453. 59-67.

12364 **Vagi, D.L.** Coinage and history of the Roman Empire. 2000 ⇒16, 11527. [R]JRS 92 (2002) 216-217 (*Sugden, Keith*).

12365 *Vismara, N.* Evidenze religiose sulla monetazione arcaica della Lycia: elementi per una prima discussione. TEuph 23 (2002) 101-127. Pl. IX.

12366 *Waner, Mira; Safrai, Ze'ev* A catalogue of coin hoards and the shelf life of coins in Palestine hoards during the Roman-Byzantine periods. LASBF 51 (2001) 305-336.

T4.3 **Jerusalem**, *archaeologia* **et historia**

12367 *Alliata, Eugenio; Pierri, Rosario* Il Monte degli Ulivi nella *Demonstratio evangelica* di EUSEBIO di Cesarea. LASBF 52 (2002) 307-320.

12368 *Alliata, Eugenio* Che cosa sappiamo (e cosa non sappiamo) della tomba di Cristo. TS(I) (2002) 34-35, 47-48.

12369 [E]**Ariel, Donald T.** Excavations at the City of David V 1978-1985: extramural areas. Qedem 40: 2000 ⇒16,11535; 17,11248. [R]ZDPV 118 (2002) 87-92 (*Weippert, Helga*).

12370 *Bahat, Dan* Identification of the gates of the Temple Mount and the 'Cave' in the early Muslim period. Cathedra 106 (2002) 61-86 Sum. 204. **H.**

12371 *Barkay, Gabriel; Fantalkin, Alexander; Tal, Oren* A late Iron Age fortress north of Jerusalem. BASOR 328 49-71.

12372 **Ben-Dov, Meir** Historical atlas of Jerusalem. [T]*Louvish, David*: NY 2002, Continuum 400 pp. $50. 0-8264-1379-X [BiTod 40,197— Senior, Donald].

12373 **Biddle, Martin** The tomb of Christ. 1999 ⇒15,11389. [R]Cathedra 105 (2002) 181-184 (*Patrich, Joseph*);

12374 Die Grabeskirche in Jerusalem. 2000 ⇒16,11543. ᴿOrthFor 16 (2002) 55-57 (*Müller, Andreas*).

12375 **Bontao-Baccarl, Stéphanie** La mausolée en *opus reticulatum* de Jérusalem: tombeau d'Hérode ou simple témoin d'un modèle romain?. Latomus 61 (2002) 67-87.

12376 *Borrmans, Maurice* Gerusalemme nella tradizione religiosa musulmana. Pace e guerra. 2002 ⇒600. 203-220.

12377 *Cabezón Martín, Agripino* Las grutas del Parque de la Independencia de Jerusalén, ¿un mithraeum? LASBF 52 (2002) 297-306.

12378 *Cobbing, Felicity* The Cedric Norman Johns archive in the collections of the Palestine Exploration Fund. PEQ 134 (2002) 169-172.

12379 **Döpp, Heinz-Martin** Die Deutung der Zerstörung Jerusalems und des Zweiten Tempels in Jahre 70 in den ersten drei Jahrhunderten n. Chr. TANZ 24: 1998 ⇒14,10614; 15,11401. ᴿVigChr 56 (2002) 305-306 (*Poorthuis, Marcel*).

12380 *Drake, R. Trywhitt* The Basilica of the Holy Sepulchre—1874. Holy Land (Autumn 2002) 2-15, 36-38.

12381 *Dumm, Demetrius* Jerusalem: political idol or sacred place?. BiTod 40 (2002) 19-24.

12382 *Engelen, Jan* Jeruzalem—de heilige stad!: een retouche. ITBT 10/7 (2002) 15-17.

12383 ᴱ**Geva, Hillel** Jewish Quarter excavations in the Old City of Jerusalem: conducted by Nahman AVIGAD, 1969-1982, 1: architecture and stratigraphy: areas A, W and X-2, final report. 2000 ⇒16, 11563. ᴿRBLit (2002)* (*Killebrew, Ann E.*).

12384 **Gonen, Rivka**, *al.*, Excavations at Efrata: a burial ground from the Intermediate and Middle Bronze Ages. IAA Reports 12: J 2001, Israel Antiquities Authority 153 pp. 965-406-076-0.

12385 *Grabbe, Lester L.* The Hellenistic city of Jerusalem. Jews in... cities. 2002 ⇒719. 6-21.

12386 *Hendrickx, Benjamin* The "abominatio desolationis", standing in the holy place: remarks on the conquest of Jerusalem and the "pact" between Muslims and Christians. APB 13 (2002) 165-176.

12387 **Hjelm, Ingrid** Jerusalem's rise to sovereignty in ancient tradition and history. K 2002, Diss. Copenhagen [StTh 57,76].

12388 *Hübner, Ulrich* Jerusalem und die Jebusiter. ᶠWEIPPERT, M.: OBO 186: 2002 ⇒133. 31-42.

12389 *Jacobson, David* Herod's Roman temple. BArR 28/2 (2002) 19-27, 60-61.

12390 *Kalimi, Isaac* The capture of Jerusalem in the Chronistic history. VT 52 (2002) 66-79 [1 Chr 11,6].

12391 **Kark, Ruth; Oren-Nordheim, Michal** Jerusalem and its environs: quarters, neighbourhoods, villages 1800-1948. J 2001, Magnes 445 pp.

12392 *Keel, Othmar* Das kanaanäische Jerusalem;

12393 Jerusalem, Heilige Stadt der drei Religionen. Die Bibel: Geschichte und Gegenwart. 2002 ⇒971. 98-99/110-111.

12394 *Kletter, Raz* Temptation to identify: Jerusalem, *mmšt*, and the *lmlk* jar stamps. ZDPV 118 (2002) 136-149.

12395 *Kloner, Amos; Zissu, Boaz* The "Caves of Simeon the Just" and "The minor Sanhedrin": two burial complexes from the second temple period in Jerusalem. FFOERSTER, G. 2002 ⇒39. 125-149.

12396   **Krüger, Jürgen** Die Grabeskirche zu Jerusalem: Geschichte—Gestalt—Bedeutung. 2000 ⇒16,11587. [R]CFr 72 (2002) 802-803 (*Gieben, Servus*).

12397   *Kuhrt, Amélie* Sennacherib's siege of Jerusalem. [F]MILLAR, F. 2002 ⇒79.13-33 [2 Kgs 18-20; 2 Chr 29-32; Isa 36-37].

12398   *Leithart, Peter J.* Where was ancient Zion?. TynB 53 (2002) 161-175.

12399   **Leppäkari, Maria** The end is a beginning: contemporary apocalyptic representations of Jerusalem. Åbo 2002, Diss. Åbo Akademi [StTh 57,77].

12400   *Lerner, Constantine* Sara Miapor: an Armenian character in The life of St. Nino and Jerusalem. Armenians in Jerusalem. Hebrew University Armenian studies 4: 2002 ⇒771. 111-119.

12401   *Luzzatto, Amos* Gerusalemme ebraica. Pace e guerra. 2002 ⇒600. 191-196.

12402   *Maarten van Lint, Theo* The poem of lamentation over the capture of Jerusalem written in 1189 by Grigor Tlay Catholicos of all Armenians. Armenians in Jerusalem. 2002 ⇒771. 121-142.

12403   **Magen, Yitzhak** The stone vessel industry in the second temple period: excavations at Hizma and the Jerusalem Temple Mount. [E]Tsfania, Levana: J 2002, Israel Exploration Society xiii; 186 pp. 965-221-048-X. Bibl. 181-186.

12404   *Manoogian, Sylvia Natalie* Libraries of Armenian Jerusalem. Armenians in Jerusalem. 2002 ⇒771. 143-155.

12405   *Marguerat, Daniel* Le conflit des interprétations en histoire: lectures juives et chrétiennes de la chute de Jérusalem. [F]HAMMANN, G. 2002 ⇒57. 249-268 [BuBB 38,90].

12406   **Mazar, Eilat** The complete guide to the Temple Mount excavations. J 2002, Shoham xvi; 120 pp. 965-90299-1-8. Bibl. 120.

12407   *Mébarki, Farah* Jerusalem: die Treppen des Herodes. WUB 23 (2002) 65.

12408   *Nagar, Yossi* Human skeletal remains from the Mamilla Cave, Jerusalem. 'Atiqot 43 (2002) 141-148.

12409   *Nowell, Irene* Jerusalem: our city of peace. BiTod 40 (2002) 12-18.

12410   *Papazian, Dennis R.* The contribution of Armenian Jerusalem to Armenians in America. Armenians in Jerusalem. Hebrew University Armenian studies 4: 2002 ⇒771. 167-191.

12411   *Patrich, Joseph* On the lost circus of Aelia Capitolina. SCI 21 (2002) 173-188;

12412   Herod's theatre in Jerusalem: a new proposal. IEJ 52 (2002) 231-9.

12413   **Peri, Oded** Christianity under Islam in Jerusalem: the question of the holy sites in early Ottoman times. 2001 ⇒17,11286. [R]BSOAS 65 (2002) 586-588 (*Finkel, Caroline*).

12414   *Reich, R.* The virtual model at the Davidson Center near the Temple Mount and the reconstruction of the royal stoa. Qad. 35/1 (2002) 48-52. **H.**;

12415   The international archaeological excavation project at the City of David during the British Mandate. Qad. 35/1 (2002) 53-57. **H.**

12416   *Reich, Ronny; Billig, Yaʿakov* Triple play: the many lives of Jerusalem's builing blocks. BArR 28/5 (2002) 40-47.

12417   *Reich, Ronny; Shukron, Eli* Reconsidering the Karstic theory as an explanation to the cutting of Hezekiah's tunnel in Jerusalem. BASOR 325 (2002) 75-80.

12418 *Reich, Ronny; Shukron, Eli* The western extramural quarter of Byzantine Jerusalem. Armenians in Jerusalem. Hebrew University Armenian studies 4: 2002 ⇒771. 193-201.

12419 *Reynolds, Susan* Fiefs and vassals in twelfth-century Jerusalem: a view from the west. Crusades 1 (2002) 29-48.

12420 *Seligman, Jon* Jerusalem's ancient walls strike again: the Knights' Palace Hotel. 'Atiqot 43 (2002) 73-85.

12421 *Sembrano, Lucio* Gerusalemme: città-sposa e sposa-città: l'inesauribile forza di un simbolo di eternità. Tempo ed eternità. 2002 ⇒ 545. 129-140.

12422 *Shanks, Hershel* Droht ein Einsturz der Südmauer des Tempelbergs in Jerusalem?. WUB 24 (2002) 78.

12423 *Silvestrini, Achille* La presenza cristiana a Gerusalemme. Pace e guerra. 2002 ⇒600. 197-202.

12424 **Tichit, Agnès** Jérusalem, ville unique. La Bible Tout Simplement: P 2002, L'Atelier 128 pp. €13.

12425 *Tilly, Michael* Unter fremder Herrschaft: Jerusalem von der Spätantike bis zur Gründung Israels. Damals 34/12 (2002) 24-30.

12426 **Tilly, Michael** Jerusalem—Nabel der Welt: Überlieferung und Funktionen von Heiligtumstraditionen im antiken Judentum. [D]*Mayer, G.*: Stu 2002, Kohlhammer ix; 307 pp. €35. 3-17-017265-4. Diss.-Habil. Mainz 2001.

12427 *Tworuschka, Udo* Angewandte Religionswissenschaft—am Beispiel der Heiligen Stätten in Jerusalem. BThZ 19 (2002) 5-24.

12428 *Wagemakers, B.* De vlucht naar Pella: een oude discussie en een nieuwe suggestie. NedThT 56/2 (2002) 89-98.

12429 *Wenning, Robert* Der Abendmahlssaal: ein historisch-archäologischer Überblick. BiKi 57 (2002) 46-49.

12430 *Zanger, Walter* The elusive Mount Zion. JBQ 30 (2002) 179-182.

12431 *Zuckerman, Constantine* Jerusalem as the center of the earth in Anania Širkac'i's Ašxarhac'oyc'. Armenians in Jerusalem. Hebrew University Armenian studies 4: 2002 ⇒771. 255-274.

T4.4 Judaea, Negeb; *situs alphabetice*

12432 **Bagatti, Bellarmino** Ancient christian villages of Judaea and the Negev. [T]*Rotondi, Paul*: SBF.CMi 42: J 2002, Franciscan Printing Pr. 231 pp. $30. 965-516-046-7. Bibl. 11-14.

12433 *Blakely, Jeffrey A.; Hardin, James W.* Southwestern Judah in the late eight century B.C.E. BASOR 326 (2002) 11-64.

12434 *Blakely, Jeffrey A.* Reconciling two maps: archaeological evidence for the kingdom of David and Solomon. BASOR 327 (2002) 49-54

12435 *Braun, Eliot* Egypt's first sojourn in Canaan;

12436 *Commenge, Catherine; Alon, David* Competitive involution and expanded horizons: exploring the nature of interaction between northern Negev and lower Egypt (c. 4500-3600 BCE). Egypt and the Levant. 2002 ⇒497. 173-189/139-153.

12437 *Golani, Amir; Segal, Dror* Redefining the onset of the early Bronze Age in the southern Canaan: new evidence of 14C dating from Ashkelon Afridar. [F]GOPHNA, R. 2002 ⇒49. 135-154.

12438 [E]**Wexler, Lior**, *al.*, Surveys and excavations of caves in the northern Judean Desert (CNJD)—1993. [T]*Glick, Don; Pommerantz, In-*

na: 'Atiqot 41. J 2002, Israel Antiquities Authority 2 vols; xv; 276; xviii; 304 pp. 965-406-149-X.

12439   *Aḥwqat*: *Finkelstein, Israel* El-Aḥwqat: a fortified sea people city?. IEJ 52 (2002) 187-199.

12440   *Arad*: *Herzog, Ze'ev* The fortress mound at Tel Arad: an interim report. TelAv 29/1 (2002) 3-109.

12441   *Ashkelon*: *Mébarki, Farah* Aschkelon: Tor der Mittelbronzezeit restauriert. WUB 23 (2002) 65-66.

12442   *Beersheba*: *Herzog, Z.* Water supply at Tel Beersheba. Qad. 35 (2002) 87-101. **H.**;

12443   *Knauf, Ernst Axel* Who destroyed Beersheba II?. [F]WEIPPERT, M.: OBO 186: 2002 ⇒133. 181-195;

12444   *Milevski, Ianir; Bankirer, Rina Y.* Excavations at Ramot Be'er Sheva', site 47. 'Atiqot 43 (2002) 1-16;

12445   *Nahshoni, Pirhiya, al.*, A chalcolithic site at Ramot Nof, Be'er Sheva'. 'Atiqot 43 (2002) 1*-24* Sum. 253. **H.**

12446   *El-Khirbe*: *Hizmi, H.* El-Khirbe—an Iron Age fortress east of Jerusalem at the edge of the desert. Qad. 35 (2002) 102-107. **H.**

12447   *'En Boqeq*: **Fischer, Moshe; Gichon, Mordechai; Tal, Oren,** *al.*, 'En Boqeq: excavations in an oasis on the Dead Sea, 2: the *officina*: an early Roman building on the Dead Sea shore. 2000 ⇒16,11652. [R]AJA 106 (2002) 346-347 (*Magness, Jodi*).

12448   *Gat*: *Ehrlich, Carl Stephan* Die Suche nach Gat und die neuen Ausgrabungen auf Tell eṣ-Ṣafi. [F]WEIPPERT, M.: OBO 186: 2002 ⇒133. 56-69.

12449   *Gaza*: **Humbert, Jean-Baptiste** Gaza Méditerranéenne: histoire et archéologie en Palestine. 2000 ⇒16,11638. [R]TEuph 23 (2002) 205-207 (*Sapin, J.*).

12450   *Gezer*: *Finkelstein, Israel* Gezer revisited and revised. TelAv 29 (2002) 262-296.

12451   *Horvat Bor*: *Israel, Y.; Erickson-Gini, T.* Meṣad Horvat Bor. BAIAS 19-20 (2001-2002) 7-17.

12452   *'Ira*: [E]**Beit-Arieh, Itzhaq** Tel 'Ira: a stronghold in the biblical Negev. 1999 ⇒15,11463. [R]BiOr 59 (2002) 630-3 (*Steiner, Margreet*).

12453   *Jericho*: **Bar-Nathan, Rachel** Hasmonean and Herodian palaces at Jericho: final reports of the 1973-1987 excavations, v.3: the pottery. J 2002, Israel Exploration Society xi; 284 pp. $68. 965-221-0-47-1. 8 pl.;

12454   **Netzer, Ehud** Hasmonean and Herodian palaces at Jericho: final reports of the 1973-1987 excavations, v.1: stratigraphy and architecture. 2001 ⇒17,11317. [R]Qad. 106 (2002) 127 (*Hirschfeld, Y.*); BAIAS 19-20 (2001-2002) 180-181 (*Rosenberg, Stephen*).

12455   *Lachisch*: *Feldman, Steven* Return to Lachish. BArR 28/3 (2002) 46-51.

12456   *Malhata*: *Ilan, Ornit* Egyptian pottery from small Tel Malhata and the interrelations between the Egyptian 'colony' in southwest Palestine and the 'Canaanite' Arad basin and central highlands. Egypt and the Levant. 2002 ⇒497. 306-322.

12457   *Masada*: *Hirschfeld, Yizhar* The monastery of Marda: Masada in the Byzantine period. BAIAS 19-20 (2001-2002) 119-156; [E]**Talmon, S.** Masada VI 1999 ⇒4096.

12458 *Masada; Herodium; Qumran*: **Laperrousaz, Ernest-Marie** Trois hauts lieux de Judée: les palais-forteresses hérodiens de Massada et de l'Herodium: le couvent essénien de Qoumrân... 2001 ⇒17, 11323. [R]DSD 9 (2002) 414-417 (*Magness, Jodi*).

12459 *Megiddo*: [E]**Finkelstein, Israel; Ussishkin, David; Halpern, Baruch** Megiddo III—the 1992-1996 seasons. 2000 ⇒16,11690; 17, 11324. [R]BASOR 327 (2002) 80-83 (*Harrison, Timothy P.*).

12460 *Moreschet-Gat*: *Levin, Yigal* The search for Moresheth-Gath: a new proposal. PEQ 134 (2002) 28-36.

12461 *Moẓa*: *Greenhut, Z.; De Groot, A.* Moẓa: a Bronze and Iron Age village west of Jerusalem. Qad. 35/1 (2002) 12-17. H.

12462 *Naḥal Tillah*: *Kansa, Eric; Levy, Thomas E.* Ceramics, identity, and the role of the state: the view from Naḥal Tillah. Egypt and the Levant. 2002 ⇒497. 190-212.

12463 *Rekhes Nafha*: *Saidel, Benjamin Adam* The excavations at Rekhes Nafha 396 in the Negev Highlands, Israel. BASOR 325 (2002) 37-63.

12464 *Timnah* (Tel Batash): **Mazar, Amihai** Timnah (Tel Batash) I: stratigraphy and architecture: text/plans and sections. 1997 ⇒13, 10662. [R]JNES 61 (2002) 151-152 (*Joffe, Alexander H.*).

12465 *Yarmut*: *Miroschedji, Pierre de* Tel Yarmut, 1999: excavations and surveys. IEJ 52 (2002) 87-95.

T4.5 Samaria, Sharon

12466 **Bagatti, Bellarmino** Ancient christian villages of Samaria. [T]*Rotondi, Paul*: SBF.CMi 39: J 2002, Franciscan Printing Pr. 244 pp. $30. 965-516-034-3. 64 pl. [RB 110,309].

12467 *Kletter, Raz* People without burials?: the lack of Iron I burials in the central highlands of Palestine. IEJ 52 (2002) 28-48.

12468 **Van der Steen, Eveline Johanna** Tribes and territories in transition: the central east Jordan Valley and surrounding regions in the Late Bronze and Early Iron Ages: a study of the sources. [D]*Noort, E.*: 2002, 258 pp. Diss. Groningen [RTL 34,594].

12469 *Yahya, Adel* A Palestinian organization works to preserve sites in the West Bank in the midst of war. NEA (BA) 65 (2002) 279-281.

12470 **Zwingenberger, Uta** Dorfkultur der frühen Eisenzeit in Mittelpalästina. OBO 180: 2001 ⇒17,11332. [R]BiOr 59 (2002) 635-638 (*Van der Steen, Eveline J.*).

12471 *Aphek*: *Feldman, Steven* Return to Aphek. BArR 28/5 (2002) 52-59;

12472 [E]**Kochavi, Moshe; Beck, Pirhiyah; Yadin, Esther** Aphek-Antipatris 1: excavation of areas A and B: the 1972-1976 seasons. 2000 ⇒16,11704. [R]BASOR 327 (2002) 84-85 (*Joffe, Alexander H.*).

12473 *Apollonia-Arsuf*: [E]**Roll, Israel; Tal, Oren** Apollonia-Arsuf: final report of the excavations, v.1: Persian and Hellenistic periods. Tel Aviv University Monographs 16: 1999 ⇒15,11529; 17,11335. [R]TEuph 24 (2002) 163-166 (*Sapin, J.*).

12474 *Beth Ha'ameq*: *Givon, Shmuel* Beth Ha'ameq—village of shepherds and farmers from the Chalcolithic period and the early Bronze Age. [F]GOPHNA, R. 2002 ⇒49. 87-106.

12475   *Caesarea M*: Cotton, Hannah M.; Eck, Werner A new inscription from Caesarea Maritima and the local elite of Caesarea Maritima. [F]FOERSTER, G.: 2002 ⇒39. 375-391;

12476   [E]**Donaldson, Terence L.** Religious rivalries and the struggle for success in Caesarea Maritima. 2000 ⇒16,11708; 17,11336. [K]RBLit (2002)* (*Royalty, Robert M.*);

12477   **Holum, K.G.; Raban, A.; Patrich, J.,** *al.*, Caesarea papers, 2: Herod's temple, the provincial governor's praetorium and granaries, the later harbor, a gold coin hoard, and other studies. 1999 ⇒ 15,11532. [R]AJA 106 (2002) 109-110 (*Burrell, Barbara*);

12478   *Patrich, J.* Caesarea: the palace of the Roman procurator and the Byzantine governor; a storage complex and the starting stalls at the Herodian stadium. Qad. 35 (2002) 66-86. **H.**;

12479   The martyrs of Caesarea: the urban context. LASBF 52 (2002) 321-346.

12480   *Dor*: Stern, Ephraim Excavated at Gorgon Dor. BArR 28/6 (2002) 50-57;

12481   *Stewart, Andrew* Geschenke für die Archäologen. WUB 25 (2002) 63-64.

12482   *'Ein Assawir*: Yannai, Eli The northern Sharon in the Chalcolithic period and the beginning of the early Bronze Age in light of the excavations at 'Ein Assawir. [F]GOPHNA, R. 2002 ⇒49. 65-85.

12483   *Ḥorvat 'Etri*: Zisu, B.; Ganor, A. Ḥorvat 'Etri: the ruins of a second temple period Jewish village on the coastal plain. Qad. 35/1 (2002) 18-27.

12484   *'Izbet Ṣarṭa*: Shanks, Hershel After excavation: what happens when the archaeologists leave?. BArR 28/3 (2002) 40-44, 61.

12485   *Lod*: Van den Brink, Edwin C.M. An Egyptian presence at the late of the late Early Bronze Age I at Tel Lod, central coastal plain, Israel. Egypt and the Levant. 2002 ⇒497. 286-305.

12486   *Ramat Hanadiv*: **Hirschfeld, Yizhar** Ramat Hanadiv excavations: final report of the 1984-1998 seasons. 2000 ⇒16,11735; 17,11344. [R]Or. 71 (2002) 326-28 (*Piccirillo, Michele*); RBLit (2002)* (*Killebrew, Ann E.*); TEuph 24 (2002) 166-167 (*Sapin, J.*).

12487   *Shechem*: **Campbell, Edward F.; Wright, G.R.H.** Shechem III: the stratigraphy and architecture of Shechem/Tell Balâtah: v.1: text; v.2: the illustrations. American Schools of Oriental Research, Archaeological Reports 6: Boston, MA 2002, American Schools of Oriental Research 2 vols; xxii; 351 pp. $175/£125. 0-89757-062-6. Bibl. v.1, 343-351; 304 fig.; vol. 2: 175 ill.

12488   *Yavneh-Yam*: Fisher, M. Yavneh-Yam 1992-1999: interim report. Qad. 35/1 (2002) 2-11. **H.**

T4.6 **Galilaea**; *Golan*

12489   **Bagatti, Bellarmino** Ancient christian villages of Galilee. [T]*Rotondi, Paul*: SBF.CMi 37: 2001 ⇒17,11347. [K]RivBib 50 (2002) 246 (*Rolla, Armando*); BiOr 59 (2002) 618-619 (*Schoors, A.*).

12490   *Bieberstein, Sabine* Maria aus Magdala, Simon der Fischer und viele andere: Jüngerinnen und Jünger aus Galiläa. WUB 24 (2002) 48-53.

12491   *Biguzzi, Giancarlo* Note di archeologia biblica. ED 55 (2002) 143-151.

12492 **Chancey, Mark A.** The myth of a gentile Galilee. MSSNTS 118: C 2002, CUP xv; 229 pp. €59.20. 0-521-81487-1. Bibl. 183-218.

12493 **Frankel, Rafael,** *al.*, Settlement dynamics and regional diversity in ancient Upper Galilee: archaeological survey of Upper Galilee. IAA Reports 14: J 2001, Israel Antiquities Authority vi; 175 pp. 965-406-141-4. Bibl. 164-173.

12494 **Grootkerk, Salomon E.** Ancient sites in Galilee: a toponymic gazetteer. Culture and history of the ancient Near East 1: 2000 ⇒16, 11752. ᴿRBLit 4 (2002) 87-90 (*Atkinson, Kenneth*).

12495 *Laurant, Sophie* Galiläa, der Garten Israels. WUB 24 (2002) 4-5.

12496 **Reed, Jonathan L.** Archaeology and the Galilean Jesus. 2000 ⇒ 16,11755. ᴿHeyJ 43 (2002) 222-223 (*Taylor, N.H.*); AThR 84 (2002) 421-422 (*Hewitt, Marsha Aileen*); CBQ 64 (2002) 389-401 (*Hoppe, Leslie J.*); BBR 12 (2002) 273-280 (*Chilton, Bruce*); RBLit (2002)* (*Kerkeslager, Allen*); JBL 121 (2002) 757-760 (*Moreland, Milton*); JAAR 70 (2002) 928-931 (*Hadley, Judith M.*).

12497 *Rosenfeld, Ben-Zion* The Galilean valleys (*beq'aoth*) from the bible to the talmud. RB 109 (2002) 66-100.

12498 **Sawicki, Marianne** Crossing Galilee: architecture of contact in the occupied land of Jesus. 2000 ⇒16,11756; 17,11352. ᴿJBL 121 (2002) 760-762 (*Moreland, Milton*).

12499 *Zangenberg, Jürgen* Dorf und Stadt im neutestamentlichen Galiläa. WUB 24 (2002) 46-47.

12500 *Bethsaida*: ᴱ**Arav, Rami; Freud, Richard A.** Bethsaida: a city by the north shore of the Sea of Galilee, 2. 1999 ⇒15,11557; 16, 11761. ᴿRBLit 4 (2002) 84-87 (*Meyers, Carol*);

12501 *Rottloff, Andrea; Schipper, Friedrich* Das hellenistisch-frührömische Bethsaida: Archäologie und Geschichte einer Stadt zur Zeit Jesu. Ment. *Josephus*. PzB 11 (2002) 127-142;

12502 *Rottloff, Andrea* Bethsaida / Et Tell: die Geschichte seiner Erforschung. PzB 11 (2002) 99-101;

12503 Ein Ausblick in die christliche Wirkungsgeschichte: Bethsaida im Licht spätantiker und mittelalterlicher Pilgerberichte. PzB 11 (2002) 149-153;

12504 *Schipper, Friedrich* Zur Geographie des Gebietes um den See Gennesaret. PzB 11 (2002) 93-95;

12505 Das eisenzeitliche Bethsaida: Archäologie und Geschichte einer Stadt am See Gennesaret zur Zeit des alten Israel. PzB 11 (2002) 103-119.

12506 *Beth-Shan*: *Agady, S., al.*, Byzantine shops in the street of the monuments at Bet Shean (Scythopolis);

12507 *Foerster, Gideon* Skythopolis—Vorposten der Dekapolis. Gadara —Gerasa. 2002 ⇒485. 72-87;

12508 *Weiss, Zeev* New light on the Rehov inscription: identifying 'The gate of the Campon' at Bet Shean <2000>. ᶠFOERSTER, G. 2002 ⇒ 39. 423-506/211-233.

12509 *Cana; Capernaum*: *Richardson, Peter* What has Cana to do with Capernaum?. NTS 48 (2002) 314-331.

12510 *Capernaum*: *Loffreda, Stanislao* Capharnaum. Holy Land (Summer, Autumn 2002) 30-45, 25-34.

12511 *Dan*: **Biran, Avraham; Ben-Dov, Rachel** Dan II: a chronicle of the excavations and the Late Bronze Age 'Mycenaean' tomb. J

2002, Nelson Glueck School of B.A. vi; 249 pp. $58. 0-87820-308-7 [RB 110,310].

12512   *Ḏrr*: *Garfinkel, Yosef; Matskevich, Zinovi* Abu Zureiq, a Wadi Rahab site in the Jezreel valley: final report of the 1962 excavations. IEJ 52 (2002) 129-166.

12513   *Hazor*: *Ben-Tor, Amnon* Tel Hazor, 2002: excavations and surveys. IEJ 52 (2002) 254-257.

12514   *Hippos*: *Segal, Arthur* Hippos wird endlich ausgegraben: archäologische Arbeiten am Ostufer vom See Gennesaret. WUB 24 (2002) 76-77.

12515   *Kinneret*: *Fritz, Volkmar; Münger, Stefan* Vorbericht über die zweite Phase der Ausgrabungen in Kinneret (Tell el-ʿOreme) am See Gennesaret, 1994-1999. ZDPV 118 (2002) 2-32;

12516   *Knauf, Ernst Axel* Kinneret and early Iron Age chronology. BN 113 (2002) 18-23.

12517   *Megiddo*: *Niemann, Hermann Michael* Wohl doch nicht Salomos Pferdeställe ... Ergebnisse der Kampagne 2000 in Megiddo. WUB 23 (2002) 66-67.

12518   *Meron*: *Feig, Nurit* Salvage excavations at Meron. ʿAtiqot 43 (2002) 87-107.

12519   *Nahal Zippori*: *Gal, Zvi* Settlement location in Nahal Zippori as a reflection of cultural diversity from the Neolithic through the early Bronze Age II-III periods. [F]GOPHNA, R. 2002 ⇒49. 45-64.

12520   *Nazareth*: **Bagatti, Bellarmino; Alliata, E.** Excavations in Nazareth, 2: from the 12th century until today. [T]*Bonanno, R.*: SBF.CMa 17: J 2002, Franciscan Printing Press 206 pp. $30. 70 fig.; 84 pl.;

12521   *Bechmann, Ulrike* Zwei Jahrtausende später: Christinnen und Christen in Nazaret. WUB 24 (2002) 54-57.

12522   *Rehov*: *Mazar, Amihai* Le cas de Tel Rehov. MoBi 146 (2002) 30-31.

12523   *Sephoris*: *Strange, James* Un sito importante: Sefforis in Galilea. Mondo della bibbia 62 (2002) 53-57;

12524   Eine Stadt des Herodes Antipas: Sepphoris. WUB 24 (2002) 22-25.

12525   *Shaʿar ha-Golan*: *Garfinkel, Yosef* Shaʿar ha-Golan, 2000-2002: excavations and surveys. IEJ 52 (2002) 258-264.

12526   *Taʿannek*: **Ziese, Mark S.** The Early Bronze Age ceramic assemblage from Tell Taʿannek, Palestine. [D]*Younker, Randall W.*: 2002 Diss. Andrews [AUSS 42,219].

12527   *Teʾo*: **Eisenberg, Emanuel,** *al.*, Tel Teʾo a Neolithic, Chalcolithic, and Early Bronze Age site in the Hula Valley. IAA Reports 13: J 2001, Israel Antiquities Authority (4) 227 pp. 965-406-142-2. Bibl. 220-227.

T4.8 *Transjordania*: **(East-)Jordan**

12528   *Edwards, Phillip C.*, *al.*, Archaeology and environment of the Dead Sea plain: preliminary results of the second season of investigations by the Joint la Trobe University / Arizona State University project. ADAJ 46 (2002) 51-92.

12529   *Graf, David* Die Dekapolis—ein Prolog. Gadara—Gerasa. 2002 ⇒485. 4-5.

12530   *Herr, Larry G.* 5,000-year-old burials discovered in Jordan. NEA (BA) 65 (2002) 282-283.

12531   *Ji, Chang-Ho C.; Lee, Jong Keun* The survey in the regions of 'Iraq
         al-Amir and Wadi al-Kafrayn, 2000. ADAJ 46 (2002) 179-195.
12532   *Kerner, Susanne* Die Dekapolis-Städte—der Versuch einer Zusam-
         menfassung. Gadara—Gerasa. 2002 ⇒485. 146-147.
12533   *Levy, Thomas E.* Tribes, metallurgy, and Edom in Iron Age Jordan.
         ACOR Newsletter 14/2 (2002) 3-5.
12534   **MacDonald, Burton** "East of the Jordan": territories and sites of
         the Hebrew scriptures. ASOR Books 6: 2000 ⇒16,11802.
         ᴿBASOR 325 (2002) 88-90 (*Dearman, J. Andrew*); WO 32 (2002)
         242-247 (*Jericke, D.*); AJA 106 (2002) 614-616 (*Naskhai, Beth
         Albert*); CBQ 64 (2002) 357-358 (*Jacobs, Paul F.*).
12535   *Ninow, Friedbert* Preliminary report on the Wadi Ash-Shkafiya sur-
         vey 2001. ADAJ 46 (2002) 151-156.
12536   *Photos-Jones, Effie, al.*, The sugar industry in the southern Jordan
         valley: an interim report on the pilot season of excavations,
         geophysical and geological surveys at Ṭawaḥin as-Sukkar and Khir-
         bat ash-Shaykh 'Isa, in Ghawr aṣ-Ṣafi. ADAJ 46 (2002) 591-614.
12537   ᴱ*Piccirillo, Michele* Ricerca storico-archeologica in Giordania XXI
         —2001. LASBF 51 (2001) 360-393.;
12538   XXII—2002. LASBF 52 (2002) 466-516.
12539   *Quintero, Leslie A.; Wilke, Philip J.; Rollefson, Gary O.* From flint
         mine to fan scraper: the late prehistoric Jafr industrial complex.
         BASOR 327 (2002) 17-48.
12540   *Savage, Stephen H.; Zamora, Kurt; Keller, Donald R.* Archaeology
         in Jordan, 2001 season. AJA 106 (2002) 435-458.
12541   *Savage, Stephen H.; Metzger, Mary L.* The Moab archaeological
         resource survey: test excavations and faunal analysis from the 2001
         field season. ADAJ 46 (2002) 107-123.
12542   *Walmsley, Alan G.* Die Dekapolis-Städte nach dem Ende des
         Römischen Reiches: Kontinuität und Wandel. Gadara—Gerasa.
         2002 ⇒485. 137-145.
12543   *Wimmer, Stefan J.* Neue Stele Ramses' II. durch Zufall gefunden.
         WUB 25 (2002) 64.

12544   **Abila**: *Mare, W. Harold* Abila und Wadi Quweilbeh—Basiliken
         und Gräber. Gadara—Gerasa. 2002 ⇒485. 46-58.
12545   **Abu al-Kharaz**: *Fischer, Peter M.* Egyptian-transjordanian interac-
         tion during predynastic and protodynastic times: the evidence from
         Tell Abu al-Kharaz, Jordan Valley. Egypt and the Levant. 2002 ⇒
         497. 323-333.
12546   **'Ajlun**: *MacKenzie, Neil D.* Ayyubid / Mamluk archaeology of the
         'Ajlun area: a preliminary typology. ADAJ 46 (2002) 615-620.
12547   **al-Baṣṣa**: *al Zaben, Ebrahim* Preliminary report on the results of
         the excavations at al-Baṣṣa / Iraq al-Amir (1996/1997). ADAJ 46
         (2002) 41*-50*. **A.**
12548   **al-Fudayn; Raḥab-al Mafraq**: *al-Husan, Abdel-Qader* The new
         archaeological discoveries of the al-Fudayn and Raḥab-al Mafraq
         excavation projects, 1991-2001. ADAJ 46 (2002) 71*-94*. **A.**
12549   **al-Jafr**: *Fujii, Sumio* A brief note on the 2001-2002 winter season
         survey of the al-Jafr basin in Southern Jordan. ADAJ 46 (2002) 41-
         49.
12550   **al-Mabrak**: *al Zaben, Ebrahim* Preliminary report on the results of
         the excavations at al-Mabrak / East 'Amman (1994). ADAJ 46
         (2002) 11*-19*. **A.**

12551   *al-Muḍaybi͑*: *Andrews, Stephen J., al.*, The Karak resources project
        1999: excavations at Khirbat al-Muḍaybi͑. ADAJ 46 (2002) 125-
        140.
12552   *al-Mudayna*: *Daviau, P.M. Michèle; Dion, Paul-Eugène* Econo-
        my-related finds from Khirbat al-Mudayna (Wadi ath-Thamad, Jor-
        dan). BASOR 328 (2002) 31-48.
12553   *al-'Umayri*: ᴱHerr, Larry G., *al.*, Madaba Plains Project 5: the
        1994 season at Tall al-'Umayri and subsequent studies. Madaba
        Plains Project series 5: Berrien Springs, Michigan 2002, Andrews
        University Press xii; 407 pp. $80. 1-883925-33-9;
12554   Madaba Plains Project 3: The 1989 season at Tell el-'Umeiri and
        vicinity and subsequent studies. Berrien Springs, MI 1997,
        Andrews Univ. Pr. x; 373 pp. 0-943872-71-5;
12555   Madaba Plains Project 4: The 1992 season at Tell el-'Umeiri and
        vicinity and subsequent studies. Berrien Springs, MI 2000,
        Andrews Univ. Pr. x; 256 pp. 0-883925-26-6;
12556   *Trenchard, Warren C.* Madaba Plains Project: Tall al-'Umayri,
        2000. AUSS 40 (2002) 105-123.
12557   *'Aqaba*: *Parker, S. Thomas* The Roman 'Aqaba project: the 2000
        campaign. ADAJ 46 (2002) 409-428.
12558   *Aroer*: *Feldman, Steven* Return to Aroer: a trip through the ages
        with the ageless Avraham Biran. BArR 28/1 (2002) 50-54.
12559   *ash-Sharah*: *Tweissi, Qais* Traditional sites of the Ma'an district /
        ash-Sharah. ADAJ 46 (2002) 159*-176*. A.
12560   *at-Tannur*: *Abu Shmeis, Adeib I.; al-Shami, Ahmad; Tarawneh,
        Khaled* The archaeological surveys in the at-Tannur Dam Basin /
        Wadi al-Ḥasa. ADAJ 46 (2002) 95*-106*. A.;
12561   *McKenzie, Judith; Reyes, Andres; Gibson, Sheila* Khirbat at-
        Tannur in the ASOR Nelson Glueck archive and the reconstruction
        of the temple. ADAJ 46 (2002) 451-476.
12562   *Bethany*: *Villeneuve, Estelle* Deux rives pour un seul baptême.
        MoBi 146 (2002) 52-53;
12563   *Waheeb, M.* Results of the excavations at Bethany east of the Jor-
        dan river: a preliminary report. ADAJ 46 (2002) 31*-40*. A.
12564   *Braq*: *Farajat, Suleiman; Marahleh, Mohammad; Falahat, Hani*
        Report on the Khirbat Braq excavations. ADAJ 46 (2002) 21*-30*.
        A.
12565   *Busayra*: **Bienkowski, Piotr** Busayra: excavations by Crystal-M.
        BENNETT 1971-1980. British Academy Monographs in Archaeol-
        ogy 13: Oxf 2002, OUP 500 pp. £99. 0-19-727012-3. 214 fig.; 648
        phot., tables.
12566   *Dhraʾ*: *Goodale, N.; Kuijt, I.; Finlayson, B.* Results from the 2001
        excavations at Dhraʾ, Jordan: chipped stone technology, typology,
        and intra-assemblage variability. Paléorient 28/1 (2002) 125-140.
12567   *el-Fukhar*: *Strange, John* Revealing the history of Tell el-Fukhar.
        ACOR Newsletter 14/2 (2002) 5-6.
12568   *ez-Zeraqon*: **Genz, Hermann** Die frühbronzezeitliche Keramik
        von Hirbet ez-Zeraqon: mit Studien zur Chronologie und funktiona-
        len Deutung frühbronzezeitlicher Keramik in der südlichen Levan-
        te. ADPV 27/2; Deutsch-jordanische Ausgrabungen in Hirbet ez-
        Zeraqon 1984-1994 Endberichte 5: Wsb 2002, Harrassowitz viii;
        166 pp. €76. 3-447-04536-1. Bibl. 133-143.

12569 *Farasa*: *Schmid, Stephan G.* The international Wadi Farasa project (IWFP): preliminary report on the 2001 season. ADAJ 46 (2002) 257-277.

12570 *Gadara*: *Hoffmann, Adolf* Topographie und Stadtgeschichte von Gadara/Umm Qais. Gadara—Gerasa. 2002 ⇒485. 98-124;

12571 *Kerner, Susanne* Gadara—schwarzweiße Stadt zwischen Adjlun und Golan. Gadara—Gerasa. 2002 ⇒485. 125-136.

12572 *Tawalbeh, Dia'eddin A.* Islamic settlement in Umm Qays (Gadara). ADAJ 46 (2002) 621-628.

12573 *Vriezen, Karel J.H.* Een antieke stad wordt zichtbaar: opgravingen in Umm Qēs (Ant. Gadara) in Jordanie. Phoenix 48 (2002) 46-60;

12574 **Weber, Thomas Maria** Gadara—Umm Qês, 1: Gadara decapolitana: Untersuchungen zur Topographie, Geschichte, Architektur und der Bildenden Kunst einer 'Polis Hellenis' im Ostjordanland. ADPV 30: Wsb 2002, Harrassowitz xi; 613 pp. €128. 3-447-0398-1-7 [RB 110,640].

12575 *Gerasa*: *Parapetti, Roberto* Gerasa und das Artemis-Heiligtum. Gadara—Gerasa. 2002 ⇒485. 23-35;

12576 *Seigne, Jacques* Comments on Jean-Pierre Braun et al.: The town plan of Gerasa in AD 2000: a revised edition (ADAJ 45, 2001);

12577 Comments on Ina Kehrberg and John Manley: New archaeological finds for the dating of the Gerasa Roman city wall (ADAJ 45, 2001). ADAJ 46 (2002) 631-633/633-637;

12578 Gerasa-Jerasch—Stadt der 1000 Säulen. Gadara—Gerasa. 2002 ⇒ 485. 6-22;

12579 *Shmeis, Adeib Abu; Waheeb, M.* Recent discoveries in the baptism site: the pottery. ADAJ 46 (2002) 561-581.

12580 *Ghassul*: *Bourke, S.J.* Teleilat Ghassul: foreign relations in the late Chalcolithic period. Egypt and the Levant. 2002 ⇒497. 154-164;

12581 The origin of social complexity in the southern Levant: new evidence from Teleilat Ghassul, Jordan. PEQ 134 (2002) 2-27.

12582 *Iraq al Amir*: *Will, E.; Larché, F.* Iraq al Amir: le château du Tobiade Hyrcan. 1991 ⇒9,13971; 11/2,b166. [R]BAIAS 19-20 (2001-2002) 157-175 (*Rosenberg, Stephen G.*).

12583 *Jabal al-Qal'a*: *Mansour, Sahar* Preliminary report of the excavations at Jabal al-Qal'a (lower terrace): the Iron Age walls. ADAJ 46 (2002) 141-150.

12584 *Uthman, Mohammad* Preliminary report of the restoration works at Jabal al-Qala'a (1/7-31/12/2001). ADAJ 46 (2002) 107*-112*. **A**.

12585 *Jabal Harun*: *Frösén, Jaakko, al.*, The 2001 Finnish Jabal Harun project: preliminary report. ADAJ 46 (2002) 391-407.

12586 *Jawa*: **Daviau, Paulette M. Michèle**, *al.*, Excavations at Tall Jawa, Jordan, 1: The Iron Age Town, 2: the Iron Age artefacts. Culture and history of the Ancient Near East 11/1-2: Lei 2002-2003. Brill 2 vols; xlii; 566 + xxiv + 372 pp. €170/$230 + €116/$157. 90-04-13012-8/12363-6. Incl. 2 CD-Rom.

12587 *Jerash*: *Kehrberg, Ina; Manley, John* The 2001 season of the Jarash city walls project: preliminary report. ADAJ 46 (2002) 197-203;

12588 *Naghaway, Aida* Umayyad Dirhams from Jarash. ADAJ 46 (2002) 127*-132*. **A**.

12589 *Seigne, Jacques* A sixth century water-powered sawmill at Jarash. ADAJ 46 (2002) 205-213.

12590   *Johfiyeh*: *Lamprichs, Roland* Tell Johfiyeh: ein eisenzeitlicher Fundplatz in Nordjordanien und seine Umgebung: erste Ergebnisse der Ausgrabungskampagne 2002. UF 34 (2002) 363-452.

12591   *Kapitolias*: *Lenzen, Cherie* Kapitolias—die vergessene Stadt im Norden. Gadara—Gerasa. 2002 ⇒485. 36-45.

12592   *Khallit ʿIsa*: *Melhem, Ismaeel; al-Husan, Abdel-Qader* Preliminary reports of the excavations and restoration at Khallit ʿIsa / Bayt Idis—the 2001 season. ADAJ 46 (2002) 51*-61*. A.

12593   *Pella*: *da Costa, Kate, al.*, New light on late antique Pella: Sydney University excavations in Area XXXV, 1991. ADAJ 46 (2002) 503-533;

12594   *Watson, Pamela* Pella—die Stadt am Jordangraben. Gadara—Gerasa. 2002 ⇒485. 59-71.

12595   *Petra*: *Akasheh, Talal S.* Ancient and modern watershed management in Petra. NEA (BA) 65 (2002) 220-224;

12596   *Augé, Christian, al.*, New excavations in the Qaṣr al-Bint area at Petra. ADAJ 46 (2002) 309-313;

12597   *Basile, Joseph J.* Two visual languages at Petra: aniconic and representational sculpture of the great temple. NEA (BA) 65 (2002) 255-258;

12598   *Bedal, Leigh-Ann* The Petra garden feasibility study, 2001. ADAJ 46 (2002) 381-389;

12599   Desert oasis: water consumption and display in the Nabataean capital. NEA (BA) 65 (2002) 225-234;

12600   *Bikai, Patricia Maynor* The churches of Byzantine Petra. NEA (BA) 65 (2002) 271-276;

12601   *Bodel, John; Karz Reid, Sara* A dedicatory inscription to the emperor TRAJAN from the small temple at Petra, Jordan. NEA (BA) 65 (2002) 249-250;

12602   *Conyers, Lawrence B.; Ernenwein, Eileen G.; Bedal, Leigh-Ann* Ground-penetrating radar discovery at Petra, Jordan. Antiquity 76 (2002) 339-340;

12603   *Egan, Emily Catherine* Stucco decoration from the south corridor of the Petra great temple: discussion and interpretation. ADAJ 46 (2002) 347-361;

12604   *Hübner, Ulrich* Ras Ḥamra bei Petra. ZDPV 118 (2002) 169-175;

12605   *Joukowsky, Martha Sharp* Ten years of excavation at the Petra great temple: a retrospective. ACOR Newsletter 14/2 (2002) 1-2;

12606   The Brown University 2001 Petra great temple excavations offer more suprises. ADAJ 46 (2002) 315-330;

12607   *Kanellopoulos, Chrysanthos* The monumental entrance to the upper market and the Trajanic inscription at Petra: the architectural context. ADAJ 46 (2002) 295-308;

12608   A new plan of Petra's city center. NEA (BA) 65 (2002) 251-254;

12609   *Karz Reid, Sara* Excavations at the Petra small temple, 2000-2001. ADAJ 46 (2002) 363-379;

12610   *Kolb, Bernhard* Excavating a Nabataean mansion. NEA (BA) 65 (2002) 260-264;

12611   *Kolb, Bernhard; Keller, Daniel* Swiss-Liechtenstein excavation at az-Zanṭur / Petra: the twelfth season. ADAJ 46 (2002) 279-293;

12612   *Lindner, Manfred; Gunsam, Elisabeth* A fortified suburb of ancient Petra: Shammasa. ADAJ 46 (2002) 225-241;

12613 *Nehmé, Laïla* La chapelle d'obodas à Pétra: rapport préliminare sur la campagne 2001. ADAJ 46 (2002) 243-256;
12614 **Taylor, Jane** Petra und das versunkene Königreich der Nabatäer. Dü 2002, Artemis & W. 220 pp. €49.90. 3-538-07136-5. Num. ill. [EuA 78,343].
12615 *Wenning, Robert* Petra in Jordanien, Zentrum der Nabatäer: eine Stadt als "religiöse Landschaft"?. Religiöse Landschaften. AOAT 301: 2002 ⇒408. 49-67.

12616 ***Philadelphia***: *Najjar, Mohammed* Rabbath Ammon—Philadelphia — Amman. Gadara—Gerasa. 2002 ⇒485. 88-97.
12617 ***QaʿAbu Ṭulayḥa***: *Fujii, Sumio* QaʿAbu Ṭulayḥa west, 2001: an interim report of the fifth season. ADAJ 46 (2002) 15-39.
12618 ***Rabbathmoab***: *Calzini Gysens, Jacqueline; Barnes, Hugh* Preliminary report on the first survey campaign at ancient ar-Rabba (Rabbathmoab / Aeropolis). ADAJ 46 (2002) 493-498.
12619 ***Ras-Irbid***: *al-Shami, Ahmad* Bayt Ras-Irbid archaeological project 2002. ADAJ 46 (2002) 61*-70*. A.
12620 ***Robatha***: *Walmsley, Alan; Barnes, Hugh* A brief ground survey of Ruwath (Robatha), South Jordan, 28 October-16 November 2000. ADAJ 46 (2002) 485-491.
12621 ***Rujm Ṭaba***: *Dolinka, Benjamin J., al.,* The Rujm Ṭaba archaeological project (RTAP): preliminary report of the 2001 field season. ADAJ 46 (2002) 429-450.
12622 ***Ṭafila-Buṣayra***: *MacDonald, Burton; Sawtell, Wayne* The Ṭafila-Buṣayra archaeological survey: phase 3 (2001). ADAJ 46 (2002) 477-484.
12623 ***Umm ar-Raṣaṣ-Kastron Mefaa***: *Piccirillo, Michele* The ecclesiastical complex of Saint Paul at Umm ar-Raṣaṣ-Kastron Mefaa. ADAJ 46 (2002) 535-559.
12624 ***Yaʾamun***: *Foran, Debra; Harrison, Timothy* Tell Yaʾamun: the 2002 season. ACOR Newsletter 14/2 (2002) 8.
12625 ***Zahrat Adh-Dhrʿ***: *Edwards, Phillip C., al.,* Zahrat Adh-Dhrʿ: a new pre-pottery neolithic A site on the Dead Sea plain in Jordan. BASOR 327 (2002) 1-15.
12626 ***Zarʿa***: *Vieweger, Dieter; Eichner, Jens; Leiverkus, Patrick* Tall Zarʿa in Wadi al-ʿArab: the 'Gadara region project'. ADAJ 46 (2002) 157-177.

T5.1 **Phoenicia**—*Libanus*, **Lebanon**; *situs mediterranei*

12627 *Copeland, Lorraine; Yazbeck, Corine* Inventory of stone age sites in Lebanon, part III, additions and revisions, 1967-2001. MUSJ 55 (1997-1998) 119-325.
12628 ᴱ**Donati Giacomoni, Paola; Uberti, Maria Luisa** Fra Cartagine e Roma: seminario di studi italo-tunisino, Bologna, 23 febbraio 2001. Epigrafia e antichità 18: Faenza 2002, Fratelli Lega 95 pp.
12629 **Lilliu, Giovanni** La civiltà preistorica e nuragica in Sardegna. AANL.M 9/15,3: R 2002, Accademia Nazionale dei Lincei 221-264 pp. 88-218-0877-7. Bibl. 254-264.
12630 **Sagona, Claudia** The archaeology of Punic Malta. Ancient Near Eastern Studies, Supplement 9: Herent 2002, Peeters 1165 pp. 90-429-0917-X.

12631   **Wardini, Elie** Lebanese place-names (Mount Lebanon and North Lebanon): a typology of regional variation and continuity. OLA 120: Lv 2002, Peeters 719 pp. 90-429-1248-0. Bibl. 683-696.

12632   *Beirut*: *Alpi, Frédéric* Un regard sur Beyrouth Byzantine (IVᵉ-VIIᵉ s.). Aram 13 (2001-2002) 313-321;

12633   *Antaki, Patricia* Le château croisé de Beyrouth: étude préliminaire. Aram 13 (2001-2002) 323-353;

12634   *Arnaud, Pascal* Beirut: commerce and trade (200 BC - AD 400). Aram 13 (2001-2002) 171-191;

12635   *Badre, Leila* The Bronze Age of Beirut: major results. Aram 13 (2001-2002) 1-26;

12636   *Curvers, Hans H.* The lower town of Beirut (1200-300 BC): a preliminary synthesis. Aram 13 (2001-2002) 51-72;

12637   **Elayi, Josette; Sayegh, H.** Un quartier du port phénicien de Beyrouth au fer III / Perse: les objets. TEuph.S 6: 1998 ⇒14,10849. ᴿTEuph 23 (2002) 198-205 (*Sapin, J.*).

12638   *Finkbeiner, Uwe* Bey 020—the Iron Age fortification. Aram 13 (2001-2002) 27-36;

12639   *Hall, Linda Jones* Berytus through the classical texts: from *colonia* to *civitas*. Aram 13 (2001-2002) 141-169;

12640   *MacAdam, Henry Innes Studia et circenses*: Beirut's Roman law school in its colonial, cultural context. Aram 13 (2001-2002) 193-226;

12641   *Núñez, Francisco J.* An approach to exchange relations in Iron Age Beirut: the ceramic evidence. Aram 13 (2001-2002) 37-49;

12642   *Perring, Dominic* Beirut in antiquity: some research directions suggested by recent excavations in the souks. Aram 13 (2001-2002) 129-140;

12643   *Seeden, Helga* Dialoguing with the past: will Beirut's past still speak to the future?. Aram 13 (2001-2002) 359-375;

12644   *Steiner, Margreet* The Hellenistic to Byzantine souk: results of the excavations at Bey 011. Aram 13 (2001-2002) 113-127;

12645   *Tarazi, Renata Ortali* Loi et pratique dans la conservation du patrimoine culturel: le cas des fouilles archéologiques dans le centre-ville de Beyrouth. Aram 13 (2001-2002) 355-358.

T5.4 **Ugarit**—*Ras Šamra*

12646   *Bordreuil, Pierre* Ein gut verwaltetes Königreich. WUB 23 (2002) 16-17.

12647   *Calvet, Yves* Das Haus des Urtenu: eine Residenz gibt ihr Geheimnis preis. WUB 23 (2002) 20-21.

12648   *Caubet, Annie* Ugarit im Louvre. WUB 23 (2002) 25-29.

12649   *Dietrich, Manfried; Loretz, Oswald* Der Untergang von Ugarit am 21. Januar 1192 v.Chr. UF 34 (2002) 53-74.

12650   *Fleming, Daniel E.* Schloen's patrimonial pyramid: explaining Bronze Age society. BASOR 328 (2002) 73-80.

12651   *Kinet, Dirk* Ein Rundgang im archäologischen Gelände von Ugarit. WUB 23 (2002) 10-15.

12652   **Lackenbacher, Sylvie** Textes akkadiens d'Ugarit: textes provenant des vingt-cinq premières campagnes. LAPO 20: P 2002, Cerf 397 pp. €33. 2-204-06701-6.

12653 *Malbran-Labat, Florence* Textes religieux et multilinguisme à Ougarit. Hethitica XV. 2002 ⇒683. 173-181.
12654 *Mallet, Joël* Ras Shamra-Ougarit (Syrie), 62ᵉ campagne, 2002: l'exploration des niveaux du Bronze moyen II (1ʳᵉ moitié du IIᵉ millénaire av. J.-C.) sous le palais nord. UF 34 (2002) 527-550.
12655 *Márquez Rowe, Ignacio* The king's men in Ugarit and society in late Bronze Age Syria. JESHO 45 (2002) 1-19.
12656 **Pardee, Dennis** Les textes rituels. Ras Shamra - Ougarit 12: 2000 ⇒16,8578; 17,11476. ᴿOLZ 97 (2002) 539-544 (*Schorch, Stefan*); UF 34 (2002) 975-977 (*Dietrich, M.; Loretz, O.*); BiOr 59 (2002) 593-595 (*Spronk, Klaas*); AuOr 20/1-2 (2002) 291-294 (*Watson, W.G.E.*);
12657 Ritual and cult at Ugarit. ᴱ*Lewis, Theodore J.*: Writings from the ancient world 10: Atlanta, GA 2002, SBL xiii; 299 pp. $30. 1-589-83-026-1. Bibl. 252-266.
12658 *Pitard, Wayne T.* Voices from the dust: the tablets from Ugarit and the bible. Mesopotamia and the bible. JSOT.S 341: 2002 ⇒458. 251-275.
12659 **Tropper, Josef** Ugaritische Gramatik. AOAT 273: 2000 ⇒16, 8587; 17,11479. ᴿBSOAS 65 (2002) 177-179 (*Gianto, Agustinus*); ZDMG 152 (2002) 185-192 (*Streck, Michael P.*).
12660 ᴱ**Watson, W.G.E.; Wyatt, N.** Handbook of Ugaritic studies. HO 1/ 39: 1999 ⇒15,11640; 17,11480. ᴿArOr 70 (2002) 91-94 (*Segert, Stanislav*); JNES 61 (2002) 221-223 (*Clemens, D.M.*).
12661 **Wright, David Pearson** Ritual in narrative: the dynamics of feasting, mourning, and retaliation rites in the Ugaritic tale of Aqhat. 2000 ⇒16,8594. ᴿCBQ 64 (2002) 561-562 (*McLaughlin, John L.*).
12662 **Wyatt, Nick** Religious texts from Ugarit. BiSe 53: 1998 ⇒14, 10905... 17,11481. ᴿJNES 61 (2002) 123-125 (*Pardee, Dennis*);
12663 L ²2002, Sheffield A. 502 pp. 0-8264-6048-8. Bibl. 450-485.
12664 *Yon, Marguerite* 70 Jahre Überraschungen aus Ugarit;
12665 Ugarit—6000 Jahre Geschichte. WUB 23 (2002) 4-5/7-9;
12666 Ugarit—eine weltoffene Handelsstadt. WUB 23 (2002) 18-19.
12667 **Zamora, José-Ángel** La vid y el vino en Ugarit. 2000 ⇒16,11873. ᴿOr. 71 (2002) 321-326 (*Heltzer, Michael*); AuOr 20/1-2 (2002) 297-298 (*Watson, W.G.E.*).

T5.5 Ebla

12668 *Archi, Alfonso* The role of women in the society of Ebla. Sex and gender. 2002 ⇒712. 1-9.
12669 *Astour, Michael C.* A reconstruction of the history of Ebla (Part 2). Eblaitica 4. 2002 ⇒474. 57-195.
12670 *Aucagne, Jean* Quelques énigmes du sémitique occidental à la lumière d'Ebla. MUSJ 55 (1997-1998) 59-87.
12671 *Dolce, Rita* Ebla after the 'fall'—some preliminary considerations on the EB IVB city. DaM 13 (2002) 11-28;
12672 Ebla et ses souverains du renouvellement de la ville protosyrienne tardive à l'épanouissement du règne amorrhéen. ᴹIMPARATI, F. 2002 ⇒61. 217-244.
ᴱ**Gordon, C.** Eblaitica 4. 2002 ⇒474.

12673 *Matthiae, Paolo* Fouilles et restaurations à Ebla en 2000-2001: le palais occidental, la résidence occidentale et l'urbanisme de la ville paléosyrienne. CRAI 2 (2002) 531-574;
12674 A preliminary note on the MB I-II fortifications system at Ebla. DaM 13 (2002) 29-51.
12675. *Pinnock, Frances* The urban landscape of old Syrian Ebla. JCS 53 (2001) 13-33.
12676 *Pomponio, Francesco* Funzionari di Ebla e di Mari. ^MIMPARATI, F. 2002 ⇒61. 653-663.
12677 *Stieglitz, Robert R.* Divine pairs in the Ebla pantheon;
12678 The deified kings of Ebla. Eblaitica 4. 2002 ⇒474. 209-14/215-22.

T5.8 **Situs efossi Syriae in ordine alphabetico**

12679 *Blum, Hartmut* Überlegungen zum Thema "Akkulturation". Brükkenland Anatolien?. 2002 ⇒453. 1-17.
12680 ^E**Bunnens, Guy** Essays on Syria in the Iron Age. Abr-n.S 7: 2000 ⇒16,387. ^RTEuph 23 (2002) 191-194 (*Elayi, J.*).
12681 **Dirven, Lucinda** The Palmyrenes of Dura-Europos: a study of religious interaction in Roman Syria. RGRW 138: 1999 ⇒15,11708; 17,11491. ^RBiOr 59 (2002) 130-134 (*Gordon, Richard*); SEL 19 (2002) 165-168 (*Scagliarini, Fiorella*).

12682 *Abu Hureyra*: **Moore, A.M.; Hillman, A.J.; Legge, A.J.** Village on the Euphrates. 2000 ⇒16,11896. ^RBiOr 59 (2002) 619-621 (*Roodenberg, J.*).
12683 *'Ain Dara*: **Stone, Elizabeth C.; Zimansky, Paul E.** The Iron Age settlement at 'Ain Dara, Syria: survey and soundings. BAR International Series 786: 1999 ⇒15,11701. ^RBASOR 325 (2002) 83-86 (*Lehmann, Gunnar*).
12684 *Alalakh*: *Hess, Richard S.* The bible and Alalakh. Mesopotamia and the bible. JSOT.S 341: 2002 ⇒458. 209-221.
12685 *Antioch O.*: ^T*Norman, A.F.*: Antioch as a centre of Hellenic culture as observed by LIBANIUS. Translated texts for historians: 2000 ⇒ 16,11901. ^RHeyJ 43 (2002) 384-386 (*Leemans, Johan*).
12686 *Bazi*: *Einwag, Berthold, al.*, Tall Bazi 1998 und 1999—die letzten Untersuchungen in der Weststadt. DaM 13 (2002) 65-88.
12687 *Bet Yerah*: *Greenberg, Raphael; Eisenberg, Emanuel* Egypt, Bet Yerah and early Canaanite urbanization. Egypt and the Levant. 2002 ⇒497. 213-222.
12688 *Brak*: *Emberling, Geoff; McDonald, Helen* Recent finds from the northern Mesopotamian city of Tell Brak. Antiquity 76 (2002) 949-950.
12689 *Carchemish*: *Klengel, Horst* Karkamis in der hethitischen Großreichszeit: ein geschichtlicher Überblick. Die Hethiter. 2002 ⇒535. 163-167.
12690 *Emar*: *Faist, Betina; Finkbeiner, Uwe* Emar: eine syrische Stadt unter hethitischer Herrschaft. Die Hethiter. 2002 ⇒535. 190-195;
12691 **Fleming, Daniel E.** Time at Emar: the cultic calendar and the rituals from the diviner's archive. Mesopotamian Civilizations 11: 2000 ⇒16,11906; 17,11502. ^ROLZ 97 (2002) 236-242 (*Pruzsinszky, Regine*);

12692 *Vita, Juan-Pablo* Warfare and the army at Emar. AltOrF 29 (2002) 113-127.

12693 *Halaf*: **Cholidis, Nadja; Martin, Lutz** Der Tell Halaf und sein Ausgräber Max Freiherr VON OPPENHEIM. B 2002, Vorderasiatisches Museum 72 pp. €20.50. 3-8053-2978-4. Num. ill. Bibl. 70-71 [RB 109,636].

12694 *Kamid el-Loz*: **Marfoe, Leon** Kamid el-Loz: settlement history of the Biqaʿ up to the Iron Age. 1998 ⇒15,11714; 16,11910. ᴿAfO 48-49 (2001-2002) 272-274 (*Tunca, Ö.*).

12695 *Munbâqa*: **Mayer, Walter** Ausgrabungen in Tall Munbâqa—Elkalte II: die Texte. 2001 ⇒17,11506. ᴿUF 34 (2002) 969-974 (*Zeeb, Frank*).

12696 *Palmyra*: **Degeorge, Gérard** Palmyra. Mü 2002, Hirmer 279 pp. €80. 3-7774-9340-6. Einf. von *Paul Veyne*; 156 ill. [EuA 79,360];

12697 Palmyre: métropole caravanière. 2001 ⇒17,11509. ᴿRH 307 (2002) 1072-1073 (*Benoist, Stéphane*);

12698 **Yon, Jean-Baptiste** Les notables de Palmyre. BAH 163: Beyrouth 2002, Inst. Français d'Archéologie du Proche-Orient vi; 378 + 11 pp. €48. 2-912738-199. Num. ill.

12699 *Qatna*: *Klingbeil, Gerald A.* Entre centro y periferia: Qatna en la investigación arqueológica e histórica reciente. DavarLogos 1 (2002) 149-162.

12700 *Tuttul*: **Miglus, Peter A.; Strommenger, Eva** Tall Bi'a/Tuttul, VIII: Stadtbefestigungen, Häuser und Tempel. WVDOG 103; Ausgrabungen in Tall Bi'a/Tuttul 8: Saarbrücken 2002, Saarbrücken Verlag (10) 141 pp. 3-930843-76-5. 134 pl. Bibl. 117-122;

12701 **Strommenger, Eva; Kohlmeyer, Kay**, *al.*, Tall Bi'a/Tuttul, III: die Schichten des 3. Jahrtausends v. Chr. im Zentralhügel E. WVDOG 101; Ausgrabungen in Tall Bi'a/Tuttul 3: Saarbrücken 2000, Saarbrücken vii; 141 pp. Bibl. 120-124.

T6.1 Mesopotamia, *generalia*

12702 *Beaulieu, Paul-Alain* W.F. ALBRIGHT & assyriology. NEA (BA) 65 (2002) 11-16.

12703 **Bottéro, Jean** La plus vieille cuisine du monde. P 2002, Audibert 203 pp. ᴿAnnales 57 (2002) 1359-1360 (*Joannès, Francis*).

12704 *Cathcart, Kevin J.* Irish contributions to the study of ancient Egypt and Mesopotamia in the nineteenth and early twentieth centuries. PIBA 25 (2002) 18-28.

12705 **Charvát, Petr** Mesopotamia before history. L ²2002 <1993>, Routledge xv; 281 pp. 0-415-25104-4. 69 fig.; 44 pl.; 3 maps. Bibl. 240-269.

12706 *Cooper, Jerrold S.* Virginity in ancient Mesopotamia. Sex and gender. 2002 ⇒712. 91-112.

12707 *Dandamayeva, M.M.* The notions 'Assyria', 'Babylonia' and 'Mesopotamia' in classical tradition. ᴹDIAKONOFF, I. 2002 ⇒27. 60-71.

12708 **Haas, Volkert** Babylonischer Liebesgarten: Erotik und Sexualität im Alten Orient. 1999 ⇒15,12085...17,11522. ᴿWO 32 (2002) 204-205 (*Röllig, Wolfgang*); OLZ 97 (2002) 527-530 (*Cholidis, Nadja*).

12709 *Hallo, William W.* Sumer and the bible: a matter of proportion. Context of scripture. 2002 ⇒326. xlix-liv.

12710 **Harris, Rivkah** Gender and aging in Mesopotamia: the *Gilgamesh* epic and other ancient literature. 2000 ⇒16,11930. [R]CBQ 64 (2002) 132-134 (*Spencer, John R.*).

12711 *Høyrup, Jens* How to educate a Kapo or reflections on the absence of a culture of mathematical problems in Ur III. Under one sky. AOAT 297: 2002 ⇒9014. 121-145.

12712 *Huot, Jean-Louis* La Mésopotamie sans la bible. MoBi 146 (2002) 19-23.

12713 *Koch-Westenholz, Ulla* Everyday life of women according to first millennium omen apodoses. Sex and gender. 2002 ⇒712. 301-309.

12714 *McCaffrey, Kathleen* Reconsidering gender ambiguity in Mesopotamia: is a beard just a beard?. Sex and gender. 2002 ⇒712. 379-391.

12715 **Potts, Daniel T.** Mesopotamian civilization: the material foundations. 1997 ⇒13,10919... 15,11723. [R]BiOr 59 (2002) 333-341 (*Van Koppen, Frans*).

[E]**Steele, John M.; Imhausen, Annette** Under one sky: astronomy and mathematics in the ancient Near East 2002 ⇒9014.

12716 *Stone, Elizabeth C.* The Ur III-Old Babylonian transition: an archaeological perspective. Iraq 64 (2002) 79-84.

12717 *Veenker, Ronald A.* Syro-Mesopotamia: the Old Babylonian period. Mesopotamia and the bible. JSOT.S 341: 2002 ⇒458. 149-167.

12718 *Warburton, David A.* Eclipses, Venus-cycles & chronology. Akkadica 123 (2002) 108-114.

12719 *Weisberg, David B.* The impact of Assyriology on biblical studies. Context of scripture. 2002 ⇒326. xliii-xlviii.

T6.5 **Situs effossi Iraq** *in ordine alphabetico*

12720 *al-Hiba*: *Ochsenschlager, Edward L.* Seeing the past in the present: twenty-five years of ethnoarchaeology at al-Hiba;

12721 *Brak*: *Oates, Joan; Oates, David* The reattribution of Middle Uruk materials at Brak. [F]HANSEN, D. 2002 ⇒58. 155-167/145-154.

12722 *Jemdet Nasr*: **Matthews, Roger** Secrets of the dark mound: Jemdet Nasr 1926-1928. Iraq archaeological reports 6: Warminster 2002, Aris & P. xiii; 162 pp. $90. 62 fig.; 48 pl.

12723 *Kumme*: *Mayer, Walter* Die Stadt *Kumme* als überregionales religiöses Zentrum. [F]DIETRICH, M. 2002 ⇒28. 329-358.

12724 *Niniveh*: **Gut, Renate Vera** Das prähistorische Ninive, 1995 ⇒11/2,b424... 17,11539. [R]AJA 106 (2002) 325-326 (*Emberling, Geoff*);

12725 *Matthiae, Paolo* La magnificenza sconosciuta di Ninive: note sullo sviluppo urbano prima di Sennacherib. AANL.R 13 (2002) 543-87.

12726 *Nuzi*: [E]**Owen, David I.; Wilhelm, Gernot** General studies and excavations at Nuzi 10/3. Studies on the civilization and culture of Nuzi and the Hurrians 12: Bethesda, MD 2002, CDL viii; 331 pp. 1-883053-68-4;

12727 Nuzi at seventy-five. 1999 ⇒15,11732. [R]AfO 48-49 (2001-2002) 198-200 (*Pruzsinszky, Regine*).

12728 *Tepe Gawra*: **Rothman, Mitchell S.** Tepe Gawra: the evolution of a small, prehistoric center in northern Iraq. University Museum Monograph 112: Ph 2002, University of Pennsylvania xxii; 494 pp. 0-924171-89-8. Bibl. 153-170.

12729 *Uruk*: [E]**Pedde, Friedhelm** Uruk: Kleinfunde, 4: Metall- und Steinobjekte im Vorderasiatischen Museum zu Berlin. Ausgrabungen in Uruk-Warka Endberichte 21: 2000 ⇒16,11956. [R]Mes. 37-38 (2002-2003) 343 (*Invernizzi, A.*);

12730 [E]**Postgate, J. Nicholas** Artefacts of complexity: tracking the Uruk in the Near East. Iraq archaeological reports 5: Wmr 2002, British School of Archaeology in Iraq vi; 258 pp. 0-85668-736-7.

T6.7 Arabia; Iran; Central Asia

12731 [E]**Cleuziou, Serge; Tosi, Maurizio; Zarins, Juris** Essays on the late prehistory of the Arabian Peninsula. Serie Orientale 93: R 2002, Istituto Italiano per l'Africa e l'Oriente 438 pp. Text arrangements by *Victoria de Castéja*.

12732 **Piccirillo, Michele** L'Arabia cristiana: dalla provincia imperiale al primo periodo islamico. Mi 2002, Jaca 259 pp. 88-16-60282-1. Bibl. 254-256.

12733 *Bertram, Jan-K.* Grenzen und Grenzüberschreitungen im Kaukasusbereich—die Trialeti-Kultur des 3./2. Jahrtausends v.Chr. Brückenland Anatolien?. 2002 ⇒453. 117-128.

12734 [E]**Boyle, Katie; Renfrew, Colin; Levine, Marsha** Ancient interactions: East and West in Eurasia. McDonald Institute Monographs: C 2002, CUP xii; 344 pp. 1-902937-19-8.

12735 *Helms, S.W.*, *al.*, The Karakalpak-Australian excavations in ancient Chorasmia: the northern frontier of the 'civilised' ancient world. ANESt 39 (2002) 3-43.

12736 *Martinez-Sève, Laurianne* La ville de Suse à l'époque hellénistique. RAr 1 (2002) 31-54.

12737 **Sürenhagen, Dietrich** Untersuchungen zur relativen Chronologie Babyloniens und angrenzender Gebiete von der ausgehenden 'Ubaidzeit bis zum Beginn der Frühdynastisch-II-Zeit, 1: Studien zur Chronostratigraphie der südbabylonischen Stadtruinen von Uruk und Ur. 1999 ⇒15,11736. [R]Mes. 37-38 (2002-2003) 341-342 (*Chiocchetti, L.*).

T7.1 Ægyptus, *generalia*

12738 *Adams, Robert McC.* Edging toward credible models: a commentary. Egypt and the Levant. 2002 ⇒497. 523-527.

12739 **Bomhard, A.S. von** The Egyptian calendar: a work for eternity. MIFAO 117: 1999 ⇒15,11743. [R]BiOr 59 (2002) 80-82 (*Spalinger, Anthony*).

12740 **Bresciani, Edda** An den Ufern des Nils: Alltagsleben zur Zeit der Pharaonen. [T]*Schareika, Helmut*: 2002, Da:Wiss 255 pp. Bibl. 246-248.

12741 **Caratini, Roger** L'égyptomanie, une imposture. P 2002, Michel 270 pp. €15.90. [R]MSR 59/2 (2002) 88-94 (*Cannuyer, Christian*).

Cathcart, K. Irish contributions to the study of ancient Egypt and Mesopotamia 2002 ⇒12704.

12742   **Clagett, M.** Ancient Egyptian science: a source book, 3: ancient Egyptian mathematics. 1999 ⇒16,11961. ᴿJNES 61 (2002) 290-291 (*Depuydt, Leo*); CEg 153-154 (2002) 177-180 (*Rampelberg, Doris*); Aeg. 81 (2001) 345-346 (*Piacentini, Patrizia*).

12743   *Hendrickx, Stan; Van den Brink, Edwin C.M.* Inventory of predynastic and early dynastic cemetery and settlement sites in the Egyptian Nile valley. Egypt and the Levant. 2002 ⇒497. 346-399.

12744   *Higginbotham, Carolyn* Travelling the ways of Horus: studying the links between Egypt and the Levant. Ment. *Albright, W.*: NEA (BA) 65 (2002) 30-34.

12745   **Hoffmann, F.** Ägypten: Kultur und Lebenswelt in griechisch-römischer Zeit: eine Darstellung nach den demotischen Quellen. 2000 ⇒16,11967. ᴿBiOr 59 (2002) 534-538 (*Martin, Cary J.*).

12746   *Levy, Thomas E.; Van den Brink, Edwin C.M.* Interaction models, Egypt and the Levantine periphery. Egypt and the Levant. 2002 ⇒497. 3-38.

12747   **Linant de Bellefonds, Louis Maurice; Goyon, Jean-Claude; Kurz, Marcel** Voyage aux mines d'or du Pharaon. n.p. 2002, Fata Morgana 277 pp. 2-85194-577-7. Composé de *Entre Nil et Mer Rouge* par *Jean-Claude Goyon*, *Un homme d'action dans l'Égypte du XIXe siècle* par *Marcel Kurz*; Bibl. 273-276.

12748   *Maeir, Aren M.* The relations between Egypt and the southern Levant during the late Iron Age: the material evidence from Egypt. Ä&L 12 (2002) 235-246.

12749   **Meskell, Lynn** Archaeologies of social life: age, sex, class et cetera in Ancient Egypt. 1999 ⇒15,11749. ᴿJESHO 45 (2002) 384-387 (*Toivari-Vitala, Jaana*);

12750   Private life in New Kingdom Egypt. Princeton, NJ 2002, Princeton Univ. Pr. xvi; 238 pp. $35. 0-691-00448-X. 62 fig.; Bibl. 215-231. ᴿAntiquity 76 (2002) 903-904 (*Strudwick, Helen*).

12751   *Miroschedji, Pierre de* The socio-political dynamics of Egyptian-Canaanite interaction in the early Bronze Age. Egypt and the Levant. 2002 ⇒497. 39-57.

12752   *Pernigotti, Sergio* La struttura dello stato nell'Egitto arcaico. Ricerche di Egittologia e di Antichità Copte 4 (2002) 35-46.

12753   **Scheidel, Walter** Death on the Nile: disease and the demography of Roman Egypt. Mn.S 228: 2001 ⇒17,11570. ᴿHZ 276 (2002) 132-133 (*Jördens, Andrea*).

12754   *Smith, Patricia* The palaeo-biological evidence for admixture between populations in the southern Levant and Egypt in the fourth to third millennia BCE. Egypt and the Levant. 2002 ⇒497. 118-128.

12755   ᴱ**Starkey, Paul; Starkey, Janet** Travellers in Egypt. L 2001, Tauris ix; 318 pp. £15. 1-86064-674-3.

12756   **Tiradritt, F.** Ancient Egypt. L 2002, British Museum Pr. 143 pp. £10. 0-7141-1950-4 [BiOr 59,521].

12757   **Vandersleyen, Claude** Ouadj our w d wr: un autre aspect de la vallée du Nil. 1999 ⇒15,11757. ᴿOLZ 97 (2002) 453-463 (*Quack, Joachim Friedrich*).

12758   *Venit, Marjorie Susan* Ancient Egyptomania: the uses of Egypt in Graeco-Roman Alexandria. ᶠHANSEN, D. 2002 ⇒58. 261-278.

12759 [E]**Vermeersch, Pierre M.** Palaeolithic quarrying sites in Upper and Middle Egypt. Egyptian Prehistory Monographs 4: Lv 2002, University Press 365 pp 90-5867-266-2. Bibl. 361-364.

12760 **Versluys, M.J.** Aegyptiaca Romana: Nilotic scenes and the Roman views of Egypt. RGRW 144: Lei 2002, Brill xv; 509 pp. €125/$149. 90-04-12440-3. Bibl. 478-489.

12761 *Vos, Julien de* À propos des *Aegyptiaca* d'Asie Mineure datés du IIe millénaire av. J.-C. Hethitica XV. 2002 ⇒683. 43-63.

12762 *Westendorf, Wolfhart* Das Ende der Unterwelt in der Amarnazeit oder: die Erde als Kugel. GöMisz 187 (2002) 101-111.

T7.2 *Luxor*, **Karnak** [East Bank]—**Thebae** [West Bank]

12763 *Leclère, François* Fouilles dans le cimetière osirien de Karnak—travaux récents. BSFE 153 (2002) 24-44.

12764 **Cabrol, A.** Les voies processionnelles de Thèbes. OLA 97: 2001 ⇒17,11579. [R]BiOr 59 (2002) 275-277 (*Karlshausen, Chr.*).

12765 **Donadoni, Sergio** Theben: heilige Stadt der Pharaonen. 2000 ⇒ 16,11980. [R]WO 32 (2002) 186-188 (*Gamer-Wallert, Ingrid*); OLZ 97 (2002) 740-744 (*Seyfried, Karl-Joachim*).

12766 **Vergnieux, Robert** Recherches sur les monuments thébains d'Amenhotep IV à l'aide d'outils informatiques: méthodes et résultats. 1999 ⇒15,11765. [R]BiOr 59 (2002) 66-68 (*Spieser, C.*).

T7.3 **Amarna**

12767 [E]**Cohen, Raymond; Westbrook, Raymond** Amarna diplomacy: the beginnings of international relations. 2000 ⇒16,11981; 17, 11581. [R]BASOR 327 (2002) 87-88 (*Rainey, Anson E.*).

12768 *Goren, Yuval; Finkelstein, Israel; Na'aman, Nadav* The seat of three disputed Canaanite rulers according to petrographic investigation of the Amarna tablets. TelAv 29 (2002) 221-237.

12769 *Kemp, Barry* Resuming the Amarna survey. EgArch 20 (2002) 10-12.

12770 *Liverani, Mario* Il 'corriere rapido' nelle lettere de El-Amarna. [M]IMPARATI, F. 2002 ⇒61. 491-496;

12771 The cautious advisers of the Amarna pharaohs. [M]CIASCA, A. 2002 ⇒15. 289-294.

12772 *Na'aman, Nadav* Dispatching Canaanite maidservants to the Pharaoh. ANESt 39 (2002) 76-82.

12773 *Rainey, Anson F.* The 'Amârjan texts a century after Flinders PET-RIE. ANESt 39 (2002) 44-75.

12774 *Van der Westhuizen, J.P.* Subject fronting in the Shechem letters. JSem 11/1 (2002) 1-22.

12775 *Waki, Mihoko* Storage in ancient Egyptian towns and cities (with a focus on Amarna). GöMisz 190 (2002) 103-112.

T7.4 **Memphis,** *Saqqara*—**Pyramides,** *Giza* (Cairo)

12776 **Arnold, Dieter,** *al.*, The pyramid complex of Senwosret III at Dah-shur: architectural studies. NY 2002, Metropolitan Museum of Art 150 pp. $100. 164 pl.; 38 fig.
12777 [E]**Bárta, Miroslav; Krejcí, Jaromír** Abusir and Saqqara in the year 2000. ArOr.S 9: 2000 ⇒17,11595. [R]JARCE 39 (2002) 254-256 (*Brand, Peter J.*).
12778 *Bogdanov, I.V.* Foreigners as pyramid temple personnel. Journal of Ancient History 242 (2002) 23-32 Sum 32. **R.**
12779 **Kanawati, Naguib,** *al.*, Tombs at Giza, Vol I: Kaiemankh (G4561) and Seshemnefer I(G4940). 2001 ⇒17,11602. [R]DiscEg 53 (2002) 87-89 (*DuQuesne, Terence*);
12780 Vol II: Seshathetep/Heti (G5150) and Seshemnefer I I(G5080). The Australian Centre for Egyptology, Reports 18: Wmr 2002, Aris & P. 68 pp. 0-85668-815-0. Num. pl., ill.
12781 *Lehner, Mark* The Pyramid Age settlement of the southern mount at Giza. JARCE 39 (2002) 27-74.
12782 *Mathieu, Bernard* Les pyramides du point de vue du défunt. [E]*Laurant, Sophie*: MoBi 145 (2002) 27-29.
12783 *O'Connor, David* Pyramid origins: a new theory. [F]HANSEN, D. 2002 ⇒58. 169-182.
12784 **Rousseau, Jean** Construire la grande pyramide. 2001 ⇒17,11608. [R]DiscEg 52 (2002) 107-113 (*Potter, Jeremy*).
12785 **Verner, Miroslav** The pyramids: their archaeology and history. L 2002, Atlantic xiv; 495 pp. £25. 1-903809-45-2. Num. ill. [R]DiscEg 53 (2002) 131-134 (*Matthews, Valerie*).

T7.5 **Delta Nili**; *Alexandria*

12786 *Butzer, Karl W.* Geoarchaeological implications of recent research in the Nile delta. Egypt and the Levant. 2002 ⇒497. 81-97.
12787 *Faltings, Dina A.* The chronological frame and social structure of Buto in the fourth millennium BCE. Egypt and the Levant. 2002 ⇒ 497. 165-170.
12788 *Kaplony, Peter* The first (certain) testimony for the city-name 'Sais'. [F]GOPHNA, R. 2002 ⇒49. 255-268.
12789 *Laurant, Sophie* Dans le delta du Nil, le royaume des pharaons de Tanis. MoBi 141 (2002) 6-13.

12790 *Alston, Richard* Reading Augustan Alexandria. Ancient West & East 1/1 (2002) 141-161.
12791 **Bernand, André; Goddio, Franck** L'Égypte engloutie: Alexan-drie. P 2002, Institut européen d'archéologie 191 pp. 28456-71067.
12792 *Empereur, Jean-Yves* Alexandrie (Égypte). BCH 126 (2002) 615-626;
12793 Du nouveau sur la topographie d'Alexandrie. CRAI 3 (2002) 921-933.
12794 [E]**Empereur, Jean-Yves** Alexandrina, 1. 1998 ⇒16,12002. [R]CEg 153-154 (2002) 346-348 (*Nachtergael, Georges*);

12795 Alexandrina, 2. Etudes Alexandrines 6: Le Caire 2002, Institut français d'Archéologie orientale viii; 349 pp. ᴿCEg 153-154 (2002) 348-351 (*Nachtergael, Georges*).

12796 *Fernández Sangrador, Jorge Juan* Alejandría. ResB 35 (2002) 55-61.

12797 **Fernández Sangrador, Jorge Juan** Los orígenes de la comunidad cristiana de Alejandría. 1994 ⇒10,12777... 12,10451. ᴿBurgos 43 (2002) 244-245 (*Fernández, Aurelio*).

12798 **Jakab, Attila** Ecclesia Alexandrina: évolution sociale et institutionnelle du christianisme alexandrin (IIe-IIIe siècles). 2001 ⇒17, 11616. ᴿCHR 88 (2002) 561-562 (*Pearson, Birger A.*); Salm 49 (2002) 497-501 (*Fernández Sangrador, Jorge Juan*).

12799 *Moioli, Maria Lauretta* La cultura scientifica in Alessandria nella prima epoca ellenistica: spunti per un discorso propedeutico. Acme 55/1 (2002) 249-259.

12800 *Taub, L.* Instruments of Alexandrian astronomy: the uses of the equinoctial rings. Science and mathematics. 2002 ⇒532. 133-149.

12801 **Venit, Marjorie Susan** Monumental tombs of ancient Alexandria: the theater of the dead. C 2002, CUP xv; 267 pp. 0-521-80659-3. Bibl. 205-222.

T7.6 *Alii situs Ægypti* alphabetice

12802 *Abousir*: **Vachala, Bretislav** Guide des sites d'Abousir. Le Caire 2002, Inst. français d'archéologie orientale 112 pp. 2-7247-0326-X [BiOr 60,615.];

12803 *Verner, Miroslav* Forty years of the Czech excavations in Abusir. ArOr 70 (2002) 415-425.

12804 **Verner, Miroslav** Abusir: realm of Osiris. Cairo 2002, The American University in Cairo Press (8) 248 pp. $49.50. 977-424-723-X. Bibl. 243-244. ᴿNEA(BA) 65 (2002) 214-215 (*Chauvet, Violaine*).

12805 *Amara*: ᴱ**Spencer, Patricia** Amara West I: the architectural report. 1997 ⇒13,10999... 15,11797. ᴿCEg 153-154 (2002) 172-177 (*Troy, Lana*);

12806 Amara West: II, the cemetery and pottery corpus. Excavation Memoir 69: L 2002, Egypt Exploration Society xii; 39 pp. 0-85698-150-8. Bibl. xi-xii.

12807 *Avaris*: **Fuscaldo, Perla** Tell El-Dab'a X: the palace district of Avaris: the pottery of the Hyksos period and the New Kingdom (Areas H/III and H/VI). 2000 ⇒16,12008. ᴿBiOr 59 (2002) 73-75 (*Aksamit, Joanna*).

12808 *Ayn al-Labakha* **Hussein, Adel** Le sanctuaire rupestre de Piyris à Ayn al-Labakha. 2000 ⇒16,12009. ᴿBiOr 59 (2002) 88-93 (*Kaper, Olaf E.*).

12809 *Dakhleh*: ᴱ**Hope, Colin A.; Bowen, Gillian E.** Dakhleh Oasis Project: monograph: preliminary reports on the 1994-1995 to 1998-1999 field seasons. Dakhleh Oasis Project, Monograph 11. Oxf 2002, Oxbow v; 349 pp. £60/$90. 1-84217-070-8.

12810 *Deir el-Medina*: *Toivari-Viitala, Jaana* A case study of ancient Egyptian marriage practices in the workman's community at Deir el-Medina during the Ramesside period. Sex and gender. 2002 ⇒ 712. 613-619.

12811 *el-ʿAjjul*: Fischer, Peter M., al., Tell el-ʿAjjul 200: second season preliminary report. Ä&L 12 (2002) 109-153.
12812 *El-Bahnasa*: Padró, J., al., Campañas del 2001-2002 en Oxirrinco (El-Bahnasa, Egipto). AuOr 20 (2002) 147-161.
12813 *el-Balamun*: **Spencer, A.J.** Excavations at Tell el-Balamun 1995-1998. 1999 ⇒15,11807...17,11626. [R]BiOr 59 (2002) 301-304 (*French, Peter*).
12814 *el-Dabʿa*: Jánosi, Peter Bericht über die im Frühjahr 2001 erfolgten Sondagen im Dorf ʿEzbet Helmi (Grabungsfläche H/I). Ä&L 12 (2002) 195-210.
12815 *Fayyum*: **Zecchi, Marco** Geografia religiosa del Fayyum: dalle origini al IV. secolo a.C. 2001 ⇒17,11632. [R]Aeg. 81 (2001) 352 (*Curto, Silvio*).
12816 *Panopolis*: [E]**Egberts, A.; Muhs, B.P.; Van der Vliet, J.** Perspectives on Panopolis: an Egyptian town from Alexander the Great to the Arab conquest. Acts internat. symposium, Leiden Dec. 1998. PLB 31: Lei 2002, Brill xix; 273 pp. €110/$128. 90-04-11753-9.
12817 *Taposiris Magna*: **Vörös, Gy.** Taposiris Magna, port of Isis: Hungarian excavations at Alexandria (1998-2001). 2001 ⇒17, 11640. [R]DiscEg 53 (2002) 123-129 (*La'da, Csaba A.*).
12818 *Umm el-Qaab*: **Dreyer, Günter**, al., Umm el-Qaab I: das prädynastische Königsgrab U-j und seine frühen Schriftzeugnisse. Archäologische Veröffentlichungen 86: 1998 ⇒14,11070; 16,12018. [R]JARCE 39 (2002) 258-263 (*Van den Brink, Edwin C.M.*).

T7.7 Antiquitates Nubiae et alibi

12819 *Burstein, Stanley M.* Ethiopia: the southern periphery of the Graeco-Roman world. Ancient West & East 1/1 (2002) 55-58.
12820 [E]**Friedman, Renée** Egypt and Nubia: gifts of the desert. L 2002, British Museum xv; 255 pp. $63. 0-7141-1954-7. Colloquium British Museum 1998.
12821 *Gophna, Ram; Van den Brink, Edwin C.M.* Core-periphery interaction between the pristine Egyptian Nagada IIIb state, late Early Bronze Age I Canaan, and terminal A-group lower Nubia: more data. Egypt and the Levant. 2002 ⇒497. 280-285.
12822 **Kirwan, Laurence** Studies on the history of late antique and christian Nubia. [E]Hägg, Tomas; Török, László; Welsby, Derek A.: CStS 748: Aldershot, Hampshire 2002, Ashgate xii; 262 pp. £57.50. 0-86078-893-8.
12823 *Lohwasser, Angelika* Eine phönizische Bronzeschale aus dem Sudan. Ä&L 12 (2002) 221-234.
12824 **Török, László** The image of the ordered world in ancient Nubian art: the construction of the Kushite mind, 800 BC-300 AD. PÄ 18: Lei 2002, Brill xix; 525 pp. €132/$154. 90-04-12306-7.

T7.9 Sinai

12825 **Anati, Emmanuel** The riddle of Mount Sinai: archaeological discoveries at Har Karkom. Studi Camuni 21: 2001 ⇒17,11641. [R]ArOr 70 (2002) 81-82 (*Vachala, Břetislav*).

12826 **Eddy, Frank W.; Wendorf, Fred**, *al.*, An archaeological investigation of the central Sinai, Egypt. 1999 ⇒15,11827. ^RAJA 106 (2002) 607-608 (*Snape, Steven*).

12827 **Meshel, Zeev** Sinai: excavations and studies. BAR intern. ser. 876: 2000 ⇒16,12025. ^RBASOR 327 (2002) 86-7 (*Gittlen, Barry M.*).

12828 ^E**Mouton, Jean-Michel** Le Sinaï de la conquête arabe à nos jours. Cahier des Annales Islamologiques 21: Le Caire 2001, Institut français d'archéologie orientale 227 pp. ^RStIsl 95 (2002) 177-180 (*Troupeau, Gérard*).

12829 *Saidel, Benjamin Adam* More than meets the eye: a reappraisal of the occupational history of Unit A at Nabi Salah in southern Sinai. BAIAS 19-20 (2001-2002) 19-27.

12830 *Stanley, Jean-Daniel* Configuration of the Egypt-to-Canaan coastal margin and north Sinai byway in the Bronze Age. Egypt and the Levant. 2002 ⇒497. 98-117.

12831 *Steel, L.*, *al.*, Late Bronze Age Gaza: prestige production at el-Moghraqa. Antiquity 76 (2002) 939-940.

12832 *Yekutieli, Yuval* Settlement and subsistence patterns in north Sinai during the fifth to third millennia BCE. Egypt and the Levant. 2002 ⇒497. 422-433.

T8.1 Anatolia *generalia*

12833 *Attoura, Hala* Aspekte der Akkulturation. Brückenland Anatolien?. 2002 ⇒453. 19-33.

12834 *Burney, Charles* Urartu and its forerunners: eastern Anatolia and Trans-Caucasia in the second and early first millennia BC. Ancient West & East 1/1 (2002) 51-54.

12835 *Dercksen, Jan Gerrit* Kultureller und wirtschaftlicher Austausch zwischen Assyrern und Anatoliern (Anfang des zweiten Jahrtausends v.Chr.). Brückenland Anatolien?. 2002 ⇒453. 35-44.

12836 *Hawkins, John David* Die Erben des Großreiches II: die archäologischen Denkmäler in den späthethitischen Kleinkönigreichen Anatoliens und Nordsyriens im Überblick (ca. 1180-700 v. Chr). Die Hethiter. 2002 ⇒535. 264-273.

12837 *Hoffner, Harry A. Jr.* Hittite-Israelite cultural parallels. Context of scripture. 2002 ⇒326. xxix-xxxiv;

12838 Before and after space, time, rank and causality. ^FPOPKO, M. 2002 ⇒91. 163-169.

12839 *Klinger, Jörg* Die Hethitologie: Genese und Perspektive eines vergleichsweise jungen Forschungszweiges. Die Hethiter. 2002 ⇒535. 26-29.

12840 *Marazzi, Massimiliano* Segni, segnari e manifestazioni scrittorie nell'Egeo e nell'Anatolia del II millennio a.C. ^FNEUMANN, G. 2002 ⇒80. 283-296.

12841 *Özgüç, Tahsin* Anatolische Fürstensitze: von der Frühbronzezeit bis zu den assyrischen Faktoreien. Die Hethiter. 2002 ⇒535. 42-45.

12842 ^E**Pouthier, Jean-Luc** La Cappadoce patrimoine chrétien. MoBi 142 (2002) 12-47.

12843 *Richter, Thomas* Zur Frage der Entlehnung syrisch-mespotamischer Kulturelemente nach Anatolien in der vor- und frühen althethitischen Zeit (19.-16. Jahrhundert v.Chr.). Brückenland Anatolien?. 2002 ⇒453. 295-322.

12844   *Wilhelm, Gernot* Anatolien zwischen Ost und West. Die Hethiter.
        2002 ⇒535. 16-17.

T8.2 Boğazköy—*Hethaei*, the Hittites

12845   *Bonatz, Dominik* Fremde "Künstler" in Ḫattuša: zur Rolle des Indi-
        viduums beim Austausch materieller Kultur in der Späten Bronze-
        zeit. Brückenland Anatolien?. 2002 ⇒453. 69-83.
12846   **Kassian, Alexei S.** Two Middle Hittite rituals mentioning [f]Ziplan-
        tawija, sister of the Hittite King [m]Tuthalija II/I/. [E]*Korolëv, Andrei
        A.*: 2000 ⇒16,12037. [R]Journal of Ancient History 240 (2002) 51-
        68 [Eng. Sum. 68] (*Sideltsev, A.V.*).
12847   *Niemeier, Wolf-Dietrich* Ḫattusa und Aḫḫijawa im Konflikt um
        Millawanda/Milet: die politische und kulturelle Rolle des mykeni-
        schen Griechenland in Westkleinasien. Die Hethiter. 2002 ⇒535.
        294-299.
12848   **Otten, Heinrich; Rüster, Christel** Textfunde von Büyükkale aus
        den Jahren 1934-1939. KBo 43: B 2002, Mann xviii; 50 pp. 3-786-
        1-2421-3.
12849   *Özgüç, Tahsin* Die Stellung der Hethiter im kulturellen Erbe der
        Türkei. Die Hethiter. 2002 ⇒535. 14-15;
12850   Frühe Bronzezeit: die Kultur der Hattier als Quelle der hethitischen
        Kultur. Die Hethiter. 2002 ⇒535. 36-41.
12851   *Seeher, Jürgen* Eine in Vergessenheit geratene Kultur gewinnt Pro-
        fil: die Erforschung der Hethiter bis 1950;
12852   Großkönigliche Residenz—Mittelpunkt staatlichen Lebens: die Pa-
        lastanlage in der hethitischen Hauptstadt Ḫattusa;
12853   Ḫattusa-Boğazköy—Hauptstadt des Reiches: die Entwicklung der
        Stadtanlage und ihr Ausbau zur Großreichsmetropole. Die Hethiter.
        2002 ⇒535. 20-25/94-99/156-163.
12854   *Yener, K. Aslihan* Excavations in Hittite heartlands: recent investi-
        gations in Late Bronze Age Anatolia. [M]GÜTERBOCK, H. 2002 ⇒54.
        1-9.

T8.3 Ephesus; Pergamon

12855   *Becker, Guido* Anhang zu "Selig, die nicht sehen und doch glau-
        ben": Privatoffenbarungen und biblische Archäologie. Theologi-
        sches 32 (2002) 21-24 [Ephesos; Emmaus].
12856   *Dray, Stephen* The problem of the historical context of scripture.
        Evangel 20 (2002) 79-81.
12857   **Murcia Ortuño, Francisco Javier** Sintaxis de las inscripciones
        griegas de Éfeso. ClByM 45: 1999 ⇒16,12041. [R]EM 70 (2002)
        353-357 (*Riaño Rufilanchas, Daniel*).
12858   [E]**Pillinger, R.,** *al.,* Efeso paleocristiana e bizantina: frühchristliches
        und byzantinisches Ephesos. Archäologische Forschungen 3;
        DÖAW.PH 282: 1999 ⇒15,11842. [R]CDios 215 (2002) 321-322
        (*Gutiérrez, J.*).

12859   *Lawall, Mark L.* Early excavations at Pergamon and the chronology
        of Rhodian amphora stamps. Hesp. 71 (2002) 295-324.

12860 *Queyrel, François* La fonction du grand autel de Pergame. REG 115 (2002) 561-590.
12861 **Radt, Wolfgang** Pergamon: Geschichte und Bauten einer antiken Metropole. 1999 ⇒15,11847; 16,12044. ^RAJA 106 (2002) 132-133 *(Ault, Bradley)*.
12862 *Schwarzer, Holger* Vereinslokale im hellenistischen und römischen Pergamon. Religiöse Vereine. STAC 13: 2002 ⇒468. 221-260.

т8.6 *Situs Anatoliae*—Turkey sites

12863 *Lampe, Peter* The Phrygian Archaeological Surface Survey Project of the University of Heidelberg and the discovery of Pepouza and Tymion. ZAC 6 (2002) 117-120.

12864 *Alacahöyük*: *Özgüç, Tahsin* Alacahöyük: ein Kultort im Kerngebiet des Reiches. Die Hethiter. 2002 ⇒535. 172-175.
Antioch P: ^E**Drew-Bear, T**. Congrès sur Antioche 2002 ⇒734.
12865 *Belkis*: *Önal, Mehmet* Rescue excavations in Belkis/Zeugma: the Dionysos room and the pit below its mosaic floor. DaM 13 (2002) 317-319.
12866 *Diyarbakir*: *Lipiński, Edward* Diyarbakir an Aramaean capital of the 9th century B.C. and its territory. ^FPOPKO, M. 2002 ⇒91. 225-239.
12867 *Kuşakli-Sarissa*: *Müller-Karpe, Andreas* Kuşakli-Sarissa: Kultort im Oberen Land. Die Hethiter. 2002 ⇒535. 176-189;
12868 Kuşaklı-Sarissa: a Hittite town in the 'upper land'. ^MGÜTERBOCK, H. 2002 ⇒54. 145-155.
12869 *Maşathöyük*: *Özgüç, Tahsin* Maşathöyük. Die Hethiter. 2002 ⇒ 535. 168-171.
12870 *Midas*: **Berndt, Dietrich** Midasstadt in Phrygien: eine sagenumwobene Stätte im anatolischen Hochland. Zaberns Bildbände zur Archäologie: Mainz 2002, Von Zabern 80 pp. €34.80. 3-8053-2855-9.
12871 *Neša*: *Özgüç, Tahsin* Neša: Beschreibung einer Stadtentwicklung. Die Hethiter. 2002 ⇒535. 152-155.
12872 *Nemrud Daği*: *Jacobs, Bruno* Bergheiligtum und Heiliger Berg: Überlegungen zur Wahl des Nemrud Daği-Gipfels als Heiligtums- und Grabstätte. Religiöse Landschaften. AOAT 301: 2002 ⇒408. 31-47.
12873 *Norşuntepe*: **Schmidt, Klaus** Norşuntepe: Kleinfunde II. Mainz 2002, Von Zabern xii; 206 pp. €128. 3-8053-2015-9. 86 tables; 16 pl.
12874 *Sardis*: **Ramage, Andrew; Craddock, Paul** King Croesus' gold: excavations at Sardis and the history of gold refining. 2000 ⇒16, 12048. ^RAJA 106 (2002) 113-114 *(Killick, David)*.
12875 *Šapinuwa*: *Süel, Aygül* Ortaköy-Šapinuwa. ^MGÜTERBOCK, H. 2002 ⇒54. 157-165.
12876 *Wilusa*: *Latacz, Joachim* Wilusa [Wilios/Troia]: Zentrum eines hethitischen Gliedstaates in Nordwest-Kleinasien. Die Hethiter. 2002 ⇒535. 196-201.

T8.9 Armenia; Urartu

12877   *Brutian, Georg* Armenology: the subject matter and methods of
        study. Armenians in Jerusalem. 2002 ⇒771. 19-31.
12878   *Mgaloblishvili, Tamila G.* The most ancient feast of Vardoba-Athe-
        nagenoba. Armenians in Jerusalem. 2002 ⇒771. 157-165.

12879   ᴱ**Biscione, Raffaele; Hmayakyan, Simon; Parmegiani, Neda** The
        north-eastern frontier Urartians and non-Urartians in the Sevan
        Lake Basin. Documenta Asiana 7: R 2002, CNR 474 pp. 88-87345-
        06-6.

T9.1 Cyprus

12880   ᴱ**Bolger, Diane; Serwint, Nancy** Engendering Aphrodite: women
        and society in ancient Cyprus. ASOR Archaeological Reports 7;
        CAARI Monographs 3: Boston 2002, American Schools of Archae-
        ological Research xvi; 457 pp. $100. 124 fig.
12881   *Karageorghis, Vassos* Some thoughts on the past, present and
        future of Cypriot studies. Ancient West & East 1/1 (2002) 34-38.
12882   **Karageorghis, Vassos** Cipro: crocevia del Mediterraneo orientale
        1600-500 a.C. Centri e monumenti dell'antichità: Mi 2002, Electa
        226 pp. 88-435-7217-2. Bibl. 218-225;
12883   Early Cyprus: crossroads of the Mediterranean. LA 2002, Getty
        Museum 231 pp. $70. 0-89236-679-6. 424 fig.;
12884   Ancient art from Cyprus in the cultural foundation of the Bank of
        Cyprus. 2001 ⇒17,11680. ᴿBiOr 59 (2002) 166-168 (*Wright,
        G.R.H.*);
12885   Ancient Cypriote art in Copenhagen: the collection of the National
        Museum of Denmark and the Ny Carlsberg Glyptotek. 2001 ⇒17,
        11681. ᴿBASOR 328 (2002) 90-92 (*Barlow, Jane A.*).
12886   ᴱ**Smith, Joanna S.** Script and seal use on Cyprus in the Bronze and
        Iron Ages. Colloquia and Conference Papers 4: Boston, MA 2002,
        Archaeological Institute of America xv; (2) 248 pp. $35/£30. 0-
        9609042-7-1. Conf. Archaeological Institute of America 1997.
12887   ᴱ**Swiny, Stuart** The earliest prehistory of Cyprus from colonization
        to exploitation. ASOR, Archaeological Reports 5: 2001 ⇒17,
        11686. ᴿBASOR 328 (2002) 81-84 (*Knapp, A. Bernard*).
12888   **Webb, Jennifer M.** Ritual architecture, iconography and practice
        in Late Bronze Age Cyprus. SIMA Pocket Book 15: 1999 ⇒15,
        11872. ᴿBiOr 59 (2002) 158-161 (*Wright, G.R.H.*).

T9.3 *Graecia*, Greece

12889   **Alcock, Susan E.** Archaeologies of the Greek past: landscape,
        monuments, and memories. The W.B. Stanford Memorial Lectures:
        C 2002, CUP xiv; 222 pp. 0-521-81355-7. Bibl. 184-212.
12890   *Bellia, Giuseppe* Viaggio, a Creta, Rodi e Patmos. Ho Theológos
        20 (2002) 143-146.
12891   **Camp, John M.** The archaeology of Athens. 2001 ⇒17,11693.
        ᴿAJA 106 (2002) 617-619 (*Glowacki, Kevin*).

12892 **Cerchiai, Luca; Jannelli, Lorena; Longo, Fausto** Città greche della Magna Grecia e della Sicilia. Venezia 2002, Arsenale 286 pp. 88-7743-278-0. Bibl. 279-282.

12893 *Etienne, Roland, al.*, Délos. BCH 126 (2002) 529-546.

12894 **French, Elizabeth** Mycenae: Agamemnon's capital: the site in its setting. Stroud, Gloucestershire 2002, Tempus 160 pp. 0-7524-1951-X. Bibl. 154-155.

12895 *Gauthier, Philippe* Rapport sur l'état et l'activité de l'École française d'Athènes pendant l'année 2001-2002. CRAI (2002) 1141-1150.

12896 **Godart, Louis** Popoli dell'Egeo: civiltà dei palazzi. Civiltà mediterranee: CinB 2002, Silvana 142 pp.

12897 **Hitchcock, Louise A.** Minoan architecture: a contextual analysis. SIMA-PB 155: Jonsered 2000, Åströms 267 pp. $38.90. 91-7081-192-X. 33 fig. [R]AJA 106 (2002) 123-124 (*Mcenroe, John C.*); BiOr 59 (2002) 153-158 (*Wright, G.R.H.*).

12898 **Lemos, Irene S.** The protogeometric Aegean: the archaeology of the late eleventh and tenth centuries BC. Oxf 2002, OUP xxiv; 319 pp. £110. 0-19-925344-7. 26 fig., pl.

12899 **Merker, Gloria S.** Corinth, 18/4: the sanctuary of Demeter and Kore: terracotta figurines of the classical, Hellenistic and Roman periods. 2000 ⇒16,12081; 17,11700. [R]RAr (2002/2) 426-428 (*Jeammet, Violaine*).

12900 **Morris, Ian** Archaeology as cultural history: words and things in Iron Age Greece. 2000 ⇒16,12083. [R]Antiquity 291 (2002) 261-262 (*Mee, Christopher*); RAr (2002/2) 424-426 (*Kistler, Erich*).

12901 **Murphy-O'Connor, Jerome** St. Paul's Corinth: texts and archaeology. ColMn [3]2002 <1983, 1992>, Liturgical xiv; 241 pp. $22. 0-8146-5303-0 [ThD 50,176—Heiser, W. Charles].

12902 *Provost, Samuel* Philippes. BCH 126 (2002) 502-518.

12903 *Provost, Samuel; Boyd, Michael* Application de la prospection géophysique à la topographie urbaine, II: Philippes, les quartiers Ouest. BCH 126 (2002) 431-488.

12904 **Rothaus, Richard M.** Corinth: the first city of Greece: an urban history of late antique cult and religion. RGRW 139: 2000 ⇒16, 12086. [R]JBL 121 (2002) 769-773 (*DeMaris, Richard E.*).

12905 **Themelis, Petros** Ηρωες και ηρωα της Αρχαιας Μεσσηνης. Βιβλιοθήκη της εν Αθήναις Αρχαιολογικής Εταιρείας 210: Athens 2000, Athens Archaeological Society x; 191 pp. 960-8145-16-3. 154 fig.; 6 pl.

12906 [E]**Wells, Berit** New research on old material from Asine and Berbati: in celebration of the fiftieth anniversary of the Swedish Institute at Athens. Skrifter Utgivna av Svenska Institutet i Athen 8/17; Acta Instituti Romani Regni Sueciae 8/17: Sto 2002, Astroms 155 pp. 91-7916-043-3.

12907 **Whitley, James** The archaeology of ancient Greece. 2001 ⇒17, 11703. [R]Antiquity 291 (2002) 262-264 (*Mee, Christopher*).

12908 [E]**Williams, Charles K., II; Bookidis, Nancy** Corinth: results of excavations conducted by The American School of Classical Studies at Athens: vol. XX: Corinth, the centenary, 1896-1996. CM 2002, Harvard Univ. Pr. xxviii (2); 475 pp. 0-87661-020-8. Bibl. xi-xxiii.

T9.4 **Creta**

12909 [E]**Chaniotis, A.** From Minoan farmers to Roman traders: sidelights on the economy of ancient Crete. 1999 ⇒15,11878; 17,11707. [R]At. 90 (2002) 678-680 (*Foraboschi, Daniele*).

12910 **Fitton, J. Lesley** Minoans. Peoples of the Past: L 2002, British Museum 224 pp. 0-7141-2140-1. Bibl. 215.

12911 [E]**Hamilakis, Yannis** Labyrinth revisited: rethinking 'Minoan' archaeology. Oxf 2002, Oxbow x; 237 pp. $45. 1-84217-061-9.

12912 **Sporn, Katja** Heiligtümer und Kulte Kretas in klassischer und hellenistischer Zeit. Heid 2002, Archäologie und G. 416 pp. €75. 3-935-289-00-6. 30 pl.; 19 tables.

12913 *Tanner, Mary* The winds of Crete: a bible study. ER 54 (2002) 455-457.

T9.6 **Urbs Roma**

12914 [E]**Augenti, Andrea** Art and archaeology of Rome: from ancient times to the baroque. 2000 ⇒16,12090. [R]Prudentia 34 (2002) 229-231 (*Wilson, Marcus*).

12915 *Bendlin, Andreas* Gemeinschaft, Öffentlichkeit und Identität: forschungsgeschichtliche Anmerkungen zu den Mustern sozialer Ordnung in Rom. Religiöse Vereine. STAC 13: 2002 ⇒468. 9-40.

12916 **Berliner, Abraham** Storia degli Ebrei a Roma: dall'antichità allo smantellamento del Ghetto. 2000 ⇒16,12092. Orig. tedesc. 1893. [R]ATT 8 (2002) 241-243 (*Ghiberti, Giuseppe*).

12917 **Bomgardner, D.L.** The story of the Roman amphitheater. 2000 ⇒ 16,12094. [R]AJA 106 (2002) 342-343 (*Futrell, Alison*).

12918 **Bonfils, Giovanni de** Roma e gli ebrei (secoli I-V). Bari 2002, Cacucci 277 pp. €20. 88-8422-166-8.

12919 **Claridge, Amanda** Rome: an Oxford archaeological guide. 1998 ⇒14,11181. [R]JRS 92 (2002) 218-219 (*Bispham, Edward*).

12920 *Dentzer, Jean-Marie* Rapport sur l'état et l'activité de l'École française de Rome pendant l'année 2001-2002. CRAI (2002) 1173-94.

12921 **Haselberger, Lothar**, *al.*, Mapping Augustan Rome. [E]*Dumser, Elisha Ann*: Journal of Roman Archaeology Suppl 50: Portsmouth 2002, Journal of Roman Archaeology 275 pp. $109.50. 1-887829-50-4. 20 fig.; 2 maps.

12922 **Junkelmann, Marcus** Das Spiel mit dem Tod: so kämpften Roms Gladiatoren. 2000 ⇒16,12106. [R]AJA 106 (2002) 343-344 (*Cerutti, Steven M.*).

12923 **Kardos, Marie-José** Lexique de topographie romaine. Topographie de Rome II: P 2002, L'Harmattan 373 pp. €29.50. 2-7475-3546-0 [Latomus 63,810—Jacques Poucet].

12924 *Martí Aixalà, Josep* Roma. ResB 35 (2002) 45-53.

12925 **Salles, C.** La Rome des Flaviens, Vespasien, Titus, Domitien. P 2002, Perrin 277 pp. 2-262-014752. Bibl.

12926 [E]**Steinby, Eva Margareta** Lexicon topographicum urbis Romae: 5 (T-Z). 1999 ⇒15,11892. [R]AJA 106 (2002) 138-139 (*Richardson, L.*); Latomus 61 (2002) 240-241 (*Debergh, Jacques*).

12927 **Vigna, Massimo** Roma: un millennio di sacralità. Saggi 73: R 2002, Sigillo 253 pp. Bibl. 241-245.

T9.7 Catacumbae

12928 **Bisconti, Fabrizio** Mestieri nelle catacombe romane: appunti sul declino dell'iconografia del reale nei cimiteri cristiani di Roma. 2000 ⇒16,12118; 17,11730. [R]Aug. 42 (2002) 502-504 (*Ghilardi, Massimiliano*).

12929 *Cappelletti, Silvia* Sulla cronologia delle catacombe giudaico-romane di Villa Torlonia. Acme 55/1 (2002) 261-278.

12930 Centocinquanta anni di tutela delle catacombe cristiane d'Italia. Città del Vaticano 2002, Pontificia Commissione di archeologia sacra. 30 pp. 88-88420-01-0. Ill.

12931 **Dorsch, Klaus-Dieter; Seeliger, Hans Reinhard** Römische Katakombenmalereien: im Spiegel des Photoarchivs Parker; Dokumentation von Zustand und Erhaltung 1864-1994. 2000 ⇒16,12120; 17,11731. [R]RQ 97 (2002) 346-347 (*Heid, Stefan*).

12932 **Fiocchi Nicolai, Vincenzo** Strutture funerarie ed edifici di culto paleocristiani di Roma dal IV al VI secolo. 2001 ⇒17,11734. [R]SMSR 68 (2002) 429-431 (*Luciani, Valentina*).

12933 *Guyon, Jean* Vereint im Tod: christliche und heidnische Gräber in den Katakomben an der Via Latina in Rom. WUB 25 (2002) 50-53.

12934 **Pergola, Philippe** Le catacombe romane: storia e topografia. Quality paperbacks 46: R 2002, Carocci 263 pp. 88-430-2164-8. Catalogo a cura di *Palmira Maria Barbini*; Bibl. 247-263.

12935 **Zimmermann, Norbert** Werkstattgruppen römischer Katakombenmalerei. JAC.E 35: Müns 2002, Aschendorff 309 pp. 3-402-8118-0. Num. pl.

T9.8 *Archaeologia paleochristiana*—early Christian archaeology

12936 [E]**Cecchelli, Margherita** Materiali e tecniche dell'edilizia paleocristiana a Roma. 2001 ⇒17,11738. [R]Aug. 42 (2002) 504-506 (*Ghilardi, Massimiliano*).

12937 **Íñiguez, José Antonio** Tratado de arqueología cristiana. Biblioteca de teología 25: Pamplona 2002, EUNSA 566 pp. 84-313-1990-9 [ActBib 79,90—Borràs, A.].

12938 *Kotansky, Roy* An early christian gold lamella for headache. Magic and ritual. RGRW 141: 2002 ⇒505. 37-46.

12939 *Leyerle, Blake* Children and disease in a sixth century monastery. [F]FOERSTER, G. 2002 ⇒39. 349-372.

12940 *Locatelli, Davide* La ripresa delle indagini archeologiche nella villa di San Pawl Milqi a Malta. [M]CIASCA, A. 2002 ⇒15. 295-318.

12941 *Provoost, Arnold* A theoretical model concerning early christian topography. [F]FOERSTER, G. 2002 39. 333-347.

12942 **Thümmel, Hans-Georg** Die Memorien für Petrus und Paulus in Rom. 1999 ⇒15,11903; 17,11745. [R]ZKG 113 (2002) 99-101 (*Blaauw, Sible de*).

12943 **Volp, Ulrich** Tod und Ritual in den christlichen Gemeinden der Antike. SVigChr 65: Lei 2002, Brill 340 pp. €85/$101. 90-041267-1-6. Bibl. 273-309.

XIX. Geographia biblica

U1.0 Geographica

12944 **Artus, Olivier** La géographie de la bible. CEv 122: P 2002, Cerf 1-61 pp. €5.79. 0222-9714.

12945 **Aujac, Germaine** ERATOSTHÈNE de Cyrène, le pionnier de la géographie: sa mesure de la circonférence terrestre. 2001 ⇒17, 11749. ᴿBAGB 61/4 (2002) 83-84 *(Briquel, Dominique)*.

12946 ᴱ**Sbordone, Franciscus; Medaglia, Silvius M.** STRABONIS geographica, 3: libri VII-IX. Scriptores graeci et latini: R 2000, Officinae Polygraphicae xxiv; 437 pp. €21.70.

12947 *Ur, Jason A.* Settlement and landscape in northern Mesopotamia: the Tell Hamoukar survey 2000-2001. Akkadica 123 (2002) 57-88.

12948 *Zadok, Ran* Contributions to Babylonian geography, prosopography and documentation. ᶠDIETRICH, M. 2002 ⇒28. 871-897.

U1.4 Atlas— maps; photographiae

12949 ᴱ**Aharoni, Yohanan,** *al.,* The Carta bible atlas. J ⁴2002, Carta 223 pp. $39. 965-220487-0.

12950 **Balossi Restelli, Francesca** Atlante storico del vicino oriente antico, 1: la formazione delle più antiche culture agricole, Fasc. 4: epipaleolitico e neolitico aceramico. ᴱ*Liverani, Mario*: R 2002, 33 pp. 88-87242-19-4. Zahlr. Ill. u. Kt.

12951 *Berggren, J.L.* PTOLEMY's maps as an introduction to ancient science. Science and mathematics. 2002 ⇒532. 36-55.

12952 *Blümel, Wolfgang* Karien im Barrington Atlas: corrigenda et addenda. Epigraphica Anatolica 34 (2002) 115-116.

12953 **Chenorkian, Robert; Harbi-Riahi, Mounira; Zoughlami, Jamel** Atlas préhistorique de la Tunisie 19: Maharès. CEFR 81: R 2002, École Française de Rome (4); 95 pp. 2-7283-0662-1.

12954 **Custer, Stewart** Stones of witness: images of the Holy Land. Greenville, SC 2002, BJU Pr. xii; 236 pp. $50.

12955 ᴱ**Dowley, Tim** Atlas of the bible and christianity. 1997 ⇒13, 11110; 14,11239. ᴿJian Dao 17 (2002) 203-204 *(Ka-Lun, Leung)*.

12956 *Goren, Haim* Sacred, but not surveyed: why was the *Survey of Western Palestine* put off until the 1870s?. Cathedra 106 (2002) 87-118 Sum. 204. **H.**

12957 ᴱᵀ**Kam-to, Choi,** *al.,* Atlas of the bible and christianity. 1999 ⇒15, 11925. ᴿJian Dao 17 (2002) 203-204 *(Ka-Lun, Leung)* [⇒12955].

12958 ᴱ**Kennedy, Hugh** An historical atlas of Islam. Lei ²2002 <1981>, Brill xx; 86 pp. €225/$295. 90-04-12235-4. With CD-Rom.

12959 **Kettermann, Günter** Atlas zur Geschichte des Islam. Da:Wiss 2001, vi; 186 pp. Einleitung von *Adel Theodor Khoury*.

12960 **Motyer, Stephen; Delf, Brian** Atlas bíblico ilustrado. M 2002, Paulinas 48 pp [EstJos 56,276—Llamas, Román].

12961 **Rodriguez-Almeida, Emilio** Formae urbis antiquae: le mappe marmoree di Roma tra la Repubblica e Settimio Severo. CEFR 305: R

2002, École Française de Rome 79 pp. €23. 2-7283-0557-9. Bibl. 77-79.

12962 **Wright, Paul H.** Atlas of bible lands. Nv 2002, Holman 160 pp [Faith & Mission 20/3,114s—David E. Lanier].

12963 [E]**Nordiguian, Lévon; Salles, Jean-François** Aux origines de l'archéologie aérienne: A. POIDEBARD (1878-1955). 2000 ⇒16,12173. [R]Journal of Ancient History 242 (2002) 228-233 (*Koshelenko, G.*).

12964 **Piccarreta, Fabio; Ceraudo, Giuseppe** Manuale di aerofotografia archeologica: metodologia, tecniche e applicazioni. 2000 ⇒16, 12174. [R]AJA 106 (2002) 482-483 (*Myers, J. Wilson*).

U1.6 Guide-books, *Führer*

12965 **Murphy-O'Connor, Jerome** La Terra Santa: guida storico-archeologica. 1996 ⇒12,10566. [R]BeO 44 (2002) 58-61 (*Sardini, Davide*).

U1.7 Onomastica

12966 **Kaswalder, Pietro Alberto** Onomastica biblica: fonti scritte e ricerca archeologica. SBF.CMi 40: J 2002, Franciscan Printing Press 544 pp. $30. 965-516-031-9.

U2.1 Geologia

12967 *Bichler, Max, al.*, Aegean thephra—an analytical approach to a controversy about chronology. A&L 12 (2002) 55-70.

12968 *Hine, Harry M.* Seismology and vulcanology in antiquity?. Science and mathematics. 2002 ⇒532. 56-75.

12969 *Manning, Sturt W., al.*, New evidence for an early date for the Aegean Late Bronze Age and Thera eruption. Antiquity 76 (2002) 733-744.

12970 **Torrence, R.; Grattan, J.** Natural disasters and cultural change. One World Archaeology 45: L 2002, Routledge xv; 352 pp. $135. 0-415-21696-6. 69 fig.; 16 tables; 27 maps.

12971 *Wirsching, Armin* Mit Schattenmessungen die Erdkrümmung erkennen und den Erdumfang berechnen. GöMisz 191 (2002) 89-99.

U2.2 *Hydrographia*; rivers, seas, salt

12972 *Al-Muheisen, Zeidoun; Tarrier, Dominique* Water in the Nabatean period. Aram 14 (2001-2002) 515-524.

12973 [E]**Amit, David; Patrich, Joseph; Hirschfeld, Yizhar** The aqueducts of Israel. Journ. of Roman Archaeology Suppl. 46: Portsmouth, RI 2002, Journ. of Rom. Arch. 459 pp. 1-8878-2946-6.

12974 *Avner, Uzi* Ancient water management in the southern Negev. Aram 14 (2001-2002) 403-421.

12975   **Bagg, Ariel M.** Assyrische Wasserbauten: Landwirtschaftliche Wasserbauten im Kernland Assyriens zwischen der 2. Hälfte des 2. und der I. Hälfte des I. Jahrtausends v. Chr. Baghdader Forschungen 24: 2000 ⇒16,12186. [R]WO 32 (2002) 256-260 (*Radner, Karen*); AfO 48-49 (2001-2002) 212-216 (*Dalley, Stephanie*).

12976   *Costa, Paolo M.* Reservoirs and accelerators. Aram 14 (2001-2002) 581-598.

12977   *Dalley, Stephanie* Water management in Assyria from the ninth to the seventh centuries BC. Aram 14 (2001-2002) 443-460.

12978   *Dight, Richard J.W.* The construction and use of canal regulators in ancient Sumer. AuOr 20 (2002) 115-122.

12979   *Dvorjetski, Estée* Thermo-mineral waters in the eastern Mediterranean basin: historical, archaeological and medicinal aspects. Aram 14 (2001-2002) 487-514.

12980   **Fagan, Garrett G.** Bathing in public in the Roman world. AA 2002, Univ. of Michigan Pr. xiii; 437 pp. $28. 0-472-08865-3. 32 pl.

12981   *Hadas, Gideon* Ein Gedi water mills. BAIAS 19-20 (2001-2002) 71-93.

12982   *Kloner, Amos* Water cisterns in Idumea, Judaea and Nabatea in the Hellenistic and early Roman periods;

12983   *Peleg, Yehuda* The stone pipeline of Susta-Hippos;

12984   *Placentini, Danila* Palmyra's springs in the epigraphic sources. Aram 14 (2001-2002) 461-485/423-441/525-534.

12985   *Reich, Ronny* They are ritual baths: immerse yourself in the ongoing Sepphoris mikveh debate. BArR 28/2 (2002) 50-55.

12986   *Scagliarini, Fiorella* The origin of the *Qanāt* system in the al-ʿUlā area and the Ĝabal ʿIkma inscriptions;

12987   *Tsuk, Tsvika* Urban water reservoirs in the land of the bible during the Bronze and Iron Ages (3000 BC - 586 BC);

12988   *Vibert-Guigue, Claude* La question de l'eau à l'époque omeyyade en Jordanie: approches iconographique et architecturale. Aram 14 (2001-2002) 569-579/377-401/535-567.

12989   [E]**Wikander, Örjan** Handbook of ancient water technology. 2000 ⇒16,12194. [R]Gn. 74 (2002) 468-470 (*Knauss, Jost*).

12990   *Zelinger, Yehiel; Oren, Shmueli* The aqueduct of the heretic's daughter: remains of the early Arab aqueduct to Ramla. [F]GOPHNA, R. 2002 ⇒49. 279-288.

U2.3 *Clima,* climate

12991   *Brown, David* The level of the Euphrates. [F]WALKER, C. 2002 ⇒ 130. 37-56.

12992   **Fitzgerald, Aloysius** The Lord of the east wind. CBQ.MS 34: Wsh 2002, The Catholic Biblical Association of America vi; 234 pp. $12. 0-915170-33-7. Bibl. 210-216.

12993   *Matthews, Roger* Zebu: harbingers of doom in Bronze Age western Asia?. Antiquity 76 (2002) 438-446.

12994   *Sanlaville, P.* Changements climatiques et évolution des plaines alluviales dans le sud du Levant durant les stades isotopiques 5 (125-75 ka) et 4 (75-55 ka). Paléorient 28/1 (2002) 15-26.

U2.5 *Fauna*, **animalia**

12995 [E]**Collins, Billie Jean** A history of the animal world in the ancient Near East. HO 1/64: Lei 2002, Brill xxii; 620 pp. $164. 90-04-12126-9. Bibl. 537-601.

12996 **Barringer, Judith M.** The hunt in ancient Greece. Baltimore 2001, Johns Hopkins Univ. Pr. xiii; 296 pp. $48. 0-8018-6656-1. 110 fig.

12997 *Bar-Yosef Mayer, Daniella E.* Egyptian-Canaanite interaction during the fourth and third millennia BCE: the shell connection. Egypt and the Levant. 2002 ⇒497. 129-135.

12998 *Beaulieu, Paul-Alain* Les animaux dans la divination en Mésopotamie. Les animaux. 2002 ⇒516. 351-365.

12999 *Black, Jeremy* Les bêtes qui parlent: les animaux dans les récits mythologiques sumériens. Les animaux. 2002 ⇒516. 367-382.

13000 *Boehmer, Rainer M.* Vom Hassek Höyük bis zum Buch Tobias: von Sägefischen und Haien im Altertum. BaghM 33 (2002) 7-43.

13001 *Bonechi, Marco* Noms d'oiseaux à Ebla: les rapaces;

13002 *Bordreuil, Pierre; Briquel-Chatonnet, Françoise* Tiglath-Phalasar I a-t-il pêché ou chassé le naḫiru?. Les animaux. 2002 ⇒516. 251-281/ 117-124.

13003 *Borowski, Oded* Animals in the literature of Syria-Palestine;

13004 Animals in the religion of Syria-Palestine;

13005 *Breniquet, Catherine* Animals in Mesopotamian art;

13006 *Brewer, Douglas* Hunting, animal husbandry and diet in ancient Egypt. A history of the animal world. HO I/64: 2002 ⇒12995. 289-306/405-424/145-168/427-456.

13007 *Calvet, Yves* Ougarit: les animaux symboliques du répertoire figuré au Bronze Récent. Les animaux. 2002 ⇒516. 447-465.

13008 *Caubet, Annie* Animals in Syro-Palestinian art. A history of the animal world. HO I/64: 2002 ⇒12995. 211-234.

13009 [E]**Ciccarese, Maria Pia** Animali simbolici: alle origini del bestiario cristiano, 1: (Agnello - Gufo). BPat 39: Bo 2002, EDB 508 pp. €33.90. 88-10-42048-9. Bibl. 463-466.

13010 *Colbow, Gudrun* Les combats d'animaux en Mésopotamie à l'époque paléo-babylonienne. Les animaux. 2002 ⇒516. 383-398.

13011 *Collins, Billie Jean* Animals in Hittite literature;

13012 Animals in the religions of ancient Anatolia. A history of the animal world. HO I/64: 2002 ⇒12995. 237-250/309-334.

13013 *Collon, Dominique* L'animal dans les échanges et les relations diplomatiques. Les animaux. 2002 ⇒516. 125-140.

13014 *Cool Root, Margaret* Animals in the art of ancient Iran. A history of the animal world. HO I/64: 2002 ⇒12995. 169-209.

13015 **De Benedetti, P.** E l'asina disse... l'uomo e gli animali secondo la sapienza di Israele. 1999 ⇒15,11953; 17,11786. [R]Hum(B) 57 (2002) 516-518 (*Bertoletti, Ilario*).

13016 *Dolce, Rita* Ébla: le bestiaire du Bronze Ancien et du Bronze Moyen: valeurs symboliques dans le domaine du sacré et de la royauté. Les animaux. 2002 ⇒516. 411-434.

13017 *Ehrenberg, Erica* The rooster in Mesopotamia. [F]HANSEN, D. 2002 ⇒58. 53-62.

13018 *Fedele, Francesco G.* L'est: la faune du Hamrîn (Iraq). Les animaux. 2002 ⇒516. 15-44.

13019 *Foster, Benjamin R.* Animals in Mesopotamian literature. A history
       of the animal world. HO I/64: 2002 ⇒12995. 271-288.
13020 *Genest, Olivette* La bible relue par les animaux. Théologiques 10/1
       (2002) 131-177.
13021 *Gilbert, Allan S.* The native fauna of the ancient Near East;
13022 Bibliography of Near Eastern zoology. A history of the animal
       world. HO I/64: 2002 ⇒12995. 3-75/493-536.
13023 *Glassner, Jean-Jacques* Signes d'écriture et classification: l'e-
       xemple des ovi-caprinés. Les animaux. 2002 ⇒516. 467-475.
13024 *Groneberg, Brigitte* Tiere als Symbole von Göttern in den frühen
       geschichtlichen Epochen Mesopotamiens: von der altsumerischen
       Zeit bis zum Ende der altbabylonischen Zeit;
13025 *Guichard, Michael* Les animaux dans la vaisselle de luxe d'un roi
       de Mari: l'exemple des gobelets céphalomorphes. Les animaux.
       2002 ⇒516. 283-320/435-446.
13026 *Gunter, Ann C.* Animals in Anatolian art;
13027 *Hesse, Brian; Wapnish, Paula* An archaezoological perspective on
       the cultural use of mammals in the Levant. A history of the animal
       world. HO I/64: 2002 ⇒12995. 79-96/457-491.
13028 **Hoffmann, Friedhelm; Steinhart, Matthias** Tiere vom Nil. 2001
       ⇒17,11793. [R]CEg 153-154 (2002) 354-56 (*Nachtergael, Georges*).
13029 *Horwitz, Liora Kolska* Fauna from the Wadi Rahab site of Abu Zu-
       reiq. IEJ 52 (2002) 167-178.
13030 *Horwitz, Liora Kolska, al.,* The archaeozoology of the three early
       Bronze Age sites in Nahal Besor, north western Negev. [F]GOPHNA,
       R. 2002 ⇒49. 107-133.
13031 *Houlihan, Patrick F.* Some instances of humor associated with
       animal riding in ancient Egypt. GöMisz 190 (2002) 35-45;
13032 Animals in Egyptian art and hieroglyphs. A history of the animal
       world. HO I/64: 2002 ⇒12995. 97-143.
13033 *Huot, Jean-Louis* Quelques réflexions, en guise de conclusion;
13034 *Joannès, Francis* Le découpage de la viande en Mésopotamie;
13035 *Lafont, Bertrand* Cheval, âne, onagre et mule dans la haute histoire
       mésopotamienne: quelques données nouvelles;
13036 *Lion, Brigitte; Michel, Cécile* Poissons et crustacés en Haute
       Mésopotamie au début du IIe millénaire av. J.-C.;
13037 *Mashkour, Marjan* L'exploitation des équidés en Asie du sud-
       ouest: l'exemple de Qabrestan, un établissement du IVe millénaire,
       au nord du plateau central iranien;
13038 Remarques complémentaires sur les vestiges fauniques du temple
       de l'E.Babbar à Larsa en Basse Mésopotamie. Les animaux. 2002
       ⇒516. 489-493/333-345/207-221/71-116/45-54/347-349.
13039 *McKay, Heather A.* Through the eyes of horses: representation of
       the horse family in the Hebrew Bible. [M]CARROLL, R.: JSOT.S 348:
       2002 ⇒13. 127-141.
13040 *Millet Albà, Adelina* Les noms d'animaux dans l'onomastique des
       archives de Mari. Les animaux. 2002 ⇒516. 477-487.
13041 *Monchot, H.; Horwitz, L.K.* Représentation squelettique au paléoli-
       thique inférieur, le site d'Holon (Israël). Paléorient 28/2 (2002) 71-
       86.
13042 **Osborn, Dale J.; Osbornová, Jana** The mammals of ancient
       Egypt. The Natural History of Egypt 4: 1998 ⇒14,11292; 16,
       12218. [R]JNES 61 (2002) 145-146 (*Brewer, Douglas J.*).

13043   *Parayre, Dominique* Les suidés dans le monde syro-mésopotamien aux époques historiques;

13044   *Pardee, Dennis* Animal sacrifice at Ugarit;

13045   Les équidés à Ougarit au Bronze récent: la perspective des textes. Les animaux. 2002 ⇒516. 141-206/321-331/223-234.

13046   *Phillips, Anthony* Animals and the torah. Essays on biblical law. JSOT.S 344: 2002 <1995> ⇒223. 127-138 [Dt 25,4; 22,1-3].

13047   *Poplin, François* Épilogue. Les animaux. 2002 ⇒516. 495-506.

13048   *Riede, Peter* 'Doch frage die Tiere, sie werden dich lehren': Tiere als Vorbilder und 'Lehrer' des Menschen im Alten Testament. Im Spiegel der Tiere. 2002 <1999> ⇒229. 1-28:

13049   Im Spiegel der Tiere: Überlegungen zum Verhältnis von Mensch und Tier in der christlich-jüdischen Tradition <2000> 29-56;

13050   Der Gerechte kennt die Bedürfnisse seiner Tiere: der mensch und die Haustiere in der Sicht des Alten Testaments <1997> 57-64;

13051   David und der Floh: Tiere und Tiervergleiche in den Samuelbüchern <1995> 65-106;

13052   Der Säugling am Loch der Kobra: zum Tierfrieden im Alten Testament. 153-164;

13053   'Denn wie der Mensch jedes Tier nennen würde, so sollte es heißen': hebräische Tiernamen und was sie uns verraten <1993> 165-212;

13054   Tiere im Alten und Neuen Testament: ein Überblick <2001> 213-246;

13055   Nachwort. 247-250;

13056   Anhang 1: alphabetische Übersicht über die Ableitung und Klassifikation der hebräischen Tiernamen <1993> 251-270;

13057   Anhang 2: Glossar der hebräischen und aramäischen Tiernamen / Tierbezeichnungen <1993> 271-288;

13058   Anhang 3: Liste der im hebräischen und griechischen Alten Testament enthaltenen Tiernamen <2001> 289-305;

13059   Anhang 4: neutestamentliche Tiernamen <2001> 306-310.

13060   *Schuegraf, Oliver; Terbuyken, Peri Johanna* "La Illa Il Allah! Aus voller Kehle jauchzten die Treiber der Kamele": zu Verbreitung und Bedeutung antiker Cameliden zwischen Kaspischem Meer, Palästina und Arabischer Halbinsel. JAC 45 (2002) 62-76.

13061   *Scurlock, JoAnn* Animals in ancient Mesopotamian religion;

13062   Animals sacrifice in ancient Mesopotamian religion. A history of the animal world. HO I/64: 2002 ⇒12995. 361-387/389-403.

13063   *Tanret, M.* Les animaux dans les archives d'Ur-Utu. Les animaux. 2002 ⇒516. 55-70.

13064   *Teeter, Emily* Animals in Egyptian literature;

13065   Animals in Egyptian religion. A history of the animal world. HO I/64: 2002 ⇒12995. 251-270/335-360.

13066   *Villard, Pierre* Le chien dans la documentation néo-assyrienne. Les animaux. 2002 ⇒516. 235-249.

13067   *Watanabe, Chikako Esther* The lion metaphor in the Mesopotamian royal context. Les animaux. 2002 ⇒516. 399-409.

13068   **Watanabe, Chikako Esther** Animal symbolism in Mesopotamia: a contextual approach. Wiener Offene Orientalistik 1: W 2002, Institut für Orientalistik der Universität Wien xv; 179 pp. 3-900-345-0-8-2. Bibl. 166-174.

13069 *Whitekettle, Richard* All creatures great and small: intermediate level taxa in Israelite zoological thought. SJOT 16 (2002) 163-183 [Gen 1,20-25; Lev 14; Dt 14].
13070 *Wilkens, Barbara* Archaeozoology westwards: the fauna of Tell Afis (Syria). Les animaux. 2002 ⇒516. 5-14.

U2.6 *Flora*; plantae biblicae et antiquae

13071 **Amigues, Suzanne** Études de botanique antique. MAIBL 25: P 2002, De Boccard xv; 501 pp. 2-87754-130-4. Préf. *Pierre Quézel*.
13072 **Armstrong, D.E.** Alcohol and altered states in ancestor veneration rituals of Zhou Dynastic China and Iron Age Palestine. Lewiston 1998, Mellen 176 pp. [R]AuOr 20/1-2 (2002) 263-266 (*Olmo Lete, Gregorio del*).
13073 **Della Bianca, Luca; Beta, Simone** Oinos: il vino nella letteratura greca. Ricerche, Lettere classiche 108: R 2002, Carocci 108 pp. 88-430-2151-6. Bibl. 107-108.
13074 *Dick Herr, Denise; Petrina Boyd, Mary* A watermelon named Abimelech. BArR 28/1 (2002) 34-37; 62 [Judg 9].
13075 *Fox, Nili S.* Fantastic figs in Jeremiah's baskets and in the ancient Near East. ProcGLM 22 (2002) 99-108 [Jer 24].
13076 *Lev-Yadun, Simcha; Weinstein-Evron, Mina* The role of Pinus Halepensis (Aleppo pine) in the landscape of early Bronze Age Megiddo. TelAv 29 (2002) 332-343.
13077 **Maillat, Jean; Maillat, Solange** Les plantes dans la bible: guide de la flore en Terre Sainte. P 1999, Désiris 302 pp. €42. 2-907653-63-6.
13078 **Manniche, Lisa** Egyptian luxuries: fragrance, aromatherapy, and cosmetics in pharaonic times. 1999 ⇒15,11975; 16,12234. [R]DiscEg 54 (2002) 133-135 (*Park, Rosalind*).
13079 [E]**Neumann-Gorsolke, Ute; Riede, Peter** Das Kleid der Erde: Pflanzen in der Lebenswelt des Alten Israel. Neuk 2002, Neuk'er 374 pp. €39. 3-7887-1818-8 [ThQ 183,87—Groß, Walter].
13080 *Rubin, Rehav* The *melagria*: on anchorites and edible roots in Judaean Desert. LASBF 52 (2002) 347-352.
13081 *Tischler, Johann* Hethitische Äpfel. [F]POPKO, M. 2002 ⇒91. 345-350.
13082 **Walsh, Carey Ellen** The fruit of the vine: viticulture in ancient Israel. HSM 60: 2000 ⇒16,12240. [R]CBQ 64 (2002) 364-365 (*Hobbs, T.R.*); RBLit 4 (2002) 90-93 (*Jordan, David J.*).

U2.8 Agricultura, alimentatio

13083 [E]**Bowman, Alan K.; Rogan, Eugene** Agriculture in Egypt from Pharaonic to modern times. PBA 96: 1999 ⇒15,11986. [R]AJA 106 (2002) 125-126 (*Adams, Colin E.P.*).
13084 *Cartwright, Caroline R.* Grape and grain: dietary evidence from an early Bronze Age store at Tell es-Sa'idiyeh, Jordan. PEQ 134 (2002) 98-117.
13085 **Cauvin, Jacques** The birth of the gods and the origins of agriculture. [T]*Watkins, Trevor*: 2000 ⇒16,12242; 17,11823. [R]BCSMS 37 (2002) 61 (*Brown, Stuart C.*).

13086 *Dahl, Jacob* Land allotments during the third dynasty of Ur. AltOrF 29 (2002) 330-338.

13087 *Enß, Elisabet; Perkams, Matthias* Symbol und Technik: Kelter und Keltern in Antike und Christentum. JAC 45 (2002) 77-121.

13088 *Lovell, J.* Shifting subsistence patterns: some ideas about the end of the chalcolithic in the southern Levant. Paléorient 28/1 (2002) 89-102.

13089 *McCreery, David W.* Bronze Age agriculture in the Dead Sea basin: the cases of Bâb edh-Dhrâ, Numeira and Tell Nimrin. FFLANAGAN, J.: JSOT.S 359: 2002 ⇒38. 250-263.

13090 **Sharon, Diane M.** Patterns of destiny: narrative structures of foundation and doom in the Hebrew Bible. DGeller, Stephen A.: WL 2002, Eisenbrauns xii; 244 pp. $29.50. 1-57506-052-3. Diss. Jewish Theol. Sem. 1995. Bibl. 209-232. RRBLit (2002)* (*Kennedy, James M.*) [Eating and drinking].

13091 *Volschenk, G.J.* Die ontwikkeling vanaf 'n horti-kulturele na 'n simplistiese agrariese ekonomie in die leefwêreld van die bybel. HTS 58 (2002) 1089-1112 [OTA 26,435];

13092 Die ontwikkeling vanaf 'n simplistiese na 'n gevorderde agraiese ekonomie in die leefwêreld van die bybel. HTS 58 (2002) 1829-1854 [OTA 26,436].

13093 *Yamauchi, Edwin M.* Banquets in the biblical world. ProcGLM 22 (2002) 147-157.

U2.9 Medicina *biblica et antiqua*

13094 E**Andorlini, Isabella** Greek Medical Papyri I. 2001 ⇒17,11835. RBiOr 59 (2002) 309-312 (*Papathomas, Amphilochios*).

13095 *Arnott, Robert* Disease and medicine in Hittite Asia Minor. The archaeology of medicine. 2002 ⇒13096. 41-52.

13096 E**Arnott, Robert** The archaeology of medicine: papers given at a session of the annual conference of the Theoretical Archaeology Group held at the University of Birmingham on 20 December 1998. BAR International Ser. 1046: Oxf 2002, Archaeopress v; 129 pp. 1-84171-427-5.

13097 **Eapen, J.** The divine physician: a study on healing in the bible. Aloor 2002, Biblia 154 pp.

13098 **Flemming, Rebecca** Medicine and the making of Roman women: gender, nature, and authority from CELSUS to GALEN. 2000 ⇒16, 12260. RJRS 92 (2002) 204-205 (*Pearcy, Lee T.*).

13099 ET**Fraisse, Anne** CASSIUS FELIX: De la médicine. CUFr Guillaume Budé: P 2002, Belles Lettres lxxxvii; (2) 260 pp. 2-251-01424-1. Bibl. lxxxiii-lxxxvii.

13100 **Geller, M.J.** West meets East: early Greek and Babylonian diagnosis. AfO 48-49 (2001-2002) 50-75.

13101 *Haussperger, Martha* Die Krankheiten des Verdauungstraktes. WO 32 (2002) 33-73.

13102 *Hiltbrunner, Otto* Die gesellschaftliche Stellung der Ärzte und ihre Rolle bei der Ausbreitung des frühen Christentums nach Asien. FGNILKA, C.: JAC.E 33: 2002 ⇒48. 197-204.

13103 E**Karenberg, A.; Leiz, Chr.** Heilkunde und Hochkultur. 2000 ⇒ 16,411. RBiOr 59 (2002) 36-39 (*Haussperger, Martha*).

13104 **Kolta, K.S.; Schwarzmann-Schafhauser, D.** Die Heilkunde im Alten Ägypten. 2000 ⇒16,12268. [R]BiOr 59 (2002) 75-77 (*Vanlathem, Marie-Paule*).

13105 [ET]**Maire, Brigitte** GARGILIUS MARTIALIS: Les remèdes tirés des légumes et des fruits. CUFr Assoc. G. Budé: P 2002, Les Belles Lettres cxx; 241 pp. 2-251-014227-6.

13106 *Nutton, V.* Ancient medicine: ASCLEPIUS transformed. Science and mathematics. 2002 ⇒532. 242-255.

13107 *Passarella, Raffaele* Medicina in allegoria: AMBROGIO, FILONE e l'arca di Noè. Tra IV e V secolo. 2002 ⇒475. 189-252.

13108 *Van der Horst, Pieter W.* The last Jewish patriarch(s) and Graeco-Roman medicine. Japheth. 2002 ⇒251. 27-36.

13109 **Zacco, Roberto** La cultura medica nell'Antico Egitto. Bo 2002, Martina 184 pp. €20. 38 ill.

U3 *Duodecim tribus*; **Israel tribes**; *land ideology; adjacent lands*

13110 **Brueggemann, Walter** The land: place as gift, promise, and challenge in biblical faith. Overtures to Biblical Theology: Mp [2]2002, Fortress xxvii; 225 pp. $18. 0-8006-3462-4. Bibl. 209-212.

13111 *Dan, Joseph* Land Israel. RGG 5. 2002 ⇒796. 53-58.

13112 *Dietrich, Walter* Wem das Land gehört: ein Beitrag zur Sozialgeschichte Israels im 6. Jahrhundert v. Chr. Theopolitik. 2002 <1997> ⇒159. 270-286.

13113 *Dujardin, Jean* La relation à la terre dans le judaïsme. CEv 121 (2002) 58-63.

13114 *Gangloff, Frédéric* Le 'pays dévasté et dépeuplé': genèse d'une idéologie biblique et d'un concept sioniste: une esquisse. BN 113 (2002) 39-50.

13115 **Gonen, Rivka** To the ends of the earth: the quest for the ten lost tribes of Israel. Northvale, NJ 2002, Aronson xxv; 206 pp. 0-7657-6146-7. Bibl. 191-195.

13116 *Grosby, Steven* Territoriality. Biblical ideas. 2002 <1995> ⇒172. 191-212.

13117 *Guolo, Renzo* Il fondamentalismo ebraico tra teologia della terra ed esilio in *Eretz Israel*. FilTeo 16 (2002) 275-294 Sum. 275.

13118 **Hartman, David** Israelis and the Jewish tradition: an ancient people debating its future. 2000 ⇒16,12280. [R]JQR 92 (2002) 609-612 (*Kellner, Menachem*).

13119 *Herrmann, Siegfried* Was bleibt von der Jahwe-Amphiktyonie?. Geschichte und Prophetie. BWANT 157: 2002 <1992> ⇒179. 89-99.

13120 **Parfitt, Tudor** The lost tribes of Israel: the history of a myth. L 2002, Weidenfeld & N. ix; 277 pp. £19. 0-297-81934-8.

13121 *Volschenk, G.J.; Van Aarde, Andries* Die historiese vraag na die land en grondbesit in Israel: die tekortkomings van die historiese kritiek. HTS 58 (2002) 212-234 [OTA 26,140].

U4.5 *Viae*, **roads, routes**

13122 [E]**Olshausen, Ekhardt; Sonnabend, Holger** Zu Wasser und zu Land: Verkehrswege in der antiken Welt. Stuttgarter Kolloquium zur historischen Geographie des Altertums 7: Stu 1999, Steiner 492 pp. €100. 3-515-08053-8. Num. ill.

13123 *Shaked, Idan* The tenth- and eleventh-century mail route from Banias to Tyre, and identification of 'The Black Watch'. Cathedra 103 (2002) 21-32 Sum. 189. **H**.

U5.0 *Ethnographia*, sociologia; *servitus*

13124 **Aguirre, Rafael** Del movimiento de Jesús a la iglesia cristiana: ensayo de exégesis sociológica del cristianismo primitivo. 1998 ⇒14, 11354; 15,12050. [R]ASEs 19 (2002) 267-271 (*Pesce, Mauro*).

13125 *Bauckham, Richard* Egalitarianism and hierarchy in the bible. God and the crisis. 2002 <1997> ⇒142. 116-127.

13126 *Berlinerblau, Jacques* The delicate flower of biblical sociology. Tracking the tribes. JSOT.S 351: 2002 ⇒455. 59-76.

13127 *Berner, Ulrich* War das frühe Christentum eine Religion?. ZNT 10 (2002) 54-60.

13128 *Bird, Frederick* Early christianity as an unorganized ecumenical religious movement;

13129 *Blasi, Anthony J.* Early christian culture as interaction;

13130 General methodological perspective. Handbook of early christianity. 2002 ⇒275. 225-246/291-308/61-78.

13131 *Bloomquist, L. Gregory* A possible direction for providing programmatic correlation of textures in socio-rhetorical analysis. Rhetorical criticism. JSNT.S 195: 2002 ⇒369. 61-96.

13132 *Bovati, Pietro* Lo straniero nella bibbia. RCI 83 (2002) 405-418, 484-503.

13133 *Braude, Benjamin* Cham et Noé: race, esclavage et exégèse entre islam, judaïsme et christianisme. Annales 57 (2001) 93-125.

13134 **Byron, Gay L.** Symbolic blackness and ethnic difference in early christian literature. L 2002, Routledge xii; 223 pp. $26. 0-415-243-68-8. Bibl. 175-203.

13135 *Carter, Warren* Vulnerable power: the Roman Empire challenged by the early christians. Handbook of early christianity. 2002 ⇒275. 453-488.

13136 *Ceresko, Anthony R.* The identity of the Indian church: a biblical perspective. Prophets and proverbs. 2002 <1997> ⇒154. 87-96.

13137 *Chalcraft, David J.* Max WEBER on the Watchtower: on the prophetic use of Shakespeare's sonnet 102 in 'Politics as a vocation'. Apocalyptic. JSPE.S 43: 2002 ⇒373. 253-270.

13138 *Combrink, Bernard* The challenges and opportunities of a socio-rhetorical commentary. Scriptura 79 (2002) 106-121.

13139 **Delacampagne, Christian** Une histoire de l'esclavage de l'antiquité à nos jours. Références. P 2002, Livre de Poche 320 pp.

13140 *Denzey, Nicola* The limits of ethnic categories. Handbook of early christianity. 2002 ⇒275. 489-507.

13141 *Dijkstra, Meindert* 'De vreemdeling die in uw steden woont': omgang met mensen van andere volken en culturen in Oud-Israël. Phoenix 48 (2002) 118-140.

13142 *Dreyer, Y.* Leadership in the world of the bible: (de)institutionalisation as an ongoing process. VeE 23 (2002) 625-641;

13143 Love-patriarchalism' in the New Testament in light of ethnography. HTS 58 (2002) 502-519 [NTAb 47,295].

13144 *Elliott, John H.* Jesus was not an egalitarian: a critique of an ana-
chronistic and idealist theory. BTB 32 (2002) 75-91.

13145 *Eltrop, Bettina* Kinder im Neuen Testament: eine sozialgeschichtliche Nachfrage. JBTh 17 (2002) 83-96.

13146 *Fischer, S.* The division of Israel's monarchy and the political situation of Lesotho. VeE 23 (2002) 353-366.

13147 *Frick, Frank S.* Norman Gottwald's 'The tribes of Yahweh' in the
context of 'second-wave' social-scientific biblical criticism. Tracking the tribes. JSOT.S 351: 2002 ⇒455. 17-34.

13148 *Fried, L.S.* The political stuggle of fifth century Judah. TEuph 24
(2002) 9-21.

13149 **Gehring, Roger W.** Hausgemeinde und Mission: die Bedeutung
antiker Häuser und Hausgemeinschaften—von Jesus bis Paulus.
BWM 9: 2000 ⇒16,12313; 17,11880. ᴿThLZ 127 (2002) 754-757
(*Schmeller, Thomas*).

13150 **Gibson, E. Leigh** The Jewish manumission inscriptions of the Bos-
porus Kingdom. TSAJ 75: 1999 ⇒15,12080...17,11881. ᴿTJT 18
(2002) 264-265 (*Kloppenborg Verbin, John S.*); JQR 92 (2002)
507-520 (*Levinskaya, Irina*).

13151 *Glancy, Jennifer A.* Family plots: burying slaves deep in historical
ground. BiblInterp 10 (2002) 57-75.

13152 **Glancy, Jennifer A.** Slavery in early christianity. Oxf 2002, OUP
xiv; 203 pp. $40. 0-19-513609-8. Bibl. 181-192. ᴿCBQ 64 (2002)
758-759 (*Harrill, J. Albert*).

13153 *Grosby, Steven* Sociological implications of the distinction between
'locality' and extended 'territory' with particular reference to the
Old Testament. Biblical ideas. 2002 <1993> ⇒172. 69-91;

13154 Borders, territory, and nationality in the ancient Near East and
Armenia. Biblical ideas. 2002 <1997> ⇒172. 120-149;

13155 The category of the primordial in the study of early christianity and
second-century Judaism <1996>;

13156 The nation of the United States and the vision of ancient Israel
<1993>. Biblical ideas. 2002 ⇒172. 166-190/213-234;

13157 Nationality and religion. Biblical ideas. 2002 <2001> ⇒172. 235-
256.

13158 **Guttenberger Ortwein, Gudrun** Status und Statusverzicht im
Neuen Testament und seiner Umwelt. NTOA 39: 1999 ⇒15,
12084; 16,12317. ᴿCBQ 64 (2002) 387-388 (*Branick, Vincent P.*).

13159 *Hanges, James Constantine* DURKHEIM and early christianity. Reappraising Durkheim. SHR 92: 2002 ⇒143-162 ⇒1031.

13160 *Harland, Philip A.* Connections with elites in the world of the early
christians. Handbook of early christianity. 2002 ⇒275. 385-408.

13161 *Hendel, Ronald S.* Israel among the nations: biblical culture in the
ancient Near East. Cultures. 2002 ⇒448. 43-75.

13162 *Hoglund, Kenneth* The material culture of the Persian period and
the sociology of the second temple period. Second temple studies
III. JSOT.S 340: 2002 ⇒296. 14-18.

13163 *Horrell, David G.* Social sciences studying formative christian phenomena: a creative movement;

13164 'Becoming christian': solidifying christian identity and content.
Handbook of early christianity. 2002 ⇒275. 3-28/309-335.

13165 **Horsley, Richard A.; Silberman, Neil Asher** The message and
the kingdom: how Jesus and Paul ignited a revolution and trans-

formed the ancient world. Mp 2002, Fortress xi; 290 pp. $18. 0-8006-3467-5. ᴿAThR 84 (2002) 774-775 (*Maier, Harry O.*).

13166 *Junco Garza, Carlos* La sagrada escritura, raíz de la solidaridad. Qol 28 (2002) 25-47.

13167 *Kee, Howard Clark* Sociological insights into the development of christian leadership roles and community formation. Handbook of early christianity. 2002 ⇒275. 337-360.

13168 *King, Philip J.; Stager, Lawrence E.* Of fathers, kings and the deity. BArR 28/2 (2002) 43-45, 62.

13169 *Kirner, Guido O.* Apostolat und Patronage, (I) methodischer Teil und Forschungsdiskussion. ZAC 6 (2002) 3-37.

13170 **Kocúr, Miroslav** National and religious identitiy in Gal 3,23-29 and Rom 10,12-21: an exegetical and theological study. R 2002, E.P.U.G. 170 pp. Extr. Diss. Gregorian. Bibl. 149-163.

13171 *Kügler, Joachim; Bechmann, Ulrike* Proexistenz in Theologie und Glaube: ein exegetischer Versuch zur Bestimmung des Verhältnisses von Pluralitätsfähigkeit und christlicher Identität. ThQ 182 (2002) 72-100.

13172 ᴱ**Laurence, Ray; Berry, Joanne** Cultural identity in the Roman Empire. 1998 ⇒14,11407; 17,11895. ᴿLatomus 61 (2002) 245-246 (*André, Jean-Marie*).

13173. *Lawrence, Louise Joy* "For truly, I tell you, they have received their reward" (Matt 6:2): investigating honor precedence and honor virtue. CBQ 64 (2002) 687-702 [Mt 5-6].

13174 **Legrand, Lucien** The bible on culture: belonging or dissenting?. 2000 ⇒16,12329; 17,11896. ᴿMiss. 30 (2002) 399-400 (*Weingartner, Robert J.*).

13175 *Levine, Baruch A.* 'Seed' versus 'womb': expressions of male dominance in Biblical Israel. Sex and gender. 2002 ⇒712. 337-343.

13176 *Lugo Rodríguez, Raúl H.* Biblia y religiosidad popular. Qol 29 (2002) 71-78.

13177 **Malina, Bruce J.** The social gospel of Jesus: the kingdom of God in Mediterranean perspective. 2001 ⇒17,11904. ᴿCBQ 64 (2002) 173-174 (*Crook, Zeba Antonin*).

13178 *Marshall, John W.; Martin, Russell* Government and public law in Galilee, Judaea, Hellenistic cities, and the Roman Empire. Handbook of early christianity. 2002 ⇒275. 409-429.

13179 **May, Michael W.** Land and power: the social dynamics of land ownership in Iron Age Israel. ᴰ**Brisco, T.** 2002, 206 pp Diss. Fort Worth [RTL 34,592].

13180 ᴱ**Männchen, Julia** Gustaf DALMAN: Arbeit und Sitte in Palästina, 8: Das häusliche Leben, Geburt, Heirat, Tod. 2001 ⇒17,11906. ᴿOLZ 97 (2002) 269-271 (*Thiel, Winfried*); ThLZ 127 (2002) 620-621 (*Tilly, Michael*).

13181 **McKnight, Scot** Turning to Jesus: the sociology of conversion in the gospels. LVL 2002, Westminster x; 214 pp. $19. 06642-25144.

13182 *McNutt, Paula M.* 'Fathers of the empty spaces' and 'strangers forever': social marginality and the construction of space. ᶠFLANAGAN, J.: JSOT.S 359: 2002 ⇒38. 30-50.

13183 **McNutt, Paula M.** Reconstructing the society of Ancient Israel. 1999 ⇒15,12106...17,11907. ᴿCTJ 37 (2002) 124-128 (*DeVries, Simon J.*); CBQ 64 (2002) 358-359 (*Miller, Robert D.*).

13184 *Meggitt, Justin J.* The first churches: social life. Biblical world, 2. 2002 ⇒273. 137-156.

13185 **Miller, Troy A.** The emergence of the concept of heresy in early christianity: the context of internal social conflict in first-century christianity and late second temple sectarianism. *DHurtado, L.W.*: 2002, 328 pp. Diss. Edinburgh [RTL 34,599].

13186 *Nielsen, Donald A.* Civilizational encounters in the development of early christianity. Handbook of early christianity. 2002 ⇒275. 267-290.

13187 **Ohler, Annemarie** The bible looks at fathers. *TKaste, Omar*: 1999 ⇒15,12112. RCBQ 64 (2002) 140-141 *(Benjamin, Don C.)*.

13188 *Osiek, Carolyn* Archaeological and architectural issues and the question of demographic and urban forms. Handbook of early christianity. 2002 ⇒275. 83-103.

13189 **Otto, Eckart** Max WEBERs Studien des antiken Judentums: historische Grundlegung einer Theorie der Moderne. Tü 2002, Mohr xii; 378 pp. €79. 3-16-147897-5.

13190 *Pilch, John J.* Interpreting the bible with the value orientations model: history and prospects. BTB 32 (2002) 92-99;

13191 The roles of woman and men in family, society and church. The roles. 2002 ⇒540. 12-26.

13192 **Pilch, John J.** Cultural tools for interpreting the good news. ColMn 2002, Liturgical 81 pp. $7. 0-8146-2826-5. Bibl. 75 [BiTod 40,403 —Senior, Donald].

13193 *Pilhofer, Peter* Die ökonomische Attraktivität christlicher Gemeinden der Frühzeit. Die frühen Christen. WUNT 145: 2002 ⇒225. 194-218.

13194 **Pleins, J. David** The social visions of the Hebrew Bible: a theological introduction. 2001 ⇒17,11913. RTheol. 105 (2002) 54-55 *(Hagedorn, Anselm C.)*; ThTo 59 (2002) 488, 490, 492-493 *(Gottwald, Norman K.)*; BBR 12 (2002) 148-150 *(Ashley, Timothy R.)*; JBL 121 (2002) 348-351 *(Dempsey, Carol J.)*.

13195 *Ravasi, Gianfranco* La bible face à l'autre, au différent, à l'étranger. Com(F) 37/1 (2002) 23-39;

13196 Immagini bibliche della città. Com(I) 183-184 (2002) 25-31.

13197 *Remus, Harold* Persecution;

13198 *Richardson, Peter; Edwards, Douglas* Jesus and Palestinian social protest: archaeological and literary perspectives;

13199 *Sanders, Jack T.* Establishing social distance between christians and both Jews and pagans;

13200 Conversion in early christianity. Handbook of early christianity. 2002 ⇒275. 431-452/247-266/361-382/619-641.

13201 **Sanders, Jack T.** Charisma, converts, competitors: society and societal factors in the success of early christianity. 2000 ⇒16, 12350. RCBQ 64 (2002) 392-394 *(Pilch, John J.)*.

13202 *Sanders, James A.* The family in the bible. BTB 32 (2002) 117-128.

13203 **Schmitt-Pridik, Ursula** Hoffnungsvolles Alter(n): praktisch-theologischer Versuch einer gerontologischen Bibelauslegung. *DKlessmann, Michael*: 2002 Diss. Wuppertal [ThRv 99/2,xi].

13204 *Schneider, Herbert* Has God ordained the subordination of wives to husbands?: problematic texts of the New Testament. The roles. 2002 ⇒540. 83-106 [Eph 5, 21-33; Col 3,18-19; 1 Tim 2,11-15; Titus 2,3-5; 1 Pet 3,1-7].

13205 *Smend, Rudolf* Der Ort des Staates im Alten Testament. Die Mitte des A.T. 2002 <1983> ⇒244. 174-187.

13206   **Snyder, Graydon F.** Inculturation of the Jesus tradition: the impact of Jesus on Jewish and Roman cultures. 1999 ⇒15,12133... 17, 11918. [R]JBL 121 (2002) 172-175 (*Vinson, Richard B.*).

13207   *Spriggs, David G.* The bible: cultural treasure or cultural obstacle?. Anvil 19/2 (2002) 119-130.

13208   *Staples, Peter* Structuralism and symbolic universes: second temple Judaism and the early christian movement. Handbook of early christianity. 2002 ⇒275. 197-221.

13209   **Stegemann, Ekkehard W.; Stegemann, Wolfgang** The Jesus movement: a social history of its first century. 1999 ⇒15,12141... 17,11920. [R]Horizons 29 (2002) 155-156 (*Cook, Michael L.*); JBL 121 (2002) 565-567 (*Oakman, Douglas E.*);

13210   Historia social del cristianismo primitivo: los inicios en el judaísmi y las comunidades cristianas en el mundo mediterráneo. [T]*Montes, Miguel*: 2001 ⇒17,11921. [R]ActBib 38/1 (2002) 60-61 (*Boada, J.*).

13211   *Stegemann, Wolfgang* War das frühe Christentum eine Religion?. ZNT 10 (2002) 61-68.

13212   *Stiebert, J.* Homosexuality in Botswana and in the Hebrew Bible: an impression. VeE 23 (2002) 196-208.

13213   **Testart, A.** L'esclave, la dette et le pouvoir: études de sociologie comparative. 2001 ⇒17,11922. [R]REA 104 (2002) 612-613 (*Annequin, Jacques*).

13214   **Theissen, Gerd** Die Religion der ersten Christen: eine Theorie des Urchristentums. [2]2001 ⇒17,11924. [R]ActBib 39 (2002) 211-212 (*Boada, J.*).

13215   *Thomsen, Marc* Two biblical models for relating to the ethnic and religious other. CThMi 29 (2002) 28-33.

13216   *Thumma, Lucas* Human person, human dignity and human society: biblical foundations and theological perspectives in the social teaching of the church. ITS 39 (2002) 219-256.

13217   *Turcotte, Paul-André* Major social scientific theories: origins, development, and contributions. Handbook of early christianity. 2002 ⇒275. 29-59.

13218   *Van Eck, E.* Socio-rhetorical interpretation in practice: recent contributions in perspective. HTS 57 (2001) 1229-53 [NTAb 46,446].

13219   *Volschenk, G.J.; Van Aarde, Andries* A social scientific study of the significance of the jubilee in the New Testament. HTS 58 (2002) 811-837 [NTAb 47,303].

13220   *Vorster, J.N.* The blood of female martyrs as the sperm of the early church. R&T 9/1-2 (2002) 8-41 [NTAb 47,347];

13221   Bodily parts vying for power: hierarchies and bodies in early christianity. Scriptura 80 (2002) 287-306 [NTAb 47,548].

13222   *Vos, C. J. A.* The dynamics of leadership. VeE 23 (2002) 776-789.

13223   *Wagner, Volker* Beobachtungen am Amt der Ältesten im alttestamentlichen Israel, 1.Teil: der Ort der Ältesten in den Epochen der Geschichte und in der Gliederung der Gesellschaft;

13224   Beobachtungen am Amt der Ältesten im alttestamentlichen Israel, 2. Teil: die Kompetenzen und Aufgaben der Ältesten im Rechtsleben und im Kult. ZAW 114 (2002) 391-411/560-576.

13225   *Watson, Duane F.* Why we need socio-rhetorical commentary and what it might look like. Rhetorical criticism. JSNT.S 195: 2002 ⇒ 369. 129-157.

13226   *Weippert, Helga* Der Lärm und die Stille: ethno-archäologische Annäherungen an das biblische Alltagsleben. Congress volume Basel
2001. VT.S 92: 2002 ⇒570. 163-184.
13227   *Wesley, Arun K.* Sacralisation and secularisation : an analysis of a
few biblical passages for possible racial overtones and ethnocentrism. AJTh 16/2 (2002) 375-395.
13228   *West, Gerald* Tribes in Africa: the impact of Norman Gottwald's
'The tribes of Yahweh' on African biblical hermeneutics (with an
emphasis on liberation and inculturation paradigms). Tracking the
tribes. JSOT.S 351: 2002 ⇒455. 85-97;
13229   Disguising defiance in ritualisms of subordination: literary and
community-based resources for recovering resistance discourse
within the dominant discourses of the bible. [F]PATTE, D. 2002 ⇒89.
194-217.

u5.3 **Commercium, oeconomica**

13230   *Belmonte Marín, J.A.* Presencia sidonia en los circuitos comerciales
del Bronce Final. RSFen 30 (2002) 3-18.
13231   **Bulgarelli, Odoardo** Il denaro alle origini delle origini. L'alingua
175: Mi 2001, Spirali 329 pp. 88-7770-586-8.
13232   **Drexhage, Hans-Joachim; Konen, Heinrich; Ruffing, Kai** Die
Wirtschaft des Römischen Reiches (1.-3. Jahrhundert): eine Einführung. Studienbücher, Geschichte der Kultur der Alten Welt: B
2002, Akademie 400 pp. €34.80. 3-05-003430-2. 12 ill.
13233   **Faist, Betina I.** Der Fernhandel des assyrischen Reiches zwischen
dem 14. und 11. Jh. v. Chr. AOAT 265: 2001 ⇒17,11936. [R]OLZ
97 (2002) 364-366 (*Saporetti, Claudio*); AfO 48-49 (2001-2002)
205-207 (*Van de Mieroop, Marc*).
13234   *Fiensy, David A.* What would you do for a living?. Handbook of
early christianity. 2002 ⇒275. 555-574.
13235   **Goddeeris, Anne** Economy and society in northern Babylonia in
the early Old Babylonian Period (ca. 2000 - 1800 BC). OLA 109:
Lv 2002, Peeters (4) 451 pp. €68. 90-429-1123-9. Bibl. 406-421.
13236   *Harland, Philip* The economy of first-century Palestine: state of the
scholarly discussion. Handbook of early christianity. 2002 ⇒275.
511-527.
13237   [E]**Hudson, Michael; Van de Mieroop, Marc** Debt and economic
renewal in the ancient Near East: colloquium Colombia University,
Nov. 1998. International Scholars Conf. on Ancient Near Eastern
Economies 3: Bethesda, MD 2002, CDL 355 pp. 1-883053-71-4.
13238   *Kyrtatas, Dimitris J.* Modes and relations of production. Handbook
of early christianity. 2002 ⇒275. 529-554.
13239   *Lampe-Densky, Sigrid* Domitia, Marcia, and the nameless smug-
gler: pearl dealers in the Roman Empire. [F]SCHOTTROFF, L. 2002 ⇒
111. 59-65.
13240   *Milevski, Ianir; Marder, Ofer; Goring Morris, A. Nigel* The circulation of asphalt in southern Canaan and Egypt during the early
Bronze Age I. [F]GOPHNA, R. 2002 ⇒49. 219-236.
13241   **Möller, Astrid** Naukratis: trade in archaic Greece. 2000 ⇒16,
12385. [R]ArOr 70 (2002) 437-439 (*Smoláriková, Květa*).

13242 *Niemeyer, Hans Georg* Aegyptiaca im Mittelmeerraum: Handelsgut der Phönizier?: zur Beschreibung eines Problems in der archäologischen Forschung. ^MCIASCA, A. 2002 ⇒15. 367-372.

13243 **Schwarz, Hertha** Soll oder Haben?: die Finanzwirtschaft kleinasiatischer Städte in der Römischen Kaiserzeit am Beispiel von Bithynien, Lykien und Ephesos (29 v.Chr.-284 n.Chr.). Bonn 2001, Habelt 516 pp. Diss. Tübingen 1999.

13244 *Tokunaga, Risa* The relations between Ancient Egypt and South Arabia through the archaeological and epigraphical evidence. Bulletin of the Society for Near Eastern Studies in Japan 45/1 (2002) 96-119 Sum. 96. **J.**

13245 *Van de Mieroop, Marc* In search of prestige: foreign contacts and the rise of an elite in early dynastic Babylonia. ^FHANSEN, D. 2002 ⇒58. 125-137.

13246 **Van Driel, Govert** Elusive silver: in search of a role for a market in an agrarian environment. Nederlands Instituut voor het Nabije Oosten te Leiden 95: Lei 2002, Nederlands Instituut voor het Nabije Oosten ix; 345 pp. $75. 90-625-8096-3.

13247 **Young, Gary Keith** Rome's eastern trade: international commerce and imperial policy, 31 BC-AD 305. 2001 ⇒17,11950. ^RRevue historique 126 (2002) 399-402 (*Sartre, Maurice*); JRS 92 (2002) 234-235 (*Adams, Colin*); Ancient West & East 1/1 (2002) 196-199 (*Alston, Richard*).

U5.7 **Nomadismus**, *ecology*; **Urbanismus**; *Demographia*

13248 **Homan, Michael M.** To your tents, O Israel!: the terminology, function, form, and symbolism of tents in the Hebrew Bible and the ancient Near East. Culture and history of the Ancient Near East 12: Lei 2002, Brill xxv; 231 pp. 90-04-12606-6. Bibl. 193-214.

13249 *Rosen, Steven A.* The evolution of pastoral nomadic systems in the southern Levante periphery. ^FGOPHNA, R. 2002 ⇒49. 23-44.

13250 **Alston, Richard** The city in Roman and Byzantine Egypt. L 2002, Routledge xvi; 479 pp. £65 0-415-23701-7. ^RDiscEg 54 (2002) 129-132 (*Papathomas, Amphilochios*).

13251 *Amiet, Pierre* À la recherche d'un modèle explicatif de la 'révolution urbaine': le rôle des nomades. RA 96 (2002) 97-102.

13252 **Greenberg, Raphael** Early urbanizations in the Levant: a regional narrative. New Approaches to Anthropological Archaeology: L 2002, Leicester University Pr. xii; 141 pp. $145. 0-7185-0230-2. Diss. Hebrew Univ. Bibl. 123-138.

13253 ^E**Hansen, Mogens Herman** A comparative study of six city-state cultures: an investigation conducted by the Copenhagen Polis Centre. DVSS.HF 27: K 2002, Reitzels 144 pp. 87-7876-316-9.

13254 *Morenz, Ludwig D.* Die 'Stadt': generische Bezeichnung und kulturelle Bedeutung im Horizont der Schriftentstehung in Sumer und Ägypten. DiscEg 54 (2002) 85-96.

13255 *Paz, Yitzhak* Fortified settlements of the EB IB and the emergence of the first urban system. TelAv 29 (2002) 238-261.

13256 **Pezzoli-Olgiati, Daria** Immagini urbane: interpretazioni religiose della città antica. OBO: FrS 2002, Universitaires xvi; 305 pp. FS 88. 3-7278-1392-X. Diss.-Habil. Zürich.

13257	*Ramazzotti, Marco* La 'rivoluzione urbana' nella Mesopotamia meridionale: replica *versus* processo. AANL.R 13 (2002) 641-752.
13258	**Sperber, Daniel** The city in Roman Palestine. 1998 ⇒14,11475. [R]RBLit (2002)* (*Graf, David F.*).
13259	*Wright, John W.* A tale of three cities: urban gates, squares and power in Iron Age II, neo-Babylonian and Achaemenid Judah. Second temple studies III. JSOT.S 340: 2002 ⇒296. 19-50.

13260	**Scheidel, Walter** Measuring sex, age and death in the Roman empire: explorations in ancient demography. 1996 ⇒12,10775... 16,12414. [R]Gn. 74 (2002) 555-556 (*Wierschowski, Lothar*).

U6 Narrationes peregrinorum et exploratorum; *loca sancta*

13261	*Adelman, Tzvi* Howard In Zion and Jerusalem: the itinerary of Rabbi Moses BASOLA. JewSt 41 (2002) 143*-149*.
13262	*Bitton-Ashkelony, Brouria* Pilgrimage in monastic culture in late antiquity. Armenians in Jerusalem. 2002 ⇒771. 1-17.
13263	[ET]**Cachey, Theodore J.** PETRARCH's guide to the Holy Land: itinerary to the sepulcher of our Lord Jesus Christ. ND 2002, Univ. of Notre Dame Pr. ix; 235 pp. $37.50. 0-268-03873-2. Biblioteca Statale, Fascimile ed. of Cremona, Deposito Libreria Civica, manuscript BB. 1.2.5 [JEH 54,553s—Piper, Alan].
13264	**Cardini, Franco** In Terrasanta: pellegrini italiani tra Medioevo e prima età moderna. Biblioteca storica: Bo 2002, Il Mulino 527 pp. [R]AFH 95 (2002) 445-447 (*Betti, Gian Luigi*).
13265	[E]**Carls, Wieland** Felix FABRI: Die Sionpilger. 1999 ⇒15,12191. [R]MÂ 108/1 (2002) 116-118 (*Monnet, Pierre*).
13266	**Coccopalmerio, Mario** Il ritorno del pellegrino: eulogie di Terra Santa. Genova 2001, Marietti 178 pp. [R]Lev. 49/3 (2002) 83-85 (*Palmisano, Antonio L.*).
13267	**Diotallevi, Ferdinando** Diario di Terrasanta, 1918-1924. [E]*Fabrizio, Daniela*: Mi 2002, Biblioteca Francescana x; 442 pp. [R]MF 102 (2002) 464-465 (*Eldarov, Giorgio*).
13268	**Donner, Herbert** Pilgerfahrt ins Heilige Land: die ältesten Berichte christlicher Palästinapilger (4.-7. Jahrhundert). Stu [2]2002, Kath. Bibelwerk 408 pp. 3-460-31842-2.
13269	*Ervine, Roberta* Changes in Armenian pilgrim attitudes between 1600 and 1857: the witness of three documents. Armenians in Jerusalem. Hebrew University Armenian studies 4: 2002 ⇒771. 81-95.
13270	**Harpur, James** Sacred tracks: 2000 years of christian pilgrimage. Berkeley, CA 2002, Univ. of California Pr. 192 pp. 0-520-23395-6. Bibl. 186-187.
13271	**Herbers, Klaus** 'Wol auf sant Jacobs straßen!': Pilgerfahrten und Zeugnisse des Jakobuskultes in Süddeutschland. Ostfildern 2002, Schwabenverlag 227 pp. €20.
13272	*Homs i Guzman, Antoni* La *Relacio de la peregrinació a Jerusalem* del Franciscà Joan LÓPEZ (1762-1781). AST 75 (2002) 171-339.
13273	*Jacobs, Andrew S.* 'The most beautiful Jewesses in the land': imperial travel in the early christian Holy Land. Religion 32 (2002) 205-225.

13274 **Janin, Hunt** Four paths to Jerusalem: Jewish, Christian, Muslim, and secular pilgrimages, 1000 BCE to 2001 CE. Jefferson, North Carolina 2002, McFarland x; 262 pp. 0-7864-1264X. Bibl. 249-57.

13275 *La Porta, Sergio* Grigor Tat'ewac'i's pilgrimage to Jerusalem. Armenians in Jerusalem. 2002 ⇒771. 97-109.

13276 **Miller, Naomi F.** Drawing on the past, an archaeologist's sketchbook. Ph 2002, University Museum 112 pp. $20. 93170-727-8.

13277 ᵀᴱ**Pfullmann, Uwe** Richard Francis BURTON: Die Goldminen von Midian: Reisen und Forschungen im biblischen Land, 1876-1877. Stu 2002, Erdmann 319 pp. €22. 3-522-60101-7 [ArOr 71,108s— Van der Heyden, Ulrich].

13278 **Seetzen, Ulrich Jasper** Unter Mönchen und Beduinen: Reisen in Palästina und angrenzenden Ländern 1805-1807. ᴱ*Lichtenberger, Achim*: Stu 2002, Erdmann 318 pp. €22. 3-522-60044-4.

13279 ᴱ**Severis, Rita C.** The diaries of Lorenzo Warriner Pease 1834-1839: an American missionary in Cyprus and his travels in the Holy Land, Asia Minor and Greece. Aldershot 2002, Ashgate 2 vols. 0-7546-3561-9. Bibl. vol. 2, 1119-1137.

13280 *Stone, Nira* Jerusalem as a point of conversion from sin to sainthood: a story of a woman pilgrim in art. Armenians in Jerusalem. Hebrew University Armenian studies 4: 2002 ⇒771. 221-230.

13281 **Wilkinson, John** Jerusalem pilgrims: before the crusades. Wmr ²2002 <1977>, Aris & P. xii; 420 pp. £28/$48. 0-85668-746-4. Bibl. 393-409.

U7 *Crucigeri*—The Crusades

13282 **Bordonove, Georges** Les Croisades et le Royaume de Jérusalem. Les Grandes Heures de l'Histoire de France: P 2002, Pygmalion 449 pp. 2-85704-766-5. Bibl. 439-443.

13283 *Gutierrez, Lucio* 'Holy wars' in history: a preamble to the crusades. PhilipSac 37 (2002) 225-247.

13284 **Kirstein, Klaus-Peter** Die lateinischen Patriarchen von Jerusalem: von der Eroberung der Heiligen Stadt durch die Kreuzfahrer 1099 bis zum Ende der Kreuzfahrerstaaten 1291. B 2002, Duncker & H. 683 pp. €88. 3-428-09964-8.

13285 **Maier, Christoph T.** Crusade propaganda and ideology: model sermons for the preaching of the cross. C 2000, CUP viii; 280 pp.

13286 ᴱ**Minervini, Laura** Cronaca del Templare di Tiro (1243-1314): la caduta degli stati crociati nel racconto di un testimone oculare. Nuovo Medioevo 59: 2000 ⇒16,12450. ᴿStMed 43 (2002) 999-1000 (*Mecacci, Enzo*).

13287 ᴱ**Pouthier, Jean-Luc** La Méditerranée des croisades. MoBi 144 (2002) 3-51.

13288 *Pringle, Denys* The fief of AIMERY of Franclieu and the estate of the abbey of St Mary of Mount Sion in the territory of Jerusalem. RB 109 (2002) 587-601.

13289 **Riley-Smith, Jonathan** What were the Crusades?. SF 2002, Ignatius xiii; 114 pp. $12. 0-89870-954-7 [ThD 50,183—Heiser, W.C.].

U8 Communitates Terrae Sanctae

13290 *Bechmann, Ulrike* Die Friedensvorschläge palästinensischer Christen müssen gehört werden!. BiKi 57 (2002) 176.
13291 **Heyer, Friedrich** 2000 Jahre Kirchengeschichte des Heiligen Landes: Märtyrer, Mönche, Mirchenväter, Kreuzfahrer, Patriarchen, Ausgräber und Pilger. 2000 ⇒16,12447; 17,11994. [R]ÖR 51 (2002) 396-397 (*Heller, Dagmar*).
13292 *Leupen, Piet* Religie en Jeruzalem: de visie van een historicus. ITBT 10/7 (2002) 11-14.
13293 **Marcus, Amy Dockser** Tempelberg und Klagemauer: die Rolle der biblische Stätten im Nahost-Konflikt. 2001 ⇒17,11998. [R]BiKi 57 (2002) 174-175 (*Niemann, Hermann Michael*).
13294 **New, David S.** Holy war: the rise of militant Christian, Jewish and Islamic fundamentalism. Jefferson, NC 2002, McFarland x; 233 pp. 0-7864-1336-0. Bibl. 207-221.
13295 *Prior, Michael* The Israel-Palestine dispute and the bible. ScrB 32 (2002) 64-79.
13296 **Reuther, R.R.; Reuther, H.J.** The wrath of Jonah: the crisis of religious nationalism in the Israeli-Palestinian conflict. Mp [2]2002, Fortress xxiv; 296 pp. $18.
13297 **Wagner, Donald E.** Dying in the land of promise: Palestinian christianity from Pentecost to 2000. 2001 ⇒17,12002. [R]OCP 68 (2002) 280-281 (*Poggi, V.*).

XX. Historia scientiae biblicae

Y1.0 History of exegesis: General

13298 **Auwers, Jean-Marie** La lettre et l'esprit: les Pères de l'église, lecteurs de la bible. ConBib 28: Bru 2002, Lumen Vitae 79 pp. €9. 2-87324-185-3.
13299 **Behr, John** Asceticism and anthropology in IRENAEUS and CLEMENT. 2000 ⇒16,12461. [R]JECS 10 (2002) 291-292 (*Gowans, Coleen Hoffman*); RSPhTh 86 (2002) 509-511 (*Meunier, Bernard*).
13300 *Bray, Gerald* The church fathers and their use of scripture. The trustworthiness of God. 2002 ⇒410. 157-174.
13301 *Buenacasa Pérez, Carles* Le patrimoine de l'église de l'Afrique romaine (1er-Ve siècles): contribution d'une recherche récente. RevSR 76 (2002) 311-321.
13302 *Butturini, Emilio* Guerra e pace nei Padri della chiesa. DSBP 33 (2002) 22-125.
13303 **Clark, Elizabeth Ann** Reading renunciation: asceticism and scripture in early christianity. 1999 ⇒15,12231...17,12005. [R]ABenR 53 (2002) 331-335 (*Rader, Rosemary*); CrSt 23 (2002) 499-501 (*Young, Frances*).
13304 *Dal Covolo, Enrico* 'Ego sum via et veritas' (Gv 14,6): argomentazioni patristiche di verità. Path 1 (2002) 221-238;
13305 Istanze di identità e di formazione sacerdotale tra Antiochia e Alessandria (secoli II-IV). VII Simposio di Tarso. 2002 ⇒587. 317-34.

13306 *Daley, Brian E.* Is patristic exegesis still usable?: reflections on the early christian interpretation of the psalms. Com(US) 29/1 (2002) 185-216.

13307 *Eber, Jochen* Die Katechese der Alten Kirche: eine Einführung; ihre Bedeutung für die Gegenwart. JETh 16 (2002) 75-97.

13308 *Edwards, Mark* Early christian biblical interpretation. Biblical world, 1. 2002 ⇒273. 333-341.

13309 **Ferrarese, Gianfranco** 'Beatum illud apostolorum concilium': Act. 15,1-35 nei Padri anteniceni. ᴰ*Grossi, V.P.*: 2002 Diss. Lateranum [RTL 34,603].

13310 **Fiedrowicz, Michael** Apologie im frühen Christentum: die Kontroverse um den christlichen Wahrheitsanspruch in den ersten Jahrhunderten. 2000 ⇒16,12472; 17,12009. ᴿGn. 74 (2002) 621-623 (*Klein, Richard*).

13311 *García Bazán, Francisco* En los comienzos de la filosofía cristiana: la actitud de los escritores eclesiásticos y de los gnósticos ante la filosofía. TyV 43 (2002) 251-268.

13312 *Giombi, Samuele* La bibbia nella storia del cristianesimo e della cultura occidentale: prospettive di lettura. La sorgente. 2002 ⇒315. 9-31.

13313 **Gounelle, Rémi** La descente du Christ aux enfers: institutionnalisation d'une croyance. 2000 ⇒16,12473; 17,12010. ᴿJECS 10 (2002) 139-141 (*Jacobs, Andrew S.*) [1 Pet 3,19-22].

13314 *Grech, Prosper* Problemi di interpretazione dell'Antico Testamento nei primi secoli. StPat 49 (2002) 25-39.

13315 **Hall, Christopher Alan** Lendo as escrituras com os pais de igreja. ᵀ*Castilho, Rubens*: 2000 ⇒16,12475. ᴿREB 62 (2002) 730-731 (*Pereira, Ney Brasil*);

13316 Learning theology with the Church Fathers. DG 2002, InterVarsity 308 pp. 0-8308-2686-6.

13317 ᴱ**Hansen, Günther Christian** Anonyme Kirchengeschichte: (Gelasius Cyzicenus, CPG 6034). GCS 9: B 2002, De Gruyter lviii; 201 pp. €68. 3-11-017437-5.

13318 **Harrisville, Roy A.; Sundberg, Walter** The bible in modern culture: Baruch SPINOZA to Brevard CHILDS. GR ²2002 <1995>, Eerdmans xiii; 349 pp. $25. 0-8028-3992-4.

13319 **Newman, John Henry** The Church of the Fathers. ᴱ*McGrath, Francis*: The Works of Cardinal John Henry Newman 5: Leominster, Herefordshire 2002, Gracewing pag. varia. 0-85244-447-8.

13320 **Reventlow, Henning Graf** Epochen der Bibelauslegung. 1990-2001, 4 vols. ⇒6,k10... 17,12023. ᴿThLZ 127 (2002) 895-897 (*Smend, Rudolf*);

13321 Epochen der Bibelauslegung, 4: von der Aufklärung bis zum 20. Jahrhundert. 2001 ⇒17,12023. ᴿThZ 58 (2002) 373-374 (*Sommer, Andreas Urs*).

13322 **Trevijano Etcheverria, Ramón** La Biblia en el cristianismo antiguo: Prenicenos, Gnósticos, Apócrifos. 2001 ⇒17,12027. ᴿAng. 79 (2002) 749-757 (*Peretto, Elio*); Salm. 49 (2002) 201-206 (*Aranda Pérez, Gonzalo*); RCatT 27/1 (2002) 244-245 (*Ricart, Ignasi*).

13323 *Van Nieuwenhove, Rik* Diversità e unità nelle scritture: la prospettiva patristica. Conc(I) 38/1 (2002) 123-133; Conc(E) 294,109-117; Conc(D) 38/1,83-90; Conc(P) 294, 100-108.

13324 *Weber, Dorothea* Dritter Bericht über lateinische Editionen und Hilfsmittel aus dem Gebiet der Patristik. ZAC 6 (2002) 215-231.

13325   EWillis, John R. The teachings of the Church Fathers. SF 2002, Ignatius xxv; 496 pp. $20. 0-89870-893-1.
13326   Ziehr, Wilhelm Die Bibel in alten und neuen Nationalkirchen. Die Bibel: Geschichte und Gegenwart. 2002 ⇒971. 214-215.

Y1.4 Patres apostolici et saeculi II—First two centuries

13327   Arnold, Eberhard The early christians in their own words. Farmington, Pa. ⁴1997, Plough xi; 367 pp. $20. RRBLit 4 (2002) 456-458 (Bauman-Martin, Betsy J.).
13328   TAyán, Juan José Padres apostólicos. Biblioteca de patrística 50: 2000 ⇒16,12499; 17,12029. RTer. 53 (2002) 297-298 (Sánchez, Manuel Diego).
13329   TBourlet, M. Apologie à Diognète; Exhortation aux Grecs. Les Pères dans la foi: P 2002, Migne 150 pp. €14. Introd. et notes par R. Minnerath [MSR 60,74—Henne, Philippe].
13330   Bradshaw, Paul F.; Johnson, Maxwell E.; Phillips, Edward The Apostolic tradition: a commentary. EAttridge, Harold W. Mp 2002, Fortress 250 pp. $47. 0-8006-6046-3.
13331   Daniélou, Jean Mensaje evangélico y cultura helenística: siglos II y III. M 2002 <1961>, Cristiandad 521 pp. €25. 84-7057-459-0.
13332   Dihle, Albrecht Θεολογια φιλοσοφουσα. FHOHEISEL, K.: JAC.E 34: 2002 ⇒59. 99-106.
13333   Hübner, Reinhard M. Der Paradox Eine: antignostischer Monarchianismus im zweiten Jahrhundert. SVigChr 50: 1999 ⇒15,12271. RZKG 113 (2002) 255-257 (Fitschen, Klaus).
13334   ELenzuni, Anna Il cristianesimo delle origini: i padri apostolici. Letture patristiche 9: 2001 ⇒17,12039. RSal. 64 (2002) 667-668 (Anoli, Boniface Mose).
13335   TLona, Horacio E. An Diognet. Kommentar zu frühchristlichen Apologeten 8: 2001 ⇒17,12081. RTThZ 111 (2002) 164-165 (Fiedrowicz, Michael).
13336   Martín, José Pablo Historiografía, religión y filosofía en el siglo II. FTREVIJANO ETCHEVERRÍA, R. 2002 ⇒122. 315-332.
13337   Panimolle, Salvatore A. Grazia divina e divinizzazione dei credenti nei Padri apostolici. DSBP 31 (2002) 27-47.
13338   Peretti, Elio Alcuni maestri del pensiero cristiano nei secoli II-III tra guerra e pace. DSBP 33 (2002) 126-195.
13339   EPrinzivalli, Emanuela, al., L'esegesi biblica cristiana nel secondo secolo. La bibbia nelle comunità antiche. 2002 ⇒286. 95-114.
13340   ESimonetti, Manlio, al., La bibbia nella comunità romana da CLEMENTE all'AMBROSIASTER;
13341   L'esegesi allegorica ad Alessandria: teorie, tecniche e finalità dell'interpretazione della sacra scrittura (I-III secolo). La bibbia nelle comunità antiche. 2002 ⇒286. 35-48/49-63.
13342   Trumbower, Jeffrey A. Rescue for the dead: the posthumous salvation of non-christians in early christianity. 2001 ⇒17,12044. RJECS 10 (2002) 542-543 (Wansink, Craig).
13343   Tugwell, Simon The Apostolic Fathers. L 2002, Continuum xii; 148 pp. £15. 0-8264-5771-1.
13344   Visonà, Giuseppe Grazia divina e divinizzazione dell'uomo negli apologisti greci: l'uomo tra natura e grazia. DSBP 31 (2002) 85-107.

13345 *Wypustek, Andrzej Calumnia magiae*: towards a new study of the relationship between Greek-Roman magic and early christianity. Charmes et sortilèges. 2002 ⇒477. 293-304.

13346 APULEIUS: [ET]**Hammerstaedt, Jürgen**, *al.*, Apuleius, de magia: Über die Magie. SAPERE 5: Da:Wiss 2002, 376 pp. €32. 3-534-14946-7.

13347 CLEMENS A: *Bianco, Maria Grazia* Grazia divina e divinizzazione dell'uomo in Clemente Alessandrino. DSBP 31 (2002) 179-195.

13348 **Choufrine, Arkadi** Gnosis, theophany, theosis: studies in Clement of Alexandria's appropriation of his background. Patristic Studies 5: NY 2002, Lang x; 230 pp. $56. 0-8204-6144-X. Bibl. 213-230.

13349 [E]**Marcovich, Miroslav** Clementis Alexandrini Paedagogus. SVigChr 61: Lei 2002, Brill xvii; 229 pp. 90-04-12470-5. Adiuvante *J.C.M. van Winden*.

13350 CLEMENS R: **Bakke, Odd Magne** "Concord and peace": a rhetorical analysis of the first letter of Clement with an emphasis on the language of unity and sedition. WUNT 2/143: 2001 ⇒17,12053. [R]RHPhR 82 (2002) 244-245 (*Grappe, Ch.*).

13351 *Bissoli, Giovanni Kindynos*—"pericolo" nella *Prima Clementis*. LASBF 51 (2001) 133-144.

13352 *Gaden, Tim* Looking to God for healing: a rereading of the Second Letter of Clement in the light of Hellenistic psychagogy. Pacifica 15/2 (2002) 154-173;

13353 "Chosen as a peculiar people": christian traditions and Hellenistic philosophy in 1 Clement. Colloquium 34/1 (2002) 35-48.

13354 *Le Boulluec, Alain* Hors la μοναρχία pas de salut: les refus de Pierre dans les *Homélies pseudo-clémentines*. Nier les dieux. 2002 ⇒ 626. 263-277.

13355 [T]**Lona, Horacio E.** Der erste Clemensbrief. Kommentar zu den apostolischen Vätern 2: 1998 ⇒14,11563... 17,12063. [R]ThRv 98 (2002) 326-327 (*Bienert, Wolfgang*).

13356 **Schmitt, Tassilo** Paroikie und Oikoumene: sozial- und mentalitätsgeschichtliche Untersuchungen zum 1. Clemensbrief. BZNT 110: B 2002, De Gruyter (10) 161 pp. €58. 3-11-017257-7. Bibl. 139-149.

13357 [T]**Spada, Domenico; Salachias, Dimitrios** Costituzioni dei Santi Apostoli per mano di Clemente. 2001 ⇒17,12070. [R]ED 55/1 (2002) 179-181 (*Deiana, Giovanni*).

13358 DIDACHE: *Löfstedt, Torsten* A message for the last days: Didache 16.1-8 and the New Testament traditions. EstB 60 (2002) 351-380.

13359 [E]**Niedźwiecki, Wojciech** Didache nauka dwunastu apostołów (Bibliografia 1883-2000) [Didaché: doctrina XII apostolorum: bibliographia (1883-2000)]. Vox Patrum 22 (2002) 639-664. **P.**

13360 *Van der Sandt, Huub* 'Do not give what is holy to the dogs' (Did 9:5d and Matt 7:6a): the eucharistic food of the Didache in its Jewish purity setting. VigChr 56 (2002) 223-246.

13361 **Van der Sandt, Huub; Flusser, David** The Didache: its Jewish sources and its place in early Judaism and Christianity. Compendia rerum Iudaicarum ad Novum Testamentum III/5; Jewish traditions in early Christian literature 5: Assen 2002, Van Gorcum xviii; 431 pp. $58. 0-8006-3471-3. Bibl. 374-404.

13362		^T**Visonà, Giuseppe** Didaché: insegnamento degli apostoli. 2000 ⇒ 16,12531; 17,12079. ^ROrpheus 23 (2002) 217-220 (*Creazzo, Tiziana*); CivCatt 153/4 (2002) 517-518 (*Cremascoli, G.*).

13363		*Ysebaert, Joseph* The so-called Coptic ointment prayer of Didache 10,8 once more. VigChr 56 (2002) 1-10.

13364		HERACLEON P: **Wucherpfennig, Ansgar** Heracleon Philologus: gnostische Johannesexegese im zweiten Jahrhundert. ^D*Klauck, H.-J.*: WUNT 142: Tü 2002, Mohr xiv; 476 pp. €99. 3-16-147658-1. Diss. Wü 2000-2001. Bibl. 415-440.
		HERMAS: *Marshall, J.* Revelation and romance: genre bending in ...Hermas and the Acts of Peter 2002 ⇒9753.

13365		**Schneider, Athanasius** "Propter sanctam ecclesiam suam": die Kirche als Geschöpf, Frau und Bau im Bussunterricht des Pastor Hermae. SEAug 67: 1999 ⇒15,12304; 17,12086. ^REThL 78 (2002) 236-237 (*Verheyden, J.*).

13366		IGNATIUS A: **Brown, Charles T.** The gospel and Ignatius of Antioch. 2000 ⇒16,12538. ^RJThS 53 (2002) 317-8 (*Stanton, Graham*).

13367		*Cohen, Shaye J.D.* Judaism without circumcision and "Judaism" without "circumcision" in Ignatius. HThR 95 (2002) 395-415.

13368		*Decrept, Étienne* Un épisode de la réforme: la course à l'édition princeps des lettres ignatiennes. RHPhR 82 (2002) 401-416.

13369		*Figura, Michael* Märtyrer durch Gottes Willen—die Deutung seines eigenen Märtyrertodes bei Ignatius von Antiochien. IKaZ 31 (2002) 332-339.

13370		**Lechner, Thomas** Ignatius adversus Valentinianos?: chronologische und theologiegeschichtliche Studien zu den Briefen des Ignatius von Antiochien. SVigChr 47: 1999 ⇒15,12308; 16,12093. ^RZKG 113 (2002) 257-260 (*Greschat, Katharina*); RSPhTh 86 (2002) 499-502 (*Meunier, Bernard*).

13371		^T**Rius-Camps, J.** Ignasi d'Antioquia: cartes. 2001 ⇒17,12095. ^RPhase 248 (2002) 180-182 (*Aldazábal, J.*); RCatT 27/1 (2002) 246-249 (*Torra, Joan*).

13372		*Rius-Camps, Josep* La comunidad cristiana del obispo de Siria, Ignacio, gravemente amenazada por los poderosos círculos docetas y judaizantes. ^FTREVIJANO ETCHEVERRÍA, R. 2002 ⇒122. 269-279.

13373		**Valls, Vicente** Aparicio Relación de los ángeles con la pasión de Cristo según San Ignacio de Antioquía. R 2002, Pontificia Univ. Sanctae Crucis Facultas Theologiae vii; 285 pp. Bibl. 265-285.

13374		IRENAEUS L: *Andía, Ysabel de* Le candélabre à sept branches image de l'église, selon Irénée de Lyon. ^FTREVIJANO ETCHEVERRÍA, R. 2002 ⇒122. 403-428.

13375		*Bondioli, Carlo Maria* Cristo mediatore nell'Adversus haereses di Sant'Ireneo. DT(P) 105 (2002) 203-224.

13376		^E**Brox, Norbert** Adversus haereses: Gegen die Häresien, V. Fontes christiani 8/5: 2001 ⇒17,12101. ^RThRv 98 (2002) 327-329 (*Jaschke, Hans-Joachim*).

13377		*Cattaneo, Enrico* Dalla Gerusalemme temporale alla Gerusalemme eterna: il senso del tempo in Ireneo di Lione. Tempo ed eternità. 2002 ⇒545. 195-216.

13378		*Norris, Richard A., Jr.* The insufficiency of scripture: *Adversus haereses* 2 and the role of scripture in Irenaeus's anti-Gnostic polemic. ^FGREER, R. 2002 ⇒51. 63-79.

Osborn, Eric Francis Irenaeus of Lyons. 2001 ⇒17,12108. ᴿRHE 97 (2002) 578-580 (*Fantino, Jacques*) [⇒.13632].

13379 *Pagels, Élaine* Irenaeus, the "Canon of Truth," and the gospel of John: "making a difference" through hermeneutics and ritual. VigChr 56 (2002) 339-371.

13380 *Peretto, Elio* Il Verbo eterno si è fatto ciò che siamo noi per farci come lui (Ireneo, *C. le eresie*, 5, prologo). DSBP 31 (2002) 137-178.

13381 **Polanco Fermandois, Rodrigo** El concepto de profecía en la teología de san Ireneo. 1999 ⇒15,12551; 17,12109. ᴿSal. 64 (2002) 166-167 (*Pasquato, Ottorino*); RSR 90 (2002) 255-256 (*Sesboüé, Bernard*).

13382 *Reed, Annette Yoshiko* εὐαγγέλιον: orality, textuality, and the christian truth in ' *Adversus Haereses*. VigChr 56 (2002) 11-46.

13383 **Sesboüé, Bernard** Tout récapituler dans le Christ: christologie et sotériologie d'Irénée de Lyon. CJJC 8: 2000 ⇒16,12547(*a*). ᴿRSPhTh 86 (2002) 507-509 (*Meunier, Bernard*); LTP 58 (2002) 378-379 (*Thibault, Annick*).

13384 JUSTINUS: **Allert, Craig D.** Revelation, truth, canon and interpretation: studies in Justin Martyr's Dialogue with Trypho. SVigChr 64: Lei 2002, Brill 90-04-12619-8. Bibl. 277-290.

13385 *Bobichon, Philippe* Autorités religieuses juives et "sectes" juives dans l'oeuvre de Justin Martyr. REAug 48 (2002) 3-22.

13386 ᴱ**D'Anna, Alberto** Pseudo-Giustino: sulla resurrezione: discorso cristiano del II secolo. 2001 ⇒17,12112. ᴿRSPhTh 86 (2002) 503-505 (*Meunier, Bernard*); JECS 10 (2002) 523-524 (*Casiday, A.M.*); Apocrypha 13 (2002) 245-256 (*Pouderon, Bernard*).

13387 **Heimgartner, Martin** Pseudojustin—über die Auferstehung: Text und Studie. PTS 54: 2001 ⇒17,12114. ᴿRHE 97 (2002) 574-578 (*Pouderon, Bernard*).

13388 **Horner, Timothy J.** "Listening to Trypho": Justin Martyr's Dialogue reconsidered. CBET 28: 2001 ⇒17,12116. ᴿSalm 49 (2002) 491-494 (*Trevijano, Ramón*); Vox Patrum 22 (2002) 588-592 (*Misiarczyk, Leszek*).

13389 *Otranto, Giorgio* Note su Paolo nel 'Dialogo con Trifone' di Giustino. VII Simposio di Tarso. 2002 ⇒587. 131-147.

13390 *Pilhofer, Peter* Moses und Bellerophontes: zur dämonischen Hermeneutik bei Justin dem Märtyrer. Die frühen Christen. WUNT 145: 2002 ⇒225. 183-193.

13391 **Rokéah, David** Justin Martyr and the Jews. Jewish and Christian Perspectives 5: Lei 2002, Brill xii; 157 pp. €57/$66. 9004-12310-5. Bibl. 135-140. ᴿVox Patrum 22 (2002) 585-7 (*Misiarczyk, Leszek*).

13392 *Sanchez, S.J.G.* Justin Martyr: un homme de son temps. SE 41 (2002) 5-29;

13393 Le manuscrit du Dialogue avec Tryphon de Justin Martyr. BLE 103 (2002) 371-382.

13394 **Sanchez, Sylvain J.G.** Justin apologiste chrétien: travaux sur le *Dialogue avec Tryphon* de Justin Martyr. CRB 50: 2000 ⇒16,12554; 17,12125. ᴿAng. 79 (2002) 461-464 (*Degórski, Bazyli*); RSPhTh 86 (2002) 502-503 (*Meunier, Bernard*); RTL 33 (2002) 577-578 (*Auwers, J.-M.*).

13395 Verheyden, Joseph Assessing gospel quotations in Justin Martyr. ᶠDELOBEL, J.: BEThL 161: 2002 ⇒24. 361-377.

13396   **Wartelle, André** Bibliographie historique et critique de saint Justin philosophe et martyr et des Apologistes du IIe siècle: 1494-1994 (avec un supplément 1995-1998). 2001 ⇒17,12045. ^RRICP 82 (2002) 219-222 (*Wolinski, Joseph*).

13397   MARCION: *Aland, Barbara* Sünde und Erlösung bei Marcion und die Konsequenz für die sog. beiden Götter Marcions. Marcion. 2002 ⇒578. 147-157.
13398   *Barton, John* Marcion revisited. Canon debate. 2002 ⇒1551. 341-354.
13399   *Bienert, Wolfgang A.* Marcion und der Antijudaismus. Marcion. 2002 ⇒578. 191-205:
13400   *Deakle, David W.* HARNACK & CERDO: a reexamination of the patristic evidence for Marcion's mentor. 177-190;
13401   *Detmers, Achim* Die Interpretation der Israel-Lehre Marcions im ersten Drittel des 20. Jahrhunderts: theologische Voraussetzungen und zeitgeschichtlicher Kontext. 275-292;
13402   *Frenschkowski, Marco* Marcion in arabischen Quellen. 39-63;
13403   *Hage, Wolfgang* Marcion bei EZNIK von Kolb. 29-37;
13404   *Kinzig, Wolfram* Ein Ketzer und sein Konstrukteur: HARNACKs Marcion. 253-274;
13405   *Löhr, Winrich* Did Marcion distinguish betwen a just god and a good god?. 131-146;
13406   *Markschies, Christoph* Die valentinianische Gnosis und Marcion— einige neue Perspektiven. Marcion. 2002 ⇒578. 159-175.
13407   *May, Gerhard* Markion/Markioniten. RGG 5. 2002 ⇒796. 834-36;
13408   Marcion ohne HARNACK. Marcion. 2002 ⇒578. 1-7.
13409   *Norelli, Enrico* Marcion: ein christlicher Philosoph oder ein Christ gegen die Philosophie?. Marcion. 2002 ⇒578. 113-130.
13410   *Regul, Jürgen* Die Bedeutung Marcions aus der Sicht heutiger kirchlicher Praxis. Marcion. 2002 ⇒578. 293-311.
13411   *Stewart-Sykes, Alistair* Bread and fish, water and wine: the Marcionite menu and the maintenance of purity;
13412   *Willing, Meike* Die neue Frage des Marcionschülers Apelles—zur Rezeption marcionitischen Gedankenguts. Marcion. 2002 ⇒578. 207-220/221-231.

13413   POLYCARP: **Berding, Kenneth** Polycarp and Paul: an analysis of their literary & theological relationship in light of Polycarp's use of biblical and extra-biblical literature. SVigChr 62: Lei 2002, Brill vii; 230 pp. €91. 90-04-12670-8. Bibl. 207-217.
13414   **Hartog, Paul** Polycarp and the New Testament: the occasion, rhetoric, theme, and unity of the epistle to the Philippians and its allusions to New Testament literature. ^DAune, David: WUNT 2/134: Tü 2002, Mohr S. x; 281 pp. €49. 31614-74198. Diss. Loyola, Chicago. Bibl. 241-61. ^REstAg 37 (2002) 598-9 (*Luis, P. de*); Salm 49 (2002) 494-497 (*Trevijano, Ramón*); WThJ 64 (2002) 415-417 (*Berding, Ken*); JBL 121 (2002) 781-783 (*Holmes, Michael W.*).
13415   ^ETStewart-Sykes, Alistair The life of Polycarp: an anonymous vita from third-century Smyrna. Sydney 2002, St Pauls 168 pp. AUS$38.50. 0-9577-4834-5.
13416   *Thompson, Leonard L.* The martyrdom of Polycarp: death in the Roman games. JR 82 (2002) 27-52.

13417   *Weidmann, Frederick W.* 'To sojourn' or 'to dwell'?: scripture and identity in the *Martyrdom of Polycarp*. ^FGREER, R. 2002 ⇒51. 29-40.

Y1.6 Origenes

13418   **Lubac, Henri de** Histoire et Esprit: l'intelligence de l'écriture d'après Origène. Oeuvres complètes 16: P 2002 <1950>, Cerf xiii; 649 pp. €39. 2-204-06761-X [RB 109,638].

13419   ^{ET}**Amacker, René; Junod, Éric** PAMPHILUS Caesariensis—EUSEBIUS Caesariensis: Apologie pour Origène: suivi de RUFIN d'Aquilée: Sur la falsification des livres d'Origène. SC 464: P 2002, Cerf 337 pp. €31. 2-204-06849-7.

13420   **Bendinelli, Guido** Il commentario a Matteo di Origene: l'ambito della metodologia scolastica dell'antichità. SEAug 60: 1997 ⇒14, 11594; 17,12136. ^RTer. 53 (2002) 600-601 (*Sánchez, Manuel Diego*); RSLR 38 (2002) 159-161 (*Vecoli, Fabrizio*).

13421   ^E**Bienert, Wolfgang A.; Kühneweg, Uwe** Origeniana Septima: Origenes in den Auseinandersetzungen des 4. Jahrhunderts. BEThL 137: 1999 ⇒15,450; 17,12137. ^RRTL 33 (2002) 104-105 (*Auwers, J.-M.*); ZKG 113 (2002) 104-107 (*Roldanus, Johannes*); RSR 90 (2002) 259-261 (*Sesboüé, Bernard*).

13422   **Castagno, Adele Monaci** Origene: dizionario. 2000 ⇒16,12567. ^RVigChr 56 (2002) 296-297 (*Roukema, Riemer*); JECS 10 (2002) 393-395 (*Casiday, A.M.*); CrSt 23 (2002) 501-503 (*Trigg, Joseph W.*); CivCatt 153/4 (2002) 416-417 (*Cremascoli, G.*).

13423   *Castagno, Adele Monaci* Sacrificio e perdono dei peccati in Origene. ASEs 19 (2002) 43-58.

13424   *Ciner, Patricia Andrea* La imaginación, los sueños y el cuerpo brillante de la preexistencia en el *Contra Ceslo* de Orígenes. Epimeleia 11 (2002) 187-195.

13425   *Cocchini, Francesca* Paolo lettore delle scritture nell'interpretazione origeniana di *1Cor* 15,25-28. VII Simposio di Tarso. 2002 ⇒ 587. 149-161.

13426   ^E**Dal Covolo, Enrico; Maritano, Mario** Omelie sull'Esodo: lettura origeniana. BSRel 174: R 2002, LAS 132 pp. €10.50. 88-213-0495-7. ^RItinerarium(Messina) 10 (2002) 271-272 (*Stelladoro, Gabriella*);

13427   Omelie sull Levitico: lettura origeniana. BSRel 181: R 2002, LAS 156 pp. 88-213-0526-0.

13428   *Danieli, Maria Ignazia* Grazia divina e divinizzazione dell'uomo in Origene. DSBP 31 (2002) 196-213.

13429   **Dawson, John David** Christian figural reading and the fashioning of identity. Berkeley 2002, Univ. of California Pr. x; 302 pp. $50. 0-520-22630-5. Bibl. 275-281. ^RJECS 10 (2002) 524-526 (*Trigg, Joseph W.*).

13430   ^{ET}**Doutreleau, Louis** Origène: homélies sur les Nombres, 3: Homélies XX-XXVIII. SC 461: 2001 ⇒17,12145. Texte latin de *W.A. Baehrens*. ^RJECS 10 (2002) 528-529 (*Bennett, Byard*).

13431   **Edwards, Mark J.** Origen against PLATO. Ashgate studies: Burlington, VT 2002, Ashgate vi; 191 pp. $70. 0-7546-1331-3. Bibl. 163-175 [ThD 50,167—Heiser, W. Charles].

13432   *Fernández Lago, José* Pozos, fuentes y ríos en la HomNum XII de Orígenes. ^FTrevijano Etcheverría, R. 2002 ⇒122. 449-467.

13433   *Fédou, Michel* Traductions. Histoire et Esprit. Oeuvres complètes [De Lubac] 16: 2002 ⇒13418. 533-618.

13434   **Hombergen, Daniel** The second Origenist controversy: a new perspective on Cyril of Scythopolis' monastic biographies as historical sources for sixth-century Origenism. StAns 132: 2001 ⇒17, 12150. ^RAug. 42 (2002) 491-497 (*Simonetti, Manlio*).

13435   *Johnson, Luke Timothy* Origen and the transformation of the mind. The future of Catholic biblical scholarship. 2002 ⇒337. 64-90.

13436   *Lubac, Henri de* Transposition origénienne <1961>;

13437   La querelle du salut d'Origène aux temps modernes <1982>;

13438   Jean Pic de la Mirandole et Pedro Garcia. Histoire et Esprit. Oeuvres complètes 16: 2002 <1977> ⇒13418. 447-454/455-526/ 527-532.

13439   *Ludlow, Morwenna* Theology and allegory: Origen and Gregory of Nyssa on the unity and diversity of scripture. International Journal of Systematic Theology 4 (2002) 45-66.

13440   **Noce, C.** Vestis varia: l'immagine della veste nell'opera di Origene. SEAug 79: R 2002, Instit. Patristicum Augustinianum 361 pp. ^E**Pizzolato, L**. Origene maestro di vita spirituale 2001 ⇒653.

13441   **Prinzivalli, Emanuela** Magister Ecclesiae: il dibattito su Origene fra III e IV secolo. SEAug 82: R 2002, Institutum Patristicum Augustinianum 234 pp. 88-7961-011-2.

13442   *Ramón Díaz, José* La verdad en el *Contra Celso* de Orígenes. ^FTrevijano Etcheverría, R. 2002 ⇒122. 429-448.

13443   ^{ET}**Ressa, Pietro** Origene: Contro Celso. Brescia 2000, Morcelliana 678 pp. €33.57. Pres. *C. Moreschini.* ^RCivCatt 153/4 (2002) 97-98 (*Cremascoli, G.*).

13444   **Rickenmann, Agnell** Sehnsucht nach Gott bei Origenes: ein Weg zur verborgenen Weisheit des Hohenliedes. Studien zur systematischen und spirituellen Theologie 30: Wü 2002, Echter xv; 527 pp. €33.80. 3-429-02293-2. Diss. Gregoriana [ActBib 11,260s—Boada, J.].

13445   *Scholten, Clemens* Psychagogischer Unterricht bei Origenes: ein Ansatz zum Verständnis des "Sitzes im Leben" der Entstehung von frühchristlichen theologischen Texten. ^FHoheisel, K.: JAC.E 34: 2002 ⇒59. 261-280.

13446   *Scott, Alan* Zoological marvel and exegetical method in Origen and the *Physiologus*. ^FGreer, R. 2002 ⇒51. 80-89.

13447   *Sieben, Hermann-Josef* Israels Wüstenwanderung (Num 33) in der Auslegung des Hieronymus und des Origenes: ein Beitrag zur Geschichte der Spiritualität und der origenistischen Streitigkeiten. ThPh 77 (2002) 1-22.

13448   ^E**Simonetti, M.** Origene: omelie sulla Genesi. R 2002, Città N. 432 pp. €45.

13449   *Somos, Robert* Origenian apoctastasis revisited. CrSt 23 (2002) 53-77.

13450   *Van den Hoek, Annewies* Assessing Philo's influence in christian Alexandria: the case of Origen. Shem. JSJ.S 74: 2002 ⇒755. 223-239.

13451   ^E**White, Cynthia** Origenes: homilies on Joshua. ^T*Bruce, J. Barbara*: FaCh 105: Wsh 2002, The Catholic University of America Pr. viii; 232 pp. $35. 0-8132-0105-5. Bibl. viii.

Y1.8 **Tertullianus**

13452 ^T**Braun, René** Tertullien: contre Marcion tome IV. ^E*Moreschini, Claudio*: SC 456: 2001 ⇒17,12167. ^RJThS 53 (2002) 328-330 (*Winterbottom, Michael*); VigChr 56 (2002) 202-207 (*Quispel, Gilles*); REAug 48 (2002) 331-334 (*Petitmengin, Pierre*).

13453 *Butterweck, Christel* Tertullian. TRE 33. 2002 ⇒799. 93-107.

13454 *Lombino, Vincenzo* La grazia in Tertulliano. DSBP 31 (2002) 108-136.

13455 *Markschies, Christoph* Montanismus. RGG 5. 2002 ⇒796. 1471-3.

13456 ^T**Micaelli, Claudio** Tertulliano: contro Ermogene. CTePa 167: R 2002, Città Nuova 131 pp. 88-311-3167-2. Bibl. 47-48.

13457 *Moreschini, Claudio* Polemica antimarcionita e speculazione teologica in Tertulliano. Marcion. 2002 ⇒578. 11-27.

13458 ^T**Moreschini, Claudio** Tertulliano: Contro gli eretici. CTePa 165: R 2002, Città N. 103 pp. €7. 88-311-3165-6. Bibl. 23.

13459 ^T**Schleyer, Dietrich** Tertullian: De praescriptione haereticorum: vom prinzipiellen Einspruch gegen die Häretiker. FC 42: Turnhout 2002, Brepols 364 pp. €41.03/35.42. 2-503-52105-3/6-1.

13460 *Thraede, Klaus* Inzest in der frühen Apologetik Tertullians. ^FHOHEISEL, K. JAC.E 34: 2002 ⇒59. 248-260.

Y2.0 *Patres graeci*—**The Greek Fathers**—*in ordine alphabetico*

13461 *Giannarelli, Elena* L'uomo, immagine di Dio, nei testi greci: linee di lettura: dal Nuovo Testamento a ORIGENE. PSV 45 (2002) 137-156 [Gen 1,26-27].

13462 *Girardi, Mario* Grazia divina e divinizzazione del cristiano nei Cappadoci. DSBP 31 (2002) 236-261.

13463 **Laporte, Jean** Les pères de l'église, 1: les pères latins, 2: les pères grecs. Initiations aux pères de l'église: 2001 ⇒17,12179. ^RRThPh 134 (2002) 89-90 (*Gounelle, Rémi*).

13464 *Metropolit Pitirim* Die Bibel und die Väter der Ostkirche. Die Bibel: Geschichte und Gegenwart. 2002 ⇒971. 130-145.

13465 *Zincone, Sergio* Grazia divina nei Padri antiocheni. DSBP 31 (2002) 262-269.

13466 AMPHILOCHIUS I: *Barkhuizen, Jan H.* Imagery in the (Greek) homilies of Amphilochius of Iconium. APB 13 (2002) 1-30.

13467 *Barkhuizen, Jan H.; Swart, G.J.* A short critical note on Amphilochius of Iconium, Homily VI.9.218-9. APB 13 (2002) 31-33 [Mt26,39].

13468 ASTERIUS S: ^T**Kinzig, Wolfram** Asterius Sophistas: Psalmenhomilien. BGrL 56-57: Stu 2002, Hiersemann 2 vols. 3-7772-0202-9. Eingeleitet... kommentiert. Bibl. v.2, 531-550.

13469 ATHANASIUS A: **Bouter, P.F.** Athanasius van Alexandrië en zijn uitleg van de Psalmen: een onderzoek naar de hermeneutiek en theologie van een psalmverklaring uit de vroege kerk. 2001 ⇒17, 12183. ^REThL 78 (2002) 240-243 (*Leemans, J.*).

13470 *Ladaria, Luis F.* Atanasio de Alejandría y la unción de Cristo (*Contro Arianos* I 47-50). ^FTREVIJANO ETCHEVERRÍA, R. 2002 ⇒122. 469-479.

13471 ᵀStockhausen, Annette von Athanasius von Alexandrien: Epistula ad Afros: Einleitung, Kommentar und Übersetzung. PTS 56: B 2002, De Gruyter x; 366 pp. 3-11-017159-7. Bibl. 307-330.

13472 ᴱᵀBrakke, David Pseudo-Athanasius on virginity. CSCO 592-593; CSCO.S 232-233: Lv 2002, Peeters 2 vols. v.1. 90-429-1080-1, v.2. 90-429-1091-7. Bibl. vol. 1, xix.

13473 CHRYSOSTOMUS: Andrén, Olof Retorisk exeges hos Johannes Chrysostomos. SEÅ 67 (2002) 145-154.

13474 Bouhot, Jean-Paul Adaptations latines de l'Homélie de Jean Chrysostome sur Pierre et Élie (CPG 4513). RBen 112 (2002) 36-71; 201-235.

13475 Brottier, Laurence La culture hellénique au service d'une meilleure compréhension des écritures: quelques exemples empruntés à l'oeuvre de Jean Chrysostome. ConnPE 86 (2002) 9-24.

13476 Campanaro, Donata Frammenti di spiritualità familiare di S. Giovanni Crisostomo nel commento al vangelo di S. Matteo. Troia (FG) 2002, Comunità in Camino [Rivista di scienze religiose 18, 224s—Salvatore Cipressa].

13477 ᵀCoco, Lucio Giovanni Crisostomo: a Stagirio tormentato da un demone. CtePa 163: R 2002, Città N. 83 pp. 88-311-3163-X. Pref. Claudio Moreschini. Bibl. 35-37.

13478 Harrison, Nonna Verna Women and the image of God according to St. John Chrysostom. ᶠWILKEN, R. 2002 ⇒136. 259-279.

13479 Hill, Robert C. St. John Chrysostom: preacher on the Old Testament. GOTR 46 (2001) 267-286.

13480 Mayer, Wendy; Allen, Pauline John Chrysostom. The Early Church Fathers: 2000 ⇒16,12624. ᴿHeyJ 43 (2002) 387-388 (Cooper, Adam G.); JR 82 (2002) 456-58 (Mitchell, Margaret M.).

13481 Mitchell, Margaret M. The heavenly trumpet: John Chrysostom and the art of Pauline interpretation. HUTh 40: 2000 ⇒16,12625. ᴿRB 109 (2002) 469-472 (Murphy-O'Connor, J.); JECS 10 (2002) 408-409 (Mayer, Wendy); ᴿBiblInterp 10 (2002) 443-446 (Riches, John); CBQ 64 (2002) 585-587 (Matera, Frank J.); LTP 58 (2002) 380-381 (Kaler, Michael);

13482 LVL 2002, Westminster xxxiii; 563 pp. $45. 0-664-22510-1 [BiTod 41,202—Senior, Donald].

13483 Pradels, Wendy Lesbos Cod. Gr. 27: the tale of a discovery;

13484 Pradels, Wendy; Brändle, Rudolf; Heimgartner, Martin The sequence and dating of the series of John Chrysostoms's Eight Discourses Adversus Iudaeos. ZAC 6 (2002) 81-89/90-116.

13485 CYRILLUS A: Cassel, J. David Cyril of Alexandria as educator. ᶠWILKEN R. 2002 ⇒136. 348-368.

13486 Russell, Norman Cyril of Alexandria. The Early Church Fathers: 2000 ⇒16,12632. ᴿHeyJ 43 (2002) 229-230 (Rousseau, Philip); JRH 26 (2002) 99-100 (Mayer, Wendy).

13487 ᴱToniolo, C. Ferrari Cyrilliana in psalmos: i frammenti del commento ai salmi di Cirillo di Alessandria nel codice Laudiano greco 42. Saggi e testi 14: 2000 ⇒16,12633; 17,12210. ᴿAevum 76 (2002) 237-238 (Visona, Giuseppe); AnCl 71 (2002) 357-358 (Schamp, Jacques); ᴿThPh 77 (2002) 567-568 (Sieben, H.-J.).

13488 CYRILLUS H: Yarnold, Edward Cyril of Jerusalem. 2000 ⇒16, 12634. ᴿHeyJ 43 (2002) 228-229 (Cooper, Adam); Theol. 105

(2002) 218-219 (*Pettersen, Alvyn*); JECS 10 (2002) 298-299 (*Holman, Susan R.*).

13489 EUSEBIUS C: ᵀ**Bardy, Gustave** Eusèbe de Césarée: histoire ecclésiastique. Sagesses Chrétiennes: P 2001, Cerf 628 pp. Introd. *François Richard.*

13490 ᵀ**Carrara, Paolo** Eusebio di Cesarea: Dimostrazione evangelica. LCPM 29: 2000 ⇒16,12635; 17,12216. ᴿAevum 76 (2002) 234-235 (*Rizzi, Marco*).

13491 ᵀ**Di Nola, Gerardo** Eusebio di Cesarea: la preparazione evangelica, libri I-II. Città del Vaticano 2001, Vaticana 327 pp.

13492 *Dochhorn, Jan* PORPHYRIUS über Sanchuniathon: quellenkritische Überlegungen zu Praep Ev 1,9,21. WO 32 (2002) 121-145.

13493 Eusébio de Cesaréia: História eclesiástica. São Paulo, 1999 Novo Secolo 347 pp.

13494 *Hollerich, Michael J.* Hebrews, Jews, and christians: Eusebius of Caesarea on the biblical basis of the two states of the christian life. ᶠWILKEN, R. 2002 ⇒136. 172-184.

13495 *Le Boulluec, Alain* Écrits 'contextés', 'inauthentiques' ou 'impies'? (Eusèbe de Césarée, *Histoire ecclésiastique*, III, 25). ᶠGEOLTRAIN, P.: BEHE.R 113: 2002 ⇒45. 153-165 [BuBB 38, 132].

13496 **Nielsen, Sylvia** Euseb von Cäsarea und das Neue Testament. ᴰ*Aland, B.*: Diss. Münster 2002 [ThLZ 128,697].

13497 *Simonetti, Manlio* Eusebio sui sacrifici pagani e giudaici. ASEs 19 (2002) 101-110.

13498 EUSTATIUS A: ᴱ**Declerck, José H.** Eustatius, Antiochenus: opera quae supersunt omnia. CChr.SG 51: Turnhout 2002, Brepols cccclxii; 286 pp. 2-503-40511-8. Bibl. x-xxv.

13499 EVAGRIUS P: *Young, Robin Darling* Appropriating Genesis and Exodus in Evagrius's *On prayer.* ᶠWILKEN, R. 2002 ⇒136. 242-258.

13500 GREGORIUS Naz: **Gautier, Francis** La retraite et le sacerdoce chez Grégoire de Nazianze. BEHE.R 114: Turnhout 2002, Brepols (4) 457 pp. 2-503-51354-9. Bibl. 425-444.

13501 ᴱ**Metreveli, Helene** Versio iberica III: Oratio XXXVIII CChr.SG 45; Corpus Nazianzenum 12: Turnhout 2001, Brepols xv; 219 pp. 2-503-40451-0.

13502 ᴱ**Otkhmezuri, Thamar** Pseudo-Nonniani in IV orationes Gregorii Nazianzeni commentari: versio iberica. CChr.SG 50; Corpus Nazianzenum 16: Turnhout 2002, Brepols lxxiv; 295 pp. 2503-40501-0.

13503 ᴱ**Schmidt, Andrea Barbara** Sancti Gregorii Nazianzeni opera: versio syriaca II: Orationes XIII, XLI. CChr.SG 47; Corpus Nazianzenum 15: Turnhout 2002, Brepols li; 172 pp. 2-503-40471-5.

13504 GREGORIUS Nys: **Capboscq, Alberto** Schönheit Gottes und des Menschen: theologische Untersuchung des Werkes In Canticum Canticorum von Gregor von Nyssa aus der Perspektive des Schönen und des Guten. RSTh 55: 2000 ⇒16,12669. ᴿThGl 92 (2002) 583-584 (*Fuchs, Gotthard*).

13505 *Coakley, Sarah* Re-thinking Gregory of Nyssa: introduction—gender, trinitarian analogies, and the pedagogy of the Song. MoTh 18 (2002) 431-443.

13506 *Daley, Brian E.* Training for 'the good ascent': Gregory of Nyssa's homily on the sixth psalm. ᶠWILKEN, R. 2002 ⇒136. 185-217.

13507 *Laird, Martin* Under Solomon's tutelage: the education of desire in the Homelies on the Song of Songs. MoTh 18 (2002) 507-525.

13508 ᴱ**Mann, Friedhelm** Lexicon Gregorianum: Wörterbuch zu den Schriften Gregors von Nyssa, 1: ἀβαρής—ἄωρος. 1999 ⇒15, 12426; 16,12671. ᴿZKG 113 (2002) 405-408 (*Wyrwa, Dietmar*); VigChr 56 (2002) 300-305 (*Leemans, Johan*);

13509 2: βαβαί-δωροφορία. Lei 2000, Brill 555 pp. €225/$276. 90-0411-450-5. ᴿVigChr 56 (2002) 300-305 (*Leemans, Johan*);

13510 3: ἔαρ-ἑωσφόρος. Lei 2001, Brill 856 pp. €225/$276. 90-0411-696-6. ᴿVigChr 56 (2002) 300-305 (*Leemans, Johan*);

13511 4: ζάλη-ἰῶτα. Lei 2002, Brill xii; 510 pp. €249. 90-0412-500-0.

13512 *Norris, Richard A., Jr.* Two trees in the midst of the garden (Genesis 2:9b): Gregory of Nyssa and the puzzle of human evil. ᶠWIL-KEN, R. 2002 ⇒136. 218-241.

13513 **Rexer, Jochen** Die Festtheologie Gregors von Nyssa: ein Beispiel der reichskirchlichen Heortologie. Patrologia 8: Fra 2002, Lang xiii; 343 pp. 3-631-50381-4. Bibl. 306-321.

13514 ᴱᵀ**Reynard, Jean** Grégoire de Nysse: sur les titres des Psaumes. SChr 466: P 2002, Cerf 574 pp. €46. 2-204-06851-9. ᴿRThPh 134 (2002) 276-277 (*Gounelle, Rémi*); REG 115 (2002) 854-856 (*Pouderon, Bernard*).

13515 ᵀ**Risch, Franz Xaver** Gregor von Nyssa: Über das Sechstagewerk: Verteidigungsschrift an seinen Bruder Petrus. BGrL 49: 1999 ⇒15, 12429; 16,12674. ᴿJAC 45 (2002) 222-227 (*Mann, Friedhelm*).

13516 *Ritter, Adolf Martin* Die Väter als Schriftausleger am Beispiel Gregors von Nyssa, *De beatitudinibus*. ZNW 93 (2002) 120-137.

13517 HIPPOLYTUS R: **Bradshaw, Paul F.; Johnson, Maxwell E.; Phillips, L. Edward** Hippolytus: the Apostolic tradition: a commentary. Hermeneia: Mp 2002, Fortress xviii; 250 pp. 0-8006-6046-3. Bibl. 225-230.

13518 **Cerrato, J.A.** Hippolytus between East and West: the commentaries and the provenance of the corpus. OTM: Oxf 2002, OUP x; 291 pp. £50. 0-19-924696-3. Bibl. 264-283.

13519 **Ducoeur, Guillaume** Brahmanisme et encratisme à Rome au IIIe siècle ap. J.C.: étude d'Elenchos I,24, 1-7 et VIII, 20, 1-3. P 2002, L'Harmattan 272 pp. 2-7475-2444-2. Bibl. 233-259.

13520 JOANNES D: **Louth, Andrew** St John Damascene: tradition and originality in Byzantine theology. Oxford Early Christian Studies: Oxf 2002, OUP xvii; 327 pp. 0-19-925238-6. Bibl. 289-305.

13521 MAXIMUS C: ᴱ**Janssens, Bart** Maximi Confessoris opera: ambigua ad Thomam una cum epistula secunda ad eundem. CChr.SG 48: Turnhout 2002, Brepols cxli; 75 pp. 2-503-40481-2. Bibl. ix-xiii.

13522 MELITO S: **Cohick, Lynn H.** The Peri Pascha attributed to Melito of Sardis: setting, purpose, and sources. BJSt 327: 2000 ⇒16, 12679. ᴿJSJ 33 (2002) 326-329 (*Schreckenberg, Heinz*).

13523 *Soto-Hay y García, Fernando* Melitón de Sardes: una aproximación a su exégesis. AnáMnesis 12/2 (2002) 37-49.

13524 ᵀ**Stewart-Sykes, Alistair** On Pascha: with the fragments of Melito and other material related to the Quartodecimans. 2001 ⇒17, 12238. ᴿCTJ 37 (2002) 156-157 (*Payton, James R.*).

13525 METHODIUS O: *Bendinelli, Guido* Grazia divina e divinizzazione dell'uomo in Metodio di Olimpo. DSBP 31 (2002) 214-235.

13526 PSEUDO-DIONYSIUS A: ᵀ**Cid Blanco, Hipólito** Pseudo Dionisio Areopagita: obras completas. Clásicas de Espiritualidad 21: M 2002, BAC 285 pp. 84-7914-615-X.

13527 ᵀ**Lilla, Salvatore** Pseudo-Dionigi l'Areopagita: La gerarchia ecclesiastica. CTePa 166: R 2002, Città N. 190 pp. 88-311-3166-4.

13528 ROMANOS M: *Trigg, Joseph W.* Romanos's biblical interpretation: drama, imagery, and attention to the text. ᶠWILKEN, R. 2002 136. 380-394.

13529 THEODORETUS C: *Hallman, Joseph M.* The communication of idioms in Theodoret's *Commentary on Hebrews.* ᶠWILKEN, R: 2002 ⇒136. 369-379 [Heb 1,2].

13530 *Hill, Robert C.* Old Testament *Questions* of Theodoret of Cyrus. GOTR 46 (2001) 57-73.

13532 *Hutter, Manfred* Die Auseinandersetzung Theodorets von Kyrrhos mit Zoroastrismus und Manichäismus. ᶠHOHEISEL, K.: JAC.E 34: 2002 ⇒59. 287-294.

13532 **Urbainczyk, Theresa** Theodoret of Cyrrhus: the bishop and the holy man. AA 2002, The University of Michigan Pr. x; 174 pp. 0-472-11266-X. Bibl. 153-163.

13533 THEODORUS M: *Kalantzis, George Duo filii* and the *Homo assumptus* in the christology of Theodore of Mopsuestia: the Greek fragments of the *Commentary on John.* EThL 78 (2002) 57-78.

Y2.4 Augustinus

13534 *Alexanderson, B.* Adnotationes criticae et interpretationes in libros Augustini *De Genesi ad litteram* et *De Genesi ad litteram, librum imperfectum.* SE 41 (2002) 113-135;

13535 Réflexions sur l'édition récente des Psalmi graduum de S. Augustin. Aug. 42 (2002) 187-204 [Ps 119-133].

13536 *Andrei, Filippo* Un frammento delle 'Enarrationes in psalmos' di Agostino alla Biblioteca Marucelliana di Firenze. Scr. 56 (2002) 316-320 [Ps 54-55].

13537 *Anoz, José* El Padre en la predicación agustiniana. Augustinus 47 (2002) 5-39.

13538 *Asiedu, F.B.A.* Pablo y la retrospectiva de Agustín sobre sí mismo: relevancia de la *epistula XXII.* Augustinus 47 (2002) 41-66.

13539 **Barros, Paulo César** "Commendatur vobis in isto pane quomodo unitatem amare debeatis": a eclesiologia eucarística nos Sermones ad populum de Agostinho de Hipona e o movimento ecumênico. TGr.T 83: R 2002, E.P.U.G. 338 pp. €21. 88-7652-916-0.

13540 *Bauer, Johannes B.* Zum Psalmentext Augustins in den Enarrationes. Textsorten. SÖAW.PH 693; VKCLK 21: 2002 ⇒697. 141-45.

13541 ᵀ**Boulding, Maria** Expositions of the Psalms, 73-98. Works of St Augustine, 3: Books 18: Hyde Park, NY 2002, New City 510 pp. $44/28. 1-56548-167-4/6-6 [ThD 49,362—Heiser, W. Charles].

13542 **Brown, Peter** Agustín de Hipona.: nueva edición con un epílogo del autor. ᵀ*Tovar, Santiago: Tovar, M. Rosa; Oldfield, John:* 2001 <1970> ⇒17,12262. ᴿRevAg 43 (2002) 429-431 (*Langa, Pedro*); CDios 215 (2002) 686-687 (*Gutiérrez, J.*);

13543 Augustine of Hippo: a biography. 2000 <1967> ⇒16,12693. ᴿPrudentia 34/1 (2002) 79-83 (*Crawford, Janet*); SvTK 78 (2002) 143-144 (*Fernbom, K.F.*); ThLZ 127 (2002) 770-72 (*Pollmann, Karla*).

13544   Burns, J. Patout From persuasion to predestination: Augustine on freedom in rational creatures. ^FWILKEN, R. 2002 ⇒136. 294-316.

13545   Dulaey, Martine L'apprentissage de l'exégèse biblique par Augustin, première partie: dans les années 386-389. REAug 48 (2002) 267-295.

13546   ^EFitzgerald, Allan D. Augustine through the ages: an encyclopedia. 1999 ⇒15,12462...17,12276. ^RRevSR 76 (2002) 105-106 (García, Jaime).

13547   ^{ET}Fuhrer, Therese Augustinus: Opera—Werke: kritische Gesamtausgabe (lateinisch-deutsch), 11: De magistro-Der Lehrer. Pd 2002, Schöningh 223 pp. €28.80. 3-506-71021-4 [EuA 79,437].

13548   ^EFürst, Alfons Augustinus—Hieronymus: Briefwechsel: epistulae mutuae. FC 41/1-2: Turnhout 2002, Brepols 2 vols; 543 pp. €67.80. 2-503-52102-9/4-5 [EuA 79,259—Hogg, Theodor].

13549   Geerlings, Wilhelm Augustinus. 1999 ⇒15,12467. ^RThGl 92 (2002) 120-122 (Fischer, Norbert);

13550   Augustinus—Leben und Werk: eine bibliographische Einführung. Pd 2002, Schöningh 212 pp. €28.80. 3-506-71020-6.

13551   Genovese, Armando S. Agostino e il Cantico dei Cantici: tra esegesi e teologia. SEAug 80: R 2002, Institutum Patristicum Augustinianum 210 pp. 88-7961-013-9. Bibl. 188-195.

13552   Gori, Franco A proposito di due articoli sull'edizione critica delle Enarrationes in psalmos 119-133 di Agostino. Aug. 42 (2002) 315-346;

13553   Genere oratorio, tradizione manoscritta et critica testuale delle Enarrationes in Psalmos predicate di Agostino. Textsorten. SÖAW. PH 693; VKCLK 21: 2002 ⇒697. 125-140.

13554   Gorman, Michael M. An unedited fragment of an Irish epitome of St. Augustine's De Genesis ad litteram <1982>;

13555   A Carolingian epitome of St. Augustine's De Genesis ad litteram. Biblical commentaries. 2002 <1983> ⇒171. 30-39/41-48.

13556   Graf, Fritz Augustine and magic. Metamorphosis. 2002 ⇒394. 87-103.

13557   Grossi, Vittorino La divinizzazione dell'uomo nella teologia di s. Agostino. DSBP 31 (2002) 322-342;

13558   L'apporto di sant'Agostino all cristologia. Cristocentrismo. 2002 ⇒437. 281-303.

13559   ^EHensellek, Werner; Schilling, Peter Specimina eines Lexicon Augustinianum (SLA), 15-16. W 2001-2002, Verlag der Österreichischen Akademie der Wissenschaften 87 + 100 pp. €22.20 + 22. 50. 3-7001-3053-8/160-7.

13560   ^THill, Edmund Augustine: On Genesis: on Genesis, a refutation of the Manichees; unfinished literal comentary on Genesis: the literal meaning of Genesis. Works of Saint Augustine 1/13: Hyde Park, NY 2002, New City 540 pp. $44. 1-56548-175-5 [ThD 50,158—Heiser, W. Charles].

13561   Hombert, Pierre-Marie Nouvelles recherches de chronologie augustinienne. EAug Antiquité 163: 2000 ⇒16,12713. ^RJAC 45 (2002) 228-231 (Marti, Heinrich).

13562   Hunter, David G. Reclaiming biblical morality: sex and salvation history in Augustine's treatment of the Hebrew saints. ^FWILKEN, R. 2002 ⇒136. 317-335.

13563   Jacobsen, Anders C. Augustin om menneskets opstandelse. DTT 65 (2002) 255-271 [1 Cor 15].

13564 *Johnson, Luke Timothy* Augustine and the demands of charity. The future of Catholic biblical scholarship. 2002 ⇒337. 91-118.

13565 **Lancel, Serge** St Augustine. ᵀ*Nevill, Antonia*: L 2002, SCM xviii; 590 pp. £25. 0-334-02886-3.

13566 *Lettieri, Gaetano* Sacrificium civitas est: sacrifici pagani e sacrificio cristiano nel "De Civitate Dei" di Agostino. ASEs 19 (2002) 127-166.

13567 *Lienhard, Joseph T.* Augustine, *Sermon* 51: St. Joseph in early christianity. ᶠWILKEN, R. 2002 ⇒136. 336-347 [Mt 1,16].

13568 ᵀ**Longobardo, Luigi** Agostino d'Ippona: il discorso del Signore sulla montagna. 2001 ⇒17,12297. ᴿAug. 42 (2002) 254-256 (*Grossi, Vittorino*); RevAg 43 (2002) 437-439 (*Jiménez, Oscar*) [Mt 5-7].

13569 ᵀ**Magazzù, Cesare; Cosentino, Augusto** Sant'Agostino: Polemica con i manichei: Contro Adimanto; Contro la lettera del fondamento di Mani; Disputa con Felice; Contro Secondino. R 2000, Città N. 723 pp. €61.97. Introd. *Giulia Sfameni Gasparro.* ᴿCivCatt 153/4 (2002) 622-623 (*Cremascoli, G.*).

13570 **Marcos, Francisco Evaristo** 'Estote ergo vos perfecti, sicut Pater vester caelestis perfectus est': doutrina teológica sobre a perfeição do Pai divino e do Cristão segundo os comentários de Santo Agostinho de Hipona ao evangelho de Mateus. ᴰ*Pastor, Félix A.*: R 2002, 156 pp. Diss. exc. Gregoriana [Mt 5,48].

13571 ᵀ**Martín, Teodoro H.; Hernández, José Maria** Agustín de Hipona: comentario a la primera carta de san Juan. Ichthys 22: S 2002, Sígueme 190 pp. 84-301-1470-X [EstAg 38,173—De Luis, P.].

13572 *Metzler, Karin* "Nimm und lies". ZAC 6 (2002) 345-347.

13573 ᵀ**Montanari, Antonio** Agostino di Ippona: l'umiltà dall'amore: il commento alla lavanda dei piedi nelle omelie 55-59 sul vangelo di Giovanni. Sapientia 7: Mi 2002, Glossa 166 pp. €14.50 [Jn 13,1-20].

13574 *Mühlenberg, Ekkehard* Wenn Augustin die Bibel unvorbereitet auslegt: Augustins Sermo 352. ᶠSMEND, R. 2002 ⇒113. 196-210.

13575 *Müller, Hildegund* Zur Struktur des patristischen Kommentars drei Beispiele aus Augustins Enarrationes in Psalmos. Der Kommentar. 2002 ⇒472. 15-31.

13576 *Neusner, Jacob* Augustine and Judaism. JJS 53 (2002) 49-65.

13577 *Pons Pons, Guillermo* La naturaleza y el cultivo de la tierra en los comentarios de San Agustín al libro del Génesis. RevAg 43 (2002) 283-307.

13578 *Popkes, Enno Edzard* "Constantissimus gratiae praedicator": Anmerkungen zur Paulusexegese Augustins. KuD 48/3 (2002) 148-71.

13579 *Primmer, Adolf* Die Edition von Augustinus, *Enarrationes in Psalmos*: eine Zwischenbilanz. Textsorten. 2002 ⇒697. 147-192.

13580 *Staubach, Nikolaus* Quattuor modis intellegi potest Hierusalem: Augustins *Civitas Dei* und der vierfache Schriftsinn. ᶠGNILKA, C.: JAC.E 33: 2002 ⇒48. 345-358.

13581 *Studer, Basil* Zur Bedeutung der Heiligen Schrift in Augustin's De Trinitate. Aug. 42 (2002) 127-147.

13582 ᴱ**Stump, E.; Kretzmann, N.** The Cambridge Companion to Augustine. 2001 ⇒17,12325. ᴿTheoria 68 (2002) 250-253 (*Yrjönsuuri, Mikko*).

13583 **Ten Boom, Wessel H.** Profetisch tegoed: de joden in Augustinus'
De civitate Dei. Kampen 2002, Kok 355 pp. €29.90. 90-435-0591-
9. Diss. [KeTh 55,163—Kooijman, Arie C.].

13584 **Toom, Tarmo** Thought clothed with sound: Augustine's christological hermeneutics in De doctrina christiana. International theological studies: contributions of Baptist scholars 4: NY 2002, Lang
277 pp. $42. 0-8204-5886-4 [ThD 50,292—Heiser, W. Charles].

13585 ᵀᴱ**Trapé, Dario** S. Agostino: polemica contro Fausto: difesa della
legge e dei profeti e di Cristo fatto uomo. Mi 2000, Res 662 pp.
€33.57. ᴿCivCatt 153/4 (2002) 196-197 (*Cremascoli, G.*).

13586 ᴱ**Van Fleteren, Frederick; Schnaubelt, Joseph C.** Augustine:
biblical exegete. 2001 ⇒17,331. ᴿRHE 97 (2002) 587-589 (*Dolbeau, François*); LouvSt 27 (2002) 182-185 (*Yates, Jonathan P.*).

13587 *Weidmann, Clemens* Zur Struktur der Enarrationes in Psalmos.
Textsorten. SÖAW.PH 693; VKCLK 21: 2002 ⇒697. 105-124.

13588 **Wills, Garry** Saint Augustine. 1999 ⇒15,12504...17,12340.
ᴿRExp 99 (2002) 119-120 (*Graves, Mike*).

Y2.5 Hieronymus

13589 *Adkin, N.* Three unidentified citations in 'Un ancien florilège hiéro-
nymien'. SE 41 (2002) 81-85 [Mt 26,24; 1 Thess 5,21].

13590 ᴱᵀ**Bejarano, Virgilio** Jerónimo: obras completas: edición bilingüe
promovida por la orden de San Jerónimo, 2: comentario a Mateo:
prólogos y prefacios a diferentes tratados: vidas de tres monjes; libro de los claros varones eclesiásticos. B.A.C. 624: M 2002, Biblioteca de Autores Cristianos xxx; 767 pp. €32.21. 84-7914-546-3
[ActBib 79,87—Vives, J.].

13591 **Bernet, Anne** Saint Jérôme. Étampes 2002, Clovis 553 pp. €22. 2-
912642-76-0 [RB 110,153].

13592 ᴱ**Canellis, Alina** S. Hieronymi presbyteri opera, 3: opera polemica,
4: altercatio Luciferiani et Orthodoxi. CChr.SL 79: 2000 ⇒16,
12744; 17,12344. ᴿRHE 97 (2002) 589-591 (*Gain, Benoît*).

13593 **Clausi, Benedetto** Ridar voce all'antico padre: l'edizione erasmia-
na delle *Lettere* di Gerolamo. Armarium 10: 2000 ⇒16,12745.
ᴿERSY 22 (2002) 81-91 (*Vessey, Mark*); VetChr 39/1 (2002) 204-
205 (*Nigro, Giovanni*).

13594 **Conring, Barbara** Hieronymus als Briefschreiber: ein Beitrag zur
spätantiken Epistolographie. 2001 ⇒17,12345. ᴿThRv 98 (2002)
116-118 (*Fürst, Alfons*); REAug 48 (2002) 198-199 (*Duval, Yves-
Marie*); ThLZ 127 (2002) 60-62 (*Haendler, Gert*); Salm 49 (2002)
501-505 (*Trevijano, Ramón*).

13595 ᴱ**Fürst, Alfons** Augustinus—Hieronymus: Briefwechsel: epistulae
mutuae. FC 41/1-2: Turnhout 2002, Brepols 2 vols; 543 pp. €67.80.
2-503-52102-9/4-5 [EuA 79,259—Hogg, Theodor].

13596 **Jeanjean, Benoît** Saint Jérôme et l'hérésie. EAug, Antiquité 161:
1999 ⇒15,12516. ᴿRSR 90 (2002) 139-140 (*Dulaey, Martine*);
ZKG 113 (2002) 110-112 (*Rebenich, Stefan*).

13597 *Kos, Stanislav* Křćanska ženidba u mišljenju i naučavanju svetog
Jeronima [Christian marriage in the thought and teachings of St.
Jerome]. Obnovljeni Život 57 (2002) 369-393 Sum. 393. **Croatian.**

13598 **Laurence, Patrick** Jérôme et le nouveau modèle feminin: la conversion à la 'vie parfaite'. EAug.Antiq. 155: 1997 ⇒13,11542; 15, 12518. ᴿRSR 90 (2002) 142-143 (*Dulaey, Martine*).

13599 *Layton, Richard A.* From 'holy passion' to sinful emotion: Jerome and the doctrine of *propassio.* ᶠWILKEN, R. 2002 ⇒136. 280-293.

13600 *Lößl, Josef* Hieronymus und EPIPHANIUS von Salamis über das Judentum ihrer Zeit. JSJ 33 (2002) 411-436.

13601 *Margetić, Lujo* Jeronimov *oppidum Stridonis.* CCP 50 (2002) 1-9. **Croatian.**

13602 *Messina, Marco Tullio* Due note su VIRGILIO in Girolamo. Tra IV e V secolo. 2002 ⇒475. 119-139 [Qoh 10,2-3; Isa 66,22-24].

13603 *Micalizzi, Lucia* Figure femminili nell'epistolario di San Girolamo. ᶠTUDDA, F. 2002 ⇒123. 183-199.

13604 *Prinzivalli, Emanuela* Il sacrificio in Girolamo. ASEs 19 (2002) 111-126.

13605 *Quezada-del Rio, Javier* El matrimonio y el sexo según las adiciones y las omisiones de San Jerónimo al libro de Tobías. Qol 29 (2002) 79-88.

13606 **Rebenich, Stefan** Jerome. The Early Church Fathers: L 2002, Routledge xi; 211 pp. $15.

13607 *Vilella, J.* Los corresponsales hispanos de Jerónimo. SE 41 (2002) 87-111.

Y2.6 Patres Latini *in ordine alphabetico*

13608 *Dolezalova, Lucie* The Cena Cypriani, or the game of endless possibilities. Der Kommentar. 2002 ⇒472. 119-130.

13609 *Geerlings, Wilhelm* Die lateinisch-patristischen Kommentare. Der Kommentar. 2002 ⇒472. 1-14.

13610 *Giorgi, Tilde* Ascesi ed esegesi nella Roma imperiale del IV secolo. Ricerche teologiche 13/1 (2002) 89-97.

Laporte, J. Les pères de l'église, 1: pères latins 2001 ⇒13463.

13611 Patrologia latina database. Alexandria, Va. 1995, Chadwyck-Healey. 5 CD-ROMs. $45. ᴿRBLit 4 (2002) 78-9 (*Thompson, John L.*).

13612 ᴱ*Prinzivalli, Emanuela, al.*, L'Occidente nel terzo secolo. La bibbia nelle comunità antiche. 2002 ⇒286. 115-128.

13613 AMBROSIUS: *Bonato, Antonio* Incidenza della grazia in sant'Ambrogio. DSBP 31 (2002) 270-321.

13614 *Fitzgerald, Allan* Ambrose at the well: De Isaac et anima. REAug 48 (2002) 79-99 [Gen 24].

13615 *Granado Bellido, Carmelo* El Espíritu y el paraíso: notas de teología ambrosiana. ᶠTREVIJANO ETCHEVERRÍA, R. 2002 ⇒122. 481-494 [Gen 2-3].

13616 **Henke, Rainer** BASILIUS und Ambrosius über das Sechstagewerk: eine vergleichende Studie. Chrêsis 7: 2000 ⇒16,12778. ᴿNatGrac 49/1 (2002) 177-179 (*Villalmonte, A.*); LTP 58 (2002) 614-617 (*Côté, Dominique*).

13617 *Marotta, Beatrice* Dal digiuno materiale al digiuno spirituale: *exempla* biblici nel *De Helia et Ieiunio* di Ambrogio. Orpheus 23 (2002) 74-89.

13618 *Passarella, Raffaele Peridrome matricis*: nota esegetica ad Ambrogio *Expos. Ps. cxviii* 19.1.2. Acme 55 (2002) 251-62 [{Ps 118,19].

13619 ANTONIUS A: **Zaffanella, Gian** Carlo Sulle orme di S. Antonio Abate: itinerario alla scoperta del monachesimo cristiano nei deserti d'Egitto. Padova 2002, Gregoriana 201 pp. Bibl. 197-199.

13620 APPONIUS: *Hamblenne, Pierre* Apponius: le moment, une patrie. Aug. 41 (2001) 425-464 [RBen 114,202—P.-M. Bogaert].

13621 BERNARDUS C: [T]**Fassetta, Raffaele**, *al.*, Bernard de Clairvaux: sermons sur le Cantique, 2 & 3: sermons 16-32 & 33-50. [E]*Leclercq, Jean, al.*,: SC 431, 452: 2000 ⇒16,12878; 17,12445. [R]LTP 58 (2002) 629-631 (*Dînca, Lucian*).

13622 CAESARIUS A: [TE]**Courreau, Joël** Césaire d'Arles: sermons sur l'Écriture: v.1, Sermons 81-105. [E]*Morin, G.*: SC 447: 2000 ⇒16, 12788; 17,12368. [R]RSR 90 (2002) 135-136 (*Dulaey, Martine*); StMed 43 (2002) 485-486 (*Cristiani, Riccardo*); [R]ZKG 113 (2002) 114-115 (*Pollmann, Karla*); LTP 58 (2002) 632-633 (*Dînca, Lucian*).

13623 CYPRIANUS: **Burns, J. Patout** Cyprian the bishop. Routledge early church monographs: L 2002, Routledge xi; 240 pp. 0-415-23849-8. Bibl. 233-234.

13624 *Rouse, Richard; McNelis, Charles* North African literary activity: a Cyprian fragment, the stichometric lists and a Donatist compendium. RHT 30 (2000) 189-233 [RBen 114,210—P.-M. Bogaert].

13625 EPHREM S: [TE]**De Francesco, Ignazio** Efrem Siro: inni pasquali. Mi 2001, Paoline 411 pp. [R]LASBF 51 (2001) 453-455 (*Pazzini, M.*).

13626 FACUNDUS H: [E]**Clément, Jean-Marie; Vander Plaetse, R.** Facundus Hermianensis: défense des trois chapitres (à Justinien), 1: livres I-II. [T]*Fraïsse-Bétoulières, Anne*: Ment. *Theodorus M.*; *Theodoretus C.*: SC 471: P 2002, Cerf 380 pp. 2-204-06855-1. Bibl. 135-138.

13627 GREGORIO de E: [E]**Pascual Torró, Joaquín** Gregorio de Elvira: comentario al Cantar de los cantares y otros tratados exegéticos. Fuentes patrísticas 13: 2000 ⇒16,12800; 17,12375. [R]Ter. 53 (2002) 299-301 (*Sánchez, Manuel Diego*).

13628 GREGORIUS M: *Christman, Angela Russell* The Spirit and the wheels: Gregory the Great on reading scripture. [F]WILKEN, R. 2002 ⇒136. 395-407.

13629 **Cremascoli, Giuseppe** L'esegesi biblica di Gregorio Magno. 2001 ⇒17,12378. [R]RivBib 50 (2002) 247-248 (*Barbaglio, Giuseppe*); CrSt 23 (2002) 827-828 (*Markus, R.A.*).

13630 [E]**Étaix, Raymond** Gregorius Magnus: homiliae in Evangelia. CChr.SL 141: 1999 ⇒15,12544...17,12379. [R]EThL 78 (2002) 248-249 (*Verheyden, J.*).

13631 **Ricci, Cristina** Mysterium dispensationis: tracce di una teologia della storia in Gregorio Magno. StAns 135: R 2002, Pont. Ateneo S. Anselmo 367 pp. €40. 88-8139-094-9. Diss. Macerata. Bibl. 311-337.

13632 IRENAEUS L: **Osborn, Eric Francis** Irenaeus of Lyons. 2001 ⇒17, 12108. [R]RHE 97 (2002) 578-580 (*Fantino, Jacques*).

13633 ISIDORUS: *Uitvlugt, Donald Jacob* The sources of Isidore's commentaries on the Pentateuch. RBen 112 (2002) 72-100.

13634 LEO M: *Cavalcanti, Elena* Il linguaggio relativo al sacrificio nei "Sermoni" di Leone Magno. ASEs 19 (2002) 201-223.

13635 *Stritzky, Maria-Barbara von* Schriftauslegung als Verkündigung: Phil. 2,6-7 in den Weihnachtspredigten Leos des Großen. RQ 97 (2002) 1-16.

13636 OROSIUS P: **Martínez Cavero, Pedro** El pensamiento histórico y antropológico de Orosio. Antigüedad y cristianismo 19: Murcia 2002, Universidad de Murcia 405 pp. Bibl. 301-321.

13637 PRUDENTIUS: *Henderson, W.J.* Similes in Prudentius' Romanus ode (Per. 10). APB 13 (2002) 143-164.

13638 SIDONIUS A: ^T**Santelia, Stefania** Sidonius Apollinaris: Carmen 24: Propempticon ad libellum. Quaderni di "Invigilata Lucernis" 16: Bari 2002, Edipuglia 164 pp. 88-7228-337-X. Bibl. 129-164.

13639 SULPICIUS Severus: ^{ET}**Senneville-Grave, Ghislaine de** Sulpice Sévère: Chroniques. SC 441: 1999 ⇒15,12562; 16,12823. ^RJAC 45 (2002) 227-228 (*Schieffer, Rudolf*).

13640 TYCONIUS P: *Alexander, James S.* Tyconius. TRE 34. 2002 ⇒800. 203-208.

13641 *Marone, Paola* Ticonio e l'autorità apostolica di Paolo. SMSR 68 (2002) 275-295.

13642 *Pollmann, Karla* Apocalypse now?!—der Kommentar des Tyconius zur Johannesoffenbarung. Der Kommentar. 2002 ⇒472. 33-54.

13643 VICTORINUS P: *Pani, Giancarlo* L'*Apocalisse* e il millenarismo di Vittorino di Petovio. SMSR 68 (2002) 43-69.

Y2.8 Documenta orientalia

13644 *Botha, Phil J.* The paradox between appearance and truth in EPHREM the Syrian's hymn "De crucifixione" IV. APB 13 (2002) 34-49.

13645 *Brock, Sebastian* JACOB of Serugh's verse homily on Tamar (Gen 38). Muséon 115 (2002) 279-315.

Y3.0 Medium aevum, *generalia*

13646 *Bataillon, Louis-Jacques* Chronique de doctrines médiévales: exégèse, prédication et morale pratique. RSPhTh 86 (2002) 145-158.

13647 *Besson, Gisèle* Pollux-Christus: lecteurs chrétiens et mythologie païenne à la fin du Moyen-Âge, d'après la tradition manuscrite du *Troisième mythographe du Vatican.* ^FGEOLTRAIN, P.: BEHE.R 113: 2002 ⇒45. 243-253 [BuBB 39,89].

13648 *Braunger, Klaus* Wenn der Geruch des Lebens in die Nase steigt... der Duft aus der Bibel—in rezeptionsgeschichtlicher Perspektive bei Klara von Assisi: zum 750. Todesjahr der Hl. Klara von Assisi (1193-1253). BN 114/115 (2002) 17-23.

13649 *Carnevale, Laura* Esegesi letterale e metafora: da TOMMASO d'Aquino alla scuola antiochena. VetChr 39 (2002) 101-114.

13650 **Dahan, Gilbert** L'exégèse chrétienne de la bible en occident médiéval, XIIe-XIVe siècle. Patrimoines: 1999 ⇒15,12572...17,12412. ^RRSPhTh 86 (2002) 145-149 (*Bataillon, Louis-Jacques*); StMed 43 (2002) 457-460 (*Donnini, Mauro*); Spec. 77 (2002) 1272-1274 (*Matter, E. Ann*).

13651 *Dinkova-Bruun, Greti* Medieval Latin poetic anthologies (VII): the biblical anthology from York Minster Library (MS. XVI Q 14). MS 64 (2002) 61-109.

13652 **Ghosh, Kantik** The Wycliffite heresy: authority and the interpretation of texts. C 2002, CUP xiv; 296 pp. £45/$65.

13653   *Gorman, Michael M.* WIGBOD and biblical studies under CHARLE-
        MAGNE. Biblical commentaries. 2002 <1997> ⇒171. 200-236;
13654   The commentary on Genesis of CLAUDIUS of Turin and biblical
        studies under LOUIS the Pious <1997>;
13655   The Visigothic commentary on Genesis in Autun 27 (S.29)
        <1997>. Biblical commentaries. 2002 ⇒171. 237-287/323-433;
13656   The oldest epitome of Augustine's *Tractatus in Euangelium Ioan-
        nis* and commentaries on the gospel of John in the early middle
        ages. Biblical commentaries. 2002 <1997> ⇒171. 435-475;
13657   The Carolingian miscellany of exegetical texts in Albi 39 and Paris
        lat. 2175. Biblical commentaries. 2002 <1997> ⇒171. 476-494.
13658   *Harris, Jennifer A.* The body as temple in the high middle ages.
        Sacrifice in religious experience. 2002 ⇒612. 233-256.
13659   **Hazard, Mark** The literal sense and the gospel of John in late-
        medieval commentary and literature. Ment. *Nicolaus L.*: Studies in
        medieval history and culture 12: NY 2002, Routledge xvii (2); 207
        pp. 0-415-94123-7. Bibl. 195-201.
13660   **Lubac, Henri de** Medieval exegesis, 2: the four senses of scripture.
        ᵀ*Macierowski, E.M.*: 2000 ⇒16,12848. ᴿTS 63 (2002) 167-169
        (*Matter, E. Ann*); IThQ 67 (2002) 77-78 (*Moloney, Raymond*);
        ABenR 53 (2002) 336-338 (*Feiss, Hugh*).
13661   **Nahmer, D. von der** Agiografia altomedievale e uso della bibbia.
        Nuovo Medioevo 48: N 2001, Liguori 443 pp.
13662   **Ocker, Christopher** Biblical poetics before humanism and Refor-
        mation. C 2002, CUP xvi; 265 pp. $60. 0521810469. Bibl. 239-62.
13663   *Passi, Sara* Il commentario inedito ai vangeli attribuito a 'WIG-
        BODUS'. StMed 43 (2002) 59-156.
13664   *Resnick, Irven M.* Ps.-Albert the Great on the physiognomy of Jesus
        and Mary. MS 64 (2002) 217-240.
13665   **Schlosser, Marianne** Lucerna in caliginoso loco: Aspekte des Pro-
        phetie-Begriffes in der scholastischen Theologie. VGI 43: 2000 ⇒
        16,12854; 17,12421. ᴿAHIg 11 (2002) 506-507 (*Reinhardt, E.*).
13666   *Trefz-Winter, Elke* Textlinguistische Verfahren als Mittel zur Fest-
        stellung inhaltlicher Differenzen: mittelalterliche christliche Mysti-
        kerinnen unter Häresieverdacht. ᶠHOHEISEL, K.: JAC.E 34: 2002 ⇒
        59. 427-436.
13667   *Verkerk, Dorothy Hoogland* Black servant, black demon: color
        ideology in the Ashburnham pentateuch. JMEMS 31 (2001) 57-77
        [RBen 114,182—P.-M. Bogaert].
13668   *Winter, Erich* Der Zielpunkt bedingt die Darstellung: altägyptische
        und mittelalterliche Typisierung der Wäge-Szene beim Totenge-
        richt. ᶠHAAG, E. 2002 ⇒55. 329-337.

            Y3.4 **Exegetae mediaevales** [Hebraei ⇒K7]

13669   AELFRICUS E: **Gneuss, Helmut** Ælfric von Eynsham und seine
        Zeit. Bayerische Akademie der Wissenschaften, Phil.-hist. Kl. Sit-
        zungsberichte 2002,1: Mü 2002, Verlag der Bayerischen Akademie
        der Wissenschaft 51 pp. 3-7696-16197. Bibl. 5-6.
13670   ALEXANDER H: *Pasquale, Gianluigi* Alessandro di Hales e la va-
        lenza salvifica veterotestamentaria. Convivium Assisiense 4/1
        (2002) 171-194.

13671 ALFRED R: ^T**Pezzini, Domenico** Alfredo di Rievaulx: Gesù dodicenne: preghiera pastorale. 2001 ⇒17,12428. ^RStPat 49 (2002) 247-248 (*Lorenzin, Tiziano*).

13672 ANSELM C: **Albanesi, Nicola** Cur Deus homo: la logica della redenzione: studio sulla teoria della soddisfazione di S. Anselmo arcivescovo di Canterbury. TGr.T 78: R 2002, E.P.U.G. 240 pp. €14. 88-7652-905-5.

13673 AQUINAS: **Baglow, Christopher T.** "Modus et forma": a new approach to the exegesis of Saint Thomas Aquinas with an application to the Lectura super epistolam ad Ephesios. AnBib 149: R 2002, E. P.I.B. (6) 290 pp. $18. 88-7653-149-1. Bibl. 277-290.

13674 *Bonino, Serge-Thomas* Le rôle des apôtres dans la communication de la Révélation, selon la Lectura super Ioannem de saint Thomas d'Aquin. BLE 103 (2002) 317-350.

13675 *Dabrowski, Wiesław* Il pensiero mariologico di san Tommaso d'Aquino nei suoi commenti alle lettere di san Paolo Apostolo. Ang. 79 (2002) 51-86.

13676 ^T**Dahan, G.** Thomas d'Aquin: commentaire de la première épître aux Corinthiens: complété par la postille sur la première épître aux Corinthiens (Chap. 7,10b au chap. 10,33). P 2002, Cerf 640 pp. €89. 2-204-06937-X.

13677 *Kerr, Fergus* Recent Thomistica: I. NBl 83 (2002) 245-251.

13678 *Levering, Matthew* Contemplating God: YHWH and being in the theology of St Thomas Aquinas. IThQ 67 (2002) 17-31;

13679 Christ's fulfillment of torah and temple: salvation according to Thomas Aquinas. ND 2002, Univ. of Notre Dame Pr. viii; 254 pp. $24. 0-268-02273-9. Bibl. 207-236.

13680 *Mróz, Miroslaw* Saint Thomas d'Aquin comme prédicateur. ACra 34 (2002) 193-226 [Lk 2,52].

13681 *Quoëx, Franck M.* Le culte dans l'ancienne alliance selon saint Thomas d'Aquin. Sedes Sapientiae 82 (2002) 53-80.

13682 **Ryan, Thomas E.** Thomas Aquinas as reader of the Psalms. 2001 ⇒17,12433. ^RSpiritus 2/1 (2002) 125-127 (*Astell, Ann W.*); ^RThom. 66 (2002) 329-332 (*Gross-Diaz, Theresa*).

13683 **Torrell, Jean-Pierre** Recherches thomasiennes: études revues et augmentées. BiblThom 52: P 2000, Vrin ii; 386 pp. €53.50;

13684 Le Christ en ses mystères: la vie et l'oeuvre de Jésus selon saint Thomas d'Aquin. 1999 ⇒15,12603...17,12434. ^RStMed 43 (2002) 237-244 (*Turrini, Mauro*).

13685 AUXILIUS: *Gorman, Michael M.* The commentary on Genesis attributed to Auxilius in MS. Monte Cassino 29. Biblical commentaries. 2002 <1983> ⇒171. 50-61.

13686 BEATO L: *Romero-Pose, Eugenio* La tradición textual del comentario a Daniel de San JERÓNIMO en los comentarios al Apocalipsis de Beato de Liébana (en torno a la tradición jeronimiana hispánica). ^FTREVIJANO ETCHEVERRÍA, R. 2002 ⇒122. 495-515.

13687 BEDA V: ^T**Foley, W. Trent: Holder, Arthur G.** Bede: a biblical miscellany. 1999 ⇒15,12605. ^RABenR 53 (2002) 221-3 (*Cristiani, Riccardo*).

13688 *Gorman, Michael M.* The commentary on the pentateuch attributed to Bede in PL 91.189-394. Biblical commentaries. 2002 <1996> ⇒ 171. 63-163.

13689 BERNARDUS C: *Birkedal Bruun, Mette* Den spirituelle topografi hos Bernhard af Clairvaux. DTT 65 (2002) 107-129.

13690 *Messa, Pietro* Uso e trasformazione del linguaggio sponsale nei *Sermones super Cantica Canticorum* di San Bernardo di Chiaravalle. Convivium Assisiense 4/1 (2002) 299-319.

13691 BONAVENTURA: **Karris, Robert J.** St. Bonaventure as biblical interpreter: his methods, wit, and wisdom. FrS 60 (2002) 159-208.

13692 BYRHRFERTH R: *Gorman, Michael M.* The glosses on BEDE's *De temporum ratione* attributed to Byrhrferth of Ramsey. Biblical commentaries. 2002 <1996> ⇒171. 175-198.

13693 CASSIANUS J: **Driver, Steven D.** John Cassian and the reading of Egyptian monastic culture. Studies in medieval history & culture 8: NY 2002, Routledge xiv; (2) 149 pp. 0-415-93668-3. Bibl. 121-44.

13694 CASSIODORUS: ᵀDonnini, Mauro Cassiodoro: le istituzioni. Fonti medievali per il terzo millennio 23: R 2001, Città N. 209 pp.

13695 CLAREMBALD A: ᴱᵀMartello, Concetto Fisica della creazione: la cosmologia di Clarembaldo di Arras: tractatulus super librum Genesis: testo traduzione e commento. Symbolon 18: 1998 ⇒15, 12610. ᴿStMed 43 (2002) 989-993 (*Finucci, Saul*).

13696 CLAUDIUS T: *Gorman, Michael M.* The commentary on Kings of Claudius of Turin and its two printed editions (Basel, 1531; Bologna, 1755). Biblical commentaries. 2002 <1997> ⇒171. 289-321.

13697 ELIPANDUS T: ᴱᵀDel Cerro Calderón, Gonzalo; Palacios Royán, José Obras de Elipando de Toledo: texto, traducción y notas. Toledo 2002, Diputación Provincial de Toledo 285 pp. 84-87100-92-9. Bibl. 257-259.

13698 EUPOLEMIUS: *Gärtner, Thomas* Zu den dichterischen Quellen und zum Text der allegorischen Bibeldichtung des Eupolemius. DA 58 (2002) 549-562.

13699 FLORUS L: ᴱFransen, Paul-Irénée; Coppieters 't Wallant, B. Florus Lugdunensis: Opera omnia: collectio ex dictis XII Patrum pars I. CChr.CM 193: Turnhout 2002, Brepols lxix; 200 pp. 2-503-04931-1.

13700 FRECHULPHUS L: ᴱAllen, Michael I. Frechulfi Lexoviensis Episcopi: opera omnia: v.1: prolegomena indices, v.2: textus. CChr.CM 169-169 A: Turnhout 2002, Brepols 2 vols.

13701 GEOFFREY A: ᵀGibbons, J. Geoffrey of Auxerre: On the Apocalypse. Cistercian Fathers 42: 2000 ⇒16,12885. ᴿCîteaux 53 (2002) 368-369 (*Campion, Eleanor*).

13702 GIORDANO P: *Delcorno, Carlo* Esegesi biblica e predicazione di Giordano da Pisa. La sorgente. 2002 ⇒315. 69-82.

13703 ᴱGrattarola, Serena Giordano da Pisa: prediche sul secondo capitolo del Genesi. 1999 ⇒15,12614; 17,12456. ᴿStMed 43 (2002) 979-980 (*Vecchio, Silvana*).

13704 GREGORIUS E: *Ayán Calvo, Juan José* La belleza del esposo: un aspecto de la cristología de Gregorio de Elvira. ᶠTREVIJANO ETCHEVERRÍA, R. 2002 ⇒122. 517-526.

13705 GREGORIUS T: *Monroe, William S. Via iustitiae*: the biblical sources of justice in Gregory of Tours. The world of Gregory of Tours. 2002 ⇒506. 99-112.

13706 GUILELMUS S-T: ᴱSpinelli, Mario Guglielmo di Saint-Thierry: Commento al Cantico dei Cantici: Opere 4. Fonti medievali 24: R 2002, Città N. 223 pp. 88-311-1027-6.

13707 HAIMO A: *Contreni, John J.* 'By lions, bishops are meant; by wolves, priests': history, exegesis, and the Carolingian church in Haimo of Auxerre's *Commentary on Ezechiel.* Francia 29/1 (2002) 29-56.

13708 HUGH F: *Mégier, Elisabeth* 'Ecclesiae sacramenta': the spiritual meaning of Old Testament history and the foundation of the church in Hugh of Fleury's 'Historia ecclesiastica'. StMed 43 (2002) 625-649.

13709 HUGH St V: *Karfíková, Lenka* Res significare habent: Exegese der Schrift und der Wirklichkeit nach Hugo von St. Viktor (+1141). Philosophical hermeneutics. WUNT 153: 2002 ⇒367. 310-322.

13710 ᴱPoirel, Dominici Hugonis de Sancto Victore: De tribus diebus. CChr.CM 177: Turnhout 2002, Brepols 265*; 102 pp. €155/142. Bibl. 15*-21*.

13711 ᴱSicard, Patricius Hugonis de Sancto Victore: De archa Noe; Libellus de formatione arche. CChr.CM 176, 176A: Turnhout 2002, Brepols 287*; 205 pp. €200/187; €73/62.

13712 IBN HAZAM: Behloul, Samuel-Martin Ibn Hazms Evangelienkritik: eine methodische Untersuchung. IPTS, Texts and Studies 50: Lei 2002, Brill xv; 276 pp. 90-04-12527-2. Bibl. 255-259.

13713 LULLUS R: ᴱTenge-Wolf, Viola Raimundi Lulli opera latina 53: tabula generalis: in Mari in Portu Tunicii in medio septembris anno MCCXCIII incepta, et in civitate Neapolis in Octavis Epiphaniae anno MCCXCIV ad finem perducta. CChr.CM 181; Raimundi Lulli Opera latina 27: Turnhout 2002, Brepols 260 pp. 2-503-04811-0.

13714 MAXIMUS C: ᵀᴱAllen, Pauline; Neil, Bronwen Maximus the Confessor and his companions: documents from exile. Oxf 2002, OUP xv; 210 pp. 0-19-829991-5. Bibl. 193-195.

13715 *Blowers, Paul M.* The world in the mirror of holy scripture: Maximus the Confessor's short hermeneutical treatise in *Ambiguum ad Joannem* 37. ᶠWILKEN, R. 2002 ⇒136. 408-426.

13716 NICHOLAS H: *Amadori, Saverio* L'*exemplum* biblico: il *Liber de exemplis sacrae scripturae* di Nicolò di Hanapes. La sorgente. 2002 ⇒315. 49-68.

13717 NICHOLAS L: ᴱKrey, Philip D.W.; Smith, Lesley J. Nicholas of Lyra: the senses of scripture. SHCT 90: 2000 ⇒16,1466; 17, 12473. ᴿJThS 53 (2002) 373-374 (*Ward, Benedicta*); BiblInterp 10 (2002) 441-443 (*Salters, Robert B.*).

13718 PETER J.O.: ᴱFlood, David Peter of John Olivi on the Acts of the Apostles. 2001 ⇒17,12476. ᴿAFH 95 (2002) 205-208 (*Iozzelli, Fortunato*).

13719 PETRUS B: ᴱHuygens, R.B.C. Peter von Blois: Tractatus duo: Conquestio de dilatione vie Ierosolimitane: Passio Raginaldi, principis Antiochie. CChr.CM 194: Turnhout 2002, Brepols 131 pp. 2-503-04941-9.

13720 QUODVULTDEUS: ᵀDattrino, L. Quodvultdeus: il libro delle promesse e delle predizioni di Dio. Città del Vaticano 2002, Vaticana 613 pp

13721 ROBERTO R: *Russo, Luigi* Ricerche sull' 'Historia Iherosolimitana' di Roberto di Reims. StMed 43 (2002) 651-691.

13722 RUFUS S: *Lucchesi, Enzo* Feuillets éditées non identifiés du *Commentaire sur l'évangile de Matthieu* attribué à Rufus de Chotep. Muséon 115 (2002) 261-277.

13723 STEPHANUS B: [E]Berlioz, Jacques; Eichenlaub, Jean-Luc Stephanus de Borbone: tractatus de diversis materiis predicabilibus: prolo-
gus, 1: de dono timoris. CChr.CM 124; Exempla Medii Aevi 1:
Turnhout 2002, Brepols xci; 638 pp. 2-503-04241-4. Bibl. vii-xiv.
13724 SYMEON: *Stylianopoulos, Theodore* Holy scripture, interpretation
and spiritual cognition in St. Symeon the new theologian. GOTR 46
(2001) 3-34.
13725 THEODORE C: *Gorman, Michael M.* Theodore of Canterbury,
HADRIAN of Nisida and Michael Lapidge. Biblical commentaries.
2002 <1996> ⇒171. 164-173.
13726 THOMAS a K: **Becker, Kenneth Michael** From the treasure-house
of scripture: an analysis of scriptural sources in De Imitatione Christi. IP 44: Turnhout 2002, Brepols 767 pp. €120. 2-503-51386-7.
Bibl. 233-255.
13727 VAN RUUSBROEC J: [E]**Alaerts, J.** Jan van Ruusbroec: Opera omnia
tomus 4: dat rijcke der ghelieven. CChr. CM 104: Turnhout 2002,
Brepols 511 pp. 2-503-04081-0. Trans. into English: *H. Rolfson,*
into Latin: *L. Surius* (1552); Bibl. 500-505.
13728 WIGBOD: *Gorman, Michael M.* The encyclopedic commentary on
Genesis prepared for CHARLEMAGNE by Wigbod. Biblical commentaries. 2002 <1982> ⇒171. 1-29.
13729 YITZHAK b. S: *Shtober, Shimon* בפירושו ארץ־ישראל של ואתריה נופיה
שמואל לספר הספרדי שמואל בן יצחק רב של [Toponymy, topography and
landscape in the commentary of R. Yitzhak Ben Shmu'el to the
book of Samuel]. BetM 170 (2002) 219-236 Sum. 287. **H.**

Y4.1 Luther

13730 *Arnold, Matthieu* ÉRASME et Luther selon Stefan Zweig: un antago-
nisme irréductible. RHPhR 82/2 (2002) 123-145.
13731 [E]**Brecht, Martin; Peters, Christian** Martin Luther: Annotierungen
zu den Werken des HIERONYMUS: AWA 8: 2000 ⇒16,12919. [R]SCJ
33 (2002) 218-219 (*Posset, Franz*); ZKG 113 (2002) 420-422
(*Basse, Michael*); Lutherjahrbuch 69 (2002) 145-146 (*Beyer,
Michael*).
13732 *Bultmann, Christoph* Luther on gender relations—just one reading
of Genesis?. CThMi 29 (2002) 424-428 [Gen 1-3].
13733 **Corsani, Bruno** Lutero e la bibbia. 2001 ⇒17,12492. [R]Sal. 64
(2002) 145-146 (*Buzzetti, Carlo*); ATT 8 (2002) 248-249 (*Ghiberti, Giuseppe*); Salm. 49 (2002) 206-207 (*Sánchez Caro, J.M.*).
13734 **Erling, Bernhard** The priesthood of all believers and Luther's
translation of 1 Peter 2:5,9. [T]*Kiecker, James G.*: Luther Digest 10
(2002) 15-20 <Lutheran Forum 33 (summer 1999) 20-29.
13735 *Espinosa, Alfonso O.* The christology of Martin Luther in the great
commentary on Galatians of 1531. [T]*Maschke, Timothy H.*: Luther
Digest 10 (2002) 21-24 <[F]MANSKE, C.L., Huntington Beach, Ten-
tatio, 1999, 59-70.
13736 **Eyjölfsson, Sigurjón Árni Guðfraedi** Marteins Lúters í ljósi túl-
kunar hans á Jóhannesarguðspjalli 1535-1540 [The theology of
Martin Luther in the light of hs interpretation of the gospel of John
1535-1540]. 2002 Diss. Reykjavik [StTh 57,79].
13737 *Helmer, Christine* Luther's trinitarian hermeneutic and the Old
Testament. MoTh 18 (2002) 49-73.

13738   *Hermsen, Edmund* Kindheitsentwürfe und Konzepte der Kindererziehung in Reformation (Martin Luther) und Pietismus (August Hermann Francke). JBTh 17 (2002) 255-290.

13739   **Kolb, Robert** Martin Luther as prophet, teacher, and hero: images of the reformer, 1520-1620. 1999 ⇒15,12637; 17,12494. ᴿBHR 64 (2002) 459-460 (*Arnold, Matthieu*).

13740   *Krey, Philip D.W.* Luther and the Apocalypse: between Christ and history. The last things. 2002 ⇒279. 135-145.

13741   **Kunze, Johannes** Erasmus und Luther: der Einfluss des Erasmus auf die Kommentierung des Galaterbriefs und der Psalmen durch Luther 1519-1521. 2000 ⇒16,12931; 17,12495. ᴿLuther 73 (2002) 162-163 (*Müller, Gerhard*).

13742   *Kvam, Kristen E.* The sweat of the brow is of many kinds: Luther on the duties of Adam and his sons. ᴱ*Moore, Rebecca E.*: Luther Digest 10 (2002) 30-32 <CThMi 24 (1997) 44-49 [Gen 3,17-19].

13743   **Lazareth, William H.** Christians in society: Luther, the bible, and social ethics. 2001 ⇒17,12496. ᴿCThMi 29 (2002) 137-138 (*Bielfeldt, Dennis*); ThTo 59 (2002) 311-312 (*Wisnefske, Ned*); JR 82 (2002) 658-660 (*Brocker, Mark S.*); WThJ 64 (2002) 426-429 (*VanDrunen, David*).

13744   Lutherbibliographie 2002. Lutherjahrbuch 69 (2002) 155-211.

13745   ᴱ**Malena, Adelisa** Martin Lutero: Degli ebrei e delle loro menzogne. Einaudi Tascabili, Saggi 789: 2000 ⇒16,12933. ᴿRSLR 38 (2002) 559-561 (*Bouchard, Giorgio*).

13746   *Mühlen, Karl-Heinz zur* Luther. RGG 5. 2002 ⇒796. 558-600.

13747   *Mühlhaus, Karl-Hermann* Law and gospel: Luther's concept and perspectives from his thinking. ThLi 25 (2002) 183-204.

13748   *Müller, Gerhard* Biblical theology and social ethics: the thought of Martin Luther. ᵀ*Vondey, Wolfgang*: Luther Digest 10 (2002) 33-34 <EvTh 59 (1999) 25-31.

13749   **Nichols, Stephen J.** Martin Luther: a guided tour of his life and thought. Phillipsburg 2002, Presbyterean and R. 240 pp. $14.

13750   **Osten-Sacken, Peter von der** Martin Luther und die Juden: neu untersucht anhand von Anton Margarithas 'Der gantz Jüdisch glaub' (1530/31). Stu 2002, Kohlhammer 351 pp. 3-17-017566-1.

13751   **Öberg, Ingemar** Bibelsyn och bibeltolkning hos Martin Luther. Sto 2002, Artos & Norma 592 pp.

13752   *Parsons, Michael* Luther and CALVIN on rape: is the crime lost in the agenda?. EvQ 74 (2002) 123-142 [Gen 34; 2 Sam 13].

13753   **Pelikan, Jaroslav; Lehman, Helmut T.** Luther's works on CD-ROM. 2001 ⇒17,12502. ᴿSCJ 33 (2002) 1126-1127 (*Sorum, Jonathan D.*).

13754   *Picardo, Gerardo* La chiesa in preghiera nei 'Dicata super psalterium' del giovane Martin Lutero. Nuova Umanità 24 (2002) 663-82.

13755   *Posset, Franz* BERNHARD von Clairvauxs Meditation zu Psalm 31,2 bei Martin Luther. Lutherjahrbuch 69 (2002) 71-78.

13756   **Steinmetz, David C.** Luther in context. GR ²2002, Academic xiii; 195 pp. $20. 0-8010-2609-1 [ThD 50,188—Heiser, W. Charles].

13757   **Stolle, Volker** Luther und Paulus: die exegetischen und hermeneutischen Grundlagen der lutherischen Rechtfertigungslehre im Paulinismus Luthers. ABG 10: Lp 2002, Evangelische 521 pp. €48. 3-374-01990-0.

13758   *Theobald, Michael* Das Magnificat in der Sicht Martin Luthers: ökumenische Perspektiven. ThGl 92 (2002) 492-507 [Lk 1,46-55].

13759 *Vial, Marc* Luther and the *Apocalypse* according to the prefaces of
       1522 and 1530. [T]*Levy, Ian Christopher*: Luther Digest 10 (2002)
       35-39 <RThPh 131 (1999) 25-37.
13760 **Wiemer, Axel** 'Mein Trost, Kampf und Sieg ist Christus': Martin
       Luthers eschatologische Theologie nach seinen Reihenpredigten zu
       1Kor 15 (1532/33). [D]*Bayer, O.*: 2002 Diss. Tübingen [ThRv 99/2,
       x].
13761 **Wöhle, Andreas H.** Luthers Freude an Gottes Gesetz: eine histori-
       sche Quellenstudie zur Oszillation des Gesetzesbegriffes Martin
       Luthers im Licht seiner alttestamentlichen Predigten. 1998 ⇒14,
       11786. [R]Luther 73 (2002) 110-111 (*Dobschütz, Detlef von*).
13762 *Zwanepol, Klaas* Luther's doctrine on the atonement in his exegesis
       of Gal. 3:13-14. Luther Digest 10 (2002) 40-42 <Luther-Bulletin 8
       (1999) 69-92.

Y4.3 Exegesis et controversia saeculi XVI

13763 **Davies, Catherine** A religion of the word: the defence of the Ref-
       ormation in the reign of Edward VI. Politics, culture and society in
       early modern Britain: Manchester 2002, Manchester Univ. Pr. xxiv;
       264 pp. $75.
13764 *Greschat, Katharina* 'Dann sind gottwilkommen, Marcion und
       Marciönin': Marcion in den reformatorischen Auseinandersetzun-
       gen um das Abendmahl. Marcion. 2002 ⇒578. 235-251.
13765 *Juhász, Gergely* The bible and the early Reformation period. Tyn-
       dale's testament. 2002 ⇒268. 25-33.
13766 **Old, Hughes Oliphant** The reading and preaching of the scriptures
       in the worship of the christian church, 4: the age of the Reforma-
       tion. GR 2002, Eerdmans 569 pp. $45. 0-8028-4775-7. [R]RBLit
       (2002)* (*Willson, Patrick*).
13767 [E]**Parker, Douglas H.** William ROYE: an exhortation to the diligent
       studye of scripture and An exposition in to the seventh chapter of
       the pistle to the Corinthians. [*Erasmus, Luther;* T]*Roye, William*] 2000 ⇒
       16,12940. [R]SCJ 33 (2002) 602-603 (*Ortwig, D.S.*).
13768 *Schmidt, Peter* Die Reformation und die Bibel: "... wir wissen, dass
       alle Wahrheit von Gott ist". Die Bibel: Geschichte und Gegenwart.
       2002 ⇒971. 164-173, 176-181.
13769 [E]**Steinmetz, David C.** Die Patristik in der Bibelexegese des 16.
       Jahrhunderts 1999. ⇒15,438...17,12509. [R]RH 126 (2002) 199-202
       (*Quantin, Jean-Louis*).
13770 *Villiers, Pieter G.R. de* Renaissance and religion: the bible in a time
       of radical change. AcTh(B) 22/2 (2002) 19-46.
13771 *Williams, D.H.* Scripture, tradition, and the church: Reformation
       and post-Reformation. The Free Church. 2002 ⇒441. 101-126.

Y4.4 Periti aetatis reformatoriae

13772 ALVAREZ B: *Léon Azcárate, Juan Luis de* Un ejemplo del uso de la
       biblia en la evangelización de América: el memorial a Felipe II
       (1588) de Bartolomé Alvarez. RevBib 63 (2001) 73-118.

13773 BUCER M: *Pellegrini, Maria Antonietta Falchi* Modelli politici e contesti storici: la *Respublica Israelis* in Martin Bucer. Il Pensiero Politico 35 (2002) 369-381.

13774 CALVIN: **Cottret, Bernard** Calvin: a biography. [T]*McDonald, Wallace*: 2000 ⇒16,12945. [R]RTR 61 (2002) 104-106 (*Bonnington, Stuart*); Augustinus 47 (2002) 471-472 (*Silva, Alvaro de*); SCJ 33 (2002) 1249-1250 (*Wildt, Kees de*).

13775 **Crouzet, Denis** Jean Calvin: vies parallèles. 2000 ⇒16,12946. [R]SCJ 33 (2002) 854-856 (*Monheit, Michael L.*).

13776 [E]**Engammare, Max** Sermons sur la Genèse, chapitres 1,1-11,4 et chapitres 11,5-20,7. Supplementa Calviniana 11/1-2: 2000 2 vols. ⇒16,12947; 17,12512. [R]BHR 64 (2002) 183-186 (*Millet, Olivier*); [R]BECh 159 (2002) 640-642 (*Trocmé, Étienne*); CTJ 37 (2002) 367-369 (*Thompson, John L.*).

13777 [E]**Feld, Helmut** Ioannis Calvini: commentariorum in Acta Apostolorum. Ioannis Calvini Opera exegetica Veteris et Novi Testamenti 12,1-2: 2001 ⇒17,12513. [R]BHR 64 (2002) 461-462 (*Moehn, Wilhelmus H.Th.*); RSLR 38 (2002) 377-379 (*Bettoni, Anna*).

13778 *Hesselink, I.J.* The role of the Holy Spirit in Calvin's doctrine of the sacraments. [F]POTGIETER, P.: AcTh(B).S 3: 2002 ⇒92. 66-88.

13779 **Moehn, Wilhelmus H.Th.** 'God calls us to his service': the relation between God and his audience in Calvin's sermons on Acts. 2001 ⇒17,12514. [R]SCJ 33 (2002) 251-252 (*Flaming, Darlene K.*).

13780 *Nicole, Roger* John Calvin's view of the extent of the atonement. Standing forth. 2002 <1985> ⇒215. 283-312;

13781 John Calvin and inerrancy. Standing forth. 2002 <1982> ⇒215. 103-132.

13782 **Pitkin, Barbara** What pure eyes could see: Calvin's doctrine of faith in its exegetical context. 1999 ⇒15,12661; 16,12949. [R]ChH 71 (2002) 412-413 (*Thompson, John L.*).

13783 *Trueman, Carl R.* The God of unconditional promise. The trustworthiness of God. 2002 ⇒410. 175-191.

13784 *Zachman, Randall C.* Gathering meaning from the context: Calvin's exegetical method. JR 82 (2002) 1-26.

13785 ERASMUS: [E]**Pabel, Hilmar Matthias; Vessey, Mark** Holy Scripture speaks: the production and reception of Erasmus' 'Paraphrases on the New Testament'. Erasmus Studies 14: Toronto 2002, Univ. of Toronto Pr. xvi; 397 pp. $80. 0-8020-3642-2. Bibl. 361-377.

13786 *Rea, Manuela* Erasmo e i giudei. SMSR 68 (2002) 297-320.

13787 FEDERICO V: *Carvelli, Simona* La *Vulgata*, i decreti tridentini e la *Iudit* di Federico della Valle. La sorgente. 2002 ⇒315. 150-161.

13788· KNOX J: *Kyle, Richard G.* Prophet of God: John Knox's self awareness. RTR 61/2 (2002) 85-101.

13789 LEFÈVRE D'ÉTAPLES: *Balley, Noëlle* Jacques Lefèvre d'Étaples (1450?-1536): un humaniste face aux apocryphes. [F]GEOLTRAIN, P.: BEHE.R 113: 2002 ⇒45. 255-262 [BuBB 39,91].

13790 MONTANO A: *Fernández Marcos, Natalio* Lenguaje arcano y lenguaje del cuerpo: la hermenéutica bíblica de Arias Montano. Sef. 62 (2002) 57-83.

13791 *Fernández Marcos, Natalio; Fernández Tejero, Emilia* De 'Elteqeh a Hita: Arias Montano, traductor de topónimos. Judaismo Hispano:

estudios en memoria di José Luis LAVAVE Riaño. [E]*Romero, E.*: M
2002, CSIC. 255-264 [RB 110,475].

13792 PARACELSUS: **Rietsch, Jean-Michel** Théorie du langage et exégèse
biblique chez Paracelse (1493-1541). Berne 2002, Lang 358 pp.
€54.80. 3-906768-86-4. Bibl. 351-358 [BCLF 641,22].

13793 SWYNNERTON T: [E]**Rex, Richard** A Reformation rhetoric: Thomas
Swynnerton's tropes and figures of scripture. 1999 ⇒15,12670; 17,
12525. [R]Rhetorica 20/1 (2002) 98-100 (*Vickers, Brian*); Reformation 6 (2001-2002) 244-245 (*MacCulloch, Diarmaid*).

13794 TYNDALE W: *Arblaster, Paul* Tyndale's posthumous reputation.
Tyndale's testament. 2002 ⇒268. 55.

13795 *Juhász, Gergely* Translating resurrection: the importance of the
Sadducees' belief in the Tyndale-Joye controversy. [F]LAMBRECHT,
J.: BEThL 165: 2002 ⇒72. 107-121.

13796 WEIGEL V: [E]**Pfefferl, Horst** Valentin Weigel: Von Betrachtungen
des Lebens Christi: vom Leben Christi: de vita Christi. Sämtliche
Schriften 7: Stu 2002, Frommann 241 pp. €218. 3-7728-1846-3.

Y4.5 *Exegesis post-reformatoria*—**Historical criticism to 1800**

13797 *Harrison, Peter* Fissare il significato della scrittura: la bibbia del
Rinascimento e le origini della modernità. Conc(I) 38/1 (2002)
134-145; Conc(E) 294,119-128; Conc(D) 38/1,90-98; Conc(P)
294, 109-119.

13798 **Raggenbass, Niklas** 'Harmonie und schwesterliche Eintracht zwischen Bibel und Vernunft': ein exegetisches Programm im Spannungsfeld von stabilitas loci und vernetzter Kommunikation: die
Benediktiner des Klosters Banz: Publizisten und Wissenschaftler in
der Aufklärungszeit. [D]*Görg, Manfred*: 2002 Diss. München [ThRv
99/2,x].

13799 BALDE J: [E]**Winter, Ulrich** Iacobus Balde: Liber epodon. BSGRT:
Mü 2002, Saur xxiii; 87 pp. 3-598-71246-4.

13800 CALOV A: **Jung, Volker** Das Ganze der Heiligen Schrift: Hermeneutik und Schriftauslegung bei Abraham Calov. CThM.ST 18:
1999 ⇒15,12674; 16,12968. [R]ThLZ 127 (2002) 491-493 (*Matthias, Markus*).

13801 CORNELIUS a L: **Noll, Raymund** Die marieologischen Grundlagen
im exegetischen Werk des Cornelius a Lapide (1567-1637).
[D]*Seybold, Michael*: 2002 Diss. Eichstätt [ThRv 99/2,v].

13802 EDWARDS J: **Brown, Robert E.** Jonathan Edwards and the bible.
Bloomington 2002, Indiana Univ. Pr. xxi; 292 pp. $35. 0-253-340-
93-4. Bibl. 271-287.

13803 ERNEST J: **Ilgner, Christoph** Die neutestamentliche Auslegungs-
lehre des Johann August Ernest (1707-1781): ein Beitrag zur Erforschung der Auklärungshermeneutik. [D]*Petzoldt, Marin*: 2002 Diss.
Leipzig [ThRv 99/2,ix].

13804 LESSING G: *Strohschneider-Kohrs, Ingrid* Lessings Hiob-Deutun-
gen im Kontext des 18. Jahrhunderts. Edith-Stein-Jahrbuch 8
(2002) 255-268.

13805 SPINOZA: *Frankel, Steven* Spinoza's dual teachings of scripture: his
solution to the quarrel between reason and revelation. AGPh 84
(2002) 273-296.

13806 **Preus, James Samuel** Spinoza and the irrelevance of biblical authority. 2001 ⇒17,12548. [R]JHP 40 (2002) 263-264 (*Frank, Daniel H.*); RStT 20/2 (2002) 76-79 (*Hughes, Aaron*); REJ 161 (2002) 532-533 (*Osier, Jean Pierre*); RStT 21/2 (2002) 77-79 (*Hughes, Aaron*).

13807 TURRETIN F: *Rehnman, Sebastian* Theistic metaphysics and biblical exegesis: Francis Turretin on the concept of God. RelSt 38 (2002) 167-186.

13808 WESLEY C: *Kimbrough, S.T.* Die Psalmlyrik Charles Wesleys: zwei Richtungen seiner Interpretation. ThFPr 28/1 (2002) 22-34.

13809 WILLIAMS R: **Byrd, James P.** The challenges of Roger Williams: religious liberty, violent persecution, and the bible. Baptists: Macon, GA 2002, Mercer Univ. Pr. xii; 286 pp. $40. 0-86554-771-8
· [ThD 50,162—Heiser, W. Charles].

13810 WOOLSTON T: **Woolston, Thomas** Six discours sur les miracles de notre Sauveur: deux traductions manuscrites du XVIIIe siècle, dont une de Mme Du Châtelet. Libre pensée et littérature clandestine 8: 2001 ⇒17,12554. [R]ETR 77 (2002) 603-604 (*Bost, Hubert*).

Y5.0 *Saeculum XIX*—Exegesis—19th century

13811 **Haynes, Stephen R.** Noah's curse: the biblical justification of American slavery. Religion in America Series: Oxf 2002, OUP xiv; 322 pp. $30. 0-19-514279-9. Bibl. 299-313 [Gen 9-11].

13812 GIRDLESTONE R: *Atherstone, Andrew* Robert Baker Girdlestone and 'God's own book'. EvQ 74 (2002) 313-332.

13813 LÜCKE F: **Christophersen, Alf** Friedrich Lücke (1791-1855), Teil 1: neutestamentl. Hermeneutik u. Exegese... Teil 2: Dokumente und Briefe. TBT 94/1-2: 1999 ⇒16,12980; 17,12577. [R]Zeitschrift für neuere Theologiegeschichte 9 (2002) 329-330 (*Wolfes, Matthias*).

13814 MÜLLER F: **Van den Bosch, Lourens P.** Friedrich Max Müller: a life devoted to the humanities. SHR 94: Lei 2002, Brill xxiv; 579 pp. 90-04-12505-1. Bibl. 547-568.

13815 NEWMAN J: **Turner, Frank Miller** John Henry Newman: the challenge to evangelical religion. NHv 2002, Yale Univ. Pr. xii; 740 pp. 0-300-09251-2.

13816 NIETZSCHE F: **Biser, Eugen** Nietzsche—Zerstörer oder Erneuerer des Christentums?. Da:Wiss 2002, 178 pp. €24.90. 3-534-16027-4. [R]ThLZ 127 (2002) 872-873 (*Petzoldt, Martin*); PLA 55 (2002) 403-405 (*Olles, Helmut*).

13817 *Campoccia, Giuseppe* Note su Nietzsche e il Nuovo Testamento. Filosofia 53/1 (2002) 85-99.

13818 **Hübner, Hans** Nietzsche und das Neue Testament. 2000 ⇒16, 1405. [R]ThLZ 127 (2002) 867-872 (*Petzoldt, Martin*).

13819 NIGHTINGALE F: [E]**McDonald, Lynn** Florence Nightingale's spiritual journey: biblical annotations, sermons and journal notes. Ontario 2001, Laurier Univ. Pr. xii; 586 pp. $85. 0-88920-366-0.

13820 ROBINSON E: **Williams, Jay G.** The times and life of Edward Robinson. SBL Biblical Scholarship in North America 19: 1999 ⇒ 15,12699. [R]RBLit 4 (2002) 486-488 (*Long, Burke O.*).

13821 TISCHENDORF C von: *Böttrich, Christfried* Tischendorf, Constantin von. TRE 33. 2002 ⇒799. 567-570.

13822   VATKE W: *Bultmann, Christoph* Vatke, Wilhelm. TRE 34. 2002
        ⇒800. 552-555.

Y5.5 *Crisi modernistica*—The Modernist Era

13823   [E]Chauvin, Ch. A. LOISY: Ecrits évangéliques: un siècle après les
        'petits livres rouges'. Textes en main: P 2002, Cerf 240 pp. €18. 2-
        204-06928-0. [R]NRTh 124 (2002) 508-509 (Joassart, B.); RThom
        102 (2002) 472-476 (*Grelot, Pierre*).
13824   Ciappa, Rosanna Rivelazione e storia: il problema ermeneutico
        nel carteggio tra Alfred LOISY e Maurice BLONDEL (febbraio-marzo
        1903). 2001 ⇒17,12594. [R]RHPhR 82 (2002) 467-69 (*Goichot, É.*).
13825   Colin, Pierre L'audace et le soupçon: la crise du modernisme dans
        le catholicisme français, 1893-1914. 1997 ⇒15,12700. [R]Annales
        57 (2002) 498-500 (*Lagrée, Michel*).
13826   Goichot, Émile Alfred LOISY et ses amis. Histoire: P 2002, Cerf
        197 pp. €21. 2-204-06895-0. Bibl. 195-196. [R]RThom 102 (2002)
        471-472 (*Grelot, Pierre*); CHR 88 (2002) 791-793 (*Talar, C.J.T.*).
13827   Loisy, Alfred L'évangile et l'église; autour d'un petit livre; Jésus et
        la tradition évangélique. 2001 ⇒17,12597. [R]REJ 161 (2002) 336-
        338 (*Mimouni, Simon C.*).
13828   *Raurell, Frederic* Posizione ambigua di DUCHESNE di fronte alla
        critica biblica dei modernisti. Laur. 43 (2002) 255-305;
13829   Duchesne i la crítica bíblica en temps del modernisme. RCatT 27
        2002 361-396.
13830   Raurell, Frederic L'antimodernisme i el Cardenal Vives i Tutó.
        Sant Pacià 71: 2000 ⇒16,12991; 17,12598. [R]Theoforum 33 (2002)
        267-268 (*Provencher, Normand*).

Y6.0 *Saeculum XX-XXI*—20th-21st Century Exegesis

13831   *Boshoff, Willem* Can 'white' South African Old Testament scholar-
        ship be African?. BOTSA 12 (2002) 1-3.
13832   Bourlot, Alberto Immagini della scrittura: 'traduzioni' della bibbia
        fra cinema e televisione. Interpretare la Bibbia oggi, 1/6: Brescia
        2002, Queriniana 198 pp. €12.50. 88-399-2456-6. Bibl. 189-194.
        [R]Asprenas 49 (2002) 453 (*Castello, Gaetano*).
13833   Capanzano, Vincent Serving the word: literalism in America from
        the pulpit to the bench. 2000 ⇒16,12993. [R]AUSS 40 (2002) 139-
        140 (*Miller, James E.*).
13834   *Johnson, Luke Timothy; Kurz, William* Opening the conversation.
        The future of Catholic biblical scholarship. 2002 ⇒337. 263-287.
13835   *Krause, Deborah; Beal, Timothy K.* Higher critics on late texts:
        reading biblical scholarship after the Holocaust. A shadow of glory.
        2002. ⇒347. 18-26.
13836   Le Roux, Jurie A story of two ways: thirty years of Old Testament
        scholarship in South Africa. OTEs.S 2: 1993 ⇒11/2,k508.
        [R]Scriptura 78 (2001) 467-478 (*Lombaard, Christo J.S.*).
13837   Lis, Marek Audiowizualny przeklad Biblii: Od translatio do trans-
        mediatio. Opolska Biblioteka Teologiczna 57: Opole 2002, Wyd.
        Teolog. Uniw. Opolskiego 156 pp. 83-88939-38-6 Bibl. 127-142.

13838 *Masenya, Madipoane* Is white South African Old Testament scholarship African?. BOTSA 12 (2002) 3-8.

13839 *Pelletier,Anne-Marie* Pour que la bible reste un livre dangereux. Etudes (2002) 335-345.

13840 *Rendtorff, Rolf* Zu den Anfängen des Biblischen Kommentars: kritische Erinnerungen. EvTh 62 (2002) 5-10.

13841 **Robin, Olivier** Le lecteur dans la bible. Lyon 2002, Profac 161 pp. €15. 2-85317-089-6. Bibl. 157-158.

13842 **Rolland, Philippe** La mode "pseudo" en exégèse: le triomphe du modernisme depuis vingt ans. P 2002, Paris 239 pp. €22. 2-85162-056-8.

13843 **Smith, Mark S.** Untold stories: the bible and Ugaritic studies in the twentieth century. 2001 ⇒17,12603. ᴿJQR 92 (2002) 314-316 (*Sasson, Jack M.*).

13844 BAGATTI B: ᴱ**Piccirillo, Michele** Un uomo di pace: Padre Bellarmino Bagatti (1905-1990). J 2002, Custodia di Terra Santa 252 pp. Studium Biblicum Franciscanum di Gerusalemme. 1 CD-Rom. Ill. [RB 110,309].

13845 BALTHASAR H von: **Ade, Edouard** Le temps de l'église: esquisse d'une théologie de l'histoire selon Hans Urs von Balthasar. TGr.T 79: R 2002, E.P.U.G. 357 pp. €20. 88-7652-907-1.

13846 BARTH K: **Aguti, A.** La questione dell'ermeneutica in Karl Barth. 2001 ⇒17,12606. ᴿTeol(Br) 27 (2002) 209-211 (*Vergottini, Marco*).

13847 **Burnett, Richard E.** Karl Barth's theological exegesis: the hermeneutical principles of the Römerbrief period. WUNT 2/145: 2001 ⇒17,12608. ᴿRTL 33 (2002) 561-564 (*Bourgine, B.*).

13848 *Gallas, Alberto* 'Jahvé ed Elohim': Gen 1-2 nell'interpretazione di Karl Barth e di alcuni suoi interlocutori. AnScR 7 (2002) 299-322.

13849 **MacDonald, Neil B.** Karl Barth and the strange new world within the bible: Barth, WITTGENSTEIN, and the metadilemmas of the Enlightenment. Carlisle 2002, Paternoster 384 pp.

13850 *Nicole, Roger* The neo-orthodox reduction. Standing forth. 2002 <1984> ⇒215. 51-77. Ment. *Brunner, E.*

13851 **Peeters, Robert Jan** Teken van de levende Christus: de openbaringsdynamische traditieopvatting van Karl Barth. Zoetermeer 2002, Boekencentrum 332 pp. €24.90. 90-239-1188-1 [ITBT 11/8, 31—Boer, Dick].

13852 **Webster, John** Karl Barth. 2000 ⇒16,13015. ᴿIThQ 67 (2002) 187-188 (*Thompson, John*); JR 82 (2002) 650-651 (*Burnett, Richard E.*).

13853 BEAUCHAMP P: *Benzi, Guido* L'esegesi figurale in Paul Beauchamp. Teol(Br) 27 (2002) 35-51.

13854 BONHOEFFER D: *Holm, Jacob* G.W.F. HEGEL's impact on Dietrich Bonhoeffer's early theology. StTh 56 (2002) 64-75.

13855 ᴱ**Weber, Manfred** Dietrich Bonhoeffer, Die Antwort auf unsere Fragen: Gedanken zur Bibel. Gü 2002, Gü 96 pp. 3-579-02332-2.

13856 BUBER M: **Bombaci, Nunzio** Ebraismo e cristianesimo a confronto nel pensiero di Martin Buber. 2001 ⇒17,12620. ᴿFilosofia 53/2 (2002) 128-131 (*Bertone, Ilaria*).

13857 *Waaijman, Kees* The hermeneutics of Buber and ROSENZWEIG. Studies in Spirituality 12 (2002) 240-268.

13858 BULTMANN R: ^E**Göckeritz, H.G.** Rudolf Bultmann—Friedrich GO-GARTEN: Briefwechsel 1921-1967: Tü 2002, Mohr S. xliv; 358 pp. €79. 3-16-147720-0.

13859 *Newlands, George M.* Rudolf Bultmann for the twenty-first century. TJT 18 (2002) 65-78.

13860 *Van Wyk, D.J.C.* Die probleem van hoe die verkondiger die verkondigde geword het: die bydrae van Rudolf Bultmann. HTS 57 (2001) 649-675 [NTAb 46,451].

13861 *Walter, Nikolaus* Was ich Rudolf Bultmann verdanke. Jesus im 21. Jahrhundert. 2002 ⇒1380. 209-225.

13862 CARROLL R: Bibliography of Robert Carroll's writings. ^MCARROLL, R.: JSOT.S 348: 2002 ⇒13. 457-462.

13863 CASSUTO U: *Rofé, Alexander* Cassuto the bible critic: his program in 1939 as viewed in 2002. BetM 171 (2002) 289-304 Sum. 384. **H.**

13864 CHOMSKY N: **Winston, Morton** On Chomsky. Wadsworth philosophers series: Belmont, CAL 2002, Wadsworth 100 pp. 0-534-5764-0-0. Bibl. 92-93.

13865 COMBRINK B: *Mouton, E.* Bernard Combrink: komeet vir die koninkryk. Scriptura 80 (2002) 149-154 [NTAb 47,436].

13866 CULLMANN O: *Arnold, Matthieu* Oscar Cullmann, théologien luthérien?. ThZ 58 (2002) 249-261.

13867 *Froehlich, Karlfried* Lebendiges Erbe: das Cullmann-Archiv Chamonix. ThZ 58 (2002) 262-274.

13868 *Lehmann, Kardinal Karl* Einheit durch Vielfalt—heute: katholische Reflexionen zum ehrenden Gedenken an Oscar Cullmann;

13869 *May, Gerhard* Oscar Cullmann und die Kirchengeschichte;

13870 *Pérès, Jacques-Noel* Oscar Cullmann, artisan de l'oecuménisme: quelques remarques sur sa réception dans le protestantisme français;

13871 *Philonenko, Marc* "Mon premier livre auquel je tiens toujours": les recherches d'Oscar Cullmann sur le Judaïsme hétérodoxe;

13872 *Reinhartz, Adele* Oscar Cullmann und sein Beitrag zur Johannes-Forschung;

13873 *Ricca, Paolo* Die Begegnung mit den Waldensern und die Spiritualität Oscar Cullmanns;

13874 *Stegemann, Ekkehard W.* Cullmanns Konzept der Heilsgeschichte in seiner Zeit;

13875 *Stendahl, Krister* Zur Situation der neutestamentlichen Exegese um 1930: Erinnerungen und Reflexionen. ThZ 58 (2002) 280-290/243-248/291-298/216-220/221-231/275-279/232-242/207-215.

13876 DELITZSCH F: *Arnold, Bill T.; Weisberg, David B.* A centennial review of Friedrich Delitzsch's 'Babel und Bibel' lectures. JBL 121 (2002) 441-457.

13877 DEURLOO K: *Siertsema, Bettine; Deenik-Moolhuizen, Jeanette* Onder professoren: 'een absoluut bijbelmannetje': interview met Karel Deurloo. ITBT 10/6 (2002) 8-10.

13878 DODD C: *Nicole, Roger* C.H. Dodd and the doctrine of propitiation. Standing forth. 2002 <1955> ⇒215. 343-385 [Dan 9,24].

13879 *Williams, John Tudno* Charles Harold Dodd—Welshman. ET 113 (2002) 270-272.

13880 DRIVER S: *Emerton, John A.* S.R. Driver as an exegete of the Old Testament. [F]SMEND, R. 2002 ⇒113. 285-295.

13881 ELIADE M: *Rennie, Bryan S.* Il n'y a pas un solution de la continuité: Eliade, historiography, and pragmatic narratology in the study of religion. Arc 30 (2002) 115-137.

13882. FRANCK, D: *Berder, Michel* Didier Franck, lecteur de saint Paul. RICP 83 (2002) 105-118.

13883 *Falque, Emmanuel* Éternel retour ou résurrection des corps?. RICP 83 (2002) 119-137 [1 Cor 15].

13884 FRYE N: *Alter, Robert* Northrop Frye between archetype and typology. Semeia 89 (2002) 9-21.

13885 GADAMER H: *Laeng, Mauro* Hans-Georg Gadamer (1900-2002): il pensiero ermeneutico di H.G. Gadamer. Rassegna di pedagogia 60 (2002) 3-4.

13886 *Le Roux, J.H.* Hans-Georg Gadamer en die Ou Testament. VeE 23 (2002) 383-392.

13887 GIRARD R: **Golsan, Richard J.** René Girard and myth: an introduction. NY 2002, Routledge vii; 237 pp. $25.

13888 **Tugnoli, Claudio** Girard: dal mito ai vangeli. 2001 ⇒ 17,12634. [R]Rivista di scienze religiose 16 (2002) 503-4 (*Di Pilato, Vincenzo*).

13889 *Valadier, Paul* René Girard revisité. Études (2002) 773-777.

13890 HENGEL M: *Frey, Jörg* Schriftenverzeichnis Martin Hengel 1999-2002. Paulus und Jakobus. WUNT 141: 2002 ⇒178. 583-587.

13891 HESCHEL A: **Dolna, Bernhard** An die Gegenwart Gottes preisgegeben: Abraham Joshua Heschel: Leben und Werk. Mainz 2001, Grünewald 383 pp.

13892 *Ehrlich, Ernst Ludwig* Abraham Heschel. [F]THOMA, C.: JudChr 20: 2002 ⇒119. 55-64.

13893 JEREMIAS J: *Lohse, Eduard* Joachim Jeremias als Ausleger des Römerbriefes. ZNW 93 (2002) 279-287.

13894 JOHNSON E: **Zagano, Phyllis; Tilley, Terrence W.** Things new and old: essays on the theology of Elizabeth A. Johnson. 1999 ⇒ 15,12743. [R]Pacifica 15 (2002) 236-238 (*Fox, Patricia*).

13895 KRAUS H: *Klappert, Bertold* Reich Gottes—Reich der Freiheit: Hans-Joachim Kraus (1918-2000) und sein Weg zur Gesamtbiblischen Theologie. ThBeitr 33 (2002) 220-231.

13896 LAGRANGE M: [E]**Couturier, Guy** Les patriarches et l'histoire: autour d'un article inédit du père M.-J. Lagrange. LeDiv: 1998 ⇒14, 11890; 15,12748. [R]LV(L) 256 (2002) 103-106 (*Abadie, Philippe*).

13897 *Montagnes, Bernard* Le Père Lagrange devant la question biblique. ScEs 54 (2002) 97-108.

13898 LÉVINAS E: *Canonico, Maria F.* L'antropologia nel pensiero di E. Lévinas. Aquinas 45/2 (2002) 113-160.

13899 *Caruana, John* Lévinas's critique of the sacred. IPQ 42 (2002) 519-534.

13900 **Cohen, Richard A.** Ethics, exegesis and philosophy: interpretation after Levinas. 2001 ⇒17,12643. [R]RStT 21/2 (2002) 84-87 (*Olthuis, James H.*).

13901 [E]**Critchley, Simon; Bernasconi, Robert** The Cambridge companion to Levinas. C 2001, CUP xxx; 292 pp. £45/16.

13902 LUBAC H. de: *Chantraine, Georges; Hercsik, Donath* Notes bibliographiques Henri de Lubac (1994-2002). Association Internationale Cardinal Henri de Lubac: Bulletin 5 (2002) 73-92.

13903   MARTINI C: *Barbieri, Gianfranco* Il card. Martini, la bibbia e la
        pastorale missionaria: la vicenda dei gruppi di ascolto della parola
        di Dio. Ambrosius 78/2 (2002) 111-115.
13904   **Crivelli, L.** Martini arcivescovo di Milano: un singolare apprendi-
        stato. CinB 2002, San Paolo 258 pp. €16.53 [RdT 43,157].
13905   MURPHY R: *Morrison, Craig E.* An essay on the life and legacy of
        Roland E. Murphy, O.Carm. CBQ 64 (2002) 624-630.
13906   MURPHY-O'CONNOR J: *McDonagh, E.* Murphy-O'Connor's bibli-
        cal apostolate. RLR 41 (2002) 221-226 [NTAb 47,23].
13907   PATTE D: *Paris, Peter J.* Praising Daniel Patte's work while await-
        ing his prophetic utterance. [F]PATTE, D. 2002 ⇒89. 158-162.
13908   RAD G von: *Le Roux, Jurie* Gerhard von Rad—'n honderd jaar.
        HTS 58 (2002) 1577-1592 [OTA 26,389].
13909   *Timm, Hermann* Ein Geschichtsbuch?: zu Gerhard von Rads Uni-
        onslektüren des Alten Testaments. ZThK 99 (2002) 147-161.
13910   RICOEUR P: **Bugaite, Elena** Linguaggio e azione nelle opere di
        Paul Ricoeur dal 1961 al 1975. TGr.Filosofia 19: R 2002, E.P.U.G.
        399 pp. €23. 88-7652-909-8.
13911   **Laughery, Gregory J.** Living hermeneutics in motion: an analysis
        and evaluation of Paul Ricoeur's contribution to biblical hermeneu-
        tics. Lanham 2002, University Press of America vii; 249 pp. 0-761-
        8-2303-4. Bibl. 215-240.
13912   ROETZEL C: *Reasoner, Mark* Calvin J. Roetzel's stereoscopic per-
        spective on Paul. [FF]ROETZEL, C: JSNT.S 221: 2002 ⇒104. 167-78.
13913   SCERBO F: *Pazzini, Massimo* Francesco Scerbo grammatico e lessi-
        cografo. [F]TUDDA, F. 2002 123. 201-211.
13914   SCHWEITZER A: *Arnold, Matthieu* Homme de coeur et de raison?:
        Albert Schweitzer, théologien. FV 101/5 (2002) 45-66.
13915   **Globokar, Roman** Verantwortung für alles, was lebt: von Albert
        Schweitzer und Hans JONAS zu einer theologischen Ethik des Le-
        bens. TGr.T 92: R 2002, E.P.U.G. 602 pp. €32. 88-7652-945-4.
13916   SOBRINO J: *Gardocki, Dariusz* The prayer of Jesus as a revelation
        of the consciousness of his sonship and his understanding of God in
        the thought of Jon Sobrino. StBob 3 (2002) 47-65 Sum. 64. P.
13917   STIER F: *Miller, Gabriele* Ein Lehrer, bei dem es was zu lernen
        gab: zum 100. Geburtstag von Fridolin Stier. Diak. 33 (2002) 287-
        292.
13918   TILLICH P: **Carey, John J.** Paulus then and now: a study of Paul
        Tillich's theological world and the continuing relevance of his
        work. Macon, GA 2002, Mercer Univ. Pr. xxii; 152 pp. $35. 0-865-
        54-681-9 [ThD 50,162—Heiser, W. Charles].
13919   VAN BUREN P: *Bellows, K.R.L.* Paul van Buren—a single-covenant
        theologian. Mishkan [Jerusalem] 36 (2002) 113-122 [NTAb 47,89].
13920   VAUX R de: *Briend, Jacques* Vaux, Roland de. TRE 34. 2002 ⇒
        800. 555-556.
13921   WEINGREEN J: *Bartlett, J.* In retrospect: Professor Jacob Wein-
        green. Search 25/3 (2002) 209-210 [NTAb 47,224].
13922   WELLHAUSEN J: *Weidner, Daniel* 'Geschichte gegen den Strich bür-
        sten': Julius Wellhausen und die jüdische 'Gegengeschichte'. ZRGG
        54 (2002) 32-61.
13923   WIESEL E: **Van den Berg, Gundula** Gebrochene Variationen: Be-
        obachtungen und Überlegungen zu Figuren der Hebräischen Bibel
        in der Rezeption von Elie Wiesel. [D]*Ebach, Jürgen*: 2002 Diss. Pa-
        derborn [ThRv 99/2,x].

13924. ZIEGLER J: *Schmitt, Armin* Erinnerungen an Joseph Ziegler (1902-
1988). WDGB 64 (2002) 441-449;
13925 BN 113 (2002) 69-78.

Y6.3 *Influxus Scripturae saeculis XX-XXI*—Survey of current outlooks

13926 *Abadie, Philippe* Bulletin d'exégèse de l'Ancien Testament: écrits et
époque postexilique. RSR 90 (2002) 231-247.
13927 *Aune, David* What bible dictionaries tell us about our discipline.
ProcGLM 22 (2002) 7-33.
13928 *Barco del Barco, Francisco J. del* A survey of Semitic studies in
Spain (1975-2000) I: Hebrew Bible, Jewish, and ancient Near East
studies. RStR 28 (2002) 131-137.
13929 *Barth, Gerhard* Über Probleme und Trends bei neutestamentlichen
Theologien. KuD 48/4 (2002) 261-275.
13930 **Brancato, Francesco** Verso il rinnovamento del trattato di escatologia: studio di escatologia cattolica dal preconcilio a oggi. Sacra
doctrina, monografie 2, Marzo-Aprile 2002, Anno 47. Bo 2002,
Studio Domenicano 199 pp. 88-7094-460-3. Bibl. 13-21.
13931 *Bultmann, Rudolf* Gedanken über die gegenwärtige theologische
Situation. NT und christliche Existenz. UTB 2316: 2002 <1958>
⇒152. 267-273.
13932· *Cardellini, Innocenzo* Ricerche attuali sull'opera deuteronomica e
deuteronomistica. RivBib 50 (2002) 209-222.
13933 *Chavalas, Mark W.* Assyrian and biblical studies: a century and a
half of tension Mesopotamia and the bible. JSOT.S 341: 2002 ⇒
458. 21-67.
13934 *Claussen, Carsten; Zimmermann, Ruben* Wie kann ich (verstehen),
wenn mich niemand anleitet? (Apg 8,31): neuere Methodenbücher
zur neutestamentlichen Exegese. ThBeitr 33 (2002) 290-301.
13935 *Ebner, Martin* Exegese des Neuen Testaments im Spannungsfeld
zwischen Religions-, Text- und Geschichtswissenschaft. ThRv 98
(2002) 365-372.
13936 **Holter, Knut** Old Testament research for Africa: a critical analysis
and annotated bibliography of African Old Testament dissertations.
Bible and Theology in Africa 3: NY 2002, Lang viii; 143 pp. 0-82-
04-5788-4 [BOTSA 13,18s—Himbaza, Innocent].
13937 *Löhr, Winrich A.* Das antike Christentum im zweiten Jahrhundert—
neue Perspektiven seiner Erforschung. ThLZ 127 (2002) 247-262.
13938 *Minissale, Antonio* Status quaestionis della ricerca sull'AT. RivBib
50 (2002) 445-453.
13939 *Moyise, S.* Intertextuality and biblical studies: a review. VeE 23
(2002) 418-431.
13940 *Okure, Teresa* Readings of the bible in Africa: a select literary survey. JKTh 10 (2002) 174-209.
13941 *Popkes, Wiard* Zum Thema 'Anti-imperiale Deutung neutestamentlicher Schriften'. ThLZ 127 (2002) 850-862.
13942 *Rainey, Anson F.* Near Eastern archaeology at the turn of the
century: a review article. RStR 28 (2002) 41-46.
13943 *Roberts, J.J.M.* The ancient Near Eastern environment. The bible
and the ANE. 2002 <1985> ⇒230. 3-43.
13944 *Rogerson, J.W.* Recent continental Old Testament literature. ET
113 (2002) 419-422.

13945   ᴱ**Saranyana, Josep-Ignasi** Teología en América Latina, 3: el siglo de las teologías latinoamericanistas: 1899-2001. M 2002, Vervuert 776 pp [REB 248, 1010].
13946   *Wischmeyer, Oda* Das Selbstverständnis der neutestamentlichen Wissenschaft in Deutschland: Bestandsaufnahme, Kritik, Perspektiven: ein Bericht auf der Grundlage eines neutestamentlichen Oberseminars. ZNT 10 (2002) 13-36.

Y7.2 *Congressus biblici*: **nuntii**, *rapports, Berichte*

13947   *Abir, Peter A.* A report of the VI plenary assembly of the Catholic Biblical Federation. ITS 39 (2002) 346-351.
13948   *Akao, John O.* 15th annual conference of the Nigerian Association for Biblical Studies, Port Harcourt, 9-12 July 2002. BOTSA 13 (2002) 16.
13949   *Benzi, Guido* Federazione biblica cattolica. PaVi 47/2 (2002) 57.
13950   *Bernabé Ubieta, Carmen* Reunión de la Asociación de biblistas españoles. Qol 30 (2002) 99-101. Salamanca, 9-11 Sept. 2002.
13951   *Cardona Ramírez, Hernán* La interpretación de la biblia en la iglesia: resonancias de un simposio. CuesTF 29 (2002) 385-395. Symposium, Vatican, Sept. 1999.
13952   *Dal Bo, Federico* Convegno: Saggezza straniera: Roma e il mondo della bibbia (Verbania, 30 gennaio-3 febbraio 2002). Materia giudaica. 2002 ⇒727. 188-189.
13953   *De Virgilio, Giuseppe* 'La parola di Dio una benedizione per tutte le nazioni': Federazione biblica cattolica: VI assemblea plenaria (Beirut, 3-12 Settembre 2002). PaVi 47/6 (2002) 34-39.
13954   Encuentro latinoamericano de expertos en pastoral bíblica: CELAM, DECAT, FEBIC LAC 4 al 8 de Marzo de 2002 Quito, Ecuador. Medellín 110 (2002) 125-132.
13955   *Haquin, A.* Colloque de Genève sur le Codex Vaticanus (B.A.V. Vat. GR. 1209). EThL 78 (2002) 303. 11 juin 2001;
13956   Analyse narrative des textes bibliques: le colloque international de Lausanne, 7-9.3.2002. EThL 78 (2002) 587.
13957   *Hoppe, Rudolf* 56. Meeting der Studiorum Novi Testamenti Societas vom 31. Juli-4. August 2001 in Montréal. BZ 46 (2002) 158-159.
13958   Konferencia: Didaché a Św. Mateusz [Conference: the Didache and Matthew]. Vox Patrum 22 (2002) 783. Tilburg 2003. **P.**
13959   *Lavik, Marta Høyland* 2002 annual meeting of the AAR/SBL, Toronto, 23-26 Nov. BOTSA 13 (2002) 16-17.
13960   *Marenco Bovone, Maria R.* IX Convegno di Studi Neotestamentari e di Letteratura Cristiana Antica: il giudeo-cristianesimo nel I e II sec. d.C.; Napoli, 13-15 settembre 2001. ATT 8 (2002) 542-548.
13961   *Milani, Marcello* XXXVII Settimana Biblica: torah e kerygma—dinamiche della tradizione nella bibbia, Roma 9-13 settembre 2002. StPat 49 (2002) 685-691.
13962   *Nigro, Giovanni* L'esegesi patristica in Italia: bilancio e prospettive di un'esperienza formativa (Trani, 6-8 giugno 2002). VetChr 39 (2002) 191-196.
13963   *Salzano, Teresa* "Noi faremo e ascolteremo" (Es 24): la vita e la torah: XXII Colloquio ebraico-cristiano. Camaldoli (Arezzo) 6-9 dicembre 2001. StPat 49 (2002) 493-498.

13964 *Shanks, Hershel* Dancing in Denver: from one scholar meeting to another. BArR 28/2 (2002) 36-41, 61.
13965 *Stendahl, Krister* Personal reflections on the GOULDER symposium;
13966 Michael GOULDER responds. Gospels according to Goulder. 2002 ⇒594. 131-136/137-152.
13967 *Van Belle, G.* Colloque: Studiorum Novi Testamenti Societas: Durham, 6-10.8.2002. EThL 78 (2002) 578-579.
13968 *Vanneste, A.* Dixième congrès des exégètes catholiques africains. EThL 78 (2002) 303. Dakar, 25-31 juillet 2001.
13969 *Vasantharao, Chilkuri* Interkulturelle Exegese der Bibel. ÖR 51 (2002) 78-81. 13. Jahrestagung der Arbeitsgemeinschaft Ökumenische Forschung (AÖF) vom 2.-4. November 2001, Univ. Hamburg.
13970 *Vitelli, Marco* Il giudeocristianesimo nel I e II sec. d.C.: notas sul IX Convegno Neotestamentario ABI. RdT 43 (2002) 411-424.
13971 *Walf, Knut* Bibel und China: ein Workshop in Taipei. Orien. 66 (2002) 59-60. The bible and Chinese culture, 5-8.1.2002, Taipei.

Y7.4 *Congressus theologici*: **nuntii**

13972 *Burggraf, Jutta* XXII simposio internacional de teología. AHIg 11 (2002) 387.
13973 *Dupont-Roc, Roselyne* Prophétisme et institutions: L'ACAT face à sa vocation: comnpte rendu des travaux des groupes sur le dossier préparatoire. Revue d'éthique et de théologie morale.Suppl. 223 (2002) 11-23.
13974 *François, W.* The 4th International Conference of the Tyndale Society: Antwerp, 30.8-3.9.2002. EThL 78 (2002) 556-557.
13975 *Kędzierski, Jacek* Chrześcijaństwo jutra: II międzynarodowy kongres teologii fundamentalnej [Christianisme de demain: IIᵉ congrès international de la théologie fondamentale]. AtK 138 (2002) 594-599. P.
13976 *Kmiecik, Violetta* Sprawozdanie z tygodnia eklezjologicznego 2001 — Sobór Bliski—Daleki (26-30 marca) [Compte-rendu de la semaine ecclésiologique 2001]. AtK 560 (2002) 189-192. P.
13977 *Kolinko, Regina Maria* Sprawozdanie z VIII międzynarodwego sympozjum o św. Józefie w San Salvador [Compte-rendu du VIII symposium sur St. Joseph]. AtK 560 (2002) 186-188. 2001. P.
13978 *Langella, Alfonso* 'Via pulchritudinis' e mariologia: cronaca del III convegno AMI (Roma 19-21 Settembre 2002). Theotokos 10/1 (2002) 97-99.
13979 *Schreijäck, Thomas* "Auf der Suche nach der Erde ohne Leid": IV. Lateinamerikanischer Ökumenischer Kongreß zur "Teología India" in Asunción/Paraguay. Orien. 66 (2002) 189/190-193.
13980 *Trapani, Valeria* VI Congresso internazionale di liturgia Roma, 31.10-3.11-2001. RivLi 89 (2002) 350-354.

Y7.6 **Reports of philological and archaeological meetings**

13981 28th archaeological congress in Israel. IEJ 52 (2002) 96-97. 24-25.3.2002, Univ. of Haifa.
13982 The 57th annual convention of the Israel Exploration Society. IEJ 52 (2002) 265.

13983   *Belfer-Cohen, Anna; Goring-Morris, Nigel* Recent developments in
         Near Eastern neolithic research. Paléorient 28/2 (2002) 143-148.
         Report on conf. 'Domesticating space: landscapes and site structure
         in the prehistoric Near East' (19-20.11.2002, Toronto).
13984   *Milano, Maria Teresa* International Organization for Qumran
         Studies, IVth Congress (Basel, 5-7 Agosto 2001);
13985   *Peri, Chiara* Convegno: le discipline orientalistiche come scienze
         storiche (Roma, 6-7 dicembre 2001). Materia giudaica. 2002 ⇒
         727. 171-173/183-184.
13986   **Pérez Jiménez, Aurelio** PLUTARCHUS redivivus: memorándum del
         II encuentro de la red temática de Plutarco (Málaga, 14-15 de junio
         de 2001) y propuesta de proyectos aprobados. Málaga 2002, Uni-
         versidad de Málaga 127 pp. 84-699-9478-6.

Y8.0 *Periti*: Scholars, personalia, organizations

13987   *Anderson, Janice Capel; Setzer, Claudia* Introduction. ^FROETZEL,
         C.: JSNT.S 221: 2002 ⇒104. 1-14.
13988   *Barbieri, Gianfranco* Il card. MARTINI, la bibbia e la pastorale mis-
         sionaria: la vicenda dei gruppi di ascolto della parola di Dio. Am-
         brosius 2 (2002) 111-115.
13989   *Bethge, Hans-Gebhard* Hans-Martin SCHENKE—Lehrer, Forscher,
         Freund. ^FSCHENKE, H.: NHS 54: 2002 ⇒108. 13-25.
13990   *Béchard, Dean* Remnants of Modernism in a postmodern age: the
         Pontifical Biblical Commission's centennial. America 3 (2002) 16-
         21.
13991   Bibliographie Ina WILLI-PLEIN. Sprache als Schlüssel. 2002 ⇒261.
         231-235.
13992   *Buchanan, Duncan* John SUGGIT: humble scholar and man of God.
         Neotest. 36 (2002) xiii-xv.
13993   *Caquot, André* Rapport sur l'état et l'activité de l'École biblique et
         archéologique française de Jérusalem pendant l'année 2001-2002.
         CRAI 3 (2002) 995-999.
13994   *Dentzer, Jean-Marie* Rapport sur l'état et l'activité de l'École fran-
         çaise de Rome pendant l'année 2001-2002. CRAI 4 (2002) 1173-
         1194.
13995   *Doelman, Jan; Snoek, Hans* Onder professoren: Niek SCHUMAN: in
         vrijheid kiezen voor traditie. ITBT 10/4 (2002) 4-6.
13996   **Dudley-Smith, Timothy** John Stott: the making of a leader. 1999
         ⇒15,12845. ^RCTJ 37 (2002) 396-399 (*Stewart, Ken*); SBET 20
         (2002) 216-218 (*Macdonald, Fergus*).
13997   *Festa, Riccardo* L'attenzione educativa ai giovani: testimonianza
         sull'applicazione del 'principio biblico dell'educazione'. Ment.
         Martini, C.: Ambrosius 2 (2002) 135-140.
13998   Fünfzig Jahre im Vetus Latina Institut: eine Ehrung für Professor
         Walter THIELE. BVLI 46 (2002) 3-5.
13999   *Garciagodoy, Juanita* An appreciation of Calvin J. Roetzel. ^FROE-
         TZEL, C.: JSNT.S 221: 2002 ⇒104. 21-24.
14000   *Gauthier, Philippe* Rapport sur l'état et l'activité de l'École fran-
         çaise d'Athènes pendant l'année 2001-2002. CRAI 4 (2002) 1141-
         1150.

14001 *Giavini, Giovanni* Da biblista a biblista: la passione per la scrittura nella lezione del cardinal MARTINI all'Università Cattolica. Ambrosius 2 (2002) 107-109.

14002 **Gordon, Cyrus Herzl** A scholar's odyssey. SBL.Biblical Scholarship in North America 20: 2000 ⇒16,13141; 17,12739. [R]RBLit 4 (2002) 483-486 (*Garber, Zev*).

14003 **Green, Barbara** Mikhail BAKHTIN and biblical scholarship: an introduction. SBL Semeia Studies 38: 2000 ⇒16,13142; 17,12740. [R]HebStud 43 (2002) 252-254 (*Walsh, Jerome T.*).

14004 *Hopper, David H.* Calvin and Macalester: a collegial appreciation. [F]ROETZEL, C.: JSNT.S 221: 2002 ⇒104. 25-29.

14005 *Hübner, Ulrich* Der deutsche Verein zur Erforschung Palästinas (1877-2002) und seine Basler Wurzeln. ThZ 58 (2002) 329-338.

14006 *Hüssler, Georg* Clemens THOMA und der Freiburger Rundbrief. [F]THOMA, C.: JudChr 20: 2002 ⇒119. 91-96.

14007 *Labouvie, Sandra* Bibliographie Ernst HAAG: [F]HAAG, E. 2002 ⇒ 55. 397-407.

14008 *Lopasso, Vincenzo* I Francescani e lo studio della bibbia in Terra Santa. Vivarium 10 (2002) 175-180.

14009 *Manns, Frederic* Faculty of biblical sciences and archeology: thanksgiving celebration. Holy Land (Spring 2002) 21-22. Studium Biblicum Franciscanum.

14010 *McNamara, Martin* The Irish Biblical Association and its publication committee. PIBA 25 (2002) 9-17.

14011 *Olmo Lete, Gregorio del* Alberto ESTRADA-VILARRASA, artista y editor: una vida ilusionada y generosa. AuOr 20 (2002) 7-12.

14012 *Painter, John* Word, theology, and community in John: Robert Kysar's contribution. [F]KYSAR, R. 2002 ⇒70. 1-17.

14013 [E]**Pozzi, Giovanni; Prodi, Paolo** I Cappuccini in Emilia-Romagna: storia di una presenza. Bo 2002, EDB 735 pp. 88-10-92805-9.

14014 *Sellew, Philip* A bibliography of the works of Calvin J. Roetzel. [F]ROETZEL, C.: JSNT.S 221: 2002 ⇒104. 15-20.

14015 *Strauss, S.A.* Pieter Potgieter as mens en teoloog: essensieel en eietyds. [F]POTGIETER, P.: AcTh(B).S 3: 2002 ⇒92. 1-16.

14016 *Terra, João Evangelista Martins* Istituto Bíblico de Roma;
14017 Istituto Bíblico de Brasília. RCB 43 (2002) 7-9/11-14.

14018 **Trimbur, Dominique** Une École française à Jérusalem: de l'École pratique d'Études bibliques des Dominicains à l'École Biblique et Archéologique Française de Jérusalem. Mémoire Dominicaine 5: P 2002, Cerf v; 153 pp. €26. 2-204-07035-1 [RB 110,159].

14019 *Van Belle, G.* Festschrift Jan LAMBRECHT. EThL 78 (2002) 562-67.
14020 *Wolff, Samuel R.* Gophna, for Gophna. [F]GOPHNA, R. 2002 ⇒49. 269-277.

14021 The word of God: a blessing for all nations: biblical pastoral ministry in a pluralistic world: final statement: the 6th plenary assembly of the Catholic Biblical Federation. ITS 39 (2002) 352-368.

14022 *Wuellner, Wilhelm* Die Rolle des Humanen in der Forschung: das Vermächtnis des Lebenswerks von Clemens Thoma im Institut für Jüdisch-Christliche Forschung in Luzern. [F]THOMA, C.: JudChr 20: 2002 ⇒119. 337-341.

14023 ΔΩΡΗΜΑ: a tribute to the A.G. Leventis Foundation on the occasion of its 20th anniversary. 2000 ⇒16,13197. [R]BASOR 326 (2002) 103-104 (*Rupp, David W.*).

Y8.5 *Periti*: **in memoriam**

14024   Abou-Ghazi, Dia Mahmoud 24.1.1924-10.4.2001 ⇒17,12765.
        [R]DiscEg 54 (2002) 105-107 (*Nibbi, Alessandra*).
14025   Angelo Tosato, biblista. Vangelo e ricchezza. 2002 ⇒246. 585-597
        (Incl. bibl.). 29.12.1938-30.4.1999.
14026   Aynard, Jeanne-Marie 1907-2002. [R]RA 95 (2001) 5-6 (*Spycket,
        Agnès*).
14027   Barthélemy, Jean-Dominique 16.5.1921-10.2.2002. [R]Newsletter
        UBS Translation... 51 (2002) 1-3 (incl. bibl.) (*Sanders, James A.*).
        Sources 28 (2002) 163-166 (*Schenker, Adrian*); [R]Istina 47(2002)
        196-197.
14028   Barth, Gerhard 31.12.1927-5.9.2002 [ThLZ 127,1134].
14029   Beauchamp, Paul 28.7.1924-23.4.2001. ⇒17,12766. [R]FilTeo 16
        (2002) 421-422 (*Vignolo, Roberto*).
14030   Bourdieu, Pierre 1.8.1930-23.1.2002. [R]Biblisches Forum (2002/1)*
        (*Lücking, Stefan*).
14031   Calderone, Philip 18.7.1926-14.4.2002.
14032   Calleja, Joseph 1946-2000.
14033   Carmel, Alex 1931-2002.
14034   Carrez, Maurice 1922-2002. [R]FV 101/5 (2002) 7-8 (*Bouttier,
        Michel*).
14035   Coulson, William Donald Edward. 17.9.1942-24.6.2001. ⇒17,
        12775. [R]AJA 106 (2002) 103-105 (*Wilkie, Nancy C.*).
14036   Ebeling, Gerhard 6.7.1912-30.9.2001 ⇒17,12777. [R]JR 82 (2002)
        347-348 (*Betz, Hans Dieter*).
14037   Federici, Tommaso 30.4.1927-13.4.2002. [R]Phase 42 (2002) 504-
        505 (*López Martín, Julián*).
14038   Fohrer, Georg 6.9.1915-4.12.2002 [ThLZ 128,242s—W. Sparn].
14039   Freeman, Geoffrey Evelyn 26.9.1921-3.12.2001. ⇒17,12781. [R]So-
        ciety for the Study of Egyptian Antiquities Newsletter, Jan. 2002, 1
        (*Miosi, Terry*).
14040   Gadamer, Hans-Georg 11.2.1900-14.3.2002. [R]Univ. 57 (2002) 422
        (*Katzschmann, Dirk*); BiLi 75 (2002) 143-144 (*Kremer, Jacob*);
        [R]EstFil 51 (2002) 299-314 (*Almarza Meñica, Juan Manuel*); RMet
        55 (2002) 905-907 (*Dahlstrom, Daniel*); Contrastes 7 (2002) 5-14
        (*Santiago Guervós, Luis de*).
14041   Giblin, Charles Homer 22.1.1928-19.1.2002. [R]AcBib 10 (2001-
        2002) 980.
14042   Gilula, Mordechai 29.1.1936-10.8.2002. [R]TelAv 29 (2002) 219-
        220 (*Sweeney, Deborah*).
14043   Guillet, Jacques 3.4.1910-28.9.2001 ⇒17,12786. [R]Christus 195
        (2002) 364-367 (*Lamarche, Paul*).
14044   Gurney, Oliver Robert 28.1.1911-11.1.2001 ⇒17,12787. [R]AfO 48-
        49 (2001-2002) 293-294 (*Black, J.A.*).
14045   Haag, Herbert 11.2.1915-23.8.2001. ⇒17,12788. [R]FrRu 9 (2002)
        75-76 (*Ehrlich, Ernst Ludwig*); BiLi 75 (2002) 64-65 (*Kalkbren-
        ner, Anton*).
14046· Huesman, John 25.10.1918-10.3.2002.
14047   Illman, Karl-Johan 27.6.1936-20.12.2002. [R]ASE 20 (2003) 243-
        244 (*Neusner, Jacob*).
14048   Karg, Norbert Viktor 27.11.1954-19.10.2001 ⇒17,12791. [R]AfO
        48-49 (2001-2002) 294-295 (*Edzard, D.O.*).

14049 Kopciowski, Elia 1921-2002.
14050 Köcher, Franz 27.12.1916-9.11.2002. ^RSef. 63 (2004) 411-417 (*Böck, Barbara*).
14051 Kunst, Hermann Ob. 6.11.1999, aet. 92. Bericht der Hermann Kunst-Stiftung 2003,7-8—Barbara Aland.
14052 Leivestad, Ragnar Skouge 1916-Jan. 2002 [TTK 74,53-54— Kvalbein, Hans; Sandvei, Bjørn Helge).
14053 Maag, Victor 17.2.1910-3.10.2002 [ThLZ 128,699].
14054 Marquardt, Friedrich-Wilhelm 2.12.1928-25.5.2002.
14055 Martin, François 1950-2001.
14056 Murnane, William J. 22.3.1945-17.11.2000 ⇒16,13233. ^RJARCE 39 (2002) 1-3 (*Van Siclen, Charles C., III*).
14057 Murphy, Roland E. 19.7.1917-20.7.2002 ⇒13905. ^REThL 78 (2002) 577 (*Collins, R.F.*).
14058 Müller, Manfred 1.6.1936-18.9.2000 ⇒16,13234. ^RAfO 48-49 (2001-2002) 295-297 (*Oelsner, Joachim*).
14059 Nardoni, Enrique 15.11.1924-28.3.2002. ^RRevBib 64 (2002) 131-136 (incl. bibl.) (*Doldán, Felipe L.*).
14060 O'Callaghan Martínez, José 7.10.1922-15.12.2001 ⇒17,12800. ^RResB 34 (2002) 72 (*Ricart, Ignasi*); Bib. 83 (2002) 593-594 (*Pisano, Stephen*); ^RAcBib 10 (2001-2002) 974-975.
14061 Pixner, Bargil 23.3.1921-6.4.2002. ^RFrRu 9 (2002) 234-235 (*Thoma, Clemens*); BiKi 57 (2002) 180 ^RBArR 28/4 (2002) 16 (*Riesner, Rainer*);
14062 *Riesner, Rainer* Wege des Messias und Stätten der Urkirche: der Beitrag von Pater Bargil Pixner OSB (1921-2002) zur Wissenschaft vom Heiligen Land. PzB 11 (2002) 87-92.
14063 Places, Edouard des 23.7.1900-19.1.2000 ⇒16,13236. ^RGn. 74 (2002) 377-379 (*Brenk, Frederick E.*).
14064 Roca-Puig, Ramon 23.3.1906-29.6.2001. ^RAeg. 81 (2001) 337-340 (*Montserrat-Torrents, J.*).
14065 Sabourin, Léopold 7.9.1919-14.1.2001 ⇒17,12808. ^RAcBib 10 (2001-2002) 977-978.
14066 Saldarini, Anthony J. 18.9.1941-16.9.2001 ⇒17,12809. ^RSIDIC 34/3-35/1 (2002) 62.
14067 Schenke, Hans-Martin 25.4.1929-4.9.2002.
14068 Schnackenburg, Rudolf 5.1.1914-28.8.2002. ^RBiLi 75 (2002) 306-307 (*Scholtissek, Klaus*); BoSm 72 (2002) 491-494 (*Dugandžić, Ivan*); ^RBVLI 46 (2002) 6.
14069 Schreiner, Josef 14.4.1922-2.5.2002. ^RBiKi 57 (2002) 180; BZ 46 (2002) 161-163 & ZAW 114 (2002) 339-341 (*Zenger, Erich*).
14070 Soisalon-Soininen, Ilmari 4.6.1917-5.10.2002. ^RBIOSCS 35 (2002) 37-39 (*Sollamo, Raija*).
14071 Stoebe, Hans Joachim 24.2.1909-27.12.2002 [ThZ 59,348ss— Neef, Heinz-Dieter).
14072 Stolz, Fritz 16.7.1942-10.12.2001 ⇒17,12813. ^RThLZ 127 (2002) 362-363 (*Dalferth, Ingolf U.*).
14073 Terrien, Samuel 27.3.1911-3.2.2002. ^REThL 78 (2002) 576 (*Collins, R.F.*).
14074 Thompson, John Arthur 24.2.1913-Dec. 2002.
14075 Trocmé, Étienne 8.11.1924-12.8.2002. ^RRHPhR 82 (2002) 387-390 (*Birmelé, André*); FV 101/5 (2002) 3-5 (*Vahanian, Gabriel*).

14076   Ventris, Michael 1922-1956. **Robinson, Andrew** The man who
        deciphered Linear B: the story of Michael Ventris. L 2002, Thames
        and H. 168 pp. 0-500-51077-6. Bibl. 160-164.
14077   Voigt, Simão 24.1.1926-24.7.02. ᴿREB 248 (2002) 965-966.
14078   Vycichl, Werner 20.1.1909-23.9.1999. ᴿAeg. 81 (2001) 341-343
        (*Lucchesi, Enzo*).
14079   Weinberg, Gladys Davidson 27.12.1909-14.1.2002. ᴿIEJ 52 (2002)
        97-98.
14080   Welch, John Joseph 16.12.1925-14.1.2002. ᴿAcBib 10 (2001-
        2002) 976; Bib. 83 (2002) 595 (*Bovati, Pietro*).

Index Alphabeticus

Auctorum

ᴰdir. dissertationis ᴱeditor ᶠFestschrift ᴹmentio ᴿrecensio ᵀtranslator/vertens

Böckler A 7679 ^{T}2836
Böhlemann P 1003
Böhler D 1526 3326
Böhm M 5739 10009 **S**
^{E}489 7637 **U** 8265
Böhmisch F ^{R}978 3479
Böke H 8401
Böll H ^{M}1702
Börker-Klähn J 12031
-**Klein D** 10156
^{E}10158 ^{T}10157
Bösen W 5316
Böttrich C 5159 5350
7325 9597 13821
^{R}150 305 5755
Braaten C 8814 ^{E}279s
L ^{R}992
Bracchi R 9406
Brachlow S ^{R}8426
Brack-Bernsen L 9166
^{R}11067
Bracke J 4314
Bradley K ^{R}11620 **R**
10698
Bradshaw P 824 5401
8464s 13330 13517
Brady C 1868 **M** ^{R}527
Braiterman Z 10159
Brakke D 10569 ^{E}51
^{ET}13472 ^{R}667 670
Brambilla F 8130
Branca P 11124
Brancato F 13930 **N**
11626
Branch R ^{R}2989 3462
3831 4185 7982
8907
Brand P 12032 ^{R}11915
12336 12777
Brandl B 12082
Brands G 12127
Brandscheidt R 2284
4574 ^{E}55
Brandt P 5682 **O** ^{E}513
S 8225
Branick V ^{R}13158
Brankaer J ^{R}1454
10595
Brant J ^{R}6272
Brashear W 10811
Brasser M 10440
Brassiani I 2374
Braude B 13133 **W**
^{T}10212

Braudel F 11674 **P**
^{E}11674
Braulik G 2929
^{D}2925 ^{R}2806
Braun B 1106 **E**
12177 12435 **J**
11830s **R** ^{T}13452
U 5466 **W** 8761
^{R}7091
Braunger K 13648
Bravo L 5317
Brawley R 7268
8575 ^{R}577 687
Braxton B 7120 7269
Bray G 7002 8365
13300 ^{E}5002s 6909
7054 **J** ^{R}2833
10932
Braybrooke M ^{R}4909
Brändle F 6194 **R**
13484
Bräuer M ^{R}764
Brecht M ^{E}13731
Brednich R ^{E}855
Breed D 7579
Breitner G 10898
Brekelmans C ^{F}10
Brelich A 148 10717
10899
Bremer J 10765
Bremmer J 5402
9740 10754 ^{E}394
9741 10628
Breniquet C 13005
Brenk F 6091
10792ss ^{R}14063
Brenner A 1580
1594 2103 8762
^{E}281 608 2179
^{R}192
Brenninckmeijer Z
3561
Břeňová K 10900
Brent A 8366
Bresciani E 9239
12740
Breslauer R 10283 **S**
10160
Bressolette M 1761
Breton S 149 ^{D}3085
9050
Brettler M 3030
8908 ^{R}2809

Breuer M 1832 2197
10044
Breuning W 10441
Brewer D 13006
^{R}13042
Breytenbach A 2505
2598 3014 3025
3334 7910
Bréchet R 6133
Briant P 11423s
Bricault L 10985
Bridge S 5018 ^{R}5298
5728
Brielmaier B ^{E}1004
Briend J 282 2465
11675 12128 13920
^{E}782s
Briffard C 2104 3181
Briggs D ^{T}4666 **R**
1762 ^{R}141 806 1257
Bright J 11208s
Brin G 10022
Brindle W 6926
Bringmann K 11627
Brink A 2632 **B** 1005
L ^{R}9441
Briquel D ^{R}12945
Chatonnet F ^{R}9118
11059 11219
Brisco T ^{D}13179
Brisman S 2165
Brisson E 1394
Brito E 1107 ^{R}1278
Britt B 4126
Britton J 9167
Bro Larsen K 9911
Broadhead E 5529 **W**
^{R}216
Broadhurst L ^{R}10530
Brock A 8729 **S** 13645
9107
Brocke C vom 7425 **E**
10442
Brocker M ^{R}13743
Brodersen K 3405
^{E}675 ^{ET}5286 10755
Brodie T 2236
Brody A 10901 11676
R ^{E}250
Broer I 4658s ^{R}4674
Broido E ^{T}11665
Broli E 969
Broline R 5847

Cavalcoli G 8405
Cavaleri P 2424
Cavalletti S 1009
Cavallo G 9414
Cavallotto S ^{TE}1399
Caviness M 3440
Cazeaux J 7912
Cazelais S ^R2017 4660
  5005 5015 6437
Cazelles H 6110 7680
Cebulj C 6198
Ceccanti M 1971
Cecchelli M ^E12936
Cecchini S 12083
Čech P 11212
Celan P ^M10326
Celsor S 1704
Cempari M 11934
Cenci A 7426
Centini M 5424
Ceraudo G 12964
Cerbelaud D 3973
  10446 11935 ^R580
  10435 10439 10447
  10465 10469 10484
  10512 10518 10536
Cerchiai L 12892
Cerdo ^M13400
Ceresko A 154 949
  2975 3168 3885
  3921 4042 4071s
  4278 4572 7851
  11185 13136
Cereti G ^E618
Ceriani S ^R11527
Cernokrak N 8473
Cernuda A 5846
Cerrato J 13518
Cerri G ^E678
Cerutti M 10605 **S**
  ^R12922
Cervantes Gabarrón J
  7556 ^R9631
Cespedes R 3082
Chacko M ^R11149
Chacón L 6341
Chadwick H 11628 **R**
  ^R11346 11377
Chakkuvarackal T
  2077s
Chalcraft D 13137
Chalier C 1596 10447
Chan M 8072

Chancey M 12492
  ^R4761
Chandezon C ^R11815
Chang H 9382
Chaniotis A ^E11799
  12909
Chantraine G 13902
Chanut C 11741
Chaplin J 8643
Chapman C 11800 **D**
  ^R234 **G** ^R118 **S**
  1527 ^R1519
Chappaz J ^E11885
Charamsa K 7614
Chardel P 1119
Chareire I ^E5468
Charette B 5117
Charlap L 8909
Charles G 5527 **J**
  5225 7572 7577 -
  Murray M ^R9637
  R ^E11737
Charlesworth J 6158
  9565s 9598 9826-
  31 9915 ^E546s
  2501 4903 9816
  9913s ^M9567
  ^R10053
Charlier P 11054
Charpilloz H 7196
Charpin D 11213
  11378 ^E87
Charron R 10647
Charry E 6511
Chartrand M 7749 -
  Burke T ^R10053
Charvát P 12705
Chatelion Counet P
  6199
Chatham J 1400
Chaudhuri S 2108
Chauveau M ^R11345
Chauvet V ^R12804
Chauvin C ^E13823
Chavalas M 11214
  13933 ^E458
Chave P ^R4923
Chavot P 4729
Chazan R ^R10449
Chávez E 3254 5696
Cheng P 8663
Chenorkian R 12953
Cheong C-S A 5915

Chepey S 9379
Cherix P 3922
Chesnutt R ^R3889
  11595
Chessex J ^M1705
Chesson M 12161
Chester A 8195 ^D8815
  S ^R6667
Cheung P 6620
Chevalier N 11731 **R**
  ^R762
Cheza M ^D1045
Chialà S 9599 ^E619
Chiaroni A 8474
Chiesa B 1833s
Childers J 5084
Childs B 4193 8862s
  H 4730
Chilton B 1870 2800
  4904-7 5191s 8266
  8475 10088 10448
  10672 ^E288 4895
  ^R4796 5669 8152
  10530 12496
Chinitz J 2633
Chiocchetti L ^R12737
Chiodi S 11055
Chirassi Colombo I
  8228
Chirilă I 155
Chiron P 9415 ^{ET}9416
Chisholm R 1305 ^R284
  798 819 2523 3957
  4191 4613 10905
  10932
Chittinappilly P 4133
Cho E 3806 **Y** 5743
  6725
Chodkiewicz M
  ^R11120
Choi J 4036 ^R10932 **P**
  ^R6739
Choksy J 11107
Cholidis N 11738
  11886 12693 ^R12708
Chomsky N 9512
  ^M13864
Chopitel J 5179
Choufrine A 13348
Chouraqui A 2709
  10047 **J** 4908
Christensen C 11936 **D**
  2892

7454-7 8578 ^{R}14057
14073
Collon D 13013
Collu M 8230 9397
Coloe M 6200 ^{R}4867
Colombo A 8231 **G**
  7750 ^{R}11922
Colón M 3565
Colpe C 9712
Colzani G 7913
C o m b a E ^{E}2 8 9 **F**
  ^{T}8696
Combes A 6394
Combet-Galland C
  7170
Comblin J 8296
Combrink B 2079
  13138 ^{M}13865
Combs W 9391
Comeau G 10370
Commenge C 12436
Compton M 6643
Comrie B ^{E}534
Condra E 7945
Conejo López-Lago M
  ^{T}4815
Cones B 8407
Conidi F ^{E}290
Coninck F de 8579
Connor G 2893
Conrad E 1123 4205
  4519 J ^{M}1706 ^{R}2990
Conradie E 1124-7
Conring B 13594
Conroy C ^{D}3051 3239
  4336
Conseca C ^{E}735
Constable T ^{R}7463
Constas N 3890
Conti B ^{E}912 **C** ^{R}18 **M**
  3508 3891 **V** 1735
Contreni J 13707
Contreras Molina F
  5907
C o n w a y C 6 2 0 1 s
  ^{R}6440
Conyers L 12602
Coogan M ^{E}107 291
  461 813
Cook E 1871 ^{T}9815 **J**
  1 1 2 8 s 1932 2749
  3 1 1 1 3 9 2 3 s ^{E}5 4 8
  ^{R}109 949 3933 4603

M 13209 **R** 7271 **S**
  1010s 9156 ^{R}4142
Cool Root M 13014
Cooper A ^{R}637 1422
  3849 13480 13488
  G 4546 **J** 2427
  1 2 7 0 6 ^{R}1 1 3 0 8
  11480 **W** ^{E}2031s
Coote R ^{R}4527
Copan P ^{E}4909
Cope O ^{E}5048
Copeland L 12627
Coppens F 12191
  12262 ^{E}731 ^{R}12190
Coppieters 't Wallant
  B ^{E}13699
Copsey R ^{R}854
Coray J 413
Corbin M 6437
Corbineau-Hoffmann
  A 1637
Cordes A 3672
Cordier P ^{T}11636
Cording R 1130
Core D 5898
Corley B 7505 ^{E}1131
  J 4 0 7 4 s ^{R}3 1 1 8
  3885 8426 **K** 8730
Corneil R ^{R}1583
C o r n e l i u s a L
  ^{M}13801 **E** 7436
  8367
Corner M ^{R}2038
Coronado F ^{E}2016
Corradino S 3367
Corral M 4452
Correia J 5558 5664
  ^{R}5011
C o r s a n i B 7 2 0 6
  13733 ^{R}8888
Corsato C ^{R}10581
  11829
Corsetti P ^{E}925
Corsini E 6203
Cortese E 4279 ^{R}374
  2996 3480 **L** ^{T}9514
Cortés E ^{D}9631
Cosaert C ^{R}7469
Cosby M 7272
Cosden D ^{R}391
Cosentino A ^{T}13569
Cosgrove C 8580
Cosi D ^{E}828

Costa A 2330 **G** ^{R}6413
  P 12976
Costecalde C ^{E}2017
C ô t é D ^{R}2 2 4 6 5 4
  10435 13616
Cothenet E ^{R}1 3 3 8
  4833 5015 5132
  6701
Cotta G 3744
Cotton H 10050 11609
  12475 ^{E}79
Cottret B 13774
Coughenour R 3892
Coulon L 12263
Coulot C 10023
Coulson W †14035
Counet P 6418
Courreau J ^{TE}13622
Court J 6100 6119
  ^{E}292 ^{R}6502 6518
Cousland J 5118 ^{R}7431
Couteau E ^{R}495 6818
Couto A 1012 2259
  ^{R}4536 500
Couturier G ^{E}13896
Cova G 3509
Cowey J ^{E}462
Cox C 3441 ^{R}285 **H**
  7914
Cozzi A 6320 8074
Córdova González E
  7448
Cöster H ^{R}1105
Craddock F 1403 5797
  P 12874
Craffert P 4731s 5469
Craig J 2607
Crainshaw J 7878 8476
Cramarossa L 7115
  7146
Cranford L ^{R}5214
  5326
Craven T ^{E}1609
Crawford J ^{R}13543 **S**
  ^{R}3 0 7 8368 9772
  9832 **T** 1841
Creach J ^{R}7899
Creason S ^{R}9115
Creazzo T ^{R}13362
Creech R 8369
Cremaschi L ^{E}619
Cremascoli G 1679
  ^{R}13362 13422 13443

Danove P 5572
Dante ᴹ1707s
Dardaillon E 11741
Dardano P 9328
Daris S ᴱ862 ᶠ21
Darnell J 9243
Darr J ᴿ5603
Darragh N ᴿ2302
Dart J 10629
Darvill T 863
Darwin C ᴹ2370 **G** 3511
Das A 8864 ᴱ1 294 ᴿ6987
Dash M 11183
Dassmann E 2528
Dassow E von 9176
Dattrino L 2289 ᵀ13720
Dauphin C 11664 ᴿ11712
Dautzenberg G ᴿ5575 7061 7065
Dauzat P 2550 ᵀ7830
Daviau P 10903 12193 12552 12586 ᴱ30
David A 9244 **R** 10990 12264 **Y** ᶠ22
Davidovitz T 10311
Davids P ᴿ7584
Davidsen O 5160
Davidson J 2260 **R** 1339 3478 7539 ᴰ2400
Davidzon I 9679 ᴿ634
Davies C 13763 **G** 2686 8968 **J** 2687 ᴿ2050 **P** 1132 2033 3379 3925 9773-6 9916 9979 10051 12265 ᴱ13 295s 9906 ᴿ693 ⁹⁹⁵⁶ **S** ᵀ10630 **W** ᴱ858 11737 11887
Davila J 2502 9917 9980 10322 ᴱ582 732 ᴿ10330 9900
Davis B 6207 7333 **D** 10904 **E** 158 1340 3926 ᴿ2628 3831 **J** 1404 2349 **S** 7751 7009 8477 ᴱ86 623s
Dawes G 4736 7377

Dawn M 6475 ᴿ604
Dawson A 5573 **J** 13429 ᴿ1520
Day J 3512 6354 10905 **P** 9070s
Dayagi-Mendels M 12266
De André F ᴹ9708
De Angelis V ᴱ464
De Ayala R ᴱ11674
De Benedetti P 2261 10163 13015
De Caen V ᴿ8910
De Cesari C 12267
De Chirico L ᴿ8201
De Claissé-Walford N 8911
De Feo F 3655
De Fiores S ᴱ625
De Floriani A 1972
De Francesco I ᵀᴱ13625
De Genaro G 6864
De Groot A 12461
De Groote M 6515
De Gruchy J ᶠ23
De Haes R 1405
De La Torre M 1133
De Lange N ᴱᵀ9005
De Luca E 8408
De Luce J ᴿ1671
De Martino S 11442 ᴱ61
De Menezes R 8865
De Mier F 4737
De Mingo Kaminou-chi A 8582
De Monticelli R 1134
De Rosa G 1479
De Santis L ᴿ5086
De Schrijver G ᴰ4133 8202
De Simone G 3607
De Stefani C ᴱᵀ1729
De Troyer K 3347 3380s 9836s ᴱ103 ᴿ7884
De Virgilio G 5062 5228 5747 7071 7253 8478 13953 ᴿ964 7758 8888
De Zan R 4194 4256

Deakle D 13400
Dearman J 4317 8016 ᴿ12534
Debanné M 7384
Debarge L ᴿ5240
Debergé P 881 1768 7616 7752s ᴱ100 583
Debergh J ᴿ12212 12926
Debidour M 11802
Debié M 654
Debray R 11939
Decker W 11822
Declerck J ᴱ13498
Declercq G 11588
Decloux S 5798
Decock P 5941
DeConick A 6208 10631
Decrept É 13368
Deeg A 1681
Deenik-Moolhuizen J 13877
Degeorge G 12696s
Degorce J ᵀ1763
Degórski B ᴿ8053 13394
Deheselle Danielle ᴿ11412
Dehn U 2872
Deiana G 7617 8232 ᴰ2965 10959 ᴿ8971 13357
Deile V 2110
Deines R ᴿ11527
Deist F 1769 11678
Dekker W ᴱ297
Del Agua A 4974 5471
Del Cerro Calderón G ᴱᵀ13697
Del Corro A 5363
Del Monte G 10855
Delacampagne C 13139
Delamarter S 9567
Delattre A 5255 ᴿ9298
Delcorno C 13702
Delf B 12960
Delhougne H ᵀ830
Delia R ᴿ12032
Delitzsch F ᴹ10507 13876
Delkurt H 1015 3927

Diez de Velasco F
10659 ^{E}396s
Dight R 12978
Dignas B 10856
DiGrazia O 2710
Dihle A 13332
Dijkstra K 11059 **M**
4270 10907 13141
DiLella A 4076
Diller C 3316
Dillmann A ^{M}9321 **R**
299 1136 5865
Dillon J 10003 ^{R}10791
M 10762
Dimant D 9603 9838
Dimonte R ^{E}1013
Dînca L 13622
Dinçol A 11443 12089
B 11443
Dingida D ^{R}1338
Dinkova-Bruun G
13651
Dion P 10903 10908
11219 12193 12552
^{F}30 ^{R}344 2807 11247
Dionysius C 7080
Diotallevi F 13267
Dipple G 6501
Diprose R 8866
Dirnbeck J 4742
Dirven L 12681
^{R}10918 **R** ^{E}466
Disse A 8913
DiTommaso L 883
9981
Dittmann-Schöne I
10721
Dixon S 11632 ^{E}11631
Dînca L ^{R}13621
Díaz Rodelas J 6929
7072 ^{E}6912 **Sariego**
J ^{R}342 -Mas P
10341
Díez Aragón R ^{T}370
del Corral F 8186
Macho A 9569
Merino L 1872
^{R}1876
Doan W 2801
Dobbeler A von 4770
^{E}6 **S von** 3407 5368
^{R}5219 5343
Dobbs-Allsopp F 4397

Dober H 10371
Dobesch G ^{E}260
Doble P 7406 ^{R}5238
Doblhofer G 11472
Dobraczynski J 6900
Dobrovolny M 8731
Dobschütz D von
^{R}13761
Docherty S 2576
^{R}6301 11608
Dochhorn J 9639
9839 13492
Docter R ^{E}733
Dodd B ^{E}7396 **C**
^{M}13878s
Dodi A 10284
Dodson A 12269
^{R}12287 **D** 5171
Doeker A 3513 8479
Doelman J 13995
Doering L 5352 8164
9654 ^{E}234 ^{R}2585
5350 5355 5360
Doglio C 6517 6607
7055s 7207
Dogniez C 4611
8969 ^{E}2180
Dognini C ^{E}467
Doherty P 11322
Dohmen C 2112
11704 ^{R}1416 1527
Dohrmann N 10164
Doignon J ^{E}3695
Dola T 7719
Dolansky Overton S
1837
Dolbeau F ^{R}13586
Dolce R 12671s
13016
Doldán F 7154
^{R}14059
Dolezalova L 13608
Dolinka B 12621
Dollfus G 937
Dolna B 13891
Dolzani M 7622
Domański A 2228
Dombrowski B 9109
Domhardt Y 926
Domínguez B ^{T}1234
García M ^{E}2000
Sanabria J ^{R}616
Donadoni S 12765

Donahue J 5533 8480
Donaldson T ^{E}12476
^{R}7091
Donati A 9493
Donati Giacomoni P
^{E}12628
Donceel R 9777
^{R}11781
Doner J ^{T}8655
Donfried K 7427
Donnat S 10994
Donnelly D ^{E}551 7155
Donner H 2941 13268
^{E}9072
Donnet D ^{R}6703
Donnini M ^{R}13650
^{T}13694
Donohue J 8481
Doorly W 2753
Doran R 3894
Doré J ^{E}8087
Dorival G 1770 3443
^{E}398 626
Dorman P 12036 **T**
8867
Dormandy R 5916
Dormeyer D 1137
^{R}5395 6749
Dorsch K 12931
Dossetti G 161
Dostoevskij ^{M}1710
Dotan A ^{E}1836
Dothan T 12195 ^{F}31
Dotolo C 7698
Doubell F 7862
Doudna G 9840
Douglas M 2822s 2846
2862 3327
Douglass H 6600 6615
Doukhan J 10453
^{D}7688
Dousse M 7917
Doutreleau L ^{ET}13430
Dov H 10165
Doveri C ^{T}2889
Dow C ^{R}1282
Dowd S 8370 ^{R}5542
5583
Dowley T ^{E}12955
Dowling E 5534 ^{R}8733
M 3974
Doxey D ^{R}11335
Doyle B 3722 4244s

Farisani E 3328
Farkasfalvy D 1344
Farmer K 1018 **W** 1533
Farnell F 5024
Farrugia E ᴿ5218 5741 11593
Fasani S 5277
Fasol A ᴰ1425
Fassberg S 9037 9110 ᴿ8996
Fassetta R ᵀ13621
Faßbeck G 3205
Faßnacht M 6841 ᴱ352
Fattorini L ᴿ4772
Fatum L ᶠ36
Faulkner N 11611
Faust A 11764 11769
Fausti S 6136
Fauth W 4513
Faü J 10024
Fava Guzzetta L 3747
Favaro G 10668
Favreau-Lilie M ᴿ735
Fayant M ᴱᵀ10815
Fazzini R 12201
Fear A ᴿ11821
Fears J ᴿ10719
Fechter F ᴿ4466
Fedele F 13018
Feder F 9299 ᴱ4319 ᴿ1963
Federici T 8484 †14037
Federico V ᴹ3366 13787
Fedou M 13433 ᴱ554
Fee G 163 1773 6735 ᶠ37
Feeser-Lichterfeld U ᴱ404
Feig N 12518
Feiler B 2470
Feiss H ᴿ13660
Felber A 9609 **H** 9246
Feld H ᴱ6137 13777
Felder C 7760 **S** 10055
Feldkämper L 977
Feldman L 2529 9681-5 10168 11499 11536s 11539 ᴱ11540 ᴿ460 9692 10912 ᵀ11538 **M** 774

S 5429 12455 12471 12558
Feldmeier R ᴿ5298 8640
Felici E 11723
Feliciano D 3749
Feliks Y 11541
Feller P 2658
Fellman J 9320s
Fellous S 2019
Fendrich H 5181
Feneberg R 5575
Fenn R 1743
Fenske W 4976 8410 ᴱ68
Fenton J 5576 ᴿ8426 **P** 10312 ᴱ10333
Fentress E ᴱ736
Ferguson E 1534 8269s 8373 ᴿ11956 **N** ᴿ7794
Fernandes L 4627
Fernandez A ᴿ12797 **D** 2379 **E** 8665 **F** ᴿ5325 **Lago J** 13432 **Marcos N** 1935-8 4398 9841 13790s ᴿ1931 **San-grador J** 10648 12796s ᴱ122 306 ᴿ12798 **Tejero E** 4398 13791 **V** 6930 7011 **-Martos J** 7761 **-Paniagua J** 5237
Fernando A 4495
Fernbom K ᴿ13543
Ferngren G ᴱ400
Ferrara A ᴿ9164 9201 **degli U C** ᴿ659 **E** ᴿ107
Ferrarese G 13309
Ferrari G 12147 12202 **L** ᵀ4812 **M** 1975 **P** ᴿ1021 7987 **S** 1699 2754 10669
Ferraro G 6112
Ferreiro A 6061
Ferrer J 4399
Ferris I 12039 **S** 8485
Ferry J 4138 4374 7625

Festa R 1019 13997
Fetzer A 5478
Feuerbach L ᴹ1672
Fewell D 3339
Fforde C ᴱ470
Fidanzio M 3569 ᴱ3579
Fiddes P 4478 8271
Fidler R 9922
Fiedler P 8486 ᴿ4843
Fiedrowicz M 3479 6092 13310 ᴿ13335
Fiensy D 4753 13234
Fierro M ᴱ710
Figal G 9395
Figueroa Jácome L ᴿ6343
Figura M 13369
Fildes A 11705
Filer J 12276 ᴿ12284
Filho J 6520
Filoramo G 7919 10571 10670 ᴱ634
Finan T ᴱ635
Fincke A 9842
Findlay J ᴿ4416 - **Wilson C** ᴿ8701
Findley G 1410
Fine S 1873
Fingernagel A 8970 ᴱ1976
Finkbeiner U 12638 12690
Finkel C ᴿ12413 **I** ᴱ71
Finkelstein I 2634 2976 11221s 11267 11284 11292 11324 11681ss 12439 12450 12768 ᴱ12459 ᴿ2976
Finlan S ᴿ7094
Finlayson B 12566
Finnern S 5025
Finney T 7509
Finsterbusch K 2896 2944
Finucci S ᴿ13695
Fiocchi Nicolai V 12932
Fiorato P 10376
Fiore B ᴿ7581
Fiorensoli D 8236 ᴱ401

Francia R 9329
Francis B ᴿ7166 **L**
    5538 8587
Franciscus A 2419
    8489
Franck D 13882s
Franco E 5578 7142
    ᴱ42
François W 13974
Frangiotti R <ed>
    11634
Frank D ᴿ13806 **K**
    ᴿ11660
Franke B 3383 **C**
    ᴿ3429
Frankel D 2690 ᴿ717 **J**
    10379 **R** 12493 **S**
    13805
Frankemölle H 7225
    8870 10455 ᴱ403
    ᴱ10456 ᴿ7201 7582
Frankfurter D 10817
    10999 ᴿ10824
Fransen P ᴱ13699
Franz A ᴱ7879 **M** 2802
    3677 -**Klauser O**
    ᴿ10255 **T** ᴱ489 7637
Franzmann M 10607
    ᴿ10646
Franzosi T ᴱ310 2237
Frassetto M 10457
Frazer J 10696
Frazier F 9687
Frechulphus L ᴹ13700
Frede H ᴱ6907 **S** 471
Fredericq-Homes D
    ᴱ25
Fredrickson D 7357
Fredriksen P 4757
    7306 10458 ᴱ308
    ᴿ9637
Freed R 12042
Freedman D 1837
    1891 2711 4613
    ᴱ806 ᴿ10952 **S** 9180
Freeman G †14039 **P**
    ᴱ738
Freer C ᴹ11736
Frei H ᴹ5821
Freitas Faria J de 8699
Freke T 4758
French E 12894 **H**
    5257 **P** ᴿ12813

Frend W ᴿ11628
Frendo A 9078
Frenkel D 3423
Frenschkowski M
    7765 8018 10818
    13402 ᴿ11870
Frerichs E ᴱ525 ᶠ40
Fretheim T 4322s
    4369 7626
Frettlöh M 7623
Freu J 11444
Freud R ᴱ12500 **S**
    ᴹ1752s 1757
    10414
Freudenthal G
    ᴿ10319
Freund A 1412
Frevel C 2202 4033
    4400
Frey A ᴱ9733 **J** 4759
    5711 5730 6114
    6162 6222ss 6737
    13890 R5340 6151
    6247 6395 6452
    9578 ᴱ225 ᴿ1227
    6471 -**Logean I**
    5172
Freyberger K 9423
Freyburger-Galland
    M ᴱ11636
Freyne S 167s 5027
    10059 ᴱ309
Friberg B 9362 **T**
    9362
Frick F 2877 13147
    P 9688
Fricke K ᴱ2063 **M**
    1020
Fricker D 4760
Frid B 10632
Fried L 4274 13148
Friedell S ᴿ10150
Friedheim E 10727
Friedlander A 1599
    7975 ᴱ138
Friedman M ᴱ151
    ᵀ10352 **R** ᴱ12820 **S**
    9845 ᴰ10143
Friedmann D 2756
Friedrich J 9079 **M**
    10459 **N** 6597
    6603
Friesen S 6521

Frilingos C ᴿ6521
    7120
Frisch A 2471
Frishman J 1482
Fritsch C 7548 **M** 4285
Fritz M ᴱ80 **V** 3000
    11224 12515 ᴿ11693
Frizzell L 4654
Froehlich K 1977
    13867
Frola M ᵀ1734
Frolov S 3145 3384
Frolova N 12348
Frosini G 5479
Frösén J 12585 E9425
Frühwald W 1721
Frydrych T 3930
Frye N 169 ᴹ1113
    1130 1147 1181
    1191 1239 1250
    1283 7622 8765
    8829 13884
Frymer-Kensky T 1600
    2691 ᴱ10460
Fuchs A 6159 11381s
    ᶠ41 ᴿ24 77 103 105
    138 153 200 327
    4659 5143 5146
    5769 6082 6152
    6372 6654 7262
    8148 8153 **E** 8772
    ᴿ1609 **G** ᴿ6883 8131
    13504 **M** 12043 **R**
    1978 **W** 7880
Fugitt S 11225
Fuglseth K 6225
Fugmann H 8667
Fuhrer T ᴱᵀ13547
Fuhs H 3931
Fujii S 12549 12617
Fuks G 11542
Fuller D 10686 **R** 6894
Fullerton J 7627
Fumagalli A 5395 **E**
    8489 **P** ᴱ9002
Fung Y 2578
Funk R 1535 4761
    10704 **W** 10619
    10633 10618
Furley W 10765
Furlong J ᴿ4013
Furnish V 310 6738
    7766 ᴿ6839 7065

Gäde G 7700
Gärtner T 13698
Gálik M 11187
Geddert T 5539
Gee J 11000
Geerlings W 13549s
 13609 ^{E}405 472 832s
Geffré C 1148ss
Gehring R 13149
Geiger A ^{M}4916 J
 3410
Gelasius C 13317
Geldbach E 2295 6426
Geljon A ^{R}228 9675
Geller M 11063 13100
 ^{R}9178 9182 S 3516
 3756 ^{D}13090
Gellner C ^{R}1702
Gelston A 4563 ^{F}44
Gempf C 6105
Gemünden P von
 ^{D}5682
Genest O 13020
Genovese A 13551
Genre G 7494
Gentili B ^{E}9427
Gentry-Akin D ^{R}8763
Gentzler E ^{E}2153
Genuyt F 6047
Genz H 12568 ^{R}11812
Geoffrey A ^{M}13701
Geoltrain P ^{F}45
George A 9181 11394
 ^{E}71 9162s ^{R}11072 L
 6440 M 3146 3171
 10464 P 3272 S
 ^{M}1711
Georgeot J 6139
Georgi D 4044 6740
Gerber D 7343 ^{R}5132
Gerdmar A 6024 7573
 ^{R}7576
Gergolet J 5850
Gerhards A 8492
 ^{E}8239
Gerhardsson B 7178
Gerlach B ^{E}9534
Gerlitz P 2331
Gershenson D 9052
Gersonides ^{M}4023
Gerstenberger E 3480
 5196 7976s
Gertel E 2874

Gertz J 2189 2509
 2610 2635 2898
 ^{R}2250
Gesche A 8083s
 ^{E}636 B 3071 P
 3897
Gestoso G 11001
Gestrich C ^{E}406
Getcha J 8493
Getty-Sullivan M
 8733
Geva H ^{E}12383
Geyer D 5580
Geyser P 8589 ^{R}4814
Gérard J ^{R}6171
Ghattas M 8055
Ghezzi B ^{E}2173
Ghi P 3827
Ghiberti G 4977
 5364 6228 9785
 12277 ^{R}7555 8300
 12916 13733
Ghilardi M ^{R}11923
 12936
Ghinatti F 9364
Ghosh K 13652
Giallanza J 8413
Giannarelli E 13461
Gianotti D 8377
Gianotto C ^{E}634
 ^{R}10641
Gianto A ^{R}12659
Giavini G 1021 7208
 14001 ^{R}278 618
 5323
Gibbal C 9330
Gibbons J ^{T}13701
Gibbs J A 5204 L
 1514 R 10176s
Gibert P 2472 5353
 7628 7920 11684
 ^{E}312s
Giblin C †14041
Gibson A 1151 E
 13150 R ^{E}314 S
 12219 12561 ^{E}869
Gichon M 12447
Gicnolo R 5581
Giebel M 10819
Gieben S ^{R}11715
 12396
Gielen M 1152 6867
 7143

Gieniusz A 7004 ^{R}183
Gierlich G 9248
Giesen H 1153 5122
 6476 ^{R}181 269 303
 1766 2168 2560
 4699 5008 5376
 5808 6262 6288
 6304 6792 6799
 6948 7367 7432
 8039 8175 11497
Gignac A 6681 6932
 7998 F ^{R}6013
Gignoux P 11109s
 ^{E}473 ^{R}9746 11110
Gijsel J 9716
Gil M 11665
Gilbert A 13021s G
 6042s ^{R}569 M 170
 1537s 3898 4004
 4045s 4079 4103
 9985 10060 ^{D}4034
 ^{F}46s ^{R}4050 Stanford
 3851
Gilboa R 2415
Giles T 10007
Gilhus I ^{R}10575
Gill D ^{R}10824 M
 12093
Giller P 10323
Gillet-Didier V 9689
Gillièron B 807
Gillihan Y 7119
Gillingham S 953 1774
 3517 11770 ^{R}681
 3478 3525 3543
Gillman A 2064 F
 ^{R}7217 7335 J 5942
 5799 ^{R}7186 N 10178
Gillmayr-Bucher S
 3518s 3571
Gilmont J 2022
Gilmour C ^{R}7431 M
 7574 ^{R}5602
Gilula M †14042
Gimeno Granero J
 3932
Gindin T 4414
Giniewski P 10465
Ginter M ^{R}8595
Giokarines K 7770
Giombi S 13312 ^{E}315
Giordani I ^{M}8357
Giordano da P 13703
 ^{M}13702

Guy L ^{R}7091
Guyon J 12933
Gündüz S 11813
Günther H ^{F}53 **M** 6870
Güterbock H ^{E}9335
^{M}54
Gygax M 11503
Gyselen R ^{E}476s
12096
Gzella H 3521

Ha J 2512
Haacker K 174 1776
4765 4766 5430
5454 5981 6648
6933ss 7012 7274
8590 10470-3 ^{E}827
2166ss
Haag E 3358 4238 ^{F}55
^{M}14007 ^{R}4470 **H**
8375 †14045
Haak R ^{E}317
Haaland G 11545
Haarmann M ^{E}11126
H a a s P 1 0 1 8 6 **V**
10862s 12708 ^{R}9350
Haase M ^{R}10999 **R**
2779
Habel N 6325 ^{E}322s
2265
Haberman B 3385
Habermas J ^{M}1193
Hackett J 8922 8924
Hadad S 12181
Hadas G 12981 **-Lebel**
M 11546
Haddad P 10187 **R**
12130
Hadidi J 11120
H a d l e y J 1 0 9 1 4
^{R}12496 **M** ^{E}29
Hadrian N ^{M}13725
Haehling R von ^{E}78
Haelewyck J 3241
3386 ^{R}9148 9577
Haemig M ^{R}56
Haendler G ^{R}7583
13594
Haensch R ^{R}9441
Haers J ^{D}8095
Haettner Blomquist T
10915
Hafemann S 8873 ^{E}558

Hage W 13403
Hagedorn A ^{R}1527
2958 13194
H a g e l i a H 8 9 7 2
^{R}1619
Hagen K ^{F}56
H a g e n b u c h n e r A
9 3 3 4 **-Dresel A**
11864
Hagene S 8822
Hagège C 9514
Hagith S ^{R}11644
Hagner D 7497 ^{E}324
^{R}5093
Hahn F 8199 8874s
^{M}5 0 6 3 ^{R}8 8 9 4 **J**
3207 10916 ^{E}408
5 5 9 **N** 4 6 1 6 **O**
1978 **S** 5259 8121
8701s **U** 7774 ^{E}325
Hahneman G 1539
Haidinger A 8970
Haidostian P 5205
Haight R 4945 8086
^{R}1517
Haimo A ^{M}13707
H a i n e s - E i t z e n K
1645
Hainthaler T ^{E}8057
^{R}635
Hainz J 6160
Halbertal M 10314
Halbfas H 2174
Halbmayr A 10662
Haldimann K 6161
6415 7093 ^{R}6109
6118 6127 6129
6132 6149 6162
6166 6172 6209
6221 6233 6240
6242 6280 6289
6303 6326 6337
6356 6396 6410
H a l i v n i D 7 7 0 3
10188
Hall C 13315s ^{E}5545
J 11504 **L** 12639
M 6601 **R** 7275 **S**
1777 5720 5726
Hallamish M 10325
Hallbaeck G ^{E}11286
^{R}1310
H a l l e n s l e b e n B

^{R}8239
Halliday M 175
Halligan J 1778 3208
11505 ^{E}296
Hallman J 13529
Hallo W 2780 12709
^{E}326
Hallof J ^{R}10981 11017
Hallotte R ^{R}31
Halpern B 3147 3761
^{E}12459 ^{R}50 **-Amaru**
B 9655
Halpérin J 2476 10474
Hamblenne P 3829
13620
Hamburger J 11948
^{R}6131
Hamel C de 979 1348
1816
Hamid-Khani S 6231
Hamidović D 9848
^{E}706
Hamilakis Y ^{E}12911
Hamilton A 3348 **G**
9549 **H** ^{E}377 **J** 2951
M 973 ^{R}29 8624 **V**
2989
Hamm M ^{E}569
Hammann G ^{F}57
Hammerling R 5260
H a m m e r s t a e d t J
^{ET}13346
Hammett J ^{R}834
Hammond D ^{R}8763 **P**
12182
Hamonville D d' ^{T}3933
Han K 5030
H a n e b u t t - B e n z E
^{E}11708
Haney K 3447 **R** 3522
^{R}270
Hanges J 13159
H a n h a r t K 5 7 1 9 **R**
2969
Hanks G 8591 **T** 8655
Hannah D 2560
Hannig R 9254
Hansberger T 3672
10189
Hansen D ^{F}58 **G** 7276
^{E}18 13317 **M** ^{E}478
13253 **N** 9302

Heil C 5049 ^{E}5033 **J**
5367 5754 6684
7027 7048 ^{R}5238 **U**
10608
Heilbronner O 10478
Heiligenthal R 4769s
^{E}6 ^{R}4878
Heilman S 10383
Heim K 3976 ^{M}2347
Heimbach-Steins M
1419
Heimerdinger J 1309
Heimgartner M 13387
13484
Heimpel W 11065
Heine B 857 **H** ^{M}1712
R ^{T}7348
Heinemann F ^{R}3931
4266 4418 7679
Heiniger E ^{R}8658
Heininger B 7477
8159
Heinsdorff C 1715
Heinz M 11232 ^{E}480
Heiser W ^{E}917
Heither T 2611
Heitzmann C ^{E}1984
Hejdánek L 1168
Hekster O 11639
Helbling D 4507
Helck H 9255
Held W 11506 12209
Helewa G 5064 6871
7882
Heller A 4914 ^{R}11413
D ^{E}1105 ^{R}13291 **E**
^{E}11950 **J** 8975 ^{E}560
K 7245
Hellerman J 8305
Hellinger M ^{E}481
Hellman M 11772
^{E}11773 ^{R}733
Hellum J ^{R}11347
Helm P 7483 8173
^{E}410
Helmer C 13737
Helms S 12735
Helou C 6115
Heltzer M 2580 2665
3343 9035 9055 ^{R}27
9065 11299 12087
12667
Helyer L 9573

Hemer C 6594
Hempel C 8976 9987
^{E}482 ^{R}164 9919
9967 10002
Hempelmann H 1169
Henao Mesa J 1025
Hendel R 2240
13161 ^{E}212 ^{R}8964
Henderson J 4362 **W**
13637
Hendrickx H 5800
12386 **S** 12283
12743
Hengel M 176ss 327
1939 4689 5982
6162 6649-52
6744-8 7013 7589
7590 8153 11507
^{D}5962 ^{E}225 638
^{M}13890
Hengstl J ^{R}11329
11472
Henke R 13616 ^{E}48
Henley J 6843
Hennig G 6046 **P**
1026ss ^{E}994
Henning K 4955
Henrich P 12154
Henriksen J ^{E}411
Henrix H 10479s
^{E}10481
Henry M 1170 6318
10326
Hensell E 5588
^{R}3111
Hensellek W ^{E}13559
Hens-Piazza G 1171
Hentrich T ^{R}10914
Henze D 6072 **M**
4508 9667
Hepner G 2513s
2514 2842
Heracleon P ^{M}13364
Heral S ^{R}11353
Heras O 5086
Herbers K 13271
Herbert E 9849s
^{E}9817 ^{R}9842
Herbordt S 12097
Herbst A 1540 1839
Hercsik D 13902
Herder J ^{M}1713
Herfort-Koch M ^{E}747
12155

Herghelegiu M 6523
Herion G 4915
Herman D 3387
Hermann W ^{R}3663
Hermanni F 8189
Hermans M ^{E}328
Hermanson E 2081
Hermant D 5031
Hermary A 12048
Hermes T ^{M}10600
10757
Hermisson H 4257s
Hermsen E 13738
Hernández J ^{T}13571 **M**
^{T}10928 **Blanco J**
^{T}1327 **Castillo R**
^{R}645
Herodes M ^{M}12389
Herodotus ^{M}3156
11279 11287 11311
Herr B ^{R}1938 9888
11700 **L** 12156
12530 ^{E}12553ss ^{R}759
M ^{E}250
Herranz Marco M
5589 5836 8703
Herrenschmidt C 457
11111
Herrmann C 12098 **G**
^{E}748 **S** 179 3148
3172 4146s 4325ss
11233s 11288 13119
W ^{R}2852
Hersche P 11951
Hershkovitz M 11850
Hertog C den 2666
2931 3004
Herz P ^{R}11658
Herzfeld N 2303
Herzog A ^{E}243 **R**
^{E}9494 **Z** 12440
12442 ^{R}11782
Heschel A ^{M}2325
10372 13891s **S**
4916 10482
Heskett R ^{R}3933
Hess R 2844 3013
3901 12684 ^{R}3321
Hesse B 13027
Hesselink I 13778
Hessenauer G 1029
Hester J 7210 7307
7437s ^{R}271 8568

Janowitz N 10822
Janowski B 2205 3209
  3665 7979 ^{D}4149 **J**
  8826
Janse M ^{E}445 **S** 2084
  5690
Jansen K 8735 -**Win-**
  keln K 9537 ^{M}3234
Janssen C 6686 7000
  ^{E}111 6685 **U** 12285
Janssens B ^{E}13521
Janz T 3329
Janzen A 5757 **D** 3340
  10066 **J** 3763 **W**
  2616 ^{F}63
Japhet S 3298s
Japp S 11775
Jarick J 3300 8827
Jaroš K 5431 8978 -
  Deckert B ^{T}11352
  11883
Jarrell R 2515
J a s c h k e H 4 9 5 7
  ^{R}13376
Jaśko A 5593
Jasnow R 9260 ^{E}2791
  ^{R}11017
Jasper D 1179
Jaspers K ^{M}1233
Jastram N ^{R}9978
Jastrow O ^{F}64
Jatho H ^{T}6719
Jauhiainen M 6604
Javierre J 4946
Jay P ^{R}8264
Jánosi P 12286 12814
Jeal R 7358 ^{R}4689
Jeammet V ^{R}12899
Jean C 9186 11068 -
  Gabriel F 5910
Jeanes G ^{R}319
Jeanjean B 13596
Jeanlin F 8503
Jeanneret L ^{T}7995
Jeanrond W 1180
Jefford C ^{R}10742
J e n k i n s A ^{R}7 8 9 3
  ^{T}11316 **C** 8174 **I**
  12053 **P** 4780
Jenner K 1958 4083
  4248
J e n n i E 8 9 2 6 s **H**
  ^{E}12287 ^{R}8947

Jennings S 11744 **T**
  6874
Jensen A 8736ss **H**
  1 3 1 0 s ^{M}1 3 1 8 **P**
  7 7 0 4 **R** 1 1 9 5 6
  ^{R}8371
Jenson P 7921 ^{R}270
  2809 **R** 8134 8828
  ^{E}279s
Jeppesen C 12288 **K**
  3523
Jeremias G ^{D}2736 **J**
  1 8 4 4 5 2 4 4 7 8 1
  5 2 1 5 5 2 6 3 8 8 7 8
  ^{E}65 ^{M}13893
Jericke D ^{R}12534
J e r i c ó B e r m e j o J
  1349
Jerome 7348 ^{M}3361
  13447 13589-607
Jersild P 8595
Jerumanis P 6236
Jervis L 5036s 6875
  7258
Jeska J 6058
Jesudasan I 5198
Jeter J 1423
Jeung R 8668
Jewett R 7006 7280
Ji C-Ho C 12531
Jimenez E 5291 **Bed-**
  man F 9931 **O**
  ^{R}13568 **Patón L**
  ^{ET}10315 **Serrano**
  A 11332
Joannes D ^{M}13520
J o a n n è s F 1 3 0 3 4
  ^{E}2783 **F** ^{R}12703
J o a s s a r t B ^{R}4 2 0
  13823
Job J ^{R}7968
Jobes K 1940 7564
J o b l i n g D 1 1 8 1 s
  11238 ^{E}336 **J** 8780
Joerg U ^{E}2068
Joffe A 11239 ^{R}378
  12464 12472 **L**
  3524
JOHANNES PAULUS II
  ^{M}10489 10559
Johansen J 9516
John F de T 2714 **V**
  5594s ^{R}5334

Johns C ^{M}12378
Johnson A 5943s **C**
  11510 **E** 1582 8781s
  13894 **L** 337 1183-7
  1 3 5 0 4 6 7 0 4 7 8 2
  5 9 8 5 7 0 7 6 7 4 6 9
  8 2 4 4 8 3 0 9 8 8 7 9
  13435 13564 13834
  ^{R}7 1 2 4 **M** 1 6 4 9
  13330 13517 ^{R}5407
  R ^{R}1836 1841 7503
  7512 9818 10932 **S**
  5325 10635 ^{E}5868 **T**
  3820 5239 ^{R}3 1 8
  3463 6451 **W** 9932 -
  DeBaufre M 5038
Johnston A ^{R}2983 **G**
  4631 **P** 7960 **R** ^{R}307
  S 9433 9627 10768
  W ^{R}662 11188
J o h n s t o n e W 2 2 0 6
  2248 3301 11957
  ^{R}3294
Jolly P 12131
Jomier J 11127
Jonaitis D ^{R}6269
Jonas H ^{M}13915
Jones A 9261 ^{E}9434 **B**
  1032 4242 ^{R}4522
  4634 **C** 11548 **D**
  11333 **F** ^{R}6820 **G**
  3149 **H** 7514 **I** ^{R}7965
  L 1487 **M** 11776 **P**
  5326 **R** ^{R}3086 **S**
  ^{E}8719
Jong I de ^{E}11279 **J de**
  11958 ^{E}11283 **L de**
  12289 **T de** 9187
Jonge H de 5481 6527
  M de 9628ss ^{R}4187
Jongeling K 9081
Jonker L 1127 1188s
  1781 3322
Jonquière T 11549
Joosse N 6338
Joosten J 1941 2120
  8928 9718 ^{T}4536
J o o s t - G a u g i e r C
  ^{R}11981
Jordaan G 2121
Jordan D 9435s ^{E}642
  ^{R}9937 13082 **M**
  8704

Karni S 8979
Karrer C 3330 **M** 7498
  8023s 8203 ᴰ3456
  5149 ᴱ105
Karris R 5759 5802
  8423 13691 ᴿ5754
  ᵀ5801
Karsten M ᵀ7583
Karz Reid S 12609
Kasher A ᴿ462 **H** 3388
  R ᴰ7895 10311
Kasiłowski P 5680
  7515 ᴱ379 ᴿ6025
Kaske C 1736
Kasper C 8376 **W** 786
  ᴱ787
Kaspi J ᴹ3388
Kasser R 9304
Kassian A 12846
Kaste O ᵀ13187
Kaswalder P 12966
  ᴿ964
Kate A ten 1959
Katsumata N ᴱ10068
Kattan A 1190
Katz P 5597 **S** 10387
  ᴱ414
K a t z s c h m a n n D
  ᴿ14040
Kaufman S 9121 9538
Kaufmann T 11962
Kavka M 10213
Kayser F 9467
Kazen T 4784
Kähler C 7782 8353
Kämmerer T 11069
  ᴿ9163
Käppeli S 10214 ᴱ119
Käsemann E ᴹ5150
Kealy J 6163 7783 **S**
  1542 ᴿ6200 6642
Kearney R 7635
Kearsley R 8275 ᴿ8144
Keathley K 1480
Keating T 8424
Keay R ᴿ6927 7295
Keck L ᴱ4655
Keddie G 4006 6141
Kędzierski J 13975
Kee H 13167 **J** 1191
  8829
Keefe D 8025

Keel O 2332 2726
  3210 10920 11687s
  12392s ᴱ567
Keen A 11453
Keenan J 8592s ᴿ672
Keener C 5087
Kehoe D ᴿ688
Kehrberg I 12587
K e l b e r W 4 7 8 5
  ᴿ4699
K e l h o f f e r J 5 7 2 8
  6876 ᴿ4704 5592
Kelle B 11240
Kellenberger E 2667
  ᴿ2993
Kellens J 9486
K e l l e r A 9 1 4 **D**
  1 2 6 1 1 1 2 5 4 0 **M**
  5859
Kellermann U ᴿ4647
K e l l e y P 1 8 4 1 **S**
  4919
Kellner M ᴿ10306
  13118
Kelly B 3282 ᴿ3344
  G ᴿ8262 **J** 8190 **M**
  ᴿ4151 11709
Kelsey C 6336
Kelter I ᴿ2357
Kemp B 12769
Kempinski A ᴹ66
Kendall D ᴱ86 623s
  R 1427
Kendel A 5482
Kennedy D 9496 **H**
  ᴱ12958 **J** ᴿ13090
K e o w n E 8 9 2 9 **G**
  3108
Kepnes S 10215
Kerber D 6237
Kerbs R 1784
Kereszty R 1351
Keréni K ᴹ10774
K e r k e s l a g e r A
  ᴿ12496
K e r n e r M 1 6 8 3 **S**
  1 2 5 3 2 1 2 5 7 1 ᴱ83
  485
Kerr A 6238 **F** 13677
  R 9081
Kessler C 10388 **E**
  2 5 3 4 ᴿ1 0 0 8 8
  10439 **Guinan A**

11070 **H** 1974 8088
  J 4 6 4 1 4 6 4 3 **K**
  ᴿ1 1 4 1 3 **R** 4 5 2 5
  4618s 9022 11337
  ᴰ2802 ᴿ3354 11261
  S ᵀ4536
Kettel J 11012
Kettenhofen E ᴿ11413
Kettermann G 12959
Keul I 10709
Keuls E 10769
Khalidi T 11160
Khalife I 11128
K h a n G 8 9 3 0 9 1 2 2
  9539 10025
Khandaker M 2366
Khazaradze N 11454
Khosroyev A 10650
Khoury A 11129s
Kiecker J ᵀ13734
Kieffer R 4786 6656
  ᴿ7576
Kieling M 4007
Kienast D 11591
Kierkegaard S ᴹ2541
  6991
Kiesow A 1605
Kieweler H 10069
Kiilunen J 5039
Kijas Z 8504
Kiley M ᴿ8423
Kilgallen J 5899 6044
  6049 ᴰ5986
Kille D 1746s
Killebrew A ᴿ12383
  12486
Killick D ᴿ12874
Kilmer A 2435
Kilpp N 2384
K i m A 9871 **B** 6753
  B-Mo 6687 **D** 8122
  E 1428 **J** 6379 7014
  8669 **S** 190 6657s
  6754ss 7031 7241
  7439 7449 **U** 8670
Kimbrough S 13808
Kimchi D 3475 ᴹ1888
Kimilike L 3936
Kindt-Siegwalt I 8354
Kinet D 10921 11241
  12651
King G 2207 **J** 1684 **K**
  8739 10572 ᴱ10573

Kokkinos N 11582
Kolarcik M 4049
K o l b B 1 2 6 1 0 s **R**
13739
Kolbe M ᴹ8504
Kolinko R 13977
Koliński R 12103
K o l l m a n n B 5 2 9 2
10770 ᴿ608 **H** 6436
Kolta K 13104
Kombi N 3526 9123
Konen H 13232
Konings J 2021 2126
ᴹ6257
Konkel A ᴿ806 **G** 1856
M 4463s ᴿ4466
Konradt M ᴱ490 ᴿ5238
Kool R 12350s
Koole J 4259
Koopmans W 1429
Koosed J 7517
Kopanias K 12055
Kopciowski E 10072
†14049
Kopcke G 12160
Koperski V 1430 5760
6758s 7108 7244 ᴱ72
ᴿ7091 7350
Koprek I 4008
Koptak P 7316
Korenjak M 9517
Kořinková J ᴿ147
Kormyscheva E 11013
K o r o l ë v A 1 2 2 9 8
ᴱ12846
Korpel M ᴱ339
Kors M 2086
Korsak M 2041
Kos S 13597
Kosch D 7162s ᴿ4863
Koschel A ᴱ491
Koshelenko G ᴿ12963
Koskenniemi E 10073
Koslowski P ᴱ643
Kosman A 10218
Kosmetatou E ᴿ12044
Kosmider B 7788
Kosmopoulou A 12056
Kosovski M 10219
Kossian A 11461
Kossman R 3389
Koster A 2828
Kot S 7015 **T** 7592

Kotansky R 10811
12938
Kotecki D 5642
Kotila M 6240
Kotjatko J 8933
Kottackal J 8706
Kottsieper I 3937
4009 9082 9124
10074 ᴿ3886 3902
3905 3911 3918
3927 3934 3938
3942 3948 3952-5
3959 3964 3975
3977 3985s 4024
4029
Kourou N 12057
K o u w e n b e r g N
ᴿ9178
Kovacs J 7078
Kowalski B 5818
6528s **T** 5125 5484
Kozar J 5699
Köber B 5065
Köcher F †14050
K ö c k e r t M 2 7 5 9
7869 ᴱ908
Köhler E 11895 **H**
2069 2127 **J** 8312s
8596
Köhlmoos M 3764
König A 4980
Köpf U 1650
Körner R 5264
Körting C 2806
Körtner U 7721 ᴱ340
1380
Köstenberger A 5001
6393 8314 ᴿ6415
7478
Kraemer R ᴱ1609
Krafeld-Daugherty M
11726
Krafft F 11965
Kraft R 1544 9368 **S**
10499 **Auchter T**
ᴿ5545
K r a f t c h i c k S 6760
7575
Krahmalkov C 9083s
Kramer J ᴱ9369
K r a m i s z e w s k a A
11966
Krammer I 4077

Kranemann B ᴱ416s **D**
8506
Krašovec J 2128 ᴱ563
Krapf M 10500
Krasowski A 1431
Krasser H 11174
Kratz R 2209s 4299
7980 ᴱ116 492
Kraus H ᴹ13895 **J** ᴿ81
M 1785 **T** 7576 **W**
6829 ᴱ105 10481
Krause D 13835 ᴿ7470
M 10598 ᴱ708 **S**
ᵀ3617
Krauss R 2637 9268
11014
K r e b e r n i k M 9189
11073s 11374 ᴱ418
Krecidlo J 6241
Kreider G ᴿ318
Kreier J 8507
Kreiml J ᴿ10432
Kreisel H ᴱ2183
Kreitzer L 1706 1717
4960 11967 ᴱ6380
Krejcí J ᴱ12777
Kremendahl D 7281
Kremer J 7147 ᴿ14040
Krentz E ᴿ9358
Kreppner F 12058
Kretzmann N ᴱ13582
Kreuzer S 1842 6973
7870 ᴱ419 1786
Krey P 13740 ᴱ13717
K r i e g C 1 0 1 3 8 **M**
5434
Krieger K 3426 7923
11550s **W** ᴿ868
Krinetzki G 2902
Krings V ᴱ674
Krispenz J 1787 3938
ᴿ3963 3976 8948
Kritzinger J 8315
Kriwaczek P 11114
Kroeger C ᴱ2175
Kroeze J 4591 8934
Kroll G 4920 **W** 6914
Kropp M 9224 11131
ᴿ5103 9150 9325
Krug J 6830
K r u g e r A 2 1 2 9 **M**
9439 **P** 3614 3814
Kruijf G de 7037

Lana I ^E493
Lancaster S 1488
Lancel S 13565
Lancellotti M 10575
  10866 12059 ^R542
  699
Lanchantin É 9749
Lanci J 1199
Landes G ^R4603
Landfester M ^E790
Landgraf J 12162
Landgrave G 5645
  6831 **Gándara D**
  5648
Landgráfová R ^R9264
Landman C 7925 **G**
  ^R6249
Landmesser C 5298
  5911 8175
Landon M 3528
Landrus H 6468
Landtsheer J de
  ^E11283
Landy F 192 4211
  4233
Lanfranchi G 11392 **P**
  11552
Lang B 2517 7180
  7639ss 7961 7981
  8245 10923 ^E809
  888s ^R2814 4907 **M**
  ^R6436 **W** 5293 5408
  8204 8508
Langa P ^R5004 9735
  13542
Lange A 4149 9789
  9872 9935 9990
  ^E303 482 ^R252 **G** 193
  8707 **N de** 10076
  ^R544 1073 **U** 8205
Langeac R de 3830
Langella A 13978
Langenhorst A 1041 **G**
  1687 4332 4947
  ^E1702
Langevin P ^D2961
Langkammer H ^D6727
Langlamet F ^R1196
Langner C 1788
Langston S 4921
Langton D 10390
Langwald M ^E1606
Lanham C ^E9497

Laniak T ^R3072 3392
Lannon J 6895
Lanzillotta L 9750
Lapatin K 12060
Laperrousaz E 12458
Lapidge M ^M13725
Lapin H 11644
Lapinkivi P 11078
Laplanche F ^E420
Laporte J 13463
Lappe W ^R9429
Laras G 4010 11511
Larché F 12582
Largo Domínguez P
  ^R3473
LaRocca-Pitts E
  2807
Larsen D 1432 8425
  M 9190 **S** 9516
Larson G 2211
Larsson G 1942 2617
  3187 3390 **T** 6247
Lasine S 7682 7789
Lasker D 10026
Lassègue M ^R9691
Latacz J 12876
Lataire B ^E72
Lategan B 1200
  7282s **L** 1433
Lathuilière P 1546
Latorre i Castillo J
  9631
Latré G ^E268
Lattke M 9576ss
Lau B 10391
Laub F ^D8751
Lauchsinger J
  ^R10069
Lauer S 10503
Laufs I ^E750
Laughery G 13911
  ^R1159 ^T5990
Laughlin J 11691
Laukkanen P 2087
Launderville D 2130
  ^R3198 4867
Laurant S 2088
  11292 12301
  12495 12789
  ^E12782
Laurence P 13598
  ^{ET}8509 **R** ^E714
  13172 **E** 6669 6925

J ^E445
Laurent F 4034 ^R328
Laurentin R 2169 4789
Laurier W 12193
Lausberg H ^M1758
LaVerdiere E 5409
  5820
Lavik M 1201 13959
Lavoie J 4031 7642
  ^R1555 4897 10024
  10536 11949
Law D 1489
Lawall M 12859
Lawrence L 13173
Lawrie D 1202
Lawson S 1434 **V**
  ^R5809
Layton B 9306 ^T10576
  R 13599
Lazarenco O 9381
Lazareth W 13743
Lazzarino del Grosso
  A 1701
Lämmlin G 3574
Läufer E 8982
Làconi M 7227
Le Blay F ^R752
Le Bon P 8831
Le Boulluec A 13354
  13495
Le Bris A 10771
Le Déaut R 782 1881
Le Rider G 12353
Le Roux J 1042 1789
  13836 13886 13908
  ^R4877
Leacock C ^E9526
Leahy A ^E114
Leanza S ^E3903
Leavitt M ^E10331
Lebacqz K 8598
LeBeau B ^E557 569
Lebrun R 10867 12105
  ^E494 683 ^R11094
Lechner T 13370
Leclant J ^E702 9270
  ^R9270
Leclerc T 4212
Leclercq J ^E13621
Leclère F 12263 12763
Lecomte C ^R690
Lecoq P 9487
Ledda G ^R1707

Lev-Yadun S 13076
Lewin A 11805 E498
L e w i s A 8 5 1 0 C
M1720 D 195 G E582
J 1547 R 7791 S
11897 R700 6759
8 6 2 1 T 1 0 9 2 4
E12657 R10962
Leyerle B 12939
Leyrer D 7371
Leyser H E1980
Légasse S 6659 6820
6915 7259
Lémonon J 4791s E539
R2010 2023 6487
6665 8902 9832
Léon Azcárate J de
13772 -Dufour X
8 1 2 2 3 8 8 8 5 9 9
M6257
Létourneau P 6251
8001
Lévinas E M1119
10216 10559 13898-
01
Lévy C E9691 R11480
11523
Li T R9084
Liapis V R10764
Libanius 12685
Libera A de E838
Lichocka B 10733
Lichtenberg R 12271
Lichtenberger A 11583
E13278 R11663 E
D7776 H 3211 7948
9873 9939 10079
D7229 8836 E345 482
542
Lichtert C 4609
Lichtheim M 11015
Liddy R R1122
LiDonnici L 10825
Lidsey J 2358
Liebenberg J 5069
10637s
Lieber L R2795 M
E10226 10393
Liebes Y 9579
Liem J 1206
Lienemann-Perrin C
8318
Lienhard F R4782 J
2184 13567 E826

Lierman J 2638
Lies L 1207 R6423
Liesen J 4087
Lietaert Peerbolte B
6531
Lieu J 3411 9132
10509s R6178 6261
6 2 8 7 1 0 6 6 7 S
1 0 6 1 0 R1 0 6 0 3
10620
Lieven A von 10577
1 0 8 2 6 1 1 0 1 6 s
R11018
Liew T 1689 5540
6252s 8671 R5592
Lightfoot J 10925 N
7500
Lightstone J 1548
10139
Ligo A 7145 V 7883
Lilla S T13527
Lilliu G 12629
Lilyquist C 12163
Lim J 983 2268 2878
L 8672 T 6689ss
9874s E499 9792
R307 4937
Limburg J 3491 3575
K 4564
Limentani G 3391
L i m e t H 1 1 3 9 3
11824 R2788
Linafelt T 3072 3392
3854 4403 E346s
R3868
Linant de Bellefonds
L 12747 P E757
L i n c o l n A 6 2 5 4 s
7284
Lind S T8961
Lindars B 6119
L i n d b e c k G 1 9 6
M1143
Lindemann A 4794
7061 8027 8881
D5627 E152 573
R2167 6886 8319
8886 8898 9744
L i n d e n N ter 984
5089
Linder A 4105
Lindner H 11555 M
12612 R 11592

Lindsay D R7298
Linetsky M E10316
Lingad C 6120
Linington S 9024
Link A 6356 C 7618
8166 -Wieczorek U
E101
Linke B R11626 11631
Linnemann E 7518
Linss W R552 7010
Linville J R1093
Lion B 13036 R125
Lipiński E 9541 11247
12866 R4452 11663
Lipschits O 3286 3345
9046
Lipscomb D M1208
Lis M 2131 13837
Liss H 4214 10356
Lissarrague F 12164
Litke J 2883
Litosseliti L E9519
Litrico L R6908
Littauer M 11814
Little D 1208
Litwak K R609 687
4687 6594 7754
Litz G 11970
Liverani M 12770s E15
12950 R478 11410
Livingston D 12303
Livingstone A R9165
Livius M6040
Livni M 3052
Livsis V E27
Liwak R E179 R4464
Ljungberg B 3073
L l e w e l y n S 9 1 3 3
9445s E4 9443s
Llop J 11394
Lloyd G 10799 -Jones
D 7039
Lo Cascio E E686
Lo Cicero C 1985
Lo L-kwong 7044
Lo Prinzi D 3994
Loader J 1549 1844
2230 3904 11293 W
4795s 5216 5639
R211
Lobato Casado A 3642
T3643
Lobrichon G 3243
3855

Lundager Jensen H
3086 10927
Lundberg M 9940
Luneau R E8087
Luomanen P 5126
R5016
Luper M R8421
Lupieri E 6533 10611
Lupu E R699
Lurie V R10043
Lurson B 11898
R11039
Lusini G 9751
Lust J 892 1821 3451
4433 4462 E10 R26
1949
Lustiger J 10511
Luter A 6534
Luther A E521 M
13767 M2061 2915
3617 3693 3744
5218 13730-62
Lutterbach H 7793
Luttikhuizen G 9752
D5970 E574
Luukkainen M E502
Luukko M 11395
Lux R 2565 2585 3905
4526
Luz U 4799 4975
5091-4 5127 5265
5410s 11191 E550
Luzarraga J 3856 6398
9877
Luzzatto A 10394
12401 S M10359
10557
Lübbe J 8985s 9941
Lücke F M13813
Lücking S 3212
R14030
Lüddeckens D 10663
Lüdemann G 4800s
5487 6026 6661
8177 M5496
Lüdorf G 11856
Lührmann D ET9723
F77 R5599
Lüken S 11972
Lüpke J von E419
Lüscher B 11018
Lütgehetmann W 6339
Lybaek L 5304

Lycan W 9521
Lygre J 5914
Lyons M R797 818
W 2503 2518
Lys D 2134

Maag V †14053
Maaijer R de R9554
Ma'ani S 9225
Maarschalk R 3765
Maarten van Lint T
12402
Mabundu Masamba
F 1045
MacAdam H 12640
MacCammon L
R8581
Macchi J E93
Maccoby H 2831
MacCormick C 3213
MacCulloch D
R13793
MacDaniel J 1435
MacDonald B 12534
12622 D 5602 E575
687 F R13996 M
7350 N 13849
Maceri F 6256
MacEwen A 3531
MacGillivray J
11735
MacGinnis J 9550
MacGinty G E2243
Macgregor A R2044
S R11400
MacGuckian M 4802
MacGuire F 7323
Mach D T3299
Machinist P E9173
Macierowski E
T13660
Macin A R5115
MacIntosh J 6089
Macías Villalobos C
E1999
Mack B 203
MacKay J R3462
Mackenzie C 2043 E
7041 I 1210 N
12546
Maclean I R386 839
J R608 T10802
Macleod D 4985 R
E503

MacMullen R 11645
MacNiccoll P 3766
Macpherson J R10691
MacQueen H E499
MacRae G 6165
Macris C 9447
Macwilliam S 4356
Madden N R8094
Maddin R 11743
Madel K 8602
Madelin H R143
Madsen C R2031 4963
Maeir A 12748
Maeland B 7140
Magarik L 4150
Magaz J E655
Magazzù C T13569
Magen Y 10018 12215
12305 12403
Maggi A 204
Maggiali L 8137
Maggioni B 1211 1355
4803 7706 8276 C
R8708
Magid S 10227 E10357
Magin C 10291
Magirius G 1046 3465
Maglioni S T10261
Magnani G 7643 8028
8092s
Magness J 9794s E40
R11781 12447 12458
Magnone P 11175
Magnoni I E353
Magonet J 4547 4592
Magrini S 1986
Magris A 10578
Maher M 3871 R3463
8526
Mahé J 10652 11462
Maia F 6257
Maier B 8427 C 3959
4335 13285 R3966 H
6535s 11973 R13165
J 3412 3713 7926
10080ss R10183
10185 11870 M
4336 P 1690 T
R3698
Maillard A 6258
Maillat J & S 13077
Maillot A 3939s
Mainberger-Ruh E
T8187

Markoe G 11250
Markschies C 8002
 9401 10601 13406
 13455
Markus R ^{R}13629
Marler S ^{R}5796
Marone P 13641
Marot C ^{M}3455
Marotta B 13617
Marquard O ^{M}10662
Marquardt F 6618
 †14054 ^{M}421 10523
Marques G ^{T}1464 V
 ^{R}1098 6674
Marquis G 1947
Marra A ^{E}770
Marrow S 6259 ^{R}6678
Marsden R 1987
Marsh C ^{R}8096
Marshall C 8603 D
 ^{R}169 E ^{E}752 G
 ^{R}4909 H 9408 ^{R}314
 7091 I 1651 4675
 7462 7287 8191
 8514 9384 ^{D}7468
 ^{E}2170 ^{R}146 556 5749
 7469 J 9753 13178
 ^{R}8836 M 3577 ^{R}8595
Martello C ^{ET}13695
Martens D 6940 E
 2760
Marti H ^{R}13561
Martin A 9580 ^{R}9470
 C ^{R}12745 D 4807
 9383 de Viviés P de
 9670 F 5992 7016
 †14055 ^{R}14 J 3578 L
 11975 12693 ^{E}1436
 M 9449 P 11976 R
 2044 13178 ^{E}7396 T
 6980 6997 7288s
 ^{R}4801 5355 7261
Martinez E ^{D}5139
 6891 Garcia J 4808
 P 12306 -Sève L
 12061 12736
Martini C 356 1047s
 3579 10514 ^{E}11722
 ^{M}1019 1054 3569
 13903 13988 13997
 14001
Martino S de 10869
Martí Aixalà J 12924

Martín Contreras E
 10229s J 13336
 Riego M ^{R}660
 6628 T ^{T}13571
 Vegas R ^{T}5620 -
 Asensio G 5993 -
 Moreno J 6260
Martínez Cavero P
 13636 de Pisón
 Liébanas R 8428
 Puche J 8697 Ruiz
 C ^{E}5266
Martone C ^{R}4508
Martuccelli P 8323
Martyn J 6762 7260
 7290 ^{R}6839
Marucci C 6612
 7795 8832
Marx A 7646 O
 ^{T}10351 T 3580
 4987
Maschke T ^{E}56
 ^{T}13735
Masciarelli M 8708
Masenya M 1215
 7796 13838 ^{R}238
Maser S ^{E}77
Mashiah R 1845
Mashkour M 13037s
Masini M 8429 8515
 ^{R}6112
Masoga A 1216
Mason A ^{E}839 R 955
 S 11556ss ^{T}11559
Masselli G 9498
Massmann L 11397
Master J 2858
Mastin B ^{R}4508
Mastrocinque A
 10579
Mateos J 5543 6142
Matera F 1437 7235
 8864 ^{E}1 294 ^{R}8304
 8572 13481
Mathauser Z 1217
Mathew A 2231
Mathews E ^{R}3103 S
 ^{R}6502
Mathewson D 1791
 6636 S 1438
Mathiesen T ^{R}749s
Mathieu B 3833
 12782 Y ^{R}328

Mathis C 3822
Mathlin T 6763
Mathys H 11512
Matjaž M 5605
Matlock R 6693 6764
Matoïan V 11857
 ^{E}12137
Matovina T ^{E}335
Matskevich Z 12512
Matson M 1792 5932
 6143 6167
Matsuoka F 1739
Mattam J ^{R}6301 8770
 10687
Matteo A 5244
Matter E ^{R}13650
 13660
Matthews C 6060 ^{E}893
 9739 ^{R}4699 5993 M
 5924 P 9559 R
 12722 12993 V 4151
 11251s ^{R}4154 10107
 12785
Matthey J 4809 5129
Matthiae G 8123 P
 3214 11398 12673s
 12725 ^{E}15
Matthias M ^{R}13800
Mattila H 5130 R
 11399
Mattingly D ^{E}504 K
 2973
Mattioli U 8647
Mattison R 8785
Mattox M ^{R}1601
Matura T 2390 8516
Maunder C ^{R}8704
Maurer A ^{R}1569 6734
 U ^{T}11916
Maximus C ^{M}13521
 13714s
May G 7135 13407s
 13869 ^{E}578 M 13179
 N 12217 R ^{R}10724
Mayemba K 5884
Mayer A 7363 B ^{E}69 C
 ^{E}777ss G ^{D}10138
 12426 ^{T}10140 R
 3414 S ^{E}2615 W
 3215 12695 12723
 13480 ^{E}9079 -
 Modena M ^{E}689 -
 Opificius R 11899
 W ^{R}13481 13486

Mehedintu V 8324
Meid W E676
Meier J 4811-4
Meijer F 6103
Meilaender G 8604
Mein A 4434
Meinhold A 209 2392
2640 2734 2737
3615 3693 3857
3942 3960s 3968
3980 3982s 3987
4649 7800s
Meiser M 5766 6766
R5219 6273
Meissner B 11753 W
8519
Mejía J 1356 7929
10516
Mekkattukunnel A
5070 5957s
Mela R R952
Melaerts H E711
Melanchthon M 7982
8674 P 1399
Melançon L R8782
Melania M8509
Melcher S 2856
Melchert C 9338 H
10871 R11453
Melczewski P 6767
Melhem I 12592
Melini A 258
Melito S M1352²ss
Mell U E5 R5321 5324
5367
Mellado P 3769
Mello A 4287 7707
ET10231
Melloni J R7877
Melo L 8431
Meloni P 7854
Melugin R R4193
Melville D 11866 S
11400
Men A 4815
Mena López M 3230
4391
Menahem ben S M3350
10311
Menchetti A 9239
Mende T 2393 E55
Mendels D 9581
10395 11513 10517
11560 R228

Mendelssohn M
M10339
Mendenhall G
R10431
Meneses R de R8088
Menestrina G 7930
R498 5425 8877
10046
Menezes R de 10928
Mengozzi A ET1692
Menirav J 10232
Menke K 8247 8709
Menken M 5453
6441
Menn E 10233
Menozzi D R11925
Mentgen G 10292
Mentzer R R3455
Menu B 3097 11344
Mercer C R579
Merceron R R11520
Mercier P 4435
Merdinger P R5405
Meredith A 5267 D
R2135
Merenlahti P 1315
Meri J 11155
Merian M the Elder
M11977 S 1961
Merino J 2311 M
E7054 Rodríguez
M T5002 5004
Merk O 1802 E105
Merkelbach R E9452
Merker G 12899
Merklein H 4816
E5006
Merkur D 1748
Merli A 2586
Merlo P 4156 10929
E10935
Meroz R 10329
Merrill E R2983 4193
4634
Merrillees R 12168
Merton T 985s
Merz A 4817 4870
4934 S E11849
Mescerskij N
M11530
Meschonnie H T2245
Meshel Z 12827
Meshorer Y 12354

Meskell L 12749s
Meskin J 10234
Messa P 13690
Messeri G 9453
Messina M 13602
Mesters C 4818 8520
Methodius O M13525
Metreveli H E13501
Metropolit Pitirim
8521 13464
Metso S 9878 9943
9992
Metternich U 9387
E382
Mettinger T 10930
Metzger B 2135 E813
M 8432 8522 12501
Metzler D 11979 K
2334s 9192 13572
E28 R326
Metzner R 6262 7404
R6128
Metzsch F von E11980
Meulenaere H de
R9276 12279
Meunier B R7359 7691
13299 13370 13383
13386 13394
Meurer G 11023 S
E2063 T 982 1049ss
1219 3059 7647
Mewe T 2102
Meyer A R6231 D
1441 J 11401 M
5607 9308 10639
E103 505 579 R
R9322 zu Capellen J
11981
Meyers C 10931
11254 E1609 R12500
E 11514 11694
D12158 R513 -
Zwiffelhoffer E
11647
Meynet R 956 1793
5010 5071s 5491
5767 5954
Meza R 5661
Mezzadri B 10773
Mébarki F 12407
12441
Mégier E 13708
Mgaloblishvili T
12878

Molla S 1705
Molnar M 5162 **P**
8138
Moloney F 211 5544
6145 6263ss 6375
^{R}6128 6288 6484 **R**
8094 ^{R}1122 13660
Moltmann J 8248
^{M}6627 7632 ^{M}8275 -
Wendel E 8744
Moltz H 3038
Moly T 8095
Mommsen T 11648
Monaco S ^{E}11507
Monari L 4450 5609
8377
Monchot H 12311
13041
Mondin B ^{R}8098
Monera A 7042
Monferrer Sala J
^{ET}3351 9645
Mongillo D 7050
Monheit M ^{R}13775
Monnet P ^{R}13265
Monroe W 13705
Monroy A 3536
Montagnes B 13897
Montagnini F 5935
7079 ^{R}617 4833
Montagu J 11837
Montanari A ^{T}13573
Montano A ^{M}13790s
Montanti C ^{R}3995
Montefiore C ^{M}10390
Monteiro E ^{E}650
Montero S 11617 ^{R}703
Montes M ^{T}13210
Montevecchi O ^{R}9471
Montfort C 5361
Montgomery H ^{E}642
Monti S 2312 2394
2441 2483
Montserrat-Torrents J
^{R}14064
Monzio Compagnoni
G 8433
Moo D 6916s 7584
Moor J de 4621 4623
^{D}1893 ^{E}1884ss
Moore A 12682 **E**
^{R}2172 **H**^{D}6593 6895
J 2360 **M** 1053 3002

^{R}2210 2788s 7789
7932 10431 **R**
6768 ^{E}13742 **S**
6848 7803 -
Jumonville R 1222
Mooren L ^{E}688 711
Mor L 1733
Mora Paz C 299 **V**
5132 5311
Morag S ^{E}689
Moral A ^{R}5816 7612
Morales A 12312 **J**
2313 4823 8524
Moran G 7709 **W**
212 2442-8 2908
2932 3022 3770
4158s
Morandini S ^{R}4903
Mordillat G 4824
More T (St) 5444
Moreau A ^{E}690 **P**
11649
Moreen V 10396
Moreland M ^{R}5016
5098 ^{R}12496
12498
Moreno García A
6446 7001 ^{E}5269
^{R}7218 7758 **J**
^{R}12291 **Martínez J**
8060
Morenz L 9135 9274
9275 10828 11025s
12222 13254
Moreschini C 1652
13457 ^{E}13452
^{T}13458
Moretti J ^{E}758
Morey J 2047
Morfino M 10237s
Morgan D 3906 **R**
4825 6168 6769
^{R}181 7819 **Gillman**
F 6102 6266 **T**
^{R}529
Morgen M 6465
Morgenstern M
10239 10397 ^{R}407
Morgenthaler C 7765
Moriconi B 6637
^{E}424
Morin G ^{E}13622
Moritz T ^{R}8820

Morla V ^{R}2410 ^{T}8781
Morley N 11297
Moro C 3984
Morolli D 9756
Morray-Jones C 10330
Morreall J 8003
Morrice W 9725
Morrill B ^{R}8534 **M**
1913
Morris C ^{E}753 10706 **I**
12900
Morrison C 3103
13905 **G** ^{R}6969 **H**
^{R}270 **M** 10085
Morrissey M 1443
Morrow W 2948
Morschauser S ^{R}7912
Morse D ^{E}383
Morselli G ^{M}1728 **M**
^{E}10349
Mortensen B 1887
Morton A 9455 **R**
^{R}5043 5739 6633
Mosala I 1749
Moscatelli L 1054
Moschetta J 4826
Moscovitz L 10240
Moseley N ^{R}2242
Moser M ^{R}6921 **P**
^{E}639
Mosetto F 6770 7126
Mosher M 9276
Mosis R 4453
Moskala J 2847 ^{R}8975
Moss A 3962 **C** 5133
Mostert W 213
Motta G 2314
Motte A 10829 ^{R}10756
Motyer A 957 4199 **J**
4200 **S** 12960
Moule C 4676
Moulinet D 915
Mounce W 7463
Mount C 5768 ^{R}6824
Mourad S 9726
Moussa A 12300
Mouton A ^{R}776 **E**
5346 7364 13865 **J**
^{E}12828
Moutsopoulos E 10775
Mouw R 4303
Mowery R 5134 ^{R}3217
Mowinckel S 4160

Naluparayil J 1794 5612 ᴱ361
Nannini D 7931
Nanos M 7293ss 7326 ᴱ6668 ᴱ7273 ᴿ552 7010
Naor B 2587
Napier D 6995
Napolitano M 9456
Nardin R 8061 ᴱ916
Nardoni E †14059 F ᵀ3075
Naré L 3986
Naro M 1795 4830 8005 ᴿ2452
Nash K 10640 P 2396
Naskhai B ᴿ12534
Nason L 7168 ᴱ278
Nasrabadi B ᴿ11780
Nasrallah L 7158
Natalini G ᵀ3559
Natoli S 6771 9457
Naudé J 8989s ᴱ581 ᴿ1947 2135 8947 9978 10123
Nauerth C ᴿ11849 11964 T 2484
Nault F 2449
Naumann-Steckner F ᴿ10878
Naumowicz J 8326
Naurath E 1056 ᴱ1057
Navarro Puerto M 5613 ᴱ5816
Nave G 5770
Naveh J 8991 12111 ᴿ9079
Navia Velasco C 5163
Navone J 2397 5073 5495 6268 11986
Navrátilová H ᴿ11367
Nayak I 7234
Naylor P 7215
Nazzaro A 6903
Nápole G 2979 3331 11255
Ndubuisi L 7159
Neagoe A 5771
Neamțu M ᴿ8052
Nebe G 6772 ᴿ9883
Nebes N ᴱ507 692
Need S 6370
Neef H 3045 ᴿ14071

Negev A ᴱ869
Negri A 3773s
Nehmé L 12613
Neil B ᴱᵀ13714
Neirynck F 5950
Nel G 8155 M 4483s 4498 4504s 8379 ᴿ4493 8684 10742 P 3908 7661 7683 ᴿ1307
Nelson R 2909 3005 ᴿ3003
Nemet-Nejat K 9193
Nemirovskaya A 9542
Nenna M ᴱ12275
Nepi A 2619 2727 ᴿ3437 ᵀ4812
Neri C ᴿ2180 U 6406
Nersinger U 8207
Nestle E 1909
Netzer A 3454 E 9797 11781 12314 12454
Neu E 9343
Neubrand M 1058 4989 6974
Neudecker R 10241
Neudorfer H ᴱ381
Neuenfeldt E 2396
Neufeld D 6548 ᴿ6537 K ᴿ4843
Neuhaus D 6773 R ᴱ508 10398
Neumann G ᶠ80 H 934 K 1225s T ᴱ209 -Gorsolke U ᴱ13079
Neuner J 1359 P 8355 ᴱ426ss
Neusner J 870 5329 10088ss 10242-9 10399 10448 10519 10672 13576 ᴱ509ss 860 4895 10091ss 10131 ᴹ4915 ᴿ14047
Neves J 5011
Nevett L 11475
Neveu F ᴿ9262
Nevill A ᵀ11377 13565

Neville D 5046 R 8096
New D 13294
Newby Z ᴿ12265
Newheart M 6269
Newlands G 13859
Newman C ᴱ362 582 4831 J 1583 7884 13319 ᴹ1472 13815
Newport J 10691 K 6549
Neyrand L ᵀᴱ3838
Newsom C 3775s
Neyrey J 6270s 6392
Négrier P 11029
Ng W 6272
Ngugi J 6057
Nguyen Manh Thu R 6123
Nibbi A 11819 ᴿ14024
Niccacci A 3909 4015 4650 ᴿ3100 8949
Nicholas H ᴹ13716 L ᴹ13717
Nichols S 13749
Nicholson E 2215 ᴿ2223 P 873 S 3124
Nickelsburg G 9615s ᶠ81 ᴿ4481
Nicklas T 1910 3424 5863 6273 6350 9727
Niclós J 3651 Albarracín J 8940
Nicol M 1444 1681
Nicolaus L ᴹ13659
Nicole É 2728 3777 R 215 1491ss 1553 4990s 7538 8178 8208 8278 8356 13780s 13850 13878
Nicolet C 216 ᴱ762 - Pierre H 12357
Nicolle C ᴱ12137
Nida E 2138
Niditch S 1653 ᴿ2983
Niebuhr K 8885 11515 ᴿ806 8330
Niedner F 4376
Niedźwiecki W ᴱ13359
Niehl F 1059 2450
Niehoff M 9692
Niehr H 9881 10934s

O'Collins G ^{D}6050
^{E}623s ^{F}86 ^{M}8041
O'Conaill S 8156
O'Connell M ^{T}832
O'Connor D 12783
^{E}11347 **F** ^{M}1730 **K**
1230 4340 4405 **M**
8941 8993
O'Day G 1446 6274
O'Donnell D 8434
O'Donovan O 1231s
3125 3910 6275
6552 6943 7035
7038 8648-51 8835
^{M}272
O'Fearghail F 5995
O'Grady J ^{E}169 **R**
^{E}11987
O'Kane M 11988 ^{E}585
^{R}11937
O'Laughlin M ^{E}4832
O'Loughlin T 2247
^{E}586 ^{R}1925
O'Mahony A ^{E}764 **K**
7440
O'Neil E ^{TE}9432
O'Neill J 218 2317
7152 7550 ^{R}7493
O'Reilly J 1911
O'Sullivan O ^{E}364
O'Toole R 5862 ^{D}5774
^{R}5801
Oakes B ^{R}8426 **E**
^{R}5339 **P** 7390s ^{E}363
^{R}7425
Oakman D 8607s
11590 ^{R}13209
Oates D 12721 **J** 9458
12721
Oberdorfer B 5496
Oberforcher R 4164 ^{R}6
287 2535 4659
10148
Oberhammer G ^{E}11176
Oberhänsli-Widmer G
10253 10308
Oberlinner L ^{D}6287
6462 ^{R}7201
Oberthür R 2451
Obler L 9523
Oborji F 5137
Obruśnik **M** 4088
Ochs P 10177 10254
^{E}2680

Ochsenschlager E
12720
Ochtendung U ^{E}111
Ocker C 13662
Ockinga B 9277
Odasso G ^{D}3629
Oded B 11258
Odell M ^{E}4416
Oden A ^{E}512 **T**
^{E}5004 5545
Odendaal M 4447
Oechslen R 10520
Oegema G 4925s
6776 7317 8836
9583 ^{E}345 ^{R}582
6476
Oehler M ^{R}5
Oehmen-Vieregge R
^{E}98
Oelkers J 7808
Oelsner J 2785
11405 ^{R}14058
Oeming C ^{T}8863 **M**
1233 3493 3584
^{E}1447 ^{T}8863
Oesch J 4596 ^{E}339
Oeste G ^{R}1629
Oettinger N 9344s
Oeyen C 6427
Ofer Y 1847s
Ofilada M ^{R}5533
Ogden D 10830 ^{R}690
10761 **G** 2142
3043 3098
Ogilvie-Herald C
2606
Ognibene S 12225
Ognibeni B 2399
^{R}4194 †14028
Oh J 2316
Ohler A 13187
Ohlhausen S 2049
Ojewole A 2400
Okoronkwo M 6085
Okoye J ^{R}387
Okure T 7419 13940
Olajubu O 6391
Olasagasti M ^{T}4861
Olbricht T 7523
9694 ^{E}553
Old H 8528 13766
Oldenhage T 5330
10400

Oldfield J ^{R}6997 8084
^{T}13542
Olinger D ^{R}7967
Oliva M ^{R}10576
Oliver G ^{E}693 **J** 1993
Oliverius J ^{R}9136
Olivi P 13718 ^{M}13718
Olivier J 12108 **G**
3594 **P** ^{R}7759
Olles H ^{R}13816
Olley J 4417
Olmo Lete G del 9088
9543 11809 14011
^{E}35 ^{R}9668 11863
13072 **Veros R del**
^{R}821
Olschewski J ^{E}98
Olsen R ^{R}832
Olshausen E ^{E}13122
Olsson B ^{E}513
Olthuis J ^{R}13900
Oltrogge D 1978
Oluseyi J 5933
Olutola P 6553
Olyan S 2809 ^{E}76
Omanson R 2143
Ombrosi O ^{T}1596
Omerzu H 6075
Ometto F 5012
Onwukeme V 5861
Oñoro Consuegra F
5824 **F** 3621 3628
3631 3652 5270
Oosterhuis T ^{R}10439
Oosting R 4284
Oppen E von 3415
Oppenheim M von
^{M}11738 12693
Oppenheimer A ^{E}514
11517
Orde K vom 3104
Oredsson D 3153
11782 ^{R}10927
Oren E ^{E}66 515 **S**
12990 **-Nordheim M**
12391
Orfali M ^{E}487
Origenes 6907 6921
7348 13430 ^{M}4316
5267 6366 7078
7314 7341 7691
9677 13418-51
Ornan T 11905

Panzram S 3218
Pao D 5997s 6778
Paolucci G E11157
Papapolychroniou E
  E9460
Papathomas A 3632
  R9470 13094 13250
Papazian D 12410
Pappalardo C 11755
Paracelsus M13792
Parambi B 5139
Parapetti R 12575
Parappally J E650
Parathanam T R202
Parayre D 13043 E516
Pardee D 10938
  12656s 12657
  13044s 9059 9089
  R9948 10929 12662
Pardes I 2233
Pardilla A 8530
Pardo I 4383
Parente F 11563
Parfitt T 10402 13120
Paris P 13907
Parisi S 5999 E123
Parisinou E 10779
  R11475
Park E R5669 J 7181 R
  R13078
Parker D 1823 1912s
  7594 E13767 R1922
  7553 G R6512 K
  R192 R 10780
  R10782 S 9090
  12557
Parke-Taylor G 4341
Parkinson R 9278
  9551 W 8030
Parmegiani N E12879
Parmentier M 7810
Parpola S 4165 11382
  11406 E712 11373
Parravicini G 8712
  11990
Parrinello R R8438
Parris D 5332
Parrot A M87 D R5019
Parry D 9882 R 2566
Parsenios G 6408
Parsons M 13752 S
  E431
Partee C 10692

Partridge R 11810
Parunak H R4178
Pascual R 2362
  Torró J E13627
Pascuzzi M 6779
  R1645 4923
Paseggi M 2539
Pasquale G 11301
  13670
Pasquato O F88
  R13381
Pasquetto V 6125
  8435 R1810 4737
  5556 5644 6135
  8429
Passarella R 13107
  13618
Passaro A 3778 3882
  E3995
Passi S 13663
Passoni dell'Acqua A
  3395 4229 R3229
Pastis J 10524
Pasto J 11584
Pastor F D13570 Ra-
  mos F R6836 6909
  7259
Pate C 7094
Patella M 6404
  R5932
Patfoort A 9390
Pathrapankal J 219s
  5217 8125
Patillon M ET9500
Patiner J R6269
Patitucci S 6076
Patrich J 11825
  12411s 12477ss
  E12973 R12373
Patrick D 7723
  R2758
Patrzynski J 6984
Pattarumadathil H
  2622
Patte D 1235 F89
  M13907
Pattee S R6886
Pattemore S 6555
Patterson S 10641
  11302
Pattie T 1824
Patton C 4166 R3202
Patzia A 815

Paul A 1555 4833
  9970 10096 R307
  499 539 741 858
  1856 3933 9688
  9690s 9792 9883
  9974 10012 11263
  11522 11539 11583 I
  4675 S 1656
Paulsell W 3585
Paupert C 8250 E11991
Pavlou T 8097
Pavúk P 12171
Pawlak L 1362
Pawlikowski J 10525
Paximadi G 3539
Payne G 6904
Payton J R13524
Paz C 1236s 5913 Y
  12172 13255
Pazzini M 3076s 4597
  8994 13913 R6671
  13625
Peabody D E5048
Peace R 6065
Pearce J E12315 S
  11596
Pearcy L R13098
Pearl C 10097
Pearson B 9617 10580
  E10530 R12798 J
  11728
Pease L 13279
Pecchioli Daddi F E61
  11231
Pečírková J R713 9640
  11066 11382 11419
Peck E 11908 W
  12067
Pedde F E12729
Peden A 9279
Pedersen N 10613 S
  7019
Pedico M 8713
Pedro de Valencia
  5269 E 4288
Peek-Horn M 4465
Peels H 3540
Peerbolte B R5212
Peeters R 13851
Pegler S R8510
Pego Puigbó A R1301
Peláez J E695
Peleg Y 1610 12316
  12983

Pruzsinszky R 9196 [R]11215 12691 12727
Pryce M [E]8535
Pryor J 9465 9729 [R]5324
Ps-Aristoteles 9416
Ps-Dionysius A [M]13526s
Puech E 7964 9091 9139s 9634 9799 9913 9948ss [R]12087
Puhvel J 226 9346s 11431
Puig i Tàrrech A 5142 [E]591
Puigdollers i Noblom R 6700
Pui-Lan K 8678
Pulikottil P 9883
Pummer R 10017
Punnakal J 4528
Punt J 1246 2092 2146 6785s 7937
Pury A de 2671 [D]3036 [E]2186 [F]93
Puthenveettil J 9386
Puthussery J 6561
Putnam R 4017
Puttkammer A 1065 3860
Pyeon Y [R]2991 4265
Pyper H 1613 3154 [E]839
Pythagoras [M]10808
Pyykkö R [E]502

Qalimi Y 10531
Qedar S 12354
Qimron E 9884
Quack J 9280 9466 10833 11033 11463 11867 [R]9254 11040 10976 11330 12757
Quaegebeur J [F]94
Quaglia R 227 1753 2551 2591ss 4499
Quaglioni D 1703 [E]615
Quantin J 1559 [R]603 13769
Quelle C 5616 **Parra** C 5166
Quenot M 11992
Quesada J 2864

Quesnel M 282 2487 6701 [E]370 782s [R]8395
Quevedo [M]4398
Queyrel A [R]12048 **F** 12860
Quezada-del Rio J 13605
Quéré F 8439
Quicke M [R]1438
Quinn J 7470 **-Miscall P** 4202
Quintero L 12539
Quiñones Benítez R 5617
Quirke S [E]9242
Quispel G [F]95 [R]13452
Quodvultdeus 13720
Quoëx F 13681

Raabe P 2051 4171
Raban A 12477
Rabello A 10358
Rabin C 8996
Rabuske I 5655
Raccah W 2961
Rachaman Y 2594
Rad G von [M]13908s
Rader R [R]13303
Radermakers J 3467 [R]5071 8439 8830
Radl W 5804
Radner E 4994 [R]10448 **K** 11406 12041 12359 [R]12975
Radt W 12861
Raeck W [R]11890
Raepsaet G 11815 - **Charlier M** [R]523 9489 11607[R] 11633
Raffaeli B 2319
Ragacs U 10532
Raggenbass N 13798
Raguin Y 8329 11194
Rahner K [M]1666
Raimondi E 2624
Raineri O [E]9323
Rainey A 8997 12773 13942

[R]11246 12767 **D** [R]840
Rainoldi F 3586
Raizen E 8998 [R]8908 **W** 8937
Raj M [R]120 2983 3729 5105
Raja A 5618 11195 **J** 5334
Rajak T 228 10098 11564 [E]52
Rakel C [R]4128
Rakocy W 6077 7308
Rakotoharintsifa A 6947
Ralte L [E]657
Ramage A 12874
Ramat P [R]534
Ramazzotti M 13257
Ramelli I 9503 11651 [ET]10803 [R]222 678 11617[sR]
Ramírez Fueyo F 7032 [R]1094 1312 5835 6005 **Kidd J** 9026 **R** 1851
Ramis Darder F 4263 4269 5167
Ramos D 3780 **F** 3587
Ramón L 4172 **Díaz J** 13442
Rampelberg D [R]12742
Ramsaran R 7392
Ramsey G 2488
Ramshaw G 8282 8536
Rand J du 6787
Raney D [R]11237
Rankin E [R]11879
Raphael [M]11981 **R** 3432
Rapp H [R]9889 9913 **U** 1614 8791
Raschzok K [D]1412
Rashbam [M]10317
Rashi 3484 [M]3651
Rashkover R 10405
Rashkow I 1586 1754 2052
Raskin J 4842
Rasmussen K 9800 **L** 7855
Rasor S 11183
Rast-Eicher A [E]135

Rese M 5498
Resnick I 13664
Ressa P ᴱᵀ13443
Retief F 7818
Reuben C 3455
Reumann J 7393
Reuter R 6702 7411
Reuther R & H 13296
Revel J ᵀ3774
Revell E 8945
Reventlow H 8167
  13320s ᴱ593 ᴿ235
  259 331 1527 2613
  2913
Rex R ᴱ13793
Rexer J 13513
Rey B 5499
Reyes A 12219 12561
Reyff S de ᴿ1724
Reymond B ᴿ799 E
  4054 ᴿ4001 S 5952
Reynard J 9696
  ᴱᵀ13514
Reynolds E 6349 6564
  F 11085 S 12419
  ᵀ11674 -Cornell R
  ᴿ1724
Rémy B 9467
Rhoads D 5620
Rhodes M 11035 P
  ᴱ195
Riaño Rufilanchas D
  ᴿ12857
Ribera-Florit J 1889
  9587 ᴱ4420 ᴿ1876
Ribichini S 12232
  ᴱ699
Ricart I ᴿ13322 14060
Ricca P 13873
Ricci C 13631 M 6079
Rice M 872 11353
Rich J ᴱ724
Richard D 7036 P
  1066 4845 6005s
  8841 W 7466 ᴰ7141
Richardson L ᴿ12926
  M ᴿ8987 ᵀᴱ8980s P
  7083 11785s 12509
  13198 ᶠ99 ᴿ10078 S
  11086
Richerd J 8440
Riches J 7819 ᴿ13481
Richey L ᵀ266

Richter H ᴿ2275 K
  ᴱ8239 R 8614 S
  2995 10614 T
  11260 12843 W
  8946
Rick A 12264
Rickenmann A
  13444
Rico C 6147
Ricoeur P 342s 1560
  ᴹ1263 1301 8588
  13910s
Ridder A 7820
Riddle J 6007
Ridgway B 12068
  ᴱ12044 D 531
Ridley R ᴿ457
Rieck J ᵀ11189
Riede P 229 3781s
  3817 13048-59
  ᴱ13079
Riedel-Spangenber-
  ger I ᴱ436
Riedl A 5272
Rieger H 8213
Riegert R 10629
Riekert S 7818
Riepl C 8946
Riera F 5805
Ries J 10615 ᴱ666
Rieske-Braun U 4846
Riesner R 5829 6285
  7526 14061 ᴿ288
  14062
Rietsch J 13792
Rietz H 8679 ᴿ9917
Riga B ᵀ4281
Rigal J ᶠ100
Rigato M 5457 5779
  5949 8747
Rigby C ᴱ311
Riggs A ᴿ1105 C
  12322
Rihll T ᴱ532
Rijksbaron A 9373
Riley G 8035 -Smith
  J 13289
Rilke R ᴹ2442
Rilloma N 2405
Rinaldi R ᴱ1988
Ring T ᵀ7261
Ringe S 5830 ᴱ332
  ᴿ8160

Ringgren H ᴱ798 819
Riniker C 8842
Ripamonti B 5273
Rippin A ᴱ11137
Risch F ᵀ13515
Riska M 9951
Risse S 10538
Ritch K ᴿ1686
Ritmeyer K & L 11993
Ritner R 11036
Ritschl D ᶠ101
Ritt H ᴰ5832
Ritter A 13516 J 9282
Rittmueller J ᴿ1436
Rius-Camps J 5551s
  5946 6008 6148
  13372 ᵀ13371
Riva F 1740
Rivas L 5227
Rives J ᴿ10109
Rivlin Y 10406
Rizzante A 3370
Rizzardi G 11164
Rizzi A 6853 ᵀ4938 B
  3588 G 2452 ᴰ3816
  L ᴱ9512 M ᴱ653
  ᴿ13490
Rizzuto A 7656
Ro H 2722 J 7885
Robbins T ᴿ10954 V
  1248 1800 5621
Roberge M ᴱ10654
Robert F 782 ᶠ102 P
  de 1249
Roberto Reims ᴹ13721
Roberts D ᴹ11709 J
  230 1659 1801 2338
  2504 2672 3258
  3542 3619 3636
  3646 3673 3783
  3810 4174ss 4216s
  4234 4249 4344
  7417 7950 7988
  9032 10940ss 11408
  13943 M 2363 6469
  R 8214 T ᴿ9358 V
  988
Robertson D ᴱ454
Robin O 13841
Robins W 1250
Robinson A 989 9553
  14076 B 899 8384
  8843 ᴿ5238 7897 E

Rothaug D ^{E}402
Rothaus R 12904
Rothenbusch R 2744
Rothman M 12728
Rothschild J ^{R}743
1876 2165 10319
10325
Rotnemer D 10401
Rotondi P ^{T}12432
12466 12489
Rotroff S ^{E}751
Rotter H ^{D}5249
Rottloff A 12501ss
Rottzoll D ^{T}2625
Rouault O 10944
Roubaud J 3862
Rouers S ^{T}7685
Rouger D 4345
Roughton N 9197
Rouiller G 7501
Roukema R 7657 8036
^{D}9711 ^{R}13422
Roure D 4093 6833
Rouse M ^{R}3074 11971
R 13624
Rousseau J 12784 P
11653 ^{R}13486
Rousset M ^{T}1652
Routledge C ^{R}12208 R
5415
Rouwez J ^{R}6812
Rouwhorst G 8540
10518
Rowe C 8140 ^{E}11654
^{R}8652 R 5623
Rowland C 4485 6031
6567ss ^{E}373 595 W
2365
Rowlands E ^{R}990
Rowlandson J ^{E}518
11358
Rowlett L 3017
Roy L 8615
Royalty R 7414
^{R}12476
Roye W ^{T}13767
Royse J ^{R}9700
Royster D 5220
Rozier G 2645
Rozzo U ^{R}891
Rödding G 2321
Röhser G 4927 7822
8846

Röll W ^{E}3728
Röllig W 9079 9093
^{E}9072 ^{R}9106 9162
12087 12708
Römer M ^{R}11323 T
2148 2218s 2491s
2646 2865 7658s
7939 10945 11116
^{E}93 124 374 2186
2996
Römheld D 3985
Rösel C 3543 H
2980 M 1516 1802
3007 4492 ^{R}769
3337
Rösener C 3089
Röwekamp G 10735
Rubens P ^{M}11999
Rubenstein J ^{T}10262
R 6822
Ruberti A 8103
Rubin L 11996 R
13080 U 11138
Rubinkiewicz R
^{D}4088
Rubiolo S 5230
Ruckstuhl E 6173
Rudman D 4018s T
4466 ^{R}4464
Rudolph D 5670 K
10581 10621
Ruffing K 13232
Rufinus ^{M}1985 ^{T}6907
A 13419
Rufus Shotep 1454
^{M}13722
Ruggieri G 233 V
^{R}669
Ruggiero F 7095
^{R}3838
Ruis-Garrido C
^{T}4724
Ruiz Cabrero L 9094
D 3622 E 3683
^{R}564 López D
5848 Pérez M
8748 Sánchez J
^{E}660 6628
Runacher C 5553
Runesson A 10101s
12234 ^{R}12188
Runia D 9697ss 9700
11519 ^{E}375 11518

^{R}106 9693 11538
^{T}9701
Runions E ^{E}20
Runnels C 11739
Running L ^{R}2050
Rupp D ^{R}14023
Ruppert L 2249 2493s
10541
Rupprecht H ^{E}9469-72
Ruprecht L ^{R}10797
Rurlander D 1367
Rusam D 9403
Rusch W ^{R}7691
Ruschmann S 6287
Rusconi C 8037
Rushton K 8795
Russell B 2702 J
12073 K ^{R}8400 N
13486 R ^{E}652 ^{R}8510
Russo A 1996 L 13721
S 9473
Russouw T 2407
Ruszkowski L 4300
Rutgers L ^{E}39 376
Ruthven J 7373
Rutishauser C 10409
Rutschowscaya M
^{R}12016
Rutter J ^{R}753 N ^{E}700
Ruwe A 9047
Ruysschaert T 5554
Ruzer S 9971 10103
Rüegger H 5653
Rühle I 3414
Rümelin C 11995
Rüpke J 10736s ^{E}12
Rüsen-Weinhold U
3456
Rüster C 12848
Rüterswörden U 2946
Ryan T 11996 13682
Ryckmans J 9227
Ryholt K 9285s
Ryken L 2054
Ryrie A ^{R}6501
Rzeuska T 12325

S aadiah G ^{M}3515
10316
Saari R 9544
Saayman W ^{R}5784
Sabar Y 9141
Sabek Y 9474

Sato M ^{R}5035
Satran D 9589 ^{E}9592
Sattler D 8337 8542
Satzinger H ^{R}9306
  9310
Sauer G 4094 ^{R}65
  4100 J ^{F}107
Saunders S 1452 8847
Sauvage P ^{E}328
Savage S 12540s
Savasta C 2455
Savon H ^{R}6907 1652
Savran G ^{R}1324
Savunen L ^{E}523
Sawicki M 5500 12498
Sawtell W 12622
Sawyer J 4218 7824
  ^{R}4634
Saxer V 8543
Sayão L 8889
Sayegh H 12637
Saz C 11754
Sänger D 7297 ^{R}269 P
  ^{R}8836
Sáenz-Badillos Á
  10294 ^{ED}10315
Sbalchiero P ^{E}846
Sbordone F ^{E}12946
Scagliarini F 12986
  ^{R}156 12681
Scaiola D 3544 3789s
  4062 ^{R}1100 1355
  1937 2520 2747
  3475 3832 3891
  4413 4661 5000
  5072 5557 6497
  6919 7218 7987
Scalabrini P 2490 7224
Scalise C ^{R}1073 P
  4346 S 9513
Scandone Matthiae G
  12235
Scanlin H 9886
Scanlon T 11826
Scanu M 7825
Scarabelli R ^{T}7555
Scarafoni P 8104 ^{E}437
Scarpa A 3791 M
  3590
Scarpi P ^{E}10835
Scarre C ^{E}519 766
Scaturchio V 8038
Scerbo F ^{M}13913

Schaab G 8141
Schaaf Y 1368 ^{R}386
Schaber J ^{E}661
Schaberg J 8749s
  8796
Schach M 3173
Schaefer K 3494
Schall U 10106
Schaller B 234 9590
  ^{D}7411
Scham S 3039
Schamp J ^{R}13487
Schams C 11263
Schapdick S 6357
Schaper J 3332
  12360
Schareika H ^{T}12740
Scharpe M ^{E}4966
Schart A ^{R}584 1527
  4651
Schattner-Rieser U
  ^{R}9012
Schatz K ^{R}5354
Schatzmann S 7161
  ^{D}6753 6904 7096
Schatzmiller J ^{R}2019
Schaube W 991
Schaudig H 9200
  11088 ^{E}28
Schauensee M de
  11841
Schädler U ^{E}747
  12155
Schäfer A 11788
  ^{E}468 B 3469 P
  7686 10414 ^{E}471
  520 767 R 3964
Schäferdiek K 2094
Schärlig A 11869
Schätzel M ^{E}53
Scheck T ^{T}6921
Scheele B 5924
Scheer T 10782
Scheffczyk L 8338
Scheffler E 5883
Scheidegger G 5169
Scheidel W 12753
  13260
Scheidgen A 5437
Scheidler M ^{E}995
Scheindlin R 10295
Schelbert G ^{R}6344
  6652 6825

Schellenberg A 2065
  4021
Schelling P 9053
Schemmel B ^{E}6491
Schenck K 7528
Schenk W ^{R}1644 5547
Schenke G ^{R}9473 H
  †14067 ^{E}10622 ^{F}108
  ^{M}13990 ^{R}6208 9732
  9734 9743 9755
  10654 L 6149
Schenker A 235 2768
  3229 4056 4281
  4290 7898 8216
  ^{D}3850 10947 ^{F}109
  ^{R}3256 7802 14028
Scherb V 10712
Scherer A 3044 3977
  ^{R}3049 3976 7904
  10905
Scherman N ^{E}10226
  10393
Scheuer M ^{R}10662
Schiavo L 5055
Schieffer R ^{R}13639
Schiff A 10143 G
  12236s
Schiffer M ^{E}768
Schiffman L 9801
  9952 9997 ^{E}769
  1876 9802 ^{R}9889
Schiffner K 1038 3174
Schiffrin D ^{E}377
Schillebeeckx E 8105s
  ^{M}8103
Schiller F 1734 ^{M}1733s
Schillhahn W ^{E}53
Schilling P ^{E}13559
Schilson A 7856 8544
Schimanowski G 6599
  9702
Schimmel A 9228
Schipper B 3234 4471
  4487s 11264 ^{E}451
  ^{R}2637 F 11696
  12501 12504s H
  ^{ET}10616
Schirmer W 11789
Schiwy G 4852
Schlaepper C 5656
Schlarb E ^{ET}9723
Schlatter A ^{M}8213
Schleiermacher F
  ^{M}6336 7474

Schürmann H ^{M}8103
Schüssler Fiorenza
[vid. Fiorenza]
Schüssler K 9311
^{E}1963
Schütte W 4551s
Schütz C 4950 8443
Schützeichel H 1369
Schwab A ^{E}723 G
3863
Schwager R 1664
Schwanda T ^{R}8425
Schwank B 6031
Schwankl O 5691
Schwantes M 4549
8618
Schwartz B 2838 D
3416 10296 11567ss
^{E}741 M 3221 9041 S
10109
Schwartzmann J 4023
Schwarz H 13243 K
^{E}610 M 12274 ^{E}723
Schwarzer H 12862
Schwarzmann-Schaf-
hauser D 13104
Schweiker W 8619
Schweitzer A 4860
^{M}13914s F 10526 S
2966
Schweizer E 4861 H
240
Schwemer A 327 6652
8153 ^{E}638 ^{R}6654 D
10879 11089 ^{R}71
Schwendemann W
3792 ^{R}2615
Schwendner G 9312
Schweyer A 11466
Schwiderski D 3337
Schwienhorst-Schön-
berger L 4024 ^{D}3547
Schwier H ^{E}10495
Schwikart G 8217 ^{E}438
Schwindt R 7365s
^{R}6128
Scibilia A 10836
Scibona C 10584 R
4548
Scippa V 3495
Scognamiglio E 1500
8848 ^{R}614 775
Scolas P ^{E}636

Scopello M 10585
Scoralick R 2812
3708 3975 3981
4557 7829 ^{R}3940
Scordato C 5440
Scott A 13446 B
3757 D 1501 I
9703 J 4678 8891
9659 ^{R}6083 L 4930
P 1254
Screech M 7830
Scriba A ^{R}4840
Scrivener F ^{M}1915
Scroggs R 6704
^{R}6839
Scullion J 1069 S
^{R}675
Scurlock J 11090
12327 13061s
Sear D 12361
Searcy E 4347
Seddik Y 11140
Seddon P ^{R}2172
7065
Sedlmeier F 4421
4454
Sedmak C 1665
Sed-Rajna G 1853
Seeanner P 6433
Seebass H 2250
2866s ^{R}2249 2523
Seeden H 12643
Seeher J 12238s
12851ss
Seeliger H 12931
Seeligmann I 4292
Seepe-Breitner A
10898
Seesengood R ^{R}7470
Seetzen U 13278
Sefati Y 11091
^{E}9201
Segal A 4931 7255
10586 11599
11790 12514 B
9953 12437 J 9142
M 3114 3336 3717
R 10713
Segalla G 5781 6335
8040 ^{R}3544 5216
6344 6364 6919
8902

Segert S 4501 4862
9803 19 67 165 525
2623 7954 9783
9796 9798 9802
9897-900 9914 9924
9974 10002 12660
Segovia 241 6328 ^{E}70
^{R}592 6298
Seibert E ^{R}3270
Seidel J 10264 ^{E}729
Seidensticker T 11141
Seidl T 3864 3872 U
12118
Seifrid M 6705 ^{E}287
Seigne J 12576ss
12589
Seijas de los R G 4220
7831 M 2924
Seiler S 3155 ^{R}3158
Seim T 5948 ^{R}6844
Seitz C 4996s ^{R}4252
7875 E 5716 M 5265
Sekine S 3946
Sela S 10319
Seland T 7318
Seligman J 12420
Sell A 7716
Sellew P 14014 ^{E}104
Sellin G ^{R}6128
Selz G 2787 9202
^{R}8978
Sembrano L 12421
Semen P 2813
Semi E 10402
Senft C 8340
Senior D 875 4694
5098s 8545
Senneville-Grave G de
^{ET}13639
Sentamu M ^{R}300
Seow C 3117 7832
Sequeri P ^{R}12019
Sermoneta H ^{E}9002
Sermonti G 10714
Serra A 5838 5854
Serrano V 5201 6011
Serroul L ^{R}7944
Serwint N ^{E}12880
Sesboué B 7833 13383
^{R}628 5235 8260
13381 13421
Setälä P ^{E}523
Setio R 2956

Singer A 10267 **C**
  ᴿ8902 **I** 10880s
  ᴹ1723 -**Avitz L**
  12174
Singor H ᴱ126
Siniscalchi C 3793
Sion O 11793
Sipilä S ᴱ1949
Siquans A ᴱ2925
Siqueira T 3639 3645
Sirat C 9005s **R** 10268
  ᶠ112
Sirboni S 5273
Sisack V 7372
Sisley J 1696
Sisson R 5057 5301
Sitaramayya K 3729
Sivatte R de 4349
  ᴿ1070 4148
Sivertsev A 11669
Sjöberg Å 2339 **M**
  ᴿ3034
Ska J 1256 2221-4
  2457 2496s 2542
  7836s 11305 ᴿ374
  2983 2996
Skarsaune O 10551
Skemp V 3361 ᴿ3360
Skierkowski M 8041
Skillen J 8653
Skinner A ᴱᵀ10415 **M**
  ᴿ5755
Sklba R 8341
Skocir J ᴱ56 ᵀ11936
Skolnik F ᴱ861
Skrzyp B 8126
Skubiszewski P ᴿ3074
  11971
Skupien Dekens C
  ᴿ3455
Sladeczek F 12004
Slattery J ᴿ4522
Slawiński H ᴿ1416
Sláma P ᵀ165
Slenczka N 9395 **R**
  243
Sleeper C 7585
Sloyan G 8546 ᴿ4780
  6868 10439
Smalley S ᴿ6187 6189
  6301 6474
Smelik K 1804 **W**
  1890

Smeltz J ᵀ11968
Smend R 244 962
  2458 2522 2769
  2997 3018 3260s
  4569 7838 7991s
  9028 11306 13205
  ᶠ113 ᴿ13320
Smiga G ᴿ6709
Smiles V 7029
Smit D 10693 **I**
  ᵀ3429 **J** 7104 7299
  P 4246
Smith A 8683 ᴿ241
  B 6794 **C** 1071
  5625 6706 ᴱ450 **D**
  1072 6012 6129
  6292 7125 ᴰ6458
  ᴿ5407 6283 **E** 8798
  H ᶠ114 **I** 6574 **J**
  1257 1997 4394
  10839 10948
  ᴱ12886 ᴿ452 515
  11852 **K** 2151 **L**
  ᴱ13717 **M** 8042
  9763 10949-52
  13843 ᴿ6283 **P**
  12754 **S** ᴿ114 **W**
  4180 10953 -
  Christopher D
  7993 ᴿ63 2766
Smolak K ᴱ697
Smoláriková K
  ᴿ11363 13241
Snape S ᴿ12826
Snavely C ᴿ323 2265
  I ᴿ816
Sneed M ᴿ4019
Snell D 2788
Snodgrass K 1258
Snoeberger M 8181
Snoek H 3805 13995
  J 4247
Snyder G 4952
  13206 **H** 1073
  ᴱ208 ᴿ10063 **J**
  3195
Snyman A 6962 **G**
  3398 **G** 7902 **S**
  1370 4359
Soards M ᴿ7347
Soares S 5558
Sobrino J 8658
  ᴹ8068 8198 13916

Socci S ᴱ599
Soderlund S ᴱ37 131
Sodi M ᴱ847
Soelle D 4864
Soeting A 6575
Soggin J 2814 7941
  11268s ᴿ205 **T**
  ᵀ1810 4772
Soisalon-Soininen I
  †14070
Sokol J 2323
Sokoloff M 9143s ᴱ50
Sokołowski M 8444
Solà T ᴿ3853
Sole L 11911
Solecka K 3947
Soler J 2674
Sollamo R ᴱ1949
  ᴿ14070
Solomon L 10416
Soloveitchik J ᴹ10409
Somekh A ᴱ10347
Somerville R 7064
Sommer A 11307
  ᴿ13321 **B** 4265
  ᴿ4187 4193 4252
  4261 4432 **M** 11270
Sommerfeld W 11092
Somos R 13449
Somville P ᴿ10815
Sonnabend H 4696
  ᴱ13122
Sonnemans H 129
  11196
Sonnet J 2225 2926
  3865
Soosai Fernando N
  6050
Sordi M ᴿ9503
Sorensen E 5294
Sorg T 8182
Sorkin D ᴱ856
Soroudi S 3262
Sorum J ᴿ13753
Soto-Hay y García F
  13523
Soucek V ᴱ935
Soulen R 817
Souletie J ᴱ1455
Souris G 9480
Sousa P de 8064
Souza E de 10697
  Nogueira P de 5679

Tannehill R ^{R}5792 5806
Tannen D ^{E}377
Tanner K ^{R}1517 4923 **M** 12913 ^{R}1105 **N** ^{R}3074 11971
Tanret M 13063 ^{R}2461
Tantlevskij I 7965
Tanzer S 6296
Tapel R 6297
Tapia Bahena T 1273
Taplin O ^{E}527
Taracha P 10885 ^{E}91
Tarawneh K 12560
Tarazi P 4679s **R** 12645
Tarocchi S 7085 ^{R}1022 5010 5750
Tarragon J de ^{R}11281
Tarrier D 12972
Taschner J 1038 2553
Taşhalan M ^{E}734
Ta-Shma I 10297
Tasioulas J ^{E}9646
Tasker D 7688
Tassin C 9999 ^{R}1455 6701
Tatian 10642 ^{M}1962
Taub L 12800
Tauberschmidt G 3950
Tauchner C 7413
Tavardon P 5203 6013
Tavares S 8183 8659
Taverner S ^{R}11527
Tavo F 6579
Tawalbeh D 12572
Tawil H 9007
Taylor B 1458 3818 ^{R}1940 **D** 9107 ^{E}605 ^{R}832 **J** 1573 4867 5785 6014s 9806 11042 12614 ^{R}6739 10718 **N** 6665 7195 7433 ^{R}4681 7091 7490 8572 8684 8769 12496
Tábet M 964 1503 3105 ^{R}564 950 1001 1100 1379 4938 7952 8429 8915 10837
Támez E 4026 6797
Tchape J 8391

Tcherikover V 11522
Tchernetska N 3917
Tchimboto B 3816
Tedeschi G 2723
Teeter E 13064s ^{R}930
Teilhard de C ^{M}2356
Teja R ^{E}665 **V** 11842
Tejerina Arias G ^{R}199
Telesko W 1998
Telford W 1806 ^{R}5542 5603
Tellbe M 6708s
Temin P ^{R}10731
Tempesta A 12175
Ten Boom W 13583
Tenge-Wolf V ^{E}13713
Terbuyken P 13060
Terian A ^{R}9688
Termini C 3795 3819 ^{E}3725
Ternes C 10786 ^{E}666
Ternynck M 8346
Terra J 3731s 3796 8143 14016s ^{E}3730
Terrien S 8897 †14073
Terrinoni U 8551
Tertullian ^{M}4514 7067 8275 13452- 60
Teshima I ^{R}10241
Testart A 13213
Testen D ^{R}9541
Teter M 2096
Tetley M 11272
Teugels L ^{R}509s 10166 10181
Tétaz J ^{E}10660
Thabut M 7665
Thackeray H 4394 11573
Thaikkattil S ^{R}5595
Thallinger J 4301
Thanner N 7689
Tharedkadavil A 2253
Thasiho Mahiniro J 10959
Thatcher A ^{R}1586 **T** 6298 ^{E}6113

Theis J 1078 5709
Theissen G 1459s 2554 2648 3166 3608 3637 3812 4293 4380 4511 4681s 4698 4868-71 4934 5281 5374 5676 5844 6032s 6347 6397 6434 6467 6978 7021 7043 7047 7132 7222 7246 7405 7535 7547 7596 7598 8184 8552 8898 13214 ^{D}8845 ^{E}601s
Thelle R 10960
Themelis P 12905
Then R ^{R}69
Theobald C 7717 ^{E}313 **M** 6299s 6923 7367 13758 ^{E}214 ^{R}7848
Theodore C ^{M}13725
Theodoretus C 2925 ^{M}3485 13529-32 13626
Theodorus M ^{M}3698 13533 13626
Theokritoff G & E ^{R}2364
Theron P 8127
Theuer G 3625 10961
Thibault A ^{R}13383
Thiede C 7554s 8256 9973 10554
Thiel J 1517 **M** ^{R}636 **W** 2998 3264 3417 **W** ^{E}179 ^{R}13180
Thiele W 4097 ^{M}13998
Thielicke H 5336
Thielman F 7022
Thiem A 12242
Thieme K ^{M}7020
Thiering B 9958 11871
Thiers C 12075
Thimmes P 5891
Thiselton A 7065
Thissen H 9291
Thom J ^{R}10824
Thoma C 10555 ^{D}10409 ^{ET}10274 ^{F}119 ^{M}14006 14022 ^{R}10032 14062

Vitelli M 13970
Vitório J 4378
Vittmann G 9295
Vitz E ^R8745
Vivaldelli G 3629
Vivas A del S 1624
Vives i Tutó J ^M13830
Viviani R 11795
Viviano B 256 ^R5298
 5576 6311 6741
 7022 **P** 4352
Viviers H 3765 3867
 ^R3852
Vílchez Líndez J 3354
Vleugels G 4999
Vlizos S 12077
Voderholzer R 11145
Voegelin E ^M383
Vogel D 2500 **H**
 ^R11400 **M** 11585 **P**
 ^E534
Vogels W 1507 2651
 3734 7841 ^R564
 2239 2711 2753
 3002 10077
Vogler W ^F127
Vogt C 12179 **E** 6492
 H ^R3641 5359
Vogüé A de ^T3191
Voigt R ^R3442 9533 **S**
 8045 †14077
Voinov V 2159
Volfing A 6131
Volgger D 2816 2960
 ^R254 2913 4466
 7181 10123 11523
Volk K 9215
Vollenweider S 257
 5508 5881 6590
 6806ss 7087 7098
 7395 7399 7401
 8046ss 8257 8854
 8900 10558 10591
 ^R7391 9463
Vollmer U 10335 ^E59
Volokhine Y 11046
 11915
Volp U 12943
Volschenk G 2841
 13091s 13121 13219
Von Wahlde U 6464
 ^D6106
Vonach A ^R3760 6974
 7984

Vondey Wolfgang
 ^{ET}2061 ^T13748
Voorwinde S 6330
 7670
Vorndran J 3681
Vorster J 13220s
Vos C 3626 3638
 3594 8347 13222
 G 7967 **J de** 3027
 12761 **J** 6711s
 6954s 7088 7103
 7185 7193 7311s
 7336 7394 9507
Voss F 7089 **M** ^R147
Vouga F 4685 5221
 8258s 8348 8901s
Voulgaris C 5857
Vörös G 12247
 12817
Vregille B de 3838
Vries A de 2676 **J de**
 2547
Vriezen K 12573
Vroom H ^D7820
Vugdelija M 5242s
Vuilleumier S
 ^E11885
Vulliamy B 5930
Vycichl W †14078

Waaijman K 3703
 13857
Waaler E 2873
Wachob W 7597
 7601
Wacholder B 9905
Wachter R 2677
Wackenheim C 7671
 M 5278
Wacker M 8804
 9625
Wade L 8288
Waerzeggers C 2790
Waetjen H 7842
 8114
Wagemakers B
 12428
Wagenaar J 4620
 9099 ^R2840
Wagner A 8956s **C**
 11757 **D** 13297 **G**
 6396 9481s **J** 6956
 V 2770 13223s

Waheeb M 12563
Wahl H 1757 ^R2553 **O**
 ^F128
Wahrman M 2368
Wai M 11198
Wainwright E 5151
 6331 ^R5083
Waite D ^E877s
Waki M 12775
Walaskay P 1465
Waldenfels H ^F129
Waldmann H 5359
Walf K 13971
Walker A 1720 **C** ^F130
 D 7252 **S** ^E11363 **W**
 7247
Wall R 1576 4686
 6018
Wallace D ^R10573 **J**
 1466 **R** 1285 3113
Walmsley A 12620
 12542
Walsh C 3868 13082 **J**
 1324 2857 ^R14003 **R**
 1286 ^E267
Walter M 6809 **N** 4885
 6054 7302 8049
 13861 ^R10035 **U**
 ^R11297
Walters S 1467 3109
Waltisberg M 9546
Waltke B ^F131
Walton J 1287 **P** ^E135
 S 4687 5789 6824
Walzer M ^M1740
Wan S 7217
Wanamaker C 7441
 ^R7062
Wander B 6019
Wandermurem M 4633
Waner M 12366
Wanke D 8260 **J** 6428
Wannenwetsch B 7034
Wansbrough H 1374s
 1375 2160 ^R4656
Wansink Craig 13342
Warburton D 12718
 ^R9244 11042 ^T9262
Ward B ^R13717 **G**
 ^R1306 **K** 8855 **T**
 1508s
Wardini E 12631
Warfield B 258

Westenholz J 9103 11099s
Westerholm S ᴰ5077 6553 ᴿ6990
Westermann C 3953 6311 7995
Westhelle V 5279
Westra L 7725
Wetzel C 1084 1829
Wetzlaugk S 8805
Wevers J 2869
Wexelman D 10336
Wexler L ᴱ12438
Weyde K 4651
Weyer M 8362
Weyermann M 1811
Wénin A 1292 2272 2599 2705 3056 3095 3471 3869 7673 ᴱ9 2254 ᴿ365 1303 2411 2651 3295 7983
Whallon W 8638
Whealey A 9671
Whedbee J 1670
Wheeler B 11150 ᵀ11151 G 2627
Whidden W 6591
White C ᴱ13451 G 9765 H 1325 ᴿ10838 10844 R 4887 5447 6104 ᶠ134
Whitehorne J ᴿ781
Whitekettle R 13069
Whitelam K 11274s 11312
Whiting R ᴱ713
Whitley J 12907
Whitlock J 1510
Whitt R ᴿ5117
Whitters M 5717
Whybray R 3954 7843
Wiarda T 5360
Wick P 8558
Wicker J ᴿ5013
Wicke-Reuter U 4099s
Wickeri P 8349 ᴱ82
Widdicombe P 7691
Widmer G ᴿ9285
Wiegard J 5845
Wiegers G ᴱ74
Wielenga B 5153s 5383

Wiemer A 13760 H 11524
Wierschowski L ᴿ13260
Wierzbicka A 5339
Wiese C ᵀ4916
Wiesehöfer J 11101
Wiesemann F 12021
Wiesmüller W 3554
Wigbod ᴹ13653 13728
Wigen T 1326
Wiggermann F 10966
Wiggins S ᴿ2656
Wigoder G ᴱ821 861
Wijngaards J 8394
Wikander Ö ᴱ12989
Wilcke C 2792 11102
Wilckens U 488 6153
Wilcox M 5790
Wild J ᶠ135
Wildermann A ᵀ10305
Wildfang R ᴱ703
Wildung D ᴱ11717
Wiles V 6811
Wiley T 2412
Wilfong T ᴿ9482 11346
Wilhelm A 260 G 9355 10664 10888 12844 ᴱ776
Wilk F 5079
Wilke A 7674
Wilken R ᶠ136
Wilkens B 13070
Wilkie N ᴿ14035
Wilkinson B 3315 D 2327 J 13281 R ᴿ12323 12336 T 11365-8
Will E 12582
Willems G 5511
Willers C 11182
Willett E 1590
Willi T 1293 3312 10126 10348 ᴿ3295 3301 3306 3308s 3321 3332ˢᴿ 11236

William L 2273
Williams C 2678 4889 11103 ᴱ12908 D 3420s 6812s 7397 13771 ᴱ441 ᴿ5798 G 3342 H 4365 ᴿ7065 J 2875 5634 13820 13879 ᴱ12022 ᵀ8188 M 2274 2652 P 3267 3801 9036 R 5170 5448 ᴹ13809 S 1378 T ᴿ350
Williamson H 4222 ᴿ76 681 2991 ᴿ4300 M ᴱ10752 P 1379 2523
Willing M 13412
Willinghöfer H ᴱ535
Willi-Plein I 261 1294 1626 2413 2555 2600 2706 3159 3802 4489 4509 8958 9042 9051 10348 11313
Willis J ᴱ13325 T 2958
Willmer H ᴿ8603
Wills A 1085 G 13588 ᴱ1408 L 10127 ᵀᴱ10128
Willson P ᴿ13766
Wilson A ᴿ7065 7396 B 6630 E 1966 G 3555 I 2928 J 8115 ᴿ8008 8026 K 12248 M ᴿ12914 R 95 667 S 6036 ᴱ99 ᴿ8633 W 7599 6071 7607 - Okamura D ᴿ1736
Wilmshurst S 5155
Wilt T 2164
Wimbush V 1295 ᴱ387
Wimmer S 12121 12249 12543
Winandy J 4291
Wingate A ᴿ8684
Winger M 7303
Wink W 8160
Winkes R 12337
Winkett L 8754
Winkler G 8559s U ᴿ491 8113 -Horacék L ᴿ10733

Situs

Esna 11017
Et-Ṭaiyiba 12339
eṭ-Ṭannur 12219
ez-Zeraqon 12568
Fara 11866
Farasa 12569
Fayyum 12815
Fray 11761
Gadara 485 12570-4
Garizim 10018
Gat 12448
Gavurkalesi 12214
Gaza 12076 12449
   12831
Gerasa 485 9426
   12575-9
Gezer 9000 12450
Ghassul 12580s
Giza 12779s
Halaf 12693
Halikarnassos 12176
   12288
Hamat 11404
Hammeh 12335
Hamoukar 12117
   12718 12947
Hamrîn 13018
Har Karkom 12825
Ḥattuša 12228 12239
   12845 12847 12852s
Hazor 9184 11203
   11338 12513
Hebron 2464ss 2472
   2486s 2489
Herodium 11582
   12314 12458
Hippos 12514
Holon 12311 13041
Horvat Bor 12451
Ḥorvat ʿEtri 12483
Horvat Teman 11910
   10883
ʾIra 12452
Iraq al Amir 12582
ʿIzbet Ṣarṭa 12484
Jabal al-Qalʿa 12583
Jabal al-Qalʿa 12584
Jabal Harun 12585
Jawa 12586
Jemdet Nasr 12722
Jerash 12587ss
Jericho 12453s
Jerusalem 13288
   12367-431

Johfiyeh 12590
Kamid el-Loz 12694
Kanatha 9423 10898
   11779 12154
   12200
Kapitolias 12591
Kato Z 12110
Khallit ʿIsa 12592
Khorsabad 12045
Kinneret 12515s
Knossos 12093
   12145
Kom Ombo 10996
Korazim 12217
Kumme 12723
Kuntillet Aǧrud 8974
   10883 11910
Kuşakli-Sarissa
   12867s
Lachisch 12455
Larsa 13038
Le Quiebre 11808
Lod 12485
Luxor 12206
Maʾahaz 12138
Malhata 12456
Mari 13025 13040
Masada 4096 10000
   11531 12457s
Maşathöyük 12869
Megiddo 3194 11801
   12459 13076
   12517
Memphis 12144
Meron 12351 12518
Messene 12905
Midas 12870
Miletos 12209
Mizpa 9210 11764
Moreschet-Gat
   12460
Moẓa 12461
Munbâqa 12695
Mycenae 12894
Nabi Salah 12829
Naḥal Tillah 12462
Nahal Zippori 12519
Nazareth 12520s
Neša 12871
Nemrud Daği 12872
Nevé Ur 12343
Nimrim 13089
Nimrud 11371

Niniveh 4520 11399
   12724s
Nir Gallim 12204
Nisya 12082 12303
Norşuntepe 12873
Numeira 13089
Nuzi 9177 12726s
Ostia 513 11767 12234
Palmyra 10919
   12696ss 12984
Panopolis 12816
Pella 6035 12428
   12593s
Petra 9442 11791
   12028 12182 12317
   12595-12615
Philadelphia 12616
Philippi 6001 9463
   12902s
Pylos 12108
QaʿAbu Ṭulayḥa 12617
Qabrestan 13037
Qaṣr ar-Rabba 9428
Qatna 12699
Qedesh 12273
Quleh 12062 12220
Rabbathmoab 12618
Raḥab-al 12548
Ramat Hanadiv 12486
Ras-Irbid 12619
Rehov 11242 12522
Rekhes Nafha 12463
Robatha 12620
Rujm Ṭaba 12621
Sais 12788
Samʾal 9146
Samaria 11579 12040
   12243
Saqqara 11873 12291
   12307s 12320 12325
   12328 12777
Sardis 8967 9478
   12874
Sarvistan 11763
Seleukeia P & T 11506
Sepphoris 12128
   12523s 12985
Shaʿar ha-Golan 12525
Shechem 12121 12487
   12774
Sheikh el-Qatrawani
   12241
Shoham 12293

Sidon 12240
Sippar 9181 12192
Soleb 12236s
Susa 11432 12115 12736
Susta-Hippos 12983
Šapinuwa 12875
Taanach 3194 12526
Ṭafila-Buṣayra 12622
Tanis 12789
Taposiris Magna 12817
Tarsus 10889

Te'o 12527
Tepe Gawra 12728
Thebes 9237 12764ss
Thessalonica 10831
Timnah 12464
Tuttul 12700s
Ugarit 12646-67 13007 13044s
ʿUmar 12151
Umm al-Rasas 11755 12623
Umm el-Qaab 12818
Ur 11841 12081 12737

Uruk 11062 12081 12729s 12737
Ur-Utu 13063
Wilusa 12876
Yaʾamun 12624
Yarmut 12465
Yavneh-Yam 12488
Yazilikaya 12238
Zahrat Adh-Dhrʿ 12625
Zaphon 13084
Zarʿa 12626
Ẓefiyya 12313
Zeugma 12122
Zizia 12227

Voces

Akkadicae

abi/apu 9020
adê 2963
g 9015
izuzzum 9016
itūlum 9016
lugalbanda 9017
rʾm 9018

Amorreae

niḫlatum 3656

Aramaicae

קרבן 9019

Graecae

ἀγᾰθός 6980
ἀγάπη 6787
ἅγιος 9379
ἀδελφοί 7289
ἀδελφός 9380
ἀδολεσχέω 9381
ἀλήθεια 8178
ἀνήρ 5746
ἀποκᾰραδοκία 9382
ἀπόστολος 6027
ἀρνίον 6510
ἀρσενοκοίτης 9383
ἀρχηγός 8034

βαπτίζω 9408
γαμῶ 9385
γῆ 6056
διακονία 9386
διδασκω 5125
δικαιοσύνη 5115
δόξα 6420
δύναμις 9387
ἐγείρεσθαι 9388
ἔθνος 10042
εἶδεν 5614
εἴδωλον 9389
ἐκλέγομαι 6237
ἐκπορεύομαι 9390
ἐπίχειρον 4342
εὐαγγέλιον 13382
εὐαγγελιστής 9391
εὐνοῦχος 7818
ἐχουσία 5573
ζάω 6767
ζωή 6767
ζωοτοιέω 6767
ἡμέρα 6561
θεραπεύω 5125
Ἰερουσαλήμ 6148
Ἰουδαῖοι 6182 6193 6264
κηρύσσω 5125
κλέπτης 9392
κόσμος 6259 9393
κτίσις 9394
κύριος 8018

λόγος 8865 9395s 11192
λοιπός 6544
μαλᾰκός 9383
μαρτυρία 9397
μυστήριον 8890
νύμφη 6510
ὀκνηρός 5394
ὁμοουσιος 9398
ὄνομα 9399
ὀπίσω 9400
παιδαγωγός 9401
παραθήκη 7453
παρθένος 9402
πίστις 6764 6800 8181 9403
πνεῦμα 6504 7508 9404
πραῢς 5245
πρόνοια 7858
σάρξ 9396
συνεργός 9405
σῶμα 9406
σωτήρ 8023 9407
τηρεῖν 6540
ὑπόκρῑσις 9384
χάρις 6802 9409
χάρισμα 7159
Χριστός 6747

Hebraicae

אב 9020

אהב 9021
אוב 9020
אכל 4653
אמה 9022
אמת 8178
במה 9023
ברית 9024
בתולה 9402
גר 9025s 13141
דבורה 9027
דבר 8865 11192
דל 3949
דמע 9935
האמין 9028
הלך 5643
המן־ 9845 9884
הנה 9029
זקן 7801
חבל 4014
חטאת 6721 9030 2697
חידה 3062
חלק 9031
חרב 1632
חרם 3009
טוב 2271
יד 9032
ישועה 4207
ישע 9033
למלך 12394

לקח 9034
מוסר 3929
מות 4246
מחיר 9035
מלט 9036
מלך 9037
ממשת 12394
מנה 4588
מרזח 4154
משא 9038
משל 9039
משפט 4207
נבלה 9040
נח 9041
נחלה/נחלת 3656
נחם 9042
נכר 9043
נפלים 10329
נשיא 2918
סד 9044
סריס 9045
עבד 9046
עברים 3106
עול 9047
עולם 4032
עלמנה 9048
ענה 9049
ענו 3620
ערך 9050

ערלה 2235
עשה 2271
פלט 9036
פרס 11872
קוה 4161
רוח 4429 8123s 8943
רחם 4068
רש 3949
שטן 9052
שוב 9051
שלום 9053
שמר 9054
שמש 9055
שפש 9055
שתק 4588

Phoeniceae

dl 9056

Ugariticae

'ap 9020
'd/db 9057
ġzr 9058
m't 9059
sākinu 9060
ṣśǵr 9061
ṯbr/ṯbrn 9062

Sacra Scriptura

Genesis

1 2277
1-2 13848
1-3 13732
1-4 7994
1-11 890 2195
  2240 2246
  2281 2316
  9660
1,1-2,4 1863
1,1-6,8 2253
1,1-27,47 10316
1,1-3 2306 2337
1,20-25 13069
1,26 2303
1,26-27 2289
  2315 8523

13461
1,26-28 2276
  7851
1,27 7338
2 13703
2-3 13615
2,1-17 2292
2,3 2305
2,6 9876
2,7 2289
2,9 13512
2,18-24 2284
2,24 8287
3 1780
3,11-14 2387
3,15 2400
  2393 8504

3,16 2399
  2407
3,17-19 13742
3,19-20 2386
3,20 2395
4 1020 1675
  1875 2414
4-11 2259
4,2-4 2513
4,8 1880 2417
5-9 2455
5,1-32 2263
6-8 9823
6,1-4 2415s
  2418
6,2-7 10156
6,3 9894

6,5-7 10267
6,13 2458 7838
  9028
6,15 9824
7-9 9894
7,16 2440
8,6-7 10476
8,7 2439
8,13 9894
9-11 13811
9,12-17 2460
9,18-29 2425
9,24-25 9823
9,27 10258
10 9659
10,1-11,9 8674s
10,6 2433

12 1614
12,1-16 2875
13-14 2220 9683
 11537
13,1-20,13 2876
14,11-20 2639
15,30-31 2765
15,32-36 2729
16-18 2690
19 2877
20 2690
20-21 3010
20,1-13 1614
 2878
21,4-9 6349
21,33-35 10218
22-24 2879ss
24,15-17 9833
25 2882
26,59 1614
27,1-11 2883s
32,1-38 2885
32,32-42 2206
33 3010 13447
35 2886

Deuteronom.

1-3 3010
1-4 2929s
1-10 2931
1,6-4,40 2206
1,19-46 2220
2,14-16 2932
2,36 2933
3 10218
3,21-22 2934
4,1-40 2935
4,32-40 2936
4,41-43 2937
5 2736 10162
5-11 2206
5,1-33 2938
5,9 2728
5,11 2732
5,16 2768
5,28-6,1 2939
5,28-29 9833
6,4 2640 2940s
6,4-5 6293
 10514
6,4-6 2942
 10231

6,4-9 2944
6,4-25 2943
6,10-25 2944
6,25 8222
7,1 1837
7,15 9879
7,25 2945
8,11-18 2234
9-10 2639
10,17-18 7646
12 8913
12-26 2739
13 2946
13,7 1843
14 2947 13069
14,1-17,13 2948
14,21 2949
14,22-29 2950
15 2951
15,2 2504
16,18-20 2902 2952
17,8-13 2952
17,8-18,22 2902
17,14-20 3127 9923
17,16-17 2953
18 2954
18,15-22 2955
18,18-19 9833
19,1-13 2937 2958
19,15 2952
19,19 2729
20 2956
21-25 2957
21,1-9 2958
21,18-21 2958 7615
21,22-23 2952
21,23 7286
22,1-3 13046
22,13-21 2958
22,22 2738
23,1 2959
24,8-9 1614
24,16 2952
24,17 7615
25,1-3 2952
25,4 13046
25,4-10 2958

25,5-10 2960s
26,1-13 2962
28 2963
28,69-30,20 2964
29-30 2206
31,1-8 2965
31,1-32,47 2206
31,28-31 2968
32 1867 2663 2967
32-33 2966
32 2968
32,8 2969s
32,43 2971
33 2972
33,8-11 9833
33,8-12 10235
33,20-21 10235
34,9 2973
34,10 2974

Josue

2 3022s 1594
6 1594
8,1-29 3024
10,12-14 3025 10296
10,12-15 2346
11 11203
15 3027
15,13-19 3026
20 1429
20-21 2886
22,9-34 3029
22 3028

Judices

1,1-20 3042
3,12-30 3043
3,16 1632
3,31 3044
4 8913 11203
4,1-5,31 3045
5 3046
5,2-31 3047
5,19 3194
6-8 3048
6-9 3049

6,1-7,14 3050
8,33-9,57 3051
9 13074
9,1-6 3052
10,1-12,15 3053s
10,16 3055
11 3010
11,29-40 3056s
13-16 3058-61 12008
13,7 9379
14 3062
15,8 3063
16,4-22 3064s
16,17 9379
17-18 3066
18,30 3067
19 8663
19-21 3035 3068s

Ruth

1,1-19 3096
1,16 3088
2 3097
2,8-9 3098
3 3099
4 2675

1 Samuel

1 3110 3112
1-7 3113
1,1-2,21 3111
2,1-10 9033
2,3 3114
2,25 3115
2,27-36 8944
3 3116
4-6 3117
4,6 3118
5-6 3119
8,11-18 3127
9,1-16 3128
13,11-14 2746
15,13-31 2746
16,1-13 3129
17 3160ss
21,9 11806
24 4379
25 3163s

55 1041
55,2-16 3454
57 3518
58 3512 3654ss
59 3518
64 3657
68 9865
68,5 3658
68,10 3659
68,31 3660
69,23-30 3661
72 3515 3662-7
73 3668s
73-80 3506
73-83 3553
73-89 3670
73,24-26 3671
74 3672
74,9 3673
75 3674 9033
75,2 3675
76 3676
78 3677
79,2-3 9873
80 3678
81 3679
82 3680
82,1-2 2504
86 3681
88 3682s
89 3515 3548
   3684s
90 3545
90-105 3507
90-106 2636
92 3686
93 3510
93,3-4 11839
94,16-23 3687
95 1396
95-99 3510
96 3688
96-99 4209
99 3689
100,3 3690
102 3584
104 3691
105 3692
106 3035
109 3693
110 3515 7503
110,4 7536
113 3694 9033

118 3695ss
   9866
118,19 13618
118,20 9854
119 3698
119-133 13535
   13552
120 1068
120-134 3699
   4206
121 3700
122 3539 3701
127 3702 9866
128 3703
129 3704 9866
130 3705
132 3515
133 3706s
135 9848
135-136 3708
137 3709
139 3710s
139-147 3698
139,21-22
   3712s
140,2 3714
146,6-9 7646
149 3715
149,6 1632
150 3716

151 3717

Job

1 11116
1,1-2,13 2545
1,1-4 4231
1,6-12 2376
1,21 2386
2,1-7 2376
2,13 3805
3 3806s
4,12-21 3808
7,7-21 1407
9-10 3809
9,27-35 3810
10 3811
14,1-15 3812
14,7-17 3813
18,11 3814
19,25-27 3815
23,3-9 3810

24 3816
27,18 3817
28 3891
38 3818
38-41 3819
40,2 3820
40,4 3821
40,6-41,26
   3822
42,17 3823

Canticum,
Song

1,1 3871
1,2 10169
   10172 10215
1,12 6398
2,8-17 3872
3,1-5 3872
3,6-11 3873
4,12-15 3874
4,13 6398
4,16 9877
6,4-7,11 3875
6,12 3875
7,6 3876
8,5-14 3877

Proverbia

1-9 3955-66
1,7 2132 3967
3 3968
3,1-12 3969s
3,6 3820
3,27-35 3971
3,34 3971
5,4 1632
8 3891
8,22-24 3972
8,22-31 3973s
8,24 2317
9,1-11 8503
10-15 3975
10,1-22,16
   3976s
11,5-6 3979
14,28-35 3980
15,27-16,9
   3981
18 3982
20,2-30 3983

22,1-24,22 3984
22,17-24,22
   3985
25-29 3986
25,21-22 3987
25,23 3988
26,1-12 3989
30 2299
30,7-9 3990
31,1-9 3991
   9674
31,10-31 3966
   3992s
31,26-31 9299
31,30 3994

Eces, **Qohelet**

3,1-15 4030
3,10-15 4031
3,11 4032s
5,9-6,6 4034
5,14 2386
6,5 4035
7,15-18 4036
9,1-12 4037
10,2-3 13602
11,1-2 4038

Sapientia Sal.

2,1-20 4059
7 3891
14,11-21 4060
16,5-14 4061
16,15-29 4062
19,21 4062

Ecus, Sirach

4,2-6,4 9299
6,32-37 3894
8,8-9 3894
15,11-18,14
   4103
16,1-16 4104
21,3 1632
24 3891
24,1-32,13 4105
27,30-28,7 4106
27,33-28,9
   10103
33,12 4107

Ezekiel

3,26 4442
1,27-2,6 4414
2-3 4441
25,8 9879
3,14-15 4443
8,17 4444
13,1-16 4445
16 4446-9
18 4379 7894
20 4450 7894
21,2-9 4414
23 4448s
23,20 1888
23,41-24,4 4414
24,15-27 4451
26,1-28,19 4452
27,1-14 4453
28,1-10 4454
28,11-19 2377
  2381 4455
32,19 8955
34 4456
34,18 1888
36,16-38 4457
37 4458
37,1-14 4459
37,8 4460
37,23 10235
39,21-29 4461
39,29 4462
40-48 4463-6
47,10 6450

Daniel

1 4504
2 2587 4505
2,41-43 4506
3,57-90 4507
4 4508
6 4509
7 4510
7,1-14 4511
7,2-14 4512
7,9-14 4513
  6547
9,24 13878
9,24-27 4514
9,25 2504
9,27 8249
11,32 10235

13 4515

Hosea

1-2 4545
1-3 4116
  4546ss
2,8-14 9852
4-11 4135
5,1-7 4549
5,8 9879
5,8-6,6 4550
5,13-15 9853
6,4 9853
6,5 4551
6,7 9853
6,9 9857
6,9-11 9853
8,6-8 9853
8,13-14 9853
9,7-9 4552
10,11 4553
11,4 9047
11,10 4535
12,1-2 4554
14,5 8222
14,6-10 4555

Joel

2,12 4557

Amos

1,3-2,5 4139
1,3-2,16 4572
1,14 4573
3,1-8 4574
3,12 4575
4,7-8 4560
5,18-20 4577
5,18-27 4578
5,24 4579
6,1 4580
7,1 4581
7,7-9 4581
8,8 4581
9,11 10235

Jonas

1 4609
2 4610

2,5 4611
3,7-8 4612

Micheas
Micah

1,1-5 1381
1,2-6 9861
1,9 9861
2-5 4620
2,1-13 4621
3,5-12 1388
4,1-5 4622
4,8-12 9862
4,14-5,8 4623
6,1-8 4624
6,15-16 9861

Nahum

1,3-6 9863
1,14 4520
2,11 9879
2,12-14 9863
3,1-7 4633
3,1-14 9863
3,4 4520

Habakkuk

1,1-17 9851
1,6 4638
2,1-20 9851
2,9-11 4639
3 4640

Soph. **Zephan.**

1,4 10936
1,12-13 9867
1,14-18 4627
1,18-22 9868
2,3-15 4520

Aggaeus
Haggai

1,1-15 4643
2,7 8883
2,20-23 4644

Zechariah

3,9 9879
1,7-6,8 4646
3,1-2 2376
3,7 8943
9-14 4524 4647
11,11 9857
11,13 5453
13,2-6 4328
13,9 9873

Malachi

1,14 9826
2,10-16 4652
3,11 4653
3,16-18 9825
3,23-24 4654

Matthaeus

1 1419
1s 5156-86
1,1-2,13 5128
1,1-25 5170
1,16 13567
1,18-24 5171
1,18-25 5172s
2 5174s
2,1-12 5129
  5176-84
2,2 5185
2,13-15 5171
  5186
2,13-23 11988
2,19-20 5171
3,1-2 1421
3,10-12 5203
3,13-17 5204
3,15 5115
4,1-11 5055
  5205-9
5-6 13173
5-7 1030 1395
  2066 5339
  13568
5,1-2 5224
5,3 5242ss
5,4-5 5245
5,17-20 1465
  5225
5,32 5247

14,46 5712
14,54 5713
14,61-64 5714
14,66-72 5713
5715
14,72 5716
15,34-36 5717
15,39 5718
15,40-41 8751
15,47 8751
16 5720
16,1-8 5721-4
8751
16,8 5725
16,8-20 5726
16,9-20 5727ss
16,14 5730

Lucas

1 5840
1ss 5834-57
1,1-4 5841s
1,26-38 5843ss
1,34 5846
1,39-56 5847
1,46-55 5848
13758
2,1-5 5849
2,1-20 5850s
8767
2,22-40 5852
2,22-50 5853
2,35 5854
2,41-52 5855
2,48 5856
2,52 13680
3,23-38 5857
4 5858
4,1-13 5055
5209 5829
5859s
4,16-30 5861
4,18 2752
4,18-19 5862
5,36-39 8790
6,1-11 5863
6,17-26 5864
6,20-49 5865
6,27-38 5227
6,29 8647
6,46 8018
7 5866

7,1-10 5867s
7,24-35 4885
7,31-35 8792
7,36-50 5869ss
7,42 5872
8,1-3 5873
8,9-10 4232
8,43-48 5874s
9,1-56 5739
9,10-17 6159
9,28-36 5367
5829 5876
9,37-43 5684
9,51-56 5878
9,52-56 5879
9,62 5880
10,17-20 5829
10,18 5881
10,25-37 5334
5739 5882s
10,29-37 1078
5884-7
10,38-42 5760
5888-91
11,16-32 5309
11,27-28 5892
11,29-32 4844
12,7-14 5893
12,13-21 1458
12,13-23 5894
12,13-24 5895
12,13-34 5896
12,22-31 5049
5897
12,27-28 8776
12,41-45 5898
13,1-5 8645
13,6-9 5899
13,11-17 1044
13,20-21 1411
8776
13,20-21 5828
14 5381
14,7-11 5900
14,20 9385
15 5901-5
15,8-9 8784
15,8-10 5828
15,10 8760
15,11-32
5906-12
5348
16 5913

16,1-8 5914
16,1-9 5915
16,1-13 5916
16,8 5917
16,19-31
5918s
17,11-19 5739
5920
17,27 9385
17,33 5921
18,1-8 5828
5922s
18,2-5 5924
18,8 5925
18,15-17 8291
19,1-10 5926
19,12-44 5927
19,40 5928
20,9-19 5378
5929
20,27-40 5930
22 5772
22-23 6167
22,7-38 5933
22,21-22 5934
22,24-38 5935
22,39-53 5829
22,43-44 1901
4444 5936
22,54-23,25
5937
23 5938
23,39-43 1464
5939
23,47 5733
23,49 8751
23,54-24,12
5940
23,55-56 8751
24 5941-7
24,1-12 8751
24,1-35 5948
24,6-8 5949
24,12 5950
24,13-35
5951s
24,27 5953
24,33-53 5954
24,34 5475
24,36-49 5955
24,45 5956
24,50-53
5957s

Joannes

1 6317 6325
6331
1,1-18 1729
6318 6324
6327-30 11186
1,3-4 6332
1,12 6243
1,12-2,12 6250
1,14 8025
1,14-17 6333
1,16 6334
1,28 6285 6335
1,35-39 8411
1,35-51 6336s
1,51 6444
2,1-11 6338s
12006
2,1-12 6249
6340 11959
2,3-4 6341
2,4 6342
2,13-22 6343
3 6344s
3-4 1715
3,1-10 8795
3,1-15 6346
3,1-16 6347
3,13 6348
3,14-16 6349
3,22-4,3 6350
3,22-30 6314
3,29 8793
4 6351s 12007
4,1 6353
4,1-42 4787
6354-8
4,1-43 6314
4,42 6246
4,44 6359
5 6360s
5-12 6185
5,1-15 8512
5,1-18 6362
5,10-47 6363
5,17-30 6364
5,18 6365
6 6128 6199
6249 6345
6366-70
6,1-14 6371
6,1-15 6159

END

STAMPA: Novembre 2005

presso la tipografia
"Giovanni Olivieri" di E. Montefoschi
ROMA • tip.olivieri@libero.it